THE
APOCALYPSE OF JOHN

STUDIES IN INTRODUCTION

WITH

A CRITICAL AND EXEGETICAL COMMENTARY

BY

ISBON T. BECKWITH, Ph.D., D.D.

FORMERLY PROFESSOR OF THE INTERPRETATION OF THE NEW TESTAMENT
IN THE GENERAL THEOLOGICAL SEMINARY, NEW YORK, AND
OF GREEK IN TRINITY COLLEGE, HARTFORD

BAKER BOOK HOUSE
Grand Rapids, Michigan

PREFACE

FOR the understanding of the Revelation of John it is essential to put one's ·self, as far as is possible, into the world of its author and of those to whom it was first addressed.   Its meaning must be sought for in the light thrown upon it by the condition and circumstances of its readers, by the author's inspired purpose, and by those current beliefs and traditions that not only influenced the fashion which his visions themselves took, but also and especially determined the form of this literary composition in which he has given a record of his visions. These facts will explain what might seem the disproportionate space which I have given to some topics in the following Introductory Studies.

The Apocalypse is the one book of the New Testament whose theme is the doctrines of the Last Things, the fulfillment of the Kingdom of God, that is, to use the common theological term, the doctrines of Eschatology.   But these had a growth, running through the periods of biblical history; and the Apocalypse, springing from the heritage of these centuries, contains much, especially as regards form, which belongs to this eschatological development.   The more fully, then, one comprehends the earlier eschatology, its history, and the prevalence of its principal conceptions, the better is one fitted to understand the Apocalypse in its leading aspects.   I have therefore given a rather long chapter to the eschatology of the Old Testament and late Jewish writers, together with that of the different parts of the New Testament.   Reference is frequently made to this to elucidate the Apocalypse.

A second topic requiring somewhat extended notice is that of the late Jewish writings called by scholars *Apocalyptic*.

v

These, broadly speaking, are visions, whether actual or assumed, of the unseen world, chiefly of the coming ages. These writings form a distinct class, with certain characteristic conceptions, forms, symbols, and methods of composition. To this class belongs the Revelation of John, which, though incomparably superior to, and in important particulars differing from, all others of the kind, yet agrees with them in many leading ideas, as well as in imagery, language, and manner of writing. There is scarcely a paragraph in the Revelation which does not receive some illumination from other writings of this group. A knowledge of the characteristics of this so-called apocalyptic literature is then indispensable in the study of the Apocalypse of John.

Two closely related topics, the Times of the Apocalypse and its primary Purpose, necessarily enter into the study of one preparing himself to read the book from the author's standpoint. Like the other books of the New Testament, the Revelation, while containing truth for all time, was immediately occasioned by a concrete, practical purpose for the Church in the age in which it was written. The relation of the Roman Empire to the Church at the close of the first century (the time of the Apocalypse), and especially the establishment of a state-religion in the emperor-worship, which plays a foremost part in the Revelation, contained within them the principle of the supreme struggle between the world and Christianity. That struggle, already beginning at the time, was viewed as destined to reach its climax in a future not very remote. The primary purpose of the Apocalypse was to help the Church to meet the conflict then and afterwards. The relation of the book to its age must therefore claim adequate space in prefatory study.

As the Apocalypse is a prophetic book, the subject of the right reading of prophecy in general presents inquiries which cannot be passed over too briefly. I have discussed certain canons for the interpretation of prophecy, recognized by present-day scholars, which may give some measure of guidance in distinguishing the transitory element from the permanent, and I have tried to show the application of such canons to some of the perplexing questions of the Revelation. The great spiritual revelations given in the Apocalypse regarding the coming of

God's kingdom are conveyed in forms of the Prophet's time; and the usefulness of his book for a subsequent age depends largely upon the separation, so far as is practicable, of the permanent from the transitory.

Criticism, technically so called, demands a considerable place in a study of the Apocalypse at the present time. For some decades now the view that the book lacks unity has attracted the support of a numerous group of scholars, and a large body of critical literature has been occupied with proposed analyses of it into different documents of widely differing authors, which supposedly have been revised and combined, perhaps through several revisions, into the present form; or, as others would maintain, the present form of the book is the result of a succession of revisions and enlargements of a single original document. These theories enter into nearly all recent discussions of the Apocalypse. The investigations upon which they are founded, carried on often with singular acuteness, are of great value in the study of the book, even if the conclusions are not always accepted. They cannot then be ignored by the interpreter or passed over in a few words. Yet they need to be tested by the methods of a strict exegesis, and especially in the light of the peculiar literary characteristics of the author of the Apocalypse. In these respects they are not infrequently found wanting. I have given in the Introduction a survey with some discussion of the representative hypotheses, and at the end of the commentary on each paragraph of the book have taken up the principal criticisms of the paragraph. In view of the prominence of the subject in recent study of the Apocalypse, it is proper to state here the position which I have taken in regard to the originality and unity of the book. As all students are aware, the author's mind was stored to a marvelous degree with the ideas, the language, and the imagery found in the Old Testament and in apocalyptic writings. The evidence of this appears on every page, one might almost say in every paragraph of a few verses. That his visions themselves should have been shaped more or less by that with which his mind was filled would be inevitable; still more would this influence be felt in any deliberate effort to describe these spiritual experiences. The Apocalyptist did not write down his visions while in a

state of ecstasy, but after all were ended.   No doubt they were
in themselves beyond the possibilities of adequate portrayal.
And as he recalls them, and seeks to describe them and put
them into systematic form, as he has done in his book, he labors
with careful deliberation and all the resources at his command
to give his readers some apprehension of the great scenes revealed to him and their significance.   In this then he becomes,
not a mechanical recorder of something seen and heard, but a
literary artist struggling to give form to inspired ideas, as do
often the poets and prophets of the Old Testament.   His portrayal becomes a carefully studied composition.   He writes in
the traditional manner of the apocalyptic, using its familiar
conceptions, its language, and its imagery.   Symbols and other
suggestions are derived very frequently from the Old Testament, sometimes from common Hebrew folk-lore, and in some
instances apparently from apocalyptic sources not preserved to
us.   There are passages in which critics are probably right in
finding traces of the influence of some unknown apocalyptic
writing — passages which, if taken by themselves, would seem
to belong to a different connection, or different historic circumstances.   But, as may be certainly concluded from the Apocalyptist's use of the Old Testament, these are very far from being
fragments incorporated into his book bodily and apart from the
connection.   Like certain passages of the prophets unmistakably before his mind in some places and shaping his representation, so these sources have suggested to him pictures or symbols,
which he transforms and applies with the utmost freedom.
Without resorting to an unjustifiable method of exegesis, paragraphs exhibiting such influence may be shown to have for the
Apocalyptist a meaning bearing directly on his theme and fitting
into the general plan which he conceives and carries out from
the beginning.   In this sense, then, I hold that the book is a
unit, the work of one mind ; that it has a wonderful plan to
which every part contributes, a plan carried out with extraordinary power to its great culmination.   But both the plan
and its execution are marked by traits which are peculiar to the
author.   I have accordingly given a paragraph to the illustration of some of the leading characteristics in what may be called
the author's literary manner, because the recognition of these

is important for the right interpretation of the book, and because a failure to recognize them is a frequent cause of the denial of its unity.

I have given in the Introduction a Summary of the Contents of the Apocalypse, embodying the interpretations adopted and showing the meaning of each division of the book in itself and its place in the plan of the whole. This chapter is designed to be read in connection with the text in order to exhibit the unity of the book and to give the reader a succinct view of the tremendous drama as it moves on from the beginning, with the forces shown at work within it, till it reaches its climax in the end.

While the work here offered is intended first of all for theological seminaries and colleges, for the clergy and other special students, I have also sought to make it helpful to that large number of readers, not professional scholars, who are interested in the Revelation and are accustomed to the use of biblical Commentaries, especially those who seek aid in fitting themselves for the instruction of maturer classes in the Bible. Accordingly I have in general translated into English matter in other languages. As more convenient for this class of readers, the English words given in the notes not infrequently cover more than the Greek words actually quoted from the text. I have in some cases retained the more familiar forms, *e.g.* the name *Jehovah*, the abbreviation 2 Es. instead of 4 Ez. for the Apocryphal book 2 Esdras. Sections likely to interest the special student only are printed in finer type. I would especially call the attention of the readers here in mind to the Summary of the Contents spoken of above, in connection with which the Revised Version should be used. For the effective use of the Summary they should prepare themselves by reading, if only superficially, the chapters in the Introduction on Eschatology, the Apocalyptic Writings, the Times and the Purpose of the Revelation, the Permanent and Transitory Elements in it. I have hoped that such a study of the Revelation, aided also by occasional reference to the discussions and notes in the Commentary proper, might suffice to show even the non-professional reader that this book of the New Testament — to many an enigma — is one of the most comprehensible, as it is one of the

most splendid, books of our Bible, and — I might also add — a
book of extraordinary literary power.

No effort has been made in the following work to give a full
bibliography for the various subjects touched upon ; but a considerable number of those publications which for one reason or
another are most noteworthy are mentioned in their respective
places.   For the Greek text on which the Commentary is based
see p. 727.

see p. 727.

                                                    I. T. B.

CONTENTS

		PAGE
PREFACE		v
ABBREVIATIONS		xiii
INTRODUCTORY STUDIES		1
I.	THE ESCHATOLOGICAL HOPE	3
	Primitive Age	4
	Patriarchal and Pre-Monarchical Age . . .	8
	Monarchical Age	16
	Exilic and Post-Exilic Age	30
	The New Testament Era	82
II.	APOCALYPTIC LITERATURE	166
	Characteristics	169
	Occasion	175
	Jewish Apocalyptic Writings	177
III.	THE TIMES OF THE APOCALYPSE OF JOHN . . .	197
IV.	THE PURPOSE	208
V.	QUESTION OF THE UNITY	216
	Critical Analyses	224
VI.	SOME CHARACTERISTICS OF THE AUTHOR'S LITERARY MANNER	239
VII.	SUMMARY OF THE CONTENTS OF THE APOCALYPSE . .	255
VIII.	PERMANENT AND TRANSITORY ELEMENTS IN THE APOCALYPSE	291
IX.	THEOLOGY OF THE APOCALYPSE	310
X.	HISTORY OF INTERPRETATION	318
XI.	EARLY CIRCULATION AND RECOGNITION . . .	337
XII.	AUTHORSHIP	343
	The Apocalypse and the Fourth Gospel . . .	353
XIII.	THE TWO JOHNS OF THE ASIAN CHURCH . . .	362
	John the Presbyter	362
	Question of John the Apostle at Ephesus . . .	366
XIV.	THE BEAST OF THE APOCALYPSE	393
	Symbol of the Roman Emperors	394
	Symbol of Antichrist	397
	Antichrist as Nero reincarnated	400
	The Second Beast	408
XV.	THE TEXT	411
COMMENTARY		417
Criticism and Textual Notes : see end of respective divisions.		
INDEX		783

xi

ABBREVIATIONS

This list is not meant to include all the works referred to, but only to make clear references which might be obscure. Other abbreviations not given here will probably be obvious in their connections. See also p. 416.

al : others, elsewhere.

Apocalyptic writings. Ap. Abr.: Apocalypse of Abraham — Ap. Bar.: Apocalypse of Baruch (Syriac) — Asc. Is.: Ascension of Isaiah — Ass. Mos.: Assumption of Moses — En.: Enoch (Ethiopic) — 2 Es.: 2 Esdras (of the Apocrypha, commonly cited 4 Ez.) — Jub.: Book of Jubilees — Od. of Sol.: Odes of Solomon — Ps. Sol.: Psalms of Solomon — Sib. Or.: Sibylline Oracles — Sl. En.: Slavonic Enoch — Test XII Pat: Testaments of the XII. Patriarchs — Test Lev: Testament of Levi, etc. — Vit. Ad.: Life of Adam and Eve.

Baldensperger: *Messian-Apok. Hoffnung*, etc. 3d ed. 1903.

Beet: *Last Things.* 1905.

Bertholet: vol. II. of Stade's *Bib. Theol. d. A. T.* 1911.

Blass: *Gram. d. neutest. Griech.* 1896.

Blj: *Commentaar op de Openbaring.* 1908.

Bouss: Bousset, *Antichrist.* Eng. tr. 1896.
  Judenthum: Religion d. Judenthums im neutest. Zeitalt. 1903.
  Jüd. Ap.: Jüdische Apokalyptik. 1903.
  Kom: Offenbarung Johannis. 2d ed. 1906.

Box: *The Ezra Apocalypse.* 1912.

Briggs, *Mess. Ap.: Messiah of the Apostles.* 1895.
  Mess. P.: Messianic Prophecy. 1886.

Bruce, *Paul: St. Paul's Conception of Christianity.* 1894.

Brückner: *Entstehung d. paulin. Christol.* 1903.

Burton: *Moods and Tenses in N. T. Greek.* 3d ed. 1898.

Buttm.: *Gram. of N. T. Greek.* Eng. tr. 1878.

Calmes: *L'Apocalypse devant la Critique.* 1907.

CB.: Cambridge Bible for Schools and Colleges.

Charles, *Eschat.: Christian Doctrine of Future Life.* 1899.
  Studies: Studies in the Apocalypse. 1913.

Cornill: *Introd. to Canon. Books of O. T.* Eng. tr. 1907.

Dalman, *Worte: Worte Jesu.* 1898.

Davidson, *Theol.: Theology of O. T.* 1904.

Deissmann: *Licht. vom Ost.* 2d and 3d ed. 1909.

Denney, *Jesus: Jesus and the Gospels.* 1908.

Dewick, *Eschat.: Primitive Christian Eschatology.* 1912.

Driver, *Introd.: Introduction to Lit. of O. T.* 7th ed. 1898.

xiii

Dobschütz : *Eschatology of the Gospels.* Eng. tr. 1910.
Drummond : *The Jewish Messiah.* 1877.
Düst. : Düsterdieck, *Offenbar. Johan.* 1865.
Edersheim : *Life and Times of the Messiah.* 8th ed. 1898.
EGT. : Expositor's Greek Testament.
En. Bib. : Encyclopaedia Biblica. 1899–1903.
Erbes : *Offenbar. Johan. kritischuntersucht.* 1891.
EV : both AV and RV.
Ewald : *Johannes' Apokalypse.* 1862.
Feine : *Jesus Christus u. Paulus.* 1902.
            Theol. d. N. T. 1910.
GMT. : Goodwin, *Moods and Tenses of Gk. Verb.* 1890.
Gunkel : *Schöpfung u. Chaos.* 1895.
Harnack, *Alt. Lit. I. : Ueberlieferung etc.,* First part of *Altchrist. Lit.* 1893.
            Chron. : Chronologie d. altchrist. Lit. 1897.
            Dogm. : Dogmengeschichte. 1890–1894.
Hast. : Hastings, Dictionary of the Bible. 1898–1904.
Haupt, *Eschat. : Eschatolog. Aussagen Jesu.* 1895.
Hausrath : *Jesus u. d. neutest. Schriftsteller.* 1906.
Hennecke : *Neutest. Apokryphen.* 1904.
Hilgenfeld : *Jüdische Apokalyptik.* 1857.
Hirscht : *Die Apok. u. ihre neueste Kritik.* 1895.
Holtzmann, *Ein. : Einleitung in d. N. T.* 3d ed. 1892.
            Mess. : Das Messian. Bewusstsein Jesu. 1907.
            Theol. : Neutest. Theol. 2d ed. 1911.
Holtzm-Bau. : Holtzmann-Bauer, *Offenbar. Johan.* 1908.
Hühn : *Messian. Weissagungen.* 1899.
ICC. : Internat. Crit. Commentary.
Jeremias : *Babylonisches im N. T.* 1905.
Jew. En. : Jewish Encyclopedia. 1901–1906.
Jülicher, *Ein. : Einleitung in d. N. T.* 6th ed. 1906.
Kabisch : *Eschatol. d. Paulus.* 1893.
Kautzsch : *Apokryphen u. Pseudepigraph. d. Alt. Test.* vol. II. 1900.
Kennedy : *St. Paul's Conception of the Last Things.* 1904.
Kühn : Kühner, *Ausführ. Gram. d. Griech. Sprache.* 3d ed. 1890–1904.
Lepin : *Jésus Messie et Fils,* etc. 3d ed. 1907.
Lietzmann : *Der Menschensohn.* 1896.
L & S. : Liddell and Scott, *Greek Lexicon.* 1883.
loc. cit. : the passage cited.
Lücke : *Einleitung in d. Offenbar. d. Johan.* 2d ed. 1852.
Mathews : *Messian. Hope in the N. T.* 1905.
Moff, *Introd. :* Moffatt, *Introduction to Lit. of N. T.* 1911.
            Rev. : Revelation, in EGT. 1910.
Muirhead : *Eschatology of Jesus.* 1904.
op. cit. : the work cited.
Orelli : *O. T. Prophecy.* Eng. tr. 1885.
Ottley : *Aspects of the O. T.* 1898.

par. : parallel passages in the Synoptic Gospels.
Peters : *The Religion of the Hebrews.* 1914.
Pfleiderer : *Das Urchristenthum.* 2d ed. 1902.
Preuschen : *Griech-Deutsch. Handwörtebuch zum N. T.* 1910.
Rauch : *Offenbar. d. Johan. untersucht,* etc. 1894.
Riehm : *Messian. Weissagung.* 2d ed. 1885.
Sabatier : *Les Origines Littéraires et la Comp. de l'Apoc.* 1888.
Salmond : *Christian Doctrine of Immortality.* 3d ed. 1897.
Schoen : *L'Origine de l'Apocalypse.* 1887.
Schürer : *Geschichte d. jüdisch. Volkes im Zeitalt. Jesu Christi.* 4th ed. 1909.
Schultz : *Alttest. Theol.* 5th ed. 1896.
Schwally : *Leben nach d. Tode.* 1892.
Schweitzer, QHG. : *Quest of Historic Jesus.* 1910 ; tr. of *von Reimarus zu Wrede.*
Smend : *Alttest. Religionsgeschichte.* 2d ed. 1899.
Smith, W. R., *Prophets : The Prophets of Israel.* 1882.
Spitta : *Offenbar. Johan. untersucht.* 1889.
Stade : *Bib. Theol. d. A. T.,* vol. I. 1905. For vol. II. see Bertholet.
Stanton : *Jewish and Christian Messiah.* 1886.
Stuart : *Commentary on the Apocalypse.* 1845.
Thayer : *Gk-Eng. Lexicon of N. T.* 1887.
Titius : *Neutest. Lehre von d. Seligkeit.* 1895–1900.
Vischer : *Die Offenbar. Johan. eine jüdisch. Apok.* 1886.
Völter : *Offenbar. Johan.* 2d ed. 1911.
    Das Problem d. Apokalypse. 1893.
Volz : *Jüdische Eschatologie.* 1903.
Weber, *System : System d. altsynagogal. palästin. Theol.* 1880.
Weiss, B., *Theol. : Bib. Theol. d. N. T.* 7th ed. 1903.
Weiss, J. : *Offenbar. Johan.* 1904.
    Paul and Jesus. Eng. tr. 1909.
    Predigt Jesu vom Reiche Gottes. 2d ed. 1900.
Wellhausen, *An. : Analyse d. Offenbar.* 1907.
    Ein. : Einleitung in d. drei erst. Evangelien. 1905.
Wendt : *Teaching of Jesus.* Eng. tr. 1897.
Wernle, *Reich. : Reichsgotteshoffnung,* etc. 1903.
Westcott : *General Survey of Hist. of Canon of N. T.* 1896.
    Introduction to Study of the Gospels. 1896.
Weyland : Omwerkings-en Compilatie-Hypothesen toegepast op de Apok. 1888.
WH, *Introd. :* Westcott and Hort, *Introd. and Appendix ;* the second part of their Greek Test.
Win : Winer, Gram. of N. T. Eng. tr. 1870.
Wrede : *Paulus.* 2d ed. 1907.
Zahn, *Ein. : Einleitung in d. N. T.* 3d ed. 1907.
    Forsch. : Forschungen zur Geschichte d. Neustest. Kanons.
    GK. : Geschichte d. Kanons. 1888–1890.
    Grundriss : Grundriss d. GK. 1901.

INTRODUCTORY STUDIES

ONE who would seek to help students of the New Testament to an understanding of the Revelation of John [1] cannot fail to be aware of the difficulty of the task. It is doubtless true that no other book, whether in sacred or profane literature, has received in whole or in part so many different interpretations. Doubtless no other book has so perplexed biblical students throughout the Christian centuries down to our own time. Its imagery and symbolism are often strange; its different parts seem to lack coherence, their significance in themselves and in their relation to one another or to a common plan is often obscure; the scenes unfolded in its visions might, if taken quite by themselves, be understood to symbolize a great variety of events or personages in the history of the nations or the Church, they might be referred to things past, things now taking place, or things yet to come. Visions like allegories lend themselves easily to very varied application. It is not surprising then that most divergent and extravagant interpretations of parts of the book have been offered with confidence and urged with a certain measure of plausibility. [2] And so in all these divergences and uncertainties it has come about that readers of the New Testament have often despaired of seizing the meaning intended. The devout reader has never failed to place among the most cherished parts of his Bible such passages as the vision of the Celestial City (chaps. 21–22), the vision of the innumerable multitude of the redeemed with God and the Lamb (chapt. 7), and the like, while yet the Revelation as a whole has seemed to remain for him a sealed book. Notwithstanding all this it may, however, be said that through the methods of biblical research

[1] On the title, see p. 417.   [2] For different modes of interpretation, see pp. 318 ff.

followed in more recent times results have been reached which, though they do not solve all the perplexing problems of the book, do nevertheless give a good measure of certainty regarding its meaning and structure in the main.   Not only is the day of fanciful interpretation past, the book is no longer an enigma.   Much as scholars may differ regarding many interesting questions pertaining to it, yet these questions do not profoundly affect the view to be taken of its fundamental scope and contents.   Whether certain portions have been incorporated from other apocalypses, whether these are of Jewish or Christian origin, whether an earlier or later date be assigned to the book, whether the author was St. John the Apostle or another John, these and similar questions may be differently answered by different scholars without materially changing our view of the great aim of the book, or even of the general features of its plan in the form in which it was received into the Sacred Canon and has been handed down to us.   Regarding its essential characteristics something approaching unanimity may be said to have been reached among the larger number of scientific interpreters.   This gain in the interpretation of the book has been won chiefly through a better apprehension of the history of its leading thoughts in the ages preceding its appearance, through a fuller study of the large class of apocalyptic literature to which it belongs in manner and form, through the critical study of sources, taking the word 'source' in a comprehensive sense, and through a clearer understanding of the nature and scope of prophecy.   This advance is a conspicuous result of applying to biblical study the historical method.   By the historical method of studying any ancient writing we mean the endeavor to realize as fully as possible the historic past out of which the work sprang.   This includes not only the circumstances which called forth the writing and its meaning for its time, but also the forces which entered into its production — the writer's characteristics and heritage, the history of his conceptions, his obligations to his predecessors, his use of traditional types and forms, in fact whatever went to make up the man as he wrote and whatever shaped the contents and form of his writing. That such a method is equally applicable to those books in which divine inspiration is a constitutive factor is unquestionable, inasmuch as the divinely illumined writer must receive his message, not magically, but through concepts which belong to his own modes of thought, and must impart it in familiar human forms. We may confidently believe that such a study is one of the ways through which the Divine Spirit, promised as a guide in truth, is ever leading the Church on to a better understanding of the word of God. If, then, we would undertake the study of the Revelation of John with the hope of reaching an interpretation in keeping with the procedure and results of sober-minded biblical research, avoiding arbitrary hypotheses, we must approach the work through certain preliminary studies. In the brief space of an Introduction the topics here referred to cannot be treated with fullness, but it is hoped that such a survey may be taken as will furnish what is requisite for entering on an intelligent prosecution of our task.

I. THE ESCHATOLOGICAL HOPE

As the central topic of the Apocalypse is the consummation of the hope of God's people we naturally begin our study with a survey, as brief as practicable, of that hope from its first recorded expression on through the ages with its changes in character and form down to its culmination in the teaching of our Lord and his Apostles and its most elaborate exhibition in this book of the Apocalypse. What we are here concerned with relates to the things of the Last Days, the final state to which the children of God, whether the individual or the people as a whole, have from age to age looked forward. In speaking of this as the *eschatological* hope, we use the term 'eschatology' in a broad sense denoting the doctrine of the Last Days in whatever form they were in any particular age conceived. While the word is sometimes taken in a limited sense in relation only to the people of God, or the nations of the world, as an organic whole and not with reference to the individual except as a part of that whole,[1] yet in its broader use it denotes the *doctrine of the End, whether the aspect be individual or general, national or universal, earthly or heavenly.*[2] When this expectation is spoken of as *messianic*, the term being taken as

---

[1] So Volz 1. [2] Cf. Davidson *Theol.* 401.

practically synonymous with *eschatological*, it must be kept in
mind that reference is not always made to the presence of the
personal Messiah, but to that final state of glory, the fully
established Kingdom of God, whether earthly or heavenly,
which forms the object of hope at the particular time under
consideration.   There are times when the figure of a personal
Messiah is wanting, or at least inconspicuous, in the anticipations of the coming kingdom.[1]   But since such anticipations
find their consummation only in the days of the Messiah, they
may be regarded appropriately as a part of the messianic hope.[2]
In tracing the growth of the eschatological hope among the
Hebrews we cannot always fix in the minuter details the characteristics of a particular age, nor the precise date at which
different phases appear or disappear, because there is often
uncertainty concerning the exact age of the historical documents, because also some of these documents contain portions
inserted at a later time and some retain traditional elements
which may be intended as figurative rather than literal.[3]   But
taking Hebrew history in its larger divisions, we may be reasonably certain regarding the nature of the eschatological expectations in the respective periods and can generally perceive the
influences which have caused the changes in the transition from
one period to another.

1. *The Primitive Age.*   In the first period of biblical history,
that contained in the first eleven chapters of the book of Genesis, we have a legendary story of a primitive age before the
separation of mankind into the tribes that formed the nations
of the earth.   As an introduction to his history of the Hebrew
people the author has here brought together a group of narratives (from what source derived, we need not here inquire)
relating to the earlier ages of the world and man, for the purpose of setting forth certain fundamental truths of religion.
And in this story of primitive humanity there are contained
two striking religious promises.   The *first* occurs in the tragedy
of Eden in the words addressed to the Serpent, 'I will put
enmity between thee and the woman, and between thy seed
and her seed; he shall bruise thy head and thou shalt bruise

---

[1] See p. 40.   [2] Cf. Stade 213.   [3] Cf. Volz 1.

his heel.'[1] The doom here uttered announces the bitter conflict to be waged through all time between the race of men and the race of the Serpent, the ever-continuing, agonizing struggle of humanity against the power of evil. At the same time there is *implied*, though not directly declared, the hope of victory for man. The evil power in the narrative, the Serpent, is the chief offender; it is upon him that the sentence falls first, and in a struggle with him ordered by God he cannot be the victor. As he grovels in the dust his head is to be crushed beneath the heel of man, who though in bitter pain does not succumb to his foe.[2] At the very threshold of his history and in the immeasurable calamity of his failure as described by the Hebrew writer, a vision of future blessing is opened to man. 'Henceforth man's gaze is no longer turned backwards in longing after a lost Paradise, but is directed hopefully to the future.'[3] The absence of all particularistic or Hebraic coloring in this narrative seems to mark it as prehistoric in its essential religious features, that is, as preserving evidence of a religious hope existing in the race out of which the Hebrews sprang. In tracing the external features of the story to an early legend we do not, it must be observed, change the religious character of the narrative. The history of man's *moral* struggle and failure does not thereby lose any of its reality and truthfulness. Rightly has this passage been called the *Protevangelium, First Gospel*, for it contains the first promise of ultimate triumph in the conflict with evil. For the same reason it may be called *messianic*, though it is doubtful whether there is any direct reference to a personal Messiah. The term 'seed of the woman' is quite general in the narrative — there is nothing to indicate a limitation. All mankind is the seed of the Mother of man.[4] And as the conflict announced is for universal humanity, so is the promise. 'The verse must not be interpreted so as to exclude those minor, though in their own sphere not less real, triumphs by which in all ages individuals have resisted the suggestions of sin and proved themselves superior to the power of evil.'[5] It is true that the promise is fully realized only in that One of the seed of the woman, who brought to nought

---

[1] 3[15]. [2] Cf. Dillmann *Kom.*, Driver *Gen. ad loc.* [3] Orelli 90.
[4] Schultz 567. [5] Driver *Gen.* 57.

him that had the power of death.[1]   The prophecy then is messianic like many others, in that it anticipates an ideal which
can be completely reached only in the Messiah and the conditions of the messianic era.

The serpent in the narrative is not the Satan of the later Scriptures.
The identification of the two belongs to a later period in Hebrew thought.
He is a demon in animal form.   Legends of demoniac animals, especially
serpents, are found elsewhere in Semitic traditions (cf. Stade *Geschichte d.
Volkes Israel* 160; Marti *Religion d. Alt. Test.* 18).   Such a legend our writer
has made use of in the story of the Fall.   The mythological serpent furnishes him a symbol of the power seducing man to evil (cf. Schultz 515).
These narratives of the 'origins' are in the form of myths current for centuries among various branches of the Semitic race.   They relate to a period
immeasurably remote from any historical record; they contain many elements which cannot be taken as actual history.   But the great truths contained in them touching God and the spiritual life of man are clear.   With
an insight, possible in that age only through divine illumination, the writer
seizes fundamental truths of religion, and taking up current narratives in a
purified form uses them as vehicles for his God-given message.   And nothing
reveals the influence of a divine inspiration more strikingly than the fact
that these narratives, when compared with the forms preserved among other
branches of the race, are seen to be so wonderfully purged of all irreligious
and immoral elements.   Such narratives then fall into the same category
as parables, allegories, figures, etc.; they are the *forms* only — the substance
is the revealed truth enshrined within them (cf. Ottley 57, Peters 183 f.).

A *second* promise belonging to this period, and opening another aspect of religious hope, is recorded in Gen. 9[25 ff.].   In the
sequel to the story of the flood, in that new beginning of human
history, Noah, the second progenitor of the race, forecasts in
poetic form the characteristics and destinies of his three sons'
descendants, the three great branches of the human family as
known to the Hebrew writers.   Here as elsewhere,[2] by what
has been called the *prophetical interpretation of history*, the destiny of a people is conceived to be determined by a blessing or
a curse pronounced upon an ancestor.   While a curse falls upon
the race of Ham and wide dominion on the earth is given to
that of Japheth, the blessing of Shem is centered in his relation
to God.   'Blessed be Jehovah, the God of Shem.'   Shem's
blessing is expressed in an outburst of praise to him who is the
author of the blessing.   The good to come to him is not speci-

[1] Heb. 2[14].   [2] Cf. the 'blessing' of Jacob, Gen. 49; that of Moses, Dt. 32.

fied — it is enough that Jehovah is his God. His blessing consists fundamentally in that peculiar relation to God ·which is not the portion of his brothers. We have not here a duplicate of the promise to Abraham, but rather one of the steps preparatory to the latter. No covenant is formed with Shem as with Abraham; there is no institution of a new national unit, no promise to Shem's seed as such, but the assurance of a special blessing to his family because they know Jehovah and have him for their God.

It is not unlikely that the precise *form* of the oracle given in this passage is influenced by the history of the Hebrews, the descendants of Shem, and reflects their consciousness of their peculiar character as the people of God. This passage, as well as that containing the final promise spoken of above, belongs to a document (J) which the author of Genesis has incorporated into his book and which doubtless dates at the earliest from a time succeeding the establishment of the Hebrew monarchy (cf. Driver *Introd.* 123, Cornill 76). Yet it is difficult to avoid the conviction that we have here a tradition belonging to a time prior to the appearance of the Hebrews in history as a people. This same document (J), in giving the story of the foundation through Abraham of a nation which should be God's peculiar people, does not *emphasize* Abraham's descent from Shem; and since Shem's descendants included many other peoples besides the Hebrews, that is, since the larger part of Shem's descendants were not among the chosen people, this prophecy regarding his race is more likely to have given perplexity to a writer of this later age, than to have originated with him. For him the beginnings of the chosen people are with Abraham. The prophecy appears to express one of the religious hopes of a race, the prehistoric ancestors of the Hebrews, which was endowed with remarkable religious apprehension and aspiration. In fact the religious conceptions of the Hebrews in historic times imply a period of prehistoric revelation from which they started and through which they reached a stage so advanced.

Such are the two hopes of this primitive period — the one altogether ideal, touching man universally, the other limited to a tribe, but beginning that course of development, through a process of selection, in which the ideal is ultimately to reach its realization. With profound insight into the divine character the writer who gathered up these traditions saw expressed here the hope of a closer relation with God in spite of the entrance of sin — a relation grounded not merely in descent but in the moral attitude of man. The blessing is, however, not thought of as independent of the family or tribe; so indi-

vidualistic a conception was impossible in that stage of society.
The special relation to God is moral but it is realized only
through membership in the family whose God is Jehovah. We
might sum up the two hopes in one, as *an aspiration toward
the sublime ideal of victory over evil, realizing itself, not in isola-
tion and individually, but in the corporate body of a family who
know and recognize God.* It was this that gave vitality and
direction to all subsequent eschatological expectation among
the Hebrews. The prophecies of a primitive revelation taken
up by them in prehistoric time gave them an outlook which
appears among almost no other people of the ancient world.
The Hebrews were almost alone among the nations in putting
their Golden Age in the future rather than in the past, though
they often, as will appear farther on, conceived that future
under earthly and temporal aspects. It is interesting to notice
that each of the promises of which we have been speaking came
to man after a failure involving the race in disaster. The Fall
in Eden at the outset, and the all-but universal wickedness that
brought on the visitation of the Flood, might have shut every
door of hope. Nothing is more characteristic of the conceptions of the Hebrew religion than this clear apprehension of
God's dealing with his children. To them that sit in the
region and shadow of death light springs up. And so through
the later history the most striking outbursts of eschatological
hope, as expressed in the prophets and in the apocalyptic
writings,[1] appear in times of national calamity.

2. *The Patriarchal and pre-Monarchical Age.* In turning
from the earlier chapters of Genesis (1–11) to the later narratives, we pass from the legendary age of the human family to
the beginnings of a historic people — the one people chosen out
of the tribes of the ancient world to be the recipient of God's
special revelation and the medium of religious knowledge to
men. The transition is too great to be readily measured in
time, but it is rapid, abrupt even, as regards the religious
aspect given in the biblical record. This is not strange, because the writer views the legendary age in the light of an
inspired perception of God's purposes from the beginning, and

---

[1] On the Apocalyptic writings see p. 166.

he sees in the early Hebrew history the immediate steps in the development of these purposes.   In our present inquiry it will suffice to take this history from its beginning to the age immediately preceding the establishment of the monarchy in the person of Saul, as constituting a single period.   For in this period the idea of a chosen people, a Kingdom of God on earth, first arises and reaches a certain definite stage in its realization. The migration of a Semitic clan from the far east into Canaan, of which the record is given in the story of Abraham, was a movement begun and carried on in the consciousness of a religious vocation.   The great leader, following what he recognized as a divine summons, led his tribe out of heathen surroundings, 'not knowing whither he went,' [1] and guided by Providence came into that land where he remained to the end a sojourner, a nomad dwelling in tents with the heirs of the promise.   But in that long trial of his faith, wonderfully endured, God, according to the narrative as given in Genesis, opened to him a vision such as has never come to another, save that given to the Son of Man in the face of his messianic work, though Abraham himself may have fallen short of its full meaning and scope.   Even if it could be shown that the patriarchs were not actual personalities, even if in the narratives concerning them we have *tribal* life given under the form of personal histories, yet the essential truth contained in our record remains the same.   The Hebrew clan, as guided by its leaders, became conscious of a special religious character and cherished these visions, dim though they may have been, of its destinies.   The promises given to Abraham, the mission committed to him, were repeated and made more definite from time to time — they were renewed to Isaac and Jacob. [2]   The process of selection, begun in Abraham, continues in the next succeeding generations, in keeping with the law of God's providence by which the fittest agent is chosen for working out a given end. [3]   Isaac is chosen, not Ishmael; Jacob, not Esau.   Israel's race thus chosen out of the tribes of men was to form the people with whom God enters into a solemn covenant; it was

---

[1] Heb. 11[8].   [2] Gen. 12[2 f., 7], 13[15 f.], 15[5], 17[1 ff.], 22[16 ff.], 26[3 f.], 28[13 ff.].
[3] Cf. Ro. 9[11] ἡ κατ' ἐκλογὴν πρόθεσις τοῦ θεοῦ, 'The divine purpose which has worked on the principle of selection,' Sanday and Headlam, *ad loc.*

to be his people and he was to be their God; it was to continue through the ages, spreading over a wide earthly domain, unnumbered in multitude, and bearing within itself blessings which all the nations of the earth should desire.

In the position and outlook of the Hebrew people as thus determined there are given at least *four* elements which are characteristic of the eschatological expectation of this period. (1) The race was to form a *nation*, a unit among the peoples, having its separate, organic, national life. The consciousness of its national character, however dim in the nomadic life of the patriarchal age, became clear through the influence of later experiences. The sufferings of common hardships in Egypt, the common trials of the exodus and the wanderings in the wilderness, the long struggle against common enemies in the conquest of Canaan, the possession of a common religious and moral law intensified the sense of unity as well as of separateness from other peoples. In spite of the jealousies and divisions that appeared among the tribes the sense of a common nationality was not lost in Israel, nor was there any widespread tendency to merge its identity in the races of kindred blood with which it was in near contact.   (2) The Hebrew nation was to possess a *land*. At first a tribe of wanderers in a land 'not its own,' it looked forward to a permanent settlement within a territory geographically defined and ultimately to become as wide in its boundaries as its people were to be numerous. To the seed which was to be as the stars in multitude was promised the land 'from the river of Egypt unto the great river, the river Euphrates.' [1] It was not until centuries after Abraham that the realization of this promise first began in the conquest of Canaan, and still several centuries later under David and Solomon that its virtual fulfillment was reached. The literal language of the promise (which belongs to the document J) was probably suggested by the actual extent of the kingdom at the time of its greatest expansion. But under this form is recorded the outlook given to the patriarchs and their descendants answering to their consciousness of their divine vocation. The possession of a large country was inseparable from their sense of their calling to become a great nation. But the

[1] Gen. 15¹⁸.

prophecies of Israel's dominion which are found in this period, though colored by the hopes of a later time, do not yet 'promise an extension which is universal. The language of the ' Blessing ' of Jacob, 'unto him shall the obedience of the peoples be,[1] contemplates not all nations, but those with which Israel comes in contact, those in or near Canaan, as is shown by the limited scope of the whole ' Blessing.' Even the far-reaching outlook pictured in Balaam's predictions[2] promises only victory over enemies and the conquest of neighboring nations. The prophetic vision is still limited in space as it is in time.[3]   (3) Over this nation and this realm the sovereign *ruler* was God. The polity was what, since Josephus[4] applied the word thus, has been called a theocracy. Other Semitic peoples also viewed their tribal god as their king.[5] And our records of the theocratic conceptions of the Hebrews in the age which we are considering doubtless reflect later ideals. Yet it seems clear that from very early times Hebrew national life was dominated to a degree not found elsewhere by a sense of the ruling presence of God. The evidence of this is seen not in isolated, occasional utterances, but in every movement, in every phase, of their history. The patriarchs, the leaders, the judges are only organs or agents of God. They act in a sense of his immediate direction.[6] The Mosaic legislation — and by this we mean those fundamental religious, moral, and civil laws which can be referred to the great Lawgiver, as contrasted with the later elaborate system which we may call Mosaic because it is an outgrowth of the law of Moses — may be said to have given the Hebrew people its organic existence as a nation; but everywhere the Law is regarded not as that of Moses, but of God. It is Jehovah's voice which is everywhere conceived to be speaking — the words are his words, his finger engraves them on the tables of stone ; Moses is but his prophet. Before the institution of the monarchy there existed in the Mosaic state no established officer or executive whose function it was *in virtue of his office* to act as the organ of God's rule. In great crises God raised up leaders and deliverers, — Moses, Joshua, the Judges, who were recognized as his immediate and special

---

[1] Gen. 49[10].   [2] Num. 23 f.   [3] Cf. pp. 301 ff.   [4] *c. Ap.* II. 16.
[5] Cf. **W. R. Smith**, *Prophets* 50.   [6] Cf. Riehm 66.

agents for meeting extraordinary needs. In its ordinary course
the foundations of national life, social and civic, as well as
religious, rested upon the recognized rule of the God of the
Covenant and the God-given law.[1] The recognition of God's
kingship carried with it a sense of his abiding presence with
his people — not only in oracles and visions, in sacred rites, in
the glory that filled the sanctuary, and in all the varied the-
ophanies recorded in their story, but especially in his living
word, which in the language of the later Deuteronomic writer
was not in heaven nor beyond the sea but in the mouth and
in the heart.[2] Moses was to the people to Godward and he
brought their causes to God.[3] We even find the direction to
'bring unto God' or to 'come near unto God' in special cases
where a witness or judge is sought.[4]   (4) The Hebrews
unlike other peoples of antiquity were conscious of a *divine
mission.* God had given them a knowledge of truth which was
to shine forth from them to lighten the world. While the consciousness of this sublime calling is clear in later times in the
writings of the prophets, it is true that in the age with which
we are here concerned its presence is seen but dimly; perhaps
it is nowhere directly expressed with certainty. Obviously
until the conception of Jehovah as merely the *tribal* god was
outgrown, until the uniqueness of Israel was fully apprehended
in the light of the uniqueness of Israel's God, the sense of such
a mission could not be pervadingly vivid. Yet it could hardly
fail to be present as an inspiring hope in the great religious
leaders when they began to perceive that Jehovah was higher
than all gods, and that he was a God of mercy and goodness
towards his people. It may be questioned how far absolute
monotheism was apprehended in this age. But what is sometimes called *practical monotheism* is contained in the beliefs of
Israel from an early time and is expressed in forms which do
not appear to be due to a late age. To the Hebrew, Jehovah
was not only the God before whom he himself had none other,
but he was the one God whom he recognized as mighty beyond
the boundaries of his own people, as mightier than all the gods

---

[1] Cf. Riehm 76.   [2] Dt. 30[12 ff.].   [3] Ex. 18[19].
[4] Ex. 21[6], 22[8], 1 Sam. 2[25]. See R.V. Most recent scholars are agreed in
translating Elohim here 'God,' not 'Judge,' as in A.V.

of the nations, as the creator of heaven and earth, the sea and
all that in them is.[1] Israel's history revealed the supremacy
of Jehovah.   The God who delivered into the hands of the
Patriarch the allied forces of Elam, overthrew the heathen
cities, Sodom and Gomorrah, sent signs and wonders into
Egypt, smote great nations and all the kingdoms of Canaan,
and gave their land for an heritage unto Israel, was for the
Hebrew a Lord above all gods.   The very covenant relation
between God and Israel, in which all the religious ideas of the
Hebrews centered, implied the isolated supremacy of Jehovah.
Of his own good pleasure he had chosen out of all the tribes
that one whom he would.[2] 'A God whose almighty rule is not
limited to that land and people in whose midst he is worshiped
is no mere national god.'[3] Almost certainly then we might
expect to find in the inspired leaders of Israel, in those who
caught a clearer vision of God and his purposes, some perception of blessings to flow out to the nations — an ideal, seized
vaguely perhaps, yet destined to become fruitful even in the
thought of that age.   Many find this doctrine of Israel's mission expressed in the words, 'Ye shall be unto me a kingdom
of priests.'[4] Israel is thought to be described here as mediating between God and the other nations, it being the function
of the priest to mediate between God and another.   It is questionable, however, whether such a thought is contained in the
words.   The aim of the passage is to describe, not Israel's
function, but its privilege as the reward of obedience, its relation to God, not to man; it shall form a kingdom whose citizens are all priests, *i.e.* are wholly consecrated to God's service
and have immediate access to him.[5] But it can hardly be
doubted that this lofty ideal is contained in the promise to
Abraham, translated in our Versions, 'In thee shall all the
families of the earth be blessed.'[6] If this is the exact meaning
of the words, we have here an explicit declaration of the doctrine afterwards fully expressed in the prophets that Israel
should become the medium of messianic blessings to the Gentiles.[7] The language of the promise should, however, in the

---

[1] Ex. 20[11].   [2] Ex. 19[5].   [3] Schultz 125.   [4] Ex. 19[6].
[5] Cf. Heb. 10[19 ff.]   See among others Knobel, Dillmann, Baentsch in Nowack's
Handkom, on Ex. 19[6]. On *kingdom* see Com. 1[6].   [6] Gen. 12[3].
[7] Cf. Is. 2[2 ff.], Zec. 8[23].

opinion of most recent scholars be rendered 'bless themselves
in thee,' *i.e.* in thy name.[1]   The nations in wishing for blessings upon themselves would wish for those possessed by
Abraham and his seed in whom they see true blessedness.
' Wherever among the nations a blessing should be uttered or
a blessing received, there would Abraham and his descendants
be made mention of as the highest type of divine blessing.'[2]
Whichever interpretation is adopted, the bearing of the passage upon Israel's mission to the Gentiles is essentially the
same.   Through the divine favor bestowed upon his people
Jehovah was to become known to the nations and the blessedness which he alone could give was to be desired by them.

The fact that in what is probably the correct interpretation of our
passage the thought is implied rather than expressed — is given in germ
only and not in clearly developed form — indicates the more certainly that
we have here an early conception rather than a reflection thrown back from
a later time.   Elements which really belong to a later period, *e.g.* the royal
glory of Judah anticipated by several centuries in the 'Blessing' of Jacob
(Gen. 49[8 ff.]) or the triumph of the king of Israel, celebrated by Balaam
(Num. 24[7]), many generations before the anointing of Saul, reveal themselves distinctly as descriptions of facts given in experience rather than as
prophecy (cf. Schultz 563, Ottley 297).   It is further to be noted that the
passages which contain the intimation here spoken of, Gen. 12[3], 18[18], 22[18],
26[4], 28[14], all belong to J, a document antedating the time of those prophets
in which this function of Israel is first distinctly expressed; cf. Driver
Introd. 15 f., 123.

While the prophecies of this period, read in the light of subsequent history, can be seen to imply in their ultimate, ideal significance the messianic
age and the Messiah, and so in this sense may be classed as messianic prophecy, there is as yet no certain reference directly to a personal Messiah.   The
obscure utterance, translated in A.V. and the text of R.V. 'till Shiloh come'
(Gen. 49[10]), has been taken by very many to point to Christ.   Scholars
differ greatly in regard to the exact meaning of the phrase, but most are
agreed that Shiloh cannot be a proper name or recognized title designating

---

[1] The promise, with slight variations in form but the same in sense, is given
in Gen. 12[3], 18[18], 22[18], 26[4], 28[14] — thrice to Abraham, and confirmed to Isaac
and Jacob.   In the first, second, and fifth places the verb is in the conjugation
Niphal and is therefore ambiguous, *i.e.* it may be reflexive ('bless themselves')
or passive ('be blessed').   In the other two cases it is in the Hithpael and is
necessarily reflexive.   The certain passages would seem to determine the sense
of the uncertain.   Hence most recent interpreters translate 'bless themselves.'
Cf. among others Dillmann, Driver, Knobel *in loc.*, Riehm 71 f. ; Schultz 570 f. ;
Briggs *Mess. P.* 89 f.

[2] Schultz 570 f.   For a similar idea cf. Gen. 48[20], 'In thee will Israel bless,
saying, God make thee as Ephraim and as Manasseh.'

the Messiah. (Cf. Driver *Gen.* 410 ff., Dillmann *ad loc.*, Briggs 95 ff., Schultz 564 ff., Westcott *Intr.* 111, Hast. IV. 500, and Cheyne in En. Bib. IV. 4469 ff.). The words of Moses, ' God will raise up unto thee a prophet like unto me ' (Dt. 18[15]), though subsequently seen to reach their ideal fulfillment in Christ (cf. Ac. 3[22]), refer *primarily* not to a particular person but to any one of a succession of prophets who should arise to meet permanently the need of the people. Israel is forbidden to resort to the heathen practices of augury and divination — a revelation is to be given to them through prophets who shall be raised up for them from time to time according to their needs. (Cf. Driver in ICC., Bertholet in Marti's *Kom. ad loc.*, Schultz 626, Ottley 299.) So also Balaam's prediction, ' There shall come forth a star out of Jacob ' (Num. 24[17]), though often understood of the Messiah, refers as the context shows to the victorious sway of Israel and its triumph over the Moabites and Edomites (cf. Gray in ICC., Knobel, Dillmann, Baentsch in Nowack's *Kom. ad loc.*).

It is evident now that among these characteristics of the life and hope of Israel in the age which we have been considering, the central one, that which conditions and gives significance to the rest, is the idea of a theocratic people, a kingdom of which God is the sovereign and in which the citizens are in covenant relation with him. God reigns over a people whom he has made his own and bound to himself in a covenant of obedience and blessing. There emerges thus in this period the idea of a *Kingdom of God* — an idea which in one form or another has ever since contained the most essential element in eschatological expectation. The eschatological hope of this period might then be defined as an *anticipation of a theocratic kingdom to be realized within national (Hebrew) and territorial (Palestinian) limits, but containing within it a blessedness which other peoples should recognize and desire.*

It should be noticed that the future to which Israel looks forward for the fulfillment of this hope is not thought of as indefinitely remote. There is nothing in the narrative to indicate that Abraham in founding the new race looked beyond the earlier generations for the full possession of the promised land and the other covenant blessings. For Jacob, predicting the destinies of his descendants in the ' latter days,' lit. ' the end of the days,' [1] that ' last time ' is not projected into a future beyond the era which is to follow upon the deliverance from Egypt and the establishment in Canaan. ' The horizon bound-

[1] Gen. 49[1].

ing his field of vision lies where, according to the promises given him, his posterity has grown into tribes and taken up its abode in the promised land.' [1] Even Moses, who gave to the kingdom its organic form and fundamental law, can hardly have looked to a far-off age for its consummation. To him, too, the complete establishment of the people with its civil and religious ordinances in their destined home, constitutes the ' end of the days,' the final, unending era. The ordinances of his law are not characterized as imperfect, temporary, typical of or preparatory to, something better. His utterances do not reveal a consciousness that this form of the kingdom was merely provisional and not final. But these limitations in the outlook of Israel's forefathers do not destroy the reality, or diminish the value, of the revelation attributed to this age. The prophecies given contained only the germ of the great truths which unfolded themselves slowly through the future and which are to reach fruition only in the consummation of the Messiah's kingdom. As in all prophecy, the abiding truth is necessarily given in local and temporal forms.[2]

3. *The Monarchical Age.* By this designation is intended the period from the institution of the monarchy down to the Babylonian captivity. In the preceding paragraph we have reviewed the leading eschatological ideas in what may be called the *formative* period of Hebrew history. The patriarchal age, the sojourn in Egypt, the years in the wilderness with the revelation at Sinai, the conquest of Canaan, and the anarchic centuries of the Judges contributed each its own factor to the preparation for the most splendid era that followed in the monarchy. After the imperfect and disappointing beginnings of the monarchy in the reign of Saul, the Hebrew kingdom under David and Solomon rose rapidly to the height of its glory and new elements entered into its eschatological hopes. In this brief period the kingdom may be said to have taken a place among the great world-powers. The condition of the neighboring nations favored its expansion, it became a military power, and its domain is said, in tradition probably not greatly exaggerated, to have reached from Egypt to the Euphrates, and to the Orontes on the north. Internally the tribes of

[1] Orelli 116.　　　　[2] See pp. 293, 301.

Israel were now welded together into at least organic unity, industry and an extensive commerce brought in great wealth, a central capital strongly fortified and splendidly adorned was established at Jerusalem, and through the building of the temple with a magnificence befitting the sole sanctuary of Jehovah and the ordering of the worship with a pure and elaborate ceremonial the political capital became also the religious center for all Israel. Zion became the home of the ark, the dwelling-place of the Most High. It was David who had raised the tribe of Judah, hitherto inconspicuous, to the headship of Israel, who had formed a great kingdom, founded an ideal capital, and had made it the shrine of the national religion by bringing up into it the ark of God. He, the warrior, the conqueror, the friend of his people, the king in whom in spite of grievous failures there were traits of the saint, more nearly than any other in Hebrew history approached the ideal ruler of God's people, and after a long reign he left the throne to his dynasty, which held it in unbroken succession more than four centuries, that is, till the overthrow of the kingdom by the Babylonians. Naturally the uniqueness of the Davidic house and of the tribe of Judah gave them a unique position in the political and religious conceptions of the Hebrew people. And this position was not *permanently* changed by the disruption in the second generation after David which resulted in the existence of two kingdoms, the northern and the southern — Israel and Judah. While the northern kingdom did not recognize the supremacy of the house of David, it does not appear to have claimed the leadership of the whole nation in either political or religious concerns. It was stronger and richer than the southern kingdom, at times it was zealous for the religion of Jehovah; in it were contained elements which contributed to the development of the national faith — in it first arose the great order of the prophets, to it belonged the labors of Elijah, Elisha, Hosea, and Amos. But on the other hand its government was throughout unstable, rebellion with change of dynasty was frequent, no one city remained continuously the seat of rule, there existed no central sanctuary, and when the kingdom was overthrown by the Assyrians and the people deported, it ceased forever to be a factor in the national or religious life of

c

the Hebrews.   The captives became merged with their heathen
captors and were as a body lost to the people of Israel.   In
striking contrast the people of the kingdom of Judah which
survived a century and a half longer, the scene of the labors of
a series of great prophets, passed through the furnace of the
Babylonian captivity purified, holding to their religion and
national hopes, prepared to return to their land with religious
conceptions fraught with momentous consequences for all time.
Hebrew history henceforth is the history of the Judæans.   The
eschatological hopes center in Judah and the house of David —
it is here that the religious development, the future of the
kingdom of God, lies.

The division of Israel into two kingdoms could not even in the northern
kingdom entirely stifle the consciousness of a unity resting in oneness of
blood and religion.   Among the prophets of the north, while it does not
appear that Elijah or Elisha touched upon the separation as one of the sins
which they rebuked, or counseled a return to union with Judah, yet Hosea
saw in the northern secession a rebellion against Jehovah and the theocratic
community.   To him the rulers were usurpers (8^4, 13^{11}).   The sanction
which God would seem to have given to the rending of the kingdom and
the appointment of the northern kings (1 K. 11^{31}, 16^2, 2 K. 9^3) is explained
by Hosea as a visitation of divine anger (13^{11}).   ' The disunion of north and
south was so great that for the sake of peace it was better to separate.   But
when the moral and spiritual decay of N. Israel had reached such a point
as in the time of Hosea, no prophet with any spiritual insight could fail to
perceive that the usurping kings lacked the divine blessing' (Cheyne, in
CB. *Hosea* 87).   In view of Hosea's declarations it is probable that he
looked for the reunion of the divided kingdom under the leadership of
Judah.   This hope is directly expressed in several passages (1^{11}, 3^5) which,
however, are by many critics (*e.g.* Stade, Cornill, W. R. Smith, Marti) referred
to a later hand.   Amos $9^{11\,ff.}$, which would show that prophet to have been
in essential agreement with Hosea, is also assigned to the hand of an editor
by many (*e.g.* Cheyne, Wellhausen, Duhm.   Driver in CB. *Joel and Amos*
119 ff. defends the passage).   In the prophets and poets of the southern
kingdom there is no recognition of two divisions in the theocratic people as
a permanent factor in the purposes of God, no consciousness of a leadership
separate from Judah or of any capital city save Jerusalem.   Israel in their
warnings and promises to a very large extent means the whole people, North
and South alike.   Their prophetic oracles are addressed to each in turn or
both in common.

The Eschatological Hopes of This Period.   This long period,
so momentous in Hebrew history, so varied in national and
religious developments, gave birth to conceptions and hopes of

great importance in the history of the kingdom of God, and in the unfolding of his purposes for his people. (1) *The theocratic king.* As the government of Israel took in this period the new form of the monarchy, so there arose in thought the new element of the theocratic king — an element destined to exert the profoundest and most far-reaching influence in eschatological hopes. As we have seen above,[1] the government of Israel in the preceding period was theocratic ; Israel had no king but Jehovah. All rule emanated directly from God ; all who exercised authority were only his organs. And in the institution of the monarchy there was no departure from this fundamental principle. Viewed from one point the institution was regarded as a falling away from the high ideal of Jehovah's sole and direct rule.[2] But God revealed the broader aspect of his purpose. The conditions of the age made necessary a visible, personal representative of the divine ruler to maintain his kingdom among the nations, and to carry it forward toward a higher realization.[3] The human kingship was not in conflict with the divine, nor even coördinate with it. The two were *in ideal* one. The theocratic king was the embodiment of the divine rule. This close relation was shown in the events of the first institution of the monarchy. It was God who chose the person to be made king; it was he who bade his prophet consecrate the chosen one as his ' anointed.'[4] He was placed over Israel by God in God's stead. He stood thus in the relation of a divine personage. Therefore while in the preceding period religious thought centers in the theocratic *people*, in this era it culminates in the theocratic *king*. Perhaps only minds of deeper insight perceived the full significance of the kingly office, but imperfectly as the ideal was realized, there was found here the germ out of which the wonderful figure of the ideal king portrayed by later prophets and poets is only a growth. The glowing colors irradiating his majestic perfections as we see him pictured in many passages in the prophets and the psalms are referred by an increasingly large number of critics to the period after the exile, but there is little in these representations which is not in germ at least implied in his theocratic character as perceived in this age. In this unique relation of

[1] P. 11.   [2] Cf. 1 S. 8[4 ff.]   [3] Cf. 1 S. 9[15 ff.]   [4] 1 S. 9[16].

the theocratic king to God and his people there is contained
what later prophets saw in the unfolded vision of the Messiah.
The figure of the personal king may fall into the background
or even disappear at times, but it emerges· again as the dominating factor in the hope of God's people, until it culminates,
transformed and spiritualized, fulfilling all prophecy, in the
person of him who is 'King of kings and Lord of lords.'[1]

(2) *The Day of Jehovah.* Another fact brought into prominence by the political and spiritual history of Israel in this
period is the expectation of the day of Jehovah, that is, Jehovah's intervention in the affairs of the world to judge his cause
and the cause of his people.[2] This expectation appears in
Amos, the earliest of the written prophets, but already as an
article of belief current among the people.[3] It was born of
Israel's relation to Jehovah as his people. They alone among
the nations were, as they believed, the object of his love and
concern ; their cause was his cause. But after the brief glory
of David and Solomon's era they were harassed by enemies
on every side ; Egypt, Syria, and Assyria, one after another,
afflicted them, and in their affliction they sighed for the day
of Jehovah,[4] when God by a signal intervention should anni-
hilate forever the power of their foes and establish his people
in everlasting peace. In the *popular* conception the coming
crisis was one of assured joy and triumph for Israel ; it was to
be the consummation of the nation's hope. The expectation
as cherished by the people at large rested on the outward and
national relation to Jehovah. His moral character was largely
overlooked. If his people kept his ordinances, if they duly
offered the sacrifices, observed the fasts and feasts, and all the
ceremonial prescriptions of the law, their part of the covenant
was performed, and they could claim that Jehovah on the other
hand should perform his. That he would do this was their
certain belief. The Day of the Lord then could be to them a
day of joy only ; to their enemies a day of confusion and
destruction. But the great prophets of the eighth and seventh

---

[1] Rev. 19[16].
[2] The use of ' day ' in this expression comes from the Hebrew use of the word
in the sense of 'day of battle,' or 'victory' ; cf. Is. 9[4]. See W. R. Smith,
Prophets 397.   [3] Cf. 5[18].   [4] Am. *loc. cit.*

centuries before Christ, whose mission was preëminently to preach the holiness and righteousness of God and the corresponding character required in his people, gave to the Day another aspect, which becomes paramount throughout this period. From the time of Amos on, it is proclaimed as a crisis in which God will manifest in the sight of the world his indignation against all iniquity, whether among the heathen or in his chosen people. The prophets found predominant in Israel corruption, civil and social, injustice, inhumanity, profligacy, greed, oppression of the poor, almost every form of moral failure, though joined with zeal in the external observances of religion. It became their special office then to correct the popular misconception of the Day of Jehovah and to proclaim it as a visitation preëminently upon the sin of Israel itself.[1] At the same time it is to be a day of judgment upon the nations [2] — not merely for their treatment of God's people, but for their offenses against the laws of universal morality.[3] Different prophets make prominent different aspects of the Day, but throughout the period it is conceived as a crisis in the affairs of Israel and the nations, the vindication of the righteous character of God. It is to be a day ' upon all that is proud and haughty and upon all that is lifted up, . . . and the loftiness of man shall be bowed down and the haughtiness of men shall be brought low, . . . and the idols shall utterly pass away. And men shall go into the caves of the rocks and into the holes of the earth from before the terror of Jehovah and from the glory of his majesty when he ariseth to shake mightily the earth.' [4] It should be noticed that, in this crisis, Jehovah himself is to come forth manifesting himself in the fullness of his power and glory. Great movements among the nations, the overthrow of kingdoms, commotions in the natural world may accompany his coming, but they do not constitute its essential character. He may employ kings and peoples as his agents, but all such agencies are unessential features in the picture — often they are absent from it. This event then is essentially different from the interventions of providence which have from time to time taken place in the past. Those might

---

[1] Cf. Am. 3², Hos. 13¹⁵ f., Is. 1²⁴ f., Zeph. 1⁴.   [2] Cf. Is. 13, Zeph. 1.
[3] Cf. W. R. Smith 134.   [4] Is. 2¹² ff.

be spoken of as *a* day of the Lord — this alone as *the* Day; it
is final, eschatological. While such a crisis necessarily implies
judgment, we do not find in this period the later idea that all
the tribes of the earth shall be gathered before Jehovah's throne
to be judged, nor is there present the later belief in a resurrection of the dead to share in the judgment.[1] The events of the
Day belong to time and earth, and are thought of as *near*.
Zephaniah's cry, ' The great day of Jehovah is near, it is near
and hasteth greatly,'[2] expresses the common expectation of the
prophets. Isaiah saw in the coming overthrow of Assyria the
precursor of the day,[3] while for Zephaniah its tokens were
found in the threatening movements of a foe commonly identified with the Scythian hordes who at this time invaded western
Asia.[4] ' The prophets wrote and spoke usually amidst very
stirring scenes. Great events were passing around them. . . .
The noise of falling empires, the desolations of the kingdom of
God, the revolutions in men's thoughts revealed to their ear
his footsteps. . . . God was so near that his full presence
which he had promised appeared imminent.'[5] Henceforth the
Coming of God, called variously ' the day of the Lord,' ' the
great day,' ' that day,' ' the day of judgment,' etc., conceived
under different forms, accompanied by different circumstances,
appears as the central event about which all eschatological
expectations range themselves. Most of the prophets contain
oracles regarding it;[6] it forms the principal theme of Zephaniah and Joel; it is fundamental in much of the later non-
canonical literature, in the teaching of our Lord and the
writers of the New Testament, and in the hope of the Christian
Church.

(3) *The Remnant.* The prophets who proclaimed the punishment to be visited upon Israel for its sins, even to the downfall
of the state and captivity among the heathen, yet foresaw that
God would not make ' a full end ' of his people.[7] The fundamental belief of the Hebrews, Jehovah is Israel's God, Israel is
Jehovah's people, could never absolutely lose its force in the

---

[1] Hos. 13¹⁴ refers to the restoration of the nation, not the resurrection of the
individual.   [2] 1¹⁴.   [3] 14²⁴⁻²⁷.
[4] Cf. Davidson in CB. *Zeph.* 98.   [5] Davidson *Theol.* 381.
[6] Cf. Is. 2¹² ᶠᶠ·, Jer. 30⁷ ᶠᶠ·, Ezk. 30, Ob.¹⁵, Zec. 14, Mal. 3.   [7] Jer. 5¹⁰.

prophets' hopes. They looked for the preservation of at least a kernel of faithful ones whom God would own as his. The idea appears first in the dramatic story of Elijah. Alone in the desert, crying in despair, ' I, even I only, am left,' there comes to him the answer of God, ' Yet will I leave me seven thousand in Israel.' [1] Amos whose ministry falls in the period doubly darkened by Israel's moral degradation and Assyria's irresistible advance toward the west, *appears* to see no gleam of hope for the nation. ' The virgin of Israel is fallen ; she shall no more rise,' [2] and it can hardly be questioned that he included the southern kingdom also in his prophecy of destruction.[3] But his very preaching implies the thought of the possible repentance and escape of at least some of his people. His call, ' Seek ye me and ye shall live,' [4] expresses the supreme motive of his work and reveals his hope of a possible remnant, even if with some we attribute to a later source the more distinct expressions of such a hope.[5] Hosea in the narrative of his faithless wife, received back again after suffering and shame had wrought repentance [6] — whether the narrative be historical or allegorical — sets forth symbolically the same hope. But it is in Isaiah that the doctrine of the Remnant becomes most prominent. Though he saw his prophecies against the northern kingdom [7] fulfilled in the Assyrian Conquest, and though he foresaw a similar destruction moving inevitably upon the kingdom of Judah,[8] yet from the outset he never lost his faith that there should be ' left therein gleanings as the shaking of an olive tree,' [9] which should form the nucleus of a new and purified people of God. Following a Hebrew custom he gives a symbolical name to a son, Shear-jashub,[10] ' a remnant shall return,' and in the narrative of his call and consecration to the prophetic work the message committed to him, proclaiming the utter waste and desolation of the land, contains also the hope of the ' holy seed ' remaining as the stock of the felled tree.[11] Even though the last clause in 6^{13} is wanting in the LXX. and may be open to suspicion, it was a correct perception of Isaiah's mission, which placed

---

[1] 1 K. $19^{14,\,18}$.   [2] 5^2.

[3] Even if with Duhm, *al.* we reject $2^{4\,f.}$, it is plain that Amos classes Israel and Judah together. Cf. 3^1, 6^1 ; W. R. Smith, *Prophets* 398, Smend 181.

[4] 5^4.   [5] *E.g.* 3^{12}, 5^{15}, 9^{8-15}. Cf. Stade, 220.   [6] 1-2.

[7] 7^8, 8^4, 17^3, $28^{1\,ff.}$.   [8] $3^{25\,f.}$, 10^{11}, $29^{1\,ff.}$.   [9] 17^6.   [10] 7^3.   [11] 6^{13}.

this factor among the words defining his divine commission.[1]
' Within the corrupt mass of Judah there ever remains a seed
of true life, a precious remnant, the preservation of which is
certain.   Beyond this the prophet sets no limit to the severity
of the troubles through which the land must pass.' [2]   Micah
does not in the parts universally accepted by critics express the
doctrine, but the record of his prophecies is too brief to justify
the belief that he did not share in the hope of his great contemporary.[3]   Jeremiah who above all other prophets is the mournful
herald of coming calamities — the destruction of Jerusalem and
the temple, the overthrow of the kingdom and the miseries of
the exile [4] — nevertheless held up to the hope of his hearers the
reverse side of the picture, the escape of a remnant.[5]   The
possibility of a better future for at least a part of his people
underlies Zephaniah's proclamation of the Day of Jehovah,[6]
as also Nahum's prophecy of the fall of Nineveh and Habakkuk's
prophecy of the overthrow of the Chaldæans.   The motive of
both Nahum and Habakkuk is to give comfort and encouragement to their people through the assurance that God is about to
destroy their enemies.   And the hope of a Remnant who will
take refuge in Jehovah,[7] a Remnant of the righteous who should
live by their faithfulness,[8] clearly pervades their prophecies,
though criticism may deny the authenticity of passages where it
is particularly expressed.[9]   Thus the prophets throughout this
period saw beyond the on-coming Day of Jehovah an Israel
within Israel surviving the great dénouement and forming the
nucleus of the kingdom of God, the heir of all its hopes and
promises.   It is to be a holy remnant disciplined through, and
redeemed out of, the fierce onset of trial.   Henceforth it is seen
that membership in a chosen race and a chosen nation is not in
itself enough to constitute membership in God's people.   It is
too much to say that we have here the beginning of the idea of
the Church as contrasted with the nation — we have rather the
germ from which one element in that idea arises.   The one
truth that, ' he is not a Jew who is one outwardly,' [10] is beginning

[1] Cf. also 1[9], 28[5].   [2] W. R. Smith 258.   [3] Cf. Stade 230.
[4] 7[12 ff.], 9[11], 13[1-11], 15[1 ff.].   [5] 23[3], 24[1 ff.], 44[28], 46[28].
[6] Cf. 2[2], even if 2[9], 3[13] be attributed to a later author.   Cf. Stade 251, Cornill
358.   [7] Nah. 1[7].   [8] Hab. 2[4].   [9] *E.g.* Nah. 1[15], Hab. 3[13].
[10] Ro. 2[28].

to make its way; the correlative truth that, 'the Gentiles are fellow-heirs and fellow-members of the body,'[1] is not yet apprehended. The racial limits are not yet outgrown. The eschatological element, however, which is contained in this hope remains under varying and expanding forms as the heritage of all subsequent ages, pictured in resplendent imagery by prophets, apostles, and evangelists; and the Church still looking on beyond the great Day of the Lord beholds in the clear light of assured hope the kingdom of God, the vast Remnant, which no man can number, ransomed from death and destruction — the kingdom of righteousness foreseen by the prophets, where God will abide with his people.

(4) *The perpetuation of the nation and of the Davidic kingdom.* In all the vicissitudes of these centuries it remained a steadfast article in the religion of at least the *people* that the relation between Jehovah and Israel could not be broken and that therefore God would defend his people against their enemies, or would not suffer them to continue permanently under foreign domination. The history of his leadings through all the past, the signal deliverances, the prosperity and glory bestowed at times assured the Hebrews as a people of their continuance in, or in case of conquest, of their restoration to, the land of their fathers. How ineradicable this *popular* expectation was is seen in the fact that the prophets from Amos on throughout the period are struggling unceasingly and with little apparent success to convince the people that the retention of Jehovah's favor and the perpetuation of the nation depend upon a thorough moral and religious reformation. Hardly less certain is it that the popular expectation always placed at the head of this kingdom of the future a prince of David's line. Any other attitude toward the leadership was scarcely conceivable. To David was due the first successful establishment of the kingdom; its most splendid era was reached in his reign and that of his son; for more than four centuries his house had held the throne continuously;[2] limitation to his line was the law of succession recognized

---

[1] Eph. 3[6].
[2] Athaliah's short usurpation is not an exception, for it was looked upon as a usurpation and it was only as the wife of one Davidic king and the mother of another that she succeeded in getting her power.

without dissentient voice.   No prophet even had suggested the
substitution of a non-Davidic prince.   'The throne of David'
had become synonymous with 'the throne of Judah.'[1]   The
striking narrative in 2 S. 7 of the everlasting covenant formed
by Jehovah with David and the promise concerning his son, 'I
will establish the throne of his kingdom forever.   I will be his
father and he shall be my son,' even if it be post-exilic in date,
formulates vividly the *popular* thought in pre-exilic times.[2]

When on the other hand we turn to inquire what were the
expectations of the *prophets*, as contrasted with the people,
regarding the nation and the kingship in the future, the question becomes a difficult one because of the tendency among
recent critics to assign much in the present form of the pre-
exilic books to post-exilic sources.   But in the absence of clear
evidence to the contrary it is reasonable to suppose as will
appear below (fine-print passage) that the prophets cherished
expectations similar to those of their countrymen and looked for
an ultimate building-up of God's people into a kingdom of
power ruled by a Davidic king, though at the same time a
kingdom and a king immeasurably above the popular idea in
moral and religious aspects.   The holiness of Jehovah which
formed the background of prophetic preaching demanded a
holy people with whom God might dwell, a holy king who
should serve as his agent and representative.   Passages then
which express the hope of an era of glory for Israel, however
much expanded and colored by the exuberant ideas of a later
time, may not unreasonably be taken to rest on implications
contained in actual utterances of the prophets.   That such
utterances, however, were less prominent among their oracles
was natural.   They were engrossed in what they saw to be an
almost impossible task — they were struggling to bring their
people to repentance and to convince them of the certainty of
divine punishment.   Naturally then they did not dwell largely
upon the prospect of deliverance or restoration.

It is doubtless true that the figure of the future king does not take so
conspicuous a place in the prophets of this period as later.   He does not

---

[1] Cf. Jer. 13[13], 22[30], 36[30].
[2] 2 S. 7 is regarded by most recent critics as post-exilic.   Cf. **Enc. Bib. IV.**
4278, Kittel, *Hist. of Heb.* II. 160, Eng. trans., Hast. IV. 389.

certainly appear as the instrumentality through which Jehovah will deliver his people or establish his kingdom. Passages in which such a function is attributed to him (*e.g.* Is. 11[4], Mich. 5[5]) are out of harmony with the usual representation and are by a large number of scholars held to be later. It is Jehovah himself who is usually represented as intervening thus in behalf of his people and kingdom. It may be assumed with scholars generally that Is. 40–66; 11[10-16] are not Isaian. The messianic Psalms, as a part of the Hebrew hymnal through the later ages, were subjected to such additions and adaptations that even those originating in this period do not furnish unquestionable evidence of the hope of his time. Objection is also urged against other passages referring to the future ruler in Israel, *e.g.* Am. 9[11], Hos. 3[5], Mic. 5[2-4], Jer. 23[5 f.], 30[9], 33[15 ff.] (so, Stade, Driver, Cornill, *al.*); yet even if such objection be accepted as established, it by no means follows, as will be seen below, that the person of a coming Davidic king was absent at this time from the hope of the prophets. Criticism in its extreme form has adopted the canon that a restoration or building up of Israel into an ideal kingdom to be ruled by an ideal king of David's line was wholly absent from the vision of the prophets before the exile. (Cf. Volz *Die vorexil. Jahweprophetie.*) This canon would exclude from our immediate inquiry not only those paragraphs which on linguistic, historical, and similar grounds are held to be later, but also all phrases and turns of expression which imply the condition of the era called in the broader sense messianic. But though the earlier conceptions of the kingdom and the person of the king may lack some of the characteristics found in the richly developed picture of a later time, it is very questionable whether this extreme position will be established as the general verdict of scholars. There are considerations which point to the opposite conclusion. (1) The prophets of this period though far above the people in religious insight were nevertheless too much men of their time to conceive of a great religion, even the religion of Jehovah, wholly apart from a nation. The world had not yet reached that conception. The *universalism* so far as it is apprehended is not that of the Church in which there is ' neither Jew nor Greek, but all are one in Christ ' (Gal. 3[28]); the national idea is not yet superseded. The predictions of the conversion of the Gentiles found in the prophets of this time (*e.g.* Is. 2[2 f.], Hab. 2[14], Zeph. 2[11]), whether belonging to this or a later era, are parts of prophecies which include the preservation of the nation of Israel. Is. 19[23-25], which Montefiore (*Hibbert Lectures*[2]; 149) calls 'the high-water mark of eighth century prophecy,' assigns to Israel the central place among the *nations* and gives it the most honorable title, ' mine inheritance.' So far from teaching or intimating that the national form is to be displaced by another, the prophets are passionately striving to save the nation by leading it to repentance; they assure Israel of the unfailing perpetuity of their state, if based on righteousness and loyalty to Jehovah. The Remnant, which, as we have seen, is an essential factor in the thought of this time, is not a new creation, it is always a residue of God's people — the Israel of old through which will be maintained God's righteous rule among men. Precisely in what way and when the Remnant may realize its purpose may not be distinctly seen, but there is no intimation that it is thought of as an invisible society apart from the forms of a state. (2) The circumstances of the years following upon the return from the exile were not fitted to *originate* expectation of an ideal kingdom ruled by a Davidic prince. A comparatively small portion of the exiles returned to a desolated land, to a city and sanctuary in ruins; the work of rebuilding the temple (declared the chief purpose of the return, Ezr. 1³) was carried on slowly, meeting apathy and opposition; as subjects of a Persian satrap the Israelites were oppressed by galling exactions; they were surrounded by hostile tribes; and if their hearts turned to the house of David for hope, they had to remember that the kingdom had rapidly declined through four inglorious reigns and had finally expired. These were not times to *give rise* to great hopes, but rather to revive and amplify for comfort and encouragement promises uttered by prophets belonging to better days.

Hosea announced the overthrow and captivity of Israel (5⁹ ᶠᶠ·), but there is also revealed to him in his personal history Jehovah's recovery of his people. Gomer, the prophet's wife, becomes the type of Israel who in exile will repent and be restored to its country (2⁷, 3¹⁻⁴). The prominence which the prophet gives to the story of Gomer may well raise the presumption that we have at least a Hosean basis in 1¹⁰ ᶠ·, 11¹⁰ ᶠ·, 14⁵⁻⁸, and similar passages foretelling a restoration. Isaiah predicts the ruin of the land, even of Judah and Jerusalem (3¹ ᶠᶠ·, 5⁵ ᶠᶠ·), but in certain prophecies also promises the protection or speedy relief of Jerusalem (10²⁴ᶠᶠ, 29⁷ ᶠ·, 31⁵). Guthe (*Das Zukunftsbild d. Jesaia*, 27 ff.) explains the conflict as follows: he attributes the former series of predictions to the prophet's earlier years when the Assyrian power threatened the destruction of both the northern and southern kingdoms, but when the catastrophe had swept away the former, leaving the latter still safe, the prophet 'believed that from the course of events he had discovered the wonderful plan of Jehovah more accurately than before and therefore changed his utterances.' Hühn also refers the difference to a change in historical circumstances. (Cf. also Cheyne, En. Bib. II. 2181.) Hackmann (*Die Zukunftserwartung d. Jesaia*) refers to a non-Isaian source the passages which declare the inviolability of Jerusalem (p. 162). Doubtless a more certain determination of the chronological order of Isaiah's oracles is essential for the solution of the problem. But whether his predictions of the ruin of Judah and Jerusalem belong to his earlier or later career, he evidently expected that the Remnant, which is so conspicuous an element in his thought, would consist, not of returned exiles but of a body of faithful ones defended and preserved within their own land. The significant name given to his son, Shear-jashub, means ' a remnant shall return,' *i.e.* to Jehovah, not from exile. In the passages unquestionably Isaian there is no reference to the Babylonian captivity. Isaiah 'uniformly regards the intervention of Jehovah in the Assyrian crisis as the supreme moment of human history and the turning point in the destinies of the kingdom of God ' (Skinner *Is.* in CB. 285). And the Remnant whose preservation he anticipates he foresees destined to form a new and purified state — a state in which the dross has been purged away, in which the judges are restored as at the first and the counselors as at the beginning (1²⁵ ᶠ· — a passage generally accepted as Isaian in substance). The designation of the magistrates here is general and without doubt includes also the Davidic king, though there is nothing to suggest the extraordinary personality of the Messiah. (Cf. Stade 229.) These expectations furnish reasonable ground for attributing to the prophet himself so sober a picture of the restored state with its purely human king as is given in 32¹⁻⁵, and for finding an Isaian element in other predictions of the ideal age.   Jeremiah, apart from the oracles attributed to him, showed his assurance of the restoration of his people in that while a prisoner in the 'court of the guard' and in the darkening hours of the siege of Jerusalem he purchased land near the city and in the transaction attended strictly to the legal formalities of witnesses and the recording of the deed (32⁶ ᶠᶠ·).   His view of his act as a prophecy addressed to his people is certainly expressed in the words, whether his or those of an editor, 'houses and fields and vineyards shall yet again be bought in this land.'   The same prophecy is contained in the vision of the baskets of figs (24, generally accepted as Jeremian), in which the good figs symbolize the captives upon whom Jehovah's pleasure rests.   'I will set mine eyes upon them for good and I will bring them again to this land' (v. 6) — words which, even if they be not those of Jeremiah, express his interpretation of the vision.   With such expression of his outlook we seem to have sufficient ground for attributing to him the substance at least of the wonderful promise of the New Covenant to be made in the coming days (31³¹ ᶠᶠ·).   But it should be noticed that the New Covenant, of which the full spiritual meaning is first set forth in the epistle to the Hebrews (8 ⁶ ᶠᶠ·), does not here contemplate a religion wholly individualistic and independent of the nation; it aims rather to show how the relation between God and his people shall abide forever, that is, when the conditions of the covenant are fulfilled in the hearts of all. (Cf. Smend 249.)   Ezekiel's prophecies of the restoration, even those given before the fall of Jerusalem (17²² ᶠᶠ·), do not belong to the period under consideration here, for he began his prophetic work in exile, after the first deportation of Hebrews to Babylon, which was the beginning of the final catastrophe.

These four great conceptions which we have considered above as dominating the religious and national thought of the *Monarchical Age* form the principal features of its outlook regarding the future of the kingdom of God.   The eschatological hope of the period may be briefly summed up as follows : *The great Day of Jehovah is near, when the God of holiness will come with might, destroying the Gentiles who have exalted themselves against him, and at the same time overwhelming with punishment for their iniquities the kingdom and nation of his chosen people. But preserving a Remnant formed of those who have continued faithful and those who have profited by the discipline of suffering,*

*he will in the end build up in Judah and Jerusalem his abiding
kingdom of righteousness and peace, where he himself will dwell
and where as foremost among the counselors and judges theocratic
kings of David's line will hold the throne.* In such a summary
it is not necessary to include every religious idea belonging to
this period which may have been influential in the eschatology
of a later time. For example, the advance in the apprehension
of theoretical monotheism must have had a profound influence
in broadening the hope of the recognition of Jehovah by the
nations of the world. How far that influence was felt in this
age cannot be fixed definitely because of the uncertainty which
in the opinion of many attaches to the date of certain parts of
our documents. The same might be said regarding the relation of the ideal Davidic king to the developed figure of the
Messiah, or the world-wide dominion of the coming kingdom.
Into the critical questions thus involved it is obviously impossible to enter here, nor is it essential. In a general view of
pre-Christian eschatology it is not fundamentally important to
determine whether these conceptions became clear before or
after the exile.

4 *The Exilic and Post-Exilic Age.* The period meant to
be covered by this designation is that extending from the
Babylonian Captivity, 586 B.C., to the final disruption of the
nation after the destruction of Jerusalem by the Romans
70 A.D. The fall of Jerusalem and the deportation of the
Hebrews by Nebuchadnezzar into the Babylonian Captivity
formed a turning-point in the destiny of God's people.
Henceforth, with the exception of the very brief period of
independence under the Maccabees, they remain to the end
the subjects of a foreign power. Their rulers, whether governors, high-priests, or so-called ' kings,' are but vassals of the
Gentiles. This foreign domination, following the succession
of the world-empires, is in turn Babylonian, Persian, Greek
(soon alternating between Greco-Syrian and Greco-Egyptian),
and Roman.[1] And the government, so far as it was in the

[1] In 538 B.C. Cyrus overthrew Babylon and established the Persian Empire ;
this in turn was overthrown by Alexander in 333 ; finally, after some eighty years
of independence under the Maccabees, through the taking of Jerusalem in 63
B.C. Judea became a tributary and afterwards a province of the Roman empire.

hands of the Hebrews, was during the greater part of the time that of a religious community rather than of a nation. In the course of this long period the process of dispersion, begun forcibly by the Assyrians and Babylonians, continued chiefly as a voluntary movement and with enormous results. The larger part of the Hebrews remained behind in Babylon and its neighborhood when by the permission of Cyrus the return from the Captivity took place, and from time to time throughout the later centuries migrations occurred to every center of the known world. Josephus, writing in the end of our period, says, 'One cannot easily find a place in the world which has not received this tribe and is not held in possession by it'[1] — a dispersion of incalculable influence in the spread of Christianity in the apostolic age. But through all these centuries Palestine continued the fatherland, Jerusalem the metropolis, of these widely scattered millions. The Holy Land, the Holy City, formed the true home of the people and their religion, though Babylon and Egypt (Alexandria) became influential centers of the life and thought of Judaism. From all quarters of the earth devout Israelites came up to the great feasts at Jerusalem;[2] every adult male wherever resident paid yearly a temple-tax of two drachms.[3]

Doubtless the two strongest forces in keeping actively alive this sense of racial oneness and of the importance of the Holy Land as the national center were the Law and the hope of a coming era of deliverance and triumph — a messianic era.[4] Ezekiel, who at Babylon in the darkness of the captivity opened up visions of a brighter future, is the exponent of both these forces, the two poles, as they are sometimes called, of the post-exilic religion. The latter factor, the messianic hope, forms the principal theme of the other great prophecies belonging to the time of the exile, those contained in Second Isaiah.[5] These prophecies have gathered up and grandly unfolded the hopes of pre-exilic times and have handed on the same through

---

[1] *Ant.* XIV. 7[2].   [2] Acts 2[9-11].   [3] Mt. 17[24], Joseph. *JB.* VII, 6[6].
[4] Cf. Baldensperger 88 ff.
[5] *Second Isaiah* is the most common designation among scholars for Is. 40–66, which are the work of a prophet or prophets later than the time of Isaiah. Whether these chapters are all to be assigned to a Deutero-Is. or in part to a Trito-Is. (Duhm, Stade, *al.*) is not important here.

the following centuries as they appear in the later prophets, in oracles inserted in earlier prophecies by later hands, and in non-canonical literature. Through nearly the whole of this period there was nothing in the external and political condition of Israel to encourage belief in a great destiny for the nation. It would be difficult to imagine a greater contrast between expectation and present reality. Yet Israel was Jehovah's people, and Jehovah's kingdom must be exalted above all the earth. This faith was inextinguishable, and became clearer with the growing perception of the oneness and holiness of God. Divine revelation, continued through a long line of prophets, foretold the ultimate triumph of God's kingdom — a triumph to which the Church is ever looking forward with sure confidence. But the truth thus given was necessarily apprehended under the familiar traditional forms, and the kingdom in which all the hope of Israel centered was consequently conceived under local and temporal aspects. Eschatological expectation in its leading features started from traditional standpoints. But other influences also came in which affected it profoundly, especially the advancing conception of the *individual* as contrasted with the *national* unit. The nation, while it stood, formed the religious unit, and the individual's worth even for himself, with his hopes and aspirations, centered in his membership in that unit. But with the downfall of the state the dignity and the value of the individual before God came into clearer consciousness. This place of the individual in religious truth is first set forth fully by the exilic prophet Ezekiel,[1] and forms perhaps his greatest contribution to religious thought, though in this as in some other respects his starting point is found in Jeremiah.[2] In the same line with this individualizing influence which arose from the changed political status of the nation was that of the Law, the more potent of the two great forces in post-exilic Judaism mentioned above. During the Captivity, and in the case of the Jews of the dispersion through this whole period, religious life was cut off from the temple-worship with its sacrificial rites; the law then, with such ordinances as might be observed everywhere, especially circumcision and the sabbath, became the outward

[1] Chapts. 18 and 23.   [2] Cf. Jer. 31[29 f.].

sign and the effectual means of union between God and his people. The law, not a particular code merely, but the whole revelation of God's will as given in command, in prophecy, in history, the perfect guide in religion and morals, becomes the object of devout veneration and love, of meditation and aspiration. It is the beauty and power of the law in this sense that forms the theme of Psalm 119.[1] Hence the teachers of the law, the scribes, become in the course of this period a more important factor than the priests — they sit in Moses' seat.[2] In these higher aspects of its relation to spiritual life the law formed the sphere and the norm of a direct personal bond between God and the *individual* soul. But this truth of man's personal worth in the divine scale advanced slowly. To make it the property of the race there was needed the creative transformation of the Master who taught us, 'the very hairs of your head are all numbered.'[3] Yet in the later years of the period under review it influenced profoundly, as will appear below, belief and eschatological expectation. Finally it should be noticed that the eschatology of this period could hardly fail to be affected by the contact of the Jews with foreign influences such as the Persian religion, and the philosophy of Greece ; at least the growth of eschatological ideas the germs of which existed among the Hebrews and other peoples in common may readily be understood to have been facilitated ; that such contact in some instances modified Hebrew thought and even introduced new elements appears unquestionable.[4]

The Eschatological Hopes of This Period. It is evident that in a period so long and of so varied influences eschatology may assume varied forms ; but it does not follow throughout a regular, harmonious advance. While in the later years there appear messianic hopes which have regard to the individual or the world rather than the nation, and other conceptions unknown in earlier times arise, yet the older forms of hope continue, modified only partially or not at all. Different tendencies exist side by side and even in the same writing. There is more or less jostling of the individual and the national, the

[1] Cf. also Ps. 19[7 ff.].
[2] Mt. 23[2.] On Scribism cf. Schultz 290 ff., Schürer II, 363 ff.   [3] Mt. 10[30].
[4] Cf. p. 79 ff.

D

local and the universal, the visible and the spiritual, the temporal and the eternal. It is therefore not possible to divide the period into parts by lines drawn chronologically. We may speak of the earlier and the later eschatology, but it must be kept in mind that we have not two sharply separated epochs in the latter of which the earlier ideas have been entirely outgrown and discarded. The expectations of the earlier part of the period are dominated by the *national* outlook and these persist; on the other hand there appear in the later centuries conceptions of a *universal* and *transcendental* character. These find expression in the apocalyptic literature and are therefore sometimes classed as *apocalyptic* eschatology; not quite accurately however, because this is not the only form of eschatology found in these writings. The period then may properly be treated as a whole, and it will be convenient to trace out first those hopes which, originating and unfolding within the limitations of a *national* outlook, continue throughout, modified to be sure in some cases but not so far transformed as to become virtually new. A later paragraph will give a survey of the expectations which belong exclusively to the *closing centuries* of the period, whether these be older conceptions radically transformed or wholly new ones.[1]

(1) *The coming of Jehovah to deliver his people and to establish his kingdom forever.* (*a*) 'Behold, Jehovah hath proclaimed unto the end of the earth, Say ye to the daughter of Zion, Behold thy salvation cometh, . . . And they shall call them The holy people, The redeemed of Jehovah.'[2] This ringing call from the midst of a people overthrown, oppressed, and scattered, sums up the *national* aspect of a hope which persists throughout this period. The hope cannot be said to have ever been literally fulfilled, but the prophecies that fostered it contain the revelation of a coming spiritual deliverance and a spiritual kingdom which were apprehended under customary forms of thought. Not the meager movement of the return inaugurated by Cyrus' command, not the brilliant era of the Maccabees answered even remotely to the expectations; yet the hope, pushed on continuously into the future as the years passed without its realization, is fundamental in the thought of these

---

[1] Cf. pp. 63 ff.   [2] Is. 62[11 f.].

centuries and appears in the prophets, earlier and later, in the Psalms, the Apocrypha, the apocalyptic writers, and in the New Testament.[1] Jehovah will come with a mighty hand and outstretched arm to gather his people out of the countries wherein they are scattered, the valleys will be exalted and the mountains and the hills made low, that his highway may be prepared. ' I will bring thy seed from the east and gather them from the west; I will say to the north, Give up; and to the south, Keep not back '[2] — words which are ever echoing on in the hope of the following years.

(b) Jerusalem, the seat of the restored kingdom, is to arise from its ruins with great splendor.[3] The temple is to be rebuilt with new glory,[4] the land will become supernaturally fruitful,[5] peace and joy will reign undisturbed with wealth and length of days, the animal kingdom will be at peace in itself and with man [6]; in short, the ideal age will be realized and continue forever. A human king does not always form a part of the picture, yet when thought of he is evidently a prince of David's house.[7] The supreme glory of the coming kingdom in the mind of the prophets is its *spiritual* perfections. God himself will dwell with his people [8] and they will walk in his statutes, they will all be righteous,[9] evil will be blotted out and deceit quenched, faith will flourish and corruption be overcome.[10]

(c) With Jehovah's deliverance of his people and the establishment of his kingdom there is joined, as an essential factor in eschatological expectation, the overthrow of the hostile nations of the world. The latter is the preparation for the former and both alike manifest Jehovah's majesty. The powers that have harassed Israel and defied God must be swept away, that the kingdom of his people may be set up in lasting security. The Day of the Lord, which in the pre-exilic prophets is first of all a visitation upon the sin of Israel,[11] becomes now predominantly an epoch of anger and retribution poured out upon the Gentiles.

[1] Cf. *inter al.* Is. 40 ff., Ezk. 36 f., Jl. 3, Ob. vv 17 ff., Zec. 8, Ps. 102$^{12-22}$, Tob. 13, Bar. 4$^{36-59}$, Sib. Or. III. 767–795, Ps. Sol. 11, Lk. 24^{21}, Ac. 1^6.
[2] Is. 43$^{5 f.}$.   [3] Is. 54$^{11 f.}$, Tob. 13$^{16 f.}$, Sib. Or. V. 420 ff.
[4] Hag. 2^9, Tob. 14^5, Sib. Or. V. 423.
[5] Ezk. 34$^{26 f.}$, Jl. 4^{18}, Am. 9^{13}, Ps. 72^{16}, En. 10^{19}, Ap. Bar. 29^5.   [6] Is. 65^{25}.
[7] Ezk. 37^{24}, Am. 9^{11}, Zec.12^8, Ps. 89$^{3 f.}$, Ps. Sol. 17^4.   [8] Ezk. 43^7, Zec. 2^{10}.
[9] Ezk. 36$^{25 ff.}$, Is. 60^{21}.   [10] 2 Es. 6$^{27 f.}$.   [11] Cf. p. 21 ff.

The overwhelming penalty of Israel's trangression has fallen in the destruction of the nation and the captivity; 'She hath received of the Lord double for all her sins.'[1] Henceforth the more lurid light of the picture falls upon the nations that have exalted themselves against Jehovah. As most of the pre-exilic prophecies contain paragraphs directed against the hostile powers of that time, so in this period similar oracles form essential portions of the utterances of Ezekiel, Second Isaiah, most of the later prophets, and many post-canonical writers.[2] As in the earlier period so in this, the coming of Jehovah's kingdom is *near at hand.* For Ezekiel it lay just beyond the downfall of Egypt which is predicted as near;[3] Second Isaiah looked for it as the sequel to Cyrus' overthrow of the Babylonian power;[4] Haggai foresaw it in the events to follow the return led by Zerubbabel and the completion of the temple;[5] the author of the book of Daniel, in the overthrow of Antiochus Epiphanes and the Greco-Syrian power;[6] the author of 2 Esdras, in the downfall of Rome.[7]

(*d*) The idea of a *second* conflict with hostile powers appears for the first time in Ezekiel.[8] With him as with the other prophets the destruction of the well-known enemies of Israel in the near future is to be followed by an era of messianic peace and felicity.[9] But according to Ezekiel after a long continuance of this messianic era, 'in the latter days,'[10] Gog of the land of Magog will come from the uttermost parts of the north leading a host made up of hordes from the north and the south and from far off parts of the earth ; they will come up against Israel and cover the land like a cloud. But Jehovah will send upon them a sword, pestilence, hailstones, fire, and brimstone; they will fall upon the mountains and in the fields, and be given to the birds and beasts to devour. It is a final rally of the powers of earth against the kingdom of God's people. These invaders from the north are taken by many to be

---

[1] Is. 40².
[2] Cf. Ezk. 25–32, Is. 47, Jl. 3, Ob. v·15, Zec. 9, En. 90¹⁸ ᶠ·, Ap. Bar. 13⁵ ᶠᶠ·, Sib. Or. III. 303–333.
[3] Ezk. 29²¹, 30³ ᶠ· ; cf. Davidson *Ezk.* in CB. 215, 217 f.   [4] Is. 44²⁴⁻²⁸.
[5] Hag. 2⁴⁻⁹.   [6] Dan. 7²³⁻²⁷. Cf. Driver in CB. *ad loc.*
[7] 2 Es. 6⁸⁻¹⁰. Cf. Rev. 19 ff.
[8] 38–39. Cf. Stade 295, Hühn 44, Briggs *Mess. P.* 283.   [9] 34–37.   [10] 38⁸, ¹⁶.

the Scythian hordes that overran and terrorized western Asia in the seventh century B.C.; but neither Gog nor Magog can be identified with any known king or land. Whatever the truth as regards the connection of the names with any historic people, the reference in Ezekiel is to an event falling after a long continuance of the messianic era, the final gathering of the nations under a great leader against the messianic kingdom and their overwhelming destruction. Such a messianic interval between a first and a second judgment of the enemies of God's kingdom does not appear elsewhere in the Old Testament, but is found sometimes in later writers.[1] Generally the Messiah's kingdom is represented as continuing in undisturbed peace forever after the one great conflict which precedes its establishment. And this conflict is oftenest conceived under forms and symbols similar to those which make up this picture in Ezekiel. The final effort of the world against the kingdom of God is represented as a united assault of the nations upon the Holy Land.[2] As eschatological figures Gog and Magog (the latter like the former a person instead of a land) appear frequently in rabbinical predictions among the enemies whom the Messiah will conquer. The 'Day of Gog' and the 'Day of Magog' are current expressions.[3] Evidently the names became traditional representations of the last assailants of the messianic kingdom, and as such they have passed into the Revelation.[4]

(e) The *redeemer*, the champion of God's people in this final crisis, is, in the expectation of the earlier part of our period, Jehovah himself. The messianic king does not appear as the instrument of deliverance. This is the representation throughout the prophets except in Daniel.[5] 'Behold, I myself, even I, will search for my sheep and will seek them out, . . . I will deliver them out of all places whither they have been scattered, . . . I will feed them upon the mountains of Israel. . . . I

---

[1] On the messianic Age as an interregnum, see p. 76.
[2] Zec. 12[2 f.], En. 56, Sib. Or. III. 663, 2 Es. 13[5 ff.], Rev. 20[6.]   [4] 20[8].
[3] Cf. Weber *System* 370 f., Volz 176, Bousset *Jud.* 206.
[5] In Dan. 12[1] Michael, the patron-angel of the Jews, appears as their champion. Is. 11[4] and Mic. 5[6], both probably post-exilic passages, refer not to the *establishment* of the kingdom, but to the kingly function of maintaining the peace of the realm against outbreaks of evil within and onsets of enemies from without.

myself will be the shepherd of my sheep.'[1]   But in later times
the destruction of hostile powers and the exaltation of God's
people are often, though not always, attributed to the Messiah.[2]

(f) Foreshadowing the advent of Jehovah and attending it,
vast movements were looked for among the peoples of the earth
and in the natural world, times of trial for the people of God,
sifting them as grain,[3] times of furious visitations upon the
Gentiles, with great portents in the earth and the heavens.
Israel learned through its own history, through bitter conflicts
with enemies, that it could enter into its state of peace and
glory only through suffering and distress; the prophetic oracles
foretold awful calamities which should sweep away the Gentile
nations ; and the universal belief that God used the operations
of nature in ever varying ways to further his purposes concerning men led to the expectation that marvels in the physical
world would attend marvels in human history.   These times
of distress as precursors and accompaniments of the coming of
the messianic era are often called the 'messianic woes,'[4] and
they become a standing feature in eschatological expectation.
Starting from the foreshadowings of the earlier prophets, later
writers, especially the apocalyptic, unfold pictures of these
pre-messianic troubles with vivid and often fantastic imagery.
The author of Isaiah 34 gives an appalling description of the
events of these days : the dissolution of the heavens; slaughter,
desolation, and war in the earth.[5]   The prophet Joel, whose
theme is the Day of Jehovah, dwells upon the coming terrors.
' Let all the inhabitants of the land tremble : for the day of
Jehovah cometh, . . . a day of clouds and thick darkness.
. . . I will show wonders in the heavens and in the earth :
blood and fire and pillars of smoke.   The sun shall be turned
into darkness and the moon into blood. . . . I will gather all

---

[1] Ezk. 34[11 ff.]   See also Is. 43[3 ff., 14 ff.], Hag. 2[21 ff.], Zec. 9[8 ff., 14 ff.], 2 Mac. 2[18],
Bar. 5[6 ff.]   [2] Cf. p. 44.   [3] Am. 9[9].

[4] As distress and sorrow are spoken of in the Scriptures under the figure of
travail-pains, so in the rabbinical writings the expression 'the birth-pains of the
Messiah,' i.e. preceding the Messiah's birth, became a current term for the last
troubles preceding the messianic era, and occurs in conjunction with the
eschatological terms Day of Gog, or Magog, the Day of Judgment. Cf. Volz 173,
Bousset Jud. 237 f.   The same figure, ὠδῖνες, travail, R.V. is found in Mt. 24[8],
Mk. 13[8].

[5] Is. 34–35 are generally referred by critics to an exilic or post-exilic source.
Cf. Driver Intr. 225 ff., G. A. Smith in Hast. II. 493.

nations and will bring them down into the valley of Jehoshaphat
and I will execute judgment upon them there.[1] It is to these
times that the words in Zechariah refer : 'It shall come to pass,
that in all the land, saith Jehovah, two parts therein shall be
cut off and die ; . . . I will bring the third part into the fire
and will refine them as silver is refined, and will try them as
gold is tried.'[2] Similarly Daniel, 'There shall be a time of
trouble, such as never was since there was a nation.'[3] In
post-canonical writers such representations abound,[4] and the
traditional pictures are taken up into the New Testament ; the
main theme in chapters 6–16 of the Revelation is the 'messianic
woes,' largely in traditional forms.[5]

(g) Allied to the idea of such precursors of the messianic
era there appears also in our period the expectation of *personal
forerunners,* who should precede the incoming of the new era.
The earliest reference to such a person occurs in Malachi:
'Behold, I will send you Elijah the prophet before the great
and terrible day of Jehovah come,'[6] and upon the basis of this
utterance the belief became general that the great prophet
would appear again before the coming of the Lord. Though
different activities were attributed to him,[7] he is generally
represented as coming to restore order, to remove wrath and
strife [8] — a function answering to the violent disorder, the
anger and variance, predicted in both civil and family life in
the times of the 'messianic woes.' Both rabbinical writers
and the New Testament give evidence of a widespread expectation of his appearing : 'They asked him, saying, How is it
that the scribes say that Elijah must first come ? And he said
unto them, Elijah indeed cometh first and restoreth all things.'[9]
In rabbinical traditions Moses also is spoken of as coming with
Elijah. In Debarim rabba, Ch. 3, God is represented as saying
to Moses, 'When I shall send the prophet Elijah ye shall both
come together.'[10] The union of these two foremost witnesses
for Jehovah, as forerunners of the messianic era, is especially

---

[1] $2^{1 f.}$, $30^{f.}$, 3^{2}.   [2] $13^{8 f.}$ [3] 12^{1}.   [4] Cf. 2 Es. 5, En. 99–100, Ap. Bar. 70.
[5] Cf. Mt. 24, Mk. 13, Lk. 21, 2 Pet. 3.   [6] 4^{5}.   [7] Cf. Volz 192.   [8] Mal. 4^{6}.
[9] Mk. $9^{11 f.}$ Cf. Mk. 6^{15}, 8^{28}, Mt. 11^{14}, Jno. $1^{21, 25}$. For numerous instances
in rabbinical writers see Weber *System* 337 f., Volz 192, Drummond 223 f.
For the fulfillment of this expectation in the person of John the Baptist cf. Mt.
11^{14}, par. With the expression 'restore all things,' cf. Ac. 3^{21}.
[10] See Weber *System* 338. Cf. Drummond 225, Volz 193.

interesting, since they appear together in the account of the Transfiguration [1] and again in the vision of Rev. 11³ ff.. Still others were spoken of as forerunners. In 2 Esdras [2] it is said that all who have been translated without tasting death will appear at the end of the troublous times, and among these Jewish tradition included not only Enoch and Elijah, but also Baruch [3] and Ezra. [4] The earlier Christian writers almost universally understood Enoch to be the associate of Elijah as one of the 'two witnesses' in Rev. 11³. [5] The answer given to our Lord, 'Some, Elijah, and others, Jeremiah,' [6] may imply the existence of a belief that the latter prophet would appear before the end. It should, however, be noticed that as far as the evidence shows, Elijah stood before all others in these expectations.

(2) *The Ideal King, the Messiah.* The hope of the former period which placed at the head of the expected state *an ideal king of David's house* [7] reaches in this period, especially in the later years, a still clearer and higher development. Whatever doubt criticism may raise regarding the pre-exilic expectation of a Messiah,[8] in the age following the exile the hope is certain and at times powerful. The central position occupied by the theocratic king in Hebrew national life throughout the centuries following the establishment of the monarchy, and on the other hand the universal existence of the monarchical form in the great world-states of these ages, make it unlikely that the Jew should have conceived the coming state under any other form. Although in many writers and at certain epochs in our period the figure of the king recedes into the background or disappears, it does not follow that the ideal state was thought of as wanting this representative of Jehovah. Silence regarding him only indicates that his agency was not always conceived to be the essential force in the great events looked for. (*a*) But in studying the course of messianic hope it is important to notice this silence, and also the advance in expectation from a theocratic *dynasty* to a single theocratic *person.* [9] In the pre-exilic period, Nahum, Zephaniah, and

---

[1] Mt. 17¹⁻⁹. [2] 6²⁶. [3] Ap. Bar. 76². [4] 2 Es. 14⁹.
[5] Cf. Bousset *Antichrist* 203 ff. [6] Mt. 16¹⁴. [7] See p. 25. [8] See p. 27.
[9] See below, *b, c.*

Habbakuk spoke more or less distinctly of the messianic era without mentioning the messianic king. So likewise in this period no mention is made of him in the eschatological utterances of Joel, Obadiah,[1] Malachi,[2] Second Isaiah,[3] and Daniel.[4] The books of the Apocrypha, though containing in most cases eschatological references, do not, with the exception of 2 Esdras, mention a personal Messiah. Among other non-canonical Jewish writings in which a Messiah is wanting are the Assumption of Moses, Slavonic Enoch, the Book of Jubilees. But as already pointed out the silence of these writers does not prove his absence from their conception of the coming kingdom.

(b) Doubtless the messianic hope in the beginning looked forward, not to one individual messianic king, but to a *succession of theocratic kings,* the unbroken perpetuation of the Davidic line, and this vaguer phase of the hope appears in our period, especially in the earlier part of it. The prophecy given in the history of David, ' Thy house and thy kingdom shall be made sure for ever before thee; thy throne shall be established for ever,'[5] belonging to the former period,[6] had in view the dynasty,

[1] In Ob. v 21 the ' saviours ' are not the Messiah but deliverers raised up like the ' Judges ' of old to free Israel from their enemies, here the Edomites, though, like all deliverers, in a sense types of Christ.

[2] In Mal. 3¹ the ' messenger ' is a forerunner sent to prepare for the coming of Jehovah, who is to come in his own person to abide in his temple among his people. Whether the ' messenger ' or ' angel ' in the second part of the verse be identified with the ' messenger ' or with the ' Lord ' in the first part, cf. R.V. ' and ' or ' even,' reference can hardly be made to the theocratic king, since the function here assigned him, whether of preparing for Jehovah's coming or sitting as his representative in a purifying judgment, is nowhere else in the prophets made a part of the Messiah's activity. Cf. Hitzig *in loc.*, Stade 334.

[3] For the ' servant of Jehovah ' in 2 Is., see pp. 49 ff. Is. 55⁴, often understood of the Messiah, refers, as most modern commentators agree, to the historical David or his house. Cf. Skinner in CB., Duhm *in loc.*

[4] The expression ' one like unto a son of man,' Dan. 7¹³, determined a subsequent designation of the Messiah, and until recent times has almost universally been taken to refer to him in person. But modern scholars are to a large extent agreed that the figure is meant to characterize not an individual person but the nature of the final kingdom of God's people. This seems to be required by the writer's own interpretation given in vv. 16–18, 22, 27, according to which the four beasts symbolize heathen world-kingdoms, and the ' son of man,' *i.e. man,* who is contrasted with the beasts, symbolizes the coming kingdom of God — ' humanity in contrast with animality.' Cf. Driver *Dan.* in CB. 102 ff. The passage is messianic in the broader sense ; the same is true of the difficult passage 9²⁴⁻²⁷, where neither the facts nor the chronology can be reconciled with an application to Christ. [5] 2 S. 7¹⁶.

[6] On the pre-exilic date of the passage cf. Cornill 197 ; but others make it post-exilic. Cf. Stade in Enc. Bib. IV. 4278.

and the same is the reference in the messianic promises in
Hosea, 'Afterward shall the children of Israel return and
seek Jehovah their God and David their king,'[1] and in Amos,
'In that day will I raise up the tabernacle of David that is
fallen, . . . and will build it as in the days of old.'[2] Jeremiah[3]
designates the coming king as David or a Branch, but the
words, 'David shall never want a man to sit upon the throne of
the house of Israel'[4] show that it is the kingly line rather than
the individual person that he has in mind.[5] The same idea is
expressed by Ezekiel, who describes the rule of the messianic
kingdom under the figure of the cedar (the Davidic house)
which shall bring forth boughs and bear fruit[6] — language which
makes clear the meaning of 'my servant David' in the prophet's
other references to the rule of the messianic era.[7] This is clearly
the meaning in Psalms 89 and 132. Also 1 Maccabees[8] and
Ecclesiasticus[9] seem to contemplate the continuance of the
Davidic dynasty rather than that of a single prince.

(c) On the other hand in the unfolding of messianic revelation the expectation of a continuance of the theocratic kingship
becomes concrete in the person of a *single ideal prince* who shall
rule the people of God — an expectation which is at last realized in the Christ that 'abideth for ever.' In post-exilic times
and especially in the apocalyptic writings this idea becomes
clear and generally prevalent. The books of Isaiah and Micah
are the earliest prophetic writings to announce distinctly this
single ideal king.[10] In the wonderful picture of the eschatological era given by the former the king is an *individual*, one whose
'name shall be called, Wonderful, Counsellor, Mighty God,
Everlasting Father, Prince of Peace.'[11] The brilliant prophecy
of the coming era in Micah[12] culminates in one individual ruler
who shall come forth out of the house of David, one who 'shall

---

[1] 3[5].

[2] 9[11].   These passages in Hos. and Am. are regarded by recent critics as post-
exilic.   [3] 23[5], 30[9], 33[15] ff..   [4] 33[17].   [5] Cf. Schultz 621.   [6] 17[23].

[7] 34[23], 37[24].   Cf. Davidson *Ezk.* in CB. XLIX. 251, Stade 294, Hühn 46.
The 'one shepherd' here means, as shown by 37[15-25], that in the messianic era
the two kingdoms Judah and Israel shall be united again.   [8] 2[57].   [9] 47[11].

[10] All the paragraphs in Is. and Mic. relative to the subject are regarded by an
increasing number of critics as post-exilic.

[11] 9[6].   The other references to the messianic king in Is. are 11[1-5], 32[1].   The
context shows that 33[17], often taken as messianic, refers to Jehovah.

[12] 5[1-9], a post-exilic passage.

stand and shall feed his flock in the strength of Jehovah.'
Haggai [1] saw in the return from the captivity the dawn of the
final era and in the Davidic leader Zerubbabel the chosen one
whom Jehovah would set as his signet, the messianic king.[2]
Zechariah's view seems to have been the same.   In the promise
'Behold, I will bring forth my Servant the Branch,' [3] the
reference is apparently to Zerubbabel as the messianic prince.[4]
Second Zechariah [5] also thinks of the coming of a single personal king whose 'dominion shall be from sea to sea and from the
River to the ends of the earth.' [6]   With this would agree certain Psalms,[7] unless with many scholars these are interpreted
of a definite historical person.[8]   Jewish apocalyptic writings
which contain this form of messianic hope are, among others,
2 Esdras,[9] the Apocalypse of Baruch,[10] Enoch,[11] Sibylline
Oracles,[12] the Psalms of Solomon.[13]   In the New Testament
there is no trace of any other expectation.   The Targums
and Jewish prayers make mention of the hope under both the
individualistic and the dynastic form.

As expectation centered more clearly in a single person and
his nature and functions came to be conceived as unique, naturally a *distinctive appellation* or *title* arose ; and since from the
beginning the king of God's people was known as 'The Lord's
Anointed ' the ideal king of the coming era came to be generally
designated as preëminently ' *The* Anointed,' or preserving the
Hebrew word ' *The* Messiah.' [14]   As the distinctive title of the coming ideal king the term does not occur in the Old Testament,[15]
but is found frequently later, as in 2 Esdras,[16] the Apocalypse
of Baruch,[17] immaterially modified in the Psalms of Solomon,[18]
and Enoch.[19]   In the Talmud, Targums, and New Testament,
as the popular designation, the name is as common as the idea.

---

[1] 2^{20} ff.   [2] Cf. Stade 315, Schultz 624.   [3] 3^8, cf. 6^{12}.
[4] Cf. Hühn 63, Stade and Schultz *ibid*.   The comparison of $6^{12\ f.}$ with 4^9 shows
that Zerubbabel is meant.
[5] By this term is meant Zech. 9–14, which, though held by some to be pre-
exilic, most critics put later than the prophet Zech.   Cf. Driver. *Intr.* 349,
Cornill 363 ff.   [6] $9^{9\ f.}$ [7] 2, 45, 72, 110.   [8] Cf. Hühn 154, Schultz 641.
[9] 12^{32}, 13^{32} ff.   [10] 29, 39 f.   [11] 46, 48, 62.   [12] III. 652.   [13] XVII.
[14] הַמָּשִׁיחַ — sometimes without the article as a proper name — in the Sept.
transliterated ὁ Μεσσίας, translated ὁ Χριστός.   Cf. Volz 213, Bousset *Jud.* 214,
Drummond 283 f.
[15] Ps. 2^2 would form an exception, if against critical opinion this were referred
to the Messiah only.   [16] 12^{32}.   [17] 29^3, 30^1.   [18] 17^{32}, 18^5.   [19] 48^{10}, 52^4.

The title Son of David, found in the Psalms of Solomon [1] and in the Talmud and Targums, is seen from the New Testament to have become common in popular use.[2] The title 'Son of God' occurs in a few instances in non-Christian writings,[3] not all of which can easily be referred to Christian revision,[4] just as the people and the king of Israel are sometimes so denominated.[5] The name 'Son of Man,' made familiar to us by its use in the Gospels, will be spoken of below.[6] Other designations such as 'the Elect One,' 'the Just,' 'the Lion' do not call for special notice here.

(d) The *function* of the Messiah is thus first of all conceived to be that of the *ruler* of the theocratic kingdom; and in keeping with the ideal character of that kingdom his rule is to be one of perfect wisdom, justice, and goodness. His agency, however, especially in the earlier part of our period, is not made prominent in determining the nature or the course of the kingdom. The kingdom can hardly be called his — it is God's.[7] Jehovah is king; the laws and ordinances are his; the messianic king is his servant. '*My servant* David (*i.e.* the Messiah) shall be king over them, . . . they shall also walk in mine ordinances and observe my statutes.'[8] So thoroughly theocratic is the idea of the state that the figure of the Messiah is that of a perfunctory ruler set over a realm already established and perfected by Jehovah.[9] This conception occurs also even in later writers. 'It will come to pass,' says the Apocalypse of Baruch, 'when all is accomplished which was to come to pass in those parts, that the Messiah will then be revealed.'[10] Generally, however, in the later years, with the growing doctrine of God's apartness from the world [11] and an increasing distinctness in the conception of the office of the messianic king, the latter became the active agent in the defense of God's people, the destroyer of their enemies, and the establisher of the perfected kingdom of God. 'When the nations become turbulent and the time of my Messiah

---

[1] 17²¹.　　　[2] Cf. Mt. 9²⁷, 12²³.　　　[3] Cf. *e.g.* 2 Es. 7²⁹, 13³²,³⁷, En. 105².
[4] Cf. Volz 213, Drummond 284 ff.　　　[5] Cf. Hos. 11¹, 2 S. 7¹⁴, Ps. 2⁷, 89²⁷.
[6] Cf. p. 124 ff.
[7] Though the expression 'kingdom of God,' 'of heaven,' βασιλεία τοῦ θεοῦ, τῶν οὐρανῶν, common in later literature, does not occur in the Old Testament, the *idea* of Jehovah's rule is universal.
[8] Ezk. 37²⁴, cf. Zec. 3⁸, Mic. 5⁴.　　　[9] Cf. p. 37.　　　[10] 29³ ᶠ·, cf. En. 90³¹⁻³⁷.
[11] Cf. Baldensperger 58 ff., Bousset *Jud.* 302 ff., Hast. Extr. 308.

is come,' says the Apocalypse of Baruch,[1] ' he will both summon
all the nations, and some of them he will spare and some of them
he will slay. . . . And it will come to pass, when he has
brought low everything that is in the world and has sat down in
peace for the age on the throne of his kingdom, that joy will
then be revealed and rest appear.' So 2 Esdras, foretelling the
conflicts of the last days and the mighty acts of the Messiah,
says, ' When he shall destroy the multitude of the nations that
are gathered together, he shall defend the people that remain.'[2]
It should however be noticed that the redemption wrought by
him is national and political — it is not an ethical and spiritual
redemption of the individual soul, though evil is to be banished
from the kingdom set up by him.[3] To his agency all the blessing and glories of the messianic age finally come to be attributed.
He will bring back the scattered Israelites,[4] and distribute them
through the land after their tribes;[5] he will make Jerusalem
more splendid than the stars and the sun and the moon; he will
build an endless tower which will touch even the clouds and be
visible to all, so that all the just may see the glory of the eternal
God;[6] he will shepherd the Lord's flock in faithfulness and
righteousness and will not suffer any among them to become
feeble in their pastures;[7] he will let no iniquity lodge among
his people.[8] In his days knowledge of the Lord will be poured
out upon the earth as the waters of the sea; he will give to his
sons the majesty of the Lord, he will open the doors of Paradise
and give to the holy ones to eat of the tree of life, and the spirit
of holiness will be upon them.[9] The radiant picture of the
fruits of his rule given in the Apocalypse of Baruch embraces
not only a society delivered from all spiritual evils but also a
physical world in which pain ceases and toil is marvelously
rewarded. 'Healing will descend in dew, and disease will
withdraw, and anxiety and anguish and lamentation will pass
from amongst men and gladness will proceed through the whole

---

[1] 72 f.   Cf. 40.
[2] 13[49], cf. 12 [32 f.], Ps. Sol. 17[22], Sib. Or. V. 108, Test. Jos. 19 ; in the N. T. Mt.
24[30 f.], 2 Thess. 2[8], Rev. 19[11-15].
[3] Is. 60[21], Ps. Sol. 17[30], Sib. Or. V. 428 ff. On the atoning ' servant ' of Jehovah
see p. 49 f.   [4] 2 Es. 13[39 ff.], Ap. Abr. 31.   [5] Ps. Sol. 17[28].
[6] Sib. Or. V. 420 ff.   [7] Ps. Sol. 17[40].   [8] *Ibid.* 17[27].
[9] Test. Lev. 18[5 ff.].

earth. And no one shall again die untimely, nor shall any adversity suddenly befall. And judgments and revilings and contentions and revenges and blood and passions and envy and hatred and whatsoever things are like these shall go into condemnation when they are removed. . . . The reapers will not grow weary, nor those that build be toilworn; for the works will of themselves speedily advance with those who do them in much tranquillity.'[1] 'The earth also will yield its fruit ten thousandfold and on one vine there will be a thousand branches, and each branch will produce a thousand clusters, and each cluster will produce a thousand grapes, and each grape will produce a cor of wine. And those who have hungered will rejoice; moreover also they will behold marvels every day.'[2]

Of the three great offices attributed to the Messiah in Christian thought, those of prophet, priest, and king, the last appears almost alone before the time of Christ. In the various activities attributed to him it is his *kingly* character that is generally thought of. Yet there are not entirely wanting traces of the belief that he would join with this character the priestly and prophetic. It is doubtful whether the title *priest* is expressly given to him anywhere in the Old Testament,[3] but a certain priestly quality seems to have attached to the person of the king with the Hebrews as among other orientals. David performed the ritual acts of sacrifice and blessing,[4] as did also Solomon,[5] and similar functions are recorded of others.[6] Not unnaturally then the theocratic king of the messianic era might be conceived as sharing in priestly prerogatives. The prophecy given in Jeremiah 30²¹ describes the prince of the messianic kingdom as one who will approach unto God, that is, without an intermediary — he will enjoy the privilege of the high-priest. The king extolled in Ps. 110, and declared 'a priest forever after the manner [RVm.] of Melchizedek,' even if not in the meaning of the author the Messiah, afterwards came to be so regarded. The argument of our Lord given in Mt. 22⁴¹ ᶠᶠ·, and that of the epistle to the Hebrews 5–7, show this to have

---

[1] 73 f.   [2] 29.
[3] Zec. 6¹³ can hardly be understood to unite the priest and the king in the person of the Messiah, for unquestionably the interpretation, ' there shall be a priest upon his throne,' RVm., is to be preferred, as shown by the following clause.   [4] 2 S. 6¹⁷ ᶠ·   [5] 1 K. 8¹⁴, 9²⁵.   [6] 1 K. 12³³, 2 K. 16¹² ᶠ·

been current opinion.[1] The author of the Testaments of the XII Patriarchs, writing in the time of the Maccabees, who were first priests and then princes, derives the Messiah from the tribe of Levi, not Judah, and makes his priestly character the more prominent,[2] but in what appears a later passage[3] his origin is traced to both tribes — he unites the priestly and the kingly. But in all these allusions to the priesthood of the Messiah what seems to be thought of is the dignity of the high-priest's office and his free approach to God. There is no mention of his making expiation for the sins of the people ; nowhere in pre-Christian literature is such a function attributed to him.[4] That appears first as a Christian doctrine in the teaching of our Lord and the writers of the New Testament,[5] where it receives its fullest exposition in the epistle to the Hebrews.

The express designation of the Messiah as a *prophet* is still more uncertain. The promise that a prophet like Moses should be raised up unto Israel, Deut. 18[15], did not primarily relate to the Messiah;[6] it is not certain that it came to be associated with him before Christian insight perceived that all the great organs of the old dispensation were united in their perfection in the person of Christ. The language of the people as given in St. John, ' This is of a truth the prophet that cometh into the world; ' and the question of the Pharisees to the Baptist, ' Art thou the prophet?'[7] show that a preëminent prophet was expected, doubtless on the ground of the Mosaic promise. And it is true that Jesus is said to have perceived that the same multitude which had proclaimed him 'the prophet' was about to take him and make him king,[8] but this does not conclusively prove an identity of 'the prophet' and the Messiah in their minds, since their purpose may have been

---

[1] Undoubtedly the psalm is messianic in the broader sense as depicting ideals which are realized only in the messianic king ; and our Lord's argument and that of the epistle to the Hebrews are cogent because based on the generally acknowledged ideal contents of the psalm. Many modern interpreters take the reference to be directly to the Messiah (Delitzsch, Hengstenberg. *al.*), others understand David himself to be meant (Ewald, Orelli, *al.*), but the larger number of recent scholars, following Hitzig, take the subject of the psalm to be one of the Maccabees, in whose persons the priestly and princely were united (Duhm, Cheyne, Hühn, *al.*).   [2] Test. Lev. 8 and 18.   [3] Test. Gad 8.
[4] See p. 49.   [5] Mt. 20[28], Mk. 10[45], Jno. 1[29], 1 Jno. 2[2], Ro. 3[25], Rev. 1[5].
[6] See p. 15.   [7] 6[14], 1[21].   [8] Jno. 6[14 f.]

indicated by other words and acts which were evoked by his 'signs,' [1] and which John, after his manner, has here omitted.[2] At all events, the identification of the two was not a prevalent idea, since in the language of both the people and the leaders they are seen to be expressly distinguished.[3] The author of the Testaments of the XII Patriarchs seems to stand. alone among Jewish writers in designating the Messiah as a prophet.[4] Yet while not looked upon as holding the distinct prophetic office, he is described as performing in his kingly character functions which belonged to the prophet. Not only was he to work miracles like the prophets, but — and this is the most essential office of the prophet — he was to come in the power of the divine Spirit to reveal God's will to men. It was declared in Isaiah [5] that the Spirit of Jehovah should rest upon him, the spirit of wisdom and understanding, the spirit of counsel, and following out this thought later writers speak of his work of bringing light to men. 'All the secrets of wisdom will come forth from the thoughts of his mouth.' [6] The Samaritans expected a Messiah who would declare unto them all things.[7] The prophetic function of revealing God was never perfectly fulfilled till he came who could say, 'He that hath seen me hath seen the Father.' [8] Both his words and his works led men to recognize him as a prophet or 'the prophet.' [9]

It is not unlikely that the expected prophet and the Messiah may in the minds of the people have stood vaguely in close combination. Disciples who had recognized Jesus as a prophet mighty in deed and word had until his death hoped he would prove the promised deliverer, the Messiah (Lk. 24[21]). It was a current belief among the Jews that when the Messiah came he would not at first be clearly manifest as such. In Justin Martyr a Jew is represented as saying, 'The Messiah, even if he has been born and is somewhere existent, is unknown and does not yet even know himself, nor has he any power until Elijah shall come and anoint him and make him known to all' (*Dial. c. Tryph.* 8); and again, 'Even if they say he has come, it is not known who he is, but when he shall have become manifest and honored, then it will be known who he is' (110). A story is preserved in the Jerusalem Talmud that the Messiah shortly after his birth was snatched away from his mother by a tempest (cf. Drummond 280). This *concealment* of the Messiah before his public manifestation in

---

[1] Jno. 7[31].   [2] Cf. Zahn *in loc.*, Stanton 127.   [3] Jno. 1[25], 7[40 f.]
[4] Test. Lev. 8.   [5] 11[2].   [6] En. 51; cf. 46[3], Test. Levi 18, Test. Jud. 24.
[7] Jno. 4[25].   [8] Jno. 14[9].   [9] Cf. Mt. 21[11], Lk. 7[16], 24[19], Jno. 9[17], Ac. 3[22].

the final era referred to elsewhere (cf. En. 62[7], 2 Es. 12[32], 13[26], the Targums; see Weber *System* 342 ff., Schürer II. 620, Volz 219, Drummond 280 f.) was made by the Jews an argument against the Messiahship of our Lord. 'When the Christ cometh,' they say, 'no one knoweth whence he is' (Jno. 7[27]).

It was not, according to the Jewish idea, a part of the Messiah's functions that he should *suffer and atone for the sin of his people*. The wonderful figure of the suffering 'servant of Jehovah' portrayed in Second Isaiah embodies more than any other conception of Old Testament prophecy the characteristics which the Gospel has taught us to attribute to the Messiah as the redeemer of the world. Interwoven with our most fundamental ideas of our Lord's person and work are the words of the prophet, 'Surely he hath borne our griefs and carried our sorrows . . . he was wounded for our trangressions, . . . the chastisement of our peace was upon him; and with his stripes we are healed.'[1] And unquestionably these words regarding the 'servant of Jehovah' are indirectly most truly prophetic of Christ, and are perfectly verified in him alone.[2] Most scholars at the present time understand the 'servant' to be a *personification* of either the faithful portion of Israel, the true Israel as contrasted with the unfaithful multitude, or the *ideal* Israel, 'who by his vicarious sufferings makes atonement for the transgressions of God's people and by his loyal fulfillment of the divine mission intrusted to him becomes the "light of the Gentiles" and the missionary of the nations, so accomplishing in his own person the ideal functions of the chosen people.'[3] It is reasonably certain that neither the prophet himself nor his pre-Christian readers associated the 'servant' with the Messiah, and such association is not found in the prophets nor in any eschatological writer before the Christian era. The references to a suffering Messiah in the rabbinical writers are generally, perhaps always, of a later date.[4] The slowness of even the

---

[1] Is. 53[4 f.]
[2] The so-called 'servant passages' (Is. 42[1-4], 49[1-6], 50[4-9], 52[13]–53[12]) have been the subject of great controversy. For a good summary of the different views see Skinner in CB. *Is. XL–LXVI.* 233 ff. Cf. also Hast. Extr. Index. On the literature of the subject see Enc. Bib. IV. 4409, Hast. Extr. 707.
[3] Ottley in Hast. II. 459.
[4] Cf. Dalman *Der leidende Messias* 66 f., Weber *System* 343 ff., Schürer II. 648 ff.

E

disciples of our Lord in learning that he could submit to being
put to death [1] and the difficulty throughout the period of New
Testament history in convincing men that 'it behooved the
Christ to suffer' [2] show that at that time there was in prevalent
Jewish belief no connection between the Messiah and the 'suffering servant.'[3]   Second Esdras [4] contains the remarkable declaration that the Messiah after a reign of glory lasting 400 years
shall die and with him all that have the breath of life, as an antecedent of the final judgment; but this has no relation to an
atoning death.[5]

(*e*) *The Nature of the Messiah.* As the direct descendant of
David the Messiah was necessarily thought of as human. The
absolute monotheism of the Hebrews forbids us to understand
the utterances of the prophets as predicating metaphysical
divinity of him, unless there is no other reasonable interpretation of their words. But such an interpretation lies near at
hand. As the supreme representative and agent of Jehovah
in the rule of his people, the one upon whom the Spirit of
Jehovah should rest in largest measure, whose reign should be
in perfect wisdom and righteousness and continue forever, he
could not be characterized in terms applicable to any other
man ; and the exuberance of oriental language could hardly fall
short of ascriptions which, taken literally, belong only to the
divine. In the loftiest characterization of him given by the
prophets, that found in Isaiah,[6] the epithets are meant to describe
him as the one in whom and through whom God worked as in
and through no other. The epithet, ' Mighty God,' whether
taken to mean ' God-like hero ' or ' Hero-God,' signalizes the
might of God which is operative in the person of the Messiah.
The name 'Everlasting Father' describes him as a king who is
forever like a father to his people.[7] The name Immanuel,
' God with us,' [8] even if taken to refer to the Messiah, can de-

---

[1] Mt. 16[22], Lk. 18[34].   [2] Acts 17[3].
[3] On our Lord's attitude toward the idea, see. p. 130.   [4] 7[28 f.].
[5] The same is true of a curious and late belief found in certain rabbinical
writers that a Messiah, the son of Joseph, *i.e.* of the tribe of Joseph, called also the
son of Ephraim, and so a Messiah of the Ten tribes, would fight against hostile
powers and die before the Messiah, son of David, should set up his kingdom for
ever. Cf. Weber *System* 346 f., Schürer II. 625, Drummond 356 f.   [6] 9[6 f.]
[7] Cf. Is. 22[21]. On the whole passage cf. Delitzsch, Duhm, Cheyne, Schultz 610,
Orelli 272 ff. On 'forever' cf. Ezk. 37[25], Dan. 2[4].   [8] Is. 7[14], 8[8].

note only God's presence through his representative. But while the prophets always thought of the Messiah as human, they conceived him to be endowed with powers and attributes which far transcended those of all other men, and their ideal could not be comprehended within the limits of their forms of thought. What they saw *dimly* could find its perfect embodiment only in him who was 'God incarnate, Man divine.' In the later years of our period there arose a clearer perception of his actual superhuman nature, as will be seen below.[1]

(3) *The relation of the kingdom and religion of Jehovah to the Gentiles in the messianic age.* The slowness of the people of Israel to learn that there is but one God, Jehovah, is seen in their frequent lapses into the worship of heathen divinities, to whom they must have attributed a real being and power. How early the truth of absolute monotheism came to be apprehended even by the religious leaders cannot be determined with certainty, because many utterances attributed to earlier writers are probably to be referred to a later source. But whatever tendencies to recognize national gods may have existed before the exile, after that period the belief is general in Israel that the gods of the heathen are no gods, that Jehovah alone is God,[2] and that he is sovereign Lord over all the world. As a result partly of this general perception of the oneness of God and his holy character and partly of movements in political history, *three* important ideas regarding the relation of the eschatological kingdom to the Gentiles — ideas doubtless already seized by the more enlightened minds — emerge in our period into clearness : (*a*) the chosen people have a mission to make Jehovah known to the Gentiles; (*b*) Jehovah must be acknowledged by all mankind ; (*c*) the messianic kingdom must embrace all peoples of the earth. (*a*) Out of the experience of the exile the author of the wonderful prophecies in Second Isaiah comes with the message, that as Jehovah has ordained prophets and priests for his people, so he has raised up his 'servant' Israel to perform the like offices for the Gentile world ; 'I will give thee for a light to the Gentiles, that thou mayest be my salvation unto the end of the earth ';[3] 'I will give thee for a covenant of the people,

---

[1] Cf. p. 73 ff. [2] Is. 44[6], 45[14]. [3] Is. 49[6].

for a light of the Gentiles; to open the blind eyes, to bring out
the prisoners from the dungeon, and them that sit in darkness
out of the prison-house.' [1] And the consciousness of this sublime mission, though in many quarters stifled by the narrow
spirit of Judaism, appears not seldom in the course of our period.
It finds expression in some of the Psalms: 'God be merciful
unto us and bless us, . . . *that* thy way may be known upon
earth, thy salvation among all nations'; [2] it appears in the
apocalyptic writers: 'The people of the great God will be to
all mortals the guide to life'; [3] it is the most potent of the
forces in the proselytism active in the last centuries of Israel's
history. This belief in God's merciful regard for the Gentiles
is nobly set forth in the book of Jonah, a poem which out of a
legend regarding the prophet brings with dramatic power the
truth that God wills the repentance of all sinners, even the
heathen, and that he himself provides for their instruction and
admonition.

(*b*) The expectation that the rule and worship of Jehovah would
be universally recognized in the eschatological age now becomes
common. Unto him 'every knee shall bow, every tongue shall
swear'; [4] his 'house shall be called a house of prayer for all
peoples'; [5] 'Jehovah will arise upon thee [Jerusalem]. . . . And
nations shall come to thy light and kings to the brightness of thy
rising.' [6] The prophet of Isaiah 60 gives a sublime picture of
the nations thronging to Jerusalem with their wealth of gold
and frankincense and herds to offer all in sacrifice to Jehovah,
and with their sons and daughters to minister before him. [7]

(*c*) And the Messiah's dominion, vaster even than the great world-
empires, which presented to the Jew an imperfect prototype
of a universal sway, is described as a dominion which should
reach from sea to sea and from the River to the ends of the
earth. [8] 'The greatness of the. kingdoms under the whole
heaven shall be given to the people of the saints of the Most
High.' [9] In non-canonical writers also the same outlook is ex-

---

[1] 42[6 f.], cf. 51[4].   [2] Ps. 67[1], cf. 96[3], 102[15].
[3] Sib. Or. III. 194 f., cf. En. 48[4], 105[1], Test. Lev. 18.   [4] Is. 45[23].
[5] 56[7].   [6] 60[2 f.], cf. 44[5].
[7] Cf. also 49[22 f.], 56[6 f.], Zec. 8[20 ff.], 14[16 ff.], Tob. 13[11], Ps. Sol. 17[31], Ap. Bar. 68[5],
Sib. Or. III. 710.   [8] Zec. 9[10].
[9] Dan. 7[27], cf. Is. 2[2-4], Ps. 22[27 f.].

pressed. 'There will come the holy ruler who will hold the scepter over the whole earth.'[1]

On the other hand, parallel with the glorious prophecy of the nations paying homage to Jehovah and their incorporation into the messianic kingdom, there runs through our whole period another and more common view. The bitter sufferings of God's people at the hands of the world-conquerors, and the degradation of the nations in morals and religion caused the Jews to regard all Gentiles as the enemies of God and doomed to merciless destruction. Fierce predictions of the outpouring of God's fury upon all the nations and their utter destruction are the prophecies predominant in the later prophets and apocalyptic writers. Jehovah's wrath will be visited upon the people of the earth through fire and sword, and through all the forces of nature; all powers will be overthrown, all the heathen will be consumed with unrelenting vengeance.[2] Intermediate between these two views and in part reconciling them are glimpses of the idea of a *remnant* which should be left among the peoples judged and which should be joined with the people of God. Visitations sent upon them should produce fruit among the Gentiles also.[3] 'It shall come to pass that every one that is left of all the nations that came against Jerusalem shall go up from year to year to worship the King, Jehovah of hosts.'[4] The universalistic ideal which recognized God's mercy for the Gentiles and looked for their admission into the messianic kingdom could not in the conditions of the post-exilic era become the *predominant* belief. The influence in the opposite direction of particularism was too powerful. The Jewish people in these centuries, as the subjects of foreign powers, formed an organized religious community rather than an actual state and their very existence as the people of God depended upon a rigorous maintenance of the laws and ordinances of their religion. This became the period of *legalism*. The Mosaic law now reached its fullest development, and observance of its ceremonial rites and prescriptions constituted the essential in loyalty to Jehovah, perhaps even more than did performance of the moral and

---

[1] Sib. Or. III. 49, cf. Ps. Sol. 17³⁰, En. 48⁵, 62⁶, Ap. Bar. 53¹⁰.
[2] Cf. Ezk. 39¹⁻²⁰, Is. 47, 63⁶, 66¹⁵, Jl. 3. Ob. vv 15 f., Zec. 14¹⁻¹⁵, Dan. 7¹¹ᶠ·, 2 Es. 13³⁷ᶠ·, Ps. Sol. 17²⁴, Ap. Bar. 40, 72⁶, Sib. Or. III. 303–651, Test. Sim. 6.
[3] Cf. Is. 19¹⁸⁻²². [4] Zec. 14¹⁶, cf. 9⁷, Jer. 12¹⁵ᶠ·, Ap. Bar. 72⁵, Test. Jud. 24.

spiritual duties enjoined. All that lay outside of this consecrated community was unclean, unholy, hateful to God. More and more the necessity of entire separation from the nations came to be felt, and there resulted the narrow, hardened exclusiveness such as is seen in the pharisaism of the New Testament era. As Israel was not yet ready for the truth that the Messiah would suffer for his people,[1] so the idea of the universality of his kingdom could not be largely fruitful till the Gospel revealed its true meaning.

(4) *The central seat of worship and rule in the messianic kingdom.* In the prophecies mentioned above it will be noticed that even where the conception of the messianic kingdom comes nearest to Christian universalism, Jerusalem is to be the center of Jehovah's worship for all nations and the seat of rule over all the earth.[2] Many peoples and strong nations will come to seek Jehovah of hosts in Jerusalem, ten men out of all the languages of the nations will take hold of the skirt of him that is a Jew, saying, We will go with you;[3] the gates of Jerusalem will not be shut day nor night that men may bring unto it the wealth of the nations;[4] in Mount Zion will be set up the throne of universal judgment;[5] 'From the whole earth they will bring incense and gifts to the house of the great God, and there will be no other house with men, . . . all the paths of the field, and the rough hills and the high mountains and the wild waves of the sea will be passable on foot and for ships in those days.'[6] The ideal is local and earthly; no other is found in the Old Testament Scriptures. Heaven as the destined abode of the saints is there unknown. A purely spiritual kingdom in which the blessed abide and reign with God in a world beyond appears first in the Apocrypha and the apocalyptic writings; but even there does not displace the idea of a national and terrestrial realm; that continues to occupy the center of eschatological outlook. The disciples who stood nearest to our Lord were slow to learn that the Messiah's kingdom is not of this world.[7] 'The numerous popular dis-

[1] See p. 49.   [2] Zec. 9[9 f.]   [3] Zec. 8[22 f.]   [4] Is. 60[11].
[5] 2 Es. 13[35 ff.], Ap. Bar. 40[1].
[6] Sib. Or. III. 772 ff. Cf. citations on p. 52, also Ezk. 17[23], Is. 61[5 f.], 66[18 ff], Ob. v 21, En. 90[33], Sib. Or. III. 718 f.   [7] Cf. Ac. 1[6].

turbances of a politico-religious nature in the time of the
Procurators (A.D. 44–66) show sufficiently the feverish expectation with which the people look forward to a miraculous
intervention of God in the course of history and to the dawn
of his kingdom on earth. How else could men like Theudas
and the Egyptian have found believers in their promises by
hundreds and thousands?' [1] — language equally applicable to
the rebellion of Bar-Cochba, whom many held to be the
Messiah.

The remarkable passages Is. 19[19], speaking of an altar to Jehovah in
Egypt, and Mal. 1[11], speaking of incense offered to Jehovah among the
Gentiles from the rising to the setting of the sun, while containing 'a
notable effort to break through the localized conception of God's kingdom'
(Orelli 318), are not at variance with the representation found everywhere
in our period regarding Jerusalem as the religious center even for foreign
nations. Such offerings are expressive of a recognition of Jehovah (akin
to the worship of an Israelite in exile) beyond Zion his chosen dwelling-
place, to which all nations will also bring their oblations, as to the sole
seat of Jehovah's abode.

But while the eschatological kingdom is thus local and earthly,
it is conceived under a form fitting the perfected reign of God
and the perfected condition of man. On through the prophets
and apocalyptic writers the picture unfolds itself with wonderful splendor. The universe of nature and man will be wholly
transformed ; the wilderness and the dry land will be glad, the
desert will rejoice and blossom as the rose, the eyes of the
blind will be opened and the ears of the deaf unstopped, the
lame will leap as a hart and the tongue of the dumb sing ;
the ransomed of Jehovah will come with singing unto Zion
and everlasting joy will be upon their heads, they will obtain
joy and gladness, and sorrow and sighing will flee away;[2] the
wolf and the lamb will feed together, the lion will eat straw
like the ox, they will not hurt nor destroy in all God's holy
mountain.[3] The apocalyptic writers following on in the line
of the prophets reproduce this picture, sometimes in varied
form only, sometimes with extravagant additions.[4] The glory
of the kingdom will be especially exhibited in the resplendency
of its capital city. Jerusalem will be builded with sapphires

[1] Schürer II. 604. [2] Is. 35. [3] 65[25].
[4] Cf. En. 10[17 ff.], 25[6], Ap. Bar. 73[2 ff.], cited on p. 45 f., Sib. Or. III. 743 ff.

and emeralds and precious stones ; its walls and towers and
battlements with pure gold; its streets will be paved with
beryl and carbuncle and stones of Ophir.[1] The hope which
inspires this glowing panegyric of Tobit breaks out in the exultant call of Baruch : 'Put off, O Jerusalem, the garment
of thy mourning and affliction, and put on the comeliness of
the glory that cometh from God for ever, . . . set a diadem
on thine head of the glory of the Everlasting. For God will
show thy brightness to every region under heaven.'[2] From
the idea of *transformation* a fervid religious imagination passes
on to the *destruction* of the heavens and the earth that now
are,[3] and to a *new creation* which shall abide for ever. 'Behold,
I create new heavens and a new earth, and the former things
shall not be remembered.'[4] 'Everything that is corruptible
will pass away, and everything that dies will depart; . . . and
the hour comes which will abide for ever, and the new world
which does not turn to corruption those who depart to its
blessedness.'[5]

In view, on the one hand, of the highly ideal glory of the
transformed Jerusalem, as pictured in these hopes, and on the
other, of the traditional belief that the earthly tabernacle was
a copy of a heavenly pattern,[6] it is easy to understand the rise
of the idea of a Jerusalem altogether heavenly, which in the
messianic age should descend upon the earth as the Holy City
of God's people, though the old idea of the renewal and glorification of the present Jerusalem still remained predominant.
Enoch[7] sees in vision the removal of the old Jerusalem, and
the bringing in of the new. The former is wrapped up, and
with all its pillars and beams and ornaments is carried away.
Then 'the Lord of the sheep brought in a new house greater
and higher than that first house, and set it up on the place of
the first; . . . all its columns were new, also the ornaments
were new and greater than those of the first old one which
he had carried away; . . . and the Lord of the sheep was
therein.' In the Apocalypse of Baruch, as the seer laments the

---

[1] Tob. 13[16] f.   [2] Bar. 5[1] ff.   Cf. Is. 54[11 f.], Ps. Sol. 17[31], Sib. Or. V. 420 ff.
[3] Is. 51[6], Jl. 2[31], Ps. 102[26 f.], 2 Es. 6[20], En. 1[6 ff.], Mt. 24[29], 2 Pet. 3[10].
[4] Is. 65[17].
[5] Ap. Bar. 44[9 ff.], cf. 32[6], Is. 66[22], 2 Es. 6 [15 f.], 7[75], 2 Pet. 3[12 f.], Rev. 21[1].
[6] Ex. 25[40], Heb. 8[5].   [7] 90[28 f.]

destruction of Jerusalem there comes to him the word of the Lord, ' Dost thou think that this is that city of which I said, On the palms of my hand have I graven thee? It is not this building which is now built in your midst; it is that which will be revealed with me, that which was prepared beforehand here from the time when I took counsel to make Paradise, and showed it to Adam before he sinned; . . . I showed it to my servant Abraham by night among the portions of the victims. And again I showed it to Moses on Mount Sinai, . . . and now, behold, it is preserved with me, as also Paradise.'[1] This idea was common in the later centuries of our period ; it appears frequently in the rabbinical writings,[2] and also in the New Testament in the expressions ' new Jerusalem ' ' heavenly Jerusalem,' ' Jerusalem that is above.'[3] Its most magnificent expression is that given in the vision of the Holy City coming down out of heaven from God as described in Rev. 21–22. While the profound spiritual insight of the New Testament writers gives to their words a meaning beyond the literal limitation, their language nevertheless shows the commonness of the idea.

It should in conclusion be noticed, however, that all the material glories, all the earthly blessings ascribed to the messianic kingdom and the new Jerusalem are only the corollary of its *spiritual* perfections. God will dwell there continually with his people, and will be unto them an everlasting light;[4] the covenant of his peace will never be removed;[5] all will be taught of Jehovah and enjoy great peace;[6] a fountain for sin and uncleanness will be opened there;[7] God will give his people a new heart, that they may walk in his statutes and keep his ordinances;[8] they will all be righteous;[9] the unclean will no more come there.[10] And this crowning characterization of ·the kingdom, as given in the prophets, continues through the post-canonical writers.[11]

---

[1] 4² ff., cf. 32² ff., 2 Es. 7²⁶, 8⁵².
[2] Cf. Weber *System* 386, the newly discovered Odes of Solomon 4³. See Dalman *Worte* 106.   [3] Rev. 3¹², 21², Heb. 12²², Gal. 4²⁶.
[4] Is. 60¹⁹, Zec. 8³, Jl. 3¹⁷.   [5] Is. 54¹⁰.   [6] 54¹³.   [7] Zec. 13¹.
[8] Ezk. 11¹⁹.   [9] Is. 60²¹.   [10] 52¹.
[11] Cf. 2 Es. 6²⁷ f., 8⁵³, En. 10²⁰ f., 69²⁹, Ps. Sol. 17³², ⁴¹, Test. Levi 18, Jub. 1¹⁷, ²³ ff., ²⁸.

(5) *The lot of those who die before the incoming of the kingdom.*
Not until late in Hebrew history does the belief, that the dead
will rise to share in the blessedness of the messianic kingdom,
emerge with clearness and obtain wide acceptance. The state
of the dead as thought of through nearly the whole period of
the Old Testament writings is one of a shadowy existence in
an underworld of darkness, from which there is no return.[1]
The dead continue to exist, but in a mode which is not called
life. In a subject about which gathered inscrutable mystery,
upon which there was no attempt to form sharply defined and
systematic ideas, the language of the prophets and poets of the
Old Testament must not be pressed with too rigorous literal-
ness, nor must we expect exact self-consistency even in a single
writer. But there is general agreement in representing the
state of the dead as in sharp contrast with all that is most
valued in life. They are cut off from communion with God
and even from his care.[2] Remembrance and knowledge of the
things of life are gone, pleasure is no more, pain and sadness
take its place;[3] princes and captives, the servant and his master, the small and the great, are alike there.[4] There are, to be
sure, traces of a somewhat different view, according to which
the distinctions of this life continue; kings occupy thrones,
they remember the king of Babylon, and greet him with taunts
as he comes down among them;[5] they are thought to have
knowledge of human affairs, and are consulted in divination.[6]
But this is the less usual view, and even this does not strongly
lighten up their unsubstantial existence. The thought which
cheered Socrates in view of his end, that in Hades he would
be in blessed communion with the great and good of all time[7]
is not found among the Hebrews; their view of death was not
brighter than that of the Homeric Achilles, who in the underworld laments: 'Speak not comfortably to me of death; I
would rather on earth do villain's service to another, one without inheritance, whose substance is but little, than be king of
all the dead.'[8] Death may be spoken of as a release from

---

[1] Job 10²¹ ᶠ·　　　　[2] Is. 38¹⁸, Ps. 6⁵, 30⁹, 88⁵, ¹¹ ᶠ, 115¹⁷, Job 10²¹ ᶠ·, 14⁷⁻¹².
[3] Job 7⁷⁻¹⁰, 14²¹ ᶠ·, Ec. 9¹⁰.　　　　[4] Job 3¹³ ᶠᶠ·, Ec. 9².
[5] Is. 14⁹ ᶠ·　Cf. Ezk. 32²¹.　　　[6] 1 S. 28⁸⁻¹⁹, Is. 8¹⁹.　　　[7] Plat. *Apol.* 40–41.
[8] *Od.* XI. 488 ff. Cf. Schultz 554 ff., Stade 183 f., Schwally *Leben nach d.*
Tode 63 ff., Salmond *Immortality* 200 ff.

trouble and pain,[1] but in the Old Testament it is not thought of as a state where the wrongs of life will be righted, iniquity punished, virtue rewarded.[2] The awards of conduct fall in this world. The rewards of the good are prosperity, long life, and a peaceful death; [3] the wicked are visited with misfortune, and with an untimely and miserable death; [4] or if the due awards do not come to a man himself, they befall his family or people, perhaps in a later generation.[5] Strange as this last mentioned allotment may seem to us with our developed sense of individuality, it did not appear so to the earlier Hebrews with whom the solidarity of the family, tribe, or people was a ruling idea.[6] The individual being lost in the larger unit, the sense of justice was not disturbed, if retribution was transferred to one's descendants or people. So late as the times of Jeremiah and Ezekiel do the worth and claims of the individual first begin to assume clearness in the religious consciousness of the Hebrews.

The hope which in time came to relieve this gloomy outlook into death did not as among the Greeks arise from a belief in an immortality of higher activity for the soul freed from the hindrances of the body,[7] but rather from a belief in a release from the prison-house, a bodily resurrection to life in all its fullness of joy and capability.[8] This belief was slow to arise because of the imperfect sense of personality just mentioned. The Hebrew was satisfied with an immortality which was realized in the continuance of his family and people. God's purposes were thought to relate to the nation and not to the individual, except as contributing to the nation's good. The good man who walked with God was conscious of the divine favor in life and at the hour of death, and having performed his part he was content to depart and leave the future with its

---

[1] Job 3[13] ff.

[2] For the later idea of a partial retribution between death and the resurrection, see p. 69 f.   [3] Ps. 91[3-16], 37[25-27], Job 5[19-26], Num. 23[10].

[4] Ps. 55[23], Job 31[2 f.], Prov. 6[15].   [5] Ex. 20[5], Num. 14[18], Lam. 5[7], Ezk. 18[2].

[6] Cf. Davidson in Hast. I. 738, Stade 285 ff., Mozley *Ruling Ideas in Early Ages* 37 ff., 87 ff.   [7] Plat. *Phaed.* 66 f., 79 ff.

[8] The intermediate state, in spite of a more comfortable hope which came to be attached to it in the latter part of our period (see p. 69 f.), still remained only an imperfect state of waiting for the complete release and recompense of the resurrection.

retributions and fortunes with God.   There is no certain
evidence of a belief in a personal resurrection until after the
exile.   There are certain passages [1] which read in the light of
later revelation seem to declare the resurrection hope ; but
when interpreted from the historical standpoint of their utterance they cannot be regarded as intended by their authors to
express this meaning.   It is obviously impossible to enter here
into the exegesis of these various passages ; it must suffice to
say that critics are now for the most part agreed that they do
not assert the doctrine of the resurrection; the language is
figurative and refers in part to the restoration of the *nation* to
a new life after its spiritual and political failure spoken of
under the figure of death,[2] and in part to temporal deliverances
of the *individual* from imminent perils or present distresses.[3]
Divine revelation in this as in other truths was progressive,[4]
and of the influences which prepared the Hebrews to receive
the doctrine some may be obscure, *e.g.* contact with other peoples, but others are manifest.   The universal belief in the
nation's restoration in the glory of the last days, the strong
consciousness that real life consisted not in a physical existence
but in spiritual union with God, these and similar factors in
religious thought must have awakened at least an *aspiration* in
the individual for a survival in death — an aspiration which in
some cases could hardly have fallen short of hope.   Leading
directly to this hope were those influences which fostered a
growth in the sense of personality, that is, a growth in the
perception that the individual member, no less than the people
as a whole, possessed worth with God and claims upon his
righteousness.   In the very fact of membership in God's people, and in the communion with God thus assured, there lay
prerogatives which gave dignity to the individual.   Also the
moral and religious law of the Mosaic system aimed at not
only the nation's relation to God, but also the spiritual life
of the individual, the rightness of individual conduct.   The
divine favor shown to the preëminently good, the stringent

---

[1] Job 19^{25} ff., Is. 53^{10}, Ezk. 37$^{1-14}$, Hos. 6^2, Ps. 16^{10} f., 17^{15}, 49^{15}.
[2] Cf. Ezk. 37^{11}, Hos. 13^1.
[3] Cf. Schultz 595 ff., Cheyne *Origin and Religious Contents of the Psalter*,
Salmond *Immortality* 237 ff., Schwally 112 ff., Enc. Bib. II, 1345 ff., III. 3956 ff.
[4] Cf. Ottley, 162 ff.

accountability for his deeds laid upon every person, the far-reaching consequences for good or for evil seen in the issues of individual acts, all tended to awaken a sense of the person's place in the regard and purposes of God.[1] But such tendencies worked slowly, especially as long as the nation existed in its integrity. When, however, in the Babylonian conquest the nation as such perished, the religious significance of the individual came to be more distinctly perceived. Ezekiel, the great prophet of the new direction in thought, gives its keynote in the words, ' What mean ye, that ye use this proverb, . . . The fathers have eaten sour grapes, and the children's teeth are set on edge ? As I live, saith the Lord Jehovah, ye shall not have occasion any more to use this proverb in Israel. Behold, all souls are mine ; as the soul of the father, so also the soul of the son, . . . the son shall not bear the iniquity of the father, neither shall the father bear the iniquity of the son.' [2] But this clear sense of personal accountability and personal retribution brought up with inevitable force the perplexing question of the inequalities of life, the suffering of the innocent, the impunity and prosperity of the wicked (the book of Job struggled with, but did not solve, the problem) ; and the righteousness of God could no longer be vindicated by an appeal to the course of this world alone ; a wider outlook was demanded to adjust the due relation between the lot of the individual and the orderings of a righteous God. It will be seen then that there lay in the religion and history of the Hebrews a factor which prepared them, though not till the later centuries, to receive the revelation of a life after death.[3] But individualism could never among the Hebrews lead to severance from the unity of God's people. In neither the old dispensation nor the new is the final felicity conceived of as apart from the Church of the redeemed. The Hebrew's life after death must be a part of that perfected life of his people in the messianic age. An incorporeal immortality entered upon immediately after death, such as the Greek anticipated,

[1] Cf. *idem* 338 ff.   [2] 18[2-4], [20].

[3] It is not necessary then to look for the *origin* of the resurrection doctrine in foreign influence, though its growth may have been accelerated by contact with the Persian religion.   See p. 81 ff.   Cf. Bousset *Jud.* 480, Volz 129 f., Fairweather in Hast. Extr. 307.

could not satisfy Hebrew aspiration.[1] As the righteous God
would glorify his people in the last days, and would gather
back the dispersed from the ends of the earth, so it came to be
an article of Jewish faith that the righteous dead also would
be raised to their retribution in the glory of the new kingdom.

In the Old Testament there are but two passages which with
unquestioned certainty announce the hope of a personal resurrection. The earlier of these, Is. 26[19] (placed by critics almost
unanimously after the exile), contemplates the resurrection of
the righteous Israelites to dwell with the righteous nation in the
' strong city ' [2] of the messianic world. No mention is made
here of the resurrection of unfaithful Israelites nor of the
Gentiles. It is expressly stated in v. 14 that the oppressors of
Israel shall not rise ; these all remain in the underworld of
the dead. The second passage, Dan. 12[2], belonging to a still
later date, though not asserting a *universal* resurrection, contains
the first recorded announcement of a resurrection of unrighteous
ones to receive their final doom. There is nothing to indicate
that the writer's outlook here extends beyond Israel, embracing
the dead generally. [3] The utterance seems to have the tone of
a truth already familiar to the readers,[4] but it is not possible
to trace with certainty the influences which in the period between the two declarations led to this widening of expectation
to include unrighteous dead. Resurrection as required for the
perfect reward of the righteous Israelite might naturally suggest the like requisite for the punishment of the unrighteous.[5]

In the following centuries the hope appears with increasing
frequency, in the non-canonical writings, and with varying
scope. [6] Sometimes the resurrection is limited to the righteous [7]
— this according to Josephus was the belief of the Pharisees ; [8]
sometimes it is spoken of as embracing all the dead [9] — this
seems to have been the popular belief in New Testament times,[10]

---

[1] The appearance of this form of hope in 4 Mac. 14[5], 16[6], 17[18], is due to
Greek influence — it is not Hebrew.   [2] 26[1 f.].   [3] Cf. Shultz 602.
[4] It may perhaps be implied in Is. 24[21 f.] ; cf. Enc. Bib. II. 1355.
[5] On the possibility of Persian influence cf. pp. 79 ff.
[6] Cf. Volz 126 ff., 237 ff., Charles *Eschatology*, Drummond 360 ff., Schürer
II. 638 ff.   [7] Cf. 2 Mac. 7[14, 36], En. 91[10], 92[3-5], Ps. Sol. 3[12], 14[9].
[8] *Ant*. XVIII. 14.
[9] 2 Es. 7[32], En. 51[1], Ap. Bar. 50 f., Sib. Or. IV. 180 ff., Test. Ben. 10.
[10] Cf. Jno. 11[24].

and according to Ac. 24¹⁵ that of the Pharisees. On the other hand the belief in either form did not make its way without opposition. Many writings are silent regarding it (*e.g.* Tobit, Judith, Wisdom, Baruch, 1 Maccabees, Jubilees) and even in New Testament times it was a subject of dispute, and was denied by the Sadducees.[1]

The question of the Corinthians anticipated by St. Paul, ' How are the dead raised, and with what manner of body do they come ? ' (1 Co. 15³⁵) appears also in the non-canonical writers of our period, but often without a clear and self-consistent answer (cf. Weber *System* 353, Volz 250 ff., Bousset *Jud.* 262). The expectation of an earthly messianic kingdom with material glories carried with it the idea of a material body made perfect and imperishable. The common view in both popular belief and the rabbinical writings was that the former earthly body was restored (2 Mac. 7¹¹, Ap. Bar. 50², En. 51¹, Sib. Or. IV. 180) ; according to one account the resurrection body was to be developed out of one of the vertebræ (cf. Weber *ibid.*, Drummond 386). On the other hand there occurs the idea of a new and different body, as the abode of the risen soul, in keeping with the renewal of the world ; ' The just will be clothed with the garment of glory, and this will be . . . a garment of life ' (En. 62¹⁵ f.) ; ' they will be as the angels ' (En. 51⁴, cf. Mk. 12²⁵). Josephus (*Bel.* II. 163, III. 374) gives it as the belief of the Pharisees that the souls of the righteous will live again in another and pure body. Even the figure of the grain of wheat, used by St. Paul (1 Co. 15³⁷), occurs in the rabbinical writings to illustrate the change in the embodiment of the risen soul (cf. Weber *ibid.*, Drummond 385). The idea of a glorified body is perhaps suggested by Dan. 12³ ; it is implied in 2 Es. 7⁹⁷, and receives its most-splendid statement in St. Paul (1 Co. 15³⁵⁻⁵⁴, Ph. 3²¹). The Apocalypse of Baruch (50 f.) gives a striking account of the body at the resurrection and its *change* into a glorified body. The seer had asked, ' In what shape will those live who live in thy day ? ' and the answer is, ' The earth will then assuredly restore the dead . . . making no change in their form, . . . for then it will be necessary to show to the living that the dead have come to life again. . . . It will come to pass when that appointed day has gone by that then shall the aspect of those who are condemned be afterwards changed, and the glory of those who are justified, . . . their splendor will be glorified in changes and the form of their face will be turned into the light of their beauty, that they may be able to acquire and receive the world which does not die ; . . . they shall be made like unto the angels and be made equal to the stars.' On the transformation see 1 Co. 15⁵¹ ff. ; cf. Charles *Ap. Bar.* p 81 ff.

Eschatological Developments in the Closing Centuries of this Period. In the preceding pages the leading eschatological

[1] Mk. 12¹⁸, Ac. 23⁸.

expectations of the Hebrews have been set forth chiefly as dominated in nature and form by the *national* idea. In some instances, *e.g.* the belief in a resurrection, it has been convenient
to trace these out in the form which they assumed in a growth
beyond these narrower limitations. In general these earlier expectations persist without fundamental change throughout our
period, as has been seen above in the frequent references to
post-canonical writings ; they are by no means superseded or
displaced by others so as to be neglected in a survey of the
eschatology of the closing years of the period. At the same
time in the later centuries influences already spoken of — such
as the loss of political independence, a clearer conception of the
nature of God and the universality of his sway, the growing
sense of the worth of the individual, contact with the beliefs of
other peoples — widened the horizon ; an outlook was attained
beyond the local, temporal, earthly, and expectation became
more spiritualized, more transcendental. There was naturally
much vagueness and inconsistency in the prevalent anticipations
of the end; the earlier and later forms were present side by
side without greatly disturbing reflection. The apocalyptic
writings, in which the later eschatological ideas are chiefly
contained, are generally compilations into which inconsistent
expectations have been brought together without serious effort
to reconcile the differences. The following paragraphs will
give a brief survey of the form which the more important
eschatological beliefs assumed in this process of growth beyond
national aspects, as well as of new factors which now arose.
These various developments of the later years are of the utmost
interest and significance as a part of the history of religious
belief, and especially because of their close relation to eschatological doctrines found in the New Testament.

(1) *The Present and the Coming Age.* It may be said that
while the earlier, traditional outlook contemplated a new
nation, the later contemplated a new world; that is, in the
earlier expectation the nation was to be delivered from and
triumph over its enemies, a kingdom of glory and universal
sway was to be set up in Palestine, Jehovah was to dwell with
his people in his temple at Jerusalem, and all nature *in its*

present order was to be renewed; whereas the later hope looked beyond all racial and even terrestrial limits to a great new world-order in contrast with this present world. Not Israel was the subject of the vision, but man universally and individually; not the restoration of the *people*, but the resurrection and immortality of the righteous *man;* not Palestine, but the new earth and the new heavens; not the hostile nations, but the powers of wickedness whether mundane or supermundane. Two clearly contrasted conceptions took their place in religious thought — the *present*, and the *coming world ;* the latter not growing out of the former by any process of natural issue or gradual change, but introduced by the sudden intervention of divine power in the cataclysm of the world-judgment, which should bring to an end the old order with everything pertaining to it, and open the way to the new. This view is concisely enunciated in 2 Esdras : 'The Most High hath not made one world, but two.' 'This present world is not the end; the full glory abideth not therein. . . . But the day of judgment shall be the end of this time and the beginning of the immortality for to come.'[1] An earlier and less distinct expression of the same view is found in the book of Daniel, where two great periods, the first that of the world-kingdoms symbolized by beasts, the second that of the saints receiving sway over all mankind, appear in immediate succession.[2] The aspect of the world's history as viewed thus is frequent in later writers, either directly expressed[3] or presupposed in their pictures of the last days ; while in the New Testament the terms, 'this world' and 'the world to come,' as the two correlatives embracing the sum of existence, become everywhere present in ethical and eschatological utterances.[4] The outlook upon this present world is throughout pessimistic. The cruel oppression of God's people by the world-powers, the triumph of evil on all sides, and the prevalence of unfaithfulness and iniquity in Israel itself bred despair. More and more the

---

[1] 7[50], 112 f.   [2] Dan. 7.

[3] Cf. Ap. Bar. 83[8], En. 16[1], 48[7], Sl. En. 65[6] ff., Sib. Or. III. 80 ff.

[4] Cf. ὁ αἰὼν οὗτος Mt. 12[32], Lk. 16[8], Ro. 12[2], Eph. 1[21] ; ὁ νῦν αἰών 1 Tim. 6[17], 2 Tim. 4[10] · ὁ αἰὼν ὁ μέλλων, ὁ ἐρχόμενος Mt. 12[32], Mk. 10[20], Eph. 1[21], Heb. 6[5]. For these technical terms in non-canonical literature cf. 2 Es. 4[27], 6[9]. 8[1], Ap. Bar. 14[13], 15[7], 48[50], En. 71[15], Sl. En. 61[2]. They are common in the rabbinical writers also ; see Weber *System* 354.

F

present order came to be regarded as hopelessly corrupt, as given over to evil powers of whom Satan was chief, and as fit only for avenging destruction ; [1] and this estimate of the present age, common in non-canonical literature of these later centuries, was also taken up into the conceptions of the New Testament writers. The term, 'this world,' 'the world,' becomes a concrete expression for the dominion of sin,[2] of which Satan is the god or ruler, which he may give to whom he will ; [3] it is a world that passeth away ; [4] it is now ·' stored up for fire, being reserved against the day of judgment and destruction of ungodly men.' [5]

(2) *The Judgment.* Between these two world-periods, closing this age and ushering in the age to come, stands the judgment, the day of Jehovah, but now not conceived as the great day of battle in which the hosts of God march against the nations hostile to Israel, or the day of punishment upon faithless Israelites.· The great act is not military, but forensic and universal. Thrones are set and the Ancient of days with attending hosts sits in judgment ; [6] before him are gathered the spirits of other orders, men of all kindreds and tongues, the dead raised again, to receive their award. The division is no longer between Israel and not-Israel, but between the righteous and the wicked, whose deeds are recorded in the opened books.[7] The *reward of the righteous* is oftenest spoken of as 'eternal life,' a term common in non-canonical literature as well as in the New Testament, and denoting participation in all the blessedness of the eternal world. The figure of light also is often used to describe the glory and blessedness of the state. The *dwelling-place* in this eternal state is oftenest thought of as on the new earth, or at least in a visible Paradise.[8] The conceptions of a world renewed and of a bodily resurrection are necessarily joined with the idea of an abode apprehended by the senses. 'I will change the earth, make it a blessing, and

---

[1] Cf. Ap. Bar. 83[10 ff.], 2 Es. 11[40 ff.], En. 80, 99 f., Jub. 10[8], Test. Dan 5.
[2] Jno. 14[17], Ro. 12[2], Eph. 2[2], 1 Co. 11[32], Ja. 4[4], 1 Jno. 5[4].
[3] 2 Co. 4[4], Eph. 6[12], Jno. 14[30], Mt. 4[9].   [4] 1 Jno. 2[17].   [5] 2 Pet. 3[7].
[6] Dan. 7[9 f.]. For the Messiah as judge see p. 75.
[7] Dan. 12[2], 2 Es. 7[31 ff.], Ap. Bar. 30, 50 f., En. 10 [11 f.], 90[20-25], Ass. Mos. 10[1-3], Sl. En. 7[1 ff.], Jude vv. 6, 14 f., Rev. 20[11-13].
[8] On the renewal of the world, see pp. 55 f.

let mine elect dwell upon it ' ; ' The earth will rejoice, the just will dwell upon it, and the elect will walk up and down in it.' [1] ' All who are godly will live again in the world (on the earth), . . . they will then see one another, beholding the lovely, gladdening sun.' [2] On the other hand the abode is sometimes placed in heaven. [3] But in a world renewed, purified of all evil, glorified, heaven and earth are merged in thought. ' The earth is heaven, heaven is the earth, the cleft is gone ; God, the Son of man, the blessed dwell together.' [4] Paradise as the abode of the blessed is sometimes placed at the ends of the earth,[5] sometimes in the *third* heaven,[6] or less definitely in the heavens. [7]

The *punishment of the unrighteous* first of all consists in exclusion from the blessings awarded to the righteous. As seen above, the resurrection in the earlier hope, and sometimes also in the later, was limited to the righteous ; the wicked remain in the underworld cut off from all the good of life ; and so the misery of their doom is sometimes characterized as the loss of all part in the blessedness of the future world. ' The sinner will not be remembered when the godly are visited ; that will be the sinner's part for ever ; but they who fear the Lord will rise to eternal life.' [8] The most common designation of their award, *death, destruction*, contains this idea of loss, but much more also. It does not signify annihilation, nor a state of unconsciousness. The spirits of the wicked, it is said, 'shall be put to death ; they shall cry and wail in a boundless void.' [9] Death, as an eschatological term, sums up all the woe of exclusion from the bliss of the saints, and all the poignant suffering of the abode of the condemned. In this sense it has passed into New Testament usage.[10] Sometimes though less commonly, the suffering spoken of is spiritual : ' They shall pine away in confusion and be consumed with shame, and shall be withered up by fears.' [11] They will lament their folly in rejecting the law of God ; [12] they will be troubled

---

[1] En. 45[5], 51[5].
[2] Sib. Or. IV. 186 ff.   Cf. En. 38[2], 62[15], Rev. 21, 2 Pet. 3[13].
[3] En. 104[2], Ass. Mos. 10[9 f.], Ap. Bar. 51[10].   [4] Volz 371.
[5] Sl. En. 42[3], En. 32[1-3], 77[3].   [6] Sl. En. 8[1].   [7] Ap. Bar. 51[11], En. 61[12].
[8] Ps. Sol. 3[11 f.], cf. *idem* 14[9 f.], En. 22[13], 99[1].   [9] En. 108[3].
[10] Cf. Ro. 2[12], Heb. 10[39].   [11] 2 Es. 7[87].   [12] Ap. Bar. 51[4].

beholding the glory of the righteous, even of those whom they have afflicted.[1] But generally it is physical pain that is foretold. The prison-house is a place of darkness, chains, and flaming fire. 'There are all sorts of tortures in that place. . . . Everywhere fire, and everywhere frost and ice, thirst and shivering, while the bonds are very cruel, and the angels fearful and merciless, bearing angry weapons, merciless torture.'[2] The pit of fire is generally present in allusions to the punishment. Its occurrence in the New Testament does not need illustration. And the suffering is unending ; no repentance, no prayers, no intercessions avail. With awful power the Apocalypse of Baruch tells of the death of hope : ' When the Most High shall bring to pass all these things, there will not there be again an opportunity for returning, nor a limit to the times, nor adjournment to the hours, nor change of ways, nor place for prayer, nor sending of petitions, nor receiving of knowledge, nor giving of love, nor place of repentance, nor supplication for offenses, nor intercession of the fathers, nor prayer of the prophets, nor help of the righteous.'[3] The same tone of hopelessness appears with appalling frequency through most of the literature of these later centuries. Some of the rabbis taught a limited punishment in the case of Israelites who were moderate offenders.[4]

The well-known name of the place of punishment, Gehenna, comes from the Hebrew name Gehinnom, the valley at Jerusalem which became a spot of special abomination, because that there kings of Judah had offered their children in sacrifice to Moloch (2 K. 16³, 21⁶). In the traditional eschatology, which looked for the establishment of the messianic kingdom at Jerusalem, this valley became a fitting place for the final punishment of Jehovah's enemies in the sight of his people, and seems to be referred to as such in Is. 66²⁴, where it is said that the triumphant Israelites should go forth and look upon the dead bodies of those that had trangressed against God, for their worm should not die, nor their fire be quenched (cf. Salmond 355 ff., Skinner in CB. *in loc.*). In the later eschatology the name designates the place of incorporeal and corporeal punishment, after the judgment, which is generally located in the underworld (Ap. Bar. 59¹⁰, 85¹³, En. 56⁸, 90²⁶, Jub. 7²⁹, Rev. 20¹⁻³). Sl. En. places it in the third heaven (10¹).

(3) *The intermediate state.* The old conception of Sheol as a place where all the dead alike are forever cut off from God and

---

[1] Wis. 5¹ ᶠ·, En. 108¹⁵.   [2] Sl. En. 10² ᶠ·   [3] 85¹².
[4] Cf. Weber *System* 327, 374, Volz 287.

the activities of life is found in these later years, but not often.[1]
A clearer perception of the individual as the object of award
and the belief in a resurrection changed the idea of Sheol, and
brought up the question of the state of the dead before the final
judgment. The answers given are not uniform, nor are they
always clear. But the view becomes generally prevalent that
at least a partial retribution is entered upon immediately after
death.[2] In 2 Esdras the brief space of seven days after death,
given to the departed that they may see the future destinies of
the righteous and the wicked, may perhaps be interpreted as
containing a belief that opportunity for repentance will be
given for this time even to the dead. But nowhere else in
apocryphal or apocalyptic literature is there clear evidence of
a belief in the possibility of change between death and the judgment; on the contrary it is said[3] that one of the torments of
the wicked is the consciousness that ' they cannot now make a
good returning, that they may live.'[4] In *rabbinical* literature
there is found the doctrine that all who have been circumcised
will ultimately be released from Sheol.[5] The great judgment,
however, is not an empty pageant, only repeating what had
already been determined; for this preliminary retribution is
not complete, it looks forward to a higher reward or a more
dreadful penalty. The preliminary aspect of the first award is
expressed in the Apocalypse of Baruch in the sentence pronounced upon the representatives of the powers of wickedness :
' Recline in anguish and rest in torment till thy last time come,
in which thou wilt come again and be tormented still more.'[6]

On the other hand the intermediate state is sometimes, especially in writings influenced by Hellenic tendencies, almost or
wholly left out of view, and what is practically the full requital
is entered upon at once after death.[7] Enoch[8] pictures the elect
dead as already in the ' garden of life ' at the coming of the
judgment day. The Paradise to which Enoch was translated

---

[1] Ecclus. $17^{27\,\text{ff.}}$, 41^4, Tob. 3^6, Bar. 2^{17}.
[2] Cf. 2 Es. $7^{78\,\text{ff.}}$, Wis. $3^{1\,\text{ff.}}$, En. $22^{4\,\text{ff.}}$, 103^7, Ap. Bar. 36^{11}, Jub. 7^{29}, 22^{22}, Sl.
En. 18^7, 40^{12}, Lk. $16^{22\,\text{f.}}$, frequent also in rabbinic literature.
[3] 2 Es. 7^{82}.   [4] See also p. 68.
[5] Cf. Weber *System* 327 f., Volz 146. For a modified doctrine in 1 Pet. see
p. 113.   [6] 36^{11}, cf. $52^{1\,\text{ff.}}$, 2 Es. $7^{87,\,95}$.
[7] Cf. Wis. 3^{1-3}, 4 Mac. 17^{18-20}. Cf. Volz 142 ff., Bousset *Jud.* 282.
[8] 61^{12}.

is described as the dwelling-place of God and the preëxistent
Messiah ; already there were there 'the patriarchs and the
righteous who from time immemorial had dwelt in that place.' [1]
The righteous Ezra also is promised translation, together with
all those who are like him, to an abode in the presence of the
heavenly Messiah, 'until the times be ended,' that is, till the
Messiah's coming.[2] It will be seen then that the ideas of Paradise were manifold. Its *location* has been spoken of above.[3]
As a place of abode it is sometimes the dwelling of God, the
patriarchs, and the righteous dead,[4] sometimes it seems identical
with heaven,[5] again it is the dwelling of the righteous after the
judgment.[6] Like the heavenly Jerusalem it was formed by
God from the beginning [7] and like that is to be revealed in the
last days.[8] Evidently it became an ideal term for a state of
rest and felicity in the presence of God and the Messiah.

(4) *The final Overthrow of the kingdom of Evil Spirits.* The
judgment is conceived as the culmination of the age-long
conflict with evil — the triumph of God not only over the
kingdoms of the world, but also and preëminently over the
kingdom of evil spirits. In the post-exilic centuries belief in
spiritual beings underwent great expansion. Angels or spirits
in unnumbered hosts were believed to perform the divine behests
through all the universe — in human affairs and in the operations
of nature. They were divided into ranks and orders in an imposing hierarchy of thrones and dominions and principalities and
powers.[9] There were angels over seasons and years, over rivers
and the seas, over the fruits of the earth, over every herb, over the
souls of men, writing down all their works and their lives.[10] So
also the evil angels and demons were grouped into an organized
kingdom under a sovereign lord. In this age for the first time
comes prominently into view the figure of one supreme ruler of
the demonic hosts, Satan, or among other names, Beliar, Beelzebub, the Devil.[11] And since, as seen above, the world came to
be regarded as given over to the dominion of evil powers, the

---

[1] 70⁴.   [2] 2 Es. 14⁹, cf. 7²⁸, 13⁵².   [3] p. 67.
[4] Cf. En. 61, 70, Jub. 8¹⁹, Lk. 23⁴³.   [5] Ap. Bar. 51¹¹.
[6] Sl. En. 9, 42³ ᶠᶠ·, Test. Levi 18, Test. Dan 5.   [7] Ap. Bar. 4³⁻⁶.
[8] 2 Es. 7³⁶, 8⁵².   [9] Col. 1¹⁶.   [10] Sl. En. 19
[11] Cf. Bousset, *Jud.* 326 ff.; Davidson in Hast. I. 93 ff.

great empires that arose one after another in history were viewed as only agencies of Satan in his enmity toward God and righteous men.   In eschatological literature these empires, either severally or collectively, as the great world-power hostile to God, are not infrequently symbolized by animals in monstrous form, such as the four beasts in Daniel,[1] the monsters of Isaiah 27 (part of a post-exilic paragraph), the eagle of 2 Esdras 11, and the first beast of the Revelation 13^{1-10}.   And the great world-rulers who waged war against God's people appear under the symbol of a monster or a part of such monster, as a horn or a head.   Thus Antiochus Epiphanes appears in the 'little horn which waxed exceeding great' in Daniel ;[2] Pompey in the dragon in the Psalms of Solomon ;[3] and as most scholars suppose, Nero in the seventh head of the Beast in the Revelation.[4]   The careers of great monarchs like Antiochus and similar tyrants who ruthlessly warred against God and his people with Satanic might and acting as Satan's agents gave rise to a typical figure which appears in later eschatological expectation, both Jewish and Christian,[5] called in Christian terminology Antichrist — a mighty world-ruler pictured with superhuman traits and exalting himself against God and warring against the saints.[6]

The dualism thus represented between God and the kingdom of evil is, however, nowhere in the Jewish religion, as in the Persian,[7] that of two nearly equal powers, the victory of one of whom over the other can be attained only through a hard conflict.   The might of Satan and his agents is always represented as only that which God in the execution of his purposes allows to be exercised ; and when the time has come he takes to himself his great power and reigns.[8]   The myriads of spiritual hosts may be pictured in the march of battle, but there is never a detailed portrayal of a combat ; the hosts of Satan are overthrown with a sudden stroke, with a breath or a word of the mouth : ' Lo, as he [the Messiah] saw the assault of the multitude that came, he neither lifted up his hand, nor held spear, nor any instrument of war ; but only I saw how that he sent out of his mouth as it had been a flood of fire, and

---

[1] 7^{3} ff.   [2] 8^{9}.   [3] 2^{25}.   [4] 13^{3}.   Cf. pp. 393 ff.
[5] 2 Es. 5^{6}, Ass. Mos. 8, Ap. Bar. 40, Sib. Or. V. 28 ff., 2 Thess. 2^{3-10}
[6] See p. 397.   [7] Cf. p. 80.   [8] Rev. 11^{17}.

out of his lips a flaming breath, and out of his tongue he cast forth sparks of the storm, . . . so that upon a sudden of an innumerable multitude nothing was to be perceived, but only dust of ashes and smell of smoke.'[1]

With the judgment comes the destruction of all the powers of wickedness, whether on the earth or in the world of spirits. Ungodly men, both the living and the dead, 'perish from before the presence of the Lord of spirits and are driven away from the face of the earth and perish for ever.'[2] 'The beasts that were past and held . . . the whole compass of the earth with grievous oppression'[3] have been destroyed one by another in historic succession, until the last is overwhelmed in the final world-catastrophe.[4] The fallen angels and evil spirits receive their doom in the pit of fire;[5] and Satan himself, dethroned and bound, is condemned to the place of torment with his fallen hosts.[6]

(5) *The Messiah and his Functions.* The widened outlook reached in many quarters in these later years is nowhere more evident than in new conceptions which now appear regarding the Messiah. A final catastrophe involving the overthrow of the whole kingdom of evil spirits, the resurrection of the dead, the renewal of the world, the passing away of the present age and the inauguration of the age to come, constitute a series of movements so vast, so transcendent, that a mere human prince, a son of David, can no longer form a central figure. Where such expectations are distinctly cherished and gain the ascendancy, the Davidic Messiah must either disappear from thought or undergo a corresponding transformation, and in fact, as already pointed out,[7] in many writings of this age he is not present. But in at least two, Enoch and 2 Esdras, which pretty certainly represent a wider circle of belief, he appears in a new and transcendent form; and in at least these two writers he receives a new name. Enoch calls him ' the Son of

---

[1] 2 Es. 13⁹ ff., cf. En. 62², Ps. Sol. 17²⁴, 2 Thess. 2⁸, Rev. 19¹⁹ f.
[2] En. 53², cf. 62⁹ f., 2 Thess. 1⁹.   [3] 2 Es. 11⁴⁰.
[4] Dan. 7, 2³⁷⁻⁴⁵, En. 52⁶, Sib. Or. III. 303–654, Rev. 17¹¹⁻¹⁸, 19²⁰.
[5] En. 10⁶, ¹³, 90²⁵, Jude v. 6, 2 Pet. 2⁴.
[6] Test. Jud. 25, Test. Levi 18, Sib. Or. III. 73, Ass. Mos. 10, Mt. 25⁴¹, Rev. 20¹⁰.
[7] p. 41.

man,' or 'that Son of man,'[1] and 2 Esdras 'the man,' or 'that man.'[2]

A superhuman, angel-like character now seems to be distinctly attributed to him, though none would venture to designate him expressly as divine. Thus *preëxistence* is ascribed to him. This idea is found as early as the LXX, which gives in Dan. 7[13], 'there came one like a son of man and he was present there as an Ancient of days,' ὡς παλαιὸς ἡμερῶν παρῆν. In Enoch it is said of the Messiah, 'Before the sun and the signs [of the zodiac] were formed, before the stars of heaven were made his name was named in the presence of the Lord of spirits.'[3] That the 'name' here, as often in Hebrew phraseology, denotes the *person* is shown in a following verse, ' He was chosen and hidden with him [God] before the world was formed.'[4] 2 Esdras speaks of his coming as that of ' one whom the Most High hath kept (preserved) unto the end of days,'[5] or 'hath kept a great season';[6] similarly some are mentioned as taken away from the evil of the world to remain with him ' until the times be ended,' that is, till his coming.[7] In the Apocalypse of Baruch[8] it is said that at the consummation of the times he 'will return in glory,' where the meaning is pretty certainly, he will return to heaven where he was before.[9] Mic. 5[2], often understood to express the Messiah's preëxistence, refers more probably to his ancient Davidic descent.[10]

This representation of the Messiah's preëxistence is thought by some (cf. Stanton in Hast. III. 355, Drummond 293) to be explained by the idea of his concealment after his human birth (see p. 48). But this explanation falls short of the conception embodied in the passages cited. Neither can the preëxistence spoken of be understood of an existence in *idea* merely, as the tabernacle with its furniture was believed to have existed with God in pattern or archetype before the earthly copies were made by Moses (Ex. 25[9, 40], Heb. 8[5]); for the reference is clearly to a *personal* existence (cf. Volz 217 ff., Bousset *Jud.* 249, Gunkel in Kautzsch 398, Edersheim I. 175 f.).

---

[1] Cf. *inter al.* 46[2, 4], 48[2], 62[7], 71[17].
[2] 13[3, 5, 12, 51]. Both En. and 2 Es. in their representations show dependence on Dan. 7[9 ff.], and it is probable that they have taken these designations from that passage, interpreted as referring to a superhuman Messiah. [3] 48[3].
[4] 48[6], cf. 62[6 f.]. [5] 12[32]. [6] 13[26]. [7] 14[9]. [8] 30[1].
[9] This interpretation is required by the context ; so, Charles *in loc.*, Ryssel in Kautzsch 423, Baldensperger 164. But Volz (37) takes the paragraph to be a Christian interpolation unconnected with the context and referring to Christ's second advent. [10] Cf. Cheyne in CB. *ad loc.*

In preëxistence itself the Messiah may not have stood alone; a kind of preëxistence seems to be thought of in the case of Moses (Ass. Mos. 1¹⁴) and of other forefathers (cf. Harnack *Dogm.* I. 98). But even if actual personal existence is meant in these cases and not mere presence in the purpose of God, the representation is less clear and certain; at all events the abiding presence of these with God is not spoken of, nor is there attributed to them a continuing personal function in union with God, as in the case of the Messiah (En. 46¹ ᶠᶠ·).

In keeping with his preëxistence, *other attributes above the human*, though not declaredly divine, are ascribed to the Messiah. He is endowed with the fullness of wisdom and righteousness, of glory and might; he is exalted above all other spiritual creatures ; he will share in the throne of God. ‘The glory of the highest will be proclaimed over him, the spirit of understanding and sanctification will rest upon him.’ ¹ ‘The Elect one stands before the Lord of spirits and his glory is for ever and ever, and his might from generation to generation.’ ² ‘The Lord of spirits seated the Elect one on the throne of his glory, and he will judge all the works of the holy ones in heaven and weigh their deeds in the balance.’ ³ ‘The kings and the mighty ones and all who possess the earth will glorify and praise and exalt him who rules over all, who had been hidden, for the Son of man was hidden before, . . . they will fall on their faces before him and worship him.’ ⁴ ‘That Son of man has appeared and has seated himself upon the throne of his glory, and all evil will vanish from before his face and cease ; but the word of that Son of man will be mighty before the Lord of spirits.’ ⁵ It is not easy to see how such a view of the Messiah’s nature and office can be harmonized with the persistent belief in his Davidic descent; but absence of strict consistency in the eschatological beliefs of a given age or even of a single writer need not present insuperable difficulty.

It is true that this picture of the Messiah’s elevation over other spiritual powers occurs chiefly in Enoch; but the later rabbinical writings, certainly in this respect not influenced by Christian belief and apparently preserving earlier Jewish teaching, show that he was not setting forth new doctrine (cf. Edersheim I. 177 f.). These portions of Enoch (the Similitudes) have been held by some to be a Christian interpolation (so, Hilgenfeld, Volkmar,

---

¹ Test. Levi 18   ² En. 49⁴.   ³ En. 61⁸.   ⁴ 62.
⁵ 69²⁹, cf. 49, 46³ ᶠᶠ·, Test. Jud. 24.

Drummond, *al.*) but this view raises great difficulty. The paragraphs in question contain no other traces of Christian influence; no reference to the historical Christ, his life, death, and resurrection, no specifically Christian doctrines such as a Christian writer inserts when he tampers with an earlier document; and on the other hand a representation such as Enoch's elevation to a kind of Messiahship ($71^{14\ ff.}$) would certainly have been modified. We are therefore probably right in holding the paragraphs to be Jewish. (Cf. Beer in Kautzsch 231, Baldensperger 17, Schürer III. 279 f.)

The Messiah now becomes the *judge* of all. In earlier writers in the judgment which shall convict the hostile nations of their wickedness and justify their destruction a forensic act preceding their punishment scarcely appears; where 'judgment,' or 'sitting in judgment' is spoken of [1] the thought is chiefly of *executing* sentence, and Jehovah is judge and executor. In the majestic scene described by Daniel [2] it is Jehovah in the likeness of 'one that was Ancient of days' who did sit and give sentence from the opened books; and this idea of the person of the judge continues through later non-Christian writers as the more common one. [3] On the other hand in the latter part of our period this function is often assigned to the Messiah. In the Apocalypse of Baruch [4] it is foretold that the leader of the hostile hosts will be taken up to Mount Zion where the Messiah 'will convict him of all his impieties, and will gather and set before him all the works of his hosts. And afterwards he will be put to death.' In similar language 2 Esdras [5] describes the Messiah's judgment: 'He shall come and speak unto them and reprove them for their wickedness and their unrighteousness, . . . he shall set them alive in his judgment, and when he hath reproved them, he shall destroy them.' In Enoch's account of the judgment not only the kings and the mighty of the earth, the sinners and the just shall appear before the Messiah's throne, but also the angels and all the spirits of evil. [6] In the New Testament this conception of the Messiah as the universal judge becomes the more usual doctrine. There is no conflict between the two ideas respecting the person of the judge; for as the Messiah is conceived to *rule* as Jehovah's representative [7] so his *judgment* is described as exercised in Jehovah's name. [8]

---

[1] *E.g.* Jl. $3^{2,\ 12}$.   [2] $7^{9\ ff.}$.   [3] Cf. 2 Es. 7^{33}, En. 47^{3}, Sib. Or. IV. 40 ff.
[4] $40^{1\ f.}$.   [5] $12^{32\ f.}$.   [6] 49^{4}, 55^{4}, 61^{8}, 62^{3}, 69^{27}.   [7] Mic. 5^{4}, Zec. 3^{8}.
[8] En. 55^{4}.

He is God's agent. Thus St. Paul characterizes the judgment as 'the day when God shall judge the secrets of men . . . by Jesus Christ'[1] and the Acts speak of a day in which God 'will judge the world . . . by the man whom he hath ordained.'[2] St. Paul and St. John then can without self-contradiction speak of the judgment as the act of God,[3] though generally attributing it to Christ.[4]

(6) *The messianic age as an Interregnum.*[5] We see in the survey above, that the two forms of eschatological hope existing side by side in the latter part of our period were the national and the universal ; the former contemplating the future of Israel, the nations of the earth in their relation to Israel, the reign of the Davidic Messiah in an earthly kingdom of righteousness and glory which should endure forever ; the latter, the world of men and spiritual beings, a universal realm in which national and earthly limitations are obliterated, the resurrection of the dead and the judgment, the heavenly Messiah, the renewal of all things and 'eternal life' in the perfection of the 'coming age.' The older, national hope, planted in a literal understanding of a long series of prophecies, was too firmly rooted to give way to the newer, transcendental, outlook, and both continued together in spite of differences and inconsistencies. But the effort to harmonize the two, to retain the hope centering in a national messianic kingdom, and at the same time the wider expectation of the 'coming world' gave rise to a view according to which the messianic age, as a period of national glory fulfilling all the promises of the prophets, is a *prelude* to the final state, an interregnum between the two æons. 'The messianic kingdom brings the national felicity, the new æon brings eternal life.'[6] The most distinct expression of this view is found in 2 Esdras.[7] When the full time has come the city (the messianic Jerusalem) will appear in the midst of great

---

[1] Ro. 2[16].   [2] 17[31].
[3] Cf. Ro. 14[10], θεοῦ is the correct reading, 3[6] ; Jno. 8[50], 5[45].
[4] For a similar identification of God and his instrument cf. Ezk. 34, where both Jehovah, vv. 11-16, and the Davidic kings, v. 23, are called the shepherd of Israel ; also Ex. 3, where both Jehovah, vv. 8, 17, and Moses, v. 10, are called Israel's deliverer.
[5] Cf. Volz 62 ff., Bousset *Jud.* 273 ff., Schürer II. 635 f., Salmond 312 f., Weber *System* 354 ff., Drummond 312 ff.   [6] Volz 64.   [7] 7[26 ff.].

wonders, the Messiah will be revealed and the saints will be in
felicity with him for a space of 400 years; afterwards the
Messiah and all that live will die,[1] the world will be turned into
its original silence for seven days; then the dead will be raised,
the world renewed, the Most High will appear on the throne of
judgment, and Paradise and the pit of torment will be opened
as the endless awards of those who are judged. In another
passage [2] 2 Esdras says that the Messiah will deliver his people
and 'make them joyful until the coming of the end, even the
day of judgment.' A similar representation is found in the
Apocalypse of Baruch [3] and probably also in Enoch,[4] where a
vision of the world's history is given in ten 'week'-periods; of
these the eighth, in which 'sinners will be given over into the
hands of the righteous,' seems to represent the messianic age[5];
while the general judgment, the destruction of the world and
the appearance of the new heavens fall in the ninth and tenth
'weeks.' In Slavonic Enoch (XXXII f.) the doctrine of an
interval of 1000 years seems to be found, as in the Revelation,
20.[6] But the idea of a messianic interregnum is less common.
It is doubtful whether it is found in the apocalyptic writers
except in these places and in Rev. 20[4], though in the late rabbinical writings a distinction between the 'days of the Messiah' and
'the coming age' is not infrequent. To the former they assign
periods varying from 40 to 2000 years — in one instance a
period of 1000 years, a *millennium*.[7] The pre-Christian existence
of this conception of the messianic age between the two æons is
interesting to the biblical student chiefly because it appears in
the doctrine of the Millennium in the Revelation,[8] a doctrine,
however, not certainly found elsewhere in the New Testament.[9]

(7) *The Reckoning of the Time until the end.*[10] The eager direction of thought toward the expected end found in much of the
later Hebrew literature of our period is not due to curious specu-

---

[1] This idea of the Messiah's death has no relation to the historic event of
Christ's death ; cf. p. 50. In the Ap. Bar. it is said that the Messiah will return
to his heavenly glory at the end of his earthly reign ; cf. p. 73.   [2] 12[34].
[3] 30[1], 40[1-3], cf. 74.   [4] 91, 93.
[5] So, Bousset *Jud.* 274 ; otherwise however, Volz 66.   [6] But see p. 184.
[7] Cf. Volz 236, Bousset *Jud.* 276, Drummond 315 ff.   [8] 20[1-6].
[9] On 1 Co. 15[23 ff.] see p. 98. For this doctrine in the O. T. see p. 36.
[10] Cf. Volz 162 ff., Bousset *Jud.* 234 ff., Drummond 200 ff.

lation about the future; it is born rather of the stress and perplexity of the times present.   The bitter bondage of God's people
to Gentile rulers, the trials of the godly among godless Israelites,
the hardness and iniquity which the weaker must endure from the
stronger, raised continually the problem of the rule of a righteous God, and faith was pointed on to a future when his ways
would be justified to men, and all evil would end.   Out of these
experiences arose ever and anon the cry, Lord, how long?[1]
The answer, characteristic of eschatological literature of whatever date, is that the end is near.   From the prophet of the first
great apocalypse, Daniel, who speaks throughout in the belief
that the times of distress are approaching their limit, to the seer
of the Revelation, whose message is of things which must come to
pass shortly,[2] the expectation is generally the same.   But before
this consummation the world must run its course fixed by God;
'The end shall be at the time appointed.'[3]   As God was said to
have fixed a measure of iniquity,[4] and the number of the saints[5]
to be filled up, so he had determined the measure of time
which must be fulfilled :   'For he hath weighed the world in the
balance ; and by measure hath he measured the times, and by
number hath he numbered the seasons; and he shall not move
nor stir them, until the said measure be fulfilled.'[6]   But the
eschatological writer conceives the generation which he addresses
to be standing already in the closing years of this measured
period ; and to set this vividly before his readers he divides the
world's history, or at least its later ages, into a definite number
of epochs in a program which discloses the final era as not far
removed.   This division of the world's history, or of the latter
portion of it, into a fixed number of periods appears first in
Daniel in the prophecies of the four kingdoms, and of the seventy
weeks,[7] the latter being an eschatological interpretation of the
seventy years of the Babylonian captivity prophesied by Jeremiah.[8]   Henceforth some such mode of computation becomes a
stereotyped feature in eschatological writings.   The numbers
commonly met with are four, seven (or its multiple seventy),
ten and twelve.   The fourfold division appears again in the

---

[1] Dan. 12⁵ ff., 2 Es. 6⁵⁹, Ap. Bar. 21¹⁹, Sib. Or. III. 55.   [2] 1¹.
[3] Dan. 11²⁷.   [4] Dan. 9²⁴, 2 Es. 12²⁵, Jub. 14¹⁶, 1 Thess. 2¹⁶.
[5] 2 Es. 4³⁶, Rev. 6¹¹.   [6] 2 Es. 4³⁶ f..   [7] 7, 9²⁴.   [8] 9².

Apocalypse of Baruch[1] and in the rabbinical writings;[2] Enoch combines the four kingdoms and the seventy weeks of Daniel in a scheme of seventy periods divided into four parts;[3] a tenfold division appears in the Sibylline Oracles IV.[4] and Enoch;[5] a twelvefold in the Apocalypse of Baruch;[6] a sevenfold in the Sibylline Oracles III.,[7] Enoch,[8] Testament of Levi,[9] the Revelation.[10] The delineation of the periods generally makes clear to which one the generation then present on the stage of history is reckoned, and thus the place of the end is shown. Sometimes also the time of the end was computed from the sum total of the years which the world is appointed to last, as determined by biblical utterances interpreted with rabbinical sublety.[11] Slavonic Enoch[12] seems to make the duration of the world 7000 years — 6000 from the creation to the judgment and 1000 for the millennium — and this number is found in the Talmud. On the other hand the view is found that the final day is not fixed, but that its advent may be hastened by the prayers of the saints and the cries of the martyrs for vengeance;[13] and later rabbinical writers[14] make its coming depend upon the repentance of Israel — a belief apparently found among the people also, as it is implied in St. Peter's discourse in the Acts 3[19] (see RV.).[15]

(8) *Persian influence in later Jewish Eschatology.* Whether Jewish eschatology in the later forms spoken of above was a direct and natural outgrowth solely from the Hebrew religion and the teaching of the prophets, or whether new elements were introduced into it from foreign beliefs, has been much debated in more recent times.[16] The question is too large to receive discussion here, nor is that essential to the purpose of the survey with which we are concerned. It will suffice to

[1] 39. [2] Cf. Volz 168.
[3] 89^{59}–90^{25}. Cf. Beer in Kautzsch 294, Charles *En.* 244.
[4] 47 ff. [5] 93, 91. [6] 53 ff. [7] 192 ff. [8] 91. [9] 17.
[10] 13, the seven heads. [11] Cf. Drummond 207 f.
[12] 33. Cf. Charles *in loc.* [13] En. 47, cf. Rev. 6[10].
[14] Cf. Weber *System* 333 f.
[15] On the 'messianic woes' as a sign of the approaching end cf. pp. 38 f.
[16] Cf. Lücke I. 58 f., Böklen *Die Verwandschaft d. jüd.-christ. mit d. pers. Eschatologie*, Charles *Eschatology*, Söderblom *La vie future d'après le Mazdéisme*, Cheyne *The Origin and relig. Contents of the Psalter*, Bousset *Jud.* 449 ff., *Die jüd. Apokaliptik* 36 ff., Baldensperger 189 ff., Hast. IV. 990, John *The Influence of Babylon. Mythol. upon the O.T.* in 'Cambridge Biblical Studies,' Jeremias *The O.T. in the Light of the Ancient East*, Eng. trans.

state certain factors which enter into the problem. Among the nations with whom the Jews in their later history were in long and close contact, only the Persians, as far as has been discovered, possessed a distinctly developed eschatology. According to the *Avesta*, the collection of the sacred books of the Persian religion (called variously Zoroastrianism, Parseeism, Mazdeism), the two principal divinities, Ormazd (Ahura Mazdah) and Ahriman (Angra Mainyu), exist in the beginning independently of each other. The former is the god of light, the creator of the world, of man and all good ; the latter, the god of darkness and the creator of all evil. The history of the world after the creation of man is the history of the conflict between these two divinities for the supremacy ; at the end of the present æon, the last of four æons (cf. Daniel's four kingdoms), the great deliverer of the world, Saoshyant (a Messiah), is raised up ; the god of evil marshals all his forces for a decisive assault upon the powers of Ormazd and is overthrown ; a universal judgment is instituted, the dead are raised, an ordeal of fire is sent upon the world, through which the good pass unharmed, while it consumes all that is evil ; the god Ahriman with his angels is cast into the abyss of torment, forever robbed of his power, and the good are admitted to the kingdom of the renewed heaven and earth to dwell in felicity with their savior Saoshyant. The parallelism with the course of this world and the final issues as conceived in Jewish eschatology is at once apparent ; and it is difficult to avoid the conviction that there is some measure of dependence. As the Avesta underwent revision sometime in the early Christian centuries, it has been contended that Persian eschatology borrowed from the Jewish, but this view is generally rejected by students of the Avesta ; at all events the more fundamental ideas contained in this representation doubtless formed a part of the original groundwork of the Avesta, as their presence in the Persian religion in pre-Christian times is established by the testimony of Theopompus (380 B.C.) as preserved in Plutarch.[1]

Circumstances in which Persian religious ideas might find their way to Hebrew acceptance are manifest. As pointed out by Bousset,[2] the Jews, who in large numbers remained behind

---

[1] *De Iside et Osiride* 47.   [2] *Jud.* 455.

in Babylon and the adjacent country after the return of their compatriots, and who came to form an influential center in the thought of later Judaism, had thus ample opportunity in the course of these centuries to come in contact with Zoroastrianism, which was now the predominant form of religion there ; and they were not unlikely to be influenced, perhaps unconsciously, by this contact, since in ethical and even theological aspects Zoroastrianism approached more nearly than did any other religion to their own. Ormazd, as a divinity of perfect goodness who should in the end triumph over all evil and become the unopposed lord of the world, was in their minds not far removed from Jehovah; and the judgment of men according to an ethical standard, the overthrow and punishment of the wicked, the sure reward of the good, and a future kingdom of righteousness, peace, and glory, were all fundamental articles of Jewish belief. The affinities therefore between the two races in religious and moral beliefs were such that a certain influence of the predominant people upon the other can be readily understood. But on the other hand this parallelism between the two eschatologies does not certainly prove a large dependence of the Hebrew upon the Persian. While subordinate factors, such as a division of the world's history into a definite number of æons, the multiplication of spiritual beings and their organization in an elaborate hierarchy, may have been adopted directly, yet the central doctrines of a universal judgment, a resurrection of at least the just, the destruction of evil powers, the reign of the Messiah, and the everlasting felicity of the redeemed in a renewed world, were expectations which might conceivably be directly developed out of the religion of the prophets. In the changed political condition of the Hebrews after the exile and with their enlarged view of the religion of Jehovah, some such development could hardly fail to take place, if they were to retain faith in their destiny as the people of God. What seems most reasonable to suppose is, that Persian ideas because of their very similarity gave a certain acceleration to the growth of what in germ was already contained in Jewish belief, and at the same time influenced the *form* taken by the growing conceptions. It is unquestionable that in many in-

G

stances foreign elements were in different ages taken up into *popular* thought among the Hebrews ; [1] but these were generally transformed and purified by the clearer religious and ethical insight of the Hebrew writers. We may not be going too far in supposing that such borrowed elements in some instances were made by the divine revealer, who works through means, an instrument for setting his revelation in clearer light. But it may be questioned whether as a historical fact the essence of a single *fundamental* truth was received by the Hebrews in this way.

5. *The New Testament Era.* This division of our subject is intended to present, in briefest possible outline, the principal eschatological teaching given in the New Testament, that is, *Christian* eschatology as related to and contrasted with the Jewish. The later developments of the latter, even if represented in writings of the same era as the New Testament Scriptures, belong distinctly to Jewish thought and have been treated in the former sections. But as in every department of religious truth, so in eschatology, the affinity between the Jewish and the Christian forms is very close, the former being the preparation for the latter. We have seen how Jewish conceptions of the Last Things grew and were modified by the course of history, and similarly we may in a general way say that the eschatological expectations of the New Testament era are but the Jewish conceptions *enlarged and transformed* by the revelation given in Christ. This relation of the Christian doctrines to their forerunners must be kept clearly before us, if we are to avoid misinterpretation of the utterances of our Lord and the New Testament writers regarding the final destiny of man and the issue of the ages. Nor can we overlook the great prominence of eschatology in the New Testament, remote as it is from the interest of our modern everyday religious thought. While that is certainly a one-sided estimate which makes the teaching of our Lord purely eschatological, solely concerned with the announcement of a kingdom coming in the near future,[2] it is nevertheless true that an eager

---

[1] Cf. Gunkel *Schöpfung u. Chaos*, Delitzsch *Babel u. Bibel.*   [2] Cf. pp. 139 ff.

outlook toward the final consummation is everywhere present as a conditioning factor in his preaching and in that of the apostles. We cannot read the New Testament with an intelligent grasp of the writers' thought without a recognition of this fact. At the same time neither in a particular writer nor in the New Testament as a whole are we to look for any complete and systematic exposition of the Last Things, expressed in precise doctrinal terms, just as we find no presentation of a *system* of theology or christology. Whatever of the doctrines of the End is given appears, not as abstract truth, but in lessons for present practical purposes, as motives to conduct, as encouragement or warning. Much that we should be glad to know of the future is left untouched, much remains at best as only an uncertain inference. It is evident that while there is agreement among the different parts of the New Testament as regards certain great fundamental expectations, yet the eschatological utterances given by various writers to meet varying occasions and circumstances must present, or at least emphasize, varying forms or aspects of eschatological hope. Within limits we may speak of a general eschatology of the New Testament, but in the following survey we shall take up separately the leading groups into which the writings fall, because only in this way can be seen the variety and scope of the views contained in the whole. And we begin properly with the eschatology of St. Paul. His epistles are nearly, if not quite, all earlier than the other books of the New Testament; we have his teaching, not at second hand, reported by others, but given in his own words; and in regard to most of these epistles a cautious criticism is disposed to accept their genuineness; St. Paul, moreover, more than any other apostle may be called the great doctor of the infant church; his influence upon its thought was everywhere felt directly or indirectly; some scholars even go so far as to find his ideas and the language coined by him to be recognized in every other New Testament book.[1]

Pauline Eschatology.[2]   *Sources.* — It is obviously impossible in the space here at command to enter into a discussion of the critical questions

[1] Holtzmann, *Theol.* II. 4.
[2] Cf. books on N. T. theology, especially Weiss, Holtzmann, Beyschlag,

concerning the genuineness of the epistles attributed to St. Paul. The following brief note regarding critical opinion must suffice. The Pauline authorship of the four great epistles, Ro., 1 Co., 2 Co., Gal., is so firmly established that no argument to the contrary is held valid by any considerable number of scholars, even among critics of an extreme tendency. Very general also in all schools of criticism, though not universal, is the acceptance of 1 Thess. More objection is raised against 2 Thess. (important in its eschatology) ; yet it is now widely acknowledged that no decisive argument against its authenticity can be found in language and style, that the apparent contradiction between 1 Thess. 5^2 and 2 Thess. $2^{8\ f.}$, may be due to difference in reference or a change of emphasis (see p. 89 on reconciliation of the two passages), that the numerous resemblances to 1 Thess. may be accounted for by a vivid recalling of the former epistle through memory or a preserved copy (cf. the recalling of the phraseology of an earlier letter in 1 Co. 5^9). There is a growing tendency in criticism at the present time to regard the arguments against the traditional view as inconclusive. Still wider is the agreement of critics now regarding Phil., which was placed among the pseudepigraphic writings by Bauer and his followers. ' Bauer's thesis that the entire epistle is post-Pauline has the approval still of only the Dutch radicals, who recognize nothing as Pauline' (Jülicher *Ein.* 108). The striking resemblances between Eph. and Col., the ecclesiology of the former and the Christology of the latter, have led many critics to reject, some the one, and some the other of these two epistles, yet none of these objections has been found so far conclusive as to gain the general acknowledgment of critical scholars. The number of those who would reject Col. has not increased of late, and while a larger number question Eph. the inconclusiveness of the objections to it seems to become more widely acknowledged in recent criticism. As regards the doctrines in question these two epistles are seen to contain, not un-Pauline ideas, but only earlier ideas more fully developed. All the above-mentioned epistles then may be taken to furnish sources for our study, and the theory of later interpolations adopted by some, cannot be carried through so completely as to affect the epistles for our present purpose. The Pastoral epistles which present greater difficulties for the critical student do not contribute eschatological teaching not found in at least some one of the other epistles, and need not therefore be used. The Pauline speeches recorded in the Acts are of course not verbatim reports, and even if representing the apostle's thought in general, can hardly be taken as evidence of teaching not found in the epistles.

St. Paul, trained in pharisaic learning and acquainted with apocalyptic writings, brought with him when he became a Christian a knowledge of the late Jewish conceptions of the Messiah ; and some inference regarding the prominence of

Stevens ; cf. also Titius *N. T.*, Pfleiderer, Vol. I, Kabisch, Feine, Brückner, Wrede *Paul*, J. Weiss *Paul*, Hausrath *Jesus* Vol. I, Kennedy *Paul*, Bruce *Paul*, Matthews *Mess.*, Beet *The Last Things*.

the messianic idea in his pre-Christian thought may be drawn from the place it occupies with him subsequently. The messianic titles, 'Christ,' that is, Messiah, and 'Lord,' occur, one or the other of them, more than 300 times in his epistles, while the name *Jesus* alone is found not more than 10 times. And his conception of the person and work of the Christ formed the center of all his religious thought as a Christian; it was this that determined the character of his eschatology. Already the doctrine of the Messiah had reached in late Jewish literature a growth in which he appears as a preëxistent heavenly person, above all created beings, endowed with divine wisdom and might, one who in the Last Days should come forth in glory to judge the world, vanquish evil, inaugurate the divine kingdom, and reign with God forever.[1] In St. Paul's doctrine of the Christ these same elements appear and are taken for granted; he does not argue to establish them, or treat them as a part of a new revelation given to him. It is probable then that this was the Messiah who in his pre-Christian days he believed would come in the fullness of time. This hope makes clear his furious persecution of the church, which preached Jesus as the Messiah; to his mind it was extreme blasphemy to think of the man, whose career had ended in an accursed death,[2] as the incarnation of that glorious one whom no might could resist and who when he came should abide forever. But when the Messiah of his faith appeared to Saul in the bright light of his glory and revealed himself as also the Jesus whom he persecuted, Saul's whole conception of the person and work of Jesus was revolutionized. He accepted with all its meaning the truth of the resurrection which the church had been proclaiming as the evidence of its faith. He saw that the Messiah of his earlier belief had come forth to earth in human form for a time and had returned to his heavenly glory. This incarnate life was an episode in the eternal life of the Christ, and the purpose of this episode, not commonly apprehended in Jewish ideas of the Messiah's work [3] now became clear; the incarnation and death of the Christ was an atonement for the sin of the world; that brief earthly sojourn of the Messiah was a preparation for the eschatological coming; it was not the coming to which

[1] pp. 74 f.   [2] Gal. 3[13].   [3] See p. 49.

Paul with all the people of God had looked forward; that still
lay in the future, that was the coming which should fulfill the
prophecies of the End and realize all eschatological hopes.
Neither St. Paul nor the other New Testament writers are
accustomed to speak of it as a *second* coming; it is with them
the coming, the Parousia. Important for St. Paul's spiritual
development and eschatology as was that meeting with the
Lord which convinced him that the heavenly Messiah had
come in the person of Jesus, still more influential in revealing
to him the nature of the glorified Christ and his work in the
world was the apostle's experience of the indwelling Christ in
the person of the Spirit. Christ, the exalted one, was the
Spirit,[1] and as Spirit dwelt in the believers and in the church,[2]
working out the life of union with him and preparing for his
coming. With the far-reaching religious consequences of the
doctrine of the indwelling Christ we are not concerned here,
except so far as it affected St. Paul's eschatology. In that
union with Christ through the Spirit lay the pledge of the
believer's resurrection and future blessedness, and of the perfection and glory of the Church. With the great revolution in
Paul's understanding and belief that came to him in and after
his conversion, some of his former conceptions of the Last
Things necessarily fell away, others were profoundly modified,
some he seems to have retained vaguely without attempting to
adjust them in every case to the hopes of his new faith. The
principal eschatological ideas expressed in his epistles may be
arranged in the following groups.

(1) *The Coming of the Lord.* This is fundamental in St.
Paul's thought. It is mentioned directly or implied throughout
as the background of teaching, of hope and warning. And
the Apostle has in mind not merely a subjective presence such
as is realized in special visitations of the Spirit, but a visible
return conceived under traditional Jewish forms. The ideas
and terms of the popular eschatology are represented most
vividly in the so-called Pauline apocalypses,[3] which belong to
the Apostle's earliest writings; but even if we suppose his

---

[1] 2 Co. 3[17 f.]   [2] Ro. 8[10 f.], 1 Co. 12[12 f.]
[3] 2 Thess. 1[7-12], 2[1-10], cf. also 1 Thess. 4[14-17].

conceptions to have become more spiritualized in later years, the essential elements are retained. The Lord will come forth suddenly attended by the heavenly hosts, at the call of the archangel and the sound of the trump the dead will rise,[1] the universal judgment will be held,[2] the redemption to which believers have been sealed [3] will be accomplished, they will be joined with Christ in his glory [4] and the kingdom of God will be established forever.[5] As in all eschatological literature, the Day of the Lord marks the transition from 'This Age' to the 'Coming Age.' Although St. Paul does not employ the latter term, his frequent use of the former shows the distinction to have been an essential part of his thought. As in the Old Testament prophets [6] and in the common belief of the apostolic age, so with St. Paul that day is looked for as near at hand; [7] he himself hoped to see it dawn.[8] Though the experiences of his later life made more distinct the consciousness that he might himself die before the parousia,[9] he did not lose his belief in its nearness.[10]

Antecedents of the Coming. The expectation of 'times of trouble,' the 'messianic woes,' which is characteristic of apocalyptic writers [11] was shared by St. Paul. Referred to in general terms elsewhere,[12] it takes definite form in the 'falling away' (ἡ ἀποστασία) and the revelation of the 'man of sin' given in the Pauline apocalypse.[13] These unmistakable signs must precede the Day of the Lord. They are not clearly described here; in fact they are referred to with the vagueness and mysteriousness usual in apocalyptic prophecy. They had already formed a part of the apostle's oral teaching among the readers. The great *Apostasy* predicted is frequently understood of a coming revolt of the Jews from God, as the 'man of sin' also is

---

[1] 1 Thess. 4[16], 3[13], 2 Thess. 1[7], 1 Co. 15[22].   [2] Ro. 2[6, 16], 14[10-12].
[3] Eph. 4[30].   [4] Col. 3[4].   [5] 1 Co. 15[24-28].   [6] See pp. 22, 36.
[7] Ro. 13[11 f.], 1 Co. 7[29], Ph. 4[5].
[8] 1 Thess. 4[15] — ἡμεῖς includes himself — 1 Co. 15[51 f.]. This expectation of the day as near does not easily fall into conformity with the prophecy that before the parousia, the fullness of the Gentiles and then all Israel should come in (Ro. 11.). But such a hope is far from impossible with a man of his fervid faith, especially in view of the wonderful scenes already enacted in demonstration of the power of the Spirit and the triumphs of the gospel already achieved.
[9] Ph. 1[20 f.], 2[17]; still stronger 2 Tim. 4[6 f.], if that be Pauline.
[10] Ph. 4[5].   [11] Cf. p. 38.   [12] 1 Co. 7[26].   [13] 2 Thess. 2[3-10].

conceived to be of Jewish origin.[1] But it is not easy to suppose
that a future lapse of the Jews from their religion should
have been a conspicuous topic in the Apostle's teaching to a
congregation mainly Gentile,[2] or that he would have especially
occupied himself with a future increase of their present harden-
ing of themselves against God seen in their general rejection of
the Messiah; [3] on the contrary he looks for a conversion of his
people as one of the events leading to the End.[4] The prediction seems rather to relate to a great lapse of Christians in the
allurements and perils of the ' last times,' the falling away of
many in the intensity of the final struggle between good and
evil.   Such an apostasy as one of the events of the 'latter
days' is mentioned elsewhere, e.g. in Daniel,[5] in later apocalyptic
literature,[6] in the Gospels,[7] in the Pastoral epistles.[8]   The *Man
of Sin* (or *lawlessness*, as given in many Mss.) whose appearance
is one of the precursors of the Lord's coming,[9] is without doubt
the Antichrist, the figure which arising in late Judaism as a
part of the popular belief regarding the End and referred to,
more or less vaguely, in apocalyptic literature becomes distinct
in the New Testament.[10]   In him as the last great enemy is
concentrated all hostility to God and the Messiah.   The description of him given by St. Paul is in part a reminiscence of
Daniel's picture of Antiochus Epiphanes, the great prototype
of subsequent pictures of the Antichrist.   He will arrogate to
himself divine honors above Jehovah himself in the temple at
Jerusalem,[11] his influence is already at work in the world,[12] but
for a little time is restrained by that mighty force for civil and
social order, the Roman Empire ($\tau\grave{o}$ $\kappa\alpha\tau\acute{e}\chi o\nu$, $\acute{o}$ $\kappa\alpha\tau\acute{e}\chi\omega\nu$, vv. 6 f.);
but when that force is removed, he will appear working in
all the power of Satan, deceiving and leading into all iniquity
those who harden themselves against a love of the truth; but

---

[1] Cf. Weiss *Theol.* 63 *b, c.*   [2] 1 Thess. 1[9], 2[14].
[3] 1 Thess. 2[15 f.], Ro. 9–10.   [4] Ro. 11[15 ff.].
[5] 9[27] ; on the meaning see Driver in CB. *in loc.* ; cf. 1 Mac. 1[11-15].
[6] En. 93[9].   [7] Mt. 24[12].   [8] 1 Tim. 4, 2 Tim. 3.   [9] 2 Thess. 2[3].
[10] See p. 398.
[11] Dan. 11[36 f.], cf. Ezk. 28[2].   The attempt of the Emperor Caligula in the year
40 A.D. to set up his statue in the temple at Jerusalem and the consequent
horror excited among the Jews may have led to the special application and
enlargement of these words of Dan. on the part of Christian prophets ; cf. Zahn
Ein. I. § 15.   [12] v. 7.

he will be destroyed by a breath from the mouth of the Lord at
the parousia.[1]

Many scholars, ancient and modern, have taken the Antichrist here to be
a false Messiah, one who arising from the Jewish people would present
himself to them as their expected Messiah. Cf. Weiss *Theol.* 63 c, Bousset
Antichrist 22 ff. The opinion that ἀνομία, ἄνομος vv. 7 f. point to an apostate
from the Jewish *law* is not supported by usage; cf. 2 Co. 6[14], Tit. 2[14]. But
one who exalted himself openly in the temple above Jehovah could not
hope to be accepted by the Jews as the Messiah foretold by the prophets.
' A pseudo-Messiah is wholly different from an anti-Messiah,' Schmiedel on
2 Thess. p. 40; cf. Holtzmann *Theol.* II. 192. For valuable discussions of
2 Thess. 2[1-12] see Bornemann in Meyer 349 ff. and 400 ff., and Wohlenberg in
Zahn *in loc.* and Excursus 170 ff.

The mention in 2 Thess. 2[3 f.] of signs preceding the parousia is regarded
by many as irreconcilable with 1 Thess. 5[1-6], where it is said that the time of
that event cannot be foreseen (Schmiedel on Thess. p. 9; Jülicher *Ein.* 50).
The apparent difference, however, disappears upon a nearer view of the
passages. In the earlier letter the writer is urging his readers to unremitting
watchfulness and preparedness for the Coming, and therefore throws the
emphasis on the suddenness and unexpectedness of the event, using two figures, the thief in the night and the birth-pains of the mother (5[3 f.]), but he
is not thinking here of the entire absence of premonitions — in the second
figure this could not be the case — but of the impossibility of foreseeing the
precise time so that preparation could be deferred. In the later letter he is
seeking to remove trouble arising among the Thessalonians from the belief
that the advent was *at the door;* and in correcting this error he throws the
emphasis on the certainty that some time must yet intervene, certain events
must happen before the end could come, as he had already told them before
he wrote the earlier epistle. These events might appear at any time and
be followed, perhaps at once, perhaps much later, by the parousia; these
might be disregarded by those who are ' saying Peace and safety,' so that
the end should come unforeseen. They are not signs which justify putting
off preparation, they do not show the precise time of the end — that is as
indeterminate as ever — but those who have fallen into practical error in
the thought that this is close at hand may be assured that it is farther off
than they had believed.

(2) *The Resurrection of the dead.* As seen above a belief in
the resurrection of the dead in a form corresponding to the
glory of the messianic age had already arisen in late Judaism.[2]
The righteous would shine forth in a glorious body like the sun
and the stars, they would be as the angels.[3] With St. Paul also
this belief was doubtless a part of his Jewish heritage; but it

---

[1] Cf. En. 62[2], 2 Es. 13[10], Is. 11[4].   [2] Cf. pp. 60 ff.
[3] En. 62[15]. Ap. Bar. 51[3, 10], 2 Es. 7[97], cf. Volz 254 f., Kautzsch 375 n.

was illuminated by his Christian experience and became one of
the central factors in his hope. His meeting with the risen
Christ on the way to Damascus gave certainty to the belief and
manifested to him the glorified body. On the other hand his
life of union with Christ through the indwelling Spirit furnished
him with a sure basis of belief in the Christian's undying life.
The Spirit giveth life and where that is there cannot be death;
and the believer's new life in the Spirit must share in that
imperishability.[1] The marvelous operations of the Spirit
already wrought in the believer's experience are but the 'first-
fruits' to be followed by the crowning issue, the swallowing up
of mortality in life.[2] And in St. Paul's thought there is no
place for an immortality of the soul apart from some form of
'body.' Life in the true sense of the term for him as for his
Hebrew predecessors includes necessarily an investiture in a
form, which, though it be not in the Apostle's thought *fleshly*,
may be called *bodily*, and an argument for immortality is for
him identical with one for a resurrection. Existence in Hades
was not life. In that great chapter of First Corinthians (15) he
has set forth his teaching about the resurrection with matchless
splendor. The earthly, visible, body must decay in death as
the seed decays — that which is sown is not quickened except it
die — but the life principle persists and will be clothed with a
new form, as is the life principle of the seed in the new plant;
that fórm will be a body different in kind from the earthly
body; there are various kinds of bodies known to our experience, and so by analogy we can conceive the existence of a body
(doubtless the Apostle used this word *body* because no other
could be found so well suited to his idea), different from those
of our experience, which shall form the investiture of the risen
life, though we cannot apprehend its nature. It will not consist of the reassembled elements of the earthly body, there will
be nothing fleshly about it — flesh and blood cannot inherit the
kingdom of God — it will be a 'spiritual body' ($\sigma\hat{\omega}\mu\alpha$ $\pi\nu\epsilon\upsilon$-
$\mu\alpha\tau\iota\kappa\acute{o}\nu$), one perfectly filled to be the *organ of the spirit*
($\pi\nu\epsilon\hat{\upsilon}\mu\alpha$).[3] Once at least such a body had been revealed to

---

[1] Ro. 8[11].   [2] 2 Co. 5[4 f], Ro. 8[23].

[3] As in $\sigma\hat{\omega}\mu\alpha$ $\psi\upsilon\chi\iota\kappa\acute{o}\nu$ the adj. does not mean *made of*, but rather *fitted to the
use of*, the $\psi\upsilon\chi\acute{\eta}$, so in the contrasted expression $\pi\nu\epsilon\upsilon\mu\alpha\tau\iota\kappa\acute{o}\nu$ cannot mean *made
of* $\pi\nu\epsilon\hat{\upsilon}\mu\alpha$.

the Apostle — in that meeting with the risen Lord — and in that revelation was given the basis of his doctrine of the resurrection of the body, whose essential characteristics he describes as 'conformed to the body of Christ's glory.'[1] He attempts no description of its nature. Such is the body with which according to St. Paul both the dead and the living will be clothed at the Lord's appearing. How much of the difficulty raised by the doctrine of the resurrection would be avoided, if the Apostle's clear teaching were intelligently read, and the reader were content to stop short of fruitless speculation just where the Apostle stopped.

The opinion is held by many (cf. Schmiedel on Col. p. 239, Holtzm. *Theol.* II. 215 ff., Pfleiderer I. 322 f.) that late in life Paul changed his view and hoped for entrance into the heavenly body and the perfect state of glory immediately after death ; and in the opinion of some he advanced to the strict consequences of this new hope, abandoning his earlier doctrines of the parousia and the resurrection, adopting, as is said, the more spiritual conceptions which appear in the Johannine writings also (but on the resurrection in these writings see p. 105). This opinion is based chiefly on 2 Co. 5[1-10], where the Apostle in contemplating the possibility of death before the parousia is thought to declare a belief that the ' house not made with hands,' that is, the heavenly body, is ready to take the place of the earthly body at the moment of dissolution (v. 1, the present in ἔχομεν is interpreted as coinciding in time with καταλυθῇ) ; and the encouragement which he finds in the thought that absence from the body makes possible presence with the Lord (vv. 6–8) is held to be incompatible with an intermediate state in the world of departed spirits and to require for its realization admission to the final perfection of the glorified state immediately after death. But while it is quite conceivable that St. Paul in the experience of a life guided by the Spirit should have grown in the understanding of truth and should have changed some of his views, it is highly improbable that one who in 1 Co. had set forth the doctrines of the parousia and the accompanying resurrection in so clear and positive a form — doctrines which he had taught for many years — could then in the short space of a few months (2 Co. cannot be separated from 1 Co. by an interval of a year) have so completely revolutionized his views and have adopted beliefs fundamentally at variance with the common Jewish and Christian expectation ;- or that if he had done so, he would not have made the change unmistakable. It is contended that the suddenness of the supposed change is made explicable by the extraordinary peril which the Apostle had encountered in the interval between the two epistles (2 Co. 1[8-10]) and which opened his eyes to the possibility of death before the parousia. But that possibility could not have been absent from the consciousness of one who before that time had passed through the great

[1] Ph. 3[21].

perils enumerated in 2 Co. 11[23 ff.]. In point of fact the doctrines of the resurrection and the parousia are expressed, apparently in this same epistle (4[14]), certainly in the Roman epistle, of later date (13[11 f.]) and in the still later Philippian epistle (3[20], 4[5]); and in the latter epistle the final transformation of the body is expressly connected with the parousia. We should therefore take the Apostle's meaning in this passage, 2 Co. 5[1-10], to be, that we faint not in the decay of the temporal, looking for the eternal (4[16-18]), for we know that, though this earthly house may be dissolved, we have as an assured possession the heavenly body which will be given us at the parousia (5[1], the present in ἔχομεν here expressing with *certainty and vividness* a fact still in the future; cf. Blass § 56, 8, Burton § 15); and then the Apostle, in dread of the disembodied state, as he contemplates the possibility of death before the Coming, finds comfort in the thought that departure from the body, whenever it may take place, will bring one nearer to the Lord (vv. 2–8). See, further, below on the *place* of the departed.

The Apostle's precise doctrine, if he had such, regarding the *place* of the departed believer before the resurrection he nowhere makes clear. It is certain that like the other New Testament writers he thinks of the ascended Christ as in the heaven of God's abode; and in two passages he apparently speaks of death as bringing the believer into that presence.[1] That such a view was found, though not usual, in late Judaism has been seen above.[2] The opinion that the Apostle intended to declare distinctly this expectation is not favored by common Jewish and Christian belief. In 2 Esdras[3] a remarkable picture is given of the righteous dead. They are not in heaven, but in the 'chambers' of the spirits, where they are guarded by angels in perfect peace, beholding in clear vision the glory of God, joying in their release from the pains of earth, hastening to behold the face of him whom in their lifetime they served, and from whom they shall finally receive their reward in glory. If St. Paul had had some such picture in his mind, he might have described the state not inaptly as being 'at home with the Lord.'[4] But we must remember that his thought was chiefly occupied with the coming end, which he always believed to be near; and so vivid was his hope of this early consummation that he passes over the interval without distinct teaching, very probably without distinct thought.

---

[1] 2 Co. 5[8], Ph. 1[23].   [2] p. 69.   [3] 7[88-98].
[4] 2 Es. in another place, 7[78], represents the soul as passing immediately at death into the presence of God.

The place of the *redeemed* is in his thought in the new kingdom yet to come, and when he speaks of the joy and glory of the 'heavenly' life he has in mind, as is true of the biblical writers in general, not the state immediately following death, but the renewed world of the messianic age. In the interval, however, before the incoming of that age, he knows that nothing can separate the believer from Christ. Even death can only bring him to the 'better state' of freer communion with the Lord, while he awaits the perfect fruition of the end. St. Paul concerns himself, not with theoretical, but with practical truth ; very likely he had for himself, certainly he gives to us, no clear doctrine of the intermediate state, beyond the all sufficient truth that the believer is in the keeping of, and in communion with, the Lord. Beyond this, speculation however natural, is curiosity, for the certain satisfaction of which we cannot look to the Bible.[1]

The *resurrection of the unrighteous* is nowhere distinctly declared by St. Paul,[2] and he is thought by some to have had no place for it in his belief,[3] for in all his utterances about the resurrection he is speaking of Christians,[4] and the sole ground of the resurrection hope of which he speaks is in the believer's union with Christ.[5] His doctrine of a universal judgment [6] would seem to imply agreement with the common Christian belief in the resurrection of all ; yet Jewish doctrine at the time varied, and he may conceivably have held with some of the Pharisees that the ungodly were judged in Hades, having no share in the resurrection. At the same time it is unsafe to draw dogmatic conclusions from the Apostle's silence ; whatever may have been the nature of his missionary preaching, he writes his epistles to Christians, and his mind is aglow with the promises of the Christian's future ; regarding the future of the wicked he maintains a reserve in striking contrast with apocalyptic writers.

---

[1] It is a false inference from the frequent use of κοιμᾶσθαι that St. Paul supposed the dead to be in a state of sleep or semiconsciousness. This euphemistic use of the word is common in Gk., Heb., and N. T. writers, where no thought of an unconscious state is present ; cf. Thayer *s.v.*, Volz 134.

[2] On Ac. 24¹⁵, see p. 115.

[3] Cf. Titius *N. T.* 51 f., Kabisch 267 ff., Beyschlag *Theol.* 268.

[4] On 1 Co. 15²², see p. 98.   [5] See p. 90.

[6] Ro. 14¹⁰, 2 Co. 5¹⁰

(3) *The Judgment.* With the coming of the Lord St. Paul
always associates, as paramount in its purpose, the judgment.
This is the one great assize which throughout Jewish and
Christian thought is placed at the end of the ages. It is universal; all, both the living and the dead, must there receive
their award.[1] Sometimes God is spoken of as the judge, sometimes Christ; the identity of the two representations is shown
in the words, 'God shall judge . . . by Jesus Christ.'[2] The
Apostle does not conceive of the Day as anticipated by a judgment passed upon the individual at his death, that is, he does
not speak of death as fixing the state of the departed; on the
other hand he is silent as regards probation after death. Here
again it must be said that he was too much occupied with the
nearness of the Coming to take into consideration the relation
of death to the great assize. The departed believer is, he is
assured, with Christ; regarding the state of the departed
unbeliever before the judgment he does not speak. He describes the award of the righteous as final, and it is with the
eternal glory and blessedness of these that he is almost exclusively concerned in his references to the issues of the judgment.
Their award is salvation,[3] eternal life,[4] glory,[5] an incorruptible
crown,[6] a reigning in life.[7] The doom of the unrighteous is
referred to much less frequently. Once only he speaks of it
as eternal;[8] but that this formed a part of his belief is the
natural inference from his general representation of the judgment as a finality, and from his usual designation of unbelievers and their destiny. He characterizes them as 'perish-
ing,'[9] and calls their future state 'death,' 'perdition,'[10] terms
whose meaning he shows by that with which he puts them in
contrast, 'life,' 'salvation.'[11] By the latter he means existence
in the full enjoyment of God's favor and in perfect communion
with him; *death* then denotes with him exclusion from such

---

[1] 2 Co. 5[10], Ro. 2[5-16].

[2] Ro. 2[16]. The share of the saints in the judgment, mentioned in 1 Co. 6[2 f.],
follows from their sharing with God in the messianic rule (cf. p. 180), as the
kingly office includes that of judge. A similar judicial function is assigned to
them in En. 95[3], Wis. 3[8]. The judgment of approval is conceived to have
already been pronounced upon the saints — judgment 'begins with the house of
God,' 1 Pet. 4[17], cf. Ezk. 9[6], Jer. 25[22].

[3] Ro. 13[11].   [4] Ro. 2[7].   [5] 2 Co. 4[17].   [6] Co. 9[25].   [7] Ro. 5[17].

[8] 2 Thess. 1[9].   [9] οἱ ἀπολύμενοι, 1 Co. 1[18].

[10] θάνατος Ro. 6[23], ἀπώλεια Ph. 3[19].   [11] ζωή, σωτηρία.

favor and communion.   We have seen above [1] that the Jewish
mind did not conceive of death as the cessation of existence,
annihilation ; and there is nothing to show that St. Paul used
the term with any other than the common Jewish significance. [2]
As regards the doctrines of *probation after death*, and a *restoration of all* (ἀποκατάστασις), if there be grounds for them, these
must be found, so far as St. Paul's writings are concerned, not
in the direct meaning of his words, but in deductions from his
general teaching about the purposes of God and the moral
nature of man — deductions which we are not justified in saying that he himself drew.   Certain passages [3] have been interpreted to contain such doctrines, but the context forbids this
interpretation, as most exegetes agree.   Further reference to
this subject will be made in another connection. [4]

Difficulty has been raised by an apparent contradiction between the doctrines of salvation and judgment as taught by St. Paul.   (Cf. Pfleiderer
I. 319 f.)   If the Christian has 'been saved through faith,' Eph. 2[8],
and if 'there is no condemnation to them that are in Christ Jesus,' Ro. 8[1],
then it is said there is no place for a judgment which shall 'render to every
man according to his works,' Ro. 2[6].   The Apostle does not take up the supposed contradiction, doubtless because he could not himself think that it
existed.   The law that the believer as well as the unbeliever shall reap that
which he soweth is everywhere recognized by him, Gal. 6[7].   Even the final
award of salvation cannot efface *all* consequences of present conduct, and
what the Apostle says of the Christian teacher's work, 1 Co. 3[12 ff.], is true
also of every Christian's life; his work may be burned, while he himself
is saved; yet it may be as one who has made his escape through fire.
Cf. Denny in EGT. on Ro. 2[6], Heinrici in Meyer on 2 Co., p. 155, Kennedy
198 ff.

(4) *The future Kingdom.*   As already seen, the doctrine of a
personal union with Christ as the source of spiritual life and
the ground of hope for the future is fundamental with St. Paul.
The religious relation then would seem to be with him purely
a matter of the individual, and to make superfluous an organized society whether Kingdom or Church.   But on the contrary the Apostle everywhere emphasizes as cardinal the doctrine of a people of God, an organized body of which every
individual Christian becomes a part and through which he is

[1] p. 58.   [2] Cf. Kennedy 118 ff.
[3] Ro. 5[18], 1 Co. 15[21 f., 28], Eph. 1[10], Ph. 2[9-11], Col. 1[20].   [4] pp. 98, 113.

joined to Christ, its living head;[1] and so the idea of a *kingdom* is as essential in his Christian eschatology as it was in the hopes of ancient Israel, though its character is changed. It is true that the express term is much less frequent with him than in the Gospels; he however uses it, and in relations which show that it was fundamental in his thought. Sometimes he speaks of the kingdom as present,[2] but generally he employs the term in an eschatological sense,[3] just as he sometimes speaks of salvation as already attained,[4] because it is ideally, or potentially present in its beginning, while the full reality lies in the future.[5] But though the term is less frequent, the idea is everywhere present; it is in the messianic kingdom that the saints are to reign with Christ;[6] it is the idea of the kingdom that underlies the use of the word Lord (κύριος, *sovereign*), found on every page of the epistles as a designation of the exalted Christ; and with the same idea in mind the Apostle speaks of Christ's preëminence over all powers and authorities.[7] In his thought, the place of the kingdom is often taken by the Church, which represents to him a people of God, not only as an organized body, but as in vital union with Christ, its supreme Lord, and filled with his presence. The identity of the Church with the kingdom in St. Paul's mind is often denied, the latter being regarded as the broader and more spiritual conception. It is of course plain that the Church as it then existed, for example, at Corinth, in Galatia, at Colossae, with all the failures and defects which called forth the Apostle's reproving epistles, no more realized the full *ideal* of the Church than did the kingdom spoken of as present realize the perfect kingdom of the future. But when his conception of the Church in its ideal, in the glory of its eschatological perfection, 'not having spot or wrinkle, holy and without blemish,' is seen, as in the Ephesian epistle, there is left no other realm to which it is subordinate or complementary. It forms the body to which Christ, he who had been seated at the right hand of God above all angelic powers, has been given as head, and which is filled with him that filleth all in all;[8] it is the community embracing the whole family of man, a

---

[1] Eph. 2[19-22], Col. 2[19], 1 Co. 12[12-27].   [2] Ro. 14[17], Col. 1[13].
[3] 1 Co. 6[9 f.], 15[50], Gal. 5[21], Eph. 5[5], 2 Thess. 1[5].   [4] Ro. 8[24], Eph. 2[5, 8]
[5] Cf. Weiss *Theol.* 96 b.   [6] Ro. 5[17], 8[17], 4[13], 1 Co. 4[8].
[7] Eph. 1[20-22], Col. 1[16-18].   [8] Eph. 1[20 ff.]

community, by whose creation and union under the one divine lordship the wisdom of God is manifested to the principalities and powers in heavenly places.[1] No clearer, grander, more spiritual idea of the kingdom can be imagined than that contained in these representations. It is possible that St. Paul designated this coming messianic rule less often as the kingdom of God, because that term or its equivalent had in his pharisaic days been associated with earthly and political glory. At all events, he saw clearly that the kingdom was to be perfectly realized only in perfectly 'serving the Lord Christ,'[2] which formed the sum of all his preaching.[3]

The *place* of the future kingdom as thought of by St. Paul, though not distinctly stated, would seem to be the renewed earth. In common with the prophets and apocalyptic writers[4] he looked for the deliverance of creation from its bondage to corruption, and for its transformation into a glory in keeping with that of the saints at the coming of the kingdom. The form of the world as it now is must pass away, creation must share in the redemption to be completed at the parousia.[5] It is difficult to find real significance in all this transformation, unless in the Apostle's mind, as in common Jewish belief, this glorified world was to be the seat of the final kingdom.[6] The same conclusion is favored by the idea of a coming of the Lord, which in Jewish thought was everywhere associated with the setting up of a kingdom upon earth, in its present or in a renewed form. The saints who at the parousia are to be caught up to meet the Lord in the air[7] are apparently to be brought with him in his escort to earth; for Christ comes to earth to hold judgment; nothing is said of a progress into the heavens, and 'the air' ($\dot{a}\eta\rho$) is never used of the heaven of God's abode, nor can it be conceived as the place of the new kingdom.[8] But

---

[1] Eph. 3[10].   [2] Col. 3[24].   [3] Cf. Feine *Jesus u. Paulus* 173 f.
[4] Cf. p. 55.   [5] Ro. 8[19-23], 1 Co. 7[31].

[6] The expression 'The Jerusalem above,' Gal. 4[26], taken from popular eschatology and denoting the Holy City now existing in heaven and ready to descend in the last days (cf. p. 56), is evidently used figuratively by the Apostle, for he never refers to it literally in speaking of the parousia and its accompanying events. It is an apt figure to set forth the superiority of the new covenant as contrasted with the old. In the same way the author of Heb. uses the phrase 'the heavenly Jerusalem,' 12[22].   [7] 1 Thess. 4[17].

[8] On 1 Thess. 4[15-18], cf. Bornemann in Meyer, Wohlenberg in Zahn, Schmiedel *Hand-Kom.* p. 28 ff.

H

there is nowhere with St. Paul a trace of the extravagant imaginings concerning the natural world which are to be found in the apocalyptic writers; [1] the whole significance of his picture of the future kingdom centers in the certainty that the saints will be with the Lord in eternal blessedness. Beyond this his prophecy has no sure word for us; and it must be kept in mind that in the prophecies of the new creation as the seat of the final kingdom and the abode of the saints in their glorified bodies, the distinction between earth and heaven practically disappears. [2]

A Millennium. On the basis of 1 Co. 15$^{20-28}$ many scholars, ancient and modern, attribute to Paul a belief, similar to that found in Jewish apocalyptic and in the Revelation of Jno., in a millennial reign of Christ between the parousia and the final consummation of the kingdom (see pp. 735 ff.). In this interpretation three steps are supposed, in the order of time: (1) the resurrection of Christ; (2) the parousia together with the resurrection of Christians, the end of this present age, and the setting up of the messianic kingdom; (3) after how long an interval is left indefinite, the resurrection of others (whether all the rest of the dead, or those only who in the interval have in the spirit-world accepted Christ), the victory of Christ over all powers hostile to God, and the delivery of the kingdom to the Father. The principal grounds urged in support of this interpretation are the following: (a) πάντες, *all*, in the words 'all shall be made alive,' v. 22, must include all men absolutely, as in the words 'in Adam all die,' the sense being that as in Adam is the *ground, cause,* of universal death, so in Christ is the *ground, cause,* of universal resurrection. (b) The words 'but each in his own order,' *i.e. company, band* (τάγμα being a military term denoting a *company, division,* of soldiers — the word itself contains no idea of orderly sequence in time), must distribute the *all* who are to be made alive into more than one company or band. Christ himself cannot be referred to as one of these bands, for he is not one of those who are raised in Christ, and further one person cannot constitute a τάγμα, *company.* (c) The first company to be raised is that of the Christians at the parousia, as shown in v. 23; the other companies must therefore arise later. (d) Verse 24 defines the period to which this later resurrection belongs; after the parousia — how long after, whether 1000 years as in Rev. is left undetermined — comes the End (or as some would take τὸ τέλος, the end of the series of resurrections). The reign of Christ, the Millennium, which began with the parousia must continue till all enemies are brought to naught, and the last enemy is death, vanquished

---

[1] Cf. p. 46.

[2] See p. 67. Such passages as 2 Co. 5^1, Col. 1^5, are sometimes taken to show that St. Paul regarded heaven as the place of the kingdom; upon the former see below; the latter refers to what is ideally present in heaven, whence Christians will receive it; cf. Haupt in Meyer *in loc.*

in the last resurrection, vv. 25 f. Then Christ delivers up the completed kingdom to the Father.

There are, however, strong objections to this interpretation: (*a*) The words ἐν χριστῷ, *in Christ*, forming one of Paul' s most frequent and characteristic terms, always denote the believer's spiritual union with Christ. The meaning of v. 22 must then be that, as death results certainly from the union with Adam, so certainly does life result from union with Christ; the second *all* then can refer to those only who are in union with Christ — it cannot refer to all men absolutely. It should further be noted that an argument upon the resurrection of *all* men would be foreign to the Apostle's purpose in this paragraph, which is solely designed to show the doubting Christians at Corinth that their resurrection is assured through their union with Christ. (*b*) The words 'each in his own order,' though following on as if intended to distribute into different groups the *all* who are to be made alive *in Christ*, are immediately shown by the writer in the added words, 'Christ the first fruits, etc.,' to distribute *all who are made alive*, including Christ, himself, and he declares that there are two divisions of these, first, Christ, called figuratively the ἀπαρχή, the first-fruits of the dead, and second, the Christians at the parousia, the argument concluding with the figure (ἀπαρχή) with which it began in v. 20. If there be any other possible subjects of a resurrection, they are entirely beyond the writer's language here. It should be added that there is nothing making it necessary or especially appropriate to find in τάγμα here a figurative use of the meaning, *military company*, though the commentators generally take it so. The same phrase, ἕκαστος ἐν τῷ ἰδίῳ τάγματι, occurs in Clem. Rom. I. 37, 41, where it can be seen from the context that the author means the appointed *station, rank*, or *place* of each one, whether the military commander, the high-priest, the layman, etc. (cf. 40, 42). The meaning of the phrase in our passage, as the writer himself explains it, would seem to be 'Christ in his God-appointed place or station; afterwards, Christians in theirs.' (*c*) There is then in the earlier part of the paragraph nothing said of a resurrection which requires for its fulfillment an indefinite period beyond the parousia; and even if the Apostle be supposed to believe in a second resurrection, we are not justified in finding it in his language here; nor is there in the words εἶτα τὸ τέλος, *then the end*, referring to the full consummation, anything which cannot be grouped with the events of the parousia as conceived by St. Paul. Elsewhere he speaks of the Advent as bringing with it the End, the series of events which belong to the completed kingdom of God; it brings the resurrection, the universal judgment (1 Co. 4[5], Ro. 2[15 f.]), the renewal of creation (Ro. 8[19 ff.]), victory over hostile powers (2 Thess. 2[8 ff.], 1[8 ff.]), and over the last of foes, death (1 Co. 15[52-54]); nowhere is there mention of a later period as bringing in the full end. The reign of Christ, whose continuance is spoken of in v. 24, does not necessarily imply a period after the Advent; already in his resurrection Christ has been raised to a kingship above created powers in this world and in the world to come (Eph. 1[20 f.], Ph. 2[9 f.]), *i.e.* the reign spoken of may consistently with the Apostle's views be placed between Christ's resurrection and the parousia (cf. Briggs *Mess. Ap.* 538 ff.). It may

well be that in this particular utterance there is in the *form* at least some
reminiscence of the apocalyptic and rabbinical doctrine of a messianic rule
before the final establishment of the kingdom. It is well to notice that
when Paul speaks of the delivery of the kingdom to the Father he can hardly
mean that all kingship then ceases with the Son, for elsewhere he speaks
of the Son as sharing the Father's throne in the eternal order (cf. passages last cited). The meaning suggested by the context and conformable
to the Apostle's general teaching is that the Son having finished his mediatorial work, having fully established the messianic dominion in the abolition
of all opposing power, will then present this completed kingdom to God
who is the 'head of Christ' (1 Co. 11³), while he continues to share with
the Father in the throne of eternal rule (cf. Weiss *Theol.* 76, c). In reading
this entire passage in Corinthians we must keep in mind that Paul sees the
End as a *whole;* with a true prophetic vision which reaches across a timeless
interval he seizes here the whole final issue summed up in one. He forms
neither for himself nor for us a program of processes and movements in a
succession of ages. Though millenniums may be conceived to intervene between one step and another in the progress of the kingdom toward its
completion, for him all is projected upon the one background of the End.
What he sees, and probably all that he would have his readers see, is the
certain, absolute triumph of the 'kingdom of Christ and of God' (Eph. 5⁵),
and the inheritance that there awaits the Christian.

Johannine Eschatology.[1] This paragraph is meant to
cover the principal eschatological ideas which appear in the
Gospel and the Epistles which bear the name of John.
Whether these books are all by one and the same author, and
how far they may be assigned to St. John, the Apostle, are
critical questions, which do not materially affect our present
inquiry ; for they form in their characteristic doctrines and
manner a single concordant group, at least so far that they
may be held to belong to one school. The Revelation is not
included in this survey, as its eschatology calls for special
treatment by itself.[2] The central doctrines of the Johannine
writings are summed up in the words of the Gospel,[3] 'These
are written that ye may believe that Jesus is the Christ, the
Son of God ; and that believing, ye may have life in his name.'
And when we see from the study of the books what the author
means by the two terms of this statement, we have here the
truths which determined the eschatological teaching through-

[1] Cf. among works on N. T. Theol. Weiss § 157, Holtzmann II. 572 ff., Beyschlag II. 462 ff., Feine 703 ff., Stevens 234 ff., *id. Johan. Theol.*; Holtzmann
Hand. Kom. IV. 198 f., Titius *N. T.* III. 8 ff.   [2] See p. 156.   [3] 20³¹.

out. On the one hand the historical person Jesus is the incarnation of the preëxistent heavenly being, the Messiah, who has come forth from his eternal glory to save the world,[1] and to set up a divine kingdom.[2] On the other hand 'eternal life' in the wide scope of Johannine use is seen to include all the blessings of the kingdom of God; and the 'belief,' in which the ground and source of that life are found, is seen to be equivalent in its essential nature to a dwelling of the believer in Christ and the indwelling of Christ in the believer, equivalent, in Pauline phraseology, to 'being in Christ.'[3] But this indwelling of Christ is realized through the presence of the Spirit.[4] In this conception of the Messiah and his work on the one hand, and on the other, of the believer's union with Christ through the Spirit together with its consequences, there is a striking agreement of the Johannine writings with the Pauline. The influence of the great apostolic teacher upon the Johannine thought becomes a plausible supposition entertained by many; but the similarity may with equal plausibility be traced to the direct teaching of the Lord and the revelation given through the experience of the life in the Spirit.

As might be expected in writings which belong to a period not earlier than the last part of the century, when the hope of a near return of the Lord was becoming a less dominant force, the emphasis is thrown more upon the present, the inner and spiritual, than upon the future, the outer and visible. The great events of the End, as conceived in traditional eschatology, are viewed as belonging to the present as well as the future, as beginning in the life that now is and anticipating that which is to come ; and it is upon their significance for the present life that the chief stress is laid. But the fundamental factors which appear in the common Christian predictions of the 'Coming Age,' that is, the parousia, the resurrection, the judgment, and the kingdom, are all found in the Johannine writings; it might be said that they constitute a kind of scheme, or programme into which has been set the practical teaching of the gospel for the life that now is; or to express it

---

[1] I. 4[14]. References are to the Gospels unless preceded by a Roman numeral indicating one of the Epistles. [2] 18[36] f., 3[3, 5]. [3] I. 5[12, 20], 15[1-7].
[4] 14[16-23].

otherwise, they may be taken as forming the background from which are projected the dominant traits of the spiritual life. This twofold aspect, a present and an eschatological, will appear as these doctrines are considered in detail.

(1) *The Kingdom.* The *idea* of the kingdom, however much spiritualized, appears as truly, though not as frequently, in the Johannine writings as elsewhere. In two most significant events in which the nature of Jesus' teaching is made the subject of special inquiry, the interview with Nicodemus and the trial before Pilate, the kingdom and the kingly office are declared expressly in word.[1] A part of the purpose of the Fourth Gospel referred to above, a purpose showing itself often in the records of the book, is to prove that Jesus is the Messiah, the Son of God, the divine *king* of whom Moses and the prophets wrote ;[2] and at the beginning and the end of Jesus' public ministry the writer accords to him the right to the *kingly* salutation.[3] The infrequency of the term, kingdom of God, in the Johannine writings as contrasted with the Synoptics has sometimes been attributed to the desire to avoid possible misconception on the part of the Roman authority. It is however chiefly due no doubt to the purpose, characteristic of these writings throughout, to set forth the high spiritual nature of all the teachings of the gospel. The idea of the 'kingdom' has resolved itself into that of 'eternal life,' the most frequent of the characteristic Johannine terms.[4] What is meant by this phrase 'eternal life' or 'life,' without the adjective, is not continued existence, but the *moral state* of perfect harmony with God, a living in union with him, an abiding in him as the branch in the vine. Such a state is life in its fullest sense, and belongs to the eternal world, as God is eternal.[5] It begins in the believer now and here. It is more commonly spoken of as present,[6] but from its very nature it is conceived of as continuing endlessly, as the union with Christ may so continue.[7] The idea thus becomes essentially equivalent to that of the kingdom, or reign, of God, which it has for

---

1 3³, ⁵, 18³⁶ ᶠ.   2 1⁴¹, ⁴⁵, ⁴⁹.   3 1⁴⁹, 12¹³.

4 ζωή αἰώνιος and the simple ζωή with equivalent sense occur some 50 times.
5 Cf. Holtzm. *Theol.* II. 578 ff., Wendt *Teaching* I. 243 ff., Stevens *Theol.* 224 ff.   6 *E.g.* 6⁴⁷, I. 3¹⁴.   7 *E.g.* 6⁵¹, 12²⁵.

the most part displaced in these writings; for eternal life in this sense is the state of perfect obedience to the will of Christ,[1] as also the state in which is given all the spiritual blessedness that in the common hope was attached to the eschatological kingdom. Imperfectly as the great ideal is realized in this world, the kingdom possesses an outward embodiment in the Church, with its visible unity,[2] with its formal rite of introduction into membership,[3] and its recognized officers.[4] But though the kingdom from its nature and its relation to eternal life must be thought of as beginning in the present, yet the recognition of a coming completion, a glory yet to be revealed, to which the present looks forward, is distinctly expressed.[5] The final triumph of the kingdom over evil does not enter so largely into the predictions of the future as in the common eschatology. In keeping with the general tenor of the writings the foreground is occupied by the victory over Satan and his domain, the world, in the present life;[6] yet here as elsewhere the present looks forward to the future completion; and the ultimate abolition of Satan's power is contemplated in those utterances which speak of the death of Christ as the casting out of the prince of this world,[7] and of his mission to destroy the works of the devil.[8] The *place* of the future kingdom seems to be thought of as in heaven. Christ, it is said, will come and receive his own unto himself, that they may be where he is.[9] The silence of the Johannine writings regarding a renewed earth is in accordance with the emphasis they everywhere throw upon the spiritual aspect of truth; but they contain no clear evidence against the belief in such renewal. In view of the prevalence of this belief in Jewish and Christian thought, and the consequent blending together of earth and heaven in the conceptions of the final state, it is doubtful whether the language which seems to point to an abode in heaven contrary to common New Testament representation can be rigorously pressed. A *Millennial* Kingdom between the parousia and the final consummation is not mentioned in the Gospel and Epistles.

---

[1] 15$^{10-14}$, I. 3^{24}.   [2] 10^{16}, 17$^{11, 20-23}$.   [3] 3^5.   [4] 21$^{15-17}$, II. 1, III. 1, 9 f.
[5] 17^{24}, I. 3^2, 2^{17}.   [6] I. 2^{13} f., 5^4 f.   [7] 12^{31}.   [8] I. 3^8.
[9] 14^3, 17^{24}.

(2) *The Coming of the Lord.* In the great farewell discourse which in the Fourth Gospel (14–16) corresponds to the apocalyptic discourse in the Synoptics, mention is made somewhat at length of a coming of the Lord to his disciples in the near future.[1] There is much difference of opinion among interpreters regarding the precise meaning of this promise.[2] It has been variously understood of (1) the appearance of the Lord after his resurrection, (2) the parousia, (3) the presence of the Holy Spirit in the believer. But (1) the brief meetings of the Lord with his disciples after the resurrection could not accomplish what he here seeks to do, remove the sorrow with which they were viewing a lasting separation from him ; [3] these few interviews could not fulfill the promise not to leave them 'orphans,' but to come and *abide* with them, and not with them only but with all who in the future should love him; [4] (2) this coming which is described as of a nature not manifest to the world [5] could not be the parousia, which like the lightning should shine from one part under the heaven unto the other, and which should separate the faithless from the faithful ; [6] (3) the only meaning which seems to suit the representation throughout is an abiding *spiritual* presence with the believer. That the presence here intended is realized through the coming of the Holy Spirit to all who love and obey Christ [7] seems to be shown by the connected utterances.[8] As he that seeth the Son seeth the Father, so he that receives the Spirit beholds Christ.[9]

Objection has been made (cf. Weiss in Meyer on 14[18], Wendt *Teaching*, II. 299) to an identification of the thought here expressed with the Pauline doctrine of Christ's presence in the person of the Holy Spirit (p. 86). It is true that the Johannine writings do not contain the exact equivalent of the statement, 'The Lord is the Spirit' (2 Co. 3[17]), and the Paraclete is distinguished from Christ as 'another' (14[16]), but in the same way the Son is distinguished from the Father (5[31 f.]) ; and since Christ's presence is

---

[1] 14[18-23], 16[16-23].

[2] Cf. Weiss, Holtzm., Meyer, Zahn *in loc.*, Stevens *Theol.* 235 f., Wendt II. 294 ff.   [3] 16[6].   [4] 14[21-23].   [5] 14[21 f.]   [6] 5[29], I. 2[28].   [7] 14[23].

[8] 14[16-18, 26], 15[26], 16[13-16], I. 3[24].

[9] Some interpret 14[3] to mean a coming at the death of an individual (cf. Holtzm. *in loc.*, Stevens *Theol.* 234), but 21[22 f.] is against this, as is also N. T. usage, which though speaking of death as a departure to be with the Lord (Phil. 1[23]), nowhere represents it as a coming of the Lord to the believer.

realized through the Spirit who comes 'in his name' (14²⁶), it is doubtful whether a clear distinction between the Johannine and the Pauline doctrines is to be maintained.

But while this spiritual coming of Christ to his Church throughout the present age stands in the foreground of Johannine thought, yet the traditional doctrine of a final, visible parousia with its attendant events is also taught. He promises to come and take his own to the place prepared for them,[1] and they are awaiting that appearance.[2] It will be seen that the references to the parousia represent it as near, within the lifetime of the readers ; also the *signs* of the End are seen in the character of the age; it is the 'last hour,' as shown by the working of antichrist already in the world.[3] The coming of antichrist before the End is referred to as a well-known belief.[4]

(3) *The Resurrection.* The resurrection in the Johannine writings is an integral part of the doctrine of eternal life ; and as that life on the one hand is a spiritual state already present, and on the other, looks forward to a future completion, so there is a present, and also an eschatological resurrection. The Christian has already passed out of death into life.[5] 'If a man keep my words he shall never see death.'[6] Death has ceased to exist for such a one. Through a spiritual resurrection the believer has entered into that life which is independent of physical death. This aspect of the resurrection is so prominent that some scholars find in the Johannine teaching no place for the doctrine of a future resurrection as an eschatological event. The passages which speak of such an event are then regarded as additions or modifications.[7] But the retention of the principal features of the common eschatology in these writings militates against so radical a process of criticism, and in fact the coexistence of the two ideas, which are but two aspects of the same idea, is found as truly, though less prominently, in St. Paul.[8] We are certainly right in taking the resurrection, as held in common Christian belief, to be a part of genuine Johannine doctrine. 'The hour cometh

---

[1] 14² f.   [2] 21²² f., I. 2²⁸.   [3] I. 2¹⁸⁻²², 4³, II. 7.
[4] On antichrist, see pp. 397 ff.   [5] 5²⁴, I. 3¹⁴.   [6] 8⁵¹, 11²⁵ f.
[7] Cf. Holtzm. *Theol.* II. 581 ff.   [8] Cf. Col. 3¹ with 1 Co. 15⁵².

in which all that are in the tombs shall hear his voice and shall
come forth.' [1]   There is, however, no reference to a 'spiritual
body' as in St. Paul.   To such an extent do traditional conceptions remain in these writings, that the resurrection of
the unrighteous also is spoken of,[2] a reëmbodiment which
would seem to be conceived as having a source different from
that of the resurrection of the righteous, as it also clearly has a
different purpose; the resurrection of the one is described as
that which *belongs to life*, that is, which arises out of the true life
begun here, and forms its necessary sequence and culmination;
the other is spoken of as that which *belongs to judgment*, that is,
to the appearing of the unrighteous before the judgment seat,[3]
where according to common belief they should in bodily form
receive their sentence.[4]   Beyond this there is nothing said of
the significance of the 'bodily' form given to the unrighteous
at the resurrection.   What relation it may have been conceived
to have to their state after the judgment is not intimated here
nor elsewhere in the New Testament.   It may quite possibly
be a reminiscence of traditional eschatology, retained without
special meaning for the Christian writer.   At all events the
interest of the New Testament writers centers entirely in the
destiny of the righteous.

(4) *The Judgment.*   Here also, as in the doctrines of eternal
life and the resurrection, there is a twofold use of the term.
On the one hand the judgment is said to be enacted in this
life; on the other, it is placed among the events of the last day.
The former aspect of the doctrine receives the stronger emphasis; and as in the case of the resurrection some scholars would
deny that there is place in genuine Johannine thought for a
general judgment at the end.[5]   'He that believeth on him is not
judged; he that believeth not hath been judged already.[6]   He
who has accepted Christ has already passed beyond judgment
and through the spiritual resurrection has entered into the
relation with God that constitutes eternal life; he who has
rejected Christ has by the very act already judged himself and

---

[1] 5^{28} f., 6^{39} f., 44, 54.   [2] 5^{29}.   [3] 12^{48}.
[4] The above seems the correct interpretation of ἀνάστασις ζωῆς, κρίσεως; cf.
Holzm. Weiss in Meyer *in loc.*
[5] Cf. Wendt *Teaching* II. 305, Holtzm. *Theol.* II. 575 ff.   [6] 3^{18}.

abides in death.[1]   On the other hand the announcement of the
great judgment of the last day, as expected in common belief,
is equally distinct.   It forms one of the events of that 'hour
when all that are in the tombs shall hear the voice of the Son
of God,'[2] and it will test the believer and the unbeliever alike.[3]
There is no real inconsistency between these two groups of
utterances.   Men are judged or are judging themselves here
and now by the attitude they take toward the truth,[4] and this
process of judging must continue till the end.   The unbeliever
may turn and reverse his judgment; the believer needs the
constant warning to 'abide in Christ' lest he be cast forth as a
branch and withered, lest he be put to shame at the Lord's
appearing.[5]   The judgment in the present life is final only so
far as the conditions on which it is based continue to be final.
The declaration contained in these two groups of passages is
another side of the truth which is expressed in the two sayings,
likewise apparently but not really contradictory, 'Whosoever is
born of God cannot sin'[6] and 'If we say that we have no sin,
the truth is not in us.'[7]   The Johannine idea of judgment
agrees then with that of St. Paul, who likewise speaks of a present
justification (which with him is a judicial act acquitting the
believer now), and a coming judgment in the great day.   The
Agent in the judgment is variously stated and in terms seemingly contradictory.   Commonly the judge is Christ; again
this is apparently denied;[8] it is declared that God is[9] and is
not[10] the judge.   The discrepancy disappears entirely, in view
of the relation of the Son to the Father,[11] and in view of the
writer's rhetorical method in presenting that side of the truth
which he means to emphasize.   These apparent contradictions
form one of the distinct characteristics of the Johannine writings, and in themselves do not furnish ground for a theory of
interpolation or redaction.   The *Award* at the judgment is,
for the righteous, eternal life in the 'abiding places' which
the Lord has gone to prepare for them, where they will
dwell with him beholding his eternal glory and transformed

---

[1] 5²⁴, 9³⁹, 12⁴⁷.   [2] 5²⁸ ᶠ·, 12⁴⁸.   [3] I. 2²⁸, 4¹⁷.   [4] 3¹⁹⁻²¹.
[5] 15⁶, I. 2²⁴, ²⁸.   [6] I. 3⁹.   [7] I. 1⁸.   [8] 12⁴⁷.   [9] 8⁵⁰, 5⁴⁵.   [10] 5²².
[11] God and Christ are united in judgment ; Christ judges as he *hears*, he does
not judge *alone*, 5³⁰, 8¹⁶.

into the divine likeness ;[1] the destiny of the unrighteous is not described ; it is however announced indirectly in the statements regarding that from which the righteous are delivered, that is, 'death,' 'perdition' ($\theta\acute{a}\nu\alpha\tau\sigma\varsigma$, $\dot{a}\pi o\lambda\acute{e}\sigma\theta\alpha\iota$). These terms do not denote non-existence, for they are used of persons still living ;[2] they sum up the negation of all that is included in eternal life as understood in the Johannine writings.[3] Beyond this negative designation there is nothing said of the state of the unrighteous after judgment.

The Eschatology of the Epistle to the Hebrews.[4] The fact which gives interest to the eschatology of the Epistle to the Hebrews is not peculiarity in its doctrines, but the extent to which the author writes in the consciousness of the future. The radiance of the coming fulfillment of the promises, or the shadow of the coming judgment, falls upon almost every paragraph of argument or exhortation. The writer reading his familiar Jewish scriptures in the light of not only Christian revelation, but also Alexandrine idealism, delights in emphasizing the unseen and future as the substance, as the real and lasting ; everything here is but a 'shadow of the good things to come,' a copy of the prototype in heaven. The Lord will come again ;[5] the day is near,[6] it will bring with it the resurrection and the judgment [7] — events evidently conceived in traditional forms though not described in sensible pictures.

Some scholars find in $9^{27\,f.}$ the doctrine that the judgment takes place immediately after death. But this cannot be the writer's meaning ; for elsewhere in the epistle he connects the final decision, whether for salvation or condemnation, with the parousia (9^{28}, $10^{23-26,\,36-38}$). The meaning in this passage is clear ; the writer in arguing that the one oblation of Christ upon the cross has made a sufficient sacrifice for sin and needs not to be repeated, enforces his reasoning by an analogy — the divine appointment for *man* is death and afterwards the judgment ; so also for *Christ*, the one death, not to be repeated, afterward the judgment ; but in his case the appearing is to *give* judgment, which for the believer issues in salvation ; in the second clause (v. 28) the writer substitutes 'salvation' for 'judgment' because the efficacy of the one death for salvation is the point under discussion. The

[1] $14^{2\,f.}$, 17^{24}, I. 3^2.   [2] 17^{12}, I. 3^{14}.   [3] Cf. pp. 102 f.
[4] Cf. among works on N. T. Theol. Weiss § 126, Holtzm. II. 332 f., Beyschlag II. 337 ff. ; Mathews *Mess.* 237 f., Enc. Bib. II. 1377.
[5] 9^{28}, 1^6.   [6] $10^{25,\,37}$.   [7] 6^2, $9^{27\,f.}$, 10^{27}, 11^{35}.

judgment of the unbeliever has no relevancy here. Similarly in 12²³, 'the spirits of just men made perfect,' some have found the doctrine of a purely spiritual resurrection taking place immediately after death. But elsewhere the writer places the perfect fulfillment of hope, the full salvation, at the End (cf. passages cited above), and there is nothing here at variance with this view, for the context and the general use of τελειόω and its cognates in the epistle show that the reference is not to the moral and spiritual perfection of the just, but to the perfection of the atonement wrought by the blood of Christ, as contrasted with the imperfect sacrifices of the Mosaic law.

God himself will be the judge,[1] the judgment is final,[2] and as it is the great assize at which all must give account, the resurrection of the unrighteous would seem to be implied.[3] The *place of the dead* before the judgment is not certainly spoken of.[4] The *reward of the righteous* is the eternal inheritance,[5] a kingdom that cannot be shaken,[6] eternal salvation[7] in the presence of God and his glory,[8] participation in the messianic rest, which is the 'sabbath-rest' of God himself.[9] The *doom of the unrighteous* is 'perdition,'[10] a term not defined more nearly, but doubtless to be taken in the general New Testament sense of the loss of all that belongs to the state of blessedness.[11] Neither here nor elsewhere in the New Testament does the word contain the idea of annihilation. But the writer dwells upon the fearfulness of punishment and the fierceness of God's wrath, which is as a consuming fire.[12] The *triumph* over the powers hostile to God is complete and final,[13] though, as elsewhere in eschatological literature, the total extinction of hostile beings is apparently not thought of; Christian eschatology simply follows in this respect the earlier forms, not carrying out the idea of triumph to its fullest consequence.

In the *great consummation* the heaven and the earth will be 'shaken,' the temporal and visible will be removed, the things

---

[1] 10³⁰, 12²³, 13⁴.   [2] 6².

[3] 6², 11³⁵ are sometimes interpreted as showing that only the righteous are raised — a plain misinterpretation.

[4] The words 'Church of the firstborn who are enrolled in heaven,' 12²³, probably refer to the Christians on earth whose names are now written in heaven; see Weiss in Meyer, and Westcott *in loc.*; cf. Lk. 10²⁰, Ph. 4³.

[5] 9¹⁵.   [6] 12²⁸.   [7] 5⁹.   [8] 12¹⁴, 2¹⁰.   [9] 4¹, ⁹ᶠ.   [10] 10³⁹.

[11] See pp. 94, 107.

[12] 10²⁶⁻³¹, 12²⁹. It is doubtful whether these passages contain a designed reference to the fires of Gehenna so often mentioned in apocalyptic writings.

[13] 2⁸, ¹⁴, 10¹³, ²⁷.

which cannot be shaken will remain;[1] that is, in a new heaven and a new earth mortality will put on immortality. Whether the writer includes in this renewal of all things the Pauline idea of a spiritual body he does not make certain. This perfected state beyond the judgment, the Coming Age,[2] is characterized as the kingdom, the City of God, the heavenly Jerusalem;[3] and in this, Christ seated at the right hand of God,[4] will rule with him forever.[5] The *place* of the eschatological kingdom is heaven.[6] This conception is a natural consequence of the two doctrines so prominent throughout the epistle, the eternal priestly service of Christ carried on in heaven, and the Christian's perfect freedom of approach to God. But the tendency must not be overlooked to blend heaven and earth wherever the idea of a renewed world is present.[7] The epistle contains no intimation of a Millennial kingdom before the last great day.

The Eschatology of the other Epistles and the Acts.[8] *St. James.*[9] The practical epistle of James makes reference to eschatological truth briefly to strengthen the suffering and tempted Christians in well-doing and to declare the doom of the wicked living in iniquity and cruelty. The passages in which the approaching end is made most of are 5^{1-6}, an apostrophic proclamation of the punishment coming upon the godless,[10] and 5^{7-11}, a message of encouragement to the oppressed Christians. The readers are living in ' the last days,'[11] the coming of Christ, the Lord of glory, is near,[12] the judgment is at the door.[13] The punishment about to break upon the ungodly is described in imagery suggested by Jewish eschatology; their riches shall be corrupted, their gold and silver rusted, their flesh consumed as by fire.[14] The destruction of this present world and the bringing in of a new creation are probably in the writer's mind here.

---

[1] $1^{11\,f.}$, 12^{26-28}.   [2] 6^5, 13^{14}.   [3] 1^8, $12^{22,\,28}$, $11^{10,\,16}$.   [4] 8^1, 12^2.
[5] 1^8.   [6] $6^{19\,f.}$, 11^{16}.   [7] Cf. p. 67.

[8] The Pastoral epistles are not included here ; a special paragraph on these is not called for, since, whether they are of Pauline authorship or not, they do not present any material departure from the Pauline eschatology as set forth above. Cf. p. 84.

[9] Cf. Weiss *Theol.* § 57 ; Commentaries on 5^{1-11}, especially Weiss, Huther, von Soden, Oesterley in EGT.; Enc. Bib. II. 1377, Hast. I. 753.

[10] On the apostrophic character of this passage cf. Weiss in Meyer *in loc.*
[11] v. 3.   [12] v. 8.   [13] vv. 9, 3–5.   [14] vv. 2 f.

But beyond the destruction of the material and visible, lies the spiritual doom of death,[1] doubtless conceived, in accordance with Christian thought generally, as that state in which all is wanting that constitutes the true life of the soul.[2] On the other hand the hope held out to the waiting Christian is the certain coming of Christ to deliver, to bestow the reward of patient endurance, to bring in such an 'end of the Lord' as was that which changed all the sufferings of Job into joy.[3] Then the crown of life will be given to them [4] in the kingdom promised to those that love God.[5] Further eschatological forecasts such as are found elsewhere are wanting in this epistle.

First Peter.[6] St. Peter, to whom this epistle is attributed (and probably with right), is commonly called the Apostle of hope, and although it may be questioned whether this virtue is not equally conspicuous elsewhere in the New Testament, yet the eschatological outlook is dominant throughout this letter. The chief aim of the letter is to encourage the kind of life and the spiritual attitude which the readers should maintain in their present severe sufferings. Naturally then the promises of the coming End·form a significant factor in the admonitions. The end of all things is at hand,[7] the readers now undergoing the test of manifold sufferings have but a little while to wait for the salvation which is ready to be revealed.[8] These present fiery trials, the raging activity of Satan,[9] seem to be regarded by the author as among the 'messianic woes' which are to usher in the Advent. These trials are sifting the Christians, distinguishing between the faithful and the unfaithful; 'judgment is beginning at the house of God,' but if the beginning with the righteous be thus severe, how much more so shall be the end with the ungodly.[10] From his exaltation at the right hand of God, above all angelic powers,[11] the Messiah is about to come forth revealing his glory,[12] bringing to his own the perfect deliverance of salvation.[13] The resurrection is not expressly mentioned, but is certainly implied in the references to the manifestation of Christ's glory, and to the judgment at which the dead as well

---

[1] 1 15, 5 20.   [2] Cf. p. 102.   [3] vv. 7-11.   [4] 1 12.   [5] 2 5.
[6] Cf. Weiss *Theol.* §§ 48-51, Mathews *Mess.* 151 ff., Hast. III 795, Enc. Bib. II. 1380.   [7] 4 7.   [8] 1 5 ff., 10, 5 10.   [9] 4 12-19, 5 8 f..   [10] 4 17 f..
[11] 1 11, 21, 3 22.   [12] 4 13, 5 1.   [13] 1 5, 9, 13.

as the living will be judged.[1] God himself (perhaps in 4[5],
Christ) is the judge.[2] The *destiny of the wicked* is referred to
only indirectly as the end which is contrasted with salvation.
The *reward of the righteous* is participation in the glory to be
revealed in Christ, a life like that of God himself in an inheritance that fadeth not away, an eternal crown of glory.[3] The
idea of the *kingdom of God*, though not spoken of under· that
name, is implied in the writer's representation of Christians as
forming a corporate body, a people, a nation. The Church constitutes the true Israel of God,[4] and in the coming realization
of its ideal its members will possess, what they now have only
potentially, royal and priestly rank; for as God's own they will
share in his kingly glory, they will reign with him, and like the
high-priest in the Mosaic system they will have perfect freedom
of access to him, offering spiritual offerings.[5] The term *inheritance* designating their future possession, when employed by so
Hebraistic a writer, is doubtless to be taken in the technical
sense of the promised messianic kingdom.[6] This is to be revealed in the last day, whether in a world purely heavenly or in
a renewed earth is not intimated. There is no place in the
writer's thought for a millennial kingdom on earth before the
End; all the events of the consummation are grouped with the
parousia.

This epistle makes a most important contribution to Christian eschatology in its teaching about Christ's activity in the
world of departed spirits. In this respect it stands alone
among the New Testament Scriptures. The other books maintain a striking reserve regarding the state of unbelievers between death and the judgment.[7] While they nowhere speak
with certainty of the possibility of a spiritual change in that
state, yet they nowhere speak of its impossibility; all their
utterances regarding the finality of probation, or the fixedness
of the lot of the wicked, relate to the state following the judgment. Their thought is so much occupied with the judgment
as near at hand, and the coming redemption of the believer,
that the present state of the unbelieving dead is lost from
view. First Peter breaks this silence, and represents Christ

[1] 4[5].   [2] 1[17], 2[23].   [3] 1[4], 4[6], 5[1, 4, 10].   [4] 2[5, 9 f.], 4[17].   [5] 2[5,9].
[6] Cf. Gal. 3[18], Heb. 9[15].   [7] On Lk. 16[19 ff.] cf. p. 151.

in the interval between his death and resurrection as preaching
the gospel to the dead, in order that they might be made the
subjects of the judgment together with the living, and that,
though they had suffered a judgment after the manner of men
universally in that they had died, they might in the final
judgment attain to a share in eternal life, which is like the life
of God, 3¹⁹⁻²⁰, 4⁵⁻⁶. While in the first passage the writer speaks
of the dead who belong to the days of Noah (a class especially
appropriate, because of their great wickedness, to illustrate the
line of thought there), in the second passage, the reference is
to the dead in general. But it should be noticed that the
writer is not concerned here with the general doctrine of
probation after death, nor is he speaking of those who had
heard the gospel and rejected it. He speaks summarily of two
classes, the one at the time of Christ's death already in the
place of departed spirits, the other still alive, both of whom are
about to be judged at the great day. The case of those who
in a future generation, that is between Christ's first and second
coming, should reject him is a subject entirely outside of his
thought.

These passages have formed the subject of much controversy, but scholars are now so largely agreed in adopting, in its main conclusions, the
interpretation given above that a detailed discussion of the exegesis does
not seem to be called for here. Interest of the dead in the Messiah's
coming, and a hope of delivery are mentioned in rabbinical writings; cf.
excerpts given by Weber *System.* 328 f., 350 f. : ' When *those who are bound*,
those in Gehinnom, saw the light of the Messiah they rejoiced to receive
him;' 'We will exult and rejoice in thee. When? When the *prisoners*
mount out of hell with the Shechinah at their head.'

Second Peter and Jude.[1] The close relation between these
two epistles, the evident dependence of one upon the other
both in contents and form, makes it fitting to take them
together in the survey of their eschatology, though 2 Peter is
much the fuller of the two. Even if 2 Peter be attributed to
the same author as 1 Peter, its similarity to Jude in some features which do not appear in 1 Peter favors this order of treatment. The critical question of the Petrine origin of 2 Peter

[1] Cf. Weiss *Theol.* § 129, Stevens *Theol.* 312 ff., Enc. Bib. III. 1377, Hast.
I. 753.

need not be entered upon here, nor the question of priority in time which arises in connection with 2 Peter and Jude. The dependence of one upon the other does not in itself settle the authorship or affect the canonical value of either. The eschatology of the epistles follows closely traditional lines. The readers are living in the 'last times.' False teachers have crept into the Church, denying Christ, rioting in corrupt living, drawing away the unstable and deriding the Christian hope. Their presence in the *last days* had been foretold ; the signs of the times then show that the end is near.[1] The Lord is about to come with his hosts,[2] the judgment like the thief in the night[3] is about to fall upon the workers of evil, 'Their sentence lingereth not.'[4] In both epistles warning of a coming visitation of divine vengeance is seen in the punishment of the fallen angels,[5] reserved in bonds under darkness unto the judgment,[6] the destruction of Sodom and Gomorrah is set forth as 'an example,'[7] and other events of history furnish the same prophecy.[8] The *promises given to the righteous* are the blessedness of salvation expressed in various terms : eternal life in the presence of the glory of God,[9] participation in the divine nature,[10] entrance into the eternal kingdom.[11] The *punishment of the ungodly* is 'The blackness of darkness reserved for them forever.'[12] Jude adopting the language of the apocalyptic writers calls it the punishment of eternal fire.[13] Its usual designation in 2 Peter is 'destruction';[14] in the latter epistle mention is also made of preliminary punishment under which the unrighteous dead are kept unto the judgment of the great day.[15] The *kingdom*, 'the eternal kingdom of our Lord and Saviour Jesus Christ,'[16] is to be consummated at the parousia, with which all the final events are connected. An earthly millennial reign preceding the final issue is not thought of. Scoffers deride the hope of the Lord's appearing, but it is the long-suffering of God towards his people[17] that delays it ; he

---

[1] P. 3³, J. 17 f. Cf. 1 Jno. 2¹⁸.　　[2] J. 14 f.　　[3] P. 3¹⁰.　　[4] P. 2³.
[5] Reference is made to the angels spoken of in Gen. 6⁴. The description of their punishment is evidently taken from En. 10 ; further use of En. is acknowledged in J. 14.　　[6] P. 2⁴, J. 6.　　[7] P. 2⁶, J. 7.　　[8] P. 2⁵, J. 5.
[9] J. 21, 24.　　[10] P. 1⁴.　　[11] P. 1¹¹.　　[12] P. 2¹⁷, J. 13.
[13] In v. 7 πυρός is pretty certainly to be joined with δίκην rather than with δεῖγμα.　　[14] 2³, ¹², 3⁷·¹⁶.　　[15] 2⁹. Cf. p. 69.　　[16] P. 1¹¹.
[17] P. 3⁹, εἰς ὑμᾶς, *to you-ward.*

wishes that all the unfaithful may come to repentance. Christians by 'holy living and godliness' can hasten the day of the Lord's appearing.[1] Second Peter describes in most vivid colors the great renewal of creation at the end. The world and all that is in it will be destroyed by fire, and there will be new heavens and a new earth, wherein only righteousness shall dwell.[2]

The Acts.[3] It does not belong to our present study to inquire into the authorship of the Acts, the nature of the sources used in its composition and similar critical problems. It may, however, be observed that the discourses contained in the book and attributed to various persons (and it is in the discourses that the principal doctrinal teaching is found), even if we should not with some scholars regard them as simply the compositions of the historian, after the manner of the speeches in Thucydides for example, are given only in brief summaries, so that the form at least is due to the historian himself ; in so far they are his, and form a part of his own presentation of his theme. But the author was master of his material from whatever manifold sources derived, and his book is a homogeneous one. If diversity of thought and belief appears, it is such as the writer supposed to belong to the different historical situations described. And he has intended to give a true picture, incomplete to be sure, but sufficient for its purpose, of the faith and work of the infant Church in the earlier decades of its existence. Our interest here is concerned solely with the principal eschatological doctrines which are contained in this portrayal of the Church's life.

The first disciples, incognizant of the Church as a body distinct from Judaism, found themselves confronted with the difficulty of adjusting the facts in the life of Jesus to their earlier belief in him as the Messiah and to their traditional expectations. Having come to accept him in the course of his earthly ministry as the one ordained of God to become the messianic deliverer and king, they were rudely thrown into

---

[1] P. 3[11 f.], cf. RV. marg., Ac. 3[19].   [2] 3[10-13], cf. p. 56.
[3] Cf. Weiss *Theol.* §§ 38–40, 42, Stevens *Theol.* 258 ff., Matthews *Mess.* 138 ff.

disappointment and despair by the crucifixion. But the resurrection restored their belief and hope; they could now ask the Lord with confidence, whether this was not the time when he would restore the kingdom to Israel.[1] After the forty days in which he spoke to them of the things concerning the kingdom of God,[2] and after the Ascension and the pentecostal gift of the Spirit, that question, so far as recorded, was never raised again. The disciples had gained a new conception of the kingdom and of the Messiah. His death, so hard for them to understand at first, and so great a stumbling-block in the way of his acceptance by the Jews as the Messiah, was now seen to be a necessity laid upon him by divine appointment.[3] Passages in the Old Testament which had not hitherto received a messianic application were now seen to be prophetic of his humiliation and death. The suffering 'servant' spoken of by Isaiah was understood to be the Messiah. This very humiliation became a proof of the Messiahship.[4] The death of the Messiah was seen to be an essential part of his appointed work.[5] But this was not the end; the brief earthly work was only preliminary. Through the resurrection and ascension God had now raised him to his full messianic dignity; exalted to the right hand of God he was now made that for which he had been ordained, 'both Lord and Christ;'[6] now the title given to Jehovah himself is also given without modification to him, he is 'Lord of all.'[7] But the consummation of his kingdom lies in the future; he must return to take to himself his sovereignty over all the world, he must come to complete his work as the deliverer and savior of his people. The outlook of the Church in consequence of this faith becomes then predominantly eschatological. Already it conceives itself to be living in the 'last days.'[8] The apostles appeal to their Jewish brethren to repent, in order that God may send forth to them the appointed Messiah to complete his work.[9] At that coming the dead will be raised, both the just and the unjust.[10] Judgment will be held and Christ will be the judge.[11] The kingdom of God[12] will be instituted with that perfect restoration of all things, in which sin will cease, as foretold by

---

[1] 1⁶. [2] 1³. [3] 4²⁸, 17³. [4] 8³²⁻³⁵, 172 f. [5] Cf. p. 85.
[6] 2³⁴⁻³⁶, 5³¹, 13³² f. [7] 10³⁶. [8] 2¹⁶ f., 3²⁴. [9] 3¹⁹⁻²¹, cf. pp. 49 ff., 130.
[10] 4², 23⁶, 24¹⁵. [11] 10⁴², 17³¹. [12] 1³, 28²³, ³¹.

the prophets.[1] The earlier Judaistic conception is gradually outgrown, and all national limitation of the expected kingdom disappears; the Messiah is the Lord and Saviour of all nations.[2] The awards of the judgment are expressed in the common New Testament terms: for the righteous, life,[3] but oftenest, salvation; for the unrighteous (whose destiny is rarely spoken of), perdition.[4] It is clear that these simple eschatological doctrines underlie all the teaching of the book, but they are brought forward with less emphasis than in most of the New Testament writings. Other doctrines, such as the 'messianic woes,' the millennium, the new heavens and the new earth, are not mentioned. The dominant message of the preaching is, Jesus is the Messiah who will bring salvation to the repentant. As regards fullness of teaching about the Last Things and the emphasis thrown upon these, the Acts is one of the least eschatological books in the New Testament.

The Eschatology of Our Lord. Inquiry into our Lord's eschatological teaching brings us face to face with the most difficult problems in the study of the New Testament. Questions regarding the sources of our knowledge and the interpretation of these, some of them questions of profound theological significance, confront us with great force, and there are many fundamental points upon which scholars have not yet reached agreement. The literature of these investigations forms a library in itself. All that we can do here is to indicate as briefly as possible grounds upon which one may reasonably base opinion and to state the essential features in the Lord's eschatological doctrine as thus exhibited.

The Lord's doctrines of the future are only the final unfolding of what he taught regarding his person, his office, and his .work, as already revealed in part in his earthly life. The whole of God's great purpose for man is bound up with the essential truths of Jesus' Messiahship and the kingdom of redemption and glory which he came to establish. His eschatology centers in the doctrine of his Messiahship. The question then whether he did in fact believe himself to be the Messiah, and in what sense, becomes fundamental in our inquiry. We cannot avoid

[1] 3²⁰ f. [2] 10³⁶, 13⁴⁷. [3] 11¹⁸, 13⁴⁸. [4] 3²³, 8²⁰.

a somewhat long discussion of it.   The subject of Jesus' messianic consciousness, or more broadly speaking, his self-consciousness, has held a prominent place in recent discussion.
Whether the consciousness of divine sonship arose out of the
consciousness of Messiahship, or the reverse, how the latter
arose and when (whether before or at the baptism, at the
Transfiguration, or at some later date, when it was first
declared), and similar questions, however much space they
occupy in a 'Life' of Christ, are not essential for our present
purpose.   In fact, we are treading on much surer ground in
speaking of his self-testimony than in speaking of the processes
of his self-consciousness.   The inquiries which concern us here
are, did he declare himself the Messiah, or assent to the language of those who so declared him, and what did he teach
regarding his Messiahship, the nature of his kingdom and its
future ?   The evidence which furnishes the answer to these
questions is found (1) chiefly in utterances recorded in the
Gospels, (2) in certain acts of the Lord's life, (3) in the
beliefs of the apostolic Church.   These will be spoken of in
order.

Our knowledge of the Lord's utterances.   Before inquiry into the Lord's
teaching about his Messiahship and the messianic kingdom, as given in the
Gospels, something should be said of the *sources* of these records.   In the
present state of critical opinion the Fourth Gospel cannot be made, with
the general consent of scholars, the basis of investigation into the Lord's
exact words.   Whether the Gospel is in whole or in part the work of
St. John, the Apostle, or of another writer, it contains, as critics of nearly
all schools agree, an interpretation or exposition of the Lord's teaching
rather than a precise verbal report.   It can hardly be questioned that the
form in which the sayings of the Lord are put is generally that of the
author; and in the broader sense of what we call form, it is probable that
the author has put into his record a meaning which in his later spiritual
enlightenment he found to be contained or implied in the Lord's teaching,
though perhaps not originally expressed there in so many words.   Critical
inquirers therefore are cautious in appealing to the testimony of this Gospel in these respects unless it is confirmed at least indirectly by other New
Testament sources.   It must, however, be said that it is just this confirmation, direct or indirect, which raises the question whether criticism has not
gone too far in minimizing the historical character of the book.   The
theory which denies to it in all its parts an apostolic source, or the character of an independent document, raises difficulties not to be set aside with a
wave of the hand.   The fact that a large part of its teaching is found in

substance, though in a much less developed form, in the synoptic record, and the fact that there is so much in the book pointing to an ultimate apostolic source, form data which cannot be permanently ignored, and cause many scholars to doubt whether the Johannine question has yet reached its final solution. It is the conviction of not a few students of keen critical instinct which is expressed by a recent writer on the subject: ' The time will come for gathering up the fragments of the Fourth Gospel which are of historic value for the story of the ministry of Jesus Christ . . . and his teaching. . . . And when it comes, our own or a later generation may find that the broken pieces which remain are neither so few nor so fragmentary as the literature of the last few years has led us to suppose.' [1]

When we turn to the record in the synoptic Gospels it is necessary first of all to recognize here also the results of the very active critical inquiries carried on in recent times.[2] Much remains to be settled in regard to the origin of the Synoptics, and the sources used iu their composition, yet it may be said that substantial agreement has been reached regarding certain fundamental points. It is established that Mark is the oldest of the three Gospels,[3] and it is also generally held that in a form not very different from that known to us it was one of the two fundamental sources used in the composition of St. Matthew and St. Luke. According to the testimony of Papias (earlier part of the second century), Mark is composed of reminiscences of the preaching of St. Peter.[4] The view that its main source goes back in some form to St. Peter is accepted as at least tenable by a large number of scholars, even among those who cannot be suspected of prejudice in favor of the Papias testimony; *e.g.* Weizsäcker, H. Holtzmann, Bacon, Jülicher.

The second fundamental source used by Matthew and Luke in common was a document, consisting chiefly, if not entirely, of discourses or sayings of Jesus. From this are derived those records of his teaching which are found in essentially the same form in both Gospels but not in Mark.[5] This assumed document formerly called Logia (*utterances*) is now generally designated by the more neutral symbol Q (German, Quelle, *source*).[6] Most scholars hold it to be older than Mark; the latter seems to have been influ-

---

[1] Brooke, *Historic Value of the Fourth Gospel* in *Camb. Bib. Essays*, 1909.

[2] On the vast literature of the subject see the various N. T. Introductions, Biblical Encyclopædias, etc. ; especially full is Moffatt *Introd. to the Lit. of N. T.*

[3] By Mk., Mt. and Lk. are meant here the books and the authors of these as they now appear.

[4] This tradition appears also in Justin, Irenæus, Clem. A. and *al.*

[5] There is no doubt that both Mt. and Lk. used minor sources in addition to these two ; but it is improbable that Mt. used Lk. or *vice versa.*

[6] It is of course supposable that the parallel, non-Marcan parts of Mt. and Lk. may not all be derived from a single document, that is, the two evangelists may have used *in common* more than one document containing sayings. Cf. Harnack *Lukas d. Arzt* 108, Allen in *Oxford Studies in the Synop. Problem* 236 ; in that case Q would be taken as a general designation of these sources as a whole ; a single document is however more commonly assumed.

enced by it and to have derived some material from it.[1]   There is reason for connecting this discourse document, at least in some form, with St. Matthew, the apostle.   Papias[2] says that 'Matthew drew up the Logia,' that is, of the Lord.   The passage has been the subject of much discussion, but scholars of widely differing schools agree that the view which connects Q in some way with the Matthæan Logia and traces back at least its oldest portions to the Apostle is probable.[3]

If now our sources, Q and Mark, go back to a Petrine and a Matthæan origin, or to any form of primitive apostolic tradition, they furnish testimony which cannot easily be set aside, especially if they concur in presenting a record which is self-consistent, and accordant with the facts of the Lord's life and the beliefs of apostolic Christianity.   This testimony must however apply with much greater force to general content of thought than to exact language; for the Lord's utterances are preserved in translation only (from Aramaic into Greek) and in a form into which they crystallized through frequent oral repetition.   Variation in the records is abundantly illustrated by a comparison of parallel sayings in the different synoptics.

On the other hand the hypothesis is strongly urged that the record of Jesus' teaching has been colored along its most fundamental lines by reading back into it the beliefs of the apostolic Church.   It must suffice to observe here (1) that a cautious historian will find great difficulty in understanding how the principal doctrines regarding the Lord's person and work, new as they were, could have come into being and have been universally accepted except through the influence of his own teaching; even the powerful personality of St. Paul could not have transformed so completely the teaching of Jesus, given to the original apostles, without leaving clearer traces of the process of transformation and also of the opposition which must necessarily have been evoked, or at least traces of essential divergences; (2) the analogy of all ancient writings which seek to carry back teaching to an authority prior to its actual origin points the way to the detection of the anachronism; we should not fail to find in the synoptic Gospels the great doctrines of apostolic Christianity set forth conspicuously and in fully developed form rather than, as is the case, incidentally and often only by implication.   Certainly the great controversies which agitated the apostolic Church, so strikingly absent from the Gospels, would have read into the Lord's sayings some clear, relevant utterances.   The effect of reading a highly developed apprehension of doctrine into the earliest form of its utterance is seen distinctly in comparing the Fourth Gospel with the Synoptics.

---

[1] Cf. Streeter in *Ox. Stud.* 165 ff.   Wellhausen, *Ein.* 73 ff., however makes Q later than Mk.; with this Jülicher, *Ein.* 322, agrees as regards the developed form of Q, while placing its primitive form before Mk.

[2] Eusebius *H. E.* III. 39[16].

[3] So, *e.g.*, B. Weiss, Sanday, Harnack, Jülicher, Wendt.

The Gospel Record of Jesus' Messianic Teaching.[1]   (1) His Messiahship. The state of the messianic hope and the conception of the Messiah in the generation to which Jesus addressed himself must have affected profoundly his attitude in speaking of his Messiahship. It has been held by some that at this time the messianic hope had become nearly extinct, or at least insignificant as a factor in religious or political thought with the Jews,[2] but this view is generally rejected. Evidence of the activity of the hope among the masses at least is seen in our Gospels, in the popular revolutions,[3] and in late apocalyptic literature.[4] Doubtless the view held at the time concerning the Messiah was not clearly defined and uniform.[5] The prophetic and spiritual character was certainly recognized.[6] Some could even wonder whether John the Baptist were not the Messiah, or the one destined to become such.[7] Yet so far as we have evidence it was everywhere believed that in his kingly office he would destroy the power of the Gentiles, deliver his people out of their hands, and establish his kingdom in visible glory, The national and political aspect is everywhere present in the picture.[8] If Jesus had shared this idea of the Messiahship, he might have come forward with the cry, 'Lo here! I am he.' This he does not do. He begins his preaching with the announcement of the coming kingdom,[9] saying nothing of himself. His acknowledgment, or assertion of his Messiahship is indirect; generally he seeks to hide it,[10] at least until the very end. There are, however, at least two instances in which he acknowledges unmistakably that he is the Christ. The first occurs at Cæsarea Philippi in connection with St. Peter's confession, 'Thou art the Christ.'[11] The Lord

---

[1] The literature is voluminous; besides works on N. T. Theol., Bible Dictionaries, etc., see the following as among the more useful: Titius *N. T.*, J. Weiss *Predigt*, Haupt *Eschat.*, Holtzm. *Mess.* (an invaluable book), Briggs *Mess. Gos.*, Bruce *Kingdom*, Baldensperger *Selbstbewusstsein*, etc., Wernle *Reich.*, Wellhausen *Ein.*, Bousset *Predigt*, Dalman *Worte*, Wendt *Teaching*, Muirhead *Eschat.*, Schweitzer *QHJ.*, Mathews *Mess.*, Lepin *Jésus*, Dewick *Eschat.*, Dobschütz *Eschat.*   [2] Bruno Bauer, Schweitzer, *al.*   [3] Cf. Acts 5[37].
[4] Ap. Bar., 2 Es., Sib Or. Cf. Bousset *Jud.* 210 f., Holtzm. *Mess.* 28, Schürer II. 601 ff.   [5] Cf. Holtzm. *Mess.* 15, Lepin *Jésus* 20 ff.
[6] Lk. 1[77], Mt. 1[21].   [7] Lk. 3[15].
[8] Cf. the 'Evangelical Canticles,' the *Magnificat*, Lk. 1[46-55], and the *Benedictus ib.* 68–79, which are derived from, or inspired by, a Jewish source and are throughout intensely Hebraistic in their view of the Messiah's office.
[9] Mk. 1[14 f.]   [10] Mt. 16[20], par.   [11] Mk. 8[29], par.

himself had called forth this confession by his question as to
whom men thought him to be, and he could not have failed to
repel the ascription, if he had in no sense regarded himself the
Christ. His failure to dissent is equivalent to assent.[1] In
strong contrast is his attitude when Peter remonstrates against
his submission to suffering.[2] Some who deny that he claimed
to be the Messiah interpret his command to tell no man of his
Messiahship (v. 30) as containing such dissent. But few
students of the Lord's life can conceive of his correcting fundamental error by a command not to speak openly about it.[3]
The second instance occurs at the trial before the Sanhedrim,
when to the high priest's question, 'Art thou the Christ?'
Jesus answers, 'I am,'[4] or according to St. Matthew[5] in words
equally affirmative, 'Thou hast said.'[6] The messianic claim
is no less certainly implied, though not so distinctly declared,
in answer to Pilate at the Roman trial,[7] also in answer to the
message of inquiry from John the Baptist, 'Art thou he?'[8] and
in answer to the request of James and John for the first place
in the kingdom.[9]

Jesus' claim to be the Messiah is attested with equal force
by his acceptance or his use of certain appellatives to which a
messianic meaning was attached either by himself or the people. The title *Son of David*, the favorite designation of the
Messiah with the people, he does not use himself, but he accepts
it in withholding signs of disapproval when it is given to him
by others, and in granting entreaties addressed to him in this
name.[10] His perplexing question to the Pharisees about the

---

[1] The strong words of benediction in answer to Peter, Mt. 16[17], are wanting
in Mk. and Lk., and are therefore rejected by many.   [2] Mk. 8[33].
[3] Cf. Holtzm. *Mess.* 21 f.   [4] Mk. 14[61 f.]   [5] 26[24].
[6] Such is the interpretation generally given to these words by the commentators. The phrase σὺ εἶπας, *thou hast said*, or its equivalent, σὺ λέγεις, ὑμεῖς
λέγετε, in answer to a direct question is found in the N. T. in the story of the
Passion only (Mt. 26[25, 64], 27[11], par., Lk. 22[70]) ; its use as a simple affirmative is
not found in Gk. writers, neither is it, as is often stated, a *common* rabbinical
formula. But it is shown by Dalman (*Worte* 253 f.) and others to occur in a
few cases in rabbinical writings expressing assent with a certain reluctance, or
out of the questioner's own mouth. This is clearly the sense in Mt. 26[25].
There is no instance of its implying denial. Cf. Holtzm. *Mess.* 30 f., Zahn
Kom. Mt. 26[25], Thayer in *Journ. Bib. Lit.* 1894.   [7] Mk. 15[2], par.
[8] Mt. 11[2 ff.], Lk. 7[18 ff.]   [9] Mt. 20[20 ff.], Mk. 10[35 ff.]
[10] Apart from the triumphal entry, on which see pp. 137, 302, cf. Mk. 10[48],
par., Mt. 9[27], 12[23], 15[22].

Davidic sonship of the Messiah [1] is taken by some as a rejection of the title for himself, and a denial of its applicability to the Messiah altogether. [2] But it is evident that the Lord is not here denying a Davidic descent of the Messiah ; he is trying to show the Pharisees out of the Scriptures that in order to constitute one the Messiah there must be not only such descent but also a relation which sets the descendant as Lord above David himself. [3] It has been seen above [4] that the title *Son of God* was applied to the theocratic people and the theocratic king, and probably also to the Messiah whom these foreshadowed. But did Jesus himself use or accept the title, and if so, was it with messianic meaning ; or is this, as some hold, a reading back of later ideas and terms into the Gospel record? The application of the title to him in the Epistles and the Fourth Gospel is too frequent to need illustration ; it is a designation adopted universally by the earliest Christian community, and this fact itself furnishes strong probability that it was used with this distinct significance in the Lord's own time. As Dr. Sanday says, ' How are we to account for the rapid growth within some 23 to 26 years of a usage already so fixed and stereotyped ? Where is the workshop in which it was fashioned, if it did not descend from Christ himself? When we think of the way in which the best authenticated records of his teaching lead us up to the very verge of the challenged expressions, it seems an altogether easier step to regard them as the natural culmination of that teaching than to seek their origin wholly outside it.' [5] The presence of the title in the Gospels is doubtless to be assigned to a correct tradition, though it is not unlikely that in some passages this may be a reflection of the more clearly defined Christology of the apostolic Church. In St. Peter's confession [6] the words, ' the Son of God,' may possibly be an addition of the author, as they are not found in the parallel accounts of Mark and Luke. In our synoptic sources this title is applied to Jesus by various persons and in various circumstances ; [7] in some cases it is used as a

[1] Mk. 12[35-37], par.
[2] Cf. Holtzm. *Theol.* I. 310 f., Wellhausen *Ein.* 93.
[3] Cf. Zahn on Mt. 22[41 ff.], Wendt *Teaching* II. 133 ff.   [4] P. 44.
[5] Hast. IV. 573.   [6] Mt. 16[16].   [7] *E.g.* Mk. 5[7], 14[61], 15[39], Mt. 14[28], 27[40].

repetition of his own words.[1] There is no instance recorded in which he directly and of his own motion gives to himself the full designation *the Son of God*, though he accepts it from the mouth of others and assents to it when questioned as to his claim to it.[2] He does, however, speak of his Sonship and God's Fatherhood, and not as men in general may so speak,[3] but in a special sense, not applicable to other men ; 'No one knoweth the Son save the Father ; neither doth any know the Father save the Son, and he to whomsoever the Son willeth to reveal him.'[4] He never places himself on a common footing with his disciples with respect to sonship ; he says 'your Father' and 'My Father,' but never 'Our Father' ; the phrase in the Paternoster is for the disciples in common with one another, not in common with him.[5] This unique Sonship is also accorded to him by the heavenly voice at the Baptism and the Transfiguration.[6] We are certainly right then in holding that the Lord declared himself the Son of God in a sense in which no other could claim that relation. But did he therein declare himself the Messiah? The wealth of meaning which the title contained for him lies beyond our present inquiry.[7] But as it sums up all the truth of his personality, it certainly contained his Messiahship. Its messianic significance for *others* is attested by the question of the high priest in which he makes the title synonymous with 'the Christ.' For Jesus himself also it contained the same messianic meaning. He assents to it before the high priest,[8] he points to himself in the parable of the vineyard[9] as Son and heir of the messianic throne.

The standing designation which Jesus gives to himself in the Gospels is *the Son of Man*. Duplicates being disregarded, it occurs some 40 times in the Synoptics and at least 11 times in St. John,[10] but elsewhere in the New Testament only

---

[1] Mt. 27[40, 43]. [2] Lk. 22[70]. [3] Mt. 6[9, 32].

[4] Mt. 11[27], Lk. 10[22]. The authenticity of this passage has been questioned, but on purely subjective grounds. It is derived from Q, and is accepted by most critics, *e.g.* Dalman, Harnack ; and so far as Jesus' unique Sonship is concerned, it is confirmed by the Marcan source, 13[32], where the words, 'neither the Son,' though wanting in some Mss., are well authenticated and are retained by nearly all critics.

[5] Cf. Weiss *Theol.*, § 17. [6] Mk. 1[11], par., 9[7] par.

[7] For an admirable article on the subject, see Sanday in Hast. IV. 570 ff.

[8] Mk. 14[61 f.], par. [9] Mt. 21[37].

[10] It is found in both Q and the Marcan document.

once.[1] Except in this single instance (in the mouth of the dying Stephen) it is used only by the Lord himself, or in repetition of his words. Its origin, choice, and meaning raise questions among the most intricate in the study of the Gospels.[2] It can be touched upon here only in the briefest way. It is certain that our sources are correct in assigning the use of the title to the Lord himself. The apostolic Church could never have originated, or have brought in from apocalyptic literature, and read back into his mouth, as some claim,[3] a term which the Church, as seen above, did not itself use ; and it is equally certain, notwithstanding contention to the contrary, that unless our Gospels are to be extensively rewritten in the interest of a theory, the Lord referred to himself in his earthly as well as his future character.

In recent discussion much attention has naturally been given to the probable form and meaning of the term in Aramaic, the language in which Jesus uttered it ;[4] and in the opinion of most philologists, υἱὸς τοῦ ἀνθρώπου, son of man, is a literal Greek translation of a term meaning man as contrasted with any other being, that is, in the Aramaic compound meaning literally son of man, the first part had entirely lost its force, so that the phrase meant simply man as a member of the human race, and was the usual, if not the only, expression for this idea. Jesus then is supposed to have used the expression when speaking of mankind at large, e.g. 'The Sabbath was made for man' (Mk. 2[27]). On the other hand he is reported in the Gospels as using it frequently, when it would not be applicable to man in general, but only to himself, e.g. 'The Son of man coming in his kingdom' (Mt. 16[28]). When the Greek translators understood it to be used in the former sense, they rendered it by simple ἄνθρωπος, man ; when in the latter sense, by ὁ υἱὸς τοῦ ἀνθρώπου, the son of man, the literal translation ; in this case they saw in it a special self-designation of the Lord, and the peculiarity of the phrase thus used, perhaps not quite clearly comprehended by the disciples themselves, may have led to its retention in a full, literal translation. We cannot affirm that the Greek translators interpret with accuracy in every instance the Lord's intention in the use of the words ; that is, there may be cases where there is room to question whether in the original he referred to man generally or to himself only (e.g. such question is raised by Lietzmann, Wellhausen, al. in Mt. 9[6], 12[8]). But such cases, if apart from

[1] Acts 7[56]. The form in Rev. has not the definite article.
[2] For bibliography see the Bib. Dictionaries, Lives of Christ, and N. T. Theologies. A vast lit. is found in periodicals and special treatises ; for some of the more important works see Hast. IV. 589 ; cf. also above p. 121 ; invaluable for the discussion of different views and lit. of the subject is Holtzm. Mess.
[3] E.g. Lietzmann, Wellhausen.
[4] Especially valuable here is Fiebig Der Menschensohn, 1901.

misinterpretation they exist at all, are too few to affect the general validity of the distinction made in our Greek sources. In nearly all places where *the son of man* occurs it is unquestionably clear that reference is made to Jesus himself. In all probability the correct translation of the term as used by the Lord in referring to himself is *The man* rather than *the Son of man*, that is, the title is not *man*, or *a man* simply, it is *the* man. If this be thought too little distinctive for a title applicable to a single person only, the same might be said of the messianic titles, the *Son of David*, and the *Son of God*, given to only one among the many descendants of David and the many sons of God. (Cf. Zahn, *Mt.* 349 ff.) It should, however, be added that we still know too little about the Aramaic spoken in Palestine at the time to say quite certainly, it had no means of reproducing the separate expressions *man* and *the son of man*, and that different Aramaic terms may not have lain behind the distinction in the Greek translation of the Lord's sayings. (Cf. Dalman, *Worte* 195.) In any event the translation, *the son of man*, cannot be due to ignorance of the exact meaning of the original, for the translation was made not by our Evangelists, but by the authors of their sources, who doubtless were as familiar with Aramaic as with Greek.

This self-designation of Jesus is nowhere explained by him ; but if the term *the son of man* is equivalent to *the man* (see above, fine print), it is parallel to, and illuminated by, a familiar biblical usage, according to which the phrase 'son of' followed by a defining noun denotes one whose essential nature, or category, is defined by the noun, *e.g.* 'sons of disobedience'[1] = the essentially disobedient, 'son of wickedness'[2] = one essentially wicked ; so 'son of man' = man, when his essential nature as man is made prominent. But in the Lord's use of the phrase the article is important. As he is *the* Son of God among many sons of God, and *the* Son of David among many sons of David, so he is *the* Son of man among many sons of men, *the* man among all men, he is *the* man who in the strictest sense can be called such, the only one in whom the race has reached its perfection.[3] The passages in which the term occurs fall, with a small number of exceptions of a neutral character, into two general groups, the one referring to present rejection, humiliation, and suffering ; the other to future glorification and power. In the former group the title is especially appropriate as contrasting the dignity of this unique being with his earthly lot ; the latter group points on to the consummate exaltation to which such a being is destined. The

---

[1] Eph. 2².   [2] Ps. 89²².   [3] Zahn *Mt.* p. 349 ff.

view that the Lord uses this title to express his lowliness and submission to man's lot, and his sympathy with all that is human (while all this is doubtless contained in the idea) overlooks the group of passages which speak of his eschatological glory. On the other hand to interpret wholly from the standpoint of the eschatological passages, confining the meaning to the apocalyptic man, the man mentioned in Daniel and other apocalyptic writers, makes it necessary to reject the passages referring to present humiliation, or to interpret these with extreme arbitrariness.

Whether the title, the Son of man, originated with the Lord himself,[1] or whether he adopted it from existing names of the Messiah, cannot be said with certainty. The very general opinion of present-day scholars [2] is that the term goes back ultimately to Dan. 7^{13}, where in reference to the eschatological kingdom the prophet speaks of ' one like unto a son of man ' coming with the clouds of heaven.[3] While this passage pretty certainly referred originally to the character of the kingdom rather than to the person of the Messiah, later it received, at least in some quarters, a messianic interpretation ; the terms, *Son of man, that man, the man,* referring to the Messiah, are found in apocalyptic literature in connections which show use of the Daniel passage,[4] though there is no evidence that this became the *general* interpretation. The Lord himself in speaking of himself under this title shows at least in one instance that the representation of the passage in Daniel was before his mind.[5] On the other hand it seems certain that *the Son of man,* or *the man,* was not in our Lord's time a *common* designation of the Messiah. Not only is evidence of this lacking,[6] but had it been commonly understood thus, he could not have applied the title to himself so often and so publicly, while at the same time maintaining such reserve in declaring his Messiahship.[7] And

---

[1] So, Zahn, Westcott, *al.*   [2] Cf. Holtzm. *Mess.* 51.

[3] Some find the source in Ps. 8^4, or in Ezek. *passim.* Gunkel followed by others seeks to trace the origin further back, into Babylonian tradition.

[4] En. 46^{1-6}, 2 Es. 13^2 ff.

[5] Mk. 14^{62}, par. If the ' Little Apocalypse ' (cf. p. 143) be attributed to Jesus, cf. also Mk. 13^{26}, par.

[6] Dalman *Worte* 197 ff.

[7] The same fact would be shown in Mt. 16^{13-17}, if the words *Son of man,* which would put the answer into the question itself, are not due to the editor ;

because he gave to the passages in Daniel a messianic meaning, it does not follow that he borrowed his favorite self-designation from this source, any more than that he borrowed the title *Son of God*, which in his self-consciousness he applied to himself, from its existing use as a designation of the messianic king. As he must have reached his consciousness of divine sonship apart from the imperfect conceptions of such sonship found in the Jewish Scriptures, so the consciousness of his perfect humanity must have arisen and found its appropriate expression apart from apocalyptic literature. It would perhaps be safest to say that he found in the prophet Dan. the designation coincident with that which naturally arose as the expression of his consciousness of his perfect humanity, *The man*, the one man in whom humanity reached its perfection; see above.

If now the explanation of the name as given above (pp. 125 f.) be correct, and the disciples did not at first see in it a messianic meaning, the question arises, whether the Lord himself attached such a meaning to it. According to our sources it seems clear that he did. The Son of man is the title by which he designates himself in that large group of passages which refer to his future coming and the fulfillment of the messianic kingdom, when he will be seen at the right hand of power and coming with the clouds of heaven,[1] when he will send forth his angels to gather out of his kingdom all that is foreign to it;[2] he designates himself by the same title in that other group of passages in which he speaks of his humiliation and suffering,[3] experiences which he regarded as part of the divinely ordered destiny of the Messiah: and still further this is the title which he takes in speaking of the mission,[4] and the powers[5] which are given to him alone among men. It is however without doubt an error to suppose the title to be with him a mere synonym of *Messiah;* it would probably be more nearly correct to take it in his use as *including* the Messiahship. He was the Messiah *because* he was the Son of man, The man, even as he was the Messiah because he was the Son of God; or rather, because he was both

they are wanting in Mk. and Lk. For a similar reason Jno. 12[34] does not furnish certain evidence.
[1] Mk. 14[62], par.   [2] Mt. 13[41].   [3] *E.g.* Mt. 8[20], Mk. 8[31], 9[31], par.
[4] Mk. 10[45], Lk. 19[10].   [5] Mk. 2[10], 2[28], par.

the Son of man and the Son of God. For him the title expressed his unique being, the one being in whom humanity reached its perfect realization and in whom at the same time divine sonship inhered. This being alone could be the Messiah, and when the Lord used the title he uttered his consciousness that he fulfilled the messianic ideal.

If in what is said above the right view has been taken of the use of the terms, the Christ, the Son of David, the Son of God, the Son of man, it is certain, notwithstanding the contention of some critics to the contrary, that Jesus accepted these titles and meant thus to express the consciousness of his Messiahship. But without doubt that which ultimately led his followers to recognize him as the Messiah was not so much his self-designation by a significant title, as the relation of his own person to his message and his work. As the central theme in his preaching was the kingdom of God, so he showed himself the central figure in that kingdom, its founder and leader. He broke the power of the prince of devils, and by that very act declared that he had brought in the kingdom of God,[1] he placed himself in his own person above the Mosaic law and laid down the qualifications for membership in the kingdom,[2] those who would belong to it must follow him,[3] he demanded absolute surrender to his will,[4] he forgave sin, he declared himself greater than the prophet, greater than the temple, greater than Solomon,[5] the prophet that had no superior was his forerunner, the Elijah who should precede the Messiah.[6]

Why Jesus, if he really regarded himself the Christ, should have so studiously avoided declaring this in explicit terms nearly all his life is not stated in our records. The view, that the one fact certainly excludes the other, is a very arbitrary reading of history; and though those who hold this view regard any possible explanation as an unwarrantable reading into the records,[7] yet most scholars fail to find a real difficulty here. If the Lord differed radically from his contemporaries in his idea of the messianic office, a premature declaration of himself would, it is easy to see, have fatally impeded his religious mission, to say nothing of the danger of provoking political revolution. Only by a slow process of enlightenment could his hearers come to see that the Son of man was truly the Messiah.

[1] Mt. 12^{28}, Lk. 11^{20}.   [2] Mt. 5–7.   [3] Mt. 8^{22}, Mk. 10^{21}.
[4] Lk. 9^{23} ff., 14^{26} f.   [5] Mt. 12$^{6, 41, 42}$.
[6] Mt. 11$^{11, 14}$; cf. Weiss *Theol.* § 13, Holtzm. *Theol.* I. 295 ff.
[7] Cf. Schweitzer *QHJ.* 220 f.

The denial on the part of certain scholars that Jesus claimed the title Messiah proceeds generally from the supposition that he must have taken it in its current, traditional acceptation, and that the adoption of it in a sense materially modified was equivalent to its rejection. The Lord's procedure here is however in keeping with his attitude toward the older revelation throughout; he rejects the partial and temporary phases, he seizes hold of, and unfolds, the essential and eternal. In at least three most characteristic particulars his break with the traditional conceptions was so complete that any messianic claim on his part was, in the mind of his Jewish contemporaries, an act of blasphemy. (1) The perception that the Messiah must suffer and die for his people, an idea at variance with every expectation inherited from the prophets, becomes a determining force in his course. Whether Jesus foresaw this from the beginning, or only later through the experiences of his life, is a question which need not detain us here.[1] But it is a striking fact, that from the epoch-making declaration of St. Peter at Cæsarea Philippi, ' Thou art the Christ,' Jesus passed immediately to teach the disciples that he must suffer and be put to death ;[2] and henceforth he sets his face unflinchingly toward Jerusalem and the cross. However or whenever he may have reached the consciousness that this was a part of his destiny, it can hardly be doubtful that he saw the applicability to himself of what the prophet, the Second Isaiah, had said concerning the suffering servant of Jehovah, though this is not directly declared in his teaching.[3] (2) He rejected entirely the Jewish conception of a political kingship to be established over the nations of the earth. In one word, ' Render unto Caesar the things that are Caesar's,'[4] he showed the remoteness of this thought from his purpose. The legions which he was able to summon to his aid were not those of the sword.[5] (3) All national limitations disappeared from his doctrine of Messiahship. His mission began, to be sure, with ' the lost sheep of the

---

[1] For various views see Holtzm. *Theol.* I. 353 ff.   [2] Mk. 8[27-31], par.
[3] Mk. 10[45] evidently contains a reminiscence of Is. 53[10-12]. The very general nature of the reference in Lk. 18[31], 22[37] to the mention of the Messiah's sufferings in the prophets favors the historicity of the statement, for a thought so prominent in apostolic teaching, if ' read back,' would probably have been made more explicit.   [4] Mk. 12[17], par.   [5] Mt. 26[52 f.].

house of Israel,' [1] but in its ultimate scope aimed to include the field which is the world. [2]   There are utterances of his, such as the answer to the Syrophœnician woman and the command to the apostles, 'Go not into the way of the Gentiles,' [3] which are sometimes taken to prove that he shared his people's idea of a purely Jewish Messiah, at least in the earlier part of his career. [4] But in Jesus' self-consciousness as the Son of God and the Son of man there must have been given the consciousness of a Messiahship which was absolutely universal.   His gospel was to be preached to all nations; [5] his disciples were to be the light of the world. [6]   The limitation at first imposed in the sphere of Jesus' own work and that of his disciples was but the natural *preparation* for the mission to all the world. [7]

But if Jesus rejected these essential elements in the Jewish doctrine of the Messiah, was there then anything left? Was he not a Messiah merely in name? By many he is thought to have appropriated to himself the office by way of *accommodation* only, suiting his self-characterization to the highest term in his people's understanding; the title was, it is said, a burden to him which he would gladly have been rid of; it has no abiding value, 'in our time it is only a requisite for missions to the Jews.' [8]   But however true it is, that the Lord, like every great originator in religious thought, must bring his message in forms already familiar to his hearers, yet he saw in the revelations of the prophets, through all that was partial and temporary, an eternal truth; [9] for him the figure of the prophetic Messiah contained a meaning not seized by the prophets themselves; for him that figure had a permanent significance.   It seems certain that it was the consciousness of his unique nature and office that led him to see in himself the Messiah and not the reverse, as some hold; [10] for it is not easy to understand how, if he had started from the prophetic conception of the Messiah, he should have so clearly distinguished the accidental features from the essential and have applied the latter only to himself; in other words, some consciousness of the latter, as

---

[1] Mt. 15²⁴.   [2] Mt. 13³⁸.   [3] Mt. 10⁵.
[4] Cf. Baldensperger *Selbstbewusstsein* ² 130 f.   See also p. 140   [5] Lk. 24⁴⁷.
[6] Mt. 5¹⁴.   [7] Cf. Wendt *Teaching* II. 197 ff.
[8] Schulz, cited by Holtzm. *Mess.* 97.   [9] Mt. 5¹⁷ ᶠ·.
[10] Cf. Holtzm. *Theol.* I. 298 ᶠᶠ·.

characteristic of his own person, must be presupposed in this application. When the consciousness of his person and work unfolded itself, he must have seen that he himself fulfilled the messianic ideal. He was conscious that he was the Son of God and the Son of man, that his mission was to suffer for men, to deliver them with an eternal salvation, to establish ·the kingdom of God and to be its Lord. All this he saw to be contained in the person and work of the Messiah of the prophets. This for him was the essential and permanent significance of the Messiahship. The majestic person, in whom the prophets dimly and distortedly saw God coming to redeem and glorify his people, was for him a real though imperfect vision of himself. He did not liken himself to the Messiah, he did not adopt the messianic rôle, he *was* the Messiah. For him all the truth of his being lay hidden in one or another of the prophetic words. And so it is with the faith of the Church. His title the Christ (the Greek term has largely superseded the Hebrew equivalent, the Messiah) sums up all that is believed of his nature and office.

(2) The Kingdom of God. Correlative with the Lord's doctrine of the Messiahship is that of the Kingdom of God. The king and his kingdom are necessarily implied the one in the other. Jesus began his public ministry by proclaiming, not himself, but the kingdom,[1] and prominent in his teaching as he soon came to make his own person, frequent as are his sayings regarding the Son of man, yet reference to the kingdom is still more frequent. We in our everyday thought have largely made the term remote and figurative, but he on the contrary in parables, in discourses, and in isolated utterances made it central in his message for the present and the future.

For βασιλεία τοῦ θεοῦ, *kingdom of God*, Mt. uses with few exceptions βασιλεία τῶν οὐρανῶν, *kingdom of heaven*, which does not occur elsewhere in the New Testament, except possibly in Jno. 3[5]. That Mt. in this is closer to the original source (so, Allen in *Ox. Stud.* 241) is improbable, for it is less likely that Mk. and the non-Mk. parts of Lk. (Q), in the considerable number of places where they have θεοῦ for the Matthæan οὐρανῶν, should have independently agreed in varying from the original, than that the

---

[1] Mk. 1[15].

variation should be due to Mt. The entire absence of the Matthæan form from the other records of the Lord's words favors the supposition that the form was not used by the Lord himself (cf. Wendt *Teaching* I. 371). In any event the general equivalence of the two forms is shown by a comparison of the parallel passages in which the forms are found. The theory that the two forms differ in reference, and that the form with οὐρανῶν always means the eschatological kingdom (cf. Allen in ICC. *Mt.* LXVII ff.) requires violence in the interpretation of such passages as Mt. 11[11] , 21[31], and the parables of the sower, the tares, and the drag-net. The same method of interpretation would make the form with θεοῦ likewise eschatological. The view that οὐρανοί is here put by metonymy for *God*, according to well-known rabbinical usage (Schürer II. 629, followed by many) is at variance with the fact that neither Mt. nor Jesus shows any reluctance to use the divine name. Most scholars take the Matthæan form to be intended to designate the heavenly origin and character of the kingdom; cf. Holtzm. *Theol.* I. 249 ff., Stevens *Theol.* 28.

We have no occasion here to enter into the manifold inquiries, historical and ethical, attaching to the Lord's use of this term; we can only notice briefly those that are most essential to our present purpose, the consideration of his eschatology. (1) He himself nowhere declares precisely what he means by the term. For this reason some suppose he must have taken it in the usual Jewish sense, as the realization of the Old Testament theocracy.[1] Such a kingdom was of course to be one of perfect righteousness, one where God's rule was absolute; but it centered, nationally and politically, in Israel. If, however, as maintained above, Jesus' conception of his Messiahship grew out of the consciousness of his unique nature as the Son of God and the Son of man, his idea of the messianic kingdom must have been free from all national determination. And this is made clear in his teaching. The conditions of membership in the kingdom have no relation to birth; they are set forth in the Beatitudes and are purely spiritual. Men should come from all corners of the earth and sit down in the kingdom, while Jews should be thrust out.[2] The early disciples, Jews as they were, found it hard to grasp this truth, but this slowness of theirs forms no sufficient evidence that the Lord had not declared the doctrine. (2) The phrase βασιλεία τοῦ θεοῦ, *kingdom of God*, can mean either the *sphere* of God's rule,

---

[1] Cf. Weiss *Theol.* § 13 b.   [2] Mt. 8[11 f.], Lk. 13[29].

his domain, or the activity of God, his *reign*.[1] Many take the
latter to be the predominant thought in Jesus' use of the expression. The reference, then, is to a spiritual condition of
perfect obedience to God, the complete sway of his will in the
hearts and conduct of men. But the idea of rule must pass
over into that of the sphere of rule. There must be, if not
now, at least in the end a *people* over whom God reigns. Not
only in the eschatological expectations of the Jews is there the
idea of a *realm* of God, but in Jesus' teaching also the objective
aspect appears distinct, as when he speaks of entrance into it,[2]
of its coming and manifestation,[3] of differences of rank in it,[4]
of eating and drinking in it.[5] (3) Much difference of opinion
exists as to whether Jesus means to declare the kingdom to
have already come in his appearing, or whether he places it
wholly in the future. The disciples are taught to pray for its
coming, and in many places the Lord clearly speaks of it as
future, identifying it with the eschatological kingdom to be
established at his parousia ; [6] this is the most frequent representation, in both the Marcan source and Q. On the other
hand there are utterances of his that appear equally clear in
declaring it already present. One of the most striking of
these is that given at the healing of the demoniac, 'If I by the
Spirit of God cast out devils, then is the kingdom of God come
to you,' that is, in so far as the power of Satan is overthrown,
the kingdom of God is introduced.[7] The very fact that the
Messiah has come implies the presence of the kingdom, at least
in some sense, in his activity. 'These acts of power are the
morning-flush of the rising day of his glory, they are indeed
proofs of the presence of the kingdom of God.' [8] The parables of the sower, the tares, the mustard seed, the drag-net, the
leaven, though opinions may differ regarding the main truth
intended, all clearly imply the presence of the kingdom before
the End. To the same effect is Jesus' answer to the Pharisees,
asking about the time of the coming, 'The kingdom of God is

---

[1] Cf. Dalman *Worte* 75 ff., Bousset *Predigt* 101, Volz 299 f.
[2] Mt. 7[21], 18[3], Lk. 13[28].   [3] Mk. 1[15], Lk. 19[11].   [4] Mt. 18[1], Lk. 7[28].
[5] Mk. 14[25], Lk. 14[15].
[6] *E.g.* Mk. 9[1], par., 14[25], Mt. 7[21], 8[11].
[7] Mt. 12[28], Lk. 11[20], a saying probably from Q. On φθάνω here cf. Zahn
Mt. in loc.   [8] Titius *N. T.* I. 184.

[already] among you.'[1] Among other passages which contain the same representation are those in which Jesus speaks
of present membership in the kingdom and present entrance
into it.[2] It is evident, though many deny the possibility of
combining the two ideas,[3] that in one sense the kingdom is
eschatological, and that in another it is already present in the
world. The relation of the two aspects to each other has been
variously expressed, as that of idea and reality, the inner and
the outer, essence and manifestation, content and form, the
time of conflict and the time of triumph. Most scholars who
recognize the Lord's habit of viewing the present, the real, and
the imperfect, in the light of the timeless, the ideal, and the
perfect, find little difficulty in accepting both conceptions of
the kingdom as belonging to his teaching.[4] But the wide
scope in his use of the term makes it difficult to give to it a
definition applicable to either aspect, if taken by itself. (4) If
now the kingdom is in any sense already present, the question
naturally arises whether our Lord associated with it even the
ideal of any present, outward form, or whether it is as yet only
an inner, spiritual state, a force ruling in the individual only.
In the Lord's Prayer the petition, Thy kingdom come, is made
more specific by the equivalent phrase, Thy will be done. The
conditions of membership in the kingdom, as set forth in the
Lord's teaching, and the blessings promised are purely spiritual.
It is therefore contended that the idea of ' kingdom ' is entirely
superseded by that of ' reign ' ; wherever God's will is done in
the heart, there his reign, his kingdom is realized. The idea
of a *people* of God disappears. It needs no argument to show
that the founding of an institution which should assume the
functions of political government in the world was foreign to
Jesus' purpose ; but unless the New Testament history is to be
entirely rewritten, it is clear that he intended his followers to
form an organized community. Distinct reference to the

---

[1] Lk. 17²¹. This probably is the correct interpretation. Cf. Weiss in Meyer,
Plummer in ICC. *in loc.*

[2] *E.g.* Mt. 11¹¹ f., 21³¹, 23¹³, Mk. 12³⁴, Lk. 7²⁸, 12³¹, 16¹⁶.

[3] Cf. Schweizer, *QHJ.* 237 f.

[4] The confidence with which critics of the extreme eschatological school deny
all allusion to a present kingdom moves Harnack to the somewhat impatient
remark, ' If any one finds it impossible to accept the teaching, The kingdom is
future and yet present, argument with him is useless,' *Sayings of Jesus* 232.

Church is found in the Gospels in St. Matthew only,[1] and here, in passages which are attributed by many to later influence; such attribution is not wholly improbable. But whether there be in the Lord's words a distinct mention of the Church or not, the formation of a community seems certain in his purposes. The disciples (afterwards made apostles) whom he gathered about him in the outset of his ministry constituted the nucleus of a community; and he sent them out, not merely to preach an eschatological kingdom,[2] but to make present followers of himself,[3] a body of disciples separate from the world, as a city set upon a hill, who should all be brethren.[4] By the initial rite of baptism these were introduced into a visible society; they observed as a distinct community rite the ordinance which contained a symbol of the new covenant inaugurated in the Lord's death (and a new covenant implied a new covenant people). That in such a society there must be those to whom, by Jesus' command, administrative functions were assigned is an inevitable inference, though in the present state of critical opinion, this cannot be said to be explicitly stated. It must however be remembered that neither the outward form nor the inner spiritual state taken by itself alone can contain in full the biblical idea of the kingdom; not Israel, merely as a people, not the Church, merely as an organized society, *is* the kingdom; neither is the rule of God in the individual soul that kingdom. The perfect kingdom is that in which both elements are united in their perfection. In our record of the Lord's words, the passages in which he identifies the Church and the kingdom, as in giving to an apostle 'the keys of the kingdom of heaven,' and in the explanation added to the parable of the tares, are attributed by many to a later source;[5] yet in this parable itself, which, as distinguished from the added explanation, may certainly be accepted as from the Lord, and likewise in the parable of the drag-net,[6] the connection between the Church and the kingdom is clearly implied. And such parables contain also the answer to the objection, that where there

---

[1] 16[18 f.], 18[17]. On these passages cf. Weiss in Meyer *in loc.*, Wendt *Teaching* II. 351 ff., Holtzm. *Theol.* I. 268 ff., Stevens *Theol.* 138 ff.
[2] Mt. 10[7].   [3] Mt. 10[32, 40, 42].   [4] Mt. 23[8].
[5] Mt. 16[19], 13[41] are wanting in Mk. and Lk. Cf. Holtzm. *Theol.* I. 270 ff.
[6] Mt. 13[47-50].

is any evil or imperfection the kingdom of God cannot be. Undoubtedly this is true of the kingdom in its ultimate state; but as God's rule in the hearts of his children is partial, so the present form of the kingdom is but a very imperfect embodiment of the ideal. The interval between the Church as it now is and the kingdom in its ideal perfection is measureless. But if there be in any sense a present kingdom, it must in every respect fall short of the kingdom to which it looks forward. Now it is the Church marred by human frailty, like every Christian character; then it will be the Church purified and triumphant.[1]

Evidence from Certain Events in the Lord's Life. In the foregoing section we have reviewed the testimony to Jesus' messianic claims furnished by utterances, his own and those of others, recorded in the Gospels. Similar testimony is borne by certain events in his life. The story of the triumphal entry into Jerusalem is accepted by most scholars as historical, and its testimony to Jesus' declaration of his Messiahship seems unquestionable. The homage of the multitude is rendered to him as the Messiah, he accepts that homage and defends those who offer it against rebuke.[2] The fact that his view of his messianic office differs from theirs is not a sufficient ground for evading the acclamation. To have denied that he came as the promised One would have been to deny the applicability of the messianic prophecy to himself. The correction of the mistaken messianic view of the multitude may in these last pressing events be left to the lesson of the passion and resurrection, now close at hand. So also the history of the crucifixion furnishes evidence which cannot by reasonable criticism be set aside. Jesus was delivered over to the Roman authority, was tried, condemned and executed as one who claimed to be the Messiah. Nowhere in the trial did he deny the charge.[3] Though in

---

[1] Cf. p. 96.

[2] Mt. 21[11] does not show this act of the people to have been simply an ovation given to a *prophet* — so, some take it; the words of the multitude express rather the ground upon which they justify the messianic acclaim of v. 9, *i.e.* Jesus' greatness as a prophet; cf. Jno. 6[14 f.].

[3] Had he denied it, no disciple could after his shameful death have ever given him the title.

his earlier ministry he had been reserved in speaking of his Messiahship, the very existence of this charge and his attitude throughout the trial show that he regarded himself the Messiah, and that he had in some way declared this so that it had become known. A course so at variance as was his with all current ideas of a Messiah could not apart from his words have led to this charge.

Evidence from the Earliest Christian Belief. The value of the earliest Christian belief as testimony to Jesus' claim to be the Messiah and to his teaching regarding his kingdom lies in what seems unquestionably to be the origin of such belief. We have seen above the universal belief of the apostolic age : Jesus, the risen and ascended Lord, is the Messiah ; he will return soon in visible glory to consummate the kingdom of God ; the judgment will be held ; and eternal life will become the inheritance of the risen believers in a realm above all national or racial limitations, above all political domain and merely earthly glory. This hope takes its character from the conception of the kingdom and the king (though neither of these express *terms* is much used outside of the Gospels), or perhaps it should rather be said, from the conception of the person and work of the Messiah in whom it all centers. But whence comes this belief that Jesus is the Messiah ? A confident answer, familiar to readers of modern theological literature, is that it arose in the early Christian community as a result of reflection upon Christ's resurrection ; that event first led the disciples to attribute to Jesus a messianic character, a thing which he himself had never claimed.[1] The convincing objection to this theory is well stated as follows : 'The rise of this belief [that Jesus is the Messiah] is altogether inexplicable, if Jesus had not himself in his lifetime acknowledged himself to his disciples as the Messiah. For it is, to be sure, conceivable that the first disciples of Jesus, whose hopes had all been shattered by his death and burial and whose views of his Messiahship had all been destroyed, should under the influence of their acquaintance with the risen Jesus have *returned* to the belief that he was the Messiah, if they

---

[1] Among well-known advocates of this view are Scholten, Bruno Bauer, Brandt, and more recently Wrede *Das Messiasgeheimniss.*

had previously acquired this belief through his utterances and course of action. But it would be wholly inexplicable that this belief should have *originated* with the disciples after the catastrophe ; one would have to suppose that these wonderful Easter experiences had produced in their souls something absolutely new in a purely magical way and without any psychological mediation.' [1] Some believed that John the Baptist had risen again in the person of Jesus,[2] but they did not on this account receive this Jesus-John as the Messiah. And when we look at the new conception of the Messiah and his kingdom everywhere existent in the apostolic Church, it is equally certain that it could not have *originated* in the minds of the disciples themselves. It was hard for them to unlearn the doctrine of a national kingdom and glory,[3] and the Messiah's resurrection and ascension could not *in themselves* transform the traditional hope ; these could at most only postpone its fulfillment. Moreover the highly spiritualized idea of the kingdom reached in the Church, as seen in St. Paul and St. John, makes it difficult to understand how the doctrine of the Lord's return should have become prominent, if it had not been taught by the Lord himself. All these considerations make it reasonably certain, that these fundamental beliefs of the apostolic Church did not *arise* by any process of reflection within the Church itself, but through the teaching of Jesus ; in other words that we have here trustworthy testimony to Jesus' teaching regarding himself and his kingdom.[4]

The Place of Eschatology in Jesus' View of His Mission. The above study of Jesus' doctrine of his Messiahship and his kingdom has been necessary because it is in that doctrine that his eschatology centers ; the contents and significance of the latter are determined by the former. But before speaking of the details of his teaching in regard to the Last Things, notice should be taken of a subject, in part anticipated above, the relative prominence of the present and the coming age in his thought. In recent New Testament study much discussion has been given to the question, whether Jesus did not regard his

---

[1] Bousset *Jesus* 77. Cf. also Holtzm. *Mess.* 37, Wellhausen *Ein.* 92.
[2] Mk. 8[28], 6[14].   [3] Mk. 10[37], Acts 1[6].   [4] See p. 120.

mission as wholly eschatological.[1] By a considerable number of scholars the question is answered emphatically in the affirmative — an answer which must materially modify the traditional view of the Life of our Lord. This interpretation of New Testament history makes Jesus in his earthly course, like John the Baptist, simply a prophet proclaiming the coming of the kingdom of God; he remains, throughout, his own forerunner. Not yet has the kingdom come, not yet is he the Messiah. The consciousness that he is *destined to become* the Messiah is a secret with him, which at first he did not intend to reveal even to his disciples. How the kingdom will come, how he will attain his Messiahship he knows not; all that he leaves in his Father's hands, but he believes the fulfillment is not far off. On that first mission of the Twelve (Mat. 10) he sends them out, expecting that before their return God will intervene with power, the new kingdom will break upon the world. In the disappointment which followed and in view of the enmity of his people he came to see that his own death was necessary, serving God's purpose, but that it could not cause his work to fail, it must be the means of bringing in the kingdom; he would soon return as the Son of man on the clouds of heaven. His mission was not to teach either about God or man's relation to God, or about human duty; he did not give men moral precepts, except only for the short interim before the End, in preparation for it (an *interimsethik*, as it is called). Thus the whole content of his teaching, according to the extreme eschatologists, was eschatological, the announcement of the coming kingdom, whose blessings, since he did little to correct current conceptions, he must have understood to be in general those commonly expected by his people.

That this will not be the permanent reading of Jesus' history can be pretty confidently asserted. We have seen above, how certain was his consciousness that he *is*, not that he is going to be, the Messiah, and that in his work the kingdom has already come to men; we have also seen that he formed his followers into a lasting community. When we turn to his lessons of

[1] Cf. J. Weiss, *Predigt*, Baldensperger *Selbst*, Schweitzer **QHJ.**, Dobschütz *Eschat.*, Holtzm. *Mess.*, Wellhausen *Ein.*, Burkitt in *Cam. Bib. Essays*, Dewick *Eschat.*

religious and moral truth we find him everywhere dealing with eternal verities, with the fatherhood of God whose love embraces every child of man, with love as the fundamental law of all human relations. It is a most striking feature in his utterances, that there is in them so little of the temporary and provisional, that they are for all time and all circumstances. Perhaps the most convincing objection to a purely eschatological interpretation of his aim is found in the fact that through all the centuries the profoundest spiritual needs of the world have been met in his person and teaching, to a large extent quite apart from his eschatology, which has fallen into the background and is often entirely overlooked. 'If eschatology is the key to all gospel questions, then it becomes the problem of problems how Christianity could go on without eschatology through so many centuries.'[1]

But on the other hand no careful student of the Gospels will make the subject of eschatology in the Lord's conceptions insignificant; on the contrary it will be seen to lie in the background of his characteristic themes, to shape the form of his utterances and to express the final meaning of his office and mission. As already seen, the outlook of the prophetic and apocalyptic writers in later Judaism is toward an approaching end; to a very large degree is this true of the Church throughout the apostolic age. And in this respect Jesus is in harmony with the movement of religious thought throughout this long period. As to how far he looked upon this end as close at hand more will be said below. The atmosphere of the age is often described as charged with eschatological expectation; and Jesus is said to have taken over from the apocalyptic its most common conceptions. It would be more strictly just to say that he laid hold of certain great eschatological truths which in the progress of divine revelation had become common property, that he purified and spiritualized these and gave them their true significance in their relation to himself. It was inevitable that he should express such truths in the forms made familiar by the prevalent apocalyptic; and yet his divergence from the apocalyptic writers is very marked. He says nothing of national and political glories in the coming kingdom, or of its sway over

[1] Dobschütz *Eschat.* 58 f.

vanquished nations; he gives no description of earthly splendors
or material blessings in the new age, he does not picture the
nature or inhabitants of the various heavens, the state of the
dead, the resurrection, or the horrors of the judgment.   There
is no evidence that he was familiar with the non-biblical apocalypses, though the leading eschatological elements contained
in them had without doubt become more or less the common
property of the time.   These he taught, not however in the
manner of the apocalyptic writers.   With the exception of the
great discourse concerning the Last Things, assigned to the
week of his passion, as he sat on Mount Olivet over against
Jerusalem, which will be noticed later on,[1] his doctrines of the
future are brought in only incidentally, with a few simple
touches, as bearing upon some topic of which he is speaking,
and yet in a way which shows that they were profoundly influential in his thought.   The truth which he taught his followers
and the divine power which he brought into their lives were
forces mighty for millenniums of earthly history, and yet it is
clear that he is everywhere pointing to a consummation, an end.
There is a sense in which his whole aim may be called eschatological, that is, his aim is the complete redemption of man,
the complete establishment of the kingdom of God; and the
realization of all this lies in the End.   But this perfect consummation of his messianic work is a *fact*, of which he is unwaver-
ingly assured from the beginning; the question of the *time* of
the final advent or the *place* of the kingdom was entirely subordinate.

As compared with late Judaism, and even with the days of the Lord's
earthly life, the eschatological attitude of mind, the outlook which viewed
things from the standpoint of the end, became more intense in the apostolic age; and naturally so, for the Messiah had now appeared and the
consummation of hope, greatly modified as the hope had become, could not
be far distant; already the 'Last Times,' which should precede the full
messianic glory, appeared to be present.   The disciples were mourning
because the Bridegroom had been taken from them, but his return could
not be long delayed (cf. Wellhausen *Ein.* 107, Dobschütz *Eschat.* 74 f.).
It is for this reason that eschatological traits are more prominent in the
later Gospel records than in the earlier, and it is not unlikely that through
the same influence the record of the Lord's words may have received in

[1] p. 143.

some cases a more distinct eschatological coloring than originally belonged to them. Matthew among the Gospels contains the most highly developed eschatology; not a few of the sayings or allusions, as here given, appear to be additions to, or modifications of, the Marcan source, or Q; next in order after Mt., as regards eschatological matter, comes Mark, and last Q. But eschatological matter is contained in all our sources, in Mark, in Q, in the matter peculiar to Mt., and in that peculiar to Lk. (cf. Streeter in *Ox. Stud.* 425 ff., Dobschütz *Eschat.* 79 ff., Sanday in *Hib. Journ.* Oct. 1911). But apart from this documentary evidence, the power of eschatology among the earliest disciples attests its certain attribution to the Lord himself. 'The beliefs of the early Church may have modified, and did modify, the records of his utterances, but it is too great a paradox to maintain that what was so central in the belief of the primitive Church was not present at least in germ in what the Master taught,' Streeter *op. cit.* 433.

The Little Apocalypse. The great discourse on the Last Things given in Mk. 13, Mt. 24, Lk. 21, and often called the Little Apocalypse, has since its critical treatment by Colani and Weizsäcker (1864) been held by many scholars to be an 'apocalyptic leaflet' (*apocalyptisches Flugblatt*) of Jewish or Jewish-Christian origin, which came into circulation shortly before the destruction of Jerusalem and which Mk. (the source of Mt. and Lk.) introduced, with the insertion of some genuine sayings of Jesus, into his Gospel.[1] It is seen to follow in its outline the conventional form of the Jewish apocalypses with their principal divisions : first, the beginning of troubles; second, the culmination of the 'messianic woes'; third, the final catastrophe, with the appearance of the Messiah, the judgment, and the completion of the ages; it predicts future events with a definiteness of detail in traditional imagery at variance with the Lord's usage as seen elsewhere; it attributes to him sayings held to be irreconcilable with one another. Such are the principal grounds for the theory mentioned. But the absence of all political and national traits shows that it cannot be a *Jewish* apocalypse; and the supposition that Mk. should have picked up and inserted in his book a *Jewish-Christian* document circulating anonymously, or pseudonymously, is so at variance with the general character of his work, that it can be adopted only when other reasonable explanations of the facts are wanting. In point of fact the hypothesis is unnecessary. The salient apocalyptic features in the discourse follow, as do the Jewish apocalypses in general, the traits found in the Old Testament, especially in Daniel (cf. Briggs 134) ; and in *so far* it might be accepted either as spoken by the Lord himself, whose words and conceptions so often attach themselves to the prophets, or as given in Q, to which some scholars refer it, or as compiled by Mk. from his sources. There is no part requiring the hypothesis of a document originating independently of these sources. On the other hand the analogy of the Lord's discourses as generally given in

---

[1] Among numerous discussions, cf. Weiffenbach *Wiederkunftsgedanke Jesu;* Briggs *Mess. Gosp.* 132 ff. ; Bacon *Journ. Bib. Lit.* Vol. XXVIII. ; Haupt *Eschat.* 21 ff. ; Spitta, *Stud. u. Krit.* 1909 ; Streeter in *Ox. Stud.* 179 ff.; Dobschütz *Eschat.* 85 ff. ; Stevens *Theol.* 152 ff.

the Gospels suggests that we have here a group of sayings spoken on various occasions; and the occurrence here of sayings found in other connections in Mt. and Lk. points in this direction, as does also the apparent mingling of different subjects, or at least the difficulty of combining in one outlook all the representations found here. Only one other long discourse is found in Mk. (chap. 4); that also has an eschatological tone and is a compilation. The close juxtaposition of the destruction of Jerusalem and the Lord's coming, found in the Little Apocalypse in all three forms of the discourse, and made especially distinct in Mt. but not occurring elsewhere in the Lord's utterances, may be due to the compiler, whether Mk. or the author of his source, who clearly connected the two events in time. To his mode of thought and expression may also be due the minute picture of future events, characteristic, not of the Q sayings, but of the apocalyptic, as may be the presence of much of the traditional imagery. Also some parts may be interpretative additions made by the compiler. This hypothesis, which regards the discourse as for the most part a group of sayings, not all originally relating to the same theme, but so interpreted, and therefore here combined and reported in familiar apocalyptic phraseology, seems to present the least difficulty.

The Principal Expectations in Jesus' Eschatology. In the foregoing pages we have considered the fundamental conceptions of Jesus which determined the nature and contents of his eschatology, that is, his messianic office, and the kingdom which he came to establish; and we have seen the place which eschatology occupied in his thoughts of his office and mission. It remains now to inquire into certain leading features, which with those already spoken of, make up the picture of the End, as it appears in his utterances.

(1) *The Parousia.* The dominating doctrines in the Lord's eschatology are those of his Coming and his future Kingdom. Regarding the former, two questions arise: what did he teach about the *nature* of his coming, and what about its *time?* The Pauline and Johannine writings speak of a coming or a presence in the Spirit, and the same idea may be alluded to in the Lord's promises, to be with his disciples, as given in St. Matthew.[1] There is a most real sense in which the Lord is continually coming to his children; and many understand this spiritual coming to include all that he intended in speaking of his parousia. In a special sense also there was a coming in the outpouring of the Spirit on the day of Pentecost, and also in

[1] 18[20], 28[20].

the resurrection, and many hold one or the other of these to
have been the parousia of which he really spoke. But after the
occurrence of the resurrection and the Pentecostal coming in
the Spirit, it is inconceivable that the Lord's sayings, if they
had originally referred to these events and had not distinctly
declared an eschatological coming, should have been so completely transformed and made to refer rarely or indirectly to
these events, but often and unmistakably to the one event of
the advent at the end of the ages. If there had occurred a
process of ' reading back,' it would have taken a direction the
reverse of that found in the Gospel record. In view of the
extraordinary spiritualization of messianic ideas in the apostolic
Church it is hard to conceive how the expectation of a future
advent could have become so intense and universal, unless
it had been awakened by the Lord himself. Upon all sound
critical principles we must attribute to him the announcement
of a coming which, whether in our Gospel records it be described
in vivid apocalyptic imagery, or alluded to only incidentally, is
a definite event, a visible advent in glory and power, ushering
in the final reign of the kingdom of God.[1] The question of the
Lord's prediction regarding the *time* of his coming is a difficult
one. He is recorded as saying that some of those listening to
him should live to see the coming of the Son of man,[2] that it
should take place before the apostles on their mission should
have gone over the cities of Israel,[3] that the generation then
present should not pass away till all was accomplished.[4] The
Lord bids his hearers to be always ready for the coming of the
Son of man.[5] The sense of such passages interpreted by the
uniform usage of the phraseology in the New Testament is so
evident, that the numerous attempts of scholars to find reference to some event other than the parousia must be regarded as
quite unsatisfactory. The same may be said of the theory of
' prophetic foreshortening' which views future events across
long intervals, as if near at hand. Whether, or not, such passages report accurately the very words of Jesus, it cannot be
doubted that they express what the disciples *understood* him to

---

[1] *E.g.* Mt. 16[27], Mk. 14[62], Lk. 9[26]. On various senses of the Coming cf.
Haupt *Eschat.* 139 ff., Stevens *Theol.* 165 ff.   [2] Mk. 9[1] par.
[3] Mt. 10[23].   [4] Mk. 13[30].   [5] Lk. 12[35-40].

foretell. The certain belief of the apostolic Church, that the great day was near, cannot be explained except on the supposition that the disciples had so understood his teaching. But an apprehension of his teaching which was radically wrong is very unlikely. His reported language in such connections may have been colored or made more precise than that actually used through the prepossession of his hearers, yet it is difficult to avoid the conclusion that he in some form spoke of his return at a time not all too remote, that he looked for an earlier consummation of his kingdom than history has shown to be realized. In this conclusion the larger number of recent scholars are coming to agree.

The supposition that this prediction is wanting in the oldest source, Q, and has been added in the later Marcan and Matthæan source (cf. Streeter in *Ox. Stud.* 424 ff.) cannot be established. It is without doubt true that eschatology is less prominent in Q, but our knowledge of that document is too meager to furnish data for certain inference in this particular doctrine; at all events eschatology is found in it and probably this very idea of the nearness of the parousia (Mt. 23$^{34-39}$ is probably a Q passage). While eschatology in general became more developed in the later documents, Mt. and Mk., yet this doctrine of the coming as near is more likely to have been eliminated than to have been added to the record of the Lord's words at a time when the parousia and its signs were delayed. An example of later modification probably due to this influence is seen in Luke's version of the parable of the talents (cf. Lk. 19$^{11-28}$ with Mt. 25$^{14-30}$, different versions of the same parable), where we have a correction of the opinion that the kingdom would appear immediately, v. 11.

It should be kept in mind that the question is historical rather than dogmatic. While we must speak with great reserve concerning the limitations of the Lord's knowledge, yet the doctrine of the incarnation carries with it a limitation in the ordinary sphere of human knowledge, as a feature of his incarnate life. There is a sphere in which life with him as with all men was a process of growth.[1] It is only in moral and spiritual truth that his oneness with the Father must be understood to raise him above all error. 'Religious perfection does not include omniscience.'[2] The fact of the final, absolute triumph of God's kingdom can never be a matter of doubt with him, but the exact time when this should be accomplished is that of a

---

[1] Lk. 2^{52}.   [2] Baldensperger 205.

historical event, dependent at least in part upon human conditions, and he declares that no man knows the day and the hour, 'not even the angels, neither the Son.'[1]

But it is doubtful whether this declared ignorance of the precise time of the parousia is irreconcilable with those other sayings which place it within the generations then present, though many scholars so regard it;[2] to many however it seems quite possible to understand the Lord to have referred in the one case to a somewhat long and indefinite *period*, in the other, to a precise date within that period. The householder knows the night is the period within which the attempts of a thief would be made, but no one can tell in what watch of the night he will come.[3] 'In putting the date at the end of this generation he gives no real date.'[4] All Jewish prophecy placed the End in close connection with the appearing of the Messiah, and it would seem almost inevitable that Jesus, who was conscious that the messianic work had begun in him, should have hoped for its consummation at no distant time. In any event we cannot too strongly emphasize the fact that the disagreement between the Lord's hope and the course of subsequent history in no way affects the essential nature of his person, or his revelation to man. 'If we keep to the letter of his words, we cannot help agreeing that he was wrong regarding the outward form of his predictions, and especially the time of God's fulfillment. But this does not involve, I am sure, any imperfection on his side, any more than his opinion about the sun as a star going round the earth, or about the Pentateuch as a book written by Moses. . . . The form of his expectation was unimportant even for himself. He left it to his Father how and when he would realize it.'[5]

Perhaps the greatest difficulty in supposing that the Lord looked for an early return lies in his knowledge of the obstacles which must hinder the growth of the divine kingdom. His profound insight into human nature

---

[1] Mk. 13[32], Mt. 24[36]. The genuineness of no saying of Jesus is more certain than this ; it could not have arisen at a time when it seemed at variance with his accepted divinity ; on the contrary there appears an effort to get rid of it. It is omitted in its connection in Lk. after 21[33], and the words ' neither the Son ' are wanting in some later Mss. of Mt.

[2] Cf. Holtzm. *Theol.* I. 401 f., Denney *Jesus* 355.

[3] Lk. 12[38-40]. Cf. Weiss *Theol.* § 33 *a*, J. Weiss, *Predigt* 71, 96 ff.

[4] Dobschütz *Eschat.* 116.   [5] *Ibid.* 184 f.

and his experience of hostility on the part of even God's chosen people made clear to him the slowness with which moral and spiritual truth must advance in the world. He does not, to be sure, say that the world should be evangelized before the parousia, but rather that the gospel must first be preached to all nations (Lk. 24⁴⁷, Mk. 13¹⁰); yet this could not mean a mere proclamation of the gospel; the slow process of 'making disciples' was intended (Mt. 28²⁰), and the Lord's anticipation of something of this slowness is seen in his words. Such expressions in the eschatological parables as 'after a long time' (Mt. 25¹⁹), 'into a far country' (Lk. 19¹²), 'my lord tarrieth' (Mt. 24⁴⁸), which clearly express this thought, may as some suppose be due to later editorial work in view of the delayed parousia (cf. Holtzm. *Theol.* I. 386 f.); yet these parables, as well as those speaking of the growth of the seed (Mk. 4), all imply a considerable lapse of time, a delay. The questionable phrases mentioned crystallize what is really contained in the parables themselves. We cannot, however, for a moment suppose that these two aspects of the future presented themselves to Jesus' mind as in perplexing conflict. His vision was steadily fixed on working the works of him that sent him; all else he left in the hands of the Father who in the exercise of his own power had fixed the times and seasons (Acts 1⁷). And in this respect he was followed by his disciples who went on through the apostolic age planting and organizing churches, laying foundations in faith and morals, as those who would build a structure for ages of earthly history, yet ever cherishing an eager expectation of a near end. Only in one church, that of the Thessalonians, do we see the hope of the near advent seriously disturbing the settled order of Christian thought and conduct; and this failure was promptly reproved by their apostle.

The *antecedents* of the Messiah's coming, as they are commonly described in apocalyptic literature, appear also in the Lord's predictions of his parousia. The 'messianic woes,' times of trouble, convulsions in the heavenly bodies and in earth, wars, terrors, persecutions, apostasy will occur as *signs* that the end is near. The details of these prophecies and the imagery, taken directly from traditional apocalyptic representations, are found only in the eschatological discourse (Mk. 13, par.), and we cannot say how far they are to be attributed to the Lord, and how far to the recorder of his sayings; yet what is essential in the doctrine of the 'messianic woes,' as a time of trouble and testing, which shall precede the Lord's appearing, is contained in other parts of our record.[1] But the parousia itself will break upon the world suddenly, as a thief in the night.[2] The two thoughts are held by many to

[1] Mt. 10¹⁷⁻²², ³⁴⁻³⁷, 23³⁴ f., Lk. 17²², 18⁷ f.   [2] Lk. 12³⁹.

be contradictory.[1] But the same juxtaposition of signs of the end and ignorance of the time appears in Jewish literature also,[2] and in St. Paul.[3] Many find this difficulty in the Lord's sayings removed by the figure used, as seen above ; the uncertainty pertains to the particular watch, not to the night as a whole. In another connection the suddenness appears to be represented as the unpreparedness of those who, like the generation of Noah, are not watchful, and blind themselves to the monitions of the signs.[4]

(2) *The Eschatological Kingdom.* Little need be added to what has already been said concerning the kingdom of the future. If, as maintained above, the kingdom was in some sense already present in the person and work of Jesus, and if it consists essentially in the reign of God's will, then it is found at least in one aspect wherever that will is the controlling force in men. It may then ever be growing in power and extent, ever coming, as a moral and social evolution, in the promotion of which men are used as God's agents ; and every child of God finds in this advancement of the kingdom, with the blessings it confers, his sufficient motive to activity for himself and others. The various parables of the growing seed and the leaven seem to represent its perfection as the last result of such a process of evolution. Many find in this process and its final outcome all that·is meant by the Lord's prophecies of a coming kingdom. But throughout apocalyptic literature and throughout Jesus' teaching there is found the representation of a great future event, a miraculous intervention of God, which apart from man's agency shall establish the kingdom in its final glory. A stone is to be 'cut out of the mountain without hands,'[5] the harvest is to come at the end of the period of growth, then the sickle is put forth.[6] God has fixed conditions which shall precede the final event,[7] but the consummation is his act alone. The idea of an invisible, spiritual state, the outcome of a gradual process of evolution, does not satisfy the terms of the Lord's prediction. Though a spiritualizing

---

[1] Cf. Holtzm. *Theol.* I. 389.   [2] Cf. Volz 171 f.   [3] Cf. p. 89.
[4] Lk. 17²⁷ ; cf. J. Weiss in Meyer *in loc.* and on Mk. 13³². Cf. p. 147.
[5] Dan. 2⁴⁵.   [6] Mk. 4²⁹.   [7] Cf. pp. 78 f.

of the conception appears in the Fourth Gospel and St. Paul, an aspect which may not improbably be traced back to the Lord himself, yet even in these writers this form does not displace that of the visible apocalyptic kingdom which shall come at the End.[1] 'The kingdom of God is not established, so long as its dominion is only recognized by individuals; it wants to be collective, universal.' [2]

The Lord does not describe the glories of the kingdom which is to come, but he assumes its blessedness. He places it not in heaven but on earth. Everywhere he speaks of its *coming*, that is, to earth ; the petition, 'Thy kingdom come,' is followed by the defining words, 'Thy will be done on earth.' The Lord does not speak specifically to his followers of their entrance into the present heaven of God's abode.[3] In this respect he follows the usual biblical and apocalyptic idea, and doubtless he has also in mind the same idea of a *renewed* world, in which the distinction between heaven and earth disappears. In one instance he refers directly to this renewal ; [4] he also uses the apocalyptic phrase, 'heaven and earth shall pass away,' [5] a phrase always associated with the idea of world-renewal.[6] How much in this may be symbol and how much literal reality we cannot say, but there is no compelling reason for resolving it altogether into the former. 'Because we have entered upon the dispensation of the Spirit, we are not reduced to the barrenness of intellectual purism ; we are not called upon to strip rudely away all that is still shrouded in symbol and metaphor. We may leave ourselves room for the expectation of a new heaven and a new earth, though we cannot guess what outward form of embodiment they may assume.' [7] As regards also the *members* of the kingdom the Lord follows the common apocalyptic representation. These are his faithful ones gathered out of a world where there are many enemies. The latter are driven from his presence into a punishment described in the conventional terms.[8] As in the apocalyptic writings, the

---

[1] Cf. p. 304.   [2] Dobschütz *Eschat.* 206.

[3] 'Lay up treasure in heaven' means, lay up there, as in a treasure house, the treasure which befits that place, whence as from a place of deposit it may be paid out to you again.   [4] Mt. 19²⁸, παλινγενεσία.   [5] Mt. 5¹⁸, Lk. 21³³.

[6] Cf. Titius *N. T.* 25, J. Weiss *Predigt* 105 ff., Bousset *Predigt* 87, Wellhausen *Ein.* 103.   [7] Sanday *Hib. Journ.* Oct. 1911, 103.

[8] Mt. 25⁴¹.

supreme foe is the prince of evil spirits, and the supreme triumph in the establishment of the kingdom is the overthrow of Satan and his hosts, and their consignment to the doom prepared for them. There is no intimation of a conquest by their conversion into friends. If these representations regarding his enemies seem hard to reconcile with the measureless love and mercy which irradiate the whole character and teaching of our Lord, we must observe that in these conventional apocalyptic forms may be expressed the terrible possibility of an unending hostility to, and separation from, God.

(3) *The Intermediate State and the Resurrection.* Little is said on these subjects in the synoptic records, but the usual apocalyptic doctrines are expressed or assumed. In answer to the Sadducees' argument against the resurrection, the Lord shows from the Old Testament scriptures that the dead are raised.[1] In one other connection also he speaks of the resurrection, and there it is mentioned as a fact which both he and his hearers accept without question.[2] It is to take place among the events of the End, and both the just and the unjust would seem to be understood as sharing in it, though this is not distinctly stated, and some suppose that the just only are thought of. The difference of opinion in Jewish, and perhaps Christian, circles regarding the share of the unjust in the resurrection has already been spoken of.[3] Their presence at the judgment is perhaps assumed in such sayings as, ' It shall be more tolerable for Tyre and Sidon, for the land of Sodom, in the day of judgment,' etc.[4] A bodily existence of the wicked after the judgment is more distinctly implied in the words, ' Fear him who is able to destroy both body and soul in hell.' [5] It is noticeable however that the Lucan account of the dispute with the Sadducees limits the reference to the righteous, to ' those who are accounted worthy to attain to that world and the resurrection of the dead.' [6] This variation from the Marcan and Matthæan accounts is perhaps due to editorial influence. It is clear that a distinction between the just and the unjust in this respect was not clearly defined in the Lord's teaching.

[1] Mt. 12¹⁸⁻²⁷, par.   [2] Lk. 14¹⁴.   [3] pp. 62, 93.   [4] Mt. 11²², ²⁴.
[5] Mt. 10²⁸. Cf. J. Weiss *Predigt* 109 ff.   [6] Lk. 20³⁵. Cf. also 14¹⁴

The nature of the *resurrection body* is alluded to in only one place, in the argument with the Sadducees, where the Lord tells them that they know not the power of God, that is, to raise the dead in a form adapted to an existence whose conditions are entirely different from those of our present bodily life, to a state where they neither marry nor are given in marriage, for the risen will be as the angels. We seem to have here reference to what St. Paul calls the 'spiritual body,'[1] and the appearances of the Lord as given in the post-resurrection history agree with this identification. These narratives are designed to show that the Lord had really returned, not as a phantom, but in a bodily form which could be apprehended by the senses, though not subject to the conditions of matter. In the source peculiar to St. Luke,[2] as also in the Johannine account,[3] there are features, such as the eating of material food, which cannot easily be reconciled with the other facts in the narratives. These may probably be regarded as traditions due to the intense realization of the identity of the risen Lord with the former Master, and the failure, notwithstanding the conflict with the appearances and disappearances recorded in the same narratives, to distinguish a 'spiritual body' from that which has 'flesh and bones.'

Concerning the subject so profoundly interesting to the later Christian world, and prominent also in late Jewish literature, the state of the soul immediately after death and before the judgment, the Lord says very little, as is true of the New Testament in general ; and this quite naturally, in view of the supposed nearness of the End, and the resurrection. What is recorded of the Lord's sayings is given in forms taken entirely from the current apocalyptic. As in the later Jewish belief, the state is not one of semiconscious existence, but of active consciousness, a capability of pleasure and pain, of a living union with God. The recompense, even if not the final one, awarded to the conduct of this present life is entered upon immediately after death. The patriarchs in the place of the departed, as living, still have God as their God,[4] the dying thief is at once admitted to paradise (not heaven, but the abode of the blessed dead).[5] The only place in which the Lord speaks

---

[1] Cf. p. 90.   [2] 24[39-43].   [3] 20[27].   [4] Mt. 12[27].   [5] Lk. 23[43].

directly of the state of the dead is in the parable of the rich man and Lazarus,[1] which represents these as passing at death, the one to suffering, the other to blessedness. There is nothing here to intimate that the award, which follows at once, anticipates the final judgment day so far as to leave no room for the latter. Doubtless the parable is to be understood according to the usual apocalyptic view, which looked upon such award as preliminary, pending the final recompense. A final judgment still awaits Tyre and Sidon, and the land of Sodom, of which the earlier doom is only anticipative.[2] But there is nothing indicating that this preliminary doom may be reversed at the end. The possibility, or impossibility, of a moral change in the interval before the judgment is not spoken of, either here or elsewhere. It should be noticed that the passage is not an exposition of dogma concerning the state of the dead, but a parable chosen from familiar beliefs to enforce a moral lesson. ' It does not take us beyond the broad fact that there is a state of being into which men pass at death, and that the divine righteousness follows them thither with moral decisions affecting their condition there and reversing antecedent estimates and circumstances.' [3]

(4) *The Judgment and its Awards.* As in all biblical and apocalyptic representations, so in Jesus' teaching, the day of judgment appears as an inseparable part of the great drama of the End. All nations will be gathered at the tribunal, both the living and the dead; [4] the smallest act will be brought into account; [5] in some sayings, God appears as the judge,[6] but oftenest Christ.[7] The *awards* of the judgment are conceived under the forms of the familiar Jewish eschatology, though there is little tendency to graphic picturing of the future state, such as is found in apocalyptic writers; only a few profoundly significant terms are used to characterize the lot of the judged. The award of the righteous is eternal life,[8] the inheritance of the kingdom prepared for them from the foundation of

---

[1] Lk. 16¹⁹⁻³¹.   [2] Mt. 11²²,²⁴. Cf. p. 69.
[3] Salmond in Hast. II. 275.   [4] Mt. 25³², 11²²,²⁴, par., 12⁴¹, par., 13⁴¹ᶠ·.
[5] Mt. 12³⁶.   [6] Mt. 10³²ᶠ·, Lk. 9²⁶, 18⁷.
[7] *E.g.* Mt. 7²²ᶠ·, 16²⁷, 25³¹ᶠ·, Lk. 13²⁷.   [8] Mk. 10³⁰.

the world,[1] immediate communion with God, 'they shall see
God.'[2]   The unrighteous go away into eternal punishment,[3]
they are cast out into outer darkness,[4] into the Gehenna of unquenchable fire.[5]   The terrible thought of an unending penalty
naturally leads students of the Lord's words to seek some trace
of a possible reversal or mitigation.   His statement regarding
the one sin of blasphemy against the Holy Spirit, which shall
not be forgiven in this age nor in that following the judgment,[6]
is thought to imply that other sins may be forgiven in the
'coming age.'   But such an interpretation is not supported by
his other utterances; on the contrary it is in conflict with these.
The words are an emphatic expression for *never*, which is used
in the Marcan parallel.[7]   Some have found in the 'few stripes'
with which the servant, ignorant of his lord's will, shall be beaten [8]
allusion to a shortening of the period of punishment.   This too
is contrary to Jesus' teaching given elsewhere, and even if
accepted, would not meet the hard case of those who having
sinned knowingly might conceivably in a future state repent.
We are without doubt compelled to accept the sayings as they
stand with all their hardness, in view of the beliefs regarding
the subject at the time, and the Lord's adoption of current
modes of expression.   These very facts, however, raise an important consideration regarding the *finality* of such utterances.
The scope of Jesus' teaching on the subject, as addressed to
men of his own time, led naturally to limitations.   He had no
occasion to touch the theme of a change of attitude in the 'coming age'; and his well-known habit of enunciating general
truths, without mentioning possible exceptions and modifications in varying circumstances, would make unlikely the
introduction of such contingent factors into his eschatological
teaching.   The general tenor of his utterances on the subject is
what we should expect.   And it is also doubtless true that this
element in his teaching is much intensified in the form in which
it is preserved by the hearers of that generation, who could
hardly have comprehended an eschatological punishment essentially different from that of current belief, or have expressed

---

[1] Mt. 25[34].   [2] Mt. 5[8].   [3] Mt. 25[46].   [4] Mt. 22[13].   [5] Mk. 9[43].
[6] Mt. 12[32].   'The age to come' does not refer to the period between death
and the judgment.   [7] 3[29].   [8] Lk. 12[48].

it in essentially different forms. The part played by the recorder is strongly illustrated in a comparison of St. Matthew with the other Synoptists. The larger number of these hard sayings are found in the former, and many of these are seen by critical examination to be additions or variations due to editorial working over of the source. Our ultimate view of the great Christian truth contained in these sayings of the Lord must be affected by the revelation which he gave concerning God's attitude toward the sons of men. But when long cycles intervene before the final judgment, we must in view of the tendency toward moral fixedness, the tendency of habit to pass into unchangeable character, conceive at least the possibility of a soul passing into a self-induced, unchangeable attitude of enmity toward God, a state of 'eternal sin.'[1] This is what would constitute eternal punishment; it is what St. John calls 'sin unto death,' that is, sin resulting in complete spiritual death.[2]

Conclusion. In closing a survey of our Lord's eschatological teaching it is well to observe that there must of necessity be much in it which we cannot clearly represent to ourselves in the forms of our modern thought. He chose the terms, the imagery, and the conceptions familiar to his age, with all their limitations and imperfections, for nothing else could have had real meaning for his hearers. Perhaps we may say that nothing could be more intelligible to us, especially in view of our biblical inheritance. The forms of the revelation given in prophecy can only very imperfectly shadow forth the realities to come. The principal function of prophecy, so far as it is predictive, is to encourage, to warn, and to guide along the way in which God is moving, and toward the end to which he would bring his people. It can never be entirely understood until it is fulfilled. But yet in these prophecies of the Lord telling of his coming, the setting up of his Kingdom, the resurrection, and the judgment, though much may be in traditional form and symbolical, this at least seems to be clearly taught by him : that there awaits the world a manifestation of his presence in the glory of a completed triumph of the cause of God over all evil, a reign of God in the world ; that a great

---

[1] Mk. 3²⁹.   [2] 1 Jno. 5¹⁶.

testing of moral issues will stand at the meeting of the ages ; that the redeemed clothed in a new form will be gathered into one people of God ; that an entrance into life, then fully realized, and into a closer union with God, will be granted to all those ' who have loved the Lord's appearing.' [1]

The Eschatology of the Revelation.   The exposition here given of the eschatology of the book of the Revelation presupposes the views adopted in regard to its composition and interpretation found in the Commentary, as well as results reached in certain later paragraphs in the Introductory Studies. While eschatological teaching is introduced in other books of the New Testament incidentally, the Revelation alone has the prophecy of the Last Things as its entire theme.   Hence the subject is unfolded here with features and details not found elsewhere.   It was natural that the Church of the first century should produce such a writing, for Christian hope centered in the coming of the kingdom of God and his Christ.   The messianic hope was the necessary offspring of the belief in an ultimate triumph of good over evil, of God over Satan, and was especially intensified in times of imperial persecution.   Such a time the Church was entering upon at the close of the century,[2] and it foresaw the advance of this persecution to the fierce conflict of the End.   The framework of Christian eschatology in general was, as repeatedly pointed out above, that of Jewish apocalyptic ; but this is especially the case in the book of the Revelation.   Yet as the conception of the Christ differs from, though growing out of, that of the Jewish Messiah, so the whole conception of the kingdom and of the final issues is permeated with a new and more spiritual idea.   The author of the Revelation does not transform traditional apocalyptic by *discarding* its elements and figures — no New Testament writer does this in a thoroughgoing way — it is not likely that he himself conceived the future altogether apart from these conventional forms ; but he adds facts of Christian revelation, and thus gives to his eschatological picture a new meaning, which must be seen to be such, when his additions are followed out to

---

[1] 2 Tim. 4⁸.   [2] See pp. 201 ff., 208 ff.

their consequence. It is not necessary to ask how far he used traditions in a purely figurative sense — that he does so in some instances cannot be questioned. The permanent meaning and value of his great panorama is spoken of elsewhere.[1]

The *time* of the End, as generally in Jewish and Christian expectation, is near at hand.[2] And yet the multiplied series of plagues, the period of Antichrist's domination, and the preliminary millennial kingdom form a sequence requiring the assumption of a long lapse of time before the final catastrophe. It is a tempting supposition that the nearness declared refers only to the beginning. But it is clear that 'the things which must shortly come to pass'[3] and 'the words of prophecy'[4] include the contents of the whole book ; with this reference to the End agrees the announcement of the Lord's coming.[5] It is not possible to bring the two representations into exact accord. The dissonance is due to the fact, frequently seen, that the Apocalyptist is following different eschatological traditions in different parts, and does not attempt to bring these into actual harmony.[6] A historical program followed with close logical sequence of time and space is foreign to the manner of our Apocalyptist, who is original and at the same time uses extensively conventional ideas. There is in this an intimation that he is conscious of using traditional conceptions in a sense not strictly literal. The prophecy of our book centers in a final catastrophe, like all apocalyptic, and the events group themselves into three classes : (1) the long series of preliminary movements ; (2) the crisis of the definitive conflict with Satan ; (3) the resurrection, the world-judgment, and the final state of the redeemed.

(1) The Preliminary Events. (*a*) *The messianic woes.*[7] This standing feature in apocalyptic prophecy appears here in the sending of divine visitations upon the world in preparation for the Great Day. These as given in our Apocalyptist's picture are the three series of the seals (chap. 6), the trumpets (8–9), and the bowls (16). These are partly natural plagues, though miraculously intensified, such as war, slaughter, famine,

---

[1] pp. 291 ff. [2] Cf. 1[1, 3], 3[11], 10[6], 22[6, 7, 10, 20]. [3] 1[1], 22[6].
[4] 1[3], 22[10]. [5] 3[11], 22[7, 12, 20]. [6] Cf. pp. 722 f., 745. [7] Cf. p. 38 f.

pestilence, earthquake, and the scorching heat of the sun; partly also they are supernatural, such as vast disturbances in the heavens, the corruption of the waters, the tortures of the hellish locusts and of the cavalry of fiend-like horses.   But all alike are sent by special intervention of God and with special eschatological purpose.   They are manifestations of his wrath, and have the twofold purpose of punishing and of leading to repentance.   As in all apocalyptic representation, the former purpose is made most distinct, yet the latter is also included.[1] They constitute a part of 'that hour which is to come upon the whole world to try them that dwell upon the earth.'[2]   The forms under which the coming visitations are represented are derived for the most part from suggestions given in the familiar plagues of the Old Testament, but the Apocalyptist does not always intend the literal meaning of his prediction, as for example in 6^{14}, where the heaven is said to be removed as a scroll rolled up, though in what follows it is seen to remain ; or in 8^{12}, where the extinction of a third part of the luminaries causes darkness for a third part of the day.[3]   (*b*) *The perse- cution of the saints.*   As elsewhere in the New Testament,[4] the last days are to be times of suffering for the Church.   The hostility of the world-power, the Roman Empire (the Beast, as first manifested), with its demand of emperor-worship, already showing itself, will increase to the end of that domination and pass on with unlimited intensity into the succeeding reign of Antichrist.   Satan through his special agents, the beast and the false prophet, and by the aid of all his servants, will wage relentless war with the woman's seed, who have the testimony of Jesus.[5]   This dread prophecy springs from the universal observation of the increasing bitterness of the conflict through which moral progress wins its victory.   But the saints who prove faithful are assured of final deliverance.[6]   (*c*) *The destruction of Rome.*   The persecution of God's people in any age by the world-empire then existing gives to the conflict thus aroused the character of a supreme trial ; and the deliverance of the saints, the triumph of the cause of God, is foreseen

---

[1] See p. 554.   [2] 3^{10}.   [3] See Com. *in loc.*
[4] Cf. Mk. 13^9 ff., Ac. 14^{22}, 2 Tim. 3^{12} f.   [5] 12^{17}, 13.
[6] 3^{10}, chapt. 7, $12^{6, 14-16}$, 14^{1-5}.

by prophets and apocalyptists to be realized only in the destruction of this great enemy, it may be Egypt, Assyria, Syria, or Rome. The Christian Apocalyptist at the end of the first century sees that a crisis in the trial of the Church was about to be precipitated in the Roman persecution, and was approaching a climax in the attempt to displace the worship of Christ by the worship of Cæsar.[1] The Roman Empire is the Beast in his earlier manifestation.[2] Naturally then the annihilation of Rome's power stands among the foremost events expected by the Apocalyptist. The fall of the imperial city forms a dominant factor in the book, and the theme of one of its most splendid passages. Already its doom is near ; the king called symbolically the sixth is now reigning ; his successor, the seventh, who will be the last, will continue but a little while ; then Rome will be utterly destroyed by Antichrist.[3]   (d) *The Coming of Antichrist.* The Roman emperors and the priesthood maintaining the emperor-worship are only the humanly endowed agents of Satan, and their removal does not end this warfare against the Churcl.. The expectation that the conflict with a hostile world-power must go on to an extreme of intensity, and the prevalent Jewish and Christian belief in the advent of a world-ruler, human yet possessing demonic powers, opened to the Apocalyptist a vision of the part to be taken by Satan's mightiest agent, the Antichrist.[4] When the Roman Empire should have fulfilled its destined period, Antichrist, the beast in his supreme manifestation, will come in the person of a demonized Nero returned from the dead,[5] and with his allies, the ten kings of the earth, will destroy the imperial city.[6] He will rule the entire earth with awful tyranny; aided by the false prophet (a wonder-working priesthood), he will demand universal worship, the extreme form of emperor-worship begun by the Roman rulers ; and he will persecute the saints unto death. He will continue through the symbolical period, three and a half years.[7]   (e) *The Conversion of Israel.* The Apocalyptist, a Christian Jew, appears to introduce a prophecy, found elsewhere in the New Testament, that in the Last Times God's ancient people will repent of their rejection

---

[1] See pp. 201 ff., 209.   [2] pp. 407 f.   [3] 14[8], 16[19], 17[1–19][5].
[4] See pp. 397 ff.   [5] See pp. 400 ff.   [6] 17[12-17].   [7] 13[3-18], 17[8, 11].

of Christ.[1] They will be moved to repentance by preachers, whose words will be enforced by great miracles wrought in their presence. This conversion of Israel seems to be placed in the reign of Antichrist. (*f*) *The overthrow of Antichrist by the Christ and the temporary imprisonment of Satan.* As the destined time of Antichrist's rule nears its end he will gather his adherents, the hosts of earth, at Harmagedon for the great battle against the Christ. The heaven will be opened and Christ will come forth as a warrior accompanied by the celestial armies ; with the sword of his mouth he will slay the nations, Antichrist's followers ; Antichrist himself and his prophet will be cast alive into hell.[2] An angel will lay hold of Satan, and binding him with a great chain will cast him into the bottomless pit where he will be bound a thousand years.[3] Christ does not appear in this scene as a being of love and compassion ; it is the day of his wrath against his enemies, proven incorrigible. The characterization is similar to that which appears repeatedly in the Gospels, especially the Fourth Gospel.[4] The Fourth Gospel, though distinctively the 'Gospel of love,' is also the Gospel of Christ's wrath, and its author often shows the disposition of a son of thunder, whether he be the Apostle or another. (*g*) *The Millennium.* After the destruction of the hostile hosts of the earth with their leaders and the binding of Satan, no foe will remain to war on the saints, and a preliminary kingdom will be set up on earth. Here the martyrs raised from the dead will reign in blessedness with Christ a thousand years (a symbolical period). The rest of the dead will not be raised till the general resurrection.[5] The seat of the millennial kingdom will be Jerusalem,[6] but unquestionably an idealized Jerusalem, not the actual historic city, unsuited to the blessedness described, and long since destroyed ; yet the celestial city, the new Jerusalem, cannot be meant; that does not descend till a later period, at the time of the entrance of the new heaven and earth (21). In the prophecy of the temporary binding of Satan, and a preliminary millennial kingdom on earth, to a share in which the martyrs

---

[1] See pp. 588 ff.   [2] 16$^{13-16}$, 19$^{11-21}$; cf. 2 Thess. 2$^{8-10}$.   [3] 20$^{1-3}$.
[4] Cf. Mt. 23$^{13-33}$, Mk. 3^5, Jno. 2$^{13-16}$, 5$^{37-46}$, 8$^{15-55}$, 9$^{39-41}$, 11^{38} RV marg.
[5] 20^5.   [6] 20^9.

only are raised, the Apocalyptist differs from the other New Testament writers; these connect all the events of the End immediately with the Lord's second coming. It is evident that he is adapting the earlier apocalyptic to one of the special purposes of his book, the exhibition of the blessed reward to be bestowed on martyrdom.[1]

(2) The Crisis of the Definitive Conflict with Satan. *The release of Satan, his last assault upon God's people, and his eternal doom.* After the thousand years of peace in the preliminary kingdom Satan will be loosed and will marshal the nations of the earth, the enemies of God, in number as the sand of the sea, who will come from afar from every quarter against the citadel of the saints, the Jerusalem of the millennial kingdom. Fire from heaven will consume the host, and Satan who deceived them will be cast into the endless tortures of hell. In connection with this battle nothing is said of any part taken by Christ. The difficulty caused by the presence in the earth of the hosts of hostile nations after they have previously been declared to be destroyed in the battle with Antichrist[2] is due to the author's use of a familiar representation in two distinct but similar connections, without attention to exact congruity.[3]

(3) The Resurrection, the World-judgment, and the Final State of the Redeemed. (*a*) *The general resurrection and judgment.* The complete triumph of God in the conflict with Satan will be followed by the resurrection of all the dead, the wicked as well as the rest of the righteous who not being of the number of the martyrs had not already been raised to a share in the millennial kingdom.[4] These all appear before the judgment throne; the sentence of the wicked is the second death, the unending doom of hell;[5] to the righteous is awarded endless life in the new Jerusalem in perfect union with God.[6] After this final judgment no change of state is contemplated. As regards *the interval between death and the resurrection*, the book is silent concerning the state of the wicked. Of the righteous dead it is said that they will enjoy a blessed rest from trouble, and their good works will be remembered in their behalf at the judgment.[7] To those who have died the martyr's

---

[1] p. 737.   [2] 16[14], 19[21].   [3] See p. 745.   [4] 20[12-13].
[5] 14[9-11], 20[15].   [6] 21[3]-22[5].   [7] See on 14[13].

M

death special honor will be given while they await resurrection to their place in the millennium; garments of heavenly glory will be given to them, while they remain in keeping beneath the heavenly altar; and they are bidden to rest from their distressful yearning for vengeance for yet a little while, when their destined number will be filled up and their prayer answered.[1] Then will come their reward in the reign of the millennium. The supposed nearness of the end accounts for the small space in the Apocalyptist's thought given to the state of the dead.

(b) *The new heaven and earth, and the new Jerusalem.* The concluding act in the drama of the End is, as generally in Jewish and Christian eschatology, the renewal of all things. A new heaven and a new earth, as befits the perfected kingdom of God, will take the place of the old; the new Jerusalem having the glory of God will descend from heaven to the new earth to form the abode of God with his people. The new Jerusalem as viewed by the Apocalyptist is not heaven, the heaven of God's dwelling as everywhere conceived in the Bible; it is the city of Jewish apocalyptic prepared from eternity and preserved in heaven to be brought down to earth after the judgment, as the place where God will dwell with his people. But in this conception of a renewed world heaven and earth are completely blended. The throne of God and the Lamb with the redeemed worshiping before them is, as seen by the Apocalyptist in the final consummation, placed indifferently in heaven and in the new Jerusalem on the new earth; or as we might say, the conception of this new Jerusalem takes the place of heaven as generally thought of.[2] How far the Apocalyptist formed to himself a clear idea of the attributes and perfections of the new state described under these figures it is impossible to say, but it is clear that the spiritual facts contained in them form for him what is most essential in his prophecies. This is seen in what he says of the nature of the kingdom, the conditions of membership in it, and the state of the saints therein. And for a true apprehension of his eschatology this must be constantly kept in mind in connection with his use of apocalyptic traits, more or less conventional, which form the outlines of his pictures. To his own mind he has thoroughly Christianized the

---

[1] See on 6[11].   [2] Cf. 7[9-15] with 21[2-3]; see also 15[2].

meaning of the traditions which he uses. The kingdom is universal, composed of every nation, kindred, and tongue of earth; [1] the gates of the city stand open to every tribe of the Israel of God, it is built upon the foundations of the Apostles of all the world; [2] its members are those who have been redeemed by the sacrificial death of Christ,[3] they have gotten the victory over Satan through the blood of the Lamb and the word of his gospel; [4] their salvation is attained only through faith in him and its steadfast maintenance;[5] they are those who keep his commandments, who follow him in all things, who keep themselves unspotted from the world, have no guile in their mouth, no fault before the throne of God.[6] But their blissful inheritance is not a good won by their own works, it is a free gift;[7] their accomplished salvation is ascribed to God and Christ,[8] it is the Lamb that has redeemed them to God.[9]

It is certainly a misinterpretation when the Apocalyptist is understood to ignore virtually faith as a primary condition of salvation and to assign the decision to works, the keeping of God's commandments, that is, to substitute a kind of Christian legalism for the doctrine of faith as found elsewhere. (So, Weizsäcker, Holtzmann, Jülicher, Swete, *al.*) Great emphasis is, to be sure, placed on ἔργα, *works;* cf. chapts. 2–3, *passim*, 14[13], 19[8]; and of the final judgment it is said, that men shall be judged according to their works, 2[23], 20[12-13], 22[12]. But equally clear is the same characterization of the judgment given by Paul, the great defender of justification by faith, cf. Ro. 2[6], 2 Co. 5[10], Col. 3[24 f.]. Works are throughout not thought of apart from the faith from which they spring and without which they are inconceivable. All difficulty is removed by the utterance of the Gospel that the work of God which men must do is faith in Christ (Jno. 6[28 f.]). To the same effect our author coördinates the commandments of God which the saints are to keep with faith in Jesus (14[12]). For the scope of the term ἔργα, *works*, see Com. on 2[2]. There is in New Testament soteriology no antithesis between faith and works except that between a living faith necessarily active and a belief which though real is inoperative in the life. This is the real antithesis discussed in the epistle of St. James. The severe stress of the times contemplated in our book explains the emphasis which the author throws on works; in the awful temptation awaiting the Church the faith of its members must manifest itself in their deeds.

The *final blessedness* of the saints is described under various forms, for the most part figures whose spiritual meaning is plain. They will cease from all sorrow and pain, God will wipe

[1] 5[9], 7[9], 15[4]. [2] 21[12-14]. [3] 1[5], 5[9], 7[14]. [4] 12[11]. [5] 14[12], 2[13].
[6] 14[4-5, 12]. [7] 21[6], 22[17]. [8] 7[10], 12[10], 19[1]; see Com. *in loc.* [9] 5[9].

away every tear from their eyes, he will dwell in the midst of them, he will be their God and they his people.[1] Their intimate spiritual communion with God and Christ is set forth in manifold figures; as sharers in the divine throne, as kings and priests,[2] they will enjoy the glory and the privilege of immediate access to God's presence; they will be joined with Christ as a woman is joined to her husband,[3] they will be the sons of God,[4] and bear the marks which show them to be wholly his,[5] — all figures expressing the closest spiritual union. The comprehensive term by which the eschatological state is expressed in the book is *life;* the saints partake of the tree of life,[6] of the water of life,[7] the same idea is contained in the eating of heavenly manna;[8] they receive the crown of life;[9] they are enrolled in the book of life.[10]   In the prominence of the term *life*, the book agrees with other New Testament writings, especially the Pauline and Johannine.

Yet in the writings of Paul and John not merely continued existence is meant, but also all the blessedness of the indwelling of the believer in God, and consequently a state already begun in this life (see pp. 94, 102); while in the Revelation the state of undying existence after the judgment seems to be chiefly thought of. A fundamental difference is found herein by some between the Revelation and the Fourth Gospel; in the latter the future life of the believer is only the continuance of what is begun here, the believer has already passed from death into life (Jno. 5[24]); while in the Revelation life is understood to be the unending state bestowed upon him at the judgment as the reward of his course here. This difference, however, though it may appear to exist in most cases, is not maintained throughout the two books. In the Fourth Gospel *life* refers in some instances to the future state entered upon at the end (cf. 5[29, 39], 6[27, 40], 12[25]); on the other hand in the Revelation the figures of the continued leading forth to the fountains, the flowing forth of the waters from the throne, the feeding with manna, the leaves ever growing for healing (7[17], 21[6], 22[1 f., 17], 2[7]), all imply a continuing spiritual *process* similar to that meant in the Gospel rather than a fixed condition beginning at the judgment. In the offer of life in 21[6], 22[17] certainly a reference to the spiritual life of the present is included. Naturally the Gospel speaks oftenest of the one aspect of life and the Revelation of the other, for the former book is chiefly concerned with the present spiritual state, and the latter with that belonging to the future world.

---

[1] 21[3-4], 7[15-17].   [2] 3[21], 5[10].   [3] 19[7-9].   [4] 21[7].   [5] 3[12], 22[4].
[6] 2[7], 22[2, 14, 19].   [7] 7[17], 21[6], 22[1, 17].   [8] 2[17].   [9] 2[10].
[10] 3[5], 13[8], 17[8], 20[12, 15], 21[27].

A word should be added on the most striking differences in eschatology, already alluded to, between the Revelation and the other New Testament writings. The appearance of the warrior Christ to battle with Antichrist at a time anterior to the general judgment and separated from it by a millennium, as described in 19^{11-21}, the silence regarding any part taken by Christ in the last conflict with Satan and in the judgment after the thousand years as described in 20^{7-15}, are at variance with prophecies of the events of the Lord's coming given elsewhere in the New Testament. The Lord's destruction of Antichrist by the word of his mouth forms a part of St. Paul's prophecy of the parousia,[1] but the 'coming' ($\pi\alpha\rhoο\upsilon\sigma\acuteι\alpha$) there spoken of must according to the uniform usage of the Apostle be understood of the advent for the general judgment and the establishment of the kingdom. And the only future coming of the Lord spoken of by other New Testament writers, apart from our book, is that with which these last events are associated in one group. What is elsewhere foreseen as immediately consecutive steps in one great movement is viewed by our Apocalyptist as consisting of parts widely separated in time however closely connected in essential relations. In visions of a future immeasurably remote variation in perspective, the occurrence of a parallax, as it were, need not cause great difficulty, especially in our book where the greater fullness of detail would make easy the separation of things elsewhere combined. In some places in his book the Apocalyptist agrees with the other writers in condensing these last events into one connected series, and in assigning to Christ a coming to judgment; cf. 1^7, $2^{7,\,10}$, 14^{14-20}, 22^{12}. In the particular chapters in which the variation spoken of occurs he views the steps separately, because he is especially interested here in a millennium as providing a reward for the martyrs; and this carries with it the premillennial overthrow of Antichrist.[2] The representation in these chapters of the last conflict and the judgment follows closely the earlier Jewish model; hence the absence of Christ from these scenes.

[1] 2 Thes. 2^8.   [2] See p. 736.

II

APOCALYPTIC LITERATURE[1]

THE Revelation of John follows, not only in form but to a considerable extent in matter also, the manner of a class of Jewish writings which were widely known and influential in the last two centuries before Christ and in the first century of our era, and which are now generally called *apocalyptic*. As regards the type of literature the Revelation is rightly placed in the same general class with these, much as it differs from them, and it cannot be correctly interpreted apart from these modes of thought and expression which greatly influenced its formal character. A knowledge of this apocalyptic literature is essential then to a right understanding of our book. In placing the Revelation of John in the class of apocalyptic writings, most of which lie outside of the canon of Holy Scripture, we do not detract from its practical value, or its canonical character. Driver's words in reference to the Book of Daniel are appropriate here : ' Just as there are Psalms both canonical and non-canonical (the so-called Psalms of Solomon), Proverbs both canonical and non-canonical (Ecclesiasticus), histories both canonical and non-canonical (I Macc.), " midrashim " both canonical (Jonah) and non-canonical (Tobit, Judith), so there are analogously Apocalypses both canonical and non-canonical ; the superiority, in each case, from a theological point of view, of the canonical work does not place it in a different literary category from the corresponding non-canonical work, or works ' (*Dan.* in CB. LXXXIV).

The noun *apocalyptic* in distinction from *prophecy* is the term now commonly used to denote that group of eschatological hopes and beliefs which have been set forth above[2] as belonging to the *latest* development of Judaism — a development in which a universal and transcendental outlook appears as the principal characteristic instead of the national and earthly.

---

[1] Cf. Lücke I, Hilgenfeld *Jüd. Apokalyptik*, Baldensperger 172 ff., Bousset *Jüd. Apok.* and *Judenthum* 230 ff., Volz 4 ff., Drummond 3 ff., Porter *Messages of the Apoc. writers*, the articles in Hast. Enc. Bib. and the Jewish Enc. For the literature dealing with each of the apocalyptic writings respectively, see p. 181, Schürer III 188 ff. 　　[2] p. 63 ff.

While the expectations of both prophecy and apocalyptic center in a coming messianic era, that is, in a final era in which the kingdom of God will be established, the former conceives this kingdom chiefly in political and earthly aspects, the latter in those that are non-political and supernatural. The main interest of the one is mundane ; of the other supermundane. The principal elements in the messianic hope of *prophecy* are the Day of Jehovah, in which punishment will be meted out to the heathen and faithless Israelites ; the deliverance of God's people from all their enemies ; the institution of Jehovah's kingdom in Palestine and the extension of its power over all the Gentiles ; the return of the scattered Israelites ; the restoration of Jerusalem in great splendor ; the presence of God in his temple ; the reign of a Davidic Messiah in an era of perfect peace and glory. On the other hand in *apocalyptic* the principal factors of the eschatological hope are the advent of the ' coming age,' spiritually perfect in contrast with this ' present age ' hopelessly corrupt ; the universal judgment, not of Jew and Gentile as such, but of the righteous and the wicked, not of men only but also of angels and spirits ; the resurrection of the dead ; the everlasting destruction of the power of Satan and his hosts ; the superhuman Messiah reigning with God in a renewed heaven and earth ; eternal life in the presence of God and the Messiah for the righteous, and for the unrighteous unending punishment in Gehenna. By *apocalyptic literature* then is generally meant those writings which contain this latter form of eschatological hope in whole or in part.

Apocalypse. ἀποκάλυψις, ἀποκαλύπτειν, a term occurring in various but kindred senses in the Septuagint and the New Testament, is common in the latter with the special significance of a *supernatural* unveiling, revelation, of divine mysteries, of the unknown and hidden things pertaining to the kingdom of God and divine truth. In 2 Co. 12$^{1-7}$ Paul uses it with reference to his ecstasies or visions; and similarly it is used in Rev. 1^1, as a descriptive title of the unveiling, the revelation, given by God of the consummation of his kingdom as recorded in this book (cf. Thayer, Westcott, *Introd.* 34 ff.). It is not here a title designating the book as *an* apocalypse, that is, as belonging to a class of books called *apocalypses*. But from the use of the word in this opening description the book came subsequently to receive the title, the *Apocalypse of John*, and pseudepigraphic writings of a later date, containing professed visions of the future, adopted the title, *e.g.* the *Apocalypse of Peter*, the *Apocalypse of*

Paul. As a name of a type of literature *apocalypse* then is subsequent to the time of our book (cf. Zahn *Ein.* II. 596). The distinction between the author's use of the word in the opening verse and that of the title given to the book in *later* time is shown by the defining words in each case; in the former the meaning is the revelation given by God of the mysteries described; in the latter the Apocalypse of, *i.e.* written by, John.

Modern writers taking the word *apocalypse* in its generic sense have applied the adjective *apocalyptic* to all writings whether Jewish or Christian which possess in common certain characteristic forms appearing in the Apocalypse of John and which contain an unveiling, a revelation, real or fictitious, of events and doctrines of the Last Things as these are conceived in the later, transcendental, eschatology spoken of above.[1] It is thus that such pre-Christian writings as the Book of Daniel, the Book of Enoch, as well as late Jewish books, *e.g.* 2 Esdras, are called apocalyptic. The word is also applied in cases where these eschatological ideas are found, though not in the form of a professed revelation, *e.g.* the Psalms of Solomon. A curious feature in many apocalyptic writings is the writer's interest in fancies pertaining to the physical universe, the phenomena of nature and the heavenly bodies; these are a part of the secrets unveiled in the alleged revelations. Considerable portions of the Book of Enoch are taken up with such subjects.[2]

The two classes of hopes styled by modern writers, the one prophetic, the other apocalyptic, clearly belong to different stages of religious thought. It is desirable therefore to give them distinct names; but it can hardly be questioned that those now in common use are not happily chosen as titles mutually exclusive; for prophecy which in its essential character, is a divine message relating to religious and ethical truth, calling to present duty, is not wanting in the writings called apocalyptic; and on the other hand apocalyptic ideas appear more or less distinctly in writings which we term prophetic. The apocalyptic writings so far as they contain a product of genuine revelation — and this is undoubtedly the case in some instances — are prophetic. But the *older* prophecy is chiefly concerned with the call to present duty, and the prediction of the future is subordinate; while *apocalyptic* prophecy, though containing a moral and religious appeal to its readers, is occupied predominantly with the future. Such writings then as the Book of Daniel, the Rev. of John, Is. 24–27, Mt. 24–25, belong to apocalyptic prophecy, that is, they are both prophetic and apocalyptic.

[1] p. 63 ff.   [2] 17–36, 72–82 ; cf. Sl. En. *passim.*

Characteristics of Apocalyptic Literature. The various writings, or parts of writings, styled apocalyptic, notwithstanding many minor differences, agree so far in certain leading features as to justify the grouping of them into a special class with a designation of its own. Of these characteristic features the most fundamental is found in the group of *eschatological* expectations and beliefs, which speaking in a general way we may say are common to the class. A survey sufficient for our purpose of this apocalyptic form of eschatology has been given above, and the distinction pointed out between the apocalyptic and the older prophecy.[1] It is *first of all* in these religious and eschatological ideas that the distinctiveness of these writings as a type of literature consists. But there are also certain other characteristics of a more external and formal kind, the recognition of which will not only define the class more clearly, but will also serve to prevent the misinterpretation of many passages found in literature of this nature.

(1) *Visions and raptures.* The highly elaborated vision, or similar mode of revelation, is the most distinctive feature in the *form* of apocalyptic literature. The subject matter is attributed by the authors to a special revelation, commonly given in visions, ecstasies, or raptures into the unseen world. It is true that in the older prophecy the vision is not only mentioned as a means of revelation, but also descriptions are given of the concrete pictures unfolded to the prophet;[2] such pictures however are brief, simple, and altogether subordinate as constitutive factors. It is in the book of Ezekiel, who at least in this respect shows a tendency toward the apocalyptic, that we first find highly elaborated visions forming an essential element of the work.[3] And this characteristic becomes more distinct and fundamental in the apocalyptic literature proper. Here the vision or rapture is a literary form wrought out with great fullness of details, often with strange symbolism and with fantastic imagery. Examples of such constitutive traits are the vision of the four beasts and that of the ram and the he-goat in Daniel;[4] the vision of the bullock, the sheep and

---

[1] p. 167.   [2] Cf. Is. 6$^{1-4}$, Am. 8^1, Jer. 1^{11,13}.
[3] Cf. the vision of the throne-chariot, 1–3, the rapture visions in 8–11, 40–48, cf. also 37$^{1-14}$.   [4] 7–8.

the seventy shepherds in Enoch [1] symbolizing human history to the establishment of the messianic kingdom ; the visions given to Enoch in a rapture through the unknown regions of the earth, through Hades and the heavens,[2] unveiling the secrets of nature, and the final abodes of the righteous and the wicked ; the vision in the Apocalypse of Baruch of the forest trees and the vine,[3] and that of the lightning-crowned cloud pouring down twelve showers of dark and bright waters,[4] symbolizing the fortunes of Israel, the ' messianic woes ' and the triumph of the Messiah ; the vision in Second Esdras of the mourning woman transfigured, symbolizing the final glorification of afflicted Zion,[5] and that of the eagle [6] picturing the final destruction of the world power, Rome ; the revelations given in a rapture through the seven heavens, which form the principal contents of Slavonic Enoch ; the visions and raptures of the Revelation of John.   It is this fundamental place of the vision, or similar mode of *unveiling* hidden things (*apocalypse*) in these writings, that has given them the *name* apocalyptic.

(2) *Mysteriousness.* It is characteristic of these writings that the revelations, or half revelations, are often given in strange, unintelligible forms.   The symbolical beasts are unimaginable monsters with their many heads and horns springing out and warring one with another ; [7] inanimate objects are represented with attributes of men and animals ; [8] the extraordinary and unnatural are preferred to the ordinary and natural. [9] Hence a standing feature is the *interpreter* explaining the visions, allegories, and symbols ; sometimes this is God himself,[10] but commonly an angel,[11] in accordance with the great prominence assigned to the agency of angels throughout this literature.[12] This element of mysteriousness is probably due, at least in part, to the thought that the great secrets treated of could be communicated only under such mysterious forms ; and notwith-

---

[1] 85–90.   [2] 17–36.   [3] 36–38.   [4] 53–74.   [5] 9–10.
[6] 11–12.   [7] Dan. 7 f., 2 Es. 11 f., Rev. 13, 17.
[8] Dan. 7[8], Ap. Bar. 36, En. 86–88, Rev. 9[1].
[9] Cf. Ap. Bar. 29, 73[6 f.], En. 10[17 ff.], 80, 2 Es. 5[4-9], Sib. Or. III. 796 ff., Rev. 5[6-8], 8[7-12], 9[3-11].   [10] Ap. Bar. 38 ff., 2 Es. 13[13 ff.].
[11] Dan. 7[16 ff.], 8[16 ff.], En. 1[2], Ap. Bar. 55 ff., 2 Es. 10[29 ff.], Rev. 1[1], 17[1].
[12] p. 70.

standing the presence of the interpreter there remains a large element of vagueness and uncertainty, of designed enigma, especially in predictions of the future. The significance of the writings in their general import was doubtless made intelligible to the readers, while many details must have been altogether obscure. It is not unlikely that even the writer himself, in order to give his picture fullness and power, or mysteriousness, sometimes introduced touches to which he did not attach a separate meaning in themselves. A specific meaning in every detail can no more be sought in an elaborate vision than in the parables of our Lord,[1] or in the ornate picture of a Homeric simile. The significance of the representation is contained in the leading factors, while details are often designed only to give life and color.

(3) *Literary Dependence.* The apocalypses are not throughout the primary sources of the material which they contain. The apocalyptist is not essentially an originator; he adopts, transforms, interprets apocalyptic matter already at hand. The prophecies of the Old Testament writers, their visions, imagery and symbolism, entered largely into these compositions, as did also popular traditions and conceptions in which were enshrined as in folk-lore, myths and fancies belonging to the Hebrews and other orientals in common. The apocalypses do not spring from the professional scribes or the official class; they are for the most part folk-literature; hence folklore, popular legends and ideas inherited or adopted from a non-Hebrew source could the more easily have found their way into this field. Thus not only the general outlines of the future age, the coming judgment, the messianic glory are stereotyped elements following out and transforming the lines of older prophecy, but also many characteristic details are only slightly varied uses of a store of traditional material from which all alike draw.[2] Each writer borrows from his predecessor and from common tradition. Examples of such dependence are the frequently recurring representations of the series of world-kingdoms determined by symbolical numbers, four, seven, etc.;

---

[1] Cf. Trench, *Notes on the Parables* III.
[2] Cf. Gunkel 225 f., Bousset, *Antichrist* 6 ff.

kings and empires under the form of animals with heads and horns symbolically numbered; the dragon-form of the arch-enemy; portents in the heavens and the earth; the emergence of the apocalyptic beasts from the sea; the trumpet-call ushering in the great day. The Book of Daniel, the first great apocalypse, established the norm which later writers followed more or less closely in certain ideas and in forms, symbols, and general structure. Very wide also was the influence of such passages as Isaiah 13–14, Ezekiel 1, 28–39, Joel 2–3, Zechariah 9–14. In some instances it is not improbable that the writer has taken over and adopted familiar pictures containing minor details which are not strictly applicable to his purpose, using the representation because of its significance as a whole.[1] Such an origin may sometimes account for traits which would otherwise give insoluble difficulty to the interpreter. It is not however to be supposed that the apocalyptist is altogether wanting in originality, or real spiritual vision. Our great apocalypses without doubt contain, if not new religious conceptions, at least new inventions of the religious imagination, probably in some cases, we may say, new forms of vision. A more mechanical dependence also appears in the writings as now extant; as they have come down to us they are nearly all seen by critical analysis to consist of *compilations* from different documents, with and without revision, and to contain additions by later hands. But of the two canonical apocalypses, the Book of Daniel is commonly regarded as essentially a unit; the unity of the Revelation of John will be discussed below.[2]

(4) *Pseudonymity.* The apocalypses, with the exception of the Rev. of John,[3] were attributed to authors of an age long past. They purport to contain revelations given to such men of antiquity as Moses, Enoch, Isaiah, Baruch, Ezra, and the like. The Revelation of John however in this as in many other respects differs from the other apocalypses. The apocalyptists were probably led to attribute their writings to some great name of the past because they were conscious that they could not speak to their generation in their own name with the power

---

[1] Cf. p. 171.   [2] pp. 216 ff.   [3] Also the Shepherd of Hermas.

of an independent prophet. The age of the great prophets had passed away. It was so far a time of spiritual decline, that no one was sent with an Isaian trumpet-call to duty ; no one could come with the cry, ' Thus saith the Lord,' and meet with believing acceptance. The apocalyptists stand on a lower plane of inspiration and mission ; their office is preëminently to hold up as motives promises of the future. Genuine visions they in some cases undoubtedly received, but the commission was not that of the direct personal preacher ; it was rather to *write* a revelation of the unfolding of God's promises made of old to his people. The roots of their prediction lie in the past,[1] and they not unnaturally then speak as if from the past. As the whole course of world-history to its consummation — a favorite theme with them — is one, they carry back to the past the visions of the end ; and the correspondence of a part of the assumed predictions with the known facts of past history, and the authority of a great name, give credibility to the forecasts of the future. This professed ancient authorship, once established as a characteristic of apocalyptic writing, came to be adopted by inferior writers and imitators as a mere literary form. But when as in the New Testament age prophecy revives again, and one like the author of the Revelation of John comes forth with the consciousness of a real prophetic commission,[2] he speaks in his own name. That writings inspired with a strong moral and religious purpose should be attributed to assumed names may seem to our modern minds inexplicable ; but such was not the case with the ancients, especially the Hebrews. First of all, the material of the apocalypses being, as seen above, largely derived from earlier sources, the writers doubtless often regarded their works not so much their own as those of some great personage of the past. The procedure seen here is not very different from the common literary device of putting into the mouths of persons of another time speeches, poetic utterances, and the like which perhaps tradition attributed to them and which were appropriate to them. At all events pseudonymity was a common literary characteristic of these centuries, and does not by any means in all cases show a disregard of truthfulness, or an intention actually to deceive in the interest of the author or his cause.

[1] Cf. p. 171.   [2] See p. 292.

Pseudonymous writings appear at this time in great numbers among the Greeks and Hebrews alike, especially at Alexandria.[1]

It should be distinctly observed that when the characteristics of apocalyptic literature mentioned above are attributed to the Book of Daniel or the Revelation of John, these books of our Bible are not robbed of their religious value or their canonical rank.   There is nothing in these features of their construction which would render their visions and revelations less real than those of Isaiah or St. Paul.   There can be no question that in many of the pseudepigraphic writings the visions described are pure inventions adopted as a part of the literary form.   But in these two books at least, the reality of a great spiritual ecstasy, of a supernatural unfolding of things seen only by the inner eye, stands upon the same ground of credibility as in the other visions and revelations of the prophets and of the New Testament.   Neither dependence upon earlier sources nor minute study in the elaboration of details in the record of the visions is in itself a mark of fictitiousness.   The greatest of the prophets derived material from their predecessors, as for example Isaiah from Amos and Hosea,[2] and Ezekiel from Jeremiah.[3]   And visions assume the forms of familiar objects ; traditional ideas and imagery give them their characteristic features.   Ezekiel's great vision in his opening chapter contains a striking combination of traditional Hebrew and Babylonian figures.[4]   The more thoroughly the mind of the seer is permeated with the imagery and symbolism of his predecessors, the more certainly would his vision in a state of ecstasy borrow leading traits from these.   In the study of the Revelation of John it will be seen that the visions are to a very large extent composed of factors evidently suggested by the Old Testament and other sources, yet transformed and brought into new combinations with the freedom of an independent seer.   It is moreover of fundamental importance in studying this book to remember that it is not a description penned while the visions were still present with the author, while he was still in a state of ecstasy ; it is a record made subsequently,

---

[1] Holtzm. *Ein.* 192 f., Jülicher 42.   [2] Cf. W. R. Smith *Prophets* 209.
[3] Cf. Davidson *Ezek.* in CB., p. xix f.   [4] Cf. Stade 290 f.

after he had left Patmos.[1] The book then is a definitely planned work to put before the readers the great revelations which had been given to the Prophet in his visions. And it is easy to understand, or rather it is scarcely possible not to suppose, that the stupendous scenes unfolded before the Seer's view defied, perhaps, his own power to grasp fully, certainly his power to portray. These revelations surpass in awful grandeur, in profound religious value and in fullness of scope, all other apocalypses, and the writer labors with all the resources which he can summon to his aid to present them to his readers with vividness and power. While the work in its fundamental conceptions must belong to his memory of his visions, yet much also both in the framework and the details must be due to his conscious effort as a literary artist struggling to give in familiar apocalyptic form and manner a presentation of the truths revealed in his ecstatic experiences. The plan, minutely organized with the structure of an elaborate outline, with intricately interwoven threads, bears frequent traces of a prophet who is working consciously to embody truth seized in an ecstasy rather than to describe symbols actually seen. Something of the same studied effort, though on an inferior plane and carried out with far less brilliancy of religious imagination, appears in the closing vision of Ezekiel (40–48) and in the Book of Daniel. The writer's conformity to a particular type of literature is not unlike that of the prophets and psalmists who adopt the forms of Hebrew poetry, or that of the authors of the Book of Job and the Song of Solomon, who have put their message in the form of lyrical drama. In none of these cases does the conscious elaboration of the form affect the canonical rank of the work.

The Occasion of the Apocalyptic Writings. The origin of the apocalyptic writings is found in the religious and political condition of the Jews in the three centuries of the period in which falls the birth of Christ. They are born of the distress, spiritual and civil, of the times. As the writers look out upon it, the world is full of wickedness, sin is triumphant, the godly are afflicted, evil spirits are mightier than the powers of goodness, the kingdom of God's people is overthrown, and a

[1] 19.

galling subjection. to Gentile rule continues from generation to generation. The present, whether for the righteous individual or for God's kingdom, is an era of great darkness, and the immediate future offers only an outlook still darker. 'For look, how much the world shall be weaker through age, so much the more shall evils increase upon them that dwell therein, . . . for the world is set in darkness and they that dwell therein are without light.'[1] Where are the blessings foretold by the fathers and the prophets, where the happiness and prosperity promised to the godly, where the glory promised to the kingdom? In these dark questionings touching the righteousness and faithfulness of God, touching the truth of the prophets, the devout Jew with invincible faith turns away from the hopeless present to the future ; he catches revelations, apocalypses, of a not far-off coming of God, of a day of deliverance and recompense, of the fulfillment of the yet unfulfilled prophecies. At the same time the historical experiences of the nation and the influence of surroundings have broadened and modified the outlook of the apocalyptist ; his vision of the future has become more spiritual, wider in scope, to a larger degree supermundane. It is in these circumstances that he appears as a prophet to bring a needed message to his time. He raises a voice of warning against the prevailing iniquity, whether in Israel or among the Gentiles, declaring the certain and awful vengeance soon to be revealed ; but chiefly he seeks to comfort and encourage the suffering and despairing. In the midst of bitter trials, and in face of those more bitter about to come, he appears with his vision of sure deliverance and final glory to revive hope, to stay up faith, to fortify endurance. He unfolds a future which shall show to Israel and the world that God is just and righteous, that he is faithful to his promises, that he is gracious to give their recompense to his righteous servants. This is the great purpose of the apocalypses in general. And the deeper the distress of the times and the more threatening the nearer future, the more glowing becomes the apocalyptic picture of the end. A tendency toward the apocalyptic in both spirit and form begins to show itself in the prophets who arose in the trials of the exilic

[1] 2 Es. 14[17 ff.].

and earlier part of the post-exilic age, but it was the time of
Antiochus Epiphanes, with its awful persecutions, that produced the first distinct apocalyptic book, so far as known to
us, the Book of Daniel. The various writings grouped together
in the Book of Enoch belong to the second and first centuries
before Christ, a period of almost unbroken trouble from internal strife, apostasy, and fierce conflict without ; the Psalms of
Solomon fall in the time of the conquest of Jerusalem by
Pompey ; the Assumption of Moses shortly before, and the
Apocalypse of Baruch and 2 Esdras shortly after, the tribulation attending the destruction of Jerusalem by Titus; the
Revelation of John in a period in which the Roman persecution of the Church had already begun, and still fiercer woes
were threatening.

The Jewish Apocalyptic Writings. *Apocalyptic tendencies in
the Old Testament prior to the Book of Daniel.* Reference has
already been made to Ezekiel as marking in some respects a
transition from the older prophetic type to the apocalyptic.
Ezekiel's activity coincides with the great crisis of the nation's
downfall in the Babylonian captivity; and while much of his
book is occupied with denunciation of Israel's sin and announcement of inevitable punishment in the doom of the nation, his
vision passes on through this calamitous period to a restoration,
a sublime redemption; and his picture, notwithstanding its
features of local and political glory after the manner of the
older prophets, is full of profound spiritual significance.[1] The
Prophet's idea of God is more transcendental, his universalism
more distinctly religious, his outlook more eschatological; he
announces clearly the religious significance of the individual, as
well as that of the nation. With him begins, as already pointed
out, the elaborate vision as a literary form, the prominence of
angels as the agents of God, the prediction of an assault by the
combined world powers (Gog and Magog) upon God's people in
the 'latter days,' the idea of a world-judgment.[2] The influence
of his conceptions and his literary manner appear widely in
the apocalypses in later times, especially in the Revelation of
John. ' If the author of the Apocalypse [of John] be a purer
poet than Ezekiel, the prophet has given him his inspiration

[1] Cf. Davidson *Ezek.* in CB. 287 ff., Stade 293 f.   [2] Cf. Stade 295.

N

and furnished him with materials for his most splendid creations.' [1]   Second Isaiah (Is. 40–66), generally placed by critics near the end of the exilic period,[2] presents an interesting comparison and contrast with the apocalypses.   Like these it is a message of consolation to Israel in affliction, promising the near coming of Jehovah to deliver; but while the promises are set in the national and local framework, the vision of the Prophet is constantly breaking through into a wider and more spiritual outlook.   In the supernatural blessings to be poured out upon the land, in the glory of God's presence with his people, in the profoundly religious universalism, in the creation of a new heaven and a new earth, briefly, in the general spirit of the prophecies, the predominating tone is that of the apocalyptic. Similar in tone is another post-Isaian passage, Is. 13–14[23] (commonly assigned to the closing years of the exile), with its picture of convulsions in the heavens, of woes and desolation in the earth, its exultation over the fall of the oppressing city. Here belongs also Is. 34–35, a paragraph of the same or a later date.   After the exile the tendency toward the apocalyptic shows itself frequently in the prophetic writings as preserved. In the visions of Jehovah's coming and the great consummation to follow, the prophecies frequently take on the general features of the late eschatological representation.   Of such a character is Is. 24–27, a vividly apocalyptic passage falling after the exile. Apocalyptic in tone and coloring is the book of Joel; such are also Obadiah vv. 15 ff., Zephaniah with its terrible picture of the consuming wrath of Jehovah in the Great Day, Zechariah 1–8 with its symbolical visions interpreted by angels, Second Zechariah (Zech. 9–14) with its prophecy of the final gathering of the nations against Jerusalem, Jehovah's intervention, the salvation of his people, and his universal recognition.

The Book of Daniel.   This book is generally placed by scholars in the closing years of Antiochus Epiphanes, that is, not far from 164 B.C.   Antiochus, king of Syria, of whose domain Judea now formed a province, had entered on the policy of unifying his kingdom by bringing all parts of it to adopt the Hellenic civilization and with this the Hellenic religion.   Such

---

[1] Davidson *op. cit.* p. xxvi.   [2] Cf. Driver *Introd.* 230 ff., Cornill 284 ff.

a policy, though received with sympathy by a party among the Jews, was of course immeasurably abhorrent to every devout adherent of the religion of Jehovah; and Antiochus soon saw that he had raised up in Judea a strong body of irreconcilable opponents, near the border of his enemies, the Ptolemies of Egypt, and that he could remove this obstacle in the way of his purposes, both internal and external, only by extirpating the Jewish religion. Accordingly he took possession of Jerusalem, plundered the temple, slew many of the people and sold many as slaves, prohibited under penalty of death all Jewish religious rites and introduced those of heathenism; on the altar of burnt-offering in the temple was erected an altar to Zeus. 'The temple was filled with riot and revelings by the heathen, who dallied with harlots, . . . and moreover brought inside things that were not befitting; and the place of sacrifice was filled with those abominable things which had been prohibited by the laws. And a man could neither keep the Sabbath, nor observe the feasts of the fathers, nor so much as confess himself to be a Jew,' 2 Macc. 6[4 ff.]. Both in Jerusalem and in the country the Jews were forced to join in the heathen sacrifices and feasts, to eat unclean food; they were martyred for circumcising their children and for even possessing a copy of the law; the books of the law were rent in pieces and burnt.[1] This was the first distinctly *religious* persecution which the Jews had suffered, the first era of martyrdom. It was in these circumstances that the prophet of the Book of Daniel brought forward his message to strengthen his countrymen in a firm adherence to their law and to console them with the certainty of an early deliverance. The unknown writer assumes as his standpoint, not his own age, but that of the Babylonian and Persian domination several centuries earlier; and he puts his exhortations and revelations in the form of narratives relating to Daniel and visions purporting to be given to the same Daniel, who is described as one of the Judean nobles carried away by Nebuchadnezzar. How much of the story of Daniel is actual history, how much tradition, and how much is derived from the author himself it is, as in the case of Job and Jonah, neither possible nor necessary to determine. From whatever sources the author derived the

[1] 1 Macc. 1–3, 2 Macc. 5–9.

external material of his work, its inner meaning and spirit are
his own; they belong to his own time, they are the word of
God sent through him to his present suffering coreligionists.
The *narratives* form the first part of the book (1–6) and on the
one hand tell how Daniel and his companions, who were subjected to trials similar to those imposed by Antiochus, such as
the eating of unhallowed food (chapt. 1), participation in
idolatrous worship (3), renunciation of prayer to their God
(6), adhered staunchly to their religion and were wonderfully
delivered and rewarded; on the other hand the narratives tell
how the Babylonian kings, Nebuchadnezzar and Belshazzar,
who like Antiochus had lifted themselves up against Jehovah,
were humbled under his hand. The *visions* form the distinctively apocalyptic part of the book (7–12). In a series of
visions essentially parallel, represented as given to Daniel and
interpreted by an angel, the course of world-history is unfolded
from the Babylonian domination to the destruction of Antiochus' power and the final consummation of the kingdom of God.
Under the symbol of beasts is represented the succession of
world-kingdoms, four in number,[1] culminating in the rule of
the 'little horn,'[2] Antiochus, whose impious character and
deeds are described with the definiteness of a contemporary.[3]
But the end of this distress is shown to be near; after three and
a half years, 'a time and times and half a time,'[4] the might of
Antiochus, the last of the anti-theocratic world-powers, will be
annihilated. Jehovah himself will come with his hosts, 'a stone
cut out of the mountain without hands'[5] will break in pieces the
world kingdom; Michael, the great prince, will stand up for the
people;[6] the judgment will be set and the books opened;[7] those
that sleep in the dust will awake, some to everlasting life and
some to shame and everlasting contempt;[8] the beast will
be slain, his dominion will be taken away and given to one
like unto a son of man,[9] that is, to the people of the saints
of the Most High;[10] and the messianic kingdom in its glory
and universality will be established forever. The share of the
saints in the messianic rule becomes a common doctrine in

---

[1] Cf. Driver in *Dan.* in CB. 94 ff.   [2] 7[8], 8[9].
[3] Cf. 7[24 f.], 8[9-14, 23-25], 9[26 f.], 11[21-45].   [4] 7[25].   [5] 2[45].   [6] 12[1].
[7] 7[10].   [8] 12[2].   [9] 7[11 ff.].   [10] 7[27].

later Jewish eschatology and passes over into New Testament writers.[1]

The three and a half years spoken of in the prophecy may be taken as an approximate reckoning of a particular historic period ; but from the analogy of apocalyptic usage, according to which numbers are oftenest symbolical, and predictions of the actual future are vague, it is more likely that the expression denotes merely a short period. There is plausibility in the view that $3\frac{1}{2}$ as a symbol of a limited period of calamity is primarily derived from an Oriental nature-myth, representing perhaps the period of winter. Cf. Gunkel *Zum religionsgesch. Verständniss* 79 ff., *Schöpfung u. Chaos* 266 f., Jeremias *Babylonisches im N. T.* 43. But at all events, whether originating with our author, or adopted by him from popular usage, the term has passed from the Book of Daniel to the Revelation of John, as a symbolical designation of the last brief but direful period of the sway of evil; Rev. 11[2], 12[6], 13[5].

Non-Canonical Apocalyptic Writings. In the following notice of the other principal apocalypses it is obviously impossible in the space at command to give a full survey of their contents, or to take up the critical questions connected with them. Only such a brief account can be given as may serve to show their general nature, and render more intelligible the frequent reference to them.[2] *Ethiopic Enoch.* The Book of Enoch, or Ethiopic Enoch, as it is called in distinction from the recently discovered Slavonic Enoch, is a collection of writings, commonly supposed to belong to the last two centuries before Christ, and ascribed to Enoch, 'the seventh from Adam.'[3] The record of Enoch's favor with God and his translation given in Genesis[4] caused Hebrew tradition to attribute to him marvelous knowledge. In his walk with God, he was made the recipient of revelations which opened to him

[1] Cf. Wis. 3[8], 5[16], Test. Dan 5[13], En. 108[12], Mt. 19[28], 1 Co. 6[2], 2 Tim. 2[12], Rev. 2[26], 3[21], 20[4].

[2] Kautzsch contains the most important of these writings, except Slavonic Enoch, in a German trans. with valuable introductions and notes. They are given in Eng. with introd. and notes in Vol. II. of the great work *The Apocrypha and Pseudepigrapha of the O. T.*, edited by Charles in conjunction with other scholars (1913) ; the introductions there given are invaluable in the study of most of the writings mentioned below. The S. P. C. K. has more recently issued a number of them in inexpensive vols., the work of Charles, Oesterley, and other Eng. authorities. Invaluable are the critical and exegetical studies of Enoch, Sl. Enoch, the Testaments of the Twelve Patriarchs, and others given by Charles in separate vols.

[3] It also contains material derived from a lost 'book of Noah,' which is mentioned in Jub. 10[13], 21[10].   [4] 5[24].

the secrets of almost limitless knowledge.   Tradition ascribed
to him the writing of 366 books.[1] It was natural then that
many pseudonymous writings should be issued in his name ;
those that have survived are doubtless but a fragment.   A
number of such writings (probably not less than three or four,
in the opinion of Charles, five) were united in one book by a
compiler before the end of the last century B.C.   Critical
students of the book differ regarding the documents into
which it is to be resolved and the respective dates of these, but
most agree in placing the oldest portions before 160 B.C. and
the latest before 64 B.C.   The so-called Similitudes (37–70),
the most valuable portion of the book, because containing the
fullest messianic doctrine, are commonly placed before the
middle of the first century B.C.   The book was the most influential of all the writings now held uncanonical.   It is frequently referred to by other apocalyptic writers and was much
used by the early Christians.   It is quoted as a work of genuine
prophecy in the Epistle of Jude (v. 14), traces of familiarity
with it seem to appear in other books of the New Testament,
especially in the Revelation, though these may possibly be due
to ideas and imagery in common currency at the time ; it is
cited as Scripture in the Epistle of Barnabas, Tertullian defended its canonicity, Irenæus, Clement of Alexandria, and
others refer to it as an authority.   But in time it passed into
disuse and disappeared from the literature known to Europeans
till in the eighteenth century it was discovered in an Ethiopic
version of the Old Testament Scriptures of the Abyssinian
Church.   This Ethiopic version was made from a Greek version
(of which some fragments have been discovered recently), and
this in turn from a Hebrew or Aramaic original.   The book
consists chiefly of revelations purporting to be given to Enoch
through visions, through journeys in the unknown regions of
the earth and the heavenly world, and through the instructions
of angels.   The subject matter embraces a very great variety
of topics.   Some of the most important are: the coming of
God to judge the world, to bless the saints and to punish
wicked men and the fallen angels ; the story of the fall of the
angels, their baleful influence in the world, their preliminary

[1] Sl. En. 23⁶.

and final punishment ; the divisions of Hades for the righteous and the wicked ; the names and offices of the archangels ; the secrets of nature with the operations of its forces, theories regarding the movements of the sun and the moon, the winds and storms, the calendar of the year, and similar themes of physical science ; the person and office of the Messiah, his preëminence above all the angels, his preëxistence, his union with God in the judgment and in the rule of the final kingdom, his endowment with the fullness of wisdom and power, his recognition by the mighty ones of earth ; the final assault of antitheocratic powers upon Jerusalem and their annihilation in the depths of hell ; the course of history from Adam to the establishment of the messianic kingdom ; the resurrection of the dead ; the renewal of the heavens, the new Jerusalem ; and the final abode of the righteous where they will dwell with God, the Messiah, and the angels. Nothing short of a full exposition of the contents of this extraordinary book can give an adequate idea of its value for the history of thought in the New Testament era. ‘ It is quite plain that this apocalypse either exerted a considerable influence on the generations immediately before and contemporary with Jesus, or at least reflects a large number of ideas which were in the minds of men of these generations and are not accounted for by the Old Testament.’ [1]

Slavonic Enoch. Another fragment, or collection of fragments, of the Enoch literature survives in the Secrets of Enoch, or Slavonic Enoch as it is called, because so far as known it exists only in a Slavonic version. The original was in Greek (perhaps parts of it in Hebrew or Aramaic). It belongs to the latest period of Judaism, perhaps the first century of our era, but to a time prior to the destruction of Jerusalem in 70 A.D. Although it was well known to Jewish and Christian writers, it passed from notice in the earlier centuries and was lost till it was brought to light again near the close of the last century. [2] The contents consist mainly of Enoch's jour-

[1] Scott *Rev.* in *The New Cent. Bib.* 16.
[2] The Slavonic versions found at that time in Russia and Serbia were first seen by Charles to be distinct from Ethiopic Enoch, and knowledge of them was introduced to Western Europe in his Eng. Ed. *The Book of the Secrets of*

neys through the seven heavens, and what he saw and heard in
each one of these, and the hortatory discourses of Enoch addressed to his sons.   The book is especially valuable as giving
the fullest presentation of the Jewish doctrine of seven heavens
and their occupants.   The abode of the fallen angels and their
leaders is placed in the heavens.   This representation throws
light on the reference found in several New Testament passages to the presence of evil powers in the heavens.[1]   In the
third heaven is Paradise with the tree of life and all that is
beautiful and glorious prepared to be the abode of the righteous, while in the far-off northern regions of the same heaven
are the places of torture prepared for the wicked.   The seventh
heaven is the abode of God, the picture of whose glory with
the orders of angels ranged about him singing the Thrice Holy
is similar to that in the Revelation.   The doctrine of a millennium seems to be taught,[2] though the passage containing it is obscure.   The days of the creation story are represented as prophetic of the world's duration, a day being
reckoned as a thousand years ; [3] after the six days, that is, after
6000 years, follows the seventh day of rest, the 1000 years
of the millennium ; then is established the eighth day at
whose beginning there will be 'a time when there is no
computation and no end ; neither years, nor months, nor weeks,
nor days, nor hours.'[4]   The book is further interesting in that
it contains a considerable number of parallelisms with the New
Testament,[5] which, though they may not be the origin of the
New Testament passages, show these to have been influenced
by ideas and forms of expression current at the time.

The Sibylline Oracles.   These are a collection of verses purporting to be uttered by the ancient Sibyl.   In heathen antiquity
the Sibyl (or the Sibyls, various opinions were held regarding

---

Enoch, 1896.   A later Germ. ed. of value is Bonwetsch, *Das slav. Henoch.* See
above, p. 181; further Volz, and Schürer III. 290 ff.
    [1] *E.g.* 'the spiritual hosts of wickedness in the heavenly places,' Eph. 6[12] ;
'there was war in heaven,' Rev. 12[7] ; cf. Col. 1[20], Lk. 10[18].
    [2] 32 f.   [3] Cf. 2 Pet. 3[8].
    [4] 33[2].   But the text and interpretation here are uncertain. Volz, 30, denies
the reference to a millennium, and takes the seventh day of rest to be similar to
the period of ' world-silence ' spoken of in 2 Es. 7[30], as preceding the awakening
to the life of the new æon.   [5] Cf. Charles, Index I.

the number) was a supposed prophetess of a bygone age, possessing inspired knowledge of the future, to whom were attributed the so-called Sibylline Oracles. The oracles purporting to be derived from this source were sent throughout the Greek and Roman world and great authority was attached to them, even in important affairs of state. In Rome special functionaries were appointed to keep the official collection in secrecy and to interpret them when needed for state purposes. Private individuals also obtained and circulated oracles supposedly Sibylline. Of these numerous oracles nothing remains except a few fragments which have been handed down through quotation in classical writers.[1] But the Sibylline Oracles known to us are of quite different origin. As early as the second century B.C. the Hellenistic Jews adopted this form of literature as a means of propagating their religion, and in later times Christian writers followed their example, making use of the Jewish Sibyllines, modifying them and adding to them. Because of the weight attaching to the Sibylline name and the ease with which the oracles could be invented and circulated the form was especially suited to this purpose, and the heathen prophetess was made to prophesy of the truths of Judaism and Christianity. Such was the origin of the Sibylline Oracles that have come down to us. They were held in repute by Christian writers of the earlier centuries and are frequently quoted by them. The gathering of them into our present collection was the work of an unknown editor, probably of the sixth century; and of this collection there exist books I–VIII and XI–XIV,[2] in all some 4000 verses in Greek hexameter (often violating however the fundamental rules of Greek prosody). They not improbably contain some paragraphs worked over by Jewish writers from a heathen source but in the main are of Hebrew and Christian origin. The part especially useful for the study of apocalyptic literature is contained in books III–V, which are generally held to be the earliest and of Hebrew authorship (though with a heathen groundwork in some passages and Christian interpolations), the oldest portions of these being not later than the second century B.C., that is, not far from the time of the Book

---

[1] See Alexandre's 1st Ed.
[2] Books XI–XIV are sometimes cited as IX–XII.

of Daniel. The contents of this part are a strange medley of prophecies relating to the histories of the various nations to their fall; predictions of the 'messianic woes'; portents and the coming judgment; warnings and admonitions; promises of the triumph of the messianic kingdom, its glory and universal sway. It will be seen that these books contain valuable documents for the illustration of pre-Christian conceptions of the messianic age and of the eschatological ideas of the time. The other books of the collection are, as most scholars are agreed, late; they are without special value for apocalyptic study.[1]

The Psalms of Solomon. Frequently classified with the apocalyptic writings, though differing from them in form and to a large extent in thought, is a collection of eighteen psalms passing under the name of Solomon (this authorship is nowhere intimated in the psalms themselves), written by one or more authors about the middle of the last century B.C. The composition of most of them, as seen by internal evidence, falls soon after Pompey's capture of Jerusalem (63 B.C.). They are preserved in Greek, but the original was undoubtedly in Hebrew. They proceed from a devout but strongly Pharisaic school, and are important not only as illustrating the religious conceptions of Pharisaism just before the time of our Lord, but also as showing the persistence of the older type of messianic expectation (quite different from that of the Similitudes of Enoch) which appears frequently in the popular mind of the New Testament era. They also furnish evidence that the expectation of the messianic kingdom and the yearning for the coming of the Messiah had at least in some quarters again become intense. Psalms XVII–XVIII are the principal messianic portion and give the most splendid picture of the person and rule of the messianic king found in the literature of this age. The writer has not in mind the restoration of a dynasty of Davidic princes but the coming of a single person, the son of

---

[1] Modern editions of the text are those of Alexandre 1841–1856, containing invaluable excursuses omitted in the 2d Ed. 1869, Friedlieb 1852, Rzach 1891 (the most valuable for the text). See above, p. 181 *a.* A Germ. trans. of VI–VIII (with parts of the remaining books) is contained in Hennecke, *N. T. Apokryphen;* introduction and notes to the latter in Hennecke, *Handbuch z. d. N. T. Apocryph.*

David, the Lord's Anointed, who will establish the kingdom in Jerusalem, driving the heathen (the Romans) and all sinners from the holy land; he will restore the dispersed and will reign in righteousness, in the fullness of wisdom and in the might of the Spirit of God; the peoples from the ends of the earth will come to behold his glory and he will rule over them. He is not explicitly described as more than man, nor as ruling forever; yet there is nothing in the hymns expressly at variance with these ideas. Traits of the apocalyptic eschatology however appear in other parts of the collection, where the universal takes the place of the national; the Day of the Lord is a world-judgment; the distinction is general between the righteous and the wicked; the recompense of the one is everlasting destruction and darkness, of the other, resurrection to eternal life — a life in the light of the Lord.[1]

The Odes of Solomon. Reference should also be made here to a collection of hymns, called The Odes of Solomon, just brought to light, which though, like the Psalms, not in the usual form of the apocalyptic writings, are as regards spirit, and in some instances also, as regards doctrine, in affinity with apocalyptic modes of thought. These Odes are mentioned in early lists in connection with the Psalms of Solomon, and five of them had already been discovered and published[2] in the last century; but near the close of the first decade of the present century a collection of 42 was found by J. R. Harris in a Syriac version[3] and published in English.[4] They are placed by Harnack between 50 B.C and 67 A.D., and according to his penetrating and cautious criticism, are Jewish hymns subsequently added to and modified by Christian hands; but the Jewish and Christian elements can to a very considerable extent be separated, and the

---

[1] 3¹⁶ᶠ·. This combination of ζωὴ αἰώνιος and φῶς has the sound of the Johannine writings. For the text of the Psalms the best editions are Gebhardt 1895, and the 2d ed. of Swete 1899. For critical study, Eng. trans. etc., Ryle and James, *The Psalms of the Pharisees* 1891 is exhaustive. See Kautzsch and Charles referred to above. For lit. see especially Schürer III 205 ff.

[2] See Ryle and James, cited above.

[3] The original was apparently Heb. or Aram.

[4] J. R. Harris, *The Odes and Psalms of Solomon, now first published from the Syriac Version.* Cambridge 1909. Harnack has given a Germ. ed. of the Odes only, *Ein jüdisch-christlich.Psalmbuch aus dem ersten Jahrhundert* 1910. See also Viteau, *Les psaumes de Salomon* 1911.

former constitute the principal part.   The Odes are especially
valuable as reflecting a phase of Jewish thought at the beginning
of the Christian era; and they reveal a certain religious attitude
not clearly seen in other Jewish writings of the time.[1]   The
tone is that of intense individualism and thoroughgoing universalism ; the Jewish national idea nowhere appears; holiness
is ethical, not ceremonial; the Messiah and the messianic kingdom are wanting.   On the other hand, there is an eschatology
embracing in its view the resurrection of the saints, the renewal
of the world, Paradise, eternal life, the kingdom of God built
upon an immovable foundation, which is the destined abode of
the holy.

The Testaments of the XII Patriarchs.   This is a book in
twelve parts in which each of the twelve Patriarchs is represented in turn as gathering his sons about him in his last hours
and giving them his final message of exhortation and prophecy ; he tells them the story of his own life (sometimes with
details added to, or differing from, the biblical account), counsels them to avoid his errors, or follow his virtues, as the case
may be, and with prophetic vision foretells the future of the
tribe and the people.   The work has been preserved in several
versions, the oldest of which is the Greek.[2]   The careful study
given to the book in recent times has established its origin ; it
is not as was long supposed the work of a Christian writer, but
in the main a Jewish work of two or more authors, with later
Christian interpolations.   The oldest parts are placed by some
in the second century B.C., the youngest Jewish parts in the
earlier half of the first century A.D.   The Christian additions
begin probably not earlier than the second century of our era.
Even if the oldest portions should not be assigned to so early
a date as that given above, yet all Jewish portions belong to a
time prior to the destruction of Jerusalem, 70 A.D.   The

---

[1] Harnack regards their discovery as epoch-making in the higher criticism of
the Fourth Gospel, because in his opinion they contain the essential factors of
the Johannine theology.   *Op. cit.* p. V. and 118 ff.

[2] Especially valuable also is the Armenian version.   All previous editions of
the text have been superseded by Charles, *The Greek Versions of the Testaments of the XII Patriarchs*, etc., 1908.   For Eng. trans., notes, etc., see his
Test. of the XII Pat. translated from the Editor's text, 1908.   See above,
p. 181; also Schürer III 339 ff.

apocalyptic parts belong to the Jewish source. The book then is an important witness to the doctrines of late Jewish eschatology. The conceptions of both the older, national, and the later, more transcendental, forms of eschatological expectation are represented in different parts of the book. 'On the one hand we hear of the destruction of Israel's enemies, the king-Messiah, the final assault of the nations, the splendor of Jerusalem, the return from captivity and the gathering of the dispersed ; on the other hand we hear of the new Jerusalem and Paradise, of the resurrection, the vanquishment of Belial and the evil spirits, of eternal blessedness and eternal perdition' (Volz 28). The book is rich in material illustrative of apocalyptic ideas, and not a few passages in the Revelation receive light from it. Very interesting in the Testament of Levi (18) is the representation that the Messiah is to spring out of the tribe of Levi and abide as a priest-king forever.[1]

The Book of Jubilees. In the form of a revelation made by 'the angel of the presence' to Moses on Mt. Sinai in the first year after the departure from Egypt, the Book of Jubilees gives a freely expanded version of the biblical story from the creation to the institution of the passover. The author is a Jew of the intense legalistic school writing near the beginning of the Christian era, whether before or after cannot be determined certainly, and his purpose is to enforce in the spirit of Pharisaism the laws, ordinances, and usages of Judaism by showing them to be divinely sanctioned and to have been observed in the very earliest time. The history contained in the book is arranged in chronological divisions based upon the recurrence of the Hebrew jubilee-year, and the writer designates the interval between two such years as a jubilee-period. It is this division of history according to jubilee-periods that gives to the book its name.[2] Written originally in Hebrew, it has come down to us in an Ethiopic version,[3] which was discovered in the last century.[4] The chief value of the work con-

---

[1] Cf. Ps. 110, Heb. 7. For lit., see above, p. 181.

[2] It is also called ' Little Genesis,' because it gives the Genesis history in an inferior, not shorter, form.

[3] This was made from a Gk. vers. ; fragments of other versions remain.

[4] See Charles, *The Book of Jubilees, translated from the Editor's Ethiopic*

sists in the light it throws on Pharisaism in the New Testament era and in its eschatology, though the latter forms an inconspicuous factor.   The author's standpoint is in the main rigidly national.   The enemies of Israel are to be destroyed ; Palestine is to be the seat of the divine kingdom which shall rule all the world ; the temple will be built up in Jerusalem and God will dwell there ; the Davidic house will reign for ever ; it is not clear whether a personal Messiah is expected. There is no distinct mention of a resurrection, though this may be implied in the 'book of life' and in the judgment of the world.[1]   A peculiar but obscure passage ($23^{30\,f.}$) seems to represent the righteous dead as raised not in body but in spirit, and thus beholding and rejoicing in the great consummation for ever.   The wider outlook of late eschatology is on the other hand not absent.   The 'great judgment' to be executed not upon nations but upon all individuals according to their walk and works, and the destruction of the earth, the renewal of all creation, for which the author looks, are parts of a world-eschatology.[2]

Second Esdras.   Besides the Book of Daniel and the Revelation of John, we have in our Bible a third apocalypse, Second Esdras, contained in the Apocrypha.[3]   This book generally supposed to have been written in Greek[4] is preserved to us in five ancient versions, Latin, Syriac, Ethiopic, Arabic, and Armenian ; of these the oldest is the Latin, which is included in the Vulgate, though not placed by the Council of Trent in the list of canonical books.   Chapts. 1–2 and 15–16, which appear in the Vulgate and in our version, are shown by other ancient versions as well as by internal evidence to be additions to the original work ; the real apocalypse, itself held by many

---

Text, 1902.   For critical study, see Rönsch, *Das Buch der Jubeläen* 1874, Charles *The Ethiopic Version of the Heb. Book of Jub.* 1895 ; see above, p. 181.
   [1] Cf. Volz 25.   [2] Cf. Volz *ibid.*
   [3] The title is taken from 1¹, 'the second book of the prophet Esdras ' ; but the more common designation is Fourth Ezra, after the Vulgate ; cf. Art. VI in the Book of Common Prayer, the canonical books, Ezra and Neh. being 1st and 2d Ez.   The name *Apocalypse of Ezra*, sometimes given to it, is unfortunate, because a late Christian apocalypse bearing that title exists ; see Tischendorf, *Apocalypses Apocryphae.*
   [4] A few quotations from the Gk. survive ; but some scholars argue for a Heb. original ; cf. Charles, *Ap. Bar.* Introd. LXXII, Gunkel in Kautzsch 333.

to be a composite work, consists of 3–14. An important paragraph is omitted in chapt. 7 between verses 35 and 36 of the Latin Mss. known to the translators of our A.V., but this fragment, discovered in the last century by R. L. Bensly,[1] and certified by Latin Mss. since found, and by other ancient versions, has been inserted in our R.V. of the Apocrypha (1894).[2] This Jewish apocalypse was written in the latter part of the first Christian century ; it belongs then to a date not far from that of the Revelation of John. It springs from a time of deepest despondency as regards both the national and the religious outlook. In the destruction of Jerusalem by the Romans the hope of Israel as a nation was cut off ; and on the other hand to the devout Jew sin and evil seemed everywhere triumphant throughout the world. In a series of visions the author of the book, impersonating the well-known Ezra of the Babylonian era, overwhelmed by the desolation of Zion and the prosperity of the oppressors, makes his complaint before God concerning the calamities of his own time ; Israel, formed to be the people of God and to possess the earth, is given over into the hands of a people (the Romans) more sinful than themselves ; and as regards the lot of the individual, the godly suffer, the wicked flourish, punishment falls upon frail man, who by the nature given him is powerless to avoid sin ; he is like the seed that perishes because it has not received the rain in due season, or is corrupted through too much rain ; there are few that will be saved. The fortunes of Israel and the course of the world had bred in the author extreme hopelessness as regards his nation and the condition of the individual. The answers therefore which in the visions of the book meet these dark perplexities are of a twofold character ; they tell of hope for the nation and hope for mankind. For the nation, the forms of the older eschatology are brought in, promising the overthrow of the hostile world-power (Rome), the coming of the Messiah, the restoration of Jerusa-

---

[1] *The Missing Fragment of the Fourth Book of Ezra* 1875.

[2] The best text of the Latin version is that given by James, *Texts and Studies* III. 2, 1895. For students dependent on Eng. sources the R.V. is indispensable. See Box, *The Ezra-Apocalypse* 1912. The ed. of Gunkel in Kautzsch is of great value. For comm., see Lupton in the ' Speaker's Com.,' Bissell in Lange ; for further works, see Schürer III 315 ff.

lem, the earthly messianic kingdom ; for the individual and mankind at large, the later eschatological forms are used, and foretell the destruction of this corrupt age, the 'coming æon,' the resurrection, the judgment, the awards of eternal life and eternal punishment meted out to every man according to his works.   Especially interesting is the author's effort to combine the older and the newer eschatologies by the introduction of an intervening messianic era of limited duration between the two æons.[1]   The book is an important example of apocalyptic literature near the time of our New Testament Apocalypse ; and it is all the more useful because the two are almost certainly independent of each other.   Some parallelisms will be pointed out in the Commentary ; here attention is called to only one, the elaborate picture of the Roman power under the form of a many-headed eagle and its annihilation upon the appearance of the lion (the Messiah) — a vision parallel with that of the beast in the Revelation.   Both are in substance derived, as are similar representations elsewhere, directly from the Book of Daniel.[2]   'The entire work is extremely rich in various material ; it can almost be called a compendium of the world of eschatological thought' (Gunkel in Kautzsch 348).   In depth of religious reflection and breadth of spiritual outlook, in imaginative force and sobriety of execution it stands far above all other non-canonical apocalypses.

The Apocalypse of Baruch.   As in the case of Enoch, so a considerable body of pseudepigraphic literature gathered round the name of Baruch, the friend and scribe of the prophet Jeremiah.[3]   Of these writings the most important are the book in the Apocrypha bearing his name, and the (Syriac) Apocalypse of Baruch.[4]   The latter, a distinctly Jewish work, and apparently of composite authorship,[5] was lost until late in the last century when it was discovered in a Syriac version (made from a lost Greek version — the original was Hebrew) and was first published in 1866.[6]   It is frequently called the

---

[1] See p. 109 f.   [2] Cf. pp. 71, 180.   [3] Jer. 36.
[4] For other books cf. Charles, *Ap. Bar.* p. XVI ff., Schürer III 313 f.
[5] Cf. Charles *op. cit.* p. LIII ff., Kautzsch 407 f.; but against this see Baldensperger 37, Kautzsch 409.
[6] The best ed. is Charles, *The Ap. of Bar.* 1896, containing the Syriac text,

Syriac Apocalypse of Baruch in distinction from a Greek work of the same name.[1] It was written not far from the same time as 2 Esdras, that is, in the latter half of the first Christian century; and in origin, scope and purpose is strikingly similar to that book, notwithstanding important differences. The author's aim is to comfort and encourage his despairing countrymen amid the calamities that had befallen the Jewish nation through the destruction of Jerusalem, and in their perplexity caused by the sight of the godly suffering and the wicked prospering. In the person of Baruch, prophesying the Babylonian captivity because of Israel's sin, and the subsequent restoration and glory of the nation, our author seeks to meet the perplexing problems which presented themselves to the devout Jew of the time then present. As in 2 Esdras, the earlier, national, and the later, universal, eschatology appear side by side. On the one hand there are prophecies of the 'messianic woes,' the divine deliverance near at hand, the messianic kingdom established forever with supernatural, earthly glories in Palestine, the Messiah's sway over all the earth; on the other hand the approaching world-judgment ('the youth of the world is past,' 85^{10}), the resurrection, the renewal of creation, the heavenly Jerusalem, the everlasting felicity of the righteous and the unending torment of the wicked. Here also as in 2 Esdras there is an earthly rule of the Messiah of limited duration, after which he (does not die, as in 2 Esdras, but) returns to his heavenly abode to reign for ever. Both these books contain a vision of the proud, corrupt, world-sway of Rome and its destruction by the Messiah. As regards formal structure the two books are alike in that they are divided into seven parts, generally with intervals of a fast of seven days.[2] Both are of value not only in interpreting the Revelation, but also in illustrating other doctrines and questions of Judaism in the New Testament era.

Eng. trans. and notes. A Germ. ed. by Ryssel is given in Kautzsch. For a valuable study of the eschatology see Volz 35 ff.

[1] This Greek *Apoc.* is a quite different book of the 2d century A.D. and of small value for eschatological study. The Gk. text is given by James, and an Eng. trans. of the Slavonic vers. by Morfill in *Texts and Studies* V. Kautzsch contains a Germ. trans. by Ryssel.

[2] Cf. the use of the no. seven in the structure of the Revelation.

The Assumption of Moses.[1]   This is a Jewish writing placed by the larger number of scholars in the earlier part of the first century A.D. It is frequently mentioned by Christian writers from the time of Clement of Alexandria, but finally disappeared till the last century, when a Latin version (made from a Gk. vers. — the original was probably Semitic) of the first part was rediscovered and published in 1861. The concluding part, still unrecovered, contained according to Origen[2] the story of Michael's dispute with the devil about the body of Moses, which is referred to in the Epistle of Jude, v. 9.[3] The portion of the book preserved is really a 'Testament' of Moses, and nothing is said in it about his assumption; that narrative was probably contained in the other part which, whether originally a second part of this book or a separate work afterwards combined with this, gave its name to the whole.[4] The subject of the surviving part is the final charge given by Moses to Joshua, in which he foretells the history of Israel down to the reign of the sons of Herod the Great, that is, to a date some time after 4 B.C. Then the prophecy passes over to the end of the times. After the 'messianic woes,' described in terms taken from the age of Antiochus Epiphanes, the kingdom of God will be revealed to all creation; God will rise up from his throne in wrath because of the persecution of his children, and with the agency of the archangel Michael, amid portents in heaven and earth, will punish the heathen and destroy their idols; the devil will be no more, and sorrow will cease; Israel will mount up in triumph over the world-power, Rome, and will be exalted to an abode of glory in the heavens whence it will look down with exultation upon its enemies. No mention is made of a Messiah, the resurrection, or an earthly kingdom in Palestine. But the value of the book does not consist in its eschatology only; it gives us from the lips of a Jew, one of a rigorous nationalistic type, an indignant denunciation, hardly less severe than that of our Lord or St. John the Baptist, of Pharisaic self-righteousness, greed, deceit, and hypocrisy. The Sadducees and scribes also

---

[1] Not to be confounded with the *Apocalypse of Moses;* see p. 195.
[2] *De princip.* III 2, 1.
[3] The best ed. containing Eng. trans. and notes is Charles, *The Ass. of Mos.* 1897. Kautzsch contains the valuable Germ. Ed. of Clemen. See also above, p. 181.   [4] Cf. Schürer III. 298, Charles in Enc. Bib. I. 234.

are denounced as the receivers of bribes, through which they are led to profane their office and pervert truth.

The Apocalypse of Abraham. This apocalypse, apparently referred to in several early writers,[1] is preserved in a Slavonic version, and was first made known to the modern world by a German translation at the end of the last century.[2] It is of Jewish origin with Christian additions, and appears to belong to the first century A.D. It consists of two parts, I–VIII, legendary, IX–XXXII, apocalyptic. The eschatology, while mainly national, contains elements of the more general form. Abraham is carried into heaven and shown the future history of Israel, its sufferings under heathen oppressors, and its final deliverance in the messianic era. The heathen tyranny of 'this age' will continue twelve 'years,' then the 'coming age' will appear. 'Messianic woes' will precede the judgment, God will send forth the Messiah to gather the dispersed Israelites in Jerusalem, and will give over their enemies to the worm and the fire prepared for them, while his people will joy in his presence forever. Nothing is said of a resurrection.

The Life of Adam and Eve. A considerable group of writings concerned with the story of Adam has been preserved. Most of these are of Christian origin, though with some Jewish groundwork (cf. Schürer III. 396 f.). Among these is a Life of Adam and Eve, so called in the Latin title, in Lat., Gk., and Slavonic recensions. There is reason for referring the groundwork of this to a Jewish source (cf. Kautzsch 510 f.) ; it is therefore of value in apocalyptic study ; cf. Volz 43. The Gk. version was published by Tischendorf in 1866 under the title 'Apocalypsis Mosis,' which is frequently used in reference to it. The Lat. version used the Gk., or the original of the Gk., working it over and adding other Adam matter. Some translators, *e.g.* Wells in Charles, Fuchs in Kautzsch, have combined the Lat. and Gk. recensions, designating some parts The Life of Adam, etc., others The Apocalypse of Moses. See further on the book, Jew. Enc. The standpoint is that of the late eschatology. The present world will continue a fixed period, 5500 years ; then will come the universal resurrection, the judgment, the damnation of Satan and his hosts, and for the righteous an eternal life of blessedness in Paradise in the presence of God. A part of Satan's torment will be caused by the sight of Adam seated on the throne from which he himself has been cast down.

[1] Cf. Lücke I. 232, Schürer III. 337.
[2] Bonwetsch, *Die Apoc. Abrahams* 1897. See also above, p. 181, on publications of S. P. C. K.

[*The Ascension of Isaiah.* Mention should be made of this writing because it is sometimes referred to in the study of Jewish apocalyptic, though in fact the apocalyptic portions are Christian. The work, preserved entire only in an Ethiopic version brought to light in the early part of the last century, is a combination of two or three separate documents: (1) a *Martyrdom* of Is., I–V, closing with the story of the *sawing asunder* of Is. often mentioned in early writers and perhaps referred to in Heb. 11^{37}; (2) an *Ascension* of Is. to the seven heavens, VI–XI, after the manner of Slav. Enoch. The first part, a Jewish composition with interpolated Christian sections, is generally placed in the first cent. A.D. or a century earlier; the second part is a Christian work not earlier than the second cent. A.D. The best ed. with text, Eng. trans., and notes, is Charles, *The Ascension of Is.* 1900. A Germ. vers. by Flemming is contained in Hennecke's *N. T. Apokryphen.* Kautzsch contains trans. of the first part. See further Schürer III. 386 ff.]

Other Apocalypses.   Besides the writings spoken of above a few others of less importance are extant. The *names* also of certain others have been preserved, and in some instances citations from these ; and from their inclusion in ancient lists of Old Testament Apocrypha, and the manner in which they are mentioned in early Christian writers, it seems probable that they were of Jewish origin, or at least contained a Jewish groundwork ; [1] such are the Apocalypse of Elijah, the Apocalypse of Zephaniah, and probably in this category, as containing apocalyptic material, should be reckoned the pseudepigraphic books bearing the name of Ezekiel, Jeremiah, and other Old Testament personages. It is evident that this form of literature was widely current among the Jews as late as the end of the first Christian century ; but with the destruction of Jerusalem in 70 A.D. and the despair that followed regarding the future, it declined rapidly and finally ceased altogether. On the other hand the messianic hope of the Christian Church, the intense expectation of the Lord's return, and the inauguration of ' the coming age ' formed a fertile soil for just this kind of writing. In the evils of ' this present world,' in the sufferings which everywhere met or threatened the new community, the Christians turned with eager look to the future. They adopted the familiar Jewish apocalypses as expressions of their hope, they found comfort and encouragement in them ; they Christianized them by working them over and adding to

[1] Cf. Schürer III. 357 ff.

them ; they wrote apocalypses of their own.   The preservation
of the Jewish apocalypses which we now possess is entirely due
to this use made of them by the Christians.   Doubtless the
great apocalypse, the Revelation of John, gave special stimulus
to such literary productions among the Christians, as the Book
of Daniel had done among the Jews.   It does not fall within
the scope of this Introduction to take up these Christian apocalypses, all of which are later than the Revelation, though they
may in some cases contain matter derived from non-canonical
sources.[1]   Among those of wholly Christian origin oftenest
mentioned are The Shepherd of Hermas, the Apocalypse of
Peter, the Apocalypse of Paul, the spurious Apocalypse of John,
a late work quite different from the New Testament book.[2]

III.   The Times of the Apocalypse of John

We have seen above [3] that it was the circumstances of their
times which caused the apocalypses to be written and which
determined important factors in their contents ; they stand in
close relation to their age.   This is equally true of the Apocalypse of John.   First of all then in an effort to apprehend its
meaning the question arises, what were the conditions in the
Roman Empire and especially in the Roman province of Asia,
where the Apocalypse originated, which can be seen to have
been chiefly influential in its production and contents.   According to the earliest external testimony the Apocalypse of John
was written in the last part of the first century ;   and the
correctness of this tradition will be shown to be reasonably certain in the following pages.   Partly from the book itself and
partly from external history it is seen that there were in this
period two great movements which touched most closely the
future destiny of Christianity, and which as the writer of the
Apocalypse shows, called forth our book and largely shaped its
contents.   These were (1) the erection of the emperor-worship

---

[1] Cf. Bousset, *The Antichrist Legend, passim.*
[2] On pseudepigraphic Christian apocalypses, see Lücke I. 213 ff., Hennecke
N. T. Apokryphen, Holtzmann *Ein.*   An Eng. trans. of some of these is given
in *Ante-Nicene Fathers.*   [3] p. 175.

into the state religion of the Roman Empire; and (2) the persecution of the Christians.

Roman Emperor-worship.[1] Strange as the ascription of divinity to an emperor may seem to our thought, yet the religious conceptions of the ancient Gentile world presented no obstacle to such apotheosis. Polytheism with its gradation of rank among the divinities made easy the deification of men, whose office, power, or achievements so far surpassed the ordinary as to appear superhuman; and ancestor-worship, common in both the east and the west, directly opened the way to an apotheosis of such men after death. An attribute of divinity attached more or less distinctly to kings, for example, the Egyptian Pharaohs claimed descent from a god and received worship in hymns sung to them in their lifetime, and Cleopatra assumed the title θεὰ νεωτέρα. Among the Greeks legendary heroes, *e.g.* Achilles and Heracles, were held to be mortals deified after death, as was Romulus among the Romans. A temple was erected to Lycurgus, the lawgiver, after his death; to Lysander, the hero of the Peloponnesian war, altars were raised in his lifetime. Alexander the Great and his successors received divine honors, coins of Antiochus bear the inscription *King Antiochus, god manifest.* But it was among the Romans that emperor-worship became an organized part of the political and religious system of the empire. More than a century before the establishment of the empire a certain deification of the *State* is found in the provinces in the payment of divine honors to the goddess Roma and the Roman governors; and such worship received a powerful impulse when the majesty of the state became personified in the emperors, who were quick to seize upon this means of strengthening their authority. Provinces and cities came to vie with one another in offering this servile adulation. Julius Cæsar boldly claimed divine honor and placed his statue among those of the gods in the temples. After his death the Senate and People decreed his *consecratio*, apotheosis, and the appearance of a comet was regarded a sign of his reception into the company of the superior divinities.

---

[1] See Boissier, *La religion romaine etc.*, Kornemann, *Zur Geschichte d. antik Herrscher-Kulte*, Wissowa, *Religion u. Kultus d. Römer*, Roscher, *Lexicon* II. 901 ff., Westcott, *Epistles of St. Jno.* 267 ff.

An altar to him was erected in the forum, and in Ephesus a temple bearing the inscription, *To the goddess Roma and the divine Julius*. A slight reaction appears in the course of his successor Augustus, who forbade the offering of divine honor to himself in Rome; yet in the provinces he sanctioned temples to himself in conjunction with the goddess Roma, and he accepted from the Senate the title *Augustus*, σεβαστός, hitherto the epithet of the gods. Upon his death he obtained by vote of the Senate the honor of *consecratio*, and a temple to him was erected on the Palatine. His worship spread rapidly in both the Asian and the western provinces, so that Philo could say, that everywhere honors were decreed to him equal to those of the Olympian gods. The cult thus established continued through the following reigns, varying somewhat in the emphasis laid upon it according to the disposition of the respective emperors, but gradually becoming an essential factor in the imperial religious system.

While the earlier emperors were content with the voluntary worship which a servile people was zealous to offer, the half-insane Caligula (A.D. 37–41) went to the extreme of demanding universal homage to his statue; but there is no evidence that an attempt was made rigorously to carry out this decree everywhere. In Alexandria the populace took advantage of it to wreak their rage on the hated Jews and a terrible persecution broke out. The same motive stirred the heathen inhabitants of Jamnia, a coast town of Palestine, to attempt forcing the worship on the Jewish population. The non-compliance of the latter being reported to Caligula, he determined to take vengeance by setting up his statue in the temple at Jerusalem. A large Roman army was put in readiness to meet the anticipated opposition; but the horror and spirit of resistance aroused throughout the Jewish world caused the emperor's friends to persuade him to recall the edict. Later he returned to his purpose, but died before it could be executed. The religious freedom granted to the Jews by former emperors was now restored to them and they were not afterwards disturbed for failure to join in the emperor-worship; they proved their loyalty in other ways.[1] No mention is made of Christians as

[1] See Schürer I. 483.

suffering with the Jews in these persecutions; in the cities spoken of they were too few to attract attention, and as yet were not distinguished by Roman authorities from the Jews. Certainly the worship of the beast, that is, the emperor-worship,[1] described in the Revelation as to be enforced upon all the world under penalty of ostracism and death (chapt. 13), cannot be connected with the age of Caligula — at that time there is nothing in accord with the picture. In other words our book cannot belong to that age. Under Nero and his successors down to Domitian, the emperor-cult continued as one of the established religious institutions, but its progress is not signalized by edicts enforcing it, or by notorious persecutions arising from it. It is in the reign of Domitian (81–96) that we reach an insistence upon the cultus more vehement and more threatening for the future. This emperor, who because of his infamous career failed to receive the honor of apotheosis from the Senate at his death, was strenuous in claiming divinity in his life; to his subordinates he became *deus et dominus, our lord and god*, though it is not clear just how far actual enforcement of his worship was carried. In the time of Trajan (98–117) there seems to have been no *universal law* enjoining the cult, for Pliny's letter asking for the emperor's instructions as to the treatment of the Christians[2] shows that their refusal to offer incense to the emperor's statue was not charged as an infraction of law; it was only made a test of Christian discipleship. However, at a time considerably before that date the rapid spread of the cult throughout the empire caused rejection of it to become in general disloyalty to the person of the emperor. Therein lay its force. In the development of the imperial policy, the value of the cultus as a governmental institution was quickly perceived. Rome allowed its conquered peoples to retain their own religions without adding the Roman. But a universal empire needed also a universal religion, and only in the worship of the state, personified in the emperor, could all subjects except Jews and Christians eagerly join. While it was the province of Asia that took up the new worship with the most fervent zeal, it flourished also in all the provinces of Europe and Africa.

[1] On the impersonation of the beast in the emperors see pp. 394 ff.
[2] See p. 205.

Its priesthood was everywhere established, and not only the *divi*, those deified by vote of the Senate after death, had everywhere their temples, priests, and festivals, but the reigning emperors also had their part in these institutions. In Asia Minor a considerable number of cities gained the special title νεωκόρος, *temple-keeper*, in reference to the cult — a title derived from the special maintenance of some heathen cult, as *e.g.* Ephesus was called the *temple-keeper* of Artemis (Ac. 19[35]). In this worship then political and religious devoteeism, state and church so to speak, became identical. The Christian Church could not fail to see the significance of the movement. As long as the Roman state did not arrogate to itself an inherent religious character Paul could speak of it as a 'minister of God,'[1] and Peter could give the injunction 'Honor the King.'[2] But when the homage belonging to God alone was demanded as due to the person of the emperor the Christian must see concentrated and culminating therein the whole conflict between the Church and the world. It is true that the picture of the *universal enforcement* of the worship, aided by its special priesthood miraculously endowed (the second beast),[3] which is given in Rev. 13, belongs to a time still in the future of the Apocalyptist, that is, the time of antichrist, when the culmination of enforcement would be reached. On the other hand it is clear that the Apocalyptist's forecast of the future grows out of his present; already the cult is a settled factor in the imperial system, with its highly organized institutions, and the Apocalyptist foresees the ultimate consequences, the awful peril which must certainly arise when the movement then present shall have reached its final development. But such a well-organized expansion of the cult as was already present was not reached before the last years of the century, that is, before the time of Domitian. The Apocalypse then could not have been written before that date.

Early Roman Persecutions.[4] While Jewish hostility to the Christians proceeded from religious grounds, that of the

---

[1] Ro. 13[4].   [2] 1 Pet. 2[17].
[3] On the significance of the second beast see pp. 408 ff.
[4] See Hardy, *Christianity and the Roman Government*, Lightfoot, *The Apostolic Fathers*, parts I. and II., Linsenmeyer, *Die Bekämpfung d. Christenthums*, etc., Ramsay, *The Church in the Roman Empire*.

Romans was due to political, social, and other non-religious causes. The Lord's words, 'Ye shall be hated of all men,' were soon fulfilled. The recognition of the Christ in Jesus, with his teaching of a religion which must supersede the Mosaic system, and which also made the Gentiles 'fellow-heirs and fellow-members of the body, and fellow-partakers of the promise,'[1] aroused at once the rancorous hatred of the Jews. On the other hand the attitude of the Christians toward the life of a heathen community made them detested and suspected. They avoided and condemned the idolatry and prevalent immorality of their fellows,[2] kept aloof from the popular festivals as un-Christian in character, and in some instances they interfered with lucrative trades;[3] they recognized an authority higher than that of the emperor and refused worship to the latter; the Master whose name they bore and to whom they offered homage had been put to death as a malefactor; their numbers were drawn chiefly from the lower ranks of society;[4] their frequent meetings in private were believed to be occasions of even such crimes as incest and the drinking of the blood of their own children. Inevitably then the Christian as such must become the object of persecution; sometimes through mob violence, as in the case of Stephen,[5] of Paul at Lystra,[6] sometimes under the cover of the forms of law, as Jesus had been condemned on the charge of treason against Cæsar.[7] The Acts show that the offense against Roman law was frequently charged as a pretext to gratify hatred; *e.g.* by the masters of the divining girl at Philippi,[8] by the populace in the seizure of Jason and others at Thessalonica,[9] in the arraignment of Paul before Gallio.[10]

The first persecution undertaken by the Roman *government* directly and of its own motion was that of Nero in the year 64, the most fiendish in its atrocities of all the Roman persecutions. According to Tacitus[11] Nero's motive was to divert the popular suspicion that he was himself the author of the great fire which had just destroyed a large part of the city; as the culprits, he brought forward the Christians, who were hated by

---

[1] Eph. 3⁶.   [2] 1 Pet. 4³ ᶠ.   [3] Cf. Ac. 16¹⁹, 19²⁴ ᶠᶠ., p. 205.
[4] 1 Co. 1²⁶.   [5] Ac. 7.   [6] Ac. 14¹⁹.   [7] Jno. 19¹².
[8] 16¹⁹ ᶠᶠ..   [9] 17⁶ ᶠ.   [10] 18¹² ᶠ..   [11] *Ann.* XV. 44.

the populace, and inflicted upon them most exquisite tortures.
They were ferreted out and a great multitude, Tacitus says,
was convicted, not so much for the crime of incendiarism, as
for hatred of the human race. It was natural when once popular rage had flamed up against them, because of alleged
responsibility for the fire, that the general hatred of them
should vent itself without restraint. The connection of Nero's
persecution with the fire, as stated by Tacitus, is questioned
by some on the ground of the silence of other writers, but the
argument from silence is so far from conclusive here that most
scholars accept the testimony of Tacitus as accurate. Under
what law procedure was instituted against the Christians is
not stated. It is not certain that the mere status of being a
Christian was declared unlawful till the very end of the century. An edict, *non licet esse Christianos*, is attributed to Nero,
but this is doubtless an anachronism. When Christianity
came to be recognized as distinct from Judaism it was of
course seen to be a *religio illicita*, since the introduction of a
new religion was forbidden. Yet Rome, because of the great
number of strange religions allowed in its conquered subjects,
was tolerant or indifferent in such matters. A Roman citizen
might not adopt a foreign religion, but the existence of a new
cult among the populace was not likely to be scrutinized
closely, unless its devotees were obnoxious in other ways.
Even down to the time of Trajan the charge against Christians
does not appear that of an unlawful religion, but rather danger
to society and disloyalty — accusations made specific in all the
monstrous forms which popular hatred could conceive. The
charge under which the Philippians covered their attack on
Paul and Silas[1] was not that of introducing a new religion,
but of urging as Jews ('these men being Jews') upon Roman
citizens a non-Roman religion. The doctrine preached might
be lawful for Jews, but not so, the accusers claimed, for the
Philippians, 'being Romans.' The harsh treatment of Christians throughout this period was legalized by the general police
power of the magistrate to punish, with whatever customary
penalties seemed good, any person supposed to be a menace to
the order of the community ; and in view of the general atti-

[1] Ac. 16[19] ff..

tude of the people toward the Christians the mere profession of the name was enough to raise suspicion against them as evildoers.[1] The nature and extent of their molestation would therefore vary with the governors at different places and times.   The great persecution of Nero was apparently confined to the city of Rome, and it is certain that his violent policy was not carried out by his immediate successors and in the provinces. Yet it could not be without its influence ; though no general persecution in the earlier following reigns is reported there must have been with the spread of Christianity individual cases of oppression and even death in different parts of the empire. The readers of the Epistle to the Hebrews had suffered severely, and had been despoiled of their possessions,[2] but the death penalty had not been visited upon their numbers.[3]

It was in the reign of the infamous Domitian (81–96) that a more active persecution was again instituted. His insistence on the offering of divine homage to himself has been mentioned above. In Christian tradition he was styled the second great persecutor of the Church, the second Nero, though the persecution of his time was different from that of Nero and lacked its atrocities. The general testimony of early Christian writers leaves no reasonable question that his reign became a time of special suffering for the Christians, though details of his measures are for the most part wanting ;[4] and this testimony is confirmed by at least one non-Christian writer. Dio Cassius[5] states that he put to death Flavius Clemens, and banished Clemens' wife, Flavia Domitilla, both relatives of his, on the charge of ἀθεότης, *sacrilege*, which in the case of Domitilla at least is shown by inscriptions and Christian tradition to have denoted profession of Christianity. Clement of Rome, contemporary with Domitian, refers to his course in the quite general words 'the sudden and repeated calamities and adversities which have befallen us.'[6] Christian writers report that he banished the Apostle John to Patmos, and while the statement may as some suppose owe its origin to

---

[1] 1 Pet. 2[12].   [2] 10[32] ff.   [3] 12[4].
[4] For a conspectus of passages relating to Domitian's persecution, see Lightfoot *St. Clement* 104 ff.   [5] *Hist. Rom.* LXVII. 14.   [6] I. 1.

Rev. 1⁹, yet there is no sufficient evidence that this was not an actual fact of history.[1] In whatever reign the Apocalypse may have been written, its author had almost certainly been an exile in Patmos.[2] Domitian's persecution did not consist in the wholesale slaughter and the atrocities instituted by Nero ; deaths were evidently inflicted in different parts of the empire, but apparently other penalties, banishment, imprisonment, confiscation of property, etc., were more usual. Domitian's motive was fear of political enemies ; and behind the religious charges against those who were executed there was unquestionably as the real cause of action a determination to get rid of persons thought to be politically dangerous.

This rigorous activity of Domitian against the Christians which made him in tradition a second Nero was not continued by his immediate successors, Nerva and Trajan. The present position and the outlook of the Christians now became less distressful. The former of these emperors is said by Dio Cassius to have restored the exiles, to have released those accused of lese-majesty and to have checked other persecutions for this cause and for adopting ' Jewish customs,' a term which may perhaps include a profession of Christianity. The attitude of Trajan (98–117) is seen from his correspondence with Pliny to have been that of leaving the Christians unmolested, so far as this could be done consistently with what appears to have now become the ordinary policy of the empire. In the province of Bithynia-Pontus, of which Pliny was governor, the Christians had become so numerous that the heathen temples began to be deserted, and the falling off in the profitable trade of providing fodder for the sacrificial animals aroused strong hostility against the new cult. In the numerous cases brought before him for trial Pliny followed the course of punishing with death those who obstinately adhered to their profession of being Christians, or if Roman citizens, they were sent to Rome. This was probably now the common policy pursued in the provinces. But doubt arose in Pliny's mind whether punishment should be administered for the mere fact of the Christian profession, even though no crimes were charged, or only for actual crimes associated with the Christian name. He had, as

See pp. 379 ff. 2 See Com. on 1⁹.

he informed the emperor, instituted an examination and found no criminal purpose in the Christian brotherhood, but only superstition.   In answer to his inquiry Trajan instructed him not to search out the Christians, nor to proceed against them upon the motion of anonymous accusers, but to punish those brought before him and proven to be Christians.   It is clear from Pliny's doubt that there was at the time no law specifically prosecuting Christians as such, but that the magistrate's general authority in police administration to suppress all dangerous elements was turned against the Christians, who were everywhere regarded as offenders against society and the national religion.   Trajan's instructions doubtless came to be known in other provinces and must have influenced the procedure of the governors.   Though many martyrdoms must have occurred, yet the emperor could not be ranked with Nero and Domitian in fierce hostility toward the Christians, and in his insistence on his prerogative of divine homage.

Now the situation of the Christians revealed in the Apocalypse is such that it can hardly be doubtful to which period the book belongs.   The limits of the Neronic persecution, which was confined to Rome, have at this time been altogether exceeded ; the hour of trial, including banishment, imprisonment, and even death, has already fallen upon the churches of Asia Minor addressed in the seven epistles.[1]   Martyrdoms have already taken place in many parts of the earth,[2] the souls of the martyrs are crying for vengeance long delayed.[3]   But this situation can hardly be supposed before the time of Domitian. On the other hand the present calamities of the Christians are everywhere in the book viewed as but the forerunner of a yet severer time of trial for the whole world in the near future. Suffering, persecution, martyrdom, advancing to the extreme, give tone to every picture of the coming days.   But the comparative relaxation of distress in both the present conditions and the outlook which we have seen to characterize the reigns of the emperors immediately succeeding Domitian make highly improbable an assignment of the book to that later period. The place then which the persecutions occupy in the motives and prophecies of the apocalyptist seems clearly to point to the

[1] 1^9, $2^{3, 13}$, $3^{8, 10}$.   [2] 18^{24}.   [3] 6^9 f.

time of Domitian. It has been seen above that the book contemplates a stage in the growth of emperor-worship not reached at an earlier date.

Other Historic Circumstances Indicative of Date. With the above indications pointing to the time of Domitian concur at least two others, also furnished by the circumstances revealed in the book. (1) The particular form of the Nero myth which has come to be pretty generally accepted as underlying the representation in chapts. 13 and 17 of the head wounded and healed, the beast that was and is not and is about to come, could not have been reached till near the end of the century.[1] (2) The condition of the Asian churches addressed in the seven epistles requires a considerably long interval after the labors of St. Paul among them, and after the epistles to the Colossians and the Ephesians, the Pastoral epistles and 1 Peter. So large a decline in religious life at Ephesus, Sardis, and Laodicea[2] is not probable in the years following soon after the apostle's foundation work there, and is at variance with the state implied in the apostolic epistles named. False teachers to be sure had appeared here at the time of those epistles, but the formation of such into a distinct school designated by a well-understood name, the Nicolaitans, and teaching widely a doctrine so well known as to need no special definition by the Apocalyptist, presents a situation of which there is no trace in the apostolic epistles, and which could arise only after a considerable lapse of time. Also the absence of any intimation pointing to the great work of Paul in Asia Minor is less explicable if that had been of recent date. Scholars who have assigned the book to the time of Nero or a date shortly after — a view held by many down to recent times — have found the principal evidence for this theory in chapts. 11 and 17. The former chapter is understood to show that Jerusalem is still standing and persecuting the prophets of God, but is about to be besieged by the Romans (70 A.D.) and with the exception of the temple to be wholly overrun by the Gentiles. And this early date is thought to be established by the writer's statement in 17[10], that the sixth emperor is reigning at the time, which might be as early as Nero, but by no method of

---

[1] See pp. 400 ff.   [2] Cf. 2[4], 3[4], 3[15 ff.].

reckoning the numbers later than Vespasian (69–79). Yet with the general acceptance of the conclusion, that the Apocalyptist in places has in some form or other made use of earlier sources, it follows that chapt. 11 ceases to fix an early date. And as regards 17[10] the writer's habit of using numbers symbolically invalidates the argument. The author's use of sources and derived material in a new sense given to it to suit his purpose, and the significance of the enumeration of the Roman emperors are discussed elsewhere.[1] Most scholars at the present time are agreed that the situation contemplated in the book is that of a period near the close of the first century, or as most would say, the last years of Domitian's reign. With this conclusion based on internal evidence agrees also the earliest external testimony, that of Irenæus,[2] who in speaking of the Apocalypse says, ' For it was seen, not long ago, but almost in our generation, near the end of Domitian's reign.' This date is given frequently in later Christian writers, who may perhaps in some instances be independent of Irenæus.

IV. The Purpose of the Apocalypse

Like the other books of the New Testament the Apocalypse was written with the practical purpose of meeting a need of the particular readers addressed, in their existing condition and in the circumstances of their own time or of the time supposedly about to come. What is said of the other books is especially applicable to the Apocalypse ; it is a ' Tract for the Times.' And if what is of permanent meaning and value in it is to be distinguished with certainty from the temporary and formal, this can be done only by studying the book first of all from the standpoint of the first readers and of the author's immediate purpose. As the first century, to whose closing years the Apocalypse belongs, advanced through the later decades the antagonism of the world to the Church assumed, as we have seen,[3] a more and more distinct form. Christianity, now spread-

---

[1] See pp. 174, 586, 704 ff.   [2] V. 30, Eusebius *H. E.* III. 18, V. 8.
[3] pp. 201 ff.

ing widely and growing in power, was by its very nature hostile to the social, moral and religious life of the time; it was making to itself bitter enemies in every rank of society, Jew and Gentile were uniting against it; and finally it ranged among the forces opposing it the power of the imperial government. The general establishment of emperor-worship as a political and religious institution of the empire brought the Christian face to face with the question of his loyalty to his lord Cæsar and his Lord Christ. The powers of evil were everywhere gathering mightily against the Church. The Roman government, which held sway virtually over all the world, was adopting a policy, more or less settled and regular, of suppressing Christianity; persecution, begun under Nero, was revived and society at large was quick to avail itself of this aid in its warfare. The leaders among the Christians could see clearly that the Church was entering upon a life-and-death struggle, a time of storm and stress, of great suffering. To meet this crisis Christians would be called to the supreme test of their faith, steadfastness and self-surrender. Of this they must be forewarned. But the Church at the time did not as a whole show preparedness to rise to the great demand in full. While in some parts it was worthy of praise for its patience and fidelity, its spiritual vigor and its readiness for martyrdom, in other parts there was lukewarmness, tolerance of corrupt teaching, and yielding to the seductiveness of surrounding immorality.[1] The Church needed a ringing call to awaken it to its highest activity. It needed also in the hour of awful trial coming upon it an assurance of its final deliverance and of the glorious reward which should be meted out to the faithful in the end. This state of things, these urgent needs of the Church, were clearly perceived by a great Christian prophet, and he saw himself commissioned by God to bring to the Church his wonderful message — a message designed on the one hand to forewarn the Church of its peril and arouse it to a purified, vigorous life; on the other, to fortify its courage and hope by revealing the ultimate destruction of the powers of evil, and the perfect consummation of the Christian hope in the establishment of the kingdom of God. Such were the circumstances calling for the voice of the

[1] See the seven epistles, chaps. 2–3.

P

prophet, and such the purpose of his book.   Putting his divine message in the form of an epistle he addressed it directly to a group of churches in Asia Minor.   He was guided to adopt this specific address, probably in part because that was the field of his own labors, the one with which he was most familiar, the one where his authority was most fully recognized ; probably in part also because this was the sphere where the various exigencies of the Church were conspicuously pressing ; here the emperor-worship took its most aggressive form, here the energetic and corrupt life of the busy Asiatic cities produced the most manifold influences subversive of Christian faith and character ; here the seven communities were, if not comprehensive examples of the life and surroundings of the whole Church, at least types of good and evil so varied as to make them in a sense representative of the world at large.   At all events it is clear, that while the message is sent specifically to a group of seven churches, it is intended for the whole Church.   Every one that hath an ear is bidden to hear what the Spirit saith to the churches ; the warnings and promises of the book are not merely local, but applicable to all Christians scattered throughout the world ; its visions and revelations are concerned with things universal.[1]

The direct relation of the book to the circumstances, and to the Christian beliefs and expectations of the time demands a somewhat fuller exposition.   This relation becomes apparent in those matters upon which emphasis is especially laid, as may be seen by a brief survey of the principal topics.   (1) As a prophet, commissioned with a special message of reproof and exhortation addressed to the people of God regarding their present spiritual state and their future steadfastness, the author devotes the foremost paragraph of his book to the searching words of the Lord of the Church given in the seven epistles (2–3) ; and the lessons of that portion are summarily reiterated in later paragraphs in view of the crises spoken of.[2] (2) The evil days upon which the Church had already entered and those still more evil now imminent were thought to form ' The Last Time,' with its trials and hopes ; the movements of the forces of evil now at work in the world were viewed as the

---

[1] See on 1[4].   [2] Cf. 7[14], 13[10], 14[4-5, 9-12], 18[4-5], 20[4], 21[8, 27], 22[12-15].

last forerunners of those final events. Hence the revelations of the book relate chiefly to things which must come to pass shortly. (3) The common belief in an intensification of 'woes' before the dawn of the Great Day made inevitable in any prophecy of the destinies awaiting the world terrible visitations, such as those of the seals, the trumpets and the bowls, whether as plagues sent upon the enemies of God or as trials to test the saints. (4) The hostility of the Roman government, now manifesting itself in measures taken to suppress Christianity, was seen by the prophet as a great weapon of Satan in his warfare against the Christ, and its advance to the bitterest conflict was clearly discerned. The Church needed — to be advised of the Satanic nature of this hostility and forewarned of its increasing activity; at the same time it needed also a vision of the final overthrow of this great adversary. Of old the world-monarchies, Assyria, Babylonia, Greco-Syria, had persecuted the people of God, and the prophets had foretold in vivid pictures their final doom; so now the Apocalyptist foresees the Roman world-power and the imperial city, at present serving to the utmost Satan's designs against the Church, ultimately swept away in utter ruin. Naturally this theme is frequently in the background of the author's thought. The activity of Satan in Rome's persecution of the Church forms the underlying motive in the great scene of chapt. 13 and the explanation of it given in 17^{8-11}; it appears also in other passages, e.g. $2^{10,\ 13}$, $12^{9,\ 12,\ 17}$, 20^2. And the punishment of Rome in its utter destruction forms the subject of the long paragraph $17-19^5$, describing in full what is announced briefly elsewhere, e.g. 14^8, 16^{19}, 11^{18}. (5) The prevalent expectation regarding Antichrist was at this time quickened by the intimations of current events. As seen elsewhere[1] the belief was common that before the end Antichrist would come as universal world-tyrant, exalting himself above God and demanding worship from all, that he would work in the power of Satan, and even Rome must be removed to make way for him. His actual appearing was still held in check, but his influence was already at work in the world.[2] Especially in one respect was seen the beginning of his advent, that is, in the demand of the Roman

---

[1] See pp. 398 f.   [2] Cf. 2 Thess. 2^7, 1 Jno. 2^{18}.

emperors that divine worship should be offered to them.   The
emperors were viewed as the representatives, in a certain sense
the impersonation, of the coming Antichrist.   And by a
strange coincidence a fancy prevailed in the closing years of
the century that one of the emperors (Nero), the one most
monstrous in his wickedness and his persecution of the Christians, would return from the dead, overthrow Rome, and establish himself as universal tyrant, making himself equal to God.[1]
Such a fancy could easily be seized by a prophet and poet as
falling in with the current expectation of the Antichrist.
Antichrist was already present in his representatives, the emperors, demanding worship from Christians and non-Christians
alike.   He would soon come in his own person in the fullness
of his power, and with extreme measures against the Church.
The emperors as they follow one after another are the respective heads of the beast which cometh up out of the abyss of
the dead ; one of them now dead will return, as a wounded
head restored, to carry to its consummation the work committed by Satan to the beast.[2]   The place occupied by ruler-
worship in the national religion at the time and in the anticipations of Antichrist naturally gives to the subject great
prominence in the Apocalyptist's admonitions and promises.
The office of the beast, his destiny, the bitterness of the conflict with him, the reward of those who in steadfast loyalty to
Christ resist his demand, are dominant thoughts throughout
the book.[3]   (6) As the crisis upon which the Church was
entering must inevitably bring with it the peril of martyrdom,
and as the Apocalyptist's exhortations frequently contemplate
the call to this extreme trial, so in one of the most striking
passages of his book he reveals to his readers the *martyr's*
peculiar reward.[4]   To this special class is reserved the blessedness of the first resurrection and the millennial reign with
Christ.[5]   In other passages also the martyrs are assured of
their special remembrance before God.[6]   (7) But while the
times make appropriate a separate message to the martyrs, the
whole body of Christians stand in need of the comforting and

[1] See pp. 400 ff.   [2] See pp. 407 f.
[3] Cf. 11[7], chapt. 13, 14[9-11], 15[2], 16[2, 10, 13], 17[8-17], 19[11-21], 20[4, 10].   [4] 20[4].
[5] See p. 736.   [6] Cf. 6[9-11], 12[11], 16[5-7], 19[2], the seven epistles *passim*.

strengthening assurance that God will carry through unfailingly his purpose to deliver his people and establish his kingdom ; that Christ is ever present with his Church, controlling in its behalf the destinies of the world, overcoming in the end every enemy ; and that through the gate of fierce struggle with the powers of evil the saints will pass to a blessed eternity of union with God and their Lord Christ. This is the supreme message to the Church in the stress of the awful days now coming to it. And this hope is revealed in nearly every chapter. It is expressed directly in the opening vision of Christ in his ascended glory, chapt. 1 ; in the epistles, 2–3 ; in the great scenes of the court of heaven, 4–5 ; in the visions of the resurrection, the judgment and the new Jerusalem, 20–22. It is implied in the manifestations of God's wrath against the wicked, and the judgments sent upon them, *e.g.* chapts. 6, 8–9, 16–18. It is vividly pictured in the anticipatory visions and hymns which are ever and anon introduced like beams of light from heaven piercing the dark scenes of divine wrath and Satanic warfare.[1]

This rapid survey will show the immediate relation of the contents of the Apocalypse to the state and circumstances of the Church at the time when it was written ; that it is a book for the years forming the close of the first century and the beginning of the second, and is addressed to the precise needs and the hopes and fears of that age. And it cannot be doubted that as it was read in the congregations of those Asiatic churches, and from them spread to other parts of the Church, it added mightily to the forces which nerved Christians to stand firm in their great trial.

In what has been said regarding the author's purpose in the Apocalypse, his own personal deliberation and choice are assumed to share in his work. It is therefore appropriate in this place to speak specifically of this factor, *the Apocalyptist's part in his writing,* the right apprehension of which must underlie all discussion of the contents and structure of the book, and its interpretation. There are two facts which are established by the study of the book itself, and which are fundamental here : (1) deliberate study in the composition of

[1] Cf. chapts. 7, 11^{15-19}, 12^{10-12}, $14^{1-5, 13}$, 15^{2-4}, 19^{6-9}.

the work ; (2) the influence of the Old Testament prophets and the apocalyptists in the book.   (1) *Deliberate study in the composition of the book.*   The author represents himself as receiving his message through visions.   Now the vision had become the standing form in which all apocalyptic writers cast their works, even those who could lay no justifiable claim to a divine revelation.[1]   Hence it is assumed by some that in our book also the visions are merely a literary device of the writer ; and this view is thought to be confirmed by the evident traces of deliberate care and study in the composition.   If however we accept the reality of the vision in the case of the Old Testament prophets and others, there appears no reason why we should not do so here.   The wonderful character of many of the scenes of our book is less easily accounted for as a product of poetic fancy, than as revealed in that strange spiritual experience which we call ecstasy, and whose actuality is recognized by most biblical scholars.   The writer's uniform representation, that revelations of this character were given to him as the source of his message, rests upon a basis as sure as his claim to the office of a prophet,[2] and we are warranted in accepting the occurrence of visions in his case, as we do in that of Isaiah, of Peter, or Paul.

But a prophet does not write while in a vision or state of ecstasy, and when he commits to writing a record of these extraordinary experiences he becomes a deliberate composer. And so we see our author laboring with all the skill and resources at his command to convey to his readers some apprehension of the marvelous revelations which had been made to him.   Stupendous scenes passing all human power to picture had been opened to his sight ; these had been shown to him not all at once but, as he himself has given us to understand, at different times and from different standpoints, and he is bidden to make a record of all that he had seen.   Things beyond man's comprehension, things which were doubtless only dimly seized by himself, he struggles to make visible, and to combine into a picture of the one great theme to which they all relate.   He uses in his task the imagery of familiar writings, he invents, he adopts and adapts from earlier sources, as an

[1] Cf. p. 169.   [2] See pp. 292 ff.

artist with a great ideal before his vision makes use of every
resource whether original or conventional, at times betraying
his consciousness that he is trying to express the inexpressible.
How far he is merely reproducing forms actually seen in his
ecstasy, and how much of his work is due to the conscious
effort to produce in his readers some visualization of what had
been perhaps vaguely presented to his spiritual eye, it is impossible to say.   This carefully studied character of the composition is seen unmistakably in the long and very complicated
plan of the book, in the relation of part to part and to the
whole, in the elaborate scheme of sevens,[1] in details looking
forward and backward, in structural repetitions.   These and
other similar features are pointed out in the Commentary.   A
striking parallel to this studied elaboration in the description
of a vision is found in Ezekiel's account of his visions of the
temple and the land of restored Israel (chaps. 40–48).   But
for all this studied effort in literary labor our book is none the
less a series of visions.   And doubtless in the course of literary
composition the author's conscious work would not always be
sharply distinguished from his ecstatic state.   A poet is often
transported with his inspiration, even though he labors with
the quantities of syllables or accents in trying to give to his
conceptions metrical form.

(2) *The influence of the Old Testament prophets and the
Apocalyptists in the book.*   The writer's mind is stored to a
remarkable degree with Old Testament prophecies, especially
those concerning the End, with Jewish eschatological tradition,
and with its language and imagery.   It was natural then that
his visions themselves should be moulded by the conceptions
thus inherent in all his thoughts of the Last Things.   Visions
take fashion from that of which the mind is full.   There is
scarcely a paragraph in the book which does not contain reminiscences of the prophets, or apocalyptic writings, as is pointed
out in the Commentary.   But it is a mistake to find herein
evidence that the visions are altogether a literary form built
up on traditional lines and not a real experience of the author.
On the other hand in the writer's effort to give form to the

[1] See p. 253 f.

mysteries revealed to him, as said above, the familiar representations given in the prophets and elsewhere must often have suggested themselves to him as the most fitting embodiment. It is of course impossible to say how much in these parallelisms is due to this effort, and how much belonged to the visions themselves ; the distinction is unimportant. The essential fact to be recognized in this characteristic of the book is the influence which this inheritance of the author's from earlier prophets and apocalyptists exerted on the contents of his visions and his manner of picturing them. The author's procedure in carrying out his great purpose will be seen in a survey of the contents of the book and its structure to be given below.[1] It is desirable to consider first two topics, (1) the question of unity, (2) certain characteristics in the author's literary manner, topics which pertain to the plan of the book and its interpretation. These are taken up in the following paragraphs.

V. The Question of the Unity of the Apocalypse

Taking the Apocalypse in its general outline the reader traces a sequence in the acts which fill up the great drama of the Last Things. The several series of precursory judgments follow one after another and are succeeded by the cycle of events which belong to the End itself. We perceive readily the relation of at least the larger parts to an ordered plan. The thread sometimes seems to be broken, but it reappears. Passing over certain portions to be noted later we see that the events move toward one great consummation as follows: the unfolding of the future, declared in the first verse, is directly entered upon in the breaking of the seven seals one after another, which closed the book of the world's destiny (5–6, 8[1]), and it continues with certain interruptions through the visions of the seven trumpets (8, 9, 11[15ff.]) and of the seven bowls of God's wrath (15, 16) ; then follow in quick succession the events of the End, that is, the vanquishment of the enemies of

---

[1] pp. 255 ff.

God, both earthly and spiritual, the resurrection, the judgment and the doom of the wicked (18–20), and finally the perfected kingdom of God in the new world (21–22$^{1-5}$). But on the other hand into this general outline there are thrown many passages, of greater or less length, whose direct relation to the main plan of the book is not apparent on the surface ; they seem to interrupt an orderly sequence ; an advancing series of events is broken in upon by matter which apparently belongs to a different context or a different chronological position. Chief among such seemingly disturbing passages are the seven epistles, concerned, not with things of the Last Days, but with the then existing condition of certain churches of Asia Minor (2–3) ; the vision of the court of heaven, pictured not with reference to a final abode of the redeemed, but as the eternal throne-room of God surrounded by the adoring company of angels (chapt. 4) ; certain anticipations such as the announcement of the End, as already come (6^{17}, 14$^{15-20}$), triumphant hymns celebrating the consummation as reached (11$^{15-18}$, 12^{10}, 19$^{6-9}$), visions of the saints in final blessedness (7$^{9-17}$, 14$^{1-5}$, 15^{2}) — all these introduced in the midst of events which belong earlier in time. Similar inappropriateness to the connection appears in the paragraphs inserted between the sixth and seventh seals (chapt. 7), and between the sixth and seventh trumpets (10–11^{14}) ; the visions of the woman and the dragon (chapt. 12), and of the beasts rising out of the sea and the earth (chapt. 13) ; the premature announcement of the fall of the great city (14^{8}). Besides this evident interruption of order and the consequent difficulty in certain passages in determining a meaning related to the context, differences in the historical situation implied and in religious ideas are also thought by some scholars to exist in various places. It is inevitable then that the unity of the book should be called in question. Theories of (1) revision and rearrangement by later hands, (2) a compilation of different documents, (3) interpolation, are offered as furnishing the readiest solution of many problems, and seem to be sustained by reasons more or less weighty.[1]

[1] For a survey of critical views, see pp. 224 ff., 237 f. The passages above enumerated do not include all those against which critical objections are raised from one quarter or another, but they are those which form the principal interruptions in a regular sequence.

The test of unity must be sought in the results of a thoroughgoing exegetical and critical study of the book itself. There are however some general and historical considerations which dispose us to ask in anticipation whether, in spite of disturbances of order and other difficulties, there may not be a consistent plan wrought out by a single mind — a plan which takes up into itself all parts of the book, as serving the author's complex purpose, though in some cases these be suggested by, or adapted from, other sources. As regards historical evidence it does not need much argument to show that in all probability our present form of the book is that which was current in the earlier part of the second century. The knowledge of it is too widely and continuously attested to leave room for serious doubt. Irenæus, whose personal knowledge reaches back into the first half of the century, attests its existence in many, some of them *ancient*, copies ; [1] and if the form known to the still earlier witness, Justin Martyr, as a book circulating among Christians and attributed to an apostle,[2] had differed from these copies, it could hardly have been so completely displaced by these later compositions that no trace of it was left. This is tantamount to saying that the present form of the book is identical with that existing (possibly we may say in at least seven copies, — one for each of the seven churches) at the end of the first century, the age to which the book belongs.[3] In view then of the different opinions concerning its structure we may say that the writer who claimed to be, and was accepted as, the author, sent it out in its present form, as either (1) a collection of independent and loosely related documents, or (2) a revision or enlargement of an older book or books, or (3) an ordered unit in which every part, however suggested to him, had in his mind a significant place in his plan. Since however the paragraphs which seem opposed to a unity are of such a kind that they could not in general be conceived to be originally documents standing alone, apart from a larger context, and since a clear dramatic sequence is, as seen above, found in the book taken as a whole, the theory of a mere collection of independent documents is inconceivable. Even if the passages in question be, as some suppose, not isolated frag-

---

[1] See p. 339.   [2] See p. 338.   [3] See p. 206 ff.

ments but parts of complete documents from which they have
been excerpted, the objection is not removed ; a writer, who
has made the other parts of his assumed collection into so
systematic a whole, could not have destroyed this order by
introducing paragraphs unrelated to the rest.   In other words
the theory demands a more general disorder in the book than
we find.   Few, to be sure, would maintain a wholly planless
collection of documents, but the objection is equally cogent
against the theory that the Apocalypse was produced by a
loose combination or commingling of different sources around
a common center, without effort to harmonize one source with
another so far as to make a united whole.

On the other hand there is strong objection to theories
which would remove the difficulties in question by the supposition of an earlier apocalypse, whether Jewish or Christian,
revised and enlarged by a late editor seeking to adapt it to
readers of his own faith and time — an editor who is assumed
to have done his work so imperfectly as to combine much disturbing and conflicting material.   This earlier apocalypse is
very commonly conceived to consist, broadly speaking, of
those parts of the present book which taken together form a
close, uninterrupted unit as shown above.   With a little skill
there may be formed from these portions a harmonious and
powerful apocalypse — one which, if the Christian features
characterizing it be not arbitrarily expunged,[1] embodies in
splendid form the same prophecies which in the Gospels are
attributed to our Lord, and which appear in the Pauline and
Petrine epistles.   In the first place then it seems impossible
that a book of this nature, so expressive of the hope of the
Church at the time and appearing in the last half of the first
century with a large number of other Christian writings,
should not, like these, have survived or been known to the
Church in the second century, especially since, according to
the supposition, it survived till late in the first century.   And,
secondly, it is incredible that a Christian writer at the end of
the century in sending out the present form of the book as a
description of visions specially given to himself should really
have used the book of another, a book doubtless as well known

[1] Cf. Vischer's hypothesis, p. 229.

to many of his contemporaries as to himself, and should have enlarged it by insertions which must have been felt to disturb the harmony and obscure the meaning of the original writing. In some instances, places more inappropriate and less likely to be chosen for the insertion of foreign matter could not be found. Or if this earlier book be supposed to be the work of the same author, it is difficult to believe that a writer, who frequently shows so keen a sense of artistic grouping and such adherence to schematic form, should in the revision of his book have done such violence to his habits of thought and composition. If the added portions contain, as some suppose, separate oracles which he wished to preserve by making them a part of his book, one able to command his material, as he shows himself elsewhere, could hardly have failed to give the enlarged composition a form as clearly a unit as was the earlier book.

What is here said would be true in part if, as has been more frequently maintained, this earlier writing were a *Jewish* apocalypse, worked over into our form of the book for Christian use. Other objections also would then arise ; the Jewish writing formed by the combination of these portions, pruned of all their Christian features (and this is done only by a most arbitrary process of erasure), would form an apocalypse more splendid than any of those preserved to us in Jewish literature, and it is hard to believe that it could have perished so completely that not even its name should anywhere be mentioned. Further, we see from the treatment of the Jewish apocalypses of Enoch, the Testaments of the Twelve Patriarchs, 2 Esdras and others, that when the Christians sought to adapt such writings to their own use, they limited themselves to the interpolation of a sentence or paragraph here and there ; [1] they did not transform them and represent them as visions given to a Christian seer of their own day.

These general considerations touching the composition of the Apocalypse are but preliminary to others more specific, to come up later in their appropriate connections. [2] *Certainly the ultimate test of unity can be reached only by the exegesis of the whole book, by a study of the author's language, literary manner, and teaching, and by a survey of the contents of the book in its*

---

[1] Cf. Lücke I. 229.   [2] See *Critical Analyses*, pp. 224 ff., and Com.

plan and several parts. The indications furnished in these various connections will be spoken of in later paragraphs and in the Commentary.

The *nature of the unity,* however, as it is understood in the present Commentary on the Apocalypse, should be distinctly stated. It is a unity consistent with a free use of material derived more or less directly from other sources, and even with the construction of whole paragraphs on the basis of such material. Reminiscences of the Old Testament appear here oftener than in any other book of the New Testament. More than half the number of verses contain allusions to the Old Testament, or imagery, figures or language therefrom ;[1] especially frequent is the use of Daniel and the apocalyptic parts of Isaiah, Ezekiel, and Zechariah ; also non-canonical apocalyptic literature has left its impress upon thought as well as upon form. There is however nothing approaching a literal transference of whole paragraphs from any *known* writer. A few examples will illustrate the author's use of passages occurring in other sources known to us. The description of the plague of the locusts (9^{2-11}) is taken from Joel 1-2 ; the plagues of the seven trumpets and the seven bowls (8-9, 16) chiefly from Exodus 7-10 ; the episode of the 'little book' (chapt. 10) from Ezk. 2-3 ; the representations of the beast (chapt. 13) from Dan. 7 ; the summons to the birds of prey ($19^{17 \text{ f.}}$) from Ezk. $39^{17 \text{ f.}}$; much of the lament over the fall of the great city (chapt. 18) from Ezk. 26-27. But a comparison of these passages in our book with the parallel portions of the Old Testament will show how remote the author is from inserting mere excerpts from other writings. He is indebted to these both in idea and language, yet he uses the material with great independence, changing, omitting, adding, in every way adapting to his own purpose. He is as far as possible from a copyist ; he writes rather as one whose memory is filled with vivid thoughts and expressions which he uses to unfold his great theme. Now his treatment of sources in these cases gives us information of the utmost value for the interpretation of other passages which may possibly be formed after apocalypses *not known* to us. Examples of portions quite generally

[1] Cf. in WH the Table of Quotations from O.T. ; Hühn, II. 234 ff.

held by recent critics to be taken from non-extant apocalypses are the episode of the staying of the winds and the sealing of Israel (7^{1-8}) ; the measuring of the temple and the history of the two witnesses (11^{1-13}) ; the dragon's persecution of the woman and her seed (chapt. 12). If now in the paragraphs mentioned above as moulded after the Old Testament we may certainly believe we have a criterion of the author's method of handling matter not original with himself, then it is clear that the supposed fragments of non-extant apocalypses, if such they are, were treated with similar freedom. These suggested forms, symbols, and imagery, but were not literally followed ; they were worked over with a mastery that adapted them to the purpose which the author had in mind. The original connection, if known, might to be sure make clear some *details* retained and obscure to us, as the figures of the olive tree and the candlestick in 11^4 are explained by the source from which they are taken, Zech. 4. But whether, for example, the prophecy of the occupation of Jerusalem by the Gentiles in 11^{1-2} is a Jewish fragment of the year 70 A.D., whether the picture of the Beast in 13^{1-10} is a fragment from the time of Caligula, Nero, or Vespasian, are questions which, though interesting from the standpoint of literary criticism, are secondary in the interpretation of the book. The ultimate inquiry must be, whether such paragraphs have a place in the author's plan and what is their significance in *his intention.* This inquiry will be considered in the respective places in the Commentary.

The use of language as bearing on unity. The presumption of the foregoing pages in favor of the unity of the Apocalypse is confirmed by the use of language found throughout the book. That in its existing form it is the product of a single mind, whether originating or working over derived material, seems to be put beyond reasonable doubt by the uniform presence of a characteristic style.[1] As regards (*a*) vocabulary, (*b*) favorite expressions, (*c*) arrangement of words in a sentence, (*d*) grammatical peculiarities and even grammatical errors, the book has among the writings of the New Testament characteristics of its

---

[1] Weyland's effort to find a peculiarity of language in certain parts is not successful. Cf. p. 231,

own, which appear with as great a uniformity as can be affirmed of any work of complex structure. It is not possible to excerpt any considerable portion which departs from this style so far as to justify its attribution to a different writer.[1]

(a) Exclusive of proper names and a few variations in the Mss., there are in the book nearly 875 different words. Something over a hundred of these (about one in eight) are not found in any other New Testament book, though most of them occur in the Septuagint or non-biblical writers. These words, not found in other New Testament writings, are largely due to peculiarity in subject matter; fully a fifth of them belong to the paragraph describing the downfall of the great city (chapt. 18), an equal number to the description of the New Jerusalem (21–22⁵), nearly 20 to the vision of the first six trumpets (8–9), nearly 10 to the vision of the seven bowls (chapt. 16), paragraphs which all fall naturally into the plan of the Apocalypse and cannot reasonably be separated as inappropriate insertions. The long paragraph of the seven epistles (2–3), dealing with common topics of everyday Christian life, contains not more than 10 such words. Most of these peculiar words are the only words used in our book for their respective ideas; that is, there are not in other parts of the book terms parallel with these, which might be taken to indicate different authors. In the few cases of parallel words,[2] these are found either in the same paragraph or distributed through paragraphs which cannot be omitted without destroying the structure of the book. In some cases[3] an unusual word is chosen because of its special appropriateness (Cf. Com. *in loc.*). There is nothing in these various usages to indicate difference of authorship. As regards the rest of the vocabulary, that which is common to our book and the other New Testament writings, no portion shows a use of terms sufficiently diverse to set it apart from others. (b) Some examples of the use of *favorite* words and expressions will likewise indicate the work of one writer throughout. The number of occurrences in each case is given after the example: αἷμα (19), ἀναβαίνω (13), ἀνοίγω (26), ἀποκτείνω (15), ἀρνίον (28), βάλλω (28), βιβλίον (23), γῆ (82), γράφω (29), δίδωμι (57), ἔθνος (23), ἐνώπιον (35), θάλασσα (26), θρόνος (46), κάθημαι (33), μέγας (80), νικάω (17), ὄνομα (37), οὐρανός (52), πίπτω (23), προσκυνέω (24), πῦρ (25), στόμα (22), ὕδωρ (18). It will be seen that these words, to which many additions might be made, occur very often, and a comparison with the other books of the New Testament will show that with perhaps the sole exception of αἷμα they occur much oftener here than elsewhere; they may then be regarded as specially characteristic of the vocabulary of the book. And their distribution is significant; of these 24 examples every chapter contains from 12 to 19,

---

[1] Upon language, grammar, etc., cf. Lücke II. 448 ff., Bousset 159 ff., Swete CXV. ff. and 311 ff.

[2] *E.g.* διάδημα and στέφανος; κυκλόθεν and κύκλῳ; μάχαιρα and ῥομφαία; πλήσσω and πατάσσω.

[3] *E.g.* βιβλαρίδιον chapt. 10, elsewhere βιβλίον; κατασφραγίζω 5¹; elsewhere σφραγίζω.

except chapt. 22 which has 8. Still more striking is the recurrence of set phrases. Examples of these, recurring sometimes with slight variation, are : λόγος τοῦ θεοῦ καὶ ἡ μαρτυρία Ἰησοῦ 1[2, 9], 6[9], 12[11, 17], 20[4] ; Κύριος ὁ θεός, ὁ παντοκράτωρ 1[8], 4[8], 11[17], 15[3], 16[7, 14], 19[6, 15], 21[22] ; οἶνος τοῦ θυμοῦ τῆς πορνείας, or τοῦ θεοῦ, or τῆς ὀργῆς 14[8, 10], 16[19], 17[2], 18[3], 19[15] ; φυλὴ καὶ γλῶσσα καὶ λαὸς καὶ ἔθνος 5[9], 7[9], 10[11], 11[9], 13[7], 14[6] ; οἱ μικροὶ καὶ οἱ μεγάλοι 11[18], 13[16], 19[5, 18], 20[12] ; ἀληθινός with πιστός, ἅγιος, or δίκαιος 3[7, 14], 6[10], 15[3], 16[7], 19[2, 11], 21[5], 22[6] ; οἱ βασιλεῖς τῆς γῆς 1[5], 6[15], 15[3], 16[14], 17[2, 18], 18[3, 9], 19[19], 21[24] ; φωνὴ μεγάλη 1[10], 5[2, 12], 6[10], 7[2, 10], 8[13], 10[3], 11[12, 15], 12[10], 14[7, 9, 15, 18], 6[1, 17], 19[1, 17], 21[3]. It will be noticed that these are distributed promiscuously through the book and that the paragraphs felt to disturb the unity share this trait of the writer in common with others.   (c) As regards the arrangement of the principal parts of a sentence the book shows extraordinary monotony. As a rule the governing word precedes the governed. The subject usually follows the verb, though there are many exceptions and these are found in every part. With far fewer variations the object follows the verb, though here too most chapters furnish one or more exceptions; attributives, that is, adjectives, adjective phrases and dependent genitives, follow the noun almost without variation, excepting ἄλλος and adjectives of number and quantity ; but μέγας which occurs 80 times is found, when attributive, only once (18[2i]) or perhaps twice (16[1]) before the noun. Variations from these principles of order, so far as they occur, are not grouped in any part of the book in such a way as to indicate different writers.   (d) In certain grammatical pecul-iarities and irregularities, the Apocalypse stands alone among writings known to us. It is not possible to take up these with any fullness here ; many will be noticed in the Commentary. (For a good summary see Bousset 159 ff.) Most of these grammatical peculiarities occur many times and are charac-teristic, not of any one section of the book, but of the whole. Some examples will suffice for the present purpose : (1) Departure from the laws of agreement in number, case, or gender : a verb singular with several connected subjects, or with a plu. subj. (8[7], 9[12]) ; a plu. vb. with neuter plu. subj. (1[19]) ; the nominative in apposition with some other case (1[15]) ; change of case or gender in an adjective or participle (11[4], 12[5], 14[19]), especially in λέγων and ἔχων (13[14], 9[14]), change to nominative in a dependent noun (7[9]). (2) Indifferent interchange of tense in the same paragraph (3[9], 11[8–18]) (3) Omission of the copula, which is as often absent as expressed. (4) The article repeated with each noun in a series, and with adjectives and adjec-tive phrases after a noun which has the article (2[19], 4[11], 3[12]), an idiom occurring with great frequency. (5) The repetition of the antecedent of a pronoun or adverb in the relative clause (3[8], 12[6]).

Critical Analyses of the Apocalypse. The unity of the Apocalypse was first made the subject of extended critical investigation in the work of Völter, *The Origin of the Apocalypse*, which appeared in 1882. As early as the seventeenth century Grotius (*Adnotationes ad N. T.* 1644), while hold-ing to the apostolic authorship of the whole, assigned different parts to different places and dates, and his view, though generally rejected, was followed by Hammond (*A Paraphrase and Annotation upon all the books of the N. T.* 1653) and a few others, *e.g.* Lackemacher and Clericus. This primitive movement toward criticism remained almost forgotten, certainly without any influential adherent, for more than a century; even Semler, the forefather of modern biblical critics, while strongly opposing the canonical value of the Apocalypse, did not attack its unity. In the early part of the nineteenth century the question was taken up anew and with a nearer approach to scientific method by Vogel (*Commentationes VII. de Apoc. Joann.* 1811–1816), who attributed certain parts to the apostle John and others to John the Presbyter. Vogel's hypothesis was not definitively accepted by any large number of scholars. Berthold (*Historisch-kritische Einleitung* 1812–1819) adopted it with reserve; Bleek at first followed it so far as to assign different parts to different dates, though maintaining unity of authorship (John the Presbyter), but subsequently he changed his view and maintained unity of date also (*Beiträge zur Evangelienkritik* 1846, *Vorlesungen über d. Ap.*, posthumously edited by Hossbach 1862, 116 ff.); De Wette in the first edition of his *Introduction* (1826) followed the earlier opinion of Bleek, but in the second edition (1830), under the influence of Ewald (*Commentarius in Ap. Johan.* 1828, *Studien u. Kritiken* 1829) returned to an energetic maintenance of the unity of the work. The unity became so far an axiom with scholars that Lücke (II. 870) could say, ' At the present time [1852] all the hypotheses of the origination of the Apocalypse from parts composed at different times by one and the same author or by several authors seem to be given up and set down as *ad acta.*' But Schleiermacher's *Introduction*, published a few years before (*Ein. in d. N. T.*, edited posthumously by Wold 1845), and regarded by Lücke as the last in the critical movement against the unity (II. 869), was destined to give at a later date a new impulse to hypotheses of division. Schleiermacher, though not giving any detailed examination of the book, set forth the theory that it is composed of a large number of visions seen by a single seer at different dates and having no relation to one another. He called attention, not to differences in historical situation and interruptions in logical order, but rather to what he considers incongruities in thought, especially as regards representations of Christ. In this he exerted an influence in much of the later criticism. Völter in 1893 says, ' The critical flame of recent times was as it were kindled by his judgment concerning the Apocalypse ' (*Problem*, p. 2). Both Weizsäcker and Völter, who revived the problem of unity in 1882, show at least in their later writings traces of Schleiermacher's leading in criticism, though not adopting his results as regards the composition of the book. Weizsäcker in the course of an article in the *Theologische Zeitung* (1882, p. 78 f.) incidentally expressed his opinion in quite general terms and without reasons: ' As regards the Apocalypse it is a question whether we are to look at it as a single document. I confess to the opinion that we have in this writing . . . a composition which in its origin is a compilation.' In this article he does not really go much beyond his predecessors, but at a later date he gives a fuller, though still very brief, statement of his view, together with reasons, as will be seen below.

Q

Völter a little later in the same year published his work referred to above, *The Origin of the Apocalypse*, and for the first time gave a discussion of the problem, which took up the various parts of the book in detail. The two scholars offered different solutions of the problem and along lines which appear on one side or the other through all subsequent criticism. Weizsäcker leads the movement in the direction of a *combination theory*, which in the form given by him conceives the author of the Apocalypse himself to have *incorporated* certain fragments into the organism of his work, though many later critics adopted a hypothesis of compilation which supposes a more or less mechanical collection of unorganized sources. Völter on the other hand maintained a theory of *revision*, according to which the present form of the book was reached through a series of versions enlarged and modified from time to time by later editors to conform it to new circumstances. Through these two scholars an overwhelming flood of critical discussion was set in motion, which has continued through these subsequent years. Their theories in the precise form advocated by them and in details are not followed; but the influence of their methods and of their critical observations appears throughout. It will be seen that in later criticism the two processes of compilation and revision are often combined. It is obviously impossible in this place to attempt any large survey of these numerous writings; the utmost that can be done is to state briefly the hypotheses advanced by the leaders in the various phases of the movement, and to make some general observations on the validity of these.

Völter. Völter's first edition was soon followed by a second, enlarged and modified, and this in turn by various others works, the last appearing in 1911. (*Entstehung d. Ap.*[2] 1885; *Die Offenbarung Johan. keine ursprünglich jüd. Ap.* 1886; various articles in theolog. journals 1886–1891; *Das Problem d. Ap.* 1893; *Die Offenbarung Johan. neu untersucht.* 1904[1], 1911[2].). In this long period of activity he frequently changes his views, though these changes relate for the most part to details and not to his characteristic propositions, *revision* and a *Christian* origin of the whole as opposed to the use of *Jewish* apocalypses as sources. According to his latest publication he finds in the Apocalypse the work of *five* different periods (p. 51). (1) the primitive Apocalypse of John (probably John Mark, certainly not the apostle or the presbyter) written in A.D. 65. This consists of 1^{4-6}, $4-9$, 11^{14-18}, $14^{1-3, \ 6-8, \ 14-20}$, 19^{1-10}. In order to reconstruct thus the primitive Apocalypse it is necessary to omit or revise the following verses, which are included in these paragraphs, but are ascribed, altogether or in part, to later hands: 4^1, $5^{6, \ 9, \ 10, \ 11-14}$, 6^{16}, 7^{9-17}, $11^{15, \ 18}$, 14^1, $19^{2 \ b, \ 3 \ b, \ 10}$. (2) (56 ff.) An appendix added A.D. 68 by the author himself and consisting of 10, 17, 18, 11^{1-13}, chapters 17 and 18 being originally inserted between 10 and 11. Here again certain verses containing the work of a reviser are to be omitted at least in part; these are 11^8, $17^{1, \ 6, \ 14}$, 18^{20}. (3) (135) A revision, consisting chiefly of an insertion made by Cerinthus in Vespasian's time (69–79 A.D.). This is composed of $12-13$, 14^{9-12}, $15-16$, $19^{11}-21^8$; here must be omitted or modified 12^{11}, 13^8, 14^{10}, 15^4, $16^{15, \ 19 \ b}$, $19^{13 \ b}$; and to prepare for this insertion, $5^{10 \ b}$, $11^{15, \ 18}$ were added. (4) (141 ff.) A revision made early in Domitian's reign (A.D. 81–96). This transferred 17–18 from the original place between 10 and 11 to its present place after 16. To facilitate this change the redactor added $16^{19 \text{ b}}$, 17^{1}, and to make the connection of the transposed passage with the following clearer he inserted $19^{2 \text{ b, 3 b}}$. To him are also due 1^{7-8}, $21^{9}-22^{21}$, except $22^{7, 12, 13, 16-20}$, and he made insertions or changes in $5^{6, 9, 11-14}$, 6^{16}, 7^{9-17}, 11^{8}, 12^{11}, 13^{8}, $14^{1, 10}$, 17^{14}. (5) (148 ff.) The final revision made late in Domitian's time consisted of the addition of the introductory parts, 1^{1-3} and $1^{9}-3^{22}$, also the insertion or change of 14^{18}, 16^{15}, 17^{6}, 19^{10}, $22^{7, 12, 13, 16-20}$.

As the principal guiding lines in his analysis of the Apocalypse, Völter finds in different parts of it want of consecutiveness, combination of discordant elements, disturbance of historical order, juxtaposition of a human and a divine Messiah and of Judaistic and universal conceptions of Christianity, and a Cerinthian distinction between a heavenly Christ and Jesus. And his reconstruction through a series of revisions is determined by the effort to reconcile differences, to separate and recombine according as harmony and historical and logical sequence are supposed to require. He has worked out his theory with wonderful ingenuity, though probably no one now will entirely accept it. But the influence of his criticism has been widely felt in later study. Some of the more important points in his argument will be noticed in the Commentary on passages with which they are concerned. Objections of a general character are: that he not only overlooks the strong evidence of the work of one mind in the book, but he finds disagreements and difficulties where none really exist, and employs an unwarranted exegesis, especially in passages touching the person and function of Christ. Further, it is very improbable that all these different recensions, superior as they were in homogeneity according to the hypothesis, should have been so completely displaced by this last one as to leave no independent trace of their existence. But apart from all other difficulties the arbitrariness of procedure in omitting and rearranging paragraphs, in erasing and modifying isolated verses and phrases in order to secure conformity to a theory, is opposed to all sound criticism. With a similar boldness in rearranging and revising it would not be difficult to show, for example, that the Epistle to the Romans in a primitive form taught the limitation of justification by faith to the Jews, and that a reviser added the parts in which the logical result of the doctrine is extended to the Gentiles.

Weizsäcker. Weizsäcker's very general utterance in favor of a composite origin of the Apocalypse, referred to above, was made more precise four years later in his *Apostolic Age (Das Apostol. Zeitalter der christ. Kirche* 1886[1], 1892[2]), in which he presents his view briefly with grounds for the same (486 ff., 358 ff.). The statement of his argument here given is based on the second edition of his work. He regards the Apocalypse as the work of an author, the unity of whose plan is maintained by the sequence of the three connected series of scenes determined by the seven seals, the seven trumpets and the seven bowls (489). Into the framework thus formed the writer has incorporated various single visions not his own and having various origins. The book then is not one grand scene moving on as a unit in itself, nor is it a series of such scenes joined to one another naturally; it is an intricate composition which holds fast an artificial thread through many digressions, and maintains the connection by allusions which refer sometimes to what has preceded, sometimes to what is yet to follow (488). The principal portions thus taken up from foreign sources are the introduction, including the seven epistles, chaps. 1–3, the conclusion in 21–22, and chapters 7, 10–11, 12, 13, 17–18. This analysis is based on the following grounds: the introduction and conclusion have no close connection with the great prophecies of the book and contain no reference to the condition and circumstances of the times reflected in these. The great prophetic portions, mentioned above as incorporations, have no relation to the three series of signs which form the framework; while the latter relate to destructive wars vaguely pictured and great movements in nature, the former draw their material from present realities, or at least touch present historical circumstances (489). As regards *form* also, these parts do not fit into the structure of the plan. Chapter 7 is inserted between the sixth and seventh seals; 11^{1-18} with its own introduction, chapt. 10, between the sixth and seventh trumpets, transfers the scene to another place. After, or within, the last trumpet scene, two great scenes independent of each other are introduced in 12 and 13, but in 14 the former thread is resumed. Chapters 17–18 come in after the seven bowls, but have no connection with these. Weizsäcker argues further that the portions which he attributes to other sources are not, as are the other portions, shown by an angel but are direct visions; these portions do not have a common origin, for example, chapter 11 sets us in Jerusalem, while 13 and 17 show no relation to a Jewish provenience (490); visions are repeated with a different meaning, for example the 144,000 are in chapt. 7 the Christian remnant of the Jews, but in chapt. 14 they are those believers who have preserved themselves especially holy through chastity; some things in the author's plan are not carried out, for example, the last three trumpets are to bring three woes, bnt only two, 9^{12}, 11^{14}, are given; there are anticipations revealing different writers, for example, 11^7 anticipates chapt. 13 (491); there are differences in dátes — while the book was written at the end of the first century, some portions, as chapts. 7, 11^{1-18}, fall before A.D. 70 (492 ff., 358 ff.). Further details will be noticed in the Commentary.

Weizsäcker's treatment of the problem is brief, being given in subordinate parts of his history, and leaves much that is requisite for completeness (Weyland says of Völter and Weizsäcker that 'they both contributed much to the solution of the problem of the Apocalypse. Each of them did it in his own way. The one gave too much, the other too little.' *Omwerkings.* etc. 53), but his criticism is masterful and has led the way for all later efforts which seek to do justice to the evidence for unity on the one hand, and for diversity on the other, that is, the theory that a single author has conceived the plan as a whole and has incorporated into this fragments, isolated visions, derived from earlier sources. Apart from objections to details, the great defect in the hypothesis, as Weizsäcker presented it, is that it fails to account for the incorporation of these large portions of the book into a plan in which they have no organic place. A writer who could conceive and carry through a plan which, these insertions being omitted, moves on so clearly and harmoniously to a great consummation, a plan so powerfully dramatic, cannot be imagined to have broken it up and overloaded it with irrelevant matter of foreign origin, to such an extent that it is lost in the accretions. Had he wished merely to give an appropriate setting for these collected prophecies, he could not be supposed to have adopted this form, which in reality fails of that purpose. This defect of Weizsäcker's is one that appears in much of the criticism following his lines. *No hypothesis which accepts the general unity of the Apocalypse and also the presence of incorporated material in it can be satisfactory, unless it furnishes reasonable grounds for assigning to all the material used a significant place in an organized whole.*

Vischer. In the same year with Weizsäcker's work referred to above (1886) criticism of the Apocalypse entered on a new stage in the appearance of Vischer's treatment of the question (*Die Offenbarung Johan, eine jüdische Apokalypse in christlicher Bearbeitung*, 1886). As the Jewish apocalypses, Enoch, 2 Esd., the Testaments of the Twelve Patriarchs and others were taken up in the first and second centuries by the Christians and received additions at their hands, so Vischer argued that the Apocalypse of John was originally a Jewish apocalypse, which was worked over by a Christian writer to adapt and recommend it to the use of his coreligionists. In this recension chapters 1–3 were prefixed in place of the original introduction, $22^{6\text{-}21}$ was added as a conclusion and numerous passages and phrases were inserted. (These occur in $5^{6,\,8,\,9\text{-}14}$, $6^{1,\,16}$, $7^{9\text{-}17}$, 9^{11}, $11^{8,\,15}$, $12^{11,\,17}$, $13^{8,\,9\text{-}10}$, $14^{1\text{-}5,\,10,\,12\text{-}13}$, 15^{3}, $16^{15,\,16}$, $17^{6,\,14}$, 18^{20}, $19^{7,\,9\text{-}10,\,11,\,13}$, $20^{4,\,6}$, $21^{5\text{-}8,\,9,\,14,\,22,\,23,\,27}$, $22^{1,\,3}$, p. 116 ff.) Harnack wrote a commendatory appendix to Vischer's brochure, and the theory was hailed widely as solving the chief difficulties of the Apocalypse. Many of Vischer's critical observations are of real value, though his theory as a whole is now no longer in favor. He founded his hypothesis on the supposition that there are running throughout the book two distinct and irreconcilable lines of thought, the one Jewish, the other Christian. He finds on the one hand a Jewish Messiah whose birth is still in the future and who is to appear merely as God's instrument of wrath for the destruction of the world; on the other hand, the Christian Messiah who has already appeared in Jesus, the Lamb who has redeemed men by his blood, and who now sits enthroned with God in heaven. In the fundamental Jewish document the messianic kingdom was confined to Jews who keep the commandments of God, while in the added parts it consists of an innumerable multitude out of every nation who are redeemed by the blood of Jesus through faith in him. In the one part God is judge, in the other Christ (71 ff.). And similarly the distinction is traced out through manifold details in representation and expectation. In the recovery of this primitive Jewish apocalypse, Vischer begins his study with chapters 11–12, which after the erasure of a few (Christian) sentences he finds to be purely Jewish and to contain the key to the whole book (31 f.). Then by a process of free excision in the preceding and following chapters he succeeds in constructing an apocalypse conformed entirely to Hebrew eschatology. He endeavors to show that the excluded passages and phrases can all be omitted without injury to the connection and in most cases to its improvement even (34 ff.). In this process the 28 instances of the mention of the Lamb are all excluded from the text (38 ff.), so are also the six instances of the name of Jesus (60 ff. The name of Jesus occurs 14 times, but 8 of these are in the introduction and conclusion, parts by the hypothesis due to the reviser), and in short everything which has a distinctively Christian character. The indication of unity furnished by language and style Vischer meets with the contention that the primitive Jewish document was written in Hebrew or Aramaic and translated into Greek by the Christian reviser, who wrote the added parts (37 f.). Vischer is much influenced by Völter; and his theory and method, widely as they differ, are open to a similar charge of arbitrariness, and disregard of the evidence for unity. Some details will be noticed in the Commentary. The difficulties arising from the assumption that such a Jewish apocalypse was entirely lost, and from a comparison of the treatment of other apocalypses by the Christians, have been spoken of above (pp. 218 ff.). Two general considerations are added here. (1) The foundation on which the hypothesis rests, the assumed coexistence of irreconcilable Jewish and Christian elements, is false. The same two elements, so far as they *actually* exist in the Apocalypse (not as they are by misinterpretation assumed to exist there) are found combined in the Gospels and the Pauline epistles. This we should expect in a Jewish-Christian writer, above all in a Christian apocalyptist, since apocalyptic ideas and forms are to so large an extent derived immediately from Jewish sources. But even if it were otherwise, the existence of incongruous ideas in the same writing without an attempt at mediation is too frequent in literature to establish in itself diversity of authorship. (2) It is pertinent to ask whether instead of beginning with chapts. 11–12 revised and made into a Jewish fragment it would not serve a saner critical process to begin with the Introduction (1–3) and follow the Christian keynote found there through the remaining chapters, where it so often reappears, and thus to deduce a Christian character for the whole; this procedure has the advantage that it does not make it necessary to expunge or revise large parts of the book as *impossible* with an original Christian apocalyptist.

Weyland.   Independently of Vischer and at the same time, the Dutch scholar, Weyland, published in the *Theologische Studien* of Utrecht (1886) a dissertation presenting a similar hypothesis, but assuming *two* Jewish sources, from which the Christian compiler drew, instead of one. This view Weyland set forth more fully two years afterwards in a work (*Omwerkings-en Compilatie-Hypothesen toegepast op de Apokalypse van Johannes* 1888) in which he also took cognizance of the hypotheses of Vischer and other later critics. He agrees essentially with Vischer as to the parts of the Apocalypse to be assigned to Jewish and Christian sources respectively, differing only in some details. But the Jewish portions he assigns to two different documents, the first of which he places about 69 A.D., the other

81 A.D. (p. 111). The work of the Christian compiler, who combined rather mechanically (p. 68), he puts in A.D. 130–140 (p. 129). İt is not necessary to give here Weyland's analysis in full. The following passages with a few modifications he assigns to his earliest Jewish source : 10, 11$^{1-13}$, 12–13, 14$^{6-11}$, 15$^{2-4}$, 19$^{11-21}$, 20, 21$^{1-8}$ (p. 176). The other portions are assigned to his later Jewish source and his Christian source in essential agreement with Vischer's table. His distinction between Jewish and Christian parts is made on grounds similar to those urged by Vischer ; he adds the absence of a fundamental thought running throughout (176 ff.) and also a peculiarity of language which he finds characteristic of the Christian redactor. As regards the use of language, he says, ' We shall not try to offer a proof of the difference in style between the different parts. This difference can be felt, at least by him who has feeling, but with great difficulty described ' (138). The critics are evidently without the ' feeling ' requisite, as they are for the most part agreed that no such diversity of style exists. Weyland's *argument* is occupied with the effort to prove a lack of unity and the presence of both Jewish and Christian elements. He does not take up in a systematic form the evidence for his theory of *two* separate Jewish documents, though in the course of his discussion he incidentally urges certain general differences, especially in dates and historical circumstances (101 ff.), and in the localities to which the visions relate (111 f.). Much of what is said above of objections to the theories and methods of Völter and Vischer is equally true of the work of Weyland. It is too arbitrary and introduces too many difficulties to be accepted as a solution of its problem. The significance of Weyland's hypothesis in the course of criticism lies in the fact that it is the beginning of recent *compilation* theories, that is, those which view the Apocalypse as a complex, formed more or less *mechanically* from a number of independent documents.

Sabatier. The fresh impulse given to criticism of the Apocalypse by Vischer's publication produced in France the two closely related studies of Sabatier and Schoen, which however reached a result directly the reverse of Vischer's hypothesis. With these critics the nucleus of the book is a *Christian* apocalypse whose author has taken up into it a series of earlier Jewish oracles. The main point in their position is similar to that of Weizsäcker, and they may be regarded as a link between him and the critics who have taken the field since the waning of the theories of Vischer and Weyland, and who maintain a form of unity with incorporated fragments. Sabatier's booklet (*Les Origines Littéraires et la Composition de l'Apocalypse de Saint Jean*, 1888) though published a year later than Schoen's, properly precedes the latter in our survey, because Schoen's study is in part based on that of Sabatier, as presented in his lectures at the École des Hautes-Études and in an article published in the *Revue Critique*, 1887. As regards the Christian origin of the book Sabatier urges that the name John, as that of the author, is decisive ; for it is incredible that the author, if the Apostle, should have sent out in his name a Jewish apocalypse, touched up with Christian passages ; or if some other Christian bearing the name had wished to adapt a Jewish apocalypse to his readers, he would merely have made brief Christian insertions and have kept for the book the great authority of the reputed Jewish writer, as was done in the case of the other apocalypses (p. 8). Considering the book as a whole, Sabatier finds clear marks of unity and Christian origin; the epistolary form appears as a framework in the introduction and the close, and is also suggested by the frequent use of the pronoun I in the body of the work; the introductory chapters 1–3, Christian in character and inseparably connected with what follows, present in accumulated form the symbolism and apocalyptic rhetoric of all the rest (p. 10 f.); the body of the work is conceived upon the basis of what is seen from the Gospels to be a traditional Christian scheme of the Last Days, the ἀρχὴ ὠδίνων, the θλῖψις μεγάλη, the τέλος, *the beginning of sorrows, the great tribulation, the End* — a scheme of the final destinies of the world here carried out in the form of an imposing drama in the three acts of the seals, the trumpets, and the bowls (p. 17 f.). But within this framework Sabatier finds portions having no relation to the context or dramatic movement, and entirely Jewish in conception and expectation; their prophecies are connected with great historic situations, their scene is placed on earth, while that of the drama itself is in heaven, and they contain duplicates of scenes given in other parts of the drama as primarily conceived (19 ff., 26 ff., 35 f.). The portions thus characterized and distinguished from the rest of the book are earlier Jewish oracles which the author of the Apocalypse has inserted in his book, as prophecies concerning the destinies of humanity. These inserted oracles are (p. 27): 11[1-13], 12–13, 14[6-20], 16[13-16], 17–19[4], 19[11-21], 20[1-10], 21[9]–22[5]; they were composed about 70 A.D., while the book itself belongs to the end of the century (p. 36). Sabatier's work is of permanent value in the study of the Apocalypse, but it exaggerates the Jewish character of the assumed insertions, overlooking the extent to which Christian apocalyptic adopts Jewish forms and conceptions; like similar theories it raises difficulty in projecting foreign material into the writer's plan in a haphazard way; and it fails to recognize the full scope and literary manner of the Apocalypse. See below, pp. 239 ff.

Schoen.   Schoen's treatment of the Apocalypse (*L'Origine de l'Apocalypse de St. Jean*, 1887) is, as already said, based on that of Sabatier and is largely in agreement with it. It emphasizes in like manner the general unity and Christian origin of the book, but confines the inserted Jewish oracles to somewhat narrower limits. These are 11[1-13], 12, 13, 18, in which however there are additions or revisions made by the Christian author, for example in 12[10-12, 13-17], 13[8-10], 18[20]; on the other hand the introduction of the Jewish oracles has in some places influenced the Christian parts, for example, chapt. 10, composed by the author to introduce the adopted oracles in general, so 17[1-6] to introduce chapt. 18, and 17[7-18] to explain the vision of chapt. 13 (132 ff.). The grounds taken both in defense of unity and Christian origin, and in the supposition of inserted Jewish oracles, are in general the same as those of Sabatier. The special significance of Schoen in reference to that form of criticism which recognizes in the Apocalypse both unity and diversity lies in the fact that he not only minimizes the incorporated material, but he also directly expresses the principle — though he does not carry this out practically into the exegesis of the difficult passages — that the Christian author gives to the borrowed oracles a new sense, that he sees in them a spiritual and symbolical force which suits them to the purpose of his great Christian apocalypse (144 f.).

Spitta. The *compilation* theory received a striking form at the hands of Spitta in a work of great fullness and subtle criticism (*Die Offenbarung des Johannes*, 1889). According to his analysis the foundation of the Apocalypse is a primitive Christian writing with which a later Christian redactor combined two separate Jewish documents (227), each of these three writings being a complete apocalypse culminating with the triumph of the people of God and the punishment of their enemies. The earliest of these, the first Jewish apocalypse, designated J^2, was written in the time of Pompey 63 B.C.; the second, the later Jewish Apocalypse, J^1, in the time of Caligula; the third, the primitive Christian Apocalypse, U (by John Mark, 502 f.), a decade before the destruction of Jerusalem. These documents were combined by a Christian redactor at the beginning of the second century, or possibly a little earlier, in Domitian's time (464, 529). The nucleus of each of these three separate sources, taken in chronological order, the reverse of the order in our Apocalypse, is formed respectively by the visions of the 7 bowls, the 7 trumpets, and the 7 seals (466, 549 ff.). A detailed exhibition of Spitta's distribution of the parts of the book among his several sources is not necessary here; it will be sufficient to indicate the passages which he places at the beginning and the close of the respective documents: U begins with address and introductory visions 1–5, and closes with 22^{8-21}; J^1 begins with the sealing of Israel 7^{1-8} and closes with the millennium, the judgment and the End 20^1–21^8; J^2 begins with 10 and closes with the new Jerusalem $21^{9\,\mathrm{ff.}}$. It is noticeable that Spitta, in contrast with Völter, Vischer, Weyland and others, joins 1–3 (with the excep-, tion of a few verses) closely with 4–5. Spitta's views will be noticed in the course of the Commentary. One who goes through the painful labor of reading his nearly 600 pages will find many valuable suggestions, but his hypothesis and the arguments advanced for it are too artificial to furnish a solution of the problems undertaken. His own anticipation (544) that he would be regarded 'hypercritical' is abundantly verified in the general opinion of later critics. It is interesting to observe that he perceives the difficulty in supposing three documents complete in themselves to have been thus broken up and interwoven with one another. He offers a solu tion which he thinks extremely *simple* ('*die denkbar einfachste*'); the redactor viewed the record of the plagues and other events before the End as a narrative, not of parallel, but of different, events; if then he wished to combine them it was necessary to insert one into the other, to make one flow out of the other, as a part of it (230 ff.). But Spitta's attempt to carry through this method of combination involves dissections and transferences as remote as possible from the *simple*. If the redactor had wished to present a unit in his book, he could not, according to Spitta's analysis, have made a worse failure; if on the other hand he had wished simply to preserve three separate documents, no plausible explanation can be offered of his process of rearrangement.

Erbes. Somewhat on the same lines with Völter, Erbes (*Die Offenbarung Johannis kritisch untersucht,* 1891) sees in the present form of the Apocalypse a *working over* of earlier Christian documents. The first of these, 12^1–13^{18}, $14^{9\,b\text{-}12}$, he assigns (184) to the year 40 A.D.; the second, the Apocalypse of St. John the Apostle (146 ff.), containing most of the remaining parts of the book, to 62 A.D.; from this second document are, however, to be excluded numerous insertions due to the final redactor who combined the two early documents. Most of these insertions are brief, consisting of a verse or two; longer insertions are 15^5–19^4, $19^{9\,b}$–20^{10}, 21^5–22^2. The final revision is assigned to 80 A.D. (In a later publication, *Der Antichrist in d. Schriften d. N. T.,* 1897, he places the final redactor possibly in the earlier part of Vespasian's time.) The value of Erbes' observations is recognized in subsequent criticism, but his hypothesis is open to objections similar to those urged against Völter's treatment of the book.

Rauch. As Völter's criticism was taken up and made the basis of a modified hypothesis by Erbes, so Vischer's theory received a new form at the hands of Rauch (*Die Offenbarung des Johannes untersucht nach ihrer Zusammensetzung u. d. Zeit ihrer Entstehung,* 1894). Though the latter in his interpretation and criticism is an eclectic, adopting from all his predecessors, yet in his results he agrees with Vischer in making our book a Jewish apocalypse with Christian additions. But in his analysis he goes even beyond Weyland; he supposes a primitive Jewish apocalypse of the year 62 A.D. (137), a continuous writing, picturing the general judgment of the world and consisting of five parts (93 f., 121): (*a*) the introductory visions (4–5); (*b*) the seal visions (6–7, $14^{1\text{-}5}$); (*c*) the trumpet visions (8–9^{21}, $11^{15\text{-}19}$); (*d*) the judgment (14^{14}–15^4, $16^{17\,b,\,18,\,19\,a,\,20}$); (*e*) the renewal of the world (19^{11}–21^8). This apocalypse was subsequently enlarged by the insertion of *five* distinct Jewish fragments — (1) $10^{1\,b,\,2\,a,\,5\text{-}7,\,4,\,9\text{-}11}$, $11^{1\text{-}13}$, $12^{1\text{-}17}$; (2) 12^{18}–13^{18}, $16^{13\text{-}16}$; (3) $14^{6\text{-}13}$; (4) 15^5–$16^{12,\,17\,a,\,21}$; (5) 17^1–19^6, 21^9–22^5 — some of them dating as early as 40 A.D. (134 f.). The Jewish apocalypse thus enlarged was then christianized in 79–81 A.D. (140) by a writer who added an introduction (1–3, except $1^{7\,b}$) and a conclusion ($22^{6\text{-}21}$), and inserted numerous verses in whole or in part, that is, all the passages possessing a specifically Christian coloring, interspersed in every chapter (except 8) throughout the book (121 ff.). Rauch's arguments against the unity and in support of the distinction between Jewish and Christian portions are the same as those of his predecessors. The five Jewish fragments assumed in his theory are determined by the supposed inappropriateness of the passages in their respective connections.

Other Forms of Analysis. In the foregoing paragraphs, the writers who have been most influential in recent criticism of the Apocalypse have been reviewed, and it will be seen that the pioneers in their respective directions are Völter, Weizsäcker (with his successors Sabatier and Schoen), Vischer, and Weyland. Other critics following similar lines of argument, some in one direction and some in another, have offered different analyses, to be sure, but their hypotheses are in reality only modifications or expansions of those of their forerunners, or oftener are combinations of these. It remains then to speak very briefly of some of the most noteworthy among these followers, or elaborators. *Schmidt (Anmerkungen über d. Composition d. Offenbarung Johannis,* 1891) distinguishes *three* principal Jewish portions: the vision of the seals (4^1–7^8); the vision of the trumpets (8^2–11^{15}) with the interpolation of a vision of Jerusalem (10^1–11^{13}); the book of the Messiah (12^1–22^5) with an interpolated vision of the fall of Rome (14^{6-20} and 17^1–19^5). With these *five* Jewish parts, of distinct origins, the oldest dating before 70 A.D., an independent Christian document of the time of Domitian, containing the seven epistles, was afterwards joined by a redactor who belongs to the early part of the second century; he also added of his own the introduction and conclusion. *Briggs (The Messiah of the Apostles,* 1895) views the book as " a collection of apocalypses of different dates issued in several successive editions. . . . In the main these apocalypses came from an early date, prior to the destruction of Jerusalem " (301). In the gradual combination of these separate documents the book passed through four editions: the first contained the apocalypses of the seals, the trumpets, and the bowls; the second added the apocalypse of the epistles; the third the apocalypses of the beasts and the dragon; in the fourth the final editor prefixed the title 1^{1-3}, and added the close 22^{18-20}. To him is due the present unity of the book; he " transposed parts of the different original apocalypses, . . . and so rearranged the whole material as best to suit the symmetry he was aiming to produce " (290). St. John the apostle was the author of the apocalypses of the epistles, the seals, and the bowls, and of all matter related thereto. The final editing was near the close of the first century, or early in the second century. *J. Weiss (Die Offenbarung d. Johan.,* 1904), makes the foundation and the larger part of the book a Christian apocalypse complete in itself, written in the latter half of the sixties (112) by a John of Asia Minor (47 ff., 112). A second document entering into the composition in its present form was a Jewish apocalypse framed in the year 70 A.D. (145) by a writer who combined several earlier visions, adding also material of his own (115 f.). This Jewish apocalypse formed the ' little book' to which the final editor refers in chapt. 10, and from which he means to say he derived certain of the prophecies following (42 f.). In the time of Domitian (6 f.) these two documents were combined by the final editor, who gave the book its present form, adapting these earlier prophecies to his own times, rearranging, interpreting, omitting parts, and adding others (39 ff.). Even those who do not accept the hypothesis of Weiss cannot fail to recognize the value of his work in the study of the Apocalypse. *Wellhausen (Analyse d. Offenbarung Johannis.* 1907) supposes the principal author, or more strictly editor, to have been a John (not the apostle) who wrote in the time of Domitian. Into the apocalypse which he framed he took up a large number of earlier sources, many of them Jewish, working them over, furnishing them with introductions and conclusions and making insertions. Most of these sources are later than the destruction of Jerusalem, but two at least, 11^{1-2} and 12^{1-17}, fall just before that event (3 f.). A later editor slightly revised this Johannine apocalypse, giving it its present form. Wellhausen does not attempt to distinguish throughout the work of these two writers, nor does he assign to the Johannine work a definitely arranged plan. The Apocalypse, he says, is not a drama but a picture-book, and though there was some effort to bring the pictures into sequence, it was unsuccessful because impossible. Various parts, for example, 11^{1-2}, 11^{3-13}, are quite isolated and are brought into their present places by one of the editors through some feature quite external. It is only by decomposition that the Apocalypse can be explained (15 f.). Wellhausen's method in both interpretation and criticism is so extravagant that his work cannot be regarded as making an important contribution to the study.   *Bousset* (*Die Offenbarung Johannis*, in Meyer's *Kom.*, 1896[1], 1906[2]), starting from Weizsäcker and Sabatier gives to the theory of unity with incorporated material a guarded and well-reasoned form which has recommended it to a wide circle of scholars, even among those who do not accept all its details. He makes our book a carefully planned apocalypse, in the composition of parts of which the author (of the time of Domitian, probably John the Presbyter) has used material derived in some instances from documents, in others from eschatological traditions handed down independently of written sources (cf. below, on Gunkel); such derived material the writer uses, not mechanically, but with the purpose of his book consciously in mind. The most important passages in which this use is seen are: 7^{1-8}, 11^{1-13}, 12, 14^{14-20}, 17, 18, $21^{9}-22^{5}$. The influence of oral tradition or written documents is probably present in some places where it is not clearly demonstrable. Bousset does not dissect sentences or verses in an attempt to distinguish different origins, nor does he *confidently* combine the incorporated material into a defined primitive document; he has carried out his hypothesis with reserve, with sanity of judgment, and — what is essential in the study of the Apocalypse, but often wanting in its critics — with keen sympathy with, and high appreciation of, his author.   *Gunkel.* The epoch-making book of Gunkel, *Creation and Chaos* (*Schöpfung und Chaos*, 1895), which sets beyond reasonable question the perpetuation and influence of oriental eschatological myths among the Hebrews through oral tradition, touches the Apocalypse chiefly in its interpretation, rather than in its literary structure; but it reaches results that have an important bearing on the critical analysis. Gunkel does not take up the Apocalypse as a whole or present any tabular analysis of it; he assumes that it contains many single visions which in their nature are independent and originally not planned with reference to one another (194); and he investigates certain parts (chiefly chapts. 12, 13, 17) according to the method of *eschatological tradition*. Starting with the principle that the real author of the material in an apocalypse is not in general the writer but a succession of generations, he finds that the writer of the Johannine Apocalypse has derived much in the form and contents of his book, not only from the Old Testament and Jewish apocalyptic writings, but also from eschatological tradition handed down orally through centuries; even in some cases where his material is parallel with that known to us through literary sources, there may be evidence that he is drawing from another form of tradition (207 ff.). Gunkel of course accedes to the Apocalyptist a degree of independence which leads to interpretation, development, combination, and arrangement of the matter handed down (253). The study of a tradition in its *history* becomes therefore fundamental; imagery and symbols found in our Apocalypse are often taken unchanged from their source, and thus many difficulties reach their solution in the form to which the representation may be ultimately traced up. This method of investigation is urged by Gunkel as correcting two procedures much in vogue, that of the excessive dissection of the text in many critical analyses, and that of seeking the explanation of a large number of symbols and figures in the events of history contemporaneous with the writer. Unquestionably Gunkel has introduced a most valuable principle in the study of the Apocalypse, though he has exaggerated its application. Bousset has made use of the method in his commentary, and also applying it in a special work on the tradition of the antichrist (*Der Antichrist in der Ueberlieferung des Judenthums, des neuen Testaments, u. der alten Kirche*, 1895) he has argued for the existence of this tradition in an oral form before the New Testament era and continuing through centuries independently of our Scriptures. The results of this inquiry he has applied in the study of some difficult passages in the Apocalypse (*e.g.* 11[1–13]).

For a convenient survey, the different critical analyses of the Apocalypse exhibited above may be divided into *three* classes (Cf. Bousset 125 ff.), though these are not sharply distinguished throughout, for the hypotheses in some cases combine the characteristics of several classes, and it is not possible to assign the critic in every instance to one of these categories to the exclusion of relation to others. Yet the following general grouping will be useful for giving greater clearness to an intricate subject. (1) The *revision* theory. In this class are ranged those hypotheses which suppose a *Grundschrift*, a primary apocalypse (according to some, Jewish, according to others, Christian), *complete in itself* and afterwards worked over through successive revisions into the present form of the book by editors, who added material of their own, or wove in some already existing material. (2) The *compilation* theory. Here belong the various hypotheses which assume a number of Jewish and Christian sources brought together by a Christian redactor more or less mechanically and lacking a close inner connection, or a relation to a plan; of course some critics of this class attribute a larger activity to the redactor than do others. (3) The *incorporation* theory, or as some call it, the *fragment* theory. This views the Apocalypse as in reality a unit in so far as it possesses a definitely organized plan, conceived and carried out by a single writer; but in the execution of this plan the writer is held to have used in *certain places* eschatological material derived from other sources (whether Jewish, Christian, or oral tradition), which he worked over more or less and adapted to his purpose. In such passages one may say that the creation is not the writer's own, but that the *use* of it is his. Critics differ as to the extent to which such material has been taken up into the book, and also as to the modification which it may have received from the writer's hands. At bottom this view attributes to the writer a procedure not fundamentally different from his use of the Old Testament. That he has used the latter constantly, that many of his passages are but a free working over of representations found there is unquestioned (cf. pp. 221 f.). In the same way he may be conceived to have appropriated ideas and representations preserved elsewhere, in oral tradition or religious writings, in cases where these are thought to embody or illustrate a sacred truth. The merit of this hypothesis is that while it does full justice to the strong evidence for unity, it provides for the presence of material which appears to have existed originally in some other connection, and it makes explicable the apparent disturbance in thought and the differences in historical situation. It is for these reasons that it has now gained the ascendency among scholars — scholars it should be observed who cannot be suspected of unfriendliness toward incisive criticism in itself. Representatives of this school are Weizsäcker, Sabatier, Schoen, H. Holtzmann, Bousset, Jülicher, Porter, Baljon, W. Bauer, Moffatt, Calmes, and many others. It may be in place to add that the present commentator considers this hypothesis to be required by sound criticism, and the following Commentary, as will be seen in the interpretation of the passages in question, proceeds on this view, though a considerable limitation as to the amount of incorporated material in the Apocalypse, and the probability of a very free handling of this on the writer's part are maintained; also special emphasis is laid on the necessity of finding in such material a meaning suited to the Apocalyptist's plan. There is a useful, but frequently overlooked, truth in the words of Pfleiderer: ' The task of the exegete consists first of all in ascertaining approximately the probable sense which the author himself connected with his visions and imagery; but what sense these may have had in their original form is a question of secondary importance, all the more certainly as the author himself probably had for the most part no distinct knowledge of this' (*Das Urchrist.*[2] II. 284).

The *traditional* theory of unity, that which denies the use of sources altogether in our book, has been defended throughout the whole period of recent criticism. Among those maintaining the unity in this absolute form are Beyschlag, Hilgenfeld, Düsterdieck, Hirscht, B. Weiss, Zahn, Warfield, Simcox (hesitatingly).

In this long period of active critical inquiry, notwithstanding the many extravagances which mark its course, the gain which has come to our knowledge of the Apocalypse is inestimable. The book has been placed in a certain light; its real aim, significance, and general structure have been settled beyond doubt; the fanciful interpretations of it, in whole or in part, which have appeared so often in an earlier time, are no longer possible. The great service which criticism has rendered toward the attainment of this result must be acknowledged by every student of the New Testament. It may be observed here that the primary fault in much of the criticism is in reality a failure to apply thoroughly the historical method of study. The book is the work of a prophet and religious poet often transported with the transcendent thoughts filling his vision, writing with the unrestrained freedom of a Hebrew in departing from ordered sequence and self-consistency, in seizing and mingling figures, in joining abruptly anticipation and retrospect, in suggesting rather than unfolding thought, and in drawing for his vehicle of expression from every part of Jewish life and literature, especially from Jewish eschatology. The Psalms furnish frequent illustration of these literary habits; and even if the presence of these features should be urged as evidence of composite structure there also, it is nevertheless true, that the Hebrew was accustomed to this mode of composition in his most familiar poetry and felt no difficulty in it. Yet the Apocalypse is treated by many of its critics very much as if it were composed in the library of a modern western scholar without freedom in the use of material, without the influence of the writer's very distinctive manner, and according to canons requiring every sentence to be coldly pruned and squared to conform to the rest. As regards the value of the data upon which the various hypotheses are based, it is significant that the critics are all agreed upon the presence of derived material in the book; beyond this there is no consensus of opinion. In this respect the state of critical opinion differs widely from that regarding the Pentateuch and some of the Jewish apocalypses (cf. Bousset 125 f.). The different critical theories mentioned above will, so far as seems necessary, be further discussed in the paragraphs on *Criticism*, appended to the respective sections of the Apocalypse, in the Commentary.

VI. Some Characteristics of the Author's Literary Manner

It is the purpose of the following paragraph to call attention to certain characteristics of the writer's manner, which are important in the study of the Apocalypse. Some of these are insignificant in themselves, but they assume especial significance, because they throw light upon difficulties which are frequently raised concerning the meaning of a phrase or passage, and concerning the structure of the outline. It is a principle which should need no affirmation, that every book must be interpreted in the light of the author's purpose and his literary manner. Now in every part of our book problems in interpretation and in the criticism of its structure present themselves which are insolvable apart from these guiding lines. The author of the Revelation does not aim to write merely a burning prophecy of the Last Things, such as might have been given in a brief apocalypse not greatly exceeding the eschatological chapters in the Gospels. (1) Such a prophecy he does indeed seek to give; but (2) he seeks also to give with that and centering in it, a vivid portrayal of the great powers, divine and satanic, in their hostility to each other and in their relation to the events that were coming on the earth; (3) his plan embraced also pictures of various other and subordinate causes and influences working in the drama of the world's future; and (4) he aims, like a true prophet, to comfort and encourage God's people in the perilous times before them and to call them to sustained fidelity in this great trial of their faith and patience. These four 'leading motives,' as they may be called, are felt throughout the vast symphony of the Apocalypse, and the writer combines and interweaves them after a manner of his own. It is imperative then to perceive clearly what the special traits of his manner are in order to get at the meaning of details and to understand his principles in the grouping of paragraphs. In his treatment of his theme the canons of literary art, as laid down by our academic methods, may be departed from; whether this is so or not, is a matter of small moment; the important inquiry with us is, what the author himself aimed at and whether his aim is carried out with consistency. And if we keep before us the manifoldness of his subject and look for a presentation of this in keeping with the writer's characteristic habits of thought and composition as revealed throughout, we shall find strong ground for maintaining a real unity in the book, that is, a unity of the kind defined above (p. 221), and, considering the prophetic and poetic nature of the work, a unity of splendid character; most of the divergencies and interruptions which are thought to contain evidence of different documentary strata disappear, and the presence of an original mind working freely with traditional material shows itself throughout. The characteristics mentioned below are those, not of a part of the book, but of the whole. Thus the conclusion to which historical and linguistic considerations led us in the former paragraph is confirmed.

In the following survey of conspicuous features in the writer's manner some will be seen to clear up the meaning of figures, symbols, and minor expressions, while others help us to see the significance intended in larger paragraphs and the office of these in the general outline. *Special attention should be given to the light to be gained from the peculiarities of single sentences and short paragraphs;* for a writer's habits of mind often reveal themselves certainly in a single sentence or passage, as in the treatment of the larger parts of his work. And so in our author some of the difficulties that are most noticeable in the sequence of thought and grouping of material, that is, some of the principal grounds of critical objection, will be seen to be but expressions of precisely the same literary habits which appear in sentences and short passages of undeniable unity.   What is here said is not to be taken as minimizing the difficulties encountered in the Apocalypse; it is rather a plea for a more rigorous application of a principle fundamental in exegesis, to criticism.   Criticism has, not without justice, been censured for a want of thoroughgoing exegesis.[1]   At all events the interpretation of the parts of the Apocalypse in which critical objections are especially raised cannot be settled off-hand by any universal canon; moreover we must in some instances be content to accept the result which seems least improbable, if we are to escape the insuperable difficulties attaching to the denial of a real unity.

The following are the principal characteristics of the writer which are especially helpful in elucidating the difficulties of the Apocalypse.   (1) Repetition, overfullness.   (*a*) This feature appears with great frequency, as shown by examples below, within a single sentence or paragraph ; (*b*) and the same habit of mind extends to the larger unit of the book, leading to similar repetition and fullness in the parts which make up the structure of the whole.   There cannot then be found in (*b*) an argument against the unity of the book.

Examples of (*a*) are: *his head, his hair, white as wool, as snow* 1^{14}, *hast received and heard* 3^3, *the heavens and the things that are therein, and the earth and the things that are therein, and the sea and the things that are therein* 10^6, *if any man desireth to hurt them . . . if any man shall desire to hurt them* 11^5, *victorious from the beast, and from his image, and from the number of his name* 15^2, *eat the flesh of kings, and the flesh of captains, and the flesh of mighty men, and the flesh of horses and of them that sit thereon, and the flesh of all men, both free and bond, and small and great* 19^{18}, cf. also 1^{18}, $3^{12, 17}$, $4^{9\,ff.}$, $5^{12\,f.}$, 6^{15}, 7^{4-8}, 9^6, $12^{2,\,5,\,8\,f.}$, $13^{5\,f.}$, 14^6, $17^{14\,f.}$, $18^{6\,f.,\,17}$, $20^{2,\,12\,f.}$, 21^3, 22^{15} — this list could be largely increased.   Examples of (*b*) are: the thrice

[1] Cf. Zahn. *Ein.* II. 605.

R

repeated series of seven visitations, those of the seals, the trumpets and the bowls; the message to the Church in a series of seven epistles, all cast in the one fixed form; repeated hymns of praise, having the same or a similar theme, $4^{8,\,11}$, $5^{9\,f.,\,12,\,13}$, $7^{10,\,12}$, $11^{15,\,17\,f.}$, $12^{10\,ff.}$, $15^{3\,f.}$, $19^{1\,f.,\,5,\,6\,ff.}$; repeated pictures of the saints in triumph, $7^{9\,ff.}$, $14^{1\,ff.}$, 15^{2}; repeated acts symbolical of the End, $14^{14-16,\,17-20}$; repetition in the description of the New Jerusalem, 21^{22-25}, 22^{3-5}; parallelisms in the Introduction and the Conclusion, 1^{1} and $22^{6,\,1\,a}$; 1^{3} and $22^{7,\,12,\,18\,f.}$; 1^{8} and 22^{13}.

(2) Closely connected with the foregoing characteristic is the introduction of brief, indefinite expressions and statements which are afterwards made specific or fuller, sometimes after an interval.   (a) Instances, either in clauses immediately connected, or in a resumption after an interval but within the same sentence or paragraph are very numerous.   (b) Here again the habit shown within the limits of a single passage appears also in the relation of more widely separated paragraphs, that is, a representation is sometimes taken up again in a later paragraph with details and enlargements.   The essential identity of (a) and (b) bears directly upon critical objections frequently urged against certain portions.

(a) Examples within closely connected clauses are: 2^{2} *thy works*, i.e. *thy toil, patience*, etc., so also in $2^{9,\,13}$ and through all the seven epistles; 2^{14} *a stumbling block*, *i.e.* partaking of idolatrous feasts, etc.; 11^{3} *my two witnesses*, *i.e.* as characterized in vv. 4 ff.; 12^{16} *the earth helped*, defined in the following parallel clause; 14^{6} *eternal gospel*, *i.e.* as given in the words of v. 7 (see Com.); 20^{9} *the camp of the saints*, *i.e.* the beloved city; similar cases are 1^{14}, 6^{4}, 7^{4-8}, $12^{8\,b,\,9}$, $13^{12\,b,\,13-15}$. Examples in which the more definite or fuller representation follows after an interruption but in the same paragraph are: 1^{4} *the seven churches*, *i.e.* those specified in v. 11; also $7^{9\,and\,13\,ff.}$; $9^{3\,and\,5\,and\,10}$; $10^{3\,a\,and\,6}$; $14^{1\,and\,4\,f.}$; $15^{1\,and\,5\,ff.}$ (b) Examples in passages more or less widely separated are: $12^{6\,and\,13-17}$; 13^{1-8} and 17^{7-17}; 14^{8} and 18; $16^{19\,b}$ and 18; 21^{1-2} and $21^{9-22^{5}}$.

(3) Interruptions in the course of thought.   Departure from logical order, already seen in some of the cases spoken of above, appears very often in the book.   This is far from a fatal objection to unity; it cannot even be regarded as a defect, in a work of fervid religious imagination, especially in one proceeding from a mind like that of a Hebrew prophet.   The Hebrew mind in general does not bind itself by the strict law of continuity, which the Greeks have taught the western world, as **witness** the Psalms, for example, or the Pauline epistles.   The

instances of this break in continuity which occur in the Apocalypse may be arranged in three groups (for examples see below): (*a*) displacement within a single paragraph, a frequent occurrence and very significant as regards the writer's manner; (*b*) the interjection of brief utterances ; (*c*) the insertion of longer episodes between portions which as parts of one series belong closely together.   Passages of this last kind are numerous, and not only disturb the casual reader, but also enter largely into the argument against the unity of the book. There are, however, several considerations which relieve the difficulty felt here.   The habit of mind which permits the displacement within a single paragraph and the insertion of parenthetical utterances, referred to above (*a*, *b*), makes altogether conceivable the author's departure from logical order and his insertion of episodes in the treatment of the larger factors which make up the outline of the book.   And if as viewed from this point these interruptions are *natural* with the author, it will be shown below that there are in his purpose *special motives* leading directly to the introduction of these episodes; so that these so far from destroying unity serve rather to prove its presence.   The particular office which such episodes perform in the general plan will be pointed out in the paragraph on *prefatory passages*.[1]   All that is sought here is to show that they fall in *naturally* as a part of the author's manner. Of these episodes there are two classes ; *first*, those containing an anticipation of the End, or of some eschatological event, as if already present before its actual entrance.   Such anticipation is characteristic of a prophet.   In a prophet's vision the end is present from the beginning.   Our Lord anticipating the final triumph sees already in his earthly days ' Satan fallen ' (Lk. 10[18]), and the prince of this world ' now cast out ' (Jno. 12[31]); St. Paul frequently speaks of salvation as already accomplished ; and thus it is that our writer in his pictures of the future sometimes changes to the present or past tense, so certain and vivid is his vision of the coming event.[2]   His tendency to look first to the result and afterward to steps preceding is seen in his repeated use of the grammatical figure *hysteron-proteron*, inversion of the logical sequence, for example, 5[2, 5] *to*

----

[1] p. 245.   [2] 11[7-13], 20[7-10].

open the book and to loose the seals; cf. 3^{17} *am rich* (the result) and *have gotten riches* (the process); 3^9 *come and worship*, etc. (the effect) *and know*, etc. (the cause); 10^4 the sealing up before the writing; 10^9 the bitter sequel before the sweetness of the taste; 12^{10} salvation, the blessed consummation, before its foundation, the establishment of the kingdom; 19^{13} the garment sprinkled with the blood of carnage before the battle. We are therefore prepared to find the habit of anticipation entering also into his program in its larger aspect.   *Second.* The second class of these episodes consists of passages, some of them of considerable length, which may be compared to a picture within a picture.   These portray in striking visions, as it were in an idealized *inset*, the persons, agencies, and forces at work in and through the great eschatological events foretold in the larger picture, they open an insight into causes and motives underlying the other scenes.

(*a*) Examples of the displacement spoken of above: 2^6 belongs with the other expressions of approval and before the censure, *i.e.* before v. 4; $6^{12\,b-14\,a}$, the celestial phenomena are inserted into the midst of the terrestrial $6^{12\,a\,and\,14\,b}$; $7^{17\,a}$ the guidance to the fountains belongs with the thirst, v. 16 *a*; 14^5 the truthfulness and faithfulness of the saints belong with their other virtues, v. 4 *ab*, and before their redemption v. 4 *c*; cf. also $1^{16\,c}$ which belongs with v. 14; 3^{10} with v. 8; $4^{5\,a}$ with v. 3 and before vv. 4, 5 *b*–6; $13^{3\,ab}$ with v. 2 *a*, whereas v. 2 *b* goes with v. 3 *c* f.; $20^{13\,ab}$ with v. 12 *a*; 20^{15} with v. 12 *d*; 19^{14} separates vv. 12 f. from vv. 15 f.; $22^{18\,f.}$ separates v. 17 from v. 20.   (*b*) For interjection of brief utterances, cf. 1^8, 8^{13}, 9^{12}, 11^{14}, $13^{9\,f.}$, 13^{18}, $14^{12\,f.}$, $16^{5,\,7}$, 16^{15}, 18^{20}, 20^6.   (*c*) The insertion of longer episodes will be fully illustrated in the following paragraph on *prefatory passages*. A single example of each class mentioned above (p. 243) is given here to show more distinctly what is meant: 7^{9-12} the vision of accomplished redemption before the events preliminary to the End have run their course; 12^{1-17} showing that Satan's hatred of the Messiah is the real force at work in the persecution of the Church.

(4) The systematic introduction of prefatory passages.   The foregoing paragraph has shown · the writer's tendency to open to the reader in certain anticipatory passages a glimpse into an issue whose actual entrance belongs to a later point in the sequence of events; it has also been shown that it is a part of his purpose to give in certain visions *lying outside of this sequence* an ideal picture of the powers and forces at work in the eschatological events described.   Now an examination of the

book will show that these two classes of interruptions in what
may be called the action of the book are introduced, one or
both of them, as a kind of prelude, at every great juncture or
critical turning-point.   It is a fixed habit of the author to
preface in this way each new stage in the march of the future,
and as the judgments preparatory to the parousia approach
their culmination these preludes assume larger proportions and
become more complex ; in some instances after the announcement of, or after the initial step in, a new series of movements,
a new prelude intervenes before the series actually begins its
course.   In this use of preludes should be noticed the splendid
alternation of light with shadow.   Before every vision of gloom
and terror the writer introduces a glimpse of the radiant glory
that lies beyond — it is a burst of harmony which lingers on with
one, whose ear is attuned, through all the hoarse tumult soon
filling the air.   The assurance of hope, the promise of the victory of the Kingdom, is offered anew with every new approach
of trial.   Herein is carried out into detail the principle that
determines the rise of the apocalyptic books in general ; see
p. 175.   Nothing could more clearly show that the supreme
purpose of the book was to cheer and sustain the readers
through the awful troubles that were coming on the world
before the sway of Antichrist and his servants should be forever broken.

The characteristic here mentioned will appear in the following brief survey which takes up in order each series in the
movements determining the outline of the book.   (1) The
commission to the seven churches, the first paragraph after the
introduction, is prefaced by a vision revealing the author of
the commission, the great Head of the Church, in the midst of
the seven churches (1^{12-20}).   (2) The eschatological movements which fill up the rest of the book are prefaced in chapters
4–5 by the revelation of the divine powers controlling the whole
destiny of the world to the end, while chapt. 5 also forms the immediate preface to the breaking of the seals.   (3) The great
turning-point reached in the breaking of the last seal (8^1) is
prefaced by the anticipative vision of God's people brought in
safety through the coming crisis (7^{9-17}).   (4) After the initial
step of the breaking of this last seal and before its sequel seen

in the seven trumpet-blasts is introduced, there comes in as a preface the symbolic act (8^{3-5}) showing that the judgments of the seven trumpet-blasts now to come are expressions of the wrath of God moved to intervention by the prayers of the saints.   (5) After the judgments of six trumpets have run their course, the crisis reached in the seventh blast (11^{15}) is introduced by the double preface bidding the prophet anew to go on with his bitter duty to the end, now certainly near at hand (10), and giving assurance of Israel's conversion in the last time (11^{1-13}).   (6) After the sounding of the seventh trumpet, here again before the sequel is introduced, that is, before the appearance of the angels with the seven bowls (15^{1}) there is brought in a preface of still greater complexity in keeping with the magnitude of the crisis; this preface consists of the following parts : (*a*) the song of praise anticipative of the end (11^{15-18}) and the symbolic occurrence showing the coming judgments to be the acts of the God of the *covenant* (11^{19}), (*b*) *first*, the allegory revealing Satan's hostility to the Christ as explaining the persecution of the Church, together with the assurance of his final downfall (12) and *second*, the symbols of his agents in these persecutions (13), (*c*) a prelude directly introducing the acts of judgment, consisting of the anticipation of the triumph of the saints (14^{1-5}), proclamations (14^{6-13}), and symbolic acts (14^{14-20}).   (7) After the *announcement* of the next series, that is, the angels with the plagues of the seven bowls (15^{1}), and before the initial step in the unfolding of the series ($15^{5\,ff}$), there is introduced as a prelude another glimpse anticipative of the final triumph (15^{2-4}).   (8) After the plagues of six bowls are accomplished and before the crisis of the last ($16^{17\,ff.}$) the place of the usual preface is taken by a brief interlude of encouragement and warning (16^{15}) looking to the trial about to break upon the world.   (9) With the plague of the seventh bowl (16^{17-21}) the long series of preparatory events beginning with the breaking of the first seal (6^{1}) is finished and now is to begin the last chapter in the divine drama, the destruction of the arch-enemies with their stronghold, and the setting up of the eternal kingdom.   This crisis is prefaced by an anticipative vision showing vividly the wickedness of the capital city of the Beast as the cause of the destruction now to be visited upon her ($17^{1-7,\ 15-18}$) and explaining the symbol of the Beast and telling of his coming overthrow (17^{8-14}). (10) The first act in the final chapter, the destruction of the great city, is not represented in vision, it is proclaimed in word and symbol ($18^{1-8,\ 21-24}$) and the lament to be uttered over it is anticipated (18^{9-19}), also the heavenly song of exultation is heard after the destruction is accomplished (19^{1-5}).   (11) The culminating movements ushered in by the appearing of the Messiah leading forth the armies of heaven for battle (19^{11-16}) are prefaced by the heavenly hallelujahs anticipative of the consummation (19^{6-8}); the battle and the final events which are inseparably connected follow one another without pause (19^{17}–22^5).

(5) The introduction of an object not previously mentioned, as if already familiar to the reader. Some passages in which this usage occurs have on this ground been held to be impossible in their present connection — the usage is thought to show either the incorporation of a fragment or a derangement in the original order. But from a number of instances virtually parallel it would appear to be a part of the writer's manner to anticipate, as if familiar, objects to be made distinct later; sometimes also expressions which, so far as appears are unfamiliar, are left unexplained. This trait in the apocalyptist is not hard to account for; he writes with all the great factors of his visions present to his mind, and it is by no means inconceivable that he should sometimes forget that he has not yet put the reader entirely on his own plane, and should introduce as if understood an idea or figure before he has reached its full presentation, or should use unfamiliar symbols and terms without explanation. This may perhaps be criticized as a literary fault, yet it is one that may occur in any imaginative work. The most striking instance of this usage occurs in 11^7 where '*the* (not *a*) beast that cometh up out of the abyss' is introduced with the article, as if known to the reader, though the reference is first made clear in $13^{1\,\mathrm{ff.}}$. But in view of other cases essentially similar the peculiarity can hardly give sufficient ground for objection to the originality of the passage in this place.[1] The following cases may be compared: '*the* seven

[1] See Com.

churches' 1^4, though v. 11 first specifies which among the Asian churches are meant; '*the* second death' 2^{11}, first made clear in 20^{14}; similar are also '*the* seven spirits' 1^4, '*the* great city' 16^{19}, '*the* great harlot' 17^1, 'my two witnesses' 11^3; the following are without subsequent explanation: '*the* morning star' 2^{28}, '*the* seven thunders' 10^3.

(6) Contradictions, abrupt changes, unimaginable conceptions. These features appear frequently and the attempt to get over the difficulties thus arising has led on the one hand to an artificial and impossible exegesis, on the other, to an extreme critical process which finds in all differences a mark of different documents. In the work of a poetic mind moving freely through a series of stupendous visions the very character of visions like that of dreams forbids us to look in all cases for rigorous self-consistency or conformity to the realities of actual life. We are prepared to find in visions inconsistencies, sudden transitions, impossible combinations. It is true that incongruities may sometimes be traceable to the reminiscence of a source which suggested his thought to the author; the eschatology of Ezekiel, for example, which greatly influenced him, has left its trace in the post-millennial gathering of the nations against the beloved city (20$^{7\,\text{ff.}}$, Ezk. 38), though according to the earlier representation (19$^{19-21}$) all earthly enemies had already been destroyed. Yet here as elsewhere the author's use of a source is, as shown above,[1] an independent one and does not destroy the unity of his plan; it is certain that there are not in these characteristics sufficient data for resolving the book into a series of excerpts put together unskillfully.

The principal cases calling for consideration will be noticed in the Commentary; it is sufficient here to give without discussion a few examples to illustrate the writer's manner in the respect spoken of. Examples of conflict are: '*Straightway I was in the Spirit*' 4^2, though the Prophet had been 'in the Spirit' from 1^{10} on; in 3^{12} there is to be a temple in the new Jerusalem, in 21^{22} there is no temple there; the grass is unhurt in 9^4 though in 8^7 it had all been destroyed; in 16^1 all the bowls are poured out upon the earth, but in vv. 8, 17 one is poured upon the sea, another upon the air; in 17^{15} waters are said to have been seen, but in v. 3 f. the Prophet sees a wilderness, not water. Examples of abrupt transition, or of the merging of different representations are: 1^{16} the right hand holding the seven stars, v. 17

[1] p. 221.

the same right hand laid assuringly on the Prophet; in 7^{15-17} the heavenly throne-room, the temple, and the pastures are combined in one picture; in 13^2 the beast with seven heads suddenly becomes a beast with one head (one mouth), then a personal ruler (his throne) and in v. 12 he is identified with one of his heads; in $17^{19\ f.}$ the heads are first mountains, then kings; in 20^{12} the two conceptions, one of a book recording men's deeds, and another of a book containing a list of those destined to life, are blended. Examples of unimaginable conceptions (in all apocalyptic literature very numerous) are: the seeing of writing within a sealed roll, a lamb taking the book and breaking the seals, the 'living creatures' holding harps, 5^{1-8}; the smiting of the luminaries followed by a diminution, not of the intensity, but of the duration of light 8^{12}; the fabulous nature of the locusts $9^{7\ ff.}$; a person clothed with the sun 12^1; a city 12,000 furlongs high 21^{16}.

(7) The use of symbols, types, and numbers employed symbolically. As in all writing which seeks to represent vividly spiritual things, especially prophecy and the literature of visions, symbolism is the instrument used most extensively in our book. Symbols, using the word in its most comprehensive scope, enter into every representation, one might almost say into every sentence. These are taken largely from the Old Testament, especially from the apocalyptic portions of the prophets, but some are derived from apocalyptic tradition handed down through other sources, some from everyday life and observation, some certainly are to be attributed to the author's invention. As with the prophets of the Old Testament[1] so here also we have symbolical *actions*.[2]   It is important to determine the meaning which the author attached to the symbols used and to avoid the fancifulness to which they easily lend themselves — a most common source of misinterpretation.   In general they are not explained by the writer. Often the meaning is clear in itself, or is made clear by the context, or by a use familiar to the readers; in some cases, however, explanatory words are added;[3] in still others the symbol is left obscure.[4] Care must be taken not to attach a mystic significance to all the details in a symbolical representation; frequently these are designed merely to embellish the picture, to give it vivid-

---

[1] *E.g.* Is. 20 $2^{ff.}$, Jer. 13^{1-7}, Ezk. $37^{16\ ff.}$, Zec. $11^{7\ ff.}$.
[2] *E.g.* $7^{2-8}, 10^{8-11}$, $11^{1\ f.,\ 19}$, 14^{1-20}, 18^{21}.
[3] *E.g.* $1^{20}, 4^5, 5^{6\ b}$, 11^8, 12^9, $17^{9\ f.,\ 12,\ 15,\ 18}$, 19^8.
[4] *E.g.* $2^{17\ b}$, 8^1, $9^{14\ f.}$, $10^{3\ b\ f.}$, 13^8, $19^{12\ b}$.

ness and power, very much as the details sometimes used to fill out a parable or a Homeric simile. It is a mistake (one, however, often met with in the interpretation of the Apocalypse) to seek, for example, a special mystical meaning for the golden girdle, the flaming eyes etc. in $1^{13\,\text{ff.}}$, for the jasper, the sardine stone, and the rainbow in 4^3, for the sun, moon, and stars in 12^2.[1] In general the context and the manner of apocalyptic writers will guide with reasonable certainty to the purpose of such details. The use of proper names and designations calls for special notice here. These are almost wholly typical except in certain places where reference is made to a distinct historical fact,[2] and in the prologue and epilogue, where the visionary element with its peculiar style is subordinate; even the names of the churches addressed in the epistles are not altogether an exception, for these are really intended to be typical of the whole Church.[3] Abaddon, Harmagedon, Gog and Magog belong solely to apocalyptic language; and in our book Babylon, Egypt, Jerusalem, Jezebel, Sion, and Sodom have a typical sense only; though the cities of Rome and Jerusalem sometimes form the theme, they are never called by their proper names; Balaam is made the type of the Nicolaitans;[4] Euphrates[5] is apparently thought of less really than typically, as a kind of horizon-line beyond which lies the unknown and dreaded East; the name Jew occurring but twice[6] seems to be in the author's mind a designation of the true child of God; children of Israel in the description of the new Jerusalem[7] is the designation of the whole people of God, and the use in that passage, taken together with the general use of proper names shown above, furnishes strong presumption that this is the meaning of the term in the only other place (apart from the historical reference in 2^{14}) in which it occurs, the much discussed passage $7^{2\,\text{ff.}}$.[8]

Numbers, except as determined by definite reference in the context, are generally symbolical; to such an extent is this the case that even in some places where they designate an exact fact, for example, the 'seven mountains' of Rome,[9] we may probably regard this a coincidence. This trait is a part of the

---

[1] See Com. *in loc.*   [2] *E.g.* 2^{13}.   [3] P. 210.   [4] $2^{14\,\text{f.}}$.   [5] 9^{14}, 16^{12}.
[6] 2^9, 3^9.   [7] 21^{12}.   [8] See Com.   [9] 17^9.

writer's inheritance.[1] The oriental mind shows a special fondness for this use of numbers; it appears alike in the Hebrew scriptures and in the records of other peoples. What primarily may have caused a sacred or symbolical character to be attached to a particular number does not belong to our present inquiry; that at all events must be more or less a matter of conjecture, for the usage in most cases took its rise in prehistoric time. But it is easy to see how in certain numbers the idea inherited by the Hebrews through their Semitic traditions should have grown. Whatever in an earlier age made 7 a sacred or typical number, it was inevitable that this character should be intensified by the importance of the week of 7 days in the Hebrew religion; similarly the number 12 must have been affected by the number of the tribes. In rabbinical and apocalyptic literature this treatment of numbers becomes especially frequent. In our writer then it is only one of the traits adopted from the general biblical and apocalyptic manner. And the particular numbers thus used by him are nearly all found with similar meaning in the Old Testament and Jewish apocalypses. The numbers oftenest employed thus in our book are 3, $3\frac{1}{2}$ (and in certain relations, its equivalent 42 or 1260), 4, 7, 10, 12, 1000 and multiples of 1000. It is not to be supposed that a specific meaning attaches invariably to a given numerical symbol, so that we could substitute this as a paraphrase in all cases; in view of the vagueness characterizing the style of visions we may presume that the writer himself did not always have a precise intention in mind. Sometimes the tradition taken up by him determined the choice of the number. An essential thing is that we should neither take the number literally, nor seek to find in it a recondite, mystical meaning. For the most part the general tenor of the representation will suggest a sufficiently definite sense.

Three, one of the most frequent numbers in the Scriptures to denote *adequateness, sufficiency,* is used in our book with the same meaning, for example the 3 plagues 9[18], the 3 woes 8[13], the effect of the earthquake 16[19]; the *third* part affected by the trumpet-blasts 8[7 ff.], 9[15] apparently denotes a large, but not the larger, part; similarly the third part of the stars 12[4]; the 3 gates in each side of the wall of the New Jerusalem 21[13] are due directly

---

[1] Cf. Lücke II. 404 ff., Enc. Bib. III. 3434 ff., Hast. III. 560 ff.

to Ezekiel 48³⁰ ᶠᶠ·, which furnishes the prototype for our author here; in
Enoch 34–36 heaven has 3 gates opening toward each of the four quarters.
The other cases in which the number occurs (6⁶, 8¹³) call for no comment here.
Three and a half, always typical, is unquestionably taken from Dan. 7²⁵,
12⁷, where the '*time and times and half a time*,' *i.e.* three and a half 'times,'
denote the last period of the triumph of evil and the oppression of God's
people, as accomplished in the rule of Antiochus, after which should come
the Great Day of Jehovah, with the destruction of the enemy and the giving of the kingdom to the saints of the Most High.   While the persecutions
of Antiochus are seen to have lasted approximately 3½ years (cf. Driver
Dan. in C. B. 93; *Introd.* 494) it is probable that the author of Dan. uses
the number typically of the indefinite but short period which he pictures as
preceding the End.   The theory is plausible that he derives the number
from Semitic tradition, that primarily it figured the three months or more
during which nature is in the grasp of frost and cold (cf. Gunkel 266 ff.,
389 ff.) and that it afterwards became a symbol of the fierce period of evil
before the last great triumph, a symbol of the time of the power of Antichrist, 'the times of the Gentiles,' Lk. 21²⁴, or more widely, the symbol of
any period of great calamity.   The common explanation of it as ' a broken
seven,' based on Dan. 9²⁷, is improbable, for the typical use of a number
grows out of its exact use with concrete objects (cf. Gunkel 267).   At all
events, whatever may have been the origin of the symbol, its significance in
Dan. is plain.   From Dan. it passes into the Talmud (cf. Volz 170) as an
eschatological number; as such it appears also in 2 Es. 5⁴, where it is said
that the destruction of the great world-power will be seen by him to whom
God grants to live 'after the third time.'   The Ms. has *post tertiam* which
unquestionably refers to the 'three times' still granted to the last hostile
world-power before its end.   The AV, *trumpet*, is from the reading *tubam*, a
corruption of *turbatum;* cf. Box *Ez. Ap. in loc.*   The ellipsis of the noun
after *tertiam* 'corresponds to the mysterious style of apocalyptic writing'
(Gunkel in Kautzsch, 359, cf. Charles *Asc. Is.* p. 29).   According to the
Ascension of Is. 4¹² the last world-power, the incarnation of Beliar, will rule
3 years, 7 months, and 27 days.   This by the Julian reckoning is equivalent
to the '1335 days' of Dan. 12¹² and is doubtless taken from that (cf. Lücke
I. 285, Charles *Asc. Is. in loc.*, Flemming in Hennecke's *Handbuch* 327).
But this number of days in Dan. 12¹² like that in 8¹⁴ is probably an *interpretation* of the original 3½ 'times' in 7²⁵, suggested to a reviser by the facts
of history.   The author of the Apocalypse in 12¹⁴ takes the primary
phrase of Daniel ' a time and times and half a time'; elsewhere he interprets 'times' as *days*, or *years*, and in the latter case gives variously 3½ years,
or the equivalent 42 months, or 1260 days, the month being reckoned as
30 days (11², ³, ⁹, ¹¹, 12⁶, 13⁵).   *But in all places the meaning seems to be the
same, the period of the last terrible sway of Satan and his agents in the world
before the second coming of the Lord.*   *Four* in the 'four living creatures' 4⁶
and *passim* is traditional; the representation of the cherubim is taken from
Ezk. (1⁵ ᶠᶠ·; an earlier tradition may lie behind Ezk.) who makes them 4 (cf.
Enoch 40), as the bearers of Jehovah's throne-car moving straight forward

into the 4 quarters of the earth. 'Four-square,' as an epithet of the Holy City, 21[16], also follows the pattern of Ezk. 48[16, 20]. The 'fourth part' given into the power of death 6[8] can hardly have any other meaning than a large but not unlimited part. The other *fours* (7[1f.] 9[14f.]) which call for notice are seen to be associated with the 4 points of the compass. *Seven,* the preëminently sacred number with the Hebrews and found also among other peoples, the one used typically in the scriptures in every conceivable relation and numberless instances, where *fullness, completeness, certainty* is thought of, is the favorite number with our author and forms one of the dominant influences in his manner. There are the 7 churches with their 7 angels, 7 stars and 7 lampstands; the 7 spirits with their 7 lamps; the Lamb with 7 eyes and 7 horns; the 7 seals, the 7 trumpets and the 7 bowls, with their respective 7 plagues; two groups of seven angels; the dragon and the Beast with their 7 heads; 7 mountains, 7 kings, 7 thunders. The number occurs 54 times; also its presence in the writer's thought is seen even where it is not expressly mentioned, *e.g.* as a constructive feature (see cases below) or as determining the number of terms in a rhetorical series (5[12], 6[15], 7[12]). It is commonly understood to be used in an exact sense in the 7 churches, the 7 kings, and the 7 mountains, though even here a symbolical meaning is possible (see Com.). In all other instances it is unquestionably typical or schematic, denoting ideal *completeness, entirety, sufficiency.* In the case of the 7 spirits, the 7 thunders, and the 7 heads of the dragon, tradition may have had some influence in determining the number (see Com. on 1[4], 10[3], 12[3]); in all other cases of its symbolical use its choice seems due to the author's fondness for the number. As a multiple of 1000 the 7000 killed in the earthquake 11[13] denote a large number but relatively to the whole population a small one, probably a tenth part (see Com.).

As a *constructive feature* the number may be made the basis of an altogether arbitrary analysis of the book (so Ewald 38 ff.), yet besides the clearly marked paragraphs of the 7 epistles, the 7 seals, the 7 trumpets, and the 7 bowls, there are others which without fancifulness can be seen to consist of 7 parts. The paragraph of the actual parousia with its culminating events, 19[11]–22[5], falls into the following 7 parts: (1) 19[11–16]; (2) 19[17–18]; (3) 19[19]–20[3]; (4) 20[4–6]; (5) 20[7–10]; (6) 20[11–15]; (7) 21[1]–22[5]. The fall of the 'great city,' 18[1]–19[5], divides itself naturally as follows: (1) the proclamation 18[1–3]; (2) the summons to the Christians 18[4–5]; (3) incitement of the spirits of vengeance 18[6–8]; (4) lament of merchants and others 18[9–19]; (5) call to heaven etc. to rejoice 18[20]; (6) the symbolical act and the cry of the angel 18[21–24]; (7) the hymn of exultation 19[1–5]. Chapter 14, which forms a single paragraph as a complex prelude to the vision of the bowls, falls into the following parts: (1) 1–5; (2) 6–7; (3) 8; (4) 9–12; (5) 13; (6) 14–16; (7) 17–20. The epilogue 22[6–20], exclusive of the benediction, is commonly divided as follows: (1) 6–7; (2) 8–9; (3) 10–15; (4) 16; (5) 17; (6) 18–19; (7) 20. (Cf. RV and WH.) The great vision of chapters 4–5 consists of *two* descriptive parts 4[1–8a], 5[1–8], and *five* hymns 4[8b, 11], 5[9f., 12, 13]. In this connection cf. also the introduction of 7 beatitudes, 1[3], 14[13], 16[15], 19[9], 20[6], 22[7, 14]. It is an interesting fact that a series of 7 is sometimes divided into 3 + 4, or 4 + 3. Thus in the 7 epistles the first 3 form one group, the last 4 another (see Com.); in the 7 seals the peculiarity of the revelation of the fifth marks the change to a new group; a similar division is indicated by the angelic cry 8[13] inserted between the fourth and fifth trumpets, and by the interlude 16[5-7] between the third and fourth bowls. Such a resolution of 7 is not a clearly established usage in other writers. (It is doubtful whether in Mt. 13 the grouping of the parables is intended as a division of 7 into 4 + 3.) The explanation of the peculiarity is not certain. The theory that 7 originally owes its sacredness to the fact that it is the sum of 3 + 4 is in itself improbable; at any rate there is no indication of this thought with our author; nowhere so far as the numbers are expressly named does he bring 7 into connection with 3 and 4, as constituent parts; and we are perhaps right in thinking that he did not attach important significance to the division, for he does not direct attention to it, and it becomes apparent only upon critical observation. Quite possibly it is a slight pause in the middle of a series due to a habit of mind seen throughout the book, a reluctance to move directly to an end through a long *unbroken* succession of steps.   *Ten*, which among all the peoples using the decimal system is found frequently as a round number for *fullness, completeness,* occurs often in this sense in the Bible and apocalyptic writers. Our book uses it in this typical significance only. The 'ten days' of tribulation 2[10] denote a period not long, but enough so to bring severe trial to the sufferers (see Com.). The other instances in which the number occurs are found in the representations of the dragon and the Beast, and in the interpretations of these (12[3], 13[1], 17[3, 7, 12, 16]); here the 10 horns are taken over from the prototype in Dan. 7[7], as a part of the tradition and are made typical of complete sway over the kings of the earth; the reference in 17[12] to 10 kings is an application of the traditional number used typically rather than an explanation of the choice of 10 as the number required by actual history. Whether the author of Dan. derived the number of the horns from Semitic tradition is not certain — that origin is possible (cf. Gunkel 332).   *Twelve* like seven possesses preëminently a sacred character with the Hebrews and is applied typically to a great variety of objects in both civil and religious matters. In most cases this is probably traceable directly to the number of the tribes. Twelve thus becomes especially appropriate as a symbol of *completeness* in whatever pertains to the theocratic people as such, and to their ideal capital city. New Testament writers still conceive of Israel as consisting of 12 tribes, nothwithstanding the disappearance of the ten (Acts 26[7], Ja. 1[1]); and Ezekiel pictures the ideal city with 12 gates (48[31 ff.]). So the author of the Apocalypse sees the eschatological Israel, which is sealed and kept faithful through the last woes, composed of the full number of tribes with the full number in each tribe, 12 tribes of 12,000 each (7[4 ff.]); he sees the new Jerusalem (21[12 ff.]) in the form of a cube, whose side measures 12,000 furlongs; it has 12 gates inscribed with the names of the 12 tribes and guarded by 12 angelic warders; it has 12 foundations bearing the names of the 12 apostles and a wall measuring 12 times 12 cubits. In the 12 fruits of the tree of life 22[2], the number, as shown by the added words, is determined by the 12 months, the meaning being that the yield continues perpetually through the year. The number is used in one other passage, 'the crown of 12 stars,' 12¹, where the reference is probably to the 12 signs of the zodiac (see Com.). *A thousand*, as in common usage everywhere, is a typical unit of enumeration where large numbers are meant, *e.g.*, '*the cattle on a thousand hills*,' Ps. 50¹⁰, '*One of a thousand*,' Job 9³. So in our book the 1000 years of the Millennium 20⁴ denote a long but limited period; and so a multiple of 1000 is used where large measures or large numbers of persons are spoken of, as in the sealing of Israel 7⁴ᶠᶠ·, the measurement of the Holy City 21¹⁶, and the number of the heavenly host 5¹¹. Its use in forming large multiples of 7 and 12 has been spoken of above.   666 and some other numbers which occur in only one connection can be spoken of most conveniently elsewhere; see p. 403, and Com. 4⁴, 9⁵, 11³, 14²⁰.

VII.   Summary of the Contents of the Apocalypse [1]

Prologue.   I. 1–8.   (1) Superscription, vv. 1–3.   (2) Exordium, vv. 4–8.   (*a*) Address and Salutation, vv. 4–6; (*b*) Proclamation of Christ's Advent — the Motto of the book, vv. 7–8.

In the *Superscription*, vv. 1–3, the writer announces the subject of his book, a revelation of things soon to come to pass. He vouches for the origin and sanction of its contents, which come from God himself through divinely ordained agencies — Christ, an angel, and the writer himself, a divinely commissioned prophet to whom the revelations of the book are shown in visions, vv. 1–2. He commends the book to be read in Christian assemblies, and enforces the injunction to heed its words by the assurance that the time is near when its prophecies shall be fulfilled, v. 3.

The *Exordium*, vv. 4–8, falls into two parts, (*a*) Address and Salutation, vv. 4–6; (*b*) Proclamation of Christ's Advent — the Motto of the book, vv. 7–8.   (*a*) The book is in the form of an epistle addressed to seven Asian churches, though intended for the whole Church.[2]   At the opening the writer adopts the stereotyped formula of address and salutation found with slight variations in all the New Testament epistles except

---

[1] Throughout this section conclusions are assumed which are reached in other parts of the Introduction and in the Commentary. The summary must be constantly supplemented by these fuller discussions.   [2] See p. 210.

Heb., James, 1 and 3 Jno. He closes (22²¹) likewise with a
benediction of the readers similar to that in nearly all the
epistles.   In the address the writer calls down upon the readers grace and peace from the divine presence; and while there
is nothing to suggest a limitation of these blessings to particular needs and times, yet the Apocalyptist has especially in mind
the coming days with their stupendous issues; the thought of
the future dominates the whole passage.   The epithets applied to God and Christ throughout appear to be derived directly from the vision of chapters IV.–V. (a passage quite
probably written before this introductory greeting) and the
divine persons are named in the same order as there.[1]   Before
the revelation of the future, that vision of chapters IV.–V.,
portraying the personages and motives working out the fulfillment
of the messianic hopes, emphasizes the divine attributes which
are closely related to such fulfillment.   So here in the opening benediction, the same attributes of God and Christ are
rehearsed, because the writer is likewise thinking of the assurance which these special attributes give to the readers regarding the revelations and promises of the book.   The blessing is
invoked (1) from God as the eternal one, one therefore who
as superior to all the changes of human history will in the end
come in his eternal kingdom, v. 4 (cf. 4⁸); (2) from the all-
searching Spirit, the revealer of the divine message to the
churches, v. 4 (cf. 4⁵, 2⁷); (3) from Jesus Christ, who opens
the sealed book of the future and gives here in the Apocalypse
a faithful revelation of the Last Days, v. 5 (cf. 5⁵), who though
once slain is now risen to a new life into which his children
will follow him, v. 5 (cf. 5⁶, ⁹ ᶠ·), and who will become supreme
Lord in the messianic kingdom — in the language of Jewish
eschatology, the Root of David, the ruler of the kings of the
earth, v. 5 (cf. 5⁵).   To him, because in his love he has redeemed us by his death and destines us for rule and priestly
privilege in his kingdom, belongs the ascription of eternal
praise, vv. 5 f. (cf. 5⁹ ᶠ·).   (b) The Proclamation of the
Lord's Advent.   The Exordium closes fittingly with a solemn
announcement of the Lord's coming, the thought of which
underlies what precedes, though not formally expressed.   The

[1] See pp. 426 f.

whole future foretold in the book centers in the parousia, a distinct announcement of which is therefore to be expected in these opening words. These verses have been called the Motto of the book, as summarizing its central theme. The proclamation of the Advent is made with striking dramatic force. The writer interrupts as it were his own words and lets his readers hear the well-known apocalyptic cry, *Lo, he comes, every eye shall see him*, to which then the writer himself responds, *Even so, Amen*, v. 7; and then, as the supreme assurance, the voice of Jehovah is heard, *I am the Eternal one, the Almighty*, one whose purpose regarding the eternal kingdom cannot fail, v. 8.

The Initial Vision. I. 9–III. 22.   Christ's appearance to the Prophet with the command (1) to send a book of all the visions revealed to him to seven Asian churches (the Church), I. 9–20; (2) to include a special message to each of these several churches, II.–III.

(1) The manifold introduction to the book (1^{1-8}) now being ended, the writer enters at once upon his theme, the revelation from God which is made to him in visions and sent with all its varied messages to the churches. While sojourning in the island of Patmos he was lifted up into a state of ecstasy on a certain Lord's-day, and heard in words clear and loud like the sound of a trumpet the command to write in a book what is to be shown to him, and to make it known to seven designated churches of Asia Minor. It is in fulfillment of this divine injunction that he now after all his visions are ended writes this book. The somewhat indefinite announcement of the Superscription (vv. 1–2), that God had sent a revelation to his servants through the writer is made more specific; it is the revelation given in these visions, a record of which he is commanded to send to the churches. At the sound of the call the Seer turns and beholds in a manifestation of overpowering splendor one like unto a son of man, who as the head of the Church sends to it the message of all the visions that are to follow. The older prophets, *e.g.* Isaiah (VI.), Jeremiah (I.), Ezekiel (I.–III.), describe visions in which they received their call; and they dwell on their *authorization and equipment* for their work.

s

But that is not the chief purpose of this vision. The simple command *Write* is in this place enough. The writer describing himself as a sharer with his readers in their afflictions and hopes, v. 9, here fixes his eye mainly on the exalted character of the great Author of the message and his intimate relation to his Church, to which the message is sent. Christ appears, portrayed in traits taken chiefly from descriptions of God and an angelic being given in the Old Testament, which are meant to picture him in dazzling glory and majesty, vv. 13–16. A symbolic meaning is not to be sought in the details, except so far as they form traits in a picture of resplendent glory, and contain current terms used in expressing divine activities.[1] Two symbols, the lampstands and the stars, figuring the churches in two different aspects, are shown, which with their context reveal, the one, the Lord's presence in his Church, the other, the might of his holding hand, vv. 12 f., 16, 20. With awe-awakening voice like the sound of many waters, v. 15, Christ declares his transcendent being and the message which in his exalted state he sends to his servants; as the eternal one, v. 17, as in his essential nature the living one, who triumphed over the grave and is Lord of life and death, v. 18, he sends this revelation which with warning and encouragement discloses things which are present in relation to their great issues, and things which shall come to pass, leading up to the End, v. 19, when his eternal purpose shall be accomplished and his kingdom of life shall be established in the complete triumph of his saints over death. While the figure of the Son of man contains reminiscences of the Jewish Messiah, the Christian conception of the exalted Christ is the predominant characteristic in the vision. Verse 20 adds an explanation of two symbols which would otherwise be obscure.

(2) The special messages to the seven churches, II.–III. The vision of the preceding chapter (1^{10-20}) while forming an introduction to the whole book, in that it defines its general scope and gives the Lord's authorization to the Prophet in his entire commission (vv. 11, 19), stands also as the immediate introduction to the group of special messages to the several churches now to follow. The head of the Church has revealed

---

[1] See p. 249.

himself as present within the Church, holding it in his sway to protect it, to chastise it, and to control its destinies.   In that character now in view of what is coming on the earth he sends to these seven churches, which are typical of the Church as a whole, these special words of exhortation, of searching reproof and approval, of fearful warning and glorious promise.   Nothing more clearly distinguishes our book from other apocalypses than does this paragraph of the seven epistles ; yet nothing is more closely in keeping with its purpose and true prophetic character.   The foremost duty of the prophets of Israel was to correct and instruct the people of God ; judgment must begin at Jerusalem.   In the eschatological chapters of the Gospels [1] the thought turns in the outset from prediction and promise to urgent exhortation.   And in general the foremost word of prophecy to Christians is, Take heed to yourselves, repent, be zealous — the most emphatic bidding to the imperfect Church. And so our author with the instinct of the genuine prophet introduces here in the foremost place these stirring words to the churches, regarding their present spiritual condition and their preparation for the coming crisis.   The cursory reader, and many critics as well,[2] may find in the insertion of the paragraph a disturbance of the orderly plan of the book, but a true insight into its nature as a message of prophecy leads us to expect just here in the outset some such direct and searching address to the Church regarding its own life.   The first concern of the Church is its own present state, its fidelity to all that the Lord requires of it ; and only thus can it prepare itself for the future.   What has been said of the destination of the book as a whole is true of the seven epistles also ; while each has its specific message for the particular church addressed, it has in the author's mind its lessons for all the others in the group, and he invariably speaks of the contents of each as, ' What the Spirit saith to the churches.'   There can be no doubt that he saw in all the revelations given to him by the Spirit, both here and elsewhere in the book, a message for other churches besides the seven, the other churches of Asia and of the world at large.

Four of the epistles (to the churches in Ephesus, Pergamum,

[1] Mk. 13, Mt. 24–25, Lk. 21.   [2] See p. 492.

Thyatira, Sardis) contain both praise and censure ; two (to the churches in Smyrna and Philadelphia) unreserved praise ; one only (to the church in Laodicea) unreserved censure. The writer shows an intimate knowledge of each of the congregations addressed. With penetrating insight he sees their faults and perils, he administers rebuke unsparingly, he threatens with the terrors of a fierce judgment, he allows no compromise with a low standard of Christian zeal and morality. But on the other hand he is also quick to see every virtue, to commend, to encourage, to strengthen. The flashes of wrath against the evils found in the churches are apt to blind us to the under-lying manifestation of love aud tenderness. The presence of love in chastisement (cf. 3^{19}) is after all the keynote of all the epistles. Gracious recognition and encouragement come first ; censure stands second. There is no irrevocable spurning of those rebuked, they are called with loving promise to repent-ance. The 'lukewarm' Laodiceans, chastised with stinging words of abhorrence, are the very ones to whom is given the most outspoken promise of intimate, loving fellowship, 3^{20}.

The most casual reader will have noticed the recurrence of certain fixed terms or elements of structure in every epistle. These are (1) 'To the angel of the church in — write' ; (2) 'These things saith he' ;[1] (3) An epithet of the speaker, Christ, taken either from the vision of I. 10–20, or from some characteristic of Christ prominent in the author's mind, as seen later, and designed in all cases to enforce the message ; (4) 'I know,' followed by a characterization of the state of the church, with praise or censure ; (5) commands, warnings, promises suited to each special case ; (6) 'He that hath an ear' etc. — an appeal to every one to heed the Spirit's message to the churches ; (7) 'To him that overcometh' etc. — an eschatological promise to the victor. The order of (6) and (7) in the last four epistles is the reverse of that followed in the first three; so that in this respect the seven fall into two groups of three and four (see p. 253). But with this uni-

---

[1] The words 'These things saith he' introducing every epistle are like the 'Thus saith the Lord' of the prophets ; a literal dictation of words is not meant, but the content of the Lord's will regarding the matter with which the prophet is commissioned.

formity of structure there is no monotony of thought ; each
epistle contemplates a different situation and brings a different word of prophecy.   The specific message of each epistle
can best be reviewed in connection with the account of the
particular church addressed, as given in the Commentary.

The Scene in the Court of Heaven, IV–V.   (1) God enthroned in heaven, and surrounded by the worshiping hosts
of the angelic hierarchy, IV.   (2) The sealed book and the
Lamb, V.

(1) The Introductory Vision (1^{10}–3^{22}), designed to prepare
the Church to meet the future foretold in the other visions,
closes with the last of the seven epistles.   The writer now
passes to that future with *the persons and forces working within
it.*   With Chapter IV begins the long series of revelations of
' things that are ' and ' things that are to come to pass,' which
grouped after the author's own manner make up a united
whole, the main contents of the book, chapters IV–XXII. 5.
The fulfillment of God's purposes concerning his kingdom is
near.   The vision here opened, consisting of two inseparably
connected parts, IV and V, furnishes the foundation and assurance of all that follows — God enthroned over all in eternal
majesty and power, IV, giving over the book of his will to
Christ, the Lamb, the revealer and fulfiller, V.   These are the
supreme ' things that are,' [1] out of which the ' things that are
to come to pass ' must flow certainly and completely in spite
of the powers of evil.   The scene which presents itself here is
one of wonderful magnificence.   Heaven is revealed under the
form of the monarch's throne-room.   Jehovah appears seated
on his throne in the splendor of many-colored light, v. 3, and
surrounded by the highest beings of his celestial court.   Before the throne the polished pavement of the royal hall
stretches out like a sea of glass, v. 6 ; lightnings and thunders,
and voices, symbols of the divine presence, proceed from the
throne ; and before it burn seven lamps of fire, symbols of the
Spirit of God.   As befits the King of kings, God is attended
by a company of angelic kings, four and twenty, seated on
thrones and wearing crowns of gold, v. 4 ; and four Living

---

[1] See Com. 1^{19}.

Creatures, the cherubim and seraphim, stand one on each of the four sides of the throne, vv. 6–8. These, the highest in the celestial hierarchy, raise continually a hymn of praise, worshiping God in his divine nature, his almighty power, and his eternal being, v. 8; while the four and twenty angelic kings respond with acts of lowliest adoration, and with an anthem glorifying God as the creator of all, vv. 9–11.

(2) In chapter V is given the second part of the vision, essential to the completion of the former part. A roll firmly sealed is seen in the hand of God seated on his throne, v. 1 — a roll containing the decrees of God concerning the Last Things, and the consummation of his kingdom, now to be revealed in the following visions. A challenge is given to the whole created world to open the roll; and no one is found worthy, v. 2. Then the Messiah, the Christ, is seen in the form of a lamb in the midst of the group assembled about the throne. He has the tokens of the fullness of power and omniscience (the seven horns and the seven eyes), at the same time he bears the mark of having once been slain, he is seen to be the victor over death. Only he, the possessor of these matchless attributes, may take the roll to open it, vv. 5–7; God's purpose regarding his kingdom of glory, dimly apprehended by the sages and prophets of old, can be fully revealed only by him who makes its accomplishment possible; its deepest meaning is seen only in him who fulfills the office of the promised Messiah, the Lion of the tribe of Judah, the Root of David, and who redeems by his death a people out of every nation to form the final kingdom and to be kings and priests unto God, vv. 5, 6, 9, 10. In the former part of the scene *creation* forms a theme of praise (4^{11}), but in this second part all thought centers in the Lamb's work of redemption. The Lamb's act of taking the roll from the hand of God, the gift to him by God of the book of the supreme decrees of the divine will now to be made known and fulfilled, v. 7, forms a dramatic crisis of most momentous significance. The scene is one of marvelous splendor. A grand anthem — the Adoration of the Lamb — at once bursts from the angelic ranks that stand nearest the throne, vv. 8–10; the hymn is caught up and wafted on antiphonally, swelling out through all the court of heaven, sung

by ten thousand times ten thousand, and thousands of thousands; through all runs the theme, worthy is the Lamb, vv. 11–12; and then the whole created world to its farthest bounds, things animate and inanimate, the living and the dead beneath the earth, take up the refrain, and echoing the hymns of both parts of the great scene, join God, who sits upon the throne, and the Lamb who stands before the throne, in one common ascription of praise, v. 13. The strains cease, the offering of homage ends, as it began, with those highest in rank and nearest the throne; the four Living Creatures respond to the hymn with their great 'Amen,' the four and twenty kings prostrate themselves in silent adoration. It may well be questioned whether Christian literature possesses anywhere a work of art more grandly conceived and executed than this twofold scene enacted in the court of heaven. We cannot fathom the experience of transport in which the prophet and poet who composed it must have been rapt as he recalled his vision and tried to give it written expression.

The representation of Christ in the form of a lamb, that was once slain, is in striking contrast, but not in conflict, with the glorious picture of the heavenly Son of man in the introductory vision (1^{10-20}). There the majesty and power of the ascended Christ are chiefly thought of ; here the fruits of his redemptive death. In its relation to the structure of the book it should be observed that this hymn, while fittingly arising here in recognition of the glory of the Lamb, at the same time forms, in keeping with the author's manner,[1] the immediate introduction to the acts which are to follow in the breaking of the seals (chapter VI).

The breaking of the first six seals of the roll, VI. The book of God's decrees concerning the coming of his kingdom, securely closed with seals which none but the Lamb can open, is now soon to be unrolled ; the promised revelation of the events of the Last Days is now to be given. It begins with the breaking of the first seal. The book cannot be *unrolled* till all the seals are broken, yet neither at the beginning nor at the end is the revelation of the contents said to be made by

[1] Cf. p. 245.

reading from the roll, nowhere is there any intimation of such reading; all is disclosed, portion by portion, in marvelous scenes, which present themselves to the Seer's eye in *visions*, unfolding in succession simultaneously with the Lamb's act in breaking the seals one after another.[1] Doubtless these visions are meant to be understood as corresponding respectively to the contents of certain parts of the book. The revelation of the *main* contents of the book must await the fully opened roll, it must form the sequel to the breaking of the last seal (8^1). All that precedes that is in a way introductory. So in one brief chapter are given with the breaking of the first six seals those preparative or premonitory manifestations which come before the *immediate forerunners* of the End. The portents, which in eschatological writings are made an essential factor as 'signs' of the coming day of judgment, fall into two classes ; in one group are phenomena which occur in the ordinary course of the world, but with increased extent and severity, such as earthquakes, famine, war, etc.; in the second group are the marvelous plagues sent by special intervention of supernatural power, such as water changed to blood, fabulous monsters of torture, etc. Broadly speaking our author may be said to have distinguished the two groups, making the first the *remoter* 'signs,' assigning them to this introductory chapter VI, and announcing them as pictured in visions which accompany the breaking of the first six seals ; while the more awful and more distinctly supernatural plagues form the judgments of the later period which follows the actual opening of the roll. In this he seems to have been guided by the form of apocalypse preserved in the Gospels (Mk. 13 par.), with which he was pretty certainly familiar, whether as there recorded, or as current in tradition. He presents then in this chapter visions of those stereotyped forms of visitation, war, slaughter, famine, earthquake, pestilence, etc., 'the beginning of woes,' as he regards them, and as they are denominated in the Gospels.[2] Such in brief are the contents of this chapter and its place in our book.

At the breaking of the first seal one of the Living Creatures utters a summons with a voice of thunder, and there appears in

---

[1] See Com. 6^1.   [2] Mk. 13^8.

obedience to the call a rider upon a white horse, with a bow and a crown, emblems of the victor in war. He symbolizes *conquest* with all the accompanying woes of captivity and subjection to a foreign foe, vv. 1–2. At the breaking of the *second* seal and in obedience to the summons of the second Living Creature there appears a rider upon a red horse, with a great sword ; his office is to take peace from the earth and cause men to slay one another. He symbolizes the *slaughter of war*, vv. 3–4. The *third* rider, with the black horse and his balance for doling out bread by weight, personifies the distress of *famine*. The grains for bread are to be sold at famine prices. Yet as none of these calamities, which form but the *beginning* of woes, can be conceived to be unlimited in its severity, so in this case the hardier plants, the olive and the vine, escape the devastation which cuts off the grain, vv. 5–6. The *fourth* rider, bearing the name *Death*, riding a pale horse and attended by his invariable companion Hades, receives authority over a large, but limited, part of the earth, and in certain specified forms of destruction. He personifies not death in general, but those particular forms of death which cut off in the sum total a vast multitude of men, *bloodshed, famine, and wild beasts*, vv. 7–8. The vision of the *fifth* seal opens a quite different scene. The souls of those who have already suffered martyrdom for the gospel's sake are seen in safe-keeping beneath the altar in the heavenly temple, and they are heard crying loudly' for the speedy coming of judgment and the avenging of their blood. But they are bidden to wait in patience yet a little while till the destined number of their fellow martyrs shall be filled up in the persecutions now threatening. They are not admitted to the full fruition of the glorified state, but they receive white robes, an emblem of the blessedness which is already bestowed upon them, vv. 9–11. This cry for vengeance is more Jewish than Christian, yet it is not conceived as wholly personal ; it contains a yearning for the triumph of the cause of God and the coming of his kingdom.[1] The vision has a place here among the other events leading up to the End, for in common apocalyptic belief the prayers of the suffering saints for judgment were efficacious in bringing in the End ;[2] and

---

[1] See Com. 6[10].   [2] Cf. En. 97[5], 104[3]. See p. 79.

further, so far as the vision tells of other persecutions yet to come, it has a place among prophecies of pre-messianic calamities. In the apocalypse of the Gospels also (Mk. 13[9]) persecution stands in the eschatological series with earthquake, famine, etc.[1] The breaking of the *sixth* seal is followed in the series of visions by a great earthquake and awful portents in the heavens. So terrible are these that they can be described only in the language and imagery currently applied in apocalyptic literature to the final dissolution of the world. In the words of stereotyped hyberbole the mountains are said to be removed from their places, the lights of heaven to be darkened, and the firmament rolled away. The dwellers upon the earth from the highest to the lowest, believing in their terror that the great day of wrath has come, flee to the caves and call upon the mountains to hide them from the presence of God and the wrath of the Lamb.[2] The whole scene of the breaking of the seals is constructed with wonderful power and artistic skill. With a few bold touches, there is in each vision put before the reader a picture of extraordinary dramatic force. The four mysterious riders, mounted on horses whose colors correspond to the horsemen's missions, and equipped with their appropriate emblems, come forth one after the other in quick succession as they are summoned in tones of thunder, and sweep across the earth triumphant in their ministry of woe. The veil is then lifted and a glimpse opened into the abode of the martyred saints, whose cry for judgment harbingers the near advent of the day of doom. And now the series reaches its climax in vast catastrophes in nature, which seem to the whole family of terror-smitten men to be mingling heaven and earth in final and complete ruin, at the bursting forth of the wrath of God and the Lamb.

Prelude to the breaking of the Seventh Seal. VII. (1) Sealing of the servants of God, vv. 1–8. (2) An anticipatory vision of the redeemed before the throne, vv. 9–17.

With the events of the sixth seal (6[12-17]) close the visitations which form the *beginning* of woes; these are preparatory to the more awful judgments which are now to sweep over the

---

[1] See Com. 6[9-11].   [2] See Com. 6[12].

world as the nearer forerunners of the End. In fact the first six chapters of the book, with the revelation of God's purpose and of the powers working in and through all, and with the events of the six seals, form a preparation for the breaking of the seventh seal (8^1), when the book of the future will be unrolled and its *main* contents (following after what may be called the introductory part, indicated by the visions of the six seals) made known, or rather enacted in the world's final drama. Just here then at the critical turn, between the six and seventh seals, the author, after his characteristic manner,[1] introduces an episode or *prelude*, designed to encourage the readers in the face of coming trial by the assurance of final deliverance and triumph. The despairing cry of the terror-stricken in the scene just closed (6^{17}) 'who is able to stand'? receives for the Christian an answer (1) in a vision of the safe-guarding of the servants of God, VII. 1–8, and (2) in an *anticipatory* vision of the redeemed gathered in heaven, after 'the great tribulation' is passed, VII. 9–17.

In the first vision of the prelude, vv. 1–8, the writer uses imagery drawn from some apocalyptic source,[2] just as he frequently applies symbols taken from Ezekiel, Zechariah, and other parts of the Old Testament. The spirits of the winds are seen about to let loose upon the earth these destructive apocalyptic agencies, but they are stayed by an angel till the seal of God shall have been stamped upon the foreheads of his servants, which like the mark set on the men of Jerusalem in the vision of Ezekiel (9^4) shall guard them from destruction in the calamities about to overwhelm the world. The sealed are, as the Apocalyptist, following his source, designates them, all the tribes of Israel, that is, the whole Church of God, for with our writer as with others of the New Testament the Church is the true 'Israel of God.' Twelve tribes are sealed, no tribe is wanting to fill up the full number; and those sealed in each several tribe are declared to number 12,000, a number typical of fullness;[3] that is, none is omitted, every member of every tribe, every individual member of the Church receives the pledge of security.

From the manner in which the scene opens we should expect

---

[1] See p. 245.   [2] See p. 533.   [3] See p. 254.

the winds to be let loose after the sealing is accomplished, but this does not occur; nor are these winds shown in the following chapters of the book to be associated with the plagues sent upon the world. The writer however is probably not conscious of any defect here. He takes over the figures from his source without attempting to show any connection with later movements, perhaps regarding these winds as symbols of destructive forces in general and so, appropriately enough, representing any or all of the trials against which the Church needs a seal of safety. Similarly he takes over from the source used the enumerating in detail of the tribes of Israel, not because he is thinking of the national Israel, but because such an enumeration vividly symbolizes the *comprehensiveness* of the guarding care of God, which in the coming woes will suffer no single servant of his to be swallowed up in the destruction of the world.

The second part of the prelude, vv. 9–17, is one of those visions characteristic of the author which like a picture within a picture open up out of nearer scenes a view of a realized ideal lying beyond. It gives *in anticipation* a glimpse into the glory that awaits the victor after the coming struggle is ended. The sealing in the former vision is the promise; the scene in this vision is the promise realized in all its fullness, when the 12 times 12,000 of the tribes of Israel, the 144,000 of the complete Church of God (cf. 14[1]), are seen in their character as an innumerable multitude redeemed out of every nation and people. The heaven represented is that of chapters IV–V. The throne-room is seen again with God enthroned there, the Lamb standing before the throne, the four Living Creatures, the Elders (the angelic kings) and all the host of angels. In the midst of these are seen the redeemed robed in white, holding palms of victory and praising God and the Lamb for their finished salvation. As in the scene of the fourth and fifth chapters, the angel hosts take up antiphonally the hymn of adoration, vv. 9–11. One of the Elders performs the familiar office of the 'interpreting angel,'[1] explaining the scene to the prophet and telling of the unending blessedness of the redeemed, vv. 13–17.

[1] See p. 170.

The first series of visions following the opening of the roll at the breaking of the last seal. VIII–IX. (1) Immediate sequel of the breaking of the seventh seal, VIII. 1–2. (2) Offering of incense on the golden altar, VIII. 3–6. (3) The visions of the first six trumpets, VIII. 7–IX. 21; (*a*) first four trumpet-visions VIII. 7–12; (*b*) the woeful cry of an eagle in mid heaven, VIII. 13; (*c*) the fifth trumpet-vision — the plague of fiendish locusts, IX. 1–12; (*d*) the sixth trumpet-vision — the plague of fiendish horses, IX. 13–21.

After the interlude formed by chapter VII, the prophet's vision returns to the breaking of the seals of the roll. The scene is still in Jehovah's throne-room, the Lamb still holds the roll. As in the earlier scene new objects and characters, not mentioned at first, were seen to be present as the vision advanced, *e.g.* the roll in God's hand, the Lamb, etc.,[1] so here the seven archangels who wait on the throne of God are now seen. The breaking of the seventh seal opens the roll; and answering to its *main* contents there is given the whole series of visions now following in our book to the end (XXII. 5). These are arranged in an organized system framed on the author's favorite number, seven. The seven archangels, or throne-angels, with their respective trumpet-blasts introduce the visions and series of visions, which with certain interludes carry out the whole revelation of the mystery of God to its accomplishment. The first six of these visions tell only of sore judgments (VIII–IX). The seventh trumpet, as will be seen below, introduces not only such a judgment, but also other events that belong to the full accomplishment of God's purpose. The agency of the archangels as the ministers of the visions, and the use of the trumpet so closely associated with august, especially eschatological, announcements, are appropriate to the superlative importance of the revelations which are to be given.

(1) The Lamb now breaks the seventh seal and trumpets are given to the seven archangels, foreboding the announcement of momentous issues. The hosts of heaven stand silent with dread suspense in anticipation of the events to follow, VIII. 1–2. (2) Throughout the long silence which follows the break-

[1] See Com. 5⁶.

ing of the seventh seal there rises from the golden altar before
the throne a cloud of incense, offered to add efficacy to the
prayers of all the saints crying for judgment ; and there follow,
with fire from the altar, hurled upon the earth, tokens that the
prayers are heard and that the wrath of God is about to fall
upon the world.   These symbols of the relation of the prayers
of God's people to the coming judgments form a fitting introduction to the trumpet visions, in the events of which the
prayers are seen to be answered.   From these tokens of God's
will the seven angels perceive that their time for action has
come ; they prepare to sound their trumpets and usher in the
threatened judgments, VIII. 3–6.   (3) The visions of the
first six trumpets, VIII. 7–IX. 21.   (*a*) In the *first four trumpet-visions* (8⁷⁻¹²) four plagues of a supernatural character, in
part parallel to the Egyptian plagues, are hurled in quick succession upon the dry land, v. 7 ; the sea, vv. 8–9 ; the other
waters, vv. 10–11 ; and the heavenly bodies, v. 12, working
devastation and horror.   In each region a large, though not
the greater, part is smitten — the effect is limited.   The suffering and terror of men, though constituting the purpose of
the visitations as punishment and warning, are not mentioned
except in the instance of the third, where the death of many
occurs incidentally.   (*b*) Between the fourth and fifth trumpet-visions an eagle flying in mid-heaven forewarns the world
that grievous woes are now to follow with the three remaining
trumpet-blasts, v. 13.   The first four plagues have fallen
directly upon a portion of the natural world, and have thus
wrought their effect upon men indirectly and to a limited
extent.   The fifth and sixth plagues, the first two woes, which
are now to come are of a specially fiendish character and attack
men directly in their persons, in the one case torturing but not
killing, in the other both torturing and killing.   (*c*) The
plague of the fifth vision (9¹⁻¹²), the first of the woes proclaimed by the eagle (8¹³), is inflicted by a swarm of hellish
locusts let loose from the nether-world and equipped with
fabulous forms and scorpion-like tails, for terrifying and tor-
menting.   They are led by the angel of hell.   By these fiendish
creatures the enemies of God are tortured without the relief of
death for the long space of five months, the length of the period

in which the ravages of the natural locusts usually occur. (*d*) The plague of the sixth trumpet-vision (9^{13-21}), the second woe, consists of an innumerable troop of fiendish horses, under the leadership of four angels prepared for the very day and hour of their work, but hitherto kept bound in the East. The horses like the locusts of the first woe are fabulous monsters; they have the head of a lion and serpent-like tails ending in a head with its sting. With the tail they inflict torture and with the mouth they spit forth, as from hell, fire, smoke, and brimstone, killing a third of mankind. The angel leaders of the host, and the riders of the horses are not direct agents in the work of the plague — this work is the office of the monsters. The plague is sent upon the unbelieving heathen world, which notwithstanding this warning continues in its idolatry and wickedness, vv. 20–21. In the successive steps of the trumpet-visions a certain climax is reached in the sixth. Though this is not the culmination, it forms the last of the *series* which with its characteristic preliminary episode (10^{1}–11^{14}) introduces the seventh and final trumpet-vision ($11^{15\ ff.}$). Hence the vast havoc assigned to its plague, the destruction of a third part of mankind ; and hence the more august opening of the vision — a voice is heard from the altar, in answer to the prayers of the saints for judgment, bidding the archangel himself to let loose upon the world the four angels with their innumerable troop of hellish horse.

Interlude between the sixth and seventh trumpet-visions. X–XI. 13. (1) Solemn announcement of the End as near ; foreboding of wrathful judgment; special message to the prophet himself. X. 1–11. (2) The Repentance of Israel, XI. 1–13. The first six trumpet-visions following one another in immediate succession have been closed ; and now before the seventh, the Apocalyptist after his manner[1] pauses and introduces an interlude which serves to prepare for the new vision and to lend impressiveness to it. The interlude consists of two parts: the first a prelude which has direct reference to the seventh trumpet-vision, forming as it were an overture to it (10^{1-11}), the second, a prophecy of an event looked for as necessary before the parousia (11^{1-13}).

[1] See p. 245 ff.

(1) The vision of this paragraph (10^{1-11}), directly preparatory to the seventh trumpet-blast, is concerned with three
agencies, the angel, the seven thunders, and the Prophet. (*a*)
An angel descending in a glory befitting his mission from God,
and assuming a position which shows his message to be addressed to the earth and the sea, that is, to the whole world,
announces with a most solemn oath that the mystery of God,
the consummation of the kingdom, is soon to be accomplished
in the period introduced by the seventh trumpet-blast, vv. 1–2,
5–7. (*b*) Accompanying the angel's cry seven thunders, with
words which the Prophet hears but is restrained from writing
down, forebode judgments of divine wrath as about to burst
upon the world among the events of the coming vision, vv. 3–4.
(*c*) As another part of his mission the angel gives to the
Prophet a message from God contained in a little scroll. The
Prophet is bidden to receive the divine word into his heart, to
appropriate it fully, in the figure here used, to eat it; but he
is forewarned that in the sequel he must find a bitter experience. As he faces the momentous issues of the last of the
trumpet-visions, with the call to new prophecies concerning
many peoples and kings, he feels the demand of his prophetic
office urging him forward with intensified force — it is as if
his commission were given to him anew — and he experiences
the sweetness of a duty in which he is the special agent of God,
the roll is sweet to the mouth; but he is forewarned that he
must find the discharge of that duty bitter also, in that he
must in the new vision utter many oracles of wrath and woe,
vv. 8–11.

(2) In the second part of the interlude (11^{1-13}) the Apocalyptist passes abruptly to a prophecy of the final repentance
of Israel. God's ancient people, the heirs of the messianic
promises, had rejected the Christ and his gospel. This attitude
of the chosen of Jehovah toward the Church of the Messiah
sorely perplexed the Jewish Christian, but he could not believe
that the Israel of the covenant was to be cast off forever and
fail of a share in the messianic kingdom. It became a clearly
announced Christian prophecy, one which our Apocalyptist
accepted in common with other New Testament writers, that
at the last Israel would be 'grafted in again' (Ro. 11^{23}) among

the people of God. And this ingathering was looked for in close proximity to the parousia ; it belonged among the events immediately preceding the End. This prophecy then could not fail of a place in a revelation of the last things written by a Jewish Christian. And the appropriate place for it is just here, before the opening of the seventh trumpet-vision which embraces the last great cycle of events.

The author clothes the prophecy in a form derived from some apocalyptic writing, unknown to us, containing predictions regarding Jerusalem and its people, just as we have seen him adapting to his use passages from the Old Testament writers, and in chapter VII some apocalyptic fragment unknown to us.[1] Jerusalem as frequently in the scriptures represents Israel, according to the common usage of denoting a nation by its capital city. Jerusalem for its sins is to be given up to the 'nations,' the punishment often inflicted upon Israel of old for its unfaithfulness. The nations shall have it in complete subjection and profane it for the whole period of 'the times of the Gentiles,' but a Remnant of faithful ones, as predicted by the prophets, shall be preserved — the sanctuary with its faithful worshipers shall be measured off as a precinct to remain untouched, vv. 1–2. God's compassion for his covenant people has however not failed. He will send two mighty prophets, who will throughout the period call Israel to repentance, v. 3. These are like the two olive trees and the candlestick in the vision of Zechariah (Zec. IV), they are but the channels through which works the might of God, v. 4. Endowed with the marvelous gifts of Elijah and Moses they will work 'in the spirit and power' of those great servants of God, preaching to Jerusalem repentance and obedience, laboring to 'restore all things' before the Lord's coming, vv. 5–6. But as preachers of righteousness and workers of fearful miracles, they will incur the deadly enmity of the wicked, and of the Beast that cometh up from the abyss, the Antichrist. And when they shall have reached the end of their destined period they will suffer shameful martyrdom, vv. 7–10. But afterwards a glorious triumph will be accorded to them in their resuscitation and exaltation into heaven in the sight of all. A great earthquake will accom-

---

[1] See pp. 533 ff., 586.

T

pany these events and destroy one tenth of the city. These
marvels sent as further monitions will strike terror into all who
escape the earthquake ; most (nine tenths) of the inhabitants
of Jerusalem will now heed the words which had been uttered
by the two prophets and will repent of their sins, vv. 11–13.
Thus the purpose of God concerning Jerusalem (Israel) will
reach its accomplishment — an event which must precede the
parousia.

The seventh trumpet-blast.   XI. 14–19.   (1) Announcement
of the third woe, that is, the calamities to follow the seventh trumpet-blast, v. 14.   (2) Sounding of the seventh
trumpet, and the outburst of joy in heaven, vv. 15–18.   (3)
Answering manifestations in heaven and in the world of
nature, v. 19.

(1) After the interlude in X–XI. 13, the Apocalyptist takes
up again the thread of the trumpet-visions broken off at the
close of chapter IX. Looking back beyond the parenthesis
formed by this interlude, he continues as if no interruption had
taken place, declaring the end of the second woe and announcing the third as soon to follow, v. 14.   (2) With these words
of transition he introduces the seventh trumpet. The sounding of this last trumpet proclaims the *period* of the end. To
this period belong all the great movements that are now to follow. Though the end itself is not to come immediately, its
certainty and nearness are proclaimed in this sounding of the
seventh trumpet. A loud hymn of praise bursts forth from
heavenly voices celebrating the incoming of the kingdom of
God, as if already present. The hymn is one of the author's
characteristic *anticipatory* outbursts of praise, uttered at the
beginning of a movement from the standpoint of the final issue.
The Kingdom of the Lord and his Anointed has come and he
will reign forever, v. 15.   The four and twenty Elders, pros-
trating themselves before God in adoration, take up the theme,
amplifying it and proclaiming the arrival of the last bitter conflict of the wrath of God with the wrath of ' the nations,' and
the time of the judgment which shall give their reward to God's
servants and destroy the destroyers of the earth, vv. 16–18.
(3) The song is followed by a twofold response *in action :*

(*a*) the ark of the covenant is revealed in the heavenly temple, symbolizing God's fulfillment of his covenant in the coming reward of his servants ; (*b*) great catastrophes burst forth upon the world, symbolizing the wrath now to be visited upon God's enemies, v. 19.

Chapters XII–XIII : As part of the preliminaries to the events which culminate in the great conflict with Satan and his agents and the overthrow of these, now to be enacted in the seventh trumpet-series, the Apocalyptist introduces here a revelation of the forces operating behind the events and the agencies employed.[1] Two visions are given, which are not intended to depict things that are about to take place as parts of the dramatic movement ; they portray ' things that are,'[2] rather than things that must come to pass, though intimations of issues following are added. The *first* (XII) reveals the cause of the persecutions which the faithful suffer and must continue to suffer in the coming distresses ; this is Satan's fierce hostility to the Messiah.   At the same time the initial defeat with which Satan meets, and his expulsion from the seat of his kingdom, as here described, assures his final downfall.   The *second* vision (XIII) gives a picture of the agent through which Satan is waging, and will wage, unrelenting war with the Messiah's followers, the saints.   This is the Beast (impersonated first in the Roman emperors and then in Antichrist), which receives all his might and authority from Satan, and which together with his helper, the second beast (impersonated in the priesthood of the ruler-worship), uses all his delegated power to accomplish Satan's purpose.

(1) *Satan's hostility to the Messiah.* XII. 1–17.   (*a*) Frustrated attempt to destroy the Messiah, vv. 1–6.   (*b*) Satan's expulsion from his seat in the lower heavens, vv. 7–12.   (*c*) Pursuit of the mother of the Messiah and persecution of the Messiah's brethren, vv. 13–17.

For the exhibition of his thought in this vision the Apocalyptist uses symbols and figures taken from some familiar legend,[3] but he explains his use of these so far as to make his meaning reasonably certain.   His procedure in this respect should guard

---

[1] See pp. 244 ff.   [2] See p. 442 f.   [3] See pp. 613 ff.

us against reading a meaning into minor unexplained traits, which are probably only touches to give vividness to the picture, whether taken over from the source, or specially added by the author himself. The vision consists of three parts.

(*a*) The first part, vv. 1–6, is enacted, so to speak, on a stage whose background is the sky. A woman is seen arrayed in all the glory of the heavenly bodies ; she is about to give birth to a child. A dragon-monster, in a form similar to that found frequently in ancient mythology, stands before her ready to devour the child at the moment of its birth ; but the child is caught away and borne up to the throne of God. As a *sequel* the Apocalyptist, anticipating the third part of his vision (vv. 13–17), and without alluding to a transition from the sky to the earth, adds the woman's flight to a refuge prepared for her in the wilderness, v. 6. The dragon in the scene is Satan, the child is the Messiah, and the woman is the people of God as existing, not in actuality, but in *idea ;* the concrete reality corresponding to this ideal is found in the Church of God, whether under the old or the new covenant, but neither of these is directly intended here. The scene is entirely ideal and such is the figure of the Messiah ; there is no relation to the Lord's earthly life,[1] no reference to the Messiah's coming into being, the Messiah in his ideal being is meant. And as the earthly Messiah is born of the people of God, so here the ideal Messiah is born of the ideal people of God, the woman, 'our mother,' as St. Paul calls her (Gal. 4[26]). And the Apocalyptist means to represent under these symbols, taken from some popular tradition, Satan's deadly hatred of the Messiah *from the beginning*, and his hatred of God's people, because of their relation to the Messiah. At the same time the scene shows the futility of that hatred ; Satan is powerless to prevent the Messiah's exaltation to joint sovereignty with God, and a refuge is provided for God's people. Definite events of history are not thought of here; so far as the vision tells of Satan's design from the outset, it relates to the past; but in the issues it relates to all time till the End.[2]   (*b*) The second part of the vision, vv. 7–12, pictures a scene entirely distinct from the former. The archangel Michael with his hosts attacks

---

[1] See p. 617.   [2] *Ibid.*

Satan in the seat of his kingdom, which is placed according to a current Jewish belief in the lower heavens.[1] Satan
and his hosts are overthrown, cast out from the center of his
dominion and hurled down to earth. This event is not the
original fall or revolt of Satan ; his place in the lower heaven
has existed hitherto (v. 8), and he has hitherto been the foe of
men before the court of God (v. 10) ; yet the event belongs to
the Apocalyptist's past, not the future.[2] The rage of Satan
over his expulsion explains his increased fury in the present as
well as the coming persecutions of the Church. The expulsion
of Satan from the seat of his kingdom is the signal for an outburst of praise from voices in heaven, as if the final triumph
were already come. The first part of the hymn, vv. 10–12 a, is
anticipatory ; the beginning of Satan's downfall assures the complete triumph of the End ; and the singers exult in the kingdom of God and his Anointed, as if now established. The
conclusion of the hymn, v. 12 b, reverts to the present and the
woe which has befallen men in Satan's wrathful presence among
them.   (c) In the third part of the vision, vv. 13–17, the
scene is on earth. Satan, baffled in his design against the
Messiah, cast out from his domain in the lower heavens,
and knowing that the time of his complete overthrow is certainly fixed, becomes the more furious in his rage against the
Messiah's mother, the people of God. The Apocalyptist continues the figures of the first part and expands the account of
the woman's flight, which was mentioned in anticipation in
v. 6. The dragon as a water-monster hurls floods of water
after the woman to sweep her away, but the earth swallows the
floods, and she is borne on eagles' wings to a refuge in the
wilderness, where she is nurtured in safety through the calamitous times preceding the end, times designated by the measure,
stereotyped in apocalyptic phraseology, of three and a half years
or 1260 days.[3] The people of God in its ideal being is divinely
preserved to the end ; the gates of hell do not prevail against
the Church. From his baffled pursuit of the woman, Satan
turns to persecute her other children, the brethren of the
Messiah. The writer here distinguishes between the ideal
people of God and the actual children of God who form the

[1] See p. 617.   [2] See p. 618.   [3] See p. 252.

present concrete reality corresponding to the ideal.   These are
the followers of Jesus, v. 17, who in this last age are exposed to
the full force of Satan's intensified rage.   But the deliverance
of the ideal mother gives sure promise of safety to her children
who keep the commandments of God and hold fast the testimony of Jesus.

(2) *The Beast, the agent of Satan in his warfare against the
saints ; and the Beast's helper, the second beast.*   XII. 18–XIII.
18.

On the place of this vision in the plan of the book see pp.
275, 279.   The Beast incidentally alluded to in XI. 7 is now
introduced and described in his form and functions.   He is the
agent of Satan in his warfare with the followers of the Messiah
($12^{17}, 13^{7}$), and from this point on he continues the dominant figure in all the anti-Christian hostilities that follow till the establishment of the millennium (20^{4}).   Satan does not appear in his
own person as an active participant till the end of the millennium
($20^{7 \text{ ff.}}$).   This agent of Satan appears here in a traditional form
designed to inspire awe and terror.   He is a monster combin-
ing parts of divers animals : he has seven heads and ten horns;
one of his heads has received a deadly wound, of which it has
been healed.   He is endowed with the full power of Satan for
his work in the world, and through him the world worships the
dragon, Satan.   His activity is twofold : he exalts himself
above God as the object of worship, which all who are not followers of the Lamb are led to render him ; and he rules every
tribe and people on earth with absolute sway, making war
against the saints and overcoming them, vv. 1–10.   In securing
the worship of the world he uses the services of a deputy, the
second beast, whom he endows with power to deceive men and
lead them to pay the homage demanded.   This second beast,
possessing attributes unlike those of his master, the first beast,
accomplishes his mission, that of deluding men and causing
them to offer divine homage to the Beast, by means of great
miracles wrought in the sight of men, and by making the image
of the Beast speak to command the worship of itself under the
penalty of death for disobedience, vv. 11–15.   The Beast's
deputy causes also men of all ranks and conditions to receive a

mark of religious devotion to the Beast, which is made essential
for participation in civil and industrial life, vv. 16–17.   The
paragraph closes with the intimation that the Beast is a symbol
of a man and bears a man's name indicated by a number, which
some may have the skill to decipher, v. 18.

It is essential to keep in mind that the Apocalyptist is not
here introducing a new act in carrying out his dramatic plan;
we have rather a vision opening up, after the author's manner,
a picture of the power which Satan uses in the last times, and
a description of the special activities of that power in warring
against God.   A fuller discussion of the symbolism and significance of the chapter is given elsewhere.[1]   It is enough to
premise here, the Beast is Satan's instrument, as represented
first in the succession of Roman emperors, symbolized by the
seven heads, and then, after the destruction of the Roman empire, as represented in Antichrist, in whom the emperor Nero
will return from the dead, symbolized by the head wounded
unto death and healed.   The worship of the Beast is the emperor-worship already demanded in the Roman empire and
destined to be carried to the extreme in worship which will be
exacted by the coming Antichrist.   The second beast symbolizes the priesthood and other functionaries, whose office it is
to establish and maintain the ruler-worship, whether in the
case of the Roman emperors, or the Antichrist.

The redeemed with the Lamb on mount Zion.   XIV. 1–5.
Over against the appalling picture of the warfare upon the
saints waged by the dragon and his agents, the beasts (XII–
XIII), the Apocalyptist now opens a vision of the final triumph
that lies beyond.   Here as throughout the book the prophecies
of darkest trial are lightened up by a glimpse into the blessedness that awaits the victor at the end.   The vision is anticipatory; it stands outside of the events moving toward the last
issue.   The whole company of the saints, symbolized by the
number 144,000 (see p. 648), now redeemed and triumphant,
are seen gathered together with the Messiah on mount Zion,
the central seat of the perfected kingdom of God on the earth.
As the worshipers of the Beast bore his mark (13^{16}), so the

[1] pp. 393 ff.

saints bear the name of God and the Lamb, whose servants they are thus shown to be; and at the same time they are thus sealed as victors (cf. 3^{12}). While the saints are thus revealed on mount Zion, an innumerable host of angels in the great throne-hall of heaven are heard singing before the throne and before the four Living Creatures and the Elders a song of praise for the saints' redemption — a song which none can learn save those who have learned by experience the blessedness of its theme, vv. 1–3. As an admonition to the readers the Apocalyptist specifies some of the virtues of the saints upon which their redemption is conditioned; these are cardinal Christian virtues, chastity, truth, ready following of the Lord, complete consecration like the first fruits which were a holy offering belonging solely to God, and to sum up all in one word, blamelessness, vv. 4–5.

Announcement of the last judgment, warning and promise. XIV. 6–20. This paragraph is prefatory to the march of events which is to begin again in chapter XV; and it also connects the remaining part of the book back with the sounding of the seventh trumpet (11^{15}). That trumpet-blast introduces the vast cycle in which God's purpose regarding his kingdom is to reach its fulfillment (10^7). But the outburst of praise which greeted the trumpet's sound (11^{15-18}) is not followed immediately in the Prophet's revelation by the actual beginning of the final movements. We have seen that the Apocalyptist first reveals in visions which form an interlude in the drama the motives and agencies at work — Satan's hostility to the Messiah and the instruments of his warfare — and in anticipation, the final triumph of the saints (XII–XIV. 5). Then the last series of plagues (XV–XVI), the third woe, predicted as part of the sequel of the sounding of the seventh trumpet (8^{13}, 11^{14}) is to form the immediate precursor of the great day of the Lord. A fitting preface, therefore, to this beginning of the End is this announcement (14^{6-20}) of the judgment, with its call of the world to repentance and with its warning and promise. The announcement is made in the most august tones and in solemn sevenfold form. It must be kept in mind that so far as the entrance of the judgment is announced the announcement is anticipatory — in prophetic style the future is made present.   (1) An angel is seen flying in mid-heaven and proclaiming to all the world the glad tidings of the near fulfillment of God's eternal purpose, and calling upon all peoples and nations to repent and worship the one true God, the creator of all, vv. 6–7.   (2) A second angel proclaims the fall of the great world-power, Rome, the instrument of Satan and the supreme earthly foe of God's people — a power whose removal forms one of the chief events in eschatological expectation, v. 8.   (3) A third angel proclaims the terrible doom that awaits the worshipers of the Beast, vv. 9–11.   (4) The Prophet himself admonishes the saints to hold steadfastly in all the coming trial to the commandments of God and their faith in Jesus, v. 12.   (5) The Prophet's admonition is enforced and the saints are strengthened for martyrdom by a voice from heaven which pronounces blessed all those who shall die in the Lord before the great day enters, v. 13.   (6) A vision of the Messiah as harvester figures the end of the world, vv. 14–16; and (7) another, under the figure of an angelic vintager, pictures the wrath of God in the destruction of the wicked, vv. 17–20.

The seven last plagues, the plagues of the bowls, the third woe.
XV–XVI.   (1) Announcement of the subject of the vision, XV. 1.   (2) Anticipatory hymn of praise, XV. 2–4.   (3) Immediate preparation for the outpouring of the plagues, XV. 5–XVI. 1.   (4) The plagues poured out, XVI. 2–21.

After the prophecies of the preceding chapter (14$^{6-20}$) proclaiming the judgment as close at hand and calling the world to repentance, there follows now the last series of visitations, the last of those terrible 'messianic woes' which in all eschatological expectation are looked for before the Great Day. The plagues of the bowls now introduced take their place as a member in the momentous series heralded by the seventh trumpet-blast (11^{15}), the cycle in which the mystery of God is to be accomplished.   They specifically prepare the readers for the two great events, the destruction of Rome (XVII–XIX. 5), which is in reality only an expansion of XVI. 19, and the conflict of the Beast with the Messiah (XIX. 11–21) to which the sixth plague looks forward. This series of plagues forms the third woe foretold in XI. 14 (cf. pp. 669 ff.).

(1) The subject of this portion of the book is announced as in a kind of *title* by a vision of seven angels having the plagues in which are finished God's wrathful visitations sent upon the world before the last great crisis, XV. 1. These words do not announce something distinct from that which follows in vv. 5 ff.; they state in a summary way the subject which begins in detail there and is unfolded from that point on through the rest of the paragraph to the end of chapter XVI. (2) Before the first step is actually taken in bringing in these terrible judgments, the Apocalyptist looks forward to the end and sees in an *anticipatory* vision the saints standing as victors in the court of heaven after the world-drama is finished, and praising God for his acts of righteous judgment. Both the thought and language of their hymn echo a familiar song of Moses ; and at the same time the hymn gives expression to the thought which forms a great factor in the theme of our book, the acts of the Lamb in revealing and establishing the righteousness of God in the judgment of the world. The hymn may therefore be called the song of Moses, and as well also the song of the Lamb. XV. 2–4. (3) The immediate *preparation* for the outpouring of the plagues now follows, XV. 5–XVI. 1, and is in keeping with the momentous character of what is about to take place. The details in the ordering of the scene and even the ornate phraseology used are chosen with a view to give majesty to the picture. The sanctuary of heaven is seen, conceived under the form of the ancient tabernacle, the shrine of God's abode with his people. From this, as from the immediate presence of God and as sent on a mission from him, come forth seven angels, perhaps the seven presence-angels, clothed in the white, glistening raiment symbolical of celestial beings, and wearing, like the Messiah in his glorified state (1^{13}), girdles of gold. Throughout the whole the agency of God himself is made conspicuous. One of the four Living Creatures, the supreme order in the heavenly hierarchy who stand nearest to God, is chosen as his intermediate agent, and hands to the seven angels vessels of gold filled with God's wrath. The tabernacle itself is filled with a cloud, symbolical of God's presence and power ;

he has entered into the sanctuary of his dwelling and abides there unapproachable till his righteous judgment of wrath has been visited on his enemies. It is his voice sounding from the tabernacle, that dismisses his ministers for their terrible work. As regards the phraseology, it is probably with the purpose spoken of above that the tabernacle receives the august designation, *the sanctuary of the tabernacle of the testimony in heaven;* God is the *God who liveth for ever and ever;* the cloud of his presence is a *cloud of glory and power.* (4) In obedience to the voice from the sanctuary, the angels go forth and pour out the bowls of God's wrath, and the ensuing plagues burst one after another upon the world, XVI. 2–21. The plagues, nearly or quite all of them, contain reminiscences of the Egyptian plagues; they resemble also, more or less closely, the series of trumpet-plagues (VIII–IX). The bowls in the case of the first four are poured out in succession upon the earth, the sea, the rivers, and the sun ; the last three, upon the kingdom of the Beast, the Euphrates and the air. But the effect of the outpouring is always manifested in an ensuing plague, which falls upon men. Even the drying up of the Euphrates, the sixth plague, is meant to open the way for a great scourge in the coming of the kings from the east ; and a second event following with the same bowl, vv. 13–14, that is, the appearance of three demons, lying spirits sent forth to work upon the kings of the whole earth, forms a part of the preparation for the world-calamity, the battle of the Great Day. The seventh plague, vv. 17–21, with its horrors undreamed of, culminates in the destruction of Babylon (Rome), in whose fall the present world order perishes and Antichrist becomes the unopposed lord of the earth. This destruction of Rome, only hinted at in these verses, v. 19, is described with fullness in the next paragraph (17^1–19^5). Two *parentheses*[1] are inserted in the course of the description of the plagues : (*a*) Between the third and fourth bowls ejaculations from the angel of the waters and the personified altar are heard (16^{5-7}) praising God, in language echoing the saints' hymn of XV. 3–4, for his righteous judgment in the plague of the waters. This praise is assigned to these two with special appropriateness. The

[1] Cf. p. 243 f.

former exults that the element over which he presides has been turned into a medium for visiting on the guilty a retribution related in kind to their offense.   The altar, the symbol of the prayers of the saints for judgment, acknowledges that in this plague the prayers are receiving their answer.   This parenthesis divides the series of seven into two groups of three and four.[1]

(*b*) In v. 15, when the agencies for gathering the hosts of the Beast for the great battle are already sent forth on their work and the dread hour cannot long be delayed, the Apocalyptist fittingly inserts, *in the name of the Lord*, a reminder of the suddenness of the advent, and a warning to the saints to be watchful and prepared.

The destruction of Rome by Antichrist.   XVII. 1–XIX. 5. (1) Introductory vision ; the woman seated on the scarlet colored beast, vv. 1–6.   (2) The angel's interpretation of the vision ; Rome and the agency of her destruction, vv. 7–18. (3) Sevenfold declaration of her ruin, XVIII. 1–XIX. 5.

After the series of plagues sent upon the world with the outpouring of the seven bowls (XVI), the last of which gives premonition of special judgment to be visited on Rome, there now follows a vision, or series of visions, announcing the coming of the crowning catastrophe in the world-order as then existing, the destruction of the imperial city, in whose fall the Roman empire vanishes and Antichrist becomes triumphant over all the earth.   The magnitude of this crisis, as viewed by the Apocalyptist, is seen in the fullness with which he announces it.   Forebodings of it have been given among his other prophecies (14[8], 16[19]), and now it is made the subject of a distinct part of the book.   (1) The Seer is carried away in the Spirit into a wilderness, where is revealed to him with full and manifold assurance the judgment of the world-capital, together with the instrumentality through which this judgment is to be accomplished.   An introductory vision pictures under the figure of a harlot seated upon a beast the guilt of Rome in her moral corruption and her fierce persecution of the saints, as the cause of her visitation, XVII. 1–6.   (2) An interpretative passage explaining the significance of the woman and the beast shows

[1] Cf. p. 254.

the former to be the symbol of Rome, and the beast with his
seven heads to be in the *first place* the symbol of the seven
Roman emperors of whom the sixth was then reigning, and in
the *second place*, in the head smitten unto death and restored
(13³), to be the symbol of Antichrist, in whom one of the emperors once slain will become reincarnate, coming from the
abyss with demonic power.   In so far as the beast is identified
with the head (the emperor) at any time impersonating him, it
may be said, with reference to his impersonation in the particular head meant in vv. 8, 11, that the beast was and is not and
is about to come.   The beast in his last impersonation, that is,
Antichrist, will with his ten vassal kings act as the instrument
of God, making desolate the imperial city and utterly burning
it with fire, vv. 7–18.   (3) (*a*) An angel radiant with heavenly
glory proclaims to all the earth the certain coming of Rome's
fall and devastation, XVIII. 1–3.   (*b*) A voice from heaven
summons God's people to flee from her allurements and the
consuming plague about to come upon her in righteous judgment, vv. 4–5.   (*c*) The same voice incites the spirits of
vengeance to do their full work, vv. 6–8.   (*d*) In a passage of
intense pathos the Apocalyptist anticipates the dirge which the
kings of the earth and others will utter as they stand in terror
far off and look upon the smoke of her burning, vv. 9–19.
(*e*) In startling contrast with this pathetic lament, the Apocalyptist throws in [1] an apostrophe to heaven, to the saints, the
apostles and the prophets, bidding them to rejoice in the judgment which God has visited upon Rome in their behalf,[2] v. 20.
(*f*) A strong angel hurls a great mill-stone into the sea, typifying her coming fall and utter disappearance from the earth,
vv. 21–24.   (*g*) After these manifold assurances of the coming
destruction, the Prophet passes over in anticipation to the end,
without allusion to the beginning or progress of the destroyer's
work; all is conceived to be finished, and a loud chorus is
heard from heaven celebrating God's righteous judgment upon
the corrupt and corrupting city, and the vengeance taken for
the blood of his servants, XIX. 1–5.   This whole paragraph
on the destruction of Rome is in its completeness, its skillful
arrangement, its adaptation of the several parts, and in its sus-

[1] Cf. pp. 243 ff.   [2] Cf. Com. 18²⁰.

tained power throughout, the work of a poet and prophet of a high order.

Sequel of the fall of Rome.   XIX. 6–XX. 6.   (1) Prophetic hymn hailing the kingdom of God, XIX. 6–10.   (2) Appearing of the warrior Messiah, XIX. 11–16.   (3) The great battle of the Messiah with Antichrist, XIX. 17–21.   (4) Imprisonment of Satan and the millennial reign of the martyrs, XX. 1–6.

(1) With the fall of Rome the present order of the world closes and the beginning of the end is now entered upon. The chorus of alleluias celebrating the triumph of God's judgment in the crisis of Rome's destruction (19^{1-5}) is now followed immediately by the alleluias of the angelic hosts, in tones of many waters and mighty thunders, *anticipating*, as if already come, the full establishment of the Kingdom of the Lord God Almighty, and the perfected union of Christ with his Church, figured in the marriage of the Lamb, vv. 6–10. (2) The vision of the Apocalyptist now passes quickly over what remains.   After this *anticipatory* hymn (19^{6-10}), he returns to the critical events which must first intervene before the final issue.   The picture is drawn with a few vigorous strokes.   The short reign of Antichrist, the head slain and restored, is passed over in keeping with this rapid movement. The prophecy of earlier visions has announced that power as God's agent in the overthrow of Rome ($17^{16\,f.}$), and as succeeding to a sway over all the earth ($17^{8,\,17}$, 13^{3-8}).   But the mysterious period of his domination is not pictured in detail in the visions of the Seer, as it is not in apocalyptic tradition.   Its general character has been shown in the prophecies of chapters XI and XIII.   In the present chapter where the action is moving swiftly to the end the Apocalyptist comes at once to that which was of supreme moment in the Christian anticipation of Antichrist, his complete annihilation by the Messiah. The warrior Messiah appears here, followed by the hosts of heaven, to meet Antichrist, who has gathered his armies at Harmagedon for the battle of the great day of God ($16^{14,\,16}$). The Messiah, true and faithful to his character as the deliverer of his people and the destroyer of their great enemy, his eyes

flashing with avenging fire, comes forth with tokens of certain victory; he rides upon a white horse, the sharp sword of his irresistible word with which he will slay all his antagonists is seen, his garments are, as it were, in anticipation stained with their blood; the armies that follow him ride on white horses and are clad in white robes, symbolical of victory.   His many crowns and the name written on his mantle proclaim him King of kings and Lord of lords, 19^{11-16}.   (3) In certain anticipation of the victory over Antichrist and of the slaughter of his hosts, and in a spirit of terrible vengeance, an angel summons the birds of prey from all quarters of the heaven to feast on the carnage of the battle now to follow.   The Seer then comes to the actual conflict upon which all events since the outpouring of the sixth and seventh bowls have been converging.   He sees the hostile hosts in array, but gives no description of a battle; nothing is said of the clash of armies, or of a hard-won victory; in fact nothing of the kind enters into the conception; all is achieved in an instant by the miraculous power of the warrior Messiah.   The two leaders are seized and hurled down to the lake of fire, and all the hosts are slain by the sword from the Messiah's mouth, vv. 17–21.   (4) The auxiliaries of Satan, that is, Rome and the imperial power, Antichrist and his adjutant the false prophet, together with all the kings of the earth with their armies, these all have been removed in the events culminating in the battle of Harmagedon. Now Satan himself robbed of his power is seized by an angel, fettered, and imprisoned in the abyss for a thousand years. At the same time the martyrs are raised from the dead and reign with Christ over the earth throughout this period, undisturbed by Satan.   In striking contrast with many apocalyptists, who with an exuberance of sensuous figures dwell upon the delights, the luxuriance, and the glories of the messianic age, our prophet describes the blessedness of the saints in a single sentence of masterly reserve: they reign with the Messiah and have the immediate access of priests to God and Christ, XX. 1–6

The End.   XX. 7–XXII. 5.   (1) The destruction of the nations in their last assault upon the citadel of God's people, and the final doom of Satan, vv. 7–10. (2) The general resurrection and judgment, vv. 11–15. (3) The new heaven and the new earth, and God's presence with his people in the new Jerusalem, XXI. 1–8. (4) The city of the new Jerusalem, XXI. 9–XXII. 5.

(1) After the long era of messianic peace on earth, the powers of evil are again let loose and gather all their forces for a final assault on God's people; the profound quiet of the millennial lull is the harbinger of the outburst in which the storm gathers up all its fury for the last great onset. Satan released from his imprisonment goes forth to the four corners of the earth to deceive and assemble for the war the nations Gog and Magog, in which are embraced under a symbolic name all the tribes of men hostile to God. These come thronging up in countless myriads from all quarters, covering the face of the whole earth, and encompass Jerusalem, the seat of the Millennial Kingdom, and the camp of the saints. But, as in the battle with Antichrist ($19^{19\,\text{ff.}}$), so here also there is no shock of armies; fire comes down from heaven consuming all the hostile hosts, and Satan himself is cast into the lake of fire, where with the Beast and the false prophet he is to be tortured forever, XX. 7–10. (2) Satan and all his hosts being now forever overthrown, the general resurrection and judgment follow, as the expected sequel. The Seer beholds a great throne resplendent in the light of divine glory, he beholds God seated thereon as judge, before whose awful majesty the earth and the heavens, as belonging to the transitory, flee away; only the eternal remains. All the dead are raised and stand before the throne, the books are opened and each is judged according to his deeds. All whose names are not found written in the book of life are cast into the lake of fire. Death, and Hades the abode of the dead, are personified in the scene, and as the last enemy to be overcome, are represented as cast into the same place of unending punishment with the others; death exists no longer as a terror to the saints. The reward of the righteous in the judgment is not spoken of in this passage, XX. 11–15. (3) After the resurrection and the judgment, but one step remains to the fulfillment of all. The great drama of the world-ages reaches its end in the bringing

in of the new heaven and the new earth.   The present earth
and heaven have passed away, and the Apocalyptist sees in
their place a new heaven and a new earth; he sees also the
holy city, Jerusalem, hitherto standing in its ideal glory before
God in heaven, now descending in splendor, as a bride adorned
for her husband, to the new earth to form the tabernacle of
God's abode among men.   Here will be perfected the union
of God and his saints; they will be his people and he will be
with them, he will take from them death and all sorrow and
pain, he will give freely to every yearning heart the water of
life, he will satisfy every soul athirst for God, the victor in the
conflict with evil will walk with him in the union of perfect
fatherhood and sonship.   But the part of the wicked will be
the lake of fire and the second death, XXI. 1–8.   (4) The
holy city, which in XXI. 2 f. was announced, in passing, as
part of the great scene of the final renewal of all things, is now
in XXI. 9–XXII. 5 described in detail.   The prominence of
a glorified Jerusalem as the center of God's kingdom in familiar eschatological expectations makes a vision of this character essential in a full revelation of the End; and the Seer conceives the city, which had hitherto been hidden in heaven,[1] as
now coming down in wonderful splendor to form the seat of
God's throne and the shrine of his abode on the new earth.
The city as it presents itself to his vision cannot be conformed
to an imaginable reality, it cannot be delineated with the
measurements and conditions of structures of men's building.
It is a divine creation, and the Apocalyptist struggles here by
the use of symbols and marvelous imagery to represent its vastness, its symmetry, and its glorious perfection.   His vision is
much influenced by Ezekiel and other prophets.   He is carried
away in an ecstasy to the top of a high mountain whence he
beholds the city coming down from heaven radiating the wonderful light of God's presence, vv. 9–11; it is reared on the
foundation of the apostles, the gate-towers of its high walls
with their angel keepers assure entrance to all the tribes of
the Israel of God from every quarter of the earth, vv. 12–14;
it is vast in its boundaries beyond all the cities of men, and in
its perfect symmetry its height is equal to its length and

_____
[1] Cf. p. 56.

U

breadth — it reaches up to God's seat in the heavens, vv.
15–17; it is built wholly of gold and precious stones, vv.
18–21; it contains no temple, for it becomes itself one vast
sanctuary through the presence of God and the Lamb; and
because of the light of that presence it has no need of sun,
or moon, or lamp, vv. 22–23; the divine light which streams
out from it will lighten the nations of the earth, and without
ceasing they will come into it, as into the temple, to offer the
homage of their costliest gifts, vv. 24–26; no wicked one, but
only those enrolled in the Lamb's book of life, may enter in,
v. 27; the water and bread of life are there, for from the
throne of God and the Lamb proceeds a life-giving river, along
whose banks grows in countless numbers the tree of life, which
yields its fruit for food continually, and its leaves will heal the
nations of all deathful diseases of the soul, XXII. 1–2; there
will be there the throne of God and the Lamb, before which
the saints will offer worship, and as priests in the immediate
presence of God, they will see his face; they will bear the
mark which shows them to be wholly his; in the light of his
presence they will need no sun nor lamp; and they will reign
for ever and ever, vv. 3–5.

The Epilogue. XXII. 6–21. The long series of visions
forming the revelation announced in chapter I. 1 is finished in
XXII. 5. The contents of the roll of seven seals are fully revealed, reaching their final chapter in the description of the
glory and bliss of the saints in the new Jerusalem. The book
proper, which the Apocalyptist is bidden to write (1^{11}) is ended,
and he now in these last verses appends his Epilogue, between
which and the Prologue, prefixed in the first chapter, there is a
clear correspondence in form and matter.[1] The book begins
and ends as an epistle ($1^{4\,ff}$, 22^{21}). The epistolary introduction and conclusion form the framework into which is set the
whole message contained in the visions. The chief purpose of
the Epilogue is to give the strongest possible sanction to the
book and to bring its message home to the hearts and con-
sciences of the readers. The several parts of this paragraph
are loosely connected; the thought and the speakers whose

[1] Cf. p. 771.

words are given change abruptly.   The angel who talks with the Seer in the vision of the new Jerusalem (21⁹ᶠᶠ) here authenticates the revelations given in the book, v. 6 *a*; the Seer himself affirms the revelation to have been given by angelic agency at the bidding of God, the inspirer of the prophets, v. 6 *b*; the Lord's own words are given, with his own voice as it were he proclaims his advent near, v. 7 *a* — the central thought of the book; the Apocalyptist declares the blessedness of those who heed the prophecies of the book, v. 7 *b*.   The author of the book vouches for his direct personal knowledge of what is recorded therein and shows how the angel affirmed his prophetic rank, vv. 8–9.   The angel, vv. 10–11, the Lord himself, vv. 12–13, and the Apocalyptist, vv. 14–15, announce the nearness of the advent with its accompaniment of doom and reward.   The Lord, again speaking with his own voice, proclaims himself, in his office as Messiah and introducer of the approaching day of God, to be the sender of this message to the churches, v. 16; and the Spirit and the Church in response lift up their prayer for his coming, v. 17.   The author affixes a solemn warning against perversion or evasion of the teaching of his prophecy, vv. 18–19; he repeats the Lord's promise of his advent, and utters his own responsive prayer, v. 20; he then closes with the usual epistolary benediction, v. 21.

VIII.   PERMANENT AND TRANSITORY ELEMENTS IN THE APOCALYPSE DISTINGUISHED

It has been shown above [1] that the purpose of the Apocalypse as immediately determined by the circumstances of the period in which it was written, and its essential character as a 'Tract for the Times,' must be kept constantly in mind in seeking to ascertain its meaning.   And as we read it, we find that the writer was influenced in every chapter by the thoughts and forms characteristic of traditional apocalyptic.   But as the centuries advanced beyond his time, the face of the world changed.   Emperor-worship (so important an integral factor

[1] Pp. 208 ff.

in the origin and contents of the book), with all it represented
as regards imperial hostility to the Church passed away, governmental persecution ceased, Christianity gained a footing as
the recognized religion of the State.   What seemed the paramount dangers to the Church, when the Apocalypse was
written, no longer existed.   The question then arises, has the
book a meaning and value for another age, our own for example,
in which the circumstances of society, and the needs and perils
of the Church are very different ?   Has it a meaning that can
be expressed in language which does not employ the conceptions, imagery and terms of the apocalyptic writings ?   The
very closeness with which its own time is aimed at in its contents would seem to render it irrelevant to a time altogether
dissimilar.   No doubt as a document of a bygone and most
interesting era in history, it is of extraordinary value.   But
what is its practical value for the faith and conduct of another
age ?   The question is complicated by the fact that its predictions, forming as they do the principal part of its contents,
were to a large extent not fulfilled.   Rome was not destroyed,
Nero did not return, Antichrist did not appear, the millennium
was not set up, the End with its stupendous events has not
come.   The clue to the solution of these difficulties, leading to
the separation of a permanent element from the temporary and
formal, is found in the real nature and characteristics of prophecy in general.

The Apocalypse as a work of prophecy.   The office of the
prophet, in abeyance for some centuries but brought back
again in one of the greatest of the order, John the Baptist,[1]
forms one of the established ministries for the 'building up of
the body of Christ.' [2]   But while there were prophets in the
apostolic Church and prophetic elements in the New Testament writings generally, the Apocalypse stands alone as a distinctively prophetic book.   Here the author claims the name
of prophet and emphasizes his special commission from God, as
the bearer of an inspired message to the Church ; [3] his stand-

[1] Mt. 11[11, 14].
[2] Cf. Eph. 3[5], 4[11], 1 Co. 12[28], 14 *passim*, Ac. 15[32], Rev. 16[6], 18[20], *al.*
[3] 22[9], 10[11], 1[1, 11, 19], 22[6, 8, 16].

ing characterization of the book is 'words of prophecy.'[1] In keeping with these claims the book is seen to be parallel in its fundamental character with the Old Testament prophecies. All alike belong to a time of stress, or special emergency ; their message relates to the cause of God as one with the cause of his people in the crisis of the age ; the messengers announce themselves as specially commissioned speakers from God. Their prophecy is first of all directed to the spiritual condition of God's people, warning them of their duty and arraigning them for their failures. On the other hand it encourages their hopes and steadfast activity through the promise of triumph, which God has in store for them in the near future. The fact that the prophecy of the Revelation is in the *apocalyptic* form does not differentiate it in its essential nature from those of the Old Testament.[2] And there is no more ground for questioning the reality of the mission from God in the case of our author, than in that of these older prophets. It is interesting to notice in this connection that the author does not, like other apocalyptists, deliver his message under an assumed name. A true prophet came in his own person, spoke in his own character as directly sent by God — his personality was important. And so the writer of our book is too clearly conscious of his missson as a prophet to admit of his putting his message in any anonymous or pseudonymous form ; he speaks to the readers as the John well known to them, while he is careful to show his credentials attesting his true prophetic office.[3]

Certain canons of prophecy and their application to the Apocalypse. The grouping of the Revelation in this broad class with the prophetic writings of the Old Testament gives certain valuable helps regarding the nature and form of the message. The contents of Old Testament prophecy, the character of its predictions, and the light thrown in that epoch and especially in the New Testament age upon their fulfillment or non-fulfillment, enable us to deduce a few simple canons for the right understanding of prophecy in general, which are applicable to the Revelation, and are of the utmost value in solving the difficulties mentioned above and in determining the permanent significance of the

[1] 1³, 22⁷, ¹⁰, ¹⁸⁻¹⁹.   [2] Cf. p. 168.   [3] 1¹, ⁹ ff, 22⁸⁻¹⁰, ¹⁶.

book. (1) The contents of a prophetic message are determined
by the circumstances, the needs, and the dominant religious
conceptions of the age to which it is addressed ; for the message is always designed to accomplish God's work in a particular historical situation. It is true that underlying all
prophecies are certain truths regarding the character of God
and his will which are in themselves independent of historical
circumstances. But these are always apprehended by the
prophet through the media of the conditions of his own time.
Such limitations are not only a necessary result of the limitations of all human agencies employed by God ; they are also
essential for the very purpose of the prophet's mission, which
is to arouse God's people to their religious duty in the special
emergency arising, and to assure them of God's good purpose
for his kingdom of the future. In the Old Testament period
the prophecies are inseparably bound up with certain political
and local institutions and ideas; Israel is the people of God
and beloved by him, while the nations, Edom, Assyria, Babylon,
and the others, are his enemies and hated by him ; 'I have loved
Jacob, but Esau I hated' (Mal. 1²); Palestine is the country,
Jerusalem the capital of God's kingdom soon to be established
in splendor; salvation is deliverance from the oppressing foreign nations ; to Israel the subject peoples of the earth will
pay homage ; the future king is an idealized descendant of
David, who will have the uttermost parts of the earth for his
possession and break the nations with a rod of iron. In the
course of Israel's history, with its varying internal conditions
and its varying relations to foreign powers, it happens that
sometimes one of these factors, sometimes another, comes more
to the front in the national life and becomes the predominant
theme in the prophecy of that epoch. 'At one time the idea of
the congregation of Jehovah appeared as the ruling idea in the
contents of the prophetic consciousness, at another time the
kingdom of God, again the theocratic kingship, again the priesthood, again the abiding presence of God in the temple' (Riehm
130). Now these ideas are not with the prophets figures or
allegories of a coming spiritual kingdom, of the Church and the
Christian life. They are held literally and form an essential
part of the subject to which the contents of the prophecy

relate. But in the light of later history, and especially, of the New Testament revelation, it is easy to see that these factors are temporary, that they do not form part of the ideal, universal, truth contained in the prophetic message. The contemporaries of the prophet could apprehend the permanent only through these transitory embodiments. The Christian reader makes the distinction. In the New Testament era the change in the idea of the kingdom of God, its place, its people, its destinies, its Savior and King, brings with it a vast change in the contents of prophecy; and there runs through the New Testament a prophetic element conformed to these Christian ideas. It is not necessary to illustrate this characteristic of Christian prophecy, or to point out the general agreement in this respect of the Revelation with the other books. But in the New Testament also the same law holds as elsewhere regarding the contents of prophecy — the topic to which a prophetic utterance relates is determined by existing conditions and beliefs. Now the gaze of the apostolic Church was turned intently to the future and the Lord's return, its outlook was eagerly eschatological. Therefore its fortunes, its struggles, fears, and hopes were viewed from the standpoint of its eschatological expectations. The elements of its eschatology were however in many instances suggested by Jewish apocalyptic ideas belonging to the times in the midst of which Christian expectations took form. Thus it comes about that there appear in Christian prophecy factors which, however much modified, are a product of Jewish eschatology. Naturally such elements play a large part in the Revelation, though they occur elsewhere; compare especially the eschatological discourses in the Gospels, also 2 Thess. 2^{1-10}, 2 Pet. 3^{7-13}. Here belong in our book the following: the prophecy of Antichrist with his demonic powers, his world-wide tyranny, his blasphemous claim of divinity; the coming of the warrior-Messiah with the armies of heaven to destroy Antichrist; the elaborate programme of pre-messianic plagues; the representation of the hostility of the world-monarchy to the people of God as a direct agency of Satan in his warfare against God; the renewal of the earth and the heavens; perhaps other prophecies also may be added to this class. It is important to observe, that these factors constitute not a form or symbol but the actual contents of the respective prophecies. They are the historical element, that which is furnished by contemporary thought and experience. And as such they are to be distinguished from the great spiritual truths of God's eternal purposes in the world, his mighty control of the movements of human society, to work out his gracious will for the sons of men. These latter are the elements of permanent meaning in the prophecy. The former, as springing out of the accidents of contemporaneous history, as the media through which our Prophet seizes his divine revelation, may safely be regarded as circumstantial and transitory; like the national and local ideas of the Old Testament prophets they do not possess final validity. The remark of Davidson (Hast. IV. 126) is especially appropriate here : ' Prophecy while maintaining its spiritual principles unchanged from age to age, by substituting one embodiment of these principles for another age after age, seems itself to instruct us how to regard these embodiments and constructions. They are provisional and transient. They sustain the faith and satisfy the religious outlook of their day, but they have no finality.'

(2) Many predictions of the prophets were not fulfilled. The central significance of prophecy is found not in the prediction of coming events of history, but in revealing the truth of God. Yet since the truth thus declared by the prophet always has its bearing, in practical and moral aspects, on the future as well as the present of God's purposes, the prophet is also a foreteller. And his predictions, that God will deal with men according to their character and conduct, are unerringly verified. The profoundest meaning of the prophetic message as a whole is fulfilled in Christ. Also important historic events, especially of the near future, are foretold ; for example, the return of Israel from exile, Jer. 29$^{10\,\text{ff.}}$; the deliverance of Jerusalem from the army of Sennacherib, Is. 37$^{33\,\text{ff.}}$; the fall of Babylon, Jer. 50–51. On the other hand the instances of unfulfilled predictions are numerous. Most familiar among such are the announcements of the great eschatological crises as near, and the pictures of the reign of David's son in an earthly kingdom of glory, over a people enriched with every felicity. Also in the forecast of events of a more ordinary

kind, a comparison of the prophecies with subsequent history shows the lack of correspondence to be frequent. A few examples will suffice: the Egyptians were not carried off captive by the Babylonians (Jer. 46), nor by the Assyrians (Is. 20); the Jews, restored from exile, did not gain possession of Edom, Gilead, and Philistia (Ob. vv. 18–20); Judah did not take captive the inhabitants of Tyre, Sidon, and Philistia (Joel 3⁴⁻⁸); Tyre was not laid waste by the Assyrians and after forty years restored to her prosperity to consecrate her wealth to Jehovah (Is. 23). The announcement in many prophecies that the great events of the End were near is attributed by many scholars to what is called the *perspective* character of prophecy; the prophet is conceived to overlook the intervening ages just as one overlooks the low-lying intervals in a landscape and views a distant mountain as near.[1] This simile, however, does not remove the actuality of the error, the observer of the landscape really supposes the mountain to be near. The illusion — not irreverently may we call it so — in the prophet's case seems rather to spring from his vivid perception of God's presence and work in the crisis of his day; he sees God operating mightily in the great world-movements taking place, he sees the moral connection of these movements with the progress of God's Kingdom, and forgetting the slowness of moral advance, he passes inevitably to the inference that the final goal is now about to be reached.

It is proper to observe that in some instances the failure of a prediction is apparent rather than real. It is sometimes clear that the fulfillment of the prophecy was *conditional*, dependent on the future conduct of those addressed. Jonah's unqualified declaration that Nineveh should be destroyed in forty days, 3⁴, was annulled by the repentance of the Ninevites. Micah predicted unconditionally that Jerusalem should be plowed as a field, 3¹²; but Hezekiah's repentance averted the fulfillment of the words, Jer. 26¹⁹. This conditional character in certain predictions, which though uttered absolutely were intended to work a moral change, and therefore left their fulfillment in suspense, is directly asserted by Jeremiah, 18⁶⁻¹⁰, and it doubtless belongs to many cases, where the issue does not correspond with the utterance. Another class of predictions only apparently showing error in the prophet occurs in the details of certain prophetic descriptions. As in similes and parables the essential thought is often for the sake of greater

[1] Cf. Orelli, 33.

vividness developed by features having no separate applicability and intended only to fill out the picture, so the prophecy of a coming event is sometimes given, not in a simple, concrete statement of the fact, but in an idealized picture drawn in detail with traits suggested by ordinary experience.   Thus the atrocities and devastation foretold in the prediction of Babylon's fall in Is. 13$^{17-18}$ were according to Babylonian records not actually realized, but they are such as often occurred in the sacking of a city; what the prophet has in view is the capture of the city in a siege, and he elaborates his portrayal of it by the use of these common accessories.   Similarly the minute geographical chart of the Assyrian march against Jerusalem, Is. 10$^{28-32}$, is only an ideal sketch of the ways open to such an army of invaders.   The predicted ignominious treatment of Jehoiakim's dead body, Jer. 22^{19}, 36^{30}, not verified by the event (2 Ch. 36^{10}; cf. LXX. 36^{8}), is a touch taken from the frequent savagery of a conqueror and is added to make vivid the prophecy of the king's death.   But while it is necessary in even the briefest notice of the fulfillment of prophecy not to overlook these classes of predictions whose non-verification is only apparent, yet these constitute only a small number in comparison with those which must be admitted not to have been realized in fact.

The effort to avoid a supposed difficulty in such unfulfilled predictions by taking them as figurative or allegorical is now generally disallowed by scholars, because that explanation can be applied to only a limited number, and does violence to the prophet's evident intention to be understood literally.   Equally indefensible is the view that the prophecies in question look forward to a time yet even now in the future, when they will be fulfilled.   The very nature of the prophet's message, as addressed to a need in a crisis actually present with the readers, would make inappropriate an announcement belonging only to a future indefinitely remote.   It is true that the *spiritual ideas* regarding God's purposes and his dealings with men may be realized at least partially again and again in the course of history and at last perfectly in the End.   But that is not what the prophet evidently means in foretelling a definite concrete event as about to come.   The prophecies regarding Assyria, Babylon, the restored glory of Jerusalem and Palestine, cannot be fulfilled, because the circumstances of the world which are presupposed cannot, we may undoubtedly say, arise again.   ' It is impossible that the evolution of the divine purpose can ever again be narrowed within the limits of the petty world of which Judah was the center, or Egypt and Assyria the extremes. . . . No sane thinker can seriously imagine for a moment that Tyre will again become the emporium of the world's commerce, or Jerusalem the seat of universal sovereignty. The forms in which Isaiah enshrined his spiritual hopes are broken and cannot be restored; they belong to an epoch of history that can never return.' Smith, *Prophets* 337.

These unfulfilled prophecies, however, cause difficulty only when we conceive the prophet to speak from a state, in which he has often been compared to a musical instrument or a pen in the hand of another. But the prophets of at least the age of written prophecy are not so represented in the Scriptures. Even in their ecstasies they retain their consciousness in activity. What St. Paul says of the Christian prophets is applicable to all : 'The spirits of the prophets are subject to the prophets,' 1 Co. 14[32]. They are not moved mechanically in either receiving or communicating truth. And they must hear and utter God's word through the medium of forms which are intelligible to themselves and to men in general. That which is especially revealed to them, that which forms the true contents of their divine message, consists of spiritual truths to be declared to men and the relation of these to the exigencies of the time. The prophet beholds the social and political movements taking place about him in the light of the revelation given to him. His supernaturally quickened perception may sometimes show him the future in which the present must issue; but his predictions must naturally be shaped by his present national and local circumstances, since it is through these that he apprehends his special revelation from God. While the final issue of God's will and purpose is made unmistakable to him, the precise manner in which this shall be accomplished is unknown to him ; often it could not be comprehended by him or by those whom he addresses. As he himself sees the future in the aspect of an issue from his present, so he must fashion his forecasts with this limited foresight. Therefore while his prophecy of the final outcome of God's will is infallible, his pictures of future historical events in which he looks for this realization of the divine purpose belong to his circumscribed vision. The frequent failure of such historical

predictions cannot therefore cause surprise, or raise real difficulty in the interpretation of prophecy.

It is well to notice the attitude of the prophets themselves
and of the New Testament writers toward an exact literal fulfillment of earlier prophetic utterances. For example, the
messianic age was, according to the predictions of Isaiah, to
follow the downfall of Assyria ; second Isaiah placed it after
the destruction of Babylon, Daniel after the overthrow of the
Græco-Syrian power, the Revelation a short time after the fall
of Rome. But the earlier prophet did not, because of the
prediction unverified in history, lose any of his authority with
his successors as an inspired messenger from God. The abiding truth regarding the kingdom of God revealed through the
prophets was accepted by the Church of the New Testament
era as independent of the local and temporal details given in
the Old Testament writings. It is clear that the prophet
himself did not make infallibility in his historical forecasts
essential to his office as the trustworthy announcer of the word
of God. This is seen in the unconcern with which the prophets
and their followers recorded earlier utterances which were
found to be at variance with after events. To quote again
from Robertson Smith, ' It is plain from the very freedom with
which Isaiah recasts the details of his predictions from time to
time — adapting them to new circumstances, introducing fresh
historical or poetic motives, and canceling obsolete features in
his older imagery — that he himself drew a clear distinction between mere accidental and dramatic details, which he knew
might be modified or wholly superseded by the march of history, and the unchanging principles of faith, which he received
as a direct revelation of Jehovah himself, and knew to be
eternal and invariable truth ' (*Prophets* 342).

The recognition of this element of fallibility in certain details
of prophecy due to the prophet's necessary relation to his
present, to his belief that the eternal ideals revealed to him are
about to be realized in forms growing out of the great world-
movements of his own day, furnishes an important factor in
the interpretation of the Revelation. The prediction of the
near downfall of the Roman world-power, the graphically
drawn picture of the destruction of the imperial city, the

accession of a half-demonic world-tyrant (Antichrist) who should soon be destroyed, and the immediate setting up of a millennial reign of the martyrs with Christ on earth, are predictions which history has not verified. But their failure cannot give difficulty in the study of the Revelation, as a book of prophecy. They are similar in origin to the predictions given by the Old Testament prophets in connection with the great crises of their time. They enshrine great truths regarding the kingdom of God; but the form in which the Apocalyptist saw the truth realized, the form in which he has clothed his revelation, is derived from events and ideas belonging to an age now past. That form is transitory, the truth is eternal. We now distinguish the one from the other. We confidently believe in the final realization of the divine ideal revealed; on the other hand, in view of what we see to be characteristic of prophecy, we do not look for anything like a literal fulfillment of predictions shaped by the facts and conditions of a transient period of history.

(3) In the above discussion it has perhaps been made sufficiently clear that the function of the prophet is not that of a writer who shall tell beforehand the history of the future. But it may be useful to speak more particularly of that point, because of its value in guarding against some prevalent misinterpretations of the Apocalypse. In one sense the prophet may be said to foresee the most distant end; he sees the certain triumph of God's kingdom over all the powers of evil, the accomplishment of God's purpose of goodness for his children, but he does not know the time — 'of that day and hour knoweth no man' — though he supposes it to be near; nor has he any vision of the *form*, in which all will be actually realized, or the far-off changes which must first take place in the world. Political and social movements of the remote future are not of interest in his immediate mission, and doubtless could not be understood by him or by those to whom he speaks. 'The Spirit of God can give certainty to the prophet concerning the nearness of historical details only in the case of those which stand in some immediate connection with the circumstances of his present, not concerning those in which this is not the case; because for the apprehension of the latter there is entirely

wanting in the prophet's consciousness every point of contact which makes it possible for the apprehension to arise ' (Riehm 104 f.). This is so because the inspiration of the prophet does not work magically, but through the media of his own consciousness and understanding. And so while definite events of the nearer future closely connected with his present, such as those mentioned above (p. 296), are foreseen by the prophet, the history of the distant future in which the cause of God's kingdom must meet entirely new conditions remains hidden. The operation of this law is abundantly illustrated on the one hand in the fulfillment of predictions relating to persons and kingdoms in the Assyrian, Babylonian, and other ages; on the other hand in the absence from the earlier writings of pictures of the exact historic conditions existing in the New Testament era.

The principle here stated of the prophet's inability to foresee incidental details in a remote future appears to be contradicted by a considerable group of passages found in the Gospels. It is there said of some act of the Lord's, or other fact recorded in the narrative, that it is a fulfillment of a saying of the prophets; e.g. Mt. 2^{23}, 4^{14}, $27^{9\ f.}$, Jno. 12^{38}, 15^{25}. Now while it is true that the meaning of prophecy as a whole is summed up in Christ, yet that is quite different from a foresight of particular occurrences in the life of Jesus. Apart from those prophecies which may be said to contain general intimations of the character and work of the true Messiah, the specific Old Testament utterances referred to in these passages in the Gospels were not originally spoken as prophecies; e.g. the words quoted in Mt. 2^{15}, as predicting the flight into Egypt, are in the original connection (Hos. 11^1) a statement of the historic fact that Israel in the beginning had been delivered out of Egypt; similarly in Jno. 3^{18}, the words quoted as predictive of Judas' baseness in betraying the Lord were uttered by the psalmist (41^9) in the midst of a bitter experience and referred to a familiar friend who had become an enemy. A certain verbal parallelism in such places led the New Testament writer to see in the words a prophecy, according to the common Jewish view which gave to every utterance and event recorded in the Old Testament a meaning of unlimited scope, especially a prophetic meaning. The relation of such utterances to their occasion, or to the context in which they occur, was entirely disregarded. It is of course evident that such an interpretation of the words of the Old Testament is not helpful in determining the scope of prophecy. A striking contradiction of the principle of limitation here maintained has been supposed to be found in the words of Zechariah, 9^9, literally describing the Lord's entry into Jerusalem just before his passion (Mt. 21^{1-9}). Now the prophet's words are a part of his picture portraying the Messiah as a king of peace; in a figure he describes him as coming, not in the pomp of a triumphal procession riding the war-horse, but in the lowly guise of one who rides the beast of peaceful life. But Jesus, conscious of his Messiahship and of the true nature of the Messiah, here deliberately appropriates *in action* this familiar and distinctive characterization of the messianic king, just as on other occasions he applies to himself delineations understood to be messianic, *e.g.* Mt. 24³⁰, 26⁶⁴, Lk. 4¹⁷ ᶠᶠ, 7²⁰⁻²³. It would be contrary to all analogy to suppose that Zechariah foresees this detail in the Lord's doings, when its significance has already been abundantly shown in the Lord's teaching.

The importance of apprehending this law of limitation in the prophet's vision is at once apparent in the interpretation of the Apocalypse; for it makes the fact clear, that the book is not a prediction of the great movements in the world and the Church in the later centuries of European history, or in the centuries which are yet to come. The question as to how many of the seals of the roll, if any, have yet been broken in the world's history, the attempt to find pictured in the visions such events as the rise of Mohammedism, the usurpations of the papacy, the Reformation, the great European wars, or to identify with figures portrayed in the book well-known historic persons [1] — these and many like inquiries all proceed from an utter misconception of the character of prophecy. It is true that events more or less parallel with the scenes here described have occurred in history, and it is quite possible that others even more closely parallel may occur in future ages; yet it is certain that these are not the actual events which the Apocalyptist sees in his visions. Nor are we justified in projecting his scenes into the still distant future hidden from him, and finding in his visions assurance that there will yet come the strange figure of Antichrist; the awful marvels of the plagues of the seals, of the trumpets and the bowls; the establishment of a thousand years' reign of the martyrs on earth; the hosts of the world marshaled by Satan in person for battle before an earthly citadel of the saints. What the book does assure us of, as a genuine work of prophecy, is the accomplishment, *under other forms* and through the ages, of those eternal purposes of God regarding his kingdom, which the Apocalyptist apprehended and proclaimed under the forms here used.

[1] See p. 330.

The prophecy of a divine intervention, by which the final crisis is introduced, is understood by many scholars to belong to this class of predictions whose fulfillment is not to be expected. The coming of God and Christ at the End with its attendant events of resurrection and judgment forms, as is urged, a cataclysm at variance with the evolutionary process of history known to us, and also at variance with the teaching of Jesus in what is assumed to be the original form of the parables which liken the Kingdom of heaven to growing seed — first the blade, then the ear, then the full-corn —, to the grain of mustard seed, and to the leaven leavening the three measures of meal (Mk. 4²⁶ ᶠᶠ·, Mt. 13¹⁸⁻³³). Thus the catastrophic establishment of the Kingdom by an objective coming of God in a return of the Lord, which is the common teaching of New Testament eschatology, is referred to the influence of traditional apocalyptic; and the idea of a spiritual coming extending through the ages is substituted. (For the Lord's teaching in these parables cf. Holtzm. *Theol.* I. 287 ff., Mathews *Mess.* 67 ff., Wendt *Teaching* I. 369 ff.) But as regards this view it may be said, that both natural science and history show the two processes, the evolutionary and the catastrophic, not to be mutually exclusive; the former is often only the preparation for the latter. So the New Testament views the kingdom of God in two aspects, as always coming and on the other hand as yet to come (cf. p. 134). We have not sufficient data for affirming positively that Christian prophecy is wrong in attributing the final establishment of the kingdom to signal acts of God's intervention. In any event the question as to God's manner of working out a result in a future, which seems immeasurably remote, is not one of pressing practical importance.

The Apocalypse to be read from the author's historical and literary standpoint. If the principles regarding the nature and characteristics of prophecy in general as stated above are well founded, we must first of all read the Apocalypse historically as we read for example an epistle of St. Paul. The Apocalyptist, as we have seen, comes with his message to the Church in the great crisis beginning near the end of the first century, when the very existence of Christianity was threatened by the imperial government, when the emperor-worship was coming into mortal combat with Christian worship, and when persecution of the Christians unto death appeared imminent throughout the world. The Apocalyptist saw in these movements the precursors of the Last Times, as did the prophets of old in the threatenings of the Assyrians, the Babylonians, and other hostile nations. In these perils he sees himself sent by God to forewarn the Church, to exhort, and to give assurance of the future. In a work whose subject is determined by these circumstances and whose literary form is shaped largely by prevalent conceptions and inherited apocalyptic imagery he shows that the long conflict between God and Satan is now becoming intense in the warfare waged against the Church by Satan's agents, the Roman emperors, that it will continue till, like the hostile world-monarchies of old, Rome is overthrown, and then that it will become still more intense in the rule of Antichrist, who forms but the sum and culmination of all that was most cruel and impious in his forerunners, the emperors. The picture in conformity with apocalyptic tradition shows series after series of marvelous plagues sent upon the world as visitations of punishment and warning. But over against all this terribleness it shows Christ, ever holding the Church in his hand, God surely working out his sovereign will, Satan overthrown, the saints redeemed in the eternal blessedness of the new Jerusalem. All this the Apocalyptist has worked out in a unified composition of wonderful power and majesty. With this origin and these motives in mind we read the book as a kind of drama, or creation of ideal literature, in which every paragraph has its meaning with reference to the outcome of the whole. There are passages which are remote from the facts of history and nature, there are obscure passages; but it is not difficult to conceive the Apocalyptist to be using all these as contributing to the plan of his book and to his purpose. Thus we read the book entirely from the author's standpoint, with his view of the significance of the events then taking place, with his understanding of the marvels and imagery of the book as *factors in his drama*, with his anticipation of the future. As regards any particular detail, we do not ask what event in future history it denotes, but rather, adopting the author's understanding of it, what office it performs in the plan of his work as a whole. The book is thus viewed not so much in its parts as in its unity, in the composition of which the author, after his own manner, not ours, has chosen and disposed all the factors so as to bear nearly or remotely on the climax of his theme — the faithful people of God brought through all their conflicts, through all the assaults of Satan, triumphant into the everlasting kingdom. An effort to show more fully the Apocalyptist's

x

meaning in the respective parts and their relation to the whole is made in the Commentary; see also the Summary, p. 255 ff.

The permanent prophetic element in the Apocalypse. But while we read the Apocalypse in its historical and literary aspects, we read it chiefly with its prophetic character in view; for as a prophecy it has its message for all time. The conditions to which the Apocalyptist addressed his book passed away; certain historical predictions failed. But there is no failure in God's revelation. What was given to the Apocalyptist, what is given to us in the book, is the permanent truth enshrined in its transitory forms; and upon this depends its practical usefulness in any age, its own or ours. It would be presumptuous to set forth as complete any statement of this underlying truth; for new experiences must disclose new factors in a divine revelation. But if we view our book in the light of older prophecies uttered in analogous crises and in the light of the general teaching of the New Testament, we can broadly summarize its leading elements somewhat as follows: the eternal God is through all the movements of history, through all the course of the world's empires, through all the ascendency of iniquitous powers, surely working out his purpose to establish his reign of righteousness, peace, and blessedness; the warfare waged by the people of God against evil strongly intrenched in power must at times become bitter in the extreme, demanding steadfastness and readiness to sacrifice all, even life itself, but God's care for his own is unfailing, they are sealed for a final deliverance in a new and divine order; the Church is in the safe-keeping of its divine Head who is ever present with it; punishment, warning, and a call to repentance come to the enemies of righteousness in the present course of the world, but in the end all opposing forces of evil will be overthrown, and the faithful, redeemed, will be admitted to the perfect life of union with God and their Lord. But these truths and whatever else of divine revelation is given to our Prophet are not apprehended by him in this abstract form. As they were intended for immediate, practical use, so they were seen and communicated concretely in connection with their time. In a later age, our own or one yet to come, entirely different conditions in the world must call for a different, though perhaps not final, representation of the great truths here embodied. *The practical usefulness of the Apocalypse* becomes apparent in these permanent elements in it. Wherever in the condition of society at large, of the Church, and of individual life, similar spiritual issues are involved, there these fundamental truths are applicable and our book brings its practical message. The Church, whose vision reaches across the ages, which in its consciousness of an endless life counts a thousand years as one day, must always find encouragement and inspiration in prophecies of the new Jerusalem, far off as the fruition may be. But the hope of that consummation ceased to be a power felt consciously and strongly by Christian people in the events of their time, when the expectation that the end was near passed away. With most Christians of to-day the things of the eschatological kingdom are shadowy and rarely thought of except in the vague trust that in some far-off æon evil will cease and good will reign supreme. If the message of the Revelation is to be used as a frequent source of practical help in the present course of the world, it must be seen to be more closely related to the conditions and emergencies of familiar experience. But this help is to be sought not in its supposed prediction of present events, but in the *application* of its permanent truths in present situations to which they are relevant. In other words the book must be used as we use any other part of the Bible. We read these first of all historically, having in view the precise situation addressed and the author's meaning as intended for that situation; but the general truth thus apprehended we apply to all other cases in which it is seen to give us instruction concerning God's will and our own conduct. We draw from the Revelation its practical message as in the use of the epistles, the histories, the parables, or any other parts of Scripture, which though written primarily with reference to specific circumstances of another time, yet reveal universal truth. This is not the place to speak at length of the practical lessons given in the book; these are too manifold and must vary with varying contingencies. A few illustrations will suffice to indicate some of the classes of practical applications to which the truths of the book properly lend themselves. In every fierce conflict between good and evil it

utters its twofold message of threatening and encouragement
to the combatants; to the warrior wearily fighting for the
right it opens a wonderful vision of God enthroned over all,
unfailingly controlling the destinies of the world and surely
bringing righteousness to a final, though perhaps long delayed,
victory.   In all the perils of the Church, in its weaknesses and
its strength, in all the calamities threatening it, Christ is shown
to be with it, walking in the midst of its candlesticks and holding it in his hand.   In vast catastrophes and disasters falling
upon men as if from an invisible hand, such as are seen in the
visions of the seals, the trumpets, and the bowls, are shown, if
not direct interventions of God, at least *symbols* of divine displeasure and revelations of an appointed cosmic order in which
natural calamities may serve a spiritual purpose.   The book
taken as a whole is preëminently one for times of stress, in
which organized government with all its civil, military, and religious powers wages war upon right, as the Roman emperors
waged war upon Christianity.   Perhaps in no event since the
age in which the Apocalypse was written has the essential character of its great conflict been more nearly paralleled than in
the world-war of the present century, the most gigantic struggle
between righteousness and governmental iniquity known to
history.   In this instance, among other parallelisms stands out
one, in which even the form is in part reproduced, the appalling
atrocities committed by one of the parties to the war in its
effort to destroy Armenian Christianity — atrocities committed
in the service of an emperor seeking to make himself a world-
ruler.   Not that the Apocalyptist is for a moment to be understood as foreseeing this, or other historical wars of later times;
what he sees is one form of the war of might upon right; and
whenever that war arises in history, his revelation of God's final
arbitrament is directly relevant.   To take another illustration
relative to movements in society, the book brings us a message
of assurance in one of the most common and disheartening results of moral conflict — the triumph of wrong.   Here the
Apocalypse shows us that the Beast may hold sway till he has
filled up the course of his seven heads, that Antichrist may ter-
rorize the world to the end of his reign, yet the cause of righteousness will at last prevail; thus it strengthens our struggling

hope in the progress of the world. If we venture to look into
the future, it is not difficult to imagine other forms of conflict
arising in the control of society, in which the message of the
book will apply. We have ceased to expect the coming of Antichrist as a ruler holding sway over all the earth and opposing
God. To the ancient world the dreaded power hostile to God
and his people appeared embodied in the world-monarchs of the
time, and naturally the climax of such hostility was looked for
in a ruler who should sum up in his own person all the might
and wickedness of his predecessors. That expectation has
passed away. No emperor will again make himself a world-
dominating power; no government will set itself the task of
exterminating the Church throughout the earth. But great
problems of social, industrial, and humanitarian right may arise,
very likely bringing righteousness into bitter conflict with
tyranny and iniquity, calling for our Prophet's exhortation to
courage and self-sacrifice and for his proclamation of divine
wrath and doom.

To these illustrations drawn from conditions in society and
the Church at large, might be added a quite different class of
examples, showing the practical usefulness of the book. It
brings aid to our vision, so dull in spiritual things, in that it
stirs our religious imagination by its wonderful picture of the
glory of God in the court of heaven, of the majesty of the ascended Christ, of the presence of the Holy Spirit in union with
the Father and the Son, and of the sublime worship which the
whole universe of created intelligences offers before the throne
of God and the Lamb. It lightens up the darkness of the
world, to which we journey through death, by its splendid
visions of the blessedness of the saints before the throne and in
the new Jerusalem; for though these visions relate to the final
state of the redeemed, after the resurrection, in the kingdom of
the end, yet Christian imagination seizes upon them as in some
way symbolizing also the rest and peace of that state after
death which St. Paul foresees, when he speaks of 'having a
desire to depart and be with Christ, for it is very far better'
(Phil. 1[23]). The warnings and promises of the seven epistles
touch practically the daily individual life in a wide round of
perils and duties. The whole portrayal of Satan's warfare

against the Church, his devices, his mighty power, his final doom, since these represent spiritual facts, can be legitimately brought by the Christian reader into a practical relation to his own spiritual experiences.   Even the three great series of miraculous visitations may furnish him with a symbol of the disasters and devastation wrought by evil in the soul, and of the poignant suffering of an offended conscience, at the same time a symbol of the wrath that remembers mercy.   These few illustrations can serve only to indicate lines along which practical uses of the book may be found.   When once we distinguish the permanent religious truths given in it from the transient embodiment in which the Prophet apprehended and expressed them, we perceive the wide range of their applicability, and the book, often regarded as one of the least practical, becomes one of the most practical books in the Bible.

IX. The Theology of the Apocalypse

The doctrine of God.   In his being and attributes the God of the Apocalypse is the same as elsewhere in the New Testament, though attention is fixed more upon certain properties of his character and withdrawn from others.   He appears chiefly as the Jehovah of the Old Testament, the eternal one, the almighty creator and ruler of the universe, the righteous judge, the Holy One, whom all in heaven and earth must obey and worship.   He is not distinctly portrayed as the God who ' so loved the world that he gave his only begotten Son '; it is nowhere in the book said ' God is love '; he is not in specific words declared to love even the righteous.   If we read the book and compare it with other parts of the New Testament, viewing only the most outstanding features in the respective representations, it might appear to belong in its conception of God to Hebrew rather than Christian thought; there might seem to be truth in the statement that ' Its doctrine of God has no exact parallel in the rest of the New Testament ' (Swete cliv).   This view however leaves out of sight certain facts essential to a comprehensive estimate.   In the first place the book is not concerned with the preaching of the gospel and the evangelizing of the world — in which God's love would be emphasized — rather, it transports us to the end of the ages, and the last attempts of Satan and his agents to destroy the work of God in his children. As regards God's relation to the unchristian world, its subject is the retribution which righteousness must inflict upon enemies remaining obdurately antagonistic to God. In so far then the thought is concentrated on one aspect of God's character, to the incidental disregard of others. Righteous judgment and wrath, from the nature of the case, figure chiefly in the portrayal of God. But in this the book does not differ fundamentally from representations of the God of the Last Times given in other writings of the New Testament. The difference consists in the greater amplitude of the picture, in keeping with the nature of the book. The character of God as manifested in the end is set forth summarily by St. Paul in precisely the same traits ; ' Or despisest thou the riches of his goodness and forbearance and long suffering ? . . . but after thy hardness and impenitent heart, treasurest up for thyself wrath in the day of wrath and revelation of the righteous judgment of God ; who will render to every man according to his works, unto them that are factious and obey not the truth, but obey unrighteousness, shall be wrath and indignation, tribulation and anguish.' Ro. 2⁴⁻⁹. Similar are the representations given in the parables of the wedding feast (Mt. 22⁷, ¹² ᶠ·), of the ten virgins (Mt. 25¹²), of the pounds (Lk. 19²⁷), and in the eschatological discourse of the Gospels (Mt. 24²⁸, ³⁰). As declaring the attribute of unrelenting wrath against the obdurate in the character of God cf. also Jno. 3³⁶, 9³⁹, 12⁴⁰, 1 Pet. 4¹⁷ ᶠ·, 2 Pet. 2⁴⁻⁹, Jude, v. 15 ; see also p. 160. In the second place, the love of God for his people, and his relation of fatherhood toward them, though not declared in express terms, are throughout contained in his attitude toward them and his acts in their behalf. It may be remarked that the actual word *love*, as applied to God's love for his children or mankind at large, does not occur in the Synoptists. That idea is expressed there by *fatherhood*, *e.g.* Mt. 5⁴⁵, while in the Fourth Gospel the latter term is almost wholly displaced by the former ; but in both the fact is explicit apart from the precise words used. So in the Apocalypse the loving care of

God for his people is as clearly manifested as his wrath against their enemies.   In fact his righteous judgment inflicted on the latter is but the converse of his love for the former, and is in effect so characterized ; cf. 11^{18}, $16^{6 \, f.}$, 19^2, $6^{9 \, ff.}$.   The establishment of the perfected kingdom in the renewed world, to which every event in the book looks forward, has for a part of its purpose the reward of those whom God loves, 11^{18}, 22^{12}.   And this love is revealed in manifold details in the course of the book. The following will serve as sufficient illustration : the perfect oneness of God and Christ in all the moral motives exhibited in the book makes the declared love of Christ for the saints (1^5, $3^{9, \, 19}$, cf. 3^{12}) an expression of God's love.   God protects and delivers the saints in the distresses and perils, 7^{1-8}, $12^{6, \, 14, \, 16}$; he will release them from all sorrow and pain, $7^{16 \, f.}$, 21^4 ; they shall have the immediate access of priests to his presence and shall share in his throne, 1^6, 5^{10}, 20^6 ; they shall dwell with him and he with them, he will be their God and they his sons, $21^{3, \, 7}$, 22^4.   But more than this, God's compassion even towards his enemies is not without trace in the book ; see pp. 554, 569. It is evident then that the difference between the Apocalyptist and the other New Testament writers lies not in an essential difference of view regarding God, but in the emphasis which the very nature of his book causes him to lay on certain aspects of the divine character.   And it follows that we cannot find here decisive indicia bearing on the question of the author's identity with any other New Testament writer.

The doctrine of Christ.   As is natural in a book of the Last Things the person and activities of Christ are chiefly those of the risen One.   Apart from his function as the bearer of testimony, that is, as revealer, which is a general term comprehending his activity after, as well as before, his resurrection, there is no specific reference to his earthly course, except to his death.   But the book stands alone in its vivid revelations of the glorified Christ.   While its doctrine does not in its essential significance go beyond that of the Fourth Gospel, where the divinity of the Logos and the eternal glory of the Son are plainly declared (*e.g.* $1^{1 \, f.}$, 17^5) or beyond the teaching of Paul (*e.g.* Col. 2^9, Phil. 2^6), yet nowhere else are found these wonderful scenes revealing to the eye and ear the majesty of Christ's ascended state, and these numerous utterances expressing in terms applicable to God alone the truth of his divine nature and power. He is seen in the first vision in a form having the semblance of man, yet glorified with attributes by which the Old Testament writers have sought to portray the glory of God; his hair is white as snow, his face shines with the dazzling light of the sun, his eyes are a flame of fire, his voice as the thunder of many waters; he announces himself as eternal, as one who though he died is the essentially living One, having all power over death, 1^{13-18}. He appears in the court of heaven as coequal with God in the adoration offered by the highest hosts of heaven and by all the world, 5^{6-14}. He is seen coming forth on the clouds as the judge and arbiter of the world, 14^{14-16}. Wearing crowns and insignia which mark him as King of kings and Lord of lords, he leads out the armies of heaven to the great battle with Antichrist, 19^{11-21}. In keeping with these scenes, attributes and prerogatives understood to belong to God only are assigned to him either alone or as joined with God; he is the Alpha and Omega, the first and the last, the beginning and the end, 22^{13}, 1^{17}, 2^8 — a designation which God also utters of himself, 1^8, cf. Is. 44^6, 48^{12}; worship is offered to him in common with God, 7^{10}, 5^{13} — a worship which angelic beings are forbidden to receive, 19^{10}; doxologies are raised to him as to God, 1^6; the throne of God is his throne, the priests of God are his priests, 3^{21}, 22^1, 20^6; life belongs essentially to him as to God, compare 1^{18} with $4^{9, 10}$. It is not necessary to add further illustration of the divine nature attributed to him by the Apocalyptist. In some instances the writer might seem to identify Christ with God without difference of person; and for the most part in the representations mentioned above the idea of a 'subordination' of the Son to the Father seems to be absent. But it is certain that the author does not confuse the person of Christ with the person of God, and equally certain that no Jewish or Christian writer thinks of a plurality of Gods. On the other hand there is a second class of passages which must be brought into comparison with those given above, if we are to gain a full view of the Apocalyptist's

Christology. Christ is designated the Son of God, 2^{18}; God is his Father, 1^6, 2^{27}, $3^{5,\,21}$, 14^1; God is his God, $3^{2,\,12}$; he receives his power to rule from God, 2^{27}; the revelation which he sends through the Prophet he receives from God, 1^1. The problem presented by these two conceptions of Christ, apparently irreconcilable, is that which appears in the New Testament generally. In the Fourth Gospel two distinct lines of thought are dominant: 'The Word was God,' 1^1, and 'The Father is greater than I,' 14^{28}. So with St. Paul; compare the declaration, 'being on an equality with God,' Phil. 2^6, with that of 1 Co. 11^3, 'The head of Christ is God.' The two conceptions of the person of Christ had come to be held singly yet clearly, but there appears as yet no attempt to reconcile them. The idea of 'subordination' was inseparable from the Lord's incarnate life and mediatorial work; the fact of his divine exaltation came to be apprehended in that process through which the Spirit guides the Church into truth. The writers of the New Testament are prophets of a spiritual revelation, not philosophic theologians, and they do not betray difficulty in holding the two views of the person of Christ in conjunction, without a clearly defined doctrine of unity. But they furnish the foundation truths upon which the Church at a later date based its precise definition of two natures in one person.

It is worth while to notice the Apocalyptist's use of personal names in designating Christ. In the prologue and the epilogue (1^{1-8}, 22^{6-21}) he uses the customary names, Jesus, Jesus Christ, or Lord Jesus. In the body of the work (1^9–22^5), the usual designation is the Lamb. Setting aside some passages where the 'testimony of Jesus' is mentioned, — a phrase in which reference may be made to Christ in both his earthly and his heavenly state ($1^{9,\,2d\,case}$, 12^{17}, 14^{12}, 17^6, 19^{10}, 20^4), we find in this part of the book the name Jesus or Christ in only five places ($1^{9,\,1st\,case}$, 11^{15}, 12^{10}, $20^{4,\,Christ,\,6}$) and in these reference is made to the *risen* Christ. Once Lord occurs and refers to the earthly Christ, 11^8. In all other cases, 28 in all, the Lamb is used, and almost without exception (the two exceptions, 7^{14}, 12^{11}, are perhaps not really such) designates the *risen* Christ, though in some instances allusion is at the same time made to the redeem-

ing death which had preceded the glorified state ($5^{6,\,9,\,12}$, 13^8).
It will be seen then that the standing personal name which the
Apocalyptist uses for the glorified Christ is the Lamb. This
is the name given to him in the most august scenes. As the
object of the worship offered by the hosts of heaven and earth,
chapts. 4–5; as the unveiler of the destinies of the ages, chapts.
5–6; as one enthroned, before whom and to whom the redeemed
render the praise of their salvation, $7^{9\,\mathrm{ff.}}$; as the controller of
the book of life, 13^8; as the Lord of the hosts on mount Zion,
14^1; as the victor over the hosts of Antichrist, 17^{14}; as the
spouse of the glorified Church, 19^7; as the temple and light of
the new Jerusalem, $21^{22\,\mathrm{f.}}$; as the sharer in the throne of God,
22^1, — Christ is called the Lamb. Nowhere in the occurrence of
the name is there evident allusion to the figure of *meekness and
gentleness* in suffering. But when the thought turns back to
the *redemption* which the risen Christ had previously wrought
by his death and to the results of his death in the victory
gained by the saints and in their spotlessness before God, the
Lamb is the only name given to Christ ($5^{6,\,9,\,12}$, 7^{14}, 12^{11}, 13^8).
In this last connection the figure is clearly that of the Lamb as
an atoning sacrifice, and is parallel with what is probably
the correct interpretation of the words of the Fourth Gospel,
'Behold the Lamb of God, that taketh away the sin of the
world,' Jno. $1^{29,\,36}$. The application to Christ of this figure of
the Lamb as an atoning sacrifice is not common in the New
Testament; outside of the passages in the Revelation and the
Fourth Gospel mentioned above it occurs only once, 1 Pet. 1^{19};
the thought in the figure of the paschal lamb, 1 Co. 5^7 is different. The representation of the Messiah as a lamb in
Enoch 90^{38}, Test. Jos. 19 is not parallel with our author's use;[1]
though it is possible that, as some suppose, there may have
existed in popular apocalyptic a portrayal of the triumphant
Messiah under the figure of a lamb. Yet it is altogether improbable that there could have been connected with such a representation the idea of a redeeming sacrifice. Whatever be the
source of the application of the figure to the triumphant Christ,
whether originating with the Apocalyptist himself, or adapted
by him from the sacrifice of the incarnate Christ, or from some

[1] See Com. 5^6.

current imagery, the scope of his use of the figure as a whole is
significant as characteristic of his mode of thinking about the
person of Christ. The Lamb is the Christ in the highest
exaltation of his divine glory ; he is likewise the Christ who
has suffered death to redeem a people unto God. The glorified
Christ and the Lamb that had been slain are not thought of
apart from each other ; and the Apocalyptist is not conscious of
any antinomy ; there is no trace of an effort to introduce a
mediating unity. The exaltation viewed as a *reward* of the
humiliation, as in Phil. $2^{8 \, f.}$, might seem to be hinted at, as for
example in the words, 'As I also overcame and sat down with
my Father in his throne,' 3^{21}, but this thought is not brought in
anywhere distinctly, as indicating cause and effect.

The doctrine of the Holy Spirit. The Apocalypse cannot be
said to present essential divergence from the Pauline Epistles
and the Fourth Gospel in its doctrine of the Spirit, though his
operations are not so much emphasized in our book, nor made so
specific. The same problems arise here regarding the personality of the Spirit, and his relations to God and Christ. The
Spirit appears to be conceived as a person, and as such to be
distinguished from God in the invocation of grace and peace
from him, 1^4, also in the seven Spirits before the throne of God,
4^5, and perhaps in the utterance added to that of the voice from
heaven, 14^{13}. The designation *seven Spirits* for the one Spirit
is due to the symbolism adopted by the author ; see Com. 1^4.
In like manner the distinction from Christ is seen in the invocation , $1^{4 \, f.}$, in the Spirit's prayer addressed to Christ for his
coming, 22^{17}. It is not to be expected that the personality of
the Spirit should be so distinctly conceived and expressed as
that of Christ whose incarnate life gives force to the idea of his
person. The Apocalyptist's conception of the unity of the
Spirit with God and Christ is shown distinctly. The Spirit is
God's Spirit, 3^1, 4^5, 5^6. He is also the Spirit of Christ, Christ
hath the seven Spirits of God, hath the seven eyes which are
the seven Spirits of God, 3^1, 5^6 ; at the close of each of the
seven epistles Christ, the speaker, though naming the Spirit as
if another person, identifies him with himself ; the words which
he gives as his are called the words of the Spirit. This con-

ception of identity and yet of distinction in the persons of God, Christ, and the Spirit is the same as that expressed by St. Paul, Ro. 8[9-11]. But when we speak of the processes of personification, identification, and distinction, we do not attribute to the author the completeness and precision of a later mode of thinking. The Apocalyptist does not feel difficulty in a certain personalizing of the Spirit, as distinct from God and Christ, while holding to the unity of God ; the relation of his conceptions of God, Christ, and the Spirit to one another and to the oneness of the divine being presented no problem to his thought, or the thought of that age. It is inconceivable that he should have viewed the Father, the Son, and the Spirit as three distinct and coördinate Gods ; it is equally clear that he placed Christ and the Spirit in an order above the highest angelic beings, above all created existences. These truths of religious faith which the Apocalyptist held singly, without the consciousness that there was needed a principal of unity, took form subsequently, when the Church entered upon the task of more precise theological statement, in the doctrine of the three persons in the unity of the Godhead. The principal *office* of the Spirit spoken of in the Apocalypse is that of revealer and inspirer. The ecstasies in which the prophetic visions are opened to the seer are due to his operations, 1[10], 4[2], 17[3], 21[10]. He is the organ of Christ's message to the churches in the seven epistles, ' Hear what the Spirit saith unto the churches,' chapts. 2–3 *passim;* and the same thought underlies the words of 22[16], as also the statement regarding God's revelation, 22[6]. The Spirit is the inspirer of the prophets, 19[10]; and in one instance he stands as the intercessor for the Church, 22[17], cf. Ro. 8[27]. The renewing and sanctifying influence of the Spirit, made prominent in the Fourth Gospel and St. Paul (*e.g.* Jno. 3[5-8], 7[38 f.], Gal. 5[22 f.]), is not directly mentioned in the Apocalypse. If, however, the allusion to the water of life, 22[1, 17], be interpreted by Jno. 7[38 f.], that thought may be contained there.

X. History of Interpretation

Both the subject matter and the form of the Apocalypse are such that the book lends itself easily to various methods of interpretation. The author is commissioned to write of things which shall come to pass after the date of his writing (1^{19}); and though the command includes also things belonging to his own present, 'the things that are,' yet these are viewed chiefly in their relation to the future. Prediction, therefore, becomes the most prominent characteristic of the book; and that which is predicted is given in the form of visions unfolded in an intricate series, with stupendous imagery, with vast movements in heaven and earth, with strange figures passing across the scene, with typical numbers and names, and with all the mysteriousness of the unreal world. Very rarely does the writer translate what is seen into the language of plain, realistic definition. Naturally then there is great room for fanciful explanations, and many hard questions arise regarding the meaning of the whole and its several parts to which manifold answers have been given. Do the Seer's visions relate to events which are to culminate in his own immediate future, or does he survey the whole destiny of the Church and the world as it is unfolded in the course of history; or still again, do all his predictions await the last great days for their fulfillment? Are the events foretold to be understood as actual, visible facts, or are they but symbols of spiritual truths and experiences? Do the visions of the seals, the trumpets, and the bowls give three parallel representations of the same events (the so-called *Recapitulation* exegesis), or do they form a continuous series each leading up to what follows? Is the reign of the thousand years a kingdom to be established on earth, or is it only a spiritual condition; did it begin with Christ's earthly life, or with the conversion of the Roman empire, or is it wholly in the future? Who or what is the Beast; is he a person, a world-ruler, or the Roman pontiff, or some great heretic and enemy of the faith, or is he only the personification of all wickedness in its hostility to God and his Church? Are the seven heads certain great historical kings, or great empires that have succeeded one another in history, or are they symbols of evil forces in the spiritual world? What is the significance of the strange numbers employed? Is the great harlot the city of Rome, pagan or papal, or the capital city of the world-kingdom at some future period, or an apostate Church? These are some of the questions which have exercised the ingenuity of interpreters in the course of the centuries, and the answers given have been determined by various influences, especially by the circumstances, political or ecclesiastical, of the interpreter's time, by his general attitude toward the interpretation of Scripture, by his view of prophecy and inspiration, by his theory of the critical analysis of the book, and by the peculiar characteristics of apocalyptic literature to which the book belongs. No attempt is made here to survey the vast body of literature which in the course of time has been occupied with the subject; it is rather the aim of the present paragraph merely to present the views of those interpreters who have most influenced their own and later times, and thus to trace in a brief outline the more important steps in the interpretation of the Revelation through the different periods of its history and in its different systems.[1]

(1) *The first four centuries.* For the purposes of the outline here intended it is convenient to group together the interpreters of the first four centuries. Like 'every scripture inspired of God' the Apocalypse was certainly meant to be to those to whom it first came 'profitable for teaching' (2 Tim. 3[16]), and so the writer must have counted on its being understood in its chief lessons. Doubtless the readers had already been instructed orally in such eschatological teaching as appears in the Gospel record of our Lord's words, and in the epistles; and if so, they possessed the norm guiding them to the general understanding of a book which likewise told of the approach of the 'times of the Gentiles,' 'the messianic woes,' and of the near appearing of Christ in his kingdom, a book which also warned and encouraged the Church in view of what was

---

[1] On the history of the interpretation of the Apoc., cf. Lücke II. 951 ff., Bleek, *Vorlesungen* 28 ff., Elliott, *Horae Apoc.* Vol. IV., Bousset, *Kom.* 49 ff., Charles, *Studies* 1 ff.

coming on the earth. That there is much in it which was not understood by them or misunderstood, can hardly be doubted, but the monitions to preparedness and steadfastness, the revelations of hope and comfort, were clear; and as long as the eschatological expectations of the apostolic age continued active, the Church was not altogether far from the author's thought in the understanding of the book; but as that expectation died away, or was transformed, the Church entered into a wilderness of wandering in its conception of this portion of Scripture, from which it is only in recent years escaping through the rise and rigorous application of the historical method of study (cf. p. 2).

Justin Martyr. The first post-apostolic writer who refers directly to the Revelation is Justin Martyr. He asserts (*Dial. c. Tryph.* 81) that it teaches a literal millennial kingdom of the saints to be established in Jerusalem, and after the thousand years the general resurrection and judgment. And it is evident from the scope of his argument that this was the common view in the middle of the second century. In this respect at least he takes the book in a realistic sense. To the other prophecies he makes no allusion.[1]

Irenæus. Although Irenæus did not write a commentary on the Revelation, he makes frequent use of it, giving an interpretation of many of its representations.[2] Like Justin he finds in the book the doctrine of chiliasm, that is, of an earthly millennial kingdom; Christ will come and after the conquest over Antichrist and his hosts, will set up his kingdom in a renewed Jerusalem, where the saints will reign with him in blessedness 1000 years, as the beginning of the incorruptible life in final glory. Then will follow the general resurrection, the judgment, and the renewal of the world. The Beast, Antichrist, is a person springing out of the tribe of Dan, in whom will be concentrated all world-power and all apostasy and hostility to God's people. While in the mind of Irenæus the Roman empire embodies the world-power hostile to God, and he sees its dissolution predicted among the events preceding

---

[1] The supposition based on Jerome *De vir. illust.* 9 that Justin and Irenæus wrote commentaries on the Apoc. is generally rejected. Cf. Lücke II. 558 ff.

[2] See especially *Adv. Hær.* V.

the advent of Christ, he does not identify Antichrist with any known Roman emperor. He suggests Λατεῖνος, Latinus, among possible explanations of 666, the number of Antichrist's name, but rejects it as he does all other precise names, interpreting the number in a highly artificial way as summing up Antichrist's essential character. The series of plagues that precede the End he takes literally of visitations similar to those sent upon Egypt. As a rule he understands the book realistically, yet in some cases a purely symbolical interpretation is given; for example, the four Living Creatures about the throne of God symbolize the functions of Christ, the lion his kingship, the calf his priesthood, the man his humanity, the eagle his prophetic office; the number four determines the number of the Gospels.[1] Irenæus is closely followed by Tertullian.

Hippolytus (bishop of Portus Romanus, died 235). Like the writers just spoken of, Hippolytus is a chiliast, but he placed the millennium in a comparatively late future, in the year 500. He takes the book of Daniel as the norm for understanding the Revelation. The first beast he identifies with the fourth beast of Daniel, which he makes the Roman empire. One of the heads will be wounded unto death in that the empire will be broken up by the ten Kings; it will then be healed in the restoration of world-sovereignty by Antichrist. Antichrist, who was represented by Antiochus Epiphanes and who will come out of the tribe of Dan, will reign 3½ years, persecuting the Church and putting to death the two Witnesses, the forerunners of the parousia (held to be Elijah and Enoch); his number may represent various names; among these Λατεῖνος is especially suggested by his headship of the restored Latin sway, but the true meaning is a mystery only to be understood in the future. The great harlot and Babylon are Rome. The woman with child is the Church continually bearing through preaching the word of God, her flight into the wilderness is the flight of the Church from the persecutions of Antichrist, the two wings of the eagle given to her are faith in Christ who stretched out his two arms on the cross. *Victorinus* (bishop of Petavium, martyred about 303). The commentary of Victo-

[1] III. 11.

Y

rinus, long known in two much worked-over recensions, has recently been recovered in what is generally accepted as a genuine form.[1] As yet only the concluding part has been published,[2] but this is sufficient to show the author's standpoint. He understands the Revelation in a literal, chiliastic, sense. He places its date in the reign of Domitian, the sixth ruler reckoned from Galba. Some time after Nerva, the seventh, at a time still in the future for Victorinus, Nero will return from the dead as the eighth. This *Nero redivivus* is the Beast and Antichrist, and his coming is near at hand. The persecutions of Victorinus' time belong to the sixth seal; with the seventh will come the End. The plagues of the bowls do not follow those of the trumpets in a continuous series, but are parallel with these, that is, they *recapitulate* these in another form. The two witnesses are Elijah and Jeremiah; the 144,000 are Jews who in the last days will be converted by the preaching of Elijah; the woman fleeing into the wilderness symbolizes believers fleeing from the hosts of Antichrist. The second beast, the false prophet, will cause the image of Antichrist to be set up in the temple at Jerusalem. The commentary of Victorinus is the first among extant commentaries to use the *Nero redivivus* myth; and its theory of *recapitulation*[3] recognizes a difficulty in the formal composition, and offers a solution adopted by many later writers.

Origen. It will be seen that with all the writers named above the earthly messianic kingdom at a date not too far distant is a dominating factor. The Revelation is taken literally. Like the Jewish apocalypses with which it has so much in common, it is understood, as in fact it was primarily intended to be, a source of comfort and encouragement in a time of fierce persecution. Naturally this aspect of it could not be overlooked, but was rather kept alive as long as the Roman empire was hostile to Christianity and bent on its extinction. But over against this realistic understanding of the Revelation, there were influences leading to an entirely different conception of its nature. The growing force of Greek thought in the Church

---

[1] Discovered by Haussleiter in the Codex Ottobonianus Lat. 3288 A.

[2] Haussleiter in *Theol. Literaturblatt* 1895.

[3] Viz. that the events do not all form a continuous series, but some scenes recapitulate the events of other scenes; cf. p. 318

was opposed to the literalism of Jewish apocalyptic, and the passage of the centuries without the appearance of the Lord to set up the looked-for kingdom led to an effort to find a non-literal meaning in the prophecies. Also the opposition to the heresy of Montanism, which made great use of the Apocalypse and gave extravagant form to its millennial teaching, caused it to be either rejected or differently interpreted. Thus a spiritualizing or allegorizing exegesis arose. The leader in this was Origen, the vehement opponent of Millenarianism. A promised commentary of his on the Revelation seems never to have been written, but his understanding of it can be seen from his theory of the interpretation of Scripture, and from his treatment of certain passages of the book found in his writings. He lays down the principle that the true meaning of prophecy is to be found only by going beyond the literal and historical sense to the spiritual; and he says specifically of the Apocalypse that the mysteries hidden in it can be understood only in this way. His whole interpretation of the book is therefore spiritual rather than literal. At a definite period the Lord will come, not visibly, but in spirit, and establish his perfected kingdom on earth. The time of his advent will coincide with the coming culmination of evil in the person of Antichrist, a future world-ruler, a child of Satan. The imagery of the visions is to be taken allegorically; for example, the seven heads of the dragon are seven deadly sins, the ten horns are serpent-like powers of sin which assail the inner life, the roll with seven seals is the Scriptures, whose meaning Christ alone can unseal; the warrior whose name is the Word of God, issuing upon a white horse from the opened heavens, is Christ, who opens heaven by giving the white light of truth to those who receive him. *Methodius* (bishop of a see, probably Olympus, in Lycia, early in the fourth century). This same spiritualizing procedure appears also in Methodius. He accepts a millennial period, as a preparation for the final blessedness, but the visions are taken allegorically. The woman with child is the Church bearing children into spiritual life, and since the true life of these is with the Spirit in heaven, they are removed from the assaults of the dragon, the devil. Methodius expressly denies that the woman's child can be Christ. The seven heads of the dragon are the chief sins, the fallen stars are false teachers who are fallen from the faith, but claim knowledge of heavenly things.

Ticonius (the exegete of the Donatists). With the reign of Constantine and the conversion of the Roman empire, Rome and a Roman emperor could no longer be regarded by the Church as the beast of the Apocalypse and Antichrist. On the other hand the persecution of the Donatist heretics by the Catholic Church led the adherents of that sect to find these antichristian powers in the rulers of what was viewed as a worldly and corrupt Church. The Donatists were of the true Church and as such were persecuted by the Satanic powers foretold in the Revelation, that is, by the Catholic hierarchy supported by the world-power. In these circumstances appeared near the end of the fourth century the epoch-making commentary of the Donatist Ticonius, a work followed in its method even by many orthodox scholars. Ticonius' commentary has not been preserved by itself, but the principal parts of it are recovered through its use by later writers.[1] His interpretation is throughout spiritualistic, he explains nothing by the events and circumstances of the age of the Apocalyptist. The millennial kingdom and the millennial reign of the saints are realized in the Church, between the first coming of Christ and the second ; Christ was the ' strong man ' who in his earthly appearance laid hold of Satan and bound him for a thousand years. Antichrist is sometimes conceived impersonally, as the personification of the sum of evil powers present in the world ; again he is represented as a definite historical person, who in the last days will be set by Satan over his kingdom in its war upon the true Church. The time will come when the true Church will be separated from the false in the sight of men ; then Antichrist will appear and continue his great persecution $3\frac{1}{2}$ years. The two Witnesses symbolize the Church preaching Christ in the two Testaments. The Beast is the world-power, the seven heads are the sum of all the kings of the earth ; the head wounded unto death and restored forms an eighth head, who is one of the seven and symbolizes the corrupt priesthood, which is of the world though claiming not to

---

[1] The chief sources for it are Beatus, Primasius, Pseudo-Augustine, and Bede. On Ticonius cf. Bousset, *Kom.* 56 ff., Swete CCV. f.

be such ; Jerusalem is the symbol of the Church, as Babylon is the symbol of the antichristian world. Ticonius is followed by Augustine,[1] in his spiritualizing method, though the latter in the application of the method avoids the heresies of the Donatists. Both writers adopt the recapitulation theory.[2]

(2) *From the fifth to the end of the fifteenth century.* What is here made the second period in the exegesis of the Apocalypse is characterized throughout the greater part of it, by the predominating influence of Ticonius and the spiritualizing method, with some following here and there of Victorinus and the realistic interpretation. But in the latter part of the period the course of events brought up again the chiliastic expectation, though in a much modified form. Two commentators of the sixth century, Andreas in the East and Primasius in the West, who wrote extended works on the Revelation, served as agents transmitting the influence of Ticonius and others of the earlier period to the following centuries.

Andreas (bishop of Cæsarea in Cappadocia), author of the fullest and best known of the Greek commentaries, defines his method as that of Origen ; the threefold sense which he finds in Scripture is (1) the literal or historical, (2) the figurative or moral, (3) the spiritual or mysterious, which contains the mysteries of the future, expressed in symbols. He makes the last predominant in the interpretation of the Apocalypse, though he sometimes refers the symbols and imagery historically to the time of the Apocalyptist. The kingdom of 1000 years, as with Ticonius and Augustine, begins with Christ's earthly life and will continue till the knowledge of him is everywhere extended, the number of years being symbolical of completeness and multitude. The first resurrection is the believer's rising from spiritual death ; Babylon represents, not Rome, but the sum of the world-powers ; the temple is the Christian Church. On the other hand, Andreas adopts in many cases the realistic interpretation ; Antichrist will arise from the tribe of Dan and fix the seat of his rule at Jerusalem ;

---

[1] Augustine did not write a commentary on the Apocalypse, but interpretations of parts of it are given in his writings, cf. especially *De civ. Dei* 20, 7 ff.

[2] For this theory see p. 322.

Andreas mentions several names and attributes as explanations given of 666, but rejects them all, holding the number a mystery not to be understood till Antichrist comes; he rejects the reference of the wounded head to Nero; the seven heads are seven historical empires of which Rome is the sixth, Constantinople the seventh; the two Witnesses are Elijah and Enoch; the first five seals relate to the past, the remaining seals and the trumpets and the bowls, to the future.

Primasius (bishop of Hadrumetum in Africa) follows yet more closely than does Andreas the spiritualizing method of Ticonius, purged of its Donatistic errors. He says expressly in his preface, that he is guided by Augustine and Ticonius; from the latter he introduces long excerpts. The general procedure of his exegesis consists in finding the abstract and universal in the concrete; reference to historical events or persons is for the most part wanting, though some realistic interpretations also occur; *e.g.* Antichrist is with him a person who will come out of Dan, the two Witnesses are Enoch and Elijah, the four angels standing at the corners of the earth are the kingdoms of Assyria, Media, Persia, and Rome. The commentaries of other writers in the first half of this period follow, often through the influence of Primasius, often directly, the leading of Ticonius with a blending of earlier interpretations. There are differences in the explanation of details, but there is no independence of traditional methods. An exception occurs in Berengaudus, a ninth century commentator. He interprets the first six seals as covering the time from Adam to the rejection of the Jews in the fall of Jerusalem; the first six trumpets are the preachers sent by God from the beginning of biblical history down to the latest defenders of the Church, the seventh trumpet represents the preachers who will come in the time of Antichrist; the horns of the beast are the barbarian tribes who destroyed the Roman empire. But in many other cases Berengaudus follows closely his predecessors. He does not appear to have exerted influence on the course of interpretation, though he may be said to have anticipated the principle of the later system which found in the Revelation prediction of the future history of the Church and the world.

Joachim (Abbot of Floris in Calabria, died 1201) made a

really new departure in the interpretation of the Apocalypse at
the end of the twelfth century, expressing a change of view
wrought by the course of history and the character of the age.
From the time of Ticonius and Augustine it had been a belief,
nearly universal, that the kingdom of the thousand years began
with the earthly appearance of Christ, or with his resurrection
and ascension ; Satan had been 'bound,' that is, his power had
been in part restrained, but he was not destroyed, Antichrist and
antichristian powers were still at work constantly in the world;
at the end of the millennial period a final manifestation of evil
in personal form would take place, with all its enmity toward
the Church.   Therefore as the ten centuries neared their end,
a general unrest and fear seized society.   Satan was about to
be loosed for the last great conflict, the time of dread persecution was at hand, after which would come the judgment and the
end of the world.   The critical period however passed by, neither Antichrist nor the Lord appeared, nothing occurred in the
experience of the Church or the world in which Christians could
see their expectations and fears realized.   This undisturbed
passage of the time of expected crisis produced first of all a
change of view in regard to the meaning of the thousand years.
Augustine centuries before had taken it as symbolical of an indefinite period, and this understanding of it now became general.   But the expectations which had been so actively aroused
were not at once allayed; great interest in the coming of the
Last Days continued, eschatological thought was busy.   The
Lord's appearance was believed to be not far off, and this foreboding was soon intensified by the condition of the Church
itself, which now entered on a period of unconcern and self-
content.   Relieved as it was from fear of the sufferings believed
to be predicted for the time now past, secure in its imperial
domination, it beheld in its present state the fulfillment of the
promises of millennial glory.   Naturally deterioration and
worldliness followed as the result in both official administration
and individual moral life.   Devout observers saw in these
forces at work in the Church the presence of Antichrist and his
agents.   Such a predominance of evil could not continue, — in
its very presence lay the presage of the End as near.   The foremost writer to interpret the Revelation in this direction was

Joachim of Floris.　Like Ticonius he views many of the prophecies as referring to his own time.　He divides the history of
the world into three periods, that of the Father, the Old Testament period, that of the Son, the New Testament period, still
continuing in Joachim's time, that of the Holy Spirit soon to
come ; the last is the time of peace and glory, when Christ will
appear again on earth — the millennium again conceived as
future and not already begun ; the number of years, however, is
not taken literally.　This coming age would be the time of the
'contemplative life,' realized in perfected monasticism.　A new
order of monks, an order of the Holy Spirit, would arise which
would 'refresh all the earth as streaming rain.'　Joachim divides
and subdivides the Apocalypse in an artificial manner, and in explaining the different divisions uses the recapitulation method.
In one part the Beast is Mohammedism, which received a deadly
wound in the Crusades but revived again partially from time to
time and is fully restored in the person of a Saracen king ; in
another part the Beast is the devil.　Of the seven kings, five of
whom are fallen, the sixth is apparently Saladin, the seventh is
Antichrist, after whose overthrow by Christ the millennial kingdom will be established ; at the end of the millennium the hosts
of Antichrist, which had fled to the remotest regions of the earth,
would return to their assault and be destroyed ; then would
come the judgment and the consummation.　The false prophet
represents the heretics of the time.　Joachim did not attack
directly the Pope, but the general corruption of the Church,
which he believed would be restored to its primitive purity and
simplicity through monasticism.　In his view, the 'papacy in its
true ideal belonged to the foundation of the Church ; it was
antichristian only in its worldliness.'[1]　Joachim's influence was
powerful in the years immediately following, especially with
the Franciscans, who held him as a prophet, and in their conflict with the Pope carried his interpretation of the Apocalypse
to an extreme.　Passages expressive of the later thought were
interpolated into his writings, books were pseudonymously attributed to him.　There arose in these years a widely spread
belief that the world was entering on the Last Days, a belief
doubtless not wholly due to Joachim's influence, but fostered

[1] Lücke II. 1010.

by it and finding expression in his writings. The demand for the reformation of the Church was growing, and the Apocalypse thus interpreted became a powerful instrument in the hands of the leaders of this movement. The Pope in his struggle with the emperor, Frederick II., had declared him to be the Beast rising out of the sea with names of blasphemy on his head; and the opponents of the Pope were quick to retort that the latter was the Antichrist foretold in the Apocalypse. With the followers of Joachim and with all who set themselves against the corruption of the Church and the hierachy it became an axiom that the Pope was the Beast, the Antichrist, and that papal Rome, or the Roman Church, was the woman sitting on the scarlet-colored beast. Their destruction was foreseen as near, many reckoned the year or the decade. Thus there entered into the study of the Revelation a conception which, untenable as it is, dominated the exegesis of the book for centuries and continued almost down to the present generation. Bousset observes with justness that 'The history of the interpretation of the Apocalypse runs on from the fourth century into the thirteenth and fourteenth chiefly under the influence of two works, the commentaries of Ticonius and Joachim of Floris.'[1]

Nicolas of Lyra (teacher of theology at Paris, died 1340). Near the end of this period there appeared for the first time in a fully developed form another view of the predictions of the Apocalypse, which was destined to be widely adopted in the following centuries, the view which regarded them as forecasting the whole course of the Church's history. Though steps had been taken in this direction by earlier interpreters, a systematic and comprehensive application of the idea appears first in Nicolas of Lyra. Abandoning the theory of recapitulation, he finds in the course of the book prediction of a continuous series of events from the apostolic age to the final consummation. The seals refer to the period extending into the reign of Domitian; in the later parts are predicted the Arian and other heresies, the spread of Mohammedism, Charlemagne, the Crusades, and other historical details; the millennium is already present; Satan is to be loosed and return again with his hosts; then will come the End.

---

[1] *Kom.* 82.

(3) *From the beginning of the sixteenth century to the present time.* The centuries here named may be taken as forming a single group in our survey, because of the presence of certain well-marked characteristics through the period taken as a whole. On the one hand the principles of interpretation which emerged in the latter part of the former period are the dominant rule with the larger number of writers quite into the nineteenth century; on the other hand, parallel with this course of opinion, there arises and grows through these years another movement which issues in the rigorous historic method of to-day — the method which most interpreters now recognize as alone legitimate. We have seen above the rise of the view that the Revelation is a prophetic epitome of the whole history of the Church and that important parts of it are directed against the Roman Church and the papacy. This antipapal aspect of it dominates a large part of the literature of the reformers and the reformed Church down to quite recent times. 'The reckoning of the thousand years' kingdom from the birth of Christ or his death and the founding of the Church, or from Constantine, as also the reference of the Antichrist of the Apocalypse to the papacy, gradually became a part of Protestant orthodoxy.'[1] Roman interpreters following the manner of their opponents easily identified the Beast and Antichrist with Luther and other leaders in the Reformation struggle, and the False Prophet with the Protestant sects. In applying the prophecies of the book to the course of history different writers according to their taste or time have seen different events and persons foretold. Place is found in the visions for the subsequent course of the Roman empire, for the invasions of the Goths and other barbarian tribes, for the Turks and their conquest of Christian lands, for the Crusades, the wars of the Reformation, the French revolution, and also for great historic figures, *e.g.* Constantine, Luther, Gustavus Adolphus, Napoleon, and so on with endless variety, as the phases of history changed and the fancy of scholars dictated. With some the recapitulation theory is adopted, each of the two series, the trumpets and the bowls, repeating and making clearer the series of the seals; but generally the three series

---

[1] Lücke II. 1018.

are viewed as unfolding a continuous history. The precise reckoning of future times and dates has fascinated many minds and has been carried out in elaborate computations. The mathematicians Napier and Whiston fixed the date of the End, the former between 1688 and 1700, the latter at 1715, which he afterwards changed to 1734 and again to a later date. Not so much a distinct system of interpretation as a special form of this *continuous-historical* theory is that of Auberlen (1854) and his followers, who see in the Apocalypse the prediction not of the historical *details* of the future, but of the decisive epochs and the spiritual forces active in the progress of the Church through its conflict with the world. The fantastic character of much of the work belonging to the whole school of interpretation here spoken of should not, however, obscure the great service of many of its adherents in grammatical, philological, and archæological investigations and in acute exegesis. Over against these two 'leading motives' — the forecasting of the future history of the Church or the world, and the reference of certain parts to the corruptions of the Roman Church — which run through this period, there appears, develops, and culminates that method of interpretation which approaches the Apocalypse and seeks to get at its meaning from the facts and circumstances of the writer's own time. A special impulse in this direction was given by the effort of writers of the Roman Church to oppose the antipapal interpretation almost universal with Protestant scholars.

Ribeira. The first writer in this movement was the learned Spanish Jesuit, Franciscus Ribeira, who published his commentary late in the sixteenth century. His position was determined by a return to the early Christian fathers. With him the first five seals relate to the age from the preaching of the Apostles to the persecution under Trajan; with the sixth seal the Apocalyptist turns to the End, with which all the rest of the book is concerned; from his own time and the nearest future his vision passed over to the Last Days with no prophecy of intervening events. The two Witnesses, Elijah and Enoch, Antichrist originating in Dan, the destruction of Babylon-Rome belong to the End. The deadly wound of the Beast healed represents Antichrist's imitation of Christ's death

and resurrection. Bousset rightly says of Ribeira and his immediate Jesuit followers that 'they labored with a comprehensive learning, with a knowledge of the fathers and the history
of the exegesis of the Apocalypse, such that their works are
not yet antiquated.' [1]

Alcasar, also a Spanish Jesuit, in a work of great fullness
(1614) divides the Apocalypse into three parts, and develops
the theory that the first and second parts (chapts. 5–11 and
chapts. 12–19) refer respectively to the conflicts of the Church
with Judaism and the heathenism of the Roman world, while
the third part (chapts. 20–22) predicts the victory and rest of
the Church in the thousand years' kingdom which began with
Constantine and will continue till the end of the world. In
the first four seals the beginnings of the gospel movement are
pictured, then in the sixth seal passing over to the year 70 and
the Jewish-Roman war the Seer describes the deliverance of
the Christians (chapt. 7), the calamity visited upon the Jewish nation (chapts. 8–9), their rejection, the opening of the
Church to the Gentiles and the destruction of Jerusalem, with
the conversion of a remnant of the Jews through the two Witnesses slain and risen, that is, the Church rising out of its persecution to a higher life (chapts. 10–11). The second part
opens with the birth of the Gentile Church from the Jewish,
the man child born of the woman, and the persecution under
Nero (chapt. 12). The vision of the bowls carries on the
story of the progress of the gospel in overcoming the Roman
world, the last chapter in which is formed by the conversion
of the empire, Constantine being the strong angel who binds
Satan. Beyond this general conception of the age closing
with Constantine, there is in Alcasar no use made of the
method spoken of above which finds in the Apocalypse the
future history of the Church; that is, he finds in the book no
prediction of world-history beyond the time of Constantine,
when the millennium began. His work is the first to attempt
a complete exposition of the entire premillennial part of the
book, as a connected and advancing whole falling within the
Apocalyptist's age and the centuries immediately following.
It becomes therefore important in the growth of a truly scien-

1 *Kom.* 92.

tific method of exegesis, in spite of its frequent misapprehension of symbols and other details.

Later writers, following in the direction of these interpreters who interpreted the book from the standpoint of the Apocalyptist's time, have become increasingly numerous in the progress of biblical study, till it may be said, unquestionably, that they hold the ascendency. The advance, however, to a consistent and comprehensive use of the method has not been made directly; many of its followers have joined with it an allegorizing, or a church-historical interpretation. Grotius, the leader among Protestant scholars who first adopted the principles of Ribeira and Alcasar, agrees with the latter in his general analysis of the Apocalypse into the three parts mentioned above, with their respective themes, but he admits into his interpretation more departures from the Apocalyptist's time, finding in the book prophecy of *details* in the reign of Constantine and of events of universal history. His commentary (1644) exerted great influence, and in addition to its philological and archæological learning, it is significant as the first among Protestant works to confute the reference of the Beast to the Pope, and as the first to call in question the *unity* of the Apocalypse,[1] a subject which assumes great importance among later interpreters. Some adherents of his school[2] limited the prophecies in their main significance to the destruction of Jerusalem, but a broader application of the method has generally prevailed. The theory of Eichhorn (1791) is especially interesting in its treatment of the book as a great historic poem picturing in dramatic form the victory of Christianity over Judaism and heathenism, symbolized respectively in Jerusalem and Rome. In the course of the succeeding years a gradual advance in criticism, in correct exegetical procedure and in the accumulation of illuminative material has definitively established the theory that the meaning of the Revelation is to be sought through the circumstances of the writer and the readers, and the directly practical purpose of the book. In this agree, in spite of important differences in other respects, most scholars of recent times.

This latest interpretation of the Revelation has been pro-

---

[1] Cf. p. 224.
[2] Abauzit 1733, Hardouin 1741, Harenberg 1759, Züllig 1834–40, *al.*

foundly affected by two facts which have been recognized only within modern times, but which are very important among the circumstances originally shaping the book and so entering as large factors into its study according to the historic method. (1) The book is now seen to belong to the somewhat large class of apocalyptic literature and to have taken much in its form and matter from this source. Lücke's monumental work was the first to exhibit with fullness this group of writings and the relation of the Revelation to them. And the application of these results has revolutionized the interpretation of much in our book. (2) The critical study of *unity*, with the generally accepted view that the Apocalyptist made more or less use of other writings, whether combining these somewhat mechanically, or working them over and fitting them into a carefully arranged design, or presenting them in a redaction, has given a new aspect to the exegesis of certain parts, if not the whole.

One other method of interpreting the Revelation should be mentioned in our outline of this period — that which conceives the Seer throughout his book, or through all except the first three chapters, to have been looking across the intervening ages to the time even for us still in the future and to have spoken only of the Last Days as thus viewed. Ribeira, as seen above, understood the Apocalyptist to pass over in the sixth seal to the time of the End. This view of the Spanish scholar was taken up and applied to other parts of the book in the last century by Maitland (1826), Kliefoth (1874), and some others; some understood the seven epistles to be addressed to the actual historic churches of the writer's time, others take them as picturing the various conditions of the Church throughout its earthly course, and still others refer even these to the eschatological era. This system of interpretation has not gained a large number of adherents.

Classification of different methods of interpretation. The different interpretations of the Apocalypse, spoken of above, have been grouped into three systems, which most English and American expositors, following Davidson's *Introduction*,[1] have designated (1) the *preterist*, which sees the chief prophecies of

[1] Vol. III.

the book fulfilled in the destruction of Jerusalem and the fall of the Roman empire. (2) The *continuous-historical*, according to which the book embraces important conditions and movements in the history of the Church and the world from the writer's age to the end of time. (3) The *futurist*, which places the events foretold entirely in the Last Days.[1] A better designation of these groups, at least of the first and third, is that current among German writers: (1) *zeitgeschichtlich*, *contemporary-historical*, (2) *kirchengeschichtlich*, *church-historical*, or *weltgeschichtlich*, *world-historical*, (3) *endgeschichtlich*, *eschatological*. Such a classification, however, is not to be carried out on rigidly fixed lines, for most of the interpreters combine, at least to some degree, elements belonging to different systems. As already pointed out, *futurists* take some parts as directly historical, *preterists* transfer parts to the Last Days, adherents of the *world-* or *church-historical* method assign parts to each of the other systems; in other words the different theories are not in practical application made mutually exclusive throughout. And in fact the nature of the book is such that no one of the systems taken in its narrow limitations to the exclusion of the others can give a just conception of the Apocalyptist's meaning. Every apocalyptic writing is grounded in the present and the past, but at the same time looks forward to the future. But not much argument is needed to show that neither the *continuous-historical*, nor the absolute *futurist* method can be adopted as the determining rule in the study of the Revelation. The book, as shown by its opening, especially the letters to the seven local churches, and by its close, is addressed to the needs of a definite historic community, its message is first of all meant directly and distinctly for that community. Its contents then cannot be understood to consist principally of pictures of medieval and modern history, or of predictions of an eschatological era removed from the readers' present by indefinite ages. Also the true conception of prophecy[2] forbids us to seek here the details of future history. On the other hand in the use of what is certainly the correct method, the *contemporary-historical*, two

---

[1] Davidson himself makes a fourth class, that of the ' extreme futurists,' who refer the first three chapters also to the last time   [2] Cf. p. 301.

mistakes have often been made: (1) the ignoring of a truly prophetic character in the book, which gives to it a spiritual outlook not realized within the limits of the history of the Roman empire; (2) the effort to extend too widely the interpretation of *symbolical* language by circumstances of the writer's era.

While the method followed in the present commentary is, as already indicated, the *contemporary-historical*, a more precise designation would be *apocalyptic-prophetic*, for the work is here regarded as possessing the marks of what it claims to be (cf. pp. 292 f.), the message of a prophet sent by God and guided by the Spirit, as truly as *e.g.* are the eschatological passages in St. Paul's epistles to the Thessalonians. But in both matter and form the prophecy is apocalytic. The prophet's thought here moves in a realm akin to that of the whole class of apocalyptic writings, and his manner as regards the general scope of his work, its formal disposition, and its language and symbols, is determined by this generic relation. This view of the book does not, however, withdraw it from the category of writings which are to be studied after the historic method; quite the contrary, it emphasizes the necessity of that method, for prophecy and apocalyptic are addressed first of all to the particular wants of the time in which they originate; they not only reflect the circumstances of their day, but their meaning and true use can be apprehended only by approaching them from the standpoint of their origin. At the same time the genuine prophetic character of our book removes it from the class of purely artificial, literary apocalypses; and even if it be seen that the author has made use in some cases of earlier apocalyptic documents, it is not hard to conceive that he has introduced such as a means for the elaboration of his wonderful visions, giving them a meaning suited to the great purpose of his work.

XI. Early Circulation of the Apocalypse and Its Recognition as Canonical [1]

No other writing of the New Testament can claim in comparison with the Apocalypse more abundant and more trustworthy evidence that it was widely known at an early date. It is also shown beyond question to have been recognized from an early time in a part of the Church, and by certain fathers in all parts of the Church, as belonging in the category of authoritative Scriptures. Many of the witnesses to these facts specify also the name of the author. But the question as to his personality, whether he be St. John the Apostle or another John, need not complicate the inquiry of the present paragraph, in which it is not fundamental. That question can be best considered separately.[2] A rapid circulation of the Apocalypse from the outset would be favored by two circumstances : it was directly addressed to seven churches and each of these would be likely to obtain a copy of a message sent specifically to itself from a prophet and teacher well known to it, and of evident authority. But it was also seen to be a message to the whole Church,[3] and its predictions and promises related to Christians everywhere in the perilous times upon which the Church was now entering. As it was heard when read in the Asian congregations, it must have stirred the profoundest emotions, and eventually copies of it could hardly fail to be carried afar in the busy intercourse of Asia Minor with the world.

The Apostolic Fathers contain no certain trace of acquaintance with the book. Some scholars have thought to find reminiscences of it in Ignatius, Barnabas, and Hermas. But the parallelisms occur in ideas which the Apocalypse has in common with earlier known writings, or are too remote to furnish evidence of acquaintance.[4] The silence of these writers does not however prove their ignorance of the book ; they have in general no occasion to quote it. Possibly in the case of Hermas

---

[1] Cf. Zahn *Geschichte d. Neutest. Kanons; Grundriss d. Geschichte etc.* ; *Forschungen zur Geschichte etc.* ; Westcott *On the Canon of the N. T.* For a survey of testimony cf. Lücke II. 516–657. A convenient summary is given by Alford *Rev. Prolegomena* 198–220 ; Speaker's Com. *Rev.* 406–426 ; Bousset *Kom.* 19–31 ; Swete CII–CXIV.   [2] See pp. 343 ff.   [3] See Com. 1⁴.
[4] Cf. Zahn *GK.* I. 954 f.

z

and The Teaching of the Twelve Apostles we might expect
some echo of it, since they speak particularly of the Last Things;
but the absence of such reminiscence from these writings is far
from convincing evidence that the book had not yet reached
Rome, or the home of The Teaching. A few years later, testimony to the book becomes direct and unquestionable. The
earliest witness comes from the near vicinity of some of the
churches to which the book was addressed. *Papias*, bishop of
Hierapolis in the early part of the second century, called by
Irenæus a companion of Polycarp (of whom Irenæus himself
was a younger contemporary) and a man of olden time, ἀρχαῖος
ἀνήρ,[1] knew the book and accepted it as inspired. His testimony is not preserved in his own words, but Andreas in his
commentary on the Apocalypse,[2] in which he shows that he had
used the writings of Papias among many other earlier writers,
reports him as bearing witness with Irenæus, Methodius, and
Hippolytus to the inspiration of the Apocalypse. Most scholars
are agreed that there is no ground to question the accuracy of
Andreas' report of Papias. *Justin Martyr*, who became a
Christian c. 133, tarried at Ephesus c. 135, and wrote his *Apol-
ogy* c. 150, and his *Dialogue with Trypho* 155–160,[3] bears unquestionable testimony in the words (*Dial.* 81), 'A certain man
among us whose name was John, one of the Apostles of Christ,
prophesied in a revelation made to him, that those who believe in
our Christ would spend a thousand years in Jerusalem, and that
after this the general . . . resurrection of all would take place
and a judgment.' Also his language regarding Satan (*Apol.*
I. 28), 'The prince of evil demons is called a serpent and Satan
and the devil as you can learn, by examination, from our writings' alludes plainly to Rev. 12^9, 20^2. For other passages
showing Justin's use of the Apocalypse see Zahn, *GK.* I. 531 ff.
Irenæus, born in Asia Minor, probably at Smyrna, c. 130–135,
presbyter and bishop at Lyons (Gaul), in his great work *Against
the Heresies*, written 181–189,[4] often quotes the Apocalypse,
sometimes as the work of 'John a disciple of the Lord,' sometimes 'John,' without nearer definition, as a person well known;
in one place (V. 30) he cites it as 'the Apocalypse' without

---

[1] Euseb. *H. E.* V. 20.   [2] See p. 325.
[3] Cf. Harnack, *Chron.* 284.   [4] Cf. *ibid.* 723.

any limiting designation, showing thus that the book was familiar to all. He mentions 'ancient copies,' thus showing its early circulation. He speaks of objections to the Gospel but nowhere of opposition to the Apocalypse. The *Epistle of the Churches at Vienne and Lyons*, written c. 177 to their brethren in Asia Minor and Phrygia in the persecution under Marcus Aurelius, shows acquaintance with the Apocalypse in a number of places, and in one instance speaks of it as Scripture. Most of this epistle is preserved in Eusebius, *HE*. V. 1 f. *Melito*, bishop of Sardis, one of the churches addressed in the Apocalypse, a prolific writer and an active personality in the affairs of the Church in Asia Minor, wrote a work on the Apocalypse c. 175. Only the title is preserved (Euseb. IV. 26), but the fact that such a work was written attests the importance attached to the Apocalypse at the time. *Theophilus*, bishop of Antioch (in Syria) in the latter part of the second century, used the Apocalypse as doctrinal authority, appealing to it in opposition to the heresy of Hermogenes.[1] *Tertullian* of Carthage, at the end of the second and the beginning of the third century, quotes extensively from the book, and appears to know of no objection to it except that of Marcion (see below). The version which he used in his quotations agreed essentially with the Vulgate of later date; it may therefore be reasonably argued that that version, since it retained its hold on the Church, was one supported by ecclesiastical use. 'Everything tends to show that the Apocalypse was acknowledged in Africa from the earliest times as canonical Scripture' (Westcott 267). Both *Clement of Alexandria*, contemporary with Tertullian, and *Origen*, also of Alexandria, a younger contemporary of Clement and the leading early critic of the canon of Scripture, followed the common tradition of the Church in accepting the book as canonical. The *Muratorian Canon*, a fragment belonging to a date near the end of the second century,[2] giving so far as it is preserved a list of the books of the New Testament which at least the western church held to be canonical, includes the Apocalypse.

This summary of testimony, which is far from exhaustive, will show that the Apocalypse within a little more than a cen-

[1] Euseb. *H. E.* IV. 24. [2] Cf. Zahn *GK*. II. 1–143, Westcott, 214 ff.

tury after its appearance became known in all parts of the
Church and was widely held to be a work of inspired authority. But this general acceptance was not undisputed. The
earliest opponent was Marcion, whose career as a religious
teacher at Rome began c. 140. He rejected the Apocalypse.
But he rejected also all the Johannine writings and the other
books of the New Testament except ten Pauline epistles and
the Pauline Gospel, his recension of Luke. His rejection of
these parts of the New Testament rested, not on historical
ground, but on divergence from his dogmatic tenets, especially
his anti-Judaism.[1] Somewhat later the so-called Alogi rejected the Apocalypse and the Gospel. The ground of this
rejection seems to have been bitter opposition to the Montanists, who supported their millenarian doctrine and their extravagant belief regarding a new outpouring of the Spirit by
appealing to these books.[2] Stuart (I. 337) makes an apt comparison in the case of Luther: 'the leading reformer had a
warm dispute with the Romanists on the subject of justification by faith alone. They appealed with all confidence to the
epistle of James as deciding against him. He, unable to overthrow their exegesis, rejected the book itself and called it in
the way of contempt *epistola staminea.*' One historical argument was adduced by the Alogi, viz. that there was no church
at Thyatira and that therefore an inspired Apostle could not
have written the epistle addressed to that church ($2^{18 \text{ ff.}}$). But
the Apocalypse itself gives evidence that one existed there at
the time of the book, if not in the time of the Alogi. Whoever the author, he would not have assumed as fact a thing
known to all to be erroneous. According to Epiphanius that
city was a center of Montanism. In sympathy with the Alogi,
as a zealous anti-Montanist the Roman presbyter Caius in the
time of Zephyrinus (bp. 199–217) wrote a Dialogue against
the Montanist Proclus in which he attributed the Apocalypse
to Cerinthus.[3] Caius accuses Cerinthus of attributing to the
apostle John the book which he had himself fabricated.[4]

---

[1] Cf. Zahn *GK.* I. 585 ff., Westcott 318 ff.   [2] Cf. Zahn I. 223 ff.
[3] Euseb. *H. E.* III. 28.
[4] The attitude of Caius toward the authenticity of the Apocalypse, obscure
in the passage in Eusebius, is made clear in certain Syriac fragments from Hip-

Caius, in impugning the apostolic origin of the Apocalypse in the interest of anti-Montanism, reviews the book and finds various discrepancies between it and other parts of the New Testament; *e.g.* the *signs* of the End contradict the Lord's words about coming as a thief in the night.[1] A more characteristic example of Caius' discrepancies is the following : hellish locusts overrun the wicked, but the Scripture says the wicked shall flourish and the saints shall be persecuted. Caius' criticism was without any considerable influence in the west; it was taken up and refuted by Hippolytus, his contemporary at Rome, a zealous defender of the Apocalypse as written by the apostle John.

Toward the middle of the third century Dionysius the Great, bishop of Alexandria, in his opposition to millenarianism and apparently influenced by Caius, took up anew the question of the authenticity of the Apocalypse; and though concluding that the John who wrote it was not the Apostle, he nevertheless accepted it as divinely inspired, thus retaining its canonical authority.[2] The criticism of so illustrious a figure in the Church as Dionysius could not fail to exert influence, especially in Egypt and the east. Following in his footsteps Eusebius, the historian, bishop of Cæsarea in the earlier half of the fourth century, saw a second John as the author of the book. The rejection of the apostolic authorship became now more frequent in the east, and in consequence the inspired authority of the book was less generally accepted there, or at least the testimony to its wide acceptance is less certain. Among those who either distinctly declared against it, or seem to have used it with reserve, were Cyril of Jerusalem, Gregory Nazianzen, Amphilochius of Iconium, Chrysostom, Theodoret. The Peshitta, the vulgate Syriac version, does not contain it, and its presence in the earliest revisions of the old Syriac is due to a later hand. Similarly the earliest forms of the Armenian and Egyptian versions seem to have lacked it. But on the other hand in common with the whole western church adherents of the traditional view are numerous in other churches

polytus published by Gwynn in *Hermathena* 1888. On Caius see Zahn *GK*. I. 222 ff. ; II. 973 ff.

[1] Cf. pp. 147, 351.   [2] For his argument on authorship see pp. 354 ff.

also, *e.g.* Ephrem Syrus, Basil of Cæsarea, Gregory of Nyssa, Epiphanius, Athanasius, Cyril of Alexandria, Didymus.[1] It is clear that the canon appearing in those versions which lacked the Apocalypse was not regarded as a final, authoritative pronouncement against the book. No synodical authority of the Church had as yet set forth a canon of the New Testament; individual opinion was restrained by no external influence save tradition and common consent. But it is not difficult to account for the rise of objections to the Apocalypse in this period; and it should be noted that the impugners of the book did not appeal to the testimony of early history. The age of persecution, to which the book was directly addressed, had passed by, the most striking prophecies had not been fulfilled, and the meaning of the book had become extremely obscure to this generation. Many might therefore hesitate to attribute it to inspiration; probably also many who have left in their writings few or no traces of using it may have accepted its canonicity, while finding it for the reasons just stated less available than the other books of the New Testament as an authority to be appealed to, or to be quoted. The absence from a great version may be due to the thought that it was not well suited to reading in the congregations, rather than to a disbelief in its inspiration. Versions were primarily works of gradual growth, and designed for use in public service.

The first action relating to the Scriptures taken by a synod is that of the council of Laodicea, not far from 360.[2] This was an assembly of certain provinces of Asia Minor. It adopted an ordinance forbidding the reading of uncanonical scriptures in public worship. And in the list of canonical books given, the Apocalypse is wanting; but that part of the decree as now extant is not generally regarded genuine,[3] though probably of early date. The third council of Carthage (397) adopted a decree regarding the Scriptures to be read in service, and the Apocalypse, in keeping with the universal opinion of the western church from earliest times, was included in the list of canonical books. The council of Constantinople

---

[1] Cf. Lücke, 628 ff.   [2] Cf. Zahn, *GK.* II. 196 ; Westcott 439 f.
[3] Cf. Zahn II. 193 ff. ; Westcott 445.

(the Quinisextine, 692) ratified the decrees of Laodicea and Carthage, notwithstanding their apparent contradiction as regards the inclusion of the Apocalypse, and thus the book was formally acknowledged a part of the New Testament of the eastern church. But the action of the various councils, it is well to remember, did not create the New Testament canon ; it only registered what had come to be recognized by the general consent of the Church. Neither such action of the councils, nor the opinion of the Church, thus formally recorded, could settle the question of authorship, purely a question of historic fact. The decision thus reached could only declare the conviction of the Church that the Apocalypse, like the other books of the canon, is the work of one who has here recorded truth apprehended through the influence of the Spirit, truth of special authority as the word of God. The fact that a part of the Church reached this recognition so slowly can raise no doubt as to its verity. A part of the Church, the western, was slow to recognize the inspired character of the epistle to the Hebrews. In each case the guiding Spirit of God led the whole Church eventually to discern the revelation of divine truth thus given to it. The two books form two of the richest treasures of the sacred canon.

XII. AUTHORSHIP [1]

Information regarding the author of the Revelation must be sought first of all in the book itself. The book is in the form of an epistle, the writer of which designates himself simply as John the servant of Christ, a brother who is one with the readers in the persecution of the time and the Christian hope

[1] Besides commentaries, encyclopedias etc., see among recent publications, Gutjahr, *Glaubwürdigkeit d. irenäischen Zengnisses*, etc. ; Schwartz, *Ueber d. Tod d. Söhne Zeb.*, in the *Abhandlungen d. könig. Gesellschaft d. Wissen. zu Göttingen*, Phil.-Hist. N. F. VII. 1904 ; Badham, *Am. Journ. of Theol.* 1899, 729 ff. ; 1904, 539 ff. ; Clemen, *Am. Journ. of Theol.* 1905, 643 ff. ; Bacon, *Fourth Gospel in Research*, etc., also articles in *Hibbert Journ.* 1903, I. 510 ff. ; 1904, II. 323 ff. ; III. 353 ff. ; Moffatt, *Introd. to Lit. of N. T.* 501 ff. ; 596 ff. ; Lightfoot, *Essays on the Work entitled Supernatural Religion;* Zahn, *Forsch.* VI. 147 ff. ; Harnack, *Chron.* 320 ff. ; 651 ff. ; Corssen, *Warum ist d. vierte Evang.* etc., in *Zeitschrift für Neutest. Wissen.* 1901 ; J. Weiss, *Offenbar.* 155 ff.; Larfeld, *Die beiden Johan. von Ephesus* ; Chapman, *John the Presbyter*, etc.

of the kingdom, $1^{1,4,9}$, 22^8. The particular John meant he nowhere specifies. Several persons bearing the name are mentioned in the New Testament, and probably others were known to the churches. But the writer assumes that his name needs no definition; he is addressing directly the churches of seven Asian cities where he is well known, where he had evidently labored for a considerable time, for he is familiar with the exact circumstances and the spiritual condition of each one of the congregations, he knows the events of their past history.[1] Reports regarding a church might be brought to a stranger, as to Paul in the case of the Colossians, but here there is a minute personal knowledge of the special surroundings, and of the present and past experiences, of churches in seven important and somewhat widely scattered cities, including the great capital city of Ephesus; and it is clear that these cities are not the whole field of the writer's labors, they are chosen out of a larger number,[2] and together represent a considerable territory in which the writer had for some time gone up and down bearing witness to the gospel. He does not enforce his message by appealing to an official station in the Church, if he held any such, as St. Paul is constantly compelled to point to his apostolic authority; and yet we feel that there is throughout, and especially manifest in chapts. 1–3 and in the epilogue, 22^{8-21}, the tone of one who speaks out of the consciousness that he is, and is acknowledged to be, a religious leader among the Christians of Proconsular Asia, and that he possesses the unquestioned right to address to these churches, and through these to others, a writing to be read in their public assemblies. He emphasizes his office as a prophet,[3] doubtless because of the peculiar character of this message as differentiated from that of his familiar preaching. He refers to his sojourn at Patmos, which if due to banishment was already known to the readers, in order to show them, as the prophets and apocalyptists frequently do, the precise circumstances in which the revelations were given to him. He is now no longer at Patmos;[4] he might have told the churches by word of mouth about his visions, but he is conscious of the divine purpose in his message

---

[1] Cf. especially $2^{2-5, 13, 19, 21}$, 3^{10}.   [2] Cf. p. 210.   [3] See pp. 292 f.
[4] See Com. 1^9.

as belonging to those beyond his reach in both space and time. There is nothing in the book to indicate that he does not continue his work in the Asian churches after his departure from Patmos. He reveals everywhere his Jewish nationality, but not a Judaizing tendency; his mind is wonderfully stored with the ideas and language of the Jewish prophets and apocalyptists, his Greek is often that of one who is thinking in the Hebrew idiom, yet his departures from correct Greek usage are pretty certainly not due to ignorance; his general correctness and his Greek vocabulary show him to have possessed an adequate command of the language. As a Christian his thought does not in its fundamentals differ from that of the other writers of the New Testament, though in some aspects it is more distinctly developed.[1]

This testimony regarding the author given in the book itself is against the view held by some,[2] that an unknown writer or editor here assumes the name John. It is argued that the extant apocalypses are all pseudonymous, that the authors have antedated their books, and sought to give them authority by the assumption of a great name of the past, as that of Enoch, Isaiah etc.; the inference is therefore drawn, that the author of this book follows the custom of his class. And this supposition is held to be required by what is claimed as established facts, viz.; that the book is an editorial compilation of various apocalyptic fragments, and that no John is known, neither the Apostle nor another, who suits the conditions of authorship presupposed in the book. In answer it should be said first of all that the Shepherd of Hermas survives as an example of a Christian apocalypse which is not pseudonymous, and further that our Apocalyptist shows himself too strongly assured of his own inspiration, as one of the now restored order of prophets, to admit of his assuming another's name to sanction his words.[3] As regards the composite structure of the Apocalypse enough is said elsewhere of the presence in the book of a single personality shaping both the language and the thought in the present form, whatever use he may have

---

[1] See pp. 310 ff., 163 f., 356 ff.
[2] So, Semler, Volkmar, Scholten, more recently Weizsäcker, Wernle, Bacon, *al.*   [3] See p. 293.

made of other material.[1] The theory of a fictitious John, impersonating either the Apostle or the so-called John the Presbyter, raises difficulties of which no satisfactory solution is given. The advocates of a pseudonymous author generally take the assumed name to impersonate the Apostle; the writer in choosing a name to give authority in his book could find none more available for his purpose than that of the foremost John known to the Church. But if at the time when the Revelation was written, the end of the first century, the Apostle was really, as tradition represents, a resident among the Asian churches, it is not conceivable that another would have addressed this letter to them in his name; nor would one have ventured to do so in the years soon following John's death; some clear evidence would be needed in the book to persuade surviving contemporaries, that it was the Apostle himself who was here speaking in a posthumous writing, and to explain why this writing had not appeared before. The writers of pseudonymous apocalypses leave no room for question as to these points; Daniel is bidden to seal his book to the time of the End, 8^{26}, $12^{4,\,9}$; compare also 2 Esd. 14^{46}, Enoch 1^2. Nothing of the kind appears in the Revelation. So far as can be shown by any designation which the author gives himself he might be another John as certainly as the Apostle, and there is no intimation that the book of an apostle, now dead, is here brought to light. Especially would some indication of this kind be needed, if there were in the younger generation in the Asian church another well-known John called the Presbyter; see pp. 362 ff. On the other hand if the view of many recent scholars be correct, that the Apostle had been martyred some fifty years before and had never resided in Asia, all the more certainly would a writer assuming identity with him be compelled so to designate himself in some way, and to explain the late appearance of the book. It is hardly necessary to point out that these considerations are of equal force against an unknown writer's use of the name of John the Presbyter.

Most scholars of all schools of criticism, though differing as to who the John was, are agreed that the book was not pseudonymous, that it was written, at least in part, by a John well

---

[1] See pp. 216 ff. ; also paragraphs on Criticism in Com.

known at the time to the Asian churches. The traditional
view that the author was John the Apostle is held by many
recent scholars.[1] The larger number of present-day critics
identify the author with John the Presbyter; some few (*e.g.*
Spitta) with John Mark. The last supposition is generally
rejected, since there is nothing in the New Testament or early
tradition associating Mark in this way with the Asian church.
Opinion will probably remain divided between John the Apostle and John the Presbyter, according to the attitude of different minds toward evidence. But it cannot be too strongly
emphasized that the question of the personality of the author
is altogether subordinate to that of the canonicity of the book
and its religious value.[2] Large parts of the Old Testament
scriptures are of undetermined authorship; not only the historical books are such, but also most of the psalms, portions of
the prophets, and other writings. And in part the same is
true of the New Testament; the writers of a third of the number of books are not announced in the books themselves, and
inquiries regarding their personalities are far from reaching a
uniform answer. But we accept, *e.g.* the priceless epistle to
the Hebrews as we do the second part of Isaiah, each from the
pen of a great unknown. And we attribute to all such portions the same authoritative character as to the rest of the
Scriptures. So the Revelation has come to us declaredly the
work of a Christian prophet, bringing its own credentials;[3]
and the Church has been guided with common consent to recognize in it a God-sent message of spiritual truths. As such
the sympathetic reader accepts the lessons of its wonderful
visions, its words of command and encouragement. In view
of these facts it would perhaps be sufficient to rest the question of authorship here. Certainly it would seem that the
question of his personal identity, as not involving the essential
truth of a part of our New Testament, might be studied with
impartiality. Unfortunately one cannot follow the various discussions of the topic with the conviction that such has been
the case. In the following brief survey of the subject a statement is given of the chief arguments which have been offered

---

[1] So, B. Weiss, Zahn, Sanday, Stanton, Reynolds, Drummond, Simcox,
Batifol, *al.*   [2] See pp. 337 ff.   [3] Cf. pp. 292 ff.

as possessing force, and some comment on these is added.
Two questions really preliminary to the inquiry, the personality of the so-called John the Presbyter, and the tradition of
John the Apostle's sojourn in Asia, are most conveniently considered elsewhere (pp. 362 ff., 366 ff.); the results of the discussion there presented are taken into account here.

Early testimony to the authorship of the Apocalypse.   In
estimating the trustworthiness of opinion regarding the authorship of the Apocalypse in the early years of its circulation, it
is necessary to take into account especially the nature of the
writing and the extent to which it was known.   It was not an
anonymous, or pseudonymous tract,[1] copies of which were
manufactured in a *statio* and sent out to the public through
the *bibliopolæ*, the *booksellers;* it was a personal letter addressed in the author's unmistakable name to those churches
in which he was well known, and it was to be read in their
assemblies.   Unquestionably it became familiar at once to the
Christians in the capital city of Ephesus and the rest of the
seven cities.   And the hearers all knew from whom the message came, as certainly as did the Corinthians in receiving a
letter from St. Paul.   Like other epistles addressed to
churches, it must have been read repeatedly, recalling the personality of the writer, whoever he might be.   It is quite conceivable that a book like the Fourth Gospel might not be so
certainly and universally associated with its author; but it is
hard to believe that a message so personal as that of the Revelation could have been wrongly attributed at, or near, the time
of its reception.   And it may reasonably be supposed that
there were at least seven copies of it in existence soon after its
first transmission.   We have evidence of a considerable circulation not long after it was written in the reference which
Irenæus makes to 'all good and ancient copies.'[2]   Irenæus
himself, in his younger years a contemporary of many of a
maturer age who were living when the book was first read in
the churches, could hardly speak of copies as *ancient*, unless
they belonged to a time very near the date of the book.   And
he shows also that discussion had arisen in those earlier years,

---

[1] Cf. p. 345 f.   [2] *Haer.* V. 30 ; Euseb. V. 8, 5.

before the time when he was writing his work against the Heresies (c. 185–190), regarding the number of the Beast, and that appeal had been made to those who had seen the author face to face. The witnesses appealed to could not have been living at the time of the writing of the book against the Heresies; the dispute then must have been of earlier date, that is, the book must have been somewhat widely known at that early date. In these circumstances it would not be easy for much uncertainty or confusion to arise, within this period, regarding the personality of the author. We know from everyday experience how short a period is that of more than fifty years in our knowledge of the authorship of a book, which has made a deep impression and has been much read by us. Particularly is this true of a writing in which the author draws special attention to his words by declaring his personality. We must therefore attach weight to this early opinion concerning the authorship of the Revelation, if it is clearly expressed and uniform.

As bearing on the value of the witness of Justin Martyr, Papias, and Irenæus, here cited, reference must be made to what is said of these writers respectively on pp. 338 f., and to the discussion of the date of Irenæus and the value of his testimony given on pp. 368 ff. The earliest testimony recorded is that of *Justin*, who lived some time at Ephesus, the center of the region to which the book was sent, at a date when the generation to which it first came had not yet passed away. He appeals to it as an acknowledged work of John the Apostle.[1] *Papias*, who belonged to that earlier generation, recognized the book, according to Andreas, as inspired, but we have no words of his showing to whom he attributed it. It is a fair presumption from the manner in which Andreas refers to Papias' view of the book, that he regarded him as agreeing with his own opinion, that the author was the Apostle;[2] at all events if Papias had expressed a divergent opinion, the historian Eusebius would certainly have stated it, since he is eager to establish the non-apostolic authorship and uses Papias' book in proof of the existence of another John, the Presbyter, to whom the Apocalypse might be attributed.[3] *Irenæus*, who

[1] *Dial. c. Tryph.* 81.　　　[2] Cf. p. 338.　　　[3] Cf. p. 362.

was a younger contemporary of Papias and Justin and who had ample opportunity for knowing the opinion prevalent in Asia from the beginning of the century, makes frequent and explicit reference to the Apocalypse as that of 'John the disciple of the Lord,' and he shows distinctly that by this term he means John the Apostle.[1] From this time on the same testimony appears generally in the fathers, *e.g.* Clement of Alexandria, Tertullian, Origen, etc. Especially valuable is the testimony of Origen as the great student and critic of the history of the New Testament books. And in none of these authorities is there argument to establish this authorship; it is assumed as acknowledged.

The opponents of the apostolic authorship in the second century, Marcion and the Alogi, did not appeal to any early testimony. Marcion accepted only the Pauline epistles and Luke, the Pauline Gospel. The Alogi rejected all the Johannine writings because the Montanists found here support for their doctrines.[2] The absence of any *historic* evidence in favor of an author other than the Apostle is shown in their absurd attribution of the Apocalypse to Cerinthus. In the third century *Caius*, presbyter at Rome, rejected the book for the same reason as did the Alogi. And this seems to have been the motive that led Eusebius in the fourth century to attribute it to John the Presbyter. Near the middle of the third century *Dionysius of Alexandria*, though taking it as inspired, assigned it on purely internal grounds to a John other than the Apostle, possibly John Mark. A fragment in Eusebius, *H.E.* VII. 24 f., preserves his argument. Holding as unquestionable the apostolic origin of the Fourth Gospel and the Epistles, he argues that the Revelation differs from these in characteristic ideas and terms, in language and grammatical idiom, and also in the author's naming of himself, though with none of the self-designations used in the Gospel. The substance of his argument against an identity of authorship in the two books, revived and widely adopted in modern times, is shown on pp. 354 ff. The presence of a second John at Ephesus he found to be indicated in the fact that two tombs of John were to be seen

---

[1] Cf. p. 368.   [2] Cf. pp. 340 f.

there.[1] *Eusebius*, notwithstanding his large acquaintance with the earlier Christian literature, was evidently unable to discover any tradition of a non-apostolic authorship of the Revelation. So much external testimony to the personality of the author, traceable back to almost contemporaneous sources, is found in the case of almost no other book of the New Testament.[2]

Internal Testimony. When we turn to the book itself and ask what evidence it furnishes, that the John who wrote it was the Apostle, there is little or nothing which possesses force enough to be considered decisive, either affirmatively or negatively. The writer does not designate himself an apostle and there is nothing in the book which could come from an apostle only; but on the other hand, nothing which we can confidently say an apostle could not have uttered. A number of intimations are pointed out as against identifying the author with the Apostle, but these are not convincing. They are as follows: (*a*) a mark of subapostolic authorship is seen in 21[14], where the writer speaks of the apostles quite objectively, as a group in which he does not reckon himself, assigning to them the dignity with which a later generation sees them clothed. And he takes the same objective attitude toward them in 18[20], where also he thinks of them all, it is said, as martyrs already in heaven. But it will be seen that the argument, if valid, would exclude the author from the number of the prophets also; yet he emphasizes his place among these.[3] For further answer to this argument see Com. on these passages. (*b*) An apostle who had heard the Lord's words recorded in Mk. 13[32] could not have written this book, whose very plan is a schematic computation of the advent. It is however enough to say that the computation of the time of the End is no more precise in the Revelation than in the immediate context of that passage in Mark, that is, in vv. 14–31; nor is it more in conflict with the Lord's words than is that passage.[4] (*c*) There is nowhere in the book any reminiscence of a personal knowl-

---

[1] On Dionys. cf. Alford 210 ff. ; Simcox *Rev.* in *Camb. Gk. Test.* XXIII. ff. ; Swete CIX. f.

[2] On the absence of the book from the Syrian canon and uncertainty in eastern opinion see pp. 341 f.   [3] See pp. 292 f.   [4] Cf. p. 149.

edge of, or intercourse with, Jesus in his earthly life.   There is, however, no appropriate place for such personal reminiscences of the author in a series of revelations in which the Christ appears only in his ascended majesty and the glory of his final triumph.   Even his death is referred to only in its relation to his great victory, and the victory of the saints in their final redemption.   It might be queried whether memories of that life in Galilee would not furnish to many critics a mark of late impersonation, as do, for example, the words of 2 Pet. 1^{17-18}.   (*d*) The words of 14^4 show that the writer was an ascetic and therefore unmarried; but according to 1 Cor. 9^5 all the apostles were married; the author then cannot be John the Apostle: So bizarre a piece of exegesis would be out of place in a serious survey of arguments, if it were not urged by critics who lay claim to scientific methods.   (*e*) The apostle to whom were spoken the words of Mk. 10^{40}, 'is not mine to give,' could not have put into the mouth of the Christ the promise of Rev. 3^{21}, 'I will give to him to sit with me in my throne.'   Here also the exegesis is at fault.   The latter passage merely individualizes the general messianic promise common from Daniel's time on, Dan. 7^{27}, that the kingdom should be given to the saints; the former declares that the place of honor in the final kingdom does not depend on the Lord's personal favor, but is already prepared by God's eternal ordering for him who is greatest in service, v. 44.   (*f*) One who heard the Lord's prophecy of the destruction of the temple, recorded in Mk. 13^2, could not have written Rev. 11^1, declaring its preservation.   But with equal force it might be argued that no one, whether apostle or another, could have written the passage in the nineties, long after the temple had been destroyed.   For further discussion of the question see Com. *in loc.*   (*g*) The author seeks to give his message the weight of his name, 'I John,' but not of an apostolic rank.   He calls himself servant of Christ, brother, companion, but not apostle; whereas Paul though using the former terms in self-designation, yet in nearly all his epistles announces his authority as an apostle.   Paul's usage, however, was not a norm to be followed necessarily by another.   He wrote his epistles in the exercise of his apostolic authority, which was frequently called in question. The author of the Revelation wrote his book in no such circumstances; his message is that of a *prophet*, it is that character which he emphasizes.[1] It is shown elsewhere (p. 368) that the title *apostle* was much less used to designate the Ephesian John even by those who distinctly witnessed to his apostleship. (*h*) The author of the Revelation is versed in the scriptures and apocalyptic literature, but the apostle John in his trial at Jerusalem was perceived (Ac. 4[13]) to be in the Jewish sense 'unlearned and ignorant.' But that judgment of the council was based on the answer of Peter, speaking for both himself and John,[2] and it shows no more rabbinical learning than might be possessed by a member of any Jewish family devoutly instructed in the Scriptures. It is questionable whether the Apocalypse reveals an author whose knowledge of the Scriptures, popular apocalyptic, and rabbinical sayings went beyond the possible attainments in such a family. We need not discuss here Mk. 1[20], Jno. 19[27], 18[16], passages often cited to show that John's family was above the humblest rank.

From this survey of the objections urged on internal grounds against the apostolic authorship of the Revelation, it may fairly be maintained that these cannot be regarded as decisive, or even as furnishing strong presumption against that authorship. In view then of the exceptional force of the external evidence, and the evidence, discussed at length below, in favor of John's activity in Asia at the end of the century,[3] there appears a reasonable degree of probability in the tradition that the book comes from the Apostle. In the contents, spirit, and impassioned language of the book, there is much that is akin to the vehement 'son of thunder,' who would call down visible judgment from heaven to consume the enemies of the Lord, Lk. 9[54]; and herein may be found some confirmation of this conclusion. But this and similar features in the character of the Apocalyptist are too common to justify any sure inference.

The Apocalypse and the Fourth Gospel. In seeking to determine the personality of the Apocalyptist, we are not immediately concerned with the relation of his book to other

---

[1] Cf. pp. 292 f.   [2] Cf. Ac. 1[15], 2[14], 3[12], 5[29].   [3] Cf. pp. 366 ff.

2 A

writings whose authorship is not certainly settled. Yet in view of the widely accepted tradition which assigns both the Fourth Gospel and the Apocalypse to one author, the question is properly noticed here. In the third century Dionysius argued on internal grounds that it was impossible to accept identity of authorship; and in recent times his argument has been taken up and expanded with a force to give it acceptance with the majority of present-day scholars. While some would accept the Gospel only as apostolic, and others the Apocalypse only, still others deny that character to both. No candid student can fail to see that the assumption of a common authorship must face a number of weighty objections; and one may well hesitate to assert categorically that these objections are inconclusive. We are accustomed to utterances to the effect that the question is definitively closed; e.g. 'It is one of the most certain theses of New Testament science that not another line from the author of the Apocalypse is preserved in the New Testament' (Jülicher 241). Yet in examining the grounds upon which such a judgment is based, the impartial investigator must acknowledge that answers to these objections, and counter-arguments also present themselves, though these too may not be conclusive. The subject presents one of those questions in New Testament criticism in which mental bent, apart from the bias of prejudgment, is chiefly influential in determining the conclusion reached. In the comparison of the two books the Apocalypse must be taken, as is maintained throughout the present commentary, to be the work of one author, who, whatever use he made of apocalyptic fragments and other material, has so completely adapted these in language and interpretation to his purpose, that the book as it lies before us is to be considered in so far a unit. The differences between the Apocalypse and the Fourth Gospel which are held to preclude identity of authorship are grouped into the following classes.

(1) *Linguistic differences.* While the Greek of the Gospel is grammatically correct, that of the Apocalypse is frequently ungrammatical,[1] *e.g.* a nom. in apposition with other cases, or

[1] Cf. p. 224.

even after a preposition, as ἀπὸ ὁ ὢν καὶ ὁ ἦν καὶ ὁ ἐρχόμενος, 1⁴; harsh changes of construction occur and lack of agreement, as 2²⁶, 3²¹, 11¹,¹⁵, 21¹⁴. Hebraisms are more frequent than in any other book of the New Testament. Favorite expressions of the Gospel appear in the Apocalypse either not at all or less often, or in a different sense; and *vice versa.*[1] These linguistic differences, many of them not perceived in a translation, but appearing in almost every paragraph in the Greek, are so striking that the reader in passing from one book to the other feels himself almost certainly in contact with a different writer. Although these peculiarities have been exaggerated by some critics, they are not to be minimized, certainly not to be overlooked. An older explanation referring grammatical and similar differences to different ages of the same writer, who learned in later years to write better Greek (Hort, Westcott, *al.*), cannot be accepted in view of the date of the Apocalypse.[2]

But there are on the other hand counter considerations which must be noticed. The departures from correct grammatical usage are not due to ignorance ; the writer shows a knowledge and command of Greek too accurate to make such a supposition tenable. Beyond question both books come from writers, or a writer, whose mode of thought and native speech are Hebraic ; and that this Hebraic manner is followed more closely in one book than in the other may conceivably be due to causes other than duality of authorship. The whole character of an apocalypse, a type of writing Jewish in origin, contents, and manner, would lead us to expect a more Hebraic style in the Revelation than in the Fourth Gospel, which is a theological interpretation of the incarnate life of Christ.[3] Moreover as the Apocalypist in the selection and arrangement of his matter shows careful observance of a fixed plan, a studied handling of his subject with reference to the production of a drama of visions, so he may be conceived to have adopted, perhaps half unconsciously, a diction and manner which he felt to be more consonant with the utterances of a prophet and ecstatic.

[1] For a survey of linguistic differences see Lücke II. 662 ff. ; and for criticism of Lücke, Stuart I. 377 ff. ; cf. also Speaker's Com. 454 ff.   [2] Cf. p. 206 ff.

[3] There is not sufficient warrant for the supposition frequently advanced that the Apocalypse takes the name Jew as a title of honor, while the Fourth Gospel takes it as one of dishonor ; see Com. 2⁹.

The Apocalyptist's choice of the form Ἱερουσαλήμ in preference to Ἱεροσόλυμα, which is used in the Gospel, seems intentional (see Com. 21^{10}) ; so the oft-recurring ἀρνίον, Lamb, to the exclusion of ἀμνός, the only form elsewhere applied to Christ in the New Testament, is a technical term consciously adopted as a fixed epithet of the Christ of heavenly glory (cf. pp. 314 ff.). Over against these differences between the two books, striking parallelisms also in a linguistic respect have been often pointed out (cf. among others Bouss. *Kom.* 177 f.). Some of the more noticeable of these are the following. Only in the Johannine writings is Christ called the Word (cf. Com. 19^{13}). His designation as the Lamb is more strongly emphasized in these writings than elsewhere in the New Testament (cf. Jno. 1$^{29, 36}$) ; in fact precisely this designation occurs elsewhere only in I Pet. 1^{19}. The figures of the water of life, springs of water, and the like, are conspicuous here, cf. Jno. 4$^{10 f., 14}$, 7^{38}, Rev. 7^{17}, 21^{6}, 22^{17}. For the figure of the shepherd cf. Jno. 10$^{1 ff., 26 f.}$, 21$^{16 f.}$, Rev. 7^{17}. For the supersession of the temple cf. Jno. 4^{21}, Rev. 21^{22}. Worthy of notice is the agreement of Jno. 19^{37} and Rev. 1^{7} in the form, varying from the LXX., of Zechariah 12^{10}, quoted in each place in connection with the crucifixion. The emphasis on the ideas of truth and falsehood, whether taken separately or in contrast with each other, so common in the Gospel and 1 Jno., appears in the Apoc. also, though the words, ἀλήθεια and ψεύστης, do not occur in the latter (cf. Com. 21^{8}). ἀληθινός, *true to the ideal,* occurs 10 times in the Apoc., 13 times in the Gospel and 1 Jno., only 5 times in the rest of the New Testament. μαρτυρία in the sense of testimony to divinely given truth is very frequent in the Apoc., Gospel, and 1 Jno., but occurs only once in the rest of the New Testament (Ac. 22^{18}). νικᾶν as a kind of technical term for complete victory over the world and Satan, occurs in the Apoc. 11 times, in the Gospel and 1 Jno. 7 times, not in precisely the same way elsewhere in the New Testament, τηρεῖν τὰς ἐντολάς, or the sing., in the Apoc. twice, in the Gospel and 1 Jno. 9 times, in the rest of the N. T. twice. τηρεῖν τὸν λόγον, or the plur., in Apoc. 4 times, the Gospel and 1 Jno. 8 times, not elsewhere in the N. T. ἑβραιστί twice in Apoc., 5 times in the Gospel, not elsewhere in the N. T.

Parallelisms such as are pointed out above, and the number could be considerably increased, furnish strong intimation that the Apocalypse, if not from the same author as the Gospel and 1 Jno., arose in common with these in a circle that was dominated by a single personality. There is plausibility in the suggestion [1] that the superior smoothness of the Greek of the Gospel and various linguistic differences are due at least in part to the employment of a Greek amanuensis. Josephus revised portions of his work in this way ; Paul wrote most of his epistles by the hand of another; and there is force in the supposition that the phraseology was sometimes influenced by the amanuensis. In

[1] Cf. Zahn, *Ein.* II. 629.

spite of the marked differences in language and style it would
appear that the Apocalypse in these respects is more closely
akin to the other writings called Johannine than to any other
books in the New Testament, and that these five books form a
group bearing clearer marks of oneness, in the aspect under
discussion here, than do any other New Testament writings not
professedly from the same author.   The phenomenon common
in literature of the production by one author of writings differing widely in diction and manner must cause hesitation in
forming a decision on these grounds alone.

(2) *Theological differences.*   (*a*) The *God* of the Apocalypse
is chiefly represented as the creator and sovereign of the universe, enthroned apart in majesty, judging the world in wrath,
not in mercy.   In the Gospel he is the Father who so loved the
world that he gave his only begotten Son.   In the one book he
appears as the Hebrew God, in the other as the Christian.   For
the most part in the Apocalypse, the aspect is that of a being
to be worshiped and feared, more than to be loved.   This difference, however, is due to the respective scopes of the two
books.   The Gospel seeks to give the complete revelation of the
character of God as manifested in the incarnate Son ; the Apocalypse is confined chiefly to one aspect of that character, that of
the righteous judge.   The difference is that between the whole
and a part.   There is no contrariety.   For further discussion·
of this point see pp. 310 ff.   (*b*) The *Christ* of the Gospel is the
revealer of God to men, the source of spiritual renewal, the
meek redeemer who lays down his life for the world.   In the
Apocalypse he is the mighty messianic prince of Jewish expectation, who rules the nations with a rod of iron.   But here
again the comparison is made from a partial view.   In the
Apocalypse, since it is the *book of judgment*, he is preëminently
the victor over the prince of this world, the punisher of obdurate
enemies, the rewarder of the faithful.   But there appear here
also and frequently the features predominant in the Gospel
characterization.   Christ is here the faithful μάρτυς, *witness*,
through whom the Christian possesses the μαρτυρία, *the testimony*,
God's revelation given in the gospel; cf. 1[5, 9], 3[14], 6[9], 12[11, 17], 19[10],
20[4].   He is the fountain of spiritual life for all who thirst, 21[6],

22^{17}.   He is the Lamb who has redeemed men by the gift of his life; cf. 1^5, 5^9, 7^{14}, 12^{11}, 14^4.   Thus the highly spiritualized conception of the nature and functions of the Messiahship given in the Gospel discloses itself in the midst of the imagery of the Apocalypse.   On the other hand the characteristics most conspicuous in the apocalyptic representation are not wanting in the Gospel, the Gospel of severity as well as the Gospel of love. These are implied in such passages as 2$^{13-16}$, 5$^{37-46}$, 7^{34}, 8$^{15-55}$, 9$^{39-41}$, 12^{31}, 16^{11}; see further p. 160.   It may be argued with force that the representations of the Christ in the two books point to a single author or at least to a group dominated by one mind.   For the two representations form a complement of each other such as is found in no other books of the New Testament.   In the Gospel we have the eternal Son who has laid aside the divine glory which he had in his union with the Father, and has become incarnate that he may give life to the world; in the Apocalypse we have throughout the same eternal Son, returned to his heavenly majesty, his redemptive work accomplished, and at the end of the ages consummating his own triumph and the triumph of his people over the powers of evil. The Logos become flesh, and the Lamb (as the latter is used in the Apocalypse; see p. 314 ff.), ideas which completely dominate their respective books, are correlative conceptions, each contains the other.   Not only does the portraiture of the one book presuppose that of the other, but also it is only in these books that the two conceptions are developed with such pervasiveness and fullness.   And it is only in these two books that we find with so frequent recurrence the Son's ' subordination ' to the Father.[1]   The view that the writer of the Fourth Gospel who had a definite conception of how the Lord spoke on earth could never have represented him as speaking after the different and sustained manner of the Apocalypse,[2] is utterly unwarranted in the case of one who had witnessed the Transfiguration and the Ascension, one who had worshiped the Lord in the awe-inspiring appearances after the resurrection,[3] and who through many years of the life in the Spirit had beheld in him ' the Lord of glory.'   (c) The *Spirit* is represented in the Apocalypse in the strange form of the seven Spirits, and his functions are

---

[1] Cf. p. 314.   [2] J. A. Robinson, *al.*   [3] Cf. Mt. 28^{17}, Jno. 21^{12}.

chiefly those of the producer of the ecstatic state and of the mediator of revelation and prophecy. He is not spoken of as the Helper, or as the agency of spiritual life, as in the Gospel, though the latter may be implied in $22^{1,17}$. There is however no actual contradiction between the two books in the doctrine of either the person or the offices of the Spirit. His manifold operations are, to be sure, made less conspicuous in the Apocalypse; this might be expected in a book more concerned with the final consequences of the spiritual life than with its agencies and processes. For the general agreement of the Apocalypse with the other books of the New Testament in the doctrine of the Spirit see pp. 316 f.

(3) *Eschatological differences.* The Gospel is almost wholly concerned with the present, not the coming, age. It speaks of judgment, resurrection, the coming of the Lord, eternal life, all as spiritual processes occurring in the present, *e.g.* 5^{21-27}, 14^{16-28}. But in the Apocalypse these terms designate instead eschatological events. In this is seen the most striking difference between the two books; they appear to be separated from each other by the widest reach of religious thought. Yet here again it is quite possible to mistake an apparent, for a real, divergence, or at least to overlook the proper limits of the difference. The chief factors of traditional eschatology which form the theme of the Apocalypse are found in the final anticipations of the Gospel also, though in a subordinate relation. And on the other hand the form of judgment, resurrection, and advent, which are conceived in the Gospel in a spiritual way, is presupposed in the spiritual relation of the faithful to their Lord in the present life as pictured in the Apocalypse.[1] In both cases it is a matter of antecedent and consequence; but in the Gospel attention is largely fixed on the former, in the Apocalypse on the latter. And a Christian Jew of the time, even the author of the Fourth Gospel, if he received visions of the Last Times and wrote a record of these, must have been dominated by the current eschatology inherited from Jewish sources, but christianized. The great difficulty lies in conceiving an author who so thoroughly spiritualized traditional beliefs as does the

[1] For fuller discussion see pp. 101 ff., 163 f.

Fourth Evangelist, to have entered so fully and with so much sympathy, as the author of the Apocalypse does, into the forms of traditional eschatology. It would however be rash, as the history of literature warns us, to affirm that a writer might not possess so great versatility, or be able to withdraw himself to so great a degree from one phase of a subject with its appropriate manner, and concentrate himself upon another and the manner belonging to it. The problem involved is analogous to that of a dramatist's power of vivid characterization. The writer of the Apocalypse shows remarkable versatility in the production of the paragraph of the seven epistles, which in its immediate aim, in its horizon and manner, differs so widely from other parts of the book as to form in the minds of many critics an argument for composite authorship.[1] Something of the same facility appears in his readiness in combining with Jewish messianic imagery the christian doctrines of faith in Jesus, and redemption from sin through his blood. A similar capability appears in the Evangelist, who, while retaining in a measure current eschatological notions, fixes his attention chiefly on the corresponding spiritual processes which are antecedent to those future events and prepare the way for them. A writer who accepted so unhesitatingly, as does the Evangelist, the literal application of utterances of the prophets to Jesus' history,[2] could hardly have rejected every form of visible consummation of the future pictured by the prophets. It seems certain that he is not seeking so much to displace accepted eschatology as to interpret its most essential character as beginning to be realized in the present spiritual life. A striking parallelism to this aim followed in the Gospel is seen in the doctrine of Antichrist in the first epistle. The common belief in the coming of the great adversary, Antichrist, as one of the chief events of the Last Times, is evidently not denied, but it is pointed out that his essential work is already begun in the present opposition to Jesus as the Christ; in a spiritual sense he has come already,[3] as in the Gospel the judgment and resurrection have in a spiritual sense already taken place.[4]

---

[1] See pp. 492 ff.   [2] Cf. 12^{38-41}, 13^{18}, 17^{12}, $19^{24, 36-37}$.
[3] Cf. $2^{18, 22}$, 4^3, also 2 Jno. 7, 2 Thess. 2^7.
[4] For a supposed difference between Rev. and Jno. as regards the term *eternal life*, and the place of faith and works in soteriology see pp. 164, 163.

Conclusion. The reader who takes up the two books in his Greek Testament in immediate succession feels inevitably as he passes from one into the other that he is in a different atmosphere, that the language, manner, presuppositions, and outlook have changed. And if he analyzes the difference in the aspects spoken of above, it may seem impossible to attribute the writings to one author. Many find it so. And yet in view of what may be said, as we have seen, in the way of explaining divergences and establishing agreements, the question comes up with force, whether the subtler affinities are not such as at least to make the attribution of the books to one author supposable. At all events we may reasonably hesitate to consider the question definitively settled in the negative. The confident, in some instances one might say the arrogant, tone of utterances often heard to the effect that all competent critics are at one in denying a unity of authorship, is certainly not warranted, though it is true that most present-day scholars hold to a diversity of authors. To say nothing of many scholars of the more conservative school, whose critical acumen it would be presumptuous to deny, a number of critics, who are remote from the suspicion of undue deference to traditionalism, accept what is essentially equivalent to a common source. Harnack [1] 'confesses to the critical heresy' which carries both books back to one author, to be sure, on the supposition that the Apocalypse is a working over of a Jewish source by the hand — not that of the Apostle — from which the Gospel comes. But our question here is oneness of authorship, not apostolicity. J. Weiss [2] says, 'However different the two writings may be, they have so much in common that it must be said that the same circle must have shared in the publication of both'; and commenting on the difficulty in supposing writings so different to have been accepted and understood by the same readers and at the same time, he adds, 'it does not help much to assign the two writings to different authors.' Weiss' theory that both books are redactions of writings of John the Presbyter does not concern the present discussion. What is of interest here is that he finds upon internal evidence that both books in their present form spring from one source, perhaps one person. Bousset [3] in his

[1] *Chron.* 675. [2] *Offenb.* 156. [3] *Kom.* 179 ; cf. also *En. Bib.* I. 199.

survey of the affinities between the Apocalypse and the other writings called Johannine finds these so clear that he concludes the books all originated in a circle which stood under the influence of one person, the Asian John, who in Bousset's view is the Presbyter. Here too the dominating influence of one personality must exclude the assumption of radically divergent views in theology, eschatology, and general religious outlook. Such theories of the books come nearer to the assumption of one writer, with freely working amanuensis, than to that of a plurality of writers possessing views mutually exclusive.[1]

XIII. THE TWO JOHNS OF THE ASIAN CHURCH

A. *John the Presbyter.* The interest of the student of the Apocalypse in the person thus designated arises from the fact that he may with plausibility be supposed to be the John well known to the Asian churches, and the author of the Apocalypse, if there are found insuperable objections to assigning this rôle to the Apostle. He is not mentioned in the New Testament. The designation, 'the Elder,' which the writer of 1 and 2 John gives himself, assumed by many to refer to him, lacks as necessary for identification the addition 'John.' The term there used is entirely vague; it might be given to an apostle (1 Pet. 5¹), it may be official, applied to one holding the common office of presbyter, or it may denote simply superior age or dignity. It is evidently a designation familiar to the readers of those epistles, but if it were meant to distinguish the writer from another of the same name, the name could hardly be omitted. There is nowhere in the literature of the second century (not even in Iren. *Hær.* IV. 27–32, nor in Papias, Euseb. III. 39, 15) evidence of the use of the term as a widely known substitute for the proper name of a particular individual. Where found it refers to one specified in the context; see p. 373.

Except in an obscure fragment of Papias, preserved in Eusebius *H.E.* III. 39, no mention of the Presbyter John is found before the fourth century. Eusebius is the first to point out the existence of such a person as evidenced by the fragment which he preserves from the introduction to Papias' book entitled Λογίων κυριακῶν ἐξηγήσεις, *Interpretations of utterances of the Lord.* The passage, so far as it need be given here, reads thus: εἰ δέ που καὶ παρηκολουθηκώς τις τοῖς πρεσβυτέροις ἔλθοι, τοὺς τῶν πρεσβυτέρων ἀνέκρινον λόγους· τί Ἀνδρέας ἢ τί Πέτρος εἶπεν ἢ τί Φίλιππος ἢ τί Θωμᾶς ἢ Ἰάκωβος ἢ τί Ἰωάννης ἢ Ματθαῖος ἤ τις ἕτερος τῶν τοῦ κυρίου

---

[1] The present commentator ventures to say that his earlier conviction of the impossibility of maintaining a unity of authorship has been much weakened by a study of the two books prolonged through many years.

μαθητῶν, ἅ τε ᾿Αριστίων καὶ ὁ πρεσβύτερος ᾿Ιωάννης οἱ τοῦ κυρίου .μαθηταὶ λέγουσιν; that is, according to the interpretation adopted below, *But furthermore, if perchance there came* [to me] *anyone who had been a hearer of the elders, I was wont to inquire about the sayings of* [these] *elders regarding what Andrew or what Peter had said, or what Philip or what Thomas or James, or what John or Matthew or any other of the Lord's disciples* [had said], *and* [I was wont to inquire] *what Aristion and the presbyter John, the disciples of the Lord,* [or according to the emendation of the text adopted below, *the disciples of John*] *are saying.* The passage has given occasion to much exegetical controversy, which can be taken up only very briefly here. (Among the works referred to on p. 343 see especially Larfeld and Chapman.) It will be seen that Papias mentions two groups of persons whose words he sought to get. He marks the transition from one group to the other by the rhetorical variation from ἤ τί to ἅ τε. The first group consists of apostles including John. The designation οἱ τοῦ κυρίου μαθηταί given to these refers without doubt to their personal relation to the Lord when he was on earth; it was the testimony of such, handed down through trustworthy intermediaries, which was of value for the purpose of Pápias. The second group consists of two persons; one Aristion, not an apostle and not known to us; the other, called the presbyter John. Our inquiry is concerned with the personality of the latter. He has quite commonly been identified with John the apostle, because he is here called, as the text stands, the disciple of the Lord, and no other John is known among the Lord's personal disciples in the New Testament, or, apart from this fragment of Papias, in the tradition of the first three centuries. The difficulty arising from the repetition of John's name in the second group is in the opinion of many explained by a difference between the two groups as regards time and place. Papias' first mentioned inquiry, τί εἶπεν κτλ. was meant to ascertain the testimony of such immediate disciples of the apostles as had lived long in Palestine and had had opportunity to hear many apostles all of whom at the time when the inquiry was made were dead except John. The inquiry spoken of in the second part, ἅ τε λέγουσιν, sought the testimony of such immediate disciples (not all necessarily *apostles*) of the Lord as were, at the time when the inquiry was made, still living and in Asia, viz. Aristion and John. The difference in tense, εἶπεν, λέγουσιν, marks the distinction. Papias himself may have heard these Asian disciples, but he seeks the report of others also who had heard them. The apostle John who lived on in Ephesus till the close of the century belongs to both groups; hence the repetition of his name. The epithet ὁ πρεσβύτερος, the *elder*, which is given to him, is then explained as a title of honor, distinguishing him from others because of his age, or as an official title to mark him as the head of the Asian church; cf. Zahn, *Ein.* II. 220, 210; Chapman 35 f., 39. Thus a distinct John ceases to many minds to be a reality. John the Presbyter is called an invention of Eusebius, because the historian was the first to interpret the passage in Papias as witnessing to his existence.

But if Papias had in mind the activities of one and the same John at different times and places, he could hardly have chosen language less likely to convey that thought. Without some more distinct note of the Apostle's place in both groups, the name in the second group; especially with the added ὁ πρεσβύτερος, must inevitably be understood of a different person. Moreover the added phrase, οἱ τοῦ κυρίου μαθηταί, *the disciples of the Lord*, in the second part further complicates the passage. It is certain that the phrase has the same meaning in both clauses, an immediate disciple of Jesus himself, such as were the apostles and others. If any variation were thought of, it must necessarily in some way be indicated; but of this there is no trace.[1] And after the preceding words, ἤ τις ἕτερος τῶν τοῦ κυρίου μαθητῶν, *or any other of the Lord's disciples*, which summarily include all disciples other than those just named, the repetition of the designation in this clause is harshly tautological. If emphatic repetition or specification were intended, there would at least be required some such addition as καὶ ἐκεῖνοι, *these also* disciples, etc.

A chronological difficulty also arises not only in identifying the second John with the former, but in denominating the second group personal disciples of the Lord. The present λέγουσιν, *are saying*, marks the disciples of the second group as still living at the time when Papias wrote. The present cannot be used here, as often, of words given in an earlier writing, for the reports here spoken of are oral — this fact Papias emphasizes in the context. And in view of the aor. εἶπεν in the parallel group, this cannot be taken as a historical present. It is true that Papias in both clauses is speaking of inquiries made in the past (ἀνέκρινον), and he might have used ἔλεγον instead of the present, but he thinks of the witness of this group as still living, they are speaking at the present time and giving the same testimony; they furnish an apt example of what he declares most valuable, τὰ παρὰ ζώσης φωνῆς καὶ μενούσης, *the deliverances of a living and abiding voice*. Now the date of Papias' book cannot be determined with certainty. Zahn, *Forsch*. VI. 112, puts it with probability c. 125–130. Harnack's argument, *Chron*. 356 f., for a date as late as 145–160 is inconclusive. But even if the earliest possible date, 125 A.D., be adopted, the Apostle was long since dead, as were all the other personal disciples of the Lord.

It can scarcely be doubted that there is some textual error in the passage as given by Eusebius. Some would omit the words altogether; so, Hausleiter, Mommsen, *al.* Others emend them; *e.g.* οἱ τῶν τοῦ κυρίου μαθητῶν μαθηταί, Abbott; οἱ τοῦ κυρίου μαθητῶν μαθηταί, Renan; οἱ τούτων μαθηταί, Bacon. This last emendation is less violent in form than the others, but it would make these two men, Aristion and John the Presbyter, who were living in the year 125, personal disciples of those just mentioned, that is of a considerable number of apostles, one of whom (James) had been dead eighty years, another (Peter) and perhaps several others, at least sixty years. The most probable emendation is that suggested in the recent work (1914) of Larfeld (see pp. 113–136), with whom the science of palæography and

---

[1] Utterly without foundation is Harnack's interpretation which makes the phrase in the second clause refer to aged Christians who had come from Palestine, and who as young children had merely seen the Lord and come into slight contact with him. *Chron*. 660.

diplomatics is a specialty. With abundant illustrations drawn from Mss. and inscriptions, he shows the methods of copyists in abbreviating proper names and also their frequent mistakes in reading such abbreviations. He cites the use of Ιων for Ιωαννου in the late usage and shows the probability of its use in early times. But ω in the Mss. is often written in a form easily mistaken for co, so that Ιων is confused with ιcον. And ιc is frequently mistaken for κ. Thus ιcον, wrongly written for ιων, abbreviation for Ιωαννου, became κον, an abbreviation occurring instead of κυ for κυριου. A copyist who had just written in the preceding clause τον κυ (= κυριου) μαθητων might easily in the second clause mistake ιων (= Ιωαννου) for κον or κυ, and write τον κυ μαθηται. The abbreviation κυ is found in most Mss. of Eusebius. It is concluded then that what Papias wrote was οἱ τοῦ Ἰωάννου μαθηταί, the disciples of John. In the text thus emended the art. before Ἰωάννου may mark him as the one just mentioned, or the well-known. Larfeld's reasoning is so plausible and the reading so completely solves the difficulties of this much disputed passage, that we may accept his emendation with considerable confidence.[1]

If this be the correct form of Papias' words, the two persons Aristion and John the Presbyter become somewhat less shadowy. They are younger contemporaries of John the apostle; they are spoken of in a way implying that they are known to the unnamed friend of Papias to whom he addressed his book, and since he doubtless intended his book for a wider circle of readers, presumably the Asian churches, they are probably known to these also. They were not conspicuous enough to have left a great impression on the churches, if we may judge from the fact that there is no mention of them, except in this writing of Papias, unless it be true, as many suppose, that much, or all, that is said of John the apostle in the Asian tradition should be referred not to the Apostle, but to the Presbyter, the two being confused in popular thought. Aristion and John are specially mentioned by Papias among his authorities because as disciples of the Apostle they were able to report what he had said. The title Presbyter given to John is assumed to be familiar to the readers, and may have been used to distinguish him from his master, the Apostle. It is probably the official term presbyter.

The term οἱ πρεσβύτεροι, the elders, in the plu., as used in the passage of Papias, cannot be official, for presbyters, found in every church, were not as such personal authorities for the words of the Lord's apostles, in the sense here intended by Papias. The term appears to be a standing one to denote men of an older generation, the fathers, who were looked upon as authoritative witnesses to the past. It occurs often in Irenæus and later writers. In itself it might include the apostles; but it is doubtful whether it was so understood. Irenæus at all events defines his use of it by the added words, disciples of the apostles; e.g. Hær. V. 5, 1; 36, 2. And Papias also, if Larfeld's emendation be adopted, uses it thus; for throughout the passage cited he is speaking of what his visitors reported from the elders, and as included

[1] Harnack expresses his approval of it as probable; Theol. Lit. Zeitung, May 23, 1914.

in such reports he refers to what they told of the words of Aristion and John the Presbyter. These two then are *elders* in the sense here intended; but they are also defined as disciples of the apostle John. We thus obtain a clue for the interpretation of the much disputed first clause, τί Ἀνδρέας κτλ. Taken by themselves, the words τί . . . εἶπεν κτλ would most naturally be regarded as in apposition with τοὺς λόγους, *I inquired about the words of the elders*, i.e. *what the elder Andrew said*, etc. Thus the elders in this connection would be identified with the apostles, and the clause is interpreted so by many. But another construction is possible, which makes the clause the object of the action contained in λόγους, *I inquired about the words of the elders in regard to the sayings of Andrew*, etc. The elders as disciples of Andrew, Peter, etc., were the proper witnesses of the sayings of these. This interpretation, required in the emended form of the second clause, is also free from chronological difficulty. If the apostles here named are the elders meant, the visitors to Papias to whom he addressed his inquiries would be contemporaries and hearers of a considerable number of apostles, some of whom had been long dead at the time when Papias must have been making his inquiries; cf. p. 364.

It must be said in conclusion that the sole explicit historical evidence for the existence of John the Presbyter, as distinguished from the Apostle, is this passage of Papias. And while we are compelled to interpret the passage as witnessing to his existence, yet there remains the extraordinary fact, not satisfactorily accounted for, that no other trace of such a person appears till about the beginning of the fourth century, when Eusebius called attention to the significance of Papias' language, though Papias' book had been well known through the centuries, when the Alogi and others were seeking for a non-apostolic authorship of the Johannine Apocalypse, and Dionysius was unable to find any evidence of a second John in Asia to whom to attribute it, except the two tombs at Ephesus; cf. p. 350. In view of these circumstances the question cannot fail to arise whether the text of Papias used by Eusebius may not have contained some other error also besides that discussed on pp. 364 ff.

B. *The tradition of John the Apostle at Ephesus.* Few traditions of early Christian history have been held to be more certainly authenticated than that of the abode of John the apostle at Ephesus in the last years of the first century. But in recent times there has been raised among students of the Johannine question an array of objections, which are accepted by many as conclusive against the truth of the tradition. The earlier criticisms of the last century, those of Lützelberger, 1840, and Keim, 1867, were generally disregarded, as not outweighing the evidence in support of the tradition. But since the publication of the De Boor fragments in 1888 (see below, pp. 381 ff.), the question has been reopened and a formidable line of argument presented against the traditional view; see works mentioned on p. 343. In a discussion of the authorship of the Apocalypse the question cannot be avoided; since if it be shown conclusively that the Apostle had not lived in

Asia Minor, the book, which distinctly connects its author with the Asian church, cannot have proceeded from his hand. It should be added, on the other hand, that even if it were certainly proved that he lived at Ephesus, his authorship of the book would not necessarily follow, since the work of another John may have been attributed to him. And it is not amiss to repeat here that the apostolic origin of a book, however important in some respects, is not in itself of such fundamental significance that the value of a part of our New Testament stands or falls with it (cf. p. 347). It would seem then that the question of an Ephesian residence of the Apostle might be studied without exaggerating or minimizing the evidence on either side.

First of all it need not be seriously questioned that there was about the time to which the Revelation belongs a person named John, whether the apostle or another, prominent in the churches of at least seven cities of Asia Minor. The book itself, which as seen above, pp. 344 f., cannot be regarded pseudonymous, bears full testimony to this fact; and even if it were pseudonymous, its assumptions must, except on suppositions that do too great violence to the structure of the book and its representations, bear the same testimony.[1] Of the other books of the New Testament it may be said that the attribution of the Fourth Gospel and the epistles to a John by the writers of the following generation, since the books bear unmistakable marks of Ephesian provenience, likewise indicates the presence there of an influential person bearing the name. The history of the Acts does not come down to so late a date. The testimony of the writers of the second century to an Asian residence of the Apostle, which will be spoken of below, even if mistaken in the matter of personal identity, furnishes evidence of a John as well known to the Asian churches. Accepting then an Asian John, and in spite of the scantiness of evidence (cf. p. 366) the presence and influence of John the Presbyter in the Asian church, we have to ask, Did the Apostle also live and labor there, or was this true of the Presbyter only, who erroneously came to be thought of as the Apostle? It is certain that only one of the name could have been *prominent* there at the time of the Apocalypse. The writer attaches no distinguishing epithet to his name, there is for the readers but one John who could address them thus (cf. pp. 344 f.). If this was the Apostle, and if the other John was there, the latter was too subordinate to be thought of by any one as the author of such an address to the seven churches. But if this John was the Presbyter, then the Apostle either had not labored there at all, or his presence and influence belonged to the past; so that at the time of the Revelation it was not necessary to guard against a possible confusion of the author with him.

It is convenient to take up first the evidence in support of the Apostle's

---

[1] Prof. Bacon, who rejects the tradition of an Asian John, makes the sojourn at Patmos a clever fiction of the pseudonymous author impersonating the Apostle ; Patmos was near enough to account for the self-styled Apostle's addressing a book to these churches ; it was remote enough to forestall any objection of the readers to the effect, that they had not known of the Apostle's being in their vicinity. *Hib. Journ.* 1904, vol. 2, 331.

abode in Asia at the time; but this must not be allowed to prejudge the argument, to be considered later, which is adduced against the tradition. The New Testament furnishes no *direct* evidence upon the subject; see further pp. 380, 390.   The earliest writer of the second century who makes explicit mention of the Apostle's sojourn in Asia is Irenæus.   His references to the presence there of one whom he designates 'John the disciple of the Lord' are so definite (*e.g.* Euseb. *H.E.* III. 23, 3 ; IV. 14, 6) and his allusion to the Apostle in this designation so clear (cf. Euseb. V. 8, 4 ; 24, 16, *Hær.* II. 22, 5, *non solum Joannem sed et alios apostolos ;* also III. 3, 4) that no doubt can be legitimately raised regarding the *fact* of his testimony; the question of its value hinges solely upon its accuracy.   The preference for the designation *disciple* instead of *apostle* found in Irenæus, Papias, and others is probably due to the fact that that term expresses more distinctly what was specially insisted on, the value of testimony given by those who had learned immediately from the Lord himself.   The same designation is given to the other apostles as well as John.   *Apostle* was applied in some cases to those who had not been of the original twelve.   Irenæus makes his reference to the Apostle clear beyond question.   There is not the slightest force in the contention (*e.g.* Bouss. *En. Bib.* I. 198, a position essentially abandoned in the last ed. of his *Kom.* 46) that the use of the term *disciple* by Irenæus indicates reference to a John not known as an apostle; cf. Chapman, 59 ff.   It is noticeable that *disciple* is the word always used in the Fourth Gospel; *apostle* as an official term does not occur there.   The sole question regarding the witness of Irenæus is then, Is it correct?   The proof of his error is regarded by many critics so convincing, that they unhesitatingly set his testimony aside.   He is conceived to have confounded throughout John the Presbyter with the Apostle, and this mistake of his is thought to have perpetuated itself, largely through his great influence, in the later writers of that and the following centuries.   That the John of whom he speaks could not have been the Apostle but must have been the other John prominent in Asia is considered certain from evidence adduced for the Apostle's martyrdom at an earlier date, and from various indications that he could not have been prominent in Asia.   Irenæus then, it is contended, is the real source of this tradition, so widely current and apparently well attested, concerning the Apostle.   If his error is established, the trustworthiness of the tradition is held to be destroyed. See works mentioned on p. 343.

It becomes then of the first importance in our inquiry to consider the *date* of Irenæus and *his sources of information*, as bearing on his credibility.   Irenæus, in the latter part of his life presbyter and bishop at Lyons in Gaul, was probably by birth an Asiatic.   At all events he had lived for a considerable time in Asia Minor and was thoroughly familiar with the church there and its traditions.   The chronology of his life cannot be fixed in detail, but some intimations point clearly to approximate dates sufficient for our purpose.   His great work, *Against the Heresies*, was written between 180 and 189 A.D.   We have from somewhere near that date; either before or after, a part of a letter of his, important for our inquiry, written to Florinus, a presbyter at Rome, who was falling into the error of Valentinianism (Euseb. *H.E.* V. 20). In this letter Irenæus speaks of his relation to Polycarp in a way which gives us some clue to the probable time of his birth. He says that while a boy, παῖς ἔτι ὤν, he was wont to hear Polycarp in lower Asia discoursing on his intercourse with John and others who had seen the Lord. He speaks of his exact remembrance of not only the personal appearance of Polycarp, his place of discoursing, his customary entrance and exit, but also of the discourses which he was wont to deliver, telling what the immediate disciples of the Lord had said regarding the Lord's work and teaching. This *teaching* of the Lord as reported by Polycarp Irenæus says he so accurately understood and remembered that he can testify to its agreement with the Scriptures. And it is this teaching which he wishes to bring back to the remembrance of the erring Florinus, who had been attending the lectures at the same time with Irenæus. It is to be noted also that throughout the passage the imperfect tense is used and other expressions showing that Irenæus is speaking of hearing Polycarp for at least some little time. He may perhaps not have been a permanent pupil of his, but the language implies something more than the casual hearing of one or two sermons, as some would contend. Now if he so clearly comprehended and remembered the Christian teaching which Polycarp was reporting, he must have been at the time when he heard Polycarp a person of considerable maturity. What he here speaks of is quite different from stories of the Lord's miracles for example, which a child might understand and remember. Therefore when he speaks of himself as being in those days a *boy*, it is clear that he uses the term as one often does in speaking of early years from the standpoint of later life — and it was in that age that Irenæus was speaking in this letter to Florinus. The broad sense in which he takes the word he makes clear by his context. In another place (*Hær.* III. 3, 4) he uses the similar but looser expression ἐν τῇ πρώτῃ ἡμῶν ἡλικίᾳ, *in our early age,* in reference to the time of his seeing Polycarp.[1] Harnack's supposition that he was a child of not more than twelve or fifteen years (*Chron.* 325) is utterly at variance with the context. What he says of his understanding and recollection of Polycarp's discourses would justify us, without doing violence to the word παῖς, in supposing him to have been at least twenty or twenty-five years old. Now Polycarp's martyrdom occurred, as most agree, in 155 A.D. (so, Harnack, Zahn, *al.*). We may therefore safely place the birth of Irenæus not far from 130 A.D., if not earlier, (Zahn dates it 115). The significance of so early a date in relation to the value of his testimony will appear below.

Harnack, who is determined at all hazards to eliminate the authority of Irenæus from the Johannine problem, has constructed an elaborate argument (*Chron.* 320 ff.) to show that as regards the personality of the John

---

[1] In Soph. *Phil.* the young warrior and ship-commander Neoptolemus is regularly called παῖς, *boy.* In Hom. *Od.* IV. 665, Telemachus, a young man about twenty, is called νέος παῖς, *a young boy.* Lightfoot, *Ignat.* I. 448, points out in late writers numerous cases of a similar term applied to persons of thirty or more years.

2 B

spoken of by Polycarp, Irenæus is not a trustworthy witness. As many critics share his view and as he puts the case against Irenæus in its strongest form, the more important points in his argument are here summarized. They may conveniently be tabulated as follows, criticism of the respective points being reserved till the conclusion. (*a*) Irenæus' work *Against the Heresies* was completed in the year 189. (*b*) The lapse of Florinus into Valentinianism could not have occurred before 190; for Irenæus wrote to the Roman bishop Victor urging his deposition and Victor's bishopric began in 190, and furthermore Florinus is not mentioned in Irenæus' work against the heresies, completed in 189. (*c*) It is unlikely that a Christian 60–70 years old should have fallen away into heresy. (*d*) If the lapse of Florinus could not have occurred before 190, and if at the time of the lapse he could not have been 60 or 70 years old, he must have been born as late as 120–130 A.D. (*e*) But the date of Florinus gives us a clue to that of Irenæus, since he must have been younger than Florinus by ten or fifteen years, probably more. For in his letter to Florinus he says εἶδον γάρ σε παῖς ἔτι ὢν ἐν τῇ κάτω Ἀσίᾳ παρὰ Πολυκάρπῳ λαμπρῶς πράσσοντα ἐν τῇ βασιλικῇ αὐλῇ καὶ πειρώμενον εὐδοκιμεῖν παρ' αὐτῷ (Euseb. *H.E.* V. 20, 5), *For while yet a boy I saw thee in lower Asia with Polycarp doing brilliantly in the royal court and striving to be held in good esteem by him.* The language implies that Florinus must have already been a pupil of Polycarp for some time when the boy Irenæus saw him ; this is especially implied in the words λαμπρῶς πράσσοντα ἐν τῇ βασιλικῇ αὐλῇ, lit. *doing brilliantly in the royal court.* The words are commonly understood to mean *taking a conspicuous position in the royal court,* though Harnack does not say what precise sense he gives them. (*f*) If now Florinus was born near 130, and Irenæus was at least 12 or 15 years younger, the birth of Irenæus is fixed at not far from 140, probably shortly before 142 (*Chron.* 329). (*g*) Irenæus then was about 13 when Polycarp died (155 A.D.). How long before this it was that he heard Polycarp in Asia is not indicated. This conclusion, that he was a young boy at the time alluded to, is confirmed by the added words, ταῦτα καὶ τότε διὰ τὸ ἔλεος τοῦ θεοῦ τὸ ἐπ' ἐμοὶ γεγονὸς σπουδαίως ἤκουον (Euseb. V. 20, 7), *these things even then through the mercy of God bestowed upon me I listened to earnestly ;* he implies that it was only through the special mercy of God granted to him that a boy so young was able to understand the discourses of Polycarp. (*h*) It cannot be urged that Irenæus' knowledge of Polycarp's words about the Apostle rests not only on that early acquaintance but also on later intercourse, since the possibility of any supposed later intercourse is certainly excluded. For the ardent interest which Irenæus felt as a boy in Polycarp's discourses would surely have impelled him later in life to seek his instructions ; but there is no trace of this, it must be that Polycarp died soon after the time alluded to. Although Irenæus is bent on influencing Florinus by appealing to the authority of Polycarp, he refers to early teaching only ; he evidently has no later teaching to cite. In the work on the heresies in speaking of his relation to Polycarp he says, ' whom I saw in my early age,' III. 3, 4, ἑωράκαμεν ; he had *seen* him, but does not claim there to have heard him. From this whole line of argument it follows as a *certain conclusion (sicheres Ergebniss)* that only as a maturing boy did Irenæus see Polycarp and hear him preach; he was never his pupil and never had association with him (p. 328). In his mistaken recollections of Polycarp's discourses he confounds John the Presbyter with the Apostle. Thus his testimony to the Apostle's residence in Asia Minor is completely eliminated, as is that of the later witnesses, since they merely echo what they had learned from Irenæus. The evidence adduced *against* John the Apostle's residence in Asia will be spoken of below.

An examination of this argument will reveal its inconclusiveness at every point. In the following comments the letters, *b, c,* etc., refer to the respective paragraphs above. As regards the date of Florinus' birth (against *b, c, d*), it is impossible to say how long before his open break with the Church and his actual deposition Florinus may have been uttering principles accordant with, or at least leaning toward, Valentinianism. Irenæus' letter to him was a friendly message written to him while he was yet acting as a presbyter in the Church; it was designed to check his advance and recall him from error. It may have preceded the open rupture and deposition by a considerable time, that is, some time before 190, the earliest date at which Irenæus could have written to Victor urging deposition. How long Florinus may have been suffered to continue in his office is wholly uncertain. The very fact of Irenæus' letter to Victor indicates some slowness on the part of the bishop to act. The absence of allusion to Florinus in the work *Against the Heresies* furnishes no evidence that his lapse had not already begun or actually taken place. Valentinianism is one of the heresies treated of, but there was no occasion to mention specifically the name of Florinus, nor of many others who were not the authors of the heresy but the followers. The assumption (*c*) is unwarranted that one would not at the age of seventy take the step toward which he had long been tending. Therefore data for the inference (*d*) that Florinus was born between 120 and 130 are entirely wanting.

In the second place, whatever may have been the date of Florinus' birth, the supposition (*e*) that Irenæus was ten or fifteen years younger is without any certain foundation. It rests on the very obscure words λαμπρῶς πράσσοντα ἐν τῇ βασιλικῇ αὐλῇ, *doing brilliantly in the royal court.* These are commonly understood to refer to some conspicuousness at the imperial court. Now even if that be the meaning, the words could quite conceivably be applied to a youth of twenty or twenty-five (the age attributed above, p. 369, to Irenæus at the time), performing some particular service in the imperial household. But there is great difficulty in taking the words in. this literal sense. There was no imperial court in lower Asia, and the attempts of some scholars to connect the reference with an imperial visit to the province of Asia[1] have failed of any probable conclusion. The position of the words as part of what appears to be one phrase, παρὰ Πολυκάρπῳ . . . παρ᾽ αὐτῷ, shows almost certainly that they are to be taken as refer-

---

[1] Cf. Zahn, *Forsch.* IV. 277 ; Lightfoot, *Contemp. Rev.* 1875, *Ignat. and Polycarp*, I. 2, 662 ff.

ring to Florinus' relation to Polycarp, and not to anything in his external situation, which in fact would have no bearing on the thought of the context. The phrase τῇ βασιλικῇ αὐλῇ then not improbably refers to some court or hall where Polycarp gave his discourses;[1] and the first phrase λαμπρῶς . . . αὐλῇ appears to be closely connected in thought with the second, πειρώμενον . . . παρ' αὐτῷ; Florinus' *brilliant career* in the Christian school was connected with his *effort to possess the esteem* of Polycarp, whose instructions he was attending, apparently in preparation for the work of a Christian teacher. There is no intimation that his age differed greatly from that of Irenæus. We have here then no data for determining the time of Irenæus' birth. The interpretation (*g*) given to the words ταῦτα . . . σπουδαίως ἤκουον is read into them; σπουδαίως ἀκούειν does not mean to *hear understandingly*, but to *listen to earnestly, give eager attention to*, an act of moral earnestness, in the power to exercise which Irenæus sees the special mercy of God toward him. The language would be appropriate in the mouth of one of any age.

The contention (*h*) that Irenæus could not have met Polycarp later in life rests wholly on the argument from silence. The assumption that Polycarp died while Irenæus was a boy, that is, before Irenæus had opportunity to seek his instructions in maturer years, requires for its support a full knowledge of the movements of Irenæus in his earlier years; we must know that there were no hindrances in the way of resorting to Polycarp, if the latter were living. But of this we know nothing. The possibility of a later intercourse is not essential to our inquiry. But while there is no certain evidence in favor of it, there is none to the contrary. It is not true, as claimed, that in trying to influence Florinus by appealing to Polycarp, Irenæus confines himself to those early reminiscences; he also refers him to the letters of Polycarp (Euseb. V. 20, 8), with which he doubtless assumes him to be acquainted. At all events the force of his appeal consists in reminding Florinus of what Florinus himself already knew of Polycarp's words learned in those early associations. Irenæus himself might conceivably have heard much from Polycarp at a later date. His silence concerning this *proves* nothing. If there is in the use of the word ἑωράκαμεν decisive force against any prolonged association with Polycarp, we must also understand the words τῶν ἑωρακότων τὸν κύριον in this letter to Florinus (Euseb. V. 20, 6) to characterize John and the rest of the apostles as those who had *seen* the Lord but had not been his pupils. From this survey of the argument advanced for the late date of Irenæus' birth and the valuelessness of his report of Polycarp's utterances in the matter under discussion, it is apparent that the contention cannot be said to be established; and the evidence in support of an earlier date which has been drawn from Irenæus' own words, as pointed out above, pp. 368 f., must claim for itself a force not hereby destroyed. The question whether facts proved in regard to John's life may not invalidate Irenæus' testimony to an Asian residence will be considered below. The fixing of Irenæus' date is

---

[1] Cf. Ac. 19⁹, Hast. IV. 822, also Harnack, *Chron.* 330.

important, not only in connection with the report of Polycarp's words, but also in relation to Irenæus' testimony in general, as will be seen.

It is necessary to notice more fully Irenæus' *sources* of information. He mentions by name only two witnesses, Polycarp and Papias. He refers often to 'the Elders,' whom he does not name, and sometimes uses the sing. 'the Elder.' This term is used by Papias and others also. It cannot designate a definitely fixed body of men, as in the case of 'the apostles'; none such existed. Irenæus shows that he generally had in mind personal disciples of the apostles, as he repeatedly adds a definition to that effect; *e.g. Hær.* II. 22, 5; V. 5, 1; 33, 3; 36, 2. In one case he uses the term of a person who was a disciple of those who were themselves disciples of the apostles; IV. 27, 1. It is evident that he refers to such as were commonly held to be competent witnesses to the apostles' words, 'the fathers.' The instances in which he alludes to the sayings of unnamed persons are numerous. It is idle to inquire what particular persons he had in mind; it was not important for his readers to know, for the description added, or the designation, *elders*, was enough to mark them as authoritative. The explanation of so frequent an appeal to others is found in what Irenæus says in the preface to his book against the heresies. He there expresses strongly his sense of inadequacy for the great task he is undertaking. It is in keeping with this spirit that he so often seeks to support himself upon the utterances of others; *e.g.* 'he that was better than we,' I. 13, 3; 'one who was before us,' III. 17, 4; 'one of the ancients,' III. 22, 3; 'a certain person before us,' IV. 41, 2; 'the Elders.' The cases of the sing. 'a certain Elder,' 'the Elder,' etc., all occur in one long paragraph, IV. 27–32, treating of the proper attitude of Christians toward the failures of Old Testament worthies, and throughout that paragraph Irenæus is reproducing the thought of a certain unnamed Elder to whom he keeps referring. It is not possible, nor is it important, to determine who this Elder is. Wherever the term is used with the definite art., 'the Elder,' the reference is to this one Elder had in mind throughout the paragraph, not to some person whose proper name has been displaced by the term as a well-known appellation. The writer of 2 and 3 Jno. could substitute 'the elder' for his personal name in writing to the narrow circle addressed where he was thus known, especially as the author of the letters would be announced by the bearers of them; but there is in this no ground for supposing that there was one, *e.g.* Papias, or Polycarp, to whom this appellation could be given throughout the Church in place of his personal name; cf. p. 362. Harnack (*Chron.* 333 ff., so, others) argues that the Elders to whom Irenæus refers are only those of Asia Minor, with whom he had himself had no personal intercourse, and that he knows of their traditions through Papias only; in other words, the Elders with him are practically synonymous with Papias. Thus Irenæus' knowledge of early tradition in the Asian church is confined to what he read in Papias and what he remembered from hearing, when a young boy, a few sermons of Polycarp. He ceases to form a trustworthy authority in any matter of the early church of Asia. But this view does as great violence to his knowledge of Asian tradition as it does to his acquaintance with

Polycarp. The radical fault of this kind of argument is that it treats Irenæus' testimony much as if he were a recluse remote in time and place from the vigorous intercourse going on throughout the Church, and writing from studies limited to one or two books. It is, to be sure, unquestionable that he used Papias' book, as he refers to him by name; and in some cases it may be plausibly conjectured that Papias was his authority for attributing a tradition to the Elders. But he read many books; he shows familiarity not only with most of the writings that make up the New Testament, but also with other letters of Polycarp besides the one preserved (Euseb. V. 20, 8), with Clement of Rome, Ignatius, Justin, Hermas; he refers often to the writings of others. It is certain that Papias was not the only one from whom he derived traditions of an earlier time. In one case, *Hær.* V. 33, 3–4, he distinguishes Papias from the Elders; after citing certain sayings of the Elders, apparently handed down orally (*quemadmodum presbyteri meminerunt . . . audisse se.*), he refers to Papias *also* as testifying to the same in writing (ταῦτα δὲ καὶ Παπίας ἐγγράφως ἐπιμαρτυρεῖ). But quite apart from his acquaintance with Christian writers, Irenæus was an influential presbyter and bishop in the western church, he was active in movements affecting the relation of the eastern and western churches to each other, he had lived for some time in Asia Minor, he had been in Rome as a delegate to the bishop from the church of Lyons and Vienne and perhaps had lived there previously; in short he was a man in immediate contact with current life and tradition throughout the Church.[1]

In connection with the faulty theory regarding the sources of Irenæus' knowledge, the further mistake is made of not distinguishing between traditions of very different kinds. When he cites the authority of the Elders to the effect, that the Lord lived to an age between forty and fifty, *Hær.* II. 22, 5, or that the Lord taught the miraculous yield of wine, wheat, and all the fruits of the ground as one of the blessings of the coming kingdom, *Hær.* V. 33, 3 f., the testimony is rejected; but we must recognize that plain, objective facts of history, lying within the ken of all, stand in a different category. Is there a single one of the most trusted modern critics and historians who may not in some instance be convicted of error in judgment or statement of fact? And it is noticeable that not one of Irenæus' appeals to the Elders relates to external facts in the history of the Church, or of the life and work of the great Christian leaders. Mis-

---

[1] The Moscow Ms. of the *Martyr. of Polycarp*, a ninth century Ms., states that he was at Rome when Polycarp was martyred at Smyrna, and that he instructed many there. Harnack wrongly argues (*Chron.* 323 f.) that the letter of the Christians at Lyons commending him to the Roman bishop Eleutherus, as if a stranger, when sent there as a delegate in 177–178, 'absolutely excludes' any previous work of teaching there. But the short fragment of the letter preserved, Euseb. V. 4, does not speak of him as unknown to Eleutherus; but as a ground for his favorable reception, the letter commends his zeal for the gospel, which quite conceivably may refer to his career at Lyons in the interval since he was at Rome, if he had been there before. At all events there is no more implication of introducing a stranger than in Paul's words, 1 Cor. 4¹⁷, 16¹⁰, recommending Timothy to the Corinthians among whom he had already labored.

takes about utterances attributed to the Lord, mistakes in such matters as the authorship of a book are conceivable enough, but a mistake about so patent a fact as that of the residence of John the apostle in Asia could not in the circumstances occur without discovery and correction.

Passing over for the time being the critical question regarding Papias, whose book Irenæus used, we have to notice more fully that which was for Iranæus in the matter of our present inquiry his chief and most trustworthy source of information. The weight of his testimony here is determined not by his dependence on the Elders or any person named, but on a wider circle of witnesses. What gives its value to his testimony is the probability that he is recording what was a matter of common notoriety. It is worth while to look at this claim more closely. The sense of brotherhood among the first Christians led to a remarkable knowledge of, and interest in, the brethren not only of the immediate community, but also of more distant congregations. The greetings and other mention of names in Paul's epistles show how real was the personality of Christian teachers and workers in the minds even of those to whom they were unknown by face. Especially general and distinct must this knowledge have been in congregations which like those of the seven Asian cities were connected by trade routes so that intercourse was easy. The New Testament bears abundant witness to the ready intercourse between churches in widely separated parts of the empire. Evidence of the active fellowship maintained by the churches in which Irenæus was presbyter and bishop, those of Vienne and Lyons, with the Christians in Asia Minor is seen in the letter of the former to the latter, giving an account of their sufferings in the persecutions under Marcus Aurelius, c. 177 A.D. Now, as we have seen, the John of the Apocalypse was a conspicuous figure recognized as an authority in the Asian church at the end of the century. His book reveals him as a striking personality, and he must have been known to young and old in the churches of the seven cities and elsewhere. And if John the *apostle*, whether he be identified with the author of the Apocalypse, or not, lived and taught among these churches, he must have been especially well known throughout the region; for the Apocalypse itself bears witness to the unique place held by the apostles in the estimation of the later Christians, 21[14], 18[20]. Churches came very early to be proud of the personal ministrations of an apostle; and at least one of the seven churches had been careful to test those who professed to be apostles, 2[2]. But John was known throughout the Church as one of the little group of foremost apostles, Gal. 2[9]; knowledge of this must have been brought to Asia by the first narrators of the gospel story. If, therefore, he went in and out among these congregations, there could have been no doubt or uncertainty in the minds of his contemporaries throughout the Asian church, about his apostolic rank. On the other hand if the John of the Apocalypse was a different person, who followed afterwards, he too as a familiar figure must in his person and non-apostolic rank have been at once recognized by the contemporaries of both as distinct from his predecessor; they could not have taken him for the apostle. Acts, sayings, and writings of the later John might be attributed to the former, but the distinction between the two *persons*, active as preachers in the churches, must remain clear in the minds of those accustomed to hear them. The merging of the two into one could arise only when the original hearers and the direct knowledge of their reminiscences had passed away. On the other hand, if the great Apostle had never lived in Asia, nor been a preacher in the churches there, it is difficult to conceive that the John known there should have been mistaken for him, and so a belief in the Apostle's presence should have arisen, until authoritative witnesses for that period were no longer at hand to correct the error. But unquestionably contemporaries of the Asian John, or Johns, survived in considerable numbers well into the time of Irenæus' mature activity; on the date of his birth see pp. 368 f. Two such are known by name, Polycarp and Papias. Polycarp, bishop of one of the seven churches, was martyred 155 A.D. at the age of eighty-six.[1] He was therefore a contemporary witness from at least the last decade of the first century till after the middle of the second, *i.e.* a time when Irenæus was some 25 years old. Papias, bishop in a city closely connected with those of the seven churches, who was the companion of Polycarp (Πολυκάρπου ἑταῖρος, Iren. *Hær.* V. 33, 4; Euseb. *H. E.* III. 39, 1) and probably of about the same age, survived to a time near the middle of the century, either before or after; cf. Harnack, *Chron.* 357. It cannot be doubted that there were many others also among the Christians of these communities, whose span of life reached at least seventy-five years and who were therefore competent witnesses from the last decade of the first century to near the middle of the second. The number of persons who in their earliest youth had seen and heard this conspicuous teacher, persons whose memories of him would have been kept vivid through older associates, and who lived on till the middle of the century must have been large. It seems inconceivable then that there should have been in the year 150 any uncertainty in these communities as to whether a certain prominent teacher was the apostle John. No phenomenon is better attested than trustworthy recollections of the identity of persons seen and heard a half century before. It is significant that Irenæus nowhere sets himself to the task of *proving* the Apostle to have sojourned in Asia; that is not one of the questions in which he appeals to the authority of the Elders or others; it is always alluded to in passing, like any other fact recognized by all. There is no intimation that the opinion needed the support of testimony and that there was any dissent from it. Papias in his introduction as quoted by Eusebius (see p. 362) distinguishes two Johns, but if there was in his book, which Irenæus knew thoroughly, any statement at variance with the belief in the residence of the Apostle in Asia, it made no impression on the mind of Irenæus. Whether such divergent opinion was actually expressed there, will be considered below. But if the Apostle was put to death many years before the time of his supposed residence in Asia, as Papias is reported in the De Boor fragment to testify, the surprising thing in connection with Irenæus' testimony is not so much that no one of many competent wit-

---

[1] *Mart. Pol.* 9. Zahn, *Forsch.* VI. 155 ff., argues for an age still older.

nesses comes forward to point out his mistake, but rather that this general popular belief, of which he is merely the recorder, could grow up without opposition or correction. Even the statement attributed to Papias in this fifth century fragment does not appear in a connection to suggest a corrective purpose. Attempts to explain how Irenæus and others could have confused John the Presbyter with the Apostle will be considered below, pp. 378 f.

We have given much space to Irenæus as a witness to the Apostle's abode in Asia because of the importance of his testimony, if trustworthy. The testimony of *other early writers* can be presented more briefly. Apart from Papias, to be spoken of later, the only writer before Irenæus to throw light on our question is *Justin Martyr*. Justin was born near the beginning of the century, he lived some time at Ephesus and was martyred at Rome c. 163–167; cf. Harnack, *Chron.* 722. Among other writings of the New Testament he studied carefully, as shown by reminiscences, the Gospels, Acts, and Galatians, books witnessing to the prominence of John among the apostles; and in his *Dialogue with Tryphon*, published between 150 and 160, but described as held primarily at Ephesus, he speaks of the Apocalypse as written by the Apostle John. (*Dial. c. Tryph.* 81; cf. Zahn *GK.*, I. 457 ff., 560 ff.). Justin was too discerning a student not to have seen that the author of the book, whoever he might be, was a prophet of the church in Asia. Therefore in accepting the book as apostolic, whether rightly or wrongly, he was accepting the Asian residence of the Apostle. He has no occasion to speak of that point specifically, but his words imply the popular belief at Ephesus. The first writer after Irenæus to furnish direct evidence is *Polycrates*, bishop of Ephesus near the end of the century. About 195 A.D. he wrote a letter to Victor, bishop of Rome, concerning the Easter controversy (Euseb. *H. E.* V. 24), in which, to show his competence to speak of the past usage of the church in Asia, he says that he is 65 years old and that among his kin there have been seven bishops. He was born therefore c. 130 and was a younger contemporary of Polycarp and Papias; and because of his age, family associations, and place of residence he may be accepted as a well-informed witness to matters in the Asian church. In enumerating many luminaries of the church there, who had died and were awaiting the resurrection, he says that John, who leaned upon the Lord's breast, had fallen asleep in Ephesus. That the descriptive epithet given to John was at the time understood of the Apostle is unquestionable.[1] It is noticeable that the form of this mention of the Apostle's relation to Asia does not seem to be a reminiscence of Irenæus' statements, but rather to be derived from some common opinion like that given by Dionysius a half century later, that the tomb of the Apostle was shown at Ephesus; cf. p. 350. The apocryphal *Acta Joannis* written late in the century, though abounding in fable, yet in placing the scene of the principal acts of the Apostle in Ephesus, may be taken as witnessing to a common

[1] It is not necessary to discuss here the view that primarily it had a different reference; cf. Scholten, *Der Apost. Johan.* ; Delff, *Das vierte Evang.*, also *Theol. Stud. u. Krit.* 1892 ; Bacon, *Fourth Gospel*, etc.

belief. The *Alogi* also of the same period furnish similar evidence indirectly; for while they seek to disprove the Apostle's authorship of the
Revelation, they accept its Asian origin, and do not impugn the popular
belief regarding its author by any argument against his Asian residence,
but by attributing the book to Cerinthus. Only *two other authorities* need
be mentioned here, the two conspicuous writers belonging to the end of
this century and the beginning of the next, Clement of Alexandria and
Tertullian of Carthage. Both speak explicitly of the Apostle's sojourn in
Asia; cf. Clem. *Quis dives* 42; *Tertull De Prescript.* 36. It will be seen
that by this time the tradition was attested by writers in all parts of the
Church, and alike by the different schools of thought. And in none of
these is there argument to establish the fact attested, there is no consciousness of a divergent opinion. It is superfluous to follow out the testimony
of later writers. That which by the end of the second century was universally witnessed to as a part of apostolic history would thereafter be generally assumed without question; and this is the case in the writings of the
following centuries.

But it is difficult to attribute the consensus of the earlier authorities to
the influence of one person, Irenæus, or of a little group associated with
him. If he was known to be in error — and we have seen the competent
witnesses to be numerous — the unquestioning agreement of so many and
widely scattered writers in the time immediately following is very difficult
to explain. At the time when the matter was one of general notoriety and not of historical research it would hardly be possible that the
writer in Gaul should constitute the principal source of information, direct
or indirect, for the rest of the world, regarding the history of the church
in Asia. But if the whole tradition is to be traced back to a mistake of
Irenæus, and perhaps a few others, we are brought to the question, How
did this error arise? And no satisfactory answer is given. The supposition is that Irenæus mistook the John of whom when a young boy he
heard Polycarp speak, that is, John the Presbyter, for the Apostle. But
the misconception of Irenæus, if such it was, would not explain the statement of Justin, whose writing antedates that of Irenæus. It is argued
that the statement attributed to Papias in the fifth century fragment,
about the early martyrdom of the Apostle, did not correct the wrong opinion of Irenæus and others, because they were already so deeply imbued
with the belief that the Ephesian John was the Apostle, that they regarded Papias' statement as a mere oversight. (Cf. Schmiedel, *En. Bib.* II.
2510). But how did they become so imbued with this error? The martyrdom of one of the foremost apostles, like that of his brother James, must
have left its trace in the Christian story told by the missionaries, at least
so far that no John laboring in Asia a half-century later could easily have
been mistaken for the Apostle. The name John was not one which in
itself must mislead. There were Christians in Asia who had once been
disciples of a great prophet John (Ac. 19[1-3]), but there is no reason to
suppose that the Baptist and the Apostle were ever confused there. It is
not easy to believe that there could have been any general confusion of the

Asian John of this late date with an apostle known to have been already martyred. If Irenæus as a young boy could make the mistake, it would have been too surely corrected to leave him imbued with the idea, or in a position to spread his mistake to many others. Still less tenable is the explanation, if Irenæus was not a young boy when he heard Polycarp; see pp. 368 f. Others find the origin of the misrepresentation in an effort to maintain for the Asian church an apostolic authority corresponding to the claim of the church in Rome in the appeal to its heritage from Paul and Peter. Irenæus is carried away with zeal for the cause of Asia and unintentionally misrepresents; so, among others Prof. Bacon, *Fourth Gospel* etc., 102, 246. Similarly others trace the error to the Gnostic controversy. Irenæus had an end to serve; in opposition to Gnosticism he wanted to prove that through connection with Polycarp he was in possession of direct apostolic tradition; without conscious dishonesty he is really making Polycarp say what he wants him to say; so, among others, Badham, *Am. Journ. of Theol.* 1904, 545 ff. But these explanations increase rather than diminish the difficulty. Although Irenæus is a 'man of peace' and in the Easter controversy pleads for due consideration of the tradition of the Eastern church, it is doubtful whether he and Justin, writing as they did from the west (Lyons, Rome) would have been misled by prejudice to exalt so unduly the eastern tradition. At all events the hypothesis assumes that they differ in the matter under discussion here from common opinion, and if there existed any ground for dissentients' believing that the Apostle had been martyred many years earlier, it would have been necessary in controversy first of all to show the error of that belief and establish the Asian residence; the consciousness of arousing dissent must have betrayed itself. This nowhere appears; the Asian sojourn is assumed as granted by all. The possibility that Irenæus and others might easily and with entire honesty confuse the Presbyter and the Apostle is said to be shown in a similar confusion of Philip 'the deacon' and Philip the apostle, which occurs in Polycrates, Clement of Alexandria, and Eusebius. But the two cases are not parallel. The two Philips are alike well-known persons in the story of the apostolic church as recorded in the New Testament; and the confusion of the two which is here spoken of occurs in writers more than a century after their time. But the supposed confusion of the two Johns would begin while the contemporaries of one or both of them were still living in the churches with which their names were connected.

Evidence against the Apostle's sojourn in Asia. The preceding pages have shown the unquestioned fact of a body of testimony defending the tradition of John the apostle's sojourn in Asia. The much questioned accuracy of that testimony has been discussed from the standpoint of the competency of the witnesses, and their probable trustworthiness. There remains yet another line of evidence which is adduced in the inquiry and which, if cogent, shows in spite of the difficulties thus raised the error of the tradition, in that the Apostle is seen to have been martyred at an earlier date and not to have sojourned in Asia at all. To many scholars this evidence appears conclusive, and whatever of truth there may be in the records of an Asian John is referred to the Presbyter. The grounds urged as establishing this conclusion are the following:

(1) The words of the Lord, Mk. 10^{39}, 'The cup which I drink ye shall drink,' etc., predict the martyr's death for both the sons of Zebedee, James and John. Jesus' prayer in the garden, 'Remove this *cup* from me,' Mk. 14^{36}, makes any other meaning impossible. Therefore at the time when Mark was written both had suffered the martyr's death. If the prophecy had been only half fulfilled in the death of James (Ac. 12^2), the author of Mark would not have inserted it; so, Wellhausen, *al.* Schwartz (p. 4), followed by others, considers the words a prophecy put into the mouth of Jesus *ex eventu*; the fact that the two brothers are reported as asking at the same time for the two places of honor, shows that they had both been martyred at the same time; doubtless Acts primarily recorded this, but was afterwards revised and given its present form under the influence of the Ephesian tradition. Thus it is seen to be an 'indisputable historic fact' that the two brothers were put to death in the year 43 or 44 A.D. The conclusion is very positive; where argument is weak, assertion must be made strong. In fact the metaphors of drinking the cup, and of baptism, here used by the Lord, are familiar figures to denote overwhelming trouble; for the former cf. Rev. 14^{10}, Ps. 75^8, Is. 51^{17}; for the latter, which compares the trouble to deep waters into which one is plunged (baptized), cf. Ps. 69^2, 124^4, Mt. 3^{11}, βαπτίσει πυρί (see Thayer *s. v.* βαπτίζω). The metaphors cannot be forced to indicate necessarily anything more than the persecution which the Lord declares his disciples must share with him, Jno. 15^{20}. His answer to those who wish to share in his glory is that they must also suffer with him (cf. Ro. 8^{17}). Doubtless the fact that in the case of James the future foretold ended in martyrdom, often leads the uncritical reader of the New Testament to suppose that a like fate probably came to John, independently of, and later than, the time of the Revelation. And in the same way we might expect a similar belief to arise in some quarters in the earlier centuries quite apart from historical evidence. But no explicit statement to that effect appears in any early *historical* writer, except the statement attributed to Papias, which is spoken of below, pp. 381 ff. The account in Ac. 12^2 may be taken as conclusive that John was not put to death at the same time with James. The two metaphors used by the Lord led to the rise of two legends; one that John was compelled to drink a cup of deadly poison, the other that he was plunged (baptized) into a vat of seething oil, but came through these ordeals unharmed. Thus the legends attest the common belief that he was not put to death as a fulfillment of the Lord's prophecy. Origen in his commentary on Mt. 20^{22} shows that with his great knowledge of Christian literature he found nothing to which the Lord's prediction in John's case could refer, except the Apostle's persecution culminating in the banishment to Patmos.

(2) The martyrdom of the Apostle is established, it is held, beyond question by the explicit statement of Papias. We are here brought to the subject repeatedly alluded to above, the testimony of Papias, who alone

among early writers, in the words attributed to him, unquestionably records the martyrdom as a historic fact. In the chronicle of Georgios Hamartolus (9th cent.) it is said of John, μαρτυρίου κατηξίωται. Παπίας γὰρ . . . ἐν τῷ δευτέρῳ λόγῳ τῶν κυριακῶν λογιων φάσκει ὅτι ὑπὸ Ἰουδαίων ἀνῃρέθη, *he was adjudged worthy of martyrdom; for Papias* . . . *in the second book of the Sayings of the Lord says that he was killed by the Jews.* The comment is added that he thus fulfilled the prophecy of the Lord. This comment may be that of the chronicler, or it may be suggested by the source from which he is drawing; at all events it shows the tendency to find a literal fulfillment of the Lord's words. Little weight was given to this fragment of Papias at the time when it was first made generally known (Nolte, *Theol. Quartalschrift* 1862, 466 ff.). But the subsequent discovery of the same fragment in a modified form (De Boor) has brought the Papian testimony into special prominence in the Johannine question, and the statement of it given in these fragments is accepted by many critics without doubt as authentic in form and accurate in regard to the historical fact.

Before speaking specially of the relation of the statement here given to the testimony of other writers, it is necessary to examine the fragments and inquire how far they furnish in themselves and in their transmission evidence of their probable authenticity as actual words of Papias. The passage in the chronicle of Georgios is given in codex Coislinianus III. 134. This codex of Georgios, though the best, differs here from all the others — there are 26 in all — which record the peaceful death of John. The passage as it appears in codex Coislin. is at once seen to be an interpolation, since the same codex cites in the context early writings to show that the Apostle died peacefully at Ephesus. And the carelessness of the interpolator, and perhaps also of the writer from whom he drew, is seen further in the added statement that Origen also in his commentary on Mt. reports John's martyrdom on the authority of the successors of the apostles. What Origen really says (*com.* on Mt. 20²²) is that tradition, not the successors of the apostles, reports that John was banished to Patmos by the Roman emperor, and that this was the martyrdom predicted for him. However, it is evident that there existed at the time of this codex, the 10th or 11th century, a statement attributed to Papias, which is here used by the interpolator to prove that the Lord's prophecy was fulfilled literally in the case of John as well as James. The interpolator's carelessness in reporting Origen deprives his reference to Papias of all value in itself as evidence of what Papias actually said; and this fact together with the divergence from accepted tradition would justify disregard of the passage, were it not for its parallelism with the more recently discovered De Boor fragment.

In 1888 De Boor brought to light a group of seven fragments contained in an Oxford Ms., Baroccianus 142, of an epitome of church history, dating from the 7th or 8th cent., among which fragments two report several statements attributed to Papias.[1] The epitome in which this group of frag-

---

[1] See *Text. u. Untersuch.* V. 2, 167 ff., also Z K G. VI. 478 ff. On the De Boor and Georgios fragments see further Harnack *Chron.* 665 f., *Alt. Lit.* 67; Zahn *Forsch.* VI. 147 ff.; Gutjahr 102 ff.; Lightfoot *Essays*, etc. 211 f.; Chap-

ments is found is a chronicle of various matters of Christian history from the beginning, compiled, as stated in the preface, from Eusebius and others; it is worked together by the epitomizer in a manner and with modifications of his own. He has made great use of the χριστιανὴ ἱστορία, *Christian History*, of Philip of Side, a work of the fifth cent., now lost; and from the language of the context it appears, as is generally agreed, that the De Boor fragments are derived from Philip as their ultimate source. Thus the report of Papias' testimony is traced back to the fifth century. The passage of interest in our inquiry reads, Παπίας ἐν τῷ δευτέρῳ λόγῳ λέγει ὅτι Ἰωάννης ὁ θεολόγος καὶ Ἰάκωβος ὁ ἀδελφὸς αὐτοῦ ὑπὸ Ἰουδαίων ἀνῃρέθησαν, *Papias in the second book says that John the divine and James his brother were killed by the Jews*. The sameness of this passage with that in Georgios Hamartolus is apparent. Both contain the words ἐν τῷ δευτέρῳ λόγῳ (λόγος for βιβλίον is unusual), also the words ὑπό Ἰουδαίων ἀνῃρέθησαν, or ἀνῃρέθη; and in the context the De Boor fragment agrees with Georgios in giving to Papias' book the inaccurate title κυριακὰ λόγια, instead of λογίων κυριακῶν ἐξηγήσεις (Euseb. III. 39, 1). Georgios omits references to James as his context is occupied entirely with John. The two passages are certainly from the same author, or one is derived from the other; at all events the primary source is pretty certainly Philip of Side. The De Boor fragment confirming that of Georgios is held to be conclusive as to Papias' testimony. De Boor's verdict is, 'There can henceforth be no doubt that Papias actually reported that the apostle John was killed by the Jews' (p. 177); and with this agrees the opinion of a large number of present-day critics.

Now if this statement was made by Papias it must carry great weight; for while he is sometimes quoted in Christian writers, whether rightly or wrongly, as saying things palpably erroneous, he could not in this case have been mistaken, since he was himself a resident in Asia at the time when the Apostle is said to have lived there. The difficulty thus raised in the conflict with what appears well-grounded tradition has called forth various suggestions in the way of solution. Many have explained the words as referring to a martyrdom of John at the end of his residence in Asia, and as occurring 'at the incitement,' not 'by the hands' of the Jews. But we cannot, without violence to the record here given, so separate the deaths of the two brothers; both are declared to have been martyred by the hands of the Jews, language appropriate to the death of James (Ac. 12²), but impossible in reference to any execution by a ruler at the end of the century in Asia Minor. But what seems conclusive against that explanation is the certainty that the Asian church, while holding the martyrdom of Polycarp among the proudly cherished memories of its history, should have left that of their great Apostle without a trace of mention or remembrance. Lightfoot (211), half approved by Harnack (*Chron.* 666), suggests that the original passage in Papias may have read somewhat thus: φάσκει ὅτι Ἰωάννης [μὲν ὑπὸ τοῦ τῶν Ῥωμαίων βασιλέως κατεδικάσθη εἰς Πάτμον, Ἰάκωβος δὲ] ὑπὸ Ἰουδαίων ἀνῃρέθη; and that the words here bracketed having been omitted by accident from the Ms. followed in Coislin. (the Georgios fragment), a copyist supplied their place with the words, καὶ Ἰάκωβος ὁ ἀδελφὸς αὐτοῦ in the Ms. from which Baroccianus comes (the De Boor fragment). Zahn. *Forsch.* VI. 147 ff., *Ein.* II. 474, avoids the difficulty by interpreting the John as the Baptist. None of these solutions have gained any general acceptance. We must admit that we have no data for conjecturing what stood in Papias, if not these precise words.

The real question is, Have we sufficient grounds to warrant the acceptance of the words as containing a genuine statement of Papias? What evidence supports its authenticity? Are there reasons for suspecting it? These are questions which we always raise before using in historical investigation any document, especially one not noticed till it had been in wide circulation for several centuries. In answer we have *assertions* of great positiveness: the words are ' of faultless authenticity, a precious remnant of actual knowledge,' Schwartz; 'It is indubitable that the works of Papias must have contained some statement of this nature,' Moffatt. But it is noticeable that scarcely a writer who speaks so positively advances any argument whatever to support authenticity, or answer objections. About all that is offered, even by those who recognize the necessity of some vindication, is that the reference in the quotation is specific to the second book of Papias, or (Bouss. *Kom.* 36) that the passage stands in an excerpt from Philip of Side with a series of Papian fragments recognized as genuine. As regards specificness of reference, it may be noted that the reference in Georgios to Origen spoken of above is equally specific — to the *Com.* on Mt.— and yet is grossly inaccurate. As regards the acknowledged genuineness of the series of Papian fragments in which this passage occurs the statement is altogether misleading. That Philip or the Epitomizer, whoever he may be, intended to put forth here a series of statements on the authority of Papias is clear, but there is nothing to show a first hand use by him of Papias' book; on the contrary, he seems in part to be following Eusebius as the source of his knowledge of Papias; cf. Chapman, 95 ff. Not only does he in the beginning of his compilation specifically mention his use of Eusebius, but the opening paragraph of the Papian passages in the De Boor fragments is condensed almost literally from Eusebius, III. 39, 1–5. One clause in it, Ἰωάννην ἕτερον ὃν καὶ πρεσβύτερον ἐκάλεσεν, cannot be from Papias, as it is taken verbally from Eusebius' argument against Irenæus. Another of the Papian sentences in the De Boor fragments speaks of Papias' error regarding the millennium; that he is here using Eusebius is seen in his adding, as does Eusebius, III. 39, 13, that Papias' error is the origin of that of Irenæus. Another of the Papian sentences in the fragments attributes to him the statement, that those raised from the dead by Christ were still living in the time of Hadrian (117–138 A.D.). It is very doubtful whether Papias with his professed care for accuracy would have stated that these persons (the art. is used, as if all were meant) were living at an age of 100 years as his own contemporaries.[1] From these instances it appears probable

---

[1] The supposition is plausible that the passage is a blunder on the part of the excerptor or compiler traceable to a misunderstanding of Quadratus quoted by Eusebius IV. 3, 1–2. See Chapman *loc. cit.*

that the compiler from whom the Papian sentences came did not make use
of Papias' book itself, and so cannot be relied upon to give the exact testimony of Papias. Not all the Papian sentences in the De Boor fragments
are traceable to Eusebius, but there is nothing to indicate a more immediate
use of Papias' book. As to the sentence important here, that regarding
John's martyrdom, the excerptor in at least one, though not very significant,
case cannot be quoting Papias exactly; the word θεολόγος was not applied
to John till after the time of Papias. But apart from the lack of evidence
to support the accuracy of the compiler in the De Boor fragments and the
suspicion inevitably raised by critical examination, there are other considerations also which compel us to pause before accepting this document as
conclusive evidence that a statement of this purport stood in Papias. Philip
of Side, to whom it is doubtless to be traced, was notoriously inaccurate.
The Christian historians, Socrates and Photius, denounce his untrustworthiness in unmeasured terms; cf. Smith & Wace, *Dict. of Christ. Biog.* And
even if the De Boor fragments be not derived from him, the chances of
error are not diminished. The chroniclers and excerptors often used their
alleged authorities through later hands, and carelessly; sometimes also with
an inaccuracy due to argumentative purposes. Nowhere is greater care in
sifting testimony called for than in the use of citations of early authorities
found in compilers of Christian traditions.

In the case of the De Boor fragment there appears the further reason for
suspicion in the divergence of its statement from the testimony of other
historical writers. The difficulty which is thus raised in the way of accepting it as correctly reporting Papias is, as no one denies, great. Can this
objection be removed by the theory of a confusion of the two Johns in the
mind of Irenæus and a few of his associates? Papias' book furnished the
source of a part of what Irenæus reported of the tradition of the Elders;
without doubt it was much used by him. How then could he, the younger
contemporary of Papias, with this book before him recording the death of
the Apostle at Jerusalem more than a century before the death of Papias,
have called the latter a pupil of the former? How could he, when near the
forties of the second century he heard Polycarp discoursing on his intercourse with John, have thought that Polycarp was speaking of a man who
had been dead a century? If in his youth he was capable of this mistake, his subsequent use of Papias' book would have corrected him. A confusion in his mind of a John (the Presbyter), a leader in the Asian church
at the end of the century, a man well known to many of his own contemporaries, with the Apostle reported by Papias as martyred in the forties of the
first century, cannot easily be attributed to him. Even if his desire to establish a direct apostolic tradition in Asia (cf. p. 379) had misled him to see
the Apostle in the Presbyter, he could not be blind to the contradictory evidence of this statement of Papias, if it existed. His maintenance of the
Apostle's Asian residence would have been conscious misrepresentation,
which Papias' book, if no other authority, would soon have exposed. Likewise as regards writers after Irenæus, it is difficult to believe that the book,
used as it was through the early centuries, if it had contained this statement

so at variance with general belief, should not have left some distinct echo, or trace of influence. Even the Alogi, while holding to the Asiatic origin of the Johannine writings, are eager to establish the non-apostolic authorship of these, yet make no use of such a statement of Papias, which would have formed for them a conclusive historical argument. Eusebius could not, to be sure, have used the statement to support his opposition to the apostolic authorship of the Revelation, because he is zealous to maintain the residence of John in Asia; but this very zeal of his for the Asian tradition would have led him to controvert the error of Papias, if the statement had stood in the copies of Papias known to him. Eusebius shows himself earnest to correct both Papias and Irenæus, where it is in the interest of his views to do so. Perhaps one further observation should be added against the authenticity of this statement in the De Boor fragment. The book of the Acts was known in Asia at the time and therefore probably to Papias. It does not then seem likely that with chapt. 12 before him he would have included John with James in the martyrdom at Jerusalem. This, however, cannot be strongly pressed, for contrary to Acts and Mt., Papias is reported, perhaps wrongly, to give a story to the effect that Judas, notwithstanding an attempt at suicide, lived on in unimaginable deformity as an example of impiety; see Lightfoot, *Apost. Fath.*, p. 523.

Considering then on the one hand the probability that the author of the De Boor fragment did not use Papias at first hand, the untrustworthiness of Philip of Side from whom the statement is derived, and also the large possibilities of error in a late compiler or chronicler; and on the other hand considering the great difficulty raised by the fragment in its relation to the history of opinion in the early centuries, we must conclude that the acceptance of its statement as historical evidence is not justified, unless strongly confirmed by other sources. A confirmation of it is found by the defenders of the fragment in those forms of testimony adduced against the Asian tradition which are discussed in paragraphs (3) and (4) below.[1]

(3) Some early martyrologies are cited as attesting the Apostle's martyrdom. The Syrian martyrology places in its list ' The apostles John and James at Jerusalem' Dec. 27, between Stephen Dec. 26, and Paul and Peter Dec. 28. The same entry stands in the Armenian martyrology, without mention of place and with unimportant variation in the order of days. The Carthaginian martyrology gives for Dec. 27, ' John the Baptist and James the apostle'; but 'the Baptist' is held to be a copyist's error for 'the Evangelist,' since John the Baptist is commemorated in the same martyrology in June. This evidence from the martyrologies is thought to be corroborated by the following authorities. The Pseudo-Cyprian tract *De Rebaptismate* (c. 250 A.D.), commenting on the Lord's

---

[1] Not all critics who deny that the John prominent in the Asian Church was the Apostle accept the De Boor fragment; *e.g.* Harnack, *Chron.* 666, says ' Papias could no more have written that John was killed by the Jews than that Paul died a natural death, unless he meant another John, the Presbyter ; but that also is not probable, since . . . the violent death of the Presbyter must have been recorded in the older literature.'

2 c

words to John and James, Mk. 10³⁹, says, 'he knew they had to be baptized not only in water but also in their own blood.' Aphraates, 'the Persian sage' (4th cent.), in his homily on persecutions, speaking of the martyrdoms of Jesus, Stephen, Peter and Paul, says 'James and John walked in the footsteps of their Master.' Clement of Alexandria (c. 165–220) speaks of the teaching of the apostles including Paul as ending in the time of Nero, *Strom.* VII. 17. The Valentinian Heracleon (c. 180 A.D.) in a passage on the confession of Christianity quoted by Clement, *Strom.* IV. 9, speaks of Christians who had died without confession before the magistrates, adding 'among whom are Matthew, Philip, Thomas, Levi and many others.' Heracleon, it is argued, would certainly have included John in this list of names, if he had died a natural death. These various testimonies are taken to furnish proof of an early and widespread tradition that the Apostle was put to death and that the belief in his sojourn in Asia was erroneous.

Before discussing this argument in detail, it is worth while to take into account certain general considerations. The Lord's words predicting suffering to James and John, soon fulfilled in the event of martyrdom in the case of James, must have led inevitably in later time to the supposition of some such fate in the case of John, especially as the New Testament records nothing to the contrary. However well established might have been the tradition, that the Apostle abode long at Ephesus, where he was supposed to have written the books attributed to him, there was in so far nothing that excluded a martyr's fate in the end. Furthermore great latitude in the use of the word *martyr* is found in the earlier centuries and continuing even into the later. Though the distinction between *confessor* and *martyr*, the latter being confined to those who had suffered death, comes to be established in the third or beginning of the fourth century, still the broader use of *martyr* occurs in late writers. We should expect then to find John reckoned among the martyrs, in either the broader or narrower sense of the word. And we might even expect legends telling of the place and manner of his martyrdom; such however are not found. The legends of the cup of poison and the caldron of oil, harmlessly endured, attest the influence of the Lord's words on tradition (cf. p. 380), and also the absence of traditions of actual killing. It is significant that critics who insist that the obscure words of Rev. 1⁹ are the sole origin of the story of John's banishment to Patmos (cf. Com. *in loc.*) are unable to trace any assertions of his martyrdom to a combination of Mk. 10³⁹ and Ac. 12². One more general observation should be made. Even if *martyrdom* be understood in its narrower sense, there is in the several testimonies presented in this paragraph (3) none, except that of the Syrian martyrology, which necessarily excludes altogether a residence of the Apostle in Asia at some time.

Having in mind these general observations, we pass to a more detailed examination of the several sources cited above as proving the Apostle's martyrdom. The large subject of the martyrologies can be touched upon only very briefly here, but enough can be shown to make evident their relation to the present question.[1] The custom of the Christians from the first of commemorating the days upon which their martyrs suffered led directly to the formation of a kind of calendar. These were local and prior to any formal œcumenical calendar of the Christian year. In time additions were made to these, including also the names of martyrs commemorated in other regions. The later lists were uncritical combinations, containing often duplications and discrepancies. The three oldest of such lists preserved are the *Dispositio Martyrum* (*Burial of the Martyrs*), the *Carthaginian Martyrology*, and the *Syrian Martyrology*. The first is part of a kind of Roman almanac, dating from 354 A.D. It is the oldest of all the lists and was much used as a source in the formation of others. The names are confined to those martyred at Rome and the vicinity. The saints of the first and second centuries are not included; it does not go back beyond 200 A.D. Even in the case of the great Roman martyrs, Paul and Peter, their martyrdom is not included, but the translation of their bones. Now important for our purpose is the fact that though designated in its title as a list of martyrs, the document contains at least two entries having no relation to martyrdom, the Nativity of the Lord, and the *Cathedra Petri*, the commemoration of Peter's founding of the Roman Episcopate. In this is seen the beginning of a tendency to broaden a so-called martyrology into a kind of ecclesiastical calendar. The Carthaginian list, which should be placed second in the order of time, is in its present form as late as the sixth century, but its principal parts are assigned to a very early date; cf. Achelis pp. 23, 27. It shows the growing tendency to include other than the local saints, *e.g.* some of the apostles, and also other days besides those of the martyrs, among these the Epiphany. It contains moreover, what becomes conspicuous in later martyrologies, a series of names grouped about the day of the Nativity; in this martyrology these are Stephen, John the Baptist, James and the Innocents. The suggestion mentioned on p. 385 that John the Evangelist has been displaced here by the Baptist through the error of a copyist is doubtful; for the Baptist appears in this Nativity cycle in many martyrologies; in the Armenian, Nestorian, Chaldean, Greek, *al.*, and the repetition of his name in the list for June is not decisive, since such duplications are common in the martyrologies; they arise either from a careless combination of earlier lists, or from a celebration of different events in the history of the same person. The third great list, the Syrian, the most important of Oriental martyrologies, is preserved in a form which dates from the fifth century, but it incorporates lists of much earlier origin. Though entitled a list of martyrs, it includes some who were such in no sense, *e.g.* Eusebius and Arius. It duplicates days, *e.g.* putting Polycarp Jan. 27 and Feb. 23, it designates Stephen an apostle, it differs from all other martyrologies in assigning a place, viz.: Jerusalem, for the martyrdom of John the apostle.

---

[1] On the martyrologies see Achelis *Die Martyrologien* in the *Abhandlung. d. könig. Gesell. d. Wissen. zu Göttingen, Phil.-hist. N. F.* 1900; Egli *Zweiter Commentar zu Wrights S. M.* in the *ZWT*, 1891, 273 ff.; also his book *Altchrist. Stud. Martyr.* etc. Zürich. 1887; Lietzmann *Die drei ält. Martyrol.*; Smith's *Dict. of Christ. Antiquities* II. 1132 ff.

Valuable as is the Syrian martyrology, it is evident that it needs to be checked by other lists. An instructive study has been given by Egli (*op. cit.*), who compares it with the Armenian, Coptic, Æthiopic, the Syrian of the Melchites, Greek, Slavic and one or two others.

An examination of the martyrologies in general reveals two facts helpful in our inquiry; first, entries not associated with martyrdom, and secondly, a tendency to group about the festival of the Nativity — whether celebrated in Dec. (Christmas) or in Jan. (the Epiphany) is immaterial in the present connection — persons standing in some special relation to the Lord; cf. Egli, *op. cit.* 279 ff. Among such occur David, the Magi, Joseph the husband of Mary, the four Evangelists, Mt., Mk., Lk., Jno. (these four all assigned to one day), but especially the five conspicuous figures Stephen, Paul and Peter, John and James. It becomes at once apparent that martyrdom is not the sole ground of selection in making up these groups. This particular Nativity-cycle of *five*, which appears in the Syrian martyrology and others, is assigned by Achelis, *op. cit.* 70 f., to a date later than that of the primitive list used by this martyrology. And it appears apart from the martyrologies in early writers also in connections where the writer is speaking, not of martyrs, but of foremost disciples; *e.g.* Gregory Nazian. *Panegyric on Basil*, Migne, *Pat.* 829; Gregory of Nyssa, *Oration on Basil, ibid.* 789. It seems reasonably certain then that the appearance of John's name in the Syrian, Armenian and other lists cannot be taken as evidence of a tradition that he was put to death; though in the broader sense of the word he would everywhere be honored as a martyr. The mention of Jerusalem in the Syrian list as the place of his martyrdom, supported by no other martyrology, is easily explained by the carelessness of the compiler of the list, who here fails to distinguish John from James; cf. his carelessness in calling Stephen an apostle.

We pass now to the early writers cited above (pp. 385 f.) as confirming the argument for the Apostle's martyrdom drawn from the martyrologies. We take these up in the order followed above. The words quoted (p. 386) from *De Rebaptismate* occur in a context, XIV–XV, which is concerned with baptism by blood; and the proof that a martyr's blood is for him a baptism, the author finds in Christ's words; first, in his words referring to his own baptism, Lk. 12⁵⁰, 'I have a baptism,' etc., and secondly, in the words addressed to James and John, Mk. 10³⁹. Now the author is concerned here, not at all with the personal history of the two disciples, but wholly with the enforcement of his argument by an utterance of the Lord's. The number of persons included is immaterial; if he had been thinking of the words as fulfilled in the case of one only, the Lord's saying would have served his argument equally well, but he takes it just as it stands, applying it rhetorically and with partial inexactness — he is not recording history. Chrysostom treats these words with precisely the same rhetorical inexactness, paraphrasing 'Ye shall be slain for my sake,' *Homilies*, on 1 Cor. XXXII. 10, though elsewhere he says John lived long after the fall of Jerusalem; *Homilies* on Mt. LXXVI. 2.

The words quoted (p. 386) from Aphraates occur in the concluding paragraph summing up his discourse. He says 'Hear ye the following names of martyrs, confessors and the persecuted'; and there follows a list of Old Testament worthies, most of whom were not slain, were not martyrs in the narrower sense; and then, after the name of Christ, the five New Testament names and an indefinite mention of others of that time and the time of Diocletian. He does not, as is sometimes said (so, Moffatt *Introd.* 606) distribute his examples into three distinct groups, classifying the five New Testament names (and so, John) as 'martyrs,' the others of the apostles as 'confessors,' and those who suffered under Diocletian as 'the persecuted.' The 'others of the Apostles' he distinctly calls 'perfect martyrs,' like Peter and Paul; and certainly he could not think of those who were put to death under Diocletian as 'the persecuted,' but not martyrs in the strict sense. He is not at all concerned with a classification of this kind, but with a comprehensive illustration of faithful sufferers. And it is noticeable that as his selection and grouping of Old Testament worthies is plainly suggested by Hebrews 11, so in the selection of the Christian names he is influenced by some prevalent usage, such as is seen above in the writings of the Gregorys (p. 388), of grouping together these five names especially connected with the Lord. But he shows his consciousness that they do not all stand on the same footing as regards actual martyrdom; he describes Stephen, Peter and Paul as *perfect* or *faithful* martyrs, but in speaking of John and James he avoids the term, saying that they followed in the footsteps of their Master, who as said in the preceding clause '*surpassed all* in affliction and confession'; that is, they followed in his steps in affliction and confession, but did not equal him, they had not both suffered unto death.

As regards the statement of Clement (p. 386), his historical carelessness is seen in the immediate context, where he makes the assertion that the public teaching of Jesus began in the time of Augustus and Tiberius, and ended in the middle of the reign of Tiberius (cf. Lk. 3[1]). In another place, *Quis dives* 42, he supports the Ephesian tradition in recording John's release from Patmos and his removal to Asia Minor. Heracleon in the words referred to (p. 386) is speaking of a distinction between real and unreal confession of Christianity, and he says that 'true confession is that made by mouth before the magistrates.' Not all have been called upon to make that confession, some have died without that trial. Among such are those named and many others. Now while Heracleon has chiefly in mind martyrdom as the result of such confession, he does not limit his definition to that, because he knew that martyrdom was not in all cases the result; other punishments were inflicted. What he is urging is readiness to meet the extreme consequences of trial before the tribunal. But if the tradition current at the time concerning John was accepted by him, the Apostle's name was not appropriate for his list. John had confessed before the magistrates and had suffered banishment as his penalty, Rev. 1[9]. We are brought to the conclusion then that the words of the authors cited above do not in any case, when rightly interpreted in the light of their context, furnish evidence that these writers supposed John to have been put to death as a martyr.

(4) A fourth line of argument is urged to prove, not directly the Apostle's martyrdom, but the error of the tradition that he abode in Asia and was a leader in the Church there at the end of the century. It is the *argument from silence.* None of the New Testament writers, it is argued, none of those of the second century, except Irenæus, Justin, and Polycrates, show any knowledge of John's sojourn in Asia. As a *general* answer to this argument it may be said that if the books of the New Testament in which knowledge of the kind could be looked for are genuine, they are all prior to the time. The Johannine writings of course cannot be taken into account here. As regards the second century literature, the three exceptions named form among the small number of writings of that period preserved a rather large body of witnesses numerically, to say nothing of the special competency of these writers, as shown above. The argument, however, must be considered more in detail.

On the assumption that the New Testament writings in question are of a late date, it is claimed that the composer of Paul's address to the elders of Ephesus, Ac. 20$^{17-35}$, would not have put so harsh an epithet as 'grievous wolves' into his description of those who were to come after him there, if John were one of these successors; furthermore there is in the address no trace of John or his influence at Ephesus. It is not necessary to point out the misapplication of the words here put into Paul's mouth, if it be that they are not a truthful record of his own language; as a denunciation of false teachers the language is similar to that which he uses in Phil. 3$^{2,\,18f.}$ But in any event we should not expect here in the supposed writer's picture of Paul's care for his churches any trace of the coming of John; the historical imagination of the author of the Acts is of a kind to guard him, even in the assumed invention of history, from allusions so false to Paul's habit of reticence regarding the labors of other apostles. A similar answer may be made to the appeal to the silence of the epistles to the Ephesians and Colossians, letters like the Apocalypse addressed to Asian churches, and also to the silence of the epistles to Timothy who was placed at Ephesus. If these are inventions of a later time, the authors show themselves in the writings clever enough to avoid so distinct an anachronism, which would be patent to all. An inventor transfers to an earlier date many things belonging to his own time, but not distinctly personal allusions, if he be even moderately skillful. Appeal is also made to 1 Peter, likewise assumed to be pseudonymous and late. The writer addressing these same Christians of Asia assumes the name of Peter to give weight to his epistle; John, it is argued, cannot have labored among them, otherwise his name would have been preferred. But that epistle is addressed to the Christians of a far wider region than the Asia of John's reputed labors, cf. 1 Pet. 1^1; and if the writer's choice of Peter's name furnishes evidence against the presence of John in Asia, it would also furnish evidence against Paul's presence in Galatia. This argument from the silence of the New Testament and other writings is said to be enforced by the fact that in the distribution of missionary labors recorded in Gal. 2^9, John recognized churches which like those of Asia were composed chiefly of Gentile converts to belong to Paul's sphere, not his own. But whatever may have been the immediate practice in carrying out that decision, Paul began his work in every place to which he came with the Jews. And Peter preached in Gentile cities; at Antioch (Gal. 2^{11}), perhaps in Galatia and other places of Pauline labors (1 Pet. 1^1, 2 Pet. 3$^{1-2}$) and probably also in Rome (1 Pet. 5^{13}). At all events at the time of John's supposed residence in Asia, Paul had been dead many years, and the whole matter of apostolic labors and oversight of the churches had changed.

Of the Christian writings outside of the New Testament the oldest is probably the epistle of the church at Rome, 1 Clement (c. 95 A.D.), written to the Corinthians as an exhortation against the divisions and other troubles which had arisen among them. This letter, it is said, assumes a certain pastoral care which would belong to Ephesus, if an apostle had been living there at the time, and especially as that city was nearer. We need not discuss how much longer was the short journey from Rome to Corinth by way of Brundusium, facilitated as it was by the active intercourse between the two cities. What is of more moment here is the fact that, quite apart from any question regarding the nature and disposition of the apostle John, the picture of the Asian church given in the Apocalypse and of the task laid upon its chief pastor, if such he was, is not of a kind that we should look to it at these times to undertake the care of other churches. But on the other hand, apart from any motive of Clement himself, it was natural that the Pauline church at Rome, following in the course of the Apostle's First Epistle to the Corinthians, which was written in part to meet the same troubles in Corinth, and which was made a part of the appeal in this letter from the church at Rome, should interest itself actively in his spiritual children there. We cannot draw from the sending of this letter any inference as to whether John was at the time living in Asia.

Of the letters of Ignatius, written when as a convict he was on his way to Rome to suffer martyrdom (c. 110–120 A.D.), one, that to the Ephesians, is held to be especially significant by its silence. While the epistle written to the Christians at Rome mentions the two great apostles whom they honored, Paul and Peter (*Rom.* IV), that to the Ephesians mentions Paul (*Eph.* XII.), but not John ; the latter seems to have no place in the memories of the writer or the readers. But the error of this inference is apparent from the context in each case. In the Roman letter Ignatius is urging the Christians there not to try to hinder his martyrdom, for which he is eager. He earnestly entreats them, he cannot, he says, give commands to them, as Peter and Paul had done. The allusion is meant to enforce his entreaty by calling up to the minds of the readers their two great martyrs ; it is an appeal to their memory of these not to oppose his sharing with the Apostles in this supreme act of discipleship. In the Ephesian letter the line of thought in the paragraph in question (XII) is entirely different. Ignatius is contrasting his present lot with the secure state of the readers. He is a convict on his way to martyrdom. Not improbably was the figure of Paul frequently present in his mind ; he was bishop of Antioch which was full of associations with the Apostle, as the seat of his labors (Ac. 11^{26})

and the center from which his great missionary tours were made.   But now especially he sees himself on the way to follow in the footsteps of the Apostle as a martyr.   And as he writes this letter in answer to the greetings of the Ephesians sent by their deputies to Smyrna, near to Ephesus, where he is halting in his journey, he is reminded that Paul also on his way to martyrdom had halted near Ephesus, at Miletus (Ac. 20^{17} ff.) and addressed words to Ephesian deputies; he expresses the thought in the words, 'Ye are the high-road of those that are on their way to die unto God.'   It is plain from these words that he thinks of Paul's last journey to Jerusalem, on which he had halted at Miletus, as only the beginning of his journey to Rome where he is eventually to be martyred.   (Cf. Zahn *Ignat.* 607.)   There would be here no reminder of John, unless he too had suffered martyrdom.   So far as the silence of this epistle is significant, it might be taken against John's death as a martyr.   It cannot be said that the epistle excludes knowledge on the writer's part of John's sojourn at Ephesus, for there is no place in the letter requiring mention of it.   But the words, 'the Christians of Ephesus who moreover were ever of one mind with the apostles' (XI), may perhaps contain reference to John with others.

Of the writings of Polycarp († c. 155 A.D.), only the letter to the Philippians is preserved.   In this he speaks of Paul and 'the rest of the apostles' (III. IX. XI), but not of John, his teacher, whom he was wont to recall in his discourses, and whose name, it is said, we should expect him to specify before that of any other apostle, if the report of Irenæus were correct.   But the reason for special allusion to Paul in a letter to the Philippians is apparent.   Paul had labored among them, and had written an epistle to them and had shown them to be the object of his strong personal affection.   An appeal to him was therefore of great weight in any exhortation addressed to them.   That this was Polycarp's motive in mentioning Paul he makes perfectly clear.   In an exhortation to the Philippians there was no more occasion for mentioning John than Peter or any other apostle.

Hegesippus, who wrote a book of 'Memoirs' near the end of the second century, says that Gnosticism did not arise till after the death of the apostles.   And he makes mention of only one witness of the time of Jesus, Symeon, as surviving into the time of Trajan.   He evidently, it is argued, knew nothing of John's reputed long life, and residence in Asia.   How far there is ground for this inference will be apparent from an examination of Hegesippus.   Only a few fragments of his work are preserved, chiefly in Eusebius.   The fragment of interest here is given in *H. E.* III. 32.   Eusebius is here recounting events in the history of the Church under Trajan, and as one of the striking events of the time, he tells on the authority of Hegesippus of the martyrdom of Symeon, the second bishop of Jerusalem, a son of Clopas (Jno. 19^{25}), a descendant of David, a nephew of Joseph, a man at the time 120 years old.   Eusebius here quotes Hegesippus as saying that Symeon had remained in peace till that time, when he was brought before the tribunal on a charge, preferred by the heretics, of being a descendant of David and a Christian; for before this the heretics [Gnostics] had not appeared, but as soon as the apostles and the first generation of Christians had passed away they came forward with great boldness and activity. In other words according to Hegesippus the apostles, or at least some of them, had lived into the time of Trajan. In so far then this author confirms the tradition of the apostle John as living till this date. In other fragments Hegesippus speaks of the persecution by the imperial government of the *descendants of David*, and of the survival of some others of the relatives of the Lord's family intq Trajan's reign. But in none of the fragments is there in themselves, or in the connection in Eusebius, any implication as to the number of witnesses surviving from the Lord's time down to this date. There is not the slightest intimation that Hegesippus knew nothing of John as a survivor till the closing years of the century.

We have thus traced the evidence adduced for the martyrdom of John and against his sojourn in Asia through its several parts, that is, the Lord's words to John and James; the alleged testimony of Papias; the testimony of the martyrologies and the writers held to be in agreement with Papias and the martyrologies; and the silence of the New Testament and certain authors of the subapostolic age and the second century. In every instance there appear good grounds for questioning the validity of the inference drawn against the tradition. And the several lines of evidence offered are not of a kind to give cumulative force to the series as a whole. On the other hand stands the almost contemporaneous evidence of the first half of the second century, which must be admitted to be strong, unless its force is broken by unquestionably strong counter-evidence. The above examination appears to show that the counter-evidence presented is not of that character. The balance of argument then leads to the conclusion that the Apostle's sojourn in Asia is probably a historic fact, and one that must be taken into account in estimating early external testimony to the authorship of the Revelation.

XIV. The Beast of the Apocalypse

Inquiry into the significance of the Beast, though belonging to the Commentary, may properly be taken up in the Introduction, since the thing symbolized forms a cardinal factor in the purpose and scope of the entire book. The figure of the Beast is derived from tradition. There ran through ancient mythologies and Hebrew folk-lore legends of a monster opposing itself to supreme powers in conflicts which symbolized the struggle of chaos against order, evil against good, death against life.[1] Some form of that myth suggested to the author of

[1] Cf. Com. 12³.

Daniel (7) the figures of the beasts of his vision, and the same source furnished, partly through the medium of Daniel and partly no doubt in other ways, our Apocalyptist's representation of Satan in the form of a dragon-monster, chapt. 12. In chapt. 13 the Beast, Satan's vicegerent in his war against God and the saints, is represented in a form similar to that given to Satan himself, but with some traits evidently drawn from Daniel, with others probably from other forms of the legend, and with still others doubtless added by the Apocalyptist himself, in accordance with his habit of modifying and adapting derived material. Details in the imagery will be spoken of more particularly in the Commentary. Traits of Daniel's four beasts are here united in one. Whether our author may not be following here the current form of the legend, and whether Daniel may not have distributed the traits among four beasts for better adaptation to his purpose to represent four kingdoms, is a question which it is not important to settle. As in some other instances when specially adapting a tradition to his purpose, the Apocalyptist adds explanatory words.[1] The explanation,[2] containing itself much that is enigmatical, is introduced in 17^{7-18}. The tradition in the mind of the writer and the special use made of it are so far cleared up by the author's explanation and by studies in comparative eschatology that scholars are now generally agreed concerning the significance of the Beast, at least in those fundamental points essential in the interpretation of the book, though there remain differences of opinion regarding certain less important aspects.

(1) *The Beast as a symbol of the Roman emperors.* Not only is the *figure* of such a monster derived from tradition, but also its application in the particular kind of conflict here thought of is traditional. A fabulous monster as a symbol of a *world-monarchy hostile to God's people* forms a familiar figure in apocalyptic. In the vision of Dan. $7^{3\,ff\cdot}$, a series of four monsters represent four successive empires, the Babylonian, the Median, the Persian, and a fourth, probably the Grecian, that of Alexander and his successors,[3] the horns of the last

---

[1] See p. 615.   [2] For the identity of the beast of 13 and that of 17 see p. 695.
[3] Cf. Driver, *Dan.* in C. B. 94 ff.

symbolizing a succession of kings culminating in Antiochus Epiphanes, ' the little horn,' 7⁸. Under the name Rahab, such a monster is a symbol of Egypt in its hostility to God and his people ; e.g. Ps. 87⁴, ' I will make mention of Rahab,' or Egypt (RV marg.); cf. Ps. 89¹⁰, Is. 30⁷ (RV), 51⁹. In Is. 27¹ three such monsters are mentioned as symbols of three world-king-doms, one of them probably Egypt, the other two perhaps Assyria and Babylonia, perhaps later kingdoms.¹ The elabo-rate vision of 2 Esd. (11) pictures the monster as a symbol of the Roman empire, and so also in Sib. Or. II. 25, the dragon is the symbol of Israel's great enemy, the Roman power in the person of Pompey. The analogy of these cases would itself suggest that our author in the use of the symbol applies it to the world-monarchy of his own time, the Roman empire, or its impersonating emperors. And in fact the very purpose of apocalyptic writings in general carries with it such contem-poraneous reference, for its aim is to encourage in the midst of sufferings inflicted by the existing world-monarchy inimical to God.² But that the Roman power impersonated in the em-perors is meant here the author shows in what he says of the Beast. In the vision of the woman seated on the scarlet-col-ored beast in chapt. 17, the beast represents the power sus-taining the existing imperial city Rome; cf. p. 695. In the interpretative verses, 17⁷ ᶠᶠ·, his seven heads are defined as a succession of kings, that is, emperors, of whom one is reigning at the time, and the city, the seat of his imperial power, is that which sitting on its seven hills is holding sway over all the earth. It appears certain then, as the larger number of inter-preters are now agreed, that the Beast so far as he is repre-sented in his seven heads symbolizes the Roman imperial power, that is, the Roman emperors, as Satan's agent in his war against the saints. The question as to the particular emperors intended is spoken of elsewhere, pp. 704 ff.

The view has been widely held that the seven heads defined as *kings*, 17¹⁰, represent not persons, but successive world-kingdoms, as do the beasts of Daniel, the word *king* being used in the sense of *kingdom*, as in Dan. 7¹⁷. The five kings, *i.e.* kingdoms, that have already fallen are then variously

¹ Cf. Delitzsch *in loc.*, Skinner in C. B.; Bertholet 291.
² See pp. 175 ff., 212 f.

identified, *e.g.* Assyria, Babylonia, Persia, Macedonia and Syria (Antiochus); or Egypt, Assyria, Babylonia, Persia, Greco-Syria; for other suggestions cf. Speaker's Com. 755. The Roman then forms the sixth kingdom, and the seventh is yet to come in the Apocalyptist's future. The Beast is distinguished from his heads; he is the power of world-monarchy in the abstract, hostile to God, and appearing in each several kingdom in succession; but in the end he will appear in his own proper person as Antichrist. He may be said to have existed in the kingdom of Antiochus Epiphanes, the prototype of Antichrist. In this sense it may be said of him, that he was, is not, and is to come, 17⁸. One of his heads may be said to have been wounded in the fall of that empire, and the wound will be healed in the coming of Antichrist. Cf. *e.g.* Hofmann *Offenb.* 228 ; Zahn *Ein.* II. 632 f. But the analogy of Dan. which the Apocalyptist has distinctly in mind here would require a succession of beasts, if a series of empires were meant ; the four empires of Dan. are represented by four separate beasts. On the other hand the heads and horns in Daniel's vision do not represent a succession of empires, but belong to a single empire, 7⁶ᶠ·, and the horns are expressly defined as kings in that empire, 7²⁴. Furthermore in Rev. the entire paragraph 17–19⁵ is concerned with the destruction of Rome ; reference to earlier monarchies would have no relation to the woman of the introductory vision, 17¹⁻⁶, in that paragraph. It seems certain that the 'kings' of 17¹⁰ are persons, not kingdoms, and that the Roman emperors are meant.

The identification of the Beast and Antichrist with the Roman emperors [1] is held by some to be inconsistent with the Christian view as expressed elsewhere in the New Testament. St. Paul, Ro. 13¹ᶠᶠ·, declares the existing governmental power, the Roman, to be ordained by God; and in 2 Thess. 2⁷ he sets the Roman power in opposition to Antichrist, saying that it is only the former that prevents the appearing of the latter. This latter passage is the only one in the New Testament expressing directly this opposition, and it is not difficult to account for it in view of the Apostle's experiences. To him the order and security of the world maintained by the Roman government represented a divine ordinance in contrast with the awful tyranny and hostility to God anticipated as to come in the reign of Antichrist. The persecutions of Nero and those of Domitian, in part already begun and in part yet threatening the Christians at the time of our book, and the growing rigor in enforcing the emperor-worship, are all subsequent to the writing of these epistles of Paul. It must also be borne in mind that to one familiar with the revolutions marking the course of Roman history it would not be difficult to conceive, as does the Apocalyptist, 17¹⁶ᶠ·, the present Roman order to be destroyed by one who had been a Roman emperor. Other New Testament passages, *e.g.* Mt. 22²¹, 1 Pet. 2¹³ᶠᶠ·, which are cited as irreconcilable with the connection of Antichrist with Rome go no further than does our author, 13⁹ᶠ·, in counseling submissive obedience to established authority. It is furthermore true that the objection here spoken of remains in reality with any theory of seven world-empires, for the Beast represented in the sixth head is in such theory the existing Roman power.

[1] On a Roman emperor as Antichrist see p. 399 ff.

(2) *The Beast as a symbol of Antichrist*. Conclusive as is the evidence that the heads of the Beast are the Roman emperors in their office as Satan's agents in the war against God's children, it is however clear that this application of the symbolism does not cover the whole significance of the Beast. Activities and attributes are assigned to him which cannot be predicated of any Roman emperor in his ordinary human personality, as is also a career falling after the destruction of the Roman empire. It is true that the prevalence of emperorworship and the practice of magic arts at the time might suggest to the author the Beast's arrogation of divine honors, and the attribution of signs and wonders to him, even if he were thought of as only a Roman emperor. But as one who, like the head wounded unto death and restored,[1] is some time to return to earth coming out of the abyss of hell, $13^{2,\ 12}$, 17^8, and who is to marshal· all the armies of the world against the spiritual hosts led out of heaven by the Messiah, 19^{11-19}, the Beast will then be more than man, he will join with his human personality a mighty demonic power. In that manifestation he will form the last great human leader of the enemies of God, he will hold a sway absolutely universal over all the earth and the kings of the earth, 13^7, $17^{13,\ 15}$; he will be worshiped universally by all that dwell on the earth, save the followers of the Lamb, 13^8; he will receive his dominion after the seventh and last of the Roman emperors has fallen, $17^{10\ f.}$; he will be the central figure upon whom will fall the vengeance of eternal fire after the last pre-millennial conflict, $19^{19\ f.}$. In all this concluding eschatological period, the period of the woeful $3\frac{1}{2}$ years, he is clearly more than a Roman emperor. He is the evident parallel of a personality which had now come to occupy a distinct place in eschatological expectation, the Antichrist. This parallelism will be the more evident from a survey of the conception of Antichrist.

The rise of the figure of Antichrist belongs to the age immediately preceding, and coincident with, the earliest years of the Christian era. It is Jewish in its origin and it is due to the growth of demonology in the late Jewish centuries. The possible influence of earlier oriental beliefs in preparing the

---

[1] On the identity of reference in these two characterizations see p. 696.

way for it need not be considered here.   The doctrine of a
supreme spirit of evil in the person of Satan had already become universal.   There now began to appear in eschatological
expectation a supremely wicked *human* figure, a person who
would come possessing world-wide imperial power, opposing
all righteousness, and exalting himself against God in the last
great crisis.   Vagueness in respect to Antichrist's relation to
Satan was necessary, especially in the earlier stages of the
idea; sometimes he is thought of as Satan in man's form and
the name Beliar, a name of Satan (2 Co. 6^{15}), is given to him,
e.g. in Sib. Or. III. 63; but he is generally regarded as distinct from Satan and acting as his great servant in the last
days; so, in 2 Thess. $2^{3\,\mathrm{ff.}}$, and in Rev.   Traces of such a combination of superhuman powers with a human personality in
the case of a historic individual are found in Daniel's description of Antiochus.   While the Prophet unquestionably refers
in the symbol of the 'little horn' to the part of Antiochus in
the eschatological events predicted, it is also plain that he conceives him to be endowed with powers more than human; cf.
$8^{9\,\mathrm{ff.},\,23\,\mathrm{ff.}}$.   He has not in mind the exact figure of Antichrist as
known later, yet he shows the tendency to regard the great
world-tyrant of the last time as possessing powers beyond the
natural man; and his description of Antiochus furnishes traits
for later pictures of Antichrist.   Subsequently the idea of the
coming in the last time of a man endowed with Satan's character and might becomes distinct in both Jewish and Christian
thought.   He is referred to in Jewish writings, *e.g.* 2 Esd. 5^6,
Sib. Or. III. 63 ff., Ap. Bar. 36 and 40.   In the New Testament, belief in his appearing is assumed as current; 'Ye have
heard that Antichrist cometh,' 1 Jno. 2^{18}; St. Paul speaks
definitely of him in his nature and work under the name of the
Man of sin, 2 Thess. $2^{3\,\mathrm{ff.}}$; he is alluded to probably in Mt.
24^{15}, Mk. 13^{14}, and possibly in Jno. 5^{43}.   He appears in other
early Christian writings, *e.g.* The Teaching of the Twelve 16;
the Ascension of Isaiah 4, frequently in the Sib. Or., in the
Christian as well as the Jewish parts.   His prominence in
Christian eschatology for centuries later is shown by Bousset,
Antichrist.[1]

[1] For the subject see Bouss. *Judenthum* 242 ff. ; Hast. III. Article *Man of Sin.*

The *name* Antichrist appears first in the New Testament, and there in the Johannine epistles only, 1 Jno. $2^{18, 22}$, 4^3, 2 Jno. 7; in the first case, $2^{18 a}$, it is evidently used as a familiar term and is taken in its popular sense; in the other cases a special spiritual application is given to the word. Outside of the New Testament the name Beliar is used in a few cases, but generally except where the influence of the New Testament is apparent some descriptive term is used instead of a proper name. As regards his nature and activities he is conceived as the embodiment of all wickedness and of supreme hostility to God, he sets himself above God as the object of worship; acting in the might of Satan he appears in a twofold rôle, that of universal tyrant with undisputed sway over all the earth, and that of the deceiver of men through signs and wonders which he has the power to perform.[1] See especially St. Paul's account, 2 Thess. $2^{3 \text{ ff.}}$. If now keeping in view this idea of Antichrist and the general expectation of his coming before the End, we read what the Apocalyptist says of the Beast, we shall see that in much which he attributes to him it is this eschatological figure that he has in mind. The union of two successive impersonations, that of a Roman emperor, or series of emperors, and that of Antichrist, in the figure of the Beast, implies a relation between the two, which though not originating with the Apocalyptist, he uses with great skill. This relation is shown in the paragraph following, which will also make clearer the full meaning of the author in the symbol of the Beast.

The connection of Antichrist with a Roman ruler does not appear with certainty in pre-Christian literature. The words ' Beliar will come from the stock of Sebaste,' Sib. Or. III. 63, are some times understood to contain the idea ($\Sigma\epsilon\beta\alpha\sigma\tau\hat{\omega}\nu$ being referred to $\sigma\epsilon\beta\alpha\sigma\tau\acute{o}\varsigma$ = Augustus; cf. Bouss. *Antichrist* 96), but this meaning is not certain. Steps leading up to such a connection can, however, be traced. The world-tyrant, who figures

---

[1] The Apocalyptist represents these miraculous powers used to deceive as exercised in part by the second beast, 13^{11-17}. But this ' other beast ' acts only with the powers which the Beast has given him as his deputy, 13^{12}. The introduction of a second beast as a mere instrument through which the Beast operates differs from the traditional representation of Antichrist, which concentrates all activity in one person; it is probably due to historic circumstances; see p. 410.

in eschatological literature, the one who in the last days is to be vanquished by divine power, is at first a historic person, the culmination of a line of rulers in a given world-monarchy. Thus the eschatological figure of the 'horn' in Dan. is the historic Antiochus of the Græco-Syrian line. The tall cedar of Ap. Bar. 36 ff., and the eagle of 2 Esd. 11, are in each case an imperial dynasty destroyed by God or the Messiah at the end of the ages. The last great enemy springs out of the line of existing world-rulers. When then the idea of Antichrist was fully developed it was an easy step to associate him in some manner with the existing Roman dynasty of world-rulers. To our Apocalyptist such association must have been directly suggested by the circumstances of his era. A Christian apocalyptist, living near the end of the first century, with a vivid memory of the awful persecution at Rome under Nero, and with the growing insistence on emperor-worship before his mind, together with all the threatening calamities of the time, could not fail to believe that the work of Antichrist had already begun, the mystery of lawlessness was already working (2 Thess. 2[7]). To a prophet at that time the soon-expected Antichrist would be only a reimbodiment and consummation of what was most atrocious in the present world-rulers. But possible fears and surmises of this kind assumed definite shape apparently in the last decades of the century through the influence of rumors spreading through the Roman world in regard to the emperor Nero.

Antichrist as a Nero reincarnated. When Nero's career of hideous crimes caused the Senate in the year 68 to condemn him to death he fled to a suburban villa and put an end to his own life. His death in this obscure place and almost alone made possible the circulation of rumors that he was not dead, but had fled; and soon after the reports assumed the definite form that he had fled to the Parthians, the dreaded barbarian hordes of the East, and that he would return thence with a large army to wreak fearful vengeance upon the Roman world. These rumors, though ridiculed by some, spread through the provinces and with amazing persistence continued into the following century. Decrees appeared as issued in his name, and two (if not more) impostors claiming to be Nero arose; one gained a large following among the Parthians; rumors of the coming of one threw Achaia and Asia Minor (the home of the Apocalypse) into great terror. These events are well attested by Roman writers,[1] and they show how widespread a hold the personality of Nero had taken upon the minds of the populace in the Roman Empire. Belief in these rumors was shared by the Jews and Christians in common with others. The Sib. Or. bear frequent testimony to this; *e.g.* IV. 119–124, 137–139 (about 80 A.D.); V. 137–154, 361–385 (latter part of the century). At first there was nothing superstitious attaching to Nero's person in these expectations, no allusion is made to a return from the dead. In the Roman writers referred to, and in the earlier Sibyllines he appears only as the well-known human tyrant. Yet there was also a certain mysteriousness about his predicted coming, and the return of one who as ruler of the world-empire had instituted a fiendish persecution of the Christians at Rome and who would, as expected, triumph over the then existing order of the world, would almost certainly be associated more or less in Christian thought with the last great enemy. Jews also whose nation had just been destroyed in the Roman wars, and who were now yearning for the messianic deliverer, would be ready to see in this monster expected as the conqueror of Rome the world-tyrant of the last days preceding Messiah's coming. That this returning Nero finally came to be invested with a supernatural character, and associated in thought with Antichrist, is abundantly attested, though it is not certain just how early this began. His identification with Antichrist is distinctly expressed in a Christian portion of the Ascension of Isaiah, 4[2], a passage possibly contemporaneous with the Apocalypse.[2] It is there said that Beliar, Antichrist, will come in the person of an unrighteous king, a murderer of his mother, by which Nero is meant; he is frequently designated as the matricidal monster in accounts of his attributes and his return. In the prophecy of his return ' from the ends of the earth ' given in Sib. Or. V. 361–385 (probably belonging to the end of the

---

[1] See Suetonius, *Nero;* Tacitus, *Hist.* I. 2, II. 8, 9 ; Dio Cassius LXIV. 9.

[2] It is placed by Charles at the end of the first century; by Flemming, in Hennecke, p. 292, either at the end of the first century or the beginning of the second.

first century) his cunning deception of men, the marvels wrought by him in nature, his ' destruction of all kings and the best of men,' form a picture plainly belonging to the Last Times. He is here demonic and, though not expressly named Antichrist, he appears to be so regarded; certainly his works are those of Antichrist. Sib.Or. V. 217 (probably of the same date) gives to his return a distinct supernatural trait; he is to be brought back ' in mid-air that all may see him.' Another trait of Antichrist is assigned him in Sib. Or. V. 33 f. (a passage placed by nearly all early in the second century); ' Then will he return making himself equal with God, but he [God] will convince him that he is not.' Such passages like the predictions of apocalyptic writings in general rest on popular traditions and beliefs, and attest an anterior existence of the Nero myth long enough to have become widely current. There appears then good ground for supposing it to have been in circulation at the end of the first century, the time of our author. And as he is frequently seen to have taken up a familiar idea and have adapted it to his use, so here he might readily picture the expected Antichrist under the form of the popularly dreaded Nero. That he has actually done so appears almost certain from the precise agreement of his characterization of the Beast with this popular belief.[1]

Some have argued that a Nero revived could not be thought of till by the lapse of time he could no longer be supposed to be alive, that is, not until one or more decades after the beginning of the second century, as he was born 37 A.D.[2] But the belief that he was still alive was far from universal in the latter part of the century, and the fear among the populace of his return from the East might long before have changed in the minds of many to a fear of his return from the dead. It was easier in that age than in our own to see in a striking work the activity of a notable personage of the past, returned among men, or to look for the return of such a person in the future. Elijah was expected by all to come again; our Apocalyptist foretells the return of Moses and Elijah in the person of the two Witnesses,

---

[1] The association of Nero with Antichrist persisted through the following centuries. Its acceptance by many is well attested; e.g. by Commodianus c. 250; the commentator Victorinus, c. 300; Sulpicius Severus, about the end of the 4th cent.; Augustine, *De civ. Dei*, c. 426.   [2] Cf. Zahn, *Ein.* II. 634.

11[3 ff.]; in Jesus, the Baptist or one of the prophets was thought by many to have come back, Mk. 6[14 ff.]. The identification of the restored head, that is, of the Beast that was, and is not and shall come, with Nero revived from the dead is put beyond question if, as seems most probable, the number of the Beast, 666, is meant to denote the name Nero.

The number of the Beast, 666, as denoting the name Nero. The designation of a name by numbers occurs in Greek popular usage of these times, and among the rabbis also it appears as a part of the so-called art of *Gematria*, which found recondite truth in the numerical value of words. (For *Gematria*, see Weber, *System*, 118; Hast. III. 566, Jew. En. *s.v.*) With the late Jews and the Greeks the letters of the alphabet were used to denote numbers; a name then could be given enigmatically in the sum of the numbers denoted by its several letters. Thus in Gen. 14[14] the number 318 was taken by the rabbis to denote Eliezer; the numbers denoted by the respective letters of that name added together form this sum. The Christian Sibylline I. 324 ff. uses 888 for the name Ἰησοῦς, Jesus. Good illustrations of this usage among the common people are found in the *graffiti*, wall scratchings, at Pompeii; *e.g.* in one, a certain woman is designated by the number 45 (or 1045), another by 545. See Deissmann, *Licht vom Ost.* 207, and the various literature there referred to. It is in the use of this method that our author gives the name of the Beast as 666. The purpose in such cases is to express the name in a veiled way, perhaps as a mere literary mannerism, perhaps as a matter of prudence. The latter would probably be the chief motive with our author, if an emperor is meant, even though one no longer living; cf. p. 405. It is not probable that the Apocalyptist would announce in words clear to every Roman hearer the return of one of the emperors as Antichrist; it is evident that he does not expect even the Christian hearers in all cases to perceive the exact personal reference; for he declares that special wisdom and understanding, σοφία, νοῦς, 13[18], are needed to interpret his utterance. In the light of the rumors and expectations regarding Nero current at the time, many must have formed conjectures as to the meaning of the number, yet no interpretation became established in tradition. Irenæus has only uncertain guesses to offer, and he thinks the Apocalyptist intended the name to remain hidden till Antichrist should come. The language, however, implies that it is discoverable by those who have the requisite wisdom; and the command, 'let him that hath understanding calculate the number,' shows that the author expects some to solve the enigma.

The word ὄνομα, *name*, would suggest reference to a person, and the added phrase, 'it is the number of a man', shows a definite personal name, and not a descriptive title to be meant. See Com. 13[18]. The problem then is to find a known person, or in view of the writer's interpretative words in 17[8-11], a Roman emperor, to whom is appropriate the rôle described there and in 13[1-8], and who at the same time bears a name the several letters of which denote numbers amounting in the sum total to 666. If we are guided solely by the lines drawn by the author himself, we must reject as explanations abstract descriptions of the character and activity of Antichrist, and the names of persons known in later history, *e.g.* Mohammed, Pope Benedict IX, Luther, and a host of others found in interpretations of the Apocalypse — all a part of the error of seeking European history in the book ; cf. pp. 301 ff. The extravagances which appear in the history of conjecture show that with skill and boldness almost any name may be made to yield the number; for some of the solutions offered, see the Speaker's Com., 687 ff., 697 ff.; Düst. 458 f., Stuart II. 453 ff., Zahn, *Ein.* II. 636 f.   The alphabet used in writing the name must be either the Greek or the Hebrew, and the author gives no intimation of the choice between these.

Solutions with Greek letters.   Efforts to find the name contained in the cryptogram must have been made by many of the earliest readers. Irenæus reports that many solutions were proposed in his time, all so far as appears using the Greek alphabet, some of these based on the reading 616 instead of 666 (see text. note *in loc.*).   He mentions three of these, only two of which were deemed worthy of much notice afterwards, τειτάν, *Titan*, and Λατεῖνος, *Latinus;* the use of the irregular ει instead of ι is paralleled in Σαβεῖνος, Φαυστεῖνος and a number of similar forms.   While Irenæus believed that the Apocalyptist intended the name to remain hidden, he preferred among the various guesses τειτάν, because among other reasons the Titan, the mythical monster who assaulted the gods, seemed a type of Antichrist.   At the same time he pointed out in favor of λατεῖνος, *Latinus,* the fact that the Latins were the rulers of the world.   This suggested connection between Antichrist and a Roman ruler is striking, and it is not impossible that in so vague a term there may have been seen by at least some an allusion to Nero.   Latinus was adopted by many in the following centuries ; among modern interpreters who adopt it are Bleek, De Wette, Düst. It is true that this word marks a relation between Antichrist and a Roman emperor, but it is general, whereas the personal name of a particular individual is required here.   Many other solutions in Greek letters have been proposed, but none of them is so far appropriate as to be largely accepted. The most plausible among these is Γάιος Καῖσαρ, *Gaius Cæsar* (Caligula), which is elaborately defended by Spitta (134 ff., 369 ff.) and Erbes (15 ff.). But this solution requires the reading 616, contrary to the weight of Ms. authority and critical opinion, and it necessitates the rejection of the author's interpretative words in 17[8, 11], which these critics then attribute to a redactor, who is also supposed to have read his own meaning into chapt. 13 and revised it accordingly ; *e.g.* vv. 6 c. and 7 c. are insertions of his.

Solutions in Hebrew letters.   It has been left to modern scholarship, so far as recorded, to discover that by the use of Hebrew letters and the transliteration of Νέρων Καῖσαρ, *Nero Cæsar*, in the form נרון קסר (the letters of which denote respectively 50, 200, 6, 50 and 100, 60, 200) we obtain the required number 666, and also the name which establishes the author's identfication of the Beast described by him with the Nero revived, as conceived in the current expectations of the time.   This solution reached in the earlier part of the last century independently by a number of scholars (Fritzsche, Benary, Hitzig, Reuss) meets the conditions of the problem so exactly that it is accepted by most scholars of the present day. Its correctness is supported by the fact that if the proper name be written Νέρω, נרו, that is, without the final consonant as in the Latin form *Nero*, the number 616 is obtained instead of 666, and thus is explained the variant reading found in some Mss. and adopted according to Irenæus by many in the second century. See text. note on 13[18]. Other interpretations obtained by the use of Hebrew characters are : Cæsar of Rome (Ewald ; this requires the reading 616) ; Cæsar of the Romans (Manchot) ; Trajan (Wabnitz) ; Völter at different times has advocated Hadrian, Trajan, Vespasian, in each case as a Nero revived ; Gunkel's proposal, *Primal Chaos* (377), also based on Hebrew letters, is derived from his theory tracing the Beast back to a Babylonian monster. Such explanations have not met with any considerable acceptance, since they do not conform to the representations in chapts. 13 and 17, and raise rather than settle difficulties.

Objections to the solution adopted above, which finds in the number the name Nero, are raised. (*a*) Our book is written in Greek, for Greek-speaking Christians, and there is no intimation that any other than the Greek alphabet was to be used in solving the problem of the number. The earliest recorded attempts at a solution, as we learn from Irenæus, were based on that alphabet. In general what is urged in this objection is true, and it explains why the name Nero should not have been *commonly* thought of in that age as connected with the number. But our author was a Jew, he thought in the forms of Hebrew idioms, he was doubtless more familiar with the art of *Gematria* as practiced by the Jews than by the Greeks, and there must have been many Jews among the Christians of the seven churches addressed in the book ; an intimation that such were contemplated among the readers occurs in the special mention of the Hebrew form of certain names ; *e.g.* 9[11], 16[16]. It would not be unnatural then that the Apocalyptist should use the Hebrew alphabet in his enigma. And this would best serve his purpose. He does not wish to name the Beast openly (see p. 403) so that it would be unmistakable to all, as *e.g.* Sib. Or. V. 21 ff. openly designates the emperors by the numbers corresponding to their initials. He will conceal it at least in part ; he is sure that some of his readers, Jews, persons familiar with the forebodings regarding Nero, will have the knowledge and understanding requisite for reading the symbol. In the troubles threatening the Christians at the hands of the imperial power it was not desirable to emphasize the announcement of the coming Antichrist as a revived Nero who should destroy the empire. It is enough for the author's purpose to make clear to the general reader that the conflict between God and Satan is now entering on its later stages, that the great adversary will employ the present world-power in a series of rulers as his agent, and then in immediate succession that agent will appear in Antichrist. The successive phases of the conflict are figured with sufficient distinctness for the less penetrating reader by the seven heads and the resuscitated head, while those to whom it is given to read the enigma will like the Apocalyptist himself see more precisely an Antichrist in the final era working in the spirit of a Nero revived and demonized. Taking the Apocalyptist's picture of the Beast's activity as a whole we can see that he is chiefly interested in foretelling the progress of Satan's warfare with the Church on to the awful culmination in which Satan will work through the mysterious personality of Antichrist. *It appears certain that the precise relation of that personality to Nero or any other historic individual is a quite subordinate point in the author's mind.* Obscurity as regards the personal reference in the number of the name, and in the wounded head, might remain for most readers, whether then or now, without the loss of the essential significance of the prophecy. Vast as is the space occupied by these two topics in the literature of the Apocalypse, it cannot be questioned that they are but details; it has happened here, as not infrequently, that attention has been riveted on a minor factor to such a degree as to confuse and obscure the understanding of the prophecy in its larger outlines.

(*b*) A second objection to the above explanation of the number 666 is found in the fact that the Hebrew form of Cæsar is קיסר, which would give the number 676. That this is the usual form of the name when written with Hebrew letters is unquestionable (cf. Zahn *Ein.* II. 636), but the form קסר in the *scriptio defectiva, i.e.* with *jod* omitted, is also attested; cf. Ewald *Apok.* 263; Buxtorf *Lex. Rabbin.* Therefore whatever caused the Apocalyptist to use the less common form, no valid objection can be found here to the Neronic explanation of the number. Why 666 should have been used instead of 676 must be a matter of conjecture, but there is plausibility in the supposition (Gunkel, 375 ff.; J. Weiss 34 f., *al*) that the number of the Beast, like his form, his many heads and horns, was a part of the designation of the monster represented in tradition. The Apocalyptist then adopting this traditional number, together with other traits of the Beast, applies it to the name Nero, an application made easy by the alternative form קסר.

The identification of the name in 13^{18} with Nero makes clear the obscure utterances in 13^3 and 17^8 regarding the head wounded unto death and restored, and the beast that was, and is not, and shall come out of the abyss. Nero is that head ; as once reigning he was, at the time of the Apocalyptist's writing he is not, that is, not living, and in Antichrist he will come again from the abyss. He was (one) of the seven and in his coming again he will be the eighth (17^{11}), that is, of these last world-rulers acting as Satan's agents. Much confusion is brought into the Apocalyptist's representation by the failure to see that he frequently identifies the Beast and his respective heads. The heads rather than the Beast himself apart from these contain in some connections the most significant features in the imagery, as do the horns in Daniel's vision, our author's chief model here, and as do also the heads and wings in the monster of 2 Esd. 11–12. This the Apocalyptist shows in the repeated reference to the restored head in chapt. 13 (3, 12, 14) and in the emphasis placed upon the heads and horns in $17^{9\ f.,\ 12}$. The Beast is not thought of in distinction from the heads ; the heads represent him and thus the two become identified. The Beast exists now in the first head, now in the second, and so on. The particular historic person, who for the time being forms one of the heads, really embodies the Beast as a whole, he *is* the Beast, in the author's thought. This identification of the head and the Beast is evident in 13^3 and 13^{12} ; in the former verse it is the deadly wound of a *head* that is healed ; in the latter verse it is said in equivalent words that the *Beast* is healed. In itself the slaying of one head would not slay the Beast, for five heads had perished, 17^{10}, and the Beast survives in the sixth. And so with apparent self-contradiction the writer says in $17^{8,\ 11}$ the Beast *is* not, that is, was not present in the world at the time of the apocalyptist's writing ; but in 17^{10} he says, one head *is ;* that is, was then present in the world. No doubt there is a certain ambiguity in this freedom of expression ; it is intelligible in an apocalyptist, who easily blends a symbol and the thing symbolized, though at variance with prosaic exactness. What the author means is apparent. He thinks of the Beast as existing, at the time of his writing, in the sixth head, but not existing as represented in a certain head then fallen. At no time in the period covered by the pre-millennial visions does the Beast cease to exist, he is always present as Satan's agent. It cannot then be said with exactness 'he is not'; but the writer so closely identifies the Beast with the head which represents him, that he can say, he was, is not, and will come, meaning that he had existed as represented in a certain head, that he does not now exist under that form, but that he will again so exist.

It may be useful to sum up in a brief statement the result of the preceding discussion of the significance of the Beast. *The Beast is Satan's agent in his warfare against the saints, as represented first in the successive Roman emperors, and then, after the destruction of the Roman empire, in Antichrist, the supreme human embodiment of demonic wickedness and power, in whom will come Nero reincarnated.* The Beast is already present in the person of the emperors, but his supreme manifestation will come with the appearing of Antichrist.

Question may be raised whether the Apocalyptist understands an absolute identification of Antichrist with Nero revived in actual person, or whether his Antichrist is not Neronic in the same sense in which the two witnesses in chapt. 11 are Elijah and Moses; see p. 595. The latter supposition might import ambiguity into the conception, but only such as characterizes apocalyptic in general. At all events in the recognition of Nero in the Beast, it is necessary to avoid the not uncommon error of misplacing the emphasis. The dominant thought in the Apocalyptist's prophecy is not that Nero shall come again, but rather that Antichrist will come, the last and most terrible manifestation of the Beast, embodying a Nero reincarnate and demonized — Antichrist, of whom no more fiendish conception can be formed than that furnished by a Nero revived according to popular fancy, and invested with superhuman power. Thus the practical unity of Satan's great agent is preserved; he is one throughout, yet he has successive impersonations, and a Roman emperor, in natural or supernatural form, constitutes each several one in turn.

The Second Beast. The figure commonly designated the second beast, though this precise term does not occur in the Apocalypse, is properly considered here, since it is only in relation to the activity of the first beast that the figure exists at all in the book. The rank and function of the 'other beast' introduced in $13^{11\,\text{ff.}}$ are stated succinctly in v. 12. He is merely the servant of the first beast, from whom he derives all his powers, and his office is the institution and enforcement of the worship of his master. The term *beast* is applied to him in 13^{11} only; elsewhere 'the beast,' a term used more than 30 times in the book, refers to the first beast, the figure of 13^{1-8}, while the second beast is denominated the *false prophet*. He accomplishes his appointed work by deceiving the world, 13^{14}, 19^{20}, and in this he is assisted by the miracles which he is empowered to

perform. He causes an image of the Beast to be made and
endows it with powers which work toward his end, 13^{15}. His
essential character is that of deceiver. And it is in this character that in one instance — and in one only — an activity is
assigned him apart from the *worship* of the Beast, though it is
wholly in the service of the Beast; an unclean spirit working
marvels goes from his mouth to move men to join in the battle
of the great day of God, $16^{13\,f.}$. As the proclaimer of a worship
professedly divine and the worker of miracles in its furtherance,
he might according to the common use of the word receive the
name *prophet* from the heathen themselves; a Christian writer
would call him, as the deluder of men in this work, a *false prophet*,
the designation which he bears elsewhere in the book, 16^{13}, 19^{20},
20^{10}. In the use of this designation the Apocalyptist appears
to give designedly, after his manner, some intimation as to the
meaning of the symbol. The distinct character and work which
are assigned to him, as what is most essential in him, and his
corresponding designation as the *false prophet*, mark his office
as precisely parallel to that of the *priesthood, or special Roman
functionaries charged with the maintenance and extension of the
emperor-worship* throughout the empire. The majority of recent
expositors agree in finding here the explanation of the symbol.
Some scholars understand it to mean the body of heathen
priests and prophets as a whole; but this gives too general a
reference, disregarding the function described here as the special
office of the False Prophet. That no particular historic person
is meant, as for example, Simon Magus, Alexander of Abon-
otichus, Apollonius of Tyana (for other names also suggested,
cf. Gunkel 348), is evident, since no known person answers even
approximately to the requirements of the description given here;
nor could any such person be assumed to perform this office in
the era of Antichrist.

A second beast as auxiliary to the first is peculiar to our
author. Hebrew folk-lore, it is true, mentions two mythical
monsters side by side, Leviathan and Behemoth; cf. Job 40–41,
2 Esd. $6^{49\,ff.}$, En. $60^{7\,ff.}$, Ap. Bar. 29^4; but these stand in no
such relation to each other as do the two beasts here. The
two characteristics of Antichrist, on the one hand the political
(that of world-tyrant), and on the other the moral (that of the

deceiver) are to a certain degree distributed by our author between two characters.   These however are not coördinate, nor
does the second beast possess certain powers wanting to the
first, so that the first must secure the help of the second to accomplish his purposes; on the contrary he himself confers the
requisite powers on the one who is to be his instrument.   This
introduction of a subaltern doubtless springs from the circumstances of the Apocalyptist's era.   The great significance of the
emperor-worship among the facts that form the background of
his book probably suggested to the Apocalyptist as a special
feature in his visions the agency of the priesthood whose office
it was to spread that worship ; cf. p. 201.   The Beast as represented in the emperors was already claiming divine honors, and
a subservient priesthood and other officials were zealous in paying
the homage demanded and in enjoining it upon the Roman
world.   The vision then figures a great movement already in
progress, one which would increase to the end of the emperors'
reign, and finally reach its culmination in the days of Antichrist.
The language of the vision points, in its immediate reference,
only to the last era.   The Beast whom the False Prophet is to
cause men to worship is characterized, $13^{12,\,14}$, as the one whose
death stroke had been healed, *i.e.* Antichrist; but it is evident
that the Apocalyptist has also in mind his own era and the
closing years of the Roman empire.   For some minor traits in
the representation of the second beast see the Commentary on
the respective passages in chapt. 13.

The use of a separate tradition is found by some in the figure of the second
beast ; so, Bouss., J. Weiss, Wellhausen, *al.*   Bouss. *Kom.* 377 f., following
Weizsäcker 498, distinguishes in Jewish tradition two separate conceptions of
the last great human opponent of God.   In the one he is a world-ruler ; in the
other he is a deceiving prophet.   And these two conceptions are held to have
had originally no connection with each other; the latter is a false Messiah
belonging to Palestine ; hence ἐκ τῆς γῆς, 13^{11}.   This latter figure our Apocalyptist has taken up and worked over into a subordinate of the first beast.
The use of an earlier source representing Antichrist in this form is thought
to explain the presence of some traits which are obscure in the account as
given in chapt. 13, but clear in the original connection ; such are the ascent
from the earth (γῆς, land of Palestine, 13^{11}), the two horns like those of a
lamb, the dragon-like speech, the mark of the Beast ; see Bouss. 366, 368.
It is not necessary, however, to resort to this theory to find an explanation
at least plausible of these obscurities ; see Commentary.   As regards the

combination of the two ideas, that of the world-deceiver and that of the world-tyrant, the same is in reality implied in Paul's account of Antichrist, 2 Thess. 2³ ᶠᶠ., for he is to come with all deceit of unrighteousness, and at the same time the world-power of Rome must be removed to make way for him; which could only be said of a greater world-power. The symbol of a beast chosen to represent the deceiving priesthood of the imperial cult is probably suggested by the symbol of the first beast; the chief and his deputy are naturally represented under forms like in kind; and the activity of the latter is only one phase of the activity of the former. For the same reason other traits in familiar descriptions of Antichrist would readily lend themselves for use in the account of the second beast. What is uppermost in the Apocalyptist's idea is not the likeness or unlikeness to the first beast, but the service rendered in the establishment of his worship.

XV. The Text [1]

The text of the Apocalypse is less certainly settled than that of any other book of the New Testament. Weiss (p. 1) enumerates in the 400 verses about 1650 variants, not including different orthographies of the same word, in the five available uncials; while in the Catholic Epistles 432 verses contain only about 1100 variants, though the number of Ms. sources and therefore the possibility of variants is considerably greater. The fact that the book did not obtain early canonical recognition throughout the Church (cf. p. 341), and was therefore less read, explains the paucity of sources and the greater carelessness of copyists. ⸶Also the grammatical errors and other peculiarities of the language led to frequent corrections or changes at the hand of the scribes. It should, however, be observed that the variants relate very largely to differences in the order of words, to the use or omission of the article or a connective, and to syntactical construction. Numerous as the variants are, and important in some respects as is the choice among them, they are not of a kind to cause uncertainty in a single paragraph taken as a whole. There is no question as regards the omission of any long passage, such as occurs, for example, in Mk. 16⁹⁻²⁰; Jno. 7⁵³–8¹¹; Ro. 16²⁵⁻²⁷.

---

[1] Cf. Scrivener-Miller, *Introd. to Criticism of N. T.* I. 320 ff.; Gregory, *Textkritik d. N. T.* I. 120 ff., 316 ff.; B. Weiss, *Die Johan. Apok.* : Bousset, *Die Offenb.* (in Meyer's *Kom.* 1906) 148 ff.; and *Zur Textkritik d. Apok.* (in *Texte u. Untersuch.* 1894); von Soden, *Die Schriften d. N. T.* I. 3, 2042 ff.

The *uncial* Mss. containing the Apocalypse entire or in part are the following : [1]

א.	Codex Sinaiticus,	IV. cent.	Petrograd.
A.	Codex Alexandrinus,	V. cent.	London.
C.	Codex Ephraemi,	V. cent.	Paris.
P.	Codex Porfirianus,	IX. cent.	Petrograd.
Q.	Codex Vaticanus, Gr. 2066, VIII. or IX. cent.		Rome.

Tischendorf cites this Ms. as B ; WH as B_2, but most editors designate it as Q, after Tregelles, to avoid confusion with B, the great Codex Vaticanus, which does not contain the Apocalypse.

[$\lrcorner$, Gimel, Codex Kosinitsanus, IX. or X. cent.

This Ms. located at Kosinitza, or by Soden at Drama, is not available, since it has not been collated or edited. Cf. Scrivener-Miller I. 377 ; Gregory I. 96 ; Soden I. 1, 104.]

א AQ contain the Apocalypse entire. C lacks 3^{19}–5^{14}; 7^{14}–17; 8^5–9^{16}; 10^{10}–11^3; 16^{13}–18^2; 19^5–22^{21}. P lacks 16^{12}–17^1; 19^{21}–20^9; 22^{6-21}.

The *cursive* Mss. containing the Apocalypse, designated by the Arabic numerals, belong to the period of the X–XVI centuries. No exact enumeration of these has been given. Scriv.-Mil. (1894) and Nestle (1899) make the number 184 and 185. Soden (1902) places it at 223. The statistical summary given by Soden, I. 1, 289, shows the paucity of Ms. sources for the Apocalypse in comparison with the other New Testament books. Taking the uncials and cursives together he finds for the Gospels 1725 ; for Acts and Catholic Epistles 520 ; for the Pauline Epistles, including Heb., 619 ; for the Apocalypse 229.

Cursive no. 1, of the 12th or 13th cent. containing the Apoc. only, with the Commentary of Andreas (see p. 325), is of particular interest, since it was the only Gk. Ms. which Erasmus had for the Apocalypse in his first edition of the Gk. Testament (1516), the first published edition after the inven-

---

[1] The symbols in ordinary use for designating the Mss. are retained here and in the Textual notes. For the new system introduced into his work by von Soden, which unquestionably has certain advantages, see his explanation, I. 1, 37 ff.

tion of printing. (The Complutensian Polyglott printed in 1514 was not published till 1522.) Verses 16–21 of chapt. 22 are wanting in this Ms., and Erasmus supplied the missing passage by translating back into Greek from the Vulgate. In other places also he adopted translations from the Latin; cf. Gregory II. 930. Though in later editions he introduced some corrections from other Gk. Mss. yet many of these translations from the Latin remained. And the Erasmian editions formed the basis of later printed editions, even of those of Stephanus, Paris, 1550, and of the Elzevirs, Leyden, 1624 and 1633, which came to be generally adopted as the so-called *Textus Receptus*. The name is due to the second Elzevir edition, whose preface contained the words, *textum ergo habes nunc ab omnibus receptum*. Thus the *Received Text*, which dominated New Testament study till the rise of the comparatively modern science of textual criticism, still contains some of these readings derived from the Latin, and not authorized by any Ms.[1]

The *ancient versions*[2] so far as they represent a text anterior to, and independent of, our extant Mss. furnish important material in constituting the text. The principal versions used in the textual criticism of the Apocalypse are: (1) The Latin, including the Old Latin (sometimes called the Itala) and the Vulgate. (2) The Syriac, including the version published by Louis de Dieu 1627, and the version published by Gwynn, 1897, 'The Apocalypse of St. John in a Syriac version hitherto unknown,' the former akin to the Harklean version, the latter to the Philoxenian. The Peshitta, *i.e.* the vulgate Syriac, does not contain the Apocalypse. (3) The Egyptian, or Coptic, including the Bohairic called also Memphitic, and the Sahidic called also Thebaic. (4) Ethiopic. (5) The Armenian.

The *citations found in the Fathers*[3] are of special value for the study of the text, since for the most part they give a text which antedates our oldest Mss.; these, however, must be used with caution, as they are often made from memory, especially

---

[1] Cf. WH. *Introd.* §§ 15, 346 ; Gregory II. 928 ff.
[2] Cf. the respective sections of the works of Gregory, Scrivener-Miller, mentioned on p. 411, also WH. *Introd.* and articles in Hast.
[3] Cf. works mentioned above.

the short citations ; moreover there is an element of uncertainty in the transmission and editing of the Mss. of the father containing the quotation. Irenæus quotes from the Apocalypse ; but most of what he quotes is preserved only in a Latin translation and the precise form of the quotation made by him is uncertain. Of special worth are citations found in Origen († c. 254), the most erudite among early Christian scholars, and a critic of the text of the Scriptures. Hippolytus († c. 237) has given a number of quotations of considerable length in his commentary on Daniel and his work on Antichrist. Especially valuable is the Latin commentator Primasius (6th cent.), as he has preserved in his work on the Apocalypse the entire text of the old Latin version. Andreas (early part of 6th cent.), the greatest of the early Greek commentators on the Apocalypse, has preserved the text which he followed.[1] Arethas (early, 10th cent.) wrote a commentary on the Apocalypse in which he incorporated large excerpts from the work of Andreas. Among others in whose writings evidence is found regarding the text of the Apocalypse are especially to be mentioned Tertullian, Cyprian, Methodius, Ticonius, Epiphanius, and Jerome.

As regards the *value of the various witnesses* to the text, it is beyond question that neither any single one of the sources nor any group of these has preserved the correct text in all cases. The Codex Sinaiticus, the oldest of the uncials, gives a text of the Apocalypse of much less value than that of some other parts of the New Testament. The highest authority for the Apocalypse is assigned to Codex Alexandrinus. With this, C is closely related, but, as pointed out above, is defective. The two late uncials P and Q are allied to each other; of the two P has preserved much the better text, but neither of them possesses high independent authority. ' P contains, in the midst of a somewhat degenerate text, so many good readings that it is entitled to an appreciable authority in doubtful cases; while the comparatively few readings of $B_2[Q]$ which rise above its generally low level of character, are such as imply a source of no distinctive value,' WH. *Introd.* § 344. Among the cur-

---

[1] His com. apart from its relation to text-criticism was of great value. 'No later commentator was able to supplant Andreas, none of his predecessors could maintain himself beside him,' von Soden, I. 1, 702.

sives, the highest authority for the Apocalypse is assigned by
critics to 95. Nos. 36 and 38 are also regarded as especially
valuable. For others which stand out above the level of the
cursives as a class, cf. Gregory I. 316 ff.

In a classification of the most frequently cited authorities
critics generally would place in a first class ℵAC 95 38, the
Vulgate (codex Fuldensis) and Syriac versions, the fathers
Prim., Cypr., Orig., Hipp., Method.; in a second class ℵ, late
correctors, PQ, most cursives, the Old Lat. Armen. and Ethiop.
versions, Andr., Ticon. Great weight must be given to the
agreement of the members of certain *groups* of authorities,
though even here there are certainly errors.[1] Among the
uncials the groups AC and ℵAC take precedence. When
ℵAC 95 vlg. Prim. agree, the highest degree of probability,
though not certainty, attaches to the reading.

It is not thought necessary to take space for printing in the
present commentary the entire text which is here adopted.
There is now a general consensus of opinion among critical
editors regarding the choice in what is most fundamental in the
larger part of variant readings. In so far, with our present
knowledge, the text may be regarded as settled in the form
given with substantial agreement in the well-known critical
editions of Ti. Ws. WH. Sod. *al.* The larger number of the
cases in which critical opinions differ are those of minor phenomena, such as variations in the order of words, in grammatical
construction, orthographies, and similar details, important in
some aspects, but not affecting the essential meaning of a passage.
The Textual Notes given below in the Commentary are made
very brief, because it is unnecessary to repeat here the critical
apparatus, which is given as fully as present knowledge permits,
in the critical editions of the text referred to above. The principal aim in the Textual Notes is to point out the more significant variants and to give, not all the evidence bearing on these,
but authorities sufficient in character and number to exhibit
the grounds for difference of opinion, and, if so be, for preference.
The reading which is preferred by the present commentator is
placed first. As a matter of value as well as interest in con-

[1] On the difficult subject of groups, cf. Weiss 96 ff.; WH. *Introd.* § 344;
Soden I. 3, 2042 ff.; Bouss. *Kom.* 151 ff.

nection with such variants, the opinions of leading critical editors are also indicated.   Variations from the *Textus Receptus* are given more attention than the subject in itself demands, because that text is for the most part followed in the authorized version, the version which is probably the one still most widely read in English, and which has entered into a vast number of works using the Revelation.

But little need be said to explain the abbreviations used in the Textual Notes.   A star affixed to a Ms. symbol marks the reading as that of the first hand, but at the same time indicates that a corrector has given another reading. — c denotes a corrector. — *al* = others. — anc com = ancient commentators or writers. — edd = most critical editors. — mrg = margin. — min = many or most cursives. — vers = versions. — vlg = Vulgate. — Prim = Primasius. — R = Textus Receptus. — RV = text of the Revisers of the Eng. Version. — Gregory = *Textkritik*, see p. 411. — Ws = B. Weiss, see p. 411.

The following refer to the critical editions, or commentaries, of the respective authors: Alf = Alford. — Blj = Baljon. — Bouss = Bousset, *Kom.*, 1906. — Düst = Düsterdieck, in Meyer's *Com.* — Holtzm-Bauer = Holtzmann-Bauer, *Offenb.*, 1908. — Lch = Lachmann. — Moff = Moffatt in Expositor's Gk. Testament. — Sod = von Soden, etc. See p. 411. — SW = Swete. — Ti = Tischendorf, *Editio octava critica major*. — Tr = Tregelles. — WH = Westcott and Hort.

COMMENTARY

Title. ΑΠΟΚΑΛΥΨΙΣ ΙΩΑΝΝΟΥ : *The Apocalypse,* or *Revelation, of John.* As with all the New Testament books, the title is not a part of the original, but was prefixed in the circulation of the book and the formation of a collection. It is derived from 1¹. This form of it, most widely supported by the earliest sources, is adopted universally by critical editors. Among later forms is that which is adopted by the AV, *the Revelation of St. John, the divine;* the epithet *the divine, the theologian,* was given to the Apostle with reference to the character of the Fourth Gospel. For the word *apocalypse,* see further on 1¹, also p. 167.

απok. Ιωανν. ℵCA several min Iren Melito (both in Euseb) Euseb Clem Or *al.* —— του αγιου is added in many min. —— The epithet θεολόγος, not attributed to Jno. before Euseb, is added in Q and most later sources.

Chapt. I. 1–3. *Superscription.* See page 255.

1. ἀποκάλυψις, *revelation:* ἀποκάλυψις and the vb. ἀποκαλύπτω denote (1) the uncovering of anything covered up, *e.g.* Ecclus. 22²², Lk. 12²; (2) the supernatural revelation of some divine truth otherwise unknown, *e.g.* Ro. 16²⁵, Gal. 1¹²; (3) the great manifestations which are to take place with the coming of the Last Days, *e.g.* Ro. 8¹⁹, 1 Co. 1⁷, 1 Pet. 1¹³, 5¹, 2 Thess. 2⁸. Here, as shown by the following words, a present unfolding of these future events to the vision of the Seer is meant, a use of

2 ᴇ   417

the noun not found elsewhere in the N. T.; for a kindred use of
the vb. cf. 1 Co. 2¹⁰. The added clause, Ἰησοῦ . . . γενέσθαι
shows that the word cannot here be understood to designate
the class of literature to which the book belongs, as in the titles
the Apocalypse of Paul, of Peter, etc. But the word here used
led to the designation of the book as the *Apocalypse of Jno.,*
and this seems to be the origin of the application of the term
apocalypse to the class of kindred writings. At all events the
use of the word as a literary designation is unknown before the
time of our book. Cf. p. 167.

The Syriac Apocalypse of Baruch bears the title 'The writing of the
Apocalypse of Baruch'; but while the original of that book, or its compilation, may belong to about the same time as the Apocalypse of Jno. the date
of the Syriac title may be much later, for there is reason to believe that the
book was written first in Heb. The Gk. version then from which the extant
Syriac version was made belongs to a later time. Cf. Kautzsch 410; Charles
Ap. Bar. XLIII. ff.

Ἰησοῦ Χριστοῦ, *of* i.e. *given by Jesus Christ:* the words ἦν
. . . ἐν τάχει show that the meaning cannot be an appearing
of Christ objectively; the gen. is subj.; on the use of the subj.
gen. with ἀποκάλυψις cf. 2 Co. 12¹, Gal. 1¹². The full form of
the title *Jesus Christ* occurs three, possibly four, times in the
book, 1¹,²,⁵, possibly 22²¹; in other places *Jesus* alone is found,
i.e. eleven or ten times. In most places it might be said that
the writer in the former is thinking of the heavenly Christ, in
the latter of the historic person Jesus; but this distinction cannot be maintained throughout; in 22¹⁶ the activity referred to
is the same as in 1¹, that of the heavenly Christ, though in one
the designation is *Jesus,* in the other *Jesus Christ.* It is perhaps better to suppose the writer to use *Jesus* in general, in keeping with his tendency to use fixed terms, and to have departed
from this designation only in the formal, elevated style of the
superscription and the invocations. Cf. Bouss. *Kom.* 176.

ἦν ἔδωκεν . . . δεῖξαι, *which God gave him to show:* the
primary source of the revelation is God the Father who reveals
through the Son (v. 5, 5⁷, Mt. 11²⁵⁻²⁷, Gal. 1¹⁵ᶠ·,¹²); as in other
things, the Son acts as his agent (Heb. 1², Ro. 2¹⁶, Jno. 1³, 5²⁷),
who does nothing of himself, cf. Jno. 8²⁸, 12⁴⁹. For the Christology, cf. pp. 312 ff. — τοῖς δούλοις αὐτοῦ, *his servants:* by

servants of God, of *Christ*, are meant sometimes those performing some special official service, as Moses, the prophets, the apostles, etc. (Rev. 10⁷, 11¹⁸, 15³, Ac. 4²⁹, Ro. 1¹, Phil. 1¹, Col. 4¹², 2 Tim. 2²⁴), sometimes believers in general. Evidently the latter is the meaning here, since the message is intended for all who should hear it read, v. 3; while the former is the meaning at the end of the verse, ' his servant John.' — αὐτοῦ, *his*, might refer to either God or Christ, but the parallel words in 22⁶ would seem to show the former to be intended. — ἃ δεῖ . . . ἐν τάχει, *things which must shortly come to pass*: the phrase defines the contents of the revelation; it is in apposition with ἀποκάλυψις, or it may be taken as the object of δεῖξαι, so RV mrg. — δεῖ, *must*: i. e. in the fulfillment of God's purpose. — ἐν τάχει, *shortly*: as everywhere in apocalyptic literature and in the N.T., the messianic kingdom with its immediate precursors is thought to be near. The revelation here given to the Apocalyptist does not relate to medieval or modern history (cf. pp. 301 ff.). It is however true that the characterization of the book given in these words does not cover all its contents; the Seer views the predictions of 20⁷–22⁵ as belonging to a period more than a thousand years in the future. Likewise such portions as the epistles to the seven churches, and chapts. 4–5 cannot be classed in the category here described. See on v. 19.

ἐσήμανεν, *signified, made known*: the relative construction is dropped. The agency of Christ spoken of in the preceding words shows that Christ is the subj. of the vb.; cf. 22¹⁶. — ἀποστείλας: sometimes, without expressed object, joined to a vb. to mark the act as carried on through an agent, *e.g.* Mt. 2¹⁶, Mk. 6¹⁷, Ac. 7¹⁴; here the intermediary is given in διά τοῦ ἀγγέλου, which, as indicated by the position of the words and by the parallel construction in 22⁶, ¹⁶, is best joined with ἀποστείλας, not with ἐσήμανεν, though the meaning is the same in either connection. Elsewhere in the N.T. the agent, if expressed with ἀποστέλλω, is in the acc., but the construction here used is supported by the similar expression πέμψας διά τῶν μαθητῶν, Mt. 11². — δούλῳ, *servant*: here said of the special service of the prophet; see above. — Ἰωάννῃ, *John*: though using the first person in the body of the work, the writer here speaks of himself objectively in the third person, a usage common in superscriptions and titles; so Jer. $1^{1-3, 4}$, En. $1^{1, 2}$, the Introductions to Herodotus and Thucydides; cf. Zahn *Ein.* II. 607. The third person furnishes no evidence that the superscription here is written by another hand; see criticism of vv. 1–3, p. 422.

The office of mediating the revelation here assigned to an angel raises an acknowledged difficulty. In the earlier part of the book the visions are shown by the Lord himself, $1^{10 ff.}$, 4^{1}; and through most of the remaining part no mention is made of any intermediate agent; the scenes appear to be opened to the Apocalyptist in his own immediate vision; if any agency were supposed, it would have to be sought in that of the Lord continued on from 4^{1}. Though angels are frequently present as a part of what is shown in the visions, it is not until we reach chapt. 17 that the act itself of showing a vision to the Seer is assigned to an angel, and it is not quite clear how much that agency includes in what then follows. The supposition (Holtzm. *al*) that the *angelus interpres*, a common figure in apocalyptic writings (*e.g.* Dan. 8^{16}, 9^{22}, Zec. 1^{9}, 2^{3}; cf. p. 170) is meant does not suit the language here used, nor is it borne out by the facts of the book, since such an interpretation is attributed to an angelic being at most but twice, 7^{14}, 17^{7}. The view (Ewald's) that the angel is present throughout acting as the agent of Christ, showing and explaining the visions, though not mentioned, is lacking entirely in evidence, and in some cases is at variance with the distinct assertion, that Christ himself is the revealer and interpreter; cf. 4^{1}, 1^{20}. The difficulty must be approached through $22^{6, 8, 16}$, where the same statement is made regarding the angel. The purpose there is to emphasize the divine ratification of the Apocalyptist's message (see notes *in loc.*); and since the angel's testimony there spoken of relates to all the visions of the book, and these receive their final seal of authority from his solemn utterance as the Lord's messenger, it is quite possible that the Seer should speak of all the visions themselves, not quite accurately to be sure, as ultimately given to him through the agency of this angel. Such an abrupt transition from Christ to his agent, or rather the blending of the two, is not difficult to understand; it is similar to that found in many places where God and his intermediary, though conceived as distinct, are also identified, *e.g.* Gen. $22^{15 f.}$, Ex. $3^{2 ff.}$, Jg. $6^{11 ff.}$ (though in the foregoing cases the reference to the angel may come from a later document, yet the writers felt no difficulty in the combination of the two ideas), also Ezk. $43^{6 f.}$, Ac. $7^{30 ff.}$, 23^{11} compared with 27^{23}. In later Jewish times and throughout the N. T. God's communication with men is almost universally represented as mediate. And so the Apocalyptist having finished the rapt recital of his visions in 22^{5}, can easily be understood to fall into the language of current belief in the unimpassioned epilogue in which he resumes the epistolary form adopted in the beginning. At all events whatever may have been its origin, this

conception of the epilogue is evidently in the writer's mind and determines
his form of expression when he turns back to write, with the same purpose
of divine ratification, these words of the Superscription, I. 1–3, the part of
his book written last, as in general with the title or preface of any book
whether in ancient or modern times; cf. the prefatory words in Jer. 1¹⁻⁸,
Lk. 1¹⁻⁴ (cf. Zahn *Ein.* II. 598, 389; Bouss. *Kom.* 182). That the writer
in his Superscription is speaking of a completed work is shown by ἐμαρτύρησεν, v. 2, and τὰ γεγραμμένα, v. 3. This variation of the Superscription
and the epilogue from the body of the book does not as some suppose
(cf. p. 422) prove diversity of authorship; on the contrary so apparent a
dissimilarity is more easily traceable to the same author than to another,
who is at pains to maintain his identity with the author of the rest of the
book.

2. ἐμαρτύρησεν, *has borne witness : i.e.* in this present book,
the Revelation; cf. 22²⁰. — τὸν λόγον κτλ. *the word of God:*
in its most general sense *the word of God* denotes any declaration, revelation, or truth coming from God. The particular
reference is to be determined by the context; here it refers to
the revelations of this book, as is shown by the following
words, 'the testimony . . . he saw.' — τὴν μαρτυρίαν κτλ.,
the testimony of, i.e. *borne by Jesus Christ:* in the N. T. the
gen. with μαρτυρία is probably always subj.; that is its use
in Rev. 1⁹, 11⁷, 12¹¹,¹⁷, 19¹⁰, 20⁴ (see notes *in loc.*). That to
which the testimony relates is generally shown by the context.
When μαρτυρία Ἰησοῦ refers to the gospel the meaning is the
truth to which Jesus bore testimony, cf. Jno. 3³² ᶠᶠ·, 8¹⁴. The
writer, here following a usage common with him (cf. p. 242),
introduces first the general expression, *the word of God,* and
then makes this more specific by the added words, *the testimony
of Jesus Christ.* In such cases καί, not *and,* but *namely, that is,*
is epexegetical, a use very frequent in the Apoc.; cf. Blass
§ 77, 7; Kühn. II. § 521, 2. — ὅσα εἶδεν, *namely of all that he
saw :* the clause is in apposition with the foregoing words and
shows that reference is made there to the revelations which
form the subject of this book and not to the Fourth Gospel
and the Epistles, as some earlier scholars have taken it, an
interpretation now generally rejected. The Apocalyptist in
prefixing the Superscription to his book already completed
(see above) defines in this verse his own part; he has borne
witness of a revelation which he describes in language repeat-

ing v. 1; it is a revelation from God mediated by the testimony of Jesus Christ, and made known to himself in visions.

3. **μακάριος**, *blessed :* there are seven of these beatitudes in the book, 1³, 14¹³, 16¹⁵, 19⁹, 20⁶, 22⁷, ¹⁴. The blessedness declared is to be attained in the coming messianic kingdom. — **ὁ ἀναγινώσκων, οἱ ἀκούοντες,** *he that readeth, those who hear :* the variation in number shows that by the first phrase the *public* reader is meant, and by the second those who hear the book read. ἀκούω here does not mean *give heed to;* that thought is expressed in the next clause, **τηροῦντες κτλ.** The Apocalyptist makes clear that his book is intended to be read in the assemblies of the churches addressed. The reading of the O. T. in the meetings of the synagogue (Ac. 15²¹) was continued in the Christian assemblies, 1 Tim. 4¹³, in which was also added from the earliest time reading of writings of the apostles, Col. 4¹⁶, 1 Thess. 5²⁷. Justin Martyr, *Apol.* I. 67, describing the Sunday services of his time says that it was customary to read the 'Memoirs' written by the apostles. — **τῆς προφητείας,** *the prophecy :* the author describes his book as that of a Christian prophet, and he emphasizes elsewhere this aspect of his work; 10¹¹, 19¹⁰, 22⁶, ⁷, ⁹, ¹⁰, ¹⁸, ¹⁹; see p. 292. — **τὰ γεγραμμένα,** *the things which have been written :* not simply the commands of the seven epistles, but the warnings and counsel which underlie the whole book. The Apocalypse is written for a distinctly practical purpose, the primary object of all prophecy. — **ὁ καιρός,** *the time :* the time of the events foretold is near; see on v. 1. The sentence gives a ground for hope in distress and for constant heed to warning. The Epilogue also contains the same admonition, 22⁷, ¹⁰⁻¹⁴.

Textual notes, vv. 2–3. After οσα, R with some min adds τε; wanting in unc. most sources, edd. — 3. τους λογους ACP min vers edd; τον λογον אQ 100 Ti. — some min and vers add ταυτης to προφητειας.

Criticism of I. 1–3. Many critics, Völter, Spitta, Sabatier, J. Weiss, *al.,* attribute this superscription to an editor, or to a later hand after the manner of the long descriptive titles prefixed to certain epistles in some Mss., cf. Ro. James in Ti. The chief grounds urged are that such a superscription is superfluous, the appropriate beginning of the book being made in vv. 4 ff.; that the Apocalyptist is spoken of objectively in v. 2; and that the agency attributed to the angel in v. 1 is at variance with the rest of the book. It is true that if the book were an epistle, pure and simple, we

should not expect anything to precede v. 4 (we might, however, if no such
words had preceded, expect at least δοῦλος θεοῦ or Χριστοῦ to be added to
Ἰωάννης in v. 4, after the analogy of the epistles generally); but as the
epistolary form is incidental, such introductory words are in place as a
preface prefixed by the author before sending forth his completed work.
Against the other objections see notes on vv. 1 and 2. Terms characteristic of the author of the book appear in this paragraph, *e.g.* δίδωμι, δείκνυμι,
μαρτυρέω and its cognates, λόγος . . . μαρτυρία, προφητεία, τηρέω with
commandments. If the use of these were a studied imitation of the author,
the striking variance regarding the agency of the angel, see above pp. 420
f., could hardly have occurred.

I. 4–8. *The Exordium.* See pp. 255 f. (1) vv. 4–6. Address
and Salutation.

4. Ἰωάννης, *John:* the writer adds nothing to define his
personality; he is evidently so well known to the churches
addressed that the name John alone is sufficient to identify
him. That he stands in some special relation to these churches
is shown not only by his intimate knowledge of their affairs,
as seen in the seven epistles, but also by the fact that he is the
chosen agent to bear this authoritative message to them. See
above, p. 344. — ταῖς ἑπτὰ . . . ἐν τῇ Ἀσίᾳ, *to the seven
churches in Asia:* Asia as always in the N. T., except perhaps
in Ac. 2⁹, is the Roman province embracing the western part
of Asia Minor. The seven churches are those specified in v.
11. On the use of the article cf. p. 247. Other churches existed in the province, *e.g.* at Colossæ, Col. 1²; Hierapolis, Col.
4¹³; Troas, 2 Co. 2¹², Ac. 20⁵; probably Miletus, Ac. 20¹⁷,
2 Tim. 4²⁰; at Magnesia and Tralles, Ignat. *Epist.*; and
doubtless at other places. See on v. 11. The choice of seven
in the address is quite certainly due to the author's fondness
for the number seven as a determining number throughout the
book; cf. pp. 253 f. He regards these seven as representing
the whole group of churches in the province; his message is
for them all. Cf. Ezekiel's selection of seven nations as representing all the Gentiles, chapts. 25–32. And it is certain
that while the book is addressed directly to a limited circle of
Asian churches, the author's purpose must also reach beyond
these to all churches throughout the world. The revelations
of the future which are given to him concern the final destinies of the whole Church and world. After the close of the

special messages, chapts. 2–3, the writer speaks throughout to Christians in terms altogether general, without thought of local limitations. The consciousness of this universal destination of the book shows itself in the repeated injunction, ' He that hath an ear let him hear what the Spirit saith to the churches'; cf. also 22⁷⁻²¹; see above, p. 210.

χάρις, εἰρήνη, *grace, peace:* combined in most of the epistolary salutations; the former denotes the divine *favor*, the latter its result, peace of soul. Elsewhere in the N. T. the Spirit is not mentioned in these salutations. With the striking Trinitarian formula used here cf. Mt. 28¹⁹, 2 Co. 13¹⁴. — ὁ ὢν . . . ἐρχόμενος, *the one who is and who was and who cometh:* this paraphrase of the divine name, describing God as the eternal one, found also in v. 8, 4⁸ and with the omission of ὁ ἐρχόμενος in 11¹⁷, 16⁵, is derived from familiar usage. In Ex. 3¹⁴ the LXX has ὁ ὤν taking the place of the name of God ; a Targum on the passage gives *qui fuit est et erit dixit mundo ;* a Targum on Dt. 32³⁹ has *ego ille, qui est, et qui fuit, et qui erit.* Wetstein and others cite similar designations of the gods in Greek writers. We might expect here ὁ ἐσόμενος, *who shall be,* but the writer substitutes ὁ ἐρχόμενος, *who cometh,* as especially appropriate to the subject of his book. ὁ ἦν is boldly used as the parallel of the two participial clauses, since the vb. has no imperfect participle form. The whole clause follows ἀπό as an indeclinable noun. This use is not found elsewhere, but is evidently adopted by the author designedly; he perhaps regards the unchangeable form more appropriate to the majesty of God and to the grandioseness of the apocalyptic style. The grammatical anomalies are not due to ignorance of Greek construction, as shown by the predominantly correct uses in the book.

τῶν ἑπτὰ πνευμάτων, *the seven Spirits:* these words raise three difficult questions : (*a*) What is meant? (*b*) Why, if the Holy Spirit is meant, is it designated as seven? (*c*) Why then placed before Christ? (*a*) The expression occurs in 3¹, 4⁵, 5⁶ also, but not elsewhere in the Scriptures or the Jewish writings. Many scholars, ancient and modern, have identified the seven spirits with the seven angels of the Presence in 8². But this is certainly wrong, for angels everywhere in the book are called distinctly angels and are seen in distinct angelic form ; but the seven Spir-

its are represented only in symbols, the seven lamps burning before the throne of God, 4⁵, and the seven eyes of the Lamb, 5⁶.
Neither when Christ is described as *he that hath the seven spirits*,
3¹, could the words be easily understood of the angels. But
conclusive is the connection in which the words stand here.
The writer is using the form of benediction customary in the
Epistles, in which the grace and peace invoked upon the readers
come only from a divine source, God and Christ; a created
being could not then be inserted as the object of such invocation. It appears certain then that the Holy Spirit is meant.
And this conclusion is borne out by 3¹, 4⁵, 5⁶. The designation
of Christ as *having* the seven Spirits, 3¹, and of the seven Spirits
as belonging to both God and Christ, 4⁵, 5⁶, is in keeping with
N. T. usage which identifies the Holy Spirit with the Spirit of
God, and the Spirit of Christ; cf. Ro. 8⁹. The representation
of the seven Spirits as seven lamps before the throne of God
and as the seven eyes of the Lamb is taken from Zec. 4²⁻¹⁰ (a
favorite passage with our author; cf. also Rev. 11⁴), where, as
the angel explains to the prophet, the same symbols represent
the Spirit of God active in the world, the eyes of God which
run through the earth, vv. 6, 10 (on that passage cf. Hitzig,
Davidson in Hast. I. 96). (*b*) In denominating the Spirit
seven Spirits, in these four places which are virtually one, the
writer departs from his own usage as well as that of others.
In all other places (13 or 14; on 19¹⁰ see note there) he speaks
of the Spirit as one. Some take the number seven to be determined by the relation of the Spirit to each several one of the
seven churches. 'The Spirit is one, yet in reference to the
seven churches there are seven Spirits, for there is one manifestation . . . of the Spirit's manifold life for each according
to the needs of each,' Swete, *The Holy Spirit in the N. T.* 274.
But this interpretation is clearly wrong; the description in 4⁵
and 5⁶ relates to what is fundamental and universal; there
is no specific reference to the seven churches. Most older and
many modern commentators have understood the phrase to denote the *sevenfold operation* of the Spirit, and find the origin of
the designation in Is. 11², which late Jewish interpreters made
the ground of attributing seven gifts to the Spirit of God (a
wrong interpretation, as only six gifts are mentioned there);

so, Targum Jonathan *in loc.* ; En. 61[11] ; so also Justin *Dial.* 87, *Cohort. ad Græcos* 32. It is true that manifoldness in the operations of the Spirit is a conception common enough, *e.g.* 1 Co. 12[4], Ro. 12[6], En. 49[3] ; and the special significance attaching to the number seven would easily lead to the designation *sevenfold* to express the fullness and perfection of the Spirit's operations, a designation which has become familiar in Christian terminology ; cf. the hymn, *Veni Creator Spiritus.* But the passages in our book are not parallel with those mentioned above ; there is here no question of the various operations of the Spirit, there is no intimation of a connection with the Isaian passage in the author's thought, or of an idea of a sevenfold character in the activities of the Spirit. It is difficult to suppose that the writer would seek to express the perfection of.the one Spirit by representing it as seven distinct Spirits.

The origin of the term must be sought elsewhere. A comparison of vv. 4–6 with chapts. 4–5 throws light upon the subject. As in the opening of the Pauline epistles the language used in the address and salutation is often determined by certain themes which appear later in the letter, so it is in our book ; the address with the benediction has the appearance of being written after the body of the work was completed ; at all events the vision of chapts. 4–5, showing the divine personages that are active in the great scenes of the book, was very vividly before the writer's mind in this opening part. But in that vision the Spirit is represented under the symbols of the lamps and the eyes, a symbolism taken directly and without essential change from Zec. 4[1–10] (see above); and *as often in the use of symbolical language, the symbol and the thing symbolized are here identified, at least so far that the writer speaks of the Seven Spirits, meaning the one Spirit represented in the seven symbols.* Now in the opening salutation, 1[4–6], having that vision of chapts. 4–5 distinctly in mind the writer takes over the same characteristic designations ; that is, the characterization of the Father given in 4[8, 11] proclaiming him in his eternity and almighty power, is reproduced in 1[4] ; that of Christ given in 5[9 f. 12], proclaiming him in his character as the messianic King of kings and the Savior who by his death and resurrection has redeemed and exalted his people, is reproduced in 1[5–6], while the symbolical designation of the Spirit given in 4^5, 5^6 is repeated here in 1^4 verbally in the phrase, the seven Spirits; in other words the phrase occurs here in the salutation as an unchanged transference from the vision, where it is due to a literal following of Zechariah in blending reality and symbol. It is highly probable that behind the seven lamps and eyes of Jehovah found in the imagery of Zechariah there lies an oriental conception taken up in modified form into Hebrew popular belief, as in the case of the seven angels in 8^2, see note there; but doubtless neither the prophet nor the Apocalyptist was conscious of that origin of the figure. It should be noticed that the article in *the seven Spirits* does not necessarily mark the phrase as a familiar term, see p. 247; in view of the close identification of the Spirit of God and God in Hebrew thought the designation is not likely to have existed as a concrete term and apart from some such symbolical connection as is found here.

(*c*) This relation of the Salutation to the vision of chapts. 4–5 explains the position of the Spirit immediately after the Father. The first part of that vision is conceived in strict Hebraic form; and the inseparable connection of the Spirit of God with God in Hebrew thought causes the Spirit to be placed in immediate association with the throne of God and before the mention of Christ. Furthermore the part of Christ in the vast scenes which are immediately to follow that vision makes natural his introduction in closest proximity to those scenes and after the other persons of the Godhead. The Salutation then follows the vision in the order of the divine persons, as well as in the designations respectively given to them. This order does not indicate a subordination of the Son to the Spirit in the author's theology. On the order cf. 1 Pet. 1^{1-2}.

5. ὁ μάρτυς ὁ πιστός, *the faithful witness:* i.e. one whose testimony can be relied on; see on 3^{14}. The appositive, as in the following words, is put in the nominative after a common usage of the author's; see p. 224. The construction is doubtless intended; perhaps the writer feels that the characteristic is expressed with more solemnity in the absolute form of an indeclinable. The term *faithful witness* stands without limitation here and might in itself refer to any revelation made

by Christ (see on v. 2), to the gospel to which he bore witness, or to the witness borne in his death (1 Tim. 6¹³). But these references are not in place here. As the blessing is here invoked from the heavenly presence, and as the two following epithets refer to the glorified Christ, evidently this epithet also is to be understood of the same activity. The writer is thinking, as in v. 2, of the revelation of the future given in this book ; cf. 22¹⁶ ᶠᶠ· It is not certain that μάρτυς is ever used in the N. T. in the sense of *martyr*, though it occurs in cases where the witness suffered death in consequence of steadfastness ; cf. 2¹³, 17⁶, Ac. 22²⁰. — ὁ **πρωτότοκος** κτλ, *the first born of the dead: i.e.* the first of the dead born through the resurrection to a new life. The language implies the future resurrection of the saints. The two clauses ὁ πρωτότοκος κτλ. and ἄρχων . . . τῆς γῆς standing together seem to show that the writer has in mind Ps. 88²⁸ LXX. (EV. 89²⁷), πρωτότοκον θήσομαι αὐτόν, ὑψηλὸν παρὰ τοῖς βασιλεῦσιν τῆς γῆς ; but the words τῶν νεκρῶν, gen. part. show that he does not take πρωτότοκος in the Heb. sense of foremost, princely rank, but rather of priority of birth into a life into which other νεκροί will follow. The language recalls the Pauline words ὅς ἐστιν ἀρχή, πρωτότοκος ἐκ τῶν νεκρῶν, Col. 1¹⁸; in the next sentence the mention of Christ's work of redemption from sin by his blood is parallel with the Pauline teaching found in the same chapt. of the Colossian epistle, vv. 14, 20. Our writer in his connection with the church at Laodicea, 3¹⁴, must have become familiar with that epistle of St. Paul ; cf. Col. 4¹⁶.

ὁ **ἄρχων** κτλ., *the ruler of the kings of the earth :* the common Jewish idea of the Messiah's rule ; he is to be King of kings and Lord of lords in the messianic kingdom, when it shall be established upon earth ; cf. 17¹⁴, 19¹⁶. In the words immediately preceding and following this clause there is found connected with this Hebraistic idea the Christian doctrine of the Messiah's redemption of his people by his death and resurrection ; cf. p. 230. — τῷ **ἀγαπῶντι** κτλ., *to him who loveth us,* etc.: the appositive construction might have been continued, making these epithets parallel with the preceding, but the thought of what Christ in his love has done and will do for his people causes the writer to throw the utterance into the form

of a doxology. For similar doxologies in this book, in which
honor is ascribed to Christ in the same terms as in ascriptions
to God, see 5¹², ¹³, 7¹⁰; and in other books 2 Tim. 4¹⁸, Heb. 13²¹
1 Pet. 4¹¹, 2 Pet. 3¹⁸. The present ἀγαπῶντι marks the continuing love which prompts to the particular acts expressed in
the aorists λύσαντι, ἐποίησεν. — λύσαντι . . . ἐν τῷ αἵματι
αὐτοῦ, *loosed by his blood:* as in the parallel passage 5⁹, Christ's
death is spoken of as a loosing from the penalty of sin. Cf.
Col. 1¹⁴, Mt. 20²⁸, Ac. 20²⁸, Gal. 3¹³, Eph. 1⁷, 1 Pet. 1¹⁹. On
the reading λούσαντι, *washed,* see below, p. 431. — ἐν here is
instrumental, denoting price ; cf. 5⁹, 1 Chron. 21²⁴.

6. ἐποίησεν: instead of ποιήσαντι, the writer breaking off
into an anacoluthon, returning to the former construction in
αὐτῷ. The clause can hardly be treated as a parenthesis (WH),
as the thought is too important a member in the period. —
βασιλείαν, ἱερεῖς, *a kingdom, priests :* the meaning is determined
from the parallel 5¹⁰, which the writer has in mind here, and
from 20⁶, passages which show that reference is made not to
the saints as forming the kingdom over which Christ now rules,
nor their present priestly character, but to the reign of the
saints and their priesthood in the messianic kingdom when it
shall be established (see notes *in loc.*). The past tense in ἐποίησεν denotes what has been ideally or potentially accomplished
in the act or purpose of God, while the actual realization is in
the future — an idiom common in the N. T.; cf. Ro. 8²⁴, ³⁰,
Eph. 2⁵, ⁸, 2 Tim. 1⁹. βασιλεία, *kingdom,* here denotes, then,
not the sphere of rule, but a *sovereign power.* This share of
the saints in the messianic rule is frequently asserted in Hebrew
eschatology, cf. Dan. 7¹⁸, ²⁷, Wis. 3⁸, En. 108¹², cf. also 1 Co. 6².
The priestly character, ἱερεῖς, *priests,* assigned to the members
of the messianic kingdom is not a prominent thought in Jewish
eschatology, though it is mentioned, cf. Is. 61⁶. It follows,
however, as the full realization of what is declared to be the
present privilege of the people of God. It is said of them in
Ex. 19⁶ that they shall be 'a kingdom of priests,' *i.e.* made up
of priests, a phrase translated in the LXX βασίλειον ἱεράτευμα,
a royal priesthood, which is followed in 1 Pet. 2⁹. The Targums give 'kings, priests,' or 'kings and priests' (Ewald,
p. 111), with which thought our author agrees, 1⁶, 5¹⁰; cf. also

Jub. 33²⁰. Whatever be the exact significance of the phrase in the Petrine use (cf. Huther *in loc.*) it is clear that Ex. 19⁶ was commonly understood to combine the two ideas of kingdom or kingship and priesthood. Since the special priestly functions of sacrifice and mediation are not attributed to the body of Christian believers except in the symbolical sense, the term evidently denotes the privilege of free, unmediated access to, and communion with, God, such as in the worship of the Hebrew ritual is permitted to the priests only. That is the significance in Ex. 19⁶. For the same thought, cf. Heb. 10¹⁹⁻²², *boldness to enter into the holy place;* Heb. 4¹⁶, Eph. 2¹⁸, *access unto the Father,* 1 Pet. 3¹⁸, though in these places the term priest is not used. In the present passage ἱερεῖς is in apposition with βασιλείαν; in 5¹⁰ the words are connected by καί. The difference is not material, for while the two ideas are formally distinct, they are in reality one; the kingship of God's people in the messianic kingdom is another aspect of their priesthood, their spiritual union with God. The latter idea is more appropriate to Christian, the former to Hebrew, eschatology. — The words ἐποίησεν κτλ., *made us a kingdom,* are correlative with ὁ ἄρχων κτλ., *ruler of the kings of the earth,* v. 5; in that verse Christ's supreme lordship in the coming messianic kingdom is declared, in this verse is shown what he in his redeeming love has provided for his children as their part in that kingdom. While there is a sense in which Christ's kingdom is already present and the members of it are now priests, that is not the thought with which the writer is concerned in this place. The sentence has sole reference to the future. — τῷ θεῷ κτλ., *to his God and Father:* the use of a single art. favors the connection of αὐτοῦ with both nouns; cf. Ro. 15⁶, 2 Co. 11³¹, Eph. 1³, 1 Pet. 1³. For the words *his God,* cf. Jno. 20¹⁷, Mt. 27⁴⁶, Eph. 1¹⁷, Heb. 1⁹. The dat. denotes the one to whom the priest's service belongs; the same relation is expressed by the gen. in 20⁶, where Christ is added. — αὐτῷ, *to him: i.e.* Christ. 'The adoration of Christ which vibrates in this doxology is one of the most impressive features of the book,' Moffatt *in loc.*

Textual Notes, vv. 4–6. a without εστιν CQ most min edd; των אA a few min; εστιν added with a, P a few min R. — 5. αγαπωντι אACQ most min edd; αγαπησαντι P many min R. — λυσαντι εκ אAC many min some vers edd; λουσαντι απο PQ most min vers R, which is in accord with other passages, cf. 7¹⁴, *washed their robes and made them white in the blood of the Lamb*, cf. also 3⁴, ¹⁸, 4⁴, 6¹¹, 22¹⁴; analogies elsewhere are Ps. 51², Is. 1¹⁶, ¹⁸, 1 Co. 6¹¹, Heb. 9¹⁴, ²², 1 Jno. 1⁷. But the weight of textual authority favors the former reading. — 6. ημας אPQ most min R edd; ημιν A some min; ημων C some vers. — βασιλειαν ιερεις אAC most min vers edd; και inserted אᶜ min some anc com; βασιλεις και ιερεις P some min R; βασιλειον ιερατευμα some min. The variety of readings attests the efforts of correctors to avoid a difficulty felt to exist in the original.

(2) vv. 7–8. Proclamation of Christ's advent — the motto of the book. See pp. 256 f.

7. This verse has been compared with Amos 1², as a sententious statement of the theme of a prophetic book placed at its opening (Düst.). The words in which the Lord's coming is announced are derived from the O. T.; the original of the first clause, *cometh with the clouds,* is Dan. 7¹³, and with variations in the preposition before the word *clouds* (μετά, ἐπί, ἐν) it becomes a common eschatological refrain; cf. Mk. 13²⁶, 14⁶², Mt. 24³⁰, 26⁶⁴, Lk. 21²⁷, 2 Es. 13³. The second part, *every eye shall see him,* etc., is taken freely from Zec. 12¹⁰, ¹².

The same combination of the passages from Dan. and Zec. is found in Mt. 24³⁰; also κόψονται πᾶσαι αἱ φυλαὶ τῆς γῆς, derived ultimately in substance from Zec. 12¹², agrees in form with Mt. 24³⁰ rather than with Zec. These facts are thought by many to show a familiarity of our author with Mt. (the reverse cannot be the case; see pp. 207 f. on the date of the Apoc.); but the possibility of the use of some current apocalyptic fragment in the composition of Mt. 24, Mk. 13 (see pp. 143 f.) may account for the agreement.

οἵτινες ἐξεκέντησαν, *who pierced: i.e.* those who put him to death, a special class included in those spoken of in the preceding clause. Many understand the Jews only to be meant; but the Romans also are likely to be included in the thought of a writer so strongly anti-Roman.

Jno. 19³⁷ also cites this passage from Zec. (12¹⁰) in connection with the crucifixion, though applied to the actual spear-thrust, and uses ἐξεκέντησαν, a correct translation of the Masoretic text, instead of κατωρχήσαντο of the LXX. The agreement is thought by many to indicate identity of authorship in the two books; cf. Zahn, *Ein.*, II. 574. But a Greek version differing from the extant LXX may have been used. The same rendering occurs in Justin 1 *Apol.* 52, *Dial.* 32. The application by two writers of the words of Zec. to the crucifixion might quite conceivably be due to a current use of prophetic passages; cf. Düst., Bouss. *in loc.*

κόψονται ἐπ' αὐτόν, *shall mourn on account of him: i.e.* on account of the terrible judgment which they associate with him at his appearing. After vbs. of emotion ἐπί with the acc. regularly denotes the object toward which the feeling is directed, cf. Mt. 15³², Lk. 23²⁸ ; but the thought here is expressed loosely. The meaning cannot be that Christ himself is the object of sorrow, nor that the sorrow is that of repentance (as in Zec.), for that idea has no place in our book in the events which follow the Advent. The sense here is the same as in Mt. 24³⁰, where however ἐπ' αὐτόν is wanting. — **πᾶσαι αἱ φυλαί,** *all the tribes:* no nation, not even the Hebrew, had accepted the Messiah ; the world as a whole rejected him, cf. Jno. 1¹⁰ ᶠ·, 1 Jno. 5¹⁹. The fulfillment of the prophecies in this verse is not described in detail in the closing scenes ; it is however summarized in 19¹¹⁻²¹. — **ναί, ἀμήν,** *even so, amen :* To the announcement of the Lord's coming given in familiar prophetic words the writer responds with strong asseveration, combining the Greek (ναί) and Heb. (ἀμήν) particles. The particles are brought together in 2 Co. 1²⁰, not elsewhere in the N. T.

8. The speaker here is God, as shown by κύριος, ὁ θεός. The words declare the sure ground of the announcement in verse 7; God the eternal one, the one who holds sway over all (παντοκράτωρ) will consummate his purpose. This abrupt introduction of God declaring some attribute or determination of his own, as a sure ground of the writer's thought in the context, finds parallels in Ps. 46¹⁰, 89³ ᶠ·. For a similar unannounced change of speaker, see below 16¹⁵, 18²⁰ ; cf. p. 244. — **τὸ ἄλφα κτλ.,** *the Alpha and the Omega :* the first and last letters of the Gk. alphabet. The formula, found also in 21⁶, 22¹³, where it is explained, *the beginning and the end,* expresses the eternity of God, as do the words here following ὁ ὢν κτλ. The same formula with the first and last letters of the Heb. alphabet occurs in the rabbis. On the thought, cf. Is. 41⁴, 44⁶, 48¹². Language essentially the same as this here applied to God is in 22¹³ applied to Christ ; see also on v. 13 and p. 313. — **ὁ ὢν κτλ.,** *he who is,* etc : see on v. 4.

Criticism of vv. 7–8. Objection to these verses is raised by Völter, Spitta, *al*, chiefly on the ground that the introduction closed with v. 6, and that these words have no appropriate connection with the context; they are held to be disturbing between vv. 4–6 and vv. 9 ff. But their place as a fitting close of the exordium is shown in the Summary, p. 256; see also notes *in loc.*

I. 9–III. 22. *The Initial Vision.* See p. 257. Christ's appearance to the Prophet with the command (1) to send a book of all the visions revealed to him to seven Asian churches (the Church) 1⁹⁻²⁰, see p. 257; (2) to include a special message to each of these several churches, chapts. 2–3, see pp. 258 ff.

I. 9. ἐγὼ Ἰωάννης, *I John :* the apocalyptic writers often mention themselves by name; cf. Dan. 8¹, 10², 2 Es. 2⁴², 3¹, En. 12³, 25². — ὁ ἀδελφὸς . . . ἐν τῇ θλίψει κτλ., *your brother and fellow-sharer in the affliction,* etc. : the writer's purpose in these words is to emphasize the feeling of close relationship between himself and his readers. It is urged by many that if he had been an apostle, he would have so designated himself here ; cf. p. 352. On the other hand his very self-effacement in the passage is viewed by some as a mark of identity with the author of the Fourth Gospel. But neither contention is of weight. The author's thought here is his oneness with his readers; the authority of his message, whatever may have been his official position, is in explicit terms here referred to Christ. The two terms ἀδελφός and συνκοινωνὸς κτλ. are connected as one, hence the art. is not repeated. — θλίψει, βασιλείᾳ, *tribulation, kingdom :* the two predominant thoughts of the book, the *tribulation* preceding the parousia, in part already begun in the persecutions, and the coming messianic *kingdom,* in both of which Christians are all alike to share, are properly brought together here. Then is added, as it were in an afterthought, the ὑπομονή, *steadfast endurance,* which must be exercised in the former as a condition of inheriting the latter; cf. 2 Tim. 2¹². The order of the three nouns which has given difficulty to some (De Wette, *al.*) is therefore natural. The close connection of the words explains the non-repetition of the art. — ἐν Ἰησοῦ, *in Jesus:* the words, like ἐν Χριστῷ, *in Christ,* so frequent in St. Paul, denote the Christian's spiritual union with Christ. It is in this union that the *endurance* is to be exercised ; and if the phrase be joined with the two other nouns also, this union is denominated

2 F

the cause of the *tribulation*, and the ground of sharing in the messianic *kingdom*.

ἐγενόμην ἐν . . . Πάτμῳ, *was* (exactly, *came to be*) *in Patmos:* γίνομαι here, as often, is virtually equivalent to εἰμί; cf. Ac. 9¹⁹, Mt. 10²⁵, Ja. 3¹⁰. The language implies that he is no longer in Patmos when he wrote this book. Patmos is a rocky, sparsely peopled island, some ten miles long and five or six miles wide, in the Ægean Sea in a southwesterly direction from Miletus. Pliny, *H.N.* IV. 12, 23, mentions it as a place of banishment. — διὰ τὸν λόγον κτλ., *because of the word of God*, etc.: these words state the occasion of the writer's being in Patmos; but they have received three different interpretations, all linguistically possible : (1) *because of*, *i.e.* in banishment for preaching, the word of God ; the view of most scholars; (2) for the sake of preaching there (Hartwig, Spitta, *al*); (3) for the purpose of receiving the visions of this book (Bleek, Düst., B. Weiss, Holtzm., Bouss., Baljon, *al*). The interpretation of the book is not affected by the choice among these views.

In favor of (3) it is urged that the term *The Word of God and the testimony of Jesus* is most naturally taken in the same sense as in the preceding context, v. 2, where the revelation of this book is meant. But if, as is almost certain, the Superscription was written after the body of the book — and this paragraph belongs to the body of the book — the usage throwing light on our passage is found not in the Superscription but in the following chapters. And there the phrase and its equivalents refer uniformly to the gospel; cf. 6⁹, 12¹⁷, 19¹⁰, 20⁴. The supposed journey to Patmos to receive the revelations has been compared with the selection of the banks of the Chebar for the visions of Ezekiel, Ezk. 1³, and the solitudes near Cumae and Arcadia for those of Hermas, *Vis.* I. 1, 3, *Sim.* IX. 1, 4. But Ezekiel was at Chebar because the Hebrew captives, of whose number he was one, had been brought there, Ezk. 1¹; and Hermas expressly mentions his rapture to the solitudes as a part of the work of the Spirit in giving him the visions. If our Apocalyptist had gone to Patmos by a similar direction, or had been rapt away thither by the spirit — cf. 17³, 21¹⁰ — he could hardly have failed to mention it in his evident effort to show fully the divine source and authorization of his message. The second view spoken of above has received little favor with scholars, because it is unlikely that the preacher would have left the great work among the Asian churches, where many a θύρα μεγάλη καὶ ἐνεργής, 1 Co. 16⁹, was open to him, to go on a mission to an insignificant islet remote from centers. The first view is suggested directly by 6⁹ and 20⁴ where the words express the ground of Christian persecution. And this interpretation is strengthened by the early tradition of the banishment of John to Patmos (Clement *Quis dives* 42, Or. *Mt.* XVI. 6, Tert. *de præscr.* 36 ; cf. Swete CLXXIII). And this tradition is not satisfactorily accounted for as derived wholly from our passage, the view of those who reject the interpretation in question; for the language of the passage does not in itself point with sufficient clearness to banishment; in fact it has been argued that if the writer had had any such banishment in mind, he could not have failed to express the thought more distinctly (De Wette). But if hé had been exiled to Patmos, it was known well to all the Asian churches, and a vague allusion is sufficiently clear to them. At all events a legend of this kind is not likely to have grown up on the basis of an expression so obscure in itself, and apart from any historic fact. A possible confusion of a different Asian John with the Apostle, whether in this tradition or in the authorship of the Apoc. or in both, need not be considered here.

10. ἐγενόμην ἐν πνεύματι, *I was in* (lit. *came to be in*) *the Spirit: i.e.* caught away by the power of the Spirit into an ecstacy; cf. 4^2, 17^3, 21^{10}. For the equivalent expression γενέσθαι ἐν ἐκστάσει cf. Ac. 22^{17}; the reverse is γενέσθαι ἐν ἑαυτῷ, cf. Ac. 12^{11}. The writer claims the ecstatic experience of the prophet; see pp. 292 f. — τῇ κυριακῇ ἡμέρᾳ, *the Lord's day:* the special observance of the first day of the week by Christians is indicated in 1 Co. 16^2, Ac. 20^7. Our passage is the earliest in which it is called the Lord's day, but the manner in which the name is used here shows it to be an established designation, and as such it occurs in the earliest post-apostolic writers; cf. Didache 14, Ignat. *Mag.* 9. That the day was so named and was celebrated because it was the day of the Lord's resurrection seems evident and is directly stated in Barnab. 15^9. Deissmann's suggestion (*Neu. Bibelst.* 45, *Licht vom Osten* 268 ff.) that as the first day of the month was called in Asia Minor the *Imperial day,* so Christians in contrast with this usage called the first day of the week after their supreme Lord, lacks support. The view of Wetstein (followed by a few scholars, *e.g.* Hort. *Ap. of Jno. I-III.* 15 f., Deissmann in En. Bib. III. 2815), that the Apocalyptist conceived himself transported to the day of Judgment, is opposed to the meaning uniformly given to the term *Lord's day* found elsewhere, and is at variance with the subject matter of the vision here introduced. — ὀπίσω μου, *behind me:* the language follows closely Ezk. 3^{12}, ἀνέλαβέν με πνεῦμα, καὶ ἤκουσα κατόπισθέν μου, καὶ

ἤκουσα φωνήν; so that no special symbolical significance is to be sought in the words *behind me*, which are appropriate to a voice coming suddenly from an unseen person. Cf. Düst. *in loc.*

φωνήν, *a voice:* there is nothing to indicate that this voice is, as some take it, the voice of an angel, or other than that of Christ who speaks in the following scene; v. 12 seems to preclude other reference. The two descriptions of the voice, as the sound of a trumpet, v. 10, and as that of many waters, v. 15, are not inconsistent, see on v. 15; nor does 4^1 compared with 5^6 require the supposition of two different persons; see on 4^1. — **ὡς σάλπιγγος,** *as of a trumpet: i.e.* loud and clear.

11. **λεγούσης:** attracted into agreement with σάλπιγγος, though referring to φωνήν; cf. λαλούσης 4^1. — **γράψον . . . καὶ πέμψον,** *write . . . and send:* the commission relates not merely to the following vision but to all those which make up the book. The content of the message is expressed here in general form, and in v. 19 more specifically, cf. p. 242. The command *write* is not to be thought of as executed while the Seer is in the ecstatic state; like the *sending* it is a real, not a visional act, and is to be performed as the Apocalyptist recalls the visions and gives them their present literary form after he has returned to his normal state. — **ταῖς ἑπτὰ ἐκκλησίαις,** *the seven churches:* for the number seven see on v. 4. It is not possible to say certainly what determined the choice of these particular churches to make up the seven. The Apocalyptist may have stood in some special relation to these, or there may have been that in their respective conditions and circumstances which made them especially suited to his purpose, or especially in need of the admonitions given; see on v. 4 and p. 210. Ramsay, *Letters* 19, points out that because of their location on an important circular route these cities were the best points to serve as centers of communication with seven different districts. The prominence of Ephesus as the capital city of the province, its geographical situation and its importance as a center of work in the apostolic Church, would explain its position at the head of the list. Beginning with this, the cities are named in geographical order: Ephesus, Smyrna, Pergamum, these three on the Roman road running north from Ephesus; and then on the road running southeast from Pergamum, Thyatira, Sardis,

Philadelphia, Laodicea. On the respective cities see on chaps. 2–3.

12. ἑπτὰ λυχνίας, *seven lampstands:* symbols of the seven churches, as explained in v. 20. The lampstand is easily made the symbol of a church through the common representation of Christians as the light of the world; cf. Mt. 5¹⁴, Phil. 2¹⁵. The writer's repeated use of Zec. 4, where the great candelabrum of the temple with its seven lamps is a conspicuous part of the imagery, accounts for the suggestion of that familiar object as a symbol of the seven churches. It is true that the temple had but one candelabrum, though with seven lights (1 K. 7⁴⁹, which mentions ten, is of doubtful authenticity, cf. En. Bib. I. 644), while there are here seven separate candelabra. The difference, however, is characteristic of the freedom of our author in adapting his material (cf. pp. 221 f.), and does not support the theory of Gunkel, *Schöpfung* 295 ff., that he derived the symbol from a mythological conception current in popular tradition; though it is not improbable, as Gunkel shows, that the different representations, seven torches, seven stars, seven eyes, and seven angels, are originally one and derived through popular tradition ultimately from a worship which viewed the seven planets as gods; see on 8². But of such an origin our writer is certainly unconscious; and the meaning with which he uses the symbol here is unquestionable.

13. Christ, portrayed in traits of superhuman glory, is now seen in the midst of the lampstands, *i.e.* in the midst of the churches. On the significance of details in the representation, see p. 258. — ὅμοιον υἱὸν ἀνθρώπου, *like unto a son of man:* that Christ is meant, and not an angel (some older com.), is shown by vv. 17 f. In the omission of the art. before υἱόν the writer agrees, not with the N. T., but with Dan. (7¹³) whom he is following in much of the description. The term occurs in one other place in the Apoc., 14¹⁴, and the acc. is used there also, though ὅμοιος in all other places in the book, 19 in all, takes the dat. The disregard of grammar here is evidently, then, designed. See on vv. 4, 5. — ἐνδεδυμένον . . . ζώνην, *clothed with a garment reaching to the feet and girt about at the breasts with a golden girdle:* this epithet, and in vv. 14–15, *his eyes,* etc., *his feet,* etc., *his voice,* etc., are taken with variations

from the description of the angelic being in Dan. 10⁵⁻⁶, and
the epithet *his head, that is, his hair*, etc., v. 14, is adapted from
the description of Jehovah in Dan. 7⁹. With this representation compare that of the angels who appear to Enoch, Slav.
En. I. 5, 'Their form shone like the sun, and their eyes were
like burning lamps, and fire came forth from their lips.' Our
writer's combination and free modification of the O. T. passages
are in keeping with his manner; cf. note on v. 12. The exalted christology of the book (cf. pp. 312 f.) makes natural
the ascription to Christ of attributes assigned to God in the
O. T. In this place the application of the description of Jehovah given in Dan. may perhaps have been suggested by the
reading of Dan. 7¹³ in the LXX, *he was there as the ancient of
days.* On the belief in the preëxistence of the Messiah see
p. 73; cf. Baldensperger 134 f. — ποδήρη, *reaching to the
feet:* the ποδήρης (sc. χιτών) was a mark of rank or dignity.
The word is used of the vesture of the high priest (Ex. 25⁶),
but also of others, *e.g.* Ezk. 9², ¹¹, Barnab. 7⁹. — περιεζωσμέ-
νον κτλ., *girt about at the breasts:* 'high girding,' like the 'garment reaching to the feet,' a mark of dignity, was characteristic
of the dress of the high priests (Joseph. *Ant.* III. 7, 2), but not
of theirs exclusively, *e.g.* Rev. 15⁶. Neither epithet, then, shows
Christ to be represented here in his priestly character, as many
com. interpret. That office of his is not mentioned in our
book.

14. κεφαλή, τρίχες, *head, hair:* the general term followed by
the more specific; cf. p. 242. — καί: not *and*, but *that is;* see
on v. 2. The clauses throughout the description are added
loosely, after the writer's manner, without strict regard to construction. — ὡς ἔριον, ὡς χιών, *as wool, as snow:* on the amplification see p. 241. — οἱ ὀφθαλμοὶ κτλ., *his eyes as a flame
of fire:* the flaming eyes generally express fierceness against
adversaries (*e.g.* Dan. 10⁶; common in classic writers also),
but sometimes also penetrating vision, cf. Ecclus. 23¹⁹; both
senses may be united here, as in 2¹⁸, 19¹².

15. χαλκολιβάνῳ: the RV translates *burnished brass,* which
expresses sufficiently well what is intended in the comparison,
though the word is uncertain in meaning, etymology, and exact
form. It is found in 2¹⁸ also, but not elsewhere.

Suidas defines it as a kind of ἤλεκτρον, *electrum*, a word however which is itself ambiguous, in some cases denoting amber, in others a compound of gold and silver; see L. & S. *s.v.* In Ezk. 1⁴ the LXX uses ἤλεκτρον, not in a way to determine its precise nature, but in connection with fire to denote a brilliantly glowing appearance. In Dan. 10⁶ the LXX reads οἱ πόδες ὡσεὶ χαλκὸς ἐξαστράπτων, *his feet were like gleaming brass;* essentially the same expression occurs in Ezk. 1⁷, the original of the imagery used in Dan. In view of these passages and the words here following, ὡς ἐν καμίνῳ κτλ., it seems clear that a brightly gleaming metal, or metallic compound, is meant. As regards gender the word is commonly taken to be neuter, but if in the following clause the reading πεπυρωμένης be adopted, the nom. is χαλκολί-βανος, fem. Cf. on the word, Thayer, Bouss. *Kom.*

πεπυρωμένης, *refined :* lit. *having passed through the fire and become purified;* cf. 3¹⁸, Job 22²⁵, Ps. 11⁷ in the LXX. The construction is the gen. abs. sc. τῆς χαλκολιβάνου. See text note p. 446. ὡς has its usual relative force, *as when refined.* If πεπυρωμένῳ is adopted, it is to be joined with χαλκολι-βάνῳ; καμίνῳ is fem. — **φωνὴ ὑδάτων κτλ.**, *voice of many waters:* *i.e.* the deep, awe-inspiring sound of masses of moving water; cf. 14², 19⁶, 2 Es. 6¹⁷, Dan. 10⁶ LXX. It is noticeable that this reference to the voice is put in the midst of the description (vv. 12–16) of what the Apocalyptist perceived *after* he had turned to behold the speaker who had called to him in the outset; it belongs therefore to what followed the words of the call in v. 11, that is, it anticipates the utterances of the rest of the vision. Such anticipation, a common trait with the writer (cf. pp. 243 f.), is easily accounted for when we remember that he is struggling to portray a series of visions now wholly past. In his vivid recollection of the scene as a whole, disregarding chronological order, he combines kindred matter ; in this case, whatever pertained to the Lord's personal manifestation — features, vesture, voice, surroundings. — The difference between v. 10 and v. 15 as regards the simile used is significant. The loud clarion of the trumpet performs an *introductory* office, it prefaces a summons, an announcement, or a brief command ; cf. 1¹⁰, 4¹, 8⁷⁻¹³, 9¹, ¹³, 10⁷, 11¹⁵ ; but the simile would be inappropriate to the utterances of the Lord's great commission here, extending to the end of the seven epistles. The tones of these utterances, like those of the angelic hymns in 14², 19⁶ are compared to the sound of many waters.

16. ἔχων κτλ.: for the looseness in construction see on v. 14. The words, *had in his right hand*, imply safe keeping, cf. Jno. 10²⁸ ; perhaps also the idea of controlling is included. In 2¹ the stronger word κρατέω, *hold fast* (cf. 2²⁵, 7¹) is substituted for ἔχω, but neither word contains in itself more than what belongs to holding in firm power. — ἀστέρας ἑπτά, *seven stars :* symbols of the seven angels of the churches, v. 20. The use of stars as an appropriate symbol in connection with the churches may have been suggested by the familiar eschatological words in Dan. 12³, *they shall shine as stars forever ;* cf. also En. 104², *ye shall shine as the lights of heaven.* But it is not unlikely that the writer having in mind the representation of the churches by their angels (v. 20) is influenced by some fancy existent in popular tradition of seven stars as seven angels ; see on 8². Whatever may be the exact meaning of the 'angels' of the churches (see on v. 20), they represent the churches in such a way that they are practically identical with these. We have then in the passage two symbols of the churches, the lampstands in the midst of which Christ is seen, and the stars which he holds in his hand. But these are really a representation under two aspects of the one fact of Christ's close relation to his Church ; the former represents his abiding presence in it, the latter his abiding power in sustaining it. The effort of some commentators to explain the holding of seven stars in the hand by supposing a garland of jewels, or a constellation bound solidly together, lays upon the interpretation of a vision the law of too strict realism ; cf. pp. 248 f.— ἐκ τοῦ στόματος κτλ., *from his mouth*, etc.: the words denote the destroying power of Christ's condemnation ; cf. 2¹⁶, 19¹⁵, Is. 11⁴, 2 Es. 13⁴, ¹⁰, Wis. 18¹⁵. The figure used combines the earlier conception of God as a warrior smiting his foes with the sword, and the later conception of annihilation by his sentence of judgment, boldly represented here as a visible accompaniment of Christ — ὄψις, *countenance* or *appearance:* the former is to be preferred ; in this enumeration of traits in detail the words of the clause are more easily understood as referring to a single one than as embracing all. — ὡς ὁ ἥλιος φαίνει κτλ. *as the sun shineth,* etc.: *i.e.* like the sun when it shineth, etc. For the brachylogy cf. Jno. 6⁵⁸, 1 Jno. 3¹². — τῇ δυνάμει, *his might:*

i.e. when not dimmed by clouds or mist. The simile denoting the dazzling splendor of Christ's countenance is from Jg. 5³¹.

17. Prostration to the earth under the overpowering influence of supernatural manifestations is a familiar feature in the narratives of visions ; cf. Ezk. 1²⁸, Dan. 8¹⁷, 10⁹, Mt. 17⁶, Ac. 26¹⁴, En. 14¹⁴. — ἔθηκεν τὴν δεξιὰν κτλ., *laid his right hand*, etc.: the act as well as the words, *fear not*, gives assurance to the Seer. A criticism which finds difficulty in adjusting the representation to that of v. 16, *holding the stars*, overlooks the abrupt changes natural in visions; cf. pp. 248 f. — ἐγώ εἰμι κτλ., *I am the first*, etc.: Many commentators connect with μὴ φοβοῦ *fear not*, after the analogy of Mt. 14²⁷, Mk. 6⁵⁰, Jno. 6²⁰ ; but in those cases ἐγώ εἰμι precedes the μὴ φοβοῦ; also the parallel in v. 8 is against such connection ; furthermore the clause probably does not give a ground for μὴ φοβοῦ, see on v. 18 at the end. — ὁ πρῶτος κτλ., *the first*, etc.: the epithet given to God in v. 8 is here ascribed to Christ (see on v. 14) and declares his existence from eternity to eternity.

18. ὁ ζῶν, *the living one:* an epithet of God, common especially in late Jewish writings and the N. T., describing him as possessing life in his essential nature. Here the words describe Christ as possessing the same inherent life; 'As the father hath life in himself, even so gave he to the Son to have life in himself,' Jno. 5²⁶. The epithet has a broader significance than the following words which speak of the resurrection ; it contains the ground of the latter. — ἐγενόμην : see on v. 9. — ἔχω τὰς κλεῖς κτλ., *I have the keys*, etc.: the words are connected closely with both the foregoing clauses, which contain the ground and the evidence of Christ's power over death ; as one who has life in himself he has power to give life (Jno. 5²⁶⁻²⁸), and in his resurrection to unending life that power has been manifested. He has power to leave in death, or to release therefrom, he has the keys of death. Here again a prerogative of God is affirmed of Christ. According to the Targums (collected by Wetstein *in loc.*) four keys were in the hands of God alone, those of life, the tombs, food, and rain; or as otherwise given, three keys, those of birth, rain, and the resurrection of the dead. For the form κλεῖς = κλεῖδας see Win. § 9, 2, *e* ; Blass § 8, 2. The expression the *keys of death* is

a part of the figure of the *gates of death*, *i.e.* of the prison-house
of the dead, or of the palace of their king, a figure common in
Greek writers from the time of Homer (*Il.* V. 646, *Od.* XIV.
156), and in the Bible (Ps. 9¹³, Is. 38¹⁰, Wis. 16¹³, Mt. 16¹⁸).
The writer's habit of amplification (cf. p. 241) appears here in
the phrase *death and Hades;* cf. 6⁸, 20¹³ ᶠ· If any distinction is
thought of, the former refers rather to the state, the latter to
the place ; or if personification is intended here, the former
refers rather to the slayer, and the latter to the ruler of the
underworld ; the gen. then is gen. poss.

This utterance of Christ, beginning with *I am the first*, etc.,
and ending with the *keys of death*, is connected by most commentators with the foregoing, as giving a ground for the in-
spiriting call, *fear not.* But the assuring touch of the Lord's
hand and the words μὴ φοβοῦ are enough. These awful utterances of divine majesty and power are fitted to increase rather
than assuage terror. Neither can the mention of the power
over death (which in reality forms only a part of the passage),
taken by commentators to point to a connection with ἔπεσα ὡς
νεκρός, *I fell as one dead*, be fittingly associated with those words,
for the words *as one dead* contain only a comparison to express
the sudden and complete prostration of the Seer, who is not in
a state of death, or unconsciousness even. The use of οὖν,
therefore, introducing the command of v. 19, shows the proper
connection of the passage ; it gives the basis of the message
which Christ bids the Seer to write to the churches. It is as
the eternal one and the Lord of life and death that he sends to
his Church the message of this book with its commands and
promises, assuring his faithful ones of the certain triumph of
his kingdom over death and all the powers of evil ; see Summary
p. 258. The office of the passage is similar to that of v. 8 ; see
note there.

19. **γράψον** κτλ., *write* etc. : the words relate to the whole book
which the Prophet is bidden to write. The command is the
same as that in v. 11, but in the repetition is made more specific, after the author's manner. — **οὖν**, *therefore:* see on v.
18. — **ἃ εἶδες καὶ ἃ εἰσὶν** κτλ., *the things which thou hast seen,*
that is, the things which are, and the things which shall come to pass
hereafter. A correct interpretation of the relation of the clauses

in this passage is of the first importance for understanding the author's definition of the scope of his book. The command is generally understood to embrace three distinct objects, *the things which thou hast seen*, referring to the preceding vision in vv. 10 ff.; *the things that are*, referring to the state of the churches spoken of in the seven epistles; and the things which are revealed in the book as yet to come to pass. But as the command in this verse is a repetition of that in v. 11, ἃ εἶδες repeats ὃ βλέπεις, and like that refers to the whole book; it must then include the things referred to in both the following clauses. The ἃ μέλλει γίνεσθαι, *the things which shall come to pass*, are made known to the writer only through the visions; and evidently the ἃ εἰσίν, *the things that are*, are not made known otherwise — what these are will be seen below. The two clauses then define what has been seen in the visions; and καί, before ἃ εἰσίν, is not *and*; it is epexegetical, *even, that is*, a use occurring in numberless cases in the book, where an appositive term makes more specific a general term; see on v. 2 and p. 242. The aor. in εἶδες then refers not merely to what is past at this moment of speaking, but to what is past at the time when the command to write is executed; cf. γράψον κτλ. 19⁹ where the perf. κεκλημένοι anticipates the yet future event of the marriage of the Lamb. The scope of the book then is here defined as revelations of two classes of objects, things that are, and things that shall come to pass. For the former see following note.

ἃ εἰσίν, *the things that are:* the class of visions designated in these words certainly *includes* things spoken of in the epistles to the churches, chapts. 2–3, which are chiefly concerned with facts then present, though the consciousness of the future underlies the whole. But the actual condition of the churches as described there was known to the writer apart from any revelation — that is not the kind of thing which forms the subject of a special divine revelation. What is made known to him in the vision is the Lord's special and direct message to the churches, his personal words of chastisement, approbation, and promise. There is however in the book much more than these two chapters that belongs to the category of things which are rather than to that of things which shall come to pass. Such is the revelation of the vision just seen, vv. 10 ff.; this is the

eternally present fact of Christ's exalted being and his relation to
his Church. So likewise the vision of the court of heaven, chapts.
4–5, reveals facts independent of time, great truths which may
always be denominated *things that are*. Chapt. 12 depicts a
power at work already at that time in the events taking place ;
much of chapt. 17 and other shorter passages are likewise to
be placed in the same category. A very considerable part of
the book has to do with a revelation of things existent, upon
which the future is conditioned. As a work of true prophecy
the book is intimately concerned with picturing the persons,
powers, and causes at work in the events that are coming on the
earth. This is an aspect of his work which the author distinctly
announces in these words here at the outset, and which differentiates it from the Jewish apocalypses in general. Failure to
recognize this as a part of the writer's aim is the cause of much
of the criticism, which rejects considerable portions of the book
as having no place in a unified plan. — Some commentators
(Ewald, DeWette, *al*) take ἃ εἰσίν in the sense of *what they
mean*, that is, what the ἃ εἶδες, interpreted to refer solely to the
preceding vision, mean as explained in v. 20. But the explanation of v. 20 touches only a part of that vision ; and moreover
the evident contrast between ἃ εἰσίν and ἃ μέλλει κτλ. is against
that interpretation. — μετὰ ταῦτα, *hereafter :* for this meaning
cf. 9¹², Jno. 13⁷.

20. The symbols of the lampstands and the stars, which appear in the vision with a meaning not as a matter of course
clear to the reader, are now explained. — τὸ μυστήριον, *as to
the mystery :* not the obj. of γράψον, nor in apposition with ἃ
εἶδες, probably not a nom. like the title of a paragraph or book
(the acc. λυχνίας is against this) ; best construed as the acc.
in apposition with οἱ ἑπτὰ . . . ἐκκλησίαι εἰσίν ; for the construction cf. 1 Tim. 2⁶, Ro. 8³, 12¹, see Blass § 81, 1, Kühn. II.
§ 406, 6. The word μυστήριον, *mystery*, denotes something secret,
hidden, which is disclosed only to special persons, or in a special
way ; among derived senses, as here, something containing a
hidden or symbolical meaning, which can be interpreted ; cf.
17⁵,⁷, Dan. 2¹⁸. See on the word Thayer *s.v.*, Stewart in Hast.
III. 465 ff. — ἐπὶ τῆς δεξιᾶς : equivalent to ἐν τῇ δεξιᾷ v. 16,
but the stars are here spoken of as resting *upon* the open hand,

cf. 5^1, 20^1. — λυχνίας: parallel with ἀστέρων; it takes ir-
regularly the case of μυστήριον. — ἄγγελοι, *angels:* the stars
symbolize the 'angels' of the churches, a term of uncertain
meaning; but the interpretation of the book is not affected by
the uncertainty, since the 'angel' is completely identified with
his church in the seven epistles.

The different explanations of 'angel' as used here may be grouped into
the following general classes: (1) The angel is the bishop, or college of
presbyters, or chief teacher, who represents the church.   In support of this
use of ἄγγελος reference is made to Mal. 2^7, 3^1; so, many commentators,
ancient and modern, among the latter Zahn, J. Weiss, Baljon.   But a decisive objection to this view appears to exist in the fact that the epistles are
in each case addressed to the angel throughout, and yet presuppose a body
of persons who are censured, praised, warned, and in general made to bear a
responsibility which could be laid upon no individual officer.   Moreover,
such a meaning of ἄγγελος has no support in Christian terminology, and is
contrary to the unvarying use of the Apocalypse.   If τὴν γυναῖκά σου were
the certain reading in 2^{20}, it would furnish strong ground for this interpretation; but see text-note *in loc.*   (2) The word is taken in its ordinary
sense, *angel*, and is explained as guardian angel, or at least, *heavenly representative.*   As such angelic patrons were assigned to persons (Mt. 18^{10}, Ac.
12^{15}) and to peoples (Dan. $10^{13, 20}$), so a church also may be conceived as
having its personal patron or representative in heaven; so, Origen, Andreas,
Bleek, B. Weiss, Porter, Moffatt, *al.*   But the first objection raised above
against No. (1) has equal force here.   Christ addresses in the epistles the
churches themselves and not an intermediary.   And moreover no ingenuity
has successfully removed the difficulty in supposing that Christ sends a
communication to certain heavenly beings through an earthly agent, the
Apocalyptist, in order to reach through these angelic representatives the
spiritual life of the churches.   (3) The angel of a church is equivalent to
the church itself, or its personified life; so, Arethas, Beatus, Lücke, De
Wette, Düst., Holtzm. *al.;* others, as Bouss, Swete, Hort, accept this view as
tenable.   This interpretation grows out of No. (2).   The highly developed
angelology of late Judaism which assumed special angels not only for persons and peoples, but also for inanimate things, is adopted by the author of
our book.   He uses the word *angel* nearly seventy times, including angel of
the winds, 7^1, of fire, 14^{18}, of the waters, 16^5, of the abyss, 9^{11}; it is not hard
then to suppose, that in a work of this poetic character, in which personification is common, he should have identified the angel and the sphere of
his activity.   Doubtless some such vague identification occurred in popular
usage, when the angel of fire, of the winds, etc., were spoken of.   It is certain that our author blends the angel and the church in the destination of
the letters and their contents; compare 1^{11} with the address and contents of
the several letters.   It is true that we have then two distinct representations
of a church, the lampstand and the angel; but the difficulty found here is

not weighty; the former may be understood to symbolize a church as having a visible, organic existence; the latter to represent it in its invisible spiritual life; the latter is not so much a *symbol* of a church as an *ideal conception* of its immanent spirit. The outward symbol of this spirit is the star, which is correlative with the lampstand (cf. Lücke II. 433). On the whole this view seems to account best for the language of the epistles and to present the least difficulty. (4) The view of Ebrard, Völter, Spitta, *al.*, that *messengers* sent from the Asian churches to John in Patmos are meant does not call for serious consideration. Such delegates could not hold the place in the Church universal which is symbolized by the stars in the hand of Christ, nor could the author be thought of as writing a letter to persons in his presence.

Criticism of v. 20. This verse has been attributed by some critics (Spitta 31 ff., Völter *Problem* 387 f., Erbes 124 f., *al.*) to a redactor, on the ground that it introduces a false explanation of the lampstands and the stars. The argument is as follows: (1) The lampstands in the vision, vv. 10 ff., do not symbolize the churches, but the seven Spirits, as shown by 4[5], and by a comparison of 2[1] with 3[1] where the lampstands are parallel with the Spirits in distinction from the stars. (2) The stars are not a symbol of the churches, but a part of the picture of Christ's glory in the vision, an ornament of his person; or they represent the luminaries that light his way when he comes as a thief in the night, 3[3]; but the churches with all the faults described in the letters could not be thought of as ornaments to the Christ or as lights to his way. Wellhausen (p. 5) argues that the lampstands cannot symbolize the churches, because the *heavenly* Christ cannot be thought of as walking about between Ephesus, Smyrna, etc. Such criticisms need only to be stated; their fancifulness is apparent. The appropriateness of the symbols to represent the churches is pointed out above in the notes on vv. 12, 16. The Apocalyptist, in conceiving the imagery of the vision, must have had distinctly in mind the significance of the symbols as given in v. 20.

Textual notes, vv. 9–19. 9. Ιησου (alone) א*CP 38 some vers edd; Χριστου is added in Q many min and vers R.—11. After λεγουσης, P some min R insert εγω ειμι το Α και το Ω ο πρωτος και ο εσχατος και; wanting in most sources edd.—13. υιον א Q many min edd; υιω ACP many min R, a correction.—μαστοις CPQ min edd; μασθοις א some min Ti; μαζοις A many min Lch.—χρυσαν א*AC edd; χρυσην א[c]PQ min R Sod.—15. πεπυρωμενης AC Lch Ws WH; -μενω. א some min and vers Blj Bouss; -μενοι PQ many min R Ti WH mrg Sod.—19. γινεσθαι א[c] A many min R Lch WH Sod *al;* γενεσθαι א*CPQ some min Ti Ws.

Chapts. II–III. *Initial Vision.* (2) Special Messages to the several Asian churches. See pp. 257, 258–261.

We have come very generally to call these seven paragraphs *epistles.* In reality they are not such. No one of them is in complete epistolary form; they are special words addressed to the respective churches individually, but included in the one common epistle (the book is in the form of a letter, cf. p. 255) sent to all the seven. From this very fact, as well as from the admonition at the close of each, Let everyone hear what the Spirit saith to the churches, it is clear that like the rest of the book each several message is also meant for all. While in each case the condition and circumstances of the particular congregation addressed are directly aimed at, there is in every 'epistle' spiritual truth for all. Every great revelation, whether O.T. prophecy, or N.T. epistle, is given in view of definite contemporary and local circumstances, but it brings in this form truth of universal significance.

II. 1–7. *The message to the Church in Ephesus.* Ephesus near the mouth of the Cayster was at this time the foremost city of Asia Minor; it formed also a prominent center of non-Christian cults. It was the 'temple-keeper of great Artemis,' Ac. 19[35], whose shrine here was one of the wonders of the world; it became one of the chief seats of the worship of the deified Roman emperors; it was the special home of magic arts, whose formulas were known as Ἐφέσια γράμματα, cf. Ac. 19[19]. In the spread of Christianity, it became an important center; St. Paul made it the seat of his long missionary work in Asia, Ac. 19[1–10]; Apollos labored there, Ac. 18[24 ff.], Timothy was placed there for a considerable time, cf. 1 and 2 Tim. *passim;* the church there was one of those to which was sent the circular letter known to us as the Epistle to the Ephesians; it was the center of the work of the John of Asia Minor. These circumstances explain, at least in part, why the epistle to that church should stand first among the seven, and why as a kind of introduction to the others it should possess certain general features; *e.g.* the emphasis on brotherly love, the first essential in any Christian society; the epithet of Christ in v. 1 and the promise in v. 7 are comprehensive and equally applicable to all the churches. The *condition* of the Ephesian church which determined the nature of the specific message sent to it was this: itinerant preachers, calling themselves apostles, known as adherents of the teaching of the Nicolaitans, had appeared there and had so far gained influence that opposition to them had cost the church a painful struggle (κόπος v. 2); it had, however, proved itself equal to its task. Whatever may have been the peculiar doctrinal error of these teachers, it would appear that they had sophistically defended unchastity and participation in idolatrous feasts, vv. 14, 20, 24. The church had tested and rejected them and had broken their hold; it was persevering still in its intolerance of evil men and its abhorrence of the Nicolaitans, v. 6. These were the circumstances in which it had won the Lord's commendation, because it had endured steadfastly, had borne trial for Christ's name, and had not grown weary in hard toil, vv. 2 f. Doubtless there were in such a community other circumstances also in which the Christians had exercised the same virtues, and the Lord's approval here expressed may be understood of these triumphs likewise. But in this rigorous struggle to maintain purity of morals and teaching in the congregation, Christian charity had suffered; the earlier spirit of free and fervid brotherly love had been checked, v. 4; with all its splendid zeal for truth and right conduct, its patient endurance and toil, the church had not risen above the inevitable danger of a certain hardness of spirit toward the erring. And so with the Lord's words of commendation comes his reproof and the command to return to its first spirit of brotherly love, the foundation virtue without which it must cease to exist, its candlestick must lose its place among the churches.

1. For the 'angel' of the church see pp. 445 f. — τάδε λέγει, *these things saith he:* see p. 260. — The twofold epithet given to Christ in this verse, taken from 1[16, 13], expresses his firm power over the churches to do with them as he will, and his watchful presence in the midst of them. The epithet is appropriate here, but in all the other epistles as well. It stands here, not with sole reference to the contents of this epistle, but is chosen apparently, because this epistle holds an introductory place at the beginning of the whole series of the epistles, which in the mind of the writer form a connected unit. In all the epistles the epithets of Christ are designed to enforce his message; at the same time they mark the oneness of the speaker with the glorified Christ, as he manifests himself elsewhere in the book, principally in the vision of 1[10 ff.], and as it were introduce him again as visibly present in connection with each epistle. — κρατῶν: stronger than ἔχων, see on 1[16]. — περιπατῶν

ἐν μέσῳ, *walking in the midst of:* the words denote constant and vigilant presence ; cf. Lev. 26¹². περιπατέω is a favorite word in the Johannine writings, occurring 17 times in the Gospel, 10 times in the Epistles, 5 times in the Apoc.

2–3. ἔργα, *works:* here, as elsewhere in the epistles, not merely deeds done, but life and conduct in general, including both outward and spiritual activities, as shown by the explanatory clauses added in each instance ; for this use of the word cf. Jno. 6²⁹. — καὶ τὸν κόπον, κτλ., *even thy toil,* etc.: in apposition with τὰ ἔργα, *thy works,* of which the whole passage to the end of v. 3 is an explanation. The 'works' of the Ephesians consist in two things, their *hard toil* (κόπον), especially in opposition to false teachers, and their *steadfast endurance* (ὑπομονήν). These two virtues are then spoken of in order more fully in the following clauses ; the κόπος, *hard toil,* is made definite in the words οὐ δύνῃ . . . ψευδεῖς, *i.e.* the active opposition to, and testing of, the false teachers ; the ὑπομονή, *steadfast endurance,* is taken up again in v. 3, ὑπομονὴν ἔχεις repeating τὴν ὑπομονήν σου of v. 2, and explained as referring to the inward state of bearing trial and of unweariedness in well-doing; in v. 3 βαστάζω, *bear,* refers rather to inward endurance of trial, in v. 2 to tolerance of something in others, as in Ro. 15¹, Ignat. *Pol.* 1. καί before ὅτι, v. 2, does not introduce a *third* activity parallel with the two preceding, but an explanation ; it is epexegetical, see on 1². — δύνῃ: this form, not occurring in Attic prose, is found in a few places in the N.T., *e.g.* Mk. 9²², Lk. 16²; cf. Blass § 23, 2. — ἐπείρασας, *hast tested:* the aor. refers to a definite past act, while the presents, δύνῃ, ἔχεις, show the present continuance of the feeling toward the Nicolaitans. — ἀποστόλους, *apostles:* the term is used here in a sense wider than in its application to the original apostles, denoting a class of itinerant missionaries bearing this name, whose existence in the Church is attested by Didache 11, also 2 Co. 11⁵, ¹³, 12¹¹. According to Ac. 20²⁹ Paul had foretold the entrance of 'grievous wolves' among the Ephesians ; false teachers appear everywhere in the apostolic Church almost simultaneously with the true. The faithful are often warned of the necessity of testing those who claim to come with messages of the Spirit; 1 Jno. 4¹, 1 Thess. 5²⁰ ᶠ·, 1 Co. 14²⁹, Mt. 7¹⁵ ᶠ·, Didache 11 f. The church at

2 G

Ephesus had done this; ἐπείρασας here = ἐδοκίμασας. Ignat. also (*Eph.* 9) commends the Ephesians because they had not suffered certain persons bringing false doctrine to sow seed among them.

4. From commendation the message now turns to reproof and warning. — ἀγάπην, *love : i.e.* love toward the brethren, so most among recent com. The virtues praised in vv. 2–3 presuppose a continuing love of Christ, while the zeal in opposing the false teachers might naturally lead to divisions and a slackening of love toward some of the brethren. This insistence in the introductory epistle upon brotherly love accords with the emphasis put upon it throughout the N. T., especially in the Johannine writings.

5. μνημόνευε, *remember :* the pres. denotes the continued act of calling to mind as an impulse to the *change* (μετανόησον), which is conceived as a single act, brought to pass once for all, and so expressed by the aor. — τὰ πρῶτα ἔργα, *the first works : i.e.* the same activities of love toward the brethren as in the beginning. — ἔρχομαι, *I will come :* the pres. here with the force of the fut., as often with this and similar vbs.; cf. Kühn. II. § 382, 6 ; Blass, § 56, 8. The *coming* here spoken of may be the parousia, which is conceived as near, or a visitation in some preliminary judgment, as in v. 22. — σοί : probably *dat. incommod.*, though possibly a Hebraism ; cf. Mt. 21⁵, Blass § 37, 5. — κινήσω κτλ., *will remove thy candlestick,* etc.: *i.e.* deprive it of its place among the churches, destroy it. Without brotherly love a church must become extinct. — λυχνίαν : the use of the word here agrees with 1²⁰ against the criticism which finds the explanation there given erroneous; see pp. 446 f. — ἐὰν μὴ μετανοήσῃς, *if thou shalt not have repented : i.e.* before the coming. The aor. subjv. with ἐάν has the force of the fut. perf.; cf. Kühn. II. § 388, A 2.

6. From reproof the message turns back again to the praiseworthy 'works' of the church spoken of in vv. 2 f. But as usual with the author (as with the author of the Fourth Gospel) repetition is joined with amplification ; the false teachers of v. 2 are here defined as belonging to the Nicolaitans, and the Lord's detestation of their teaching is emphasized. On the Nicolaitans see on v. 14.

7. ὁ ἔχων οὖς κτλ., *he that hath an ear*, etc.: every individual member of the Church is bidden to heed the message of the epistle. — τὸ πνεῦμα λέγει, *the Spirit saith:* the words attributed to Christ from v. 1 throughout the epistle are here attributed to the Spirit.   Christ speaks to the Prophet through the Spirit; the Spirit is his (cf. 3¹, 5⁶) and is here identified with him; cf. Ro. 8⁹, see also p. 316.   It is noticeable in this sentence, which appears in all the epistles, that whether the words be taken as those of Christ or as an appeal thrown in by the writer in his own person, the representation changes, in so far as the exalted person of the Son of man pictured in the vision and speaking in the rest of the epistle is now conceived as having given his message through the Spirit rather than in oral words spoken directly to the prophet.   It is as if the writer exchanged the visional representation, suited to an apocalyptist, for the customary one of a prophet; and accordingly adapting his language to his practical purpose, he substitutes the ordinary term, the Spirit, for the visional symbol, the seven Spirits. — τῷ νικῶντι, *to him that overcometh:* this phrase occurs in all the epistles and without specification of a particular object of conflict; it is to be understood of final victory over all spiritual foes, including of course the special evil denounced in each epistle respectively. — φαγεῖν . . . ζωῆς, *to eat of the tree of life:* the promise to the victor is everlasting life (cf. Gen. 3²²) in the messianic kingdom.   This promise, like the epithet of Christ in v. 1, does not have specific reference to the circumstances of the Ephesians, it is applicable to all alike; and it is placed appropriately in this introductory epistle as fundamental to the promises in all the others.   Eating of the tree of life, as spoken of in the story of Eden, becomes a common feature in descriptions of the eschatological state; cf. 22², Ezk. 47¹², 2 Es. 8⁵², Test. Lev. 18, En. 25, 4 f.   The tree is represented as now in the Garden of God, to which the saints will be admitted in the messianic age.

Textual notes, vv. 1–5.   The titles of the epistles vary in the Mss.   The principal difference is in the art. after αγγελω: (1) τω αγγελω της εν . . . εκκλησιας; (2) τω αγγελω τω εν . . . εκκλησιας (*the church-angel in*, etc.); (1) is the form for all seven epistles in אPQ and most other sources; in three epistles, 2¹², 3¹, 3⁷, it is the only form supported by the Mss. and is adopted for all by most of the recent edd. But (2) has good authority, especially in three epistles, 2^1 AC Prim, 2^8 A min, 2^{18} A Prim, and is adopted in these three epistles by Lch WH Sw. There are some slighter variations in the Mss. and the exact form of the original must remain questionable. Probably the epistles were uniform in this respect. Cf. Ws 64 f., Zahn *Ein.* II. 620, WH *Select Readings* 136 f. — 2. Q some min and vers R add σου to κοπον; generally omitted, σου after υπομονην belonging to the one compound phrase explaining εργα. — A omits και before οτι, but see Com. *in loc.* — 5. Q most min some vers Prim add ταχυ after σοι; R ταχει.

II. 8–11. *The message to the church in Smyrna.* Smyrna, north of Ephesus, at the head of a deep gulf of the Ægean, was in wealth, commercial importance, and splendor one of the foremost cities of Asia Minor. It was a seat of the emperor-worship, with which the Christians must come into conflict; and a Jewish element existed among its inhabitants, bitterly hostile to the Christians and strong enough to exert influence with the Roman authority. Hence the church there was in special peril. Already it was suffering (θλίψιν 9), perhaps through various persecutions, certainly through the calumnies of the Jews (βλασφημίαν 9). These, though possessing no power to inflict punishment, were quick to bring slanderous accusations against the Christians before the Roman courts, as their fellow countrymen had done in the case of the Lord (Jno. 19^{12}) and Paul (Ac. 24^5). Here at Smyrna a little later they joined in 'ungovernable wrath' with the Gentile mob in calling for the death of Polycarp, bishop of the church there; they assisted with their own hands in his martyrdom, and prevented the Christians from getting possession of his body (Mart. of Pol. 12 f., 17 f.). Whether through Jewish calumnies alone, or through other influences also, some of the Christians at Smyrna were already facing imprisonment, and even the martyr's death was possible, v. 10. The Christians there were poor and this increased their helplessness; but withal the Lord declares they are rich in their spiritual state (v. 9) and he encourages them to fidelity, even to the extremity of death, by the promise of the crown of life. He has for this church praise alone.

8. **ὁ πρῶτος** κτλ., *the first* etc.: see on $1^{17\ f.}$, from which this epithet of Christ is taken. In this epistle the close connection of the epithet with the condition of those addressed is apparent.

In view of possible martyrdom the Smyrnæans are to be encouraged by the remembrance that Christ himself, the eternal one, shared the martyr's death, but revived again.

9. After οἶδα, *I know*, the analogy of the other epistles, except that to Pergamum, would lead us to expect τὰ ἔργα σου, *thy works*, for which there is indeed some authority, see text-note. — θλῖψιν, *tribulation:* the context shows that persecution of some kind is meant; the meaning cannot be restricted to the sufferings of poverty. That the poverty of the Smyrnæan Christians was due to the confiscation of their property and so was a part of their persecution (the view of some com.) is without intimation here, though it is conceivable. — πλούσιος, *rich:* i.e. in spiritual possessions, cf. 3^{18}, 2 Co. 6^{10}, Mt. 6^{20}. For the writer's habit of inserting a parenthesis see p. 243. — βλασφημίαν, *reviling, calumny:* What the calumnious charges were is not indicated, but they were evidently of a kind to expose the Christians to the penalties of the Roman law. — ἑαυτούς : for this use of the reflex. pron. in the acc. with an infin., especially εἶναι, whose subject is the same as that of the governing word (λεγόντων), cf. 3^9, Ac. 5^{36}, 8^9 ; see Blass § 72, 2. Usually a certain emphasis is given to the pron., but that is not the case here. — οὐκ εἰσίν *they are not :* 'He is not a Jew who is one outwardly,' Ro. $2^{28\,f.}$ Throughout the book the Christian is with the writer the true Jew ; with him Christians constitute the 'Israel of God,' as with Paul (Gal. 6^{16}), and he writes as himself a Jew, with a jealous claim of the name for those who form the true people of God.

In this use of the name Jew, the writer is said by many scholars to stand in contrast with the author of the Fourth Gospel, with whom *the Jews* is the designation of the foes of Jesus and his disciples, though of the same nationality. But however weighty may be the objections to identity of authorship in the two books (see pp. 354 ff.), it is doubtful whether a fundamental difference in the use of this name can be maintained. The author of the Fourth Gospel writing far from Palestine and the days of Jesus' earthly life, and dealing often with events in which the mass of the Jewish people with their rulers and leaders manifested their hostility to Jesus, uses the national name, though himself a Jew, with reference to the general attitude, as one might naturally do in addressing another people, and especially when the popular distinction between Jew and Christian had become marked. But a writer who says, ' salvation is of the Jews,' 4^{22}, who speaks of an 'Israelite indeed,' *i.e.* a true Israelite, 1⁴⁷, and of 'the Jews that believed' 8³¹, who denies by implication that certain of the Jews are truly the children of Abraham 8³⁷⁻⁴⁴ (the real sense of this passage is not materially affected whether we read in v. 39 ἐστέ or ἦτε, cf. Zahn *Kom. in loc.*), agrees essentially in the matter here spoken of with the author of the Apocalypse.

συναγωγὴ τοῦ σατανᾶ, *a synagogue of Satan:* so also in 3⁹. Instead of being as they called themselves and were doubtless known, a synagogue, a congregation of Jews, which would be 'the congregation of Jehovah' (ἡ συναγωγὴ Κυρίου, Num. 16³, 20⁴), as also they probably called themselves, they were really a synagogue serving Satan (cf. Jno. 8⁴⁴), whom they served in this persecution of the Christians.

10. If μηδέν be read instead of μή (see text-note) the full construction is μηδὲν τούτων ἅ. — ὁ διάβολος, *the devil :* the real author of the persecutions is Satan, working through his servants the Jews and the Romans. — ἐξ ὑμῶν : this substitute for the indef. pron. with part. gen. occurs as subj. or obj. of a vb. ; cf. 3⁹, 11⁹, Lk. 11⁴⁹, see Blass § 35, 4. — ἵνα πειρασθῆτε, *that ye may be tried :* it is God's purpose that they may be *tested* in their trials. Some take it of Satan's purpose to *tempt* them to fall ; both thoughts may be included. — ἕξετε . . . δέκα, *ye shall have tribulation ten days :* in the circumstances known to the writer the imprisonment appears inevitable (μέλλει βάλλειν), but it is to continue for a fixed time of not great length. On the symbolical number ten see p. 254. If ἔχητε be read instead of ἕξετε, it is parallel with πειρασθῆτε, expressing purpose ; but that reading is inferior as regards sense and authorities ; see text. note. — ἡμερῶν : we should expect the acc. which in fact occurs as a variant ; the gen. with vbs. denotes not *duration* of time, but a period to some point in which an event belongs ; that is the meaning of τοῦ λοιποῦ Gal. 6¹⁷, Eph. 6¹⁰, probably also of the reading of D*Ac. 1³ which omits διά before ἡμερῶν. In this place ἡμερῶν may be a gen. of measure after θλίψιν, *a tribulation of ten days;* cf. Lk. 2⁴⁴, Kühn. II. 353, 3. — γίνου πιστὸς κτλ., *show thyself faithful* etc.: *i.e.* be ready to meet the extreme penalty of death, if it should come to that, as was possible and as had been the case at Pergamum, v. 13. — τὸν στέφανον τῆς ζωῆς, *the crown of*

life : i.e. everlasting life as the crown, the reward, of victory.
The phrase occurs also in Ja. 1¹². The crown occurs só often
in antiquity as a mark of royalty, honor, a prize of victory, etc.,
that it is unnecessary to seek (so, some com.) for a local origin
of the metaphor, *i.e.* in the games celebrated at Smyrna. The
metaphorical use of the word is common ; with the Hebrews
it denotes honor, dignity, *e.g.* Ps. 8⁵, 103⁴, Job 31³⁶, Wis. 5¹⁶ ;
in the N. T. it often denotes the eschatological reward of
victory over evil ; *e.g.* 1 Co. 9²⁵, 2 Tim. 4⁸, Ja. 1¹². The
reference in the context to struggle and victory shows that to
be the meaning here and in 3¹¹.

11. See on v. 7. — **ἐκ :** denoting properly the source whence
the effect proceeds, and so the agency or instrument ; see Thayer
s.v. II. 5 ; Kühn. § 430, 2, 3. — **τοῦ θανάτου τοῦ δευτέρου,** *the
second death:* the first is the natural death to which all are subject ; the second, the eternal death to which the condemned are
given over at the judgment, 20⁶, ¹⁴, 21⁸. This designation of it
occurs also in the Targums (see Wetstein), but our writer does
not assume a full comprehension of the term on his readers'
part ; he therefore explains it in 20¹⁴, 21⁸. The promise in this
epistle is determined directly by the peril of the readers. They
are in danger of the martyr's death here, but life eternal awaits
them as their reward ; after this first death, the second can
have no power to harm them. The reward promised here is the
same as that of the former epistle, v. 7 ; but while it is there
spoken of in its general aspect, here it is viewed in special contrast with the martyr's death, and with reference to delivery
from the horrors of the second death.

Textual notes, vv. 8–10.   8. See on v. 1. — 9. Before θλιψιν, ℵ Q most min
some vers and anc com. R read τα εργα και, in agreement with the other
epistles except v. 13 ; wanting in ACP some vers Prim edd ; but Sod inserts in brackets. The evidence for the words in v. 13 is similar, but ℵ also
omits them there. — 10. μη ACQ some min Lch Tr Ws WH Blj *al;* μηδεν
ℵ P most min some vers and anc com. R Ti Sod, the more difficult reading.
— εξετε ℵ Q most min vers. R Ti Ws Sod Blj *al;* εχητε A some min Prim
WH *al,* probably conformed to πειρασθητε by a copyist. — ημερων ℵACP
min edd ; ημερας Q most min, a copyist's change to an easier construction.

II. 12–17. *The message to the Church in Pergamum.* Perga-

mum, or Pergamus (the neuter is the more common form in

authors and inscriptions), in a northeasterly direction from Smyrna, in the valley of the Caicus, though less important as a commercial center, was in political and religious significance, in wealth and in the beauty of its public buildings, a rival of Ephesus. It possessed shrines of Zeus, Athene, Dionysos, and Asklepios. Of the last, the god of healing, its shrine, with its college of medical priests, formed a center for the gathering of sufferers from all quarters. But what is of special importance for the interpretation of this epistle, it was the foremost seat of the worship of the Roman emperors. In this city as the first place in the Asian province a temple had been consecrated (29 A.D.) to the 'divine Augustus and the goddess Roma,' and Pergamum continued to lead in this cult. Attitude toward this worship was made in time a test of loyalty to Cæsar. Pergamum therefore became in the vision of the Apocalyptist a very center of Satan's devices against the Church, for the Asian Christians the seat of 'Satan's throne,' v. 13. In spite however of the powerful temptation to deny the faith, the church there had thus far stood firm. One member at least, Antipas, had fallen a martyr (v. 13), and the Lord bestows upon the church its meed of praise.

But the Nicolaitans, the same false teachers who had appeared in other churches (Ephesus, Thyatira) with their lax doctrine regarding fornication and sharing in idol feasts, were active in Pergamum also; and the church here, with all its steadfast loyalty to the name of Christ, had not taken the same rigorous stand against these teachers as had the Ephesians (vv. 2, 6). The possibility of regarding such laxity with a degree of leniency cannot be judged altogether by the ideal Christian standard. The congregations were made up chiefly of converts from the Gentiles, with whom fornication was for the most part looked upon as a matter of indifference, and was likely to be excused by sophistical arguments, cf. v. 24, Eph. 5⁶. And also in such communities it was difficult for Christians to continue social intercourse with their non-Christian friends without partaking, at least at a meal in a friend's house, of food which in its preparation for the market, or by some table-rite had been consecrated to a god. Questions about both of these practices must have arisen in most Gentile congregations, and teachers

who found arguments for their excuse were likely to gain
hearers. St. Paul discusses both subjects in the First Epistle
to the Corinthians (chaps. 5, 6¹²⁻²⁰, 8) and one of them in his
circular letter sent to some of these Asian churches (Eph.
5³⁻¹⁴). Apparently the influence of the lax teaching had not
become so great at Pergamum as at Thyatira; at all events, the
threats are less severe, cf. vv. 21 ff.; but there were among the
Pergamene Christians those who held the false views, even
if they had not carried them out into practice, and the church
suffered these to remain in its numbers (ἔχεις v. 14). It is to
meet the peril thus arising that this message is sent. The
church is bidden to repent of its leniency. Though some
might condone, or find arguments to defend, the practices in
question, the sentence of the Lord's lips, 'the sword of his
mouth,' condemns them, and in some signal visitation he will
cut off those (αὐτῶν v. 16) who thus offend. The candlestick
of the church might remain in its place, but this visitation of
some of its members will fall as a penalty upon the whole congregation. The purpose of the warning is of course to lead
the Pergamene church to heal the fault itself and to avert
the visitation. If there were Jews at Pergamum, as there
probably were, their part in the affairs of the Christians was not
such as to call for mention in the epistle.

12. ὁ ἔχων τὴν ῥομφαίαν κτλ., *he that hath the sword*, etc. :
this epithet of Christ, taken from 1¹⁶ (see note there) and expressing the destroying power of his sentence of condemnation
is chosen with special reference to the visitation threatened in
v. 16.

13. ὁ θρόνος τοῦ σατανᾶ, *Satan's throne:* the principal interpretations of this phrase as applied to Pergamum derive its
meaning from some one of the following circumstances : (1)
The conspicuousness of the city as a seat of pagan worship. It
contained temples of at least four of the most prominent Greek
divinities (see above), who were also represented on its coins.
(2) Its prominence as the place of the worship of Asklepios,
with his title 'Savior,' and his symbol, the serpent, which would
remind the Christians of Satan (cf. 12⁹, 20²). (3) The existence on its acropolis of the marvelous altar-platform of Zeus, a
work of enormous dimensions and splendid sculptures, which

might suggest a 'throne' of the god, *i.e.* in Christian thought, a demon, Satan.   (4) The martyrdom of Antipas, which revealed a fierceness of Satan's power not yet, so far as recorded in these epistles, seen in other Asian cities.   (5) The prominence of Pergamum in the emperor-worship.   It was here that this worship first appeared in the Asian province, and the city seems to have retained a leading influence in the cult.   This explanation is probably to be preferred and is adopted by many recent interpreters, because it agrees with the importance which the book assigns to the emperor-worship, as an agency of Satan's power, and because the other explanations give to Pergamum, in the respects spoken of, a prominence which the Christians, and especially our author, would not be likely to assign to it. The reference of the phrase to the worship of Asklepios at Pergamum is adopted by a considerable number of scholars, but this worship was highly developed elsewhere, *e.g.* at Epidauros ; and neither a writer of so wide an outlook as our Apocalyptist, nor the Christians generally in Asia Minor are likely to have attached such superior significance to the Asklepian cult as to call a seat of it the *center* of Satan's rule.   The words at the end of the verse, 'where Satan dwells,' have essentially the same sense as these words, 'where Satan's throne is,' and the repetition in the two different relations indicates reference to a power which is now testing the church in the midst of it, and which was active in the past in effecting the death of Antipas. These activities are most easily understood of a power seeking to maintain the emperor-worship.   See on the phrase En. Bib. III. 3658.

κρατεῖς, *art holding fast:* in spite of a power calling to the denial of their discipleship, probably the insistence on emperor-worship, the Pergamene Christians had not denied the name of Christ, but were holding fast to it, as that of their Lord and Master. — οὐκ ἠρνήσω κτλ., *didst not deny,* etc. : the aor. refers to a specific incident in the past.   The Church, under a special stress of trial in the presence of Satan's power, had shown the same steadfastness as now.   While there may already have been other martyrdoms in the Asian cities, these were probably not numerous, as no intimations to that effect appear in the epistles. The martyrdom of Antipas may have been due to an outbreak

of mob violence (so, Zahn *Ein.* II. 612 f.) ; but if throughout
the verse reference is made to one and the same temptation, the
call to recognize the emperor-worship, his death was probably
an act of some sort of judicial sentence. This, however, would
not prove that it had already become the settled course of the
imperial government to enforce the cult by the execution of all
who evaded it. Nothing is known of Antipas beyond what
is here given. Legends that he was bishop of Pergamum, that
he was burned to death in a brazen bull, etc., are without
value. — πίστιν μου, *faith in me:* gen. obj., cf. Ro. 3²², Gal. 2¹⁶.
— 'Αντίπας : in the text here adopted, taken as indeclinable in
the gen. depending on ἡμέραις ; the appos. ὁ μάρτυς is put in
the nom. after the writer's manner, cf. p. 224. If with some
authorities ἐν αἷς be inserted after ἡμέραις, 'Αντίπας is nom.—
μάρτυς, *witness:* see on 1⁵.

14. From praise the message now turns to censure. — ἔχεις
ἐκεῖ κτλ., *thou hast there,* etc. : the language shows that the
persons meant are not teachers from abroad as at Ephesus
(v. 2), but members of the congregation itself, whose presence
is tolerated. — τὴν διδαχὴν Βαλαάμ, *the teaching of Balaam :*
the teaching, which countenances fornication and participation
in idolatrous feasts, is like that which Balaam gave to Balak,
counseling him by these enticements to ensnare Israel to its
destruction. In Num. 25¹ ᶠᶠ· (belonging to document JE) no
mention is made of the agency of Balaam in the seduction of
Israel ; it is excluded by his attitude as described in the earlier
part of the narrative. But in Num. 31¹⁶ (belonging to document P) the course of the Moabites is attributed to his counsel.
— τῷ Βαλάκ : the dat. is a Hebraism, or popular idiom (if the
correct reading) instead of acc.; see Blass § 34,2, footnote 2. —
σκάνδαλον, *a stumbling-block :* the word characterizes the deadly
consequences of the teaching.

15. οὕτως ἔχεις καὶ σύ, *so hast thou also :* the teaching of the
Nicolaitans is thus declared to be identical with the ' teaching
of Balaam,' *i.e.* it countenances fornication and partaking of
idolatrous feasts ; and it is the same as that of Jezebel's followers at Thyatira as defined in v. 20. Our author is wholly concerned with the *practical* error which has appeared in the three
churches at Ephesus, Pergamum, and Thyatira, perhaps else-

where also. No allusion is made to a dogmatic or philosophical system ; perhaps none existed, but if so, it is without importance for the understanding of these epistles (cf. Blj. 60). The use of διδαχή does not show, as some maintain, that a doctrinal system was held, for the same word is used of Balaam's counsel. On the use here made of the example of Balaam cf. 2 Pet. 2¹⁵, Jude v. 11.

Some have held the Nicolaitans to be Pauline, or ultra-Pauline Christians; so, e.g. Van Manen in En. Bib. III. 3410; but certainly they could not themselves claim, or by others be held, to be followers of Paul, the teaching of whose epistles on at least one of these practical questions was well known in the Asian churches, cf. Eph. 5³⁻⁶, Col. 3⁵⁻⁸. Nicolaitans are mentioned by Irenæus, Tertullian, and other early writers; cf. Hast. III. 547, Bouss. *Kom.* on v. 6. They are said to have derived their name from Nicolas of Antioch, one of the seven mentioned in Ac. 6⁵, supposed to have apostatized, and their teaching is associated with that of the Gnostics. But all this is uncertain and throws no real light on the Nicolaitans of this earlier age ; of these latter we have no knowledge beyond that given in our book. The purely symbolical interpretation of the name based upon a supposed identity of the Greek word Nicolaos with the Heb. Balaam is not supported by certain etymology and is too artificial; see Hast. III. 547. There is no good ground for not regarding the name historical; cf. Zahn *Ein.* II. 623 f. Swete on v. 6.

16. μετανόησον, *repent : i.e.* of their tolerance of the false teaching. — ἔρχομαι, *I will come :* see on v. 5. Some special visitation of judgment seems to be meant. — αὐτῶν, *them :* the destructive judgment will fall directly upon those who hold the teaching of Balaam, but in this visitation of its members the church will suffer punishment for failure to repent of its leniency. — τῇ ῥομφαίᾳ κτλ., *the sword of my mouth :* see on v. 12, and 1¹⁶.

17. See on v. 7. — τῷ νικῶντι κτλ., *to him that overcometh,* etc. : here again, though the promise is universal, its form is determined by the circumstances of those addressed in this epistle. Those who resist the temptation to join in the pagan banquet shall in the messianic kingdom share in the feast of heavenly manna. The particular blessing promised is one found elsewhere in Jewish eschatology. A pot of manna was stored up as a memorial in the ark (Ex. 16³²⁻³⁴, Heb. 9⁴), and according to Hebrew tradition, when the temple was destroyed,

Jeremiah (2 Macc. 2⁴ ᶠᶠ·) or an angel (Ap. Bar. 6⁵⁻¹⁰) rescued
the ark and other sacred objects, and they were miraculously
hidden in the earth to be preserved till the messianic time,
when they would be restored. And feeding on manna became
one of the promised blessings to be given in the messianic
kingdom. 'In that time the treasures of manna will fall
again from above, and they will eat thereof in those years,'
Ap. Bar. 29⁸. The same thought occurs in the rabbinical
writings (cf. Volz 350), and is evidently referred to in Sib.
Or. Proem. 87 ; III. 746. The idea is the source of the symbol used by the Apocalyptist in this verse. A reference of the
promise to the eucharist, or to the grace of Christ sustaining
the Christian in trial (so, some of the older com.) is impossible ; the promise here, as well as in all the epistles, relates to
the reward in the messianic kingdom, when the final victory
shall have been won. — κεκρυμμένου, *hidden:* it is now hidden,
but will be revealed in the coming age. The gen. is part., the
only case of this use in the N. T. with a vb. of giving ; Win.
§ 30, 7 *b* ; Blass § 36, 1, footnote.

ψῆφον λευκήν *κτλ.*, *a white stone,* etc. : As in all the promises,
the gift here spoken of belongs to the eschatological state, and
as will be seen below (fine print) it is a promise of defense
against hostile powers ; an amulet containing as its secret inscription the victor's own new name will be bestowed upon
him to give him power against every enemy. St. Paul borrows the figure of the Christian's panoply of defense in the
conflicts of the present life from contemporary warfare (Eph.
6¹¹ ᶠᶠ·) ; but an apocalyptist more naturally takes the symbol
of power and security in the future kingdom from familiar
beliefs and practices regarding *supernatural* means of defense.
The victor's new name characteristic of his new state will be
given to him on a pebble, whose color befits his victory and
glory, but none save himself will know that name written on
the stone. Thus he will have a secret charm which will give
him power against every assailant and avert every evil. Without, beyond the pale of the messianic kingdom, will be fornicators and idolators (22¹⁵), as here at Pergamum now ; but he
who comes off victor over these present temptations will be
rewarded by immunity from every allurement to evil. The

promise then, like that of the manna in the preceding clause, has a relation to the present circumstances of the readers. The choice of the victor's own new name (denoting his new state), instead of some other formula, as the secret inscription for the amulet, may be suggested by the fact that none but the redeemed himself can fully know his blessedness in the future state; at all events his defense in that state will be found in himself, in his new character and condition.

This promise, ' I will give him a white stone,' etc., has received many different explanations. The following considerations will be helpful in avoiding some untenable interpretations offered and in finding a clue to the probable meaning. (1) $\psi\hat{\eta}\phi os$ is a small, smooth stone, usually a *pebble*, such as was used in voting or counting; sometimes it is a gem. (2) White in the Apocalypse is usually the color belonging to victory and glory. (3) The name written on the pebble is known, not to others, not even to fellow-victors, but only to the individual to whom it is given. It cannot then be any of the names of God, or Christ, for these are known to all, except the secret name of Christ spoken of in 19^{12}, but that is there said to be known only to Christ himself. It cannot be Christ's new name spoken of in 3^{12}, for that is promised to all victors alike, as are the other names mentioned in that verse. It is clear from the emphatic form of the expression used that this absolute secrecy of the name is an important characteristic. (4) What is written on the pebble is the name of a *person*, not a mere formula; this is indicated by the word $\check{o}\nu o\mu a$ (not $\gamma\rho\acute{a}\mu\mu a\tau a$, cf. Ἐφέσια γράμ-ματα, p. 447), and by the similar phrase in 3^{12}. In view of what is said above (no. 3) this can hardly be other than a name given to the victor himself, as declared in the word $\kappa a\iota\nu\acute{o}\nu$; a new and secret name is given to him. The practical identity of the name and the personality in biblical thought leads to the familiar representation of the bestowal of a *new* name upon entrance into a new state or character. ' Thou shalt be called by a new name,' Is. 62^{2}, cf. 65^{15}, Gen. 32^{28}, Rev. 3^{12}. So the victor when he enters into the glorified state of membership in the messianic kingdom receives a new name.

What now is the meaning when this new name is said to be given as a secret one, inscribed on a white pebble? Various answers have been given. (*a*) The judges in the Greek courts used black pebbles for a vote of condemnation, white for acquittal; hence the victor's acquittal in the day of judgment is symbolized. (*b*) At the games tickets were given to the victors, entitling them to food at public expense, and admitting them to royal banquets; hence admission to the heavenly feast of manna is meant. (*c*) A rabbinic tradition tells of the falling of pearls together with the manna; as a reminiscence of that tradition the author connects the two objects here somewhat mechanically. (*d*) The symbol is taken from the jewels engraved with the names of the twelve tribes and set in

Aaron's breastplate (Ex. 28^{17} $^{ff.}$), or from the Urim (Ex. 28^{30}), assumed to be a diamond engraved with the name of Jehovah and set in the breastplate of the high priest; the priestly dignity of the victors is therefore denoted. (*e*) It was common to engrave various things on small stones; the pebble then is used here merely as means of giving to the victor his new name, and has in itself no significance. (*f*) Apart from objections which may be urged against details in these several explanations of the symbol, they all fail to combine the characteristics pointed out above as essential in the author's description, *i.e.* the whiteness of the pebbles, the victor's name as a new one, and the emphasis on secrecy. The emphasized *secret name* points to the probable explanation. A strong belief in the power of a *divine* name in invocations, adjurations, and incantations was everywhere current in the ancient world, among the Hebrews as well as among other peoples. Solomon's seal engraven with a name of God gave him power over demons (cf. En. Bib. IV. 4690). Also a magic power was attributed to other names and formulas. But the value of the mystical name or words was often thought to depend upon its being kept secret, lest others should make use of it. Such magical words were written on pieces of leather, small metallic plates, and probably on small stones; cf. Heitmüller *Im namen Jesu;* Jeremias *Bab. im N. T.* 104 ff.; Hast. III. 211, IV. 604, Extra vol. 640 f. This prevalence of magical practices suggests the origin of the symbol used here; the Apocalyptist takes it from a usage familiar to all his readers. A white pebble emblematic of victory, engraved with the victor's new and hidden name, will be given to him marking his entrance into his new state of being, and bestowing upon him a talismanic power against every evil. The interpretation has so strong probability in its favor that it is adopted with slight variations by most among recent commentators; so, Bouss. Holtzm-Bauer, Moffatt, Swete, *al.*

Textual *notes,* vv. 12–16. On the address see on v. 1.—13. On the insertion of τα εργα σου after οιδα see on v. 2.— After ημεραις, QP most min some vers R insert αις, or εν αις, apparently a correction, Αντιπας being considered nom. For Αντιπας, some, Zahn Blj Sw would substitute Αντιπα, gen.— After πιστος, AC some min Ti Ws Rv add μου; WH Sod bracket.— ος before απεκτανθη, omitted in some min.— 14. τω before βαλακ, AC some min edd; wanting in ℵ; τον PQ ℵ^c.— 15. ομοιως ACQ most vers edd; ο μισω some min R.— 16. ουν wanting in ℵ P many min R.

II. 18–29. *The message to the church in Thyatira.* Thyatira,

southeast of Pergamum, between the latter and Sardis, though less conspicuous in political and religious history than most of the cities which make up the seven, was an important industrial center. Foremost among its industries was that of dyeing and manufacturing woolen goods. Lydia, 'a seller of purple,' who appears in the story of Paul's work at Philippi (Ac. 16^{14} $^{f.}$), was probably an agent of a Thyatiran establishment. The guild of dyers was prominent, and numerous other guilds of craftsmen existed here, as seen from inscriptions. The church, perhaps planted by St. Paul or some of his fellow-missioners in the course of his long stay in Asia (Ac. 19¹⁰), was doubtless, like the other churches, predominantly Gentile in its composition. The Jewish element in the community is not mentioned in the epistle.

From its beginning the Thyatiran church had grown in love and fidelity, in its ministration to the brethren, and patient endurance of trial. For these virtues the Lord bestows upon it his meed of praise (v. 19); and after the correction of the particular failure censured in the epistle, his strongest admonition for the future is to hold fast in its course till he comes again (vv. 24 f.). But the same erroneous teaching of the Nicolaitans regarding fornication and idolatrous feasts which had appeared elsewhere had gained a still stronger hold here. While its advocates were promptly silenced at Ephesus, and a comparatively small number of its adherents were tolerated among the brethren at Pergamum, here at Thyatira it was authoritatively taught by one claiming the inspired gift of prophecy and therefore possessing great influence with the Christians (see on v. 20). The self-styled prophetess had, in spite of distinct warning, carried on her work now for a considerable time (v. 21) with the sufferance of the church (ἀφεῖς v. 20), and had gained a body of adherents who were following out the teaching into practice (v. 22). The prophetic claim and the powerful influence of this leader gave to the false teaching here at Thyatira a significance which it had not assumed in the other cities. This fact is what differentiates this epistle from the others aimed against Nicolaitanism, and what causes the wrathful tone of the epistle, from the epithet of Christ in the opening to the promise with its peculiar nature at the end (see on vv. 20, 27). The aim of the epistle is to strengthen the imperiled church, to summon the fallen members to repentance, and to threaten the impenitent, both the ' prophetess ' and her followers, with a signal visitation of judgment, which shall vindicate, in the sight of the scandalized churches, the Lord's abhorrence of the evil at Thyatira (vv. 22 f.). Doubtless many of the Christians belonged to the

guilds at Thyatira, and as feasts having a more or less idolatrous character were held in connection with these, and as the
temptation to unchastity might be increased through such
association, it is evident that these brethren would be in special
peril. There is, however, nothing in the epistle to indicate
that the great question here brought before the church was, as
some suppose (Ramsay, *al*), withdrawal from membership in
the guilds. The exhortation is rather to hold fast to Christian
fidelity and purity, as most of the brethren had hitherto done,
in the face of the strong temptation which must beset them in
their necessary connection with an unchristian society. The
treatment which the church itself should extend to the erring is
not specified ; the Lord's discipline of these, in case of continued impenitence, is announced in the threatened visitation
(vv. 22 f.).

18. ὁ υἱὸς τοῦ θεοῦ, *the Son of God:* this title of Christ is not
used elsewhere in the book, though it is implied in v. 27, 3⁵, *al*.
Its choice here as a title of the Messiah is probably due to its
presence in the passage, Ps. 2⁷⁻⁹, which the writer has in mind
as about to be used, v. 27.—ὁ ἔχων τοὺς ὀφθαλμοὺς κτλ., *whose
eyes are* etc.: the epithet, taken from 1¹⁴ ᶠ·, has in view the
teaching of the ' prophetess' at Thyatira ; the Lord's keen,
fierce vision penetrates its falseness, and he will tread its adherents beneath his feet. — χαλκολιβάνῳ, *burnished brass :* see on 1¹⁵.

19. τὰ ἔργα, *thy works ;* see on v. 2. — καὶ τὴν ἀγάπην κτλ.,
even thy love etc.: the words define the ' works ' (on καί, *namely,
even*, see on 1²), and there are not four distinct classes mentioned, but two, *love* and *faithfulness* (πίστιν), spoken of first in
general terms, then viewed in their specific aspects as shown
in the *appositional* clauses immediately added (καί before
διακονίαν *even*), love manifesting itself in *ministration* to the
brethren's needs (διακονίαν, cf. Ac. 11²⁹, 1 Co. 16¹⁵) and faithfulness showing itself in *steadfast endurance* of trial (ὑπομονήν).
And in these Christian activities the Thyatiran church was still
increasing ; its 'last works are more than the first.' The particular form and source of trial, in which its steadfastness was
shown, are not indicated.

20. The high praise of the church precedes severe censure.
— ἀφεῖς : peculiar contraction for ἀφίεις, see Blass § 23, 7. —

2 H

τὴν γυναῖκα(without σοῦ), *the woman :* this reading is to be preferred (see p. 471), but if with some authorities σοῦ be added, the rendering is *thy wife*, explained by most as the wife of the 'angel' of the church, *i.e.* its head, or bishop; against this see on 1²⁰. But some understand the pron. to refer to the church personified and the form of expression to be taken directly from the words 'Jezebel, his wife' in the story of Ahab, moved to evil by his wife, 1 K. 21²⁵ (cf. Alford *in loc.*), an interpretation which may certainly be rejected.

Jezebel here is not a figurative term for a party or movement, it designates an actual person, as shown in vv. 22 f. where her distinction from her followers is clear. The *name* however, like Balaam in v. 14, is probably symbolical (cf. p. 250), and characterizes the woman as like Ahab's queen, who was notorious for her support of idolatry in Israel (1 K. 18⁴·¹⁹) and, as our author here interprets 2 K. 9²², for her adultery. — ἡ λέγουσα : for the nom. see p. 224. — προφῆτιν, *a prophetess :* prophets take a very high rank in the apostolic Church; they are specially inspired messengers from God, like the prophets of the O. T.; they are often mentioned, *e.g.* Ac. 11²⁷, 13¹, 1 Co. 12²⁸, Eph. 4¹¹; on their office see especially 1 Co. 14 *passim*. The prophetic gift was exercised by women as well as men. Our author insistently claims the prophet's character; see pp. 292 f. It is easy then to understand the indignation felt toward this woman who claimed to come with special divine authority for her corrupt teaching, who not improbably had come into direct personal conflict with our writer in his earlier work among the Asian churches (see on v. 21), and who had been able to maintain her ground now for some time and gather about her a band of followers. The woman was evidently a member of the church. The theory of some (following Schürer) that she was a priestess of the Chaldæan 'Sibyl who had a temple at Thyatira does not suit the facts presupposed here; her teaching is assumed to be within the church, and the church is held responsible for her activity (ἀφεῖς) ; the epistle, like the others, has to do with members of the church only. Cf. Bouss. *in loc.* — πορνεῦσαι κτλ. ; *to commit fornication* etc.: this definition of her teaching shows the error to be the same Nicolaitanism which had appeared elsewhere.

21. **ἔδωκα αὐτῇ χρόνον κτλ.**, *I gave her time* etc.: a definite event of the past is in view here, whether the warning was given by some special visitation, by the writer himself in his work at Thyatira, or in some other way, is not intimated; the reference may be known to the Thyatiran readers. — **ἵνα μετανοήσῃ**: for this use of *ἵνα* with subjv. instead of the infin. after a noun, common in the N. T., see Burton § 216: Blass § 69, 5. — **οὐ θέλει**, *she willeth not:* she still continues her course.

22. **βάλλω**: the pres. used to express a fut. vividly (Blass § 56, 8; Burton § 15), as shown by *μετανοήσουσιν*. — **εἰς κλίνην**, *into a bed:* a visitation is threatened, a bed of sickness in contrast with the bed of adultery. For *κλίνη*, *a bed of sickness*, in connection with *βάλλω* cf. Mt. 9², Mk. 7³⁰; perhaps a Heb. idiom; so, Charles *Studies* 98 f. — **μετ᾿ αὐτῆς**, *with her:* After *μοιχεύω* the acc. is used of the sharer in the act of adultery, cf. Jer. 3⁹, Mt. 5²⁸; the construction with *μετά* found with *πορνεύω*, 17², 18³ does not seem to occur with this vb. The meaning of the phrase is then, apparently, those who follow her course in committing adultery. Some com. (Alford *al.*) take *μοιχεύω* here in the figurative sense, common in the Scriptures, of unfaithfulness to God, idolatry, and so including both faults spoken of here; but some addition would be essential to make a figurative meaning clear in a context which deals wholly with the literal sense. — **θλίψιν**, *tribulation:* some severe judgment of suffering is meant. — **τῶν ἔργων αὐτῆς**, *her works:* works springing from her influence.

23. **τὰ τέκνα αὐτῆς**, *her children:* generally interpreted her followers. But these are referred to in the preceding sentence, and there is a marked distinction between the two sentences, especially in the punishments threatened; that of the 'children' is severer than that of the 'prophetess.' It is better therefore to take the word, like the other terms in the passage, literally; the woman's children are to be smitten with death to add to her punishment (so, Ewald, Bouss. Blj. *al.*). The children born of her adulteries are probably thought of. This part of her punishment has been thought to be suggested by the slaughter of Ahab's sons, 2 K. 10⁷; but that event is not associated in the narrative with vengeance upon Jezebel. We might rather seek a parallel, as regards both cause and motive,

in the smiting of the child of David and Bathsheba; cf. v. 23 with 2 Sam. 12¹⁴. — ἐν θανάτῳ, *with death*, or *pestilence :* the former, after the analogy of the Heb. idiom, an intensive expression, *utterly slay ;* for the meaning *pestilence*, cf. 6⁸, Jer. 14¹², Ezk. 33²⁷. — γνώσονται πᾶσαι κτλ., *all the churches shall know* etc. ; the state of things at Thyatira was widely known and called for a manifestation of the Lord's displeasure. — ὁ ἐρευνῶν κτλ., *he that searcheth* etc.: from Jer. 17¹⁰, cf. Ps. 7⁹. Such evil as that at Thyatira is not hidden from the Lord, and each one in the church there will receive of him according to his deeds. An epithet of Jehovah is here applied to Christ. — ἑκάστῳ κατὰ τὰ ἔργα ὑμῶν, *to each according to your works :* both reward and punishment are included, but the latter is principally thought of in this connection. The description of Christ given in this verse is in agreement with the epithet of v. 18 and the promise of v. 27.

24. From the searching words of v. 23 the Lord turns back (cf. the message to the Ephesians, v. 6), to encourage those who have not yielded to the libertine teaching. With words inspiring confidence and hope he assures them of his approval, if they keep their present state of love and fidelity till he comes again. — ὑμῖν, τοῖς λοιποῖς, *to you, the rest :* strongly emphasized in contrast with those who held the Nicolaitan error. — οὐκ ἔγνωσαν τὰ βαθέα τοῦ σατανᾶ, *have not known the depths of Satan :* as shown by ὡς λέγουσιν, the writer is in this phrase quoting from language current with the libertine teachers, and apparently used by them to characterize their own knowledge of ' the deep things.' Some suppose that their actual phrase was either simply ' the deep things ', or ' the deep things of God ' (cf. 1 Co. 2¹⁰), and that our writer *in irony* either adds ' of Satan ' or turns their phrase ' the deep things of God ' into ' the deep things of Satan ', somewhat as in v. 9 he turns the self-designation of the Jews into ' a synagogue of Satan.' But this is against the natural sense of the language, and would require some such indication of the turn given to the original words as appears in v. 9. The entire phrase is to be attributed to the Nicolaitans ; and from the context it is clear that they used it in defense of their position. The precise form of their argument can only be conjectured. Knowledge of deep things was

a frequent boast of the Gnostics of a later time; but we obtain
from that source no light on the precise reasoning of the Nicolaitans. The fanaticism that the Christian cannot sin was
found among the Asian churches (cf. 1 Jno. 1¹⁰, 3¹⁰), and the
Nicolaitans may have argued that by entering into the strong-
holds of Satan, by 'knowing his depths,' the Christian could
demonstrate Satan's powerlessness in his case; or that the real
nature of sin could only be known in this way; or that actual
spiritual strength was gained by this personal contact with evil.
Cf. Bouss., Moffatt, *in loc.*, Völter *Offenb.* 167 f., Zahn *Ein.*
II. 65. Some light on their reasoning may perhaps be derived
from that of the Corinthians, among whom the question of
sharing in idolatrous feasts had arisen. Those who prided
themselves on their 'knowledge' and 'strength' to see the
harmlessness of such participation defended it in their own
case, arguing that those who had scruples, the 'weaker' brethren, beholding their participation would be built up in knowledge and strength. (In 1 Co. 8¹⁰ οἰκοδομηθήσεται is an ironical
repetition of the argument of the 'strong'; cf. Schmiedel,
Bachmann in Zahn's *Kom.* Plummer in ICC. *in loc.*) — οὐ βάλλω
. . . βάρος, *I put upon you none other burden*, or *weighty admonition:* What is the correlative of *other* — other than what?
Most com. find here a direct reference to the so-called *apostolic
decree*, Ac. 15²⁸ ᶠ⁻. The meaning then is that no restriction of
their Christian freedom is imposed upon the Thyatirans, beyond
the commands which are there given, and which they now observe, viz.: to abstain from things offered to idols and from
fornication. It is true that these prohibitions are foremost in
this epistle, and that the words used here may be thought to
contain a kind of reminiscence of that decree, though in fact
only one keyword of this sentence, βάρος, occurs there. But
strong objections to this interpretation present themselves.
The question arising here at Thyatira is too remote from that
before the apostolic Council to recall that decree ; the persons
addressed, the faithful, do not appear to have been perplexed
as to the restriction of their Christian freedom. Moreover, the
word ἄλλο here is, according to this interpretation, altogether
isolated, and would require the addition of something to show
reference to the decree, or to topics so remote from the context

as v. 20. It would seem necessary, then, to seek the correlative of ἄλλο in the near context, and since it cannot appropriately be found in vv. 21 ff. (efforts to find it there, De Wette *in loc.*, hardly call for discussion), it must be sought in what follows. After ἄλλος with a negative, instead of the usual construction *i.e.* the gen., ἤ, πλήν with the gen., etc., an independent clause is sometimes found introduced by πλήν, cf. Xen. *An.* I. 8, 20 ; Æsch. *Pr.* 258, or similarly by ἀλλά, cf. Hom. *Od.* XI. 559 (cf. the peculiar elliptical expression with εἰ μή, Jno. 6²²). That gives the simplest explanation of the present case ; *i.e. other than* that contained in the clause introduced by πλήν. *Burden*, then, is not the proper rendering of βάρος, which, like its adj. βαρύς, does not always denote something felt to be burdensome, but often what is *weighty*, or *important*, cf. Mt. 23²³, 1 Thess. 2⁶, 2 Co. 10¹⁰, Plut. *Perikles* 37. The meaning here would then be, *I put upon you none other weighty admonition than this : Hold fast what you have.* For the reference in the last phrase see on v. 25. The words, while enjoining continued fidelity, at the same time relieve the anxiety which might naturally be awakened by the stern utterances of vv. 22–23. — βάλλω, *put :* not so strong as *cast, throw ;* cf. Jno. 13², Ja. 3³.

25. ὃ ἔχετε, *that which you have :* their present state of Christian integrity ; cf. κράτει ὃ ἔχεις with the same meaning, 3¹¹. — κρατήσατε : the pres. might be expected, but the aor. views the act simply as a fact without reference to its continuance; cf. Jno. 15⁴, Win. § 43.4.

26–27. In this and the following epistles the order of the promise and the admonition to hear (v. 29) is the reverse of that in the three preceding epistles; see p. 260. — ὁ νικῶν : nom. absolute, repeated in αὐτῷ to suit the construction. — τὰ ἔργα μου, *my works :* those of God's commandments, a term in the author's mind in his use of τηρῶν. — ἐξουσίαν ἐπὶ τῶν ἐθνῶν, *authority over the Gentiles:* the familiar prophecy that the Messiah's followers shall share in his eschatological rule ; see on 1⁶. The particular aspect of that rule here thought of is described in the words ' with a rod of iron,' etc., taken with slight variation from Ps. 2⁹, which the Apocalyptist refers to the Messiah, according to the traditional interpretation; cf. 12⁵, 19¹⁵. The Messiah will shatter the power of

all his enemies. The fierce character of the promise here
is determined by the general tone of the letter, due to the
fact that the evil has appeared at Thyatira in an extreme form;
its principal advocate has usurped within the Church itself the
office of a prophet inspired by God; see on v. 20. — ὡς τὰ
σκεύη κτλ., *as the vessels of the potter are broken to shivers:* the
clause is best joined closely with the preceding to show that
the dominion is to be destructive, *i.e.* of enemies. Cf. RV.
It is possible to take the words as a separate clause, τὰ ἔθνη
being understood as the subj. of the vb., *they are broken as a
potter's vessels* (RV mrg.); but we should expect the fut. conforming to ποιμανεῖ; see text. note.

28. ὡς κἀγὼ εἴληφα κτλ., *as I also received*, etc.: the power
which the Messiah will give to his people to break the enemy
in pieces is one which he received from the Father; see p. 314.
— τὸν ἀστέρα τὸν πρωινόν, *the morning star:* this obscure
symbol is perhaps derived from the familiar apocalyptic saying
that in the messianic kingdom the righteous shall shine as the
stars; cf. Dan. 12³, 2 Es. 7⁹⁷, En. 104². It refers then to the
glory which shall be given to the victor; and its mention here
is perhaps suggested by the former clause; the victor's share
in the Messiah's conquest over his enemies may suggest the
glory that is to follow. The star of the *morning* may be specified as being thought the brightest; cf. Job 38⁷. In 22¹⁶
Christ himself is the morning star; see note there. The meaning cannot be, as some take it, that he will give himself to the
victor, a conception not possible in our Apocalyptist's idea of
the eschatological kingdom. For various earlier explanations,
generally rejected, see Düst., Alford *in loc.* Quite possibly
the symbol is derived from some popular religious or eschatological idea not elsewhere preserved.

Textual notes, vv. 18–27. 18. See on v. 1. — αυτου after οφθαλμους, wanting in A some min, omitted by Lch Ws, bracketed by WH. — φλογα
A C Q P R most edd; φλοξ ℵ Ti Blj. — 20. A Q some min and vers add
σου after γυναικα; wanting ℵ C P most min and vers, omitted by nearly all
edd. The addition of σου may be a mechanical error of the copyist through
the influence of the σου occurring four times in the preceding words (Ws.
p. 132), or it may be due to a copyist who identified the 'angel' with the
bishop; some refer it to a reminiscence of 1 K. 21²⁵ (see Com. *in loc.*) The evidence from both textual sources and exegesis seems to be decisive against it.

For defence of the reading see Zahn *Ein.* II. 620 f. — 22. αυτης after εργων, nearly all sources edd ; αυτων A some vers R. — βαλλω A C P most min edd ; βαλω (fut.) א Q some min and vers R. — 27. συντριβεται א A C many min R edd ; συντριβησεται P Q many min, a correction to conform with ποιμανει.

III.   1–6. *The message to the church in Sardis.*   Sardis in Lydia, south of Thyatira, at the meeting of numerous Roman commercial routes, was an ancient city, a seat of rule under successive kingdoms and famed for its wealth.   Though it had long since fallen from this high position, yet under Roman dominion it had become an important industrial center ; its manufactures of woolen and dyed goods, like those of Thyatira, were well known.   It was made one of the seats of the Roman provincial courts, and it vied with other Asian cities for the honor of erecting a temple for the emperor-worship.   The church at Sardis, so far as appears from the epistle, was untroubled in both its external relations, and its internal state. Nothing is said of hostility on the part of the Jewish element in the community, nothing of the tribulation or endurance spoken of in all the other epistles except that to the Laodiceans ; and though Sardian Christians had fallen into immorality (v. 4), this is not attributed to the influence of Nicolaitan teachers in the church.   This very freedom from the struggles forced upon the churches generally, and the hereditary Lydian character famed for its softness and love of luxury (cf. Aesch. *Pers.* 41, Hdt. I. 155) may account for the deep spiritual apathy into which the Sardian church had sunk.   'The atmosphere of an old pagan city, heavy with the immoral traditions of eight centuries, was unfavorable to the growth of her spiritual life' (Swete LX.).   The church is described as *dead* (v. 1), as spiritually asleep, not as totally extinct, for it is not conceived to be beyond the appeal to arouse itself to a living activity (v. 2).   Even those few members who had kept themselves from the immorality prevailing in such a community (v. 4) do not seem to be entirely exempt from this general characterization of the church; their firmness is acknowledged and its fitting reward is promised, but they are not commended for a vigorous Christian life fruitful beyond themselves.   With the exception of these guarded words of approval and promise, the message is one of severe censure.   Its purpose is to awaken into renewed life, in an important Asian center, a church now in danger of utter extinction.

1. The epithet of Christ is twofold, as in most of the epistles. The first part, 'that hath the seven Spirits,' is a reminiscence of the words of 1⁴, but in the form which these words receive in 5⁶ also, expressing the relation of the Spirit to Christ. (See on 2⁷, also p. 316.) The second part, 'that hath the seven stars,' is from 1¹⁶. Each part of the epithet has its special reference to the contents of the message following. He, whose eyes (*i.e.* the all-penetrating Spirit, see on 5⁶) behold all things, pierces through the delusive complacency of the Sardian church and tells them in terrible words that their works fall short in the judgment of God (v. 2), that their claim to be a living church is but nominal ; they are in reality as asleep and in imminent peril of utter spiritual death (vv. 1–2). He that hath the seven stars in his hand, he that hath the Church in his keeping to do with it as he will (see on 1¹⁶), warns the Sardians that unless they repent he will come upon them suddenly with judgment, at an unexpected hour (v. 3) ; but on the other hand the victor is assured of safety and reward in the End (v. 5). — τὰ ἑπτὰ πνεύματα, *the seven Spirits :* For this designation of the Holy Spirit see on 1⁴. — ἔργα, *works :* see on 2². Reference is here made to spiritual state as described in the following clause. — ὄνομα ὅτι κτλ., *a name that thou livest :* the name is contrasted with the reality ; for this use of the word cf. Hdt. VII. 138. — νεκρός, *dead :* not a state of complete spiritual death, which would exclude ἔμελλον ἀποθανεῖν, *about to die ;* cf. Eph. 5¹⁴, 'Awake thou that sleepest, and arise from the dead.'

2. γίνου, *show thyself, be.* For the use of γίνομαι with the partic. forming a periphrasis see Buttm. p. 308, Kühn. II. § 353, 4, A. 3. As there is nothing to indicate a change of subject the command is to be understood as addressed to all, including those mentioned in v. 4, to throw off apathy and be watchful. — στήρισον : on this form of the aor. see Blass § 16, 2. — τὰ λοιπά, *the rest :* what still remains in contrast with the *dead ;* both persons and the elements of Christian character are included. But even these are in peril of spiritual death. On τὰ λοιπά with defining rel. clause cf. 2²⁴. — ἔμελλον : the

imperf. seems to be used like the epistolary aor., but see
Burton § 28. — τὰ ἔργα, *thy works:* their characteristic spiritual life and activity as a whole. The line of argument here
makes more probable a reference to the general character and
condition of the church as a whole than to a short-coming in
every individual virtue, and so favors the reading of the art.
with ἔργα (see text. note); without the art. the sense would
be ' I have not found any works of thine, any Christian activity,
fully carried out ' (RV text). — πεπληρωμένα, *fulfilled, perfected* (RV): the word implies a measure or standard to
which the present character of the church has failed to come
up. The sentence contains a litotes ; 'have not found fulfilled' = 'have found a failure'; the works of the church are
in the judgment of God a failure. On the litotes cf. 1 Co. 10⁵
where *not pleased = displeased.* — ἐνώπιον τοῦ θεοῦ, *before God :*
i.e. in God's judgment, contrasted with the self-complacency
of the Sardians. — μου, *my:* see on αὐτοῦ, *his,* 1⁶. The word
marks the oneness of Christ's judgment of the church with
that of the Father ; cf. the same oneness in the acknowledgment of the victor in v. 5.

3. πῶς, *how:* loose use of πῶς, equivalent to *what.* Some
take it strictly as denoting the *manner, i.e.* the zeal with which
they received the Christian instruction given to them ; but
τήρει, *keep,* said of keeping what one has, points rather to the
matter, what they received. Cf. the use of οὕτως, the adv. in
place of the pron. 1 Co. 15¹¹, Eph. 4²⁰. — εἴληφας : the close connection with ἤκουσας seems to require this to be taken as the
aoristic perf. as in 5⁷, cf. Blass § 59, 4, Burton §§ 80 and 88.
— τήρει, μετανόησον, *keep (sc.* it), *repent:* the pres. of continued action, the aor. of a single act. — ἐὰν οὖν, *if therefore :*
i.e. in response to such a call to repentance. — ἥξω κτλ., *I will
come,* etc.: a special visitation may be meant as in 2²² ⁻ᶠ, or the
eschatological coming ; the latter is the meaning in the other
places where this comparison with a thief is used (16¹⁵, Mt.
24⁴³, Lk. 12³⁹, 1 Thess. 5², 2 Pet. 3¹⁰), but with a figure taken
from so familiar experience, that cannot be altogether decisive
for the present passage. — ὥραν : for the acc. in this word to
denote the time at which something occurs, see Blass § 34, 8 ;
it is common in classical Gk. also, cf. Kühn. II. 410, 5, A. 15.

4. The severe tone of the message is here softened by the recognition of those members of the Sardian church, few in number, who have kept themselves free from the taint of the surrounding pagan society. — ὀνόματα, *names : i.e.* persons ; cf. 11¹³, Ac. 1¹⁵. — οὐκ ἐμόλυναν κτλ., *have not defiled,* etc. : have not sullied their Christian character. It is doubtful whether the significance of the figure should be limited to unchastity, as many take it ; the language in 7¹⁴, 22¹⁴ would suggest rather contamination in general, suffered through yielding in contact with the life in Sardis ; cf. Jude 23. — περιπατήσουσιν μετ' ἐμοῦ, *shall walk (about) with me :* the words express intimate fellowship with the Lord, as companions in the messianic kingdom. — ἐν λευκοῖς, *in white :* white garments, especially appropriate here as symbolical of purity, are a standing characteristic of the blessed and of heavenly beings, as garments of glory ; cf. 7⁹,¹³, Dan. 7⁹, Mt. 28³ ; cf. also on garments of glory 2 Es. 2³⁹, En. 62¹⁵, Slav. En. 22⁸. No special reference, as *e.g.* to the priesthood of the redeemed, or the resurrection body, is to be sought here. In this passage, as in v. 20 and 2¹⁰, an eschatological promise is introduced before that connected with the formula ὁ νικῶν, *he that overcometh.* — ἄξιοι, *worthy: i.e.* to receive the gift of God, a gift of his grace, not the wage of works, Eph. 2⁸.

5. From the recognition of the few unsullied ones in the Sardian church the Lord turns to every one who in the end shall prove himself a victor over evil. The promise in its opening words is similar to that given to the 'few' of v. 4. But the close companionship contained in the words 'walk about with me' is not declared in the general words 'shall be arrayed in white raiment.' The part of the promise given in these words is especially appropriate to the victor over the corruption of the life at Sardis. Two other blessings are specified in the promise : (*a*) an indelible place in the book of eternal life, in contrast with the spiritual death into which the Sardians are now sinking, v. 1 ; (*b*) an acknowledgment of the victor's name, *i.e.* as a follower of Christ, before God and the angels in the day of judgment, in contrast with the judgment of condemnation now falling upon the readers' failure, v. 2. — οὕτως, *thus :* if this be the correct reading, it is best taken, *in this manner, i.e.* in

the manner spoken of in the words, 'in white'; these words
are then to be considered as added afterward in apposition with
οὕτως to make definite the meaning.

Some render οὕτως *likewise*, the victor likewise, as well as the unsullied,
shall be clothed in white; but in that case ὁμοίως, or ὡσαύτως would be used;
and this would imply a certain distinction between the ὁ νικῶν and the unsullied, whereas the latter must be included in the former; moreover any
blending of the class introduced by the formula ὁ νικῶν with the preceding
sentence is at variance with the usage of all the other epistles. The difficulty would be avoided if with many com. we could understand οὕτως to
repeat the partic. νικῶν, *thus*, *i.e.* as being a conqueror, a use common in
classical Gk. and found also in the N. T., *e.g.* Ac. 20¹¹, 27¹⁷. But this use
of οὕτως belongs to a predicate partic., which has the nature of an adv.; it
does not occur with the partic. preceded by the art. which is a substantive;
for the repetition of this substantive partic. οὗτος or ἐκεῖνος is used, *e.g.* Mt.
10²², Jno. 15⁵, cf. Buttm. p. 306, Win. § 23, 4. These difficulties raise the
question whether in spite of superior authority for οὕτως (see text. note)
the reading οὗτος should not be adopted.

τῆς βίβλου τῆς ζωῆς, *the book of life:* the idea of a book, or
books, containing the names of those who are to be members of
the kingdom of glory, or a record of men's deeds which shall
determine their destiny at the judgment, is too common in the
Scriptures and apocalyptic writings to need illustration (cf.
Bouss. *Judenthum* 247); for the Rev. cf. 13⁸, 17⁸, 20¹², ¹⁵, 21²⁷.
To keep the name of one in this book is to assure him of eternal
life. For the applicability to the Sardians of this part of the
promise see above. — ὁμολογήσω κτλ., *will acknowledge his name*,
etc.: the words are a reminiscence, almost a quotation, of the
saying of the Lord which is recorded in the Gospels, Mt. 10³²,
Lk. 12⁸, 9²⁶, Mk. 8³⁸. The meaning is, as seen from the Gospels, that the Lord will acknowledge his followers when he
comes with the angelic hosts in the day of judgment. The saying is such as would often be repeated and recorded; we cannot
infer from the passage an acquaintance with our written Gospels on the Apocalyptist's part, however probable such acquaintance may be. On the relation of this part of the promise to
v. 2 see above.

Textual notes vv. 1–5. 1. See on 2¹. — 2. εμελλον אACP most min edd;
some min R read μελλει. — τα before εργα א PQ most min R Ti Blj Sod *al*,
wanting in A C Ws WH *al*; see Com. *in loc.* — μου after θεου, Unc most min

edd ; wanting in some min and vers R. — 3. After the first ηξω, ℵ Q most min some vers R add επι σε ; wanting in ACP most edd. — γνως ACP most min R many edd ; γνωση ℵQ many min Ti Tr WH mrg. — 5. ουτως ℵ*AC most min vers edd; ουτος ℵᶜPQ many min R Sod *al.*

III. 7–13.   *The message to the church in Philadelphia.*

Philadelphia, southeast of Sardis, a meeting point of great routes from the latter city, from the coast, and from inner parts of the province on the northeast and southeast, and itself situated in the midst of a fertile region, was a city of wealth and commercial importance. Its geographical position, which gave it access to so large a territory, is supposed by some to be alluded to in the 'open door' spoken of in the epistle (v. 8), but this is probably a misinterpretation (see note *in loc.*).   The church there is described as possessing little power (v. 8), *i.e.* as regards numbers, or wealth, or members of influence in the community, but its spiritual life receives the Lord's praise, with no addition of censure.   The Jews were actively hostile to the church, and certain movements instituted against it in the past had apparently been instigated by them.   But the Christians had met the trial with fidelity to the name of the Lord and with patient endurance (vv. 8, 10).   The enemies of the church were not within, in the person of false teachers, they were without ; and so far as appears from the epistle they were chiefly Jews.

The purpose of the message is first of all to forewarn the Christians of the great trial, the 'messianic woes,' soon to come upon all the earth, to exhort them to hold fast in their fidelity, and to encourage them with promises of the future — promises of their sure deliverance (v. 10), of their certain admission into the messianic kingdom (v. 7), of an eternally enduring place in that kingdom, and an open recognition of them as the people of God and the Messiah (v. 12).   At the same time the readers are assured that the Jews themselves, or at least some of them, who are now their bitterest opponents will in the end come to do them homage as the beloved of the Messiah (v. 9).   This epistle is singularly interesting in that it touches the question which must have perplexed every Christian Jew, the attitude of God's ancient people toward Christianity, and their ultimate relation to the coming kingdom of the Messiah.   St. Paul in the epistle to the Romans had discussed the subject at considerable length (chaps. 9–11). Our author here takes it up from a different standpoint, and in a single concrete case; yet this case is viewed in an eschatological light and thus becomes typical of a whole class (see on v. 9, and 11¹⁻¹³). The subject forms a prominent topic in this, the most distinctly eschatological of the seven epistles. A glimpse is opened into the attitude of the Jews, arrogant in their claim to be the people of God and heirs of the Davidic kingdom of glory, contemning Jesus as a false Messiah (see on v. 7) and persecuting those that confessed his name. Over against this picture stands the Lord announcing himself the true Messiah, who bears the key of David's house, that is, supreme power over the messianic kingdom to admit or exclude whom he will; to his own the door will be open and none, no Jew, no scribe nor Pharisee, as now (Mt. 23¹³) will be able to shut it (v.8). At the same time, in language borrowed from the prophets, foretelling that the Gentiles shall come to bow themselves at the feet of Israel, the Lord declares to his faithful ones that in the last days a remnant of Jews will come to honor them, and recognizing him as the true Messiah will recognize them as the special objects of his love (v. 9). As Lord of that coming kingdom he will write upon the final victors those names which will show that they, and not the unbelieving Jews, belong to Jehovah as the true people of God, to the new Jerusalem, and to the glorified messianic king (v. 12).

7. On the 'Angel,' see on 1²⁰. — ὁ ἅγιος, *the Holy One:* the title elsewhere in the book given to God (4⁸, 6¹⁰) is here attributed to Christ, and as shown by the added words, 'he that hath the key of David,' etc., it is used as a designation of him in his messianic character; ὁ ἅγιος, ὅr ὁ ἅγιος τοῦ θεοῦ, *the holy one*, or *the holy one of God*, was one of the recognized titles of the Messiah; cf. Mk. 1²⁴, Lk. 4³⁴, Jno. 6⁶⁹, 1 Jno. 2²⁰, Clem. Rm. 23⁵, cf. also Ac. 4²⁷, ³⁰. It characterizes him, not in his sinlessness, but as the one especially set apart, belonging exclusively, to God; as 'the anointed one' he is uniquely 'the consecrated one.' The interpretation in the EV misses the messianic reference. — ὁ ἀληθινός, *the true one: i.e.* the true Messiah. Here as in general ἀληθινός is to be distinguished from ἀληθής;

the latter denotes what is *truthful*, the former what is *genuine*, *true to the idea;* here the one who is truly 'the holy one,' the true Messiah, as distinguished from a false one; cf. 'the true light,' 'the true God,' Jno. 1⁹, 1 Jno. 5²⁰. The word is frequent in the Johannine writings, occurring 23 times, in the rest of the N. T. 5 times. — ὁ ἔχων κτλ., *he that hath the key,* etc.: the epithet is taken from Is. 22²², where the words refer to Eliakim, who is to receive the key as the chief steward of the royal household ; as the king's representative he is authorized to exercise full administrative power in the palace in the king's name (cf. Mt. 16¹⁹). The passage in Isaiah appears to have received a messianic interpretation with the Jews, and it is used here to express the Lord's supreme power in the messianic kingdom to open or close its door as he will; cf. Heb. 3⁶, Mt. 28¹⁸. The 'key of David' is the key of David's house, *i.e.* the Messiah's kingdom. The epithet given to Christ at the opening of this epistle, like that in the following epistle, v. 14, and in part also in the preceding one, v. 1, is not taken from the vision of 1²⁰ ᶠᶠ·, but from a thought prominent in the author's mind and expressed elsewhere in the book ; Christ is the Davidic Messiah, who will receive his own to share in his kingdom, cf. 2²⁶, 3²¹, 5⁵, 19¹¹⁻¹⁶, 20⁴, 22¹⁶. The close connection of the epithet with the topic of the epistle is apparent. While the Jews, whose hostility is prominently in view, denied that Jesus was the Messiah, and claimed that they alone, and not his followers, could have part in the final kingdom of David, these opening words on the contrary declare the Lord's true Messiahship, and his power in the coming reign of glory to open the door to his own and to close it to the self-styled 'children of the kingdom.'

8. σοῦ τὰ ἔργα, *thy works:* for the meaning of 'works' see on 2². The special meaning is given in the clause ὅτι μικρὰν κτλ., *namely that thou hast little power and yet,* etc. The intervening words ἰδοὺ δέδωκα κτλ., *behold I have set before thee,* etc., form a parenthesis.

This punctuation, adopted by most com., is certainly correct, for in all the epistles in which the formula οἶδά σου τὰ ἔργα, vague in itself, occurs there follow explanatory words, either a clause introduced by ὅτι, or nouns in apposition. The connection of the ὅτι clause with the sentence immediately preceding, and giving a reason (Düst.), yields no proper sense, especially in view of the words ἦν οὐδεὶς . . . αὐτήν. The same may be said of the connection of the clause with v. 9 to introduce a ground for what is prophesied.

θύραν ἠνεῳγμένην, *a door opened :* the figure of an open door is used in the N. T. to denote (1) opportunity for an effective preaching of the gospel, cf. 1 Co. 16⁹, 2 Co. 2¹², Col. 4³; (2) an admission into a place or state, cf. Rev. 3²⁰, 4¹, Acc. 14²⁷, Jno. 10⁷, ⁹. The first use is spoken of as a Pauline contribution to Christian phraseology (Deissmann, *Licht v. Osten* 225, thinks he took it from some popular Gk. usage), but the figure is one that suggests itself so readily that its origin need not be attributed to any single writer. We are pretty certainly right in taking the words here in the *second* sense ; the Lord promises to the Philadelphians as a reward of their fidelity a sure entrance into his kingdom, he has put before them an open door, which no one can shut.

Many com. suppose the first sense to be intended here, the meaning being then that the Lord will open to the Philadelphians an opportunity to win many converts, and as some take it from the Jews, whose accession to their church is thought to be predicted in v. 9. But such a reference to future missionary activity of the church is singularly out of place, thrust in as a parenthesis between the parts of a sentence concerned with a commendation of the church for its steadfastness in the past. In fact the work of spreading the gospel is not one of the activities urged upon the Church in these epistles, nor is it indeed in the book in general; and naturally so, since the author's chief purpose is to help the Church to pass through the great trials about breaking upon it. On the other hand the *second* meaning is appropriate and is suggested by the context; the recognition of the fidelity of the Philadelphian church, expressed summarily in the words, *I know thy works*, leads easily to an immediate announcement of the final reward of their fidelity in an assured admission into the Messiah's kingdom. This interpretation is confirmed by several considerations. (*a*) The words, *I have set before thee a door opened which no one can shut*, are evidently adapted from the preceding verse; they describe this act as one of those acts of opening and shutting there spoken of, *i.e.* as an act belonging to the eschatological kingdom. (*b*) The emphatic words, *no one can shut*, refer clearly to opposition to that which is offered in the promise of the open door; this is most easily understood of Jewish hostility, which would shut out all Gentiles from the messianic kingdom. (*c*) The strongly marked eschatological tone of this epistle favors this interpretation. The prophecy of v. 9 is likewise probably to be understood to relate to the Last Days; see note there.

δέδωκα, *have set*, lit. *have given:* the word is chosen to suit what is promised as a *gift.* — αὐτήν : repeating pleonastically the rel. ἥν, a Heb. idiom common in the N. T., see Blass § 50, 4, Win § 22, 4, *b.* — ὅτι . . . δύναμιν κτλ.: *namely that thou hast little* (not *a* little) *power,* etc.: explaining τὰ ἔργα, *thy works;* see above. The words μικρὰν ἔχεις δύναμιν could not alone form a part of the τὰ ἔργα, as this phrase is used in the epistles ; they are subordinate to the following, the sense being, *though thou hast little power, yet thou didst keep my word,* etc. For this use of καί connecting clauses as coördinate where one of them is really subordinate and where καίτοι might be expected see Kühn. II. 521, 4, Thayer *s.v.* I. 2, e. — μικράν, *little :* said, not of spiritual weakness, for the church is praised throughout, but with reference to its opponents ; it is perhaps small in numbers, or in members of wealth, or influence. — ἐτήρησας, οὐκ ἠρνήσω, *didst keep, didst not deny:* the aor. shows that a definite past event is meant, some experience of trial brought upon the church, probably through the Jews, as the context would suggest.

9. Mention of persecution on the part of the Jews leads directly to the prophecy that some of those who are now the bitterest enemies of the Christians will come to do homage to them and acknowledge that they are the beloved of the Christ. For the language 'synagogue of Satan,' 'say they are Jews and are not,' see on 2⁹. — διδῶ, *I give :* for the form, instead of δίδωμι, see Blass § 23, 3, WH. *Select Readings,* p. 167. The word is appropriate because the homage will come as a gift from God. The obj. of the vb. is not given in full in this clause ; the thought is completed, with changed construction, in the clause ποιήσω αὐτοὺς κτλ., *I will make them to come,* etc. — ἐκ τῆς συναγωγῆς : for this idiom, equivalent to *some of the synagogue,* etc., see on 2¹⁰. — τῶν λεγόντων : in apposition with συναγωγῆς. — ἑαυτούς : see on 2⁹. — ποιήσω αὐτοὺς κτλ., *I will make them come,* etc.: this prophecy, like the utterance regarding the open door in v. 8, is to be understood of events belonging to the Last Days. In form the words echo those of the prophets telling of the coming of the Gentiles to do homage to the people of Israel and acknowledge Israel's God, when the final kingdom of glory shall be set up in the land. 'The sons

2 ɪ

of them that afflicted thee shall come bending unto thee; and all they that despised thee shall bow themselves down at the soles of thy feet,' Is. 60¹⁴; 'They shall fall down unto thee . . . saying God is in thee,' Is. 45¹⁴; cf. also Is. 2³, 49²³, Zec. 8²⁰ ᶠᶠ·, Ps. 72⁹. The prophetic utterances telling of the Gentiles' acknowledgment of Jehovah and Israel in the last times suggest to the Apocalyptist fitting words for the familiar N. T. prophecy that Israel, now an enemy, will in the end be gathered into the Church. See pp. 588.ff. The promise here is addressed directly to the church at Philadelphia. But as a part of what the Spirit saith in all the epistles to the Church universal, it is typical; it has a general significance, as follows from its eschatological nature; it looks forward to the time when the whole Church is about to be brought into the messianic kingdom.

Many com. take the prophecy to mean that a large number of Jews are about to be added to the Philadelphian church as a result of the missionary activity thought to be referred to in v. 8. But apart from the probable misinterpretation of that passage (see note there), the words here adopted from the prophets were current eschatological language, and the description here given of the humble homage to be paid is hardly appropriate in reference to a congregation of Christian brethren. Paul's language, 1 Co. 14²⁵, πεσὼν ἐπὶ πρόσωπον προσκυνήσει, cited to prove the appropriateness, is quite different; he is speaking of an adoration of God, not of the Corinthian congregation. But, as pointed out above, the predominant eschatological tone of the epistle, and the absence from all the epistles of reference to contemporaneous work of evangelization is opposed to the interpretation. Ignatius in his epistle to the Philadelphians, written in the next generation, warns them against the error of Judaistic teaching (chapt. 6), and this is thought by some to show the presence of a large number of Jews in the church there, perhaps brought in by missionary activity. The inference, however, is not justified, for he also warns them urgently against divisions, but at the same time says he found no divisions among them (chapt. 3). The two evils were such as were likely to befall any of the churches addressed and Ignatius not improbably saw special danger of them at Philadelphia.

ἵνα ἥξουσιν, γνῶσιν: for ἵνα with fut. ind. or a subjv. in place of an infin. see Blass § 65, 2, Burton § 205. — ἐγὼ ἠγάπησά σε, *I have loved thee:* perhaps a reminiscence of Is. 43⁴. The aor. is used from the standpoint of the convinced Jew who at the end looks back upon the present period; and the love of

Christ is viewed as an act without reference to its continuance ;
see on 2²⁵. ἐγώ is emphatic — I, the true Messiah.

10. τὸν λόγον τῆς ὑπομονῆς μου, *the word of my steadfastness :*
the meaning is clearly the loyal steadfastness of the Philadelphians, shown in certain persecutions which they had suffered ;
but the precise construction is not certain. The two nouns
may form a compound expression, the pron. μοῦ depending on
the whole : *my steadfastness-command, i.e.* my command to be
steadfast. Or better perhaps μοῦ may be joined with ὑπομονῆς,
the meaning being the word enjoining Christ's steadfastness,
either that like his, or that which he requires; cf. τὴν ὑπομονὴν
τοῦ Χριστοῦ, 2 Thess. 3⁵, which has the same ambiguity. For
other constructions hardly calling for discussion here see Düst.,
Alford. — τηρήσω, *I will keep :* corresponding with ἐτήρησας,
thou didst keep. — ἐκ τῆς ὥρας τοῦ πειρασμοῦ κτλ., *from the
hour of trial,* etc. : in the interpretation of this difficult sentence it should be observed, (1) that πειρασμός, πειράζω, *trial,
try,* always include the idea of *testing.* (2) This idea of testing
shows that the words ἡ οἰκουμένη ὅλη, *the whole world,* upon
which the trial is to come, refer, not to the physical world,
but to men ; *all mankind* is meant, as in 12⁹. (3) The second
clause, *to try them that dwell on the earth,* which merely repeats
the first (after the writer's manner, cf. p. 241), must be understood likewise of mankind universally, Christians and non-
Christians alike. The phrase οἱ κατοικοῦντες ἐπὶ τῆς γῆς, *those
that dwell on the earth,* is common in apocalyptic writings, and
for the most part refers to the wicked (because the 'world' at
large is thought of as hostile to God); sometimes the good are
meant, as in En. 37², 40⁶ ; sometimes all mankind, as in En. 70¹ ;
so here. It appears, then, a certain inference that the trial
spoken of in our passage is that of the distresses, the 'messianic woes,' foretold in the following visions as coming upon the
world before the parousia. These are not to test the saints
only ; our author distinctly recognizes the 'woes' as testing
the wicked also, and as designed to lead to repentance, see on
9²⁰, cf. also 11¹³, 16¹¹. Does the promise then mean that the
Philadelphians, or any of the saints, are to be exempted from
these trials ? Elsewhere our book, like the eschatological chapters in the Gospels, represents the 'woes' as coming on all the

saints alike; cf. 7¹⁴, 13¹⁰, 14¹², Mt. 24⁷⁻¹³, ²², par.   And this is
implied in the case of the Philadelphians in the immediate context; the words 'hold fast, that no one take thy crown,' the
condition of the promise 'he that overcometh,' etc., imply the
continuance of the struggle till the Lord comes.   In fact the
language of the promise, 'keep thee from the hour,' etc., if
taken strictly, does not mean the contrary; the ὥρα, the *hour*,
the *period*, or *season*, of the woes is one from which none could
be kept, all living must pass through it.   The true meaning of
the promise is suggested by the analogous words, Jno. 17¹⁵,
'I pray not that thou shouldest take them from the world, but
that thou shouldest keep them from the evil one' (τηρήσῃς
αὐτοὺς ἐκ τοῦ πονηροῦ), *i.e.* safe from the power of Satan, which
will continually assail them.   The Philadelphians and those
who have shown the same Christian steadfastness are promised
that they shall be carried in safety through the great trial, they
shall not fall.   For ὥρα, *hour*, = *a period* or *season*, cf. Jno. 5³⁵,
16², 1 Jno. 2¹⁸.

To the above interpretation the objection is raised (Bouss. Blj. *al*) that
testing can be understood of Christians only, and that therefore the trial
spoken of must refer to some predicted calamity which will try the saints,
not the world, such as the reign of the Beast, or the Roman persecutions.
From this trial the Philadelphians are promised exemption, while the saints
in general, to whom the words 'those that dwell on the earth' are specifically referred, must pass through it.   The Philadelphians have already
stood their fiery test and will be spared the stress and storm about to come
upon the others.   Answer to this argument is contained in what is said
above.   The further objection to the interpretation adopted above is made,
that the promise would contain nothing as the peculiar reward apparently
offered to the Philadelphians.   But the language does not imply any reward
peculiar to the Philadelphians as contrasted with others who had shown like
fidelity; the persons addressed are, as in all the epistles, typical, and the
same promise would be expected in the case of any whose present steadfastness made them worthy of this assured succor in the severe trial of the
future.

11. ἔρχομαι ταχύ, *I come quickly:* the keynote of the book.
It comes in with warning to the unfaithful and with encouragement to the faithful; the latter is intended here, the time of
patient endurance is short.—ὃ ἔχεις, *what thou hast:* see on
2²⁵. —στέφανον, *crown:* see on 2¹⁰.

12. ὁ νικῶν : nom. abs. repeated in αὐτόν, which conforms to the construction. — στῦλον, *a pillar ;* the reference here, as in the promise to the victor in all the epistles, is to the eschatological kingdom, not to the present; this is further shown by the mention of the new Jerusalem and the new name. The temple then and the pillar are figurative, and all reference to the historic Church or to office and position in it (so, some older com.) is excluded. The pillar is a common symbol of that which supports, cf. Gal. 2⁹, 1 Tim. 3¹⁵, a use, however, inappropriate here in reference to the heavenly temple. It is also used of that which is itself firmly fixed, Jer. 1¹⁸. The added words, *shall go out no more,* show this to be the meaning here; cf. Is. 22²³, 56⁵. There is nothing to indicate that the idea of the beauty of the column which some com. find here is thought of. The frequency and severity of earthquakes at Philadelphia (Strabo XIII. 628) might lend force to the figure in this place, but it is doubtful whether it was thus directly suggested. — οὐ μὴ ἐξέλθῃ, ἐπ' αὐτόν, *he shall not go out, upon him:* a return from the figure to the person. Some, however, suppose the figure of the pillar to be continued still ; *it shall not be removed, upon it.* The latter understanding of the words would lend itself more easily to the view that the figure of writing the name is derived from a local religious custom, according to which the provincial priest of the emperor-worship at the close of his year of office erected in the temple precinct' his statue, and inscribed upon it his name, and that of his father and his home, and the date of his office. The victor's priestly character might thus be indicated (Bouss. Moffatt). But the inscription here given is too dissimilar, and the circumstances of the victor entering triumphantly into the eternal kingdom are too unlike those of the priest passing out of all relation to the temple, to justify a comparison. Besides, there is in the context no allusion to the priestly character of the victor. (Cf. Blj. *in loc.*)

γράψω ἐπ' αὐτὸν τὸ ὄνομα κτλ., *I will write upon him the name,* etc.: the significance of the figure is shown by the following words, 'the name of the city . . . the new Jerusalem' ; the victor is marked as belonging to, as a citizen of, the new Jerusalem, so the other clauses mean that he will bear names which will mark him as *belonging to* God and Christ. There is in the passage no intimation of a talismanic power in the name, such as is found elsewhere : see on 2^{17}. For the inscription of the name of God and of Christ on the saints cf. $14^1, 22^4$; cf. also the name of the beast written upon his followers to mark them as his, $13^{17}, 14^{17}$. The fullness of this utterance declaring that the victor shall be marked as belonging to God, to the messianic city, and to the Messiah in his perfected glory, sets him in emphatic contrast with the assumptions of his present Jewish persecutors. On the new Jerusalem cf. $21^{2, 10 \text{ ff.}}$; see pp. 55 ff. — ἡ καταβαίνουσα : for the nom. see p. 224. — τὸ ὄνομά μου τὸ καινόν, *my new name :* the new name cannot be any of those now known ; it must be that which belongs to him in the *new* state of his completed messianic work, doubtless the name 'which no one knoweth but himself,' 19^{12} (see note there and on 2^{17}). The newness of the capital city and of Christ's name is made prominent, because the promise is wholly concerned with the new order of the messianic age. — τοῦ θεοῦ μου, *my God :* the repetition of the words with each phrase emphasizes the certainty of the Lord's promise. ' *His* God will bestow upon *his* servants the glory belonging to them,' Blj. 53. For μοῦ, *my*, in the phrase cf. v. 2 ; see on 1^6.

Textual notes. vv. 7–12. 7. On the address see on 2^1. — ο αγιος ο αληθινος CPQ most min and vers R edd ; ο αληθινος ο αγιος אAWHmrg. — For Δαυειδ, some min give αδου, a conjecture from 1^{18}. — C some min R WHmrg read κλειει for κλειων. — 8. ηνεωγμενην אP many min edd ; ανεωγμενην ACQ most min R Sw. — αυτην wanting in א. — 9. διδω AC most edd ; διδωμι PQ min R Sod.; δεδωκα א. — ηξουσιν, προσκυνησουσιν אACP many min edd ; ηξωσιν, προσκυνησωσιν Q some min R Sod. — 12. η καταβαινουσα אACP min edd ; η καταβαινει Q many min ; της καταβαινουσης אᶜ many min.

III. 14–22. *The message to the church in Laodicea.* Laodicea in Phrygia southeast of Philadelphia in the valley of the Lycus (a tributary of the Meander), located at the junction of several branches of the great trade-road from Ephesus to the East, was an important commercial city ; it was also the judicial seat of the district, it formed a center of banking operations and carried on extensive manufacturing in articles made from the native wool famous for its glossy black. Its large wealth is shown in its refusal of the imperial grant made to the cities of

this region, which had been visited by a disastrous earthquake
in 60 A.D.   A Jewish element of strength existed in the community, but nothing is said in the epistle of their attitude
toward the Christians.   Asklepios was worshipped at Laodicea,
and the school of physicians connected with his temple was well
known.   It has been conjectured that they had repute as
oculists ; at all events the ' Phrygian powder ' (τέφρα Φρυγία),
a remedy for weak eyes, must have been known, if not manufactured there.   These circumstances of the community may in
some particulars have suggested the phraseology of the epistle
to the church there (see on v. 17).   The church at Laodicea
formed with its near neighbors at Hierapolis and Colossæ the
little group of churches known to us through the epistles of St.
Paul (Col. 2¹, 4¹³, ¹⁵, ¹⁶).   He directed that two of his epistles
should be sent to Laodicea (Col. 4¹⁶), the Colossian epistle,
and another which has been lost unless it survives in the so-
called epistle to the Ephesians.   (On this church see Lightfoot,
Col. pp. 1–70).

At the time of the writing of our book the Laodicean church,
so far as the epistle shows, was not troubled with persecutions
from without, nor with false teachers within.   What called for
this special message was the lukewarm condition of the church,
which receives the Lord's censure unqualified by any commendation.   At Sardis, which stands next to Laodicea in the severe
judgment pronounced upon it, there were a few members of the
church who had maintained an integrity duly recognized by
the Lord.   At Laodicea the entire church is sharply censured.
The geographical position of Laodicea on the roads connecting the seven churches may explain why it stands last in the
list, yet this place falls in with the writer's habit of introducing
praise before censure (see p. 260).   The particular phase of
the church's lukewarmness taken up in the message is indifference to higher spiritual attainment, its complete satisfaction
with its present condition.   In its own eyes it already possesses
all the spiritual gifts of knowledge and Christian character
— it is rich and in need of nothing (v. 17).   Out of this the
most hopeless of spiritual states the Lord seeks to arouse the
church by sharp words of censure, even by an expression of
loathing (v. 16).   The language used in the beginning would

imply that their doom was already sealed; 'I am about to spew thee out of my mouth.' Yet the Lord turns to counsel, as if there were still hope (v. 18), and then lest the church should be borne down by despair begotten by his stinging reproof, he passes on to words of love and a promise of tenderest favor (vv. 19–20). The epithet of Christ in v. 14, and the promise to the victor in v. 21 do not seem to be suggested directly by the condition of the Laodiceans; they are appropriate in any of the epistles. But as in the case of the corresponding parts of the opening epistle (see on $2^{1,7}$), they have through their fundamental character a place especially fitting in the epistle that closes the series.

14. ὁ ἀμήν, *the Amen:* the Heb. adv. *Amen* used in different relations in the Scriptures (cf. En. Bib. I, Hast. I, *s.v.*) expresses the idea of *affirmation, verity.* With the art. it becomes a substantive (2 Co. 1^{20}), and it is here a personal designation, denoting the one in whom verity is personified; cf. Is. 65^{16}, 'the God of Amen' (LXX τὸν θεὸν τὸν ἀληθινόν). Some find in our passage a reminiscence of the Lord's frequent use of the phrase 'verily I say' etc. The designation as used here is made specific in the words immediately added in apposition; the *verity* referred to is that of the *witness,* who is trustworthy (πιστός) and true to the ideal of a witness (ἀληθινός, see on v. 7). This part of the epithet applied to Christ is meant to guarantee the certain truth of the revelation given by him, whether in this epistle or elsewhere in the book. Cf. 1^5, $19^{9, 11}$, 21^5, 22^6.

ἡ ἀρχὴ τῆς κτίσεως, *the beginning of the creation:* grammatically these words can mean the first of created existences, cf. ἀρχὴ τέκνων, Gen. 49^3, Dt. 21^{17}. But that interpretation, adopted by many, is at variance with the Christology of our author, which makes Christ eternal (1^{18}, 2^8), and distinguishes him from every created thing as the object of worship paid to him in common with the Father (5^{13}), while worship of an angelic being is forbidden (19^{10}). The words mean rather *the one from whom creation took its beginning,* i.e. through whom it came into being; not the creator as the primary source, for that is God in our book (4^{11}, 10^6), as elsewhere in the Scriptures, but the creative agent of God, as in Jno. 1^3, Col. 1^{16},

Heb. 1². The agreement with the epistle to the Colossians in the doctrine here given is probably not accidental, since that epistle must have been well known in the churches of the valley of the Lycus; see on 1⁵.

For a similar use of ἀρχή = αἰτία, the 'incipient cause' see Wis. 12¹⁶, where strength is called δικαιοσύνης ἀρχή; ibid. 14²⁷, the worship of idols is παντὸς ἀρχὴ κακοῦ καὶ αἰτία; cf. also ibid. 6¹⁷, 14¹²; for other examples cf. Thayer s.v. Compare also the parallel use of τέλος, Ro. 10⁴, said of Christ who brings to an end law as a means of attaining righteousness. Some take ἀρχή in our passage to mean Head, Lord; but for that idea ἄρχων would be used, cf. 1⁵. See on the passage Holtzm. Theol. I. 546 f.; Weiss Theol. 556.

Since Christ's creative relation to the world does not form one of the topics of this epistle, or of the book in general, these words are probably meant to express the *preëxistence* of Christ before all creation (cf. Holtzm. *Theol.* I. 547), *i.e.*, one aspect of that eternal existence emphasized in his self-designation, cf. 1¹⁷, 2⁸, 21⁶, 22¹³. The words then, like the fuller phrase, ' I am the beginning and the end,' assert the majesty of the Lord in his eternal being, and so they form a part of the epithet which stands fittingly at the opening of any of the epistles, but especially of this one in which the series is brought to an end; cf. p. 488.

15. **τὰ ἔργα**, *thy works:* explained by the following clause; see on 2¹. — φυχρός, ζεστός, *cold, hot:* the figures are meant to give vividness to the principal figure, *lukewarmness*, describing the condition of the Laodiceans. It is therefore unnecessary to inquire (so, some com.) precisely who are meant by the 'cold,' whether unbelievers, active enemies, backsliding Christians, etc.; the word characterizes persons indifferent about their religious state; but there is more hope of arousing such than those who, like the Laodiceans, believing themselves already rich in Christian gifts, are in a state of complacency. Hence the wish ' would that thou wert cold.' — For the use of ὄφελον in a wish see Blass § 63, 5; Burton § 27.

16. **οὕτως**, *so, therefore:* repeated in the following ὅτι clause. For this use of οὕτως cf. Ro. 1¹⁵, L & S. *s.v.* — χλιαρός, *lukewarm:* the precise meaning of the figure as used here is made clear in vv. 17–18. The Laodiceans are not altogether indif-

ferent to their spiritual state, they are not ' dead ' like most of
the church at Sardis, but they are entirely satisfied with themselves and their low plane of Christian attainment, they flatter
themselves that they are ' good Christians' and have no spiritual
lack. Hence they are *lukewarm* toward the call to vigorous spiritual activity. — μέλλω σε ἐμέσαι, *I will spew thee out :* the words
have the sound of final rejection as already fixed, but the assurance of love still continuing in chastisement, and the exhortation to repentance and zealousness given in v. 19 show that the
language is meant to awaken the Laodiceans to their imminent
danger. The strong figure of tepid water causing nausea is
used to open their eyes to the Lord's abhorrence of their present attitude.

17. πλούσιος, *rich :* reference is made, not to material wealth,
but to the spiritual state; this interpretation is required by the
following words οὐκ οἶδας κτλ., *thou dost not know,* etc., which are
meant to set the real in contrast with the supposed state, and
which are entirely figurative. The persons addressed are not
the citizens of Laodicea in general, famed for their wealth, but
the Christians, who may, or may not, have been rich. — πεπλού-
τηκα; for the hysteron-proteron see p. 243. — σὺ εἶ ὁ ταλαίπωρος κτλ., *thou art the wretched,* etc.: *i.e.* thou (emphatic), with all
thy supposed spiritual riches, art really the poor man. The art.
is generic; cf. Jno. 3¹⁰, Blass § 47, 3. — ταλαίπωρος, ἐλεεινός
κτλ., *wretched, pitiable,* etc.: general words, here with reference
to spiritual condition. — τυφλός, *blind :* often used of mental
blindness, *e.g.* Mt. 23¹⁷, and perhaps chosen here in anticipation
of the figure of ' eye-salve ' in v. 18; the inability of the Laodiceans to see their poverty is meant. — γυμνός, *naked :* cf. 16¹⁵.
The figure completes the picture of the actual poverty.

18. ἀγοράσαι παρ' ἐμοῦ κτλ., *buy of me,* etc.; cf. Is. 55¹. —
πεπυρωμένον, *refined :* see on 1¹⁵. — ἱμάτια λευκά, *white garments :*
possibly the figure is suggested by contrast with the black,
glossy garments manufactured at Laodicea (Ramsay), though
in that case we should expect in the following purpose clause
reference to such garments rather than to nakedness. — κολλού-
ριον, *eyesalve :* to be joined with ἀγοράσαι, not with ἐγχρῖσαι.
The figure is probably taken from the use of the well-known
' Phrygian powder ' at Laodicea (Ramsay). The ' gold,' ' gar-

ments,' 'eyesalve' correspond respectively with 'poor,' 'naked,' 'blind' of v. 17. A special symbolic significance is not to be sought in the several substantives; the meaning is simply that the great spiritual need is to be supplied by the gift of the Lord. — ἐγχρῖσαι : infin. of purpose parallel with the ἵνα clauses in the preceding, a change made in anticipation of the clause ἵνα βλέπῃς which is subordinate to ἐγχρῖσαι.

19. The tone of the message changes abruptly. The Lord assures the Laodiceans that his words of severe rebuke are the utterances of his chastening love, which seeks to train its object; cf. Prov. 3¹², Heb. 12⁶. — ἐγώ: emphatic; the way of the Lord is contrasted with that of others. — παιδεύω, train, discipline. — ζήλευε, be zealous : in contrast with their lukewarmness.

20. ἔστηκα ἐπὶ τὴν θύραν κτλ., I stand at the door, etc.: The exhortation of the preceding verse is enforced by the announcement of the Lord's Advent ; he is already before the gate; cf. Ja. 5⁹, Mt. 24³³, Lk. 12³⁶, Mk. 13²⁹. The eschatological reference of this sentence is made clear by the next clause, 'I will sup with thee' (see below), by the analogy of the other epistles, and by the language of the passages cited — this interpretation is generally adapted by recent com. The popular representation of Christ knocking at the door of men's hearts, though containing a great truth (Lk. 19¹⁰), is not what is intended here. — ἐάν τις ἀκούσῃ κτλ., if any one hear, etc.: the Lord wishes to find his children ready to receive him when he comes; with those who open the door at his call he will enter into the most intimate fellowship. — δειπνήσω μετ' αὐτοῦ κτλ., I will sup with him, etc.: eating together is a common symbol of close companionship in the messianic kingdom (cf. Volz 331); cf. Lk. 22³⁰, Mt. 26²⁹, Mk. 14²⁵, 'They will eat with that Son of man,' En. 62¹⁴. Here the Messiah is represented as coming to the houses of his people (cf. Jno. 14²³). The promise continues the language of love and encouragement begun in v. 19. The symbol is altogether eschatological; there is no reference to the eucharist. — αὐτός: an emphatic he ; cf. Blass § 48, 1.

21. ὁ νικῶν: on the nom. see on 2²⁶. — δώσω αὐτῷ καθίσαι κτλ., I will give to him to sit, etc.: the familiar prophecy, that in the final kingdom the saints shall share in the Messiah's rule; see on 1⁶. The reward here set before the victor is the highest

possible dignity in the final kingdom. This promise then stands
with special appropriateness at the close of the series of epistles.
— τῷ θρόνῳ μου, *my throne:* this is also the Father's throne which
Christ shares, cf. 22¹. — ὡς κἀγὼ ἐνίκησα κτλ., *as I also overcame,*
etc.; the exaltation of Christ also is the reward of his victory; cf.
ἐγὼ νενίκηκα τὸν κόσμον, Jno. 16³³.   The Apocalyptist here in
vv. 20–21 brings together the two promises of eating with the
Messiah and sharing his rule, as does Lk. 22²⁹ ᶠ·.

Textual notes, vv. 14–20. 14. For the address see on 2¹. — Λαοδικια ℵAC
most edd; Λαοδικεια P Q Sod RV.   The latter is the form in Gk. writers
and inscriptions.   R with cursive 1 has Λαοδικεων.— Before αληθινος, ℵC min
insert o, bracketed by WH, omitted by most edd. — 17. ουδεν AC min most
edd; ουδενος ℵPQ min R Sod. — ελεεινος ℵPQ min R most edd; ελεινος AC
WH Sw. — 18. εγχρισαι (to be taken as infin., not imperat. as Ti accents it)
ℵAC min edd; εγχρισον P many min R. — 19. ζηλευε ACQ min edd;
ζηλωσον ℵPR. — 20. Before εισελευσομαι, ℵQ min Ti WHmrg Blj *al* insert
και, used through influence of Heb. idiom to introduce conclusion, cf.
Blass § 77, 6.

Criticism of chapts. II–III.   The extensive critical discussion which has
arisen over these chapters can be seen sufficiently for the present purpose in
a brief summary. Most critics are agreed that these seven epistles could never
have been seven detached letters sent to separate churches.   They are clearly
seen to belong together as parts of a single document or paragaph constructed by one author on a uniform plan (see p. 260); no one of them
is in complete epistolary form; and they are too brief to have formed in
each case an entire epistle, or to have been preserved and gathered up into
the carefully organized whole found here.   Nor on the other hand could
this group of letters have formed by itself an independent document existing apart from a setting, or framework.   It needs introduction and itself
points forward to some larger composition telling of the last things.   The
critical theories which attribute these two chapters in whole or in part to a
redactor or compiler, whether inserting here his own composition or taking material from some other document, may be grouped into two general
classes.

(1) The chapters were added by the last reviser of the Apocalypse to
adapt an earlier form or certain earlier documents to his special use, he was
himself the author of this part; so, Weizsäcker, Vischer, Völter, Pfleiderer,
Weyland, *al.*   In support of this view the principal arguments urged are :
(*a*) The epistles are of a hortatory character and not connected in form
with the plan of the book, nor in contents with the subject matter of the
visions which make up the book.   A sufficient answer to this objection is
that spoken of above (p. 259), the appropriateness, we might almost say the
necessity, of some such preliminary message to the Church to prepare it in
its spiritual state for the events foretold in the visions.   (*b*) The chapters

contain traces of an age later than other parts of the book ; *e.g.* monarchical episcopacy (the angels of the churches) ; the Lord's day, a term, it is said, unknown in this sense so early ; the Nicolaitans, a later school of Gnostics (cf. Völter, *Problem* 396 ff.). But the untenableness of this contention is shown in the notes on $1^{10, \ 20}$, $2^{14 \ f.}$. (*c*) The author of the epistles uses epithets and thoughts found in, sometimes made clear only through, other parts of the book (see for examples (*c*) in paragraph (2), below) ; thus showing that he had before him the rest of the book in complete form ; so, Völter, *Problem* 399 f., Vischer, 34, *al.* But this phenomenon tends to establish identity rather than diversity of authorship ; we see one mind expressing the great thoughts and using the imagery of the book as a whole. On the writer's habit of anticipation see p. 247. Especially difficult is it, except on the supposition of identity of authorship, to explain the selection from other parts of the book of the epithets given to Christ, which are appropriate in their places (see notes *in loc.*), but not always seen on the surface to be so.

(2) Other critics refer the epistles, in what they suppose to have been their original form, to one of the *earlier documents*, from which the author of our book has taken them and revised them for his present use; so, Spitta followed in the main by Erbes, Wellhausen, J. Weiss, *al.* The argument in its main lines runs as follows : The epistles are addressed, as shown by the opening of each, solely to the seven churches, and their contents are concerned with the special states and duties of these churches and with no others. As such they formed the introduction to a comparatively brief apocalyptic message sent to the narrow circle of these seven churches. The earlier date of this part is apparent. The churches addressed are, according to the epistles, facing internal troubles and troubles from the Jews, such as might have arisen *before* the Roman persecutions, but of these latter, so prominent in the book in its present form, nothing is known in the epistles (see J. Weiss, 38 f.). This earlier and purely local writing was transformed by a redactor to adapt it to reading before the whole Church (cf. Spitta, 41 ff.). The traces of his hand are apparent. (*a*) There is in the epistles no place for appeals or promises to the Church at large. Moreover, the promises to the victor at the close of the several epistles have no relation to the contents of the respective epistles or the condition of the particular church; these appeals and promises then are to be attributed to the reviser. (*b*) The words ' What the Spirit saith ' found in every epistle as describing its contents are too objective to suit the speech of a prophet in a state of ecstasy; they have the sound of a writer in a later generation, who is enforcing the word of an older prophet (J. Weiss, 37). (*c*) The promises at the close of the letters contain many reminiscences of later passages in the book; *e.g.* compare 2^7 with 22^2; 2^{11} with 20^{14}, 21^8; 2^{28} with 22^{16}; 3^{21} with 22^1. In answer to these arguments in support of (2), it is enough to refer to what has already been said. The seven churches are used typically and each epistle has beyond its local message a purpose for the whole Church (see pp. 209 f., 259) ; nothing short of a purely arbitrary expunging of essential parts can leave a form fundamentally different.

That the various promises in the epistles are especially appropriate to their places has been shown in the notes (*in loc.*). For evidence that the epistles take cognizance of Roman hostility to the Christians see pp. 206, 452 f, 458. Internal troubles occupy the foremost place in the epistles, because the Church must prepare itself for coming trouble by the correction of present evils. On the presence in the epistles of thoughts found in other parts of the book, see p. 493.

Sufficient grounds for accepting the epistles as an integral part of the plan and work of the author of our book may be briefly tabulated as follows: the appropriateness of such a paragraph in this place (cf. p. 259); agreement with the rest of the book in language, *i.e.* as regards vocabulary and grammatical construction, including syntactical errors (cf. pp. 222 ff.); agreement in thought and symbolism (besides the passages cited above, p. 493, compare 2^{17} with 19^{12}; $2^{26\,f.}$ with 20^4; 3^5 with 13^8, 20^{15}; 3^{12} with 21^{10}; the list could be increased); agreement in the combination of Jewish and Christian messianic conceptions; difficulty in supposing a passage of such spiritual and literary power to have been written by a mere compiler, or in supposing the chapters to have been wrenched out of some other setting and fitted into the present place. Bousset sums up his judgment as follows: 'Since the efforts to reconstruct a convincing Christian Ur-apocalypse are to be considered as having failed, there remains hardly anything else but to identify the author of the epistles with the writer who wrote the Apocalypse in its present form,' *Kom.* 128. This verdict agrees with some of the older representatives of the critical school, *e.g.* Sabatier and Schoen, and expresses what we may probably say is the growing tendency of cautious criticism at the present day.

Chapts. IV.–V. *The scene in the Court of Heaven.* See p. 261.

(1) God enthroned in heaven, and surrounded by the worshiping hosts of the angelic hierarchy. Chapt. 4.

1. μετὰ ταῦτα εἶδον, *after these things I saw:* this phrase, used also in $7^{1,\,9}$, 15^5, 18^1 (cf. μετὰ ταῦτα ἤκουσα 19^1), introduces a new vision, or at least a separate part of a vision, whereas καὶ ἰδού, καὶ εἶδον introduce a subordinate part of one and the same vision. The length of interval between two visions is not shown, as it is in 2 Es.; and it is doubtful whether this phrase can be pressed to indicate strictly the chronological order in which the visions were received ; for example, the insertion of the visions of $7^{1–17}$ between the sixth and seventh seals is not improbably due to the author's method of arranging in an organized literary plan visions received at different times. — **θύρα ἠνεῳγμένη,** *a door opened in heaven:* the door set open in the vault of the sky, here conceived as a solid firmament, is not

an opening through which the Seer might look from earth into
heaven; that idea would be expressed by the phrase, 'the
heavens were opened,' cf. Ezk. 1¹, Ac. 7⁵⁶, 10¹¹, Ap. Bar.
22¹; it is that to which the Seer is to come up (ἀνάβα), and either
pass through into the heavens, as does Enoch in Slav. En.
21-24, or stand before it beholding what is within, as do Enoch
in En. 14¹⁵⁻²⁵ and Levi in Test. Lev. 5.　For the nom. θύρα,
φωνή, with ἰδού, a common idiom in the N. T., see Blass § 33,
2, footnote, Buttm. p. 139. — ἡ φωνὴ κτλ., the voice, etc.: the
voice is identified with that which spoke in 1¹⁰; it is the voice
of Christ, see note there.　The introduction of Christ here as
the agent showing a vision (δείξω) of which he himself forms a
part, the Lamb (5⁶ᶠᶠ·), has raised difficulty with many com.;
but his function here is quite different from that of the angel,
for example, who carries the prophet away and shows him a
vision, as in 17³, 21¹⁰; he does not appear here, only his voice
is heard sounding out of heaven and summoning the prophet
up from earth; after the Seer's rapture, i.e. in the actual
vision itself, Christ does not take the part of one showing a
vision.　His words, 'I will show thee what must come to pass,'
are first fulfilled in the Lamb's act of breaking the seals.　This
passage then is not opposed to the reference of the voice of 1¹⁰
to Christ, as some com. suppose, see note on 1¹⁰.　At the same
time Christ's agency in the revelations of the book is here represented in the same way as in 1¹; it is through him that they
are all given, directly or indirectly; δείξω here repeats δεῖξαι
of 1¹. — λαλούσης: belonging with ἥν is attracted into the
construction of σάλπιγγος. — λέγων: with φωνή, const. ad. sens.
— ἀνάβα: for ἀνάβηθι, see Blass § 23, 4. — μετὰ ταῦτα, hereafter: as in 1¹⁹, which shows that the words are to be joined
with γενέσθαι, not with εὐθέως κτλ., as WH punctuate.

2.　εὐθέως ἐγενόμην ἐν πνεύματι, straightway I (came to be)
was in the Spirit: the language would seem to imply the beginning
of an ecstasy, whereas the Prophet has been represented in
such a state from 1¹⁰ on; it was in this state that he saw the
open door, and heard the voice (v. 1).　No author or compiler
even, who wrote as introductory to the vision verse 1, with its
implied ecstasy, could intend in the words of v. 2 the beginning
of an ecstasy.　The words are meant to include the immediate

sequel of the summons, that is, the Seer's rapture in the Spirit
into heaven, as well as the continuance of the ecstasy in which
he received the revelations following. But the thought is
expressed in a condensed form ; the Prophet is intent upon emphasizing the fact that all befell him under the influence of the
Spirit. Similar cases in which the influence of the Spirit
already present is again spoken of as if just beginning are
pointed out ; cf. Ezk. $11^{1,5}$, En. $71^{1,5}$. There is no intimation
(as some take it) that a mightier force of the Spirit comes
upon the Seer here, as if such were thought to be needed to lift
him to heaven. The language of this verse furnishes no evidence
that this was the beginning of the book (see p. 531). Spitta's
emendation and interpretation (63 f.) ἐφερόμην for ἐγενόμην,
'I was carried away by the wind,' are of value only as an illustration of the critic's manner. — θρόνος ἔκειτο κτλ., *a throne
stood in heaven*, etc.: heaven now opens before the Seer under
the form of a vast throne-room. The central figure is God
enthroned in great glory, surrounded by his court of angelic
principalities and powers in varying orders. The leading
features of the scene are those found in Is. $6^{1\,ff.}$, Ezk. 1^{26-28},
Dan. $7^{9\,f.}$, 1 K. 22^{19}, En. 39–40, Slav. En. 20–22, and elsewhere;
but they are here combined and handled with the power of a
master hand. No attempt is made to describe the person of
God; the glory of his form manifests itself in brilliant vari-
colored light, according to the Hebrew conception of Jehovah
dwelling in light (1 Tim. 6^{16}) and covering himself with light
as with a garment (Ps. 104^2).

3. ὁ καθήμενος, *he that sat:* in a passage conceived entirely
after the manner of the Heb. vision, the writer conforms to the
customary style of later times in avoiding the name of God; he
does not himself share this reluctance, as elsewhere with this
scene in mind he uses the name unhesitatingly, cf. $7^{10,\ 15}$, 12^5,
19^4. — ὅμοιος ὁράσει λίθῳ ἰάσπιδι κτλ., *like in appearance to a
jasper stone*, etc.: the language is meant to express merely the
splendor of the light in which the prophet beholds God manifested and encircled. In Ezk. 1^{26-28} God and his throne are
seen in the brilliancy of glowing metal (LXX ἤλεκτρον), of fire
and brightness round about; the 'terrible crystal' (v. 22), the
sapphire and the rainbow contribute to the 'glory of Jehovah'

(v. 28); in Ex. 24¹⁰ God appears above a work of sapphire; in
Dan. 7⁹ his raiment is white as snow, his throne fiery flames;
in En. 14 his raiment shines more brightly than the sun, from
beneath his throne come streams of flaming fire; in Slav. En. 22
his face is like metal glowing in the fire and emitting sparks.
In all such representations the meaning of the symbolism is
clear — it is an attempt to give God a visible appearance of
glory suited to his being. A special significance is not to be
sought in each particular element or color. So in our passage
the interpretation which finds in the precious stones a fiery red
typifying the wrath of God, etc., a sea-green typifying the
mercy of God, or the water of baptism, and so on through a
series of guesses (cf. Düst. *in loc.*), imports meanings which
the analogy of symbolical representations shows to be entirely
foreign to the writer's thought. In this place it is especially
necessary to keep in mind this *general* significance of the
symbolism, because it is not certain just what stones or what
colors are represented here by the gems named. Jasper as used
here cannot be our jasper, a dull opaque, cheap stone, red,
yellow, brown, or green. Many identify the jasper of this
passage with the opal, some with the diamond. The sardius is
commonly, but by no means unquestionably, identified with
our cornelian. The smaragd, usually identified with the
emerald (so, EV)is by some regarded as a brilliant rock-crystal
showing prismatic colors. The whole subject of the relation of
the precious stones named in the N. T. to those of the O. T.,
to those of classical antiquity, and of modern mineralogy is
one of great obscurity. For a compendious discussion of the
subject see Hast. and En. Bib. on *Precious Stones*, and also the
separate articles on particular stones. Fortunately the interpretation here is not affected by our ignorance of these details.

Ἶρις κυκλόθεν τοῦ θρόνου, *a rainbow round about the throne :*
taken from Ezk. 1²⁸, ἶρις being used instead of τόξον of the
LXX. The word κυκλόθεν, *round about*, seems to show that a
complete circle, a halo, is meant (Cf. 10¹, L & S. *s.v.*), though
the passage in Ezk. and the common use of the word would
suggest rather the segment of a circle overarching the throne.
The bow is here taken from Ezk. as an element of splendor;
there is no reference, as some understand it, to God's covenant

2 K

with his people, of which the rainbow was regarded a token, Gen. 9⁸ ff. — ὅμοιος (with ἶρις): only here an adj. of two endings; see Blass § 11, 1. — σμαραγδίνῳ: sc. λίθῳ. On the color see above.

4. The vision of the Seer passes on to the angelic orders who are gathered as courtiers about the heavenly King, forming the assembly of his council or ministers. Rabbinic writers speak of angelic powers as forming in the presence of God a senate or council to whom he communicates his decrees, and with whom he confers even (cf. Weber *System* 170 f.). Some idea of that kind appears also in Gen. 1²⁶, 3²² ('Let us' and 'one of us'); in Is. 24²³ such an assembly is conceived and the heavenly beings constituting it are called 'Elders' (cf. RV mrg., LXX, πρεσβύτεροι); in Slav. En. 4¹ the same word is used of certain angels, though the text there is not quite certain; cf. also οὐ πρέσβυς οὐδὲ ἄγγελος Is. 63⁹. The four and twenty 'Elders' of our passage are angelic kings, a rank in the heavenly hierarchy, though they are not elsewhere mentioned in the precise form and number here given. That they are kings is shown in the fact that they sit on thrones and wear crowns. As such they form an appropriate feature in a picture of the court of the King of kings. 'Thrones' are mentioned in Col. 1¹⁶ in the enumeration of the different orders of the angelic hierachy. The number twenty-four has no parallel in Jewish literature, and it is likely that the author derives it from some representation current in popular tradition, but not elsewhere recorded. — πρεσβυτέρους, στεφάνους; the construction changes, as if εἶδον had been used instead of ἰδού.

The four and twenty 'elders' have formed the subject of much discussion among interpreters. But it seems certain that as the cherubim, the seven lamps of fire and other details in the scene are taken from Hebrew tradition, so these are. And as the traditions mentioned pretty certainly owe their ultimate origin to an earlier oriental source, the same is probably true here. In the early polytheistic religion of the East, the stars, the planets, etc., are gods; but as this astro-mythological tradition passes on in popular acceptance, it is transformed among the monotheistic Hebrews, and these gods become angels. Of course, as in the use of all such traditions, the original meaning is lost from the knowledge of the later Hebrew writers; and thus the Apocalyptist takes up the merely formal elements of popular belief as a symbol in conceiving and expressing his thought.

Gunkel (*Schöpfung* 308) cites Diodorus Siculus II. 31 as saying that the
Babylonians distinguished besides the signs of the Zodiac twenty-four
stars of which half stand in the northern heavens, half in the southern, and
called these the judges of the world. There may conceivably be in this belief some trace of a tradition similar to that from which sprang the popular
fancy of twenty-four angelic kings as sharers in the court of heaven (see on
8²). Some such explanation of the symbol is adopted by many of the most
recent expositors. Earlier interpreters, some also among the more recent,
make the 'elders' idealized figures representing the twelve apostles and the
twelve patriarchs combined, and so the Church in its totality. But a conception of the apostles and patriarchs coördinately combined in such a way
as to be symbolized by the number twenty-four is entirely foreign to our
book, as to the N. T. in general. The Church is not composite, it is one
Israel of God. Moreover, in a scene conceived throughout on the traditional lines of Hebrew angelology, and representing in this part the
heavenly hosts apart from creation, there is no place for idealized or glorified human beings. The Church is first referred to in 5⁹ and then objectively, as distinct from those in the heavenly court. (The RV represents
the correct text in 5⁹.) According to another view the twenty-four 'elders'
represent the twenty-four courses of Aaronic priests; 1 Chron. 24⁷⁻¹⁹. But
there is nothing to suggest these except the number twenty-four. The
'elders' do not perform priestly offices; their offering of worship (4¹⁰ ᶠᶠ·, 5⁸ ᶠᶠ·)
is an act in which every created thing shares, 5¹³. See on the subject
Gunkel 302 ff., Jeremias 12 f., Bouss., Holtzm-Bau. Blj. Moffatt *in loc.*

5. The description returns to the throne and its nearer accessories. — ἀστραπαὶ κτλ. *lightnings*, etc. : imagery often used
to denote the presence of the awful power and majesty of God,
e.g. 8⁵, 11¹⁹, 16¹⁸, Ezk. 1¹³, Ps. 18¹³⁻¹⁵, Job 37²⁻⁵. With our
passage cf. En. 14¹⁹, 'From underneath the throne came
streams of flaming fire.' By the 'voices' are meant the roar
and furious noise of a tempest. — ἑπτὰ λαμπάδες πυρός, *seven
lamps of fire :* sc. ἦσαν; the copula is omitted, as often. The
symbol is taken with modification from Zec. 4² ᶠᶠ· (cf. also Ezk.
1¹³), where as here it is explained as referring to the Spirit of
God. See on 1⁴. It is probable that behind the symbol lies
the earlier mythological conception of seven torches representing the seven planet-gods, but that origin is forgotten in the
O. T. writer as well as here. The formal element of the tradition is taken up as a convenient symbol of the Spirit, as the
all-searching eye of God ; see on 5⁶ and 8².

6. ὡς θάλασσα . . . κρυστάλλῳ, *as it were a glassy sea like
crystal :* cf. 15². The words describe the brilliant splendor of

the pavement of the great throne-room. In the theophany recorded in Ex. 24[10], there was under the feet of God ' as it were
a paved work of sapphire stone ' ; cf. Ezk. 1[26]. A heavenly
house whose ' ground work was of crystal' is described in En.
14. The representation of this pavement as a sea lay near at
hand, for the notion of a sea in the heavens, ' the waters above
the firmament' (Gen. 1[7]), was common ; cf. Slav. En. 3[3],
' They placed me in the first heaven and showed me a very
great sea, greater than the earthly sea ' ; cf. also Jub. 2[4], En.
54[8]. The likeness of the sea and the sky in appearance suggests the idea. There is no connection between the figure of
our passage and the river of life in 22[1] (Düst.) ; nor is there
here any special symbolical meaning. For some fanciful interpretations see Alford in loc.

ἐν μέσῳ τοῦ θρόνου κτλ., in the midst of the throne, etc. : the
Seer in his description passes on to the highest order of angelic
beings, who apparently stand nearest the throne. These are
conceived for the most part after the manner of the cherubim
as pictured in Ezk. 1[4 ff.], but the figures of the seraphim given
in Is. 6[2 f.] are also present in the mind of the Seer. He has
greatly simplified the representation of Ezk., making it clearer,
and has combined, with the skill of an independent artist, the
elements thus derived from tradition. The freedom and skill
with which he here treats the sources used is worthy of notice,
because of the light thus thrown on his relation to derived material in general. He takes the name ζῶα, Living Creatures,
directly from Ezk. 1[5], but whether he intends to designate the
beings distinctly as the cherubim, as Ezk. does (10[20]), or simply
to represent the highest order of angels by combining known
traits of different orders, is not quite certain. There are four
as in Ezk., and like the cherubim in the prophet's picture (10[12])
they are full of eyes, indicative of unlimited intelligence ; they
have severally the face of the lion, the ox (see on v. 7), man,
and the eagle, that is, of the highest orders of earthly creatures ; but while in Ezk. each one of the cherubim has four
faces (1[6, 10]), in our author the four faces are distributed among
the Living Creatures severally. Each being has six wings, a
feature taken like the words of their hymn (v. 8) from the
seraphim of Isaiah (6[2]) ; the cherubim of Ezk. have each four

wings (1^6). In Ezk. the cherubim are the winged supporters
of Jehovah's throne-car, upon which they bear him as he moves
through all the world in his self-manifestation. The principal
function of the Living Creatures, as given in our book, is that
of attending as the highest order of angels before God in the
throne-room of his glory, and leading in the adoration paid to
God and the Lamb ; cf. vv. 8 f., 5^{8-10}, 19^4.

Here again caution must be taken against the interpretations
which find a symbolical intention in each several Creature and
each face. The writer saw in the figures of Ezk. and Is. a
representation of the highest angelic attendants before Jehovah,
and he adopts these in their general characteristics as appropriate in his great picture of God enthroned amid the heavenly
hierarchy. With his picture compare Slav. En. 21, 'The
cherubim and seraphim standing about the throne, the six-
winged and many-eyed ones, do not depart, standing before
the Lord's face, doing his will, and cover his whole throne,
singing with gentle voice before the Lord's face, Holy, holy,
holy, Lord Ruler of Sabaoth, heavens and earth are full of thy
glory.' The supposition of many scholars that the cherubim
personify the power of God immanent in nature is not warranted by the activities assigned them in Jewish literature.
(On the cherubim and their functions see Schultz *Theol.* 483 ff.,
Weber *System* 163 f., Hast. and En. Bib. *s.v.*) And the same
is true of the Living Creatures in the Apocalypse. As regards
these latter it is noticeable that the whole created world is
distinctly contrasted with them, 5^{13}. There is magnificence in
the picture which some com. find here — a vision of heaven
with the Church (the twenty-four Elders) and the world of
creation (the cherubim) represented ideally before the throne
of God. But we are undoubtedly right in rejecting such a
view of the scene (see p. 499). The figures which throng
the court of heaven are the traditional orders of heavenly
beings, among whom none *personify* God's people or the
created universe. And even if such an ideal abstraction were
conceivable with our author, he would pretty surely show the
significance of his innovation by the addition of interpretative
words, as in 1^{20}, 4^5, 5^6. — The obscure words ἐν μέσῳ . . . κύκλῳ
τοῦ θρόνου are best taken to mean that the Creatures stand one

at the middle of each of the four sides of the throne. While
ἐν μέσῳ is found in Ezk. (1⁵), the words καὶ κύκλῳ τοῦ θρόνου
do not occur there; they are wanting in some minuscules —
doubtless a copyist's correction to relieve a difficulty.

7. ὅμοιον λέοντι *like a lion:* the Living Creatures in Ezk.
are described as having in general, with whatever peculiarities,
the human form (1⁵); so here the likeness to the lion, the ox,
etc., is to be understood, not of the form throughout, but of the
face, as shown by ἔχων . . . ἀνθρώπου in the third case. ζῷον
includes both man and beast, θηρίον the latter only. — μόσχῳ,
ox: EV, *calf.* In Ezk. 1¹⁰ the LXX use μόσχος to translate
שׁוֹר, which is there understood of a full-grown ox or bullock.
— ἔχων: *const. ad sens.,* as also in v. 8.

8. ζῷα : the subj. of γέμουσιν, or possibly with ἦν to be supplied with ἔχων. — ἓν καθ᾽ ἕν, ἀνά : emphatic distributive (cf.
Blass §§ 51, 5 ; 45, 3), lit. *having each one of them six wings
apiece (ἀνά).* — κυκλόθεν καὶ ἔσωθεν, *round about and within:*
Ezk. 10¹² points to the probable meaning : round about the
body (cf. v. 6, 'full of eyes before and behind') and within *i.e.*
on the under side of the wings. The all-seeing intelligence of
the Creatures is meant. The lack of a strict contrast between
κυκλόθεν and ἔσωθεν seems to be the origin of the reading κυκλόθεν καὶ ἔξωθεν καὶ ἔσωθεν found in some sources ; κυκλόθεν is
then joined to the preceding words ; 'they had six wings round
about, and were full of eyes without and within.' — ἀνάπαυσιν
οὐκ ἔχουσιν κτλ., *they rest not,* etc.: ceaseless songs of praise
form a common feature in apocalyptic descriptions of heaven ;
e.g. 'Those who sleep not bless thee, they stand before thy
glory and bless, praise and extol, saying, Holy, holy, holy is
the Lord of spirits,' En. 39¹²; cf. *idem* 61¹², Test. Lev. 3⁸, Slav.
En. 19⁶, 21¹ (quoted in note on v. 6). The Trisagion of our
passage is the hymn of the Seraphim in Is. 6³, but modified here
to introduce attributes of God made prominent in the book,
παντοκράτωρ and ὁ ἦν καὶ ὁ ὢν κτλ. — ἅγιος, *holy:* the word is
to be taken here according to Heb. usage to denote the sacredness of God's being, his apartness from all created things ; 'it
expresses the distance and awful contrast between the divine
and the human . . . it included every distinctive character of
Godhead,' Smith *Prophets* 224 f.; cf. Schultz *Theol.* 463 ff.

The theme of the hymn is the majesty of God in his divine
being, his almightiness, and his eternity.　For the phrase ὁ ἦν
κτλ., see on 1⁸.

9–11.　The company of Elders take up and carry forward
the great antiphon, offering lowliest homage to God and praising him in his glory and power as the creator of all things.
— ὅταν δώσουσιν; the fut. ind. with ὅταν is rare; see Win.
§ 42, 5, b; Buttm. p. 222.　The fut., with which πεσοῦνται, etc.,
correspond, is probably to be taken with a frequentative force,
after the analogy of the Heb. imperf.: 'Whenever the Living
Creatures give glory . . . the Elders fall,' etc. (AV); so, many
com., among the more recent, Düst. Holtzm.-Bauer, Blj. Swete.
As such it must be classed among the writer's grammatical
errors.　Others give the fut. its usual force, so, RV; in that
case the writer is thinking of the continuance through the future
of what is now going on; 'Whenever the Living Creatures
shall give glory,' etc. — a sense which in this connection seems
hardly possible. — δώσουσιν δόξαν καὶ τιμήν, *give glory and
honor:* primarily to acknowledge the glory and honor which
inhere in God, to praise him for his glory and honor; whereas
διδόναι εὐχαριστίαν is to offer the thanks which come from man.

The numerous repetitions in the phraseology of these verses
are characteristic of the writer; cf. p. 241. — βαλοῦσιν τοὺς
στεφάνους κτλ., *cast their crowns*, etc.: an act acknowledging
that all their kingly dignity is subordinate to God. — ὁ κύριος,
ὁ θεός: nom. for voc. as often in classical Gk. and in the N. T.;
see Blass § 33, 4. — λαβεῖν δόξαν, *receive glory :* see above on
'give glory.' — τήν, before δόξαν etc.: the art. specifies the glory,
etc., as those which are ascribed to God.— ὅτι σὺ ἔκτισας τὰ
πάντα, *because thou didst create all things :* the hymn of the Elders
goes beyond a mere repetition of that of the Living Creatures;
it adds as a ground of praise God's work in creation, a frequent
theme in Heb. psalmody; *e.g.* Ps. 33⁶⁻⁹, 102²⁵, 136⁵ᶠᶠ. — διὰ τὸ
θέλημά σου ἦσαν, *because of thy will they were :* the words do
not describe the process of coming into being ; that is expressed
in the following word ἐκτίσθησαν, *were created.*　In this first
clause the imperf. is used because existence is thought of
vividly as an accomplished fact in response to God's will; 'thou
didst will, they were.'　Cf. Gen. 1³, 'Let there be light and

there was light.' There is no idea (so, some com.) of a *poten-tial* existence in ἦσαν prior to the reality of ἐκτίσθησαν. The two clauses contain a hysteron-proteron; or the second may be taken as a more specific statement of what was stated indefi-nitely in the first, in which case καί is epexegetical, *that is, yea.* Both are common traits of the author's manner; see pp. 243, 242.

Textual notes, chapt. 4. 1. λεγων ℵAQ min edd; λεγουσα ℵ°P min R. — 2. Before ευθεως, P some min and vers R insert και, to avoid asyndeton. — 3. σαρδιω ℵAQ edd; σαρδινω P some min R. — 4. θρονους (after θρονου) ℵA min Lch Ti Ws WHmrg. *al;* θρονοι PQ many min R WH Sod *al.* — 5. α εισιν ℵ°P min most edd; α εστιν A Lch Ws; αι εισιν (or εισι) Q min R RV *al.* — 6. και κυκλω του θρονου wanting in some min and vers. — 7. εχων AQ min most edd; εχον ℵP min R Lch Sod. — For ανθρωπον, P some min R read ανθρωπος. — 8. Before και εσωθεν, Q some min insert και εξωθεν; some min read εξωθεν instead of εσωθεν. — For γεμουσιν, some min R have γεμοντα. — 9. δωσουσιν AP min R edd; δωσωσιν ℵQ min Bouss; δωσιν some min. — 10. προσκυνουσι in R seems to be due to Erasmus, who wrote thus either through error, or to conform to his reading βαλλουσιν. — For βαλουσιν (fut.), ℵQ some min R read βαλλουσιν. — 11. For ησαν, P some min R read εισι; Q some min read ουκ ησαν κτλ.; *they were not, and were created.*

(2) Chapt. V. Second part of the scene in the Court of Heaven. See pp. 261 f. The sealed book and the Lamb. 5¹⁻¹⁴.

1. The opening words of this the second part of the vision make clear the significance which the former part (chapt. 4) has in the plan of our book. The roll in the hand of God furnishes the key. God, the eternal and almighty one, as pic-tured there in awful splendor, now in this roll presents before the angelic ranks assembled around him in his throne-room the decrees of his will regarding the consummation of his kingdom. The events that are to follow — the things written in the roll — are the working out of that sovereign will, which is now to move on in irresistible might accomplishing its eternal decree. Thus is revealed the strong foundation of the Christian's hope for the future, his ground of assurance through all the events that are coming on the earth.— **εἶδον ἐπὶ τὴν δεξιάν,** *I saw in the right hand:* the imagery of the roll in the hand of God is taken from Ezk. 2⁹ ᶠ. The roll is better understood as held in the hand than resting on the open palm; for the use of ἐπί cf. 20¹. — **βιβλίον,** *a book:* primarily a *little book,* but in use the diminu-

tive force has disappeared (cf. Kühn. I § 330, 4, A. 4), and the
word when denoting a volume becomes equivalent to βίβλος,
and is employed more frequently in the N. T. than the latter.
When the diminutive is to be specified, some other form is used ;
cf. βιβλαρίδιον 10². There seems no necessity for assigning to
the book here any other than the usual form of a roll, the
form specified in Ezk. (κεφαλίς), which is before our author's
mind. As regards the *contents* of the roll it appears certain,
as scholars for the most part are now agreed, that it contains the counsels of God which are revealed in the following
visions ; it is the book of these last things in the destiny
of the world and the people of God now to be unfolded.
These have been sealed, *i.e.* hidden (cf. Is. 29¹¹, Dan. 8²⁶), but
now the seals are to be broken and all is to be revealed ; cf.
22¹⁰, Slav. En. 33⁸. Such a revelation is promised in the summons given to the Apocalyptist (4¹) ; and he must in the outset have conceived the manifestation of God in the court of
heaven to stand in direct relation to this unfolding of the
future ; hence the representation of his grief when no one is
found to open the book (v. 4). That this formed the contents
of the roll is placed beyond question in that the revelations
given are directly connected with the breaking of the seals.
The book then in its contents is quite different from those
mentioned in 3⁵, 20¹². This is a book of the future of the
world and mankind. A similar book is mentioned in many
places. The idea is closely related to that of a heavenly pattern
followed in all that is done on earth as the working out of
God's will (Ex. 25⁹, ⁴⁰, Eph. 2¹⁰ ; on the latter passage see
Haupt in Meyer's *Kom.*; Ewald in Zahn's *Kom.*). For mention of such a book see Dan. 10²¹, 2 Es. 6²⁰, En. 93¹⁻³, 103²,
106¹⁹, 108⁷, Jub. 5¹³, 23³². 'These books contain the secrets of
the future, and the opening of the books signifies the fulfillment of the hidden things,' Volz. 94.

Interpretations which find in the roll the O. T., or the O. T. and the
N. T., written the one within, the other without, and numerous symbolical
interpretations remote from the evident relation of the roll to the contents
of the Apocalypse, are fanciful and need not be considered here. For
various views of the kind see the Speaker's Com. *in loc.* Some understand
the roll to be the Testament of God, the document in which he assures his

people, as shown in the visions, of their *inheritance* of the heavenly kingdom, according to the common N. T. representation of Christians as the
'heirs of God'; so, Zahn *Ein.* II. 600, followed by J. Weiss 57 ff., Blj. *in loc.*
This view is suggested by the Roman custom of sealing a will with seven
seals. But the great frequency of seven with our author as a symbol of
completeness is sufficient to explain its use here. It is not easy to bring
the first six seals and the events connected with the breaking of these into
any relation to a sealed testament, or an inheritance. The author nowhere
intimates any relation, or any idea of a testament as symbolized by the roll.
Inheritance is mentioned but once in the book (21⁷) and then not in a way
to indicate allusion to the roll as guaranteeing it. But the analogy of the
books referred to above suggests that the whole book, each part as denoted
by its seal, has for its contents a prophecy of the future.

γεγραμμένον . . . ὄπισθεν, *written within and upon the back:*
the writing was ordinarily confined to the inner side of a roll,
but sometimes was also extended over to the outer side or back.
Here as in Ezk. fullness of contents is indicated. Some of the
writing on the back of the roll, even when rolled up, would be
visible ; that within though not visible is assumed as a matter
of course.

The words ἔσωθεν, ὄπισθεν, *within, on the back*, are both joined by almost
all interpreters with γεγραμμένον according to the representation in Ezk.
Zahn (*Ein.* II. 608) separates them, interpreting 'written within, and
sealed on the back,' on the ground that ἔξωθεν rather than ὄπισθεν would be
required for a proper correlation to ἔσωθεν. But ἔσωθεν would then be
quite superfluous, for a roll is of course written within; and ὄπισθεν, taken
with κατεσφραγισμένον, would likewise be so, if the book was in the ordinary
form of the roll; but on Zahn's view of the *form*, and the sealing see below,
p. 507. However, the compound ὀπισθόγραφος, used to describe a roll
written on both sides (see L and S. *s.v.*), shows the appropriateness of
ὄπισθεν as a correlative here. The value of the words for the sentence is
lost unless they are taken to denote fullness of contents.

κατεσφραγισμένον κτλ., *sealed with seven seals:* the compound
vb. *sealed up* is stronger than the simple vb. σφραγίζειν, the
usual term, and like the number of seals marks the security of
the sealing, appropriate in the case of a roll which none but
the Lamb is worthy to open. The question as to how the roll
could be formed, and how the seven seals could be affixed, so
as to make possible, as is supposed to be implied in chapt. 6,
the opening and reading of seven different parts one after
another, as each of the seals was broken, is one which has

greatly exercised the ingenuity of commentators. (For various guesses see Düst.) But there is nothing in the description to indicate that the roll was peculiar in its construction, or that it was sealed in any other than the usual way. We can safely assume, that if any variation essential to the symbolism had entered into the author's conception, it would at least be intimated in the description. As to the difficulty raised, it should be observed that in connection with the breaking of the respective seals, nothing is said of an actual opening of the roll, or a part of it, nor of *reading* from it. The events which accompany the breaking of the seals one after another, as described in chaps. 6 and 8, though these form the contents of the respective portions of the roll, are not represented as read from it ; on the contrary they are dramatic scenes vividly enacted before the Seer's vision in conformity with what is written in these several portions. See further p. 515.

The view that the book consisted of separate leaves fastened together after the manner of a codex, or modern book, wrapped with cords to which were affixed seals on the side of the book turned away from the Seer, 'the back' (ὄπισθεν), is urged by Zahn (*Ein.* II. 608) ; it is contended that the words ἐπὶ τὴν δεξιάν are appropriate to an object in book form, but not to a roll which could be held on the open hand only by an act of balancing not supposable here ; that ἐν τῇ δεξιᾷ would be required as in 10², ⁸, Ezk. 2⁹. But it is doubtful whether these words can be pressed to specify the flat, open hand ; cf. 20¹ ἐπὶ τὴν χεῖρα where the key of the abyss and a great chain cannot be thought of as lying on the open palm. It is further urged that ἀνοῖξαι points to the opening of a codex, that for opening a roll, ἀνειλεῖν (Ezk. 2¹⁰), ἀνελίσσειν (cf. Rev. 6¹⁴) or ἀναπτύσσειν (Lk. 4¹⁷) would be used. But ἀνοῖξαι is evidently chosen here with special reference to the breaking of the seals, cf. ἀνοῖξαι τὰς σφραγῖδας, v. 9 ; for ἀνοίγνυμι in this latter connection cf. Eur. *I. A.* 325, Dem. 1048, Xen. *Laced.* 6⁴.

2. The uniqueness of the office of the Lamb in opening the book is set forth with dramatic force by the unavailing challenge to the whole universe to find one worthy of the service, and by the grief of the Prophet.— ἄγγελον ἰσχυρόν, *a mighty angel :* one whose call could reach to the farthest limits of the universe, cf. 10³.— ἄξιος, *worthy :* one of mighty strength to break the seals and unroll the book is not needed, but a being whose rank and office give him before God worthiness to perform this supreme service in regard to the divine decrees.

Worthiness and ability are here identical, hence ἐδύνατο, *was able*, v. 3 ; cf. Mt. 3¹¹ where ἱκανός, *able*, is identical with the ἄξιος, *worthy*, of Jno. 1²⁷. The *opening* here spoken of, the revelation of God's purposes, includes also their fulfillment. Mere disclosures of the future are vouchsafed to a prophet ; ' The Lord Jehovah will do nothing except he reveal his secret unto his servants the prophets ' Am. 3⁷. But the complete revelation of God's will concerning the consummation of his kingdom includes the agency of its fulfillment. Only he who holds the Messiah's rank and has performed the Messiah's office of redemption can show the whole divine will carried out to its fulfillment. —ἀνοῖξαι, λῦσαι · hysteron-proteron.

3. ἐδύνατο, *was able:* see on v. 2. — ἐν τῷ οὐρανῷ κτλ., *in heaven*, etc.: for this threefold division of creation, an emphatic designation of the whole universe, cf. Phil. 2¹⁰, Ex. 20⁴. — οὐδέ, οὔτε : if this be the correct reading (see text. note), οὐδέ is continuative, *and not, nor*, while οὔτε is disjunctive, *neither;* see Blass § 77, 10 ; Kühn. II, § 535, 2, c. — βλέπειν, *look: i.e.* into its contents.

4. ἔκλαιον, *wept:* because, the roll being unopened, the promise of 4¹ seems to be void.

5. εἷς ἐκ τῶν πρεσβυτέρων, *one of the Elders:* no symbolical significance is apparent in the selection of one of the Elders as the speaker. It is a part of the Apocalyptist's art to bring variety into his descriptions by the use of manifold agencies (De Wette) ; cf. 6¹ ᶠᶠ·, 7¹³ ᶠ·, 8¹³, 9¹³, 10⁴· ⁸, 11¹⁵, 14⁶, 16¹, 17¹, *al.* — ἐνίκησεν, *hath overcome:* has come off victorious over Satan and death, as in 3²¹ ; cf. also the use of νικᾶν throughout the book, where the Christian is the subject, *e.g.* 2⁷· ¹¹ ᵉᵗᶜ·, 12¹², 15². The infin. ἀνοῖξαι, *to open*, then expresses result, *so that;* as a result of his victory and his consequent redemption he is deemed worthy to open the seals. This meaning is made clear by v. 9, ' Thou art worthy to open the seals, because thou wast slain and didst purchase,' etc. The interpretation *hast prevailed, got the might, to open*, adopted by some, gives to νικᾶν a sense contrary to the usage of the book, and not certainly supported elsewhere. — ὁ λέων ὁ ἐκ τῆς φυλῆς κτλ., *the Lion of the tribe of Judah*, etc.: Christ is here designated under known titles of the Jewish Messiah ; (1) as the Lion of the tribe of Judah, a title taken

from Gen. 49⁴, and descriptive of his kingly might; also in
2 Es. 11³⁷, 12³¹ the Messiah appears as a lion; (2) as the Root
of David (*i.e.* a Branch from his root), a title taken from Is.
11¹‚¹⁰, cf. Rev. 22¹⁶, 2 Es. 12³², Ecclus. 47²², and descriptive of
his headship in the final Davidic kingdom.   Also in 2 Es. *loc.
cit.* the two titles are brought together as here.   But both in
this sentence, *i.e.* in ἐνίκησεν, *hath overcome*, and more fully in
vv. 6, 9, 12, the Christian conception of the Messiah's office is
introduced in conjunction with the Jewish, and the emphasis
is thrown on the former.   Christ in the work here spoken of
as the revealer and consummator of God's will acts in his office
as the Messiah of the whole of God's people, both Jewish and
Christian; but the crowning act of his messianic work is his
redemption by his death of a people gathered out of every tribe
and nation to be a kingdom and priests unto God (cf. vv. 9–
10).   Here as elsewhere with our author the Christian idea is
the preponderating factor, though Jewish forms and conceptions are retained.

   6. New features, the roll, v. 1, the Lamb in this verse, the
myriads of angel hosts, v. 11, are gradually introduced as the
vision unfolds itself.   Christ appears here, not in the glory of
the earlier vision (1¹⁰ ᶠᶠ·), but as a lamb bearing the mark of
the death through which he has passed.   It is this death with
its redemptive results that fits him for the office of opening the
roll.   In the visions that follow this scene he is generally
spoken of as the Lamb; not until his appearance in 19¹¹ ᶠᶠ·,
leading forth his hosts to battle, is he again represented in a
form similar to that of the first vision. — ἐν μέσῳ τοῦ θρόνου
κτλ., *in the midst of the throne*, etc.: an obscure phrase, but
unless we insist on attributing to the Apocalyptist a precise
diagram probably not thought of, the words are best understood to mean simply in the very midst of the group formed
round the throne by the other beings. — ἀρνίον, *a lamb:* the
diminutive force is not to be pressed.   The word, not found
elsewhere in the N. T., except in the plural in a quite different
sense (Jno. 21¹⁵), is one of the set terms of the Apocalypse.
For fuller discussion of its use see pp. 314 ff.   While it is
here, as elsewhere in the book, a designation of the glorified
Christ, that aspect of it which marks him as having passed

through an expiatory death and thereby bringing eternal blessings to his people is emphasized throughout this scene. The Lamb once slain is contained in ἐνίκησεν, v. 5, and forms the very heart of the whole scene. The attempt of Vischer and his followers to expunge the idea (see p. 230) destroys the entire paragraph; it is criticism run riot.

ἑστηκὸς κτλ., *standing*, etc.: the lamb stands alive bearing visible marks of having been slain. — ἔχων κέρατα ἑπτά, *having seven horns:* the horn is a common biblical symbol of power, and as such occurs frequently in the Apocalypse; *e.g.* 12³, 13¹, 17³, ¹². Here *fullness* of power is indicated by the number seven; see p. 253. The lamb symbolizing the Messiah in En. 90³⁸ has 'great horns.' — ὀφθαλμοὺς ἑπτά, κτλ., *seven eyes, which are the seven Spirits*, etc.: this trait is taken from Zec. 4¹⁰, and denotes, as there explained, omniscience — the eyes of Christ behold and scrutinize all things. The fullness of power and the omniscience attributed to the Lamb in this verse form essentials in his office in opening the roll, *i.e.* as revealer and consummator of God's purpose in the events that are to come to pass. The seven Spirits (the Holy Spirit; see on 1⁴) are the Spirits of God (τοῦ θεοῦ) and at the same time they are the eyes, the Spirits, of the Lamb. The Spirit is the Spirit of God and of Christ alike, Ro. 8⁹; see on 3¹. In 4⁵ the presence of the Spirit is represented by the lamps of fire before the throne; here it is symbolized by the eyes of the Lamb. The one symbol figures the relation to God in the apartness of the celestial throne-room, the other the relation to Christ active in the world.

ἀποστελλόμενα εἰς πᾶσαν τὴν γῆν, *sent forth into all the earth:* said of the Spirits. The characterization is taken from Zec. 4¹⁰, but the vb. ἀποστέλλεσθαι is here substituted for ἐπιβλέπειν (LXX) and indicates reference to πνεύματα rather than to ὀφθαλμούς. The reading ἀπεσταλμένοι (see text. notes) might refer to πνεύματα or to ὀφθαλμούς; the gender would not be decisive (*constr. ad sens.*), but the perf. is less appropriate here, since the activity is always continuing. The art. might be expected with ἀποστελλόμενα; its absence is made an objection to that reading; so, B. Weiss *Apok.* 112 f.; and it is in fact found in some sources. But it is not indispensable; without

it the partic. is predicate rather than attrib., the sense being,
the eyes are, symbolize, the Spirits when these are sent forth.

The combination of the lion and the lamb in this scene is said by some,
e.g. Vischer and his followers, to be impossible. The might to open the
book, the conquest, assigned to the lion are inappropriate to a lamb. Bousset also finds difficulty in the representation and suggests (*Kom.* 259) a
mythological influence here. Comparing Marduk's appearance among the
gods in the Babylonian creation-myth, following Gunkel, he suggests the
possibility that there may be taken up here and worked over some elements
from a mythological tradition telling of an assembly of the gods perplexed
by their inability to perform. a certain great task (vv. 2 ff.), when there
suddenly appears in the midst a new and powerful divinity, fresh from a
mighty victory over demonic power (v. 5) and equipped with the magic
might thus won to open the book of fate, to bring to an end the old order
of the world, and to enter on the new world-rule. Jeremias also (15 ff.)
finds this incongruity in the picture and explains it by the introduction of
elements from a cosmological myth. But it hardly seems necessary to go
so far afield to explain an incongruity which does not exist, if the author
of the Apocalypse may be assumed to be familiar with the Christian doctrine that the Christ is one who must needs suffer, and yet one to whom all
authority hath been given in heaven and on earth.

7. εἴληφεν : *sc.* τὸ βιβλίον; the perf. is aoristic ; cf. Blass
§ 59, 4 ; Burton § 80. The Lamb receives the book from the
hand of God ; cf. 1¹, ' The revelation . . . which God gave him
to show.'

8. ἔχοντες ἔκαστος κτλ., *holding each one*, etc.: the words
are commonly referred to the Elders only, as the act described
is thought to be more appropriate to them ; but the Living
Creatures may also be included. — αἴ, *which :* the antecedent is
θυμιαμάτων, *incense*, the pron. being attracted, as often, into
agreement with the predicate ; or the words φιάλας . . . θυμιαμάτων may be taken as a compound expression, *bowls of incense*,
the first noun determining the gender of the relative. — αἱ
προσευχαὶ τῶν ἁγίων, *the prayers of the saints:* the incense is,
i.e. symbolizes, the prayers. The use of incense primarily
belonging to a worship inspired by anthropomorphism became
a constant feature of Hebrew ritual to give efficacy, as an
acceptable offering, to the worship accompanied by it, and to
symbolize the sweet odor of prayer rising to God ; cf. Dt. 33¹⁰
(RV mrg.), Ps. 141², Gen. 8²¹. As angels were thought to present the prayers of the saints to God (cf. Tob. 12¹², ¹⁵, Test. Dan.

6²), so here they present the incense symbolical of prayer ; cf. 8³. The service as shown distinctly by 8³ is that of angels, not of idealized representatives of the saints ; there is then nothing here to support the view that the Elders are representatives of the Church in the great heavenly scene ; see on 4⁴. The saints here spoken of are the Christians, often so denominated in the Apocalypse, as elsewhere in the N.T., *e.g.* 8³,⁴, 11¹⁸, 13⁷,¹⁰. The saints are not to be thought of as present there in the court of heaven, for their prayers would not then be presented by others in their behalf.

The introduction of the prayers of the saints here is strange. This part of the scene is heavenly and includes nothing earthly; the latter is introduced first in v. 13, in distinction from this part; and the theme of all the utterances in the scene is praise, not prayer (προσευχή is not praise, but supplication), and the utterances of the saints are included among those mentioned in v. 13. These words 'which is the prayers of the saints' are very probably a gloss brought in from 8³. If genuine, they probably refer to supplications of the saints for the speedy accomplishment of God's will concerning the kingdom, as in 8³, 6¹⁰ — an idea, however, not in keeping with anything else in the scene.

9–10. **καινήν**, *new:* an epithet of songs expressive of gratitude for new mercies ; it is frequent in the Psalms, *e.g.* 33³, 40³, 96¹ ; cf. Is. 42¹⁰. It is especially appropriate when the cause of God is about to enter on a new stage ; cf. 14³. — **ὅτι ἐσφάγης** κτλ., *because thou wast slain,* etc.: the ground of worthiness to open the roll is here declared to be the redemptive work of Christ, who by his death has purchased a people out of every nation to reign as kings and priests in the messianic kingdom. — **ἠγόρασας . . . ἐν τῷ αἵματί σου**, *hast purchased by thy blood:* cf. 1⁵. The author agrees with other N. T. writers in viewing the death of Christ under the figure of a purchase of a people which shall belong ·to God (τῷ θεῷ, *unto God*); cf. Ac. 20²⁸, 1 Co. 6²⁰, 7²³, 1 Pet. 1¹⁸ᶠ·, 2 Pet. 2¹. The object of the vb. ἠγόρασας, *hast purchased,* is *men, a people,* to be supplied from the words ἐκ φυλῆς κτλ. (The AV 'us' and the corresponding 'we shall reign' are from an incorrect text. See text. note). — **ἐκ πάσης φυλῆς** κτλ., *from every tribe,* etc.: a frequent expression in the book ; *e.g.* 7⁹, 11⁹, 13⁷, cf. also Dan. 3⁴, 5¹⁹, 2 Es. 3⁷. — **ἐποίησας,** *hast made:* as often in the book, the

hymn of praise anticipates the finished result ; see on 1⁶, also
p. 243. — τῷ θεῷ, *to God:* belonging to God as his peculiar
people. — βασιλείαν, *a kingdom:* the explanatory words βασιλεύσουσιν κτλ., show that an active meaning is intended, *a
reigning power,* equivalent to *kings;* see on 1⁶. —ἐπὶ τῆς γῆς,
upon the earth : in a passage embracing the whole scope of God's
purpose regarding his people and kingdom, the reference is
better understood of the new earth (21¹, 22⁵) rather than of the
millennial reign, 20⁶.

11–12. The other hosts of heaven, standing beyond the inner
circle of the higher orders, now take up the anthem. — ὁ ἀριθμὸς κτλ., *the number,* etc.: for this formula denoting a countless multitude cf. 9¹⁶, Dan. 7¹⁰, En. 14²², 40¹, 71⁸. — λέγοντες :
the partic. is loosely added as if the nom. had preceded ; see
p. 224. — ἄξιον κτλ., *worthy is the Lamb,* etc.: *i.e.* worthy to
receive the adoration and praise expressed in the hymn. In
the preceding hymn, vv. 9–10, the ground of praise is Christ's
death and the blessings thereby brought to his people. Here
also that death is emphasized as a ground of praise (τὸ ἐσφαγ-
μένον, *that was slain*), but other grounds are added, Christ's
power, wisdom, etc. The analogy of other doxologies, *e.g.* 1⁶,
4¹¹, 7¹², shows that the meaning here is not that Christ is worthy
to receive what God has given him, might, etc., but as in 4¹¹ to
receive adoration for the might, etc., which he possesses. See
on 4⁹,¹¹. — τήν : not repeated with the nouns following δύναμιν,
because the substantives are regarded as forming a single complex expression. The art. specifies them as those that belong
to Christ. — πλοῦτον, *riches:* cf. Eph. 3⁸, ʻthe unsearchable
riches of Christ.' — εὐλογίαν, *blessing: i.e.,* praise. The word,
like εὐχαριστίαν in 4⁹, expresses what is offered to Christ on
man's part ; this is, at least in thought, distinguishable from
the acknowledgment of what he possesses in himself, his power,
wisdom, glory, etc. The distinction is made clear in the doxology in 1 Chron. 29¹¹ ᶠᶠ·, with which this hymn is in several
terms parallel.

13. Beyond the court of heaven now the whole created
world to its farthest limits, to its deepest recesses, responds in
an epode to the strophes and antistrophes of the angel choruses.
While the hymns of the first part of the scene are addressed to

2 L

Him that sitteth upon the throne, and those of the second, to
the Lamb, these concluding strains join both in one common
ascription of praise. See p. 263. For greater emphasis the
writer adds to the customary threefold division of creation
(see on v. 3) a fourth, ' on the sea.' In these words as also in
the following phrase, ' and all things that are in them ' (in
itself superfluous after the πᾶν κτίσμα κτλ.) he perhaps has in
his mind Ps. 146⁶, ' who made heaven and earth, the sea, and
all that in them is,' or perhaps the Song of the Three Children,
the *Benedicite, omnia opera Domini*, in which, after the things
of the heavens and the earth, the things of the sea are called
upon to praise and magnify the Lord. That wonderful can-
ticle furnishes a complete commentary on our passage. The
antiphonal structure of the paragraph, vv. 9–13, makes it clear
that the heavenly beings of vv. 9–12 are not included in the
πᾶν κτίσμα ὃ ἐν τῷ οὐρανῷ of v. 13.

14. The great act of homage closes as it began, with the
angels nearest the throne, in the Amen of the Living Creatures
and the mute adoration of the four and twenty Elders. In the
antiphonal singing, in the Amen, and in the silent worship at
the end, we not improbably have some reflection of usages in
the public worship of the Church at the time.

Textual notes, Chapt. 5¹⁻¹¹. 1. εσωθεν APQ min edd; א Orig. read
εμπροσθεν, probably through the influence of Ezk. 2¹⁰, and to secure a
literal correlative to οπισθεν. — οπισθεν אA many min and vers most edd;
QP many min and vers anc com Bouss read εξωθεν. — 3. ουδε before επι
της γης and υποκατω, AP many min R Lch Tr WH Ws RV; ουτε א (the
second clause is wanting in א) Q most min Ti WHmrg Sod. — ουτε
before βλεπειν, most sources and edd, but AP some min R Bouss Sw read
ουδε. See Ws *Ap.* 114 f. — 6. εστηκος APQ min most edd; εστηκως א some
min Tr Ti WHmrg Bouss. — αποστελλομενα Q some min and anc com
Blj (in *Com.* p. 75) Bouss Alf; απεσταλμενοι A WH Lch Ws RV Sod *al*;
απεσταλμενα א some min R Ti WHmrg.; some min insert τα before the
partic. See Ws 112 f. — 9. With ηγορασας τω θεω, אPQ most min R add
ημας; wanting in A, omitted by edd, because in v. 10 αυτους and the third
person of the vb., too well supported to be questioned, show that it cannot
be read. See Ws p. 108. — 10. βασιλειαν אA some vers and anc com most
edd; βασιλεις Q min vers R Sod. — βασιλευσουσιν אP most min and vers Ti
Ws Blj Bouss Sod *al*; βασιλευουσιν AQ many min Lch WH RV Sw. The
pres., if taken strictly, meaning that the reign is now going on, is impossible with the Apocalyptist. — 11. Before φωνην, אQ many min vers Ti
WHmrg Blj *al* insert ως.

Chap. **VI.** *The breaking of the first six seals.*　See pp. 263 ff.
The scene which is now introduced stands in the same structural relation to the vision of the Lamb in chap. 5, as does the
inditing of the seven epistles to the vision of the Son of man in
the first scene; the divine agent is first portrayed in his person,
then he appears in the special action appropriate to this preliminary revelation.　The Lamb in proceeding to break the
seals begins his work as revealer.　But neither in this chapt. as
the seals are broken one by one, nor in 8^1, when the last seal is
broken and the volume may then be unrolled, is anything said
of opening the book and reading from it.　Yet in each instance,
what immediately follows is unquestionably meant to correspond to a particular part of the contents of the roll.　The
Seer does not read from the book in the customary words, ' It
shall come to pass, that,' etc.; instead he beholds the prophesied
event itself immediately enacted in vision, and thus the
prophecy is given with the more powerful dramatic force.　If
the contents of the book were not intended to be represented in
these various events, the whole imagery of the roll in the hand
of God, and the process of breaking the seals carried on in so
close dramatic connection with the scenes enacted, would lose
significance and only confuse thought.　Even after all the seals
are broken (8^1), as well as in the successive preparatory steps,
the contents of the book are made known only through this
visible fulfillment in scenes shown to the Seer.　In 2 Es. $6^{20\ ff.}$
also the prophecies of a book are revealed not by reading but by
the events that follow its opening.　It is said there, ' The books
shall be opened and all shall see '; then follows immediately, as
the result of the opening, pre-messianic portents taking place
before the eyes of the beholders.　The books there spoken of,
like that of the Apocalypse, contain prophecies of marvels; they
are not the books of the last judgment, for that does not follow
(cf. Gunkel in Kautzsch *in loc*).　There is then no real ground
for the difficulty raised by many regarding the form of the
book and the opening of its separate seals (see on 5^1).
The judgments predicted in this chapt., the sword, famine,
pestilence, earthquake, are those connected everywhere in
apocalyptic literature with the last days, and are here regarded
as the *beginning* of woes.　They are then in the Seer's vision a

part of the visitations to be sent upon men ; he means to say
that he beholds all the scenes (except that of vv. 9–11, which
he locates specifically) enacted *on earth.* They are not a kind
of symbolical tableau pictured on the heavens. The Seer is,
to be sure, in heaven, or before its open door (4¹), but he beholds these scenes taking place on earth. This is shown most
distinctly in the description of the effects of the earthquake in
vv. 12–17, but the same is evidently the meaning in the other
visions of the chapt. ; the conqueror is seen going on with his
conquests, the riders are seen advancing across the earth with
calamities in their wake. The comprehension of earth within
the scope of the Seer's vision, while he is himself in heaven,
about which difficulty has been raised, belongs to the nature
of visions, in which natural limitations are disregarded.

1. **μίαν,** *one :* indefinite as to which one. There is nothing
to intimate conformity in the order of the seals with that of the
Living Creatures in 4⁷, or any correspondence between the
nature of the respective horsemen and the faces of the Creatures (so, some of the older com.). — **ἑνὸς . . . ζῴων,** *one of the
Living Creatures :* there does not appear any special significance
in attributing the summonses to these, except as they are the
highest agents of God's will ; in the plagues of the trumpets
and the bowls, the seven angels are the agents, 8⁶, 16¹ ; see on
5⁵. — **φωνῇ** : dat. of man. is the preferable reading. If *φωνή*
be read it follows the author's common usage with appos., see
p. 224 ; but see text. note. — **ἔρχου,** *come:* this summons, repeated in the following verses, is, as most among recent com.
are agreed, addressed to the several horsemen, as shown by
their immediate appearance in each case in response to the call.
Many have supposed the Seer to be addressed ; so, the copyists
who in some Mss. add *καὶ ἴδε, and see* (cf. AV). But the summons to him together with his immediate response was given at
the opening of the vision, 4¹ ; a fourfold repetition of the call
in this place would be without motive, and there is no response
on his part given here ; nor is the summons given in v. 12,
where it would be expected, if it were addressed to the Seer.
Still less tenable is the view (*e.g.* Alford, Swete) that Christ is
addressed, a view based on the erroneous supposition that the
Living Creatures represent nature (see on 4⁶), and so here

yearning for the final redemption of creation (Ro. 8$^{22\,f.}$) they join with the Church in the prayer for the Lord's coming (cf. 22^{17}). But the scenes with which the summons here stands connected are entirely different from the final renewal of creation.

2. The imagery of the four variously colored horses is suggested by Zec. 6$^{1-8}$, where they represent the ministers who go forth to do God's will in the earth, and are, at least in part, ministers of destructive judgments. That the Heb. prophet took the figures from some popular tradition is not improbable. Whether their origin goes back ultimately to a representation in which they figured the four quarters of the heavens, or the four seasons, and were conformed in color to certain heavenly bodies, as some suppose (cf. Gunkel *Schöpfung* 122, 125; Jeremias 24 f.) is not important here, since that origin, if such it was, did not affect the use of the figures by the prophet, or the Apocalyptist. A trace of the derived character of the imagery with our author appears in the fact that the horses are mentioned before their riders, though entirely subordinate in significance. The Apocalyptist in taking over the imagery from Zec. modifies it freely after his custom, and gives it greater clearness. A single horse takes the place of the pair and chariot in the vision of Zec., the horses are not ministers of God, but bearers of his ministers, and their color is conformed to the character of the rider, and so made important in the symbolism, while in Zec. it is doubtful whether it has special significance. Three of the horsemen are brought distinctly into connection with the three sore judgments, war, famine, and pestilence, frequently grouped together, especially in Jeremiah (*e.g.* 14^{12}, 24^{10}, 42^{17}), while the fourth, on the white horse, is placed first and made part of the symbol of *conquest*, not elsewhere with certainty mentioned in the list of God's punitive judgments.

The first rider unquestionably symbolizes the *victorious warrior* (see p. 264); the bow declares him a warrior, his progress of victory is declared in the words 'conquering and to conquer,' and is also symbolized by his crown and the color of his horse. But who is this victor? The white horse and the crown are supposed by many commentators to identify him with the Christ, who appears thus equipped at the end riding forth with his hosts to battle, $19^{11\,ff.}$. Confirmation of this view is thought to be found in the fact that no calamities such as follow the other riders are mentioned here ; and further a triumph of the cause of Christ appears to be promised in the apocalyptic discourse of the Gospels (Mk. 13^{10}) before the 'beginning of woes.' But the white horse and the crown are marks of any one riding forth to victory in war. The advancing conquest of an enemy carries with it invariably its calamities, the sufferings are multiform and too evident to need specification, they are not mentioned in connection with the triumph of the Beast in 13^7. Whether or not the utterance attributed to the Lord in Mk. 13^{10} regarding the preaching of the gospel ($\kappa\eta\rho\upsilon\chi\theta\tilde{\eta}\nu\alpha\iota$ not $\nu\iota\kappa\tilde{\eta}\sigma\alpha\iota$) to all the world stands there in the right connection, it is clear from the whole course of events in the Apocalypse that the author agrees with the common N. T. eschatology, which is represented in the form of the apocalyptic utterance recorded in Mt. 24^{14} and which puts the fulfillment of the gospel mission before the parousia and not before the 'beginning of woes.' Equally inconclusive is the above line of argument when used to show that the victor symbolizes, not Christ, but his cause, or the cause of God. It is hardly conceivable that Christ should be represented here as the Lamb in the court of heaven breaking the seals and at the same time by that act revealing himself as a figure coming into view from another quarter and in another form in response to a summons from an archangel. But however that may be, there is no place in the dramatic plan of our book for the supposed triumph till the long series of judgments have been fulfilled, unless it be in anticipation ; but such anticipatory passages, which are frequent in the book, always stand in a quite different relation to their context; they are never (not even in $6^{12\,ff.}$) made, as would be the case here, a member of a closely connected series, without indication of a difference in standpoint. Here, however, the contrary indication is found ; the four riders are most naturally taken to constitute a uniform group as do the other groups, the four horses of Zec. and the four Living Creatures ; that is, the first rider, like the three others, is the personification of a judgment to be sent upon the earth. In this interpretation are agreed the larger number of most recent com. (*e.g.* Holtzm., Bouss., Wellhausen, Moffatt, Swete) as well as some among earlier com. (*e.g.* Bengel, De Wette).

Whether this conqueror be understood as the personification of conquest in general, or of the conquest of the West by the hordes of Parthians from the East, of whose invasion the Roman world was at this time in dread, the difference is not fundamental. Since the bow was the special weapon of the Parthians and they were famed as horsemen, many scholars suppose them to be designated here ; that is, their invasion is to be one of the punishments sent by God in the last days. The figure of the bow is, however, not decisive, for it is frequently mentioned alone, especially in the poetic books, as the emblem of the warrior ; *e.g.* Jer. 51⁵⁶, Hos. 1⁵, Hab. 3⁹, Ps. 45⁵. The parallelism with the three following riders would favor reference to the personification of conquest in general. At all events the general calamities of conquest are thought of and not the specific horror of slaughter in battle, which is represented by the second rider. The two symbols are not identical. Unless the writer drew the four figures from some lost source, based upon the same symbolism which appears in Zec., the addition of conquest to the three oft-mentioned punishments, the sword, famine, and pestilence, is original with him ; though Jer. sometimes adds to these as a fourth, captivity (*e.g.* 15², 21⁷, 29¹⁷ ᶠ·), which may be understood to be uppermost in the thought of conquest. — στέφανος, *a crown:* see on 2¹⁰. — καὶ ἵνα νικήσῃ, *and to conquer :* he is seen in the vision conquering, and he is to continue his victories.

3-4. See p. 265. The second rider, as shown by the sword, the color of his horse, and the mission to take peace from the earth, symbolizes war, or more precisely, the slaughter of war. As in the case of the two riders following and probably in the first also, the representation is purely symbolical, without reference to any particular event of the history of the time. — ἵνα σφάξουσιν : parallel with λαβεῖν as subj. of ἐδόθη. For this use of ἵνα with fut. ind., more commonly with a subjv., in the N. T. see Burton § 211.

5-6. See p. 265. The scales for weighing carried in the

hand, and the announcement of the extreme dearness of grain, show that the rider personifies famine; the black horse also fitly represents the ensuing distress. — ζυγόν, *a balance:* the expression to *eat bread by weight* denotes famine (Ezk. 4¹⁶, Lev. 26²⁶), though the *price* of grain as announced here is fixed by measure rather than by weight. — ὡς φωνήν, *as it were a voice:* this use of ὡς, giving a certain vagueness or mysteriousness to a phrase, is one of the characteristics of the writer's style; *e.g.* 8¹, 14³, 19¹, ⁶; cf. Bouss. on 4⁶.   Nothing shows from whom the voice comes; the only important thing is that it comes from the heavenly presence; if from the Living Creatures, we should expect ἐξ instead of ἐν μέσῳ, *in the midst of;* certainly the view (Düst. Alf. *al*) that it is associated with the Living Creatures because they represent the natural world rests upon a misconception, see on 4⁶.   The words 'a measure of wheat for a denarius,' etc., are not meant to fix a limit beyond which the famine or the price of grain might not go ('See that thou furnish a measure for a denarius,' Alford, Swete) and so protect the sufferer; for the price named is so enormous, perhaps twelve times the ordinary rate, that the words as a benevolent limitation would be ironical.   The ordinary rate at Rome in the time of Cicero (*Verr.* III. 81; for the evidence of the Mishna in the second cent. see Hast. III, 432) was a denarius for twelve measures of wheat; and barley cost half as much.   Apparently in Asia Minor at the time of the Apocalypse the relative cost of the grains was three to one. — χοῖνιξ, *a choenix, a measure:* about a quart. — δηναρίου, *for a denarius:* the denarius at its best was equal to about 18 cents (cf. Hast. III, 432), but with Nero and afterwards it was debased.   It was the wages of a day-laborer (cf. Mt. 20²), who could thus earn enough in a day to buy at these famine prices a quart of wheaten flour, or three quarts of barley meal.

τὸ ἔλαιον . . . ἀδικήσῃς, *hurt not the oil and the wine:* these words have given much difficulty to interpreters.   According to many com. the writer's purpose is to give a tone of peculiar hardness to the picture of the famine by leaving oil and wine, luxuries, cheap, while the bare necessities of life are beyond the reach of the poor.   But such emphasis on the advantage possessed by the rich can hardly be attributed to the writer in this

series of universal visitations; and moreover the place of oil
and wine in domestic economy is mistaken, as will be seen
below.　In seeking the meaning it may be observed : (1) the
plagues foretold in the breaking of the first six seals are, as
pointed out above (pp. 264 f.), such as occur with greater or
less severity in the natural order of events, and are introductory to the more dreadful calamities following the breaking of
the seventh seal (8¹) ; they are therefore *limited* in their operation.　The limitation thus implied in all is directly expressed
in the fourth (v. 8) ; so in this case the exemption of the oil
and wine might in itself be regarded as having no other significance than the setting of bounds to the operation of the famine.　(2) ' Corn and oil and wine ' is the standing formula for
designating the nutritive products of the earth, whether with
reference to times of plenty or dearth; *e.g.* Dt. 7¹³, 11¹⁴, 28⁵¹;
2 Chron. 32²⁸ ; Neh. 5¹¹ ; Hos. 2⁸, ²² ; Joel 2¹⁹ ; Hag. 1¹¹.　These
were the staple food supplies grown in the biblical lands.　They
were all essential to the normal life of those countries, they were
none of them really luxuries.　A quite natural characterization
of a limited famine might therefore be the exemption of one or
two of these articles.　(3) A drought is often severe enough
to destroy grain entirely (though in the famine here foreseen
all of the grain even is not destroyed ; some is left for market),
while the olive and the vine with their deeper roots are not
seriously affected.　The great famine which sent the sons of
Jacob to Egypt to buy grain had continued a considerable time
when they were still able to take with them a present of the
fruits of the land (Gen. 43¹¹).　Such a famine in which the
grain perished while the olive and the vine escaped must have
been familiar to every dweller in those drought-frequented
lands.　(4) It is then a supposition close at hand that our
author in the words, ' Hurt not the olive-oil,' etc., *intends merely
a limitation in the severity of the famine, and that he draws the
form of the limitation from familiar experience, without any reference to the comparative importance of the different articles, or a
symbolical meaning,* just as *e.g.* he takes from current experience
the limit of five months set to the torments of the locusts in 9⁵ ;
see note there. — **ἀδικήσῃς** : on the use of *ἀδικεῖν* for injury to
vegetable life, cf. 7³, 9⁴.

If the above interpretation be correct, there is no necessity for seeking a reference to some particular historical famine, *e.g.* that in the time of Claudius, 62 A.D. The exemption of the oil and wine has received recently an explanation from contemporaneous history which has been approved by a number of scholars (*e.g.* Bouss. Moffat). Reinach (*Rev. Archéol.* 1901, 350 ff.) finds here allusion to an event in the time of Domitian, who according to Suetonius issued in the year 92 an edict, in the interest of the Italian wine-growers, ordering half the vineyards in the provinces to be destroyed. The opposition to the edict in Asia Minor became so violent that it was withdrawn before its execution had begun; the vineyards were spared. Now the Apocalyptist, it is argued, had these recent events in mind; as an ascetic he approved the edict and was displeased at its withdrawal; and in framing this vision he introduced into it the preservation of the vine in ironical contrast with the destruction of the necessities of life. But to say nothing of the assumption regarding the Apocalyptist's attitude toward the edict, Reinach's supposition leaves quite out of account the exemption of the oil, which must also be accounted for. Oil was not a luxury and here it is made equally important with the wine, in fact stands before it. It should further be noted that the edict had no relation to a famine; the sparing of the vines by its withdrawal would not, then, have in the author's mind any association with a famine picture. The view has not been widely accepted even among scholars who most strongly emphasize, not to say sometimes exaggerate, the traces of contemporaneous events in the apocalyptic pictures.

7–8. See p. 265. The fourth rider personifies the vast destruction of human life by sword, famine, pestilence, and wild beasts, God's ' four sore judgments,' standing forms of visitation found grouped together elsewhere, *e.g.* Ezk. 14^{21}, 5^{17}, Jer. $15^{2\,f.}$, Lv. 26^{22-26}. The judgment here described does not include a mere repetition of those of the second and third seals. The second rider represents slaughter *in battle;* here all forms of death by the sword are meant, such as might occur in great numbers in an unsettled and tyrannical society. The third rider's operations are described as affecting the vegetable world and thus inflicting suffering on men, but not necessarily death ; here the havoc of famine in the destruction of human life is meant. These broader and more calamitous ravages of the sword and famine are appropriately reserved to this place to be grouped with the deathful plagues of pestilence and wildbeasts, as the special instruments of the fourth rider, Death. The rider here does not personify death in general, but only the particular operations of death wrought through the fourfold instrumentalities mentioned.

χλωρός, *pale:* a modification of the 'grizzled' in Zec. 6³. The word, denoting the pallor of death and not strictly appropriate to a horse, is transferred from the rider. — ὁ καθήμενος : nom. abs. repeated in αὐτῷ; cf. 2²⁶. — θάνατος, *death :* the word cannot here mean *pestilence,* as it does at the end of the verse ; this is shown by the combination of death and Hades in which the words as elsewhere are practically synonymous ; cf. 1¹⁸, 20¹³,¹⁴, Is. 28¹⁵, Hos. 13¹⁴ ; also his office here includes more than the work of pestilence. — ᾅδης, *Hades :* on the combination with death see on 1¹⁸. It is not important to ask whether Hades is mounted ; he is certainly not thought of as a fifth rider coördinate with the other four (so, Spitta, 296). — ἐδόθη αὐτοῖς, *was given to them: i.e.* to Death and Hades. If αὐτῷ be read (see text. note) it may refer to the former, the words καὶ ᾅδης . . . αὐτοῦ forming a parenthesis, or the sing. may be used because the two are thought of as one ; for the interchange of sing. and pl. see on αὐτῶν, v. 17. — τὸ τέταρτον, *the fourth part :* the ravages were very great but *limited ;* not half or even a third of the whole population of the earth is affected ; see p. 253. — ἐν, ὑπό : the former denotes the instrument and is more appropriate to inanimate things ; the latter, subordinate agency ; cf. L and S. *s. v.* A. II. 1. — ῥομφαίᾳ : a distinction from μάχαιρα v. 4 is not to be insisted on here ; the words are often used interchangeably, see Thayer, *s. v.* — θανάτῳ, *pestilence:* the LXX frequently use θάνατος to translate דֶּבֶר, *pestilence, e.g.* Jer. 14¹², 24¹⁰, Lv. 26²⁵ ; that is the meaning here, since a special form of death is meant, as shown by connection with the other substantives.

9. See p. 265. The writer's tendency to divide a series of seven into groups of 4 + 3 or 3 + 4 (see p. 254) appears here. Four plagues are grouped together as represented by the four riders. The plague of the earthquake (vv. 12–17) which belongs in the same category is severed from these by the introduction in this place of a vision of the martyrs, beginning the group of three (the vision of the seventh seal begins in 8¹). The scene here introduced is appropriate in a revelation of things that precede the extreme visitations of the End and the parousia ; for it tells of the prayers of the persecuted for judgment, a recognized influence in bringing in the End (cf. Lk.

18⁷, see p. 79), and it foretells persecutions still to come, which according to the Gospel tradition the Lord grouped with the plagues as forming the events which must needs first come to pass, Mk. 13⁷⁻⁹. It is moreover the Apocalyptist's habit to introduce into every series of predicted sufferings, encouragement for the martyr. The cry heard here comes from those who have already been slain for the testimony of Jesus, *i.e.* from Christian martyrs. The largeness of the events described in all the visions of the seals shows that more than a few isolated cases of martyrdom are meant. The readiest explanation of the reference is found in Nero's persecution. Another persecution is threatening, it is not far off (v. 11 'a little time'); that under Domitian seems to be indicated by the various conditions of the book; see pp. 205 f.

ὑποκάτω τοῦ θυσιαστηρίου, *under the altar :* this must be the altar in heaven, distinctly placed there in other passages, *e.g.* 8³, ⁵, 14¹⁸, and not that in the earthly temple at Jerusalem. Even if the latter had been standing at the time, a Christian writer could not have pictured that as the abode of the souls of the martyred saints. Only once in the book (11¹) is the earthly altar meant, and then the reference is made clear by connected words. The conception of heaven under the form of God's temple is common not only in the Apocalypse but elsewhere ; *e.g.* 11¹⁹, 14¹⁵, ¹⁷, 15⁵, ⁸ ; Ps. 18⁶, Hab. 2²⁰, Mic. 1², Test. Lev. 18⁶. As God was of old thought to dwell with his people in his earthly temple, so naturally heaven as his dwelling-place came to be thought of as his temple, as well as his kingly palace and the seat of his throne. The two conceptions are merged in one in the vision of the Apocalyptist without any distinct separation. The combination furnishes no difficulty, as maintained by some ; it occurs elsewhere, *e.g.* Is. 6¹, Ps. 11⁴, 29⁹ ᶠ·, Song of the Three Children 31, 33, Test. Lev. 5¹. Nor is it necessary to inquire whether the altar was in the outset represented in God's throne-room in chapt. 4 (another difficulty raised by criticism); it is doubtless not thought of there. Like the roll in the hand of God, the figure of the Lamb and the myriads of angels, it comes into view, or at least into notice, as the vision grows or changes after the manner of visions ; see on 5¹¹.

For the general significance of our passage it is not important
to determine whether the altar here spoken of represented the
altar of burnt-offering, or that of incense; on the two altars
see on 11[1]. Most scholars understand it of the former, because
that is thought to explain more easily the representation of the
souls of the martyrs as in safe-keeping beneath the altar. In
the ritual of sacrifice the blood of the victim, *i.e.* its life (Lev.
17[11]), was poured out at the base of the altar of burnt-offering,
Lev. 4[7]. So the life, the soul, of the martyr, whose blood was
a sacrifice offered to God (cf. Phil. 2[17], 2 Tim. 4[6]) might be
thought of as laid at the base of the altar of burnt-offering. In
this way the belief may have easily arisen that the souls of the
martyrs were in safe-keeping under the altar of burnt-offering
in heaven. (But see fine print below.) Similar is a belief
found in the rabbis of the second cent., as quoted by Weber
(*System* 322 ff.): God comforting Moses at his death says, ' I
will conduct thee up to the highest heaven and cause thee to
dwell under the throne of my glory,' Debar. rabba 11; so in
Schabbath 152 b, ' The souls of the righteous are kept under
the throne of glory.' Some who understand the altar of incense
to be meant in our passage attribute to it " characteristics belonging to the earthly altar of burnt-offering" (Charles, *Ap.
Stud.* 178) and so explain in the same way the language here
used of the abode of the martyrs.

Some scholars take the heavenly altar throughout the book to be the
altar of incense, finding no place for an altar of burnt-offering; so, De
Wette, Bleck, *al.* The view has recently been elaborately defended by
Charles, *Ap. Stud.* 161 ff. In fact our present passage is the only one
which seems to point distinctly to the altar of burnt-offering, and that
merely as explaining the place of the martyrs' abode. In 8[3], where two
altars are supposed by many to be distinguished, the second is perhaps
better taken to be only a more definite specification of the first; see note
there. It will be noticed that in all places in the book, where the heavenly
altar is spoken of, it is connected more or less directly with the execution
of judgment for which the saints are praying; and on the other hand these
prayers of the saints for judgment are in the book symbolized by, or connected with the offering of, incense (5[8], 8[3, 4]). It is not improbable therefore
that the altar in our passage should be taken as the altar of incense, and
that this relation of the incense to the prayers of the martyrs should then
furnish the explanation of this designation of their abode, while awaiting
the judgment; *i.e.* they are, in the mind of the writer, associated with that
altar from which goes up the incense of their prayers for judgment.

τὴν μαρτυρίαν, *the testimony :* not the testimony which they had borne in preaching, but that which they had received from Jesus. The other passages in which this expression is joined as here with ὁ λόγος τοῦ θεοῦ, *the word of God* (1², ⁹, 20⁴, cf. 12¹⁷) leave no doubt that Ἰησοῦ, *of Jesus,* is implied; that is, the testimony which Jesus bore is meant (see on 1²), and the phrase makes the preceding words more specific; καί is epexegetical, *even.* The whole expression, *the word of God, even the testimony borne by Jesus,* denotes the divine revelation which Jesus had given in the gospel; it is on account of *holding* that, that the Christians were martyred. The words ἣν εἶχον, *which they had, i.e. held* are appropriate to that which the Christians had received (cf. 12¹⁷, Jno. 5³⁸, 14²¹), but not to a testimony which they had borne; this latter interpretation found in many com. certainly cannot be maintained.

10. The cry of the martyrs for the avenging of their blood falls below the prayer of St. Stephen, 'Lay not this sin to their charge,' Ac. 7⁶⁰, but it is uttered in the consciousness that their cause is one with that of the 'holy and true' God invoked; it is a cry for just judgment (κρίνεις); it is also a cry, like that of the whole Church (22¹⁷), for the speedy coming of the kingdom. Such a cry of suffering righteousness sent up to heaven is of frequent occurrence; *e.g.* Ps. 79⁵⁻¹⁰, Lk. 18⁷, Heb. 12²⁴, En. 9³, ¹⁰, 22⁵, 2 Es. 4³⁵. The parallelism between the passage in 2 Es. and these verses of our book is so striking that a common literary origin is not improbable. The feeling which thus expresses itself is not a mere thirst for revenge, it is in part at least a protest of righteousness against iniquity. — ὁ δεσπότης: nom. for voc. — ὁ ἅγιος καὶ ἀληθινός, *the holy and true one :* God is appealed to in his character of apartness from all evil, his absolute holiness, which cannot tolerate the iniquity perpetrated, and as one who is true to that ideal of holiness (see on 3⁷). The words might be understood to be addressed to Christ; but the analogy of similar prayers referred to above points rather to God as the person invoked. — ἐκδικεῖς, ἐκ: for the repetition of the preposition cf. 19²; frequent in the LXX. — τῶν κατοικούντων κτλ., *those that dwell on the earth : the world,* in its hostility to God; see on 3¹⁰.

11. White garments are given to the martyrs (see on 3⁴ ᶠ·);

already they are *in part* accorded the glory of the reward, but
they are not thought of as transferred from 'beneath the altar'
to the immediate presence of God.   That full fruition is not in
our book granted to any before the Millennium.   The raiment
of white is understood by some to be the glorified body given
to the martyrs as a peculiar reward before the resurrection (cf.
Bouss. *Jud.* 265); but white raiment is too common a figure to
be used in so specific a sense without some further definition.
The glorified body would for the martyrs seem rather to belong
to the 'first resurrection' (20⁶) to which they attain at the
Millennium. — ἀναπαύσωνται, *should rest :* the word does not
in itself express the idea of blessedness; it denotes rest from
toil, weariness, pain, etc.; here, as shown by the following
words, the martyrs' rest from their present distressful yearning
and crying for the coming judgment.   In the gift of the
heavenly raiment, *i.e.* in the bestowal of a blessedness symbolized by such raiment, and in the promise of a consummation
near at hand, they are to await the end in blessed patience. —
If the fut. ind. be read here (see text. note) see on 3⁹ for its use
with ἵνα. — πληρωθῶσιν, *be fulfilled :   i.e.* till the number of
their fellow martyrs be filled up, a modification of the familiar
belief that the coming of the end was conditioned on the filling
up of a predestined number of the elect; cf. 2 Es. 4³⁶, Ap.
Bar. 30²; cf. also the Book of Common Prayer, 'We pray thee
shortly to accomplish the number of thine elect and to hasten
thy kingdom.' — καὶ οἱ σύνδουλοι αὐτῶν, *their fellow-servants
also :* made more specific by the following words (καί before
οἱ ἀδελφοί is epexegetical), *even their brethren who are about to
be slain.*

12.   See p. 266.   The breaking of the sixth seal introduces a
vision of a violent earthquake, accompanied by vast disturbances in the whole world of the heavens.   The details of the
scene, even the language, are with a few exceptions derived
from the stereotyped forms found widely current in apocalyptic
descriptions of the end.   These the author has taken and skill-
fully combined into an apalling spectacle.   And with his usual
freedom he does not, like his predecessors, make these portents
the *immediate* introduction to, or accompaniment of, the Great
Day of the Lord — that is yet later in the plan of his book —

rather he makes them the last and most powerful of those
'signs' which form the *beginning* of woes, one of the series
prophetic of the more dreadful calamities which are to follow
when the seventh seal shall be broken. The chief difficulty in
the interpretation of this vision has arisen from two causes.
(1) Many interpreters have failed to give their proper value
and nothing more to the words, 'the great day has còme'
(v. 17), which are not those of the Seer announcing an actual
fact ; they are the language of terror-stricken men who mis-
interpret the portents around them, as signs that the last day
is actually breaking upon them.   (2) Stereotyped imagery and
forms of expression describing in hyperbole earthquakes and
other convulsions in nature have in the criticism of the Apocalypse been understood as the Seer's literal description of what
he is beholding ; he is understood to see the rolling up of the
firmament and the removal of the mountains as actually taking
place in this vision.   But the writer himself shows that he is
speaking in hyperbole.   He could not declare literally that
every mountain was removed, and in the next sentence describe
men as seeking to hide themselves in the mountains and calling
to the rocks to fall upon them and hide them.   The imagery of
the vision is scarcely more exaggerated than that occurring
frequently in Hebrew poetry to describe a violent disturbance
in nature ; the moving of the mountains, the trembling of the
heavens, the bowing of the heavens, etc., are familiar figures.
The author is here clearly using current apocalyptic language
and describing great natural convulsions, which, though tra-
ditionally connected with the final catastrophe, he places in a
series of plagues belonging all alike to the *forerunners* of the
last calamities.

σεισμός, *earthquake :* a frequent factor among the signs of
the end ; *e.g.* Is. 2¹⁹, 29⁶, Hag. 2⁶, 2 Es. 6¹⁶, Mk. 13⁸, par. —
ὁ ἥλιος ἐγένετο μέλας κτλ., *the sun became black*, etc. : cf. Joel
2¹⁰, 'The earth quaketh, the heavens tremble, the sun and the
moon are darkened, and the stars withdraw their shining' ; cf.
also Ezk. 32⁷ ⁱ·, Is. 13¹⁰, Amos 8⁹, Mk. 13²⁴ ⁱ·. — σάκκος τρίχινος,
sackcloth of hair : the garb of mourning.   Cf. Is. 50³, 'I clothe
the heavens with blackness and I make sackcloth their covering.' — ἡ σελήνη ἐγένετο ὡς αἷμα, *the moon became as blood :* cf.

Joel 2³¹, Ac. 2²⁰, Ass. Mos. 10⁵. The figure is doubtless drawn from the reddish appearance of the moon in an eclipse, or when obscured by certain atmospheric conditions. 13. οἱ ἀστέρες ἔπεσαν, *the stars fell:* cf. Mk. 13²⁵, par. — ὡς συκῆ κτλ., *as a fig tree casteth,* etc. : adapted from Is. 34⁴, 'as a fading leaf from the fig tree' ; cf. also Nah. 3¹². 14. ὁ οὐρανὸς ἀπεχωρίσθη κτλ., *the heaven was removed,* etc. : the sky, regarded as a flexible material expanse, is conceived to be withdrawn by being rolled up like the roll of a book. 'The heaven shall be rolled together as a scroll,' Is. 34⁴ ; cf. Sib. Or. III. 82. The word ἀποχωρίζειν does not denote a splitting, or rending in pieces (so, some com.), but a removal to another place. For the passing of the heavens cf. 21¹, Mk. 13³¹, par., Ps. 102²⁶, 2 Pet. 3¹⁰. — πᾶν ὄρος κτλ., *every mountain,* etc. : cf. 16²⁰. A literal parallel to the carrying away of the mountains and the islands from their places is not found in apocalyptic writings, but the representation is doubtless suggested by the familiar effects of earthquake and volcanic disturbance, in which mountains are shattered and islands disappear. Cf. 'The mountains skipped like rams,' Ps. 114⁴ ; 'all the hills moved to and fro,' Jer. 4²⁴. 15–16. οἱ βασιλεῖς κτλ., *the kings,* etc. : these seven classes are meant to include every rank and condition of men from the highest to the lowest. — οἱ μεγιστᾶνες, *the princes,* or *nobles:* i.e. those high in civil rank (cf. 18²³, Mk. 6²¹), while the χιλίαρχοι, *chief captains,* are the military tribunes, lit. commanders of a thousand, cf. 19¹⁸, Mk. 6²¹. — ἔκρυψαν ἑαυτοὺς κτλ., *hid themselves,* etc.: cf. Is. 2¹⁹, 'Men shall go into the caves of the rocks, and into the holes of the earth, from before the terror of Jehovah, and from the glory of his majesty, when he ariseth to shake mightily the earth' ; cf. also Is. 2¹⁰,²¹. — λέγουσιν τοῖς ὄρεσιν κτλ., *they say to the mountains,* etc. : derived from Hos. 10⁸, 'They shall say to the mountains, Cover us ; and to the hills, Fall on us'; cf. Lk. 23²⁰. — ἀπὸ τῆς ὀργῆς τοῦ ἀρνίου, *from the wrath of the Lamb:* the feeling of terror expressed here is the same as that spoken of in 1⁷, 'All the tribes of the earth shall mourn because of him.' The Apocalypse, as the book of judgment, makes emphatic the affection of divine wrath in Christ. He is appropriately recognized as

2 M

joined with God in the approaching visitation. In putting into the mouth of the speakers the title, the Lamb, the author uses it in the sense which it has as one of the special terms of the book (see pp. 314 ff.) and not as a designation of Christ in a character of gentleness or meekness. There is then no inappropriateness in the wrath here attributed to him ; see below.

These words are rejected by some critics (Vischer, 40; Völter, *Offenb.* 23 ; J. Weiss 64) on the ground that the Lamb is not in this scene in the court of heaven represented as a judge, that wrath is incongruous in a lamb that has been slain, and that the sing. αὐτοῦ, v. 17, found in some Mss. shows God alone to have been mentioned. With regard to the reading of the sing. in v. 17 see below. What is said above is sufficient to show the appropriateness of the words here.

17. As pointed out above the utterance of this verse is the mistaken cry of men in terror caused by the portents which are bursting upon them. At this place in his plan the author himself cannot be understood to declare that the last day has already come. — ἡ ἡμέρα ἡ μεγάλη, *the great day :* for this standing designation of the judgment day in eschatological language, see p. 22. — αὐτῶν *their : i.e.* of God and the Lamb. If the sing. αὐτοῦ, *his,* found in some Mss., be adopted, it may refer to the Lamb alone, the Lamb's wrath because of the hostility of the world being the thought uppermost in mind ; or while both God and the Lamb are thought of, the sing. may be used because their wrath is conceived as one, see on αὐτοῖς, v. 8, also the use of the sing., 22³, 1 Thess. 3¹¹, 2 Thess. 2¹⁶ ; others still would refer the pron. in the sing. to God alone. See text. note. — τίς δύναται σταθῆναι, *who is able to stand :* suggested by Nah. 1⁶, 'who can stand before his indignation ; and who can abide in the fierceness of his anger ?' cf. Mal. 3².

Textual notes, Chapt. 6¹⁻¹⁷. 1. φωνη ACQ, which some min many edd take as nom.; but the use of ως and the position after λεγοντος make the nom. extremely harsh.   Some min Ws WH Sod Sw *al* take it as a dat. φωνῇ. P some min R read φωνης ; א some min φωνην. — ερχου (without και ιδε) ACP many min some vers all recent edd RV ; אQ many min and vers add και ιδε ; but Q omits this in v. 3 ; the source of και βλεπε in R is uncertain. — 4. אᶜA some min Lch RVmrg omit εκ before της γης. — σφαξουσιν AC min edd ; σφαξωσιν אPQ min R. — 8. αυτοις (after εδοθη) אACP min vers R nearly all edd ; αυτω Q min vers Bouss Moff, see on v. 17. — 11. αναπαυσωνται אC min R most edd RV ; αναπαυσονται AQP min WH Bouss Sw. —

πληρωθωσιν AC min vers most edd; πληρωσωσιν אPQ min Tr Ti Sod *al;* but the ellipsis of τον δρομον, or τον αριθμον supposed with this reading is too violent. The source of πληρωσονται R is uncertain. — 16. πεσετε אCQ min R RVmrg edd; πεσατε AP min Lch WH WS Sw, this form also is 2 aor., cf. Kühn I § 226, 2, A 2. — 17. αυτων אC min vers Ti Tr WH Blj Sod Sw RV; αυτου APQ min vers R Lch Ws Bouss Moff. The more appropriate αυτων might easily be changed by a copyist to αυτου through the supposition that the οργης of this verse was merely a repetition of οργης in the preceding sentence, the principal thought then centering in the wrath of the Lamb. In view of this repetition of οργης, it may well be questioned whether the change of an original sing. to a pl. would not be harder than the reverse.

Criticism of Chapts. 4–6. The three parts of the scene given in these three chapts. respectively, God enthroned in glory, the book of destiny and the Messiah who shall open it, and the breaking of the seals, are so closely bound together that the integrity of the paragraph *as a whole* is unquestionable. The principal objections raised here by critics relate to (1) the connection with the preceding, or (2) with the following part of the book, (3) the Christian origin of the paragraph, and (4) the presence of certain words or phrases and in one instance a passage of several verses.

(1) The words εὐθέως ἐγενόμην ἐν πνεύματι 4² are taken to be at variance with 1¹⁰ and with the situation implied throughout 1¹⁰–3²² (see on 4¹⁻²), and to show that the Apocalypse began here, a few introductory words about the author having preceded. Further traces of a different author are urged: θύρα ἠνεῳγμένη ἐν τῷ οὐρανῷ implies that the heaven was hitherto closed, whereas the appearance of the glorified Christ 1¹⁰ ᶠᶠ· can only be conceived to have taken place in the heavens; the voice in 4¹ cannot be the same as that of 1¹⁰, therefore the words ἡ πρώτη . . . μετ᾽ ἐμοῦ must be due to a reviser trying to bring this paragraph into connection with a context primarily foreign to it. These are the principal grounds against a connection of these chapts. with the foregoing urged by Vischer (77) and his followers. So far as this criticism calls for consideration it has been met in the notes on 4¹.

(2) The vision of the sixth seal 6¹²⁻¹⁷, it is argued, ushers in the last day, so that now there remain only the judgment and eternal life; this vision then cannot introduce the events of 7¹⁻⁸ and many other later portions which have no place in those final scenes; so, Spitta 80 ff., 302, who makes the original Apocalypse end with a brief appendix to the sixth seal, including 8¹, 7⁹⁻¹⁶, and one or two other short sections. The misinterpretation of 6¹²⁻¹⁷ on which this theory rests is shown in the Com. on these verses.

(3) Critics who regard the book a working-over of one or more Jewish apocalypses find in this paragraph numerous traces of a non-Christian origin; see Vischer 79 ff., 55 ff., Weyland 88 f. Chapt. 4, it is argued, is throughout Jewish, containing nothing distinctively Christian. Besides this negative evidence, elements are found in that and the other chapts. which are at variance with a Christian origin; *e.g.* God, not Christ, is the one who is to

come 4[8] ; the Spirit is seven, not one 4[5], the martyrs are not martyrs of
Christ and do not appeal to him, their thirst for vengeance is unchristian
6[9 f.]; in chapt. 5 there are two Messiahs, one the Lamb brought in by the
Christian reviser, the other the lion, the Jewish hero who conquers by his
might, but with whom the idea of a redemptive death is not associated. Of
these arguments only the last calls for comment. The others have been
sufficiently noticed in the Com. on the respective passages. The hypothesis
of two Messiahs here is a part of the general theory that the book contains
a combination of irreconcilable Jewish and Christian elements. See on
this theory pp. 229, 230, 509, 511. Its maintenance in this paragraph
makes necessary, in order to get rid of the Christian elements, a process of
excision in the text so violent that it is approved by few critics. Even
Spitta (58 ff.), who finds two Jewish apocalypses worked into the book,
accepts chapts. 4–6 as an integral part of the Christian Apocalypse begun in
chapts. 1–3.

(4) The word ἀρνίον is in all places in these chapts. attributed by Vischer
and his followers to a reviser, as is necessary for maintaining the theory of
an original Jewish apocalypse here. Other sentences or phrases, not fundamentally important, have been rejected on different grounds; *e.g.* ἅ εἰσιν
... τοῦ θεοῦ 4[5]; αἵ εἰσιν ... τῶν ἁγίων 5[8] (on this passage see notes *in loc.*);
ἀπὸ τῆς ὀργῆς τοῦ ἀρνίου 6[17]. The important passage 5[9-14] is rejected by the
school of Vischer through the exigencies of their theory, cf. Vischer 55 ff.;
in part also, *i.e.* vv. 11–14, it is rejected by others; so, Völter *Offenb.* 14, Erbes
50, because in these verses the praises of the angels and creation are not,
like those of the Living Creatures 9–10, grounded on the Lamb's worthiness to open the book, *i.e.* they are not called forth by the circumstances of
the context, but by the general worthiness of God and the Lamb to receive
homage. Such a canon of criticism, which would exclude all broadening
of scope or variation in the course of a hymn, would leave few hymns, especially Hebrew psalms, intact. On excisions see further, p. 530.

These objections to the general integrity of chapts. 4–6 and their appropriateness in this place are not conclusive enough to have gained a wide
assent. The congruity of the paragraph with the author's plan (see pp.
261, 443 f.), its fitness as a splendid development of the motives underlying
the preceding chapts., its agreement with those chapts. in its messianic
conceptions, in its exalted christology, its manner and language, all produce
the conviction that we have at work here the same mind and with the same
conceptions as in the opening part. In this opinion are agreed the large
majority of recent scholars of differing schools.

Chap. VII. *Prelude to the breaking of the seventh seal.*
See pp. 266 ff. (1) Sealing of the servants of God, vv. 1–8.
(2) An anticipatory vision of the redeemed before the throne,
vv. 9–17.

The opening of the seals of the roll has proceeded in unbroken order to this point in our book, when there is inserted

here between the sixth and seventh seals a paragraph containing two short visions which at first sight seem to have no relation to each other nor to the course of events described in the
context.   The first shows an earthly scene in which the seal of
God is set on the twelve tribes of Israel (vv. 1–8); the second,
an innumerable throng out of every nation standing before the
heavenly throne, clad in festal raiment, and offering an exultant
hymn of homage to God and the Lamb (vv. 9–17).   Unquestionably this chapter is not a part of the vision of the sixth
seal.   That vision formed one of a series of plagues, and the
description of these was in each case complete in itself; the
subject-matter of this chapter is of a quite different character.
A transition is moreover indicated by the formula μετὰ τοῦτο
εἶδον, *After this I saw*, which regularly marks a change (see
on 4[1]) ; its use here (vv. 1, 9) shows that these two visions are
distinct from the preceding and from each other.   The exact
meaning of the two visions, their relation to each other, and
their insertion in this place raise exegetical and critical questions upon which scholars are very much at variance.   The
saying of Vischer (46) that 'good grounds may be urged for
every explanation, yet every one is weighted with insurmount-
able difficulties' is an overstatement; yet it is true that no
explanation can·be offered to which at least plausible objections
may not be made.   The explanation here given is that which
on the whole does least injustice to the details presented, and
at the same time conforms best to the author's conceptions and
characteristic manner, as seen elsewhere.   It is a misfortune in
the study of the passage that it has in many quarters been
viewed in too isolated an aspect.

(1) vv.· 1–8. (*a*) In the interpretation of the first vision
of the chapt. certain difficulties will be removed by the recognition of· what appears to be clearly established, that the
Apocalyptist here uses in the matter and the symbolism some
source not elsewhere preserved to us.   At the opening of the
vision four angels are seen at the four corners of the earth
holding back the winds; by the loud command of a fifth angel
who bears the seal of God they are bidden to stay the winds
from their sweep of destruction across the earth till the servants of God have been sealed.   Such a brief staying of deadly

forces for the safeguarding of certain persons or things to be exempt from destruction is found in several striking cases. In Ezk. 9⁴ ᶠᶠ· the ministers of slaughter in Jerusalem are held back till a mark is set on those to whom they may not come near. A parallel still closer is found in Ap. Bar. 6⁴ ᶠᶠ·; four angels are seen standing with torches of fire at the four corners of Jerusalem, while a fifth angel descends from heaven and bids them stay the destruction of the city till he has hidden in the earth the sacred articles of the temple. So again in En. 66 f.; the Seer in his vision of the deluge beholds the angels, who are about to let loose the waters upon the earth, holding them back for a time for the building of the ark. Now in all these parallels, except in our passage, the destructive powers are seen after the enforced pause to execute their destined works. But in our book the four winds whose work is stayed for the sealing only do not appear again. They are declared to be held back only for a definite interval; then their destructive work is expected to begin. We should most naturally look for it after the breaking of the seventh seal. But none of the plagues or catastrophes which follow in the later chapters are said to proceed from these winds, or are in anyway associated with them. The supposition then seems inevitable that the author is here adapting figures from some familiar source which forcibly picture his thought, just as we see him adapting O.T. sources to his use, though as regards exact form he has in this case been less careful to bring his source in all its details into strict harmony with the imagery of the later scenes. The thought uppermost with him here is the staying of coming evils by divine ordering till God's servants have been sealed. See further p. 538. The view that a source has been used here is further indicated in the remaining part of the vision to which these introductory verses (1–3) lead up; this will appear below (under *b* and *c*).

(*b*) Who are the servants of God for whose sealing the winds are stayed? They are specified as belonging to the twelve tribes of Israel. And if we confine our view to the present passage, Israel appears to be used literally of the Jewish people. A Christian writer may speak of the Church as the Israel of God (Gal. 6¹⁶), or as the twelve tribes of Israel

(James 1¹), adopting the comprehensive title of God's ancient
people as a whole.　Yet if he were writing independently,
without borrowing imagery from some Jewish archetype, it is
hardly possible that he should carry out the idea of identity to
a detailed division of the Church into twelve families answering severally to the twelve tribes of Israel.　And even if for
greater vividness he should transfer to the Church the tribal
divisions in idea, he would certainly adopt the ideal list of the
tribes rather than fashion one so anomalous as is here given
(see on vv. 5 ff.).　It seems most probable then, as the larger
number of critical scholars agree, that the author in this paragraph had in mind some apocalyptic source, in which a calamity threatening the people of Israel was to be stayed until certain chosen ones should be safeguarded from its operations.
This conclusion does not however determine the sense in which
he *applies* the symbolism; that this could not in its original
sense be taken up into a Christian apocalypse is evident.　Who
then, in the author's intention, are the 144,000 that are to be
sealed ?　The answer which, in spite of some difficulty raised,
is most conformable to the conceptions of the N.T. in general,
as well as those of the Apocalyptist — the one that does least
violence to the universalistic spirit of the book — is that they are
the whole body of the Church, Jewish and Gentile alike; so, many
scholars both ancient and modern.　(For other interpretations
see pp. 536 f.)　St. Paul everywhere conceives the Church
to be the true Israel, and Christians to be the true Jews
(*e.g.* Ro. 2²⁹, Gal. 6¹⁶); with St. James the Christians are the
twelve tribes (1¹, cf. Soden *Kom.* 176 ff.); for the same thought
elsewhere, cf. 1 Pet. 1¹, 2⁹; Hermas *Sim.* IX. 17¹.　So with our
author the Christian is the true Jew (2⁹, 3⁹), the city of the
Church triumphant is called Jerusalem, and its gates, whose
superscriptions designate those who are to enter through each,
bear the names of the twelve tribes of Israel (20⁹, 21². ¹²).　The
description, then, of the safeguarding of the Church under the
figure of the sealing of Israel as a whole gives in itself no difficulty.
And that this is the author's meaning he seems to show certainly by the mention of the 144,000 in 14¹, where they are seen
to be the whole body of triumphant Christians (see note there).
The absence of the article in that place is urged against the

identity of those with the persons of our passage (cf. Düst.), but on the contrary its omission is in keeping with the visionary style, see p. 650. The principal difficulty in the identification of Israel with the Church in our passage lies, as seen above, in the special enumeration of the tribes. But it must be kept in mind that the Apocalyptist conceivably follows his source more closely here than is his wont. In adopting the four riders from Zec. (see on 2^6), the four Living Creatures from Ezk. (see on 4^6), the two olive trees from Zec. (see p. 593), and similar imagery borrowed from the O.T., he modifies his source materially; but apparently in this instant less modification is introduced. He may have seen in the specification of the twelve tribes, which he found in his source, a strong expression of *completeness*, which is an essential part of his thought here; he therefore retains it as not foreign to his purpose, having in mind the fullness of the spiritual, not the national, Israel. For the emphasis shown on completeness here, see on v. 4.

A sealing of the saints in this place is in the opinion of some critics open to the objection that it belongs before the visitations of the earlier visions (cf. Spitta, 80 f.). But while it might have preceded these, it is introduced here with finer dramatic effect; for those judgments are but preliminary; the supreme trials, those for which God's special safeguarding is needed, are to come now with the breaking of the seventh seal. Like the anticipatory vision of final triumph in vv. 9–17, as will be seen below, the sealing is most appropriate immediately before the opening of the events which form the main chapters in the picture of the future.

Other views concerning the persons sealed. (1) They are *Jewish* Christians, whereas the multitude in vv. 9–17 are Christians of all nations alike, including Jews; so, many com., *e.g.* Bengel, Stuart, Düst. But no satisfactory explanation is given of the safeguarding of the Jewish Christians in distinction from others; none is indicated here, nor does our author, though a Jew, anywhere intimate that a preference or advantage is granted to the Jew. (2) They are the chosen 'Remnant' of Israel who have accepted Jesus as the Messiah; the author of the paragraph is a Judaistic Christian, with whom the Messiah is sent to Israel only; the *true* Israelites are those Jews who have accepted him, they only form the true Christians; this limited number, 144,000 out of the twelve tribes, are sealed for deliverance in the coming distresses (cf. *e.g.* Völter *Offenb.* 28 f.). That might conceivably have been the thought of the original source; but that meaning could not be attributed to the author of the Revelation in its present form; with him a national limitation of the messianic kingdom has altogether disappeared. (3) They are the Israelites who shall ultimately be grafted into the people of God (Ro. 11). Israel now rejecting Christ is hardened and cast off, but in the end a remnant of each tribe shall be converted; so, *e.g.* Bouss. Baljon. Attractive as this interpretation is, it is however open to what appears conclusive objection. The hope of the final conversion of Israel, at least in part, appears in 3⁹, 11¹³ (see notes *in loc*), but there is not in the present passage, as in those places, any intimation that the writer has in mind the *conversion* or bringing back of those now regarded as enemies (2⁹); the language here like that in Ezk. 9⁴ contemplates the safe-guarding of those who are now faithful 'servants of God.' This interpretation moreover, like all those that refer the words to the literal Israel, fails to give due force to the mention of the 144,000 in 14¹, see p. 535. (4) They are a small number chosen out of the Church because of their purity (14⁴) and destined to be delivered from the last plagues; gathered under the guidance of the Lamb on mount Sion (14¹), they will behold untouched the last dreadful events, while the mass of Christians (vv. 9–17) will fall in martyrdom; so, J. Weiss, 65 ff. But so far as this vision itself (vv. 1–8) shows — and it appears complete in itself — there is no intimation of a selection on certain undefined grounds, or of a deliverance of a part preliminary to the complete triumph of all in the end; the sealing is for all the 'servants of God' (see on v. 4) and designed to secure one common safe-guarding of all.

(*c*) What now is meant by the sealing? The seal is a mark of authentication (Ro. 4¹¹), or a means of security (Rev. 5¹, 20³). In our passage both these ideas may be included; *i.e.* in contrast with the mark of the beast set on his followers and showing them to belong to him (13¹⁶ ᶠ·), the seal of God may authenticate his servants as his; but the predominant thought here is that the seal, like the mark set on the chosen ones of Jerusalem in the closely parallel scene in Ezk., is a token or pledge of security. This is shown by the language of v. 3 staying the winds from their destructive work till the seal has been set on God's servants. This general meaning is unquestioned and has been assumed in the foregoing paragraph (*b*). But a more precise definition is needed. From what are the servants of God to be preserved? The most common answer of interpreters, both ancient and modern, is, From the plagues that are now to come upon the earth after the breaking of the seventh seal. If we limit our view to the present passage, the meaning would clearly be that the sealed are to be preserved from the ravages of the winds, which we should expect to see released as soon as the sealing is accomplished. The language of v. 3, and the analogy of the parallels mentioned above (in *a*) show pretty certainly that that was the meaning in the source which the author is following. But as seen in his use of the O. T., he freely adapts derived imagery to his own conceptions (see p. 221) ; we must then look beyond the prototype to ascertain exactly the sense intended in a borrowed symbol. Now in the eschatology of the N. T. in general and especially in our book the Last Times are distinctly made times of suffering and peril for God's servants ; cf. the eschatological discourse in the Gospels (Mk. 13, par.), and in our book the forewarning of the need of endurance, 13^{10}, 14^{12}, the prophecy of coming martyrdoms 6^{11}, the limitation of the promises to the victors in the seven epistles, and similar forebodings of distress (see on 3^{10}). And the relation of the scenes of chapt. 7 to the breaking of the last seal, which ushers in the whole cycle of events to the end, gives to this pledge of security a sense appropriate to the Christian's trial in these events. It seems clear that the servants of God are not to be exempted from the coming plagues throughout, though some of these are specifically limited to God's enemies, *e.g.* those of chapts. 9 and 16. The meaning is rather that in the awful calamities of the last days and the doom of the world, the saints, like the elect in Ezekiel's vision, are to be saved from destruction, and though they must suffer, many of them even unto death, they will finally be brought in safety out of all the woe into the eternal kingdom ; so, many recent com. *e.g.* Bouss. Baljon, Moff.

Düst. takes the sealing to denote security against apostasy. But this falls short of its scope. Fidelity unto the end is of course implied as a condition, but the thought is broader, including the *result*, salvation. Charles (*Studies*, 120 ff.) makes the sole purpose of sealing security against *demonic* agencies, as in 9^4 it is expressly stated to exempt from the torments of the demonic locusts; some of the plagues which from their nature must affect all alike, *e.g.* those of 8^{7-12}, Charles treats as interpolated (*ibid.*, 146 ff.). But at this point, where the pause is made for the purpose of safeguarding against the effects of opening the seventh seal, the pledge must, as indicated here and in the parallels mentioned, be understood to secure against all the effects, unless some special limitation is intimated; and the destructive forces set in operation at the breaking of the seventh seal, the overwhelming movements in heaven and earth, in face of which the Apocalyptist is seeking to encourage the Christians, are by no means due entirely to demonic agencies.

(2) vv. 9–17. The second vision of the chapt. reveals an innumerable company before the throne in heaven praising God and the Lamb for their finished salvation. Who now are the white-robed throng and to what place in the eschatological period does this scene belong? Are they redeemed *Gentile* Christians as contrasted with those of Israel in vv. 4–8 ? Some com. have taken them so. But the language shows them to be of all peoples, without distinction. Are they *martyrs* who have passed through death triumphantly and are seen thus in heavenly glory at the end? So, many com. *e.g.* B. Weiss, Bouss. Or if martyrs, do they form the remainder to be added to those 'beneath the altar' (6⁹⁻¹¹), and with these to be admitted to the final glory *before* the judgment? So, Ewald. Or still again are they the *whole company of the redeemed* out of every tribe of men, who shall stand glorified before God in the final blessedness after the judgment? So most earlier and the larger number of modern scholars take them. This interpretation seems certainly correct. The redeemed here are those who come out of every nation and tribe, a frequent expression in our book to denote mankind universally, Jew and Gentile alike (*e.g.* 5⁹, 13⁷, 17¹⁵); and they are here in no way distinguished as martyrs. These latter are described as ' those who have been slain for the word of God ' (6⁹), and 'those who have been beheaded for the testimony of Jesus' (20⁴); but the multitude in this vision are those who 'have washed their robes in the blood of the Lamb' (v. 14), a characterization of all saints alike; cf. 1⁵, 5⁹. The vision then is a revelation of the whole Church brought in safety through the great tribulation into the blessedness of its finished salvation. The passage is parallel with others which picture the felicity of all the saints in the consummation after the judgment. Such a revelation is given in 14¹⁻⁵ and 15²⁻⁴; there also, not the martyrs only are meant, but all the redeemed of the earth (14³), all who have gotten the victory over the beast (15²).

Viewed apart from the Apocalyptist's manner the interruption of the breaking of the seals at this point and the insertion of a vision apparently so out of place would be inexplicable. The incongruity is, however, only apparent. It is the author's habit, followed almost universally, to introduce at a great crisis or turning-point just such an anticipatory passage as this, looking beyond the immediate connection to the great outcome at the end. It is in pursuance of his art in throwing light into his darkest pictures. His aim is in each new instance to encourage his readers in the face of the calamities foretold. This principle of literary structure, one of the author's finest characteristics, has been fully shown above, pp. 244 ff. At the juncture which we reach at this point in his revelation we should therefore expect just such an anticipatory scene as we find here. The seventh seal is about to be broken ; with that the roll will be opened and the long series of awful judgments and portents leading up to Christ's final triumph will begin its course. But before the terror of it all overwhelms the reader, the Apocalyptist opens to him a glimpse into the glory and blessedness which lie beyond for him who can endure unto the end.

It will be seen, then, that the two visions of this chapt., with all the dissimilarities, relate to the same persons, the whole body of the Church, though seen in different stages of its experience. The first views the great conflict before the Church from its beginning, and pledges the guarding care of God which shall bring his faithful servants through the calamities awaiting them. The second anticipates the scene of triumph when all is finished, when the accomplished 'salvation' is the theme of the heavenly song (v. 10). The first is the promise; the second is the promise fulfilled. Viewed in this light, in relation to the events now about to be unfolded, the whole episode forms a passage of great splendor in the drama of our book.

Many scholars regard it as settled beyond question that the two visions cannot refer to the same persons; the one body numbers definitely 144,000, the other is innumerable ; the one is composed of Israelites only, the other of men of all nations; the one is just facing tribulation, the other has already passed beyond it; etc. But if the view taken above of the real meaning of each vision is correct, these objections lose their force. As regards numbers it is to be noticed that the Apocalyptist in the vision of the sealing is not speaking of a *selection*, whether great or small, out of the tribes of

Israel; the idea which he is emphasizing is the completeness of the number, all the servants of God are to be sealed (v. 3), and he hears the number when the sealing is finished; all the twelve tribes have been sealed and in each tribe the number is complete; see on v. 4. Between this symbolic expression of completeness in the first vision and the actual innumerable throng in the second there is no contradiction. The other points urged against identity are met in what has been said above.

(1) First part of the Prelude. The Sealing of the Servants of God, 7¹⁻⁸. See pp. 266, 532 ff.

1. μετὰ τοῦτο εἶδον, *after this I saw:* for this formula marking a change of vision see on 4¹. — τέσσαρας ἀγγέλους, *four angels:* ' the spirits of the winds ' are meant; cf. ' the angel of the waters,' 16⁵; see pp. 70, 445. The figure of the *four* winds as destructive agencies, or as connected with portents, is a familiar one; cf. Jer. 49³⁶, Dan. 7², Zec. 6⁵. The winds appear as a stereotyped factor in eschatological imagery; cf. Dan. *loc. cit.;* see also Bouss. *Antichrist* 246 ff., Gunkel *Schöpfung* 327 ff. As such they were doubtless used in the source followed by the Apocalyptist here; see pp. 533 f. — δένδρον, *tree:* cf. v. 3. The trees seem to be singled out as being especially exposed to the force of the winds. The construction changes to the acc. to express that *against* which the force is directed, while the gen. in the preceding nouns denotes that *upon* whose surface the winds blow. If πᾶν be read here, it signifies, after the negative vb., *any,* cf. 9⁴, Blass § 51, 2 ; Win. § 26, 1.

2. ἀπὸ ἀνατολῆς ἡλίου, *from the east:* lit. the sun-rising. Why this direction is specified is not certain; perhaps it is merely a picturesque feature (Blj.), perhaps it is a reminiscence of Ezk. 43⁴, where the glory of Jehovah, whose messenger in our passage brings the seal of salvation, is said to come from the east (Völter *Offenb.* 25). — ζῶντος, *living:* this epithet of God, frequent in later Jewish writings (see on 1¹⁸), is used appropriately where the sure accomplishment of his purpose for his people is thought of; cf. 10⁶, 15⁷, — οἷς, αὐτοῖς : see on 3⁸.

3. σφραγίσωμεν, *we shall have sealed:* the pl. includes with the speaker his helpers in the work of sealing. The omission of ἄν with the subjv. after ἄχρι, infrequent in classical Gk. (GMT. 620), is the rule in the N. T., see Blass § 65, 10. — τοὺς δούλους, *the servants:* reference is made, not to a select number, but to all God's servants, to whom belongs by his promise the pledge of security. — ἐπὶ τῶν μετώπων, *upon their foreheads:* taken directly from Ezk. 9⁴. The seal corresponds to the *mark* (σημεῖον) there set upon those who are to be delivered. The followers of the Beast also bear a mark (χάραγμα, never σφραγίς) in their foreheads, 13¹⁶. What the mark of the seal is, is not important; 14¹ would suggest that it is the name of God; so in Is. 44⁵ (RVmrg.) it is said that one shall 'write on his hand, Unto Jehovah,' in allusion to the branding of a slave with his owner's name; cf. also Hdt. II. 113. A reference to baptism, found by some, is impossible in this connection; moreover the figure is never applied to baptism in the N.T., though occurring in post-apostolic writings.

4. ἤκουσα, *I heard:* the number is too large for the Seer to count. — ἐσφραγισμένοι ἐκ πάσης φυλῆς, *sealed from every tribe: i.e.* there were sealed ones from every tribe, not 144,000 from every tribe, a sense which the words in themselves might have, but vv. 5–8 show that not to be the meaning intended. The words are added to emphasize the fact that every tribe is included. And the number 12,000 in the following enumeration, whether due to the Apocalyptist or found in his source, is as used here intended to symbolize completeness (see p. 254); every member of every tribe of God's children receives his pledge of security from destruction. The unnecessary naming of each several tribe, together with the repeated number 12,000, emphasizes in the strongest possible way the inclusion of every member of God's people. — The nom. ἐσφραγισμένοι in the appos. phrase follows the author's usage.

5–8. The list of tribes given here is probably due to the source, rather than to the Apocalyptist himself. The order of the tribes need not be especially considered here. Nineteen different arrangements of the names are found in the O.T., with none of which does this list agree. For a good tabular view of these see Hast. IV. 811; see also En. Bib. IV. 5208. Geographical or maternal relations determine the arrangement in many of the lists, but in others are disregarded. The list in this chapt. does not in its present form show a clear principle of order, but the same may be said of others. There are in this list two striking peculiarities. (1) The omission of the tribe of Dan. The explanation of this on the ground that the tribe had long been extinct (De Wette, Ewald, *al.*) is insufficient, since this is true of other tribes also. The theory, that an original Δαν in the Ms. was through a copyist's error displaced by Μαν and this then was taken for a contraction of Μανασση (Spitta, *al.*), is fanciful and is generally rejected. The explanation of Irenæus (V. 30, 2) that Dan was omitted because it was believed that Antichrist would come from that tribe appears in many early com. and is widely accepted among recent scholars (*e.g.* Erbes. Bouss. Blj. J. Weiss, Moff. Swete). This belief appears to have arisen from a rabbinical interpretation of such passages as Gen. 49^{17}, Jer. 8^{16}; it is expressed in Test. Dan. 6^1, and was evidently well known in the early centuries. There is therefore much evidence that the tribe of Dan was held in disfavor. (See Bouss. *Antichrist* 171 ff.; En. Bib. I. 997.) A Jewish or a Jewish-Christian apocalyptist might therefore have thought that it had lost its claim to a place in the messianic kingdom, and that another of the families appearing in the tribal lists should be substituted in its stead to fill up the number twelve. The name is omitted together with Zebulun, or evaded, in 1 Chron. 7^{12} (see Hast. II. 130, under Aher, En. Bib. I. 996, n. 4). It is noticeable that other names also are omitted from one or more of the lists, *e.g.* Simeon, Dt. 33, Jg. 5; in the latter place Judah also; Gad and Asher in 1 Chron. 27. (2) Another peculiarity in the list is the presence of both Manasseh and Joseph, though the former is included in the latter. This occurs in no other list. The name of Dan being omitted, the author of the list fills up the number by the choice of one of the two names, Ephraim and Manasseh, sons of Joseph, which appear in many of the lists. Ephraim may perhaps have been thought less suitable, because it is so often used as the designation of the ten northern tribes.

(2) The second part of the Prelude. An anticipatory vision of the redeemed before the throne, 7$^{9-17}$. See pp. 268, 539 f.

9. μετὰ ταῦτα εἶδον, *after these things I saw:* see on v. 1. — ὅν, αὐτόν: see on 3^8. — ἐκ παντὸς ἔθνους κτλ., *from every nation,* etc. : for this standing expression of the universality of the

final kingdom see on 5⁹. — ἑστῶτες, περιβεβλημένους : both referring to ὄχλος, an irregularity in construction characteristic of the author. — ἐνώπιον τοῦ θρόνου κτλ., *before the throne*, etc.: the picture of the throne-room and the various orders of angels as given in chapts. 4–5 reappears here in detail, vv. 9, 11, 13; hence the mention of the Lamb, which some critics regard as interpolated, is strictly in place. The language in vv. 15 ff., 'Shall spread his tabernacle over them,' etc., belongs rather to the renewed earth as the abode of the blessed, as in chapt. 21; heaven and earth are blended as often in eschatological representations. — στολὰς λευκάς κτλ., *white robes*, etc.: these are marks of festal rejoicing, especially in victory. For the use of palm branches cf. Jno. 12¹³, 1 Macc. 13⁵¹, 2 Macc. 10⁷.

10. σωτηρία τῷ θεῷ ἡμῶν κτλ., *salvation to our God*, etc.: as in 12¹⁰, 19¹, reference is made to the accomplished salvation of the saints; this is the foremost theme of praise. The form of expression ascribes the work of salvation to God and the Lamb, as in v. 12 the same idiom expresses a recognition of wisdom, etc., as belonging to God; see on 4⁹,¹¹.

11–12. The angel hosts join in rejoicing over the salvation of men, cf. Lk. 15¹⁰. With the initial *amen* they affirm in liturgical manner the praise just uttered by the redeemed, and at the same time show that in the following sevenfold doxology each several ascription to God, though quite general in itself, is uttered with special reference to the final salvation. Upon the wisdom and power of God in the work of redemption, cf. Eph. 3¹⁰, 1¹⁹. With this doxology compare that of 5¹².

13. ἀπεκρίθη, *answered:* no question is implied to which answer is made; the word is used here, as often in the LXX and the N.T., in imitation of the Heb. idiom, to introduce an utterance called forth by something which has preceded ; see Thayer, *s.v.* 2. — No special symbolical meaning is to be attached to the choice of an Elder as the speaker ; see on 5⁵. For the dialogue form in introducing the explanation of a vision, cf. Am. 7⁸, 8², Jer. 1¹¹,¹³, 24³, Zec. 4².

14. εἴρηκα : aoristic perf., see on 5⁷. — κύριέ μου, *my Lord :* the words express a sense of subordinateness in the speaker, but imply nothing as to whether the person addressed is human or superhuman. — σὺ οἶδας, *thou knowest :* the pron. is

emphatic ; ignorance on the Seer's part is implied. Until the
vision is explained he cannot certainly recognize in the heavenly throng those whom he had in the first vision seen sealed.
This ignorance of the Seer does not furnish an argument (so,
Vischer 50) against the identity of the two companies. — οἱ
ἐρχόμενοι, *those who come:* the explanation of Düst., *those who
are now coming,* as if said from the standpoint of present experience is against the connection. The part. with the art.
forms a noun, *the comers,* and the pres. expresses simply the
idea of the vb. without reference to time (cf. Burton § 123,
Blass § 58, 4 at the end) ; the time is determined by the context, which in this case shows the act to have already taken
place at the time anticipated in the vision ; οἱ ἐλθόντες, *those
who have come,* might have been used. Cf. τοὺς νικῶντας 15²,
ὁ πλανῶν 20¹⁰. The theory of J. Weiss (70) that in the
original apocalypse the idea was, Those who are now marching
in festal procession to meet the Messiah requires violent
changes in the text. — τῆς θλίψεως τῆς μεγάλης, *the great tribulation :* in view of chapt. 7 as a preparation for all that follows
the breaking of the last seal, the tribulation spoken of is best
understood of the whole series of woes, which are to come
before the end : there is nothing which points to any one particular distress. Cf. Mt. 24²¹. — ἔπλυναν κτλ., *they have washed
their garments,* etc. : cf. 22¹⁴, Heb. 9¹⁴, 1 Jno. 1⁷, 'The blood of
Jesus his Son cleanseth us from all sin' ; see on Rev. 1⁵. The
language describes all Christians alike ; there is nothing to
show special reference to martyrs ; see pp. 539 f.

15. διὰ τοῦτο, *therefore : i.e.* because they are purified from
all sin. — λατρεύουσιν, *serve:* the word denotes here the ritual
service of the temple ; cf. Heb. 8⁵. All the redeemed are
priests (5¹⁰) ; they may approach near to God and perform the
sacred service in the heavenly sanctuary, which only priests
might enter. For the heavenly temple, see on 6⁹. — σκηνώσει ἐπ'
αὐτούς, *shall spread his tabernacle over them :* σκηνοῦν *to fix one's
tent,* followed by μετά, ἐν, means *to dwell among,* cf. 21³, Jno. 1¹⁴ ;
here it is used with ἐπί, because the tabernacle of God's abode
with his people is at the same time a covering of protection
spread over them. This representation belongs to the dwelling
of God upon the new earth (21³), rather than to the throne-

2 N

room ; see on v. 9. The tense here changes to the fut. The
Seer, at first beholding what stands before him in vision, now
becomes the prophet speaking from the standpoint of the
present and foretelling the future. This latter character is
maintained through the following verses, which also have in
view the abode of the saints upon the renewed earth. It is
noticeable that v. 15 combines the three places of the redeemed
— the heavenly throne-room, the heavenly temple, and the
renewed earth ; and the last sentence of the verse unites in the
subj. ('he that sitteth on the *throne*') and the pred. ('shall
spread his tabernacle,' etc.) the two abodes of God. Readiness
to blend different aspects of the same thing must be recognized
as a characteristic of our Apocalyptist, and must be taken into
account in estimating some of the difficulties raised by critics
regarding the structure of the book.

16–17. The prophecies here uttered, taken with some modification from the O. T. promises of the blessedness awaiting
Israel on its restoration from captivity, were especially suited
to bring comfort to the Christians in their sufferings and persecutions. The source of most of the passage is Is. 49^{10}, 'They
shall not hunger nor thirst ; neither shall the heat nor sun
smite them ; for he that hath mercy on them will lead them,
even by springs of water will he guide them.' — οὐδὲ πᾶν καῦμα,
nor any burning: cf. Ps. 121^6. For πᾶν, see on v. 1. — τὸ
ἀρνίον ποιμανεῖ, *the Lamb shall be their shepherd :* Christ as the
shepherd of his people is a favorite figure in the Johannine
writings ; cf. Jno. 10, 21$^{15-17}$. For the figure in the O. T., cf.
Ps. 23$^{1-2}$, Ezk. 34^{23}. — ἀνὰ μέσον, *in the midst of:* commonly the
phrase means *between, e.g.* 1 Co. 6^5 ; but here apparently equivalent to ἐν μέσῳ, *in the midst of,* as in the LXX, Jos. 19^1 ; the
Lamb stands, not at one side, but in the foremost place *before
the middle of the throne ;* see on 5^6. — ζωῆς πηγὰς ὑδάτων, *life's
water-springs:* a frequent figure in the Johannine books ; *e.g.*
21^6, 22$^{1, 17}$, Jno. 4^{14} ; cf. also ἄρτος τῆς ζωῆς, *bread of life,* Jno.
6^{35}. The figures denote that which gives life, Jno. 4^{14}. ζωῆς is
made emphatic by its position between the preposition and its
case, cf. Buttm. p. 343. The gen. may depend on ὑδάτων ; the
peculiarity in order is then like that in σαρκὸς ἀπόθεσις ῥύπου,
1 Pet. 3^{21} ; or it may depend upon the compound expression

παγὰς ὑδάτων, *water-springs.* — ἐξαλείψει κτλ., *shall wipe away every tear,* etc., cf. 21⁴; taken from Is. 25⁸. 'Words like these of vv. 15–17 must sound as a divine music in the ears of the persecuted. God will comfort as a mother comforts' (Baljon).

Textual notes, 7¹⁻¹⁷. 1. Before δενδρον, τι is read in CQ most min Pr Lch Tr Alf Ws Sod RV; אP some min R Ti WH Blj Sw read παν, which however may be due to 9⁴ 21²⁷; cf. Ws p 125; A reads επι δενδρον. — 2. Instead of ανατολης, A Ws Lch WHmrg read ανατολων; see Ws 109. — 3. αχρι אACP edd; αχρις ου Q many min R; αχρις αν some min. — 4. A omits ηκουσα . . . εσφραγισμενων. — Instead of εσφραγισμενοι, Q many min read εσφραγισμενων. — 5–8. אACPQ most min edd read εσφραγισμενοι at the beginning and the end of the list, *i.e.* with Ιουδα and Βενιαμειν, but omit it with the other names; some min R insert it with each name. A few min have Dan instead of Gad. א omits Dan and 'Simeon, and transposes Joseph and Benjamin. — 9. A some vers Prim Lch Ws Moff omit και ιδου, reading οχλον for οχλος. — εστωτες אAP min R nearly all edd; εστωτας Q many min Alf Ws; εστωτων C. — περιβεβλημενους אACQ min edd; περιβεβλημενοι אcP some min R. — φοινικες אcACP min nearly all edd; φοινικας אQ many min Ti. — 11. ειστηκεισαν אAPQ most edd, but אAP have ι for ει in the augment, a spelling due to copyists, adopted by WH; R has εστηκεσαν, of uncertain origin. — 14. της before θλιψεως and μεγαλης is omitted in A Lch. — 17. ζωης אAPQ min edd; ζωσας some min R.

Criticism of Chapt. 7. The apparent absence in this chapt. of relation to the context, the dissimilarity in the two visions of which it is composed, and the special Jewish aspect of the first of these present difficulties, for the solution of which different critics have offered characteristic theories. The fundamental questions involved have been considered above. If the interpretation there given is correct, it meets the problems of the passage without raising the greater difficulties involved in theories of excision and redaction. In addition to what is there urged on *exegetical* grounds for the unity of the chapt. and its appropriateness in this place, due weight should be given to the agreement with the rest of the book not only in language and grammatical peculiarities (cf. pp. 222 ff.) but in eschatology and christology. It will be enough to note here the theories of representative critics. (1) vv. 1–8. The Jewish form of this passage, acknowledged by all scholars, is made by Vischer a part of the argument for his theory that the book was primarily a Jewish apocalypse (see pp. 229 f.). Having eliminated all the Christian elements from chapts. 1–6, he connects this passage directly with the breaking of the seven seals. Between the sixth and seventh seals a turning-point is reached; the 'messianic woes' are about to end, and the Messiah will then come to establish the earthly kingdom expected in Jewish eschatology. At this juncture, therefore, the tribes of Israel are marked with the seal as those who are to share in this glory (46 ff.). Spitta (80 ff.) finds here the beginning of the first Jewish apocalypse, which the Christian redactor, according to his view, used in the composition of his book. Spitta sees in the passage no connection with chapts. 1–6, nor with vv. 9–17. J. Weiss (65 ff.) takes the passage to have been primarily the work of a Jewish Christian; it referred to the elect of Israel, *i.e.* those who should become Christians before the end, those who by the seal were distinguished from the rest of Israel as the true servants of God, and were thus marked as destined to be saved from wrath in the judgment. This original vision has here been transformed by a later editor and made to represent certain ·elect Christians, a small number, who shall escape martyrdom and the last and direst plagues.

(2) vv. 9–17. This passage, in its present form at least, is distinctly Christian. Vischer acknowledges that τὸ ἀρνίον, *the Lamb*, cannot here be eliminated and he holds the passage, like 14$^{1-5}$, to be unquestionably Christian in its origin. It therefore has no place in his original Jewish apocalypse, and is unsuited to the present connection; it is an addition made by a Christian editor to remove difficulty caused to him by vv. 1–8, which limit the sealed servants of God to the tribes of Israel (46 ff.). Völter also makes the vision a later addition; it does not suit the connection here, the multitude before the throne cannot be identified with the 144,000; as with Vischer, the passage is due to one who with the spread of the Church saw that the elect could not be limited to a small number from the people of the Jews (*Offenb.* 27 f.). On the other hand Spitta takes these verses as a part of his Christian Ur-apocalypse; it has no connection with vv. 1–8, and belongs to the triumph of the end which will follow the breaking of the seventh seal; 8^1 is then transferred in Spitta's plan so as to precede these verses, and the apocalypse ended with a few verses added from later chapters. According to this theory, the *preparatory* part of the book, consisting of the first six chapts., which would lead one to expect a large and complex apocalypse to follow, suddenly culminates with a very brief conclusion. Weyland (150 ff.), agreeing with Vischer in the theory of an original Jewish apocalypse, differs from him in erasing from vv. 8–17 all Christian traces, and all the other elements at variance with a literal interpretation of vv. 1–8, and so makes the remainder of vv. 9–17 a prophecy of an exact fulfillment of what is promised in vv. 1–8. Erbes (50 ff.) removes the difference between the two passages by the reverse process; he eliminates the Jewish elements from the first part by dropping out vv. 4–8, making both parts Christian; vv. 9–12 then contain the fulfillment of vv. 1–3. Erbes rejects vv. 13–17 also. According to J. Weiss (68 ff.) this second vision referred primarily to the whole Church gathered together out of every nation after its victory, not in heaven, but on earth and moving in festal procession, perhaps to meet the coming Messiah; but in the present form the editor has changed the scene to heaven and the persons to martyrs, who have passed through death to the heavenly presence.

Chapts. VIII–IX.   *The first series of visions following the opening of the roll at the breaking of the last seal.*   See pp. 269 f.

(1) The immediate sequel of the breaking of the seal, 8^{1-2}.
See p. 269.   (2) The offering of incense on the golden altar
of heaven, 8^{3-6}.   See p. 270.   (3) The vision of the first six
trumpets, 8^{7}–9^{21}.   See pp. 270 f.   (*a*) The first four trumpet-visions, 8^{7-12};   (*b*) the woeful cry of an eagle in mid-
heaven, 8^{13};   (*c*) the fifth trumpet-vision, the plague of demonic
locusts, 9^{1-12};   (*d*) the sixth trumpet-vision, the plague of
fiendish horses, 9^{13-21}.

By the breaking of the seventh seal the roll of destiny is now
at length opened.   But not even here, when the book is open,
nor in chapt. 6 when the six preliminary seals are successively
broken, is anything said of actually reading from the roll a
description or prophecy of the coming events.   Its prophetic
contents are instead revealed dramatically in the visions which
follow the breaking of the seals and correspond to the respective portions of the roll; see on 5^{1}, 6^{1}.   We have seen that the
visions of the earlier seals (chapt. 6) tell of those more ordinary judgments, war, famine, etc., the *beginnings* of woes, which
are only preparatory to the last times (see p. 264); but now
that the roll is opened we have in the corresponding visions
the whole vast cycle of the last things which follow the beginnings of woes, *i.e.* the awful plagues which more immediately
precede the end, the appearance of the supreme forces of evil,
the final conflict, and all the other events issuing in the consummation of the kingdom.   The main contents of the roll as
contrasted with what may be called its preface, disclosed in
the first six seal-visions, must include according to common
apocalyptic expectation such a series of vast movements before
the actual end.   And the august scenes of the introduction to
our book as given in the first five chapts. show a work of
these large proportions to have been contemplated in the
Apocalyptist's plan.   We should expect then at this point not
an immediate entrance of the end (so, some com., see pp. 572,
531), but what we find, only the great movements more directly
leading up to it.

(1) Immediate sequel of breaking the seventh seal, 8^{1-2}.   See
above, also p. 269.   **1. ὅταν**: this use of ὅταν instead of ὅτε
(cf. $6^{1, 3, 5, \text{etc.}}$) with a past ind. when a single, not iterative, act
is meant lacks support; if retained, it is probably a late inac-

curacy; see Blass § 65⁹. The cases cited in Burton § 316 are not parallel. — ἤνοιξεν, *he opened:* the subj. of the vb. is the Lamb, as in chapt. 6. Chapter 7 is parenthetical, and the scene of the heavenly throne-room with God and the Lamb as represented in chapts. 4–6 is here continued. — ἐγένετο σιγή, *there followed a silence:* such a pause of profound stillness gives striking dramatic effect to the opening of the scene. The long silence is interpreted by most com., probably with right, to signify the awe and dread with which the heavenly hosts await the events now coming upon the earth; they stand mute before the revelations of the opened book of destiny; cf. Dan. 4¹⁹ (RV). Possibly, however, reference may be made merely to the staying of the trumpet-blasts till the service of incense-offering shall have been accomplished. The angels receive the trumpets at the opening of the scene, but they stay the use of them till the tokens in the earth (v. 5) show that the prayers of the saints have been graciously received. See further p. 572.

Interpretations which make the silence a symbol of the eternal rest of the saints following the end, or the millennium, or similar states in the destiny of the Church, are at variance with the situation; it is a silence in heaven, *i.e.* of the heavenly hosts, and precedes chronologically the events of the trumpet-blasts, in other words, the whole series of last things. Some (B. Weiss, *al.*) find in the silence a symbol of a temporary cessation in the revelations given to the Seer. But the close connection with vv. 2 ff. shows that such a cessation does not occur; the formula for a new vision, μετὰ ταῦτα εἶδον (see on 4¹) is not used to introduce any of these verses. Charles (*Studies* 154 f.) explains the silence as one enjoined upon the hosts of heaven, an arrest of their praises, in order that the prayers of the suffering saints on earth, which concern God more than the psalmody of the angelic orders, may be heard before him. But whether or not the prayers of men may be thought to take precedence of the praises of angels, place for both has already been found in connection with the breaking of the seals; 5⁹, 6¹⁰.

ἡμίωρον, *half an hour:* in a drama of events moving so rapidly, this would seem to denote a long pause. It is one in which there is rising to God incense for the prayers of the whole company of the saints pleading for his coming to judgment.

2. τοὺς ἑπτὰ ἀγγέλους, *the seven angels:* the art. shows that certain angels well known by this designation are meant; and this is made specific by the added words; they are the seven

who stand before God, *i.e.* the seven archangels of familiar
Jewish angelology; cf. Tob. 12^{15}, 'I am Raphael, one' of the
seven holy angels which present the prayers of the saints, and
go in before the glory of the Holy One.' For other mention
of these see *e.g.* En. 81^5, 90$^{21\,f.}$, Test. Lev. 3^5; in En. 20 their
names are given (in the Gk. text); among these the most
familiar are Michael and Gabriel, cf. Lk. 1^{19}, 'I am Gabriel
that stand in the presence of God.' The angels are not said
to *enter* here; they are already present as part of the host
attending on God in the throne-room. The mention of them
here for the first time is not at variance with the earlier representation (see p. 571); it is rather the appearance of another
detail as the scene in the visionary manner gradually develops,
just as the roll, the Lamb, etc., are not thought of at first, but
later, as the vision advances. See on 5^6.

The Jewish doctrine of an order of angels, consisting of seven, standing
higher than the others and in a nearer relation to God, is thought by many
to be traceable *historically* to an early Oriental belief in seven *planet-gods.*
Hebrew monotheism in taking up such a tradition transformed the gods into
angels. Cf. Gunkel *Schöpfung* 294 ff.; Bouss. *Jud.* 319 ff., Moff. on Rev. 1^{20}.
But while there are probable grounds for this supposition, it is certain that
the Apocalyptist has no thought of such an origin; he bases his representation here as elsewhere on familiar Jewish beliefs and traditions. While
the seven Spirits, seven stars, seven eyes, seven lamps, etc., may have sprung
primarily from a single conception of Oriental polytheism, there is no such
connection in his thought. Certainly there is no identification of the seven
angels of this passage with the seven Spirits of 1^4, 4^5, 5^6; see notes *in loc.*

ἐδόθησαν αὐτοῖς κτλ., *there were given to them*, etc.: the angels
as first seen do not hold the trumpets; these are given to them
as the first step in the unfolding of the scene. The act portends
momentous announcements; these however are delayed by the
interlude of the incense-offering, vv. 3–5.

(2) Offering of incense on the heavenly altar, 8$^{3-6}$. See
pp. 549, 270. This prelude to the seven trumpet-blasts given
in these verses expresses the familiar thought, the agency of
the prayers of the saints in bringing in the judgment of the
world and the fulfillment of the kingdom; see on 6$^{9\,f.}$. That
the prayers here referred to are the cries of the saints for judgment, as in 6$^{9\,f.}$, is shown in vv. 4–5 in the immediate connection
of the prayers with the manifestation of God's wrath and the

tokens of his judgments coming on the earth. The same connection is intended in the allusion to the altar in 9^{13}, 14^{18}. The events that follow this episode of incense-offering, as one trumpet after another sounds, are the answer to these prayers of the suffering, expectant Church.

3. ἄλλος ἄγγελος, *another angel:* for the variety of agents see on 5^5. — ἐπί: *at;* for the meaning of ἐπί cf. Amos 9^1, Ac. 5^{23}, cf. also ἐπάνω 2 Chron. 26^{19}. — τοῦ θυσιαστηρίου, *the altar:* whether the altar of the first clause (3^a) be identified with the golden altar at the end of the verse (3^b), or distinguished from it, the significance of the angel's act and of what takes place afterwards is not affected. The angel makes the offering on the golden altar of incense to help the prayers of the saints, and the sequel (v. 4) represents the relation of these prayers to the coming events.

The altar mentioned at the beginning of v. 3 and in v. 5 is taken by many to represent in the heavenly temple the altar of burnt-offering in distinction from the golden altar of incense spoken of at the end of v. 3. The acts of the angel, then, as explained by the late temple ritual (cf. Schürer II. 354 f.), are as follows: he comes first to the altar of burnt-offering in the temple court, from which he takes coals of fire (cf. Lev. 16^{12}, Num. 16^{46}), then passing within he casts these upon the altar of incense and burns the incense thereon; then returning to the altar of burnt-offering he fills the censer with coals, and hurls these upon the earth. Thus the Apocalyptist is supposed to conceive of heaven under the form of the earthly temple with its two altars and complete in all its parts — a conception then held by some critics to be in conflict with the idea of the throne-room in chapts. 4–6 (see p. 571) and so the work of a different author. The grounds for this understanding of the altar in vv. 3^a and 5 are (*a*) that the word when used without added specification always refers to the altar of burnt-offering; (*b*) that the phrase 'the golden one before the throne,' added to the word in 3^b shows the altar there meant to be different from that of 3 . These grounds are, however, not conclusive. In 14^{18} and 16^7 the mention of the altar appears to allude to the prayers of the saints (see notes there), but these are connected in the author's thought with incense, cf. 5^8, $8^{3\,f.}$; so that the meaning there is best taken to be the altar of incense, and yet there is no specification added; and this reference is confirmed by a comparison of 14^{18} (see note there) with 9^{13} — the altars are probably the same, and the latter (9^{13}) is the golden altar of incense. The altar in 8^5 also is better referred to the altar of incense, see note there. As regards the second ground (*b*), our author's tendency to use an indefinite term and afterwards make it definite by repetition in more specific form (see p. 242) renders reference to two different altars uncertain. But it must be added

that even if both altars are thought of in our passage, there is no conflict
with chaps. 4–6 affecting the unity of the book, for the merging of the two
ideas, the temple and the seat of God's throne, as well as the transition of
the one idea into the other, is too easy and well attested in poetic, especially
apocalyptic, conceptions to furnish critical difficulty. Cf. pp. 524 f.

λιβανωτόν *censer:* elsewhere the word denotes *incense*, but
the epithet *golden* shows that the instrument is meant here.
Tradition assigned censers of gold to Solomon's temple, 1 K. 7⁵⁰,
those of brass to the tabernacle, Ex. 38³. — πολλά, *much:* because the incense is to accompany the prayers which are rising
from all the saints, the marytrs (6⁹ ᶠ·) and all the living as well.
— δώσει: *give, i.e. offer.* For δίδωμι in connection with offerings
cf. Lk. 2²⁴, Rev. 4⁹. For the fut. ind. with ἵνα see on 3⁹.
— ταῖς προσευχαῖς, *in behalf of,* i.e. *to help, the prayers:* dat.
commodi; see on 5⁸. The incense, viewed as an offering pleas-
ing to God, makes the prayers thus accompanied more acceptable to him.   There is in our passage no idea of a mediatorial
service of the angel, as of one through whom the prayers are
presented to God; the prayers are rising directly to God from
the whole Church; but they are enforced, so to speak, by the
accompanying incense.   A mediatorial service is attributed to
angels in the Apocrypha and pseudepigraphic writings (cf.
Tob. 12¹², ¹⁵, En. 9³, Test. Lev. 3⁵ *al*) but not in the N. T.
Such a doctrine is not supposable in our book in which the
priesthood of all believers, *i.e.* their immediate access to God,
is strongly emphasized. — τὸ θυσιαστήριον . . . θρόνου, *the
golden altar before the throne:* cf. 9¹³ ; the altar of incense, as
shown by the word *golden;* cf. Ex. 30¹ ᶠᶠ·, Lev. 4¹⁷.

4. ἀνέβη, ταῖς προσευχαῖς ἐνώπιον κτλ., *went up, before God,
in behalf of the prayers:* see on v. 3.

5. The offering of incense is now followed by assurance of
answers to the prayers of the saints.   Fire from the heavenly
altar cast upon the earth and the accompanying disturbances in
nature symbolize the wrath of God about to visit the world in
judgment.   Similar tokens are given with the seventh trumpet-
blast 11¹⁹, and the emptying of the seventh bowl 16¹⁸. The
scene is in part parallel with Ezekiel's vision (10²), in which
coals of fire from between the cherubim are scattered over
Jerusalem in token of God's judgment.   The immediate connec-

tion in our passage between the portents and the prayers with which the incense is offered favors the interpretation of the altar in this verse as that upon which the incense was burned. — εἴληφεν, *took :* aoristic perf.; see Blass § 59, 4, Burton § 80. The word is thought by some interpreters to imply that the angel had laid aside the censer and now takes it up again. The inference is, however, not certain; the pleonastic use of λαμβάνειν, common in the partic. (Kühn II. § 486, 6, A 10) seems to occur in the finite forms also, cf. Mt. 15²⁶, Jno. 19²³; see Blass § 74, 3; cf. also the pleonastic use of *take* in colloquial English. — τοῦ πυρός, *the fire :* that of the burning incense, if that altar be meant. — ἔβαλεν, *cast :* the obj. of the vb. is the fire, or the censer filled with fire; the difference is immaterial. — φωναί, *voices :* as in 4⁵, the noises of the storm.

6. The seven angels perceive the meaning of the portents, and know that the time for their part in the great drama is reached; they prepare to sound their trumpets and usher in the judgments which shall fulfill the prayers of God's people. — ἵνα σαλπίσωσιν: for ἵνα with subjv. instead of an obj. infin. see Blass § 68, 1; Burton §§ 211–212.

(3) Vision of the first six trumpets, 8⁷–9²¹. See pp. 549, 270.

The seven archangels now sounding their trumpets one after another introduce a series of visions which taken together reveal the coming events to the end. Whether certain great episodes which interrupt the sequence, *e.g.* 10¹–11¹³, are to be taken as parts of particular trumpet-visions need not be considered here. The first six trumpet-visions are occupied wholly with plagues; the seventh is so occupied in part. This preponderance given to visitations of God's anger is characteristic of apocalyptic literature in general, which belonging as it does to times of persecution emphasizes the vengeance of God upon the enemies of his people. Moreover in the Last Times, as viewed in our Apocalypse, the Lord's utterance, 'The gospel must first be preached unto all nations,' Mk. 13¹⁰, is thought of as already fulfilled. The judgments foreseen are those sent upon the world as now finally arrayed in hostility to that gospel. There are not wanting however intimations that a purpose of mercy persists through all. Israel's conversion is still aimed at (see on 3^9) and the possibility of repentance in all as the result of warning judgments is implied; cf. $9^{20\ f.}$, 16^9; pp. 311 f.　The *forms* of the plagues described here are similar in part to those sent upon Egypt — for all time types of God's punishment of his enemies — and in part to other calamities elsewhere predicted for the Last Times.　But the parallelism of the plagues of our book with these is not exact; here, as everywhere, a suggestion in passing through our Apocalyptist's vision receives transformations and additions; it is a suggestion only.

The seven trumpet-visions like those of the seven seals (see on 6^9) fall into two groups of $4 + 3$, and here as there the sixth and seventh visions are separated by a long episode (10^1-11^{13}).　A division into two groups of $4 + 3$ is marked by the insertion of 8^{13}; the distinction appears also in the subject-matter.　The plagues of the first four fall directly upon the *natural* world, the earth, the sea, the rivers and fountains, and the luminaries; the indirect effect upon men, though thought of, is barely mentioned.　But in the remaining three the judgments are sent *directly* upon men, or the effect upon men is especially emphasized.　The seventh vision differs in other respects also from those of the first group (see on 11^{15}).　Only within limits is a *gradation* to be observed in the progress of the judgments.　Comparing the three series, those of the seals, the trumpets, and the bowls, we find the first to consist in only ordinary and natural phenomena, though of severity, while in the second and third series a supernatural element is added, and the suffering is wider and severer than in the first.　In the third series as compared with the second the fierceness of God's wrath is more distinctly insisted on as present, and the anger of men against God in their torments becomes violent.　But it is evident that the plagues are not thought of as increasing in severity regularly toward a final climax; their effect is rather made to consist in the cumulative force of inevitable succession.

(3, a)　The first four trumpets, 8^{7-12}.　See pp. 549, 270. These *first four* trumpet-visions virtually form a single four-fold vision; they follow one another in quick succession and introduce a group of portents which affect mankind through the awful disasters wrought miraculously in the realms of the

earth and the heavens. The third part smitten in each case
represents the vast reach of the calamity, at the same time a
limit is set; the larger part is reserved to a later stage in the
history. The points of similarity between these plagues and
those sent upon Egypt make it unnecessary to seek for suggestions of the scenes, as some com. do, in historical storms, volcanic eruptions, etc., known to have occurred in the first century in the regions of the Mediterranean, especially as these do
not furnish a sufficiently close parallelism. The very nature
of the disasters is such that the Christians and their enemies
alike would be involved in the effects (see on 3^{10}). It is doubtful, however, whether this consequence is in the author's mind.
His purpose is to give a powerful picture of calamity sent upon
mankind at large through awful miracles in nature, as a part of
the 'messianic woes.' The absence of strict realism, natural
enough in visions, is apparent in the illogical results introduced. The darkening of a part of the luminaries diminishes,
not the intensity, but the duration of light; a single burning
star falls upon a third part of all the rivers and fountains of
the earth; fire burns amid a rain of hail and blood. Clearly a
strict relation of cause and effect is not in the mind of the
Apocalyptist here; he is intent on describing a marvelous
scene as a whole, without attention to realistic details.

7. The storm of mingled hail and fire is parallel to that of
the Egyptian plague of hail, Ex. $9^{23\,\text{ff.}}$; cf. Ps. 18^{13}. The addition of blood here may be suggested by the first Egyptian
plague, Ex. $7^{17\,\text{ff.}}$; cf. also Joel 2^{30}. A rain of fire and blood
is included among eschatological portents in Sib. Or. V. 377 f.
— ἐν: frequent with μίγνυμι in the sense *among* (cf. Kühn. II,
§ 425, 1, A 1) is here *with;* the usual construction is with σύν,
μετά, or the simple dat. — τὸ τρίτον, *the third part* : see p. 251,
also above, p. 555. — τῆς γῆς, *the earth:* the surface of the
earth with what was upon it is meant. The trees and grass
are therefore included, but the writer after his manner (cf. p.
242) adds to the general term a specification of certain particulars. Therefore 'all the green grass' refers, not to that of
the whole earth, but to that of the third part here spoken of,
and the words of 9^4 offer no difficulty (see p. 572); cf. v. 10
where similarly the limitation of the springs of the waters to a

third part of the whole is intended, but not distinctly mentioned; see note there.

8–9. The turning of water into blood in this the second plague, and the destruction of the fish are taken from the first Egyptian plague; Ex. 7¹⁷ ᶠᶠ·. — ὡς ὄρος κτλ., *as it were a great mountain*, etc. : a burning mass as large as a mountain is hurled out of the heavens into the sea. The fire consumes the ships; the effect upon the waters attributed to it in the vision is perhaps traceable to the frequent juxtaposition of fire and blood in imagery of this kind; see on v. 7. A suggestion of the imagery in this vision is not to be sought, as some suppose, in the great eruption of Vesuvius, 79 A.D., or the volcanic disturbances in the Ægean islands, as at Thera. The phenomena are dissimilar. In part parallel with the representation here is En. 18¹³, 'I saw there seven stars like great burning mountains'; cf. En. 21³, also Sib. Or. V. 158, 'Then shall come a great star from heaven into the divine sea.' — τὰ ἔχοντα : appos. to κτισμάτων; for the nom., see p. 224. — διεφθάρησαν : the pl. is probably due to the nearness of πλοίων.

10–11. The corruption of the drinking-water is also taken from the first Egyptian plague, but the means used, wormwood, is suggested by its familiar use as a symbol of divine punishment; cf. Jer. 9¹⁵, 'I will feed them with wormwood, and give them water of gall to drink,' cf. also Jer. 33¹⁵, Lam. 3¹⁵·¹⁹. A parallel to the falling star is pointed out in Persian eschatology, in which the star Gurzihar falls as a sign of the last catastrophe (Böklen, 87, 90; Völter, *Offenb.* 30). Cf. also Sib. Or. V. 158, quoted above on v. 8. To suppose the star to have burst into dust, so as to be scattered over many waters (Bouss. Holtzm.-Bau., *al*) is to insist on a realism wanting throughout the four plagues; see p. 556. — τὰς πηγὰς τῶν ὑδάτων, *the springs of the waters*: not all of the springs — though the expression would imply this — but only a third part, as shown by v. 11, *the third part of the waters became wormwood*. — τὸ ὄνομα κτλ., *the name*, etc. : the star is named from its effect. — ἐγένετο εἰς ἄψινθον, *became wormwood*: the waters became impregnated with wormwood; the words, *died of the waters*, show that they were not changed into wormwood (so, Swete). — πολλοὶ ἀπέθανον, *many died*: wormwood is not a poison, though poisonous effects were sometimes attributed to it, cf. Jer. 9¹⁵. It is not said here that all who drank of the waters died; they all suffered and with *many* the suffering resulted in death. In all these four plagues the punishment, not the death, of men is aimed at ; the death of those mentioned here is only incidental. This plague like the others works its effect upon a third part of that upon which it is sent, the waters ; and thus as a dread sign it touches all men, not a third part only. The analogy between this plague and the others of this series of four would be destroyed, if a *third part* of men were said to have died. There is therefore no ground for the supposition (J. Weiss, 75) that the writer has substituted πολλοί for τὸ τρίτον to avoid anticipation of the sixth plague in which a third part of men is killed, 9¹⁸. See p. 572.

12. The fourth plague is taken from the Egyptian plague of darkness, Ex. 10²¹ ᶠᶠ·; cf. also Is. 13¹⁰, Joel 2³¹, Am. 8⁹. The power of the plague consists in the horror of absolute darkness displacing for a considerable time the full light of day and the partial light of the night. — ἵνα σκοτισθῇ : grammatically this could be taken as a purpose clause (RV), but the analogy of the other members in this fourfold series shows that *result* is intended (AV). For ἵνα with subjv. or fut. ind. in a clause expressing result see Blass § 69, 3, end. — τὸ τρίτον αὐτῆς, *for the third part of it :* on the inconsequence of this result see p. 556. The diminution of the intensity of the light by one third would not constitute a plague analogous to the others in severity.

(3, b). The woeful cry of an eagle in mid-heaven, 8¹³. See pp. 549, 270. The introduction of the eagle's proclamation marks in a formal way the division of the seven trumpet-visions into two groups of 4 + 3 ; it also falls in with the author's fondness for inserting an interlude at transitional points; see pp. 254, 244 ff. The first four trumpet-visions are, to be sure, visions of woe, but the forewarning cry sent forth here to all the world indicates that the woes now coming are especially grievous. We reach here a transition in the character and the scope of the plagues. The first four are sent directly upon a part of the world of nature, and upon men indirectly ; and though fraught with warning to all men, they actually inflict

suffering on only a part; or in the fourth the suffering is only
temporary. But the fifth and sixth plagues (chapt. 9) are sent
directly upon the persons of men; they assail the whole world
of God's enemies and are of a peculiarly poignant and demonic
character. Of the three woes announced by the eagle (v. 13)
the Apocalyptist does not in the seventh trumpet-vision distinctly name the third; but if, as is probably true, it is found
in the series of visitations represented by the bowl-plagues
taken as a whole (chapt. 16, see notes there), that woe would
belong in general characteristics with the first and second woes,
those of the fifth and sixth trumpet-visions, rather than with
the plagues of the first four trumpet visions (8^{7-12}).

ἐνός : used as the indef. art.; cf. 9^{13}, 18^{21}, 19^{17}; see Blass
§ 45, 2. — ἀετοῦ κτλ., *eagle*, etc.: the herald of the proclamation
is the strongest of birds, flying in mid-heaven where all can see
him, and crying with a loud voice which all can hear. For the
eagle as a messenger, cf. Ap. Bar. 77^{19}. — ἐν μεσουρανήματι,
in mid-heaven: cf. $14^6, 19^{17}$. — οὐαί, *woe:* uttered thrice conform-
ably to the three woes which are to come. — τοὺς κατοικοῦντας
ἐπὶ τῆς γῆς, *those that dwell on the earth:* not all are meant,
but the wicked, as seen from $9^{4, 20}$; see on 3^{10}. The acc. here
and in 12^{12} after the exclamation οὐαί is wholly irregular and
cannot be explained; the dat. is the regular construction, *e.g.*
Mt. 23^{23}, Lk. 6^{24}; see Blass § 37, 3. — τῆς σάλπιγγος : the sing.
because the word defines φωνῶν with adjectival force, *the blasts
of the trumpet*, i.e. *the trumpet-blasts.*

Textual notes, 8^{1-13}. 1. οταν AC edd; οτε ℵPQ min Ŕ (as in all the
parallels in chapt. 6) Bouss. — 3. του θυσιαστηριου (before εχων) ℵCQ min
edd; το θυσιαστηριον AP some min R. — δωσει ℵAC most edd; δωση PQ
min R Sod Bouss. — 9. διεφθαρησαν ℵAP min edd; διεφθαρη Q min R. —
13. αετου ℵAQ most min and vers edd; αγγελου P some min arm R. —
πετομενου most sources edd; πετωμενου Q some min R. — τους κατοικουντας
ℵQ most min edd; τοις κατοικουσιν AP some min R.

(3, c) Fifth trumpet-vision ; the plague of demonic locusts,
9^{1-12}. See pp. 549, 270. Locusts, which form one of the most
dreadful scourges of the East, flying in dense swarms that
spread over many miles of the heavens and darken the sun, and
settling on large areas of the earth, where' the young devour
every shred of green before them, are often mentioned in the

Scriptures as the instruments of God's anger. They form one of the Egyptian plagues, Ex. $10^{12\,\mathrm{ff.}}$; and the prophet Joel, chapts. 1–2, in a passage of terrible power describes a visitation from them as a harbinger of the great day of the Lord. It is from this passage of the prophet that our Apocalyptist takes the suggestion of the form of the woe in this the fifth trumpet-vision, as one of the nearer forerunners of the end. This significance of the locust-plague and a few details in the description are clearly derived from the O. T. prophet, but all else is different. The locusts of this vision are fabulous creatures, they touch no green thing, they attack men only, they come out of hell and they torture with hellish stings. Their characteristics are in part taken with fantastic exaggeration from those of the natural locusts ; some of the features are not improbably derived from mythological fancies preserved in popular tradition. The use which the Apocalyptist makes of the suggestions of the prophet Joel from which he starts, and his complete transformation of the nature and activity of the locusts, are highly illuminative of his freedom in treating derived imagery.

1. ἀστέρα . . . γῆν, *I saw a star which had fallen from heaven to the earth :* the seer does not speak of beholding the star fall ; the important thing with him is what follows the fall. The abrupt transition from the form of a star to that of a person, without mention of it, is in accord with our author's manner ; see pp. 248 f. The stars moving in wonderful order across the sky were quite naturally thought of by primitive peoples as divinities, or at least living beings ; hence the prevalence of star-worship. The belief that they possessed a conscious personal nature was accepted in popular Jewish cosmology, cf. Jg. 5^{20}, Job 38^7 ; even if in these cases the word be taken as merely a poetic figure, yet the figure attests the early popular conception. This belief is most distinctly expressed in Enoch ; cf. 21^6, ' These are of the number of the stars of heaven which have transgressed the commandment of the Lord and are bound here till ten thousand years, the time entailed by their sins, are consummated ' ; cf. 90^{24}, $18^{15\,\mathrm{f.}}$; also Jude v. 13. The star of our passage is an agent sent from heaven in the service of God ; cf. 20^1. The identification of him with Satan, based on

a comparison of Lk. 10¹⁸ with Rev. 12⁹ (so, Alford, *al*) is certainly wrong; Satan nowhere appears in the book as an agent employed by God to carry out a divine ordering, such as the sending of this plague upon the world. The *form* in which the star is conceived as he receives the key is evidently that of a man; the same representation occurs in En. 88¹, ʻ He seized that first star . . . and bound it hand and footʼ; cf. 86¹ ff., where the stars appear as animals. — ἡ κλεὶς τοῦ φρέατος τῆς ἀβύσσου, *the key of the pit of the abyss: ἄβυσσος*, the *abyss*, is the underworld; in a few instances used in a general sense equivalent to Sheol, *e.g.* Ro. 10⁷, Ps. 71²⁰; then specifically of the abode or prison of evil spirits, *e.g.* Lk. 8³¹, so in this chapt. and elsewhere in Rev., cf. 11⁷, 20¹, ³. — φρέαρ, lit. *well* or *cistern*, is the *pit itself*, as in Ps. 55²³, 69¹⁵; this suits the exact meaning of the word better than *chasm* or *shaft*, *i.e.* communicating with the abyss, as some take it. The abyss is represented as closed and locked; cf. 20¹, ³, Slav. En. 42¹, ʻ I saw the key-holders and guards of the gates of hell.ʼ

2–3. The language of v. 2ᵃ is a reminiscence of Ex. 19¹⁸; that of v. 2ᵇ, of Joel 2¹⁰. — καπνός, *smoke: i.e.* from the fires of Gehenna. The meaning is not, as some take it, that the dense swarm of locusts forms a smoke-like cloud darkening the sun, for these come *out of the smoke.* — If αὐτοῖς instead of αὐταῖς is adopted, the mas. is used because the locusts are thought of as the personal agents of God. — ἐξουσία, *power:* the particular power meant, that of torment, is described more fully in vv. 5, 10. — οἱ σκορπίοι τῆς γῆς, *the scorpions of the earth:* the scorpions meant are of the kind known to men, while the locusts are demonic.

4. The marvelous nature of the locusts appears in the object of their attack; unlike the ordinary locust they do not ravage vegetation, they assail men only. — ἵνα ἀδικήσουσιν : for the construction see on 8⁶. — οὐδὲ πᾶν δένδρον, *nor any tree:* the particular specification of the trees, already included in the general term, *green thing* (cf. 7¹, ³, 8⁷), seems less appropriate here; it is perhaps the retention of a stereotyped form in which the tree is mentioned as the most conspicuous. — εἰ μή, *except:* for this elliptical use of εἰ μή without influence on the construction, see Burton §§ 471, 274. — τοὺς ἀνθρώπους οἵτινες, κτλ.,

2ο

such men as have not the seal, etc.: *i.e.* all except the saints; cf. 7¹⁻⁸.

5–6. The relief of death is denied to the tormented. — ἵνα ἀποκτείνωσιν, βασανισθήσονται: for the construction, see on 8⁶. — μῆνας πέντε, *five months :* visitations of locusts in the East are confined to the warm, dry season, about five months, favorable for the development of the eggs. While these may occur at any time in the course of this period, the monsters of the vision work their torment continuously throughout the whole time. — With v. 6 cf. Job 3²¹.

7. The plague of the locusts is described briefly in vv. 1–6, with reference to their origin and their power to torment. The Apocalyptist now in vv. 7–11 adds a more detailed description of the form of the monsters, their terrible array, and their manner of torture. Some repetition is inevitable (but see on v. 10). Their actual torture as in vv. 3–6 is in their sting, but the other attributes here assigned them are meant to be significant as increasing the terror they produce. — ὁμοιώματα, *forms, shapes :* properly *forms* made in the likeness of something; cf. Ro. 1²³, Phil. 2⁷. In appearance the locusts are like war-horses, a comparison taken directly from Joel 2⁴; but a certain resemblance is often fancied to exist between the head of a locust and that of a horse, and the hard thorax of the insect might suggest the breast-shield (προστερνίδιον) of the war-horse. There is an Arab saying often quoted in illustration of our passage to the effect that the locust has a head like a horse, a breast like a lion, feet like a camel, a body like a serpent, and antennae like the hair of a maiden. Also the Italian *cavalletta, locust,* is referred to as expressing the fancied likeness to a horse, *cavallo.* — στέφανοι *crowns :* it is difficult to connect this feature with any belonging to the natural locust; a glistening, yellowish-green protuberance on the thorax (De Wette, *al*) could hardly suggest it. Like the human face and the scorpion-like tail it is probably an invention of fancy to give terribleness to the appearance of the monsters.

8–9. τρίχας, *hair :* not improbably suggested by the antennae of the locust; see quotation above on v. 7. — ὀδόντες, λεόντων, *teeth, of a lion :* taken from Joel 1⁶, and suggested by the voracity of the locust in devouring vegetation. — θώρακας, *breast-plates:* see on v. 7. — ἡ φωνὴ τῶν πτερύγων κτλ., *the sound of their wings,* etc.: the loud rushing sound made by the wings of a swiftly flying swarm of locusts is often spoken of; it suggests the comparison with a host of chariots driving to battle, adopted here directly from Joel 2⁵. — ἵππων: the word seems superfluous here, and is rejected by many (Ewald, Bouss. *al*); τρεχόντων may have seemed to a copyist inappropriate to ἁρμάτων. But Swete cites ἅρματα τριακόσια ἵππων, I Kings 12²⁴ ᵇ, LXX.

10. This is not a mere repetition of vv. 3, 5; the scorpion-like tails with stings are here mentioned as the equipment of the locusts for inflicting the torture there attributed to them; so far as stated in vv. 3, 5 the scorpion-like sting might be inflicted by some other organ. — μῆνας πέντε, *five months:* see on v. 5.

11. The likeness of the host of supernatural locusts to an advancing army dominates the preceding representation; appropriately then they are conceived to have a commander, and one who adds to the terribleness of the array, the angel of hell. — ἔχουσιν βασιλέα τὸν ἄγγελον, *they have the angel as king,* or *a king,* viz. *the angel:* the difference is not material. With a quite different thought the author of Prov. 30²⁷ says, The locusts have no king. — τὸν ἄγγελον τῆς ἀβύσσου, *the angel of the abyss:* not Satan, who does not appear at this stage in the history of the book, but the angel who is over the pit; the abyss like everything else has its special angel presiding over it; see pp. 70, 445. — For *the abyss* see on v. 1. — Ἀβαδδών, *Abaddon:* the word meaning *destruction,* or *place of destruction,* becomes a proper name equivalent to Sheol, Hades (*e.g.* Job 26⁶, Prov. 15¹¹); it is such in cases where personification is intended (*e.g.* Job 28²²), as Death and Hades are personified in our book, cf. 6⁸. The Apocalyptist gives the name to the angel of hell and translates it into Greek by Ἀπολλύων (partic. of ἀπόλλυμι), *Apollyon, Destroyer.* Compare the giving of the name *Wormwood,* as expressive of the effect to be wrought, 8¹¹. Some (Bouss. Holtzm.-Bauer, *al.*) find in the name Apollyon an indirect allusion also to the god Apollo, one of whose symbols was the locust and to whom plagues and destruction were in some cases attributed (see Roscher, *Lex. d. Griech.*

u. Röm. Mythol. s.v.); this, however, to say the least seems uncertain.

12. Cf. 8¹³, 11¹⁴. — ἡ οὐαί: the exclamation οὐαί used substantively would naturally take the neut. art. It appears with a designation of gender in our author only, and as fem. The peculiarity is generally explained as due to the presence of some such equivalent as θλῖψις or ταλαιπωρία in the writer's thought; see Thayer *s.v.*; Win. § 27, 6, note 2. — ἡ μία: *the first;* for this meaning cf. Mt. 28¹, Blass § 45, 1. — ἀπῆλθεν, *is past:* not now at the time of the author's writing; he speaks from the standpoint of the future, inserting this comment to mark the end of the description of the first woe. — ἔρχεται: the wholly irregular sing. is possibly to be justified by the fact that the vb. precedes its subject; see Win. § 58, 4, note 1, Kühn. II, § 367, 1–2. But this construction does not occur in the N. T.; it is poetic and chiefly confined to εἶναι and γίγνεσθαι. The word οὐαί cannot be regarded as neut. here (so, B. Weiss, *al*); such a change of gender is not supposable in clauses so closely connected. The reading is probably an error of the writer or a copyist.

(3, d) Sixth trumpet-vision; the plague of fiendish horses, 9¹³⁻²¹. See pp. 549, 271. In the plague of the sixth trumpet-vision, the second woe, the Apocalyptist as before takes a suggestion from familiar eschatology. The irruption of a mighty army riding upon horses forms one of the striking predictions of Ezekiel's prophecy (38¹⁴ ᶠᶠ·), and from his time on an invasion of a fierce host becomes a standing event in visions of the Last Days; *e.g.* Is. 5²⁶ ᶠᶠ·, Jer. 1¹⁴ ᶠᶠ·, 6²² ᶠ·, Joel 3⁹ ᶠᶠ·, Zec. 14², 2 Es. 13³⁴, En. 90¹⁶, Sib. Or. III. 663. But the horse appears as an essential figure in the late Jewish pictures of an invading host; *e.g.* Is. 5²⁸, Jer. 4¹³, 47³, 50⁴², Ezk. 26⁷, ¹⁰, Hab. 1⁸, Ass. Mos. 3¹. These representations, then, furnish what may be regarded as the origin of the Apocalyptist's vision in this passage. In so far as these invasions described in earlier apocalyptists relate to the events of the end, the plague is commonly thought of as sent upon God's people and not as here upon their enemies. But that is the case also with the plague of the locusts. It is only the general form of eschatological calamity that furnishes the Apocalyptist with his type. The application of the figure,

as often with him, is quite different from its primary use. He
finds in the familiar eschatological imagery of the irruption of
a fierce *cavalry* host an example of a calamity set for the last
time, and he takes the most conspicuous figure, the horse, and
transforms it into a fiendish monster, as he had done with the
locusts. The fabulous form and activity which he gives to
these instruments of God's anger are doubtlesss the product
of his own fancy, or perhaps may in part be suggested by some
figure preserved in popular mythology.

The fear prevailing in the first century B.C. and later of an
invasion of the Roman empire by the Parthian hordes from
beyond the Euphrates caused apocalyptists of this period to
associate the eschatological invaders with these ; they placed
the home of the armies of the Last Days in the East, as in an
earlier time it had been placed in the north (Jer. 6^{22}, Ezk. 38^{15});
cf. En. 56$^{5\,f.}$, 'In those days the angels shall return and hurl
themselves to the east upon the Parthians and Medes ; they
shall stir up the kings . . . and they [the kings] shall go up
and tread under foot the land of His elect ones.' It is probably this association of these eschatological hosts with the
Parthians of the East that furnishes to our Apocalyptist the
subordinate feature of his vision, the location of the troop of
horses on the banks of the Euphrates, v. 14. To find in vv. 13–
19, as many scholars do, a fantastic description of a Parthian
invasion, actual or feared, is to exaggerate the relation of the
imagery of the Apocalypse to contemporary history. If that
were intended, the horsemen would form the principal figures ;
but they are barely mentioned, no activity in the infliction of
the plague is attributed to them, and there is no allusion to
the characteristics of the Parthians. The fabulous horses with
their marvelous powers (vv. 17–19) are alone the agents of the
plague. The location of the host at the Euphrates is the only
feature distinctly traceable to the popular dread of the Parthians. (Cf. Gunkel 216 f.)

13. φωνὴν . . . τοῦ θεοῦ, *a voice from the horns of the golden
altar which is before God :* the altar here designated as the altar
of incense (see on 8^3) is that especially associated with the
prayers of all the saints in the introduction to the trumpet-
visions (8$^{3-5}$). Thus the command which comes forth from its

horns, *i.e.* its corners, is represented as in answer to those cries for judgment ; cf. 6⁹, 8³ ᶠᶠ·, 14¹⁸, 16⁷. The connection between the command given and the prayers is made more vivid by the poetic personification of the altar, which as in 16⁷ utters its voice; the latter passage shows that the voice is not that of God, God is addressed there. The command is of course understood as in accord with God's will. — μίαν : indef. art.; see on 8¹³.

14. Only in this vision does the angel-trumpeter become an actor in the event to follow. In the first woe an angel-star is made the immediate agent (v. 2); here in keeping with the paramount significance of the vision (see p. 271) the office is performed by one of the seven archangels. — λέγοντα : instead of λέγουσαν, construct. ad. sens. —ὁ ἔχων : for the nom. see p. 224. — τοὺς τέσσαρας ἀγγέλους, *the four angels :* these angels are evidently the leaders of the invading host of horses, though not distinctly so designated; this is implied in their being loosed, and especially in the fact that the purpose for which they are said to be loosed, the destruction of a third part of men (v. 15), is executed by the host (v. 18), *i. e.,* they are identified with the host which they marshal. The monsters of this woe then, like those of the first (v. 11), are under supernatural leadership. — δεδεμένους, *bound :* as ministers of God's purpose they are kept bound till the divinely appointed time for their work has come ; cf. what is said of the winds in 7¹⁻³. — τῷ ποταμῷ τῷ μεγάλῳ, *the great river :* a standing epithet of the Euphrates, cf. Gen. 15¹⁸, Dt. 1⁷, Jos. 1⁴, Rev. 16¹². — Εὐφράτῃ, *Euphrates :* cf. 16¹². The Euphrates, the great river of Assyria and Babylonia, the chief enemies of Israel, is in the prophets put by metonymy for these countries to designate the place whence punishment would be sent by God; cf. Is. 7²⁰, 8⁷, Jer. 46¹⁰. It also formed the Roman empire's eastern boundary, from beyond which the dreaded Parthians would come. Hence it came to figure in eschatological imagery.

The four angels at the Euphrates. It is clear that the author does not identify these angels with those of 7¹; their place, condition, and function are different. The article however marks them as familiar figures. A difficulty arises also from the number four; it has no significance so far as is indicated in the account of·the host of horses; it would be appropriate to a host moving out into the four quarters of the earth, rather than to one coming in one direction, *i.e.* into the western world from the East; for this latter a single leader would be expected, as in the case of the locusts (v. 11). It seems probable that the writer has taken this feature of four angels from a familiar apocalyptic tradition in which four destructive powers, *i.e.* angels, winds, or the like, come forth from, or go forth into, the four quarters of the earth. The influence of other forms of the tradition appears in 7¹ ᶠᶠ· and elsewhere, *e.g.* Zec. 6¹⁻⁸, Dan. 7², Ap. Bar. 6⁴. But the prevalent expectation of an irruption of the Parthian hordes in the period to which our book belongs might easily lead an apocalyptist to identify these destructive angels or powers with the leaders of the Parthians, and so to place them not at the four corners of the earth, but at the Euphrates (see above). This identification was probably not original with our author, since the angels of punishment are found associated with the Parthians in En. 56⁵ (quoted on v. 12). Iselin in *Theol. Zeitschr. aus d. Schweitz* 1887, I. 64 cites from a Syriac Apoc. of Ezra (published by Baethgen) the following passage parallel to ours: 'A voice was heard, Let the four kings be loosed who are bound by the great river Euphrates, who shall destroy a third part of men. And they were loosed and there was a great uproar.' But this cannot be taken as a source wholly independent of our Apocalypse; see Spitta, 97 ff.

15. οἱ ἡτοιμασμένοι εἰς τὴν ὥραν κτλ., *those who had been made ready for the hour*, etc.: the precision with which the very moment has been fixed is emphasized by the series of time designations. It was a cardinal doctrine with apocalyptic writers, that God has fixed the precise time of every event; cf. En. 92² 'The Holy and Great One has appointed days for all things.' See Volz 165. — τήν: the art. is not repeated, since the nouns form a single compound phrase; cf. 5¹². — ἵνα ἀποκτείνωσιν : see on 8⁶. — τὸ τρίτον, *the third part :* the part to be affected by this visitation, as with the first four trumpet-visions, is a third, *i.e.* a large, but not the greater part ; see p. 251.

16. The angel-leaders drop out of sight, because it is the horses that constitute the real plague. — τοῦ ἱππικοῦ, *the cavalry :* τὸ ἱππικόν is a substantive denoting a *cavalry force ;* here the writer has in mind the horses rather than the horsemen ; the latter, so far as mentioned, take no part in what follows. — ἤκουσα, *I heard :* see on 7⁴.

17–18. The Seer passes to a description of the monsters and their equipment for their deadly work ; cf. vv. 7 ff. in the structure of the vision of the locusts. — ἐν τῇ ὁράσει, *in the vision:* a superfluous addition to εἶδον, *I saw,* not occurring elsewhere in the book, but frequent in Dan. *e.g.* 7², 8². — ἔχοντας θώρακας, *having breastplates:* the words refer, not to the horsemen only but to the horses also ; cf. the description of the locusts in v. 9 ; the words οὕτως εἶδον τοὺς ἵππους, *thus I saw the horses,* point to some added words descriptive of the horses as well as the horsemen. It is noticeable that the horsemen wear defensive armor only, in keeping with their subordinate rôle. The colors of their breastplates are made to correspond with the fire, smoke, and brimstone breathed forth by the horses. The correspondence in the two series shows that the dark blue of the hyacinth is meant to be parallel with the bluish color of smoke. — ὡς κεφαλαὶ λεόντων, *as the heads of lions:* a part of the terror-inspiring appearance of the monsters. — ἐκ τῶν στομάτων κτλ., *out of their mouths proceedeth fire,* etc. : cf. Job 41¹⁹ ᶠᶠ·. Fire-breathing monsters are common figures in mythology. The fire and brimstone here mark the hellish nature of the horses ; cf. 14¹⁰, 19²⁰, 21⁸, En. 67⁶.

19. ἡ γὰρ ἐξουσία κτλ., *for their power,* etc.: these words explain why the whole service assigned the horses, viz. the slaughter of a third part of men (v. 15), is performed by what proceeds from their mouths; it is because (γάρ) their power to *kill* resides wholly in their mouths. — καὶ ἐν ταῖς οὐραῖς, *and in their tails:* in these words closely joined with the preceding, as if a part of the explanation of the slaughter, the writer really passes to a new feature in the plague of the horses, one of which there has thus far been no mention. The mention of the power to kill residing in the mouth of the horses carries the writer's thought on to the other power, viz. to torture, which resides in the tail, and he blends the two in the common reference to the ἐξουσία, the *power* of the horses. We should expect a distinct sentence for the second thought. Since the whole number to be slain, a third part of mankind (v. 15), is said to have been slain by the mouth of the monsters (v. 18), it is plain that the serpent-like tails do not kill; their injury (ἀδικοῦσιν, cf. ἀδικῆσαι v. 10) is the torture of the serpent's sting. The monsters of the first woe torture only (v. 6); those of the second both torture and kill ; but slaughter is the

chief purpose for which they are sent (v. 15); hence it holds the first place in the description of the woe. — ἔχουσαι κεφαλάς, *having heads:* the tail ends in a serpent's head with its sting.

The feature of the serpent-like tails given to the horses has been referred to various origins. It is taken to be an allusion to the Parthian custom of binding the hair of the horse's tail in a way which gave it a snake-like appearance (Spitta 340), or it is suggested by the giants in the relief of the great altar at Pergamum (see on 2¹³), which have legs in the form of serpents (Holtzm. *al*), or by an enemy skilled in shooting their arrows behind them in flight (Bengel, *al*), or by the so-called *Amphisbaena*, which with a serpent's head at each end moved in either direction (Ewald, *al*). For other such explanations, equally far-fetched and inapplicable, see Düst. Alford, Speaker's Com. The monster is purely a fabulous creature, either of the Apocalyptist's fancy, or more probably taken from some mythological figure. A close parallel is found in the Chimaera, widely represented on vases, coins, etc., a fire-spouting monster, in which the fore part was a lion and the hinder part a serpent; see Preller, *Griech. Mythol.* II. 82 ff.

20–21. Notwithstanding the warning given in the plague, those who are not slain repent neither of their idolatry (v. 20) nor of their immorality (v. 21). In our book, as in all apocalyptic writings, the punitive purpose of the visitations is paramount, yet in some cases, as here, there is also implied a purpose to warn and lead to repentance; see pp. 554, 312. — οἱ λοιποί, *the rest:* all the survivors are unrepentant, as were also those who perished; the plague, then, like that of the locusts, was sent only upon the unbelieving world, and v. 20 shows that the *idolatrous* world is meant. The Apocalyptist has in mind the Gentile world as a whole; the Jews scattered among the Gentiles are absent from his thought here. The problem of Israel's attitude toward the gospel he meets elsewhere; see on 3⁹ and 11¹⁻¹³. — ταῖς πληγαῖς ταύταις, *these plagues:* a repetition of the words of v. 18; the plagues of fire, smoke, and brimstone are meant. — If οὐδέ be read before μετενόησαν (first case), the meaning may perhaps be that the supernatural warning did *not even* lead men to renounce their false gods, though these were but the creation of their own hands, and unreasonable objects of worship. οὔτε, adopted by some, has no proper correlative. Probably the reading οὐ is to be adopted. — μετενόησαν ἐκ: the thought of *turning away from* is implied; cf. 2²¹ ᶠ·, 16¹¹. — τῶν ἔργων τῶν χειρῶν αὐτῶν κτλ., *the works of their hands*, etc.: the nature and folly of idolatry are set forth in the stereotyped terms of Jewish writers; cf. Dt. 4²⁸, Ps. 115⁴ ᶠᶠ·, 135¹⁵ ᶠᶠ·, Dan. 5²³, En. 99⁶ ᶠ·, Sib. Or. V. 80 ff. — ἵνα προσκυνήσουσιν: equivalent to infin. of result; see on 8¹². — δαιμόνια, *demons:* that heathen divinities were demons was a common Jewish and Christian thought; cf. Ps. 106³⁷, Bar. 4⁷, 1 Co. 10²⁰. — In verse 21 the writer gives a summary statement of the heathen immorality generally associated with idolatry, taking the three fundamental vices named in the decalogue, murder, unchastity, and theft. The insertion of *sorcery* here in the same list with the vices named is explained by its wide prevalence with its trickery and allurement to all kinds of evil. It is frequently mentioned in conjunction with vice; cf. 21⁸, 22¹⁵, Gal. 5²⁰, Nah. 3⁴, Mal. 3⁵.

Textual notes, 9²⁻²¹. 2. εσκοτισθη ℵPQ min R many edd; εσκοτωθη A some min Ti Ws WH *al.* — 3. αυτοις (after εδοθη) ℵQ Ti Ws *al*; αυταις AP min R WH *al.* — 4. αδικησουσιν A 36 Ti WH Sod *al*; αδικησωσιν ℵPQ min R Ws *al.* — After ανθρωπους, some min R add μονους. — 5. βασανισθησονται ℵAP min edd; βασανισθωσι Q most min R. — 10. κεντρα, και εν κτλ. ℵAPQ min vers edd; R following som min and vers inserts ην after κεντρα and omits και, joining εν ταις ουραις to the foregoing; και is then inserted before η εξουσια. — η εξουσια αυτων ℵAP min vers edd; εξουσιαν εχουσιν Q some min; these variations in v. 10 arose from the failure to see that the words και εν ταις ουραις . . . μηνας πεντε combine two distinct thoughts: the power of the locusts to injure is in their tails, and their power is to be exercised five months. See Bouss *in loc.* — 12. ερχεται ℵA many min edd; ερχονται PQ many min R. — 13. τεσσαρων (before κερατων), PQ most min some vers R most edd; omitted in ℵᶜA some min and vers WH RV *al.* — 20. ου (before μετενοησαν) most min WH Blj RV Bouss Holtzm *al*; ουδε ℵQ some min and vers Ti Ws WHmrg Sw Alf; ουτε AP some min R Lch Sod WHmrg. — φαρμακιων APQ Ti Ws WHmrg Bouss Sw *al*; φαρμακων ℵC min Tr WH Sod RV.

Criticism of chapts. 8–9. Criticism of this paragraph has occupied itself chiefly with two questions: (1) its connection with the preceding part of the book; (2) its unity. (1) The argument against a connection with the foregoing chapts. has been most fully set forth by Spitta (86 ff.). It will be enough, then, to take up the question as presented by him. It will be remembered that in his view our book is a combination of a primitive Christian apocalypse and two Jewish apocalypses. This paragraph of the trumpet-visions, 8²–9²¹, with its introduction, as he regards it, 7¹⁻⁸, has no connection with chapts. 1–6, and, like Vischer, he assigns it to a Jewish source; he makes his first Jewish source begin here. (He transposes 8¹, making it introduce 7^{9-17}, a part of his Christian apocalypse, which he completes by appending to the latter passage $19^{9\ b-10}$ and most of 22^{8-21}.) Chapts. 1–6, with the exception of a few sentences, Spitta views as a connected composition of *Christian* origin, but 8^2-9^{21} he finds certainly Jewish; its introduction, 7^{1-8}, is declaredly concerned with the tribes of Israel only; and in the whole record of the trumpet-visions there is no trace of a Christian writer, all is purely Jewish (82, 90). But this is an inadequate statement. While this passage contains nothing distinctively Christian as contrasted with Jewish, the reverse is also true; it is one which might proceed from any Christian apocalyptist, whose mind is filled with traditional eschatological conceptions. Other objections offered by Spitta to a connection with chapts. 1–6 are: (*a*) that the plagues of the trumpet-visions fall only on the unrighteous [a statement not demonstrable of the first four], while those of chapt. 6 fall on both righteous and unrighteous. Those of the trumpet-visions ally themselves closely to the Egyptian plagues [not true of them all]; while the others are allied to the Lord's eschatological discourse. But even if the differences thus wrongly stated actually existed throughout, the inference of difference in authorship would not be established. (*b*) While according to 6^{13} the stars have already fallen to the earth and the heavens have been removed, this paragraph assumes the existence of everything in the heavens in the usual order till at the sound of the fourth trumpet (8^{12}) a third part of all the luminaries is darkened; in general the upheaval of the world in 6^{12-14} is such that the whole series of plagues in chapts. 8–9 is inconceivable. But the error in exegesis here is shown in the notes on $6^{13\ f.}$ (*c*) In $8^{2\ ff.}$ heaven is represented entirely under the form of the temple with its altars, furniture, and priests; in chapt. 4 it is a throne-room with no place for the appurtenances of the temple, or the temple service. But the error of the inference that the two representations cannot proceed from one author has been pointed out on pp. 524 f., 553. (*d*) The seven archangels who figure most prominently in this paragraph are not found among the heavenly hosts as described in chapts. 4–5. But that no distinction as regards origin between the two parts can be established by that fact is shown in the notes on 8^2.

(2) The arguments against the unity of chapts. 8–9 have been most fully set forth by J. Weiss (74 ff.). He argues that this portion of the primitive apocalypse consisted of a series of 'three woes' ($8^{13\ ff.}$) and that the later editor inserted the first four trumpet-visions, 8^{7-12}, in order to fill out a series of seven and establish symmetry with the sections of the seven seals and the seven bowls. The seven angels of 8^1 are, then, his addition. The grounds urged in support of this theory are: (*a*) there is a marked difference between the first four trumpet-visions (8^{7-12}) and the last three. In the former there is a certain monotony and repetition, without actual progress in the action; while the three 'woe-visions' possess variety and newness, and form an advance in the development of a plan. But even if this difference, which to say the least is largely imaginary, really existed, it would by no means establish diversity of origin; variety and progressive development in the course of a work are not inconsistent with monotony

in an earlier part. There is a somewhat similar difference between the first four and the last three of the visions of the bowls, 16^2 ff., and in fact between the earlier and later portions of our book as a whole. (*b*) There is a lack of agreement between the two series; in the second the locusts are forbidden to touch the grass (9^4), but in the first all the grass was burnt up (8^7). But this is a misinterpretation, as shown in notes on 8^7. (*c*) In 8^{11}, instead of an original 'one third' of mankind, which conformity with the other plagues of this fourfold series would require, the editor substitutes 'many' in order to avoid introducing here a result which forms a part of the second 'woe' (9^{18}) in the source which he is revising. The error in interpretation here is pointed out in the notes on 8^{11}. (*d*) The first four trumpet-visions are described as objective events which actually take place at the trumpet-blasts, the phrases 'I saw' and 'I heard,' *i.e.* in vision, do not occur; while in the fifth and sixth visions the fiction of a vision is retained (from the source) in the 'I saw,' 9^1, and 'I heard,' 9^{13}. But this dropping of the 'I saw' and 'I heard' occurs elsewhere in the opening of a vision or distinct part of a vision, where change of authorship is not supposable; *e.g.* $12^{7, 13}$, $14^{8 f.}$, 18^{21}. So also in the vision of the bowls, 16^2 ff., 'I heard' is used in vv. 5–7 but not in vv. 9, 11, 17; 'I saw' is inserted in v. 13 but not in the other visions. (*e*) The angels appear in 8^2, between the breaking of the seal and the incense scene, without taking any part in the action; their part does not come in till v. 6; thus v. 2 is seen to be a part of the editor's revision in forming a seven series. But on the contrary the angels do take at once an important part in the dramatic effect intended. The appearance of the seven archangels here at the opening of the scene and the giving of the trumpets to them, with the momentous events thus portended, form the background of the incense scene; it presages great issues with which the prayers of the saints are at once presumed to stand immediately connected. Without this feature the opening of the vision would greatly lose in clearness and impressiveness. (*f*) The breaking of the last seal and the tokens of divine anger when fire is cast upon the earth lead us to expect the immediate coming of the great day of wrath, the judgment itself portended in $6^{16 f.}$, but instead there follows another series of plagues, no severer than those of the seal-visions. But it is a mistake to connect the end *immediately* with the breaking of the seventh seal. We expect here momentous events, to be sure, but a whole cycle of movements must intervene before the entrance of the final catastrophe; see p. 549.

Charles (*Studies* 145 ff.) adopts the arguments of Weiss against 8^{7-12}. He finds also an additional objection to the passage based on his view that the sealing in 7^{1-8} is meant to secure against *demonic* plagues; such plagues, then, should follow at once after the sealing; there is no place for the intervening four plagues, which are not demonic in character. Omitting, then, 8^{7-12} and the words 'before God' in 8^2, he changes 'seven angels' to 'three angels' and 'seven trumpets' to 'three trumpets' in vv. 2, 6, and transfers v. 2, putting it before v. 6. But, to say nothing of the violence of these changes, probably few will accept the view upon which this objection is based, *i.e.* that the sealing in 7^{1-8} refers solely to *demonic* plagues; see 538 f.

These various objections cannot be regarded as furnishing a valid argument against the unity of chapts. 8–9 ; and the changes and transpositions made necessary in the omission of 8⁷⁻¹² are so violent that they cannot be justified without strong reasons. On the other hand, as shown above (see pp. 267 f., 549, and notes *in loc.*), the paragraph may without violence to exegesis be seen to be constructed by the author, in correspondence with the parallel sections of the seals and the bowls, on the framework of his favorite number seven. On these grounds most scholars, even those most ready to welcome criticism, if reasonably supported, accept this part as a unit in itself and as suited to its place in the plan of the book. That the Apocalyptist in the climax of the last three of the trumpet-visions may have been influenced by some source containing visions of three ' woes ' is conceivable ; but the supposition is not necessary to a natural exegesis or criticism of the paragraph.

X.–XI. 13. *Interlude between the sixth and seventh trumpet-visions.* See pp. 271 ff. (1) First Part, 10¹⁻¹¹. See p. 272. (2) Second Part, 11¹⁻¹³. See pp. 272 ff.

The sixth trumpet-vision introduced in 9¹³ ends with 9²¹. That paragraph, like those of the preceding visions, has described the whole course of its 'woe,' in its nature and effects, and vv. 20–21 show that the account reaches its completion there. A new vision evidently begins here with chapt. 10. The Seer has changed his place from heaven (4¹) to earth, though he does not mention the change (see on 10¹); new agents are introduced and a new set of themes looking forward to the events of the seventh trumpet-vision. But that vision does not begin till 11¹⁵. The sequence of the trumpet-visions then is interrupted by the insertion of this interlude, 10¹–11¹³. We have seen above that at great turning-points, or before the entrance of the culminating movement in a series, the author is wont to pause and introduce a prelude to the new revelations about to be given. It is thus that he introduced chapt. 7 as a prelude to the breaking of the last seal in the seal-series. Full illustration of this habit of the Apocalyptist's is given on pp. 244 ff. In the present place we stand before the last of the trumpet-blasts, the one about to usher in the period to which belong the Last Things. Here then the characteristic prelude is to be expected ; if it were wanting, the Apocalyptist would be felt to be inconsistent with himself. The special significance of the two parts of the prelude is spoken of below.

(1) The First Part of the Interlude, prefatory to the seventh trumpet-vision, 10¹⁻¹¹. See above and p. 272; (*a*) the announcement of the end as near, vv. 1–3 a, 5–7; (*b*) foreboding of wrathful judgment, vv. 3 b–4; (*c*) message to the Prophet, vv. 8–11.

There are three agencies presented in this paragraph; the angel, the seven thunders, and the Prophet. These all look forward to the seventh trumpet-vision. (*a*) An *angel* descending in great splendor, bearing attributes which mark him as the messenger of God, taking his stand on land and sea as indicative of a message to all the earth, with a loud voice and the right hand uplifted to heaven, announces with the most solemn form of oath taken before God, the Eternal One, the Creator of all, that the divine purpose will in the period to be introduced by the seventh trumpet-blast be accomplished without longer delay. In his hand also he bears a message sent from God to the Prophet, vv. 1–2, 5–7. (*b*) *Seven thunders* utter words which the Prophet understands and is about to write down, but a voice from heaven forbids this. What are the seven thunders, what did they utter, why is the Seer forbidden to record the utterances and what is the meaning of the episode for this connection? The number seven may conceivably be chosen by the author himself in conformity with his habit of designating things by sevens; but the article here makes this improbable. The thunders are definitely specified as *the* seven and are apparently known to the readers as such, since no explanation is added. The words are best explained as taken from some expression current in popular usage. (See more fully pp. 577 f.). But to whatever origin the use of the art. is to be assigned, the seven, whose number is that of fullness and completeness, are probably chosen here to suit the momentousness of the coming events. Now in all other prefatory passages in which thunders occur (8⁵, 11¹⁹, 16¹⁸) they form a premonition of judgments of divine wrath; that then is probably the significance here. Such judgments are about to follow among the events of the seventh trumpet-vision. This therefore may pretty certainly be taken as *the substance of their utterances and to embrace all that is aimed at in these verses*, 3–4. Cf. Wis. 19¹³, 'Upon the sinners came the punishments not

without the tokens that were given beforehand by the force of
the thunders.' As in v. 1 the accompaniments and attributes
assigned to the angel are meant to give glory to his appearing,
so here apparently the Apocalyptist seeks to give impressiveness
to the warning of the thunders by representing them as speaking in awful utterances intelligible to a hearer. The conception
seems to have no other purpose than the heightening of dramatic effect. But in the record of his vision, the precise words
fancied to be uttered, as it were, by the thunders are not essential; the significance of the imagery is clear to the readers;
and to have introduced actual words would have been at
variance with the writer's manner. Thunders and 'voices' of
storms are frequently employed in the book as symbolical
announcements, but nowhere (not even in 19^6, see note there)
are words cited as spoken by these. The writer seems to have
been reluctant to attribute to them specific words. He may in
a highly dramatic vision conceive himself to hear articulate
utterances from them and to be moved to record these; but at
the same time he is conscious of this feeling of reluctance, a
feeling which in the ecstasy of the vision assumes an objective
reality as a voice from heaven bidding him to seal up the words,
i.e., as he explains, not to write them. See further pp. 577 f.

(c) God's message to the Prophet and the nature of his prophecy
in the seventh trumpet-vision are vividly symbolized in what
is said of eating the little roll in vv. 8–11. To eat the word of
God is to receive it into the heart and make it one's own, to be
so permeated with it that it becomes the controlling power
within; cf. Jer. 15^{16}, 20^9, Job 23^{12}. The symbolism in our passage is taken directly from Ezk. 2^8–3^3, with characteristic variation. The Hebrew prophet about to be sent on his mission
sees a hand put forth to him holding a roll, and he hears the
voice of God, 'Eat this roll and go, speak unto the house of
Israel'; then he ate, and "it was in his mouth as honey for
sweetness." Thus far the Apocalyptist follows the prophet
closely. Then he introduces the new feature: 'When I had
eaten it, my belly was made bitter'; and this for his purpose
is the most significant part of the symbolism (see p. 579).
The *possibility* of this effect of the eating exists in the case of
Ezekiel's roll, as implied in the words, 'there were written

therein lamentations and mourning and woe' (2^{10}); but this does not seem to be thought of at first. The allusion in 3^{14} to 'bitterness' — wanting in the LXX — springs from a subsequent perception. It was doubtless the words of woe written in the roll that suggested to the Apocalyptist the special applicability of Ezekiel's vision to his own office in uttering the prophecies of the seventh trumpet-vision and led him to add this figure of a bitter sequel to the eating, upon which he lays the stronger emphasis. The prophecies which he is about to announce are, as the thunders had foreboded, full of wrath and calamity. Sweet as it was to be a messenger of God, to feel in his heart that closeness with God enjoyed by one whom he makes his prophet, the execution of his office was fraught with bitterness in the announcement of the awful oracles which form so large a part of these prophecies. The sweetness of the roll is referred by many to the reception of joyful revelations, such as the triumph over Satan, or the final blessedness of saints; the roll then is partly sweet and partly bitter. This interpretation is however not in so close conformity with the account given; it is not said that one part is sweet, another bitter; it is one and the same roll, the whole, that produces both effects. It is sweet or bitter according to the different aspects of the Prophet's activity.

The view that the little roll contains the revelations to be given in the seventh trumpet-vision, or that it brings a new prophetic commission to the Apocalyptist presents difficulties which are shown below (pp. 578 f.). That the contents of the roll appropriated in eating are in some way associated with the author's prophetic office is made clear by v. 11, closely connected with v. 10 (see note on v. 10), in the words 'Thou must prophesy.' The natural significance of the figure of eating and of the effects attributed to the act indicates that it is the prophet's own state and his experience in the performance of his office that are intended in the representation. The conclusion then which most readily suggests itself is that the roll contains God's command (v. 11, δεῖ, *thou must*) to prophesy. This privilege, this duty, the Prophet must take into himself, he must appropriate it, his heart must be permeated with it. But this is not his first call to the prophetic office, nor is it a

renewal of his commission ; he has been prophesying through-
out ($\pi\acute{\alpha}\lambda\iota\nu$, *again*, v. 11).   The message is rather such as comes
to every servant of God facing a great crisis.   The call to
duty which the Prophet has been unswervingly following since
the first command, ' Write ' (1^{19}), is here overwhelmingly *intensified*, as he stands before the supreme events of the seventh
trumpet-vision (see p. 579) ; and at the same time he is forewarned that his mission must carry with it proclamations of
woe.

The seven thunders.   This term is thought by many to be formed by the
author himself in conformity with the seven Spirits, the seven churches, the
seven stars, etc., as a part of the ' apocalyptic machinery ' (Alford).   But in
all these cases the art. is traceable to a familiar conception, or at least the
reason for its use is apparent.   Ewald's suggestion that the thunders of all
the seven heavens are meant presupposes ' the thunders of the seven
heavens ' to be a familiar thought ; but it does not occur in Heb. literature.
The sevenfold introduction of the voice of God in thunder in Ps. 29^{3-9} is
taken by many (Züllig, Hengstenberg, *al*) to be the origin of the expression ;
but that passage is not likely to have given currency to *the seven thunders* as
a familiar phrase ; on the contrary the sevenfold number there is more
probably due to the occurrence of seven thunders in some popular usage.
The supposition of such usage most easily explains the language of vv. 3–4.
The episode of the thunders with their mysterious utterances and the
injunction given to the Seer to leave them unrecorded is unquestionably
obscure, and no explanation offered can claim for itself more than a reasonable degree of probability.   The view has found favor with many scholars
(Weizsäcker, Pfleiderer, Bouss., Holtzm.-Bau., Baljon Moff., *al*) that in vv.
3–4 the author had in mind some apocalyptic source containing seven
thunder-visions, which was well known to his readers and which he *begins*
to use in this chapt.   *The* seven thunders are the thunders of that apocalypse ; their utterances also belong to the same source.   But deciding afterwards not to use these thunder-visions themselves the Apocalyptist justifies
the omission as in obedience to a special injunction from heaven.   But
while it is quite conceivable that the seven thunders may have figured in
some familiar apocalypse, there are strong objections to this hypothesis
regarding our writer's use of it in the way suggested.   (*a*) The author of
our book unquestionably shows careful prearrangement and reflection in
the composition of his record of his visions (cf. p. 175), and it cannot be
doubted that he subjected so complex a work to revision before giving it to
his readers.   There is then no place in it for a topic found, immediately
upon its introduction, to be unsuitable.   (*b*) Nor is there place in it for a
sentence whose object is to explain the omission of parts of a source used.
In view of the freedom with which the writer treats without explanation
passages in the canonical prophets, it is not likely that he would feel it

2 P

necessary to justify the same freedom in using a source of the kind supposed.

As regards the utterances of the thunders, the argument (Alford, Swete, *al*) that it is futile to inquire about these, since the Prophet is bidden to seal them up and the contents therefore cannot be known, is far from conclusive. They are intended to form a significant factor in the prelude, one whose general purport is to be apprehended by the readers; otherwise we may be sure they would not have been introduced. But all interpretations are to be rejected which are not directly suggested by the context or other parts of the book, as *e.g.* that they are the announcement of the final judgment (B. Weiss), of the blessed mysteries of the world to come (Hofmann), the echoes of the loud voice of the angel (Spitta), the proclamation of the fall of Rome (Ewald). As pointed out above (p. 574) the analogy of the other prefatory passages in which thunders occur and in which they are premonitions of God's anger about to burst forth in judgment, guides unmistakably to the conclusion that such is their purpose here in the prelude to a vision which abounds in exhibitions of divine wrath. To find in the injunction against recording the utterances a designed intimation that our book contains only a part of the revelations given to the Apocalyptist (so, Swete, *al*, following some ancient com.) is at variance with the general impression given by the book, and with the description the author gives of it in 1^2, as embracing ὅσα εἶδεν, *all that he saw*. If such a comment on the limitation of the book were conceivable, the place for it would be, not here, but in the prologue or epilogue; cf. the comment on the Fourth Gospel in Jno. 21^{25}.

The little roll. The *contents* of the scroll are identified by some with the oracle concerning Jerusalem, 11^{1-8}. Many others understand it to contain all the remaining revelations of the book, beginning with chapt. 11 or chapt. 12. (See p. 606.) In the latter case it is entirely distinct from the great roll of chapt. 5, whose revelations are now supposed to be ended, or it is included in that roll, forming another part of it and making known to the Seer these following oracles as contained therein. There is, however, strong objection to the interpretation of the roll as containing the subject-matter of the visions now to follow. (*a*) On the supposition that the revelations of the little roll are *distinct* from those of the great roll of the seven seals, the contents of the latter must end with the sixth trumpet-vision at 9^{21}. But the scene in the court of heaven (chapts. 4–5), when the Lamb takes the roll to break the seals, and especially the hymns of praise declaring the grounds of his worthiness to open the book, show that the contents of that roll are understood to include the consummation of the kingdom. That whole scene is inconceivable if the roll were thought to contain only two series of pre-messianic woes (chapts. 6, 8 f.). This conclusion is further established by the fact that the seven trumpet-visions, the last of which includes the end ($10^{6 \, f.}$, 11^{15-18}) are shown by the breaking of the seventh seal ($8^{1 \, f.}$) to be a part of the contents of the great roll. (*b*) The supposition that the remaining visions (chapts. 11 ff.), as the contents of the little roll, are *included* in the great roll, forming as it were a book within a book, raises equal difficulty. While the contents of the seventh trumpet-visions are, as just seen, introduced in a way to show connection with the great roll, there is no intimation of a relation to the *little* roll; this roll is not mentioned afterwards. The revelations of the later parts of the book are introduced in the same way as those of the earlier parts; and there is nothing to indicate that they are thought of as a giving forth on the Prophet's part of revelations imparted to him by eating the roll. In fact the figure of eating the roll is itself not appropriate to such a representation. It is to be noted that in Ezekiel's case the roll does not contain the messages which he is to deliver. These are to be given to him in the future, cf. 3¹⁰, ¹⁷ ᶠᶠ., ²⁷; and as he goes on in the performance of his office, his messages are seen from the subsequent chapts. to be imparted to him in each case by special revelation. The roll given to him to eat contains the word of God commanding him to fulfill obediently the call and commission which had already been given to him (2⁴⁻⁷), to receive that word and make it the impelling force within him. When the roll is described as containing lamentation and woe (3¹⁰), the language is meant to characterize the prophet's duty as woeful since he is sent to a rebellious people, who will not hear. The words express also the mournful character which the prophet's message must have for those to whom he. is sent. We infer then that the contents of the little scroll given to the Apocalyptist is the command of God urging him on with intensified force to his prophetic work in face of the momentous issues now to follow (see p. 576).

But it is clear that the part of the symbolism which is most significant with the Apocalyptist is the bitter effect of the eating. This constitutes the change which he introduces into Ezekiel's vision (see p. 575 f.); this has the emphatic place in the angel's words (v. 9); and in the words of both the angel and the Prophet (vv. 9–10) sweetness is attributed to the reception into the mouth, it is only momentary, while the permanent effect is bitterness; and in vv. 10 f. it is the bitterness of the roll that is immediately connected with the Prophet's coming activity. The chief office of the symbol then is to give warning that the seventh trumpet-vision must contain prophecies of bitter woe. The view held by many that the gift of the scroll to the Seer symbolizes the gift of a new prophetic commission, making as it were a new beginning here, is perhaps sufficiently met in what has been said. The commission given in the outset, 1¹¹, ¹⁹, covers the revelations of the whole book. There is no intimation that that commission is to cease with the sixth trumpet-vision, or that the seventh is not as truly included in it as all that precedes. The words of v. 11, ' Thou must prophesy again, cited in support of the view, no more imply an end of the first commission and the gift of a new one than does the repetition of the command ' write ' 2¹, 14¹³, 19⁹, 21⁵.

X. 1. See pp. 271 f., 573 f. **εἶδον,** *I saw:* the Apocalyptist has, as it were unconsciously, changed his place from heaven (4¹) to earth again ; though this is not announced, it is clear that he is no longer in heaven ; the angel descends from heaven and stands upon the earth when the Seer goes to him to take the roll (vv. 8 f.), and the voice which directs the Seer comes to him *from* heaven (vv. 4, 8). The sudden change is characteristic of visions (see p. 607). — ἄλλον ἄγγελον ἰσχυρόν, *another strong angel:* a contrast may be intended with the trumpet-angel of 9^{13}, or the angels of the preceding part of the book in general, or possibly with the 'strong angel' of 5^2. A similar indefiniteness occurs in 14^6. For the introduction of new persons, see on 5^5. — περιβεβλημένον νεφέλην κτλ., *arrayed in a cloud*, etc. : the majesty of the angel's appearance is conformed to his mission as a messenger from God. *Clouds* are the chariot of God (Ps. 104^3), the Lord's coming is to be with clouds (1^7); the *bow* forms an element in the glory of God's throne-room (4^3, cf. Ezk. 1^{28}) ; the *face shining as the sun* is an attribute of the glorified Christ (1^{16}, cf. Mt. 17^2), as are also the *feet glowing like fire* (1^{15}). A special significance is not to be sought in these several attributes of the angel. They serve to give him an appearance of heavenly glory. They do not however furnish ground for identifying him with Christ (so, many earlier com.) ; the unvarying use of the word *angel* in the Apocalypse is against such a supposition, as is also the oath in v. 6, which would be inappropriate to Christ. — ἡ ἶρις : the construct. changes to the nom. The art. is generic, as with ἡ γῆ, ὁ ἥλιος, when the genus consists of a single object ; cf. Blass § 46, 5 ; H. A. § 659 a. — πόδες, *feet:* the comparison with στῦλοι, *pillars*, implies that the word here includes the leg, as χείρ, *hand*, often includes the arm.

2. βιβλαρίδιον, *a little scroll :* a diminutive form not found elsewhere. Apparently the word is meant to distinguish this roll from the great roll of chapt. 5 — ἠνεῳγμένην, *open:* this feature is taken from Ezk. 2^{10}, and as the epithet is repeated in v. 8 it is evidently meant to be significant, yet no use is made of it. No allusion is made to an exhibition of the contents of the scroll. Apparently the writer has in mind merely a mark of distinction from the great roll which was closely sealed. — τὸν δεξιὸν ἐπὶ τῆς θαλάσσης κτλ., *his right foot upon the sea*, etc.: instead of *one foot upon the sea*, etc., to give precision to the picture ; no other motive for the specification of the right foot

is intimated in the context. The angel bestrides land and
sea, and cries with a loud voice, because his message is addressed to the whole world. — τῆς θαλάσσης, *the sea :* a reference to the Mediterranean cannot be insisted on here (Ewald,
Spitta) ; *sea and land* form here, as often, a comprehensive
phrase for the whole earth; cf. v. 6, 7², 12², 14⁷.

3. ὥσπερ λέων μυκᾶται, *as a lion roareth: μυκᾶσθαι* generally of the lowing or bellowing of cattle, is also used of the
roaring of the lion, see L and S. *s.v.* The comparison refers
to loudness, and does not imply, as many take it, that the
angel utters a warning cry *without articulate words.* Such a
representation is less suitable to the angel, as it is to God
whose voice is compared to the roaring of the lion, Am. 3⁸,
Hos. 11¹⁰. Our writer's habit of using an indefinite expression
which he afterwards defines or expands (see p. 242) makes it
easy to find in v. 6 the words uttered. The language of v. 5a,
repeating that of v. 2, connects the two passages closely. The
intervention of vv. 3b–4 is not against this supposition ; see
pp. 242, 574. — On the seven thunders and their utterances,
see pp. 272, 574 f., 577 f. — ἑαυτῶν, *their : i. e.* those which
they utter. In Jno. 12²⁸ ᶠ· the sound of articulate words is
heard by some as the noise of thunder. The reflex. here is
equivalent to the pers. pron., cf. Mt. 21⁸, Lk. 11²¹.

4. φωνὴν ἐκ τοῦ οὐρανοῦ, *a voice from heaven:* this may be
the voice of God, or that of Christ, who had in the outset given
the command to write, 1¹¹, ¹⁹. — σφράγισον, *seal up:* the term
is apparently taken from Dan. 12⁴, ⁹, where the prophet is
bidden to keep his visions secret till the end. His book was
already written and its contents were to be concealed by sealing the roll. In our passage the word is used figuratively, the
words have not been written ; the meaning is explained immediately in the added command, ' Write them not.' Here the
idea of keeping the utterances of the thunders secret is not so
much thought of as the omission of them from the record of
the vision. The reluctance of the Seer to attribute specific
words to the thunders is thus referred to a prohibition from
heaven ; see p. 575.

5–6. See p. 575. After the mention of the thunders, the
writer returns to the mission of the angel, relating definitely

his solemn announcement, and the purpose of the scroll which
he bore. — ἦρεν τὴν χεῖρα . . . οὐρανόν, *lifted up his right hand
to heaven:* the customary gesture in taking an oath before God
who dwells in heaven ; cf. Dan. 12⁷, Gen. 14²², Dt. 32⁴⁰. The
scene here and the form of the oath are taken from Dan. 12⁷,
but to God's eternity appealed to in that scene there is added
here his attribute as creator of all. These two attributes are
taken up in the respective hymns of 4⁸, ¹¹, and are especially
appropriate here ; the Eternal One and the Creator of all will
surely accomplish the eternal purpose which he had in creating
the world. — χρόνος οὐκέτι ἔσται, *there shall be delay no longer:*
i.e. beyond the days ushered in by the seventh trumpet-blast.
Earlier and some recent com. interpret, *time shall be no longer,*
a thought found, *e.g.* in Slav. En. 33², 65⁷. But the contrast
in v. 7 and the passage in Dan. here imitated show that the
angel's assurance is meant to answer the longing cry characteristic of apocalyptic writings, 'Lord, how long?' (cf. 6¹⁰). For
this sense of χρόνος see L and S. *s.v.*; cf. also χρονίζειν Mt. 24⁴⁸,
Heb. 10³⁷.

The interpretation, 'There shall be delay no longer, except in the days
of the voice of the seventh angel, and then the mystery shall be fulfilled'
(see punctuation of WHmrg), is as regards language, if not impossible,
extremely forced; and the announcement of the days of the seventh trumpet-
vision as a period of delay is not supposable here, nor is it consistent with
the hymns that follow the trumpet blast in 11¹⁵⁻¹⁸.

7. ἐν ταῖς ἡμέραις . . . ἀγγέλου, *in the days of the sounding
of the seventh angel:* the *period* (cf. Thayer, *s.v.* 4) belonging
to, introduced by, the seventh trumpet is meant. In the
course of that period the mystery of God will be accomplished.
The trumpet-visions are conceived to extend over periods of
time; this in the case of the fifth was at least five months (9⁵).
— ὅταν μέλλῃ σαλπίζειν, *when he shall sound,* or *shall have
sounded:* not *shall begin to sound* (AV), nor *is about to sound*
(RV), a prophecy contrary to the subsequent facts of the book.
μέλλω with the infin. forms a periphrastic fut.; cf. Blass
§ 62, 4. The words repeat the phrase, *the days of the angel,*
i.e. the days, the period, which shall come when he shall sound.
— καὶ ἐτελέσθη: the idiom is Hebraic, καί corresponding to

vav consec. with a perf. in apod. The meaning is, *shall be fulfilled*. — τὸ μυστήριον τοῦ θεοῦ, *the mystery of God*: the purpose
of God to bring his kingdom to its consummation — a purpose
hidden from the world but in the end to be fully revealed in
its accomplishment. μυστήριον, *mystery*, is often used in the
N. T. of a plan or purpose of God, for a time hidden, or only
partially revealed, but eventually made fully manifest, especially
God's purpose of salvation in Christ, *e.g.* Ro. 16²⁵, 1 Co. 2⁷.
St. Paul uses the word of the incorporation of the Gentiles
into the people of God, *e.g.* Eph. 3⁴ ᶠᶠ·. In our passage it is the
one great purpose which includes all others, the full salvation
of the saints in the perfected kingdom. — ὡς εὐηγγέλισεν κτλ.,
as he declared good tidings, etc. : *i.e.* according to the good
tidings which he declared to the prophets. The prophets meant
may be those of the O. T. (Düst. De Wette, *al*), or the Christian prophets (Bouss. Moff. *al*). The latter are meant by the
word in most places in our book, and the Apocalyptist is likely
to have had in mind the prevalent Christian expectation of the
parousia as near. For the acc. instead of the dat. with εὐαγγελίζειν see Thayer, *s.v.* I.

8. See p. 575. The second part of the angel's mission, the
delivery of God's message to the Prophet, now begins. — ἡ φωνὴ
κτλ., *the voice*, etc. : the one mentioned in v. 4. The construction here is harsh, though the sense is clear ; φωνή stands without
a vb. Perhaps the construction first thought of was λαλοῦσα
ἦν, but the partic. being attracted into agreement with ἥν, the
copula was omitted (the form λαλοῦσα in some Mss. is probably a correction) ; or possibly φωνή was thought of as nom.
abs. and the writer intended to continue ἦν ἤκουσα . . . ἤκουσα
πάλιν λαλοῦσαν, but the second ἤκουσα was omitted by mistake
either of the writer himself or a copyist.

9–10. See pp. 272, 576 f., 578 f. — λέγων δοῦναι : for the
infin. with λέγειν containing a request or command cf. Ac. 21²¹;
see Blass § 72, 5. — The order of the effects of the eating is
reversed in the two verses ; in v. 9 the bitterness is put first
because the emphasis is thrown on it. The order in v. 10 is
commonly explained by the natural order in eating ; but it is
better referred to the purpose to bring the bitterness into immediate connection with the words to follow in v. 10, which

show wherein the bitterness will arise, *i.e.* in bringing to many peoples, nations, etc., prophecies containing grievous woes. — **11.** λέγουσιν, *they say:* possibly the pl. refers to the voice from heaven and the angel (B. Weiss), but more probably it is used indefinitely, equivalent to a passive; see Kühn. II. § 352, c; H. A. § 602, c. Doubtless heavenly speakers are meant. — δεῖ, *thou must:* not a new commission to the prophet; see pp. 577, 579. — πάλιν, *again:* not in contrast with some other writer whose document the Apocalyptist is going to repeat (J. Weiss, *al*), nor in contrast with the O. T. prophets (Bengel, *al*), but in contrast with the Apocalyptist's prophecies given in the former part of the book. The new prophecies which he must utter are those that follow. — ἐπί: best taken in the sense of *concerning;* cf. Jno. 12¹⁶. — λαοῖς . . . γλώσσαις, *peoples and nations and tongues:* see on 9⁵. The Apocalyptist here adds βασιλεῦσιν, *kings,* which are really included in the preceding general terms; he emphasizes the rulers as distinguished from their peoples, perhaps having in mind such prophecies as 16¹⁴, 17¹⁰⁻¹⁷.

Textual notes, 10¹⁻¹¹. — 1. αλλον ℵAC edd; wanting in PQ many min. — η, before ιρις, ℵACQ edd; wanting in P many min R. — κεφαλην AC min edd; κεφαλης ℵPQ min R Sod. — 2. εχων ℵACPQ min edd; ειχεν many min R. — 3. αι, before επτα, wanting in ℵ* some min. arm. — 5. την δεξιαν wanting in A some min and vers R. — 6. και την θαλασσαν . . . αυτη wanting in ℵ*A some min and vers; WH bracket. — 7. ετελεσθη ℵACP most min edd; τελεσθη Q many min R. — Instead of δουλους, some min R read δουλοις. — 8. λαλουσαν, λεγουσαν ℵACPQ some min edd; λαλουσα, λεγουσα most min R. accepted as alternative form by Sod Blj Bouss. — 9. δουναι ℵACQ most min edd; δος some min R. — 11. λεγουσιν ℵAQ many min vers edd; λεγει P many min and vers R.

(2) XI. 1–13. *The second part of the Interlude between the sixth and seventh trumpet-visions : the repentance of Israel.* See pp. 272 ff., 573. (*a*) The chastisement of Jerusalem (Israel), vv. 1–2. (*b*) The mission of the two Witnesses (prophets) sent to it, vv. 3–12. (*c*) Its final repentance, v. 13.

This paragraph, 11¹⁻¹³, the second part of the interlude, contains a vision to which it is confessedly difficult to assign a meaning and place appropriate in our book. Taken as it stands it is a prophecy of the divine chastisement of Jerusalem, and its

repentance in the last times. Because of its grievous sins
Jerusalem will be given over into the hands of the Gentiles the
punishment often announced by the prophets and often actually
inflicted in the course of history. But God's love and mercy
are not entirely turned away from the holy city. The prophets
had foretold the salvation of a Remnant (see p. 22); so here
the temple and a remnant of faithful ones are marked off as
preserved from the chastisement, and two great prophets will
be sent to preach repentance to the people throughout the
period of Gentile domination. In spite of the marvelous powers
with which the prophets are seen to be endowed, the people will
for a time refuse to receive their message; but in the end, after
Antichrist has slain the prophets, after the glorious revival of
these and their exaltation into heaven in the sight of their
enemies, and after a destructive earthquake — signs sent as
further monitions — all the people who have escaped death in
the earthquake will be startled into conviction and repent of
their sins.

It is certain that such an oracle understood literally could
not be attributed to a Christian prophet. It is not necessary
to cite the words ascribed to our Lord concerning the destruction
of the temple (Mk. 13²), which may be of later origin (though
there is good ground for accepting them; cf. Ac. 6¹⁴), or
which might be unknown to the writer of this prophecy. Quite
apart from that utterance, the whole cycle of events described
lies entirely outside of Christian eschatology, as represented
elsewhere in the Apocalypse and other N. T. books. Nothing
is known there of a preservation of the temple from Gentile
desecration. The outlook of the Christian world was directed
to the early return of the Lord, with no anticipation of one or
more great forerunners who should come to prepare the way
for him. The sending of two prophets in the character of
Elijah and Moses (see pp. 593 ff.) to preach repentance, the
martyrdom of these through Antichrist (the Beast), their
revival and exaltation into heaven, form a series of eschatological events which has no parallel in Christian thought.

The passage has been taken by many allegorically: Jerusalem
is the Church, the temple and the outer courts are respectively
the faithful and faithless Christians, the two Witnesses are the

testimony borne by the whole body of Christian teachers, saints, and martyrs. But there is in the passage itself no intimation that such was the author's meaning. It is true that Christians are sometimes compared to God's temple, but it is *a* temple that is spoken of, a shrine within which he dwells (cf. 1 Co. 3^{16}, 2 Co. 6^{16}), not the temple at Jerusalem, which is never used to symbolize Christians or the Church; and when Jerusalem designates the Church, it is always the heavenly, not the earthly, city that is meant (cf. Gal. 4^{26}, Heb. 12^{22}). The details of the prophecy, especially vv. 1–2, 8, 13, make clear that primarily the actual Jerusalem was meant. The allegorical explanation is happily rejected by most among recent expositors, as belonging to a form of exegesis which reads into the Apocalypse anything to which a figurative parallel can be found there.

But unless we adopt the theory that the paragraph was inserted here between the sixth and seventh trumpet-visions by accident or an unintelligent compiler, we must conclude that it has a meaning and place here consistent with Christian eschatological thought and the Apocalyptist's manner as seen elsewhere. The visitation sent upon Jerusalem and its repentance suggest as symbols an appropriate eschatological meaning. But as regards the form of the prophecy, viewed as a symbol of an eschatological hope, it is difficult to assign it in *the first instance* to the origination of a Christian apocalyptist. Its facts are not in accord with the history of Jerusalem at the time of the Judæo-Roman War (67–70 A.D.); and at the date of the Apocalypse, the end of the century, when the temple had long since been completely destroyed, the Apocalyptist, if writing independently and forming his own symbolism, could hardly have conceived such a picture, or have introduced as essential traits expectations which were, as seen above, so remote from Christian thought. It can hardly be doubted that the author has made use here of some apocalyptic source unknown to us, taking his symbolism therefrom, and adapting it to his present purpose. We have already seen his indebtedness as regards form to familiar sources; *e.g.* 10$^{8-11}$ is founded on Ezk.; 9$^{2-11}$ on Joel; 7$^{1-8}$ on an unknown source. Most critics of recent times are agreed that such is the primary origin of much which is given in this passage, 11^{1-13}. Improbable as it is that a Christian prophet would, uninfluenced by any archetype, embody his expectation in such a form as this, yet he may easily be conceived to give his interpretation to some existing source, and take this over as the groundwork of his symbolism. In spite of its divergence from the historical circumstances of the writer's own time, we have seen the source of 7^{1-8} used in this way; a striking case of similar character is also found in 12^{1-6}, where a borrowed symbolism is applied to the Messiah quite at variance with the historic course of the Lord's life (see pp. 613, 617). It is a plausible conjecture that the supposed apocalyptic source which furnished the symbolism of our paragraph was written by a Jew in view of some threatened conquest of Jerusalem by Gentiles, that the author predicted the preservation of the sanctuary and a nucleus of faithful Israelites, the mission of the two prophets, their martyrdom, their heavenly triumph, and the repentance of the Jerusalemites, all as literal prophecy of events leading up to the coming of the Messiah. The significance which the author of our book attaches to the prophecy and the use he makes of it, as contrasted with its original meaning, will be spoken of below (pp. 588 ff.).

Spitta (417 ff.) holds that the source was written in view of the historic situation which followed the conquest of Jerusalem by Pompey, 63 B.C.; at that time the temple though desecrated was spared, and afterwards purified. It is to remain undefiled through the period of Gentile domination. In this period the two prophets will be sent to preach repentance to the Gentiles; the scene of their preaching will be Rome, where they will die (a natural death) when their mission is ended; after death their bodies will continue to work terror and prevent men from burying them; they will then be revived and exalted into heaven, and a large number of Gentiles will be converted to the Jewish religion. Everything in the present form of the passage at variance with this view of the source is attributed by Spitta to the Christian redactor who inserts the document here. The theory is interesting as an example of a not uncommon method of criticism. It is unnecessary to discuss seriously so arbitrary a treatment of the text, to say nothing of impossible exegesis. Most critics find the origin of the source, at least of vv. 1–2, in the times of the Judæo-Roman war (67–70 A.D.), which ended in the fall of Jerusalem; its author foresees the capture of the city, but predicts the preservation of the temple and a remnant of faithful Jews. Some place the document definitely between May and August of the year 70, on the ground that the peril of the city has become extreme and hope of deliverance must now be limited to the temple. There is, however, nothing in the passage to show an advanced stage of the war; the certain conquest of the city as the outcome of a conflict with Rome might have been anticipated by any careful observer even before hostilities had begun. Wellhausen (*Skizzen u. Vorarb.* VI. 221 ff.), followed by Bouss. Blj., *al*, holds vv. 1–2 to belong to an 'eschatological leaflet' written by a Zealot in the last months of the war. At this time the powerful party of the Zealots, who took an important part in the war, had its headquarters in the temple and its inner courts (Joseph. *B. J.* IV. 3, 7 ff., *al*); and an adherent of that party is supposed to have written the leaflet in this hour of distress, predicting the final safety of the Zealots, designated 'the worshipers' from their special relation to the temple. But the language used here does not go beyond the common idea of the sanctity of a temple as an asylum; and as the Zealots encouraged the people at large to continue in the temple worship (Joseph. *B. J.* V. 1, 3; cf. Ewald *Geschichte*[3] VI. 759 f.) the term 'the worshipers' would form no specific designation of the Zealots. The term itself is against the theory; see pp. 598 ff. Some critics refer vv. 1–2 and vv. 3–13 respectively to two different sources, chiefly on the ground that the former represents a historic fact, Jerusalem besieged and destroyed, the latter an eschatological expectation in which the city is conceived to be still standing. But it should be observed that Jerusalem is not represented in vv. 1–2 as destroyed, but as conquered and profaned. Bouss. (335 ff.) attributes vv. 3–13 to an earlier apocalypse especially concerned with the Antichrist legend, the two parts being afterwards combined by a writer from whom our Apocalyptist takes with modification the present form. These and similar theories, some of them ingenious, are interesting as studies in literary history. But they do not go far in settling the meaning which our author attaches to the oracle in the form which he gives. His procedure in other cases assures us that he has modified his source to any extent necessary for his purpose, and that he uses it in a sense concordant with the plan of his book, and in a sense which may be distinctly at variance with its original sense.

The significance and place of the prophecy in our book. It appears reasonably certain that in the thought of our author Jerusalem here represents Israel as a whole. A nation's capital is everywhere freely used to denote the nation itself. So in the Psalms and the Prophets Jerusalem is often spoken of where the writer has in mind all that the city represents; and so St. Paul speaks of 'Jerusalem that now is' (Gal. 4[25]), meaning the whole Heb. people organized under the Mosaic covenant; cf. Mt. 23[37], Ps. 137[5 f.], Is. 40[1 f.] The local Jerusalem and its people in distinction from the nation as a whole are nowhere the subject of special concern in Christian thought, nor do they occupy any special place in Christian eschatology.

But the repentance of the *people of Israel* in the last days was
a clearly expressed hope among Christians. The Church must
often have asked with perplexity, What is to become of God's
ancient people in the future of the new covenant? Are they
to continue alienated to the end and to be excluded from a
share in the Messiah's kingdom? The prophecies which foretold the restoration of the dispersed tribes and the sharing of
all Israel in the glories of the final Davidic kingdom must
have suggested to many Jewish Christians the hope of an
ingathering of their people. The Lord himself, in a connection
not unlike the present, when reproaching the Jews for rejecting the prophets sent to them, had declared that at his second
coming they would repent and rejoice in him as the Messiah,
Mt. 23[34-39]. St. Paul had discussed the subject with fullness
and intense earnestness (Ro. chapts. 9–11), and while finding
as yet only a remnant preserved (the temple and its worshipers
of our passage), he had foreseen the incoming of Israel as a
whole at the last. St. Peter also is represented in Ac. 3[19 ff.] as
looking for the repentance of his people before the messianic
time. Hope of this conversion seems to be expressed by our
author in 3[9] (see note there). And it will be noticed that in
all these references to Israel's repentance, this is brought into
close proximity to the End. This is what Paul means in the
words, ' What shall the receiving of them be but life from the
dead ? ' *i.e.* the resurrection and the establishment of the final
kingdom, Ro. 11[15]. If now this hope was general, and was
shared by our author, it could hardly fail to receive a distinct
place in a book concerned with the last things. And no more
appropriate place for it could be found than here before the
seventh trumpet-vision which embraces the last great cycle of
events. It stands in one of the author's interludes, because it
does not properly belong to the drama of the trumpet-visions,
since these are occupied with great world movements in the
earth and among the nations, to which the repentance of God's
ancient people bears no direct relation. It forms properly a
part of the prelude to the seventh trumpet-vision, because, as
was believed, it would be followed closely by the End. The
repentance of Israel is expressed in general terms ; the recognition of Christ as Messiah is not specifically mentioned. But

in this respect the paragraph agrees with the book in general ;
express reference to Jewish recognition of the Lord's Messiahship appears only in 3⁹. That the author, however, thinks of
it as included in the great spiritual conversion at the End is
beyond question. What has brought the divine chastisement
upon Israel is their sin in all its forms, including that of rejecting Christ (see on v. 8) ; so their repentance embraces this sin
with the others. If the above interpretation be correct, this
vision has a certain analogy to that of the sealing in chapt.
7¹⁻⁸. Both are interludes, they stand apart from the main
course of dramatic movement, they form pictures apart from
that of the immediate context. And the former assures the
reader of the final safety of the whole Church, the latter assures
him of the final safety of Israel. The details of the prophecy
must be considered more fully in their primary significance
and in their application.

*The delivery of Jerusalem into the hands of the Gentiles and
the preservation of the temple with its worshipers*, vv. 1–2. The
Jerusalem here spoken of is, as v. 2 shows, not the heavenly,
but the earthly, city. The measurement commanded is indicative of preservation (see on v. 1). The temple meant is the
earthly sanctuary, the altar is the altar of burnt-offering in the
court of the priests before the temple-edifice, the 'worshipers'
are the faithful people who worship in the courts before the
great altar. As has happened often in the course of its history
Jerusalem (representative of Israel) is given up to the Gentiles
in punishment for its sins. But a remnant, the true Israelites,
shall finally be preserved from perdition (Ro. 11⁴ᶠ·). See further notes on vv. 1–2.

The two Witnesses ; (*a*) their work and its place, vv. 3–6.
The two men who will be sent by God are called μάρτυρες,
Witnesses. They are *prophets*, as they are expressly called in
v. 10, and their work, as designated in vv. 3, 6, is that of the
prophet. They may properly be called God's witnesses, because sent by him to bear witness to the truth which they proclaim. The word and its cognates are favorite terms in the
Johannine writings ; its use here is probably due to the author
rather than his source. The prophets will appear wearing
sackcloth (v. 3), the garment of mourning and penitence (cf.

Joel 1¹³, Jon. 3⁵, Mt. 11²¹), and the course of the narrative
points to that as the character of their preaching. As in general with the prophets of the Great Day, their message will
consist of denunciations of Israel's sin, the call to repentance,
and the threatening of judgment; cf. Joel 1⁸⁻²⁰, Mt. 3¹⁻¹²,
Ac. 3¹⁹⁻²³. The prophets will carry on their mission throughout the period during which Jerusalem is trodden down by
the Gentiles, three and a half years (vv. 2–3), the symbolical
period of calamity (see p. 252). Whoever the two prophets
may be in the source, in the meaning of the Apocalyptist they
are Christian prophets — no others· are conceivable with him
(see p. 595 f.) — and he must think of their message as addressed to Israel from the standpoint of the Christian Jew, as
are the parallel messages of Peter (Ac. 2²²⁻⁴⁰, 3¹²⁻²⁶) and of
Paul (Ro. chapts. 9–11). That Israel's sin in rejecting Christ
is included in the Apocalyptist's thought, and that he viewed
the two prophets as Christians he shows in the words of v. 8,
'where their Lord was crucified,' which are an addition of his
to the source. Jerusalem is certainly represented in the vision
as the place of the prophets' labors. The words 'the great
city,' v. 8, do not show Rome to be meant (so Spitta, al); for
this term see note *in loc.* That Jerusalem is the scene is shown
not merely by the added words of v. 8, but first of all by the
close connection between v. 3 and vv. 1–2; the coming of the
Witnesses (v. 3) is introduced in immediate sequence with
the events transpiring at Jerusalem (vv. 1–2), without any
intimation of a change of place. Also the final outcome of
God's dealing with the city as given in v. 13, the sparing of
nine tenths of it, and the conversion of most of its people, cannot be harmonized with the character and destiny of Rome as
presented everywhere else in the book.

(*b*) The martyrdom and resuscitation of the Witnesses, vv.
7–12. When the two prophets have finished their appointed
time they will be slain by the beast that cometh out of the
abyss. But the ignominious treatment of their dead bodies
will be suddenly ended and the rejoicing over their death
changed to fright by the revival of the prophets and their
exaltation into heaven. This part of the prophecy is evidently
taken over, with divergences, from the source; but the space

it occupies in the paragraph shows that it is not a mere detail retained to fill out the picture. The description of the beast as the one that cometh up out of the abyss of hell shows that the familiar figure of Antichrist is meant (see pp. 397 ff.). The episode of the prophecy belongs then to a period extending into his era (whether precisely coinciding with it in its beginning is not important). Antichrist will have destroyed Rome, 17^{16}, 18^{8-24}. His authority, whose central seat is no longer thought of, will have been extended over all peoples and nations, and he will suffer no opposition to his worship (13^{15}). Jerusalem will be occupied by the hosts of his followers. On the presence of these powers in Jerusalem cf. Ps. Sol. 2^{19-25}, 'The nations reproached Jerusalem, trampling it down. . . . Delay not, O God, to turn the pride of the dragon into dishonor.' Objection has been raised to the representation of the beast and the Gentiles as hostile to the Witnesses. The argument is that the Witnesses are sent to Jerusalem; they cannot then incur the hatred of the Gentiles, nor suffer death through Antichrist whose seat is in Rome. It will be seen from what has just been said that this objection is based on a situation altogether different from that here presupposed. While the mission to the Jews is the aspect in which the work of the Witnesses is presented here, their denunciations of evil are universal, their rebukes and the wonders wrought by them (vv. 5–6) must fall on the nations, the followers of Antichrist, who as conquerors occupy the city. *Tormentors* of these also they will prove themselves as described in v. 10; and they will draw upon themselves the deadly enmity of the Beast whose worship they must denounce. The resuscitation of the Witnesses and their assumption into heaven is intended, doubtless in the source as well as here, to form a marvelous vindication in the sight of all men of God's messengers rejected and martyred.

(c) The repentance of Jerusalem (Israel), v. 13. The preaching of the Witnesses, enforced by their resuscitation and exaltation into heaven following their martyrdom, is still further enforced by a great earthquake. Nine tenths of the people are terror-stricken and aroused to repentance. Their repentance is signified in the peculiar idiomatic expression *give glory to God*, which is used to denote acknowledgment of error and turning from it (see on v. 13). That the preaching of the Witnesses has in the end its influence in moving the people to repentance is implied in the narrative as a whole, but more distinctly in this idiomatic phrase, which denotes a real spiritual change. Israel's repentance of its rejection of the Christ, though not specified, must in the thought of the Apocalyptist be included here. Thus the prophecy contained in the symbol of the preservation of the temple and its worshipers will be fulfilled. The purpose of God in temporarily casting off Jerusalem (cf. Ro. chapt. 11), in sending his two prophets, and in working his marvels, will be attained, while the visitations sent upon the Gentiles will have failed; cf. 9^{21}, 16^9.

The personality of the two Witnesses. The figures of the two Witnesses, taken over from the source, with whatever modification, are partially defined or at least dimly outlined in what are probably additions by the Apocalyptist. They are first described in v. 4 (see note *in loc.*) in their relation to God, and the imagery is taken with variation from Zec. 4^{2-14}. In the vision of Zec. two olive trees (symbolizing probably Zerubbabel and Joshua) feed their oil into a bowl, whence it is conveyed to the lamps of a single lampstand. The olive trees represent the channels through which God supplies his power for the work to be done. The Apocalyptist in adopting the figure introduces two lampstands instead of one, thus conforming it more closely to his use, and blends these in significance with the olive trees, *i.e.* the lampstands and the olive trees alike symbolize the channels through which the might of God is to work. The comparison is clearly not meant to designate the Witnesses as Zerubbabel and Joshua, for the latter are not preachers of repentance, nor have they the powers attributed in vv. 5–6 to the Witnesses. The language is meant rather to describe the Witnesses as *the agents of God working in the might which he supplies.* From the description of the Witnesses in their relation to God, the writer proceeds to designate them more distinctly in their personalities (vv. 5–6). It is a reasonable conjecture that the personal names of the two Witnesses were given in the source, but the Apocalyptist for a special reason (see p. 595) prefers to designate them by certain activities in familiar usage associated with them. The powers of

2 Q

shutting up the heavens that it rain not, of turning the waters into blood, etc., are those that appear as striking activities in the histories of Elijah and Moses (see notes on vv. 5–6). So also the function of calling to repentance here assigned to the Witnesses is that of Elijah, who according to Jewish expectation should return as the forerunner and great moral reformer before the day of the Lord. This expectation regarding Elijah, expressed first in Mal. 4⁵ᶠ·, is widely attested in the N. T. and rabbinical writings (cf. Mt. 17¹⁰ᶠ·, par., Mk. 6¹⁵, par.; see also Weber, *System*, 337 f.). It is doubtless the origin of the representation in this prophecy. While the special office of preaching repentance in the pre-messianic time was not attributed to Moses, yet he appears in Jewish tradition among the expected forerunners of the Messiah. The promise of a prophet like unto Moses (Dt. 18¹⁵) came to be interpreted sometimes of a return of Moses himself. This expectation is expressly stated in rabbinical literature (see Weber, in ref. above), and probably in the original form of Sib. Or. V. 256 (see Kautzsch *in loc.*, Volz 49). That Moses and Elijah were grouped together with special significance appears from the history of the Transfiguration (Mk. 9² ᶠᶠ·). The one name sometimes seems to suggest the other; thus they are brought together in Mal. 4⁴ ᶠ· and frequently in rabbinical tradition (cf. Weber, as above; also Edersheim *Life and Times*, etc., II. 706 ff.). The rabbinical belief in their association as forerunners of the Messiah was probably current also in popular eschatology, whence it was taken up into the source of our passage. It is further to be noted that the last end of the Witnesses, as described in v. 12, is like that accorded to Moses and Elijah in Jewish tradition; like these, the two Witnesses are glorified by exaltation into heaven. Earlier Heb. history records the death and burial of Moses in the land of Moab, Dt. 34⁵ ᶠ·. But as Elijah was taken up into heaven (2 K. 2¹⁻¹²) so also according to later tradition was Moses. This belief is implied in the rabbinic legend of the taking of his soul at death up to a dwelling-place under God's throne (see p. 525), but it is directly attested in the fragments of the Assumption of Moses, which are preserved in early writers; cf. also Jude v. 9 (see Charles, *Assump. of Mos.* 105–110, Hast. III. 450). It appears certain, then, that the two Witnesses are Elijah and Moses, who as forerunners of the great day are to perform the office elsewhere in the Scriptures assigned to the former only. The early commentators understand the second of the two Witnesses to be Enoch rather than Moses, because he, like Elijah, is recorded in Scripture to have been translated, Heb. 11⁵, Ecclus. 44¹⁶. But the description in vv. 5–6 is inappropriate to Enoch, and modern scholars are for the most part agreed in rejecting that reference.

But in what sense, now, can our Apocalyptist, a Christian writer, have taken up the return of Elijah and Moses in the last days? It is noticeable that he does not expressly give these names to the two prophets; in one aspect he describes them by a figure belonging to other names (Zerubbabel and Joshua); the powers which he attributes to them, following in the one case the story of Elijah (vv. 5–6 a), in the other that of Moses (v. 6 b), he assigns to both in common. We are led, then, to the conclusion that he has not in mind the reappearance of the historical personages themselves, but rather prophets who shall *perform the function* assigned to Elijah and Moses in Heb. tradition. Even if not familiar with the Lord's interpretation of the prophecy regarding Elijah as fulfilled in John the Baptist (Mt. 17¹⁰⁻¹³), yet as a Jewish Christian who saw in Jesus the fulfillment of prophecy, he must have recognized in many predictions an impersonal reference to agents who should act in the 'spirit and power' (Lk. 1¹⁷) of former servants of God, and perform the offices of these. So here we may take the Apocalyptist to have adopted the prediction of his source in the sense of the sending of two great prophets in the last times, who in the spirit and power of Elijah and Moses should call Israel to repentance.

But while the *duality* of the Witnesses in the source is thus accounted for, it is doubtful whether its presence there covers wholly the significance which the Apocalyptist attaches to it. He seems to give prominence to it; cf. vv. 3, 4, 10. The familiar grouping together of Moses and Elijah spoken of above, *i.e.* of the great lawgiver and the foremost of the prophets, is only another aspect of the truth contained in the frequent phrase, ' the law and the prophets,' which comprehends the sum of all revelation and commandment given to Israel. The for-

mula embraces the unquestioned authority to which appeal is
made for the enforcement of duty (Mt. 7¹²) or the sanction of
truth (Lk. 24²⁷). It is quite natural, then, that our Apocalyptist, Jewish Christian as he is, should be impressed by this
representation in his source, and should take it up and emphasize it as a prophecy of the authority which both the law and
the prophets will give to the message of the Witnesses whose
office it will be to call Israel to repentance in the last times.
The prophets whom he foresees will come in the character, not
of Elijah only, but of Moses as well. In view of the word
μάρτυρες, *witnesses*, we almost catch a reminiscence of St. Paul's
words urged in his great plea to the Jew for the Christian doctrine of righteousness before God, Ro. 3²¹, μαρτυρουμένη ὑπὸ
τοῦ νόμου καὶ τῶν προφητῶν, *being witnessed by the law and the
prophets*. This supposition, it should be observed, is quite different from the attribution of an allegorical meaning to the
Apocalyptist's words. He conceives the Witnesses as actual
persons, whose work and destiny he portrays with details as
objective realities. There is no trace of an intended allegory
representing a general power or influence at work in the
Church.

XI. 1. See pp. 584 ff., 590. The Apocalyptist in passing to
the second part of the interlude introduces a new vision without the usual phrase καὶ εἶδον, *and I saw*, or similar mark of
transition (see on 4¹). A voice addresses him, not as a mere
beholder, but as an actor; for such symbolic actions, frequent
with the O.T. prophets, cf. Is. 20², Jer. 13⁴, Ezk. 24³, cf. also
Ac. 21¹¹. But the Apocalyptist is not represented as actually
carrying out the measuring; the significant fact is the declaration of God's will. — ἐδόθη, *there was given: i.e.* by a divine
agent, whether the angel of the preceding vision or another is
not important. — κάλαμος, *a reed:* a measuring rod, as in 21¹⁵, ¹⁶,
Ezk. 40³, ⁶. — ῥάβδῳ, *a staff:* cf. Mt. 10¹⁰, par., Heb. 11²¹. The
comparison refers to length. — λέγων: a harsh construction,
the partic. referring to the agent of ἐδόθη, as if ἔδωκεν had
been used. The command is that of God, though uttered by
an agent. — ἔγειρε: for the frequent intrans. use as a sum-

mons, *up*, cf. Mt. 9⁵, Mk. 2¹¹, Eph. 5¹⁴. — μέτρησον, *measure:* the imagery is suggested by Ezk. chapts. 40–43 (or perhaps by Zec. 2² ᶠᶠ·), though a different meaning is attached to it. The determining of dimensions, as in 21¹⁵, Ezk. 40⁵ ᶠᶠ·, cannot be meant; that idea has no place here. The meaning is shown by the contrast in v. 2 to be the symbol of preservation; the measurement marks off the sphere whose bounds the devastation or profanation of the enemy may not cross; Zec. 2¹⁻⁵ is interpreted by some, though probably not rightly, as supporting this meaning of the symbol. In some places, *e.g.* 2 K. 21¹³, Is. 34¹¹, Lam. 2⁸, the measuring-line and plummet are symbols of destruction, and many older com. (so also Erbes 71 ff.) take that to be the meaning here; but the contrast of the *unmeasured* in v. 2, which is to be trodden down by the Gentiles, makes that interpretation untenable. — τὸν ναόν, *the temple:* the temple-edifice itself is meant here, as distinguished from the various courts connected with it. This is the meaning of ναός everywhere in the N. T. except possibly Mt. 27⁵; but probably there also. For the whole sacred precinct including the courts ἱερόν is used; if ναός were used in that sense here, it would necessarily include the *outer court*, which, however, is expressly excluded from the measuring, v. 2. — τὸ θυσιαστήριον, *the altar:* the exact reference of the word here is important in the interpretation of the following words. Most scholars, doubtless with right, refer it to the altar of burnt-offering, standing in the priests' court, outside of the temple-edifice. But some understand the altar of incense to be meant, which stood within the temple-edifice, in the Holy place before the Holy of holies. The measuring of the latter altar would, however, be superfluous, as it is included in the measurement of the ναός. Moreover, whatever may be true of the heavenly temple (see on 8³), when the altar of the earthly temple is spoken of without any defining word, the altar of burnt-offering is always meant. This, in the religious history of the Hebrews and in the temple-worship, was *the* altar. In the passage in Ezk. also, which suggested the imagery used here, the altar of burnt-offering is meant (43¹³ ᶠᶠ·).

τοὺς προσκυνοῦντας ἐν αὐτῷ, *those that worship thereat*, or *therein:* the idea of *measuring* the worshipers furnishes no real

difficulty, for the significance of the figure, *preserving*, is in the
writer's mind.   The phrase ἐν αὐτῷ may in itself mean *therein*,
in the temple, or *thereat*, at or near the altar.   The position of
the phrase favors the latter.   For this use of ἐν cf. Mt 6⁵,
Lk. 13⁴, also the frequent phrase ἐν δεξιᾷ, *e.g.* Ro. 8³⁴, Eph. 1²⁰;
cf. the Homeric ἐν ποταμῷ *Il.* XVIII. 521, *Od.* V. 466; see Win.
§ 48, 1, c.   Probably in all such cases the noun is primarily
thought of as including the sphere belonging, or adjacent, to it.
If now the altar of burnt-offering is meant, the *worshipers*
spoken of are doubtless the people, those to whom were allotted
the courts directly in front of the altar, *i.e.* the courts of the
Israelites or men's court, and the women's court; the court of
the Gentiles could not be included.   The people thus assembled
within sight of the great altar and its service are properly
spoken of as worshiping *at* the altar; cf. 2 K. 18²², ' Ye shall
worship before this altar,' Is. 36⁷, 2 Chron. 32¹².   The precise
force of the vb. should also be observed.   προσκυνεῖν denotes
worship, and is the appropriate word for those in the court of
the worshipers.   If *priestly service* were meant, we should
expect λατρύειν, or λειτουργεῖν.   It is true that this part of the
temple was the allotted place of worship for all Israel, and so
all Jews might be thought to be included in the measuring
symbolical of preservation (so, some com.), but that cannot be
meant, for Jerusalem itself is given up to the Gentiles, and v. 13
also shows that the godless Israelites are not included.   The
true worshipers, the faithful Israelites, must be meant.   What
is intended is a picture of God's abiding love and mercy toward
his people; he has not cast them off.   A remnant (Ezk. 14²²,
Ro. 11⁴ ᶠ·) shall be kept in safety — a symbol of the repentance
and salvation recorded in v. 13.   If on the other hand the
altar of incense is meant here, or if we interpret, ' in it,' *i.e.* in
the ναός, the temple-edifice, then the *worshipers*, the preserved,
must be the priests only, for no others were permitted to enter
the Holy place.   Such a prophecy is not conceivable with our
author, unless he has in mind all Christians as forming a priesthood (so, some com.).   Though Christians are priests (1⁶, 5¹⁰)
the supposition that the whole body of the Church is meant
here only introduces confusion into the passage; this single
phrase cannot be taken by itself allegorically, while the rest,

Jerusalem, the conquering Gentiles, the outer court, etc., receive
a literal interpretation; see p. 585.

2. τὴν αὐλὴν . . . ναοῦ, *the outer court of the temple:* the
so-called court of the Gentiles. ἡ ἔξωθεν αὐλή = ἡ ἐξωτέρα
αὐλή, cf. Ezk. 10⁵. Grammatically ναοῦ might depend upon
either αὐλήν or ἔξωθεν ; the meaning in the former case is the
outer court belonging to the temple, *i.e.* the court of the
Gentiles; in the latter case, the court which is outside of
the ναός, the temple-edifice, *i.e.* the priest's court; but the court
containing the altar would in that case be given up to the invaders, which is precluded by the measuring. — ἔκβαλε ἔξωθεν,
cast out: the meaning is shown by the added words, *measure it
not;* that part is to be cast out from a share in that which is to
be preserved. — ἐδόθη, *hath been given:* the tense refers to that
which has already been fixed in the will of God.   The subj. of
the vb. is ἡ αὐλή, or perhaps the following clause with καί,
taken as equivalent to an infin., after the Heb. idiom; cf. v. 3,
δώσω καὶ κτλ., see Thayer δίδωμι III. — τὴν πόλιν τὴν ἁγίαν,
the holy city: for this designation of Jerusalem cf. Neh. 11¹,
Is. 48², Mt. 4⁵. — πατήσουσιν, *shall tread under foot:* Jerusalem
will be subjugated and profaned, but not utterly destroyed; its
existence is presupposed in vv. 3–13. — μῆνας τεσσαράκοντα
δύο, *forty two months:* 42 months = 1260 days = 3½ years, the
conventional apocalyptic period of the domination of evil before
the End, the 'times of the Gentiles'; cf. Lk. 21²⁴ 'Jerusalem
shall be trodden down of the Gentiles until the times of the
Gentiles be fulfilled.'   See p. 252.

3. The Apocalyptist passes to the prophesying of the two
Witnesses, vv. 3–12.   See pp. 584, 590 ff., 593. — δώσω,
I will give: the subj. of the vb. is God.   The abrupt introduction of God is the easier here, because in vv. 1–2 it is really
God who is speaking through his agent.   There is nothing to
suggest Christ as the speaker (so, many com.); the reference
to witnesses of Christ in 2¹³, 17⁶ is not sufficient to establish
that meaning here. — The obj. of δώσω is contained in the
clause καὶ κτλ., instead of δώσω μάρτυσιν προφητεύειν, *I will
give, send, my witnesses to prophesy;* see on v. 2. — προφη-
τεύσουσιν, *shall prophesy:* prophesy is here used in its primary
sense of declaring an inspired message from God; cf. 1 Co. 14

passim. The warning call to repentance is meant. — ἡμέρας χιλίας διακοσίας ἑξήκοντα, *a thousand two hundred and threescore days:* see on v. 2. — περιβεβλημένοι σάκκους, *clothed in sackcloth:* indicative of the topic of their preaching; see p. 591.

4. This verse is thrown in in the form of a parenthesis descriptive of the two prophets as acting in the power of God. It is so distinctly in keeping with the author's manner, that it may probably be regarded as an addition of his to the source; see p. 593. — αἱ δύο, *the two:* the art. marks them as the two well known from their mention in Zec. (4^{2-14}). Whether there may not lie behind the imagery of Zec. some popular representation which he has taken up and applied, as Gunkel supposes (128 ff.), is not important for the interpretation of the symbol. — αἱ ἐνώπιον . . . ἑστῶτες, *which stand before the Lord of the earth:* the epithet is taken from Zec. 4^{14}, and marks the immediate relation of the Witnesses to the almighty ruler of the earth, whose servants they are in their prophetic work. — ἑστῶτες: the use of the mas. after the fem. art. is very harsh; the writer's thought passes suddenly from the symbol to the persons symbolized.

5. πῦρ ἐκπορεύεται κτλ., *fire proceedeth out of their mouth,* etc.: the representation is derived from the story of Elijah, 2 K. 1^{10}, where, however, the fire comes from heaven at Elijah's bidding. In Ecclus. 48^1 the *word* of Elijah is compared to fire, as is that of Jeremiah in Jer. 5^{14}. The Apocalyptist taking up the metaphor applies it as a reality to the Witnesses. That he has Elijah in mind is shown by v. 6a. — καὶ εἴ τις θελήσῃ . . . ἀποκτανθῆναι, *yea, if anyone shall desire to hurt them, in this manner must he be killed:* the words repeat for emphasis the thought of the preceding sentence. Perhaps θέλει should be read as in the first sentence; in either case the supposition relates to the future and εἰ with the subjv. does not differ from ἐάν with the subjv.; see Burton § 253. — οὕτως, *in this manner:* by fire.

6. Probably another addition of the Apocalyptist to his source ; see on v. 4. — ἔξουσίαν κλεῖσαι κτλ., *power to shut the heaven,* etc. : this attribute also is taken from the story of Elijah, cf. 1 K. 17^1, Ecclus. 48^3, Lk. 4^{25}, Jas. 5^{17}. According to 1 K. 18^1 the heaven was shut till the third year, *i.e.* less

than three full years ; but Jewish tradition, followed in Lk.
and James, substituted three and a half, the number symbolical
of a calamitous period. The Apocalyptist adopts the same (cf.
v. 3), in conformity with the period supposed throughout the
context. — ἐξουσίαν ἐπὶ τῶν ὑδάτων κτλ., *power over the waters*,
etc. : this attribute is taken from the history of Moses, Ex. 7²⁰ ;
the added words, *to smite the earth with every plague*, as seen
from their close connection with the preceding, refer summarily to the power of Moses in the infliction of all the Egyptian
plagues.

7. See pp. 591 f. The Witnesses are secure from the
attacks of enemies till they have fulfilled their prophetic mission, *i.e.* to the end of the period determined by God ; then
they fall as martyrs. — τὸ θηρίον, *the beast: i.e.* Antichrist ; see
pp. 397 ff. The beast is here introduced with the art. as well
known ; this has raised difficulty among critics unnecessarily.
The beast of Dan. 7⁷ᶠ·, the 'abomination spoken of by Daniel
the prophet' (Mt. 24¹⁵), had become a familiar representation
of Antichrist.   As such it not improbably stood in the source
used by the Apocalyptist, and could be taken over without
further definition, as well understood by the readers.   It is not
then an anticipation of chapt. 13, introduced prematurely ;
rather, what is introduced here incidentally is there, in its
proper place in the author's plan, taken up and shown fully in
its character and operations. — ποιήσει μετ᾽ αὐτῶν πόλεμον,
shall make war with them: said figuratively of hostile assault.
The same expression is used in 12¹⁷, where there can be no
question of contending armies ; cf. also πολεμεῖν, 2¹⁶, in reference to a small group of Nicolaitan teachers.   For πόλεμος in
the sense of a single combat, see L and S. *s.v.*

8. The denial of burial was felt by Jew and Gentile alike
to be the extreme act of indignity ; cf. 1 K. 21²⁴, Jer. 8¹ ᶠ·, 14¹⁶,
also Sophocles, *Ant. passim.* — τὸ πτῶμα αὐτῶν: strict accuracy
would require the pl. (as in some Mss.), but the sing. is sometimes used when the noun denotes that which each one of a
number of persons possesses severally ; cf. στόματος v. 5, κεφα-
λήν Ac. 18⁶ ; see Blass § 33, 4.   The vb. *sc.* ἐστί or κεῖται is
omitted. — τῆς πόλεως τῆς μεγάλης, *the great city:* Jerusalem
is certainly meant; see p. 591.   Elsewhere in the book the

term refers to Rome ; cf. 14⁸, 16¹⁹, chapts. 17–18 *passim*. But
the expression is one whose reference must be determined by
the connection. Jerusalem is so called in Sib. Or. V. 154,
226, 413 ; cf. also Jer. 22⁸. In connection with the description of it given in this verse, the writer might hesitate to call
it the holy city. — ἥτις καλεῖται κτλ., *which is called*, etc. : the
second part of the verse declares the sinfulness of Jerusalem
which causes it to be given up to the Gentiles. — πνευματικῶς,
spiritually : *i.e.* in a mystical sense, in contrast with *literally* ;
cf. Thayer, *s.v.* — Jerusalem is called Sodom in Is. 1¹⁰ ; cf.
also Dt. 32³², Jer. 23¹⁴, Ezk. 16⁴⁶, ⁴⁹. Sodom and Gomorrah are
the synonyms of extreme wickedness ; cf. Mt. 10¹⁵, 11²³. The
name Egypt is not given to Jerusalem in the O.T., but in the
state of sinfulness here thought of the city might receive this
name, typical of the enemy of God's people. — ὅπου . . . ἐσταυ-
ρώθη, *where their Lord was crucified* : the connection suggests
that these words are not meant to define more clearly the place
referred to, but to specify one of the sins of Jerusalem, which
led to its chastisement. — καί (before ὁ κύριος), *also* : the Witnesses will suffer in the same place as did *also* their Lord.

9. βλέπουσιν : the subj. is contained in the partitive expression ἐκ τῶν λαῶν κτλ. ; see on 2¹⁰. — τῶν λαῶν καὶ φυλῶν κτλ.,
peoples and tribes, etc. ; see on 5⁹. This general expression for
all peoples includes Jews as well as Gentiles. The ' nations '
to whom Jerusalem is given over are taken to represent all
Gentiles, as the Jewish inhabitants are representative of the
Jewish people as a whole. — ἡμέρας τρεῖς καὶ ἥμισυ, *three and a
half days* : the number is used in its symbolical sense, denoting
calamity, as always in the book ; see p. 252. In a country
where burial regularly took place on the day of death the time
of exposure and indignity would be regarded long.

10. οἱ κατοικοῦντες ἐπὶ τῆς γῆς, *those that dwell on the earth* :
this stereotyped phrase has its bad sense here, *the wicked* ; see
on 3¹⁰. The writer's tendency to repetition (see p. 241) is
seen in the use of the same words again at the end of the verse.
The persons meant are the same as those spoken of in v. 9, and
they are thought of as representing the world of the ungodly
at large. — χαίρουσιν κτλ., *rejoice*, etc. : the two prophets will
torment the people of Jerusalem, Gentiles as well as faithless

Jews, by their denunciations (v. 3) and their fearful miracles
(vv. 5–6), and all these, described in their ungodly character
as 'dwellers on the earth,' will rejoice over deliverance from
their torments (see p. 592); 'the world will rejoice' (Jno.
16²⁰), and men will send presents to one another in token of
their joy; cf. Neh. 8¹⁰, ¹², Esth. 9¹⁹, ²².

11–12. The martyrdom and ignominious treatment of the
Witnesses are succeeded by a triumphant vindication in their
revival and exaltation into heaven.— πνεῦμα . . . τοὺς πόδας,
*the breath of life from God entered into them, and they stood upon
their feet:* the language follows closely Ezk. 37¹⁰; cf. also 2 K.
13²¹. For πνεῦμα ζωῆς, the *breath of life;* cf. Gen. 6¹⁷. —
εἰσῆλθεν, *entered into:* in vv. 3, 7 the writer uses the fut. as
prophesying, and in vv. 9–10 the pres., for greater vividness,
with the same force; in vv. 11–13 he changes to the aor., as
narrating what he had already seen and heard in vision.— If
ἐν be read before αὐτοῖς, its use is peculiar, especially after a
compound with εἰς; but cf. Lk. 9⁴⁶; result after motion is
thought of, see Blass § 41, 1; Win. § 50, 4, a. — The resuscitation of the Witnesses takes place, not after three days, but
after three and a half; and the scene of this and the assumption into heaven is a public place in the midst of the city and
in the sight of all the people. The representation then is not
parallel to the resurrection and ascension of the Lord, and cannot be traced to that as its origin (so, some com.). It is probably taken from the author's source, and its ultimate origin
may easily be traced to the resuscitation described in Ezk. 37¹⁰,
and the ascension of Elijah, 2 K. 2¹¹. — ἤκουσαν, *they heard:*
cf. Jno. 5²⁸, 'All that are in the tombs shall hear his voice.'
But the reading ἤκουσα κτλ., *I heard a voice saying unto them,*
gives a better sense and is more in keeping with the author's
usage; cf. 6¹, ³, ⁵, ⁷, 12¹⁰, 18⁴, 21³.

13. See pp. 584, 592. A comparatively small portion of
the city, one tenth, is destroyed and apparently a corresponding
part of the people. The rest of the city is spared, the rest of
the people are aroused to repentance. — ὀνόματα ἀνθρώπων,
lit. *names of men: i.e.* persons. For ὄνομα in the sense of
person cf. 3⁴, Ac. 1¹⁵. Deissmann, *Neu. Bibelstud.* p. 24, gives
examples from papyri. It is especially used thus in enumera-

tions, persons being numbered by name; cf. Num. 1[2, 20, 28]. —
οἱ λοιποί, *the rest*: strict literalism would find here Gentiles as
well as Jews; but a conversion of the followers of Antichrist
is foreign to our book. The Apocalyptist with the purpose of
the paragraph in mind forgets the aliens present in the city;
both in the tenth destroyed and in the nine tenths delivered,
he is thinking of only the normal inhabitants, the Jews. —
ἔδωκαν δόξαν τῷ θεῷ, *gave glory to God*: a peculiar idiomatic
phrase denoting repentance; the meaning is to pay the honor
due to God by changing one's attitude and confessing, speaking,
or doing, the truth as the truth of God; cf. 16[9], Jno. 9[24], Jos. 7[19],
Jer. 13[16], 1 Es. 9[8], cf. 1 Pet. 2[12]. — τῷ θεῷ τοῦ οὐρανοῦ, *the God
of heaven*: the term, found in the N. T. here and 16[11] only, is
frequent in late Jewish writings, *e.g.* Dan. 2[18], Jon. 1[9], Ezr. 1[2],
Tob. 10[11]; see Bouss. *Judenthum* 306. It came to be used as
expressive of the transcendant majesty of God, without reference to a contrast with false gods. There is in our passage no
implication of turning from idols to the true God. There is
then no ground for Wellhausen's contention (*Analys.* 16) that
it is absurd to speak of the conversion of *Jews* to the God of
heaven, that the language can be used of Gentiles only, and
that therefore Rome rather than Jerusalem must be the city
spoken of here.

Textual notes, 11[1-12]. 1. Before λεγων, ℵ[c]Q many min (cf. AV) insert
εισστηκει ο αγγελος. — 2. Instead of εξωθεν before του ναου, ℵ some min R
Sod read εσωθεν. — 3. περιβεβλημενοι ℵ[c]C min R edd; περιβεβλημενους
ℵ*APQ min Tr WH. — 4. For εστωτες ℵ[c]P many min R read εστωσαι, a correction. — 5. θεληση 5b ℵA most edd; θελει CPQ most minWH mrg
Bouss. — 8. το πτωμα ACQ most min edd; τα πτωματα ℵP many min R. —
For αυτων after κυριος, one min R read ημων. — 9. For βλεπουσιν, some
vers Prim R read βλεψουσιν. — αφιουσιν ℵACP min edd; αφησουσιν Q many
min R. — 10. χαιρουσιν nearly all sources edd; χαρησονται some min Prim;
χαρουσιν R, uncertain source. — ευφραινονται ℵACP min edd; ευφραν-
θησονται Q some min R. — πεμψουσιν ℵ[c]AC many min R Ws Sod WH *al;*
πεμπουσιν ℵ*P some min Ti Blj Bouss. — 11. εν αυτοις A some min most
edd; εν is wanting in CP some min Tr Sod, bracketed by WH; εις αυτους
ℵQ many min; επ αυτους some min R. — 12. ηκουσαν ℵ*ACP min R most
edd; ηκουσα ℵ[c]Q many min some vers De Wet Düst Alf Bouss *al.*

Criticism of 10–11[13]. The fundamental difficulties raised in criticism of
this part of the Apocalypse have been considered above in the interpretation, as they are in reality exegetical problems. The entire passage is re-

garded by many as foreign to the plan of the book in this place and as the work of a different hand; so *e.g.* Spitta, Weyland, Wellhausen, J. Weiss, *al.* The seventh trumpet-vision and the third woe ($11^{14\,f.}$) must, it is urged, follow directly after the sixth vision and the second woe, *i.e.* immediately after 9^{21}; this paragraph breaks the sequence and in subject-matter has no connection with the preceding or the following. But for the appropriateness of the passage in this place see pp. 244 ff., 573, 588 ff. In addition to what is there said of the conformity of the structure to the author's manner, it should be observed that in characteristic language and phraseology the passage agrees with the other parts of the book; see pp. 222 ff. Also two special considerations should be noticed. (1) The words of the angel in 10^7 announcing the nearness of the Last Days and of the seventh trumpet-blast show that the paragraph, at least in its present form, is designed to stand between a series of six trumpet-visions and a seventh as the last; likewise the expressions 'another angel' 10^1, and 'prophesy again' 10^{11}, look back to some such connection as the preceding. If the theory of an editorial addition is to be maintained here, these words and phrases must be expunged, a process for which there is no ground apart from the theory itself. An editor feeling the necessity of establishing a connection which he saw to be wanting in the original form would have been likely to make the links more conspicuous. (2) The paragraph is not complete in itself, it could not have formed an 'eschatological leaflet' which has been caught up and preserved here; and that an editor should have excerpted it from its original position in another document and have inserted it between two trumpet-visions is to say the least extremely unlikely. A plausible motive for such a procedure has not been suggested.

Further arguments adduced for a different origin of the paragraph are: (*a*) 11^{1-2} was written before the year 70; but the first chapts. of the book as late as the end of the century. But it has been shown on other grounds that the Apocalyptist has in his symbolism here drawn from some earlier source in the same way as he uses throughout the O. T. writers; see pp. 584 ff. (*b*) The supposed use of an apocalypse of seven thunders (10^3) has been spoken of above; pp. 577 f. (*c*) The Seer is on earth, no longer in heaven. But see on 10^1. (*d*) From being a mere beholder he has become an active agent, 11^1. But it is doubtful whether he really becomes an actor, see on 11^1; in any case the variation is not significant.

Spitta (104 ff.) finds here the beginning of his second Jewish document, J^2. Weyland (154) makes this the beginning of the first of his two Jewish documents; he thinks that if the Christian redactor who combined the documents had perceived this document to be prior in time to that used in the preceding chapts., he would have placed it first and have given us a better book. J. Weiss also (146) assigns the passage to his Jewish apocalypse Q, which he finds to have been used in the earlier chapts. But the presence of Jewish elements is to be expected in any apocalypse; the type of literature is Jewish in origin and a Christian apocalyptist follows Jewish archetypes, especially the O. T., in forms and symbolism. Völter (*Offenb.* 76 f.) takes the paragraph, including chapts. 17–18, which he transfers to

a place between chapts. 10 and 11, to be a later addition inserted into the
primitive apocalypse by the Christian author himself, thus forming a later
edition.   Sabatier (22 ff.) regards chapt. 10 as merely a 'literary ornament'
conceived by the Apocalyptist to introduce the prophecies, of chapts. 11–14,
18, a series of Jewish fragments of which he makes use; these form the
contents of the 'little roll' which the Seer eats.   Similarly Bouss. (314 f.)
takes the vision of chapt. 10 as a digression by which the author introduces
the later oracles — the 'little roll' contains all the oracles that follow, beginning with chapt. 12 — at the same time he by this means binds together
the preceding and the following parts of his book and prevents a disorder
into which the visions through their numerousness threaten to fall.   But
against this view of the 'little roll' see pp. 578 f.

XI. 14-19.   *The sounding of the seventh trumpet.*   See pp.
274 f.   (1) The announcement of the third woe, v. 14 ; (2) the
sounding of the trumpet and the outburst of joy in heaven, vv.
15–18; (3) answering manifestations in heaven and in the world
of nature, v. 19.

The scope of the seventh trumpet-vision.   It is a frequent mis-
reading of the author's plan to find in it the promise of the
End as destined to follow at once upon the sounding of the
seventh trumpet.   The English versions also of 7^{10} give to
the reader this misleading suggestion.   On the contrary, the
seventh trumpet introduces, not a single vision merely, but a
long series reaching to and including the End.   The song of
praise which bursts forth from heaven upon the sounding of
the trumpet hails this signal as announcing the consummation
of the kingdom, but the third woe and all the other events
which enter into the last act of the drama must intervene before that consummation is reached.   The scope of this vision
is shown in 10^7 rightly interpreted; the mystery of God will
be accomplished, not at the sounding of the trumpet, but 'in
the days,' *i.e.* in the *period* belonging to, introduced by, it (see
note there).   The great cycle of events which follow now upon
the sounding of the trumpet make up the complex of the seventh and last trumpet-vision, or more properly series of visions.

Connection with the earlier trumpet-visions.   In resuming the
sequence of the trumpet-visions the writer thinks of the interlude, chapts. 10–11^{13}, as a parenthesis without effect upon the
orderly arrangement of the visions.   The same introductory

formula, ὁ . . . ἄγγελος ἐσάλπισεν, the . . . angel sounded, is
used as with the former visions, cf. 8[8, 10, 12], etc.; so also the
third woe is announced in essentially the same words as the
second, 'the . . . woe is past, behold the . . . woe cometh,'
cf. 9[12]. This characteristic feature in the composition of the
book occurs in the record of the seal-visions. After the interlude (chapt. 7) between the sixth and seventh seals, the writer
continues, as if unconscious of an interruption of the sequence,
with the fixed formula, 'when he had opened the . . . seal,'
cf. 6[3, 5, 7], etc. (see note, 8[1]). For the writer's habit of introducing such parentheses see pp. 244 ff. The scene of the
vision of these verses is again in the court of heaven, as in
chapts. 4 ff. The change in the Seer's position from earth to
heaven and the reverse occurs repeatedly in the course of the
following visions; e.g. he is on earth in 17[3], 18[1], but in 15[2 ff.] in
heaven. The transition is natural in visions, and is not especially mentioned — it is not important for the interpretation.

The third woe. Two difficulties present themselves here. (1) In the corresponding announcement in 9[12], the words follow immediately after the
first and at the entrance of the second woe, marking the transition from
one woe to the other. It is therefore urged by many interpreters that the
words 'a second woe is past,' v. 14, must stand immediately after the second woe, declaring its close. Two alternatives are then offered by those
who insist on this immediate connection. (a) The second woe beginning
with 9[13] extends to 11[13] (so, Bleek, Düst., Swete, al); the first words of 11[14]
refer then to 11[13]. But the aim and outcome of God's dealings with Jerusalem in 11[1-13] (see pp. 588 ff.) make it impossible to class these with the
'woes' sent upon the world at large as described in 8[13]. We cannot be
wrong in making the second woe end with 9[21] (see p. 573). (b) According
to the other alternative, 11[14] originally followed 9[21] immediately, the intervening passage, chapts. 10–11[13], being a later insertion. But against this
supposition see pp. 604 ff. We therefore take the words 'the second woe is
past' to refer certainly to the record of the woe as finished in 9[21], and the
words 'the third woe cometh' as announcing a woe of which the account
is to be expected in the seventh trumpet-vision. In so far v. 14 might
appropriately have stood immediately after 9[21]; but it may with equal pro-
priety stand in its present position. As the Apocalyptist at the beginning
of chapt. 8 resumes the connection with chapt. 6, picturing the details of
that former scene vividly present, as if unconscious of the interlude of
chapt. 7, so here, disregarding the parenthesis of chapts. 10–11[13], he continues in immediate sequence with chapt. 9. With our writer's tendency
to use set forms of phraseology, it is possible even to find special reason for
the present position of the words; it appears from 8[13] and 9[12 f.] that he

couples inseparably the announcement of the coming woe and the trumpet-blast, and that they are therefore kept together in our passage and put in the only place where the sounding of the trumpet could stand.

(2) A second difficulty is found in the author's supposed disregard of his announcement of a third woe. The first and second woes follow immediately after their respective trumpet-blasts, $9^{1\,ff.,\,13\,ff.}$ We should therefore expect immediately after the trumpet-blast of v. 15 some great calamity to be sent upon the world corresponding to the first and second woes, but this does not occur; in the opinion of many the third woe is altogether wanting. But while the fifth and sixth trumpet-visions are *wholly* occupied with their respective woes, and these therefore follow at once upon the sounding of the trumpet, the seventh vision is of much broader scope (see above), including the third woe as only one of its events; the place of this among these events is therefore not determined by the analogy of the first and second woes. The word ταχύ, *quickly*, used in the announcement of the third woe, occurs six times in the book, and never in the sense of *immediately*. That the third woe should be altogether wanting cannot be supposed upon any theory of the composition of the book. The emphasis put upon its prediction (8^{13}, 9^{12}, 11^{14}) makes its omission as improbable as would be the dropping out of one of the members in the seal or trumpet series. The writer does not attach the specific title 'woe' to the visitation which in the course of the visions forms the third woe, and so he leaves room for uncertainty regarding the precise calamity meant. Yet it appears most probable that the plagues of the seven bowls (chapt. 16) are intended. The grounds for this conclusion can best be shown in the interpretation of that passage; see pp. 669 ff.

(1) The announcement of the third woe, 11^{14}. See pp. 606, 607 f. This verse connects the following paragraph with what precedes the interlude, chapts. 10–11^{13} (see p. 606), and should therefore not be printed, as in some editions, as a continuation of the latter paragraph. On language see on 9^{12}.

(2) The sounding of the trumpet and the outburst of praise, vv. 15–18. See pp. 606, 274.

15. φωναί, *voices:* no particular class of the angelic host is specified as the singers in this verse ; only the heavenly source of the hymn is thought of ; for similar indefiniteness, cf. 12^{10}, $19^{1,\,6}$. The attribution of this verse to the four Living Creatures, and the effort to find in the two parts of the hymn (v. 15 and vv. 17–18) respective representatives of creation and the Church (so, Ewald, Swete, *al*) have no support in the passage. Against the view that in the angelic hierarchy the Living Creatures represent creation, and the Elders the Church, see pp. 501, 499.— λέγοντες : *construct. ad sens.* — ἐγένετο ἱ

βασιλεία τοῦ κόσμου κτλ., *the kingdom of the world is become*, etc.:
God's sovereign rule over the world is in the end completely
established ; the power of ' the prince of this world ' (Jno.
12³¹) will then be destroyed. — τοῦ Χριστοῦ αὐτοῦ, *of his Christ: i.e.*
the Anointed ; cf. 12¹⁰, Ac. 4²⁶, Lk. 2²⁶, 9²⁰, Ps. Sol. 18⁵, ⁷. —
βασιλεύσει εἰς τοὺς αἰῶνας, *he shall reign for ever :* suggested
by Dan. 2⁴⁴, 7²⁷. The subj. of the vb. is God, to be supplied
from τοῦ κυρίου ἡμῶν ; see v. 17. But the joint sovereignty of
Christ is implied in the preceding words. If the words τοῦ
Χριστοῦ αὐτοῦ were an editorial insertion to add Christ's joint
sovereignty (see p. 612), the interpolator would hardly have
failed to change the vb. to the pl.

16–18. On the twenty-four Elders, see on 4⁴. Their hymn
is an amplification of that of v. 15. Here, as in 1⁸, 4⁸, the
attributes of God specified are his omnipotence and eternity ;
these are directly related to his act here celebrated, the accomplishment of his eternally purposed kingdom. But the ὁ ἐρχόμενος of the former passages is omitted, because in the time now
reached in anticipation he has already come. — εἴληφας . . .
μεγάλην, *thou hast taken thy great power :* the power which God
has permitted Satan to hold over the world he has now taken
to himself. — ἐβασίλευσας, *hast entered on thy rule :* repeating
the thought of the preceding words. The aor. here is inceptive, as frequently with this vb., see Kühn, II. § 386, 5 ; cf.
19⁶, 2 Sam. 16⁸. The Gk. idiom takes here the aor., the past
moment being thought of when the reign began, lit. *didst begin
to reign,* whereas the Eng. idiom uses the perf., *hast become
king;* cf. Burton § 52 ; cf. the aorists ἐγένετο v. 15, ὠργίσθησαν
v. 18.

The EV here, *hast reigned* (AV), *didst reign* (RV) are unfortunate. — τὰ ἔθνη ὠργίσθησαν, *the nations have become wroth :*
reference is made to the culmination of Gentile wrath against
God, which is everywhere in apocalyptic writings a feature of
the last fierce assault made upon God's power by his enemies ;
in our book it appears in 16¹³ ᶠᶠ·, 20⁸ ᶠ· In ἐβασίλευσας, ὠργίσθησαν we have a reminiscence of Ps. 99¹, κύριος ἐβασίλευσεν,
ὀργιζέσθωσαν λαοί. With our passage, cf. Ps. 2¹, ⁵, ¹². — τοῖς
δούλοις . . . τὸ ὄνομά σου, *thy servants . . . those that fear thy
name:* the punctuation here is not certain, but the connection

2 R

is probably, *thy servants, namely the prophets and the saints, even those that fear thy name.* While the compound phrase *his servants the prophets* is common and occurs once in our book (10⁷), the immediate combination of the words here is not thus established with certainty. δοῦλος, *servant*, in the Apocalypse as elsewhere is far oftener used of the Christian in general than of the prophet in particular. καί before τοῖς φοβουμένοις is taken by some to point necessarily to a separate class, but the use of epexegetical καί is especially characteristic of the author. The frequent use of οἱ φοβούμενοι to denote Gentiles who as proselytes attached themselves to the Jewish synagogues (*e.g.* Ac. 13¹⁶) has led some interpreters to take the two terms οἱ ἅγιοι and οἱ φοβούμενοι as meaning here Jewish and Gentile Christians respectively; so, Bouss., Blj., unless, as they would prefer, καί be omitted. But a division of Christians into two such classes is wholly foreign to our author. For οἱ φοβούμενοι in the sense adopted above, cf. 19⁵, Lk. 1⁵⁰, Ps. Sol. 13¹¹. The redundancy in the passage is characteristic of the author ; cf. p. 241. — τοῖς προφήταις καὶ τοῖς ἁγίοις, *the prophets and the saints ;* cf. 16⁶, 18²⁴. For the elliptical construction equivalent to ' the prophets and the rest of the saints,' see on 16¹⁹. The mention of the prophets as a special class of the saints is in accordance with the great dignity which the author attaches to the prophetic office ; see p. 292. A distinction between the Jewish and the Christian prophets is not thought of here.— τοῖς μικροῖς καὶ τοῖς μεγάλοις, *the small and the great :* cf. 13¹⁶, 19⁵, ¹⁸, 20¹². If the acc. be read, it would be attributed to in-attention to the preceding construction, the writer continuing as if he had been using the acc. — τοὺς διαφθείροντας τὴν γῆν, *those that destroy the earth :* the writer probably has Rome especially in mind ; cf. 19², ἥτις ἔφθειρεν τὴν γῆν.

(3) Answering manifestations, v. 19. See pp. 606, 274.

The outburst of praise in anticipation of the End is followed by two manifestations symbolizing certain aspects of God's coming in his kingdom, the disclosure of the ark of the covenant in the heavenly temple, and awful catastrophes in nature. The significance of the latter is clear ; as seen repeatedly in the book, God's wrathful judgment upon his enemies is symbolized, cf. 8⁵, 10³, 16¹⁸. The symbol of the ark is referred by some to

the Jewish tradition regarding the hiding of the ark at the
time of the Babylonian destruction of Jerusalem, and its promised restoration as one of the events of the messianic age.   For
this tradition, see on 2^{17} (also Bouss. *Judenthum* 227, Volz 340).
Its disclosure here is therefore a token that the messianic
kingdom has come.   This explanation is attractive, and is
adopted by Ewald, Holtzm.-Bau., Bouss., Blj. *al.*   But while
the use of the symbol here may perhaps have been suggested
by this tradition, it is difficult to find the significance of the
symbol in the presence of a sign of the messianic time.   The
sounding of the seventh trumpet has given full assurance of
the End, already its arrival is celebrated in the hymn of
praise ; we hardly look at this point for further confirmation
of its presence ; at all events the expectation contained in this
tradition is not sufficiently prominent in Jewish eschatology to
account for its being singled out as the one sign that the
messianic age had come.   On the other hand the manifestations
in v. 19 appear to be immediately connected with the hymn of
praise ; they form as it were a response to it in action ; this is
plain in the connection between the disturbances in nature and
the wrath of God visited upon the destroyers of the earth;
therefore in the other symbol of the verse we look for some
aspect of God's act in taking to himself his kingdom.   It lies
near at hand then to find in the disclosure of the ark of the
covenant a symbolical manifestation of God's faithful fulfillment of his covenant with his people (so De Wette, Düst., many
others).   The two parts of v. 19 correspond then with the two
parts of v. 18; God has fulfilled his covenant in giving his
servants their reward, his wrathful judgment symbolized by
the turmoil in nature has come upon the destroyers of the
earth.   This verse is often taken as introductory to chapt. 12 ;
but its connection with that scene, which forms a new and
quite distinct vision, is much less immediate than with the
preceding.

Textual notes, 11^{15-18}.   15. λεγοντες AQ many min most edd; λεγουσαι
ℵCP most min R Tr Sod. — In place of the sing. εγενετο η βασιλεια, R with
one or two min has the pl. — 16. οι καθηνται ℵ* CQ many min Tr Ti Blj
Sod WHmrg *al;* καθημενοι AP many min R Lch Alf WH Ws *al.* — 17. R
with some min and vers adds και ο ερχομενος after ο ην. — 18. και before τοις

φοβουμένοις is wanting in a few min Bouss; omission favored by Balj in Com. p. 126. — τοῖς μικροῖς κτλ. ℵᶜPQ min R Ti Ws Alf Sod Bouss *al*; τοὺς μικροὺς κτλ. ℵ* AC Lch Tr WH RV Sw al.

Criticism of 11¹⁴⁻¹⁹. The majority of critics, both those who accept the interlude, chapts. 10–11¹³, as the work of the Apocalyptist, and those who refer it to another (see pp. 604 ff.), agree in assigning 11¹⁴⁻¹⁹ to our author. The relation of these verses to other parts of the book has been frequently pointed out (cf. Düst. Bouss. Blj.). Some of the more noticeable points of contact are the following. Verse 15 a looks back to the seven trumpet-visions of chapts. 8–9; v. 15b looks forward to 12¹⁰ ᶠᶠ.; v. 16 is a reminiscence of 4⁴, 5⁸, ¹⁴; vv. 17–18 anticipate parts of chapts. 13–20, as follows: the wrath of the Gentiles, chapt. 13; the wrath of God, chapt. 19; the judgment of the dead and the reward of the righteous, chapt. 20; the destruction of the destroyers of the earth, chapt. 18. As regards language every verse contains characteristic expressions or idioms of other parts of the book (cf. Bouss. 334). These facts furnish evidence bearing not only on the attribution of the passage to our Apocalyptist, but also upon the general unity of the book.

Vischer (18 f.) and his followers refer the verses to a Jewish apocalypse. The distinctively Christian words καὶ τοῦ Χριστοῦ αὐτοῦ, v. 15, are deleted, on the ground that the vb., βασιλεύει, is put in the sing. Evidence of Jewish origin is found in τοῖς φοβουμένοις, v. 18, which is taken to denote necessarily Jewish proselytes. But see notes above on these verses. Spitta joins 15 a with v. 19 and makes the passage form thus the connecting link between 10⁷ and 12¹, continuing thus the trumpet series belonging to his Jewish document J¹. Verse 19 cannot, he thinks, be joined with 15 b–18, the latter enacting a heavenly scene, while v. 19 relates to the earthly temple, as shown by κιβωτὸς κτλ.; the words ἐν τῷ οὐρανῷ are accordingly to be erased. In the first part of his book (p. 120) Spitta thinks it certain that vv. 15–18 cannot be referred to either of his Jewish documents, their source must unquestionably be Christian; but later on (pp. 583 ff.) he concludes that καὶ τοῦ Χριστοῦ αὐτοῦ, the whole of v. 16, and τῶν νεκρῶν κριθῆναι, v. 18, must be deleted and the rest of vv. 15 b–18 must form a part of his Jewish document J². Some critics (*e.g.* Volter) who accept 11¹⁴⁻¹⁹ as part of the primitive Christian Apocalypse agree with Spitta in omitting one or more of the short phrases mentioned above.

XII–XIII.   On the place of these two chapters in the plan of the book see p. 275.

XII. 1–17. *Satan's hostility to the Messiah.* See p. 275; (1) frustrated attempt to destroy the Messiah, vv. 1–6; (2) expulsion from the heavens, vv. 7–12; (3) pursuit of the mother

of the Messiah and persecution of the Messiah's brethren, vv.
13–17.

The use of a popular tradition in the imagery of the vision. In
the interpretation of this difficult chapt. it is essential to recognize, what may be regarded as established, that the Apocalyptist
has clothed his thought here in a form adopted from some
legend or myth familiar in Jewish folk-lore. That the Hebrew people retained as part of their common Semitic heritage
legends, more or less transformed, regarding creation, the heavenly bodies, etc., is a matter of general knowledge. And the
poets and prophets of the O. T. drew illustrations from these
as from any part of the store of popular thought and fancy.
We have seen in our book symbols and representations derived
from the prophets, who took them up as figures from current
fancy, though in their ultimate origin they may be traceable to
an early mythological source; such *e.g.* are the figures of the
horses $6^{2\,ff.}$ (see note there), and of the seven eyes, the seven
lamps, etc. (see on 8^2). It seems beyond question that something of the kind occurs in this chapt. A survey of the representation in all its details from the first appearance of the woman
in the sky (v. 1) to her final rescue on an eagle's wings and
through the friendly help of the earth, which opens its mouth
and swallows the floods shot forth from the mouth of the water-
monster, makes the mythological character unmistakable. It
is all very remote from an *original* creation of the Christian, or
even the Jewish, mind. The author makes plain that the child
is the Messiah (see on v. 2), but it is not conceivable that a
Christian writer in picturing Satan's assaults upon Christ
should *spontaneously* invent a story so at variance with the history of Jesus in all its parts. The birth of Christ, the earthly
career, the triumph over Satan's temptation, the ascension, as
parts of that history, are wholly different from what is represented in this scene. But we can easily understand that an
author ready as is our Apocalyptist to take up figures from
familiar sources should have seen in some popular tradition a
convenient symbol of Satan's attempt to destroy the Messiah
and his people.

Now there occur in antiquity widespread myths which present, some in one point and some in others, striking resem-

blances to this passage — a dragon's conflict with heavenly powers, a divine mother fleeing from the attempts of a god who seeks to destroy the child to be born of her, and the escape of the woman and the child (see fine print). These myths are primitive representations of the conflict of light and darkness, life and death in the natural world, of good and evil. As such they might spring up independently among different peoples, or in the easy migration of myths might spread and undergo modification. It is a reasonable supposition that the Hebrews also should have retained or taken up some similar legend embodying phases of the fundamental conflict between good and evil, between God and Satan, with promise of sure triumph of the good. And if such a legend existed there, it was natural that the Apocalyptist should, as in other cases, have drawn symbols from it. That the conception should receive among the Hebrews a form different from that found elsewhere would be inevitable. In view of our writer's usual procedure it is also likely that he has himself modified his material freely. Whatever reminiscences of the O. T. may be found in this passage, it is not possible to determine whether these are the coloring given to the myth by the Apocalyptist, or by its transmission through Hebrew tradition. The special value for the interpreter of the Apocalypse in recognizing the relation of the chapt. to a popular legend lies in the guidance to a more certain distinction between what is fundamental and what is merely incidental and formal.

There are in our chapt. some details (which will be noticed in their respective places) to which parallels of greater or less closeness are found in Heb. writings. Many interpreters account for the present representation by a combination of these; so e.g. Düst. Spitta, the older com. generally. But the picture as a whole is something far different from a composition of such elements. The origin of our passage is found by some in a tradition preserved in the Jerusalem Talmud (Beracoth II. 5) where it is said that the Messiah, born at Bethlehem on the day of the destruction of the temple, was snatched away from his mother by a storm of wind. But this is only an outgrowth of a belief that the Messiah, though already born, was as yet hidden (see p. 48). There are wanting here the essential features of our passage — the superhuman mother, the birth in the heavens, the rapture to the throne of God, the dragon's attempt upon the child's life, the persecution of the mother and the other children. The origin of the symbolism is found by some, following Dieterich (*Abraxas*), in the Greek myth of the birth of Apollo. The goddess Leto was with child by Zeus, and when she reached the time of her delivery she was pursued by the dragon 'Python, who sought to kill her and her child. But at the bidding of Zeus, Boreas brought Leto to Poseidon, who provided her a place of refuge in the island of Ortygia, where she brought forth the child, the god Apollo. Python returned to Parnassus, whither Apollo hastened four days after his birth and slew the dragon (the war in heaven of our passage). It is pointed out that the Leto myth was well known in Asia Minor, the home of the Apocalypse. But striking as is the parallelism in some respects, the difference is fundamental; the most essential feature of our chapt. is wanting in this myth, Satan's continued activity in persecuting the woman and her other children (the people of God) after his initial defeat. Gunkel (379 ff.) traces the source back to the Babylonian creation-myth and the conflict of Tiamat, the water-monster, with the newly-born god Marduk, the god of light, destined to be the supreme god. Völter (*Offenb.* 91 ff.) seeks the original in Persian mythology, and the conflict between Ormazd, the supreme spirit of good, and Ahriman, the supreme spirit of evil, who strive with each other for 'the great royal Glory,' a heavenly splendor represented as personal and betokening the supreme rule. Ahriman sends a dragon-monster with three heads to capture the 'Glory,' which flees to a lake and finds refuge and nurture with a water-spirit, who foils the dragon's purpose. Völter finds also some minor parallels here. But there is nothing parallel to what is essential in our chapt. — a child who is the object of hatred; here the woman is persecuted because of hatred of her child; in the myth the 'Glory' is pursued because it is the supreme treasure to be possessed. Bousset (354 ff.) finds similarities in Egyptian mythology, in which Hathor (Isis), the mother of the gods, is persecuted by a dragon and flees to an island, where hidden and in solitude she rears her child (Horus). After he is grown the child slays the dragon by his magic arts.

A survey of such myths, the details of which cannot be entered upon here, is interesting as showing resemblances and also important differences in the myths when compared among themselves and with the Apocalypse. But apart from essential divergences from our passage, there is sufficient reason for believing that the Apocalyptist has not drawn material immediately from any of these sources. Jewish Christian as he is, he would not for his symbolism go directly to the form of a myth current among the heathen; as in other cases, so here he has probably drawn from familiar Jewish folk-lore, whatever be the ultimate origin of the popular legend.

Satan's attempt to destroy the Messiah, vv. 1–6. In taking imagery in this chapt. from a popular source, the Apocalyptist, as in some other instances (*e.g.* 1^{20}), intimates his departure from the traditional understanding of the symbols by adding explanatory words. The epithet in v. 5, *who shall rule*, etc., derived from Ps. 2^9 (LXX) and used as a messianic designation in 2^{27}, 19^{15}, shows that the child in this scene is the Messiah (see on 2²⁷). The dragon is defined (v. 9) as Satan. The woman is not so explicitly defined, but in designating her as the mother of the Messiah, and at the same time as the mother of Christians (v. 17), the writer shows unmistakably that he intends the reader to see in her what St. Paul (Gal. 4²⁶) calls 'our Mother,' the ideal people of God (see on vv. 1, 13). The scene is enacted, not in the heaven of God's abode, but in the visible firmament, where are the stars which the dragon sweeps to the earth. The superhuman mother is adorned with the glory of the sun and other heavenly bodies, ornaments presumably suggested by the legend. The dragon is in the form of the familiar mythological monster with many heads; and he wears crowns symbolical of his world-dominion; his might and fury are exhibited as he drags from their places a third part of the stars with the coils of his tail and dashes them to the earth. The mother's travail pains mark the arrival of the time of delivery, and the dragon stands before her ready to destroy the child; but the child is caught away to the securest refuge and the most exalted messianic dignity — the heaven of God's presence and his throne. In this issue is represented the central thought of this part of the vision, *Satan foiled in his attempt to destroy the Messiah.* The flight of the woman is added (v. 6), not as forming a significant factor in this first scene, in which it plays no part; it is spoken of in anticipation of the later step in Satan's activity, described in the third scene of the chapt. (vv. 13–17), which the Apocalyptist has in mind from the outset, and for which he is here preparing the way. These words of v. 6 are not to be interpreted as describing the woman's descent to the earth; but with a certain confusion of ideas the Apocalyptist has in mind here the place and events of vv. 14–16.

The drama of these verses (1–6) is altogether transcendental, it is enacted in the sky, the characters are all symbolical, the figures and the general dramatic movement are suggested by the legend before the Apocalyptist's mind. A clear recognition of the writer's main purpose here and of the origin of the symbols used will relieve the greatest difficulty in the passage, *i.e.* that a Christian writer who accepted on the one hand the story of Christ's life from his birth to the Ascension, and on the other, the preëxistence of the Messiah (see p. 313), should introduce a representation of the Messiah's birth and rapture into heaven so irreconcilable in all respects with the Lord's earthly history. But that history is remote from the author's present contemplation. The Messiah of this scene is not the historic Jesus, the woman is not the Virgin Mary. The Apocalyptist's central thought here is a wholly ideal conception, independent of time and every concrete manifestation; it is the thought of Satan's futile hostility toward the Messiah *from the beginning;* and he sees a symbol of this in a familiar legend of a divine child of a divine mother, exposed at the very moment of birth to a superhuman enemy, but caught away to enduring triumph. The writer is not reflecting upon a moment when the preëxistent Messiah came into being, nor upon the Lord's earthly life. His vision is independent of these limitations. It may be vague and not in all respects easily reconcilable with his general doctrine of the Messiah. But these characteristics are not surprising in a Jewish prophet and apocalyptist. The writer's use of derived symbolism independently of historic circumstances has been seen above in 11^{1-2} (see p. 587).

The war in heaven and Satan's expulsion, vv. 7–12. A distinct act in the drama of the vision is introduced here, which incorporates as fundamentals two ideas regarding Satan current in Jewish belief. (1) The seat of Satan's kingdom and the abode of evil spirits were sometimes placed in one of the lower heavens. Thus in Sl. En. 7 and 18 the evil spirits are shown in the second and fifth heavens; in Asc. Is. 10^{29} the firmament is called the dwelling of the prince of this world, cf. *id.* 7^9, 11^{23}. The idea is reflected in Eph. 2^2, 'the prince of the power of the air,' cf. Lk. 10^{18}. (2) Satan was sometimes represented as having access to God's presence, and appearing there in his character of the arch-enemy of men as their *accuser,* or *calumniator, e.g.* Job $1^{6\,\mathrm{ff.}}$, Zec. $3^{1\,\mathrm{ff.}}$, Jub. 1^{20}, En. 40^7; so also in rabbinic theology. This idea led to the use of ὁ διάβολος, the *accuser,* in the LXX as a translation of the appellative of Satan, and thus the term became common as a proper name in the N.T. (see on v. 10). These verses, 7–12, tell of Satan's expulsion from the seat of his kingdom, and the end of his activity in calumniating the saints before God. This conquest is another of the divine acts in breaking the power of the great adversary of God and his people, it is another harbinger of the complete defeat in the end. The scene has no relation to the ' fall of Satan,' conceived as the apostasy of an angel of light; he is already, before the war in heaven here described, the foe of God, the prince of evil hosts, the accuser of the brethren (see p. 276). Neither is the war in heaven represented as a sequel to the attempt on the Messiah (vv. 1–6). The view, common among interpreters, that the Apocalyptist means to picture Satan as turning here to assault heaven in wrath over his failure to destroy the Messiah is not warranted by any intimation of such a connection. The opening words of the passage represent rather Michael and his angels as initiating the war; Satan and his angels are mentioned in the second place; contrast $20^{7\,\text{ff}}$. If such a relation to the first part of the chapt. were intended, we should expect it to be in some way shown, as the relation of the third part to the second is shown in vv. 12, 13. The war in heaven is a separate and parallel event in the conflict with Satan's power. Its position in time is not indicated. That the Apocalyptist thinks of it as past is evident, for Satan is already venting his rage in the persecutions of the Messiah's brethren which have now begun; see pp. 619 f. For the interpretation of the chapt. it is not essential to determine whether the war in heaven is taken from the same legend as the attempt on the Messiah. The one appears to be quite independent of the other. By whatever source suggested the war with its issue is introduced as an explanation of Satan's fury in these last times and a sure prediction of his final overthrow. Akin, though not exactly parallel, to the representation in these verses is the expulsion of Satanail and his angels from heaven in Sl. En. 29^4; cf. Is. $14^{12\,\text{ff}}$. An assault upon the powers of heaven ending with the overthrow of the assailants is a familiar theme in ancient mythology; cf. the battle of the Titans.

Satan's persecution of the woman and her other children, vv. 13–17. The third part of the chapt. for which the other two form a preparation represents Satan foiled in his persecution of the Messiah's mother, and turning his wrath upon her other children. The scene is now on earth. This is not the beginning of Satan's activity among men, but now earth be-

comes the sphere of his intensified malice. His rage here
reaches its height, because he has failed in his design against
the Messiah, he has been cast out with his hosts from his dominion in the heavens, and he sees that he has but a little time
before his final overthrow. The woman at first seen in the sky
now appears on the earth. The Apocalyptist assumes the
change without speaking of the transition (cf. p. 616). The
contrariety is not relieved by supposing different documents combined here, or an interpolated document concerning
the war in heaven (see p. 632). The first two parts of the
chapt. look forward to just such a scene on earth as this to complete their meaning, *i.e.* the significance of those events for the
Christians in their present distresses and in those which form
the subject of the later visions. The abruptness of the change
is not unlike that which occurs in the Seer's position in 10^1;
see p. 607. But in this case the appearance of the woman in
different places in two closely connected scenes requires mention
of a transition the less, because of the wholly ideal character of
the woman who is assumed to be present in a way wherever
the concrete reality exists. As in the first scene she is not the
Jewish people, so here she is not the visible Christian Church;
in both cases she is the *ideal* people of God, the Church in
its broadest, transcendental sense, to which the Messiah and
Christians alike belong, and she is present in idea wherever
they are; see on vv. 1, 13.

The woman is caught up on an eagle's wings, the earth swallows
the flood which the dragon belches forth to sweep her away,
figures doubtless taken over by the Apocalyptist, with whatever
variation, from the legend. The meaning is plain; the ideal
people is delivered and kept in safety till the times of calamity,
'the times of the Gentiles,' are past (vv. 6, 14; cf. p. 252).
But the actual earthly children of the ideal mother, the followers
of Jesus, remain to suffer the persecutions of Satan. A distinction is thus made between the ideal people, as if a separate
entity, and the individuals that form that entity, so that what
befalls the children does not befall the mother. This distinction is, however, formal rather than real. In reality the safety
of the mother carries with it the promise and pledge of the
ultimate safety of the children; for the two are inseparable, so

that only in thought is the fortune of the children different from that of the mother. A similar separation in thought between the ideal entity and the individuals forming it occurs in 19⁷ ᶠᶠ·, where they that are bidden to the marriage, Christians, are distinguished from the bride, the people of God. For other views concerning the interpretation of the chapt. see notes below.

The purpose of the visions of this chapt. It appears unquestionable that the principal events portrayed in this chapt. are not things which must first come to pass in the future. With a Christian writer the birth of the Messiah has already taken place. So also Satan's expulsion from his dominion in the lower heavens, so far as it is thought of with reference to time, is viewed as past. But as with the birth of the Messiah, so here a definite historic event is not what is distinctly before the mind of the author; his thought is concerned with the *present reality*, the fierceness of Satan's rage, which is explained by the defeat he has already begun to suffer. That defeat is thought of only in its ideal occurrence, represented in a vivid symbolical picture, quite apart from any actual event; cf. on the birth of the Messiah p. 617. Satan is already coursing the earth ' with great wrath,' he is now the prince of this world, he is now persecuting ' the other children of the woman,' the followers of Christ; the Beast his agent (the Roman emperors) has already begun his war with the saints (13⁷). The heavenly song, vv. 10–12, connecting Satan's expulsion with the arrival of the kingdom is anticipatory, like those of 11¹⁵⁻¹⁸. The purpose of the chapt. then is to be taken as a revelation of ' things that are ' (see pp. 442 ff.) — causes and agencies already at work in the world and about to manifest themselves in other forms and with greater power in the coming conflicts. The scenes explain the true cause of the present distresses and those yet to come, while at the same time they presage the certain outcome in the deliverance of the saints. It is not the purpose of the chapt., as it is sometimes understood, to give a picture of the two antagonists, Christ and Satan, who are about to contend with each other in the scenes of the later visions; for in the visions given here the Messiah plays but a passive part; he appears as a child only, miraculously delivered from Satan's attempt, and not at all

among the powers opposing Satan.   Nor is the chapt. meant to
encourage the Christians by *reminding* them that Satan's conqueror has been born, and is now awaiting in heaven the
divinely ordered time to come forth to action (a common interpretation); for in this particular paragraph nothing is said of
his return or of his conflict with and victory over Satan.   The
Apocalyptist is wholly occupied with Satan's deadly hostility
toward the Messiah, and his baffled designs.   It is that hostility
which explains all the awful distresses, present and future, inflicted upon Christ's followers by Satan's agents, the powers of
the world; while the defeat of Satan pictured in each of the
three scenes forecasts his complete overthrow in the end.

(1) Frustrated attempt to destroy the Messiah.   12$^{1-6}$.   See
pp. 612, 275 f., 615 f.

The new vision begins without the usual introductory
phrase ; see on 4^1. — σημεῖον μέγα, *a great wonder:* σημεῖον is
primarily a *mark*, or *sign*, by which a thing is known, often an
indication of something about to happen ; but often, as here, a
strange phenomenon or prodigy, in which sense it is joined as
a synonym with τέρας, ' signs and wonders,' cf. Mt. 24^{24}, Jno.
4^{48}, Ac. 5^{12} ; for its sense here, *wonder*, cf. also 15^1, 16^{14}, 19^{20},
Lk. 21^{11}, Jno. 9^{16}. — ἐν τῷ οὐρανῷ, *in the heaven :* i.e. the sky,
as shown by the presence of the stars, v. 4. — γυνή, *a woman:*
as a heavenly figure and as the mother of Christians (v.17) as
well as of the Messiah, the woman cannot be the earthly
mother of our Lord ; few even among Mariolaters maintain
that.   There is here no relation to the Lord's incarnate life
(see p. 613).   Neither can she be in this verse the Church of
the O.T. of which Christ is born after the flesh (so, Bleek,
De Wet. Düst. Alf., many others), for it is one and the same
person who appears here and in vv. 13 ff.   She is the heavenly
representative of the people of God, the *ideal* Zion, which so
far as it is embodied in concrete realities is represented alike
by the people of the old and the new covenants (see p. 616).
Such a distinction between the ideal and the real, as if separate
entities (see p. 619), is natural with a Jewish writer, since
in Jewish thought all earthly things have their heavenly
counterpart or archetype.   With our writer there is only one

true Israel, embracing alike the Jewish and the Christian Church ; cf. 3⁹, 11¹⁹, 15⁵, 21¹²⁻¹⁴. For the ideal Zion represented as the *mother* of God's people, cf. Is. 54¹, 66⁷⁻⁹, Gal. 4²⁶, 2 Es. 10⁷. As the Messiah is born of Israel, so he is appropriately made the child of this ideal woman. The representation of Israel as the *mother of the Messiah* is possibly contained in Mic. 5³. In 2 Es. 9⁴³⁻⁴⁵, 10⁴⁴⁻⁴⁶, often cited as parallel, the son cannot be the Messiah. Micah 4⁹ ᶠᶠ·, representing Zion as crying out like a woman in travail and destined to go forth to 'dwell in the field,' but at last to be rescued, is taken by many com. to furnish the principal traits of the scene in this chapt. But the birth of the divine child, the attempt of Satan to destroy it, and its rescue, the principal traits in this scene, have no parallel in Micah ; and the exile of the daughter of Zion from Jerusalem, her capture by her enemies, and her deportation to Babylon are not parallel to the fortunes of the woman as pictured in our chapt. The figure of a woman crying out in travail is too common in Scripture to furnish evidence of dependence. Here the cries merely mark the arrival of the time for the birth of the child, *i.e.* the time for the dragon to appear for the destruction of the child. No special symbolism, such as Israel's long history of suffering before the advent of Christ (so, some com.) is contained in the words ; all such historic reference is remote from the purely idealistic passage.

περιβεβλημένη τὸν ἥλιον κτλ., *clothed with the sun*, etc.: a realistic picture of the figure is not easily formed. The woman is arrayed in the dazzling glory of the heavenly bodies in conformity with her divine dignity ; no further significance is to be sought in the ornaments ; cf. 1¹⁶, Ps. 104², Song of Sol. 6¹⁰, also the description of Wisdom, Wis. 7²⁹, 'She is fairer than the sun, and above all the constellations of the stars,' Test. Naph. 5⁴ ᶠ·, 'When Levi became as the sun, a young man gave him twelve branches of palm ; and Judah was bright as the moon and under his feet were twelve rays' (Kautzsch, 487). Whatever of similarity is found in Joseph's dream (Gen. 37⁹) regarding the sun, moon, etc., that passage could not have directly suggested the figure of this scene (so, many com.). for the ideas symbolized are wholly unlike. The woman's coronet

of twelve stars may possibly contain an allusion to the twelve
tribes of Israel, but it is doubtless taken over from the source
and goes back ultimately to the twelve signs of the zodiac.
2. ἔχουσα : sc. ἐστι ; ἔχουσά ἐστι = ἔχει, see Blass § 62, 2,
Burton § 20.—κράζει ὠδίνουσα, *crieth out in the pains of travail:*
see on v. 1.—βασανιζομένη τεκεῖν, *tormented in bearing :* the
infin. is irregular ; it seems to be used as equiv. to the infin.
with τῷ, with or without a prep., defining the manner or cause
of the general term βασανιζομένη. The idea of *desire* governing the infin. can hardly be implied in the partic. (so, Burton
§ 389). The phrase βασανιζομένη τεκεῖν is synonymous with
ὠδίνουσα, repeating it with καί epexegetical.

3–4. δράκων μέγας, *a great dragon:* the dragon, a huge
serpent-like monster, often a water-monster, is a familiar object
under somewhat varied forms in all ancient mythologies. It
appears in Heb. folk-lore, and is mentioned in the O.T. as
Leviathan, Rahab, Behemoth, a serpent, a dragon ; cf. Job 7[12],
Ps. 74[14], 89[10], Is. 27[1], 51[9], Ezk. 32[2], Am. 9[3] (cf. Gunkel 29 ff.).
It is generally the embodiment of an evil power, and in late
Heb. fancy becomes, in the form of the serpent of Eden, identified with Satan ; cf. Wis. 2[24], Sl. En. 31, Ap. Mos. 17 ; so also
in rabbinic demonology (see Weber *System* 210 ff.). With
our author here and 20[2] the dragon, the old serpent, and
the devil are synonymous. The close relation in apocalyptic literature between Satan, Antichrist, and a monster
representing the world-power causes the traits of one to appear
in descriptions of the others; hence the similarity between the
dragon of our passage and the beast of chapt. 13 ; see notes
there. The description of the dragon given here conforms in
part to common tradition, as seen in extra-biblical representations, and in part is taken from the beasts of Dan. chapt. 7 ;
but the Apocalyptist apparently adds traits. The many heads
form a frequent feature, *e.g.* in the Lernaean Hydra, the Persian dragon mentioned on p. 615, Leviathan, Ps. 74[14]. The
huge coils with which the dragon sweeps the stars from the sky
are a common trait. The fiery red color may be traditional,
cf. Hom. *Il.* II, 308, δράκων δαφοινός, or it may be given here
to denote the dragon's murderous character ; cf. 6[4], Jno. 8[44].
The number seven assigned to the heads is found in a Babylo-

nian myth (see Gunkel, 361), but its introduction here is more likely due to the Apocalyptist's fondness for seven as a number of fullness. Some derive the number from Dan. 7⁴⁻⁷, where the *sum* of the heads is seven, one of the beasts having four; but this is artificial. The seven crowns are added to symbolize the fullness of Satan's power as prince of this world. The ten horns are taken from Dan. 7⁷, the horn being a common symbol of might, and the number ten denoting fullness (see p. 254). The question raised regarding the distribution of ten horns among seven heads (De Wet. Düst. *al*) does not in a vision of this character call for discussion. The dragon's act in hurling the stars to the earth appears to be suggested by Dan. 8¹⁰, though the specification of a third part must be due to the Apocalyptist; cf. chapt. 8 *passim*, 9¹⁵, ¹⁸.

5–6. **υἱόν, ἄρσενα,** *a son, a male child:* the redundancy is extraordinary; there may be a reminiscence of Jer. 20¹⁵, a *man-child,* lit. a *male son;* so, many comm. Possibly the author wrote ἔτεκεν ἄρσεν(α), as in v. 13, an expression frequent in the LXX, cf. Ex. 2², Jer. 20¹⁵; and υἱόν was added as a gloss. — **ὃς μέλλει κτλ.,** *who shall rule,* etc.: for the words as a designation of the Messiah see on 2²⁷. — **πάντα τὰ ἔθνη,** *all the Gentiles:* reference is made in the common terms of Jewish eschatology to the Messiah's complete domination over all his enemies, when his kingdom shall be established. — **πρὸς τὸν θρόνον αὐτοῦ,** *to his throne: i.e.* the throne of God. The words are added to emphasize the completeness of Satan's failure; the Messiah, so far from being destroyed, is caught up to a share in God's throne. The sentence would lose in force, if (as with Spitta 132) the phrase were rejected. — On the significance of verse 6 see pp. 616, 619. — **ὅπου, ἐκεῖ :** for the Hebraistic addition of a demonstrative after a relative see on 3⁸. — **ἡμέρας . . . ἑξήκοντα,** *1260 days:* the stereotyped phrase for the period of calamity in the last days, as in 11³; see p. 252.

(2) Satan's expulsion from the heavens, vv. 7–12. See pp. 276, 612, 617 f. The archangel Michael is the special patron of Israel, he is their 'prince,' Dan. 10²¹; he is their defender in the troubles of the last days, Dan. 12¹, 'At that time shall Michael stand up, the great prince, who standeth for the children of thy people.' He is therefore appropriately the

leader of the angel hosts here in the war against the arch-
enemy of God's people. The Messiah of the preceding scene
does not appear here in that office, because there is no connection of sequence with that scene (see p. 618), and especially
because it would be contrary to Jewish and Christian eschatological expectations that the Messiah should intervene before
the final conflicts, or, in our book, before the millennium. Cf.
Volz 222. — τοῦ πολεμῆσαι : the meaning here is clear, but the
construction is uncertain. Some supply ἐγένετο with ὁ Μιχ. in
the sense of *arose ;* the infin. then expresses purpose ; so, B.
Weiss, Blj. *al.* It is perhaps simpler to take the infin. as an
appositional gen. (Burton § 400, H. A. § 729 g), defining πόλεμος ; so Buttm. p. 268. The noms. Μιχαήλ κτλ., instead of
the acc. would then be set down as among the author's grammatical irregularities. Perhaps there is some error in the text.

8–9. οὐκ ἴσχυσαν, *were not able: i.e.* to overcome, *prevailed
not,* EV; cf. Gen. 32²⁵, Ps. 129². If the sing. be read here, the
vb. agrees with the principal subj., the dragon. — οὐδὲ τόπος
εὑρέθη κτλ., *neither was their place found,* etc.: this indefinite
statement is made specific by the following words of v. 9. —
δράκων, ὄφις, *dragon, serpent:* the words are synonymous here.
— ὁ ὄφις ὁ ἀρχαῖος, *the old serpent:* referring to the story of
Eden. The following words, the Devil and Satan, are added
to make certain the sense in which the Apocalyptist has taken
up the familiar figure of the dragon; see p. 616. — ὁ πλανῶν
κτλ., *the deceiver of the whole world:* cf. 20¹⁰. Satan is denominated in this paragraph by two characteristic acts in his hostility to men ; he is the *beguiler* of the world, and he is the
calumniator of God's servants before the divine presence (v.
10) ; for the former cf. 20³, ⁸, ¹⁰, 2 Co. 2¹¹, 11³, 1 Tim. 2¹⁴ ; for
the latter see p. 617. Both activities are brought together in
Jub. 1²⁰ also.

10. The expulsion of Satan from the seat of his dominion in
the heavens assures his complete overthrow in the end, and
calls forth one of those outbursts of praise common in the book
(see pp. 244 ff.), celebrating the future triumph as if present.
The hymn is anticipatory, the kingdom of God and the Messiah is not yet established, Satan is still to carry on his work in
the earth. The contents and spirit of the hymn are consonant

2 s

with the leading purpose of the chapt., *i.e.* the assurance of the Church of its final deliverance from the distresses inflicted upon it by the wrath of Satan. The second part of the hymn (v. 12) bewails the other aspect of Satan's expulsion from the heavens, his increased rage in the persecution of the saints till his power is destroyed. The singers are heavenly beings, but are not designated more precisely; see on 11¹⁵. They are not the saints, for these are not represented in the book as being in heaven before the end. The term 'our brethren' may be used appropriately by the angels with reference to the saints on earth, for they are the fellow-servants of these, as declared in 19¹⁰. The general expression 'in heaven' is unsuited to the martyrs beneath the altar; if, as some suppose, these were meant to be understood as the singers, they would probably be definitely specified as in 6⁹.

ἡ σωτηρία κτλ., *the salvation*, etc.: the whole work of God's *salvation* is now accomplished, he has taken to himself his full *power* (cf. 11¹⁷), his *kingdom* has come. — τοῦ θεοῦ, *of God:* the words are to be joined with each of the three preceding nouns. — τοῦ Χριστοῦ αὐτοῦ, *his Christ:* see on 11¹⁵. — ὁ κατήγωρ, *the accuser:* see above. This form of the word instead of κατήγορος is not found in the authors, but the papyri show it to have been used in the Gk. of popular speech; so διάκων is found as a popular form of διάκονος; see Deissmann, *Licht vom Ost.* 61 f. — τῶν ἀδελφῶν ἡμῶν, *our brethren:* the fellow-servants of God on earth are meant; see above. — ὁ κατηγορῶν . . . νυκτός, *who accused . . . day and night:* lit. *the one accusing, i.e.* before he was cast out. The *incessant* activity of Satan here spoken of is not mentioned elsewhere in the Scriptures, but appears in rabbinic writings.

11. This verse reminds the Church, struggling against Satan, of the source and condition of victory. The saints whose triumph is here anticipated will have overcome through the blood of the Lamb (who by his blood loosed them from their sins, 1⁵), and through the power of the divine word to which they have borne testimony; and they will have proved steadfast in the face of death. The redemptive power of Christ's death is meant here as in 1⁵, 5⁹, 7¹⁴; cf. also Jno. 1²⁹, 1 Jno. 1⁷. The frequent connection of μαρτυρία with λόγος θεοῦ in the book

(1$^{2, 9}$, 6^9, 20^4) shows that λόγον here means the word of God; and as the gen. with μαρτυρία is subj. (see on 1^2, 6^9), the expression *the word of their testimony* is to be understood, *the word of God to which they have borne testimony*, whether in life or by their death. The power here attributed to the word of God is the same as in Jno. 8$^{31 \text{ f.}, 51}$, 15^3, *al.* — διά : better translated *through* or *by* than *because of.* The distinction between the acc. and the gen. with διά virtually disappears when as here a directly active cause is meant; cf. 13^{14}, Mt. 15^6, Jno. 6^{57}, 15^3, Eph. 4^{18}; cf. Holtzm.-Bau. *in loc.* There is no contradiction between the two conquests over Satan, that of this verse and that of vv. 8–9, as some maintain (Spitta 357, Völter *Offenb.* 79, J. Weiss 80). The one following Jewish conceptions represents his expulsion from his seat in the heavens, and shows the cause of his increased activity in the earth; the other announces the spiritual triumph of the individual Christian over him in this activity of his in the earth. The close juxtaposition of the Jewish and Christian ideas is similar to that in chapt. 5. The verse has a distinct Johannine character in thought (see reff. above) and in vocabulary (*e.g.* νικᾶν, λόγος, μαρτυρία, ἀγαπᾶν).

12. οἱ ἐν αὐτοῖς σκηνοῦντες, *ye who dwell therein:* cf. 13^6. The angels are meant; departed saints are not yet dwellers in heaven. — οὐαὶ τὴν γῆν, *woe to the earth:* the expression 'the earth and the sea' is a comprehensive term for the whole terrestrial world (see on 10^2), as the sphere of Satan's activity. The *inhabitants* of the world are meant; there is no idea here of operations in the physical world. For the acc. after οὐαί see on 8^{13}. This descent of Satan to the earth is taken by many (*e.g.* Bouss. 297, J. Weiss 79 ff.) to form the third 'woe' announced in 8^{13}, 11^{14}. The words οὐαὶ τὴν γῆν compared with οὐαὶ . . . τῆς γῆς, 8^{13}, are thought to confirm this view. But οὐαί is too common an exclamation to furnish any ground for a conclusion, and τὴν γῆν in this passage has not the same reference as the expression τοὺς κατοικοῦντας ἐπὶ τῆς γῆς in 8^{13}; see below. There are two objections which seem conclusive against finding in the event here described the third 'woe.' (1) Our paragraph is wholly concerned with Satan's hostility to the people of God and the calamities he inflicts upon them;

there is no allusion to the godless; whereas the three woes announced in 8¹³ are calamities to be sent upon the non-Christian world, as seen in the first two (chapt. 9); see on 8¹³, 3¹⁰. (2) The trumpet-woes predicted in 8¹³ all lie in the Apocalyptist's future, but this expulsion of Satan, in the past; see pp. 618 f.

κατέβη, *has gone down:* the word has raised objection as if implying a freedom inconsistent with the violence expressed in ἐβλήθη, *has been cast,* vv. 9, 13. It is doubtful whether the difference is due to transference of an Aramaic idiom (Ewald, Gunkel). What is thought of in the use of the word is the simple *fact* of the descent with its consequences, not the antecedent cause, or the manner of the descent. — εἰδὼς . . . ἔχει, *knowing that he hath but a short time:* now that Satan is expelled from his throne in the heavens, he knows that the end must come soon with the appearing of the Messiah, and his rage is intensified accordingly. The ' short time ' is relative, not absolute; the words do not place this event in the future.

(3) Persecution of the Mother of the Messiah and her children, vv. 13–17. See pp. 277 f., 612, 618 ff.

The Apocalyptist here takes up and expands what he had mentioned in v. 6 summarily and in anticipation of this scene. For this feature in the Apocalyptist's manner see p. 242. The scene here is on the earth. The exact correspondence of this passage (vv. 13–16) with v. 6 makes it certain that two different events cannot be referred to, and that the woman of this passage must be the same as in vv. 1–6. She cannot, then, be the Christian Church (many older com.), for in that case it could not be said that the Messiah was born of her. Neither can she be the Church of the old covenant (many modern com. *e.g.* Ewald, Bleek, Düst.), for that Church cannot, except in a most unnatural sense, be called the mother of the followers of Jesus (v. 17); nor was that Church destined to be kept in safety to the end; it vanished away with the incoming of a better covenant. The woman is the *ideal* people of God of both the old and new covenants alike; see on v. 1.

The woman's persecution and escape are taken by many to be based on the story of Israel's deliverance from Egypt; so, *e.g.* Ewald, Bleek, De Wet. Düst. Spitta, Alf. Israel flees from the Egyptians, the dry land opens a way for them through the threatening waters, and they find a refuge in the wilderness where they are nurtured through the destined time. Their deliverance is even described in Ex. 19⁴ as an act of God's, bearing them away on eagles' wings. But the figure of bearing on eagles' wings seems to have been a current simile, cf. Dt. 32¹¹, Is. 40³¹, Ass. Mos. 108; and for the gift of wings for flight cf. Jer. 48⁹. The details of the story of Israel's escape from Egypt are too dissimilar to suggest the imagery of a dragon-monster pursuing the woman and spouting forth floods of water into the air, and the earth opening its caverns and swallowing up the waters. Among recent scholars most are agreed that the Apocalyptist has taken his imagery from some familiar legend; see pp. 613 ff.

In the symbol of the woman's flight many scholars suppose that reference is made to the flight of the Christians of Jerusalem across the Jordan to Pella in the time of the Judæo-Roman War, as recorded by Euseb. *H. E.* III. 5; so, Ewald followed by many. This reference to a part of the Church removes the difficulty otherwise thought to be raised by the identification of the children with the mother, v. 17; the 'other children' are the other Christians in distinction from the Jerusalem Church. But this interpretation limits the symbolism unwarrantably. The woman who flees here is the one who bore the child (v. 13), the Messiah; and throughout the chapt. she represents the whole people of God. The Church at Jerusalem is not the mother of the Messiah; it is nowhere spoken of as the mother of the other churches, or of the Christians as a body. So far as mentioned, it plays no conspicuous part in the thought of the later apostolic age. The entire scene here is ideal and general; allusion to a specific historic occurrence in the fortunes of that congregation has no place in the vision. Upon the supposed difficulty of the identification of the children with the mother see p. 619.

14. ἐδόθησαν πτέρυγες κτλ., *there were given wings*, etc.: God's care for the woman is made prominent. He provides the means for her escape, and in a place made ready for her in the desert, which though it offers security is barren of support, he furnishes succour for her. — τοῦ ἀετοῦ, the *eagle :* the art. is better taken as generic than as referring to an eagle mentioned in the legend; it is not the author's manner to point so distinctly to a source when extra-biblical. — ὅπου, ἐκεῖ: see on v. 6. — καιρὸν καὶ καιροὺς κτλ., *a time and times*, etc.: three and a half times = three and a half years = 1260 days; see on v. 6.

15-17. The scene enacted in vv. 15–16 is doubtless taken from the legend without material variation. In this connection a real, historical event is not symbolized, but the purely ideal effort of Satan to destroy the whole entity of God's people, and his defeat. — ὠργίσθη, *waxed wroth :* Satan becomes the more enraged against the woman because of her escape, and turns his rage upon her children, the followers of Jesus. Thus is explained the ultimate cause of the persecution which the Church suffers. — τῶν λοιπῶν τοῦ σπέρματος αὐτῆς, *the rest of her seed :* there may be here a reminiscence of Gen. 3¹⁵, 'enmity between thee and the woman, between thy seed and her seed' (J. Weiss, 138). The *rest* of the seed must be those who are distinguished from the child of vv. 5, 13, for no other is spoken of. And these remaining children are defined as adherents of Jesus. The term *the rest*, not the indefinite *other*, implies that the whole body of Christians in general are meant, not those who are contrasted with the church of Jerusalem, see p. 629; not Gentile Christians as contrasted with Jewish (so, Düst. *al*). — ἐχόντων . . . 'Ιησοῦ, *hold fast the testimony of Jesus :* the testimony of Jesus is that which he bore (see on 1²), the truth which he taught; and since these words repeat and explain the less explicit words preceding, *keep the commandments of God*, the meaning of ἔχειν in this place must be *hold fast*, not *possess* merely; see Thayer *s.v.* I. d. By these added words the Apocalyptist shows in what sense he uses the familiar figure of the 'seed of the woman.'

Textual notes, 12²⁻¹⁷. 2. και, before κραζει, אC some vers most edd; wanting in APQ most min R Sod. — 4. For ἕστηκεν, WH read ἔστηκεν, taking the form here and in Jno. 8⁴⁴ as an imperf. of στήκω; see their *Introd.* Am. ed. p. 312. — 5. αρσενα (or αρρενα) אPQ most min R Ws (see *Ap.* p. 97) Blj Sod *al;* αρσεν AC Lch Tr Ti WH *al.* If υιον be omitted as a gloss (see Com.), the neut. might naturally have been used. — 7. του πολεμησαι ACP many min most edd; του is wanting in אQ many min Ti; see Ws *Apok.* p. 120; R has επολεμησαν without authority. — 8. ισχυσαν אCP min R Ti Blj Sod Alf *al;* ισχυσεν A many min Ws WH Bouss *al;* ισχυον Q. — 10. κατηγωρ A Lch Ti Ws WH Alf *al;* κατηγορος most sources R RV Sod *al.* — 12. Before την γην, R inserts τοις κατοικουσι, following one or two min and some anc com. — 17. For Ιησου, R reads του Ιησου Χριστου, so Prim and some Mss. of the vlg, without Ms. authority.

Criticism of 12¹⁻¹⁷. Criticism of this chapt. has centered in two subjects : (1) the strangeness in the representation of the Messiah and his birth; (2) the unity of the chapt. (1) Vischer (19 ff.) finds here one of his strongest proofs that the book was primarily a Jewish apocalypse. His argument is as follows : the book is wholly concerned with things of the future, the past has no place in the Seer's view; therefore this narrative of the birth of the Messiah could not belong to the work of a Christian, for whom that birth is already past. And further the narrative has no points of similarity with the history of Jesus; neither is it conformable to the Christian expectations of the Lord's second coming. But all difficulty disappears with the supposition of a Jewish apocalypse; the forerunners of the Messiah have appeared (11³ ᶠᶠ·), the holy city has been purified by a divine visitation and prepared for its Messiah (11¹³); the seventh trumpet promising the end has sounded, and now the Messiah is born (12¹⁻⁵). But he is not to appear at once; in Jewish expectation he was to remain hidden for a time. In the second part of the chapt. the representation of Satan as the *accuser* of men before God is Jewish, not Christian. In the third part the flight of the woman, the personified people of Israel, represents some future event in which Israel as a body and the Messiah will be safe from Satan's assaults, and he will turn his wrath against the rest of the Jews, the other seed of the woman, who remain in his power. In carrying through this theory the Christian elements v. 11 and the last clause of v. 17 must be deleted.

Many other critics (Weyland, Pfleiderer, Sabatier, Schoen, Spitta, J. Weiss, Wellhausen, *al*) though differing widely from Vischer in other respects agree in attributing the picture of the Messiah's birth and the woman's flight to a Jewish document. A favorite hypothesis makes the passage an oracle designed to encourage the Jews in the distresses of the Judæo-Roman war by the assurance that the Messiah, already born or about to be born, but hidden for a time in heaven, will soon come as deliverer.

To all theories which view the chapt. as part of a Jewish document incorporated here there is the fundamental objection that the picture of the Messiah and his birth is at variance with the whole Jewish messianic expectation. The rabbinic legend of a Messiah carried away at birth to a hidden place is too late and obscure to be accepted as a probable origin (see p. 614). But in any event the representation in these verses is not Jewish. A Messiah born in the heavens of a superhuman mother, saved at the moment of birth only by miracle from the assaults of Satan, and caught away to the throne of God, is wholly unlike the expected son of David. Even if we suppose the Jewish writer to have borrowed symbols from some current mythological fancy, the paragraph taken as a prophecy, or as a representation of the past, is as difficult to explain from the Jewish standpoint as from the Christian.

On the other hand, the view long prevalent among the interpreters that the scene in vv. 1–5 represents the Lord's birth and ascension raises the insuperable difficulty of its disagreement with the accepted facts of the Gospels (see p. 613). Völter (*Offenb.* 96 ff.) holds the chapt. to be Christian, not Jewish, and he finds it a part of an assumed apocalypse of Cerinthus, whose doctrine was that the heavenly Christ descended and united himself with Jesus, but again withdrew from him so that only Jesus, not the Christ, suffered and died. The opening of the chapt. then pictures the Christ after he had been born of the heavenly woman, and had descended and united himself with Jesus at the baptism, as now again withdrawing to heaven to avoid the dangers which threatened him from Satan through the Roman

power. The theory does not call for discussion. Völter agrees with others
in supposing that the Apocalyptist's fancy is influenced by mythological
tradition.

Since Gunkel's epoch-making study scholars have tended more and more
to find the solution of the difficulties of the chapt., not in the incorporation
of an alien document, but in the use of symbols derived from some legend
current in ancient mythology and familiar in Jewish tradition. From such
a source the Apocalyptist seems to have taken the forms in which he here
embodies his revelation, shaping these to his use and giving thus a scene
which has a fitting place in his plan (see pp. 612 ff., 620). This view
is essentially that which is adopted by the larger number of most recent
scholars; so, Bouss., Holtzm.-Bau., Blj., Porter, Moff., *al.*

(2) The principal objection urged against *the unity* of the chapt. is
based on the account of the woman's flight, which is given twice, vv. 6
and 13–16. In the first instance it is spoken of in connection with the scene
in the sky, without mention of a descent to earth, though the words, *the
wilderness*, imply the earth. In the second instance it is distinctly placed
on the earth. Some critics therefore omit v. 6 as an *editorial* addition,
e.g. Spitta, J. Weiss. Others make vv. 13–16 an editorial working over of
v. 6; so Weizsäcker, Völter (*Problem*). Wellhausen (*Analys.* 18 ff.) proposes
a theory of two parallel documents with a *common* ending; A, consisting of
vv. 1–6, from which the redactor has omitted mention of the woman's descent
and the dragon's expulsion; B, consisting of vv. 7–14, in which there was
originally mention of the eagle, the entrance of the woman and the child,
and of the rapture of the child to heaven — these have been omitted by the
redactor; vv. 15–17 formed the common ending of both the variant documents A and B; vv. 10–12 stood in neither document, they were added by
the redactor. The theory is interesting as illustrative of what may be
seriously proposed in the way of criticism. J. Weiss (135) omits the war
in heaven as having no connection with the other parts of the chapt., also
vv. 6 and 13 which were added by the editor to facilitate transition. The
scene of vv. 1–5 is, he thinks, probably not the heavens, but earth, as in
vv. 14–17; these two passages, vv. 1–5, 14–17, formed the original document.

If the views taken in the Com. above regarding the interpretation of the
chapt. be correct, the real difficulties are much less serious than those raised
by the suppositions underlying most of the critical hypotheses. That the
Apocalyptist should fail to mention the woman's descent to earth in connection with v. 6 cannot raise insoluble difficulty (see pp. 616, 619);
that he should first allude to a subject briefly and afterwards take it up
more fully is one of his characteristics (see pp. 242 ff.). It should be noted
that the third part of the chapt., vv. 13–17, could not follow immediately
after v. 5, for an essential condition determining the character of the third
part is furnished by the second part, vv. 7–9, Satan's expulsion from his
throne in the heavens with all its consequences. But it is not unnatural
that the Apocalyptist should have closed the first part with some anticipatory allusion (v. 6) to its sequel, the flight and safety of the woman.
The first and second parts of the chapt. lead up to the third as expressing

the chief purpose of the paragraph; not unfittingly then they each conclude
with a statement, vv. 6, 12, anticipating that part. In so far the structure
of the chapt. seems to be the work of one mind.

XII. 18–XIII. 18. *The Beast, the agent of Satan in his war-fare against the saints; and the Beast's helper, the second beast.*

In this chapt. the Apocalyptist passes immediately to the
vision revealing the agency used by Satan in this war against
the children of the woman which has just been announced in
the preceding sentence (v. 17). For the place of the chapt.
in the plan of the book, see pp. 275 f. For the symbol of the
Beast and its significance, see pp. 393 ff., 407 ff.

XII. 18. ἐστάθην, *I stood:* with this reading the words are
joined immediately with 13¹; see AV. The Seer in his vision
takes his stand in full view of the sea, whence the Beast arises.
On the specification of the Seer's apparent place, cf. Ezk. 40²,
Dan. 8². If ἐστάθη, *he stood,* be read, Satan is represented as
standing by the sea to summon the Beast his agent in the war
now to be carried on. See text. note.

XIII. 1. For the words 'I stood,' etc., or 'he stood,' in
some editions assigned to this verse, see above. — ἐκ τῆς θαλάσσης ἀναβαῖνον, *coming up out of the sea:* the rising out of the
sea, though taken directly from Dan. 7³, is doubtless ultimately
derived from the earlier form of the myth of the beast as a
sea-monster (a Leviathan); similarly the eagle-monster in
2 Es. 11 comes up from the sea. Since the figure as used by
the Apocalyptist refers first of all to the Roman power, the
coming from the sea would be especially appropriate in the
view of one looking from the coast of Asia Minor across
the Mediterranean, and most com. regard the language as
chosen with that thought; but the representation is more
probably purely traditional. In the other places in the book
where the origin of the Beast is spoken of (11⁷, 17⁸) he comes
from the 'abyss,' *i.e.* hell, see on 9¹; not that the sea is the
gate of the abyss, nor (so, Gunkel 360 f.) that the sea and
the abyss are synonymous here. But there is no contradiction
in the two representations, as many critics find. Here the
author is concerned with the picture of the *symbol*, the Beast
figured after traditional conceptions; in the other places the

actual person is meant in whom hellish power is embodied. See p. 697. — **κέρατα δέκα**, *ten horns:* elsewhere (12³, 17³, ⁷) the heads are mentioned before the horns. Possibly the reversal of the order may be due to the emergence of the horns first as the Beast rises out of the water (so, many com.) ; but since the idea of a gradual emergence does not seem to be intimated in the context, it is more likely that the purpose is variation from the description of the dragon in chapt. 12 ; on variety with the author, see on 5⁵. — **κεφαλὰς ἑπτά**, *seven heads:* the number seven is probably due to the Apocalyptist for conformity with his representation of seven emperors as filling out the number of Roman rulers ; see p. 706 ff.

ἐπὶ τῶν κεράτων . . . διαδήματα, *on his horns ten diadems:* in the picture of the dragon, chapt. 12, the crowns are assigned to the heads ; the seven crowns there are a mark of Satan's complete kingly power as the prince of this world ; here in Satan's deputy, the Beast, though the heads symbolize kings as seen from 17¹⁰, that significance is not specially marked by the presence of crowns, it is assumed. The conspicuous feature of the heads here is the name of blasphemy, as the author's thought is here concentrated on the blasphemous claims of divinity which these kings make. This trait of the name of blasphemy on the heads is doubtless one of the touches which the Apocalyptist himself gives to the traditional figure. On the other hand the *horns*, which in the dragon (12³) were a mere symbol of Satan's power, are here the symbol of a number of kings who are to aid Satan's deputy in the end (17¹⁰ ꜰꜰ·), and crowns are assigned them to designate them specially as kings, as with the twenty-four Elders in 4⁴. The ten horns are taken directly from Dan. 7, where they form a prominent part of the imagery, and the kingly significance is emphasized there. The feature in our passage is not a mere pictorial detail retained from Dan. (so, Moff. *al*) ; it is made by our author to have important meaning as a symbol of the allies to be joined with the returning Nero in the destruction of Rome ; see pp. 699 f. The διάδημα, *diadem*, is a mark of kingly rank, cf. 19¹² ; for στέφανος, *crown*, in the same sense cf. 4⁴, 14¹⁴, though the latter is oftener the mark of victory. See Thayer on the two words.

ὀνόματα βλασφημίας, *names of blasphemy:* reference is made
to the titles taken by the Roman emperors in their assumption
of divine honors; see pp. 198 ff. *Divus, divine,* became the
common epithet of deceased emperors; θεός, *god,* affixed to
their names appears often in inscriptions; even the common
title *Augustus,* in the Gk. form σεβαστός (Ac. 25²¹), contained
the idea of religious reverence. The distinction between the
two readings, sing. and pl. (see text. note), is not important,
for the latter probably refers to the one name repeated on each
head; cf. the pl. in the seven diadems 12³.

2. The beast here pictured combines attributes of the first
three beasts of Dan. (7² ᶠᶠ·, cf. also Hos. 13⁷ ᶠ·); the fourth
beast of Dan. is represented in the ten horns. There is no
intimation that special significance is attached to the respective
animals; the purpose is to give the monster an appearance of
might and terribleness—such is the power Satan is using
against the Church. — ἔδωκεν αὐτῷ κτλ., *the dragon gave to him,*
etc.: the Beast receives all his power from Satan, the Roman
emperors and Antichrist are only Satan's deputies. — αὐτοῦ,
his: i.e. Satan's; cf. 2¹³. Grammatically the word could refer
to the Beast, but the purpose here is to show that the
Beast is Satan's vicegerent ; the power and throne are really
Satan's.

3. μίαν: the acc. through the force of εἶδον continued from
v. 1. — ἐσφαγμένην εἰς θάνατον, *smitten* (lit. *slain*) *unto death:*
the meaning is not that the Beast, having received a mortal
wound in one of his heads, is healed and survives notwithstanding the loss of that head ; the head itself is seen as one
that had been slain and then restored, precisely as in 5⁶ the
Lamb bears the mark of having once been slain. If the Beast
and the heads be viewed apart, as they may be in thought, it
is evident that the loss of one head did not involve the death of
the Beast, for he is seen from 17¹⁰ to have survived the loss
of five heads. On the other hand in the second part of this
verse and in v. 12 the Beast himself is spoken of as having
received a mortal wound. It is clear that the Apocalyptist
sometimes identifies the Beast and the head in which he is in
a particular instance represented ; see p. 407. The heads
symbolize Roman emperors, and of these the only one who

could in any sense be said to be restored after having been slain was the Nero of the belief current at the end of the century. This particular figure of a head slain and restored, used here to symbolize the Neronic Antichrist, may be an addition made by the Apocalyptist himself, influenced by the expectation current at the time, or it may possibly be traditional ; something of the kind appears in the Lernæan Hydra, in which two heads sprang up in place of one cut off.

ἐθαύμασεν ὅλη ἡ γῆ, *the whole earth wondered :* what is said of the Beast in these words and in the following verses is best understood of his final impersonation in Antichrist. While the wonder he excites, his royal sway, his blasphemy, the worship rendered to him, are all to a certain extent true of the Roman emperors, yet the universality and absoluteness here emphasized belong to the supreme manifestation expected in Antichrist, the head restored at the end. The wonder spoken of in this verse is immediately connected with the revival of the slain head, *i.e.* as seen in the Neronic Antichrist ; the time of his sway, $3\frac{1}{2}$ years (v. 5), is the stereotyped measure of Antichrist's rule (see on 11[3]) ; also the exact parallelism between v. 8 and 17[8] points to this identification. — ὀπίσω τοῦ θηρίου, *after the Beast :* they are drawn after him in wonder as followers ; cf. Jno. 12[19], Ac. 5[37], 1 Tim. 5[15].

4. The worship of the Beast is the worship of Satan, who has endowed him with all his power. The rendering of divine homage to the Beast is here spoken of summarily; it is related more fully in the following part of the chapt., especially in the account of the office of the second beast. — τῷ δράκοντι: in the Apoc. as elsewhere προσκυνεῖν is followed by either the acc. or the dat. — τίς ὅμοιος κτλ.: *who is like ?* etc.: the words are an echo of language frequently used in praising God; *e.g.* Ex. 15[11], Ps. 35[10], 113[5].

5. στόμα λαλοῦν μεγάλα, *a mouth speaking great things :* taken from Dan. 7[8, 20, 25]. The *great,* i.e. *proud, things* are blasphemies as explained by the next word and more fully in v. 6; καί before βλασφημίας is better rendered *even.* — ποιῆσαι, *to do :* i.e. to work his work or will. For this absolute use of ποιεῖν cf. Dan. 8[12, 24], 11[28, 30, 32]. The acc. μῆνας then denotes duration. Some take ποιῆσαι in the sense of *spend* with expressions of

time; μῆνας is then the obj.; cf. Ac. 20³, Ja. 4¹³, so EV. *continue.*
The former interpretation is that of most com.

6. The Beast's blasphemy against God and the hosts of
heaven is suggested by Dan. 7²⁵, 8¹⁰. This verse amplifies the
general statement in v. 5 a, from which it is separated by 5 b;
for such amplification and interruption of sequence as characteristic of the author see pp. 241 ff. — τὴν σκηνὴν αὐτοῦ, *his
tabernacle:* the heavenly, not the earthly, as seen from the
following words. — τοὺς . . . σκηνοῦντας, *those who dwell in
heaven:* the words are in apposition with σκηνήν, *tabernacle,* and
explain that by the name of the place those who occupy the
place are meant. If καί, *and,* the easier reading, be adopted,
there are three objects of blasphemy, God, heaven, and the
heavenly host (AV).

7. ποιῆσαι πόλεμον κτλ., *to make war,* etc.: the persecution
of the Church is described thus in language taken from Dan. 7²¹.
— ἐπὶ πᾶσαν φυλὴν κτλ., *over every tribe,* etc.: for the universality
of the Beast's sway cf. Dan. 7²³; and for the formula used see
on 5⁹.

8. From the might and blasphemy of the Beast the Apocalyptist passes to the divine honor which all, save the faithful
followers of the Lamb, will pay to him. — οὗ τὸ ὄνομα: the
sing. is used with reference to an implied distributive, ἕκαστος,
after the collective πάντες; see RV. — αὐτοῦ: for the Heb.
pleonasm see on 3⁸. — τῷ βιβλίῳ τῆς ζωῆς, *the book of life:* see
on 3⁵. It is here as in 21²⁷ (though τοῦ ἀρνίου there is rejected
by some critics) called the Lamb's book; the authority of the
Lamb over the book is also implied in 3⁵. — τοῦ ἀρνίου τοῦ
ἐσφαγμένου, *the Lamb slain:* the words are rejected by many
critics, as not found elsewhere in connection with the book of
life and not especially called for here. They have, however, a
purpose here; they emphasize the fact that only those refuse to
worship the Beast who are ready to follow the Lamb that
suffered even unto death, and so preserve their names from
being blotted out of his book, see 3⁵. — ἐσφαγμένου, *slain:* the
perf. here as in v. 3, 5⁶ does not differ from the aor.; the past
act, not the continuing result, is thought of; cf. Blass § 59, 3;
Burton § 80. The translation *that was slain* (AV) is better
than *that hath been slain* (RV). — ἀπὸ καταβολῆς κόσμου, *from*

the foundation of the world: the term is frequent; cf. Mt. 25³⁴, Lk. 11⁵⁰, Jno. 17²⁴. The phrase is to be joined, not with ἐσφαγμένου, *slain* (AV), but with γέγραπται, *hath been written* (RV), as shown by the precisely parallel words in 17⁸. The names of the faithful are enrolled from the beginning in the book of life.

9–10. As a fitting close to the paragraph which describes the character of the Beast, his office and sway, the Apocalyptist adds a forewarning of the endurance and fidelity which will be demanded in these trials. If captivity or martyrdom by the sword awaits the readers, they must be ready to meet these tests of their steadfastness, they must not attempt to resist by force the persecution inflicted by the Beast. The writer calls special attention to his warning by the familiar formula, ' If any man hath an ear,' etc., used often in the N. T. and elsewhere in our book; see the close of the seven epistles in chapts. 2–3. — εἴ τις εἰς αἰχμαλωσίαν . . . ὑπάγει, *if any man is for captivity,* etc.: *i.e.* if any man is destined to captivity, to captivity he *goes* (will go) submissively, as a Christian. The words of this verse are a reminiscence of Jer. 15², though the sense there is different. The admonitory words at the beginning and the end of vv. 9–10 show that the whole passage is a warning to the readers regarding their steadfastness and the avoidance of force in resisting persecution. The connection therefore, as well as the weight of Ms. authority, is against reading ἀπάγει after (the first) αἰχμαλωσίαν, *leadeth into captivity* (cf. AV), as if the author meant to console his readers with the promise that the persecutors shall suffer retribution, like in kind to that which he inflicts. Some adopt this reading ἀπάγει after the first αἰχμαλωσίαν and interpret, if any one rise up in actual war against the Beast and try to take his forces captive, he will only bring suffering on himself (cf. Bouss. *in loc.*). But for that sense αὐτός would be required before ὑπάγει, just as the emphatic αὐτόν is used in the following sentence. The two clauses, εἴ τις κτλ., *if any man,* etc., in v. 10, are not precisely parallel; the former enjoins readiness for destined suffering; the latter declares the folly of resistance. — εἴ τις . . . ἀποκτενεῖ κτλ., *if any man shall kill,* etc.: *i.e.* if one shall draw the sword against the persecutor. Cf. Mt. 26⁵², ' They that

take the sword shall perish by the sword.' — ὧδέ ἐστιν ἡ
ὑπομενὴ κτλ., *here is the steadfastness*, etc.: in these trials is
the place for Christian steadfastness, etc., they will be required
here; cf. v. 18, 14¹², 17⁹. — πίστις, *faith:* so, EV; but *faithfulness* better suits the connection; for this meaning cf. 2¹⁹, Mt. 23²³,
Gal. 5²².

11. The writer now turns to the nature and office of the
second beast, the agency employed by the first beast in enforcing the religious homage which he exacts of all men. So important a place does the emperor-worship hold in the Church's
conflict with the world at the time and in the anticipation of
the near future, that the Apocalyptist represents its ministers
under a special symbolical form, the second beast. See pp. 408 ff.
This second beast accomplishes his work by deceit and trickery
(vv. 13–15), and by the establishment of a kind of civic ostracism against the incompliant (vv. 16–17).

ἀναβαῖνον ἐκ τῆς γῆς, *coming up out of the earth:* the second
beast, impersonating the ministers of the emperor-worship, is
appropriately represented under an aspect quite different from
that of the first beast. He lacks the marks of ferocity and
power ; he speaks with the persuasive guile of the serpent who
deceived Eve ; his horns, which in common symbolism denote
power, are not ten, but only the two horns of a young lamb ;
he comes up, not from the sea, like the traditional monster of
terrible power, but from the earth. It is doubtful whether the
ascent from the earth has any other purpose than contrast with
the first beast. The *two* horns of the lamb (the specification of
the number shows it to be important) can hardly be taken (so,
many com.) as an intended equivalent of the proverbial 'sheep's
clothing,' Mt. 7¹⁵; in number and in meaning they show the
second beast altogether wanting the might and terribleness of
the first. The dragon-like speech, as intimated by words attributed to the beast in v. 14 (see note there), seems to refer to
luring *argument*, the form of expression being suggested by the
story of the dragon, the serpent, in Eden ; thus the second
beast's speech is contrasted with the first beast's loud blasphemy
against all heavenly things; the ἐλάλει ὡς δράκων is contrasted
with the λαλοῦν μεγάλα, v. 5.

12. τὴν ἐξουσίαν πᾶσαν, *all the authority:* i.e. the full

authority of the first beast delegated for this particular work.
— ἐνώπιον αὐτοῦ, *before him:* the second beast performs his
appointed service as in the presence of his master; cf. Lk. 1⁷⁵,
1 K. 17¹. — ἵνα προσκυνήσουσιν : for the construct. see on 3⁹.
— οὗ ἐθεραπεύθη κτλ., *whose death-stroke was healed.* Reference is here made to the future culmination of ruler-worship
as it will be rendered to the Beast represented in the restored
head, *i.e.* the Neronic Antichrist. In these words the Beast is
identified with the head impersonating him. — οὗ, αὐτοῦ : see
on v. 8.

13–14. Cf. 2 Thess. 2⁹, ' Whose coming is according to the
working of Satan with all power and signs and lying wonders
and with all deceit of unrighteousness.' Cf. also Mk. 13²².
The Apocalyptist in describing the operations of the second
beast may have had in mind the wonders wrought by heathen
magic. On the miracle of calling fire from heaven cf. 2 K. 1¹⁰,¹²,
Lk. 9⁵⁴. — ἵνα ποιῇ : essentially equiv. to ὥστε with infin., see
Blass § 69, 3 ; Burton § 222. — διὰ τὰ σημεῖα, *through the
wonders:* for the use of διά see on 12¹¹. — λέγων . . . ποιῆσαι
εἰκόνα κτλ., *bidding . . . to make an image,* etc. In this command is expressed the sole function of the second beast, the
enforcement of divine homage to the first beast through the
worship of his image, as the Roman world was bidden to worship the statue of the emperor. This sentence contains also
the *argument* with which the priesthood urges the worship, the
miraculous revivification of the head that had been slain. The
wonders also which they will perform will give force to their
words, especially the artifice by which the image itself will be
made to speak and threaten with death those who refuse to
offer the worship. — In this verse again the Beast and the head
are identified (see on v. 3). — τὴν πληγὴν τῆς μαχαίρης, *the
stroke of the sword:* the words are appropriate to Nero's death
by his own sword. — ἔζησεν, *lived:* lived again ; the meaning
here is not that the Beast himself continued to live notwithstanding the slaying of one of his heads (though this in itself
was true), but that so far as he was identified with a certain
head he ceased to exist in that impersonation with the death of
that head, and *lived again* with its resuscitation, *i.e.* in the Nero
reincarnate in Antichrist. For ζάω in the sense of ἀναζάω, *live*

again, not infrequent, cf. 20⁴, ⁵, Mt. 9¹⁸, Ro. 14⁹.   The aor. is inceptive.

15. The second beast gives life to the image and causes it to speak and command worship to be addressed to itself under penalty of death to the disobedient. Legends of statues assuming the functions of life are familiar in antiquity, and even in the hagiology of the Christian Church. Simon Magus boasted *ego statuas moveri feci et animavi exanima* (Clem, *Recog*. III. 47). Magic and ventriloquism made such marvels common ; but the Christians attributed these to the presence of demonic power. — αὐτῷ, *to him :* the second beast.   For this reading see text. note. — ἐάν : instead of ἄν after relatives, frequent in the N. T. ; see Blass § 26, 4 ; Win. § 42, 6. — ἀποκτανθῶσιν : if ἵνα is not expressed (see text. note) it is to be supplied in thought. — τῇ εἰκόνι τοῦ θηρίου, *the image of the Beast :* the repetition is characteristic of the author.

16. τοὺς μικροὺς καὶ τοὺς μεγάλους κτλ., *the small and the great*, etc.: for this formula emphasizing universality, see on 11¹⁸. — ἵνα δῶσιν αὐτοῖς : the subj. of the vb. may be indefinite, cf. 10¹¹, 16¹⁵, *that one give them a mark ;* or αὐτοῖς may be taken with reflexive force, *that they give themselves a mark*, see H. A. § 684 a. — χάραγμα, *a mark :* the mark is explained in v. 17 as consisting of the name of the Beast, or what is equivalent, the number of his name.   This mark indicates loyal devotion to the Beast ; it is set where it could not easily be hid, on the forehead or the right hand, and it is made requisite for the essentials of social and industrial life, buying and selling.   The origin of the representation seems to be the practice occurring among devotees of a god of branding themselves with a mark indicative of their relation to the god; cf. Is. 44⁵ (RV mrg.), see on 7³.   Ptolemy Philadelphus compelled certain Alexandrian Jews to receive the mark of Dionysos (3 Macc. 2²⁹). Numerous illustrations are collected by Wetstein on Gal. 6¹⁷; cf. also Lightfoot on the same.   Some find the origin of the symbol used here in the Roman coinage, bearing the name or likeness of the emperor, which must be used in trading.   But the mark here spoken of is one impressed on the person, not on some instrument of exchange.   Deissmann (*Neu. Bibelst.* 68 ff.) finds the origin in the stamp containing the name and date of

2 T

the emperor which must be affixed to documents in commercial transactions. At all events the meaning of the symbol is clear; all must openly show themselves loyal worshipers of the Beast, or be debarred from the ordinary relations of civic life. There is no evidence that an edict of the kind was actually issued in the establishment of the emperor-worship.

17–18. Upon the Number of the Beast, see pp. 403 ff. — If καί be read before ἵνα μή τις, it coördinates its sentence with ἵνα δῶσιν; both depend on ποιεῖ. — ὧδε κτλ., *here*, etc.: see on v. 11. — σοφία, *wisdom: i.e.* understanding, skill, in solving the problem of the number; cf. Dan. 9²². — ψηφισάτω, *calculate*: the agreement of the number and the name is to be ascertained by *calculating* the sum of the value of the letters which form the name (see p. 405). — ἀριθμὸς γὰρ κτλ., *for it is a man's number:* the words encourage calculation by giving a certain clew to the solution; the number of the Beast is the number, or what is the same thing, furnishes the name, of a man. Some interpreters (Düst. Holtzm.-Bau. Gunkel, *al.*) urge against this interpretation that τινός or ἑνός would be required with ἀνθρώπου; but the addition is not necessary, for though a certain definite person be thought of (Nero), he may be spoken of indefinitely. The alternative interpretation offered takes the phrase, after the analogy of a man's measure in 21¹⁷, to mean such as is in common use among men; so that the task of computation is shown to be only one of ordinary human calculation. But the words in that sense would not aid in the solution of the problem, for the Beast's name could be anything, the sum of whose letters amounts to 666, however unlike names known to men. It is reasonably certain that the phrase should be taken after the analogy of the similar phrases in the context, the number of the name, the number of the Beast, and his number. It means then the number denoting a man. The phrase contains a mysterious hint that there is a man, whose name gives the number 666, whose name then is the name of the Beast. The calculation spoken of must start with the man's name. It can hardly be doubted that the Apocalyptist assumes in some of his readers a knowledge, however vaguely or secretly held, of the expectations regarding the **return of Nero.**

Textual notes. 12¹⁸-13¹⁸. 12¹⁸. εσταθην PQ most min several vers R
Ti Alf Blj Sod Moff Bouss¹⁸⁹⁶ *al*; εσταθη אAC many min and vers Lch
Tr WH Ws Bouss¹⁹⁰⁶ RV *al*. It is difficult to decide between the two
readings; fortunately no important question in interpretation is affected.
While the Ms. evidence favors the second reading, the first seems preferable on exegetical grounds. If the dragon takes his stand on the shore, it
must be for the purpose of calling up from the sea his agent, the Beast; but
nothing is said of such a summons, and no command is uttered here; contrast the summonses in chapt. 6 and the command in 16¹. The dragon does
not appear in the following vision; his departure from the scene and the
conclusion of the vision of chapt. 12 seem to be intended in the words, ' he
went away,' etc. 12¹⁷. On the other hand the act expressed in the word is
appropriate to the Seer, who thus specifies his nearness to the scene of the
Beast's appearance, as he alludes to his position in 4², 17³, 21¹⁰. — 13¹. R
without authority adopts the order κεφαλας επτα και κερατα δεκα. — ονοματα
א AQ min vers most edd; ονομα CP min vers R Sod Blj. — 3. R inserts
ειδον before μιαν, so one min and some Mss. of the Vlg. — εθαυμασεν אPQ
most min Ti Blj Sod RV; εθαυμασθη A some min R most edd; εθαυμα-
στωθη C. — R with some min inserts εν before ολη η γη. — 5. ποιησαι
without added obj. ACP min vers edd; א adds ο θελει; Q most min add
πολεμον. — 6. אᶜPQ many min vers R Bouss add και before τους; wanting in
א* AC most min vers most edd. — 7. The words και εδοθη . . . νικησαι αυτους
are wanting in ACP some min; WH bracket; nearly all edd retain them
following אQ most min vers. The omission might easily occur through
oversight, since two consecutive sentences begin here with the same words,
και εδοθη αυτω. — 8. ον, before ου, C. Iren. nearly all edd; אPQ min
vers R Sod. — το ονομα ACQ min edd, see Ws *Ap.* 105; τα ονοματα אP some
min and vers R. — αυτου AC most edd; αυτων אᶜPQ min. 10. After the
first αιχμαλωσιαν, some min and some Mss. of the Vlg Iren Prim Bouss
add απαγει; wanting in nearly all sources and edd; R reads συναγει with
some anc com, without Ms. authority. — 15. After εδοθη, א QPᶜ nearly
all min edd read αυτω; αυτη ACP* Lch WH RV. On αυτη Westcott re-
marks that it is impossible to interpret it; and Hort suggests that τη γη
may have been lost after αυτη, reference being made to ' the spirit of the
earth as given to the image of the Beast' (Notes on *Select* Readings) — a
suggestion which hardly calls for comment. — ποιηση most sources and
edd; ποιησει א some min Tr mrg WH mrg *al*. See translation in RV mrg.
— ινα, before οσοι or αποκτανθωσιν, AP some min and anc com R Ws
(see *Ap.* 116) Bouss RV *al*; wanting in אQ many min Iren Ti; bracketed
by Alf WH Sod *al*. Its omission, whether by the author or a copyist, is
an oversight, as it is required with αποκτανθωσιν. — 17. και, before ινα
μη, אᶜAPQ most min vers R Ws Sod RV *al*; wanting in א*C some min
vers Iren Prim Lch Ti Blj; bracketed by Alf WH Bouss Sw Moff *al*. —
18. Nearly all sources have the number 666; 616 is given in C two min
Ticonius. Iren. (*Haer.* V. 30) mentions certain of his time who adopted
the latter reading, but states that 666 is the number of all the oldest
and best sources; see Zahn *Ein.* II. 637.

Criticism of 12¹⁸–13¹⁸. The connection of chapt. 13 with 12¹⁷, as exhibiting the instrument and the manner of Satan's war against the seed of the woman, is so clear that nearly all critics are agreed in making the chapt. a continuance of what is there begun, even though the paragraph of which this is a part is regarded by some as not belonging originally to the Apocalypse. Many following Vischer (85) trace the chapt. to a Jewish apocalypse; so, Spitta, Schoen, J. Weiss, Wellhausen, *al.* It is written, as is argued, entirely in a Jewish spirit, without original Christian traces; it pictures Jewish horror of emperor-worship and a hatred of Rome as persecutor and conqueror of the Jewish people; the characterization of Rome as a deadly enemy is not Christian, it is not found elsewhere in the N. T., not even in the seven epistles, a Christian part of the Apocalypse; the Jewish character of the chapt. is seen especially in the abhorrence of the Roman coins bearing the image of the emperor (v. 17), which it was sinful to touch; the chapt. contains nothing distinctly Christian; vv. 9–10 containing the specifically Christian terms ὑπομονή and πίστις, and the words 'the Lamb that was slain,' v. 8, are additions of the redactor, as shown by their inappropriateness to the context.

But the inconclusiveness of this argument, so far as it relates to vv. 8, 9–10, 17 is shown above in the Com. For the alleged non-Christian attitude toward Rome see p. 396. It is an error to find a contradiction in this respect between this chapt. and the seven epistles. It is true that these do not make special mention of Rome's hostility; they speak specifically of the perils and enmities encountered in the respective congregations, because the Prophet is seeking in this way to prepare the several churches, through victory over the dangers immediately present with them and especially those inhering in their present spiritual state, to meet the great trial now threatening the Church at large; that thought forms the background of the admonitions given. But the part which the hostility of the Roman power is to play in the trial is well known, the presence of a Satanic agency as already at work in the imperial arrogation of divine honor is probably alluded to in 2¹³ (see note there). At all events the later portions of the book, setting forth Roman agency in the great trial, are only a continuation and unfolding of the Prophet's message to the churches; in other words chapt. 13 is just as truly a part of the message to the seven churches as are the seven epistles, and no difficulty can arise from the author's deferring to this place specific mention of a fact which lies behind all the epistles and concerns all the churche⸱ As regards the attitude of Rome toward Christians, there is nothing in the picture of the Beast's enmity to God's people which is inappropriate in the mouth of a Christian; see p. 494. Moreover there is, quite apart from the Christian passages, exscinded without sufficient reason, a rather clear intimation that the writer has in mind here the Christians rather than Jews; the prominence given in the chapt. to the insistence on emperor-worship and the perils of disobedience reflect Christian rather than Jewish experiences; see p. 199.

Critics who do not accept the chapt. as an originally planned part of the Apocalypse have offered different hypotheses concerning its origin and redaction. Spitta (134 ff., 362 ff.) makes the Beast a single person and identifies him with Caligula whose history presents certain striking parallelisms. This identification forms the norm for Spitta's treatment of the whole passage. He exscinds not only the Christian allusions in vv. 8, 9–10, but also the mention of the wounded head healed (v. 3), and all other allusions to Nero, of whom the original form of the oracle knew nothing; these all are additions of the redactor, who following chapt. 17 identified the Beast with Nero, and worked over chapt. 13 to make it conform with chapt. 17. The πληγὴ θανάτου was primarily the deadly sickness from which Caligula recovered. The number of the Beast was 616 = Γάιος καῖσαρ (Caligula) but since the redactor could not apply that number to Nero he changed it to 666, which by the use of Heb. letters and the *scriptio defectiva* could give the name Nero. The second beast, who by his magic arts furthered the paying of divine homage to Caligula, was Simon Magus. The original form of the passage then was purely Jewish representing the trials under Caligula. This document a Christian editor of the second century worked over into the present form. Völter (*Offenb.* 100 ff.) makes the chapt. a part of the large paragraph which he supposes Cerinthus to have inserted in the Apocalypse ; see pp. 226 f. Chapt. 17, which according to Völter's theory belonged to an Appendix added by the original Christian apocalyptist himself, was a few years afterwards seen by Cerinthus to contain unfulfilled prophecies, *e.g.* the return of Nero as the Beast. Cerinthus therefore prepared chapt. 13 as a kind of recension of chapt. 17. The tenth horn is Vespasian in whose reign the Roman empire (the Beast) recovered from the troubles of the interregnum (the deadly wound). In him Nero, the wounded head, returned from the dead. Cerinthus obtained the number 666 by writing the Gk. word θηρίον with Heb. letters; but by the use of Heb. letters this number could be made to yield Titus Flavius Vespasianus Augustus ; and at the same time Caesar Nero. Vespasian therefore is the Beast, and at the same time Nero *redivivus*. J. Weiss (92 ff., 139 ff.) takes the beast-vision, 13$^{1-7}$, to be a doublet of the dragon-vision in chapt. 12, since the office of both is ποιῆσαι πόλεμον μετὰ τῶν ἁγίων. The two traditions existing separately are here placed side by side, either by the apocalyptist of Q (Weiss' Jewish document) or by the later redactor, without effort to work them over into one. In seeking to recover the form which the passage had in Q, several parts must be omitted as additions of the last redactor; in v. 3 the head wounded and healed, in v. 6 the words 'those who dwell in the heaven,' v. 8 which speaks of the emperor-worship, vv. 9–10 containing an exhortation inappropriate here. The second beast is a figure transformed from a false Messiah or false prophet, mentioned in the original Christian apocalypse. Wellhausen (*Anal.* 21 ff.) sees in the chapt. an extensive working over of a Jewish source in which the Beast represented the Roman empire, the *imperium*, and not an emperor, to which was given power to war against the Jews and overcome them in the 3½ years' war. In that earlier form the oracle contained no mention of *Nero redivivus*, of a second beast, a false prophet, nor even of an image of the emperor. Verses 3a, 7b–9, 10a, 14–15, 18, and sundry other traits in the passage are the work of one or more redactors. The original of the second beast was the *alter ego* of the *imperium*, which was conceived to represent the full power of the imperium in the provinces, as the imperium itself had its seat in the city of Rome. As no plastic likeness of the abstract imperium (as distinguished from an emperor) can be formed, this *alter ego* was thought of as the εἰκών of the imperium, just as Jesus is the εἰκών of God. This part of the vision (vv. 11 ff.) primarily ran thus: 'I saw a likeness (= an *alter ego*) of the Beast in the country (the provinces in contrast with the city of Rome) which exercises the full power of the Beast in his stead and compels the inhabitants of the provinces to worship the Beast' (*Anal.* 23). Quite at variance with this primary representation, a redactor read into the *alter ego* the idea of a false prophet who should precede Antichrist, as Elijah precedes the true Messiah, vv. 13, 14.

It must suffice here to present certain general considerations regarding these and kindred hypotheses, without taking up details in argument. (1) The respective excisions and reconstructions which are a *sine-qua-non* for the maintenance of the hypotheses are not, on grounds apart from the presuppositions of the particular theory advocated, established with such certainty as to gain the general assent of critical opinion; they are frequently altogether arbitrary, and disregard both the natural exegesis of the chapt. and the author's manner of composition. For the correctness of this statement reference must be made to the interpretation presented in different parts of the Com. (2) A clear recognition of the author's purpose in the chapt. and the place it occupies in his plan, of the free use he makes of traditional symbolism, and of his latitude in the application of current beliefs, leaves the passage without insuperable difficulty as an original part of a Christian apocalypse written near the end of the century, and as consonant with other parts of the book. (3) The excerpting, the unskillful combining and working over of material, the failure to adjust matter to a unified scheme, which are required in these hypotheses, presuppose a method of composition so artificial that it becomes probable only when supported by incontestible evidence, or when no other theory reasonably accounts for the phenomena.

XIV. 1–5. *The redeemed with the Lamb on mount Zion.* See p. 279.

The 144,000, and mount Zion. The vision of the Messiah with a great company of the redeemed on mount Zion is suggested by prophecies of the last days familiar from the writings of the prophets and apocalyptists; *e.g.* Joel 2³², ' Whosoever shall call on the name of the Lord shall be delivered; for in mount Zion and in Jerusalem there shall be those that escape'; 2 Es. 2⁴² ᶠ·, 'I saw upon the mount Zion a great multitude whom I could not number, . . . and in the midst of them there was a young man of a high stature, taller than all the rest, and upon every one of their heads he set crowns ' ; *idem* 13³⁵ ᶠᶠ·, Is. 24²³, Mic. 4⁷, Jub. 1²⁸. (1) *Mount Zion*, synonymous with Jerusalem, is one of the standing terms to designate the central seat of the eschatological kingdom ; and like Jerusalem, it sometimes has an ideal, though earthly, significance not identical with the local Zion of history ; it belongs to the *renewed* earth as the holy place in the new kingdom ; but its location is thought of vaguely, cf. 2 Es. 10⁵³ ᶠ·, 13³⁶, En. 90²⁹. (On the distinction of the eschatological from the familiar geographical Zion, see Volz 372 f.) Much as Christian thought, especially Christian hymnology, has identified new Jerusalem and mount Zion with heaven itself, these terms are not used in the Scriptures and apocalyptic writers to denote the celestial abode of God. The ' mount Zion, the city of the living God, the heavenly Jerusalem ' in Heb. 12²², the ' Jerusalem that is above ' in Gal. 4²⁶, denote the perfect archetype or pattern of the earthly, which in Heb. thought now exists in heaven, and in the end is to descend in full realization ; they are not designations of heaven the place of God and his hosts. In our book the new Jerusalem is distinctly located on the renewed earth (chaps. 21–22), and the ' beloved city ' of the millennial period is also upon earth (20⁹). The vision of these verses, 1–5, has not to do with any experience of the 144,000 leading up to the end. It pictures them in a triumph that is final ; their trial is past, they have been redeemed, they bear the names that mark them as final victors ; cf. 3¹². It is certain then that the author in this passage uses the term mount Zion in the sense found everywhere in apocalyptic writings, denoting, not heaven (so, many com.), but the seat of the messianic kingdom. The opinion that the place of the faithful seen here is to be distinguished from the Jerusalem of the renewed earth (so, Bouss., Blj., *al.*) rests upon the supposition, (*a*) that the new earth and the new Jerusalem do not appear till a later place in the drama of the book (21¹ ᶠᶠ·, ¹⁰), and (*b*) that the 144,000 are a special class of the saints, who receive a reward before the general resurrection, and the beatification of all, as do the martyrs in the millennium. But (*a*) the vision is wholly anticipatory, like that of 7⁹ ᶠᶠ·, and does not intimate any order in the sequence of events ; it is simply a vision of the End. (See p. 246.) (b) It will be seen below that the 144,000 are to be taken as identical with the body of the redeemed as a whole ; they do not form a select part. There is in this case no mention of a distinction between a first and a general resurrection ; contrast 20⁵.)

(2) *The 144,000.* These are in v. 3 identified with the redeemed ; the words there added are not οἳ ἠγοράσθησαν, *who were redeemed,* but the appositional phrase οἱ ἠγορασμένοι, *the redeemed,* as if the whole body of the redeemed, and not a particular class among them, were meant. On the other hand in vv. 4–5 they are described in language which is interpreted by a large number of scholars as limiting them to a select class (so, Düst., Holtzm., Blj., and many others). The argument is as follows: (a) The word ἀπαρχή, *first-fruits,* likens them to the first fruits of the ground which are offered to God (Dt. 26¹⁻¹¹, Lv. 23¹⁰⁻¹⁴), and which are only the beginning of the ingathering that is to follow. This use of the word to designate the first in the order of time occurs in a figurative sense in Ro. 16¹⁵, 1 Co. 15²⁰, *al.* (b) The moral qualities attributed to the 144,000 mark them as distinguished for their holiness, especially their asceticism ; they are celibates (παρθένοι, v. 4). Asceticism, it is argued, is encouraged in early Christian teaching (Mt. 19¹², 1 Co. 7²⁵⁻⁴⁰), and by this time had become widespread ; a higher degree of sanctity is attributed to the unmarried (cf. Ign. *Pol.* 5). (c) This evidence of a chosen company among the saints is confirmed by the absence of the article in the first mention of the 144,000 ; if those spoken of before in 7¹⁻⁸, whether as the chosen of Israel or the whole body of Christians, were meant in this place, the art. must have been used. The conclusion then is that the 144,000 are a select class of the saints who by the practice of Christian virtues, especially asceticism, have won for themselves a preëminent place, and like the martyrs will receive a particular reward before the final judgment. Comparison of the 144,000 with the sharers in the millennium does not suggest identity ; the characteristics are altogether different, cf. vv. 4–5 with 20⁴. They are here seen in the enjoyment of their special reward in the presence of the Messiah on

mount Zion, an eschatological but earthly center in the messianic kingdom.

But the grounds urged in support of the above interpretation are far from convincing. (*a*) The *first-fruits*, ἀπαρχή, bear a twofold relation; viewed with reference to the husbandman's ingathering they are the first, others come after; but viewed as an offering to God they stand alone; they are the part chosen out as a holy thing, consecrated and belonging to God, and are not in this relation followed by others; they constitute the whole. Jeremiah (2³) using the term figuratively calls Israel 'holiness unto Jehovah, the first-fruits'; it is chosen out of the tribes of men as the part holy unto God and belongs wholly to him. The prophet has here no thought of other nations who may later be joined with God's people. Cf. Ezk. 48⁸, ¹⁰, ²⁰, where the area wholly consecrated to God is called ἀπαρχή; there is no thought here of a later addition to be made to that part. In the same way James (1¹⁸) describes the whole body of Christians as 'a kind of first-fruits.' That the author of our passage has in mind this relation of the first-fruits he shows by adding the words 'unto God and the Lamb'; he is speaking of that which forms the hallowed offering belonging wholly to God. If he had in mind the other relation, that of priority in time, meaning that the 144,000 are the first in a continuing series, we should expect 'the first-fruits of the saints,' as in 1 Co. 15²⁰, 'the first-fruits of them that sleep'; cf. 1 Co. 16¹⁵, Ro. 16⁵. (*b*) The meaning of παρθένοι, *virgins*, must be determined by the words with which it is directly connected, μετὰ γυναικῶν οὐκ ἐμολύνθησαν, *were not defiled with women* — words which cannot refer to conjugal intercourse, for μολύνω, *defile*, when used figuratively, always contains the idea of sin, and nowhere in the Scriptures is there trace of such a thought regarding marriage. Ceremonial uncleanness might be thought to follow coition (Lv. 15¹⁸), but the word characterizing it, ἀκάθαρτος, does not necessarily imply sin. These words of v. 4 can therefore only refer to adultery or fornication. The following words, παρθένοι γάρ εἰσιν, *for they are virgins*, like ἄμωμοί εἰσιν, v. 5, express the *permanent* character of the 144,000 (the change to the present tense should be noticed) and explain how they escaped pollution; it is not because they were celibates, but because they are *chaste in fixed principle of character* (see further on v. 4). That the word παρθένος, *virgin*, in this figurative sense might be applied even to the married seems to be attested by Ign. *Smyr.* 13, τὰς παρθένους τὰς λεγομένας χήρας, which Lightfoot interprets, 'the widows whom I call virgins because of their purity and devotion.' (*c*) The absence of the art. in the first mention of the 144,000 shows only that the writer does not here specifically point out the identity of these with those before mentioned (7¹⁻⁸), though he may have the same persons in mind. The indefiniteness is characteristic of visions; *e.g.* in 17³ 'a woman' is the one before mentioned in v. 1; in 15² 'a sea of glass' is that mentioned in 4⁶; in 14¹⁴ the 'one like unto a son of man' is the one mentioned in 1¹³. Further objection to finding in the 144,000 a select class of the saints arises in the departure from the author's usage which would thus be presented. These anticipatory passages, whether visions or songs of praise, always relate to the people of God as a whole; and since this vision of triumph (vv. 1–5) stands over against the great war of Satan upon the whole Church, it would fail of the usual purpose of such passages, if its promise were limited to the small portion contained in the ascetics and unmarried.

It appears therefore clearly preferable to identify the 144,000 with the whole body of the sealed and redeemed (chapt. 7) and to see in the vision a revelation of their final triumph shown to them in anticipation to encourage them in face of the conflict with Satan and his agents just described (see pp. 244 ff.). For the number 144,000 as symbolical of the whole people of God see pp. 535, 254. The words, 'the redeemed,' define the *state* of these; then with an admonitory purpose the Apocalyptist in vv. 4–5 describes, in terms of the cardinal Christian virtues, the character they had maintained in life; they were wholly consecrated to God, they everywhere followed Christ as their leader, they were chaste, and no untruth was found in them; they are spotless. Two virtues, purity and truth, are singled out for mention, probably because of the prevalence of impurity and untruth in surrounding heathen society. Similarly St. Paul, 1 Thess. 4³ ff., in exhorting to complete sanctification, warns specifically against the two heathen vices of impurity and avarice. The opposites of the two virtues named in our passage, chastity and truth, appear in 21⁸ in the list of attributes which exclude from inheritance of the kingdom; cf. also 21²⁷. It is evident that in none of these passages is the order of attributes meant to indicate relative importance.

XIV. 1.   On mount Zion and the 144,000 see above. — τὸ ἀρνίον, *the Lamb:* for the use of the title *the Lamb*, see pp. 314 ff. — ἔχουσαι τὸ ὄνομα κτλ., *having the name*, etc.: the name set on the forehead is not to be distinguished from the seal of 7³; the seal is thought of as consisting of the name, as the mark of the Beast consists of his name, or its equivalent, 13¹⁷. For the significance of the mark see on 13¹⁷. The words set the redeemed in contrast with the worshipers of the Beast, who bear his name; at the same time there is here a reminiscence of 3¹²; the bearing of the name is a token of victory; cf. 22⁴. — τὸ ὄνομα αὐτοῦ, *his name:* the name of the Lamb is here placed before that of God because of the prominence of the Lamb in the sentence.

2–3. The prophet from his position on the earth hears the song sung in the court of heaven. The representation given in chapts. 4–5 of the great throne-room in heaven reappears incidentally in different places throughout the book; cf. 7¹¹,¹⁷, 11¹⁶, 19⁴, 21³,⁵. Who the singers are is left indefinite, as in 11¹⁵, 12¹⁰, 19¹⁶. They are not the Living Creatures and the Elders as in 5⁸ ᶠᶠ·, for they are distinguished from these in v. 3. Apparently they are the innumerable hosts of angels as in 5¹¹, 7¹¹; the similes of the many waters and the thunder refer to the loudness of a song sung by great multitudes, cf. 19⁶. In 7⁹ ᶠ·, 15² ᶠ· the saints themselves sing the hymn of praise, but here they must first *learn* the song from others (v. 3). That they are not the singers (though some com. interpret so) is clear from the fact that they are on mount Zion, but the hymn is sung in heaven. That the redeemed should sing the praise of their redemption is implied in their *learning* the song, but that is not mentioned. What is meant here is the joy in heaven over the salvation of the saints; cf. 7¹¹, Lk. 15¹⁰. — ᾠδὴν καινήν, *a new song:* see on 5⁹. That the theme of the song is the now accomplished salvation of the saints is evident from the meaning of the vision. — οὐδεὶς ἐδύνατο μαθεῖν κτλ., *no man could learn the song*, etc.: none but those who themselves experienced the blessedness of the salvation attained could learn to sing its praise duly.

4–5. Over against the promise contained in vv. 1–3 the Apocalyptist in these verses sets as an admonition to his readers the character of those who attain the promise. — οἱ . . . ἐμολύνθησαν, *who were not defiled*, etc.: many take the words to be wholly metaphorical, some understanding spiritual purity in general, freedom from all contamination from sin (cf. 2 Co. 11²), others, avoidance of idolatry, which is frequently spoken of as adultery toward God. But the addition of the specific words μετὰ γυναικῶν, *with women*, excludes such figurative interpretation; the sentence must be taken literally, as most recent interpreters agree. See further p. 649. — The past tense in the vbs. of these verses refers to the time prior to the gathering of the saints on mount Zion, *i.e.* the time of their earthly life; the presents εἰσίν, to their fixed, essential character. — παρθένοι γάρ εἰσιν, *for they are virgins:* the words account for (γάρ, *for*) the avoidance of pollution; the saints had been kept from it in their earthly life, because the principle of chastity is an essential trait of their character, they are pure in heart. For the application of παρθένος, *virgin*, to men, see L and S., Thayer, *s.v.*

οἱ ἀκολουθοῦντες, *the followers:* the partic. with the art. is equivalent to a noun, and the time of its action is determined by the context; cf. Burton § 123, H.A. § 966. The vb., of which this phrase is the pred. and οὗτοι the subj., is omitted; it is probably ἦσαν rather than εἰσίν, since the two other οὗτοι clauses with which this is parallel have the principal vbs. in the past tense; the three clauses refer to the past of the saints, which led to their present glorified state; *these were followers of the Lamb in all his ways.* The vb. changes to the pres. in the dependent clause, *whithersoever he goeth*, because the paths of Christ's leading are thought of as absolute, without reference to time. For the presents εἰσίν see above. The language here does not refer specifically to the martyr's death (so, some com.), but to perfect discipleship; it echoes words frequent in the Lord's utterances, *e.g.* Mt. 19²¹, Mk. 8³⁴, Lk. 5²⁷, Jno. 12²⁶.

— ὅπου ἂν κτλ.: if ὑπάγει is read here, the indic. is wholly irregular; see Blass § 65, 7.— ἠγοράσθησαν κτλ., *were redeemed*, etc.: this is not a mere repetition of οἱ ἠγορασμένοι in v. 3 (see below); the paramount thought here is in the predicate ἀπαρχή, *first-fruits;* they were redeemed from among men to be like the first-fruits wholly consecrated to God. As in the connected clauses it is their character that is spoken of. For ἀπαρχή, *first-fruits*, see pp. 648 f.— οὐχ εὑρέθη ψεῦδος κτλ., *no lie was found*, etc.: cf. 21²⁷, 22¹⁵. For the emphasis laid on truth cf. Jno. 8⁴⁴, 1 Pet. 2²², Ps. 32², Zeph. 3¹³, Mal. 2⁶.— ἄμωμοί εἰσιν, *they are faultless:* this epithet sums up in one word the description of the perfect character of those who are seen with the Lamb on mount Zion; cf. Eph. 1⁴, Col. 1²².

Textual notes, 14¹⁻⁵. 1. P some min R omit το before αρνιον.— R with P one min omits αυτου και το ονομα.— 2. Instead of η φωνη ην ηκουσα, P a few min R read φωνην ηκουσα; R then with a few min omits ως before κιθαρωδων.— 3. ως, before ωδην καινην, AC many min R RV many edd; wanting in אPQ many min Ti Ws Blj; Sod brackets.— 4. Before οι ακολουθουντες, Q most min some vers R insert εισιν; wanting in אACP some min edd.— υπαγη אPQ most min R most edd; υπαγει AC some min Lch WH al.— 5. R with a few min reads δολος instead of ψευδος.— After αμωμοι, γαρ is added in אQ most min and vers R Ti Blj; wanting in ACP some min and vers most edd.— R with some Mss. of the vlg adds ενωπιον του θρονου του θεου after εισιν.

Criticism of 14¹⁻⁵. This passage is pronounced by some critics one of the most enigmatical in the book. The chief objections urged are the following. (*a*) Want of connection with the context. The gathering of the 144,000 with the Lamb on mount Zion stands in no sequence with the activities of the Beast in the preceding chapt., or with the coming judgment announced in vv. 6–20; so, *e.g.* Vischer 54. (*b*) Irreconcilability with 7¹⁻⁸. There the 144,000 are the servants of God universally (7³), here they are those only who are especially distinguished by their holiness, in particular their chastity; there they bear the seal or name of God; here they bear the name of the Lamb also; so, *e.g.* Völter, *Problem*, 231. (*c*) Inconsistencies within the passage itself. In v. 1 the scene is on mount Zion, in v. 3 in heaven; the song of praise should be sung, not by unnamed angels, but by the redeemed themselves, as in 15³ᶠ·; the 144,000 are defined several times, partly in identical terms repeated (οἱ ἠγορασμένοι and οἳ ἠγοράσθησαν), partly in divergent terms — all irregularities, which show the presence of several hands; so, Wellhausen *Anal.* 23.

The principal theories offered regarding the origin of the passage may be summarized briefly. (1) The passage is the work of a Christian redactor who added it to give a wider interpretation of 7¹⁻⁸; there the delivered are 144,000 chosen out of Israel, but a Christian could not see in that the whole number of the redeemed, and he here seeks to show that the 144,000 there spoken of are only a selection out of the host of believers; so, *e.g.* Vischer 52. (2) A redactor has worked over the primitive Christian passage which he found here. It was he that added 7⁹⁻¹⁷ to show that the 144,000, the chosen of Israel, spoken of in 7¹⁻⁸ as the whole of the elect, were only a part; in the same way here he seeks to give a broader scope to the original of this passage which in v. 1 spoke of the redeemed as 144,000; he adds vv. 4–5 and represents that 144,000 as only a part, the élite, chosen because of their asceticism and peculiar obedience; so Völter, *Problem*, 231 f. J. Weiss (94 f., 65 f.) finds here a working over of a passage contained in the original Johannine Apocalypse in which the 144,000, Jewish Christians, the sealed of Israel (7¹⁻⁸), were represented as standing loyal to the Lamb, the true Messiah, in the last days when the false prophet, or the false Messiah, appears in Israel (chapt. 13); but the redactor to whom the present form is due transformed the 144,000, identifying them with a small part of the Church, those who in the last days, when most of the Christians fall in martyrdom, are led by the Lamb to mount Zion and there preserved from the final calamities. (3) One or two Jewish documents have been worked over here by a Christian redactor. Spitta (142 ff.) refers the original to his Jewish document J¹. To recover the original oracle he substitutes in v. 1 θεοῦ ζῶντος‧ for αὐτοῦ καὶ . . . πατρός, and interprets ἀρνίον (omitting the art.) of a Jewish leader, perhaps Gamaliel; he omits vv. 2–3, καὶ τῷ ἀρνίῳ after τῷ θεῷ v. 4, and brackets οἱ ἀκολουθοῦντες . . . ὑπάγῃ v. 4. Weyland (160 ff.) refers vv. 2–3 to his Jewish source *Aleph*, the rest of the passage to a redactor.

The difficulties raised in the above criticism and made the ground of these different hypotheses have, it is believed, been sufficiently met in the Com., pp. 646 ff., and in the Summary (Introd. p. 279). They arise from a disregard of the Apocalyptist's habit of inserting anticipatory passages, and from the misinterpretation of the 144,000 as a select part of the saints in contrast with the whole Church. Bouss. (382 f.) has pointed out traces of the author of the Apocalypse as a whole which are found in nearly every verse of our passage. The following parallelisms may be noted: v. 2 and 1¹⁵, 19⁶; v. 3 a and 5⁹, chapt. 4; v. 3 b and 19¹²; v. 4 b and 7¹⁷; v. 4 c and 5⁹ ⁴.

XIV. 6–20. *Announcement of the last judgment, warning, and promise.* See pp. 280 f.

6–7. In these verses the first of a series of angels introduced in the visions of this chapt. announces the glad tidings that God's eternal purpose is about to be fulfilled, the judgment is at hand; and all the world is summoned to repent and worship God. - ἄλλον ἄγγελον, *another angel:* the contrast in ἄλλον, *another*, is not clear. Perhaps the angel singers in vv. 2–3 are thought of, or perhaps a contrast is intended with the angels in general who have hitherto appeared; see on 10¹, where a similar ambiguity occurs. The specification of a *different* angel is attributable to the author's fondness for variety in the persons introduced; see on 5⁵. Neither of the explanations suggested offers serious difficulty; and the word cannot be taken to furnish ground for violent critical procedure (see p. 666). It is grammatically possible to take ἄλλον, *another*, as a pronoun in contrast with the Lamb; *I saw another*, viz.: *an angel flying*, etc. (Völter); but in that sense the word ' another ' is more than superfluous. The supposition that the Lamb in vv. 1–5 is thought of as an archangel with whom this angel is contrasted is at variance with the author's christology. The omission of ἄλλον after some Mss. raises the greater difficulty of accounting for its insertion in this connection. — ἐν μεσουρανήματι, *in mid-heaven:* in the sight and hearing of all, as the call is addressed to all; cf. 8¹³.

εὐαγγέλιον, *glad tidings:* the article is not prefixed, and the reference is not to the gospel. What the tidings are is shown by λέγων κτλ., *saying*, etc., *i.e.* the announcement that God's eternal purpose regarding his people is about to be accomplished, the judgment is near; cf. εὐηγγέλισεν, 10⁷. A comparison of v. 7 with 10⁷ shows that the glad message here spoken of is not the offer of grace implied in the call to repentance (so, some comm.). — αἰώνιον, *eternal:* existing from eternity. The epithet belongs to the divine purpose rather than to the tidings; it is transferred to the latter; these are called eternal because their subject is such. — εὐαγγελίσαι : for the infin. with ἔχειν cf. Jno. 16¹², Lk. 7⁴⁰. — ἐπί : not found elsewhere with εὐαγγελίζειν; perhaps the angel's call is thought of as sent forth *over* the dwellers on the earth. — τοὺς καθημένους ἐπὶ τῆς γῆς : not different from τοὺς κατοικοῦντας κτλ., which is found elsewhere. See on 3¹⁰. — καὶ ἐπὶ πᾶν ἔθνος κτλ., *even unto every nation*, etc.: the words repeat with emphatic comprehensiveness ' those that dwell on the earth '; hence καί should be translated *even*. — δότε αὐτῷ δόξαν, *give him glory:* for this expression meaning *repent* see on 11¹³. — ἦλθεν ἡ ὥρα, *the hour has come:* i.e. is close at hand. While the announcement of the judgment brings good tidings to the saints, it is a call to the world to fear God and repent. — τῷ ποιήσαντι τὸν οὐρανὸν κτλ., *him who made the heaven*, etc.: the ground for worshiping God is here found in his character as creator of all, as in 4^{11}, Ac. 4^{24}, 14^{15}; see on 4^{11}. The language of natural theology is appropriate in an appeal to all the world, including the heathen. — πηγὰς ὑδάτων, *springs of waters*: for this addition to the comprehensive formula, 'the heavens and the earth and the sea,' cf. 8^{10}, 16^4.

8. The second angel proclaims the judgment upon Rome. Special mention of Rome's fall is demanded because of its prominence among eschatological events and among the predictions of the book, chaps. 17–19^5. See p. 158. Babylon formed the ancient parallel of Rome; it was the capital of a world-empire, it was famous for its luxury and moral corruption, above all it was the powerful foe of God's people. And as Edom became a name for the Roman empire (see Weber, *System*, 348 ff.), so Babylon became the mystic name for the city of Rome; *e.g.* Sib. Or. V. 143, 159, Ap. Bar. 11^1, 67^7, Rev. 14^8, 16^{19}, 17^5, $18^{2, 10, 21}$, probably 1 Pet. 5^{13}. That Rome is meant in the passages in Rev. is made clear by chaps. 17–18; see p. 690. Babylon is always called *great* in Rev.; cf. also Dan. 4^{30}. — ἔπεσεν, *has fallen*: cf. 18^2. The language is taken directly from Is. 21^9; cf. Jer. 50^2, 51^8. Here, as in the O. T. passages, the past tense is prophetic. — ἢ ἐκ τοῦ οἴνου κτλ., *that hath made all nations to drink of the wine*, etc.: the cause of Rome's punishment which is mentioned here is as in $17^{2, 4}$ her corruption of the nations of the world; but see on 17^6. — τοῦ οἴνου . . . πορνείας, *the wine of the wrath of her fornication:* cf. 18^3. The expression blends two distinct ideas: (1) the wine which the courtesan Rome gives to intoxicate and seduce to fornication, cf. $17^{2, 4}$, Jer. 51^7 — reference is made to Rome's enticement of the nations to idolatry and all manner of corruption; (2) the cup of God's wrath, which he gives those to drink whom he will terribly punish, cf. v. 10, 16^{19}; this figure is common in the O. T., *e.g.* Jer. 25^{15}, 'take this cup of the wine of wrath at my hand and cause all the nations to whom I send thee to drink it,' cf. Job 21^{20}, Ps. 75^8, Is. 51^{17}, Jer. 49^{12}; primarily the figure does not refer to disagreeableness of taste, but to the maddening effects — these God uses as his punishment. In our passage the cup is described fully as both that which Rome uses to entice, and the cup of God's wrath.

9. In view of the coming judgment and the call of the world to worship God (vv. 6–7), a third angel utters warning of the terrible punishment that must fall on those that worship the Beast, vv. 9–11. Thus the Apocalyptist touches directly one of the perils prominent in the historic background of his book, the worship of the emperors. Upon the worship of the Beast, his mark, etc., see 13⁸⁻¹⁷.— ἐπὶ τοῦ μετώπου, τὴν χεῖρα: the change of case after ἐπί is striking, but not significant; μέτωπον stands in the gen. (pl.) in 7³, 9⁴, 14¹, 22⁴; in the acc. (sing.) in 13¹⁶, 17⁵, 20⁴; χείρ stands in the gen. in 13¹⁶, in the acc. in 20¹, ⁴.

10. καί, before αὐτός : best taken as introducing the apodosis ; cf. Kühn. II. § 524, 1. A. 2, Blass § 77, 6 ; it emphasizes the correspondence of the prot. and the apod., *if he worship, he shall also suffer punishment*. Against connection with the pron., *he also* (RV) is the fact that there is nothing with which the pron. is properly contrasted. For αὐτός as emphatic *he*, see Blass § 48, 1. — οἴνου τοῦ θυμοῦ κτλ., *wine of the wrath of God:* see on v. 8. — κεκερασμένου ἀκράτου, *poured out* (lit. *mixed*) *unmixed:* the full strength of the wine is emphasized. The contradiction in the literal meaning of the words is relieved by the fact that κεράννυμι came to be used in the sense of *pour out, i.e.* into the cups ; in common practice water was always mixed with the wine, and in the ordinary use of the word to denote the filling of the cups for drinking the preliminary process of mixing was easily forgotten. The same oxymoron occurs in Aristoph. *Eccl.* 1123, κέρασον ἄκρατον. — θυμοῦ, ὀργῆς, *wrath, anger:* the former refers more to vehement, furious activity ; the latter to the cause, the settled feeling of righteous indignation. See Trench *Syn.* 130 ff. — ἐν πυρὶ καὶ θείῳ, *with fire and brimstone:* cf. 19²⁰, 20¹⁰, 21⁸. Unending torture in fire is the punishment everywhere in apocalyptic literature assigned to Satan and his followers ; see p. 68. On the picture of vv. 10–11, cf. Is. 34⁹⁻¹⁰. — ἐνώπιον τῶν ἀγγέλων κτλ., *in the presence of the angels*, etc.: the idea is common in

2 u

apocalyptic literature that the punishment of the wicked is made more grievous because they can behold the bliss of the righteous and the heavenly beings; cf. En. 27³, 'In the last days there shall be upon them the spectacle of righteous judgment in the presence of the righteous for ever'; cf. En. 108¹⁵, 2 Es. 7³⁶, ⁸³⁻⁸⁷, Ap. Bar. 30⁴, 51⁵ ᶠ·, Lk. 16²³. — ἁγίων, *holy:* for the word applied to angels as an epithet of dignity, cf. Mk. 8³⁸, Lk. 9²⁶, Ac. 10²²; frequent in En. *e.g.* 20¹⁻⁸, 21⁵, ⁹. — ἐνώπιον τοῦ ἀρνίου, *in the presence of the Lamb:* the place of the Lamb after the angels has led some critics to reject this phrase; see p. 666. But in 2 Es. 7⁸³⁻⁸⁷, where as here the torment of the wicked in the sight of the blessed is described, 'the glory of the Most High' is placed after all the rest as the most grievous of the sights. So here special emphasis falls upon the mention of the Lamb at the end of the sentence, as if the most poignant factor in the pain of the wicked would be the sight of the triumph of the Lamb, against whom as worshipers of the Beast they had made war. The supposition that the phrase 'in the presence of the angels' may be a late Jewish paraphrase for 'in the presence of God' (cf. Bouss. *in loc.*) is not supported in cases where reference is made to God as distinct from other heavenly beings; *i.e.* there is not authority for taking this clause to be equivalent to 'in the presence of God and the Lamb.'

11. ὁ καπνὸς κτλ., *the smoke of their torment,* etc.; cf. 19³. — οὐκ ἔχουσιν . . . νυκτός, *they have no rest day and night:* cf. 4⁸. — οἱ προσκυνοῦντες κτλ., *those that worship the Beast,* etc.: the three clauses of the opening sentence of the message (v.9) are repeated at the end to enforce upon the readers the warning against the sin whose punishment has just been described.

12–13. The warning addressed to all the world against the worship of the Beast is followed in these verses by special admonition and encouragement to the saints. In the supreme peril of the short period intervening before the judgment they are called to steadfastness; at the same time they are assured of blessedness in the event of a martyr's death. The call to steadfastness, as in 13⁹⁻¹⁰, comes from the Prophet himself; the promise of blessedness comes with all the solemn warranty of a voice from heaven. — ὧδε ἡ ὑπομονὴ κτλ., *here is the steadfastness of the saints:* see on 13¹⁰. ὧδε, *here,* refers to the trials laid upon the saints in the enforcement of the worship of the Beast. — οἱ τηροῦντες : for the irregular nom. in the appos., see p. 224. — τὴν πίστιν ᾿Ιησοῦ, *faith in Jesus:* the gen. is obj. The words make more specific the preceding ; the commands of God are summed up in a living faith in Jesus ; cf. Jno. 6²⁹. The added word ᾿Ιησοῦ shows that πίστις here is *faith*, as in 2¹³, and not *fidelity*, as in 13¹⁰. — For τηρεῖν πίστιν, cf. 2 Tim. 4⁷. The steadfastness to which the faithful are called must in the Beast's sway bring many to the martyr's death ; the Prophet's vision therefore passes immediately (v. 13) to the certain blessedness of those who shall suffer thus. He hears a voice from heaven proclaiming it, and bidding him to write the assurance as a part of the message of his book. The language here is general, blessednesss is promised to all who die in the Lord ; but it is thus that assurance is given to the martyrs, to whom, as the connection shows, the promise is applied. In fact, most of those dying in the reign of the Beast would fall as martyrs. This interpretation which takes the message of v. 13 to be addressed to the Church with special reference to the great conflict threatening it at the time, and here in the context made the occasion of the angel's warning and the Prophet's exhortation, seems certainly correct. The word ἀπάρτι, *from henceforth*, is then joined directly with οἱ ἀποθνή-σκοντες, *those who die ;* position also favors this connection ; so, many com., *e.g.* Hofmann, Bouss., Blj., Holtzm.-Bau., Swete. For a different interpretation, see p. 661. The message de-clares also wherein those shall be blessed who shall fall in the great crisis intervening before the judgment ; they will rest from their troubles, the troubles suffered through steadfastness in the trial, and their works, *i.e.* their firm fidelity to the commandments of God and a living faith in Jesus, will as it were accompany them to appear in their behalf at the bar of judgment. — This limited application which the Apocalyptist makes of the words uttered from heaven cannot however ob-scure the *universal* truth contained in them. To the world of all time comes the divine assurance, Blessed are all those who shall die in the Lord from henceforth through the ages till the Great Day, in that they shall rest from their trials in the certain confidence that their obedience and faith will be remem-

bered in the last assize. For the repetition of the command,
'Write,' to emphasize the message, cf. 19⁹, 21⁵. For the beatitudes of the book, see on 1³. — ἐν κυρίῳ, *in the Lord: i.e.* in
spiritual union with Christ ; a Pauline phrase, cf. 1 Co. 15¹⁸,
1 Thess. 4¹⁶.

ναί, λέγει τὸ πνεῦμα, *yea, saith the Spirit:* confirming and
explaining the preceding utterance. Here, as in the seven
epistles, the Spirit and the speaker of the preceding words, God
or Christ, seem to be identified. What to the Apocalyptist is
an audible voice, to the Prophet is the Spirit speaking within.
See on 2⁷. — ἵνα ἀναπαήσονται, *in that they shall rest:* the
phrase, as shown by the parallel in 22¹⁴, is best connected as
epexegetical with μακάριοι repeated in thought from the preceding clause : *yea, blessed in that they shall rest.* An epexegetical clause with ἵνα, instead of an infin. or ὅτι clause, is
common in the N. T., especially in Jno., after a demonstrat. or
noun ; it occurs also in other relations, as in Jno. 8⁵⁶. See
Blass § 69, 6, Burton §§ 215–217. The rest of the saints is
their respite from trouble, and their state is contrasted with
that of the wicked described in vv. 9–11. Nothing is implied
regarding their place ; but cf. 6⁹⁻¹¹. — τῶν κόπων, *their labors:*
the word κόπος implies painfulness, and is used here with reference to the sufferings and persecutions of the saints. — τὰ
ἔργα, *their works:* not mere deeds are meant, but also spiritual
attitude ; the steadfastness and faith of v. 9 are included ; see
on 2². — ἀκολουθεῖ μετ᾽ αὐτῶν, *follow with them:* for μετά after
ἀκολουθεῖν instead of the usual construction, the dat. without
preposition, cf. 6⁸. Their works, in the sense defined above,
accompany the saints to the judgment and win for them their
award of approval ; cf. 2 Es. 7³⁵, 'The work shall follow and
the reward shall be showed, and good deeds shall awake,'—
said of the judgment scene ; ·ep. of Barn. 4¹², 'If he be good,
his righteousness shall lead the way before him,' cf. also
1 Tim. 5²⁴. Another form of the same idea is the treasure of
good works stored up for the judgment ; cf. 2 Es. 7⁷⁷, Mt. 6²⁰.
— γάρ, *for:* the clause gives the assurance of the preceding
utterance. If the fruits of their good works were lost to the
saints in death, the mere release from trouble could not be pronounced blessed ; the departed saints will be blessed because

their ' works ' will win for them approval at the judgment-
bar.

An interpretation of v. 13 different from that given above is adopted by
a large number of com., *e.g.* De Wette, Düst., Holtzm., Moff. They join
ἀπάρτι, *from henceforth*, with μακάριοι, *blessed*, and interpret, *blessed from now
on*, because the judgment and the beatification of the saints are immediately
at hand, and may be spoken of as if already come; cf. ἀπάρτι in Mt. 26⁶⁴.
Reference is then understood to be made to the dead in general, both those
already dead and those who shall die in the short interval before the judgment; the verse has no special relation to the distresses alluded to in the
context, nor to the martyrs. But the position of ἀπάρτι is strongly against
that connection; and the blessedness is here in the context referred, not to
the nearness of the Advent, but to rest from suffering and sure confidence regarding the judgment. Further, there is no reason why in anticipation of
the blessedness of the kingdom as near special mention should be made of
the dead in distinction from the living, for there is nowhere in the book
trace of a difficulty such as arose among the Thessalonians, the fear that
the dead might at the parousia fail of a full share in the new kingdom,
1 Thess. 4¹³⁻¹⁸; and if that difficulty were thought of, we should expect it
to be met here, as there, by assurance of the resurrection of the dead. —
Some join ἀπάρτι with the following sentence; *from henceforth . . . they
shall rest;* cf. RVmrg. But in that case it would be placed after ναί, which
stands at the beginning of its clause. Most among modern interpreters
reject that punctuation.

14. The announcement of the coming end now closes with
two simple visions which picture the judgment under symbols
frequently used with this significance in eschatological prophecy,
the harvest and the vintage, vv. 14–20. The visions put in
vivid dramatic form these familiar similes, and are not meant
to predict events which are to take place at this point in the
order of the last things, for much must yet intervene before
the end; they form rather the culminating part of this paragraph (vv. 6–20), which after the episodes of chaps. 12–14⁵,
announces *in anticipation* the coming of the great catastrophe.
Such an announcement stands appropriately here before the
movements which are now to precede more immediately the
last issues (see p. 280); it is altogether anticipatory, and as
such furnishes no difficulty by its presence at this point in the
book (see pp. 667 f.). What is here proclaimed is fully revealed later in its proper chronological place, chaps. 19–20.
In bringing together the figures of the harvest and the vintage,

and in the language, the Apocalyptist follows closely Joel 3[13], 'Put ye in the sickle, for the harvest is ripe; come tread ye, for the winepress is full, the vats overflow; for their wickedness is great.' For the harvest as an eschatological figure cf. Mt. 13[39], 'The harvest is the end of the world,' Mk. 4[29], Jer. 51[33], Hos. 6[11], 2 Es. 4[35], Ap. Bar. 70[2]. The figure is comprehensive, including in a word the whole process of the winding up of the ages, and the recompense of both the good and the bad. It is contrary to the use of the figure elsewhere and without justification in the present context to take the grain harvest of these verses to refer to the righteous only in contrast with the wicked, the subjects of the following verses, 17–20 (so, some com.). Both the tares and the wheat are present at the harvest time, Mt. 13[30]. The relation between these two visions is a different one, as will be seen below (on v. 17). The description of the harvester shows him unquestionably to be the Messiah. The representation of one like a son of man appearing on a cloud is taken directly from the familiar figure of the Messiah derived from Dan. 7[13], and could apply to no other; cf. 1[7, 13], Mt. 24[30], 26[64] par. The crown also marks the messianic King (cf. 19[12]); it might be taken (so, some com.) as the victor's crown; but the scene here is one of judgment, and the harvester is the royal judge, not a warrior. The language of v. 15, 'another angel,' and the fact that the harvester acts at the command of an angel are thought by some interpreters (*e.g.* Bleek, De Wette, Ewald) to forbid a reference to the Messiah; the harvester is then understood to be an archangel, or an angel acting as the Messiah's representative. But these objections do not, as will be seen (on v. 15), possess sufficient force to warrant setting aside the messianic interpretation. — ὅμοιον υἱόν: for the irregular construct. see on 1[13]. — ἔχων: for the nom. see p. 224.

15. ἄλλος ἄγγελος, *another angel:* the angel of this verse is easily understood to be contrasted, not with the person of the preceding verse, the Messiah, but with the first three angels, vv. 6–9. As those proclaim the coming of the judgment, this one brings the command of God for its execution (B. Weiss). The Apocalyptist introduces a large number of *dramatis personae;* 'another angel,' 'a second angel,' or similar expression, occurs more than twenty times in the book; and sometimes the

contrast is not with one mentioned in the immediate context, *e.g.* v. 6, 10¹. — ἐκ τοῦ ναοῦ, *from the temple:* here again heaven is conceived as a temple; see on 6⁹. The words are specially significant here. The temple is the dwelling-place of God, and the angel is thus distinctly represented as God's messenger; the command given to the Messiah is not the angel's, but God's; the Christ acts at God's bidding; 'The Son can do nothing of himself,' Jno. 5¹⁹; the time for the entrance of the judgment the Father has set in his own power, Ac. 1⁷, cf. Mt. 24³⁶. Thus the difficulty spoken of above (on v. 14) is removed. — πέμψον, *send:* with this use of πέμπειν cf. ἀποστέλλειν Mk. 4²⁹, ἐξαπο-στέλλειν Joel 3¹³. — ἐξηράνθη, *has become dried up: i.e. is fully ripe;* it is high time to reap. The aor. is inceptive.

17. In the vision of the vintage which now follows, vv. 17–20, the principal feature, as in its original, Joel 3¹³, is contained, not in the ingathering of the grapes, but in the treading of the winepress. The crushing of the grapes in the press, and especially the staining of the feet and garments of the treaders with the red juices, the 'blood of the grapes' (Gen. 49¹¹), became a familiar figure for the utter trampling down of enemies and furious vengeance. Hence this symbol of God's wrath visited upon the wicked; cf. Is. 63²⁻⁴, 'Wherefore art thou red in thine apparel, and thy garments like him that treadeth in the winevat? . . . I trod them in mine anger, and trampled them in my wrath; and their lifeblood is sprinkled upon my garments, and I have stained all my raiment. For the day of vengeance was in my heart'; cf. Joel 3¹³, Lam. 1¹⁵, Rev. 19¹⁵. The meaning of the second vision is clear; it pictures, not the judgment as a whole, but God's vengeance visited upon the wicked. It is then not parallel with the first, which, as seen above, figures the whole judgment, as it affects the righteous and the wicked alike. We have in the two visions, as often with the author, first a general fact or statement, then a detail or part (see p. 242). Similarly at the opening of the paragraph we have the announcement of the judgment as a whole, vv. 6–7; then the judgment upon Rome and the worshipers of the Beast, vv. 8–11. If this relation of the two visions to each other is observed, the difficulty of a supposed coördination of an angel with Christ in the harvesting (see pp. 667 ff.) is

removed. The Christ is the judge whose function extends to the whole judgment; an angel is made the agent of the execution of God's wrath on the wicked. So in the picture of the general judgment of the good and bad alike given in Mt. 13, it is the angels that are sent to punish the wicked, vv. 41 f., 49 f. The function of the 'angels of punishment' is mentioned frequently in En., *e.g.* 53³, 56¹. — ἐκ τοῦ ναοῦ, *from the temple:* the angel of the vintage also comes from the dwelling-place of God, showing that he is God's agent; see on v. 15. — καὶ αὐτός, *he also:* like the Messiah, v. 14. — δρέπανον, *a sickle:* the δρέπανον was a *reaping-hook,* used alike for reaping, and for pruning the vine and cutting off the clusters at the vintage.

18–19. In the introduction of still another angel to give the word for action this vision is in conformity with the first (v. 15), but there is here an added detail; he comes from the altar, upon which was offered the incense accompanying the prayers of the saints for judgment. Thus it is shown that the prayers are about to be answered; see on 8³. — ὁ ἔχων ἐξουσίαν κτλ., *he that hath power over fire:* for the angels of the different elements see p. 445. Why this particular angel should be deputed as the messenger is not certain; presumably it is because he is identified, or at least associated, with the fire of the incense burnt in behalf of the prayers of the saints. Cf. 8³ ᶠᶠ·, 9¹⁸, 16⁷. — πέμψον: see on v. 15. — τὴν ληνὸν . . . θεοῦ, *the winepress of the wrath of God:* see on v. 17. — τὸν μέγαν: the change of gender is peculiar. While ληνός is sometimes masc., it is likely that the author changes to that use here, because he has in mind what is here symbolized by the press and is expressed in the intervening words, τοῦ θυμοῦ τοῦ θεοῦ.

20. ἔξωθεν τῆς πόλεως, *without the city:* the great slaughter of God's enemies in the last day is placed by Joel (3¹²) in the valley of Jehoshaphat, whose location, however, cannot be identified; but the prophet appears to have in mind throughout that chapt. the vicinity of Jerusalem. In Zec. 14⁴ Jehovah appears against his enemies on the mount of Olives. Cf. also Dan. 11⁴⁵, 2 Es. 13³⁴ ᶠ·, Ap. Bar. 40¹, Sib. Or. III. 667 f., Rev. 20⁹. A final assault upon God's people by the assembled forces of their enemies, and the overthrow of these, are the

common predictions of the apocalyptic writings (see pp. 35 ff.),
and this event is thought of as taking place near Jerusalem.
The Apocalyptist appears to have this tradition in mind in the
use of the words 'without the city.' The words, unless they
are merely a traditional apocalyptic phrase retained without
precise thought of locality, refer to the Jerusalem of 20⁹, not
the new Jerusalem; see pp. 646 ff. It is not necessary to suppose some document containing the phrase to be used here;
see pp. 667 f. — ἄχρι . . . τῶν ἵππων, *unto the bridles of the
horses:* the awfulness of the slaughter is expressed by a hyperbole, which occurs elsewhere; cf. En. 100²ᶠ·, 'From dawn till
sunset they shall slay one another ; and the horse shall walk
up to the breast in the blood of sinners, and the chariot shall
be submerged to its height.' A similar passage is cited from
Mandæan eschatology: 'The horse of the king of heaven
wades in blood up to the saddle, and the blood reaches to his
nostrils' (cf. Wellhausen, *Anal.* 24). The hyperbole is also
found in rabbinical writings; see Schürer I. 695. — ἀπὸ σταδίων χιλίων ἑξακοσίων, *for a distance of a thousand and six hundred furlongs:* the measure is without doubt symbolical ; as the
measure of a field deeply covered with the blood of the slain it
is inconceivably vast. That significance is clear and is probably all that is meant. It is not possible to say why the number
1600 is chosen; presumably the Apocalyptist has in mind a
large multiple of four (400 × 4) as a symbol of fullness; see
p. 252. Such conjectures as that the length of Palestine (a not
very close approximation), or the familiar expression 'from
Dan to Beersheba,' suggests it, or the length of the Red Sea —
these and similar guesses are altogether fanciful. For other
conjectures equally far-fetched see De Wette, the Speaker's
Com., *al. in loc.* — For the use of ἀπό with measures of distance
cf. Jno. 11¹⁸, 21⁸; see Thayer *s.v.* I. 4, a.

Textual notes, 14⁶⁻¹⁹. 6. αλλον ℵᶜACP some min most vers edd; wanting in ℵ*Q most min. — 8. R with one min some vers omits δευτερος. —
αγγελος wanting in ℵ* one min ; WH bracket. — 9. R with vlg and some
other vers omits αλλος. — 10. των, with αγιων αγγελων, AQ most min R Ws
(*Ap.* 127) Alf Blj Bouss WHmrg; wanting in ℵCP some min Lch Ti WH
Sod *al.* — 12. R with some min inserts ωδε before οι τηρουντες. — 13. ανα-
παησονται ℵAC edd; αναπαυσονται Q many min ; αναπαυσωνται P many min
R Sod. — γαρ ℵACP some min and vers edd; δε most min and vers R. —

14. υιον אAQ many min edd; υιω C many min R Ws (*Ap.* 136) Alf. —
18. ο before εχων, AC some vers Lch Ws (*Ap.* 106) Alf RV *al*; bracketed
by Tr WH Bouss *al*; wanting in אPQ min R Ti Sod *al.* — 19. τον μεγαν
ACPQ many min most edd; την μεγαλην א many min R RV.

Criticism of 14⁶⁻²⁰. (1) Vv. 6–13. Of the widely varying opinions of
critics regarding vv. 6–13, the following are representative. Völter (*Problem* 233 ff.) connects vv. 6–7 directly with his original form of vv. 1–3, as
a part of the primitive Christian apocalypse; both passages reveal in the
face of coming judgment an act of God's grace; in vv. 1–3 toward the children of his covenant, in vv. 6–7 toward the heathen, who may repent in the
coming visitations. Verse 8, declaring the judgment upon Rome, is repeated in the full picture of chapt. 18; both therefore cannot be original
and preference is given to 14⁸; vv. 9–13 are out of place because after the
judgment of Rome has already begun (vv. 8, 14–20), and after the redeemed
are already safe in mount Zion (vv. 1–3), warning against the worship of
the Beast would come too late; these verses are probably interpolated by
the author of chapt. 18. J. Weiss (95 f.) assigns vv. 6–7 to the primitive
Johannine apocalypse, but refers vv. 8, 9–13 to a redactor. In v. 6 he
changes ἄγγελον to ἄετον, which he sets in contrast with the eagle of 13⁸,
thus explaining ἄλλον; see Com. Spitta (148 ff.) finds here a much revised
fragment from his Jewish document J¹, and connects it with chapt. 13;
v. 8 must be from the redactor, because such an announcement of the fall
of Babylon without previous allusion or intimation of the meaning is out
of place here; the larger part of vv. 10–11 must be omitted, as containing
a repetition from v. 9, and as being unintelligible except from the description of Babylon's judgment which is not given till later, chapts. 17–18;
vv. 12–13 must be rejected because such words of comfort to Christians do
not belong between the warning to worshipers of the Beast (9–11) and the
representation of the judgment (vv. 14–20). By these omissions all Christian touches are removed from the passage. The difficulty in the word
'other' in v. 6 Spitta removes as follows: the angel of v. 6 is contrasted
with an angel mentioned in the original form of vv. 1–5; the redactor, however, in revising those verses omitted the reference to the angel, but forgot
to revise v. 6 to make it conform. Vischer connects the passage directly
with chapt. 13 as a part of his Jewish apocalypse. He omits vv. 12–13 as
unsuited to the context (see above on Spitta), and further objects, the
phraseology of these verses is a repetition of the Christian passage 13⁹⁻¹⁰,
such words as πίστις and ὑπομονή being found only in the Christian additions to the book; in v. 10 καὶ ἐνώπιον τοῦ ἀρνίου is to be rejected as only
a cumbersome appendage to the sentence. The Christian features being
thus removed, the rest of the paragraph is Jewish. If it had been Christian, the command in v. 7, 'Fear God,' etc., would have enjoined also a
recognition of Jesus as the Messiah. Pfleiderer agrees with Vischer in
most respects, but connects these vv. directly with 10¹⁻⁷. Sabatier also
thinks that a Jewish oracle is incorporated here. Weyland, omitting vv. 8,
12–13, assigns the passage to his Jewish document *Beth.*

This survey of leading critical opinions with their wide range of diver-gences and contradictions makes clear the difficulty of establishing any theory of composition of such a kind and on such grounds as here urged. On the other hand, the theory of a substantial unity of the passage and its appropriateness here is supported by a legitimate exegesis and a due regard to the author's manner; see Summary, pp. 280 f., and Com. Its oneness of authorship with the book as a whole is confirmed, as in case of vv. 1–5, by the frequent traces of the hand that appears elsewhere; compare v. 6 with 5⁹, 7⁹, 8¹³, 10⁷ (εὐαγγέλιον, εὐηγγέλισεν, see Com.), 10¹¹, 11⁹, 13⁷; v. 7 with 5², 10⁶; v. 8 with 16¹⁹, 17⁵, 18³; v. 9 with 13 *passim*, 16², 19²⁰, 20⁴; v. 10 with 16¹⁹, 18³, ⁶, 19¹⁵, ²⁰, 20¹⁰, 21⁸; v. 11 with 4⁸, 19³; v. 12 with 12¹⁷, 13¹⁰; v. 13 with 2⁷, 22¹⁷, and the close of the seven epistles.

(2) vv. 14–20. These verses are taken by many critics to announce the judgment as introduced at this point in the order of events in the book. After this then there would seem to be no place for a continuation of the pre-messianic plagues (chapt. 16), the destruction of Rome (chapts. 17–19), and the last conflict (19¹¹⁻²¹). The solution of the difficulty thus raised is sought by most critics in the supposition that the passage stood originally at the end of another apocalypse, or of an earlier form of our Apocalypse. Some indications of ,a different connection are thought to be found; *e.g.* the obscure words 'without the city,' v. 20; the appearance of 'another angel,' v. 15, in contrast with the Messiah of v. 14; 'another angel' in vv. 17 f. as a harvester coördinate with the Messiah, as it were a second judge of the earth (see Com. *in loc.*). The passage then, it is supposed, (*a*) may have been taken up here by our Apocalyptist, without observance of his orderly plan, as one among isolated oracles incorporated; (*b*) or it may have stood as the close of an earlier form of our Apocalypse, the later inconsistent chapts. of the book being additions by another hand; (*c*) or it may be used by our author as referring to only a part of the judgment; or a preliminary judgment. Some follow Vischer in assigning the passage to a Jewish document, *e.g.* Pfleiderer, Sabatier, Spitta, Weyland; others make the original to have been Christian, *e.g.* Volter, Erbes, J. Weiss. Bousset supposes that the author has here used an apocalyptic fragment, and has worked it over from a representation of the final judgment into that of a preliminary judgment; and in transforming the world-judgment into a subordinate one he has transformed the world-judge, the Messiah, into an angel; *i.e.* the person of v. 14 is with him an angel, hence 'another angel' in vv. 15, 17. The fragment perhaps followed that used in 11¹⁻¹³, which ended with the punishment of Jerusalem; a judgment of those 'without the city' might then have followed naturally in the fragment, and the Apocalyptist has retained that expression unchanged in v. 20.

But the vision certainly cannot be understood to describe a preliminary judgment, which is to take place before the final doom. The universal use of the figures employed here shows that the judgment here symbolized is the great judgment of the last day. See pp. 661 f. On the other hand all interpretations of the passage which rest upon theories of Jewish apocalypses as the basis of the book, or of extensive redactions of a **primi-**

tive Christian apocalypse, only increase the supposed difficulties. The Apocalyptist who gave us the present form of the book could not have seen in these two visions a full revelation of the last days; those days included in his expectation many events not mentioned here, *e.g.* the reward of the righteous, the resurrection, and the final glory. To suppose that the author should take over, as an isolated fragment, the close of some apocalypse, and then continue in his book with a series of events which must precede the End chronologically, or to suppose that a redactor, while leaving unrevised a vision of the End here, should add a new story of the End as yet to come are suppositions which imply in our book a purely mechanical method of composition at variance with the fact everywhere apparent. It must be that the visions are not meant to represent the End as entering here. For the significance of the passage in this connection, and for the phrases to which objection is raised, see Summary, pp. 280 f., and the Com. *in loc.* As regards the form of the visions and some of the details it is plain that traditional representations are followed (see Com.) Whether a familiar apocalyptic fragment may in the use of any phrase have been before the author's mind is a question whose importance may easily be exaggerated.

XV.–XVI. — *The seven last plagues, the plagues of the bowls — the third woe.* See pp. 281 ff.

The last plagues. As in all such prophecies, these plagues are sent as punishments ; the bowls are bowls of God's wrath (15^1, 16^1), poured out on those who bear the mark of the Beast or are otherwise characterized as the enemies of God, *e.g.* $16^{2, 6, 9}$. At the same time there is not wanting here the thought that the plagues have a relation to the call to repentance (14^7), and that the possibility of their enforcing this call forms also a part of the divine motive in the visitation ; this is implied in the Apocalyptist's express mention of the failure to repent on the part of those who are thus visited, $16^{9, 11}$; see on 9^{20}. The righteous and the wicked alike might seem exposed to the horrors of some of the plagues, *e.g.* the third and the fourth, but the Apocalyptist is here wholly concerned with the punishment of the wicked, and the righteous are left out of sight. The disregard of logical necessity is not surprising in visions. The context makes clear that only the wicked are thought of. The plagues follow one another in close succession ; the world is now moving quickly toward the judgment. It is doubtful whether the Apocalyptist means to emphasize especially a difference in severity between this series of visitations and those of the seal and trumpet series, though these are of wider extent in their effects. The fifth and sixth plagues of the trumpet-series (chapt. 9) would be thought as agonizing as any in this series. The culminating effect of this series added to the others, as well as of the advancing steps within the series itself, is found in the overwhelming force of accumulated woe, as blow follows blow ; see p. 555. The significance of the plagues as a manifestation of God's wrath is more distinctly expressed in this series than in either of the other two.

The seven bowl-plagues as the third woe. The absence of a distinct designation of the third woe in the seventh trumpet-series gives perplexity to the casual reader of the Revelation, as well as to the critic. In 8^{13}, in the midst of the trumpet-visions, an angel proclaims to all the world that three 'woes' for those that dwell on the earth shall follow, each in turn, the sounding of the last three trumpets. The first two of these follow at once (chapt. 9) upon the sounding of the two succeeding trumpets (the fifth and sixth in the order of the trumpet-series from the beginning), and the certain coming of the third is again announced twice, 9^{12}, 11^{14}. The important place which the three woes occupy in the author's plan is evident; they are the last three great calamities in the course of the 'tribulations' sent upon the world before the final issue. As the seventh trumpet is the last and ushers in the movements which are to follow to the end (10^7), so its 'woe,' the third, is to form the closing scene in the pre-messianic visitations. It is inconceivable then that the third woe should (as some suppose) be wanting in the Apocalyptist's portrayal of the events following the sounding of the seventh trumpet, though no particular visitation is, as in the case of the first two, expressly designated by this term. But its general character and the place to be given to it are indicated by the announcements of it and by the account of the two other woes. Like the first and second woes, it would be a terrible supernatural agency working in the visible world and inflicting agony and horror on the enemies of God ; and it would stand as the last of such agencies before the parousia. Like the others, it would be primarily punitive in its purpose, but at the same time there would be present a divine motive to lead to repentance — a motive however not realized; see pp. 554, 668. These conditions are fulfilled completely in the bowl-plagues, but in no other event of the seventh trumpet-period. The occurrences mentioned in 11^{19}, or 12^{12}, taken by some interpreters as forming the third woe, do not possess the character nor hold the place required. See, further, on 12^{12}, and p. 672.

While the first and second woes consist each of a single plague, this third, as the last, the one in which the wrath of God is finished (15^1) is sevenfold; it is thus symbolized as complete. It takes its place as the seventh in the full list of seven trumpet plagues. The difficulty in the remoteness of the bowl-visions from the announcement, 'Behold the third woe cometh quickly,' 11^{14}, has been spoken of in part above, pp. 607 f. In fact it is apparent rather than real; for all that intervenes between that announcement and the introduction of this paragraph is in reality preparatory to the events now to come in the seventh trumpet-period. Chaps. 12–13 are episodic (see pp. 275 f.); $11^{15 b–19}$ and $14^{1–5}$ are anticipative hymns; $14^{6–20}$ is a prefatory announcement of the future judgment (see notes *in loc.*). After the announcement of 11^{14}, the first actual movement which takes place in the earth and directly touches those for whom the three woes are proclaimed (8^{13}) is this very outburst of the bowl-plagues. For the use of the word ταχύ, *quickly*, in 11^{14} see p. 608. It is not difficult to see why the close of the bowl-series is not followed, as in the case of the first and second woes (9^{12}, 11^{14}), by the announcement, 'The third woe is past,' for what follows here immediately, chaps. 17–19^5, is only a fuller expansion of a part of the bowl-series, *i.e.* of 16^{19}; the new paragraph is really a part of. the third woe, and continues with the activities of the angels of the bowl-series; see on 16^{17}, 17^1. In the first woe the Apocalyptist added in $9^{7–11}$ a fuller description of what was given in the earlier part (see notes *in loc.*); so here the destruction of Rome announced in 16^{19} is, because of its importance in the author's eschatology, expanded fully in the following chaps. Similarly what is seen in the sixth plague, $16^{12–16}$, is the preparation for the great conflict described in $19^{11–21}$; the latter is the completion of the plague here announced; see pp. 281, 284 — it is a part of the third woe. And here too an angel of the bowl-series is the intermediary, 19^{9-10}.

The recognition of the bowl-plagues as the third woe has important bearing on the question of the composition of the Apocalypse. According to this interpretation the program of the three woes, interwoven with the trumpet-series which was introduced in chapt. 8, is completed in a manner which accords with the first two woes in nature and purpose, and which gives to the series the climax anticipated in the outset. Thus the bowl-series not only looks back to the members with which it is organically connected; it also looks forward to two crowning events now to follow, the destruction of Rome and the battle of the Great Day. The whole portion of the book which is thus, in its outline at least, brought into one scheme, chapts. 8–19, can be reasonably regarded in its present form as the work of only one hand.

The relation of the bowl-plagues to the Egyptian plagues and to those of the trumpet-series. Each one of the bowl-plagues may be seen to contain some reminiscence of the Egyptian plagues, yet only in the first and third, the noisome sore and the changing of the drinking water into blood, is there close imitation (cf. Ex. 9^{10}, $7^{20\,f.}$). For the most part the suggestions evidently derived from the Mosaic miracles are taken up and used with free modification. The Egyptian plague of blood (Ex. 7^{20}) furnishes the starting-point of both the second and the third bowl-plagues; but in the latter series a plague of the sea is introduced, as in 8^8, in distinction from the rivers and fountains; and the blood of the sea is here coagulated and decaying. The fifth bowl-plague is suggested in part by the Egyptian plague of darkness (Ex. 10^{22}), but here the principal effect is not alone the horror of the darkness, but the accompanying physical tortures. Possibly the Egyptian plague of darkness, interpreted as due to a smiting of the sun, as in 8^{12}, may have suggested also the fourth bowl-plague, though the effect here is entirely different. In the sixth plague the single feature of the drying up of the waters to afford a passage goes back ultimately to Ex. 14^{21}; the essential part of the plague is entirely dissimilar. The thunder, lightning, and hail in the seventh plague are perhaps suggested by Ex. 9^{23-25}, but in the bowl-plague these are altogether subordinate to the other effects. Such a comparison with the Egyptian plagues is of value as showing the probable sources of various factors in the bowl-plagues, and at the same time the great freedom of the author in using suggestions.

A comparison of the bowl-series with that of the trumpets (chapts. 8–9) is made clear by a tabular conspectus.

The Trumpet-Series	The Bowl-Series
1. Hail, fire, and blood; a third part of the trees are destroyed.	The bowl poured upon the earth; the noisome sore.
2. A third part of the sea becomes blood.	The whole sea becomes blood, coagulated and decaying.
3. A third part of the drinking water becomes wormwood.	The drinking water becomes blood.
4. A third part of the sun, moon, and stars darkened.	The sun smites with fire.
5. Hellish locusts.	Darkness with tortures.
6. Myriads of hellish horse from the Euphrates.	The Euphrates dried up for passage of kings from the east; demons gather the kings of the earth for battle.
7.	Great convulsions in nature; Babylon and the other cities of the nations destroyed.

It will be seen from this table that there are close resemblances between the two schemes. In the first four members in each series, the plague touches directly the earth, the sea, the drinking waters, and the sun respectively, and in the same order. There is in both series the same departure from the Egyptian plagues in the insertion of a plague of the sea, and this stands second in each series and before the plague of the rivers and fountains. In the sixth member in each a plague comes from the Euphrates. There can be no question, then, that the bowl-series is influenced by the trumpet-series. But there are striking differences between the two. In the trumpet-series the seventh member is wanting. Some would put here the lightnings, etc., of 11¹⁹, counting these the seventh plague, because the seventh trumpet has sounded just before, 11⁵. But these commotions announced in 11¹⁹ are the conventional symbols of God's wrath, which in this connection is about to be visited on the wicked in fulfilment of his covenant, see notes *in loc.* As a plague in the trumpet-series they would not form visitations parallel with the terrible tortures of the fifth and sixth plagues in that series; they could not form the third woe; see p. 669. Furthermore it is clear from the table that no one of the bowl-series is an exact duplicate of any member of the trumpet-series. In the sixth the scourge of the Parthian hordes (see on 9¹⁴) shows its influence in both series, but in the trumpet member the relation of these to the war on the Beast is wanting, as is also the important factor of the demons sent forth to gather the kings to battle. Of the bowl-series the first (the noisome sore), the fourth, a part of the sixth, and the important part of the seventh (the fall of Rome), have no parallels in the trumpet-series. The fifth member of the trumpet-series has nothing akin to it in the other series.

Taking into account now the data furnished in these comparisons we reach the pretty certain conclusion that as regards the *essential nature* of the plagues the bowl-series cannot be said to have derived anything from the trumpet-series, as independent of the Egyptian; the striking resemblance in form and order pointed out above does not relate to significant features. Therefore the view of many critics that the bowl-series is an imitation of the trumpet-series added by a later hand (see pp. 689 f.) is improbable. The divergence of the bowl-series from that of the trumpets in the introduction of dissimilar matter, and in the omission of matter contained in the earlier series, is too great to warrant a hypothesis of imitation. The resemblances which appear in the comparison are accounted for more certainly by the supposition that the author of both series is the same person, who starts from the familiar Egyptian plagues, modifying his material freely, and following in the second series to some extent the form and outline which he had already adopted in the first. See p. 690.

XV. 1. See p. 282. This verse announces in a summary way the subject which, beginning in v. 5, is carried out in full to the end of the paragraph (16^{21}). It forms a descriptive title of the entire section, as 17^{1b} announces the topic of chaps. 17–19^5. Verses 5–6 in which the angels are first seen coming from the opened tabernacle do not form a repetition of this verse, which is not meant to announce the actual entrance of the angels at this point. The office of v. 1 as a kind of title-leaf of the vision might doubtless have been made clearer, but this lack cannot, in view of our Apocalyptist's manner, warrant a theory of different documents combined here by a redactor (see p. 688). The method of structure does not differ essentially from the writer's habit of introducing a general or comprehensive statement of what is afterward taken up in fuller detail; cf. 8^2, 12^6, 21^2, see p. 242. — **ἄλλο σημεῖον, μέγα, κτλ.**, *another wonder, great and marvelous :* a contrast with chapt. 14 may be intended, but better with the σημεῖον μέγα of 12^1. See note there for the meaning of σημεῖον. — **μέγα καὶ θαυμαστόν**, *great and marvelous :* not merely the appearance of the angels is meant, but all that follows to the end of the vision, 16^{21}. — **ἔχοντας πληγάς**, *having plagues :* i.e. having the duty of inflicting the plagues ; for ἔχω in this relation, see Thayer *s.v.* I. 2, k. The interpretation, having the bowls which contain the plagues, is not sufficiently comprehensive. — **ἑπτά**, *seven :* the complete number, see p. 670. Cf. Lv. $26^{18,\ 21,\ 24,\ 28}$. — **τὰς ἐσχάτας**, *the last :* the last in the series of plagues sent upon the world before the End. The

words are appositional and emphatic ; the following words,
'for in them is finished,' etc., explain why these are the last;
in them the wrath of God, as operative in the pre-messianic
punishments, reaches its end, the world remains impenitent
through all, and with the close of these is ripe for judgment.
It is not meant that God's wrath against his enemies will no
longer exist ; the bowl-plagues do not include the final judgment. — ἐτελέσθη : prophetic aorist.

2–4. See p. 282.   These verses contain one of the author's
anticipatory hymns sung as it were from the standpoint of the
end of a great movement which is about to begin ; see pp.
244 ff.   The saints are foreseen standing in the throne-room of
heaven after all is past, and praising God for his judgments.
While the language is general and includes all God's judgments on the wicked, there is special reference to the bowl-
plagues in which such judgments are finished.   As an anticipatory hymn the passage can cause no difficulty on the ground
of disturbing the connection; see p. 688 f. — ὡς θάλασσαν
ὑαλίνην, as it were a sea of glass: i.e. what appeared like a
glassy sea.   For the meaning, see on 4⁶. — μεμιγμένην πυρί,
mingled with fire : perhaps the flashing light reflected from the
glass-like pavement of the throne-room is meant.   As the
representation of a sea in the heavens, common in apocalyptic
imagery, is traceable to the appearance of the sky and the
clouds, the figure of the fire may perhaps go back ultimately
to the lightnings (Bouss.) ; at all events it is here merely a
factor in the splendor of the scene ; no symbolical meaning,
such as the presence of God's anger (so, many com.) is probable: A reference to the Red Sea (so, some) is purely fanciful ;
see below on The Song of Moses, p. 676 ff. — τοὺς νικῶντας :
the timeless present, the victors ; see on 14⁴. — καὶ ἐκ τῆς εἰκόνος
κτλ., that is, over his image, etc. : the words make more specific
the general expression ἐκ τοῦ θηρίου, over the Beast.   The prep.
ἐκ, from, is used with reference to the idea of coming off victorious from.   The meaning of the words is that these had not
worshiped the image of the Beast nor received as a mark the
number of his name ; cf. 13¹⁶⁻¹⁷. — ἑστῶτας ἐπὶ τὴν θάλασσαν,
standing upon the sea : not by, for the pavement before the
throne is referred to ; see on v. 2. — κιθάρας τοῦ θεοῦ, harps of

God: such as belong to the heavenly worship ; cf. 5⁸, 14²,
1 Chron. 16⁴², ὄργανα τῶν ᾠδῶν τοῦ θεοῦ. — τὴν ᾠδὴν Μωυσέως
κτλ., *the song of Moses and the Lamb:* see pp. 282, 676 ff. —
τοῦ δούλου τοῦ θεοῦ, *the servant of God:* a common epithet of
Moses ; cf. Ex. 14³¹, Jos. 14⁷, 1 Chron. 6⁴⁹, Dan. 9¹¹. See on
1¹. — μεγάλα . . . τὰ ἔργα σου, *great and marvelous are thy
works;* cf. Ps. 111², 139¹⁴. The hymn is made up of utterances
from the O. T. — κύριε . . . παντοκράτωρ, *O Lord God, the
Almighty:* cf. Am. 4¹³ LXX, Rev. 4⁸, 11¹⁷, 16⁷, *al.* The epithet
is especially appropriate here, where God's great works of
judgment are spoken of. — δίκαιαι . . . αἱ ὁδοί σου, *righteous
and true are thy ways;* cf. Dt. 32⁴, ⁴¹, Ps. 145¹⁷. — ὁ βασιλεὺς
τῶν ἐθνῶν, *thou king of the nations:* cf. Jer. 10⁷. The reading
ὁ β. τῶν αἰώνων, *king of the ages,* RV, means the ruler of the
world periods and all that belongs to them, whether the present, or the coming eternal æon which follows the parousia. —
τίς οὐ μὴ φοβηθῇ, *who shall not fear?* Jer. 10⁷. For οὐ μή with
aor. subjv. equivalent to emphatic fut., see Blass § 64, 5, Burton
§ 172. — δοξάσει τὸ ὄνομά σου, *glorify thy name:* cf. Ps. 86⁹.
— ὅσιος, *holy;* cf. Dt. 32⁴ LXX. God's holiness is given as a
reason (ὅτι, *for*) for fearing and glorifying his name ; but the
holiness here meant is not God's sinlessness, a thought foreign
to this connection ; it is his unapproachable majesty and
power ; cf. 16⁵. These are the only places in the N. T. where
the word is applied to God. For this meaning of *holiness,* cf.
Ps. 99³, 111⁹; see Skinner in Hast. II. 397. — πάντα τὰ ἔθνη
. . . ἐνώπιόν σου, *all nations shall come and worship before thee;*
cf. Ps. 86⁹. The prediction that the nations shall come and
worship before God, uttered here by the saints after the judgment, is of the same character as those of 20⁸ and 22² (said of
the nations though they had already been declared to be
destroyed, 19²¹). Such prophecies are taken over verbally
from the current Jewish expectations regarding the attitude of
the nations toward Jehovah and his people in the messianic
age ; cf. Is. 2²⁻⁴, 66²³ ; see pp. 52, 54. Without strict consistency the Apocalyptist uses these familiar prophecies to
declare the absolutely universal recognition of God in the
End ; see p. 161. The second ὅτι (*for*) clause establishes the
negative implied in the question by asserting the opposite ;

none shall fail to fear and glorify thy name, for all shall come, etc. The third ὅτι (*for*) clause gives the reason why all shall come and worship, *i.e.* because of the manifestation of God's righteous acts of judgment.

The song of Moses and the Lamb. The difficult question of the meaning of this title given to the hymn of the victorious saints must be approached through the interpretation of the hymn itself (vv. 3-4). The subject of praise as given in the first words is God's wondrous works; but this general term is made definite in the words immediately following. God's wondrous works as seen in his righteous and true ways are meant, and still more specifically at the end of the song, those righteous acts of judgment manifested in the sight of all. The word ἀληθινός, *true*, means here, as in general, *true to the ideal character* (see on 3⁷), and the two words, 'righteous' and 'true,' are closely connected; God is true to his character as a righteous judge. Now, that the righteous judgment meant here is the punishment of God's enemies is shown by the fact that it is these plagues sent upon the wicked which call forth the hymn in this place. And the ascriptions to the *righteous and true God*, repeating the language of the hymn and inserted in the following vision of the plagues, 16⁵⁻⁷, put this meaning beyond question. Compare also 19², ¹¹, where true and righteous judgments are spoken of with similar reference. There is nowhere in these two chapts. (15-16) allusion to a judgment awarding blessedness to the saints. The hymn then, like 16⁵⁻⁷, 19², is a song of praise for the just judgments visited upon the enemies of God's people. It corresponds with the prayers of the saints in 6¹⁰, 8³⁻⁵. See on 6¹⁰.

The common interpretation of the hymn, which makes it a song of praise for deliverance on the part of the saints, is entirely without support in the hymn itself; the saints say nothing of themselves or their victory, the whole is concerned with the acts of God with reference to the wicked. Very different are the songs celebrating the deliverance of the saints; cf. 7⁹ ff., 11¹⁷ f., 12¹⁰ ff., 14² f.. This song might have been put into the mouth of the angels, as in 19¹⁻³; instead it is assigned to the victorious saints; these form a fitting choir to sing of God's judgments upon their persecutors. They might have added words of exultation over their own victory, but of that there is nothing in the hymn.

The interpretation of the passage as a song of rejoicing over deliverance is based on the meaning wrongly given to its designation as the song of Moses and the song of the Lamb, and on the meaning also wrongly given to the representation of the singers as standing on (the shore of) a glassy sea. As Moses and Israel sang their song of deliverance by the Red Sea (Ex. 15), so the saints are thought to stand by the crystal sea in heaven victorious over the Beast, and led or taught by the Lamb sing their song of salvation. Or, as some take it, they sing the song whose subject is Moses and the Lamb, *i.e.* the deeds wrought by God through these. Of this, however, there is nothing in the contents of the hymn. The sea of glass in v. 2

is certainly the same as in 4⁶, the dazzling pavement of the court of heaven, a part of the splendor of the scene; there is no possible comparison with the Red Sea (on the words 'mingled with fire' see p. 674). The title 'The song of Moses,' etc., does not explain the hymn; the meaning of the title is rather to be sought through that of the hymn, which is clear.

The song of Moses is generally understood to allude to that of Ex. 15. There is, to be sure, a certain parallelism in the circumstances; vengeance is taken and God's people are delivered, and in each case the righteousness of God can be seen. Something of the same parallelism might, however, be found in the song of Deborah, Jg. 5, or in that of David, 2 S. 22. If the hymn of our passage be compared with that of Ex. 15, an essential difference appears. Here the wonders of God are viewed as exhibiting his truth to his righteous character, and as thus leading all nations to worship him. But in the song of the Israelites there is not a word of his truth and righteousness in the punishment inflicted; the keynote of that song is 'Jehovah is a man of war' (v. 3), with swift power he dashes in pieces his enemies, and the nations are struck with terror and trembling before him. Moreover in the hymn of the saints there is no certain verbal reminiscence of the passage in Exodus. It seems improbable then that this hymn contains any allusion to the song of deliverance at the Red Sea. On the other hand, the parallelism with the song of Moses in Dt. 32 is striking. After the exordium of that poem, verse 4 lays down the thesis upon which all the following words are based (cf. Driver ICC. *in loc.*): 'All his ways are justice: a God of faithfulness and without iniquity, just and right is he.' This parallelism is striking in the LXX: ἀληθινὰ τὰ ἔργα αὐτοῦ, καὶ πᾶσαι αἱ ὁδοὶ αὐτοῦ κρίσεις· θεὸς πιστός, καὶ οὐκ ἔστιν ἀδικία· δίκαιος καὶ ὅσιος Κύριος. And again in the conclusion, v. 43, an effect is declared to be wrought upon the nations by God's acts of judgment similar to that spoken of in the hymn of the saints: 'Praise his people, ye nations,' RVmrg; see Driver *in loc.* It is true that much of the phraseology of the Apocalyptist's hymn is also found scattered through other parts of the O. T., but the title, Song of Moses, points to none of these, and none of them combines so many expressions of which we have reminiscences here. It is moreover to be noticed that, while Ex. 15 is the song of Israel as well as the song of Moses, the Deuteronomic song is expressly described as *the song of Moses*, as one which he wrote and spoke and taught to the people, Dt. 31¹⁹, ²², ³⁰, 32⁴⁴. It seems reasonably clear therefore that the Apocalyptist had the Deuteronomic song in mind, and that as he followed that poem in thought and phraseology in framing the song of the saints, he meant also to give to the latter this familiar title, which should call attention to the identity of theme in the two songs.

As a further designation of the Apocalyptist's hymn, 'The Song of the Lamb' is added. The position of λέγοντες, *saying*, after both designations and introducing the words of the hymn, shows that the writer had not in mind two separate hymns, of which the second, that of the Lamb, has been omitted (so, some; cf. p. 689), but that the words given form the song of the Lamb as well as that of Moses. In seeking the sense in which the hymn can be called thus, we must, as before, start from the hymn itself. The meaning then seems to be clearly this: as the hymn declaring the righteousness of God shown in punishment is called the song of Moses because its thought and language are uttered by Moses in his well-known song, so it it called the song of the Lamb, because it is also, as it were, uttered by the Lamb, not in words but in the acts that form an essential part of this whole revelation of the last things. The Revelation is a book of God's righteous judgment upon the powers of evil, and the Lamb is the foremost agent in the revelation and execution of this judgment; he breaks the seals of the roll telling of the righteous acts of God through the whole period of the last times till the end; he, called Faithful and True, judging and warring in righteousness (19¹¹), leads the armies of heaven in the great conflict with the Beast and his hosts; he is the harvester at the end of the world (14¹⁴ᶠ·).   The connection denoted by καί, *and*, between the two titles of the song would be clearer in our idiom if we translated, *which is also the song of the Lamb* (cf. Ac. 13⁹). The thought of the Apocalyptist in this twofold descriptive title is evident: the righteous acts of God's judgment hymned by the saints in his presence after all is finished are but the consummation of what Moses and the Lamb, the old and the new dispensations, had declared. The hymn is certainly conceived to be sung after all is consummated, for the saints are not represented in the book as admitted to the court of God's presence in heaven before the end. Moreover, the singers are *the* victors, all those who come off victorious over the Beast, an issue not decided till the Beast is overthrown. The apparent future events of v. 4 are not against this; see note there. While the bowl-plagues preceding the end are the immediate occasion of the introduction of the anticipatory hymn, this contemplates also the final sequel of what is thus begun.

XV. 5. The plagues announced in v. 1 are about to begin. The immediate preparation is described in 15⁵–16¹. See p. 282. Cf. the preparation for the trumpet-plagues, 8²⁻⁶. — ἠνοίγη ὁ **ναός**, *the sanctuary was opened:* once before, the opening of the sanctuary has been made a detail in the scene ; in 11¹⁹ it was to reveal the ark of God's covenant; here it is for the exit of the seven angels, as coming from the immediate presence of God. The *sanctuary* meant here is defined by the following appositional gen. The tabernacle of the wilderness was called the 'tabernacle of the testimony' (*e.g.* Ex. 38²¹, Num. 10¹¹, Ac. 7⁴⁴), because it contained the ark, or the tables, of the testimony, the ten commandments, which declared the nature and will of God. See Hast. IV. 725, Westcott *Heb.* 235. For the critical difficulty raised by the first appearance of the angels here, thought to be at variance with the announcement of v. 1, see note there.

6–8. οἱ ἑπτὰ ἄγγελοι, *the seven angels:* the art. probably designates them as those mentioned in v. 1, though possibly the seven presence-angels are meant as in 8². — ἔχοντες . . . πληγάς, *having the seven plagues :* not the bowls containing the plagues, for these are given to them afterwards, v. 7. For the meaning, see on v. 1. — λίνον, *linen :* the word commonly means *flax,* but sometimes as here *linen clothes,* for which βύσσινος is used elsewhere in Rev. If the reading λίθον be adopted, it would refer to *precious stones* worn as ornament ; cf. 17⁴, 18¹⁶, Ezk. 28¹³. The white, glistening raiment does not mark the angels as priests (so, some com.), but as celestial beings ; see on 3⁴. Their service is not priestly. — ἔν . . . ζώων, *one of the four Living Creatures :* for the assignment of the service to one of these, see p. 282. — φιάλας, *bowls :* the φιάλη was a shallow bowl-shaped vessel used especially for drinking and libations. — The cloud or smoke is a familiar symbol of the presence of God in glory and power ; cf. Ex. 19¹⁸, Is. 6⁴, Ezk. 10⁴. — οὐδεὶς ἐδύνατο εἰσελθεῖν κτλ., *no one was able to enter into the sanctuary,* etc.: there does not appear any certain intimation that the unapproachableness of God here emphasized is associated with his wrath, as many com. take it ; it is rather due to the awfulness of his manifested presence, as in Ex. 24¹⁶, 40³⁴⁻³⁸, 1 K. 8¹⁰ ᶠ·, 2 Chron. 5¹³ ᶠ·, 7¹ᶠ· In these O. T. passages reference is made to this special manifestation for a limited time. So here God's presence in the tabernacle in the cloud of his glory is coexistent with the course of the plagues ; these proceed from, and are wrought by, his power, specifically mentioned here ; he is present in his sanctuary *in operation* till his purpose of judgment is accomplished. The sanctuary becomes filled (ἐγεμίσθη incept. aor.) with the cloud of his glory at the beginning and continues thus till the plagues are finished ; cf. 16¹⁷, 'a loud voice from the sanctuary saying, It is done.'

XVI. 1. μεγάλης φωνῆς, *a great voice:* that of God, as shown by 15⁸. The angels have received the bowls but await the command of God to begin their service, as do the harvester and the vintager in 14¹⁴⁻²⁰. Thus all is linked directly to

God. — εἰς τὴν γῆν, *into the earth:* the departure from the command in the case of the fourth and seventh angels, who pour their bowls upon the sun and the air, vv. 8, 17, is only apparent ; the bowls are poured upon that from which plagues come upon the dwellers on the earth.

2–3. The bowls are now poured out one after another and their plagues fall upon the worshipers of the Beast, vv. 2–21. See pp. 283 f., 668 ff. — The first plague is like the Egyptian plague of boils ; Ex. 9[10]. The victims of the scourge are declared to be the worshipers of the Beast ; that this is true of the other plagues is clear, though not expressly stated. — With the second plague which turns the sea into blood, cf. Ex. 7[20 f.], and the second trumpet-plague, 8[8 f.] Here the whole sea is changed to the coagulated and decaying blood of the dead, and all marine life perishes ; but the corresponding trumpet-plague affects only a third part of the sea and its life. — ζωῆς : gen. of quality.

4–7. The third plague turns the drinking water into blood ; cf. Ex. 7[20]. The corresponding trumpet-plague turns it into wormwood (8[11]). There is here a certain retribution in kind, which evokes praise from the angel who presides over the waters (see p. 445). The words celebrating the justice and holiness of God in this judgment are an echo of 15[3 f.], and have the same meaning (see note there). The same is also true of the words of the personified altar, v. 7. — For the parenthesis, vv. 5–7, see p. 283. — ἐγένετο, v. 4 : the subj. is τὰ ὕδατα. — ὁ ὢν καὶ ὁ ἦν, *who art and who wast :* see on 1[4]. The addition ὁ ἐρχόμενος, *who art to come,* found in 1[4, 8], 4[8], is omitted here, because the End is now anticipated as so near that God can be thought of as already come ; see on 11[17]. — ὁ ὅσιος, *thou Holy One :* a voc. For the meaning, see on 15[4]. — ἁγίων καὶ προφητῶν, *saints and prophets :* cf. 11[18], 18[24] ; the former refers to Christians in general, the latter particularizes a class among these. For the use of καί, *and,* in such a connection, cf. Mk. 16[7], Ac. 1[14]. — ἤκουσα τοῦ θυσιαστηρίου κτλ., *I heard the altar saying,* etc.: the altar is personified. Reference may be made here to the martyrs, whose souls are beneath the altar (6[9]), or to the saints whose prayers for judgment are accompanied by the incense offered on the altar 8[3–5]. In either case the meaning is that God is praised, because the prayer of the saints for judgment is answered in this plague. — ἀληθιναὶ καὶ δίκαιαι κτλ., *true and righteous*, etc. : echoing 15³. — Verses 5–6 are suggested naturally by the character of the retribution in this plague ; and that ascription in praise of God's just judgment leads to this response of the personified altar in a similar tone (v. 7). As regards formal structure the passage divides the seven plagues into two groups of three and four — one of the Apocalyptist's characteristics ; see p. 253. It is noticeable that in the first three the preposition after ἐξέχεεν, *poured out*, is εἰς, *into ;* in the last four ἐπί, *upon.*

8–9. In the fourth plague power is given to the sun to scorch men with great heat. They see the hand of God in this and the other plagues, and so far from repenting are hardened to blasphemy ; see p. 668. With this result of the plague contrast that of the visitations recorded in 11¹³. — αὐτῷ, *it:* the sun, not the angel, as shown by the analogy of the other plagues. — καῦμα μέγα : acc. of kindred meaning ; see Blass § 34, 3, Win. § 32, 2. δοῦναι : infin. of result ; see Blass § 69, 3 ; Burton § 371. On this phrase, 'give God glory,' see on 11¹³.

10–11. The fifth bowl is poured out on the seat of the Beast's power and a plague of supernatural darkness (cf. Ex. 10²²) spreads over the whole Roman empire. Men gnaw their tongues in their distress. — τοῦ πόνου, *the distress:* the use of the art. and the sing. as distinguished from the pl. in the next clause (τῶν πόνων) indicate that the particular distress caused by the darkness is meant. But darkness alone does not cause physical pain, such as is here described. The meaning apparently is that the preternatural darkness causing distress and terror intensifies the pain suffered from the other plagues ; these are conceived to continue present in the later visitations, as is seen from the pl. 'these plagues,' v. 9, and the words 'their pains and sores,' v. 11, where ἑλκῶν, *sores*, refers to the first plague, v. 2. For a vivid picture of the torment caused by the Egyptian darkness see Wis. chapt. 17. Spitta (170 f.) exaggerating the difficulty in attributing pain to the darkness supposes this plague to be an awkward imitation of 9²⁻¹¹ ; the pain, he thinks, is that inflicted by the sting of the locusts, and the darkness that caused by the vast swarms of the locusts, likened to smoke and darkening the sun. — τῶν πόνων, καὶ τῶν ἑλκῶν, *their pains, and their sores:* the use of καί, *and*, adding a clause which particularizes a part (τῶν ἑλκῶν) of the whole (τῶν πόνων) is the same as in the words, 'the saints and the prophets,' v. 6. — The impenitence and blasphemy which persisted through four visitations (v. 9) are here noted as persisting still through five (v. 11).

12. The sixth bowl is poured out on the Euphrates and this is dried up, that a passage may be prepared for the kings from the East. Three demons in the form of frogs come forth from the mouth of the dragon, the Beast, and the false prophet, to gather together the kings of the whole earth for the battle of the great day of God; these are gathered together into the place called Harmagedon, vv. 12–16. That this plague differs from the others is apparent. The others visit upon men the pain and torture of marvelous operations and convulsions in nature; but in the sixth there is no such effect. In this respect this plague bears a relation to the others similar to that of the fifth seal (6⁹ ᶠ·) to the other members of its series; it looks forward, and contributes to a coming result. The immediate effects of the outpouring of the sixth bowl help to bring in calamities which are to fall on Rome and the whole world.

The drying up of the Euphrates, that a way might be opened for the scattered Israelites to return from the East, is prophesied in Is. 11¹⁵ ᶠ·, 2 Es. 13⁴⁷; the Jordan became dry before the Israelites entering Canaan, Jos. 3¹³⁻¹⁷. The ultimate origin of these miracles of history and prophecy is the miracle at the Red Sea (Ex. 14²¹ ᶠ·), as is seen from Is. 11¹⁶. So the Apocalyptist here sees the great barrier that held back the hordes of the East removed by the drying up of the Euphrates. Unquestionably he has in view here, as in the sixth trumpet-vision (9¹⁴ ᶠᶠ·), to which the sixth bowl-vision is in part parallel, the coming of the Parthian hosts widely dreaded in the Roman world, and now forming one of the eschatological events connected with the expected return of Nero; see on 9¹⁴ and pp. 400 ff.

13–14. In the second part of the sixth bowl-vision the dragon and his two subalterns, as seen in chaps. 12–13, are introduced. Nothing is said of their entrance, or of the place

where they are seen ; the only important fact is that from them
proceed the demons who are to work the marvel of causing the
kings of the whole world to unite in the service of the Beast
and to come together into one place in readiness for the battle
of the great day. The kings of this passage are distinguished
from those of v. 12; those of v. 12 are the kings of the East,
those of this passage are the kings of the whole world, who
will be allied with the Beast in a future event lying beyond
the events of this bowl-plague. What is here described is only
the *preparation* for the great battle (19¹¹ ᶠᶠ·). These kings of
the whole world are identical with those spoken of in 17¹²⁻¹⁴,
where the symbolical number *ten* is given to them (see p. 669),
and where their function in the war with the Lamb is the same
as that described here. Their united gift of their service to
the Beast is here attributed to the influence of the three
demons; in 17¹⁷ it is said to be wrought by God. But there
is no necessary disagreement; the vision of the lying spirit
sent by Jehovah to entice Ahab to battle, 1 K. 22¹⁹⁻²², furnishes a precise parallel. This vision of the sixth bowl combines two distinct traditions, that of a Parthian host coming
with the returning Nero to conquer the Roman world (v. 12),
and that of the great assault of the united kings of the earth
upon God's people in the last days (vv. 13–14; see on 14²⁰ and
p. 36). It might be supposed that the Apocalyptist in the first
part (v. 12) has in mind solely the destruction of Rome by the
Neronic Antichrist and his Parthian allies, an event falling
within the period of the bowl-plagues; while in the second
part (vv. 13–14) he is looking forward to the later event, the
final battle with the Messiah described in 19¹¹ ᶠᶠ·. But it is
doubtful whether he here conceives a historic program for
the future so distinctly articulated; certainly in 17¹²⁻¹⁷ a distinction is not made between two classes of the Beast's allies.

πνεύματα τρία : we might expect a pred. partic. ἐκπορευόμενα;
its place is supplied by the rel. clause, ἃ ἐκπορεύεται. — ὡς βά-
τραχοι, *like frogs:* i.e. in form. The loathsome appearance of
the frog makes the representation appropriate ; possibly it is
suggested by the Egyptian plague, Ex. 8⁶, but this seems
remote. It is more likely that the idea is taken from some
mythological tradition. The frog figures in Persian mythology

(Völter *Offenb.* 114). A certain parallel to this passage is found in Hermas *Vis.* IV. 1, 6, where fiery locusts are seen coming out of the mouth of a fabulous beast. — εἰσὶν γὰρ πνεύματα κτλ., *for there exist spirits of demons which work miracles*, or *for they are spirits of demons working miracles :* of the two constructions possible the second takes the words as explaining the designation ' unclean spirits ' ; they are so called because they are the spirits of demons, etc. But the familiar term does not need explanation, and this clause can hardly be said to add anything not contained in the designation itself. The first construction takes the words as explaining the power of the spirits, *for there are spirits that work miracles.* This latter is perhaps better as giving due significance to ποιοῦντα σημεῖα. The sentence εἰσὶν γὰρ . . . σημεῖα is parenthetical. The rel. clause ἃ ἐκπορεύεται κτλ., *which go forth*, etc., should be joined directly with πνεύματα τρία, *three spirits*, since some statement of the purpose of the appearance of these is needed, and the words εἶδον ἐκ κτλ. need completion. — These spirits, like the second beast 13¹³ ᶠ., work miracles to deceive ; thus they influence the kings to further the cause of the Beast. — πόλεμον : for the meaning, *battle*, cf. 9⁸. — τῆς ἡμέρας κτλ., *the great day:* not the destruction of Rome, but the later event, the day of the Lord's coming to the battle with the Beast.

15. The gathering of all the forces of the Beast for battle will open to the saints the supreme crisis. The mention of it moves the Apocalyptist to interject, in the name of the Lord, a warning that the day will come suddenly, when not looked for, as a thief in the night, and that the Christian must be watchful and ready. Such a warning in the midst of these prophecies is altogether appropriate, and it falls in with the writer's tendency to insert ejaculatory parentheses, see p. 244. There is then no ground for the theory of an interpolation or gloss ; so, Spitta, Völter, *al.* — ἔρχομαι ὡς κλέπτης, *I come as a thief:* see on 3³. — μακάριος, *blessed :* see on 1³. — ἵνα μὴ γυμνὸς κτλ., *that he may not walk naked*, etc. : the Christian will remain steadfast and prepared, as one who watching by night guards his garments, that he may have them at hand for need.

16. συνήγαγεν αὐτούς, *they gathered them together :* the subj. of the vb. is the spirits of v. 13. The kings of the earth are

assembled with their hosts in readiness for the battle, which
is to take place later, 19¹¹ ᶠᶠ·—'Ἀρμαγεδών, *Harmagedon:* on
the form of the word, see text. notes. The name here given
to the place where Satan's hosts are gathered and where doubtless the battle of 19¹¹ ᶠᶠ· is conceived to occur is unquestionably
purely mystical, whatever its origin. It is unknown to Heb.
literature, and it would be contrary to the Apocalyptist's use
of proper names to identify it, in its eschatological application,
with any place so called. See p. 250. He pronounces the
name to be Hebrew, but does not as in the case of Abaddon
(9¹¹) translate it, or explain it. He knows that most of his
readers, for whom a Heb. word must be translated, cannot
connect with it a specific meaning as regards locality or ety-
mological significance. We are therefore justified in inferring
that he does not attach importance to the name itself, but uses
it, whether inventing it or receiving it from tradition, merely
to give a certain precision to his picture. It is then an imaginary name for designating the scene of the great battle
between Antichrist and the Messiah.

As regards the origin of the name, the solution which has met with the
widest acceptance with scholars makes it a compound of הַר, *mountain*, and
the proper name מְגִדּוֹן, *Megiddo* (Greek Μαγεδδών, or Μαγεδών, among various
forms) the stronghold in the valley of Esdraelon near which, 'by the waters
of Megiddo' (Jg. 5¹⁹), Israel gained a decisive victory over the kings of
Canaan — a 'victory celebrated forever afterwards in the song of Deborah,
Jg. chapt. 5. The designation 'Mount Megiddo' thus derived is open to
the objection that the region is not a mountain, but a vast plain. The
Apocalyptist may however have started from the eschatological prophecy
which placed the slaughter of the nations in their last assault upon God's
people on 'the mountains of Israel,' Ezk. 38⁸⁻²¹, 39², ⁴, ¹⁷. It is noticeable
that in his prelude to the great battle he follows this very part of Ezk. ;
see on 19¹⁷ ᶠᶠ·. He may then be supposed to define the indefinite term 'the
mountains' by adding the name Megiddo, famed in Israel's history as the
place where Jehovah's enemies perished, Jg. 5³¹. But it must be acknowledged that this explanation is not free from artificiality. There is plausibility in the view (Gunkel 265 f. *al*) that the name is taken from some
apocalyptic myth current in tradition. For other explanations, which
have however not met with much favor, see En. Bib. I. 310 ; Hast. II. 304.

17. The seventh bowl is poured upon the air, and vast convulsions follow in the heavens and the earth. An earthquake
such as the world had never known before tears Rome into

three parts and overthrows the other cities of the nations; the cup of the fierceness of God's wrath is given to Rome, she is overwhelmed in a ruin only implied here, but announced in full in the next paragraph (17–19⁵). Hail of inconceivable magnitude falls upon men, who continue still impenitent, and blaspheme God because of the severity of the plague. Both in the vastness of the phenomena and in the fullness of style the Apocalyptist seeks to give to this bowl-plague a character conformed to its place as the last in the last series. Seven times he introduces the word μέγας, *great*, accumulation and repetition mark the phraseology (vv. 18, 19), the calamities surpass all that is known in the experience of men ; see p. 249. The visitation of Babylon (Rome) occupies a central place in the plague; with the fall of the capital city of the world-empire, the present order will be closed and Antichrist will assume universal sway. The significance of Rome's destruction (see p. 158) leads the Apocalyptist to present the subject in the powerful picture that follows (chapts. 17–19⁵).

φωνὴ μεγάλη, *a great voice :* that of God, as shown by ἀπὸ τοῦ θρόνου, *from the throne.* It was God's voice that in the outset sent the angels forth on their commission (v. 1), and now when the last bowl has been poured out, his voice is again heard declaring that his command is in this last plague accomplished. The word γέγονεν, *it is done* (cf. 21⁶, Lk. 14²²), *anticipates* the outcome of the plague in which the wrath of God is finished (see on 15¹). — **τοῦ ναοῦ, τοῦ θρόνου**, *the sanctuary, the throne :* the same blending of the heavenly sanctuary and Jehovah's throne-room appears here as in other places in the book, see p. 524.

18–19. **φωναί**, *voices :* see on 4⁵. — **οὕτω μέγας**, *so mighty* (RV): a repetition of τηλικοῦτος, *so great,* for emphasis; see on v. 17. — **ἡ πόλις ἡ μεγάλη**, *the great city :* cf. 17¹⁸, chapt. 18 *passim.* The context shows that Babylon (Rome) is meant; cf. 14⁸, chapts. 17–18. A reference to Jerusalem, as some take it, is altogether foreign to the bowl-plagues; the punishment of Jerusalem by earthquake and the repentance of its people have been given already in chapt. 11. The mention of 'the cities of the nations' and of Babylon in the following words does not imply that 'the great city' is distinguished from these

and must therefore be Jerusalem.   What is said of the great
city and the cities of the nations in v. 19 a is merely a part of
the description of the unprecedented violence of the earthquake; the effect on Rome, the foremost city, is mentioned
first, and then the cities of the nations in general are spoken of.
The former is not wholly destroyed, but rent into three parts;
the latter are completely overthrown.   This use of a simple
connective, *and*, in passing from a particular case to the rest of
the same class, where the relation would be expressed more
exactly by the words 'and the others' is an idiom not peculiar
to Greek; for its use in the N. T. cf. Rev. 18²⁴, Ac. 5²⁹,
Gal. 6¹⁶; see Blass § 81, 1, Win. § 58, 7, *b*, note.   From
speaking of the great earthquake, in which Rome apparently
suffered less severely than the other cities, the Apocalyptist
passes in v. 19 b to the special visitation sent upon her as the
supreme object of vengeance in this plague-series; she is
remembered before God and the cup of the fierceness of his
wrath is given her to drink — language evidently referring to
something beyond the effects of the earthquake, lighter in her
case than in the others; it implies the extremity of punishment
inflicted upon her, cf. 18⁶.   She herself is made to drink the
cup of wrath, which she has given to men and thereby according
to 18² ᶠ·, 14⁸ wrought her own utter ruin.   This special punishment of Rome is only alluded to here in passing, because it is
made the theme of a special paragraph, that which follows. —
We have not then in the book two disagreeing representations
of Rome's destruction, as some insist, one in this passage
attributing it to an earthquake, the other, in 17¹⁶, 18⁸, attributing it to fire and other plagues. — δοῦναι: epexeget. infin.; see
Burton § 375. — τοῦ οἴνου τοῦ θυμοῦ κτλ., *the wine of the wrath*,
etc.: see on 14⁸, ¹⁰.

20-21.   After allusion to the special vengeance on Rome
(v. 19 b), the Apocalyptist returns in these verses to the convulsions in nature.   For the separation of connected thoughts,
as common with the author, see p. 244. — πᾶσα νῆσος ἔφυγεν
κτλ., *every island fled away*, etc.: the language alludes to the
sinking of islands, etc., in violent earthquakes, not to the final
dissolution of the world expected at the end; the reign of Antichrist has yet to intervene.   See on 6¹⁴. — ὡς ταλαντιαία,

about the weight of a talent: the talent as a weight varied
greatly among different peoples and at different times, from
near sixty to more than double that number of pounds.   All
that is intended here is hailstones of inconceivable hugeness.

Textual notes, 15²–16¹⁷.   15² ᶠᶠ. R with some min inserts εκ του χαραγμα-
τος αυτου before εκ του αριθμου. — 3. των εθνων א°APQ most min vers edd;
των αιωνων א*C some min vers WH RV (probably due to 1 Tim. 1¹⁷) ; R
has των αγιων without Ms. authority. — 6. οι before εχοντες AC most min
RV edd; wanting in אPQ some min R; WH bracket. — λινον PQ most min
and vers R most edd ; λιθον AC some min vlg. Lch WH RV *al.;* καθαρον is
against λιθον, which is not supported by Ezk. 28¹³ LXX, nor by χρυσιον
καθαρον 21¹⁸; א has λινους.

16² ᶠᶠ. R with some min reads επι instead of εις before την γην. — 3. ζωης
AC one min vers edd ; ζωσα אPQ min vers R Sod. — 4. For εγενετο, A a few
min Prim Lch WHmrg *al* read εγενοντο. — 6. πιειν אPQ min most edd ; πειν
AC Ws Ti WH *al,* a contracted form; see Blass § 6, 5. — 7. Before του
θυσιαστηριον, R inserts αλλου εκ, similarly some Mss. of vlg. — 12. ανατολης
אCQ most min edd ; ανατολων A some min R Ws WHmrg RV. — 16. Ἁρ-
μαγεδών (Harmagedon).   The aspirate, not determined by the uncials,
appears in many min some vers and anc com, and is adopted by most edd,
the first syllable being identified with הַר; cf. WH *Introd.* 313.   The aspirate is wanting in some min and vers, some Mss. of vlg R.   The ending
-εδων, with single δ, is supported by אA many min and vers, and is adopted
by nearly all edd; R with Q some min and vers has -εδδων. WH reads ᵃΑρ
Μαγεδών. The shorter reading Μαγεδων, without the prefix, is found in Q
some min and vers. — 17. R with some min has εις instead of επι before τον
αερα.

Criticism of chapts. 15–16.   The principal objections urged in criticism of
these chapts. are the following.   (1) The paragraph as a whole is out of
place here.   After the appearance of the Son of man and the judgments
of the harvest and the vintage, *i.e.* after the end is reached (14¹⁴⁻²⁰), there
is no room for the seven plagues which are preliminary to the end; so,
Erbes, Weyland, Wellhausen, J. Weiss, *al.*   The series is a mere parallel
of the trumpet-plagues, and was added by another hand in imitation of
those. — But the announcement of the judgment in chapt. 14 does not proclaim it as entering at that point; those visions are anticipatory.   See
pp. 280, 661.   As regards parallelism with the trumpet-series see p. 690.
(2) Verse 15¹ in which the seven angels are seen in heaven having the seven
plagues is at variance with 15⁵ ᶠ., which represents them as first appearing
later, when the temple opens to give them exit.   A redactor is here combining or working over derived material; so, Weyland, Erbes, *al.*   But the
very difficulty of the verse in its relation to 15⁵ raises doubt as to its insertion by any hand other than that of the author of the paragraph as a whole.
See further, p. 673.   (3) A song of victory praising God for accomplished
judgment (15²⁻⁴) interrupts the connection between vv. 1 and 5; it does

not belong here with plagues, but after a scene of deliverance; allusion to victory over the Beast is alien to the context; the words 'the song of the Lamb' have no significance here. Spitta (157 ff.) expunging, as the additions of a redactor, all reference to the Beast and the Lamb makes the passage (15^{2-4}) a part of his Jewish document J^2 and an immediate continuation of 14^{20}; it was a song of deliverance at the Red Sea, but the redactor christianized it and transferred the scene to heaven, combining the Red Sea with the crystal sea of 4^6; the victorious Israelites, with the Elders having harps in 5^8; and the song of Moses, with the song of the Elders praising the Lamb in 5^9. Erbes (94 f., 101) makes the hymn a part of his early Christian apocalypse. A separate song of the Lamb, found in the original, is omitted here by the redactor, because it seemed to him out of place after he had inserted the bowl-plagues; he transferred it in part to 5^{11-13}. Völter, who makes chapts. 15–16 a part of his Cerinthian addition, takes the hymn, interpreted as a song of martyrs in heaven who have fallen in recent persecutions, to be introduced here as a sign for the beginning of the last plagues. The mention of the song of the Lamb is redactional, since the Lamb would not be put after Moses, and since no song of the Lamb follows (*Problem* 225 ff.). — But the appropriateness of the passage in this place as one of the author's anticipatory hymns is shown above; see notes on 15^2, also pp. 282, 244 ff. And with the recognition of this relation of the passage to the writer's habit, the principal ground for the minor points in this criticism disappears. The excisions, rearrangements, and interpretations proposed, in order to fit the paragraph into another document or place, are too arbitrary to have furnished any widely accepted theory of reconstruction. The objections regarding the song of the Lamb have been noticed above, pp. 677 f.

The reviser's introduction of the bowl-series is variously explained by critics. According to Völter (*Problem* 253 ff.) the bowl-plagues are a part of his Cerinthian addition to the Apocalypse. The trumpet-plagues were intended, in the primitive form of the book, as the forerunner of the end, but the author of the Cerinthian insertion, writing in the reign of Domitian, had interpolated a picture of his own times (12^{12-17}, 13); therefore the seven trumpet-plagues represented for him a time long past and could not serve as steps leading immediately to the judgment; a new series of plagues must therefore be introduced to precede the end. Hence the redactor inserts here this imitation of the trumpet-plagues. Weyland (164) agrees with Völter as regards the imitation of the trumpet-plagues and the reason for the insertion of a new series here. He assigns the trumpet-plagues to his Jewish source *Aleph*, and makes the bowl-series the work of the Christian redactor. Erbes (94 ff.) takes the bowl-series as a part of the addition which in his theory was made to the Apocalypse in the year 80; it is superfluous after the trumpet-plagues of which it is an imitation; but it was added for the purpose of filling up a gap in the manifestation of God's wrath, now that the parousia was still delayed. The redactor reveals his want of skill; *e.g.* in 16^{13} in placing Satan and his two agents on equal footing, though the Beast had already been made his plenipotentiary (13^2),

2y

and therefore the three frogs would more appropriately come only from his mouth. J. Weiss (99) denies to chapts. 15–16 a place in the original Apocalypse, because such a plague-series after 14^{14-20} comes too late, and because the frequent allusion to the Beast-vision of chapt. 13 shows these chapts. (15–16) to be a part of the same Jewish document Q. The subdued pictures of the end given in 14^{14-20} did not satisfy the redactor's hot desire for vengeance and judgment; he therefore makes a new start in the bowl-plagues leading up to a representation of the end in pictures of a different style.

The views given above represent the principal types of criticism concerned with these verses (15^5–16^{21}). What has been said on p. 689 in answer to the criticism there spoken of is in part applicable here also. As regards parallelism between the two series of the trumpets and the bowls, the following observations may be made. (1) The parallelism is not so close as is sometimes assumed; no two plague scenes in the two series are precisely alike, and where there is not complete dissimilarity the variation is nevertheless material. (2) Both series are for the larger part based on the Egyptian plagues, which naturally came to form for all time symbols of visitations of God's wrath upon his enemies. It would not be strange, then, that one and the same author should take his start from these in introducing into his book two different series of plagues; nor would it be strange that an author should introduce more than one series of symbols to express the same thing, as *e.g.* the author of Dan. symbolizes the empire under the two sets of figures, the great image and the beasts (chapts. 2 and 7). There is in itself no reason why both series of plagues should not be attributed to one author. (3) We might expect a third series of plagues to be added, because of the importance of the number three with the author, as a number for fullness and largeness; cf. chapt. 8 *passim*, 9^{18}, 12^4, 14^{6-9}, 16^{13-19}. And if the view taken in the Com., pp. 668 ff., be correct, that the bowl-plagues form the 'third woe,' it is impossible to attribute the series to another author; see p. 671. See further on the parallelism between the two series, pp. 671 ff.

XVII–XIX. 5. *The destruction of Rome by Antichrist.* See pp. 284 ff. (1) Introductory vision; the woman seated on the scarlet-colored beast, 17^{1-6}.

The short vision introducing the prophecy of the destruction of Rome represents the imperial city under the figure of a woman with all the appurtenances of great luxury and corruption. That Rome is meant in the figure is made clear by the definition in v. 18. With this agree the woman's name, Babylon, worn on her frontlet (see on 14^8), her seat upon seven hills (v. 9), and her evident identification with the great world-city throughout chapt. 18. The figurative designation *harlot*

is frequently applied to Jerusalem and Israel to denote the
falling away from Jehovah into idolatry, *e.g.* Is. 1²¹, Ezk. 16¹⁵,
Hos. 2⁵. Tyre and Nineveh, Is. 23¹⁷, Nah. 3⁴, receive the name,
because they have corrupted the kingdoms of the world. The
description in v. 4 and chapt. 18 shows that the figure as used
here includes all Rome's wicked luxury and her allurement to
godlessness and immorality. As a further trait in the picture
of the woman's guilt it is added (v. 6) that she is drunken
with the blood of God's servants. This last is the most significant feature in the symbol, as explaining the ruin about to
fall on the great city; cf. 18⁶, ²⁰, ²⁴, 19². The purple and scarlet
in which the woman is clothed do not symbolize her bloody
character (so, many com.); the immediate connection with the
gold and jewels in the description of her adornment shows that
the luxury of her attire is meant, as in 18¹⁶. The representation of the woman as sitting on the beast (the imperial power)
is intended to show the oneness of the imperial city in its corruption and bloodguiltiness with the imperial power on which
it rests. All its character is only an expression of that power,
which serves as Satan's agent. The beast of this scene is in
the mind of the Apocalyptist identified with the one represented
in chapt. 13 (see p. 695), even if it had primarily a different
origin. It is possible that, as some suppose (cf. Gunkel 365),
the author may have derived the suggestion of the figure of a
woman seated on a beast from familiar mythology; the representation of a divinity borne by an animal was common.
However, the question of such an origin is unimportant in the
interpretation, since the Apocalyptist makes clear the meaning
of both figures and the relation between them.

1–2. εἷς ἐκ τῶν ἑπτὰ κτλ., *one of the seven angels that had the
seven bowls :* since the vision of Rome's destruction is an amplification of what is announced summarily among the judgments
of the seven bowls (16¹⁹), one of the angels of those judgments
appears here appropriately as an intermediary in showing and
explaining the vision. Here for the first time in the book
appears an *interpreting angel*, a figure common in apocalyptic
(see p. 170). For the representation of Rome as a harlot see
above. — τῆς καθημένης . . . πολλῶν, *that sitteth on many
waters :* for ἐπί, on, meaning *on the shore of*, cf. Jno. 21¹, 2 K. 2⁷;

cf. the French *sur mer*, said of places by the sea. The phrase here is taken from Jer. 51¹³, where allusion is made to the numerous canals distributing the waters of the Euphrates through the country about Babylon. To the Apocalyptist Rome is Babylon (see on 14⁸), and he applies to the former words of the prophets uttered regarding the latter. This epithet is taken over and applied to Rome, not because it has any parallel in Rome's location, but because the Apocalyptist sees in it a symbol of the many nations which form the foundation and strength of Rome's power (v. 15), as the waters in the plain of Babylon form the very condition of her existence; cf. Jer. 50³⁸ ᶠ·. The figure does not refer to the nations rising like the waters to overwhelm her, as in Is. 8⁷ ᶠ· (so, many com.), for that idea does not appear in the imagery of the chapt. The two representations of the woman as seated by the waters and upon the beast are not at variance with each other; the former is a geographical figure and the language is adapted to an actual city and its location, the latter is a symbol of the capital city and its relation to the imperial power on which it rests. The same juxtaposition of a geographical and a political idea appears in vv. 9 f., in the mountains and the kings.— τοῦ οἴνου τῆς πορνείας, *the wine of her fornication:* the wine which she uses as a means of seduction.

3. The Prophet is caught away in spirit, as in 1¹⁰, 4², 21¹⁰, and in this instance into a wilderness. The wilderness is taken by many com. to be typical of the utter destruction to which Rome is to be reduced. But the actual destruction of Rome, or the desolation following, is not exhibited in this vision; so far as Rome is here shown to the Seer, she appears in the splendor of her power and luxury. A solitary region was a fitting place for visions; cf. the visions of Moses Ex. 3¹ ᶠᶠ·, of Ezra 2 Es. 9²³ ᶠᶠ·, of Hermas *Vis.* I. 1ʼ, 3; III. 1, 3. It is doubtful whether anything more is intended than the variety sought by the author; see 5⁵. In his different ecstacies the Seer beholds himself on earth, 1¹⁰, 10⁸ ᶠ·; in heaven, 4¹; on the sea-shore, 12¹⁸; on a mountain top, 21¹⁰; and here in the wilderness. Wilderness as used in the Scriptures does not necessarily denote a dry and barren place, it is often an uncultivated region with little or no settled population; so that, even if the place of the woman

were meant, there would be no difficulty in the presence of
'many waters'; cf. 'the wilderness of the sea,' Is. 21¹. —
κόκκινον, *scarlet colored*: this color, similar to that of the dragon
(12³), is not elsewhere attributed to the Beast; possibly the
color of the trappings is meant (De Wette, *al*), but there is
nothing to indicate this limitation.   Neither is there anything
to point to it as symbolical of the blood of the martyrs (Düst.,
al).   Its connection in the same sentence with the names of
blasphemy and the numerous heads and horns would seem to
make it one of the attributes which give terribleness to the
beast's appearance. — γέμοντα : *construct. ad. sens.* — ὀνόματα :
the acc. after γέμειν is irregular; cf. τὰ ἀκάθαρτα, v. 4.   See
Blass § 36, 4 ; Win. § 30, 8, *b*.   The 'names of blasphemy'
refer to the blasphemous titles assumed by the emperors ; see
on 13¹.   If ἔχων be read here, see p. 224 for the irregularity.

4. The several articles of the woman's adornment are not
symbolical; they picture the splendor of her luxury. — ποτήριον
χρυσοῦν κτλ., *a golden cup*, etc.: the golden cup, beautiful to
look upon, and supposedly full of wine which the woman offers
to her votaries, is in reality filled with abominations.   The
words figure all the gross corruption of the world-city.   The
imagery is in part suggested by Jer. 51⁷. — τὰ ἀκάθαρτα : for
the acc. see on v. 3.

5. ἐπὶ τὸ μέτωπον, *upon her forehead*: after the manner of the
Roman courtesans (Seneca Rhetor, *Controv.* I. 2 ; Juvenal VI.
123), the woman bore on her head-band her name, or an inscription which declared her personality and character ; she is
Babylon the Great, the mother of harlots, etc. — μυστήριον,
a mystery: something which contains a hidden meaning.   The
word may be taken as part of the inscription, in apposition with
the words following (EV), or as part of the preceding clause
in apposition with ὄνομα, name ; in either case it signifies that
the name is to be understood *mystically*, not literally ; cf. πνευματικῶς, 11⁸. — ἡ μήτηρ κτλ., *the mother of harlots*, etc.: Rome
as the μητρόπολις, *the metropolis, the mother-city*, of the earth, is
viewed as the source and furtherer of all the abominations of
the earth.

6. Rome's sin reaches its culmination in the martyrdom of
God's people.   The woman is drunken with the blood of the

saints.   This is the chief count in her indictment, calling for the judgment of destruction, which forms the subject of the paragraph.   There are two charges against Rome, the martyrdom of the saints, and her corruption and corrupting influence. For the language of the second charge cf. Nah. 3^{1-4}; for the combination of the two charges cf. Sib. Or. V. 160–171.   It is arbitrary to assign the two charges to two different authors; so, J. Weiss 31. — μεθύουσαν ἐκ τοῦ αἵματος, *drunken with the blood:* for the expression cf. Is. 34^7, 49^{26}, En. 62^{12}, also Pliny *H. N.* XIV. 28, cited among other cases by Wetstein *in loc.* The figure includes two ideas, vastness of slaughter, and the maddening effect of the same upon the perpetrator. — καὶ ἐκ . . . ᾽Ιησοῦ, *even . . . of the witnesses of Jesus:* after his manner (see p. 242), the author uses first the quite general designation ἅγιοι, *saints,* applicable to the people of the old and new covenants alike, and then he adds the specific designation showing that Christians are meant.   Those who were martyred at Rome by Nero are probably especially in mind, cf. 16^6. Many following Vischer attribute this second clause καὶ . . . ᾽Ιησοῦ to a redactor, on the ground that the two clauses must refer to two distinct classes of persons, as shown by καί *and;* with a Christian writer, ἅγιοι, *saints,* and μάρτυρες ᾽Ιησοῦ, *witnesses of Jesus,* would have the same meaning; therefore the first must be assigned to a Jewish document, to which a redactor has given a Christian coloring by adding the second clause.   But this theory disregards the practice of the writer referred to above.   καί here is *even.*   Cf. the juxtaposition of ἅγιοι and ἀδελφοί Col. 1^1. — μαρτύρων, *witnesses:* for the use of the word in the book see on 2^{13}.

(2) The angel's interpretation of the introductory vision. 17^{7-18}.   See pp. 284 f., 406 ff.

The ' angel-interpreter,' whose office is characteristic of apocalyptic literature (see on v. 1), now explains the introductory vision, both in its present significance and in the final issues contained in it.   As the judgment upon the woman is the subject of the revelation promised in the outset, v. 1, and as she is the principal figure in the vision (vv. 1–6), we might expect her to occupy the first and chief place in this interpretation.   On the contrary the angel speaks first and chiefly of the beast that carries her.   But the critical objection raised on this account (see p. 709) is not justified, for in point of fact the judgment of the woman, *i.e.* of Rome, does occupy the larger part of the paragraph taken as a whole (17^1–19^5).   Besides what is said of it in these verses, it forms the subject of 18^1–19^5, to which this part is preparatory.   As regards the subordinate place of the woman in these interpretative verses (7–18), it must be noted that the being and destiny of the woman (the capital city) have no significance apart from the beast (the imperial power impersonated in the emperors); and the judgment which is to come upon her can be shown only through the explanation of the beast, who in his final manifestation is to be the agent of that judgment.   A single sentence and a few intimations suffice to reveal her present significance.   The revelation of her future destiny is joined inseparably with the revelation of the future of the beast.   Moreover the beast represents a complex agency active not only in the judgment of the woman, but in the events that follow till the millennium. Necessarily then prominence is given to him in the angel's interpretation.   The woman is distinctly explained as the imperial city, v. 18; see also p. 690.   The beast of these explanatory verses is declared (v. 7) to be the same as that of vv. 3–6; and it is evident that the writer identifies it with the Beast of chapt. 13, whatever differences critics may find among the three (see pp. 709, 710).   This identification is shown by the names of blasphemy, the seven heads and ten horns, the revivification, in which the two agree, and by the language describing the wonder which the revivification awakens among men (cf. 17^8 with $13^{3,\,8}$).   These verses (7–18) furnish then an explanation of what is said of the Beast in chapt. 13, and the two passages mutually throw light upon each other.

It is not surprising that the explanation of the Beast is in part enigmatical; in symbolical representation the symbol and the reality are in the nature of the case often blended; and when the thing symbolized comes to occupy in turn different and even dissimilar situations, ambiguity is likely to occur. In this case the Beast appears at one time to represent a single person, and again seven (or eight) distinct persons in succession.   He is frequently identified with the head which at a particular time represents him; see pp. 406 f. But he is always a concrete *person*, not a figure for an abstract power, as *e.g.* the force of evil. While in the explanation given in these verses the heads are said to represent a *succession* of kings arising one after another (17^{10}), they appear in the vision of chapt. 13 as a group among the attributes of the Beast, as if existing simultaneously. This, however, is only the necessary consequence of picturing a whole era in a tableau, as it were, as is common in visional portrayals, rather than in narrative or dramatic form. Thus the ten horns are seen grouped with the seven heads, but they symbolize kings who belong to a time subsequent to at least six of these (17^{12}). So the fourth beast and the ten horns in Daniel's vision (7^7), the different parts of the image seen by Nebuchadnezzar (2^{32}), the twelve wings of the eagle in 2 Es. $11^{1\,f.}$, furnish groups of objects appearing simultaneously, though symbolizing things which are successive in time (Dan. $7^{23\,f.}$, $2^{37\,ff.}$, 2 Es. 12^{14}). In chapt. 13 Satan's agent is portrayed without reference to the successive phases of his manifestation at different times and in different persons; while here in chapt. 17, in the interpretation of what was there seen, the historic sequence of the factors of the vision is pointed out.

It seems unquestionable that the idea expressed in the words ' the beast was and is not and shall come,' 17^8, is the same as that denoted in the symbolical vision by the head smitten unto death and healed, 13^3. The language is similar, and the effect of the restoration in each case is described in closely parallel terms (see above). Moreover, an interpretation of that symbol in chapt. 13 is to be expected here ; for the marvel of the head forms one of the most significant features of that vision, it is mentioned as essential three times ($13^{3,\,12,\,14}$), and its obscurity is not relieved by any parallel in apocalyptic tradition. The other important features, the heads and the horns, are here interpreted ; an interpretation of the marvelous head could not then be wanting. Taking then the two passages together we see that the head slain and revived is one in the line of kings who had already died, and that its restoration represents a kind of revivification of that king, as one in whom the Beast will appear after the sixth and seventh kings have

ceased to exist, 17¹⁰ ᶠ·. See pp. 407 f. But the Apocalyptist
is careful to add words which are fundamental in the expression of his thought as regards this revived head ; he is to
' come up out of the abyss,' language which interpreted by the
author's use throughout (9¹, ², ¹¹, 11⁷, 20¹, ³) means that he will
come up from the place of demons. He is not revived in the
mere human nature of his former existence, he comes in
demonic form and with demonic powers. The figure which
the Apocalyptist has in mind here becomes clear in the light
of the common Christian view of *Antichrist*, and the expectation of his coming ; see pp. 397 ff. With that thought before
his mind the author introduces a significant variation in interpreting here the vision of chapt. 13. There the Beast, a purely
symbolical figure, is said to come up out of the sea, as do the
beasts in Daniel's vision (7³) and the eagle in 2 Es. (11¹), a
conception probably going back to the ultimate origin of the
beast in popular mythology as a monster of the sea ; see on
12³. But the actual *person* symbolized by the restored head,
the demonic king reincarnate in Antichrist, could not be
represented as coming out of the sea ; he comes from the abode
of demons, ' the abyss.' For further points in the angel's
interpretation, see pp. 698 ff.

   7. For general notes on the following paragraph (vv. 7–18),
see (2) p. 694, and the pp. there referred to. — ἐρῶ σοι τὸ
μυστήριον κτλ., *I will tell thee the mystery*, etc.: it is clear from
what follows that the mystery which the angel promises to
explain includes more than the mere symbolical meaning of the
woman and the beast; it includes the whole subject of the
paragraph 17¹–19⁵, *i.e.* the judgment of the great harlot. From
the promise in v. 1 and from that given here, what is expected
and what really follows is the punishment of destruction, which
comes upon the woman for the crimes exhibited in the opening
vv., 1–6. This forms the theme unfolded variously and with
great force to the end. The criticism (see p. 709) that the
Apocalyptist after introducing the theme, ' the mystery of the
woman,' v. 7, then drops it and returns to it only casually in
v. 16, rests upon a misconception of the scope of the paragraph
as a whole. The Beast is introduced as an essential part of the
explanation, because he with his confederates is the agent by

whom the punishment of the woman is executed. His own
end is only briefly alluded to, vv. 11, 14 ; that forms the subject of a later paragraph (19^{11-21}). At the same time, so
important is the figure of the Beast in the oracles of the book,
that the author brings in here, as it were incidentally, the
explanation necessary for understanding the imagery of chapt.
13. That there should be amplification beyond what belongs
directly to the main subject is only characteristic of a mind
moving in the manner of a Hebrew prophet.

8. For the meaning of what is said of the Beast, see pp.
400 ff., 406 ff. — τὸ ὄνομα: for the sing., see on 11^8. — ἀπὸ
καταβολῆς κόσμου, *from the foundation of the world:* see on 13^8.
— βλεπόντων: instead of βλέποντες through the influence of ὧν.
The cause of the wonder which shall seize all is the *return* of the
Beast, and all that is implied in the resuscitation of the Nero
who once was. The wonder includes homage and adherence,
as in $13^{3\ f.}$

9. ὧδε . . . σοφίαν, *here is the mind that hath wisdom:* see
on 13^{18}. — ἑπτὰ ὄρη, *seven mountains :* as the woman symbolizes
Rome, the seven mountains upon which she sits are without
doubt Rome's seven hills, which form one of the most familiar
characterizations of the imperial city. The word ὄρος does not
necessarily denote a lofty eminence ; cf. Mt. 5^1, 15^{29}, Jno. 6^{15}.
The Latin uses both *collis* and *mons* in reference to the seven
hills. A symbolical interpretation of *mountain* as a seat of
power (some older interpreters) is inapplicable here ; there are
not seven seats of power. The local allusion is too plain to be
doubted. The twofold interpretation of the heads, as mountains and as kings, has raised unnecessary difficulty (see p.
710). Rome, the capital city, and the emperors, as inseparably connected, are both before the Apocalyptist's mind, and it
is natural that he should see in so conspicuous a feature in the
imagery as the seven heads a reference to both. The number
seven coincides with the familiar epithet of Rome as seven-
hilled, and readily suggests a parallelism between the heads
and the local city. The thought is expressed parenthetically
before the chief significance of the symbol, the seven kings.
Such a parenthesis would not then be strange even if it served
no special purpose ; but in fact it shows who the kings are

that are to be spoken of — they are the kings of Rome (Völter *Offenb.* 66 f.). For the combination of the local and political aspects of the city, see on v. 2. — ὅπου, ἐπ' αὐτῶν : for the pleonasm, see on 12⁶.

10–11. For the seven kings and the short time of the seventh, see pp. 704 ff. For the Beast that was and is not is an eighth king, see pp. 406 f., 708. — βασιλεῖς ἑπτά εἰσιν, *they are seven kings:* the seven heads symbolize seven kings, emperors of Rome. — ἔπεσαν, *are fallen:* this word is not inappropriate to the death of the five emperors (so, Alford, *al*) ; it alludes to the eminent rank of those whose death is declared, cf. 2 S. 3³⁸, 'a prince and a great man is fallen.' — καὶ αὐτὸς ὄγδοός ἐστιν, *even he is an eighth : i.e.* an eighth king, or worldruler, not an eighth head (see p. 708). For αὐτός as an emphatic *he,* see Blass § 48, 1. — καί, *even :* the position forbids joining with ὄγδοός, an eighth *also,* as well as one of an earlier order. — ἐκ τῶν ἑπτά, *of the seven ;* perhaps equivalent to *one of the seven,* cf. Ac. 21⁸, Mt. 26⁷³ ; see Thayer εἰμί, V. 3, a. But elsewhere the author uses εἶς ἐκ τῶν κτλ., *e.g.* v. 1, 5⁵, 6¹ ; he may have thought the latter implied too absolute identity between the historic Nero and the Nero incarnate in Antichrist, and therefore chose the less precise expression. — εἰς ἀπώλειαν κτλ., *he goeth to perdition :* Antichrist will be destroyed by the Messiah, 19¹¹⁻²¹.

12–13. μίαν ὥραν, *one hour:* a short time is meant. The ten kings receive their authority and their kingdoms from God, that they may serve as the helpers of Antichrist in the destruction of Rome, vv. 16–17. Their power is coterminous with that of Antichrist (μετὰ τοῦ θηρίου), which is of short duration ; they perish with him, 19¹⁹⁻²¹. — μίαν γνώμην ἔχουσιν, *have one mind :* they are unanimous in giving their power to the Beast and in assisting him in his war against the Lamb and in the destruction of Rome.

The ten horns, as a feature of the Beast, are derived directly from Dan. 7⁷, ²⁴, and they are not a mere detail of that picture taken over as a whole (so, some com.), for other features of the description given there are not retained. These have special meaning for the Apocalyptist's idea. But the figure is applied differently here. There the horns represent a series of kings arising one after another in the last world-empire (the Græco-Syrian) ; that series is represented in our book by the seven heads, while the horns symbolize, not Roman rulers, but kings whose dominions are to be given them in the last days simultaneously with one another and with Antichrist. They have not yet received their kingdoms (v. 12). The difference is characteristic of the author's independence in using figures derived from other sources.

The number ten is of course symbolical, signifying completeness (see pp. 250 f., 254), and the author's purpose is to show how Antichrist when he comes will obtain power over all nations and peoples (13^7) ; all kings, those of kingdoms large or small, near or remote, will yield their power with one consent to him as their supreme lord, for God will put it into their hearts to do so, vv. 13, 17. Rigorous literalism might raise difficulty here as regards the number. Ten is meant to symbolize all, yet Rome, if we follow chronological order, is not included — it is first overthrown by Antichrist and his allies before his rule is all-complete. But evidently the Apocalyptist means to express here merely the fullness of Antichrist's power, and his destruction of the present world-order ; chronological detail is not thought of. In the identification of the ten kings there is no ground for making a distinction between the horns of 13^1 and those of 17^{12}, and referring the former to Roman emperors (so, Düst. *al*) ; neither emperors nor Roman provincial governors (so, many) can be meant ; such a reference is too narrow, the number is all-comprehensive. For the same reason an identification with satraps of Parthian provinces, who should come as confederates with Nero (so, DeWet. Bleek, *al*) cannot be maintained, though it is doubtless true that the belief in Nero's coming with these auxiliaries to take vengeance on Rome influenced the Apocalyptist's application of the symbol. *The ten kings are purely eschatological figures representing the totality of the powers of all nations on the earth which are to be made subservient to Antichrist.*

14. οὗτοι, *these:* the Beast and his confederates are meant, as shown by 19^{19} ; cf. v. 16. The Apocalyptist's thought here passes to the final conflict between Antichrist and the Messiah, 19^{11-21}. The mention of that war and the overthrow of Anti-

christ appears inappropriate in a paragraph concerned with the
Beast's destruction of Rome, and not with the war against
the saints.   It is also argued by some that a declaration of the
Beast's overthrow cannot properly precede that of his assault
on Rome.   The verse is therefore rejected by many ; so, Vischer,
Wellhausen, Bouss., *al.*   But the parenthesis — for such it is
— is not inexplicable here.   The mention in v. 13 of the gift
of their power to the Beast on the part of the nations leads the
author's thought quite characteristically to the supreme service
in which the combined force is to be used, the war with the
Lamb, and to the final result, the Beast's overthrow.   This forms
for the readers the subject of the highest interest, and the
assurance of the final triumph of the saints conforms to the
author's habit of forestalling the dark predictions of trial by
promises of final deliverance.   After the parenthesis the Apocalyptist turns back to the main subject, the punishment of the
woman and the part which the Beast and his confederates are
to perform in that issue, vv. 16 f.   If parentheses, sudden turns
of thought and anticipation, can find no original place in a
writing of this kind, not only our book, but the N. T. generally,
and especially St. Paul's epistles, must be extensively rewritten.

ὅτι κύριος κτλ., *because he is Lord of lords*, etc.: the supreme
lordship of the Lamb gives assurance of his victory over the
Beast.   Titles similar to these given to the Lamb here and in
19[16] occur frequently as applied to God; cf. Dt. 10[17], Ps. 136[3],
Dan. 2[47], 11[36]; for the occurrence in late Jewish writings see
Bouss. *Judenthum*, 306.   They are also applied in Babylonian
mythology to Marduk. — οἱ μετ' αὐτοῦ κτλ., *and those with him*,
etc.: *sc.* νικήσουσιν ; *those with him shall conquer, as being called,
and elect and faithful ;* such cannot fail.   The phrase corresponds
to the words 'Lord of lords,' etc., which give the assurance of
the Lamb's victory.   The saints of earth are not mentioned in
19[11 ff.] as forming a part of the Lamb's army, but their share in
the conflict is implied in the words of this verse, 'those with
him.'   And in the promise of victory over the Beast, mention
of the share of the saints would be expected; cf. 2[26 f.], 12[11].
This interpretation, that of many scholars, *e.g.* De Wet., Düst.,
RV, Moff., Swete, seems certainly correct.   The other interpretation, which supplies εἰσίν, *those with him are called and elect,*

etc. (AV, Bengel, Bouss., Holtzm., *al*), gives a statement having no direct connection with the topic of the sentence, victory over the Beast in the final battle which he will attempt. — The words κλητοί, ἐκλεκτοί, *called, chosen*, the latter not found elsewhere in Rev., contain a Pauline reminiscence; cf. also Mt. 20¹⁶, 22¹⁴.

15. After the parenthesis of v. 14, the interpretation returns to the symbol of the woman, Rome, and the vastness of her power; this is contributed to her by all the nations of the earth, as life was given to Babylon by the waters of the plain about her. But all this power is to be swept away. — τὰ ὕδατα κτλ., *the waters which thou sawest:* the Seer does not in vv. 2 ff. mention the waters among the things seen; their presence is inferred from v. 1. The interpretation of the waters as a symbol of peoples follows O. T. usage; cf. Is. 8⁷, Jer. 47². This verse gives a further hint as to who the woman is; she is one who sits as queen over many nations and peoples.

16-17. The acts described are those of persons; the Apocalyptist has in mind the persons symbolized by the Beast and the horns. — τὰς σάρκας αὐτῆς φάγονται, *shall eat her flesh:* a figure taken from the ravening of wild beasts, and frequently used to denote the utter destruction of men by their fellows; cf. Ps. 27², Jer. 10²⁵, Mic. 3³, Zeph. 3³. — αὐτὴν κατακαύσουσιν, *shall burn her utterly:* i.e. the city, which is symbolized by the woman. The destruction of Rome foretold summarily in this verse is taken up again and amplified with great dramatic force in the concluding and larger part of the paragraph, 18¹⁻ 19⁵. — ὁ γὰρ θεὸς κτλ., *for God put it into their hearts*, etc.: the marvel of Rome's overthrow by the combined forces of the earth is possible, for it is God who thus works out his will; and he moves the nations to forsake their differences, and with one accord to give their power to the Beast till God's purpose is accomplished. — ἔδωκεν, *did put it into their hearts:* the act is yet in the future, but the aor. tense marks it as past with reference to the time when the events of v. 16 shall take place. — τὰς καρδίας αὐτῶν, *their hearts:* i.e. the hearts of the ten kings, as shown by δοῦναι τὴν βασιλείαν κτλ., *give their kingdom to the Beast.* — τὴν γνώμην αὐτοῦ, *his mind:* the mind, i.e. purpose, or will, of God. What that will is, is explained by the

following words, viz. : that with one mind they should give
their power to the Beast till God's word is fulfilled. Some,
following Bengel (so, Ewald, De Wet., Bouss., *al*), refer the
pronoun in the phrase *his mind* to the Beast. But in that case
we should expect θηρίον to be inserted here rather than in the
later clause δοῦναι κτλ. The mention of the Beast in v. 16 is
too remote to admit of reference to that word instead of the
near word θεός. For the meaning of γνώμη cf. Ac. 20³, Philem.
14 ; and for its use of God's will cf. Ign. *Rom.* 8³, *Sm.* 6². —
ποιῆσαι μίαν γνώμην, *to execute a common purpose: i.e.* the purpose of giving their power to the Beast, as explained in the
following words. Cf. v. 13, where the *entertainment* of the purpose is spoken of (ἔχουσιν) ; here its *execution* (ποιῆσαι) is
meant. — ἄχρι τελεσθήσονται κτλ., *until the words of God should
be accomplished:* the nations remain the vassals of the Beast till
the great battle, 19¹⁹ ᶠᶠ. The 'words of God' then include more
than the overthrow of Rome ; the prophecies of the last events
till the overthrow of Antichrist seem to be meant.

18. The interpretation of the vision closes with the clear
statement of what had already been hinted (vv. 9, 15, see notes
there), that the woman symbolizes the capital city of the world,
i.e. Rome.

The destruction of Rome by Antichrist and his vassals. — The
judgment upon Rome, the present embodiment of God-opposing power, the relentless persecutor of the saints and the
corrupter of the earth, forms one of the foremost acts in the
eschatological fulfillment. And the Beast and his activities
are introduced here revealing the agency and manner of God's
execution of her doom. God will employ the supreme terrestrial power of evil to work out his counsel. Rome will be
destroyed by the Neronic Antichrist as the agent of God's
will, vv. 16–17. The rise of this conception is not difficult to
understand. Internecine war as an organ of God in destroying
his enemies in the last times was predicted in the O. T. prophecies ; cf. Ezk. 38²¹, Hag. 2²², Zec. 14¹³. Allied to such prediction, but more akin to that of our book, was the prophecy
that the 'little horn,' the prototype of Antichrist, would obtain
his power by destroying his predecessors, with whose line he
was connected, Dan. 7⁸, ²⁴ ᶠ. And the removal of the power of

great Rome as a condition of Antichrist's appearance and full activity was an expectation found among the Christians, 2 Thess. 2^{3-8}. The possibility of the overthrow of the existing power of Rome, and the manner of its accomplishment, were contained in the belief, widespread in the latter part of the century, that Nero would return from the East with a host of Parthian confederates to avenge himself upon the imperial city. It was but one step further to the particular form of belief that lies in the background of the Apocalyptist's representation. He has taken his imagery from the expectation, whose existence may be regarded as established (see pp. 400 ff.), that in the Nero, coming now, not from the East, but from the dead, and endowed with demonic powers, the expected Antichrist would be embodied.

The Seven Kings of 17^{10-11}. As the Beast represents the Roman empire impersonated in its emperors, it is clear that the seven kings, symbolized by the Beast's seven heads, are meant to represent, whether historically or symbolically, the Roman rulers from the beginning to the end. (For the view that seven world-empires are meant, see pp. 395 f.). The words have been commonly taken to be historical, and any attempt to identify the kings respectively numbered must, as most are agreed, begin with the beginning of the empire. But we meet at once two factors which have introduced uncertainty into the reckoning. Scholars are divided on the questions as to whether Julius Cæsar or Augustus should be regarded as the first emperor, and whether we should count or omit the three emperors Galba, Otho, and Vitellius, who in the anarchy of 68–69 A.D. held the throne one after another, but were not universally recognized. A tabular view will show the numerical place of the first eight emperors according to the different modes of reckoning.

Cæsar . . .	1	1		
Augustus. .	2	2	1	1
Tiberius . .	3	3	2	2
Caligula . .	4	4	3	3
Claudius . .	5	5	4	4
Nero . . .	6	6	5	5
Galba . .	7		6	
Otho . .	8		7	
Vitellius .			8	
Vespasian .		7		6
Titus . . .		8		7
Domitian . .				8

According to the starting-point, and the retention or omission of the three emperors named, the sixth emperor, reigning at the time of the utterance in v. 10, is variously identified with Nero, Galba, or Vespasian. Nominally the empire began with Augustus, and Roman writers are cited (*e.g.* Tac. *Ann.* I. 1, *Hist.* I. 1) as dating the empire from him; most scholars begin with him in reckoning the seven. But Cæsar was virtually emperor, claimed the title *imperator*, and is frequently reckoned the first in Roman and Jewish writers, *e.g.* Suetonius *Lives of the Twelve Cæsars;* Sib. Or. V. 12; Joseph. *Ant.* XVIII. 2, 2, *idem, al;* 2 Es. 12^{15}. There is then good authority for beginning with him.

It must at least be acknowledged that we have in ancient writers no unquestionable guidance in the reckoning. Cf. Stuart II. 445 ff.; Lücke II. 839 ff.

The omission of the three emperors between Nero and Vespasian, those of the so-called interregnum, affords an easy method of avoiding the identification of the sixth king with Galba, which upon any supposition is impossible; apart from other difficulties, our book is later than Nero or Galba, neither of these can be the sixth king, in whose time the author is writing. But the omission of these three is a very questionable procedure. It is conceivable that a writer in the time of Galba, or Vespasian even, might hesitate to reckon the three in the same category as their predecessors; but it is extremely doubtful whether an apocalyptist near the end of the century, and not closely concerned with political history, would make such a distinction. The three rulers held the office and title of emperor, Suetonius, the contemporary of the Apocalyptist, gives them a place in his *Lives of the Twelve Cæsars*, Josephus unhesitatingly places them in the same list (*e.g. Bell. Jud.* IV. 9, 2), they are included with the other emperors without qualification in Sib. Or. V. 35. It requires then a certain degree of arbitrariness to avoid making the sixth king either Nero or Galba. But if we accept the influence of the Nero myth in the Apocalypse, as we seem compelled to do (see pp. 401 ff.), a date for the present form of the book later than Vespasian must be assumed, since the time between Nero and Vespasian, less than two years, is insufficient for the prevalence of that superstition. Both internal and external evidence point to a date not earlier than Domitian (see pp. 206 ff.). In spite of the arbitrariness spoken of in the treatment of the three names, many recent scholars omit them and beginning with Augustus make Vespasian the sixth king. Thus the Apocalyptist would seem to say that he is writing in the time of Vespasian, but his book bears evidence of being not earlier than Domitian. Some have sought to remove the discrepancy thus arising by the supposition that the author, as apocalyptists are wont to do, sets himself back into the time of Vespasian, and gives in the form of prophecy history already past at his own date (so, Weyland 167; Moff. 319, *al*). But such antedated prophecies are always put into the mouth of an assumed person of the past; so, *e.g.* the prophecies of Daniel, Enoch, etc. There is nowhere in the book a hint of such an assumption. This explanation is accepted by few. The more common explanation of the difficulty is that the words in v. 10 'five are fallen, the one is, the other is not yet come' belong to an oracle of the time of Vespasian, or as some would say of an earlier emperor, and that our author, writing in Domitian's time, has taken this up and incorporated it into his prophecy (so, Bouss., Blj., Holtzm-Bau., J. Weiss, *al*). But this solution is open to strong objection. Whatever adaptation of sources may be presumed in the interpretation which the author is here giving of his vision, it cannot be questioned that the time relations, whether present, past, or future, under which the heads are spoken of in v. 10, are the same as those of the beast in vv. 8, 11; in other words the *is* must refer throughout to the time of the speaker's present. Our author does not make mechanical insertions. It is

2 z

certainly unwarranted to find in his words, 'one is,' any other meaning than that the sixth king is reigning at the actual time of his writing. Some find traces of revision of an earlier oracle in v. 11; in the words 'he is an eighth and is of the seven' there is thought to be found an effort to remove a difficulty. The supposed Vespasian oracle here incorporated limited the number of kings to seven, of whom Titus would be the last; but the Apocalyptist, living under Domitian, in order to bring the oracle into accord with history, *i.e.* to prevent the number seven from being exceeded, resorts to the myth of a revived Nero, and adds the words 'he is one of the seven,' thus making Domitian not really an eighth, since he is only one of the seven now returned. Domitian then is the reincarnated Nero; so, Harnack, *Chron.* I. 245 f., Holtzm.-Bau. 404, J. Weiss 32. But the view that the Apocalyptist sees in Domitian a revived Nero is certainly wrong. The wounded head restored, Nero revived, is the Beast which is not present at the time of the Apocalyptist's writing, but he is to come from the abyss, and with the vassal kings destroy the Roman power (v. 16); he is also to lead out the armies of earth against the Messiah (19[14], [19]). These are functions which would not be assigned to Domitian. On the relation of Domitian to Nero, cf. Bouss. 416, Blj. 180 f.

According to any interpretation which conforms strictly to the requirements of the context, it is a clearly determined point in our passage, that the king denominated the sixth is reigning at the time of the utterance of v. 10. But by no method of reckoning is it possible to assign an emperor reigning near the end of the century a place as the sixth in the chronological order of the Roman rulers. Nor has any theory of an incorporated earlier oracle been proposed which can claim general assent. We are brought then inevitably to the question whether the current methods of identifying the seven emperors do not proceed on a wrong supposition. It will be helpful in considering that question to notice what the author's purpose is in the mention of the number of the kings, and how this same purpose has been met in other apocalyptic writings. Throughout the ages the cry of God's people, yearning in their persecutions at the hands of a world power for the deliverer of the great day of the Lord, had been, 'When cometh the end?' And it was the office of the apocalyptic prophet to encourage the sufferers and to show that the last days were not far off. The time was fixed in the counsel of God, but the world must first run its destined course. The æon of the present order came to be conceived as divided into stereotyped periods, certain definite numbers of ages, world-empires, reigns, etc., which must be fulfilled; and intimations were frequently given of the number yet remaining before the end should be reached; see pp. 77 ff. The favorite numbers in such world-divisions were 4, 7, 10, and 12. In Dan. the schematic numbers were 4 and 10; and the fourth world-kingdom and the end of the 10 reigns have already been reached, the last days are at hand. In 2 Es. the number of the ages is 12, of which $10\frac{1}{2}$ or $9\frac{1}{2}$ were already passed, 14[11] (the uncertainty in the text is not important in our inquiry). The Ap. Bar. also forms its vision of world-periods on the basis of 12 as the schematic number, 52 ff.; 10 periods are passed, the eleventh is present, 67. *The Apocalypse of weeks*, En. 91, 93, divides history into 10 periods, of which the seventh is already come. And so with our Apocalypse the sixth reign in the series of 7 reigns which make up the history of the last world-kingdom is present; there remains only one more before the end of the present world-kingdom and the coming of Antichrist. The one purpose of all the apocalyptists in these numbers and computations is to declare the nearness of the end. What kings have preceded is for the Apocalyptist's message to his readers unimportant; it is enough for them to know that only one is to follow before the end of the then present world-kingdom is reached.

Now, it is important to determine whether these enumerations of world-periods, kingdoms, sovereigns, etc., as presented in apocalyptic writings, are intended to conform closely with actual history, or whether they are not schemes adjusted to traditional numbers, and designed to give a certain definiteness to eschatological predictions. A very slight examination will show that the apocalyptists are not historians, and that their schedules of numbers, in which they represent the course of the world, do not appear to be derived from history, but rather to be adopted from familiar numerical symbols to which history is made to conform. Neither the apocalyptists nor their readers were interested in a careful tabulation of a remote past; their interest lay in their own age and the future to which it was leading. So Daniel's four empires are seen to be at variance with actual history; see Driver, *Dan.* 94 ff.; En. Bib. I. 1007 f. His aim is to show the movement of the ages toward the final consummation as *near*, to exhibit in the eschatological kingdom the culmination of a divine order. He adopts for his purpose the traditional notion of four world-ages, which appears also in Persian, Greek, Roman, and rabbinic tradition. For its use in other apocalypses cf. 2 Es. 11[39], Ap. Bar. 39, En. 89–90. Likewise the 10 horns, the 10 kings of the last empire in Dan., though perhaps referring to a particular line of kings, cannot be identified with the same number of actual persons. The number is schematic; it is used thus in Sib. Or. IV. 47 ff., En. 93, 91, and in this use is taken up by our Apocalyptist in the 10 horns. The number 12 assigned to the kings of the last kingdom represented by the wings of the eagle in 2 Es. 11 is equally unhistorical; the efforts to identify these with the same number of sovereigns have proved fruitless; it is certain that the number there is taken from a familiar typical use, as it is in 2 Es. 14[11], Ap. Bar. 53 ff., Ap. Abr. 29; cf. Volz, 168; Bouss. *Judenthum*, 253. Now the exact parallelism between these eschatological computations and the reckoning of seven kings in our chapt. suggests that the same usage is adopted here. We have here the same schematic representation of a succession of periods, *i.e.* reigns, of which the one then present is shown to be near the end of the existing æon. The choice of 7 as a symbol of completeness, which to a remarkable degree dominates our Apocalypse (see pp. 253 f.), would, even if an invention of the author, be only conformable to the general usage of the book; but the idea of 7 world-periods and 7 rulers is found, if not in Jewish literature, yet in Babylonian, Persian, and Greek tradition. There is also in our passage the same difficulty as in the other apocalypses in identifying the typical number with that of history; an arbitrary reckoning or an artificial explanation must be resorted to in order to bring the statement into conformity with the date of the book. It is moreover doubtful whether an apocalyptist and a Jew of the provinces would be nicely thoughtful to follow the exact succession of Roman rulers, or in speaking of the Roman state as a God-opposing power would have been careful to distinguish between the empire, beginning with Cæsar or Augustus, and the form of government preceding it. A striking illustration of an apocalyptist's subordidation of historical accuracy to a dramatic purpose is seen in the errors of Ap. Bar. 1^1, 6^1, which were committed in face of the knowledge of the facts of the O. T. history which the author shows; see Charles, *Ap. Bar.*, pp. 1 f.; Kautzsch on 1^1.

In view of these considerations we are brought to the conclusion that *the number seven here is purely symbolical, that the Apocalyptist means to represent the Roman power as a historic whole.* From beginning to end it is, as impersonated in its rulers, the enemy of God's people. But the period of its last sovereign is not thought to be already reached, the parousia is not so immediately at hand. Yet the universal belief of the apostolic age, and the uniform representation of our book, place that event not far off. The sixth reign in the series of seven may easily be conceived to be present, and the last can continue only 'a little while'; after that, the reign of Antichrist, short though it be, must claim its allotted space before the Messiah appears. As in the apocalypses mentioned above, a late number in the series, but not the last, is already reached. *Who this sixth king, the one reigning at the time, is, whether Vespasian, Domitian, or another, must be determined solely by the evidence which the book gives elsewhere of its date.* Our passage is not history, but a simple piece of eschatological symbolism, like those in the other apocalypses. And the words, 'even he is an eighth' (v. 11), are not a revision of an earlier oracle of 7 kings made by a redactor living under an eighth (see p. 705); they describe Antichrist not as an eighth head but as an eighth world-ruler coming up after the 7 world-rulers impersonated in the Roman emperors have fulfilled their course. The Roman empire must fill out its destined place in history, it must have its complete tale of kings denoted by the typical number 7; then Antichrist comes, who succeeds the Roman power which he destroys; he forms an eighth ruler added to the seventh, just as the 'little horn' (Antiochus) in Dan. forms an eleventh added to the tenth ($7^{8,\,24}$), but at the same time he is 'of the 7,' inasmuch as he is one of the 7 (Nero) reincarnate.

Textual notes. 17^{1-17}. **1.** Before υδατων and πολλων, Q most min R insert των; wanting in אAP many min edd. — **3.** γεμοντα ονοματα א*AP Lch Ti WH RV *al*; γεμον τα ονοματα Alf Ws *al*; γεμον ονοματα א᷍Q many min Blj Sod; γεμον ονοματων many min anc com R. — εχον Q most min R Ws Alf Blj Sod *al*; εχοντα אP Ti WHmrg; εχων A min WH Bouss. — **4.** Instead of τα ακαθαρτα, R has ακαθαρτητος without Ms. authority. — **8.** υπαγειν אPQ min vers R many edd; υπαγει A some min Ws WH *al.* — Instead of και παρεσται, R reads καιπερ εστιν, origin uncertain.

— 13. For διδοασιν, R without authority reads διαδιδωσουσιν. — 16. For και before το θηριον, R reads επι without Ms. authority, so some Mss. of vlg. — 17. For τελεσθησονται οι λογοι, R reads τελεσθη τα ρηματα, uncertain origin.

Criticism of chapt. 17. The criticism of this chapt. is closely connected with that of chapt. 13. Most of those who see in the latter the working over of an original Jewish document hold the same view regarding chapt. 17. The argument also upon which the principal weight is laid is essentially the same. It is enough here to refer to pp. 644 ff. for the argument and some comments upon it. This general question as to a Jewish original has however become subordinate in critical discussion to questions as to the relation of the two chapts. to each other, and the composite character of chapt. 17. *Against oneness of authorship* the following points of difference between the two chapts. have been urged as decisive. In 17 the Beast comes from the abyss, in 13 from the sea; in 17 it is the Beast that is full of names of blasphemy, in 13 it is the 7 heads; in 17 the 10 horns are helpers of the Beast, in 13 no such office is assigned them ; in 17 the heads represent mountains and kings, in 13 no such interpretation is found; in 17 the Beast wars against the Lamb, in 13 against the saints. In 13 nothing is said of 7 kings of whom 5 are fallen, one is and one is yet to come, nothing of an eighth identified with the Beast, nothing of the woman, who is conspicuous in 17; and, on the other hand, in 17 nothing is said of the dragon with whom the Beast is associated in 13. This argument is given most fully by Völter *Problem* 199 f. But these differences, if not trivial, involve no contradiction such as to establish diversity of authorship. In all comparison of the two chapts. it must be borne in mind that their respective places in the author's plan are entirely different. The earlier chapt. pictures the great agent which Satan uses in his war against the saints ; the latter chapt. is concerned with the destruction of Rome, showing her guilt and the agency used by God in her judgment. (See pp. 278, 284 f., also Com. on the chapts.) With all the similarity in the symbols, there must therefore be differences in the details which are represented and emphasized. See further, pp. 695, 697.

The principal objections to the unity of chapt. 17 are represented in the following argument of Spitta (180 ff.), whom many follow. He refers vv. 7–18 to a redactor. After the description of the woman in vv. 1–6, we should expect, he argues, the revelation of her judgment, as promised in v. 1, but on the contrary we have in vv. 7–18 an extended exposition of what is meant by the figures of the woman and of the beast which carries her. And in this paragraph itself, vv. 7–18, we should expect the woman to occupy the first place, as she does in the opening verses of the chapt. and in the promise of v. 7 ; but the reverse is the case; a long notice of the beast follows without a syllable in regard to the woman before v. 15, and then after casual allusions in vv. 15, 16, verse 18 brings in at last the identification of the woman, which is expected after v. 7. Even in vv. 1–6, the hand of a redactor shows itself ; the beast upon which the woman sits

(v. 3) is introduced without the article, and therefore cannot refer to the one mentioned before in chapt. 13; moreover such a monster, a hideous combination of the four beasts of Dan., would not be suitable as a riding-horse (*Reitthier*) for a woman dressed out with exceeding luxuriousness. Originally the beast of this picture had no relation to the beast of many heads and horns, full of blasphemous names (13¹); these attributes were added to convert this beast into that of chapt. 13. The words 'drunken with the blood of the saints,' v. 6, are seen to be an addition of the redactor, since chapts. 18-19, interpolations being omitted, show that the cause of Rome's punishment is not the martyrdom of the saints, but her immorality. — Objections to vv. 9, 11, 14 have been raised by a considerable number of critics. The twofold interpretation of the 7 heads in v. 9, the singular numbering of the last king as an eighth and also one of the 7 in v. 11, and the mention of the war against the Lamb in v. 14 are thought to present unquestionable evidence of a redactor's work. For the discussion of these passages, see Com. *in loc.*

J. Weiss (27 ff.) sees in the chapt. three strata of tradition and inter-pretation. (1) The first version was from the hand of a writer in the time of the sixth emperor, *i.e.* Nero, Galba, or Vespasian. He represented Rome under the form of a luxurious woman, the courtesan of kings. The beast was the symbol of the Roman empire, the 7 heads represented the 7 empe-rors of whom the last was yet to come, and his short reign would be followed by the destruction of Rome, which would be wrought by God himself through all manner of plagues, 18⁸, 19²; there was no thought of the agency of the beast and the 10 horns in the destruction. Rome is punished as the corrupter of the nations, 18³, ⁷, ⁹, ²³; all references to an enmity toward God's people as the cause of her visitation belong to a later hand. (2) This first source was worked over by a writer in the same or the next reign. Evidence of the reviser's work is seen in his artificial number-ing of the kings, v. 8, in his exaltation of the figure of the beast into the first place, whereas in no. 1 it was subordinate, and in his identification of the beast with the eighth king. This writer specifies the manner in which Rome is to be destroyed. Antichrist is to appear as the enemy of Rome, and her destroyer. Nero will return from the East with a host of Parthian allies to war against Rome. The city will be destroyed by the heathen world-power, Antichrist, in the person of Nero, aided by his vassals the 10 kings. (3) This version, no. 2, was finally taken up by our Apocalyptist, and through additions made to refer to the circumstances of his own time. To the tale of Rome's sins was now added the persecution of the saints, 17⁶, 18²⁴, 19²ᵇ; the beast is now described as making war with the Lamb and his followers, v. 14; the beast is no longer a future character, he is present in Domitian, to whose time the third redactor probably belongs; this redactor sees in Domitian, *Nero redivivus*, who ascended from the abyss.

It is impossible here to enter into a full discussion of these and other less noteworthy criticisms. But it is believed that the principal difficulties upon which they rest have been sufficiently met in the Summary and Com. We must recognize the freedom with which the Apocalyptist everywhere uses thought and imagery suggested by traditional sources, and the independence with which he interprets and adapts material to his purposes. A legitimate exegesis seems to establish an appropriate meaning throughout the chapt. and to make unnecessary and improbable theories of a radical working over and combination of fragments from various documents — especially as the grounds on which such theories rest not infrequently necessitate an exegesis wholly unwarranted.

(3) Sevenfold declaration of Rome's ruin, 18^1-19^5. See pp. 284 f.

After the prefatory chapt. (17), in which Rome's sin is pictured, and God's agents in her judgment are made known, the Apocalyptist comes now in chapt. 18 to the crisis of her destruction. He does not portray the assault of her enemies coming against her, or the strokes of the plagues as they fall upon her. He proclaims rather the inevitableness of her just doom and the completeness of her overthrow and devastation. The exordium and close of this great paragraph form a setting accordant with the transcendent significance of the event now foretold in the drama of the end. An angel descending from heaven with a glory that lightens all the earth and with a mighty voice *begins* the prophecy (vv. 1–3). Its *issue* in a perfect fulfillment and in the triumph of God's righteousness is celebrated with corresponding majesty in heaven; a great chorus in which are joined all the celestial hosts, the angels, the four and twenty Elders, and the four Living Creatures, raises its threefold Alleluia in Jehovah's throne-hall, and a voice from the throne calls upon all the servants of God upon earth to lift up their antiphon of praise (19^{1-5}).

In three separate aspects Rome's utter ruin is declared. Her place in the earth becomes a desolate waste, and haunt of demons and foul creatures (18^2); her political and commercial power perishes, the kings and traders of the earth proclaim the extinction of all her might and riches (18^{9-19}); all signs of her social and domestic life vanish (18^{21-23}). Viewed in detail the passage will be seen to consist of seven distinct parts. (1) The angel's announcement of Rome's certain fall, 18^{1-3}. (2) A warning to God's people to flee from the impending doom, 18^{4-5}. (3) An incitement of the spirits of vengeance to do their full work, 18^{6-8}. (4) A dirge over the

ruin of so great power and riches, 18⁹⁻¹⁹. (5) An outburst
of exultation at God's act of vengeance, 18²⁰. (6) A symbolic
act of a mighty angel figuring Rome's sudden and complete
disappearance, 18²¹⁻²⁴. (7) The loud chorus in heaven celebrating God's judgment upon the great corrupter of the earth
and the persecutor of his servants, 19¹⁻⁵. For further features
in the formal structure of the paragraph see p. 724. — As
the great cities of old were in their corruptness and hostility
to God's people prototypes of Rome, so the utterances of the
O. T. prophets relating to the punishment of these naturally
furnish to the Apocalyptist his model, and in fact much of his
matter and language in his oracle concerning the Babylon of
the Christian age. This parallelism will be pointed out in the
notes below.

XVIII. 1.   See above. — ἄλλον ἄγγελον, *another angel:* probably in contrast with the angel of chapt. 17. See on 5⁵. —
ἐξουσίαν μεγάλην, *great power:* the reference here is, apparently,
not to the exercise of *authority* (RV), but to the *power* of the
angel to utter his message so that all might hear, as indicated
by ἐν ἰσχυρᾷ φωνῇ, *with a strong voice;* cf. 5², 10¹. For this
use of ἐξουσία cf. 9³, ¹⁰, ¹⁹. — ἡ γῆ ἐφωτίσθη κτλ., *the earth was
lightened with his glory:* cf. Ezk. 43², 'The earth shined with
his glory.' Brilliant light is a standing attribute of a heavenly
being; cf. 1 Tim. 6¹⁶, 'dwelling in light unapproachable.' See
on 4³. The angel is endowed with attributes befitting his
mission.

2. ἔπεσεν Βαβυλὼν κτλ., *fallen is Babylon:* the language in
which Babylon's fall is proclaimed in the O. T. prophets is used
to prophesy the fall of Rome; cf. Is. 21⁹, chapt. 47, Jer. chapts.
50–51. See on 14⁸. The past tense is prophetic, expressing
the certainty of the future event; Rome had not yet fallen. —
ἐγένετο κατοικητήριον δαιμονίων κτλ., *has become a habitation of
demons,* etc.: the description follows conventional figures used
in the prophecies of the devastation of Babylon, Edom, and
Nineveh; cf. Is. 13¹⁹⁻²², 34¹¹⁻¹⁵, Jer. 50³⁹, 51³⁷, Zeph. 2¹⁵, Bar.
4³⁵. — φυλακὴ παντὸς πνεύματος, *a hold of every unclean spirit:*
the exact sense of φυλακή here is not certain. The meaning
prison, i.e. as a place where the unclean spirits and birds are
confined (so, Düst. Bleek, Holtzm. many others), or a place to

which they are banished (so, Ewald, De Wet. *al*), seems hardly
appropriate. Possibly the meaning is a *place of watching*,
where the demons and birds of prey watch for their victims
(so, Holtzm.-Bau., *al*); but this does not seem appropriate, at
least to the demons. If the clause φυλακὴ πνεύματος is precisely parallel with the preceding, as the repetition of δαιμόνιον
in πνεῦμα ἀκάθαρτον indicates, φυλακή is parallel with κατοικητήριον, and has probably the same meaning essentially; the
meaning, then, may be a place where the unclean spirits and
birds are kept safe, unmolested, they *live undisturbed there.*
For φυλάσσειν, φυλακή of the act of keeping free from disturb·
ance see L. & S. *s.v.*

3. The cause of Rome's judgment given here is her corrupting influence. Other causes, her overweening pride (v. 7) and
her martyrdom of the saints (v. 24), are not mentioned; the
Apocalyptist is here merely repeating the language and thought
of 14^8. — ἐκ τοῦ οἴνου κτλ., *of the wine of the wrath*, etc.: see on
14^8. — πέπωκαν, *have drunk:* cf. $14^{8, 10}$, 17^2, and the O. T. passages cited in note on 14^8. Not only is the analogy of all the
parallels against the reading πέπτωκαν, *have fallen* (RV. see
text. note), but it is doubtful whether the use of πίπτειν in
such a connection is supported; the Christian's fall from steadfastness, of which the word is used figuratively (1 Co. 10^{12}),
is not parallel to the deterioration of a corrupt heathen people.
— οἱ βασιλεῖς . . . ἐπόρνευσαν, *the kings . . . have committed
fornication:* cf. 17^2. For the meaning see p. 691. — ἐκ τῆς δυνάμεως τοῦ στρήνους αὐτῆς, *through the power of her luxuriousness*, or, *wantonness:* for the words στρῆνος and στρηνιάω, $18^{3, 7, 9}$
(καταστρηνιάω, 1 Tim. 5^{11}), not found elsewhere in the N. T.,
we have no precise equivalents; they contain the idea of excessive luxury and self-indulgence with accompanying arrogance and wanton exercise of strength. Rome's demand for
luxuries has enriched the merchants and at the same time made
them partakers of her wantonness and arrogance. The accumulation of wealth in itself is not what is here made a ground of
indictment. — δυνάμεως, *power:* the luxuriousness of Rome is
spoken of as an actual power, which has worked to the enrich-
ment of the traders. The translation *abundance* (so, some, AV)
is not warranted.

4-5. See p. 711. The certainty of Rome's visitation is emphasized by a warning to God's people uttered by God himself or Christ ('my people') to flee from the city lest they fall into her sins and share in her plagues. The language is taken from Jer. 51⁴⁵ (wanting in the LXX, as known to us); cf. also Jer. 51⁶, 50⁸, Is. 48²⁰, 53¹¹. — ἐκολλήθησαν ἄχρι τοῦ οὐρανοῦ, *have reached unto heaven:* the meaning is that Rome's sins form a vast pile which reaches unto heaven. The figure is suggested by Jer. 51⁹, 'her judgment reacheth unto heaven, and is lifted up even to the skies'; cf. Ezra 9⁶. The use of κολλᾶσθαι is peculiar; cases cited as parallel, *e.g.* Ac. 9²⁶, Lk. 10¹¹, are not the same. The thought is not that the sins *cleave to* the skies, but rather that they *cleave to one another*, forming a mass reaching unto (ἄχρι) heaven. See RVmarg. — τὰ ἀδικήματα: both the acc. and the gen. are used after μνημονεύειν; see Blass § 36, 6; Win. § 30, 10, c.

6-8. See p. 711. From the warning given to the saints the voice turns to the spirits of vengeance, and bids them to exact of Rome the full penalty of her guilt. The mention of God in the third person, vv. 5, 8, does not show a change of speaker. The persons addressed are not mentioned; the passage is rhetorical in form, proclaiming the certainty of vengeance and its cause. — ἀπόδοτε αὐτῇ . . . ἀπέδωκεν, *render unto her as also she herself rendered:* the words echo Jer. 50¹⁵; cf. also Jer. 50²⁹, 51²⁴, ⁵⁶, Ps. 137⁸. On the vindictiveness of the language see p. 723. The word ἀπέδωκεν is used for rhetorical correspondence with ἀπόδοτε and not in its exact sense; for it refers to a *deed* on Rome's part, not a *requital ;* cf. Ps. 137⁸, LXX. ἀποδιδόναι, which characterizes punishment as a *paying back,* is often used of suffering in return for suffering inflicted, cf. Ro. 12¹⁷, 1 Thess. 5¹⁵, 2 Thess. 4¹⁴, 1 Pet. 3⁹. It is therefore understood here more appropriately of Rome's punishment for her persecution of the Christians than for her corruption of the nations. The reference, then, is to the martyrdom of the saints, as in v. 24 and 19² ᵇ. The second clause 'in the cup which she has mingled,' etc., is as the language shows parallel in thought with v. 3, 14⁸, 17⁴, referring to the corruption of the nations and the drinking of the cup of God's wrath in return. A third clause, v. 7, speaks of Rome's impious pride. The three clauses then give in brief the three causes of God's wrath against Rome which are mentioned in different parts of the paragraph; see p. 723. — διπλώσατε τὰ διπλᾶ, *double [unto her] the double:* requite her in double measure, a conventional expression for *full requital;* cf. Is. 40², Jer. 16¹⁸, 17¹⁸, Ex. 22⁴, ⁷, ⁹. — ὅσα : acc. of kindred meaning; cf. Ro. 6¹⁰, Gal. 2²⁰. — ἐστρηνίασεν, *hath waxed wanton:* see on v. 3. — κάθημαι βασίλισσα κτλ., *I sit a queen,* etc.: Rome like Babylon and Tyre exalted herself above God ; cf. Is. 47⁷⁻⁹, 'I am and there is none else beside me; I shall not sit as a widow . . . but these two things shall come to thee in a moment in one day,' etc.; cf. also Ezek. 28², Zeph. 2¹⁵, Sib. Or. V. 173. — ἐν μιᾷ ἡμέρᾳ, *in one day:* like μιᾷ ὥρᾳ, *in one hour,* vv. 10, 16, 19, a symbolical term for suddenness.

9-10. See p. 711. From the proclamation of Rome's certain doom the Apocalyptist passes on to the dirge which the kings, the merchants, and seafarers of all the earth will utter, lamenting the complete ruin of the great city, vv. 9-19. — κλαύσουσιν . . . οἱ βασιλεῖς κτλ., *the kings of the earth will weep,* etc.: taken from the lament over Tyre, Ezk. 26¹⁶ ᶠ·, cf. also 27³⁵. For the attitude of the kings as contrasted with that declared in 17¹⁶, see pp. 722 f. — οἱ μετ' αὐτῆς . . . στρηνιάσαντες, *who committed fornication with her and lived wantonly:* for the meaning of the first phrase see p. 690 ; for the second see on v. 3. — τὸν καπνὸν τῆς πυρώσεως αὐτῆς, *the smoke of her burning:* while other plagues are mentioned (v. 8), destruction by fire forms the chief feature in the prophecies of Rome's ruin; vv. 8, 17, 19³, 17¹⁶; cf. Is. 34¹⁰, Ezk. 28¹⁸.

11. The lament of the merchants and seafarers is taken from the dirge over the fall of Tyre in Ezk. 27²⁸⁻³⁶. There is a double strain in the sorrow of the merchants; they lament their loss of trade, v. 11, then the utter destruction of so great treasure, vv. 16 f. The same character seems to be intended in the chant of the seafarers in the two clauses of 19 *c*, 'wherein all that had their ships in the sea were made rich' and 'in one hour is she laid waste.'

12-14. The catalogue of wares furnished to Rome illustrates the luxury of her life and the vastness of her commerce. The list is formed in imitation of Ezk. 27⁵⁻²⁴, most of the articles are mentioned there; cf. also Ezk. 16⁹⁻¹³. There are seven groups; (1) precious metals, precious stones and pearls, (2) rich cloths, (3) thyine wood and ornamental vessels of ivory, of choice wood and of brass, iron, and marble, (4) aromatic articles, (5) articles of food, (6) chattels of beasts, horses and chariots, and slaves, (7) choice fruits.   Groups 1, 2, and 5 consist of four members each; (1) gold, silver, precious stones and pearls; (2) fine linen, purple stuffs, silk, and scarlet stuffs; (5) wine, oil, fine flour, and wheat.   Probably this is intended in group 6, for horses and chariots as inseparable form one object of luxury, and the two designations of slaves refer to a single thing (see below).   If in v. 13 ἄμωμον, *amomum* (RV mrg, *spice* RV text, wanting in AV), be omitted, as in some sources (see text. note), group 4 also has four members.   In group 3 the second σκεῦος, *vessel*, is followed by four designations of material, precious wood, brass, iron, and marble.   This observance of numbers in the construction of the passage is unquestionable.   See further p. 724. — πᾶν ξύλον θύϊνον, *all thyine wood:* this probably means every variety of the wood, or perhaps better, as suiting the connection, all articles made of it.   Thyine is a hard, dark wood; it was used for costly furniture.   See En. Bib. IV. 5066.   The construction here changes to the acc., but returns to the gen. in ἵππων, v. 13, and then again to the acc. in ψυχάς; evidently for the sake of variety. — σιδήρου, *iron:* ornamental vessels are meant, as the position in a list of such shows.   Artistic goblets of iron are mentioned as votive offerings.   See Smith, *Bib. Dict. s.v.* — ἄμωμον, *amomum:* a perfume or ointment made from an oriental plant of the name, whose identification is uncertain.   It is better to transfer the word without translation.   See Enc. Bib. I. 145. — θυμιάματα, λίβανον, *incense, frankincense:* the former is a general term for substances, frequently a mixture of various substances, burnt for the production of odors, and as an offering in religious ceremonial; the latter is the fragrant gum of certain trees, and was used as incense, or an important ingredient in compounding incense.   For the composition of the incense to be used in the Hebrew ritual see Ex. 30[34-37]. — μύρον, *ointment:* a fragrant, costly ointment; cf. Mt. 26[7].

κτήνη, *beasts*, or *cattle:* as here used the word is distinguished from πρόβατα, *sheep*, and ἵππων, *horses;* it may refer to other domestic animals in general, or perhaps to beasts of burden as in Lk. 10³⁴, Ac. 23²⁴. — σώματα, *slaves*: for this use of the word see Thayer, *s.v.* 1, *c*, L & S. *s.v.* II. — καὶ ψυχὰς ἀνθρώπων, *even bondmen*, lit. *persons of men:* this phrase also is used with the meaning *slaves;* cf. Num. 31³⁵, Ezk. 27¹³, 1 Ch. 5²¹ (ψυχὰς ἀνδρῶν). Neither here nor elsewhere is there anything to indicate a difference between the two terms, as denoting different classes of slaves. Numerous suggestions of a distinction have been made, but they are arbitrary, without foundation in our passage or in the use of the terms elsewhere. The second term repeating the first is a reminiscence of Ezk. 27¹³; as seen above, that chapt. of Ezk. was before the author's mind throughout this passage. Whether he felt the first term too vague and added the second to make the meaning specific, or whether he added it simply as a reminiscence of his source, is not important. At all events, since both terms have the same reference, καί is *even* rather than *and* (EV). For ψυχή, *soul = person*, see Thayer, *s.v.* 1, *c.*, *e.g.* Ac. 27³⁷, 'We were in all . . . 276 souls.' — πάντα τὰ λιπαρὰ κτλ., *all things that are dainty*, etc.: a summary phrase including the foregoing and similar objects. — εὑρήσουσιν, *they shall find:* the construction changes abruptly from the second person to the impersonal third.

15–16. See on v. 11.　　　17–19. A lament of the seafarers is added, as in the Apocalyptist's source, Ezk., chapt. 27, from which the form also is in part taken (vv. 29–36). For the form and character of the lament see further on v. 11 and p. 724. — κυβερνήτης, *shipmaster:* properly the steersman, who had also the command over the other seamen. He was subordinate to the ναύκληρος, the supreme commander; cf. Ac. 27¹¹, where both words are found. The ναῦται are the *sailors* in the narrow sense of the term. — πᾶς ὁ ἐπὶ τόπον πλέων, *every one that saileth any whither* (Alf., RV), lit. *saileth to a place:* some, following De Wette, take the phrase to mean *coasters*, citing in support Ac. 27², τοὺς κατὰ τὴν 'Ασίαν τόπους, *the places along the coast of Asia*. But the two phrases are far from parallel. The expression used here is so peculiar that an error in the text is probable. The conjecture of πόντον for τόπον, *every one that saileth upon the sea*, is plausible; see text. note. If that was the original form, perhaps it was suggested by Ezk. 27²⁹, 'all the pilots of the sea.' — ὅσοι τὴν θάλασσαν ἐργάζονται, *as many as do business on the sea:* cf. Ps. 107²³. The phrase corresponds to ἐργάζεσθαι τὴν γῆν, *to work, till the earth;* both occur in extra-biblical writers. In itself the phrase would include *fishers,* but such allusion here is inappropriate to the context, which is occupied with Rome's commerce. — τίς ὁμοία κτλ., *what* [city] *is like the great city?:* no equal is left. Cf. Ezk. 27³². — ἔβαλον χοῦν κτλ., *they cast dust on their heads:* from Ezk. 27³⁰. — ἐκ τῆς τιμιότητος, *by reason of her costliness:* through the greatness of her costly trade. Cf. Ezk. 27³³.

20. See p. 711. These words cannot be assigned to the voice of v. 4 (so, some com.); if that were intended some identifying expression would be required after the long intervening passage, vv. 9–19; cf. the connection of 4¹ with 1¹⁰. It is rather the Prophet himself who speaks. For the apostrophe to heaven cf. 12¹², Is. 44²³, 49¹³, Jer. 51⁴⁸. The analogy of these passages shows that *heaven* in this verse is not to be understood (so, some com.) as an address to departed saints and apostles supposed to be in heaven. — οἱ ἅγιοι κτλ., *ye saints,* etc.: the apostrophe turns from heaven to the saints, apostles, etc., a separate object of address; nothing is implied as to where these are, or whether they are living or dead. The first words refer to all saints alike, the following clauses to special classes of these, *i.e.* the apostles and prophets; see on 11¹⁸. — κρίμα ὑμῶν, *your judgment, i.e.* the judgment of their cause.

This verse is rejected by many critics as interrupting the connection between the prophecies of the foregoing verses and that of vv. 21 ff. The criticism, however, proceeds from a misapprehension of the real sequence here. The verse forms the close of the passages vv. 9–20 formulating in anticipation the feelings with which the catastrophe proclaimed in vv. 1–8 will be greeted, when it shall have taken place. Verses 9–19 describe the sorrow of the world; v. 20 expresses the exultation of the Church. In this last verse the Apocalyptist might have introduced the saints themselves uttering their words of exultation; instead, however, he comes forward himself with prophetic power and sanction calling them to acclamation. The sudden introduction of his own words is in accord with his manner;

cf. 13⁹⁻¹⁰, ¹⁸, 14¹². This long passage (vv. 9–20), anticipating
the sequel of the catastrophe, being finished, the Apocalyptist
returns, v. 21, to the time of vv. 4–8, and brings in another
part of the prophecy of Rome's fall.

21–24. See p. 712. By a symbolic act an angel proclaims
Rome's sudden and utter disappearance from the earth, accompanying his act with a chant of doom. The angel's symbolical
act is suggested by Jer. 51⁶³ᶠ·; cf. Neh. 9¹¹. For similar
dramatic prophecy cf. Ac. 21¹¹, Is. 20, Jer. 13, Ezk. 4. While
vv. 9–19 tell of the ruin of Rome in its relation to the world
at large, as represented in its political power and commerce,
these verses have reference to the extinction of its internal
state, as represented in its pleasures, in the labors of its craftsmen, and in its family life. See further on the passage
p. 724. — εἰς: indef. art.; see on 8¹³. — ἄγγελος ἰσχυρός, *a
strong angel :* cf. 5², 10¹. — ὀρμήματι, *with mighty force :* the rare
word ὄρμημα appears to be used here in the sense of ὀρμή, a
violent onset made, *e.g.*, by an attacking army, and so the
violent impulse given to an object. — φωνὴ κιθαρῳδῶν κτλ., *the
sound of harpers,* etc.: the song of judgment in these verses,
22–23, is taken from Jer. 25¹⁰; cf. Is. 24⁸, Jer. 7³⁴, 16⁹, Ezk. 26¹³.
The speaker turns abruptly here to direct address, but comes
back to the third person in v. 24; so after the third person in
vv. 11–13, the second person is introduced in v. 14. Such
changes do not indicate a different hand (so, some critics); it
is a common occurrence in the psalms and the prophets, *e.g.*
Ps. 52⁴⁻⁶, 62³⁻⁴, 81¹⁰⁻¹², Ezk. 32¹¹⁻¹², Am. 6³⁻⁷. — φωνὴ μύλου
κτλ., *the sound of a mill,* etc.: no grain shall be ground; there
shall be no sign of what sustains life. — οἱ μεγιστᾶνες τῆς γῆς,
the great ones of the earth : cf. 6¹⁵, Mk. 6²¹. There is an idea
of arrogance implied. Rome has made the merchants who
traded with her like herself in their wanton pride, cf. v. 7.
There are then three reasons given in 23 *b*–24 for the judgment
of the great city: (1) she has raised up in the earth magnates
who wantonly exalt themselves, (2) she has led all the nations
astray by her seductions, (3) she has martyred the saints. See
on vv. 6–7. The second ὅτι (*for*) clause in v. 23 is coördinate
with the first, not subordinate to it. In these clauses the
tense changes to the past; the prophet, as often, speaks from

the standpoint of the accomplished prophecy. — φαρμακίᾳ, *sorcery:* used figuratively, with the same meaning as the wine of her fornication, v. 3, 14⁸. — αἷμα προφητῶν κτλ., *the blood of prophets*, etc.: cf. 16⁶, 17⁶, 18²⁰, 19²ᵇ. — προφητῶν καὶ ἁγίων, *prophets and saints : i.e.* prophets and other saints; see on 16¹⁹. — πάντων τῶν ἐσφαγμένων, *all that have been slain :* not all martyrdoms had occurred at Rome, but upon her as the head of the world-empire is laid the guilt of all; cf. the indictment uttered by the Lord against Jerusalem and that generation, Lk. 13³³, Mt. 23³⁵ ᶠ·.

XIX. 1. See p. 712. The prophecies of the fall of great Babylon have culminated in the symbolic act of the angel, and the long paragraph (17¹–19⁵) now closes fittingly with an anticipative chorus in which all the heavenly hosts join in praising God for the just judgment visited upon the corrupter of the earth and the slayer of God's servants, 19¹⁻⁵. The keynote of the song is given in the opening word *Alleluia*, praise Jehovah, the Hebrew liturgical exclamation taken over into Christian hymnody. And the song ends with the same word repeated as an antiphon ; it is uttered again by the Elders and the Living Creatures, added to their Amen in response to the angelic hymn. As the promised subject of the vision was τὸ κρίμα τῆς πόρνης τῆς μεγάλης, *the judgment of the great harlot,* 17¹, so the hymn celebrates the accomplishment of the prophecy in answering words, ἔκρινεν τὴν πόρνην τὴν μεγάλην, *he hath judged the great harlot,* 19². The utterance of praise given here is similar in thought and language to that which was anticipated before the beginning of the last plagues, 15³⁻⁴, but more exultant. And in augustness of ceremonial, and in part in construction, it is parallel with the hymns of chapt. 5. Here as there the scene is in the great throne-hall of Jehovah, with all the orders of heavenly beings ranged before and round about the Almighty ; in both scenes the higher and lower orders sing antiphonally, in both the four Living Creatures and the four and twenty Elders prostrate themselves in worship before the throne ; in both the four Living Creatures join in the Amen ; in the former scene all creation adds its response to the song in heaven, here a voice calls upon the saints of earth likewise to add their antiphon of praise. The majesty of the scene and the power of the scene and the power of the ' heavenly Te Deum,' as it is sometimes called, befit the marvelous event of Rome's destruction, which is conceived to have been accomplished, and which opens the last great act of the drama before the millennium. The entire thought of vv. 1–5 is so closely concerned with God's act in the fall of Rome, that these verses are unquestionably to be joined with the preceding paragraph, rather than made (as some take them) a part of an introduction to the following. ἀλληλούϊα, *alleluia* : praise ye Jehovah ; cf. the psalms *passim*, *e.g.* the opening of 111–113, 146–150 ; in the N. T. found only in this chapt. vv. 3, 4, 6. — σωτηρία, *salvation:* the word includes here more than the deliverance of the saints ; it is the safeguarding, the maintenance in triumph, of the whole cause of God's kingdom with its blessedness. See Düst. on 12¹⁰. — τοῦ θεοῦ ἡμῶν, *sc.* εἰσί, *are our God's:* as explained in the following verse, they are by the judgment of Rome vindicated as his.

2–3. ἀληθιναὶ καὶ δίκαιαι, *true and righteous:* see on 15³. — ἐν τῇ πορνείᾳ αὐτῆς, *with her fornication:* for the meaning, see p. 690. — εἴρηκαν, *said :* aoristic perf.; see on 5⁷. — ὁ καπνὸς αὐτῆς ἀναβαίνει κτλ., *her smoke goeth up for ever and ever:* cf. Is. 34¹⁰. The words are those of the Seer, who points to the unquenchable smoke rising as the accompaniment to the song and the proof of its truth.

4–5. πρεσβύτεροι, ζῶα, *Elders, Living Creatures:* see on 4⁴, ⁶. — φωνὴ ἀπὸ τοῦ θρόνου, *a voice from the throne :* from the immediate presence of God, apparently from one of the Living Creatures, who stand nearest to the throne and act as God's special agents ; cf. 5⁶, 6¹, ³, ⁵, ⁷, 15⁷. The words ' our God ' show that the voice of God is not meant. The command is addressed to the saints on earth ; the words οἱ φοβούμενοι αὐτόν, οἱ μικροὶ κτλ., *ye who fear him, the small and the great*, are common designations of men, not of heavenly beings. The Church on earth is bidden to add its song of praise to that of the heavenly choir ; see note on v. 1. The passage combines Pss. 134¹ and 115¹³. — αἰνεῖτε τῷ θεῷ : the Gk. translation of *Alleluia;* the command here is equivalent to ' Sing Alleluia to our God.' — τῷ θεῷ : the dat. instead of the acc. after αἰνεῖν is

3 A

not found elsewhere in the N. T., but occurs in the LXX, *e.g.*
Jer. 20¹³, 1 Chron. 16³⁶, 2 Chron. 20¹⁹.

Textual notes, 18¹–19⁵. 18¹. R with a few min omits αλλον before αγγε-
λον. — 2. For ισχυρα φωνη, R without authority reads ισχυι, φωνη μεγαλη.
— 3. του οινου אQ most min and vers R edd; wanting in AC some vers Lch
Alf; bracketed by W H *al.* See Ws *Ap.* 97. — πεπωκ- (*have drunk*) P most
min vers R most edd; πεπτωκ- (*are fallen*) אACQ some min and vers Tr
WH RV. In spite of the superior Ms. authority for the latter, most scholars
regard it an error, perhaps due to conformation with επεσεν, v. 2. Sense and
14⁸ seem to require the former. Cf. Ws *Ap.* 137. — 5. For εκολληθησαν, R
reads ηκολουθησαν, without authority. — 6. After απεδωκεν, R adds υμιν with
some min and vers anc com; wanting in most sources. — 13. και αμωμον
א*ACP many min vers anc com edd; wanting in אᶜQ most min some vers
and anc com R. The noun repeats the last three syllables of κινναμωμον,
which might account for its insertion or omission. The tendency here to
form groups of four (see Com. vv. 12–14) favors its omission; so, Bouss.
— 14. ευρησουσιν אACP some min and vers edd; ευρης or ευρησεις Q most
min; R with one min has ευρησης. — 17. επι τοπον πλεων אACQ most min
vers edd; R has επι των πλοιων ο ομιλος, so a few min some anc com. The
conjecture ποντον for τοπον (Nestle), supported by Prim. *omnis super mare
navigans*, is plausible; so, Blj Gwynn Moff. See Com. — 19. R with a few
min some anc com omits τα before πλοια. — 20. και οι before αποστολοι, most
sources edd; wanting in C a few min some anc com some Mss. of vlg R. —
23. φανη (1 aor. subjv. act., see Blass § 16, 3) is the accentuation adopted
by most edd; R some edd give φανη̣, 2 aor. subjv. pass. — 24. αιμα אACP
some min and anc com R most edd; αιματα Q most min some anc com
Ti RV.

19¹⁻⁵. For αλληλουια, WH (see their *Introd.* p. 313) write αλληλουιά, in
conformity with the Heb. — After δοξα, R with some min and vers inserts
και η τιμη. — του θεου most sources edd; some min vers and anc com have
τω θεω, adopted by R, which with one min prefixes κυριω. — 5. απο ACQ
many min edd; εκ אP many min R Ti.

Criticism of chapt. 18. The principal arguments urged in the criticism of
this chapt. are the following: (1) In chapt. 18 the kings of the earth be-
wail the fall of Rome, vv. 9 f.; but according to 17¹⁶ it is they who with
the Beast have wrought her ruin. Yet, though this difference is unquestionable, it is of a kind appearing elsewhere in the book and not in itself
indicative of a difference in authorship. In chapt. 18 the writer prophesying the utter ruin of Rome uses almost in verbal quotation the O. T. prophecies of the fall of Babylon and Tyre (see Com.), which in dramatic form
represented the kings lamenting the destruction of so much splendor and
riches. The interest of those O. T. passages for our Apocalyptist lies wholly
in the utterances as declaring the completeness of the ruin. In chapt. 17
he is concerned with the *agency* by which the ruin is wrought, and he takes
the form of his prophecy from the current expectation of the Neronic Anti-

christ and his vassals. Thus he blends two traditions: the one that of
Heb. eschatology, as represented in the prophets, with the Gentile nations
witnessing the overthrow of Israel's enemies; the other that of the more
transcendental expectation of Antichrist subjecting all the world to his
sway. It is not strange that an apocalyptist in his constant use of traditional symbolism should not be rigorously consistent, since he is conscious
that his symbols do not contain an exact historical program of the future.
The combination of differing traditions is similar to that which appears in
16^{12-16} (see note there). Cf. also the apparently conflicting prophecies
mentioned in the note on ' all nations shall come and worship,' 15^4.

(2) The destruction of Rome is attributed in chapt. 18 to the direct and
instantaneous act of God, v. 8, v. 10 'in one hour'; there is no allusion to
the Beast, the Neronic Antichrist, and his vassals the ten kings, to whom
all is attributed in 17^{16}. There is, however, no disagreement here. The
Beast and his forces are only the instrument or a part of it, which God uses
for Rome's destruction. Cf. Am. 3^6, 'Shall evil befall a city, and Jehovah
hath not done it?' Cf. Ezk. $24^{7\,f.}$, where an act spoken of is declared in
two consecutive sentences to be that of Jerusalem and that of God. Bousset (425) points out that in the prophecies of the Sib. Or., e.g. IV. 130–139,
V. 361–379, marvelous visitations sent from God upon Rome are combined
with the ruin wrought by the returning Nero. For the meaning of ' one
hour' see on v. 8.

(3) The cause of Rome's destruction is her corruption of the nations,
vv. 3, 23; nothing is said primarily of her enmity toward God's people;
17^6, $18^{20,\,24}$, $19^{2\,b}$ are redactional additions (so, e.g. J. Weiss, 119). But the
rejection of these verses is not certainly supported by reasons independent
of a theory of redaction (see notes in loc.); it is true that they could be
omitted and a complete whole would remain. But the same might be said
of v. 7, which gives another cause of God's wrath against Rome. Verse 6 a
is probably parallel with the above-named verses in referring to vengeance
for wrongs done to God's servants (see note there). Verses 6–7 appear to
sum up three causes operative in Rome's judgment; her persecution of
God's people, her corruption of the nations, and her impious pride. In the
expansion of the theme in 17^1–19^5, while the first and third causes are
mentioned somewhat incidentally, the second is presented with fullness;
probably because that is the case in the O. T. oracles which the Apocalyptist uses as his models here. An instructive parallel is seen in the book
of Nahum. Nineveh's corruption and corrupting inflence upon the nations
(3^4) form the great indictment against her; her oppression of God's people,
doubtless the thought uppermost in the mind of the prophet, is alluded to
only incidentally, 1^{13}.

(4) The violent hatred of Rome manifested is not Christian; it is suitable to a Jew with the deadly enemy of his nation in mind. The lament of
the traders, betraying a touch of grief at the destruction of such rich treasures, is more appropriate to a Jew than a Christian of the time (so,
Pfleiderer, Schoen, al). It might perhaps be said in answer that the object
of the vindictiveness shown is not persons, but a corrupt and anti-Christian

capital. At all events the tone of the passage is not foreign to the Christian utterances of the time; see on 6[10]. The enumeration of the treasures in the dirge is part of the picture taken over from the lament for Tyre, and expresses the feeling of the traders, not of the Apocalyptist. As regards the absence of specific Christian terms, which is also urged in this connection, it should be borne in mind that the Christian character of a passage, closely formed throughout on O. T. models, is determined not so much by the insertion of Christian phraseology as by the setting given to it.

Most critics suppose a Jewish source as the foundation of the chapt.; so, Vischer, Pfleiderer, Weyland, Sabatier, Schoen, Wellhausen, al. J. Weiss, omitting assumed Christian interpolations, makes it a part of his Jewish source Q, which a redactor has in the present form of the book combined with the Johannine Apocalypse; the author of the primary document knew nothing of Rome's hostility to his people, he mourns for her destruction, while acknowledging its justness because of her wickedness. Bousset assigns the chapt. to an assumed source of Vespasian's time, whether Jewish or Christian is uncertain (see pp. 705 f.). Erbes refers the whole paragraph (chapts. 17–19[4]), as a unit, to his Christian redactor of the year 80. Völter also takes the two chapts. as a unit and of Christian origin.

There is a sense in which it can without question be said that the chapt. goes back to a Heb. original, for to a degree true of no other chapt. in the book it is a mosaic of passages derived directly from the O. T. Nearly every verse is immediately suggested thus, as has been shown in the Com. But certain characteristics point strongly to our Apocalyptist as the composer. The author of chapts. 18–19[5] has special fondness for the number seven as a constructive feature; the paragraph is formed of seven distinct parts (see p. 711), and the list of choice objects in the merchants' lament gives seven distinct groups (see p. 716). Likewise the numbers three and four are unquestionably influential in the composition. In chapt. 18, for *three,* cf. the three classes in vv. 2 *b,* 24, the three nouns in 8 *a,* 16 *a,* 16 *b,* the three groups who utter laments; for *four,* cf. the four objects in several of the groups in vv. 12–14 (see p. 716), the four classes in vv. 17, 20, 22. There is also a tendency to follow a schematic form in the use of phrases which recalls the structure of the seven epistles. Thus each of the groups of utterances which fill out the paragraph closes with a 'for' clause; in chapt. 18, vv. 3, 5, 8, 10, 17, 19, 20, 23; in chapt. 19, v. 2. Each division of the lament contains the threefold refrain, (*a*) 'standing afar off,' (*b*) 'saying, Woe, woe, the great city,' (*c*) 'for in one hour,' etc., vv. 10, 15 f., 17–19. In the proclamation of the angel, vv. 21 ff., the refrain, 'no more at all,' is introduced at the end of each part, six times in all. These characteristics of the passage, so marked in the Apocalyptist elsewhere, seem to point pretty certainly to him as the composer. And with this agrees the ejaculatory insertion in v. 20 (see note there). The unusual nature of the subject explains the presence of a large number of words not found elsewhere in the book (also urged as a ground of criticism); most of these are found in the O. T. passages here imitated. The appropriateness, or we may say the necessity, of some such paragraph in this place seems beyond doubt. —

The criticism of 19¹⁻⁵, though those verses form a part of the preceding paragraph, can be taken up most conveniently in connection with chapt. 19 as a whole; see pp. 741 f.

XIX. 6–XX. 6. *Sequel to the fall of Rome.* See pp. 286 f.

(1) Prophetic hymn hailing the kingdom of God, as if present, 19⁶⁻¹⁰. The angelic hymn here introduced, like those of 11¹⁵ ⁿ., 12¹⁰ ⁿ., is wholly proleptic; much is yet to intervene before the marriage of the Lamb and the establishment of the kingdom. The hymn is not a response, as some take it (so, Spitta, *al*), to the call of v. 5, which is addressed to the saints of earth (see note there). The singers here are the hosts of heaven; cf. 5¹¹, 12¹⁰, 19¹. Not only do the similes of the many waters and the mighty thunders, as used of the voices of a multitude elsewhere in the book, point to heavenly voices (14², 1¹⁵, 6¹), but the prophetic announcement concerning the kingdom of God and the marriage of the Lamb is meant as an assurance given to the saints of earth; it must then come from heaven. And in the solemn confirmation of the words, which is added in v. 9, they are declared those of God. The theme of the hymn, like that of vv. 1–5, is occasioned by the fall of Rome; but while those verses form a song of exultation over the judgment accomplished, the thought here is wholly concerned with the end to which that crisis leads on; the one hymn looks backward, the other forward. The distinction is indicated by the ὅτι, *for*, clauses, vv. 2, 7, which give the ground of the outburst of praise in the respective cases; in the former it is because God has judged Rome, in the latter it is because the marriage of the Lamb has come. These verses (6–8) then should not in the formal analysis of the book be joined with the foregoing, as if a part of the same group of hymns (so, many com.). The transition to a new, though allied, part of the paragraph is marked by the words, καὶ ἤκουσα . . . πολλοῦ, *and I heard the voice of a great multitude*, as new divisions are introduced by καὶ εἶδον, *and I saw*, vv. 11, 17, 19, and 20¹,⁴.

6. λέγοντες, *saying:* the partic. (whatever form be adopted: see text. note) belongs, as in v. 1, with ὄχλου, *multitude;* the words of the following hymn are not uttered by the waters and thunders; the *sounds* (φωνήν) of these are similes to describe

the multitudinousness of the voices.   For the irregular nom. λέγοντες see p. 224. — ἀλληλούια, *Alleluia :* see on v. 1. — ἐβασίλευσεν, *hath become king :* the aor. is inceptive, and like the others in the passage is used where the English idiom uses the perf.   See Burton § 52.   While God's supreme lordship over the universe is everywhere assumed in Heb. and Christian thought, in a special eschatological sense he is said to *become king,* when his perfected kingdom shall have been established, and all opposing powers of evil destroyed; *e.g.* 11¹⁵, ¹⁷, 12¹⁰, Mt. 6¹⁰, 1 Co. 15²⁴.   All is anticipatory here, and reference is made, as in ' the marriage of the Lamb,' not to the millennium (20⁴⁻⁶), but to the consummation described in 20¹¹-22⁵.

7–8.   If the reading δώσομεν be adopted, the speakers turn from the hortatory form to the declarative. — ὁ γάμος τοῦ ἀρνίου, *the marriage of the Lamb :* the relation of God and his people is frequently expressed in the O. T. under the figure of marriage, and the thought passed over into Christian usage to figure the relation of Christ and his Church; *e.g.* Is. 54¹⁻⁶, Jer. 31³², Ezk. 16⁸, Mt. 25¹⁻¹⁰, Mk. 2¹⁹, 2 Co. 11², Eph. 5³².   In this passage the reference is to Christ's entrance into the state of perfect union with his Church in the consummation of all things.   The two grounds of exultation given in the hymn, the establishment of the kingdom of God, and the marriage of the Lamb, are in reality one fact viewed in two aspects. — ἡ γυνὴ αὐτοῦ, *his wife :* the espoused one who is to become his wife.   For the use of γυνή instead of νύμφη cf. 21⁹, Gen. 29²⁰. The vision of the Bride in her glory is given in 21⁹-22⁵, where, however, the figure of the bride is transferred to the new Jerusalem.   As Jerusalem and the people of Israel are frequently identified in speech (see pp. 588 f.), so in the Apocalyptist's vision of the renewed world, the people of God and their capital city, *i.e.* the Church and the new Jerusalem, are so closely connected that the figure designating the one may be transferred to the other. — Düst. points out that the promises offered under various figures to the individual at the close of the seven epistles (chapts. 2–3) are here set before the whole Church, under the figure of the marriage of the Lamb.

καὶ ἐδόθη κτλ., *yea, it hath been given to her to array herself,* etc. : the clause is explanatory of the preparation mentioned in

the preceding verse. The shining raiment belonging to celestial beings (see on 3⁴) is appropriate to the Bride, the Church,
in her glorified state here anticipated. The attire of the Bride
in its pure glory stands out in contrast with that of the woman
seated on the scarlet-colored beast, 17⁴. The word *give* is
significant here ; only by the gift of God can the Church attire
herself fittingly for the Lamb. — ἵνα περιβάληται : for a clause
with ἵνα as subj. see Burton § 211, Blass § 69, 5. — τὰ δικαιώ-
ματα τῶν ἁγίων, *the righteous acts of the saints :* the words explain what is meant by the fine linen in the Church's bridal
attire. For the meaning of δικαίωμα cf. 15⁴, Bar. 2¹⁹ (τὰ δικαιώ-
ματα τῶν πατέρων), probably Ro. 5¹⁸ ; contrast ἀδίκημα, 18⁵.
The pl. is against interpreting δικαίωμα as equivalent to
δικαιοσύνη, in the Pauline sense of *justification,* as some take
it (so, B. Weiss, *al*). The sentence, which has the sound of a
commentator's explanation, is regarded by most critics, perhaps
not wrongly, as a gloss.

9. καὶ λέγει, *and he saith :* the speaker must be the angel of
chapt. 17, who is thought of as still present with the Seer. We
should expect here some such identification of the subj. as is
given in connecting the speaker of 4¹ with that of 1¹⁰. But
the sudden introduction of his words, as if he had been mentioned in the context, is relieved by the fact that the whole
paragraph, 17¹–19⁵, belongs to what he promises (17¹) to show ;
his presence, then, is assumed to the end of the paragraph, and
may be conceived to continue in this, its immediate sequel.
The indefiniteness of the speaker does not justify a theory of
interpolation (see p. 742) ; so mechanical a use of sources is
contrary to the author's manner.

The relation of this verse to the context is clear. Since, as
seen above, a distinct paragraph, though one closely allied as
a sequel, begins in v. 6, the phrase 'these words' is to be
understood as referring to the hymn just preceding, *i.e.* to its
central theme, the heralding of the coming kingdom and the
marriage of the Lamb. The angel's utterance, then, has a significance similar to that of the angel in 10⁵ ᶠᶠ· before the opening of the last trumpet-series ; both give solemn assurance of
the fulfillment of the supreme Christian hope. And the two
utterances in this verse relate to that end ; blessed are they

that attain to it, and God's word avouches the prophecy of its advent.

γράψον, *write:* the command is meant to give emphasis to the following beatitude; cf. 14¹³, 21⁵. — τὸ δεῖπνον τοῦ γάμου, *the marriage supper;* for the figure of the wedding feast as here applied cf. Mt. 22² ᶠᶠ·, 25¹⁰. The invited guests are in the figure distinguished from the Bride, though in reality the two are identical. — The words καὶ λέγει, *and he saith,* are repeated with the introduction of a distinct thought, as in 22⁹⁻¹⁰. — οὗτοι οἱ λόγοι κτλ., *these words are true,* etc.: cf. 21⁵, 22⁶. The declaration gives solemn assurance of the truth of the foregoing prophecy of the kingdom. The meaning is clear, though the exact construction is uncertain. If with the weight of authority the art. is not inserted before ἀληθινοί, perhaps the preferable construction is, *these words are true* [*words*] *of God;* other constructions given are, *these are true words of God* (so, RV; but this disregards the art. before λόγοι); *these words are true,* they are *God's.* The AV, *these are the true sayings of God,* would require the art. before ἀληθινοί. Bouss. avoids the difficulty by rejecting τοῦ θεοῦ, for which he finds support in their absence from 21⁵, and their uncertain position in the Mss.; see text. note. — τοῦ θεοῦ, *of God:* the words of the hymn are those of angels, but they are properly called those of God, because the prophecies contained in them come from God. Objection to the passage (so, Spitta) cannot be found in the language.

10. Cf. 22⁸ ᶠ· If this verse is retained (see p. 742), the Seer must be understood to be overwhelmed with the awe inspired by the wonderful vision opened in the hymn, and by the presence of the messenger from heaven declaring the prophecies to be the veritable words of God himself. For his impulse to prostrate himself before the visitant, cf. Jos. 5¹⁴, Jg. 13²⁰, Ac. 10²⁵, 16²⁹. The supposition that the Seer mistakes the angel for Christ (Düst. *al*) is entirely without support; it is true that in former instances the command γράψον, *write,* had come from Christ or a voice from heaven, but here the words, 'and he saith,' introducing the speaker without qualification show that the Seer recognizes in him the person who had been talking with him before, *i.e.* the angel. — The angel sees in the Apocalyptist's act a homage that belongs to God alone, and

reproves him. With this scene cf. Asc. of Is. 7^{21}–8^5, ' I fell on
my face to worship him, but the angel who guided me did not
permit it, but said to me, Worship neither angel nor throne,
which belong to the six heavens . . . I am not thy Lord,
but thy companion.' It is possible that, as some suppose, the
Apocalyptist intends in this verse and in $22^{8\,f.}$ to reprove a
tendency to angel worship which existed in Asia Minor; see
Lightfoot, *Col.* 101 ff., and on Col. 2^{18}. — The fact that the
Seer hears hymns sung by heavenly hosts and falls at the feet
of an angel furnishes no ground for the supposition (J. Weiss)
that his position is suddenly changed here from earth to
heaven; cf. *e.g.* 10^9, $15^{2\,ff.}$. — ὅρα μή : for the ellipsis of ποιήσῃς
see Blass § 81, 1. — σύνδουλός σου, *a fellow-servant with thee :*
the angels are servants of God like the Apocalyptist and Christians in general; cf. ' our brethren,' 12^{10}. — τῶν ἐχόντων τὴν
μαρτυρίαν ᾽Ιησοῦ, *those who have the testimony of Jesus : i.e.* the
truth revealed by Jesus; see on 1^2. Christians in general are
meant, as seen from 12^{17}, 6^9.

ἡ γὰρ μαρτυρία . . . προφητείας, *for the testimony of Jesus is
the Spirit of prophecy :* this sentence is meant to explain how
the term *fellow-servant* can be applied to both the angel and the
Seer. The meaning of the obscure utterance can be reached
only by holding closely to the literal sense of the terms. The
Spirit of prophecy is the Spirit of God working in and through
the prophet, the divinely inspired activity of the prophet (cf.
1 Co. 12^{10}, 2 Pet. 1^{21}) ; then that which is here declared identical with it must also be an *activity;* μαρτυρία must denote the
work of testifying as in 11^7, Jno. 1^7. The work of Jesus, *i.e.*
of the Spirit of Jesus, in testifying is meant ; and in this connection reference must be made to his testifying in and through
Christians, who are spoken of in the preceding sentence. The
two activities, that of the prophet and that of the Christian in
general, are then those of one and the same Spirit ; cf. 1 Pet.
1^{11}, ' the Spirit of Christ which was in them [the prophets]
. . . when it testified.' For the Holy Spirit as the Spirit of
Jesus, or Christ, cf. Ac. 16^7, Ro. 8^9, Phil. 1^{19} ; see on 2^7. The
sentence then means, *The true Christian and the prophet are
the agents in and through whom the same Spirit of Jesus is testifying : they are fellow-servants in this relation to a common*

Lord. In 22⁸ ᶠ·, where the *prophetic* activity of the angel is
the thing chiefly thought of, it is directly pertinent to show
that the angel and the prophet John are fellow-servants by
reason of their common prophetic service (see note there).
But in the earlier part of this verse (19¹⁰) there seems to be
no allusion to the prophetic character of the angel ; the Seer
does not prostrate himself before him because he is a prophet,
but because he is the august messenger from God confirming
the prophecies of the heavenly hymn, and the angel bases his
reproof on the fact that he himself is only a servant of God
like all Christians.   There is here no intimation of a particular kind of service, prophetic or other, in which their work is
in common.   This explanatory sentence, 'for the testimony of
Jesus is the Spirit of prophecy,' appears therefore inappropriate
here, and even if the rest of the verse be retained, this part is
almost certainly a gloss added by one who had 22⁸ ᶠ· in mind.
See p. 742.   A common interpretation makes this sentence a
comment added by the Apocalyptist, or another, to show that
by the words 'the testimony of Jesus' in the former sentence
is meant 'the spirit of prophecy' ; those Christians who have
the testimony of Jesus in this sense, *i.e.* those who are prophets,
are intended there, it is only with such that the angel is a
fellow-servant.   But this does violence to the language and
does not avoid the inappropriateness spoken of above.

(2) The appearing of the warrior Messiah, 19¹¹⁻¹⁶. See pp.
286 f.   The representation of the Messiah given in
these verses follows closely traditional Jewish eschatology.
The Heb. prophets saw Jehovah coming forth as a 'man of
war' dashing in pieces his enemies, and establishing his kingdom over all the nations in the last days ; *e.g.* Is. 13⁴, 31⁴, Ezk.
chapts. 38–39, Joel chapt. 3, Zec. 14³.   But as the person of the
Messiah became more and more a distinct figure in Jewish
expectation, the office of overcoming and destroying the last
enemies was assigned to him likewise.   Anticipation of this
activity as a messianic office occurs, *e.g.* Is. 11⁴.   But in later
writers the Messiah appears clearly as the great defender of
God's cause in the last conflict ; cf. 2 Thess. 2⁸, Ap. Bar. 72,
'When the nations become turbulent and the time of my
Messiah is come, he shall summon all the nations, and some of

them he shall spare and some of them he shall slay.'   In 2 Es.
chapt. 13 a multitude of men are gathered from the four winds
to make war against him, but are destroyed by the breath of
his mouth ; Test. Dan. 5¹³, 'He shall make war against Beliar ';
Sib. Or. V. 108 f., ' Then a king sent from God . . . shall
destroy all the mighty kings.'   For kindred representations,
cf. also 2 Es. 11³⁷ ᶠᶠ·, 12³³, Ap. Bar. 39⁷⁻⁴⁰, En. 46⁴ ᶠᶠ·, Sib. Or.
V. 414 ff., Ps. Sol. 17²⁷.   Weber, *System* 365, cites from the Targums to the same effect.— The representation of the Messiah
in this passage of the Apocalypse (19¹¹⁻¹⁶) is held by many
to be at variance with that of the Gospels and other N. T.
writings (see p. 742).   But the Apocalyptist is not here concerned with the Messiah's work as a whole, but only with the
last great conflict with Antichrist and his hosts in their assault
upon the Messiah himself and his people.   It is the day of the
revelation of wrath and of the destruction of the powers of
incorrigible evil.   The picture is drawn on traditional lines
and accords not only with the general tenor of the book, but
also with the representations of the N. T. elsewhere ; cf.
Mt. 25⁴¹ ᶠᶠ·, Ro. 2⁵, 2 Thess. 1⁷ ᶠᶠ·, 2⁸, Jude vv. 13–15 ;   see pp.
310 f.

The mention of an army accompanying the Messiah in this
warfare might seem peculiar ; usually he destroys his opponents
miraculously, cf. 2 Thess. 2⁸, Is. 11⁴, 2 Es. 12¹, 13¹⁰ ᶠ·, ' He sent
out of his mouth as it had been a flood of fire, and out of his
lips a flaming breath, and out of his tongue he cast forth sparks
of the storm.   And these . . . fell upon the assault of the
multitude ' ; Ps. Sol. 17²⁷, ' He shall destroy the godless nations
with the word of his mouth.'   But our passage is in reality not
at variance with these representations.   The armies that follow
the Messiah are mounted on white horses, and clad in white
garments, symbols of victory ; they are not in armor and they
take no part in the action.   The nations are slain with the
sword that proceeds from the Messiah's mouth, vv. 15, 21.
The familiar figure of the sword of the mouth referring to the
word (cf. Heb. 4¹²) symbolizes here the death-dealing power of
the words uttered by the Messiah against his foes.   A striking
illustration of our passage is found in Wis. 18¹⁵ ᶠ·, ' Thine all-
powerful word leaped from heaven out of the royal throne, a

stern warrior, into the midst of the doomed land, bearing as a
sharp sword thine unfeigned commandment.' Cf. also Rev. 2¹⁶,
Hos. 6⁵, Is. 49². — The sword of his mouth, his word, is the
one weapon of the Messiah in this battle, and it is therefore
quite pertinent that the writer should among the different
familiar names of the Christ choose as one of his designations
in this portrayal the name given in v. 13 *b*, The *Word* of God.
The rejection of that sentence (13 *b*) by many critics, as inappropriate in this place, is therefore unwarranted ; see p. 742.
Without doubt the name is taken from the Johannine doctrine
of the Logos, current in the home of the Apocalypse, and it is
used here in a sense different from that of the Fourth Gospel;
but this freedom in the use of a figure or a name is one of the
most common characteristics of the writer ; cf. 12¹⁻⁵, ¹⁷, 19⁷,
where the people of God are represented respectively as the
mother of the Messiah, his brethren, and his bride ; or 19⁷
and 21⁹ ᶠ·, where the figure of the Lamb's bride symbolizes
respectively the people of God and the new Jerusalem.

11–12. ἵππος λευκός, *a white horse :* the color symbolizes the
victory anticipated ; cf. 6². — πιστὸς καὶ ἀληθινός, *faithful and
true : i.e.* to the ideal character of the Messiah, said here with
special reference to what is required of him in this battle with
Antichrist.   The name is already made familiar (καλούμενος)
in 3¹⁴ ; cf. also 3⁷, 1⁵. — ἐν δικαιοσύνῃ κρίνει κτλ.: *in righteousness doth he judge,* etc. : taken from Is. 11³⁻⁵. The judgment
here meant, as defined in the following words, is that of making
war on the forces of the Beast.   Cf. Sib. Or. III. 689, 'God
shall judge all with war and sword.' — οἱ δὲ ὀφθαλμοὶ κτλ.,
and his eyes are a flame of fire: cf. 1⁴, 2¹⁸. — διαδήματα πολλά,
many crowns: since he is King of kings, v. 16 ; cf. the many
crowns of the dragon and the Beast, 12³, 13¹. — ἔχων ὄνομα
κτλ., *he hath a name which no one knoweth,* etc.: cf. 2¹⁷, 3¹². The
characteristic given to the Messiah in these words is based on
the current belief in the marvelous power of a secret name ;
see p. 463.   In this hidden name, though not in this alone,
the Messiah possesses a power to subdue his enemies miraculously.   Cf. En. 69¹⁴, 'This one requested Michael to show him
the hidden name, that he might enunciate it in the oath, so
that those might quake before that name and oath' ; Asc. Is. 9⁵,

'Thou canst not hear his name till thou shalt have ascended out of this body.' For the supernatural power of the divine name cf. Ecclus. 47¹⁸, The Prayer of Manasses, 3. The name of the Messiah here spoken of cannot be any of the names given to him in current usage; see on v. 13.

13. βεβαμμένον αἵματι, *dipped in blood :* the words are suggested by Is. 63¹, and refer here to the blood of the enemies to be slain in battle. In this connection there can be no reference to the blood of the cross; the epithet is proleptic, as is the symbolism of the white horses and the white robes of the Messiah's followers. The certain triumph is in the mind of the Apocalyptist, and causes him to disregard chronological sequence. Wellhausen's objection (*Anal.* 30) that the blood-stained raiment is out of place before the end of the battle ignores this, one of the commonest features in the author's manner. — κέκληται τὸ ὄνομα κτλ., *his name is called the Word of God :* for the appropriateness of the name in this place see p. 732. This clause is by many held to be inconsistent with v. 12 c, *a name which no one knoweth*, and is rejected as a gloss, added to define the hidden name. But three different names are specified in the passage, vv. 11, 13, 16, and the names currently given to the Messiah were numerous; see p. 43. The writer of v. 12 c supposes a name different from any of these, and one kept hidden. In view of what is said there, a glossist could not select one from the familiar list as the hidden name, and expressly declare it well-known; for he does not, after the manner of an interpreter, use the word ἐστί, his name *is*, but κέκληται, *is called, i.e.* is one in familiar use. He cannot in this sentence be speaking of the hidden name.

14–16. ἵπποις λευκοῖς, *white horses :* symbolical of the victory anticipated; see p. 731. — ἐκ τοῦ στόματος . . . ὀξεῖα, *from his mouth . . . a sharp sword :* see p. 732. — αὐτός : in both cases an emphatic *he.* — ποιμανεῖ . . . σιδηρᾷ, *shall rule them with a rod of iron :* see on 2²⁷. — πατεῖ τὴν ληνὸν κτλ., *he treadeth the press,* etc.: it is *he* that executeth the vengeance. For the figure see on 14¹⁷. — οἴνου, *of the wine :* to be joined with the words following, as shown by 14¹⁰, 16¹⁹. — καὶ ἐπὶ τὸν μηρόν, *that is, upon his thigh : καί,* epexegetical. The words make more specific the preceding general term; the name is, written upon that part of the mantle that falls over the thigh, and in the case of a rider is especially conspicuous. There does not appear sufficient ground for the interpretation 'on his girdle,' Düst. *al.* — βασιλεὺς βασιλέων κτλ., *King of kings*, etc.: cf. 1 Tim. 6¹⁵. See on 17¹⁴.

(3) The great battle of the Messiah with Antichrist, 19¹⁷⁻²¹. See pp. 286 f.   17–18.   This *prelude to the battle* is suggested by Ezekiel's prophecy of the assault of the nations upon God's people in the last days, and the overthrow of Gog with his hosts upon the mountains of Israel.   The prophet is there bidden to call all the birds and beasts to assemble from every quarter and sate themselves on the flesh and blood of the slain (39¹⁷⁻²⁰).   The Apocalyptist in part follows his source verbally, and in part varies from it with characteristic freedom.   The enumeration of the victims, including every rank and condition of men (v. 18), is given in a formula similar to that used in 6¹⁵, 13¹⁶.   The redundancy is noticeable. — ἕνα : indef. art. ; see on 8¹³. — ἑστῶτα ἐν τῷ ἡλίῳ, *standing in the sun :* where all the birds of prey would behold him; but why this specific phrase is chosen to express that idea is uncertain.   Possibly some traditional representation may be contained in it. — τὸ δεῖπνον τοῦ θεοῦ, *the supper of God : i.e.* made, or given, by God ; cf. Ezk. 39¹⁹, '*my* sacrifice,' said of the prototype of this feast.

19–21.   These verses announce in the fewest possible words the *great battle of Harmagedon* and its results.   See p. 286 f. — συνηγμένα, *gathered together :* as described in 16¹³⁻¹⁴ ; see note there. — τοῦ στρατεύματος αὐτοῦ, *his army :* on the part taken by the Messiah's army see p. 731. — ἐπιάσθη τὸ θηρίον, *the Beast was taken :* the fate of Antichrist as given in this passage is different from that allotted to him elsewhere in eschatological writings.   In 2 Thess. 2⁸ he is slain by the breath of the Lord ; in Ap. Bar. 40 he is bound and brought before the Messiah, who puts him to death ; in Sib. Or. III. 73 he is burnt up.   Here the Apocalyptist sees him delivered over to the same punishment as is finally awarded to Satan himself, whose representative he is ; just as in chapt. 13 a similar form and appearance are given to him. — ὁ ψευδοπροφήτης, *the false prophet :* the description of his work added in the following

words identifies the 'false prophet' of this passage and 16¹³
with the second beast of chapt. 13. While the language repeats
that of 13¹³⁻¹⁷, and shows the justice of joining the false prophet
and the Beast in a common doom, it likewise serves to warn
the readers anew against the emperor-worship and its priesthood. — ἐνώπιον αὐτοῦ, *before him :* see on 13¹². — τὴν λίμνην
τοῦ πυρός, *the lake of fire :* cf. 20¹⁰, ¹⁴, ¹⁵, 21⁸, 14¹⁰· The idea of
a hell of fire, as a place of final punishment, found among other
peoples and common in later Jewish thought, was retained in
Christian eschatology ; see p. 68. On brimstone see on 21⁸. —
τῆς καιομένης : if this reading be adopted, the grammatical
inaccuracy is due to the intervening gen. τοῦ πυρός. See text.
note. — τῇ ῥομφαίᾳ . . . ἐκ τοῦ στόματος, *the sword from his
mouth :* see p. 731.

(4) The imprisonment of Satan and the Millennial reign of
the martyrs, 20¹⁻⁶. See p. 287. A temporary binding
of Satan, and a Millennial reign of the risen martyrs before
the final kingdom, as described in this passage, do not appear elsewhere in the book nor in the Bible (on 1 Co. 15²⁴ ᶠ·,
see p. 98). But the doctrine of a partial realization of
God's kingdom, and its continuance for a limited period before the era of its complete establishment, becomes common
in late Jewish belief, as seen in the apocalyptic writers.
This idea arose in the effort to mediate between two different
forms of eschatological outlook. The earlier Hebrew hope
was fixed on an earthly kingdom centering in Palestine,
and ruled by Jehovah himself. But in the later eschatology
the kingdom becomes transcendental and universal, its realm
embraces the renewed heavens and earth, its members include
the risen saints. Between these two stands the somewhat
vaguely apprehended idea of an earthly messianic kingdom of
limited duration, preliminary to the perfect consummation of
the end. This conception is contained in this passage of the
Revelation in its own peculiar form ; it appears in a different
and less definite form elsewhere, *e.g.* 2 Es. 7²⁸ ᶠ·, 12³⁴, En. 91¹²,
Ap. Bar. 40³. For a kindred idea in Ezekiel, see pp. 36 f.,
76 f. Our Apocalyptist in taking up the idea stands alone in
limiting the sharers in this kingdom to a special class of the
saints, the risen martyrs, thus introducing a first resurrection

to be followed by that of the remaining saints at the general judgment, vv. 4–5. The duration of this intermediate kingdom, when mentioned in apocalyptic writings, is always expressed in some symbolical measure. It is here made a thousand years, a number found elsewhere also in tradition ; a long period is meant.

The representation of Satan first bound and then released for a brief period which is to end in his final doom is not found in earlier literature, Jewish or Christian.. That it is entirely new with our author is however improbable. Something of the kind is implied in the very idea of an intermediate kingdom, before whose establishment the powers of evil must at least be restrained ; and on the other hand the last great assault of the nations, everywhere expected among the immediate antecedents of God's final triumph, presupposes the removal of that restraint. Not quite parallel with this idea, but somewhat akin to it, and perhaps aiding in its growth, is that of the seizure of evil angels and spirits, and their reservation in prison or chains for their final punishment, as frequently found in later Jewish eschatology. Thus in En. 10⁴⁻⁶ Azazel, a leader among the fallen angels, and in Jewish angelology a figure somewhat akin to Satan, is to be bound and imprisoned in darkness for an indefinite period, but at the day of judgment to be brought forth and cast into the fire. For kindred representations, cf. En. 21¹⁻¹⁰, 54⁵ ᶠ·, Jub. 5¹⁰, Sl. En. 7¹ ; cf. also 2 Pet. 2⁴, Jude v. 6, Is. 24²¹ ᶠ·

A closer parallel to our passage is found in Persian eschatology, where in the conflict between the supreme spirits of good and evil in the last days the dragon (cf. v. 2) Azhi Dahaka is conquered and kept bound for a period, but afterwards becomes free again and is slain (cf. Völter *Offenb.* 125). There is much plausibility in the theory that there lies behind such representations a common tradition. That Persian eschatology contained ideas in common with popular beliefs and apocalyptic conceptions held among the Jews of later times is well known, see pp. 79 ff. It would not be strange, then, if some such legend regarding the dragon as that given above should have been circulated in popular Jewish apocalyptic, and have been taken up by our author and transformed, as we have seen him in other instances using current traditions.

It is not difficult to understand how conceptions regarding an intermediate kingdom, if existing in popular apocalyptic, should have entered into the visions of our Prophet. For membership in that kingdom, with its security from the power of Satan and the blessedness of reigning with the Messiah, must present itself to his mind as a gift of God's supreme favor. And what reward more glorious than that could be imagined for the martyrs, who in Christian thought and especially in this book stand foremost in the favor of God? The Revelation is specifically a book for the martyrs; everywhere the author seeks to fortify those who are facing persecution in the time then present with them and in the awful future till the doom of Antichrist. Current ideas of an earthly reign of the Messiah and the restraint of evil powers would furnish him a vision of the form in which steadfastness unto death shall receive its special reward. It is thus, we may believe, that under the influence of his dominant idea of the glory of martyrdom, transforming in his vision expectations cherished in contemporary apocalyptic, he sees the intermediate kingdom set up and the martyrs alone admitted to it. In other words, the millennial vision of this passage appears to be an outgrowth of familiar eschatological ideas transformed and glorified through the faith that God has a special guerdon laid up for the martyr.

The author's purpose in this vision furnishes the clue to the correct interpretation of the Millennium as an element in Christian eschatology. Its place in his thought he makes clear in limiting a share in it to the martyrs. These few verses standing alone in biblical utterances, and apparently deriving their *format* contents from an external source, have given occasion for controversy running through centuries and for vast practical delusions. Yet the chief aim of the author is clear. *He seeks to set forth under a striking apocalyptic form the assurance that the martyr's steadfastness wins for him the special favor of his Lord, and the highest life in union with God and Christ.* That is the meaning of the passage *for us.* When once we apprehend the fact that the essential truth of prophecy, as distinguished from its form, is not the revelation of a chronological program in the world's history, we cease to find here the prediction of an *eschatological era,* however closely the Apocalyptist himself may have associated form and substance;

3 B

see pp. 293 ff., 299, 301 ff. The dispensational limit under which the Seer here apprehends his truth may, or may not, be an integral element in it for him ; yet for us, viewed in the light of the nature and course of prophetic revelation, the essential truth, which, stripped of its apocalyptic form, is expressed in the vision of the martyr's millennial glory, is that which is given in our Lord's saying, ' He that loseth his life for my sake shall find it,' Mt. 10[39].

A large school of interpreters from early times have given to this passage a non-literal meaning. The view which under considerably differing forms has been most widely advocated from Augustine on is that the first resurrection here spoken of is the spiritual renewal of the Christian, and the preliminary kingdom is the reign of Christ in those thus renewed, or in his Church ; the kingdom began at Christ's appearing ; Satan's power has been restrained, especially through the redemptive death of Christ, but not yet entirely destroyed ; the thousand years are a period symbolically measured, continuing to the last great conflict with Satan and followed by the general resurrection, the judgment, and the perfected state of the redeemed. The fundamental fault of the interpretations which follow even remotely this theory is that they mistake the nature of apocalyptic prophecy, and read into the vision of our Apocalyptist here a meaning of which he gives no intimation and which is at variance with his language. Apocalyptic prophecy is not allegory, and in our passage it is not possible upon any sound principles of exegesis to take the first resurrection as different *in kind* from that of 'the rest,' v. 5, which is described in vv. 12-13. Nor can the age-long struggle of the Church militant, or any partially improved condition of human society, answer to the picture of the millennial reign of the risen martyrs, glorious in its privileges and undisturbed by Satan now banished from the world. Recent scholars are very generally agreed in rejecting such interpretations as impossible.

1-3. τὴν κλεῖν τῆς ἀβύσσου, *the key of the abyss :* cf. 9[1]. — ἐπὶ τὴν χεῖρα : as in 5[1], the prep. is probably not to be distinguished from ἐν, with the dat. ; cf. 1[20], where ἐπὶ τῆς δεξιᾶς is used to repeat ἐν τῇ δεξιᾷ, v. 16. — ὁ ὄφις ὁ ἀρχαῖος κτλ., *the old serpent,* etc.: the dragon and the serpent, which are common in eschatological myths, are here, as generally in late Jewish demonology, expressly identified with Satan ; cf. 12[9]. For the nom. in the appos. see p. 224. — ἔκλεισεν καὶ ἐσφράγισεν κτλ., *locked and sealed it over him :* for sealing to give special security cf. Dan. 6[17], Prayer of Manas. 4, Mt. 27[66]. — ἵνα μὴ πλανήσῃ κτλ., *that he should not deceive the nations,*

etc. : the purpose of Satan's imprisonment is to prevent his
activity in misleading the nations to war against the saints
(v. 8); they are secure against his wiles throughout the Millennium. The punishment of torture to be inflicted upon him
comes later, v. 10. — τὰ ἔθνη, *the nations:* the nations are here,
as in v. 8, conceived to exist still, though according to 19²¹ they
had been destroyed. For this retention of conflicting ideas see
on 15⁴, also pp. 722 f., 745. — δεῖ λυθῆναι, *he must be loosed:*
Satan must in the ordering of God be released for the great
conflict, which according to eschatological tradition was still
to come.

4. εἶδον θρόνους κτλ., *I saw thrones,* etc.: the vision and the
language are suggested by Dan. 7⁹,¹⁰,²². — ἐκάθισαν . . . ἐδόθη
αὐτοῖς, *they sat upon them and judgment was given unto them:* it
is not clear who occupy the thrones and administer judgment,
nor what act of judgment is meant. Two views are maintained. (1) God and a heavenly assessor, or assessors, in judgment, occupy the thrones and award to the martyrs their place
in the millennial kingdom. (2) The martyrs are seated on the
thrones, and it is given them to rule and judge the nations
of the earth. The second appears to be preferable. The co-
sovereignty of the risen martyrs with Christ through the
thousand years is the one dominant thought of the passage.
If the author meant here to speak also of their entrance on the
millennial state, as an award of judgment, we should expect
specific mention of God or Christ, or both, as the awarders, as
in 2²⁶, 3²¹, 20¹¹ ᶠ·; there is nothing in the book or elsewhere to
suggest any others as the vicegerents of God set to make an
award of this kind. But the words, 'judgment,' *i.e.* the function of judging, ' was *given* to them,' would be inappropriate to
a company to which God belonged. On the other hand, αὐτοῖς
must refer to the subj. of the vb., or to αὐτούς, the thrones
thought of as identical with the occupants; the second clause
could not then mean, an award was given by the occupants of
the thrones to the *saints.* Lk. 22³⁰, Mt. 19²⁸, 'Ye shall sit on
thrones judging the twelve tribes of Israel,' where ruling and
judging are essentially synonymous, support the view that the
subj. of the vb. is the martyrs. Judging is inseparably joined
with ruling. The martyrs occupy thrones, and the power of

judging, ruling, the nations is given to them.   Cf. 2²⁶, 1 Co. 6².
This general statement of the first sentence is then repeated
and amplified by the rest of the verse.   In regard to the nations
remaining as the objects of such rule see on v. 3. — τὰς ψυχὰς
κτλ., *the souls of those that had been beheaded*, etc.: in 6⁹ the
Seer had beheld under the heavenly altar the souls of those
already martyred ; their number has now been filled up (6¹¹),
and they are all admitted to their reward.   The acc. depends
upon εἶδον. — πεπελεκισμένων, *beheaded : i.e.* by the ax.   The
word denoting a mode of execution at this time generally superseded in the empire by the use of the sword has here the sense
of *slain.* — διὰ τὴν μαρτυρίαν Ἰησοῦ, *because of the testimony of
Jesus:* for the gospel's sake·; see on 1².   The phrase is general
and includes all Christian martyrs ; while the following words,
καὶ οἵτινες οὐ προσεκύνησαν κτλ., *and such as worshiped not the
Beast*, etc., specify a particular class among these.   For clauses
of this kind connected by καί, *and*, see on 16⁶.   The words
must refer to actual martyrs, since all who refused homage to
the Beast were put to death, 13¹⁵ ; also ἔζησαν, which as v. 5
shows must mean *lived again*, makes it clear that these words
do not (as some take them) refer to such as remained alive till
the millennium.   This particular class of martyrs is brought
forward with emphasis in order to assure the readers of the
glory awaiting those who remain steadfast in the great temptation to emperor-worship; cf. 13¹⁴⁻¹⁷. — ἔζησαν, *lived :* for ζάω,
equivalent to ἀναζάω, *live again*, a frequent use, cf. v. 5, 1¹⁸, 2⁸;
see on 13¹⁴.   The new spiritual life in Christ cannot be thought
of here ; the context shows that the revival from physical death
is meant.   See p. 738. — The Apocalyptist is here concerned
with the risen martyrs only.   The faithful remaining alive at
the time are entirely outside of the present vision; nothing is
said or implied in regard to them.

5-6. οἱ λοιποί, *the rest:* all except the martyrs, both the
righteous and the unrighteous.   'The rest' cannot be understood of the unrighteous only, on the supposition that all the
righteous had already risen in the first resurrection ; for v. 4
limits the millennial kingdom to the martyred ; further, the
scrutiny of the books, vv. 12, 15, to determine the issue of judgment, implies the presence of the righteous as well as the un-

righteous at the general resurrection. — ἡ ἀνάστασις ἡ πρώτη, *the first resurrection: i.e.* the resurrection of the martyrs, as contrasted with that of all others at the general resurrection ; there is no thought of two resurrections of the same persons. — μακάριος, *blessed:* see on 1³. — ἅγιος, *holy:* wholly set apart and belonging to God. — ὁ δεύτερος θάνατος, *the second death :* see on 2¹¹. — ἔσονται ἱερεῖς κτλ., *they shall be priests*, etc.: cf. 1⁶, 5¹⁰, Is. 61⁶. Reference is made to freedom of access to God and Christ ; see on 1⁶. The thought of a priesthood forming a medium of blessings to the nations (so, some com.) has no place in the context.

Textual notes, 19⁶–20⁴. 19⁶. λεγοντες Q most min some anc com Ws WHmrg Alf Bouss *al* ; λεγοντων AP some min and anc com Tr Ti WH Blj Sod *al* ; λεγουσων ℵ ; λεγοντας some min R. The first is not easily accounted for, unless original. See Ws *Ap*. 137. — αλληλουια, see on v. 1. — 7. αγαλλιωμεν ℵAP some min edd ; αγαλλιωμεθα Q most min R. — δωμεν ℵ*Q many min anc com R Ti WHmrg Sod Bouss RV *al* ; δωσομεν ℵᶜA Lch WH Ws Alf *al* ; δωσωμεν P some min Sw *al*. — 9. Before αληθινοι, A some min Ws Lch WHmrg Alf insert οι ; wanting in most sources and edd. — του θεου in nearly all sources is placed before εισιν, but after it in ℵ* some min R, and before αληθινοι in ℵᶜ some min. — 11. καλουμενος wanting in AP many min some vers ; bracketed by Alf WH *al*. — 13. βεβαμμενον AQ most min anc com R most edd ; περιρεραμμενον ℵ* Ti ; περιρεραντισμενον ℵᶜ ; ρεραντισμενον P some min WH RV. See WH *Notes on Select Readings, in loc*. — 17. After δειπνον, R with a few min some vers adds του μεγαλου. — 20. της καιομενης ℵAP Prim most edd ; την καιομενην Q all min R Alf Bouss Sod, probably a correction. See Ws *Ap*. 137. — 21. For εξελθουση, R reads εκπορευομενη, uncertain origin.

20¹. For κλειν R reads κλειδα, with some min and anc com. See Blass § 8, 1 ; Win § 9, 2, *e*. — 2. ο οφις ο αρχαιος A Lch Tr Ti Ws WH *al* ; τον οφιν κτλ ℵQ all min anc com R RV WHmrg Bouss Sod. — 3. After εκλεισεν, R adds αυτον, with a few min. — 4. For το θηριον R, with some min reads τω θηριω.

Criticism of 19¹–20⁶. 19¹⁻⁸. The larger number of critics connect this passage, or at least vv. 1–3, directly with chapts. 17–18, though with various omissions. Most of those who assume the presence of Jewish documents in the book make the passage a part of one of these ; so Vischer, Weyland, Pfleiderer, J. Weiss, *al*. These all omit, as Christian interpolations, 19²ᵇ, like the corresponding reference to martyrs in 17⁶, 18²⁰, ²⁴ ; so also the mention of the Lamb in v. 7. The excisions of Spitta (192 ff.), who assigns the passage as a whole to his Jewish document J², are characteristic ; in v. 1, ὄχλου πολλοῦ, because superfluous ; in v. 2, ἐξεδίκησεν . . . δεύτερον εἴρηκαν ἀλληλούια, because referring to martyrs at Rome ; v. 4, because it is a repetition of a redactor's error in 5[8], where the prostration of the Elders and Living Creatures, while holding harps and bowls in their hands, is inconceivable. Völter (*Offenb.* 47) and Erbes (102), though assigning parts of the passage to an interpolator, make it as a whole Christian, and connect it, the former with 14[20], the latter with chapt. 18. Schoen (138) joins it with 16[24] as part of the primitive Christian plan. J. Weiss (120 f.) thinks that in vv. 4–10 the Seer represents himself in heaven, whereas in the context he is on earth; Weiss therefore makes vv. 4–10 an interpolation, while assigning the chapt. as a whole to his Jewish source Q.

19[9–10]. Numerous objections are raised by critics against these verses: the introduction of an indefinite speaker; the insertion of the verses between two passages, the exultant hymn and the appearing of the warrior Messiah, with which they are thought to have no connection; inappropriateness of the declaration 'these words are true,' which belongs at the *close* of the book, and is actually found there (22[6]); the inexplicableness of the Seer's act of worship in 22[8], if occurring and reproved here; the exact duplication of these verses in 22[6, 8f.]; the misinterpretation of 22[9] contained in the explanatory clause added at the end of v. 10, ἡ γὰρ μαρτυρία κτλ. — These objections have been noticed in the Com. It does not appear that v. 9 is open to valid criticism. Some of the objections to v. 10, however, must be acknowledged of weight. The Seer's impulse to offer worship to an angel is explainable at the close of the book (see note there). If it occurred at any earlier place, it would seem more natural in the presence of one of the twenty-four Elders in 7[13 ff.], or of the awe-inspiring angel of chapt. 10, or in the case of the angel of this scene, at his first appearing in 17[1]. In the particular juncture of this passage there appears no so extraordinary manifestation as to account for it. Furthermore, there is no sufficient explanation of the act of homage in 22[8], if forbidden here. The conclusion, then, suggests itself inevitably that the present passage, v. 10, has crept into the text from the latter; it is inserted as a sequel to οὗτοι οἱ λόγοι ἀληθινοί here, as it so stands in 22[6–8]. And this conclusion is confirmed by the exact repetition here of much of the language of that passage, and by the almost certain supposition that the words ἡ γὰρ μαρτυρία κτλ. in this verse are a comment inappropriate here and suggested by 22[9]. See Com.

19[11–16]. Objection is raised to the representation of the warrior Messiah here as at variance with the Christ of the N. T.; the passage therefore, the assumed Christian additions being omitted, is referred to a Jewish document; so, Vischer, Spitta, Weyland, J. Weiss, *al.* Völter who makes it Christian assigns it to his Cerinthian addition. Many critics reject the mention of the name 'The Word of God,' v. 12 *b*, as inconsistent with v. 12 *c*, and brought in from the Johannine doctrine of the Logos, without any appropriate relation to the context. These objections have been spoken of in the Com.

19[17–21]. Critics for the most part agree in joining this passage with vv. 11–16, and assigning it to the respective sources assumed for those verses.

20[1–6]. Vischer (68 ff.) raises a number of objections to vv. 4–6. The millennial reign of the saints is not clear, since there can be no subjects, all men except the saints having been destroyed in the battle against the Messiah, 19²¹. Further objection is raised to the general judgment; at the first resurrection all martyrs are raised, but in this number would be included all the faithful, since all who refuse to worship the Beast are martyred (13¹⁵); all saints then share in the millennial kingdom and only the wicked are not raised in this first resurrection; why then another judgment? Why do not the messianic kingdom and world renewal follow the battle at once? Why an interregnum? Spitta (208 ff.), in part for the reasons given by Vischer and in part on other grounds, refers vv. 4–7 to a redactor; the context (20¹⁻³, ⁸ ff.) belongs according to him to his Jewish source J¹, but these verses cannot belong there, as they contain Christian allusions; moreover a twofold resurrection is unknown to Jewish apocalyptic and O. T. tradition. The indefiniteness of the persons seated on the thrones points to an original connection in which this was clear. Erbes (109), rejecting from his primitive apocalypse a twofold resurrection and a preliminary kingdom of the martyrs, refers the whole passage 20¹⁻¹⁰ to his redaction of the year 80.

The principal grounds upon which these various criticisms of our paragraph, 19¹–20⁶, are based have been touched upon in the Com. Apart from details there discussed, there are two general lines of argument which appear to establish the place of the paragraph, with perhaps the exception of a short sentence or two, in the original work of the Apocalyptist from whom the book as a whole has come. (1) The passage as a whole and in its parts agrees with the author's plan, his leading thoughts and his manner, as seen in the Summary (pp. 286 f.) and in the Com. After the fall of Rome, just such a sequel is demanded with its note of triumph and anticipation of the end thus begun, with its swift overthrow of the beasts, Satan's earthly agents, hitherto central figures, and with some special promise for those who are faithful even to martyrdom. And it is not supposable that the form of the sequel here given has displaced another. It is true that the reign of the martyrs in a preliminary kingdom is peculiar to this passage; but it is not in actual contradiction with the author's eschatology as given elsewhere; see pp. 165, 735 ff. (2) In language, idioms, and grammatical mannerisms the paragraph agrees with the book in general; and, what is significant, almost every verse shows parallelism with other parts of the book, as may be seen from the following examples, which could be multiplied. In chapt. 19 compare v. 1 with 7⁹, ¹⁰, ¹², 12¹⁰; v. 2 with 15³, 16¹⁷, 17¹, ⁵; v. 3 with 14¹¹; vv. 1–5 with 5⁶⁻¹⁴ (see p. 720); v. 6 with 6¹, 14², 11¹⁷; v. 7 with 21⁹ ᶠᶠ·; v. 8 with 18¹⁶; v. 11 with 6¹⁻², 3¹⁴; v. 12 with 2¹⁸, ¹⁷; v. 15 with 1¹⁶, 2²⁷, 14¹⁹; v. 16 with 17¹⁴; v. 19 with 16¹⁴; v. 20 with 3¹¹⁻¹⁷. — In chapt. 20 compare v. 1 with 9¹; v. 2 with 12⁹; v. 4 with 6⁹; v. 6 with 2¹¹, 1⁶, 5¹⁰.

XX. 7–XXII. 5. *The End.* See pp. 287 ff.

(1) The destruction of the nations in their last assault upon the citadel of God's people; and the final doom of Satan,

20⁷⁻¹⁰. See p. 288. After the lapse of the long period of peace assigned to the preliminary messianic kingdom, Satan as predicted is now released for his last attempt on the kingdom of God. The vision of the gathering of the nations in a final assault on the holy city, and their utter destruction, is shaped by traditional Jewish eschatology. Such an onset of Israel's enemies in the last days with their complete overthrow is prophesied by Ezk. (chapts. 38–39), and appears frequently in later apocalyptic writers (see on 14²⁰ and p. 35). Thus in 2 Es. 13⁵ ff., 'Lo, there was gathered together a multitude of men, out of number, from the four winds of heaven, to make war ; . . . upon a sudden of an innumerable multitude nothing was to be perceived, but only dust of ashes and smell of smoke' ; Sib. Or. III. 663 ff., 'The kings of the nations shall throw themselves against this land in troops, . . . in a ring round the city the accursed kings shall place each one his throne, with his infidel people by him, . . . and judgment shall come upon them from the mighty God and all shall perish . . . from heaven shall fall fiery swords,' etc. ; cf. also 2 Es. 13³⁴, En. 56⁵⁻⁸, 90¹³⁻¹⁵, Test. Jos. 19⁸. Numerous similar allusions occur in the Targums also ; see Weber *System* 369 ff. The chronological place of this assault of the nations, whether before or after the messianic kingdom is introduced, varies in different authors ; in Ezk. as here it follows it (see Volz 175 f.). The names Gog and Magog here given to these hostile nations meet us first in Ezk. (38²), where the former denotes the prince, the latter his land ; but in later apocalyptic writers they became frequent as symbolical names of the nations who in the last days should rise up to war against God and his people ; see p. 36. Quite probably the names, like the war itself, go back to an earlier tradition. —The agency of Satan in leading this hostile movement of the nations is peculiar to our author. This is in keeping with the greater distinctness given to the personality of Satan in the N. T. generally, and especially in our book. In Ezk. it is God himself who brings the nations against his land for the purpose of their destruction (38¹⁶), according to a common idea that God punishes the defiantly wicked by leading them into a heinous sin in which their ruin is complete. It is noticeable that in this conflict between

God and Satan and in the events that follow, the Messiah is not mentioned, whereas in the battle with Antichrist (19¹⁹ ᶠᶠ·) it was he who came forth to meet Satan's agents. In this last dread encounter in which Satan puts forth his supreme force against God, God himself intervenes with death and destruction hurled down from heaven.

The close dependence of the Apocalyptist's prophecy upon current Jewish expectation of such an assault of the nations at the end furnishes the solution of the difficulty already mentioned (see on v. 3 and 15⁴). The victory described in 19¹⁹⁻²¹ over Antichrist and his subjects, who included all the kingdoms of the world (13⁷ ᶠ·), seems to leave no place for the hostile armies of this passage. But the two visions· are entirely distinct. In the former the Apocalyptist is concerned with the completeness of the Messiah's triumph, and the establishment of the millennial kingdom holding power over all the earth. While in the picture there drawn all enemies are destroyed, the emphasis is not laid so much upon the extinction of the nations' existence as upon the defeat of Antichrist and the establishment of the Messiah's sway. But in the present vision the great onset of the nations, which forms a central act in familiar conceptions of the end, is the more essential part, and the thought of the Apocalyptist is wholly fixed upon that event as pictured in tradition. Two different aspects of one Jewish tradition furnish the form of the two visions, and dominate respectively each in turn. The incongruity between the two in this respect lies therefore entirely beyond the Apocalyptist's notice ; he is not for the time being thinking of the visions in their relation to each other, they form two separate chapters in his revelation. A similar concurrence of discordant representations appears in the relation of the kings to the destruction of Rome ; see p. 723. We have to bear in mind that we are dealing with the ecstasies of a Seer and poet whose pictures in the two instances are independently of each other influenced by conventional forms. Inconsistencies of this nature cannot then properly cause serious difficulty for the interpreter or the critic. See p. 769.

7–8. λυθήσεται, *shall be loosed :* on the release of Satan, see pp. 735 f. In vv. 7–8 the author uses the future, speaking as a prophet, but in vv. 9–10 a the past, as if reporting what he had seen in vision, turning back to the fut. in v. 10 b. — πλανῆσαι, *to deceive* : Satan's power as represented in the book, whether exercised directly or indirectly, consists in deceiving men and leading them to become his tools in his war against God ; cf. vv. 3, 10, 12⁹, 13¹⁴, 19²⁰. — ταῖς τέσσαρσι γωνίαις κτλ., *the four corners of the earth* : cf. 7¹, Is. 11¹². — On Gog and Magog, see p. 744. — ὧν, αὐτῶν : for the pleonasm, see on 3⁸.

9.   ἀνέβησαν, *they went up* : Jerusalem, the seat of the millennial kingdom that rules all the world, is ' the middle of the earth ' (Ezk. 38¹²), to attack which the hostile armies march up from all quarters. — ἐπὶ τὸ πλάτος τῆς γῆς, *over the breadth of the earth* : they cover the whole surface of the earth, a hyperbole like ' their number is as the sand of the sea,' v. 8. — τὴν παρεμβολήν, *the camp* : the word, denoting a military camp, is the standing term for the encampment, the halting place, of the Israelites in the wilderness, *e.g.* Ex. 16¹³, Dt. 23¹⁴.   So here it may denote simply the abiding place of God's people, or its use may be suggested by the approach of attacking armies.   It is doubtless identical in meaning with the following phrase, ' the beloved city.'   The saints are not represented here as an army prepared for battle ; it is doubtful whether they are thought of as encamped around the city (so, some com.); they take no part in repelling the attack of the nations. — τὴν πόλιν, *the city* : the city of the millennial kingdom, an earthly Jerusalem, is meant.   The traditional conception of Jewish eschatology followed throughout the passage requires this interpretation ; and the connection with vv. 4–6 implies the same.   This is not the new Jerusalem, which does not descend till the bringing in of the new earth (21²) ; yet an idealized city must be imagined, one meet to be the capital of the millennial realm.   The Jerusalem of historic time cannot be thought of, and in a world so idealistic as that of the millennium a realistic world-capital is not to be sought.   But to find here an allegory of a spiritual Jerusalem attacked by the power of sin is to abandon consistent exegesis. — ἠγαπημένην, *beloved* : for this epithet applied to Jerusalem, cf. Ecclus. 24¹¹, Ps. 78⁶⁸, 87². — κατέβη πῦρ κτλ., *fire came down out of heaven,* etc. : the Apocalyptist follows his

source; cf. Ezk. 39⁶, 'I will send a fire on Magog'; cf. also
Ezk. 38²², Sib. Or. III. 673 (cited on p. 744), 691. 'While
the hosts are thus consumed, Satan like his adjutants, the
Beast and the false prophet, is consigned at once upon his
defeat to his punishment, v. 10, 19²⁰. This is the lake of fire
in conformity with the doctrine of Jewish eschatology·; cf. v.
15, 14¹⁰.

10. ὁ πλανῶν : for the pres. partic. with the art. made equivalent to an imperf. by the context, see on 14⁴. — ἐβλήθη εἰς
τὴν λίμνην κτλ., *was cast into the lake of fire:* Satan first cast
down from his throne in the heaven (12⁹), then bound and
imprisoned for a thousand years (20² ᶠ·), now receives his final
doom.

(2) The general resurrection and judgment. 20¹¹⁻¹⁵. See
pp. 287 f. The judgment scene as described here follows
in its essentials the other Scriptures and apocalyptic writers ;
e.g. Mt. 25³¹⁻⁴⁶, Ro. 14¹⁰, 2 Co. 5¹⁰, 2 Es. 7³³ ᶠᶠ·, En. 90²⁰⁻²⁷, 'I
saw till a throne was erected in the pleasant land, and the
Lord of the sheep sat himself thereon ; and the other took the
sealed books and opened those books before the Lord of the
sheep. . . . And I saw at that time how a like abyss was opened
in the midst of the earth full of fire, and they brought those
blinded sheep, and they were all judged and found guilty and
cast into this fiery abyss, and they burned . . . and I saw those
sheep burning.' The simplicity and restraint of the picture
drawn by our Apocalyptist in this scene, as well as in the
account of the last battle, vv. 7–10, stands in characteristic
contrast with the gruesomeness found in some other apocalypses, and in some medieval artists and poets. The place of
the throne and the judgment is not indicated. The throne of
the court of heaven described in 4² ᶠᶠ· is probably not meant ;
into that heavenly court the wicked would not be admitted,
even for judgment. Evidently the precise place is not thought
of. ' In· the last judgment the categories of space and time
fall away ' (Baljon *in loc.*). God alone appears as judge,
Christ is not mentioned. This is natural here, since the
Apocalyptist is following throughout this scene distinctively
Jewish models. The part of Christ is for the time being
dropped out of sight. Elsewhere the author recognizes clearly

Christ's office in this connection, cf. 2[7, 10], 14[14 ff.], 22[12], passages
which taken by themselves might exclude God's share in the
judgment.   Nor is there a conflict between this verse and
Jno. 5[22], which cannot be taken to mean that the author of the
Fourth Gospel dissented from the universal Christian doctrine
of God also as judge of the world ; cf. Jno. 5[45], 8[50], 12[26].
St. Paul also speaks at one time of the judgment seat of Christ,
at another of that of God ; cf. 2 Co. 5[10], Ro. 14[10].

11. **εἶδον θρόνον,** *I saw a throne :* cf. Dan. 7[9], Is. 6[1]. — **λευκόν,**
white : in keeping with the divine glory of the judge. — **τὸν**
καθήμενον κτλ., *him that sat upon it :* for the form of expression
cf. chapts. 4–5 *passim.*   The reference here is to God, not
Christ.   The Apocalyptist speaks as a Hebrew using the peri-
phrase instead of the name of God ; but see on 4[3]. — **ἔφυγεν ἡ**
γῆ κτλ., *the earth and the heaven fled away :* the world that now
is is represented as *removed* to give place to the new heaven and
the new earth (21[1]) ; for a similar representation cf. En. 90[28 f.].
According to another current belief the present world is to be
burnt up ; cf. 2 Pet. 3[10–13].   For still another view cf. En. 45[4],
' I will *transform* the heaven . . . I will transform the earth.'
See pp. 56, 749 f.

12. **τοὺς νεκρούς,** *the dead :* the living are not mentioned,
for after the battle of vv. 7–10 none are living except the saints
of the millennial kingdom, and their judgment has already
taken place.   A resurrection in bodily form is assumed according
to universal Jewish and Christian belief. — **τοὺς μεγάλους κτλ.,**
the great and the small, etc.: cf. 11[18], 13[16], 19[5, 18]. — **βιβλία, ἄλλο**
βιβλίον, *books, another book :* see on 3[5].   The former contain the
record of men's deeds, whether good or bad, which form the
ground of judgment ; the latter contains the list of those
destined to life.   There is no incongruity between the two
ideas, for the deeds determine whether names are inserted in
the book of life. — **τὰ ἔργα,** *their deeds :* for the comprehensive
meaning of the term see on 3[2].

13. The writer, in keeping with a common habit of his (see
pp. 242, 243), here turns back to a fuller statement of the appearing of the dead before the throne (12 a) ; all the recep-
tacles of the dead give up those contained in them.   The words
belong before the opening of the books and the judgment ; and,

because of their introduction in this later place, mention of the
judgment is here repeated. — **ἔδωκεν ἡ θάλασσα** κτλ., *the sea
gave up the dead*, etc.: the mention of the sea in distinction
from Hades might imply that the souls of those who had met
death by drowning were not thought to come into the place of
departed spirits; and Wetstein cites from Achilles Tatius (fifth
cent. A.D.) showing the existence of such a belief; but it is
hardly possible to attribute this thought to our author. The
abhorrent fate of those whose unburied bodies were carried
about in the sea, or devoured by the fish, would account for the
particular mention of these as restored at the resurrection;
cf. En. 61⁵, cited below. — **ὁ θάνατος καὶ ὁ ἅδης**, *death and
Hades:* cf. 6⁸; see on 1¹⁸. — With this verse cf. 2 Es. 7³²,
'The earth shall restore those that are asleep in her, and so
shall the dust those that dwell therein in silence, and the secret
places shall deliver those souls that were committed unto
them'; En. 61⁵, 'These measures shall reveal all the secrets of
the depths . . . and those who have been devoured by the fish
of the sea, that they may return'; 51¹, 'In those days shall the
earth also give back that which has been intrusted to it, and
Sheol also shall give back that which it has received, and hell
shall give back that which it owes.'

14. Death and Hades are here personified and doomed to
punishment, a conception due to the connection thought to
exist between death and sin; at the same time, the deliverance
of the saints from all future fear of death is thought of; cf. 21⁴,
Heb. 2¹⁵, 1 Co. 15²⁶, 'The last enemy that shall be brought to
naught is death.' — **ὁ θάνατος ὁ δεύτερος**, *the second death:* cf.
v. 6, 2¹¹, 21⁸. The second death is here defined as (consignment to) the lake of fire; the first is the physical death common
to all.

15. This verse announces the sentence decreed for all the
condemned. The award of those destined to life is not mentioned here; it forms the subject of the following paragraph.
On this latter theme the Apocalyptist dwells at greater length
and with deep but restrained fervor.

(3) The new heaven and the new earth; and God's presence
with his people in the new Jerusalem, 21¹⁻⁸. See p. 288.
In this prophecy of the new world and its conditions the Apoc-

alyptist uses the familiar language and imagery of O. T. eschatology.   The passage is largely made up of reminiscences of
biblical apocalyptic.   Yet the writer, with his customary command of suggested figures and words, has combined these into
a whole of wonderful simplicity, harmony, and power.   The
most striking feature in this vision of the bliss of the saints is
its spirituality.   The glory and the blessedness of the reward
promised to the saints consists in the presence of God and perfect communion with him, the satisfaction of every yearning
for the divine life of the soul, and the absence of death, sorrow,
and sin. — The question, frequently raised among earlier commentators, whether the new world is to be a *renovation* of that
now existing, or a different one brought in in place of the old
previously removed or destroyed, is one with which apocalyptic
prophecy from its nature is not concerned.   In v. 1, as in 20¹¹,
the language suggests a prior removal of the old; in 21⁵ the
words, 'I make all things new,' would more naturally denote a
renovation of that now existing.   But it is wholly improbable
that the Apocalyptist has in mind any distinct thought of the
process; it is the result that fills his vision.   It is certain that
his language cannot be taken to describe systematically a future
cosmic event.   See on 20¹¹.

1.   ἀπῆλθαν, *were passed away :* as announced in 20¹¹. —
ἡ θάλασσα οὐκ ἔστιν ἔτι, *the sea is no more :* some have taken
these words as parallel with the preceding clause, οὐκ ἔστιν ἔτι,
repeating ἀπῆλθαν; the sense then would be, the heavens, the
earth, and the sea of the first world have passed away, and
nothing would be implied as to an absence of the sea from the
new world (so, Düst. *al*).   But in that case we should expect
ἦν instead of ἔστιν, and a repetition of πρώτη as with γῆ; moreover, when the author adds θάλασσα to οὐρανός and γῆ for
emphatic comprehensiveness, he joins the three in one clause;
cf. 5¹³, 10⁶, 14⁷.   Most scholars are agreed that the Apocalyptist
means, there is no sea in the new order seen in his vision.   He
nowhere explains the absence of the sea from the new earth; it
must therefore be accounted for by some common thought regarding the sea, which makes its presence inappropriate.   A kindred idea is found elsewhere in apocalyptic writings; *e.g.* Sib.
Or. V. 447. 'In the last time the sea shall be dry'; Ass. Mos.

10⁶, 'The sea shall retire into the abyss.' The consuming of
the sea is frequently mentioned in connection with the burning
up of the world; *e.g.* Sib. Or. V. 158 f., 'A great star shall
come from heaven into the divine sea, and shall burn up the
deep sea'; Test. Lev. 4¹. For many other examples see Bouss.
Antichrist 238 f. Some find here an echo of a popular fancy
connected with the primitive oriental myth of the Creator's
conflict with a sea-monster, such as appears in the allusions to
the dragon, Rahab and Leviathan; cf. Is. 27¹, 51⁹, Job 26¹³ (so,
Moff., *al*, Bouss.¹⁸⁹⁶, rejected in the ed.¹⁹⁰⁶). But there is in
the eschatological allusions to the sea cited above no intimation
that a sea-monster is thought of, as in these latter passages
referred to. The most probable supposition (Ewald, *al*) traces
the idea to the dread of the sea felt by the ancient world, whose
means of coping with its dangers were inferior. The violence
and treachery of the sea, its unrest 'casting up mire and dirt,'
made it an element out of place in the untroubled earth of the
new order; cf. Is. 57²⁰, Ps. 107²⁵⁻²⁸, Ezk. 28⁸.

2–4. Cf. v. 10, 3¹². — ἐκ, ἀπό, *out of, from :* the former refers
to the place of origin, the latter to the divine originator. —
ὡς νύμφην, *as a bride :* the figure of the bride, which in 19⁷ is
applied to the people of God, represents here the seat of their
abode, the new Jerusalem. See on 19⁷. — ἡ σκηνὴ τοῦ θεοῦ
κτλ., *the tabernacle of God*, etc.: cf. 7¹⁵, Ezk. 37²⁷, Zec. 2¹⁰, 8⁸,
2 Co. 6¹⁶. The new Jerusalem, like the tabernacle in the wilderness, is to be the place of God's abode with his people. —
For the promises of the passage cf. 7¹⁷, Is. 25⁸, 35¹⁰, 65¹⁹, Hos.
13¹⁴. — πόνος, *pain :* probably physical pain is meant, as in 16¹⁰ ᶠ.
— τὰ πρῶτα ἀπῆλθαν, *the first things have passed away :* cf.
2 Co. 5¹⁷. The language here, as also in the words of v. 5,
'I make all things new,' is a comprehensive summary of all that
is contained in the announcement of v. 1; at the same time, the
connection suggests a special reference to sorrow, death, and
pain as belonging to the things which will have passed away.

5–6. ὁ καθήμενος ἐπὶ τῷ θρόνῳ: in this phrase the gen. is
generally used in Rev.; for the dat. cf. 7¹⁰, 19⁴. The Mss. vary.
— καινὰ ποιῶ πάντα, *I make all things new :* cf. 2 Co. 5¹⁷, Is.
43¹⁸ ᶠ. — γράψον, *write :* the object of the vb. is the revelation
contained in vv. 1–5; ὅτι is best taken as *for.* With renewed

emphasis (see on 'write,' 19⁹) God bids the Prophet to bring
to the Church the promise of supreme blessedness offered in
the new earth and the new Jerusalem, and God himself with
solemn asseveration vouches for the truth of the revelation. —
ὅτι οὗτοι οἱ λόγοι κτλ., *for these words*, etc.: reference is made
to the whole revelation given in vv. 1–5. — πιστοὶ καὶ ἀληθινοί,
faithful, i.e. *trustworthy, and true:* cf. 22⁶. ἀληθινός is here
equivalent to ἀληθής; see Thayer, *s.v.* — γέγοναν, *it is done:*
literally *they*, *i.e.* the words, *have come to pass;* cf. γέγονεν, 16¹⁷.
The renewal of all things, and the future blessedness of the
saints, resting as they do on the solemn assurance of the eternal
God himself, the Alpha and the Omega, the beginning and the
end of all, may be spoken of as if already come to pass.   The
aoristic ending of the perf. γέγοναν is rare; see Blass § 21, 3,
Win. § 13, 2, *c.*   The correction γέγονα introduced into many
Mss. is taken as equivalent to εἰμί and made the copula with
the following words, ἐγώ, τὸ ἄλφα κτλ.; but the word itself
(lit. *have come to be*), and 1⁸, 22¹³, are against the emendation.
— τῷ διψῶντι κτλ., *unto him that is athirst I will give*, etc.: cf.
7¹⁷, 22¹·¹⁷.   For the figure of thirst used often to express an
earnest sense of spiritual need, especially a yearning for communion with God, cf. Is. 55¹, 44³, Ps. 42¹ᶠ·, 63¹.

7. The promise of v. 6, ' Unto him that thirsteth,' etc., is in
this verse repeated in another form, ' I will be his God, and he
shall be my son'; the thirst for God will be satisfied in the
relation of perfect sonship with God.   The language of v. 6 *b*
is strikingly Johannine; cf. Jno. 4¹⁰, ¹⁴ 7³⁷ᶠ·, cf. also Rev. 7¹⁷,
22¹⁷.   But v. 7 shows traces of the Pauline style; κληρονομεῖν
is a favorite Pauline idea, as is also the sonship of the believer.
The close relation to God denoted in our passage by the latter
term is expressed elsewhere in the Johannine writings by τέκνον
(cf. Jno. 1¹², 1 Jno. 3¹·², 5²), and in our book by ἱερεύς, see on
1⁶. — ὁ νικῶν, *he that overcometh:* the words echo the close of
the seven epistles, chaps. 2–3, and remind the readers anew
of the stern conflict which must precede entrance on the wonderful inheritance here promised. — With the words ' He shall
be my son,' cf. 2 S. 7¹⁴.

8. Over against the inheritance of the saints is set the lot of
the wicked, who are characterized here by epithets, of which

some have special reference to circumstances of the time, others
are common designations of the heathen, as used elsewhere in
the N. T. The first epithet δειλοῖς, *cowardly*, in contrast with
steadfast, which is necessary to 'him that overcometh,' refers to
those who through fear evade the persecutions now assailing
and threatening the Church. — ἀπίστοις, *faithless*, or, *unbelieving :* in this connection the former, meaning those who prove
faithless in trial, is better; the other epithets denote special
classes, and it is likely that such is intended in this word rather
than the general class of the unbelieving, to which those referred
to in all the other epithets belong. — ἐβδελυγμένοις, *abominable :*
perhaps those who join in the abominable emperor-worship
(cf. Ro. 2²²), or perhaps more broadly those guilty of heathen
immorality in general, cf. v. 27, 17⁴ᶠ·, Tit. 1¹⁶. — The following
classes, murderers, fornicators, sorcerers, idolaters, are common
in descriptions of the heathen. — πᾶσι τοῖς ψευδέσιν, *all liars :*
the false. Falseness is frequently stigmatized in the book, cf.
2², 3⁹, 14⁵, 21⁸·²⁷, 22¹⁵, in keeping with the Johannine emphasis
on truth. In the use of epithets applied to the wicked compare
this verse with 22¹⁵. — For the lake of fire as the second death
see on 20¹⁴. — πυρὶ καὶ θείῳ, *fire and brimstone :* brimstone mingled with fire is a familiar figure as an instrument of God's
wrath; cf. Ps. 11⁶, Is. 30³³, Ezk. 38²², Rev. 14¹⁰, 19²⁰. The use
is probably derived from the story of the overthrow of Sodom
and Gomorrah, Gen. 19²⁴, upon which God is said to have rained
fire and brimstone. That representation may perhaps be due
to the abundance of sulphur in the region ; perhaps to the smell
of ozone, which the ancients sometimes referred to sulphur,
perceived in violent discharges of lightning.

Textual notes, 20⁸–21⁷. 20⁸. R with many min omits τον before πολεμον,
and αυτων after αριθμος. — 9. The words απο του θεου are inserted before or
after εκ του ουρανου in אᶜPQ most min vers R, probably through the influence
of 21²; wanting in A most other sources edd. — 12. For θρονου, R with some
min has θεου. — 14. The words η λιμνη του πυρος are added after δευτερος
εστιν in nearly all sources and edd; wanting in some min vers Prim R.
The entire sentence ουτος ο θανατος . . . πυρος is omitted by some min vers
anc com Moff *al*, bracketed by Bouss.
    21². R with some Mss. of the vlg inserts εγω Ιωαννης with ειδον. —
3. θρονου אA Iren vlg some anc com nearly all edd; ουρανου PQ most min
vers anc com Prim R Sod. — λαος PQ many min and vers anc com Ws

3 c

WHmrg Bouss *al*; λαοι אA some min Iren some anc com most edd. The pl. may have arisen through the influence of αυτοι; see Ws *Ap.* 101. — After μετ᾽ αυτων εσται, many edd follow אQ most min and vers in omitting the words θεος αυτων or αυτων θεος which are found in AP some min and vers Iren R Ws WHmrg RV *al.* They may be due to a reminiscence of such passages as Jer 24⁷, 31³³; cf Heb 8¹⁰. — 4. οτι, before τα πρωτα, אQ most min and vers most edd; wanting in AP some min Lch WH RV *al.* — 6. γεγοναν אᶜ A Iren nearly all edd; γεγονα א*QP most min vers some anc com Sod *al*, probably a correction due to the unusualness of the aoristic ending in the perf., see Com.; R has γεγονε, apparently a conjecture. — Before το αλφα, A some min anc com R Ws Alf insert ειμι; wanting in most sources and edd. — 7. R with a few min inserts the art. before υιος.

Criticism of 20⁷–21⁸. The close connection of this paragraph with the preceding in the programme of events, and the natural sequence within the paragraph itself, have caused most critics to recognize here an immediate continuation of 20¹⁻⁶, and to assign the passage as a whole, minor excisions being disregarded, to the same source, Jewish or Christian, supposed to be found in the foregoing. Vischer and his school make it, of course, Jewish, as wanting in specifically Christian elements. Spitta, who refers 20⁴⁻⁷ to the redactor, makes 20⁸–21¹ the continuation of 20¹⁻³. In 21 he sees a conflict between vv. 2 and 9; in the former the Seer beholds the new Jerusalem descending, but in the latter v. he must be taken to the top of a high mountain to see it. (See p. 768). Spitta assigns 21²⁻⁴ to the redactor, but 21⁹ ff. to his Jewish source, J², in which it continues 19⁸; 21⁵⁻⁷ belong in part to the redactor, in part to J¹. Völter assigns the paragraph to his Cerinthian insertion, and finds a Christian tone throughout. Erbes, omitting 20⁴⁻⁶, makes 20¹⁻¹⁰ a continuation of his addition (Christian) of the year 80; but 20¹¹–21⁴ he assigns to the primitive Johannine Apocalypse, where it continues 19⁹. J. Weiss finds in 20⁷–21⁴, some minor portions being omitted, a continuation of 20¹⁻⁶, and a part of the primitive Johannine source. — Some critics (Vischer, J. Weiss, *al*) reject 21⁵⁻⁸. The chief objections raised are as follows: it is strange that God himself should be introduced as a speaker, instead of Jesus or an angel; that one sitting on the throne of heaven should asseverate the truth of his utterances, that further utterances should be introduced by και λέγει, και εἶπεν, a manner elsewhere belonging, it is claimed, to the redactor; such expressions as the command γράψον, ὁ νικῶν, κληρονομεῖν ταῦτα, echo his phraseology. The whole passage has the sound of an imitator seeking to give authority to his prophecy. See Vischer, 65 ff., J. Weiss, 108 f. The inconclusiveness of these objections hardly needs to be pointed out in detail. They have not been acknowledged by critics generally as calling for discussion. Charles, discussing the order in chapts. 20⁴–22, proposes an elaborate scheme of rearrangement in this part of the book. The theory can be noticed to better advantage in connection with the criticism of 21⁹–22⁵; see p. 770.

Our paragraph (20⁷–21⁸) taken as a whole is undeniably Jewish in form. The author uses the conceptions and language of the prophets and later

apocalyptic writings. But this is true of apocalyptic writing in general
and is wholly compatible with a Jewish-Christian authorship. St. Paul's
eschatological passage in 2 Thess. 2^{3-12} is thoroughly Jewish; if the word
Jesus be omitted in v. 8, with some ancient authorities, there is not a distinctively Christian trace in the paragraph. The integrity of our paragraph
is supported by the ordered combination of its parts; these, the final victory over Satan, the general resurrection and judgment, and the union with
God in a renewed world, make up in sequence the fulfillment of the eschatological hope. No considerable part can be held superfluous, and if the
freedom of apocalyptic usage be taken into account no inconsistency appears; no passage requires a forced exegesis to support it in its place (see
Com.). The necessity of such a paragraph, as the culmination of the plan
which has shaped the literary development of the book from the beginning,
need not be pointed out; and its composition by the author of our Apocalypse appears probable from its conformity with his thought and manner.
The presence of his hand will be seen from the numerous parallelisms with
other parts of the book. In chapt. 20 compare v. 8 with 12^9, 7^1, 16^{14}; v. 9
with 13^{13}; v. 10 with 19^{20}, 14^{10}, 16^{13}; v. 11 with 20^4, $5^{1,\ 7,\ 13}$, 16^{20}, 12^8, v. 12
with 2^{23}, 22^{12}; v. 13 with 1^{18}, 6^8; v. 14 with 2^{11}, 21^{19}; v. 15 with 3^5. — In
chapt. 21 compare v. 2 with 11^2, 21^{10}, 22^{19}, 19^7; v. 3 with 10^4, 11^{12}, 7^{15}; v. 4
with 7^{17}; v. 5 with 19^9, 22^6; v. 6 with 16^{17}, 1^8, 22^{13}, 7^{17}; v. 8 with 22^{15}, 19^{20}.

(4) The city of the new Jerusalem. 21^9–22^5. See pp. 287,
289 f. This vision of the holy city is shaped throughout by
the eschatological imagery contained in the prophets and apocalyptists. In the earlier Hebrew expectation of the final era
Jerusalem, which should form the center of Israel's dominion
over all nations, and the temple at Jerusalem were to be built
up in great magnificence. The splendor of the renewed city
and temple is set forth in marvelous imagery; cf. Is. $54^{11\ f.}$,
60^{13}, Tobit $13^{16\ f.}$, 14^5, Hag. 2^{7-9}. But as seen above (pp.
54 ff.) when eschatological ideas became more transcendental,
a new heaven and a new earth came to be looked for, and a
new Jerusalem, already existing in ideal perfection in heaven
and ready to descend upon the new earth, becomes an established factor in visions of the end. To the description of this
new Jerusalem are transferred all the splendors of the earthly
Jerusalem predicted in the earlier eschatological writers. The
details in the picture of the holy city and its relation to the
nations, as given in our passage, are derived chiefly from
Isaiah and Ezekiel, as will be pointed out below.

In this passage (21^9–22^5) is given in full a vision of the city

whose descent has been declared in passing in v. 2.   As the
sequel to the judgment scene of chapt. 20¹¹⁻¹⁵ in its relation to
the reward of the righteous, the Prophet has introduced in
21¹⁻⁸ a summary statement of the new order of the world ; a
voice from heaven has proclaimed the coming of God to abide
with his people, and has foretold their blessedness in a perfected union with God.   The city of the new Jerusalem itself,
as spoken of there, is a subordinate part of the larger picture
of the new world ; it is there mentioned, as it were only incidentally, as the *place* of what forms the chief theme of that
passage, the reward of the saints in the presence of God among
them.   But now in these verses, 21⁹–22⁵, the Apocalyptist
comes on to tell of his vision of the city in all its perfection
and splendor — a theme which could not be wanting in an
extended apocalypse of the final bliss of the saints.   These
verses then do not, as some critics suppose, contain a duplication of what has already been revealed in v. 2, but rather the
actual vision which was there only briefly mentioned to serve
the purpose then in hand.   See more fully, p. 768 f.

XXI. 9.   **εἶς ἐκ τῶν ἑπτὰ ἀγγέλων κτλ.**, *one of the seven
angels*, etc. : why the office of showing the holy city should be
assigned to one of the angels of the seven last plagues is not
made clear.   But the close parallelism in language between
21⁹ ᶠ· and 17¹, ³, the introductory words in their respective
visions, intimates that the new Jerusalem, the capital city of
God's perfected kingdom, is thought of as contrasted with the
great city (Rome) that had reigned over the kings of the earth
(17¹⁸) ; the Bride is contrasted with the woman on the scarlet
beast.   Hence an angel of the same class, not necessarily the
same angel, appropriately appears here as the ministrant.   See
on 17¹. — **τῶν γεμόντων κτλ.**, *full of the seven last plagues :* the
reference of the partic. to the angels, *who were laden with the
plagues*, so, some, *e.g.* RV, involves too great violence in the
use of the word γέμειν ; pretty certainly it refers to the bowls.
The grammatical error is due to the prominence of τῶν ἑπτὰ
. . . ἐχόντων.   For the use of the pres. partic., see on 14⁴. —
τὴν νύμφην, *the Bride :* properly the betrothed ; the 'marriage
of the Lamb' is thought of as not having yet actually taken

place, though close at hand. Therefore τὴν γυναῖκα, *the wife*, is used proleptically, the one who is to be the wife. See on 19⁷. — Noticeable in this vision is the frequent mention of the Lamb.

10. In vv. 10–17 the Apocalyptist describes the city in its general aspect, telling of the divine light emanating from it, of its walls, its gates, and its measurements. This part of the description is derived mainly from Ezekiel's vision of the new temple, which is to form the central object in the kingdom of the last times, chapts. 40–48. Like the Hebrew prophet (Ezk. 40²) the Seer is carried away to the top of a high mountain, whence the vision is opened before him. He is borne thither in a state of ecstasy ; the words ' in the Spirit' have the same meaning as Ezekiel's phrase ' in the visions of God ' ; the ecstasy is that into which the Seer is raised by the Spirit. Cf. 1¹⁰, 4², 17³. — ἐκ τοῦ οὐρανοῦ ἀπὸ τοῦ θεοῦ, *out of heaven from God :* see on v. 2.

The form Ἱερουσαλήμ (a not quite accurate transliteration of the Heb.) is found uniformly in the LXX, but alternates in the N. T. with Ἱεροσόλυμα (Hellenistic mistranslation, ἱερός and Σόλυμα. See En. Bib. II. 2409), some writers using both forms indifferently. But in Mk. and the Fourth Gospel the latter only occurs, while Heb. and Rev. have the former only ; in these two books, Heb. and Rev., the name refers to the heavenly city. In the five places in the N. T. (Gal. 4²⁶, Heb. 12²², Rev. 3¹², 21², ¹⁰), where the heavenly city is mentioned by name the first form only is used, *i.e.* the Heb., instead of the inaccurate form of current Gentile usage. Paul in Gal., though using uniformly the second form in speaking of the historic city, changes to the first to designate the heavenly city ; Gal. 4²⁵ can hardly be said to be at variance with this statement, for the form there is evidently determined by that of the following verse which contains the controlling thought. There seems then to have been a tendency to use the Hebraic form in speaking of the heavenly city (cf. Lightfoot, on Gal. 4²⁶) ; and this use would be especially expected in a description of the heavenly city following closely the Heb. prophets. It therefore seems far from certain, as some suppose, that the difference between Rev. and the Fourth Gospel in the use of this proper name indicates diversity of authorship, however cogent other reasons may be for maintaining such diversity.

11. ἔχουσαν τὴν δόξαν τοῦ θεοῦ, *having the glory of God :* cf. Ezk. 43⁵, ' Behold the glory of Jehovah filled the house ' ; Is. 60¹, ' The glory of Jehovah is risen upon thee.' Before entering on his description of the city in its material aspects, the

Apocalyptist speaks of that which must strike his vision first, and which gives to the descending Jerusalem its supreme splendor, the presence of God manifested in the effulgence of wonderful light. For the divine glory exhibited in brilliant light, see on 4³, 18¹. — ὁ φωστὴρ αὐτῆς, *its light: i.e.* the light which it emitted. φωστήρ is that which gives light ; here the luminary which the city constitutes (αὐτῆς) ; cf. Phil. 2¹⁵. For the 'jasper' stone, see on 4³. — κρυσταλλίζοντι, 'of crystalline brightness and transparency,' Thayer, *s.v.* Cf. 4⁶, 22¹.

12–13. In vv. 12–17 the Apocalyptist describes the walls, the gates and the measurements of the city, following mainly Ezk. — ἔχουσα : the partic. refers to πόλις which is in the writer's thought, the construction changing loosely to the nom. — The twelve gates, three on each side and bearing the names of the twelve tribes of Israel, are taken directly from Ezk. 48³¹ ᶠᶠ· In Ezekiel's vision each several tribe has its own gate of entrance into the city, as it has its full share allotted to it in the distribution of the land, 48¹⁻²⁰ ; so likewise in the new Jerusalem each tribe of the whole Israel of God (cf. 7¹⁻⁸) is assured of its right of equal approach into the place of God's presence. — ἐπὶ τοῖς πυλῶσιν ἀγγέλους δώδεκα, *at the gates twelve angels:* the angels stand upon (ἐπί) the gate towers, one at each gate, as watchers; cf. Is. 62⁶, 2 Chron. 8¹⁴. This feature does not appear in Ezekiel's picture. The walls, the gates, and the watchmen are things which belong to the conception of a perfect city, and as such they appear here ; a defense against the entrance of evil, as some interpret, is not to be pressed, as nothing of the kind is intimated in the context. For the same reason, the order of the points of the compass, E N S W, is not to be taken as having special significance ; it follows Ezk. 42¹⁶ ᶠᶠ· instead of 48³¹ ᶠᶠ· — ἀπό: lit. *from.* The city is described as *seen from* the standpoint of the Seer ; cf. H. A. 788 c, Kühn II. § 447 C.

14. ἔχων : the author's tendency to use the partic. in this form (see p. 224) favors the retention of this reading in spite of the grammatical error. — θεμελίους, *foundations:* cf. Is. 28¹⁶, Heb. 11¹⁰. The number twelve assigned to the foundation stones not only conforms to the prominence of that number in this vision, denoting here the *completeness* of the substructure

of the wall, but is especially chosen with reference to the twelve
apostles in their office of laying the foundations of the Church;
cf. Eph. 2²⁰, 'built upon the foundation of the apostles and
prophets.' St. Paul emphasizes his function of laying foundations, 1 Co. 3¹⁰, Ro. 15²⁰. Cf. also the Lord's words, Mt. 16¹⁸.
The term 'the twelve apostles' is used here in its official
sense designating the body of the apostles as a whole; the
individuals, whether the original twelve, or whether including
St. Paul and others added to the number, are not thought of.
This corporate reference of 'The Twelve' must have been
common, as may be inferred from its use in cases where a
smaller number must be actually understood; cf. 1 Co. 15⁵,
where only eleven, or according to Jno. 20²⁴, only ten made up
the number. Even in the Gospels it is doubtful whether the
whole twelve are always thought of in the use of the term, *e.g.*
Lk. 9¹². A Roman parallel has been frequently pointed out;
decemviri and *centumviri* came to be used as official terms without regard to the precise number. The dignity here ascribed
to the apostles does not in itself indicate, as many contend
(see pp. 351 ff.), a non-apostolic writer, or one looking back
upon the apostles in the light with which a later generation
invested them. This consciousness of their fundamental importance on the part of the apostles, yet without a trace of
presumptuousness, appears elsewhere; cf. 1 Co. 12²⁸, 4⁹, 9¹,
Eph. 2²⁰, Mt. 19²⁸, Jno. 17¹⁸, ²⁰. — τοῦ ἀρνίου, *of the Lamb:* the
celestial city is distinctively the city of the Lamb in his transcendent glory; cf. 21⁹, ²², ²³, ²⁷, 22¹, ³. (See pp. 314 ff.)
Hence the apostles, whose names are inscribed on the foundations, are designated as those of the Lamb.

15–16. The reed in the hand of the angel and his act of
measurement are suggested by Ezk. 40³ ᶠᶠ· The angel apparently does not measure the gates, as from v. 15 we should
expect him to do. This detail in the language of v. 15 is retained from Ezekiel, where it is carried out in full, 40⁶ ᶠᶠ· —
τετράγωνος, *foursquare:* more exactly, *quadrangular.* Cf. Ezk.
48²⁰. — ἐμέτρησεν τὴν πόλιν, *he measured the city:* 'the city'
here and in v. 16 is commonly understood to be distinguished
from the wall, *i.e.* the inner part of the city is meant without
including the encircling wall. But the author's very common

habit of first introducing a comprehensive term and then defining it more specifically by clauses added with καί, *and* (epexegetical ; see p. 242) suggests that usage here, since there is no apparent motive for distinguishing the city from its wall. In such a picture as is given here the two most naturally form a single idea. If it were not so, we should almost certainly find some intimation of a reason for the distinction. We may infer then that the height of the *wall* is included in the statement of the height of 'the city' in v. 16. See further on v. 17, on the measurement of the wall. — ἐπὶ σταδίων : to denote the limit in measuring the acc. would be expected ; see Win. § 49 on ἐπί. The gen. however is not unexampled ; cf. Xen. *An.* VII. 8. 14, ὁ δὲ τοῖχος ἦν ἐπ' ὀκτὼ πλίνθων. — σταδίων δώδεκα χιλιάδων, *12,000 furlongs:* this 1500 miles might be the measurement of each of the four sides, or of the whole compass of the city ; doubtless the former, as indicated by the following words. In either case the number, the multiple of twelve by a thousand, is symbolical of completeness and immensity (see p. 254). Rabbinical writers interpret Zec. 9¹ to mean that the future Jerusalem would extend as far as Damascus. — τὸ ὕψος αὐτῆς, *its height :* the city is seen as an exact cube. Doubtless this feature is intended to express perfect symmetry. In Ezekiel symmetry is made prominent. Possibly the cubical form is suggested (so, many com.) by that of the Holy of holies in the temple (1 K. 6²⁰), to which the new Jerusalem answers as the special place of God's presence. Reference is frequently made in this connection to the rabbinical fancy given in Baba bathra 75, 2, that the future Jerusalem would be a cube twelve miles high. A city 1500 miles high, as in our passage, while unimaginable, is no more so than a pearl large enough to form the whole of a vast gate-tower, or gold transparent as glass (v. 21). The Apocalyptist, regardless of architectural reality, is struggling to express by symbols the vastness, the perfect symmetry, and the splendor of the new Jerusalem. Perhaps the great height of the city figures the blending of heaven and earth in the new world. Cf. the prediction in Sib. Or. V. 251 f., that in the last days the walls of Jerusalem will reach as far as Joppa and 'up to the darkling clouds' ; also *ibid.* 424 ff., where it is said that the city will have a 'tower touching the very clouds and seen of all, so that all the faithful and all the righteous may see the glory of the invisible God.'

17. The measure of the wall, 144 (12 × 12) cubits, about 216 feet, is understood by most interpreters to refer to height. The indefinite expression would most naturally be taken of length or height, and the former is excluded here. In a picture so remote from the actual the difference between the height of the wall and that of the enclosed city cannot in itself be decisive against this interpretation. Yet in the connection here, the difficulty arising in that reference is undeniable. The wall and its gates are prominent features in the portrayal of the city; the former is mentioned no less than six times, and is called 'great and high'; but as the wall of a city 1500 miles high it would be infinitesimally low. If the idea of the cube is to be preserved, a wall of this height must be left altogether out of mention. Some explanation of the disproportion would seem to be required. In Ezk., followed so closely in the present vision, the *thickness* of the wall is measured (40^5, 42^{20}); and if 'the city' in vv. 15 f. includes the wall, the height is given there (see note above). It would appear preferable then to understand this measurement to refer to thickness. — μέτρον ἀνθρώπου, *man's measure;* 'he measured its walls 144 cubits, man's measure, which is angel's measure.' The phrase μέτρον κτλ. is in apposition with the foregoing clause; cf. Win. § 59, 9, *b.* The measuring here is performed by an angel, but the Apocalyptist will have his readers understand that the dimensions given in these marvelous figures are determined by the standards in common use among men. There is an absoluteness in symbolical figures and measurements — those of men and angels are the same.

18. In vv. 18–21 the precious materials of which the city is made are enumerated. The details are suggested by Is. $54^{11\,f.}$, Tob. $13^{16\,f.}$; see p. 755. The wall is of jasper, and the city itself of gold clear as glass; the crystal-like nature of the gold denotes its purity and its brilliant radiation of light, the light effects being especially characteristic of the divine city. (See on 4^3.) — ἐνδώμησις, *building;* lit. the act of building into, or that which is built into, something; probably the *material* is

meant which is built into the wall, that of which it is made.
The word is found elsewhere only in Joseph. *Ant.* XV. 9, 6,
where it is used of a wall built into the sea as a breakwater.
Some understand it in our passage as the lower part of the
wall built into the foundation; but in that case we should
expect τοῦ θεμελίου instead of τοῦ τείχους.

19–20. The foundation stones are conceived as visible. In
the first sentence the foundations as a whole (the force of the
pl.). are said to be adorned with precious stones; how this
adornment is carried out in detail is explained in the following
appositional passage (the asyndeton is noticeable), in which
each one of the twelve parts of the foundation is shown to consist of its own particular stone. No special mystical sense is
to be assigned to the several stones; the writer's purpose is to
give to the appearance of the city the greatest possible richness
and splendor of light and color which could be exhibited by
the materials known in familiar imagery. The ornamentation
of Aaron's breastplate, Ex. 28[17 ff.], 39[10 ff.], forms the *locus classicus*
for lists of the precious stones, and is used at least in part here,
as in Ezk. 28[13]. The identification of the stones is in some
cases doubtful, in some impossible. See on 4[3]. On the precious
stones themselves, and the comparison of the several lists, see
En. Bib. IV. 4803 ff., Hast. IV. 619 ff.

21. The great gate-towers, the most conspicuous part of the
wall, are of pearl, each one being formed of a single pearl.
Wetstein quotes from Baba bathra, 75, 1, the rabbinic prophecy,
'God will bring gems and pearls thirty cubits long and wide,
and will hollow these out to the height of twenty cubits and
to the breadth of ten cubits, and place them in the gates of
Jerusalem.' — ἀνὰ εἷς ἕκαστος: for this distributive expression see Win. § 37, 3; Blass § 39, 2. — ἡ πλατεῖα, *the street:*
used collectively for all the streets, or, perhaps better, as
referring to the one broad street characteristic of an oriental
city.

22–23. The Apocalyptist, dwelling on the glories of the city,
is still thinking of outward and visible things. The presence
of God and the Lamb is here spoken of, not with reference to a
spiritual union of the saints with them (quite different is the
purpose in v. 3); but as explaining the absence of a temple in

the city and its independence of all ordinary means of illumination. In Ezekiel's vision of the future Jerusalem the temple forms the principal object; likewise in Jewish eschatology in general it is an essential part of the glorified city, *e.g.* Is. 44²⁸, 60¹³. Its absence in the vision of our Apocalyptist echoes the Christian thought of Jno. 4²¹'²³. No temple-building is needed, for the presence of God and the Lamb makes every place where they are a sanctuary, and the whole new Jerusalem is filled with their presence. — οὐ χρείαν ἔχει τοῦ ἡλίου κτλ., *hath no need of the sun*, etc.: from Is. 60¹⁹ᶠ. The apparent distribution here between God and the Lamb of different functions in giving light to the city is rhetorical rather than real; in 22⁵ it is God who displaces the 'lamp.' The presence of God and the Lamb, who are thought of together, makes unnecessary all other sources of illumination, whether sun, moon, or lamp. On ἡ δόξα τοῦ θεοῦ, *the glory of God*, see on v. 11.

24–26. In these verses the Apocalyptist describes the attitude of the Gentile nations of all the earth toward Jehovah in the seat of his kingdom, the new Jerusalem. The writer uses figures and language taken over verbally from the prophets, which presuppose the continuance of Gentile peoples on the earth after the establishment of the eschatological era. What he means to express in these purely conventional terms is clear, *i.e.* the *universality* of the knowledge and sway of God, and of the homage which will be paid to him. On the difficulty raised here by the existence of Gentile nations in the renewed earth, after the events of 19²¹ and after the judgment, see pp. 769 f., 745. — περιπατήσουσιν . . . τοῦ φωτός, *the nations shall walk by its light:* cf. Is. 60³, 'Nations shall come to thy light, and kings to the brightness of thy rising.' — οἱ βασιλεῖς τῆς γῆς κτλ., *the kings of the earth bring their glory into it:* cf. Ps. 72¹⁰, 'The kings of Tarshish and of the isles shall render tribute; the kings of Sheba and Seba shall offer gifts'; Is. 60⁵, Tob. 13¹¹, Ps. Sol. 17³⁴. — οἱ πυλῶνες αὐτῆς κτλ., *the gates thereof shall not be shut by day:* from Is. 60¹¹. Offerings may be brought in continually. — νὺξ γὰρ κτλ., *for there shall be no night there:* a parenthesis thrown in to explain why day only is mentioned in the preceding clause, instead of the full phrase *day and night*, as given in Is. — τὴν δόξαν . . . τῶν ἐθνῶν, *the glory and the honor*

of the nations: those choicest treasures of theirs, the possession
of which is counted a glory and honor.

27. From the nations coming up to the holy city with offerings of homage, the Apocalyptist turns in contrast to such as
may not enter; cf. v. 8, 22¹⁵. The idea is that of Is. 52¹, Ezk. 44⁹.
For the presence of such in the new earth see on vv. 24 ff. —
ποιῶν βδέλυγμα κτλ., *doeth an abomination and a lie:* the mas.
without the art. (see text. note) can be joined with the neuter
expression πᾶν κοινόν, because the latter implies a *person,* who
is made unclean; see B. Weiss *in loc.* — εἰ μὴ οἱ γεγραμμένοι
κτλ., *but only those who are written,* etc.: *s.c.* may enter. For
the brachylogy see Burton § 274, Win. § 67, 1, *e.* — τῷ βιβλίῳ
κτλ., *the Lamb's book of life:* see on 13⁸.

22¹. Hitherto in the vision (21⁹·ᶠᶠ·) the Apocalyptist has
spoken of the visible splendors of the new Jerusalem and its
relation, as the abode of God, to the nations of the earth. He
now comes in 22¹⁻⁵ to that which nourishes and gladdens the
life of God's servants therein. The river of life, whose streams
make glad the city of God (Ps. 46⁴), flows out from the throne
through the midst of the city. This feature accords with the
river of Eden, Gen. 2¹⁰; but the details are directly suggested
by the waters which in Ezekiel's vision issue from under the
temple and flow forth to heal the waters of the Dead Sea, and
to give life whithersoever they come, 47¹⁻¹²; cf. also Zec. 14⁸,
' It shall come to pass in that day that living waters shall go
out from Jerusalem.' The effect of the waters in regions beyond
the city, spoken of in Ezekiel's vision, does not appear to be
thought of here; the passage is chiefly concerned with what
affects the spiritual life of God's servants. For the significance
of the waters here cf. v. 17, 21⁶, 7¹⁷, Jno. 4¹⁴. Students of the
origins of eschatological imagery find a primitive connection of
the idea of the river of paradise with the Milky Way, and of the
twelve gates of the heavenly Jerusalem with the signs of the
zodiac; cf. Bouss. 447 ff.; Gressmann *Ursprung d. isr.-jüd.
Eschatol.* These conjectures are interesting in a historical
study; but our Apocalyptist and the O. T. writers from whom
his imagery is taken are without doubt unconscious of such
primitive connections, if they exist. — τοῦ θρόνου τοῦ ἀρνίου,
the throne of the Lamb: cf. v. 3, 3²¹.

2. **ἐν μέσῳ τῆς πλατείας αὐτῆς**, *in the midst of the street thereof:* it is probably best to take these words as a part of v. 1, and as referring, not to the position of the throne (in that case we should expect the art. to be repeated), but to the flowing forth of the waters, 'proceeding out . . . in the midst of the street thereof'; so, a number of com. following Matthæi (see RV, WH.). Otherwise the new and distinct object of the next sentence, the tree of life, would be introduced without the connective *καί, and*, or the repetition of the vb., a construction opposed to the author's uniform usage. Moreover, in Ezekiel's vision (47¹⁻¹²), closely followed here, the waters are seen flowing first from the temple (answering to God's throne here), and out through the courts (answering to the city about the throne, v. 3). But as regards the place of the trees, the river alone is there spoken of, there is no allusion to the street of the city. Most com., however, join the phrase with v. 2, and interpret, 'In the midst of the street thereof and on either side of the river was the tree,' etc. Or some (Ewald, Düst., *al*) govern *ποταμοῦ* by *ἐν μέσῳ*, 'between the street and the river, on this side and that'; but this would imply two streets, one on either side of the river, with a tree-grown space between each street and the river; the sing. 'street' is against this. In any case the general representation is clear; a broad street and a river run through the city, and along the course grow numerous trees.

The tree of life is another traditional feature of paradise; cf. 2⁷, Gen. 2⁹, 2 Es. 7⁵³, 8⁵², En. 25² ᶠᶠ·, Sl. En. 8³ ᶠ·. The description in our passage follows almost *verbatim* Ezk. 47¹², 'By the river upon the bank thereof, on this side and on that side, shall grow every tree for food, whose leaf shall not wither, neither shall the fruit thereof fail; it shall bring forth new fruit every month, because the waters thereof issue out of the sanctuary; and the fruit thereof shall be for food, and the leaf thereof for healing.' — **ἐντεῦθεν καὶ ἐκεῖθεν**: equivalent to the *ἔνθεν καὶ ἔνθεν* of Ezk. 47¹², LXX. — **ξύλον**, *tree:* used collectively; there are multitudes of trees. — **ποιῶν, ἀποδιδούς**: if the mas. be adopted, it would be supported by the looseness of construction frequent with the author. — **καρποὺς δώδεκα**, *twelve crops of fruit:* as explained by the following words, and

by Ezekiel's phrase, 'it shall bring forth new fruit every month.'
— τὰ φύλλα κτλ., *the leaves, for the healing of the nations:*
spiritual healing is meant. The *fruit* of the tree is doubtless,
as in Ezk., thought of as food for dwellers in the city, though
that is not mentioned here. Cf. En. 25⁵, 'Its fruit shall be
for food to the elect'; Test. Lev. 18¹¹. The familiar use of
the leaves of plants as medicines doubtless suggests to Ezk. this
attribute of the trees in his prophecy. For the healing properties of the tree of life cf. 2 Es. 7¹²³, Ap. Mos. 6². For the
presence in the new earth of those in need of healing see on
21²⁴ ᶠᶠ·.

3–4. πᾶν κατάθεμα κτλ., *there shall be no more curse*, or
accursed thing: at this point in the description of the holy city
and the blessedness of the saints, mention of the absence of any
curse, as an unconnected statement, does not seem in place. It
is probably to be taken as part of a thought in the context here.
If it looks forward to the next sentence, the meaning would be,
there will be no accursed thing to prevent the presence of God
(cf. Jos. 7¹²), but his throne will be there, before which his
servants will worship undisturbed. But we should then expect
δέ, instead of καί, to introduce the next clause. A thought
better suited to this place is obtained by joining the words with
the former verse; the tree of life will heal the nations, and
there will be no more a curse of God resting upon them. In
either interpretation the words are not a mere doublet of 21²⁷;
see on v. 5 and p. 770. — αὐτοῦ, αὐτῷ, *his, him:* God, not the
Lamb, is meant. The writer uses the sing. because he is thinking of God as supreme, as in 11¹⁵; cf. 1 Co. 11³. But equal
worship is offered to the Lamb, as seen from 5¹³. — λατρεύ-
σουσιν, *shall serve:* offer worship; cf. 7¹⁵. — ὄψονται τὸ πρόσωπον αὐτοῦ, *shall see his face:* cf. Ps. 17¹⁵, Mt. 5⁸, 1 Jno. 3². —
τὸ ὄνομα αὐτοῦ κτλ., *his name shall be on their foreheads:* cf. 14¹;
see on 13¹⁶ for the meaning. — In these last verses, what for the
saints forms the supreme felicity is reached, immediate presence
with God and the Lamb.

5. νὺξ οὐκ ἔσται ἔτι, *there shall be night no more:* the words
occur in 21²⁵; but the purpose there is to explain a limitation
in the preceding sentence (see note there); here the delight-
someness of the city is meant. See following note. — οὐκ

ἔχουσιν χρείαν κτλ., *they need no light of lamp*, etc.; here again
there is repetition, cf. 21²³, but the relation is different. In
21²³ the words are introduced to explain the unusualness of the
city in certain particulars, its want of the ordinary means of
illumination; here, in vv. 2–5, the Apocalyptist is telling of the
delightsome life of the citizens, one of whose joys it is that they
need no sun nor lamp, because of the light of the divine glory
present with them.   These three repetitions, in vv. 3 *a* and 5,
of parts of 21²³, ²⁵, ²⁷, do not therefore form a legitimate ground
of objection to unity of authorship here; see p. 770. — If φῶς
be read before ἡλίου, it must depend upon οὐκ ἔχουσιν, *they have
no light of the sun.* — βασιλεύσουσιν κτλ., *they shall reign*, etc.:
the description of the blessedness of the saints in the new
Jerusalem closes with the prophecy of their unending reign in
the kingdom of God.   With this prophecy close the visions
of the book.   This form, which the promise receives in the
beginnings of apocalyptic writings, cf. Dan. 7²⁷, it retains
throughout; cf. 1⁶, 3²¹, 5¹⁰, Lk. 22³⁰, Ro. 5¹⁷.   The spiritual
fact denoted by this sovereignty, in which, according to apocalyptic figure, the saints are to share, is expressed *for us* in our
Lord's words, ' My kingdom is not of this world . . . every one
that is of the truth obeyeth my voice,' Jno. 18³⁶ ᶠ., and the complementary utterance, ' the truth shall make you free,' Jno. 8³².

Textual Notes, 21⁹–22⁵.   21⁹. των γεμοντων ℵ*AP some min most edd;
τας γεμουσας Q most min R Alf Ws (see *Ap.* 137) *al*, probably a correction.
— 10. After πολιν, some min R insert την μεγαλην. — 12. For εχουσα, before
τειχος, R with a few min reads εχουσαν τε. — The words και επι . . . δωδεκα
are wanting in A. — 14. εχων APQ (wanting in ℵ*) some min most edd;
εχον ℵᶜ most min R Ws Sod. — 15. R with some min and vers omits μετρον
before καλαμον. — Q most min omit και το τειχος αυτης. — 16. επι σταδιων
ℵP many min R most edd; επι σταδιους AQ many min Lch Ws Alf WHmrg
al. — 21. For διαυγης, R reads διαφανης. — 23. Before αυτη, some
min insert εν. — 24. R with one min some anc com adds των σωζομενων
after εθνη. — After δοξαν, Q many min some vers and anc com R add και
την τιμην. — 27. Instead of κοινον, R reads κοινουν, without authority. —
ποιων ℵA most min edd; ποιουν PQ some min and anc com R, due to conformation to κοινον. — Before ποιων, the art. is wanting in ℵᶜA some min
Lch Ws Alf Sod *al*; bracketed by WH Bouss Sw *al*. It is inserted in ℵ*
most min Ti Tr RV *al*, probably a correction to relieve the hard expression
κοινον και ποιων βδελυγμα, but see Com. See Ws *Ap.* 5 and 85. — 22¹. Before ποταμον, R with many min has καθαρον. — 2. εντευθεν και εκειθεν AQ

(wanting in P) most min edd; ενθεν και ενθεν ℵ; εντευθεν και εντευθεν some min R. — ποιουν ℵQ most min R most edd; ποιων A min Ti Bouss. — αποδιδους ℵQ many min Tr Ti WHmrg Sod Bouss al; αποδιδουν A many min R Ws Alf WH al. See Ws Ap. 113. — 5. ετι ℵAP min vers anc com edd; εκει some min and vers anc com R. — Before λυχνον, ℵA some min and vers most edd insert φωτος; wanting in PQ most min R; bracketed by Alf Sod al. — Before ηλιον, ℵ many min vers R most edd read φωτος; AP some min WH al read φως, probably a copyist's mistake. — ηλιου is wanting in Q many min.

Criticism of 21⁹–22⁵. Apart from minor objections raised against certain words and phrases, the grounds for criticism of this paragraph are found in three particulars. (1) It is said to duplicate 21¹⁻⁸, introducing as a new subject a vision of what has already been seen. The Apocalyptist has seen the new Jerusalem descending from heaven, and has heard a voice from the throne declaring the blessedness which awaits the dwellers there. Nothing further is now to be expected. Therefore the appearing of an angel, 21⁹ ff., taking the Seer to the top of a high mountain to behold the city descending, together with its great glories, must be a later addition, or a fragment, which the author of the Apocalypse in its present form has incorporated without the changes necessary to adapt it properly to its context; so, Weyland, Völter, Erbes, Sabatier, J. Weiss, al.

The answer to this criticism is twofold. In the first place a writer whose visions of a renewed world and God's presence with his people follow so closely the traditional Jewish pictures could not fail to portray the visible glories of the future Jerusalem, a favorite theme in the O. T. prophets and other apocalyptists. And he expressly states that his vision included a view of the city adorned in this outward splendor, 21². Some description of this must then be expected in the record of his visions; but nothing of the kind appears in vv. 3–8. The glory there spoken of very briefly is wholly spiritual and personal. And it may be noticed also that in the structure of the book the great powers and motives entering into the course of action are represented in great tableaux as it were. Such are the scenes of Jehovah and the Lamb in the court of heaven, chaps. 4–5; of the woman and the dragon, chapt. 12; of the Beast and his adjutant, chapt. 13; of Rome and her fall, chaps. 17–18. In a book with such a literary structure, a revelation of the glories of the new Jerusalem, to which all hope has been directed from the beginning, could not be wanting. The loss of such a vision as this would diminish the symmetry of the book. — In the second place, as regards the bringing in of the passage, the author follows a manner seen elsewhere in the book. Thus in 15¹ he announces the theme of the vision of which he is to tell; then in 15⁵ f. the vision itself is introduced as if not already announced. Analogous is the vision of chapt. 18 completing what in a summary way had been announced in 19¹⁶ (see note there), and had been promised in 17¹. Cf. also the vision of 12¹⁻⁶, afterwards expanded in 12¹³⁻¹⁷. So here in 21² the Apocalyptist alludes incidentally to the new Jerusalem as a part of what he is foretelling, and then in vv. 9 ff. gives the vision of the city itself. The theme of vv. 1–8 is the supreme *religious significance* of the new order which centers in the Jerusalem to be shown in the later passage. See p. 756. It must not be forgotten that the author in the arrangement of the record of his visions, which were received at different times, must frequently have in mind, and may allude to, something to be fully introduced later. If this is a part of his manner, it must be acknowledged, even if the rigorous critic pronounces it a defect.

(2) The vision in some of its details is said to be inconsistent with the general situation supposed in it. The last judgment has taken place, all evil has been overcome and consigned to its final punishment, the new earth and the new Jerusalem have been brought in. On the other hand, without the gates of the holy city there remain the Gentiles, who shall come to Jerusalem with their offerings, 21$^{24-26}$; there remain the common and unclean who may not enter and who are yet to be healed by the leaves of the tree of life, 21^{27}, 22^{2}, cf. 22^{15}. The paragraph (21^{9}–22^{5}) is therefore regarded by many as a slightly changed Jewish document, which together with the other features of traditional Jewish eschatology retains also these representations of the heathen who still remain in the earth as the subjects of God's people in the messianic kingdom; see pp. 51 ff., 54. So, many critics, *e.g.* Vischer, Pfleiderer, Spitta, Sabatier, J. Weiss. The redactor in adopting the document made some Christian additions, but was not careful to revise it to bring it into harmony with its position. These additions made by the redactor consist chiefly in the mention of the Lamb; these are said to be dragged in at the end of their clauses, thus betraying themselves as appended later with a special purpose; they could be omitted without detriment to the construction. Such are found in 21$^{9, 14, 22, 23, 27}$, 22$^{1, 3}$. The mention of the apostles 21^{14} is a Christian addition.

But if the borrower of the Jewish document had felt the necessity of making at least eight additions to give it a Christian tone and suit it to a place in the book, he could hardly have failed to remove these references to the heathen in 21$^{24-27}$, 22^{2}, which would immediately present themselves to a reviser as at variance with the rest of the Apocalyptist's picture; a glance at the passages will show that they could be omitted as easily as the critic omits the allusions to the Lamb and the apostles. Their presence furnishes evidence against, rather than for, a redactor's work. As regards the excision of allusions to the Lamb, on the ground of a loose connection with their clauses, it is interesting to apply the same principle to some of the N. T. epistles. In 2 Thess. *e.g. Jesus, Jesus Christ* and a few phrases containing these words could with equal ease be omitted and leave a perfect sentence in 1$^{7, 8, 12}$, 2$^{1, 8, 14, 16}$, 3$^{5, 6, 12}$, the word *Lord* being referred to God; there would remain then in the epistle nothing distinctively Christian except the salutation and blessing. So in Titus, the Christian phrases in 2^{13}, 3^{6} could be as easily expunged and with the same effect as regards the Christian character of the epistle. An adequate solution of the difficulty in these allusions to the heathen in our paragraph is found in the writer's use throughout the passage of familiar language and imagery occuring in

3 D

the prophets and other Jewish writers. His picture is drawn on conventional lines. The terms and figures are those used everywhere in descriptions of the complete triumph of the messianic kingdom over all the earth in the last days. Incongruities of the kind appearing here lie for the time being entirely beyond the Apocalyptist's thought. The usage is similar to that found in 6^{14}; there also the conventional language of apocalyptic is employed, which if taken strictly, would declare the removal of the heavens and the earth, though these are in the following visions seen to be in existence; see note there. See pp. 722, 745.

Charles, *An Attempt to recover the Original Order of the Text of Rev. xx. 4–xxii.* 1915, seeks to remove the discrepancy in question here by a theory of two distinct cities descending from heaven, and by a corresponding rearrangement of the text in chapts. 20–22. His view is that the Apocalyptist John died after carrying his work to 20^3, but left notes for its completion. These notes contained a vision of a new Jerusalem which should descend and form the capital of the kingdom in the preliminary reign of the thousand years before the end. During the time of that city the heathen exist in the earth and are referred to in verses belonging to that vision, 21^{24-27}, $22^{2, 15}$. But the notes left by the Apocalyptist contained also another vision, one of a second Jerusalem which was to come down with the new heaven and the new earth after the judgment. In the world to which this second city belongs, there would be no sorrow nor sin. These notes left by the Apocalyptist were put together and appended to 20^3, by an unintelligent literary executor, in our present form, which confuses the two cities; a rearrangement of the text however restores the cities as distinct, and removes the difficulty under consideration. Charles rearranges the text as follows: for the vision to which the first Jerusalem belongs, 20^{1-3}, $21^9–22^{1-2, 14-15, 17}$, 20^{4-10}; for that to which the second city belongs, 20^{11-15}, $21^{5 a, 4 d, 5 b, 6 a}$, $21^{1-4 a b c}$, 22^{3-5}. The rest of the contents is arranged, $21^{6 b c-8}$, $22^{6-7, 16, 13, 12, 10, 11, 18, 19, 8, 9, 20, 21}$. Without taking up in particular the difficulties raised by this theory, it will perhaps be enough to observe: the allusions to the continued existence of evil in 21^{24-27}, 22^2 are of an altogether incidental nature, and probably most scholars would find their presence more easily explained by the writer's use of traditional figures without thought of exact consistency, than by a theory requiring so violent a rearrangement, and presupposing the Apocalyptist's death and the mistakes of a literary executor.

(3) There are striking repetitions in the paragraph; 21^{23} is repeated in $22^{5 b}$; 21^{25} in $22^{5 a}$; 21^{27} in $22^{3 a}$; a fact taken as certain evidence of a redactor's hand. But it should be observed that repetition is one of the most common phenomena in Heb. writers; *e.g.* in the chapt. which the author has distinctly in mind throughout this passage, Is. 60, there are similar repetitions. Cf. 1 b with 2 b, 19 b; 4 c with 9 b; 5 b with 11 b; 19 with 20. Moreover in our passage the repetitions are in no case mere duplications; the repeated sentence is brought in for a different purpose; see Com. on the respective passages.

In addition to answers offered above and in the Com. to the critical

objections, and besides what has been said regarding the necessity of such
a vision in the book (pp. 768 f.), attention may be called, in support of
the paragraph, to numerous examples showing parallelism with other parts
of the book and indicating the work of the same hand. In chapt. 21 com-
pare v. 9 with 17^1; v. 10 with 17^8, 11^2, 3^{12}, 21^2; v. 11 with 15^8, 4^6, 22^1; v. 12
with 14^1, 19^{16}; v. 15 with 11^1; v. 17 with 13^{18}; v. 19 with 17^4, $18^{12, 16}$;
v. 22 with 1^8, 4^8, 11^{17}, 16^7; v. 23 with 18^1; v. 27 with 21^8, 22^{15}, 13^8, 17^8. —
In chapt. 22 compare v. 1 with 21^6; v. 4 with 7^{15}, 14^1, 17^5.

XXII. 6–21. *The Epilogue.* See pp. 290 f. The purpose
of the Epilogue is clear. It sets forth in varied and solemn
form the divine authority of the book; it reiterates the great
assurance which gives their significance to its prophecies, the
certainty of the Lord's coming; it solemnly bids the hearers to
give heed, for their encouragement and warning, to the message which God has thus sent to his Church. But while all
this is clear, there are *formal* difficulties in the details; the
thoughts are loosely connected, ejaculatory utterances are thrown
in, there are repetitions and interruptions; also the person
whose words are given cannot always be identified with certainty. Yet these irregularities do not obscure the general
significance; and they are characteristic of the author; see
pp. 241 ff. They do not furnish unquestionable ground for
critical objection, or for a rearrangement of the text; see pp.
781 f.

It is useful to survey more minutely the principal thoughts
of the Epilogue in comparison with the Prologue, 1^{1-8}, since
the Prologue, as probably the last part of the book to be written
(see pp. 420 f., 426 f.), was pretty certainly influenced by the
Conclusion in matter and form. In both alike the revelation
is authenticated in the most solemn manner; it comes from
God himself (22^6, 1^1), and from Jesus (22^{16}, 1^1), through angelic agency ($22^{6, 16}$, 1^1). It is a message of genuine prophecy,
$22^{6, 9, 10, 18 f.}$, 1^3. The author of the book is the John well known
to the seven churches, 22^8, $1^{1, 4, 9}$, but duly commissioned as a
prophet, $22^{8 f., 10}$, $1^{1, 9-11}$. The book, given with these most certain sanctions, is to be read in the churches, $22^{18, 16}$, $1^{3, 11}$. Its
messages encourage the faithful with the promise of sure reward,
$22^{7, 12, 14}$, 1^3, and warn the unfaithful and unbelieving of impend-

ing retribution, 22^11 f., 18 f., 1^7. The coming of the Lord is near, 22^7, 10, 12, 20, 1^3. The central divine figure is he who was known in the historic Jesus, but is to come in the majesty of the ascended Christ, 22^16, 12 f., 1^5, 7. Of the thoughts in the Epilogue which do not appear in the Prologue, the most striking — one most natural in response to the reiterated promise of the Lord's advent — is the yearning cry of the Apocalyptist and the Church, echoing the Christian ejaculation current at the time, Marana tha, *Our Lord, come,* 22^20, 17.

XXII. 6. εἶπέν μοι, *he said unto me :* as there is no intimation of a change in the speaker, the subj. here must be the angel who is present and active throughout the preceding paragraph; cf. 21^9 ff., 15, 22^1. — οὗτοι οἱ λόγοι, *these words :* the λόγοι, *words,* include, not only the actual *utterances,* but the whole revelation given in the vision. And while reference is here made directly to what is revealed in the vision immediately preceding (21^9–22^5), it is clear that all is included which is presupposed and culminates in that vision of the coming of the new Jerusalem, that is, the revelations of the whole book ; this is shown by the general scope of the following clauses, and especially by the express designation, ' the words of the prophecy of this book.' The Epilogue beginning here is therefore that of the whole book, whose truth the angel attests. — πιστοὶ καὶ ἀληθινοί, *faithful and true :* see on 21^5. — ὁ θεὸς . . . προφητῶν, *the God of the spirits of the prophets :* the meaning is made clear by 19^10, where ' the spirit of prophecy' is the Holy Spirit in its activity of inspiring prophecy. The spirits of the prophets thus inspired are meant here ; cf. 1 Co. 14^32. There is no allusion here in the plural to the term ' seven Spirits,' 1^4 (so, some com.), since in that case the full form of a designation so peculiar would be required. The phrase ' Lord of the spirits,' *i.e.* Lord of the angels and other spiritual beings, is common in En., *e.g.* chapts. 37–71 *passim,* and some com. find in the words of our verse an amplification of that expression ; so, Bouss. Blj. But the words here added show that the divinely illumined spirits of the prophets are meant. The purpose of this sentence is to authenticate the book as a genuine work of prophecy ; God who controls the inspiration of the prophets

has inspired his angel and the Apocalyptist to show his servants what must shortly come to pass.

ἀπέστειλεν τὸν ἄγγελον κτλ., *hath sent his angel*, etc. : the
connection here, especially the phrase, ' what must shortly come
to pass,' compared with 1¹ shows that the designated activity
of the angel refers to the revelations of the book in general
and not merely to those of the last vision, 21⁹–22⁵, though the
special office of an angel in showing a vision is not mentioned
till we reach 17¹.   The disagreement cannot however furnish
sure ground for criticism of the paragraph ; see p. 781.
While the revelations in the course of the book are described
as received in various ways, *i.e.* as directly from Christ, as
seen in a state of ecstasy, as heard from heavenly voices, etc.,
yet in late Jewish thought an angel as the intermediary in
God's communication with men becomes so prominent a figure
that such may be thought of, perhaps vaguely, as also present
in any form of revelation.   So here the Apocalyptist in looking back upon his visions as a whole may characterize them as
mediated by an angel, even in cases where such agency has not
been specifically mentioned.   A vision may be received in an
ecstasy, and at the same time an angel intermediary may be
thought of, as in 17¹ ᶠᶠ·   What is expressly stated in these last
visions concerning an angel's office may in the Apocalyptist's
thought be associated with the earlier visions and ecstasies.
With the language of our verse agrees also that of v. 16 and 1¹.
The allusion here is not to be limited to the office of the ' angel
interpreter,' common in apocalyptic.   See pp. 420 f. — The
utterance in this second part of the verse, ' God hath sent his
angel,' etc., is probably not a continuation of the angel's words,
but rather those of the Apocalyptist himself, as in 1¹; at this
point the words are not necessary as an address to him, they
are more appropriate as an assurance given by him to his
readers.   For the connection of the first three utterances, vv.
6–7, by *and*, see end of note on v. 7. — τοῖς δούλοις, *his servants :* the members of ' the churches,' as in v. 16.

7. ἰδοὺ ἔρχομαι ταχύ, *behold, I come quickly :* this announcement of the Lord's, answering to the yearning of the Church,
is given as if he himself were speaking with his own voice, as
in vv. 12, 16, 16¹⁵.   The words might have been introduced as

a quotation, as in v. 20; instead the Lord is heard as it were speaking directly, as the prophets sometimes introduce an utterance of God's without the customary, 'saith the Lord,' *e.g.* Is. 16¹⁰ ᵉⁿᵈ, 61⁸, cf. Rev. 1⁸. — μακάριος ὁ τηρῶν κτλ., *blessed is he that keepeth the words,* etc. : this utterance is best understood to be that of the Apocalyptist, as in 1³. The expression, ' this book,' is less appropriate to Christ speaking from heaven than to the author contemplating before him the book he has now finished and is about to send to his readers, as in vv. 18–19. In vv. 9–10 the angel, standing beside the author, uses the same expression, but if this sentence were meant as his, it would more fittingly follow the opening sentence of v. 6. — ὁ τηρῶν τοὺς λόγους, *he that keepeth the words : heedeth the message given.* — τοῦ βιβλίου τούτου, *this book :* the book as a whole lies before the author finished; he has only to add its Conclusion in these verses, 6–21, and then its Superscription 1¹⁻³, and Exordium 1⁴⁻⁸. For the book as a work of prophecy, see p. 292. — These two verses, 6–7, contain four distinct messages to the reader regarding the book. (1) The angelic sanction given to the truth of the book. (2) The solemn affirmation of the Apocalyptist that it is God, the inspirer of prophecy, who has herein revealed to his servants the things which must shortly come to pass. (3) The assurance given, as it were, by Christ's own voice from heaven, that the central promise of the book, the Lord's coming, is about to be fulfilled. (4) A warning to heed the prophetic truth of the book. The first three utterances, probably to be assigned to three distinct speakers, are linked together rather mechanically by *and*, as it were in a tabular form.

8–9. κἀγὼ Ἰωάννης ὁ ἀκούων κτλ., *and I John am he that heard,* etc.: while vv. 6–7 give the superhuman guaranties of the book, the author in these verses assures his readers that he, the John who is well known to them and who wrote the book, is himself the very one who saw and heard what is contained therein; thus the book is authenticated on the human side. — ταῦτα, *these things :* all the revelations of the book are meant. — ὅτε ἤκουσα . . . ἔπεσα κτλ., *when I heard . . . I fell down,* etc. : since the arrangement of the several parts of the Epilogue is loose, the precise moment of this act of vehement

impulse is not determined by the place of the sentence in the
paragraph ; it does not naturally follow the giving of the summary passage vv. 6–7, which is composed of the utterances of
several speakers deliberately combined. But the meaning is
clear ; at the close of all the visions culminating in the glory
of the new Jerusalem, the Apocalyptist, overawed by the revelations and by the announcement of the angel, whose words set
the seal of divine sanction on the whole series of prophecies,
prostrates himself, as was not unnatural, to offer homage to so
exalted a visitant. The angel forbids the homage, since he is
only a fellow-servant with the Apocalyptist and other prophets,
and with all Christians who heed the message of the book.
The purpose of the passage is to attest with emphasis the *prophetic* rank of the author. For further comment on the episode, see on 19^{10} and p. 742.

10–11. Verses 10–13 repeat the assurance that the end is
near, but the repetition is meant to enforce the encouragement
and warning given. The angel is still the speaker in vv. 10–11,
as shown by καὶ λέγει, *and he saith*, repeating the same words
of v. 9 ; cf. the use of the phrase in 19$^{9\,f.}$, 21^{5}, also καὶ εἶπεν,
22^{6}. The language of the command given is suggested by
Dan. 8^{26}, 12$^{4,\,9}$, where the prophet supposedly writing centuries
earlier than the time of the events referred to in the prophecies
is bidden to seal up the oracles, to keep them hidden till the
time of their fulfillment; thus their appearance first in the
time of Antiochus is explained. Here the reverse is the case.
The Seer is bidden not to seal up the prophecy; the time is
near, already the Church needs the message of consolation and
warning which it is admonished to receive. — ὁ ἀδικῶν ἀδικη-
σάτω ἔτι, *he that is unrighteous, let him do unrighteousness still:*
the words are a reminiscence of Dan. 12^{10}, which also follows
the command in regard to the sealing up of the book ; cf. also
Ezk. 3^{27}. There is a tone of irony in the utterance ; the time
is short, no change in the wicked is to be looked for, let him
continue in his wickedness, if he will ; his penalty will soon
fall. This is the tone generally in apocalyptic. The second
clause is an encouragement to the righteous to remain steadfast, since the end is near. — ἔτι, *still:* denoting the continuance of a state or act, not, *yet more* (so, some, RV mrg), denot-

ing an increase in degree ; only with a comparative word has
ἔτι this latter force. The aorists here are not inceptive, they
denote rather a state or continued activity, which is regularly
expressed by the pres., but which the Gk. sometimes views
simply as a fact, or whole, without regard to continuance, and
expresses by the aor. ; see H. A. § 836 a, GMT. § 56. The
variant δικαιωθήτω, which some approve and interpret, *let him
become still more righteous*, while more in accord with the other
clauses as regards the form of the word, is at variance with the
force of ἔτι.

12-13. The angel's announcement in vv. 10-11 is followed
in these verses by a similar announcement with its promise and
warning from Christ himself, whose words are again introduced,
as if he were speaking in person ; see on v. 7. — ὁ μισθός μου
μετ᾽ ἐμοῦ, *my reward is with me:* a reminiscence of Is. 40¹⁰, 62¹¹.
— ἀποδοῦναι ἑκάστῳ κτλ., *to render to each one according to his
work:* cf. 2²³, Ro. 2²⁶, Ps. 62¹². The words are meant for both
the righteous and the wicked. These two clauses, ὁ μισθός
κτλ., and ἀποδοῦναι κτλ., are found combined as here in Clem.
Rom. 34³ ; the author of the latter may perhaps have been
familiar with the Apocalypse. — ἐγὼ τὸ ἄλφα κτλ., *I am the
Alpha and the Omega*, etc.: *i.e.* the Eternal one ; see on 1⁸.
The language which is applied to God in 1⁸, 21⁶, is used here,
as in 1¹⁷, 2⁸, to describe the person of Christ ; see on 1¹⁷. The
words of v. 13 seem designed to give solemn assurance of v. 12 ;
it is as the Eternal one that Christ is to judge and give to each
according to his works. On Christ as judge in the Apocalypse
see p. 747.

14-15. The blessedness of the saints and the doom of the
wicked are set over against each other. The speaker may be
Christ, but probably the Apocalyptist, to whom belongs generally, in the Epilogue and elsewhere, the office of applying
personally to the readers the truth revealed. — οἱ πλύνοντες
τὰς στολὰς αὐτῶν, *they that wash their robes:* cf. 3⁴, 7¹⁴, also
1 Co. 6¹¹. The variant οἱ ποιοῦντες τὰς ἐντολὰς αὐτοῦ, *they that
do his commandments*, makes equally good sense ; cf. 12¹⁷, 14¹³.
Though τηρεῖν is commonly used with ἐντολή, a frequent Johannine phrase, yet ποιεῖν also occurs, cf. 1 Jno. 5². — ἵνα ἔσται,
εἰσέλθωσιν: the clauses may be taken as expressing purpose

(Blass § 65, 2), or result (Burton § 218); for interchange of
subjv. and fut. ind. see Burton § 199. — ἐξουσία ἐπὶ τὸ ξύλον
κτλ., *right to the tree of life*: lit. *power over, i.e.* to eat of the
fruit. For ἐξουσία ἐπί with acc. = *power over*, cf. 6⁸, 13⁷, 16⁹,
Lk. 9¹. The tree of life growing in the midst of the new Jerusalem is meant here, cf. v. 2. — πυλῶσιν: a peculiar use of the
instrumental dat.; see Win. § 31, 7; Blass § 38, 1. For the
gates see 21¹²ᶠ. — ἔξω, *without*: outside of the holy city. This
verse is closely parallel with 21⁸; see note there; cf. also 21²⁷.
— κύνες, *dogs*: a frequent term denoting a base, malicious
person, cf. Phil. 3², Ps. 22¹⁶,²⁰, 2 K. 8¹³. Some (Düst., *al*) supply here the imperat. instead of the ind.; 'out, ye dogs.' If
that were intended the vb. could hardly be omitted; and further, the suggested presence of such persons in the city, or their
effort to enter, is impossible. For the existence of the wicked
on the earth see p. 745.

16. In this verse is added the last and most solemn attesta-
tion of the book, the Lord's words, spoken, as it were, directly
with his own voice, as in vv. 7, 12. It is he, the historic Jesus,
he the Messiah of David's line, he the morning star about to
bring in the eternal day of the new kingdom, who has sent his
angel to bear witness to the Prophet of these revelations for the
Church. — Ἰησοῦς, *Jesus*: there is an emphasis on the name,
as that of the historic person known to the Church. It is
noticeable that in almost every one of the fourteen places where
the name Jesus is used in the book it is in connection with the
office of witnessing or revealing; and in every case in the book
where that office of Christ is spoken of he is designated by this
name. The Fourth Gospel gives a similar prominence to revelation in the earthly work of Jesus. — τὸν ἄγγελόν μου κτλ.,
my angel, etc.: here, as in v. 6, all the revelations of the book
are conceived to be mediated by an angel; see note there. —
ὑμῖν, *you*: the pl. is peculiar; it is best explained as referring
to the prophets in general, of whom John is one, cf. vv. 6, 9. —
ἐπί, *for*: for this meaning of ἐπί with the dat. cf. Eph. 2¹⁰, see
Kühn. II. § 438, ii. f. — ταῖς ἐκκλησίαις, *the churches*: the
seven churches of Asia, to which the Revelation is addressed.
That the message is meant ultimately for the whole Church is
unquestionable; see on 1⁴. — ῥίζα *root*: as defined by the fol-

lowing word, in the Heb. sense of that which springs from the
root, *scion;* cf. Is. 53², 11¹⁰, Ecclus. 47²². The character of
Christ as the Messiah is spoken of because it is in that office
that he sends to his people, the Church, this message of the
fulfillment of all the messianic hopes. — ὁ ἀστήρ, *the star:*
a familiar Heb. symbol of the expected Davidic King, cf. Num.
24¹⁷, 'There shall come forth a star out of Jacob'; this is undoubtedly the source from which the figure is taken in late
Jewish writings, cf. Test. Lev. 18³, Test. Jud. 24¹, though the
symbol may have been derived primarily from Babylonian as-
trology. The symbol of the *morning* star may refer to superior
brightness; but in this connection, in which the thought of
the advent is predominant (cf. especially the response in v. 17),
it seems to denote the one who is to bring in the perfect day of
God. See on 2²⁸.

17. In yearning response to the words of the Lord, the
Spirit speaking through the Prophet, *i.e.* the Prophet as moved
by the Spirit, and the Church, lift up their prayer: Come. —
ἡ νύμφη, *the Bride:* the figure is used here of the Church on
earth, still waiting for its marriage with the Lamb; see on 19⁷.
— ὁ ἀκούων, *he that heareth:* every one who shall hear the book
read in the assemblies of the Christians (see on 1³) is exhorted
to join in the prayer for the Lord's advent. — ὁ διψῶν κτλ.,
he that is athirst, etc.: the Apocalyptist has still before his
mind the congregation, to whose members he has just appealed;
and he turns from the theme of the advent with a sudden cry
to every one among them who is spiritually athirst to come and
take freely the water of life which Christ offers. For the
figures used see on v. 1 and 21⁶. The sudden turn in this
verse of the Apocalyptist to direct exhortation of the hearers
is similar to that in 13⁹ ᶠ·, 14¹³ ᶠ·.

18–19. After the manifold sanctions of his book, as given in
the preceding parts of the paragraph, the Apocalyptist, in a
tone in keeping with its divine authority thus attested, now
adds a solemn warning against any changes by addition or
omission. His words are a reminiscence of Dt. 4², 'Ye shall
not add unto the word which I command you, neither shall ye
diminish from it'; cf. also Dt. 12³², Jer. 26². The warning is
addressed to the *hearer* (παντὶ τῷ ἀκούοντι), before whom the

book is read in the congregation, not to a copyist; it is therefore certainly to be understood, like Moses' injunction regarding the law in Dt., to refer to *perversion* of the divine truth
enjoined, such as might arise through some distorting addition
made in the thought of the listener, or through some willful
evasion. The severity of the threat uttered has raised objection to the passage, as if it were aimed at a verbal fixedness,
the letter rather than the spirit, and as if at variance with our
author's freedom in the use of the O. T. But this character is
due to the *form ;* this follows the words of Dt., and what seems
to have become the conventional manner of safeguarding the
integrity of a book. In illustration of such a usage a striking
passage is quoted from the pseudepigraphic Aristeas, 311, in
reference to the story of the translation of the Septuagint;
' When the whole company expressed their approval, they bade
them pronounce a curse *in accordance with their custom* upon
any one who should make any alterations, either by adding anything or changing in any way whatever any of the words which
had been written, or making any omission.' Other similar
efforts to preserve the integrity of a writing are seen ; *e.g.* En.
104[10-13], Sl. En. 48[6-9], Joseph. *c Ap.* I. 42. See Bouss. *Judenthum* 125. The speaker here is certainly the Apocalyptist, not
the Lord, as some interpret. After the august utterance of
v. 16 and the response in v. 17, a passage of this character, if
assigned to the Lord, would form an anticlimax not supposable.
— τῆς προφητείας, *the prophecy :* the prophetic character of
the book is again emphasized ; in this lies the justification of
the threat uttered. — ἀπὸ τοῦ ξύλου, ἐκ τῆς πόλεως, *from the
tree, out of the city :* in the literal sense of the language, the
offender is spoken of as if he had possessed a certain part of the
tree and the city, which part will be severed from the rest and
taken away — it will come to naught. — τῶν γεγραμμένων κτλ.,
even the things which are written in this book : i.e. the tree of life
and the city, as described in 21[10]–22[5] ; a share in the tree of
life and the holy city summarizes all the blessedness promised
in the book to the saints. These words are in apposition with
τοῦ ξύλου . . . ἁγίας.

20. This utterance of the Lord is not spoken directly by
him, as in vv. 7, 12, 16, but quoted from him by the Apoc-

alyptist. — ὁ **μαρτυρῶν ταῦτα**, *he who testifieth these things :* the reference is, not to *μαρτυρῶ*, *I testify*, v. 18, but to 'the testimony of Jesus Christ,' spoken of in 1² (see note there); the revelations given in the contents of the whole book are meant. — **ἀμήν**, *Amen : so be it* — a part of the Apocalyptist's response to the promise of the advent as near. — **ἔρχου κτλ.**, *Come, Lord Jesus :* Gk. version of the current Christian ejaculation, Marana tha (Aramaic); cf. 1 Co. 16²². See Hast. III. 242.

21. The book opens as an epistle, 1⁴ ᶠᶠ·; it now closes with a benediction similar to that which in one form or another appears at the end of all the Pauline epistles. It is an epistle which incorporates the record of the revelations given to the author. The benediction begins with the unvarying Pauline phrase (cf. also Heb. 13²⁵), *ἡ χάρις, the grace.* Among the different endings of the benediction presented by the variant readings (see text. note), those which are to be preferred are unlike any found in the epistles.

Textual notes, 22⁶⁻²¹. 6. O, before *κυριος*, אA some min R edd; wanting in PQ most min WHmrg. — For *των πνευματων των προφητων*, R with some min and vers reads *των αγιων προφητων.* — 7. R. with some min and vers omits *και* before *ιδου.* — 11. For *ρυπαρος*, R has *ρυπων.* — *ρυπανθητω* א min most edd; *ρυπαρευθητω* Q many min Alf WHmrg *al*; R has *ρυπωσατω* without authority. — *δικαιοσυνην ποιησατω* אAQ many min vers edd; *δικαιω-θητω* some min R, which seems to be due to conformation to the other vbs. But the epistle from Vienne and Lyons to the churches of Asia, 2ᵈ cent., see Euseb. *HE.* V. 1, has this form in a free citation of this passage; see Zahn *GK.* I. p. 201. — 14. *πλυνοντες τας στολας αυτων* אA some min vers anc com most edd; *ποιουντες τας εντολας αυτου* Q most min vers anc com R Bouss Sod *al.* See Ws *Ap.* p. 10, also Com. — 16. *επι* אQ most min R edd; *εν* A some min Lch Ws WHmrg *al.* — For *πρωινος*, R has *ορθρινος.* This and the following variations of R in vv. 17–18 are translations from the vlg (see p. 413). — 17. For *ερχου*, *ερχεσθω*, R has *ελθε*, *ελθετω.* — 18. For *μαρτυρω εγω*, R has *συμμαρτυρουμαι γαρ.* — 19. Before *των γεγραμμενων*, R with vlg has *και.* — 20. R with some min has *ναι* before *ερχου.* — 21. After *κυριου*, some min and vers R have *ημων.* — After *Ιησου*, Q many min vers R Sod *al* add *Χριστου*; bracketed by WH; wanting in אA most edd. — There are six variants of the phrase *μετα κτλ.* Only the following call for notice here; *μετα παντων των αγιων* Q many min vers anc com Bouss Sod; *μετα των αγιων* א vers Tr Alf WH RV Blj *al*; *μετα παντων* A vers Lch Ti Ws *al.* There is no conclusive reason for preference among these. The reading of R, *μετα παντων υμων*, is a translation from the vlg. See Nestle *Einführung*² p. 125 f.; Hast. IV. 733. — *αμην* is added at the end in אQ many min and vers R RV

Sod; wanting in A many min most edd. — The subscription αποκαλυψις Ιωαννου is given in אA; wanting in Q most min.

Criticism of 22⁶⁻²¹. Grounds of criticism have been found in this paragraph in the multiplicity of unconnected thoughts, in the interruptions and repetitions, and in the abrupt introduction of new speakers. But see p. 771, also the Com. in detail. Further critical contentions are: (*a*) The agency of the angel is out of place, as in the primitive form of the Apocalypse the Seer receives his revelations directly from Christ; so, Spitta, J. Weiss, many others; but see pp. 773, 420 f. (*b*) In vv. 18–19 a redactor is trying to canonize his own words through Johannine authority; Erbes, *al*; but see Com. *in loc.* (*c*) Reminiscences of other passages, or parallelisms, betray the hand of a redactor; for example (Spitta 221 ff.), v. 6 is derived from v. 16 and 1¹⁻³; v. 7 is derived from vv. 10, 12, 20; v. 9 is repeated from 19¹⁰; similarly, according to Völter, *Offenb.* 142 ff., v. 7 is a reminiscence of 16¹⁵, 19¹⁰ ᵉⁿᵈ; vv. 8–9 imitate 19¹⁰; vv. 14–15 imitate 21⁷⁻⁸. But these parallelisms (with the probable exception of vv. 8–9 and 19¹⁰, upon which see Com. *in loc.*) are of a kind that indicates, not an imitator or interpolator, but a single author, whose thoughts and characteristics naturally appear repeatedly in different, but appropriate, connections.

The more important among the critical theories proposed are as follows: Vischer (34) makes the paragraph the work of a Christian redactor, combining without order sayings which he attributes to the Apocalyptist and to Jesus. Spitta (222 ff.) thinks that the passage in its *primary* part is the conclusion of the original Christian Apocalypse, corresponding to the epistolary form of the opening of the book. But numerous additions were made by the redactor; of these the principal are vv. 6–7, 9, 14–15, 17 a b, 18 b–20 a. Weyland (174 f.), on the other hand, finds here the conclusion of his Jewish document *Alpha*, to which the Christian redactor has added 7 a, 12–13, 16–21, and some short phrases. Völter (*Offenb.* 142 ff., 148 ff.) assigns the primary form of the Epilogue to a redactor, who wrote in Domitian's time, perhaps in the early part of it; to him belong vv. 6, 8–9, 10–11, 14–15, 21. But a later redactor, writing in the end of Domitian's reign, or perhaps in Trajan's, added vv. 7, 12–13, 16–20. Erbes (118 ff.) refers the whole conclusion, 22⁶⁻²¹, to his Apocalypse of the year 62 A.D., except vv. 18–19, which may belong to a later editor. J. Weiss (108 ff.) thinks the passage contains a remnant of the original conclusion of the Johannine writing addressed to the seven churches, but that this has been transformed and enlarged by a redactor. He suggests as the Johannine part vv. 8 a, 11 (introduced by the first phrase of 10) –14 a, 15–16, 20–21. It will be noticed that, except in the case of vv. 18–19, there is not unanimity regarding the verses to be assigned to a redactor.

Another method of meeting the difficulties of the passage, starting from the opinion that these are due to a derangement of the original order of the text, proposes a rearrangement. The nature and scope of this procedure are sufficiently shown in the theories of Moffatt and Charles. The former arranges as follows: vv. 8–9, 6–7, 10–11, 14–16, 13, 12, 17, [18–19], 20–21.

The arrangement proposed by Charles is given on p. 770. In regard to these critical hypotheses, whether of redaction or rearrangement, it must, on the one hand, be borne in mind that displacements in order through accident, or the intention of a copyist, are frequent phenomena, as are also the changes of revisers; and if these processes are clearly indicated in our paragraph, or if the supposition is requisite for the solution of the problem presented, there need not be great hesitation in accepting at least some theory of the kind above mentioned. But, on the other hand, it has been seen to be characteristic of our author to depart from logical order, to introduce parenthetical utterances of a different speaker, and to make abrupt transitions (see pp. 241 ff.). Probably an easier solution of the difficulties arising is found in these usages of the writer than in a theory of redaction, or in a conjectural rearrangement. Unquestionably a writer possessing the literary skill, and the sense of symmetry shown conspicuously in some parts of our book, must have appended to his work a Conclusion, either such as the present Epilogue, or one which this has displaced. That the Epilogue here given was written by the author of the Prologue seems evident from the correspondence in language and thought, see p. 771. That the peculiarities and even the difficulties are those belonging to our Apocalyptist's manner confirms the belief that we have his original Conclusion preserved in this paragraph. It should be observed that the general purpose of the Epilogue in the plan of the book, and the meaning of its several parts, are not materially affected by the critical questions raised.

INDEX

I. Greek Words[1]

ἄβυσσος, 561
ἅγιος, 478, 502
ἀκολουθέω, 660
ἀληθινός, 478
ἄλλος ἄγγελος, 662
ἄλλος, πλήν, 470
ἄμωμον, 716
ἄν, omitted with subjv., 541
ἀνὰ μέσον, 546
ἄξιος, 507
ἀπαρχή, 648
ἀποδιδωμι, 714
ἀποκάλυψις, 417
ἀποκρίνομαι, 544
ἀποστέλλω, 419
ἀποχωρίζομαι, 529
ἀρνίον, 509
ἀρχή, 488

βαθέα τοῦ σατανᾶ, 468
βάρος, 469
βασιλεία, 429
βιβλαρίδιον, 580
βιβλίον, 504

γίνομαι, for εἰμί, 434
γυνή, for νύμφη, 726

δειλός, 753
δηνάριον, 520
διά, with acc. and gen., 627, 640

διάβολος, 617
διάδημα, 634
δίδωμι, 553
δίδωμι δόξαν θεῷ, 604
δικαίωμα, 727
δοῦλος, 419
δρέπανον, 664

ἑαυτούς, with infin., 453
ἔχειρε, intrans., 596
εἰ, with subjv., 600
εἰρήνη, 424
εἷς, as indef. art., 559
ἓν καθ᾽ ἕν, 502
ἐν κυρίῳ, 660
ἐνώπιον, 640
ἐξ, with gen. for part. gen., 454
ἐξουσίᾳ, 712
ἔργα, 449
εὐαγγέλιον, 655
Ἐφέσια γράμματα, 447
ἔχω, with infin., 655

ζάω, for ἀναζάω, 640
ζυγός, 520

ἡμίωρον, 550

θάνατος, 523
θεὸς τοῦ οὐρανοῦ, 604
θυμός, ὀργή, 657
θύρα ἠνεῳγμένη, 480, 494

[1] This list is not intended to include all the words and idioms noticed in the Commentary, much less to exhibit the vocabulary of the Apocalypse.

ἱερεῖς, 429
Ἱεροσόλυμα, Ἱερουσαλήμ, 356, 757
ἵνα clause as subj., 727
ἵνα, with result clause, 558
ἵνα, with subjv. or fut. ind. for infin.,
   467, 482, 519, 554, 640

καί, epexegetical, 421, 438, 527, 636,
   733
καί, Hebraistic, 582
καί, in ellipsis, 610
καί, in passing from whole to a part,
   680, 694, 718
καί, in passing from a part to whole,
   687
καί, with apodosis, 657
καί, with clause, for infin., 599
κάλαμος, 596
καταβολῆς κόσμου, ἀπό, 637
κατήγωρ, 626
κεράννυμι ἄκρατον, 657
κλίνη, 467
κόκκινος, 693
κολλάομαι, 714
κόπος, 660

λαμβάνω, pleonastic, 554
λατρεύω, 598
λιβανωτός, 553
λίνον, 679
λόγος τοῦ θεοῦ, 421
λόγος ὑπομονῆς, 483

μαρτυρία, with gen., 421
μάρτυς, 428
μέλλω, with infin. for fut., 582
μολύνω, 649, 652
μόσχος, 502
μυκάομαι, 581
μυστήριον, 444, 583, 693

νεκρός, 473
νικάω, 508

ὁ ἦν, 355, 424
ὅμοιος, with acc., 437
ὄνομα, 473, 475, 603, 651
ὄπισθεν, 506
ὅπου ἄν, with ind., 653
ὅρμημα, 719
ὅρος, 698
ὅσιος, 675
ὅταν, with ind., 503, 549
οὐαί, construction after, 559
οὐαί, ἡ, 564
οὕτως, repeating partic., 476
ὄφις, 625, 738

πᾶν, after a negative, 541
παρεμβολή, 746
παρθένος, 649, 652
πέμπω, 663
περιπατέω, 449, 475
πίστις, 639, 659
πνευματικῶς, 602
ποδήρης, 438
ποιέω, 636
πόλεμος, 601
προφῆτις, 466
πρωτότοκος, 428
πῶς, instead of ὅ τι, 474

ῥάβδος, 596

σάκκος, 600
σημεῖον, 621
σοφία, 642
στρηνιάω, στρῆνος, 713
σφραγίζω, 581
σῶμα, 717
σωτηρία, 726

ταχύ, 608

υἱὸς ἀνθρώπου, 437
υἱὸς τοῦ θεοῦ, 465

φιάλη, 679
φοβούμενοι, οἱ, 610
φρέαρ, 561
φυλακή, 712
φωνή ὑδάτων, 439

χαλκολιβάνῳ, 438

χάρις, 424
χοῖνιξ, 520
Χριστὸς αὐτοῦ, 609
χρόνος, 582
ψυχαὶ ἀνθρώπων, 717
ὥρα, 484

II. SUBJECTS

Abaddon, 563
Abraham, Apocalypse of, 195
Abraham, significance of story, 9; conscious of mission, 9
Acta Johannis, 377
Acts, book of, eschatology, 115
Adam and Eve, Life of, 195
Alcasar, 332
Alleluia, 721
Alogi, 340, 350, 378
Alpha and Omega, 432
Altar, in earthly temple, 597; heavenly altar, 524, 552; souls of martyrs beneath it, 524; altar personified, 680
Amen, the, 488
Amulet, 462, 463
Andreas, 325
Angel, of abyss, 563; angel as agent in the revelations of Apoc., 420, 773; angel interpreter, 170, 691
Angels, of the seven churches, 445; angels as a council of God, 498; as mediators, 553; present prayers of the saints, 511; joy in salvation of men, 544; angels of punishment, 664; worship of angels, 728, 729, 775
Angelology, 70, 445
Animals, demonic, 6; symbols of monarchies, 71

Antichrist, 71, 88, 159, 160, 397; connection with a Roman ruler, 399; a Nero reincarnated, 400, 406, 408
Anticipation, 247
Anticipatory passages, preludes, and interludes, 245
Antipas, 458, 459
Aphraates, 386, 388
Apocalypse, meaning of term, 167, 417, 418
Apocalypse, the, author's manner, some characteristics of, 239; repetition, 241; indefinite expressions afterwards explained, 242; interruptions, brief interjections, 243; prefatory passages, 243, 244; hysteron-proteron, 243; anticipation, 247; sudden changes, 248; use of symbols, 249; proper names as symbols, 250
Apocalypse, the, composition of, careful study in, 214, 174, 175; influence of O. T. and apocalyptic writers, 215, 221, 238, see Sources, Criticism, and Unity; the book to be read from author's historic and literary standpoint, 208, 239, 304, see Motives
Apocalypse, the, date, 206, 207; purpose, 208; addressed to whole

3 E

Church, 210, 423; relation to its time, 210

Apocalypse, the, early circulation and recognition, 337; Apostolic Fathers and other early writers, 337; opponents, 340; absence from some versions, 341; this absence explained, 343; action of councils, 342

Apocalypse, the, eschatology, 156; relation to tradition, 156, 162; variation from other N. T. books, 165

Apocalypse, the, and Fourth Gospel, 353; differences, linguistic, 354; theological, 357; eschatological, 359; conclusion, 361

Apocalypse, the, as prophecy, 292, 306, 422; contents of prophecy determined by contemporaneous circumstances, 294; the principle applied to the Apoc., 295; unfulfilled predictions, 296; prophecy not history written beforehand, 301; application to the Apoc., 303; catastrophic and evolutionary, 304; permanent significance of the Apoc., 291, 306; practical usefulness, 307

Apocalyptic, as distinguished from prophecy, 166, 168; eschatological hopes of, 167; apocalyptic opposed to evolutionary, 304

Apocalyptic literature, 166; characteristics of, 169; visions and raptures, 169; mysteriousness, 170; literary dependence, 171; pseudonimity, 172; studied conformity to type as affecting canonical rank of a book, 174; occasion, 175, 8; apocalyptic tendencies in O. T. before Daniel, 177; non-canonical apocalypses, 181, see under respective authors; Christian use of, 196; Christian apocalypses, 197

Apostles, 449; the twelve, 759
Appositive, in nom., 224, 427
Archangels, the seven, 551
Aristion, 363, 365
Ark, the, hidden, 461, 611
Article, the, 224, 227; absence of, 650
Augustine, 325, 326, 327
Authorship, of the Apoc., testimony of the book, 343; author a Jew, 345; book not pseudonymous, 173, 293, 345, 367; question of author's identity with the Apostle John subordinate in importance, 347; early external testimony, 348; internal testimony, 351; conclusion 353

Babylon, Rome called so, 656
Balaam, doctrine of, identical with Nicolaitanism, 459
Baruch, the Apocalypse of, 192
Battle, of Antichrist with the Messiah, 734
Beast, of the Apoc., 393; figure traditional, 393; symbol of Roman emperors, 394; of Antichrist, 397; Antichrist a Nero reincarnated, 400, 406, 408; number of the Beast, 403; Beast identified with one of his heads, 406, 635; summary definition, 407; second beast, 408
Beast, mark of, 641
Beast, from the sea, from the abyss, 633, 697
Beatitudes, of the Apoc., 422
Beelzebub, Beliar, 70
Berengaudus, 326
Blessings, of an ancestor, 6, 7, 14
Book, of life, 476
Book, the sealed, see Roll
Books, in judgment, 66, 476, 748
Bousset, critical theory of, 236, see paragraphs on criticism in Com., passim

Briggs, critical theory of, 235
Brimstone, 753

Caius, 340, 350
Captivity, Babylonian, influence on Jewish eschatology, 30
Change, of speaker, 432; of place, 579, 607; of tense, 576; of case after preposition, 657
Characteristics, of Apocalyptist's manner, 239
Christology, of Apoc., 312
Church, the whole, addressed in the Apoc., 210, 423; the Church the true Israel, 535
Clement, of Alexandria, 339, 350, 378, 386, 389; of Rome, 391
Clouds, in imagery, 580, 679
Coming age, as an eschatological term, 64; see Kingdom of God
Coming of Christ, see Parousia
Coming of Jehovah, to deliver his people and establish his kingdom, 34, see Deliverer
Contents, of the Apoc., 255
Conversion, of Israel, see Israel, final conversion
Criticism, of the Apoc., 216; critical analyses, 224; classification of theories, 237; service rendered by criticism, 238
Criticism of respective parts of the Apoc., 1^{1-3}, 422; 1^{7-8}, 433; 1^{20}, 446; 2–3, 492; 4–6, 531; 7, 547; 8–9, 570; $10-11^{13}$, 604; 11^{14-19}, 612; 12^{1-17}, 630; $12^{18}-13^{18}$, 644; 14^{1-5}, 653; 14^{6-20}, 666; 15–16, 688; 17, 709; 18, 722; $19^{1}-20^{6}$, 741; $20^{7}-21^{8}$, 754; $21^{9}-22^{5}$, 768; 22^{6-21}, 781
Crown, metaphorical use of, 455

Dan, tribe of, source of Antichrist, 543
Daniel, book of, 178; first great apocalypse, 172

Date, of the Apoc., 206, 207
David, uniqueness in Heb. history, 17
Davidic king, 26, 28, 30, 40; dynasty, rather than individual king, perpetuated, 40
Davidic kingdom, perpetuated, 25; expectation of the people, 25; of the prophets, 26, 27, 28
Dead, Christ among the, 112; mentioned in the rabbis, 113
Dead, the, state of, in Heb. thought, 58, 68, 69; in the N. T., 95, 108, 112, 152, 161; possibility of change, 69, 112, 154; question of finality of utterances, 154
Death, meaning of, 67, 94, 108, 109
Death, punished, 749
De Boor fragments, 381
Deliverer, of the nation, in earlier thought, God, 27, 37, 44; in later thought, the Messiah, 38, 44
Demonology, 70
Demons, heathen divinities regarded such, 570; demonic animals, 6
Demonstrative, repeating relative pleonostically, 481
De Rebaptismate, 385, 388
Derived material, see Sources
Dionysius, the Great, 341, 350
Disciple, instead of apostle, 368
Disturbances, before the Day of the Lord, see Messianic woes
Donatists, 324
Doxologies, 429
Dragon Myth, 614, 623
Dramatis personae, variations in, 508
Drunken, with blood, 694
Dualism, between God and evil powers, 71
Dwell, those that dwell on the earth, 483
Dynasty, theocratic, 41

Elder, the, the Elders, in Irenaeus and others, 363, 373

Elders, the twenty-four in the Apoc., 498
Emperor-worship, 198
End, the, 743; time of, see Time
Enemies, of God, destroyed, 20, 21, 29, 35
Enoch, Ethiopic, 181; Slavonic, 183
Ephesus, 447
Epilogue, 771; compared with prologue, 771
Erbes, 234; see paragraphs on criticism in Com. *passim*
Eschatological age, glories of, 35, 45, 55, 57; kingdom, earthly, 54; influences broadening outlook, 64; eschatological hopes of apocalyptic and prophecy contrasted, 167; eschatological events spiritualized, 101, 104, 105, 106, 144, 149. *See also* Kingdom of God
Eschatology, defined, 3
Eschatology, of primitive age, 4, 8; patriarchal and pre-monarchical age, 8, 15; Monarchical age, 16, 18, 29; exilic and post-exilic age, 30 (earlier centuries, 33, later centuries, 63); New Testament era, 82; Pauline, 83; Johannine, 100; epistle to the Heb., 108; James, 110; 1 Peter, 111; 2 Peter and Jude, 113; Acts, 115; our Lord's doctrine, 117; the Apocalypse, 156
Eschatology, place of, in Jesus' view of his mission, 139, see Jesus
Eschatological discourse in the Gospels, 143
Eternal life, 102
Euphrates, 566; the four angels at, 566; dried up, 682
Eusebius, as witness to authorship of the Apoc., 341, 351, 385
Evil spirits, kingdom of, overthrown, 70, 72, 103, 109
Evolutionary, as opposed to apocalyptic, 304
Ezra, Fourth, see Second Esdras

False prophet, see Second beast
Fire, punishment in, 68, 657
First-fruits, 648, 649
Forerunners, of the Messiah, 39
Fourth Gospel, as report of Jesus' words, 118
Frogs, 683

Gehenna, 68
Gentiles, relation to messianic kingdom, 51; recognize Jehovah and come to Jerusalem to worship, 52, 54; contrary view, 53, see Nationalism; saints rule over Gentiles, 429, 470
Georgios Hamartolus, 381
Give glory to God, idiomatic, 681
God of heaven, 604
God's presence with his people, 749
Gog and Magog, 37, 744
Gospels, sources of, 119
Grammatical irregularities in the Apoc., 224, 354, 424, 437
Grotius, 333
Gunkel, 236, see paragraphs on criticism in Com. *passim*

Harlot, figurative use of word, 690
Harmagedon, 685
Harvester, vision of, 661
Heads, of beasts, a succession of rulers, 696
Heaven, in O. T. not destined abode of the saints, 54; sometimes so in later writers, 67, 70
Heaven and earth, blended in the renewed world, 67, 98, 103, 110, 162
Hebrew nation, perpetuation of, 25, 34, see Nationalism
Hebrews, epistle to, eschatology, 108
Hegesippus, 392
Heracleon, 386, 389
Hippolytus, 321
Historical method, defined, 2

History, coloring earlier predictions, 7, 14

Holy land, *see* Land

Horn, as symbol, 510; the ten horns, 699

Horsemen, the four, 517

Horses, the plague of, 564

Hysteron-proteron, 243

Ignatius, 391

Incense, accompaniment, or symbol, of prayer, 511, 553

Inconsistency, in use of a tradition, 745

Indefinite expressions, afterwards made definite, 242

Individual, growth of idea, 32, 60; influenced by law, 33; influence of Ezekiel, 32, 61

Interimsethik, 140

Interludes, 244

Intermediate state, *see* Dead, the state of; sometimes not thought of, 69

Interpretation of the Apoc., difficulties in, 1; progress in, 2; history of, 318; first four centuries, 319; from fifth to end of fifteenth century, 325; from sixteenth century to present time, 330; classification of methods, 334

Interpreting angel, 170, 691

Interruption, interjection of brief utterances, 243, 244

Irenaeus, 320, 338, 348, 368; his date and trustworthiness, 368; sources of his information regarding the Ephesian John, 368, 373

Isaiah, Ascension of, 196

Israel, final conversion of, 159, 482, 589, 592

James, epistle of, eschatology, 110

Jerusalem, called the great city, 601; in Jewish hope, seat of the escha-tological kingdom, 30, 35, 54; seat of millennial kingdom, 160

Jerusalem, the heavenly, 56, 97, 110, 162. *See* New Jerusalem.

Jesus, his doctrine of the kingdom of God, 132; the kingdom both present and future, 134; relation to the Church, 135

Jesus, eschatology of, 117; its relation to his Messiahship, 117; place of eschatology in his view of his mission, 139; principal eschatological expectations, 144; summary statement of his eschatological teaching, 155. *See also* on his Messiahship and Doctrine of the kingdom

Jesus, Messiahship of, 117; his messianic consciousness, 118, 129, 131, 132; our knowledge of his utterances, 118; the Gospel sources, 121; his acceptance of messianic titles, 122; his use of title, Son of man, 124; his messianic work, 129; his early silence regarding his Messiahship, 129; departure from traditional ideas of the Messiah, 130; not the Messiah in name only, 131; evidence of messianic claims furnished by events in his life, 137; evidence from early christian belief, 138

Jew, use of name in the Apoc., 453

Jews, final conversion of, *see* Israel

Jezebel, 466

Joachim, 326

Johannine writings, eschatology, 100; agreement with Pauline, 101, 104, 107, 163, 164; relation to traditional eschatology, 101; two-fold aspect of eschatological terms, 101, *see* Eschatological events spiritualized

John the Apostle, at Ephesus, 366; evidence from tradition, 367;

Irenaeus, 368, *see* Irenaeus; Justin, Polycrates and others, 377; the Apostle confused with the Presbyter, 375, 378; argument against the Apostle's sojourn at Ephesus, 379; prophecy of Mk. 10^{39}, 380; Papias, 380; Martyrologies and other witnesses, 385; silence of N. T. and second century writers, 390; conclusion, 393

John the Apostle, his martyrdom, 380 ff.

John, the Presbyter, 362

Jonah, purpose of the book, 52

Jubilees, Book of, 189

Judah, tribe of, leader in religious history, 17

Jude, epistle of, eschatology, 113

Judging, synonymous with ruling, 739

Judgment, the, 66, 87, 94, 106, 108, 110, 111, 114, 116, 153, 161; awards in, 67, 94, 107, 109, 110, 111, 114, 117, 153, 161, 163, 187; the judge, 75, 94, 107, 109, 116, 165, 747

Justin Martyr, 320, 338, 349, 377

Key, of David, 479; keys of death, 441

King, future ideal, 26; *see also* Theocratic king, and Messiah

Kings, saints called so, 429

Kingdom, the eschatological, its place according to christian eschatology, 97, 103, 110, 115, 150, 162; for its place in Heb. expectation, *see* Jerusalem

Kingdom of God, the idea, emergence, 9, 11, 15; presence in monarchical age, 19; in exilic and post-exilic age, 32, 34; in N. T. era, 87, 95, 102, 110, 111, 112, 114, 116, 132, 149, 162

Kingdom of God and the Church, 96, 103, 112, 135

Kingdom of God, present and future, 96, 102, 134, 149

Kingdom of heaven, the term in Mt., 132

Kingdoms of Israel, northern and southern contrasted, 17

Lake, of fire, 735

Land, a, possession of, in Heb. eschatology, 10, 25, 30

Language, of the Apoc., 223, *see* Grammatical irregularities

Laodicea, 486

Law, the, influence of, in Babylonian captivity, 31, 32

Legalism, period of, 53

Legendary period, in biblical history, 4, 5, 6

Life, 90, 94, 102, 164

Lion, of tribe of Judah, 508; figure of, joined with that of a lamb, 511

Litotes, 474

Little Apocalypse, 143

Living Creatures, the four, in the Apoc., 500

Locusts, the plague of, 559

Lord's day, the, 435

Lücke, 334

Lyons and Vienne, epistle of the churches at, 339

Manna, in messianic kingdom, 461

Man of sin, 88, *see* Antichrist

Marcion, 340, 350

Marriage of the Lamb, 725, 726

Martyr, use of the term, 386, 428

Martyrs, judging and ruling, 739

Measurement, mark of preservation, 597

Melito, 339

Mercy of God, present in punishment, 312, 554, 569

Messenger, in Malachi, 41

Messiah, growth of idea, 26, 29, 40, 44, 72, 85, 101, 116, 186; the

Messiah not always present in eschatological hope, 5, 14, 41, 72; names of, 43, 72, 478, 732; Messiah, not at first thought of as superhuman, 50; later, as preëxistent, 73; other superhuman attributes, 74

Messiah, functions of, 44; as priest, 46, 189; as prophet, 47; as judge, 75, see Judgment; as defender of his nation, 730, see Deliverer; as sufferer for sins of his people, 47, 49, 85, 116, 130, 429

Messiah, hidden, 48; snatched away at birth, 48; put to death after reign of glory, 50

Messiah, son of Joseph, distinguished from Messiah, son of David, 50

Messiahship of Jesus, see Jesus

Messianic interregnum, 37, 76, see Millennium

Messianic woes, 38, 87, 111, 148, 157

Messianic, as synonym of eschatological, 4

Methodius, 323

Millenarianism, 320 ff., 327

Millennium, 37, 76, 98, 103, 110, 112, 114, 160, 184, 735

Mission, Hebrews conscious of, 9, 12, 51

Monarchies, agents of Satan, 71

Monotheism, 12, 51

Morning star, 471

Moses, Apocalypse of, 195; Assumption of, 194

Mother, the, of the Messiah, 616, 621, 628

Motives, four leading, in the Apoc., 240

Mount Zion, 647

Muratorian Canon, 339

Mystery, meaning of, 444, 583

Name, new and secret, 461, 462; Christ's unknown name, 732;

names written on the victor, 485; names of blasphemy, 198, 635; proper names as symbols, 250

Nation, Heb. perpetuation of, 25

Nationalism, in Heb. eschatology, 10, 20, 23, 25; gradually yields to universalism, 34, 52, 54, 64, 189; disappears in christian eschatology, 97, 101, 112, 117, 130, 163

Nations, Gentile, come to new Jerusalem to worship, 675

Nearness, supposed, of messianic age, 15, 22, 36, 87, 92, 105, 108, 110, 111, 114, 116, 145, 157

New covenant, 29

New heavens and earth, 56, 97, 103, 110, 115, 150, 162, 749

New Jerusalem, 56, 162, 189, 486, 755; measurements of, 759 ff.

New name, see Name

New song, 512

Nicolaitans, 450, 459, 464, 468

Nicolas of Lyra, 329

Number, of elect, to be filled up, 527

Numbers, symbolical, 250

Origen, 322, 339, 350

Oxymoron, 657

Palm branches, tokens of rejoicing, 544

Papias, 338, 349, 362, see De Boor fragments

Paradise, location, 67; meaning, 70

Parentheses, interjection of brief utterances, 244

Parousia, 86, 104, 108, 110, 111, 114, 116, 144, 165, 304, 331. See Day of the Lord, Judgment, Nearness

Parthians, 519, 565, 567, 704

Participle, with article, as noun, 545

Patmos, Apocalyptist's sojourn there, 434

Paul, his inherited view of the Messiah, 84; revolutionized on the journey to Damascus and by the experiences of the life in the Spirit, 85, 86; his eschatology, 86

Pauline epistles, 84; apocalypses, 86

Perfect, aoristic, 474, 511, 544

Pergamum, 455; as seat of Satan's throne, 457

Permanent significance of the Apoc., 291

Persecution, of saints in the last days, 158; Roman persecutions, 201

Persian influence in Jewish eschatology, 79

Peter, First, eschatology, 111; the End prominent, 111; Christ preaching to the dead, 112

Peter, Second, and Jude, relation of the two epistles to each other, 113; eschatology, 114

Philadelphia, 477

Pillar, in the temple, the victor as such, 485

Place, of righteous dead, 91, 92, 512; see Paradise, the Dead

Place, Seer's change of, 692

Plague, of bowls, 668; relation to the Egyptian, 671. See Third Woe

Polycarp, 369, 376, 392

Polycrates, 377

Pope, the, as Antichrist, 329, 330, 331, 333

Popular tradition, used in prophets and apocalyptists, 499, 517, 551, see Sources

Practical usefulness of the Apoc., 303

Prayers of saints for judgment, 526, 551

Preludes, in the structure of the Apoc., 244, 245

Present and coming ages, 64, 87

Priesthood, of emperor-worship, 639, see Second beast

Priests, the saints as such, 13, 112, 429, 741

Primasius, 326, 414

Promises, earliest religious, 4, 6, 8

Prophecy, see the Apoc. as prophecy

Prophet, his vision limited, 301

Protevangelium, 5

Punishment, in presence of the angels, 657; angels of punishment, 664

Punishment, of the wicked, in Jewish eschatology, generally physical, 68; sometimes spiritual, 67; unending, 68, 69; limited in the rabbis, 69. See the Dead, Judgment, awards of.

Purpose, of the Apoc., 208

Rauch, critical theory of, 234

Recapitulation theory, 322

Redeemed, on Mount Zion, 144,000, 648

Redundancy, 241

Remnant, doctrine of, 22, 27, 28

Restoration, of Israel, 28

Resurrection body, 63, 89, 106, 152

Resurrection of the dead, lateness of the belief, 58; growth of belief, 60; the doctrine in the N. T., 87, 89, 105, 108, 111, 151, 161

Resurrection, the general, 747

Resurrection, of unrighteous, 62, 93, 106, 151, 161

Ribeira, 331

Roll, the little, 575, 578

Roll, the sealed, 504, 507; not read, 507, 515, 519

Rome, destruction of, 158, 690, 703, 711

Root, of David, 509

Sabatier, 231; see paragraphs on criticism in Com. passim

Saints, reign of, 767

Salvation, 721

Sardis, 472

Satan, ruler of this world, 66; of evil spirits, 70; calumniator of men, 617; imprisoned and released, 160, 735; final doom, 161, 743;

hostility to the Messiah, 612, 615; seat of his kingdom, in the heavens, 617; expulsion therefrom, 617; his persecution of the mother of the Messiah, 618

Schmidt, critical theory of, 235

Schoen, 232, *see* paragraphs on criticism in Com. *passim*

Sea, in heaven, 500, 674; sea gives up its dead, 749; no sea in the new earth, 751

Sealing of the saints, 534

Second assault of hostile powers on the people of God, 36, 161, 743

Second beast, 408, 639

Second death, 161, 455

Second Esdras, Fourth Ezra, 190

Second Isaiah, 31

Second Zechariah, 43

Selection, a principle in religious history, 9

Serpent, in Eden, 6

Seven, frequency in the Apoc., 253; as a constructive feature, 253; seven divided into 3+4, 254; seven churches, why this number, 423; choice of these particular churches, 210, 436; seven epistles, 258, 446, *see* respective cities; seven heads of the Beast as mountains, 698; seven kings of Rome, 704; seven lamps, 425, 499, 510, 551; seven Spirits, 424, 473, 510

Sibylline Oracles, 184

Signs, of the end, 87, 89, 105, 111, 114, 148, 351

Singular, for plural, 523, 530, 601

Smyrna, 452

Solomon, Odes of, 187; Psalms of, 186

Son of man, in Daniel, 41

Son, the, of man, as name of the Messiah, 72; its use by Jesus, 124

Song, of Moses and the Lamb, 676

Sorcery, 570; at Ephesus, 447

Sources, used by the Apocalyptist, with or without modification, 171, 174, 215, 221, 437, 496, 499, 517, 527, 533, 536, 555, 560, 575, 593, 613, 615, 671, 699, *al. passim*

Spirit of prophecy, 729

Spitta, 233, *see* paragraphs on criticism in Com. *passim*

Star, as a person, 560

Stones, precious, 497

Studied composition of the Apoc., 174, 175, 214

Suffering servant in Isaiah, 49; *see* Messiah as sufferer for sin

Summary, of contents of the Apoc., 255

Superscription of the Apoc., written last, 421

Sword, of the mouth, 731

Symbolic acts, 719

Symbols, use of in the Apoc., 249; significance of details, not to be exaggerated, 249, 251

Tabernacle, of testimony, 678

Talent, 688

Te Deum, the heavenly, 721

Temple, heaven as, 524, 545, 552

Tertullian, 339, 350, 378

Testaments of the Twelve Patriarchs, 188

Testimony, of Jesus, 421, 526

Theocracy, 11

Theocratic king, 19, 26, 30, 40, 42

Theology of the Apoc., 310; doctrine of God, 310; of Christ, 312; of the Holy Spirit, 316

Theophilus, 339

Things that are, 443, 261, 275, 620

Third woe, the, 607, 627, 669

This age, 64

Throne room, in heaven, 496, 498, 500, 539, 651, 674, *see* Temple

Thunders and lightnings, as symbols, 499, 553, 574, 578, 610

Thyatira, 463

Ticonius, 324

Time of the end, 77; computation of, 78, 331; fixed measure of iniquity, fixed number of saints, to be filled up, 78, 527; also time, not fixed, influenced by prayers of saints and martyrs, by repentance of Israel, 79, 116; hastened by holy living, 115. *See* Nearness

Times of events, fixed by God, 567

Transcendental outlook, in Jewish eschatology, 34, 64, 65

Tree, of life, 451, 765

Tribes, the twelve, list of in the Apoc., 542

Twelve apostles, the, 759

Unity of the Apocalypse, 216; historical evidence, 218; general objections to theories of compilation and enlargement, 218; ultimate test of unity, 220, 240; nature of unity, as understood in present Com., 221; language, as bearing on unity, 222; author's manner and aim, as bearing on unity, 239. *See* Criticism and Critical Analyses

Universal, in distinction from national,

in eschatology, 27, 52, 64, 166, *see* Nationalism

Victorinus, 321

Vintage, vision of, 661, 663

Vischer, 229, *see* paragraphs on criticism in Com. *passim*

Völter, 225, 226, *see* paragraphs on criticism in Com. *passim*

War, in heaven, 617, 624

Warrior Messiah, 730

Water, of life, 764; waters, as symbol, 702

Weiss, J., 235, *see* paragraphs on criticism in Com. *passim*

Weizsäcker, 225, 227, *see* paragraphs on criticism in Com. *passim*

Weyland, 230, *see* paragraphs on criticism in Com. *passim*

White, garments, 475, 544, 679; white stone, 462

Winds, in eschatological imagery, 541

Wine, of God's wrath, 656

Witnesses, the two in Chap. 11, 590

Word of God, name of the Messiah, 732

World, this, meaning of term, 66

Wrath, of the Lamb, 529, 160

twin brooks series BOOKS IN THE SERIES

THE ACTS OF THE APOSTLES ....Richard B. Rackham
APOSTOLIC AND POST-APOSTOLIC TIMES (Goppelt) ....Robert A. Guelich, tr.
THE APOSTOLIC FATHERS ....J. B. Lightfoot
THE ATONEMENT OF CHRIST ....Francis Turrettin
THE AUTHORITY OF THE OLD TESTAMENT ....John Bright
BACKGROUNDS TO DISPENSATIONALISM ....Clarence B. Bass
BASIC CHRISTIAN DOCTRINES ....Carl F. H. Henry
THE BASIC IDEAS OF CALVINISM ....H. Henry Meeter
THE CALVINISTIC CONCEPT OF CULTURE ....H. Van Til
CHRISTIAN APPROACH TO PHILOSOPHY ....W. C. Young
CHRISTIAN PERSONAL ETHICS ....Carl F. H. Henry
COMMENTARY ON DANIEL (Jerome) ....Gleason L. Archer, Jr., tr.
THE DAYS OF HIS FLESH ....David Smith
DISCIPLING THE NATIONS ....Richard DeRidder
THE DOCTRINE OF GOD ....Herman Bavinck
EDUCATIONAL IDEALS IN THE ANCIENT WORLD ....Wm. Barclay
THE EPISTLE OF JAMES ....Joseph B. Mayor
EUSEBIUS' ECCLESIASTICAL HISTORY
FUNDAMENTALS OF THE FAITH ....Carl F. H. Henry, ed.
GOD-CENTERED EVANGELISM ....R. B. Kuiper
GENERAL PHILOSOPHY ....D. Elton Trueblood
THE GRACE OF LAW ....Ernest F. Kevan
THE HIGHER CRITICISM OF THE PENTATEUCH ....William Henry Green
THE HISTORY OF CHRISTIAN DOCTRINES ....Louis Berkhof
THE HISTORY OF DOCTRINES ....Reinhold Seeberg
THE HISTORY OF THE JEWISH NATION ....Alfred Edersheim
HISTORY OF PREACHING ....E. C. Dargan
LIGHT FROM THE ANCIENT EAST ....Adolf Deissmann
NOTES ON THE MIRACLES OF OUR LORD ....R. C. Trench
NOTES ON THE PARABLES OF OUR LORD ....R. C. Trench
OUR REASONABLE FAITH (Bavinck) ....Henry Zylstra, tr.
PAUL, APOSTLE OF LIBERTY ....R. N. Longnecker
PHILOSOPHY OF RELIGION ....D. Elton Trueblood
PROPHETS AND THE PROMISE ....W. J. Beecher
REASONS FOR FAITH ....John H. Gerstner
THE REFORMATION ....Hans J. Hillebrand, ed.
REFORMED DOGMATICS (Wollebius, Voetius, Turretin) ....J. Beardslee, ed., tr.
REFORMED DOGMATICS ....Heinrich Heppe
REVELATION AND INSPIRATION ....James Orr
REVELATION AND THE BIBLE ....Carl F. H. Henry
ROMAN SOCIETY AND ROMAN LAW IN THE NEW TESTAMENT ......A. N. Sherwin-White
THE ROOT OF FUNDAMENTALISM ....Ernest R. Sandeen
THE SERVANT-MESSIAH ....T. W. Manson
STORY OF RELIGION IN AMERICA ....Wm. W. Sweet
THE TESTS OF LIFE (third edition) ....Robert Law
THEOLOGY OF THE MAJOR SECTS ....John H. Gerstner
VARIETIES OF CHRISTIAN APOLOGETICS ....B. Ramm
THE VOYAGE AND SHIPWRECK OF ST. PAUL (fourth edition) ....James Smith
THE VIRGIN BIRTH ....J. G. Machen
A COMPANION TO THE STUDY OF ST. AUGUSTINE ....Roy W. Battenhouse, ed.
STUDIES IN THE GOSPELS ....R. C. Trench
THE HISTORY OF THE RELIGION OF ISRAEL ....John Howard Raven
THE HISTORY OF CHRISTIAN DOCTRINE (revised edition) ....E. H. Klotsche
THE EPISTLES OF JUDE ....Joseph B. Mayor
THEORIES OF REVELATI... ....H. D. McDonald
STUDIES IN THE BOOK OF DANIEL ....Robert Dick Wilson
THE UNITY OF THE BOOK OF GENESIS ....William Henry Green
THE APOCALYPSE OF JOHN ....Isbon T. Beckwith
CHRIST THE MEANING OF HISTORY ....Hendrikus Berkhof